The Professional's Handbook of
Financial Risk Management

The Professional's Handbook of Financial Risk Management

Edited by Marc Lore and Lev Borodovsky

Endorsed by the Global Association of Risk Professionals

OXFORD AUCKLAND BOSTON JOHANNESBURG MELBOURNE NEW DELHI

Butterworth-Heinemann
Linacre House, Jordan Hill, Oxford OX2 8DP
225 Wildwood Avenue, Woburn, MA 01801–2041
A division of Reed Educational and Professional Publishing Ltd

℞ A member of the Reed Elsevier plc group

First published 2000

British Library Cataloguing in Publication Data
The professional's handbook of financial risk management
  1 Risk management   2 Investments – Management
  I Lore, Marc   II Borodovsky, Lev
  332.6

Library of Congress Cataloguing in Publication Data
The professional's handbook of financial risk management/edited by Marc Lore and
  Lev Borodovsky.
  p.cm.
  Includes bibliographical references and index.
  ISBN 0 7506 41118
  1 Risk management   2 Finance   I Lore, Marc   II Borodovsky, Lev.
  HD61 1.P76
  658.15'5—dc21   99–088517

ISBN 0 7506 4111 8

Typeset by AccComputing, Castle Cary, Somerset
Printed and bound in Great Britain

Contents

Foreword

The role and importance of the risk management process (and by definition the professional risk manager) has evolved dramatically over the past several years. Until recently risk management was actually either only risk reporting or primarily a reactive function. The limited risk management tasks and technology support that did exist were usually assigned to ex-traders or product controllers with little or no support from the rest of business. The term *professional risk manager* was virtually unheard of in all but the largest and most sophisticated organizations. Only after a series of well-publicised losses and the accompanying failure of the firms involved did the need for sophisticated, proactive and comprehensive financial risk management processes become widely accepted.

The new world of the professional risk manager is one that begins in the boardroom rather than the back office. The risk management process and professionals are now recognized as not only protecting the organization against unexpected losses, but also fundamental to the efficient allocation of capital to optimize the returns on risk. The professional risk manager, when properly supported and utilized, truly provides added value to the organization.

A number of risk books were published in the latter half of the 1990s. They addressed the history of risk, how it evolved, the psychological factors that caused individuals to be good or bad risk takers and a myriad of other topics. Unfortunately, few books were written on the proper management of the growing population and complexity of risks confronting institutions. Marc Lore, Lev Borodovsky and their colleagues in the Global Association of Risk Professionals recognized this void and this book is their first attempt to fill in some of the blank spaces.

KPMG is pleased to the be the primary sponsor of GARP's *The Professional's Handbook of Financial Risk Management*. We believe that this volume offers the reader practical, real world insights into leading edge practices for the management of financial risk regardless of the size and sophistication of their own organization. For those contemplating a career in risk management, the authors of this text are practising financial risk managers who provide knowledgeable insights concerning their rapidly maturing profession.

No one volume can ever hope to be the ultimate last word on a topic that is evolving as rapidly as the field of financial risk management. However, we expect that this collection of articles, written by leading industry professionals who understand the risk management process, will become the industry standard reference text. We hope that after reviewing their work you will agree.

Martin E. Titus, Jr
Chairman, KPMG GlobeRisk®

Preface

Risk management encompasses a broad array of concepts and techniques, some of which may be quantified, while others must be treated in a more subjective manner. The financial fiascos of recent years have made it clear that a successful risk manager must respect both the intuitive and technical aspects (the 'art' and the 'science') of the discipline. But no matter what types of methods are used, the key to risk management is delivering the risk information in a timely and succinct fashion, while ensuring that key decision makers have the time, the tools, and the incentive to act upon it. Too often the key decision makers receive information that is either too complex to understand or too large to process. In fact, Gerald Corrigan, former President of the New York Federal Reserve, described risk management as 'getting the right information to the right people at the right time'.

History has taught us time and time again that senior decision makers become so overwhelmed with VaR reports, complex models, and unnecessary formalism that they fail to account for the most fundamental of risks. An integral part of the risk manager's job therefore is to present risk information to the decision maker in a format which not only highlights the main points but also directs the decision maker to the most appropriate course of action. A number of financial debacles in 1998, such as LTCM, are quite representative of this problem. Risk managers must work proactively to discover new ways of looking at risk and embrace a 'common sense' approach to delivering this information.

As a profession, risk management needs to evolve beyond its traditional role of calculating and assessing risk to actually making effective use of the results. This entails the risk manager examining and presenting results from the perspective of the decision maker, bearing in mind the knowledge base of the decision maker. It will be essential over the next few years for the risk manager's focus to shift from calculation to presentation and delivery.

However, presenting the right information to the right people is not enough. The information must also be timely. The deadliest type of risk is that which we don't recognize in time. Correlations that appear stable break down, and a VaR model that explains earnings volatility for years can suddenly go awry. It is an overwhelming and counterproductive task for risk managers to attempt to foresee all the potential risks that an organization will be exposed to before they arise. The key is to be able to separate those risks that may hurt an institution from those that may destroy it, and deliver that information before it is too late.

In summary, in order for risk management to truly add value to an organization, the risk information must be utilized in such a way as to influence or alter the business decision-making process. This can only be accomplished if the appropriate information is presented in a concise and well-defined manner to the key decision makers of the firm on a timely basis.

Editors: Marc Lore and Lev Borodovsky
Co-ordinating Editor: Nawal K. Roy
Assistant Editors: Lakshman Chandra and Michael Hanrahan

About GARP

The Global Association of Risk Professionals (GARP) is a not-for-profit, independent organization of over 10 000 financial risk management practitioners and researchers from over 90 countries. GARP was founded by Marc Lore and Lev Borodovsky in 1996. They felt that the financial risk management profession should extend beyond the risk control departments of financial institutions. GARP is now a diverse international association of professionals from a variety of backgrounds and organizations who share a common interest in the field.

GARP's mission is to serve its members by facilitating the exchange of information, developing educational programs, and promoting standards in the area of financial risk management. GARP members discuss risk management techniques and standards, critique current practices and regulation, and help bring forth potential risks in the financial markets to the attention of other members and the public. GARP seeks to provide open forums for discussion and access to information such as events, publications, consulting and software services, jobs, Internet sites, etc. To join GARP visit the web site at www.garp.com

Contributors

EDITORS

- **Marc Lore**

Executive Vice President and Head of Firm-Wide Risk Management and Control, Sanwa Bank International, City Place House, PO Box 245, 55 Basinghall St, London EC2V 5DJ, UK

- **Lev Borodovsky**

Director, Risk Measurement and Management Dept, Credit Suisse First Boston, 11 Madison Avenue, New York, NY 10010-3629, USA

Co-ordinating Editor

- **Nawal K. Roy**

Associate Vice President, Credit Suisse First Boston, 11 Madison Avenue, New York, NY 10010-3629, USA

Assistant Editors

- **Lakshman Chandra**

Business Manager, Risk Management Group, Sanwa Bank International, City Place House, PO Box 245, 55 Basinghall St, London EC2V 5DJ, UK

- **Michael Hanrahan**

Assistant Vice President, Head of Risk Policy, Sanwa Bank International, City Place House, PO Box 245, 55 Basinghall St, London EC2V 5DJ, UK

CONTRIBUTORS

- **Philip Best**

Risk specialist, The Capital Markets Company, Clements House, 14–18 Gresham St, London, EC2V 7JE, UK

- **Michel Crouhy**

Senior Vice President, Market Risk Management, Canadian Imperial Bank of Commerce, 161 Bay Street, Toronto, Ontario M5J 2S8, Canada

- **Mark Deans**

Head of Risk Management and Regulation, Sanwa Bank International, 55 Basinghall Street, London, EC2V 5DJ, UK

- **Thomas Donahoe**

Director, MetLife, 334 Madison Avenue, Area 2, Convent Station, NJ 07961, USA

- **Robert E. Fiedler**

Head of Treasury and Liquidity Risk, Methodology and Policy Group Market Risk Management, Deutsche Bank AG, D-60262 Frankfurt, Germany

- **Andrew Fishman**

Principal Consultant, The Capital Markets Company, Clements House, 14–18 Gresham St, London, EC2V 7JE, UK

- **Dan Galai**
Abe Gray Professor, Finance and Administration, Hebrew University, School of Business Administration in Jerusalem, Israel
- **Teri L. Geske**
Senior Vice President, Product Development, Capital Management Sciences, 11766 Wilshire Blvd, Suite 300, Los Angeles, CA 90025, USA
- **Kostas Giannopoulos**
Senior Lecturer in Finance, Westminster Business School, University of Westminster, 309 Regent St, London W1R 8AL, UK
- **Michael Haubenstock**
PricewaterhouseCoopers LLP, 1177 Avenue of the Americas, New York, NY 10036, USA
- **Ian Hawkins**
Assistant Director, Global Derivatives and Fixed Income, Westdeutsche Landesbank Girozentrale, 1211 Avenue of the Americas, New York, NY 10036, USA
- **Alvin Kuruc**
Senior Vice President, Infinity, a SunGard Company, 640 Clyde Court, Mountain View, CA 04043, USA
- **Alan Laubsch**
Partner, RiskMetrics Group, 44 Wall Street, New York, NY 10005, USA
- **François-Serge Lhabitant**
Director, UBS Ag, Aeschenplatz 6, 4002 Basel, Switzerland, and Assistant Professor of Finance, Thunderbird, the American Graduate School of International Management, Glendale, USA
- **Allan M. Malz**
Partner, RiskMetrics Group, 44 Wall St, NY 10005, USA
- **Bob Mark**
Executive Vice President, Canadian Imperial Bank of Commerce, 161 Bay Street, Toronto, Ontario, M5J 2S8, Canada
- **Frank Morisano**
Director, PricewaterhouseCoopers LLP, 1177 Avenue of the Americas, New York, NY 10036, USA
- **Wesley Phoa**
Associate, Quantitative Research, Capital Strategy Research, 11100 Santa Monica Boulevard, Los Angeles, CA 90025, USA
- **Mattia L. Rattaggi**
Corporate Risk Control, UBS, AG, Pelikanstrasse 6, PO Box 8090, Zurich, Switzerland
- **Richard Sage, FRM**
Director, Enron Europe, Flat 1, 25 Bedford Street, London WC2E 9EQ
- **P. K. Satish, CFA**
Managing Director, Head of Financial Engineering and Research, Askari Risk Management Solutions, State St Bank & Trust Company, 100 Avenue of the Americas, 5th Floor, New York, NY 10013, USA
- **Richard K. Skora**
President, Skora & Company Inc., 26 Broadway, Suite 400, New York, NY 10004, USA
- **Grant Thain**
Senior Vice President, Risk Management, Citizens Power LLC, 160 Federal Street, Boston, MA 02110, USA

- **Shyam Venkat**

Partner, PricewaterhouseCoopers LLP, 1177 Avenue of the Americas, New York, NY 10036, USA

- **Kurt S. Wilhelm, FRM, CFA**

National Bank Examiner, Comptroller of the Currency, 250 E St SW, Washington, DC 20219, USA

- **Deborah L. Williams**

Co-founder and Research Director, Meridien Research, 2020 Commonwealth Avenue, Newton, MA 02466, USA

- **Duncan Wilson**

Partner, Global Risk Management Practice, Ernst & Young, Rolls House, 7 Rolls Building, Fetter Lane, London EC4A 1NH, UK

Acknowledgements

We would like to thank our wives Carolyn and Lisa for all their tremendous help, support, and patience. We also wish to thank all the authors who have contributed to this book. Special thanks go to Nawal Roy for his superb effort in pulling this project together and always keeping it on track, as well as his remarkable assistance with the editing process. We wish to thank Michael Hanrahan and Lakshman Chandra for writing the Introduction and their help in editing. Finally we would like to thank all GARP's members for their continued support.

Marc Lore
Lev Borodovsky

Introduction

The purpose of this book is to provide risk professionals with the latest standards that represent best practice in the risk industry. The book has been created with the risk practitioner in mind. While no undertaking of this size can be devoid of theory, especially considering the ongoing changes and advances within the profession itself, the heart of this book is aimed at providing practising risk managers with usable and sensible information that will assist them in their day-to-day work.

The successful growth of GARP, the Global Association of Risk Professionals, has brought together thousands of risk professionals and has enabled the sharing of ideas and knowledge throughout the risk community. The existence of this forum has also made apparent that despite the growing size and importance of risk management in the financial world, there is no book in the marketplace that covers the wide array of topics that a risk manager can encounter on a daily basis in a manner that suits the practitioner. Rather, the practitioner is besieged by books that are theoretical in nature. While such books contain valuable insights that are critical to the advancement of our profession, most risk professionals are never able to utilize and test the concepts within them.

Consequently, a familiar theme has emerged at various GARP meetings and conferences that a risk handbook needs to be created to provide risk practitioners with knowledge of the practices that other risk professionals have employed at their own jobs. This is especially important considering the evolving nature of risk management that can be characterized by the continuous refinement and improvement of risk management techniques, which have been driven by the increasingly complex financial environment.

One of the challenges of this book has been to design its contents so that it can cover the vast area that a risk manager encounters in his or her job and at the same time be an aid to both the experienced and the more novice risk professional. Obviously, this is no easy task. While great care has been taken to include material on as many topics that a risk manager might, and even should, encounter at his or her job, it is impossible to provide answers to every single question that one might have. This is especially difficult considering the very nature of the risk management profession, as there are very few single answers that can automatically be applied to problems with any certainty. The risk management function in an organization should be a fully integrated one. While it is independent in its authority from other areas within the bank, it is at the same time dependent on them in that it receives and synthesizes information, information which is critical to its own operations, from these other areas.

Consequently, the decisions made by risk managers can impact on the entire firm. The risk manager, therefore, must tailor solutions that are appropriate considering the circumstances of the institution in which he or she is working, the impact that the solution might have on other areas of the organization, and the practical considerations associated with implementation that must be factored into any chosen decision.

This handbook has thus been designed to delve into the various roles of the risk management function. Rather than describing every possible role in exhaustive detail, the authors have attempted to provide a story line for each of the discussed topics, including practical issues that a risk manager needs to consider when tackling the subject, possible solutions to difficulties that might be encountered, background knowledge that is essential to know, and more intricate practices and techniques that are being used. By providing these fundamentals, the novice risk professional can gain a thorough understanding of the topic in question while the more experienced professional can use some of the more advanced concepts within the book. Thus the book can be used to broaden one's own knowledge of the risk world, both by familiarizing oneself with areas in which the risk manager lacks experience and by enhancing one's knowledge in areas in which one already has expertise.

When starting this project we thought long and hard as to how we could condense the myriad ideas and topics which risk management has come to represent. We realized early on that the growth in risk management ideas and techniques over the last few years meant that we could not possibly explain them all in detail in one book. However, we have attempted to outline all the main areas of risk management to the point where a risk manager can have a clear idea of the concepts being explained. It is hoped that these will fire the thought processes to the point where a competent risk manager could tailor the ideas to arrive at an effective solution for their own particular problem.

One of the obstacles we faced in bringing this book together was to decide on the level of detail for each chapter. This included the decision as to whether or not each chapter should include practical examples of the ideas being described and what it would take practically to implement the ideas. It was felt, however, that the essence of the book would be best served by not restricting the authors to a set format for their particular chapter. The range of topics is so diverse that it would not be practical in many cases to stick to a required format. It was also felt that the character of the book would benefit from a 'free form' style, which essentially meant giving the authors a topic and letting them loose. This also makes the book more interesting from the reader's perspective and allowed the authors to write in a style with which they were comfortable.

Therefore as well as a book that is diverse in the range of topics covered we have one with a range of perspectives towards the topics being covered. This is a facet that we think will distinguish this book from other broad-ranging risk management books. Each author has taken a different view of how his or her topic should be covered. This in turn allows us to get a feel for the many ways in which we can approach a problem in the risk management realm. Some authors have taken a high-level approach, which may befit some topics, while others have gone into the detail.

In addition, there are a number of chapters that outline approaches we should take to any risk management problem. For example, Deborah Williams' excellent chapter on enterprise risk management technologies gives us a good grounding on the approach to take in implementing a systems-based solution to a risk management problem.

As well as providing practical solutions this book also covers many topics which practitioners in the financial sector would not necessarily ever encounter. We are sure that readers will find these insights into areas outside their normal everyday environments to be both interesting and informative. For any practitioners who think the subtleties of interest rate risk are complicated, we would recommend a read of Grant Thain's chapter on energy risk management!

As mentioned earlier, we could not hope to impose limits on the authors of this book while allowing them free reign to explore their particular topic. For this reason we feel that a glossary of terms for this book would not necessarily be useful. Different authors may interpret the same term in many different ways, and therefore we would ask that the reader be careful to understand the context in which a particular phrase is being used. All authors have been quite clear in defining ambiguous words or phrases, whether formally or within the body of the text, so the reader should not have too much difficulty in understanding the scope in which phrases are being used.

Rather than one writer compiling the works of various authors or research papers it was felt that the best approach to producing a practical risk management guide was to let the practitioners write it themselves. Using the extensive base of contacts that was available from the GARP membership, leaders in each field were asked to produce a chapter encapsulating their knowledge and giving it a practical edge. Condensing their vast knowledge into one chapter was by no means an easy feat when we consider that all our contributors could quite easily produce a whole book on their specialist subject. Naturally *The Professional's Handbook of Financial Risk Management* would not have come about without their efforts and a willingness or even eagerness to share their ideas and concepts.

It should be noted that every effort was made to select people from across the risk management spectrum, from insurance and banking to the regulatory bodies and also the corporations and utility firms who are the main end-users of financial products. Each sector has its own view on risk management and this diverse outlook is well represented throughout the book.

All authors are leaders in their field who between them have the experience and knowledge, both practical and theoretical, to produce the definitive risk management guide. When asking the contributors to partake in this project we were quite overwhelmed by the enthusiasm with which they took up the cause. It is essential for those of us in the risk management arena to share knowledge and disseminate what we know in order to assist each other in our one common aim of mitigating risk. This book demonstrates how the risk management profession has come of age in realizing that we have to help each other to do our jobs effectively. This is best illustrated by the manner in which all our authors contrived to ensure we understand their subject matter, thus guaranteeing that we can use their solutions to our problems.

Editorial team

Part 1

Foundation of risk management

Derivatives basics

ALLAN M. MALZ

Introduction

Derivative assets are assets whose values are determined by the value of some other asset, called the **underlying**. There are two common types of derivative contracts, those patterned on **forwards** and on **options**. Derivatives based on forwards have **linear** payoffs, meaning their payoffs move one-for-one with changes in the underlying price. Such contracts are generally relatively easy to understand, value, and manage. Derivatives based on options have **non-linear** payoffs, meaning their payoffs may move proportionally more or less than the underlying price. Such contracts can be quite difficult to understand, value, and manage.

The goal of this chapter is to describe the main types of derivatives currently in use, and to provide some understanding of the standard models used to value these instruments and manage their risks. There is a vast and growing variety of derivative products – among recent innovations are credit and energy-related derivatives. We will focus on the most widely used instruments and on some basic analytical concepts which we hope will improve readers' understanding of any derivatives issues they confront.

Because a model of derivative prices often starts out from a view of how the underlying asset price moves over time, the chapter begins with an introduction to the 'standard view' of asset price behavior, and a survey of how asset prices actually behave. An understanding of these issues will be helpful later in the chapter, when we discuss the limitations of some of the benchmark models employed in derivatives pricing.

The chapter then proceeds to a description of forwards, futures and options. The following sections provide an introduction to the **Black–Scholes model**. Rather than focusing primarily on the theory underlying the model, we focus on the option market conventions the model has fostered, particularly the use of **implied volatility** as a metric for option pricing and the use of the so-called 'greeks' as the key concepts in option risk management.

In recent years, much attention has focused on differences between the predictions of benchmark option pricing models and the actual patterns of option prices, particularly the **volatility smile**, and we describe these anomalies. This chapter concludes with a sections discussing certain option combinations, **risk reversals** and **strangles**, by means of which the market 'trades' the smile.

Behavior of asset prices

Efficient markets hypothesis

The efficient market approach to explaining asset prices views them as the present values of the income streams they generate. Efficient market theory implies that all available information regarding future asset prices is impounded in current asset prices. It provides a useful starting point for analyzing derivatives.

One implication of market efficiency is that asset returns follow a **random walk**. The motion of the asset price has two parts, a **drift rate**, that is, a deterministic rate at which the asset price is expected to change over time, and a **variance rate**, that is, a random change in the asset price, also proportional to the time elapsed, and also unobservable. The variance rate has a mean of zero and a per-period variance equal to a parameter σ, called the **volatility**. This assumption implies that the percent changes in the asset price are normally distributed with a mean equal to the drift rate and a variance equal to σ^2.

The random walk hypothesis is widely used in financial modeling and has several implications:

- The percent change in the asset price over the next time interval is independent of both the percent change over the last time interval and the level of the asset price. The random walk is sometimes described as 'memoryless' for this reason. There is no tendency for an up move to be followed by another up move, or by a down move. That means that the asset price can only have a non-stochastic trend equal to the drift rate, and does not revert to the historical mean or other 'correct' level. If the assumption were true, technical analysis would be irrelevant.
- Precisely because of this lack of memory, the asset price tends over time to wander further and further from any starting point. The proportional distance the asset price can be expected to wander randomly over a discrete time interval τ is the volatility times the square root of the time interval, $\sigma\sqrt{\tau}$.
- Asset prices are continuous; they move in small steps, but do not jump. Over a given time interval, they may wander quite a distance from where they started, but they do it by moving a little each day.
- Asset returns are normally distributed with a mean equal to the drift rate and a standard deviation equal to the volatility. The return distribution is the same each period.

The Black–Scholes model assumes that volatility can be different for different asset prices, but is a constant for a particular asset. That implies that asset prices are **homoskedastic**, showing no tendency towards 'volatility bunching'. A wild day in the markets is as likely to be followed by a quiet day as by another wild day.

An asset price following geometric Brownian motion can be thought of as having an urge to wander away from any starting point, but not in any particular direction. The volatility parameter can be thought of as a scaling factor for that urge to wander. Figure 1.1 illustrates its properties with six possible time paths over a year of an asset price, the sterling–dollar exchange rate, with a starting value of USD 1.60, an annual volatility of 12%, and an expected rate of return of zero.

Empirical research on asset price behavior

While the random walk is a perfectly serviceable first approximation to the behavior of asset prices, in reality, it is only an approximation. Even though most widely

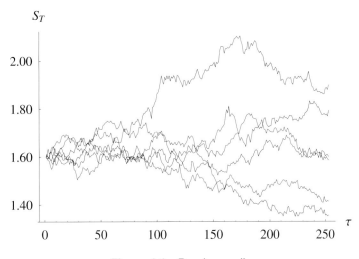

Figure 1.1 Random walk.

traded cash asset returns are close to normal, they display small but important 'non-normalities'. In particular, the frequency and direction of large moves in asset prices, which are very important in risk management, can be quite different in real-life markets than the random walk model predicts. Moreover, a few cash assets behave very differently from a random walk.

The random walk hypothesis on which the Black–Scholes model is based is a good first approximation to the behavior of most asset prices most of the time. However, even nominal asset returns that are quite close to normally distributed display small but important deviations from normality. The option price patterns discussed below reveal how market participants perceive the distribution of future asset prices. Empirical studies of the stochastic properties of nominal returns focus on the behavior of realized asset prices. The two approaches largely agree.

Kurtosis

The **kurtosis** or **leptokurtosis** (literally, 'fat tails') of a distribution is a measure of the frequency of large positive or negative asset returns. Specifically, it measures the frequency of large squared deviations from the mean. The distribution of asset returns will show high kurtosis if asset returns which are far above or below the mean occur relatively often, regardless of whether they are mostly above, mostly below, or both above and below the mean return.

Kurtosis is measured in comparison with the normal distribution, which has a coefficient of kurtosis of exactly 3. If the kurtosis of an asset return distribution is significantly higher than 3, it indicates that large-magnitude returns occur more frequently than in a normal distribution. In other words, a coefficient of kurtosis well over 3 is inconsistent with the assumption that returns are normal. Figure 1.2 compares a kurtotic distribution with a normal distribution with the same variance.

Skewness

The skewness of a distribution is a measure of the frequency with which large returns in a particular direction occur. An asset which displays large negative returns more

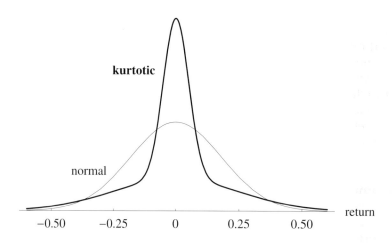

Figure 1.2   Kurtosis.

frequently than large positive returns is said to have a return distribution skewed to the left or to have a 'fat left tail'. An asset which displays large positive returns more frequently than large negative returns is said to have a return distribution skewed to the right or to have a 'fat right tail'. The normal distribution is symmetrical, that is, its coefficient of skewness is exactly zero. Thus a significantly positive or negative skewness coefficient is inconsistent with the assumption that returns are normal.

Figure 1.3 compares a skewed, but non-kurtotic, distribution with a normal distribution with the same variance. Table 1.1 presents estimates of the kurtosis and skewness of some widely traded assets. All the assets displayed have significant positive or negative skewness, and most also have a coefficient of kurtosis significantly greater than 3.0.

The exchange rates of the Mexican peso and Thai baht *vis-à-vis* the dollar have the largest coefficients of kurtosis. They are examples of intermittently fixed exchange

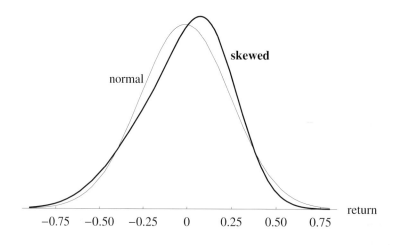

Figure 1.3   Skewness.

rates, which are kept within very narrow fluctuation limits by the monetary authorities. Typically, fixed exchange rates are a temporary phenomenon, lasting decades in rare cases, but only a few years in most. When a fixed exchange rate can no longer be sustained, the rate is either adjusted to new fixed level (for example, the European Monetary System in the 1980s and 1990s and the Bretton Woods system until 1971) or permitted to 'float', that is, find a free-market price (for example, most emerging market currencies). In either case, the return pattern of the currency is one of extremely low returns during the fixed-rate period and extremely large positive or negative returns when the fixed rate is abandoned, leading to extremely high kurtosis.

The return patterns of intermittently pegged exchange rates also diminishes the forecasting power of forward exchange rates for these currencies, a phenomenon known as **regime-switching** or the **peso problem**. The term 'peso problem' has its origin in experience with spot and forward rates on the Mexican peso in the 1970s. Observers were puzzled by the fact that forward rates for years 'predicted' a significant short-term depreciation of the peso *vis-à-vis* the US dollar, although the peso–dollar exchange rate was fixed. One proposed solution was that the exchange rate peg was not perfectly credible, so market participants expected a switch to a new, lower value of the peso with a positive probability. In the event, the peso has in fact been periodically permitted to float, invariably depreciating sharply.

Autocorrelation of returns

The distribution of many asset returns is not only kurtotic and skewed. The return distribution may also change over time and successive returns may not be independent of one another. These phenomena will be reflected in the **serial correlation** or **autocorrelation** of returns. Table 1.1 displays evidence that asset returns are not typically independently and identically distributed. The rightmost column displays a statistic which measures the likelihood that there is serial correlation between returns on a given day and returns on the same asset during the prior five trading days. High values of this statistic indicate a high likelihood that returns are autocorrelated.

Table 1.1 Statistical properties of selected daily asset returns

Asset	Standard deviation	Skewness	Kurtosis	Autocorrelation
Dollar–Swiss franc	0.0069	0.347	2.485	6.0
Dollar–yen	0.0078	0.660	6.181	8.0
Dollar–Mexican peso	0.0132	−3.015	65.947	56.7
Dollar–Thai baht	0.0080	−0.461	25.879	87.4
Crude oil	0.0204	0.249	4.681	41.1
Gold	0.0065	−0.165	4.983	21.3
Nikkei 225 average	0.0138	0.213	3.131	26.3
S&P 500 average	0.0087	−0.578	8.391	25.6

Forwards, futures and swaps

Forwards and forward prices

In a **forward** contract, one party agrees to deliver a specified amount of a specified commodity – the underlying asset – to the other at a specified date in the future (the maturity date of the contract) at a specified price (the **forward price**). The commodity may be a commodity in the narrow sense, e.g. gold or wheat, or a financial asset, e.g. foreign exchange or shares. The price of the underlying asset for immediate (rather than future) delivery is called the **cash** or **spot price**.

The party obliged to deliver the commodity is said to have a **short position** and the party obliged to take delivery of the commodity and pay the forward price for it is said to have a **long position**.

A party with no obligation offsetting the forward contract is said to have an **open position**. A party with an open position is sometimes called a **speculator**. A party with an obligation offsetting the forward contract is said to have a **covered position**. A party with a closed position is sometimes called a **hedger**.

The market sets forward prices so there are no cash flows – no money changes hands – until maturity. The payoff at maturity is the difference between forward price, which is set contractually in the market at initiation, and the future cash price, which is learned at maturity. Thus the long position gets $S_T - F_{t,T}$ and the short gets $F_{t,T} - S_T$, where $T - t$ is the maturity, in years, of the forward contract (for example, $T = 1/12$ for a one-month forward), S_T is the price of the underlying asset on the maturity date, and $F_{t,T}$ is the forward price agreed at time t for delivery at time T. Figure 1.4 illustrates with a dollar forward against sterling, initiated at a forward outright rate (see below) of USD 1.60. Note that the payoff is *linearly* related to the terminal value S_T of the underlying exchange rate, that is, it is a constant multiple, in this case unity, of S_T.

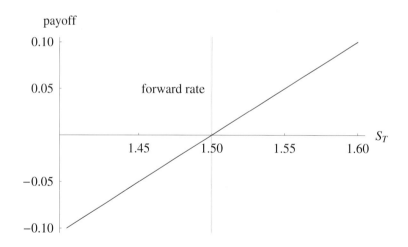

Figure 1.4 Payoff on a long forward.

No-arbitrage conditions for forward prices

One condition for markets to be termed efficient is the absence of **arbitrage**. The term 'arbitrage' has been used in two very different senses which it is important to distinguish:

● To carry out arbitrage in the first sense, one would simultaneously execute a set of transactions which have zero net cash flow now, but have a non-zero probability of a positive payoff without risk, i.e. with a zero probability of a negative payoff in the future.

- Arbitrage in the second sense is related to a model of how asset prices behave. To perform arbitrage in this sense, one carries out a set of transactions with a zero net cash flow now and a positive expected value at some date in the future.

Derivative assets, e.g. forwards, can often be constructed from combinations of underlying assets. Such constructed assets are called **synthetic assets**.

Covered parity or **cost-of-carry** relations are relations are between the prices of forward and underlying assets. These relations are enforced by arbitrage and tell us how to determine arbitrage-based forward asset prices.

Throughout this discussion, we will assume that there are no transactions costs or taxes, that markets are in session around the clock, that nominal interest rates are positive, and that unlimited short sales are possible. These assumptions are fairly innocuous: in the international financial markets, transactions costs typically are quite low for most standard financial instruments, and most of the instruments discussed here are not taxed, since they are conducted in the Euromarkets or on organized exchanges.

Cost-of-carry with no dividends

The mechanics of covered parity are somewhat different in different markets, depending on what instruments are most actively traded. The simplest case is that of a fictitious commodity which has no convenience value, no storage and insurance cost, and pays out no interest, dividends, or other cash flows. The only cost of holding the commodity is then the opportunity cost of funding the position.

Imagine creating a long forward payoff synthetically. It might be needed by a dealer hedging a short forward position:

- Buy the commodity with borrowed funds, paying S_t for one unit of the commodity borrowed at $r_{t,T}$, the $T-t$-year annually compounded spot interest rate at time t. Like a forward, this set of transactions has a net cash flow of zero.
- At time T, repay the loan and sell the commodity. The net cash flow is $S_T - [1 + r_{t,T}(T-t)]S_t$.

This strategy is called a **synthetic long forward**.

Similarly, in a **synthetic short forward**, you borrow the commodity and sell it, lending the funds at rate $r_{t,T}$: the net cash flow now is zero. At time T, buy the commodity at price S_T and return it: the net cash flow is $[1 + r_{t,T}(T-t)]S_t - S_T$.

The payoff on this synthetic long or short forward must equal that of a forward contract: $S_T - [1 + r_{t,T}(T-t)]S_t = S_T - F_{t,T}$. If it were greater (smaller), one could make a riskless profit by taking a short (long) forward position and creating a synthetic long (short) forward. This implies that the forward price is equal to the future value of the current spot price, i.e. the long must commit to paying the financing cost of the position: $F_{t,T} = [1 + r_{t,T}(T-t)]S_t$.

Two things are noteworthy about this cost-of-carry formula. First, the unknown future commodity price is irrelevant to the determination of the forward price and has dropped out. Second, the forward price must be higher than the spot price, since the interest rate $r_{t,T}$ is positive.

Short positions can be readily taken in most financial asset markets. However, in some commodity markets, short positions cannot be taken and thus synthetic short forwards cannot be constructed in sufficient volume to eliminate arbitrage entirely. Even, in that case, arbitrage is only possible in one direction, and the no-arbitrage condition becomes an inequality: $F_{t,T} \leqslant [1 + r_{t,T}(T-t)]S_t$.

Cost-of-carry with a known dividend

If the commodity pays dividends or a return d_T (expressed as a percent per period of the commodity price, discretely compounded), which is known in advance, the analysis becomes slightly more complicated. You can think of $d_{t,T}$ as the dividend rate per 'share' of the asset: a share of IBM receives a dividend, an equity index unit receives a basket of dividends, $100 of par value of a bond receives a coupon, etc. The d_T may be negative for some assets: you receive a bill for storage and insurance costs, not a dividend check, on your 100 ounces of platinum. The amount of dividends received over $T-t$ years in currency units is $d_{t,T}S_t(T-t)$.

The synthetic long forward position is still constructed the same way, but in this case the accrued dividend will be received at time T in addition to the commodity price. The net cash flow is $S_T + d_{t,T}S_t(T-t) - [1 + r_{t,T}(T-t)]S_t$. The no-arbitrage condition is now

$$S_T - F_{t,T} = S_T - [1 + (r_{t,T} - d_{t,T})(T-t)]S_t.$$

The forward price will be lower, the higher the dividends paid:
$F_{t,T} = [1 + (r_{t,T} - d_{t,T})(T-t)S_t$.

The forward price may be greater than, less than or equal to than the spot price if there is a dividend. The long's implied financing cost is reduced by the dividend received.

Foreign exchange

Forward foreign exchange is foreign currency deliverable in the future. Its price is called **forward exchange rate** or the **forward outright rate**, and the differential of the forward minus the spot exchange rate is called the **swap rate** (not to be confused with the rate on plain-vanilla interest rate swaps).

To apply the general mechanics of a forward transaction described above to this case, let $r_{t,T}$ and $r_{t,T}^*$ represent the domestic and foreign money-market interest rates. The spot and forward outright exchange rates are S_t and $F_{t,T}$, expressed in domestic currency units per foreign currency unit.

To create a synthetic long forward,

- Borrow $S_t/(1 + r_{t,T}^*\tau)$ domestic currency units at rate $r_{t,T}$ and buy $1/(1 + r_{t,T}^*\tau)$ foreign currency units. Deposit the foreign currency proceeds at rate $r_{t,T}^*$. There is no net cash outlay now.
- At time T, the foreign currency deposit has grown to one foreign currency unit, and you must repay the borrowed

$$\frac{S_t(1 + r_{t,T}\tau)}{1 + r_{t,T}^*\tau}$$

including interest. This implies that the forward rate is

$$F_{t,T} = \frac{1 + r_{t,T}\tau}{1 + r_{t,T}^*\tau} S_t$$

Here is a numerical example of this relationship. Suppose the Euro-dollar spot exchange rate today is USD 1.02 per Euro. Note that we are treating the US dollar as the domestic and the Euro as the foreign currency. Suppose further that the US 1-year deposit rate is 5.75% and that the 1-year Euro deposit rate is 3.0%. The 1-year forward outright rate must then be

$$\frac{1.0575}{1.03} \, 1.02 = 1.0472$$

Typically, forward foreign exchange rates are quoted not as outright rates but in terms of **forward points**. The points are a positive or negative quantity which is added to the spot rate to arrive at the forward outright rate, usually after dividing by a standard factor such as 10 000. In our example, the 1-year points amount to $10\,000 \cdot (1.0472 - 1.02) = 272$. If Euro deposit rates were above rather than below US rates, the points would be negative.

Gold leasing

Market participants can borrow and lend gold in the gold lease market. Typical lenders of gold in the lease market are entities with large stocks of physical gold on which they wish to earn a rate of return, such as central banks. Typical borrowers of gold are gold dealing desks.

Suppose you are a bank intermediating in the gold market. Let the spot gold price (in US dollars) be $S_t = 275.00$, let the US dollar 6-month deposit rate be 5.6% and let the 6-month gold lease rate be 2% per annum. The 6-month forward gold price must then be

$$F_{t,T} = \left(1 + \frac{0.056 - 0.02}{2}\right) \cdot 275 = 279.95$$

The gold lease rate plays the role of the dividend rate in our framework.

A mining company sells 1000 ounces gold forward for delivery in 6 months at the market price of USD 279.95. You now have a long forward position to hedge, which you can do in several ways. You can use the futures market, but perhaps the delivery dates do not coincide with the forward. Alternatively, you can lease gold from a central bank for 6 months and sell it immediately in the spot market at a price of USD 275.00, investing the proceeds (USD 275 000) in a 6-month deposit at 5.6%. Note that there is no net cash flow now.

In 6 months, these contracts are settled. First, you take delivery of forward gold from the miner and immediately return it to the central bank along with a wire transfer of USD 2750. You redeem the deposit, now grown to USD 282 700, from the bank and pay USD 279 950 to the miner.

As noted above, it is often difficult to take short positions in physical commodities. The role of the lease market is to create the possibility of shorting gold. Borrowing gold creates a 'temporary long' for the hedger, an obligation to divest himself of gold 6 months hence, which can be used to construct the synthetic short forward needed to offset the customer business.

Futures

Futures are similar to forwards in all except two important and related respects. First, futures trade on organized commodity exchanges. Forwards, in contrast, trade

over-the-counter, that is, as simple bilateral transactions, conducted as a rule by telephone, without posted prices. Second, a forward contract involves only one cash flow, at the maturity of the contract, while futures contracts generally require interim cash flows prior to maturity.

The most important consequence of the restriction of futures contracts to organized exchanges is the radical reduction of credit risk by introducing a **clearinghouse** as the counterparty to each contract. The clearinghouse, composed of exchange members, becomes the counterparty to each contract and provides a guarantee of performance: in practice, default on exchange-traded futures and options is exceedingly rare. Over-the-counter contracts are between two individual counterparties and have as much or as little credit risk as those counterparties.

Clearinghouses bring other advantages as well, such as consolidating payment and delivery obligations of participants with positions in many different contracts. In order to preserve these advantages, exchanges offer only a limited number of contract types and maturities. For example, contracts expire on fixed dates that may or may not coincide precisely with the needs of participants. While there is much standardization in over-the-counter markets, it is possible in principle to enter into obligations with any maturity date. It is always possible to unwind a futures position via an offsetting transaction, while over-the-counter contracts can be offset at a reasonable price only if there is a liquid market in the offsetting transaction. Settlement of futures contracts may be by net cash amounts or by delivery of the underlying.

In order to guarantee performance while limiting risk to exchange members, the clearinghouse requires performance bond from each counterparty. At the initiation of a contract, both counterparties put up **initial** or **original margin** to cover potential default losses. Both parties put up margin because at the time a contract is initiated, it is not known whether the terminal spot price will favor the long or the short. Each day, at that day's closing price, one counterparty will have gained and the other will have lost a precisely offsetting amount. The loser for that day is obliged to increase his margin account and the gainer is permitted to reduce his margin account by an amount, called **variation margin**, determined by the exchange on the basis of the change in the futures price. Both counterparties earn a short-term rate of interest on their margin accounts.

Margining introduces an importance difference between the structure of futures and forwards. If the contract declines in value, the long will be putting larger and larger amounts into an account that earns essentially the overnight rate, while the short will progressively reduce his money market position. Thus the value of the futures, in contrast to that of a forward, will depend not only on the expected future price of the underlying asset, but also on expected future short-term interest rates and on their correlation with future prices of the underlying asset. The price of a futures contract may therefore be higher or lower than the price of a congruent forward contract. In practice, however, the differences are very small.

Futures prices are expressed in currency units, with a minimum price movement called a **tick size**. In other words, futures prices cannot be any positive number, but must be rounded off to the nearest tick. For example, the underlying for the Eurodollar futures contract on the Chicago Mercantile Exchange (CME) is a three-month USD 1 000 000 deposit at Libor. Prices are expressed as 100 minus the Libor rate at futures contract expiry, so a price of 95.00 corresponds to a terminal Libor rate of 5%. The tick size is one basis point (0.01). The value of one tick is the increment in simple interest resulting from a rise of one basis point: USD $1\,000\,000 \cdot 0.0001 \cdot \frac{90}{360} = 25$. Another example is the Chicago Board of Trade (CBOT) US Treasury bond futures contract. The underlying is a T-bond with a face value of USD 100 000 and a minimum remaining maturity of 15 years. Prices are in percent of par, and the tick size is $\frac{1}{32}$ of a percentage point of par.

The difference between a futures price and the cash price of the commodity is called the **basis** and **basis risk** is the risk that the basis will change unpredictably. The qualification 'unpredictably' is important: futures and cash prices converge as the expiry date nears, so part of the change in basis is predictable. For market participants using futures to manage exposures in the cash markets, basis risk is the risk that their hedges will offset only a smaller part of losses in the underlying asset.

At expiration, counterparties with a short position are obliged to make **delivery** to the exchange, while the exchange is obliged to make delivery to the longs. The **deliverable** commodities, that is, the assets which the short can deliver to the long to settle the futures contract, are carefully defined. **Squeezes** occur when a large part of the supply of a deliverable commodity is concentrated in a few hands. The shorts can then be forced to pay a high price for the deliverable in order to avoid defaulting on the futures contract.

In most futures markets, a futures contract will be **cash settled** by having the short or long make a cash payment based on the difference between the futures price at which the contract was initiated and the cash price at expiry. In practice, margining will have seen to it that the contract is already largely cash settled by the expiration date, so only a relatively small cash payment must be made on the expiration date itself.

The CBOT bond futures contract has a number of complicating features that make it difficult to understand and have provided opportunities for a generation of traders:

- In order to make many different bonds deliverable and thus avoid squeezes, the contract permits a large class of long-term US Treasury bonds to be delivered into the futures. To make these bonds at least remotely equally attractive to deliver, the exchange establishes **conversion factors** for each deliverable bond and each futures contract. The futures settlement is then based on the **invoice price**, which is equal to the futures price times the conversion factor of the bond being delivered (plus accrued interest, if any, attached to the delivered bond).
- Invoice prices can be calculated prior to expiry using current futures prices. On any trading day, the cash flows generated by buying a deliverable bond in the cash market, selling a futures contract and delivering the purchased bond into the contract can be calculated. This set of transactions is called a **long basis** position. Of course, delivery will not be made until contract maturity, but the bond that maximizes the return on a long basis position, called the **implied repo rate**, given today's futures and bond prices, is called the **cheapest-to-deliver**.
- Additional complications arise from the T-bond contract's delivery schedule. A short can deliver throughout the contract's expiry month, even though the contract does not expire until the third week of the month. Delivery is a three-day procedure: the short first declares to the exchange her intent to deliver, specifies on the next day which bond she will deliver, and actually delivers the bond on the next day.

Forward interest rates and swaps

Term structure of interest rates

The term structure of interest rates is determined in part by expectations of future short-term interest rates, exchange rates, inflation, and the real economy, and therefore provides information on these expectations. Unfortunately, most of the term structure of interest rates is unobservable, in contrast to prices of most assets, such as spot exchange rates or stock-index futures, prices of which are directly observable. The term structure is difficult to describe because fixed-income investments differ widely in the structure of their cash flows. Any one issuer will have debt outstanding for only a relative handful of maturities. Also, most bonds with original maturities longer than a year or two are coupon bonds, so their yields are affected not only by the underlying term structure of interest rates, but by the accident of coupon size.

Spot and forward interest rates

To compensate for these gaps and distortions, one can try to build a standard representation of the term structure using observable interest rates. This is typically done in terms of prices and interest rates of **discount bonds**, fixed-income investments with only one payment at maturity, and **spot** or **zero coupon interest rates**, or interest rates on notional discount bonds of different maturities. The spot interest rate is the constant annual rate at which a fixed-income investment's value must grow starting at time to reach $1 at a future. The **spot** or **zero coupon curve** is a function relating spot interest rates to the time to maturity. Most of the zero-coupon curve cannot be observed directly, with two major exceptions: bank deposit rates and short-term government bonds, which are generally discount paper.

A **forward interest** rate is an interest rate contracted today to be paid from one future date called the **settlement date** to a still later future date called the maturity date. The **forward curve** relates forward rates of a given time to maturity to the time to settlement. There is thus a distinct forward curve for each time to maturity. For example, the 3-month forward curve is the curve relating the rates on forward 3-month deposits to the future date on which the deposits settle. Any forward rate can be derived from a set of spot rates via arbitrage arguments by identifying the set of deposits or discount bonds which will lock in a rate prevailing from one future date to another, without any current cash outlay.

Forward rate agreements

Forward rate agreements (FRAs) are forwards on time deposits. In a FRA, one party agrees to pay a specific interest rate on a Eurodeposit of a specified currency, maturity, and amount, beginning at a specified date in the future. FRA prices are defined as the spot rate the buyer agrees to pay on a notional deposit of a given maturity on a given settlement date. Usually, the reference rate is Libor. For example, a 3 × 6 (spoken '3 by 6') Japanese yen FRA on ¥ 100 000 000 can be thought of as a commitment by one counterparty to pay another the difference between the contracted FRA rate and the realized level of the reference rate on a ¥ 100 000 000 deposit.

Suppose the three-month and six-month Swiss franc Libor rates are respectively

3.55% and 3.45%. Say Bank A takes the long side and Bank B takes the short side of a DM 10 000 000 3 × 6 FRA on 1 January at a rate of 3.30%, and suppose three-month DM Libor is 3.50%. If the FRA were settled by delivery, Bank A would place a three-month deposit with Bank B at a rate of 3.30%. It could then close out its position by taking a deposit at the going rate of 3.50%, gaining $0.002 \times \frac{90}{360} \times 10\,000\,000 = 5000$ marks when the deposits mature on 1 June.

FRAs are generally cash-settled by the difference between the amount the notional deposit would earn at the FRA rate and the amount it would earn at the realized Libor or other reference rate, discounted back to the settlement date. The FRA is cash-settled by Bank B paying Bank A the present value of DM 5000 on 1 March. With a discount factor of $1.045 \times \frac{90}{360} = 1.01125$, that comes to DM 4944.38.

Swaps and forward swaps

A **plain vanilla interest rate swap** is an agreement between two counterparties to exchange a stream of fixed interest rate payments for a stream of floating interest rate payments. Both streams are denominated in the same currency and are based on a notional principal amount. The notional principal is not exchanged. The design of a swap has three features that determine its price: the maturity of the swap, the maturity of the floating rate, and the frequency of payments. We will assume for expository purposes that the latter two features coincide, e.g. if the swap design is fixed against six-month Libor, then payments are exchanged semiannually.

At initiation, the price of a plain-vanilla swap is set so its current value – the net value of the two interest payment streams, fixed and floating – is zero. The swap can be seen as a portfolio which, from the point of view of the payer of fixed interest (called the 'payer' in market parlance) is long a fixed-rate bond and short a floating-rate bond, both in the amount of the notional principal. The payer of floating-rate interest (called the 'receiver' in market parlance) is long the floater and short the fixed-rate bond.

The price of a swap is usually quoted as the **swap rate**, that is, as the yield to maturity on a notional par bond. What determines this rate? A floating-rate bond always trades at par at the time it is issued. The fixed-rate bond, which represents the payer's commitment in the swap, must then also trade at par if the swap is to have an initial value of zero. In other words, the swap rate is the market-adjusted yield to maturity on a par bond.

Swap rates are also often quoted as a spread over the government bond with a maturity closest to that of the swap. This spread, called the swap-Treasury spread, is almost invariably positive, but varies widely in response to factors such as liquidity and risk appetites in the fixed-income markets.

A **forward swap** is an agreement between two counterparties to commence a swap at some future settlement date. As in the case of a cash swap, the forward swap rate is the market-adjusted par rate on a coupon bond issued at the settlement date. The rate on a forward swap can be calculated from forward rates or spot rates.

The expectations hypothesis of the term structure

In fixed-income markets, the efficient markets hypothesis is called the **expectations hypothesis** of the term structure. As is the case for efficient markets models of other asset prices, the expectations hypothesis can be readily formulated in terms of the forward interest rate, the price at which a future interest rate exposure can be locked in. Forward interest rates are often interpreted as a forecast of the future spot interest rate. Equivalently, the term premium or the slope of the term structure – the spread of a long-term rate over a short-term rate – can be interpreted as a forecast of changes in future short-term rates. The interpretation of forward rates as forecasts implies that an increase in the spread between long- and short-term rates predicts a rise in both short- and long-term rates.

The forecasting performance of forward rates with respect to short-term rates has generally been better than that for long-term rates. Central banks in industrialized countries generally adopt a short-term interest rate as an intermediate target, but they also attempt to reduce short-term fluctuations in interest rates. Rather than immediately raising or lowering interest rates quickly by a large amount to adjust them to changes in economic conditions, they change them in small increments over a long period of time. This practice, called interest rate smoothing, results in protracted periods in which the direction and likelihood, but not the precise timing, of the next change in the target interest rate can be guessed with some accuracy, reducing the error in market predictions of short-term rates generally.

Central banks' interest rate smoothing improves the forecasting power of short-term interest rate futures and forwards at short forecasting horizons. This is in contrast to forwards on foreign exchange, which tend to predict better at long horizons. At longer horizons, the ability of forward interest rates to predict future short-term deteriorates. Forward rates have less ability to predict turning points in central banks' monetary stance than to predict the direction of the next move in an already established stance.

Option basics

Option terminology

A **call option** is a contract giving the owner the right, but not the obligation, to purchase, at expiration, an amount of an asset at a specified price called the **strike** or **exercise price**. A **put option** is a contract giving the owner the right, but not the obligation, to sell, at expiration, an amount of an asset at the exercise price. The amount of the underlying asset is called the **notional principal** or **underlying amount**. The price of the option contract is called the **option premium**.

The issuer of the option contract is called the **writer** and is said to have the **short** position. The owner of the option is said to be **long**. Figure 1.5 illustrates the payoff profile at maturity of a long position in a European call on one pound sterling against the dollar with an exercise price of USD 1.60.

There are thus several ways to be long an asset:

- long the spot asset
- long a forward on the asset
- long a call on the asset
- short a put on the asset

There are many types of options. A **European option** can be exercised only at expiration. An **American option** can be exercised at any time between initiation of the contract and expiration.

A **standard** or **plain vanilla option** has no additional contractual features. An

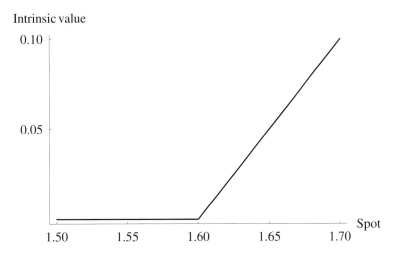

Figure 1.5   Payoff on a European call option.

exotic option has additional features affecting the payoff. Some examples of exotics are

- **Barrier options**, in which the option contract is initiated or cancelled if the asset's cash price reaches a specified level.
- **Average rate options**, for which the option payoff is based on the average spot price over the duration of the option contract rather than spot price at the time of exercise.
- **Binary options**, which have a lump sum option payoff if the spot price is above (call) or below (put) the exercise price at maturity.

Currency options have an added twist: a domestic currency put is also a foreign currency put. For example, if I give you the right to buy one pound sterling for USD 1.60 in three months, I also give you the right to sell USD 1.60 at £0.625 per dollar.

Intrinsic value, moneyness and exercise

The **intrinsic value** of a call option is the larger of the exercise price minus the current asset price or zero. The intrinsic value of a put is the larger of the current asset price minus the exercise or zero. Denoting the exercise price by X, the intrinsic value of a call is $S_t - X$ and that of a put is $X - S_t$.

Intrinsic value can also be thought of as the value of an option if it were expiring or exercised today. By definition, intrinsic value is always greater than or equal to zero. For this reason, the owner of an option is said to enjoy limited liability, meaning that the worst-case outcome for the owner of the option is to throw it away valueless and unexercised.

The intrinsic value of an option is often described by its **moneyness**:

- If intrinsic value is positive, the option is said to be **in-the-money**.
- If the exchange rate is below the exchange rate, a call option is said to be **out-of-the-money**.
- If the intrinsic value is zero, the option is said to be **at-the-money**.

If intrinsic value is positive at maturity, the owner of the option will **exercise** it, that is, call the underlying away from the writer. Figure 1.6 illustrates these definitions for a European sterling call with an exercise price of USD 1.60.

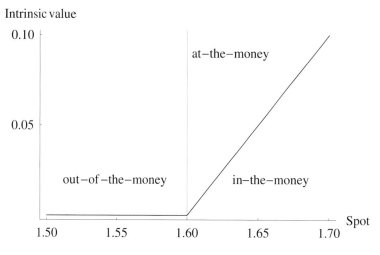

Figure 1.6   Moneyness.

Owning a call option or selling a put option on an asset is like being long the asset. Owning a deep in-the-money call option on the dollar is like being long an amount of the asset that is close to the notional underlying value of the option. Owning a deep out-of-the-money call option on the dollar is like being long an amount of the asset that is much smaller than the notional underlying value of the option.

Valuation basics

Distribution- and preference-free restrictions on plain-vanilla option prices

Options have an asymmetric payoff profile at maturity: a change in the exchange rate at expiration may or may not translate into an equal change in option value. The difficulty in valuing options and managing option risks arises from the asymmetry in the option payoff. Options have an asymmetric payoff profile at maturity: a change in the exchange rate at expiration may or may not translate into an equal change in option value. In contrast, the payoff on a forward increases one-for-one with the exchange rate.

In this section, we study some of the many true statements about option prices that do not depend on a model. These facts, sometimes called distribution- and preference-free restrictions on option prices, meaning that they don't depend on assumptions about the probability distribution of the exchange rate or about market participants' positions or risk appetites. They are also called arbitrage restrictions to signal the reliance of these propositions on no-arbitrage arguments.

Here is one of the simplest examples of such a proposition:

- **No plain vanilla option European or American put or call, can have a negative value**: Of course not: the owner enjoys limited liability.

Another pair of 'obvious' restrictions is:

- **A plain vanilla European or American call option cannot be worth more than the current cash price of the asset**. The exercise price can be no lower than zero, so the benefit of exercising can be no greater than the cash price.
- **A plain vanilla European or American put option cannot be worth more than the exercise price**. The cash price can be no lower than zero, so the benefit of exercising can be no greater than the exercise price.

Buying a deep out-of-the-money call is often likened to buying a lottery ticket. The call has a potentially unlimited payoff if the asset appreciates significantly. On the other hand, the call is cheap, so if the asset fails to appreciate significantly, the loss is relatively small. This helps us to understand the strategy of a famous investor who in mid-1995 bought deep out-of-the-money calls on a large dollar amount against the Japanese yen (yen puts) at very low cost and with very little price risk. The dollar subsequently appreciated sharply against the yen, so the option position was then equivalent to having a long cash position in nearly the full notional underlying amount of dollars.

The following restrictions pertain to sets of options which are identical in every respect – time to maturity, underlying currency pair, European or American style – except their exercise prices:

- **A plain-vanilla European or American call option must be worth more than a similar option with a lower exercise price**.
- **A plain-vanilla European or American put option must be worth more than a similar option with a higher exercise price**.

We will state a less obvious, but very important, restriction:

- **A plain-vanilla European put or call option is a convex function of the exercise price**.

To understand this restriction, think about two European calls with different exercise prices. Now introduce a third call option with an exercise price midway between the exercise prices of the first two calls. The market value of this third option cannot be greater than the average value of the first two.

Current value of an option

Prior to expiration, an option is usually worth at least its intrinsic value. As an example, consider an at-the-money option. Assume a 50% probability the exchange rate rises USD 0.01 and a 50% probability that the rate falls USD 0.01 by the expiration date. The expected value of changes in the exchange rate is $0.5 \cdot 0.01 + 0.5 \cdot (-1.01) = 0$. The expected value of changes in the option's value is $0.5 \cdot 0.01 + 0.5 \cdot 0 = -0.005$. Because of the asymmetry of option payoff, only the possibility of a rising rate affects a call option's value.

Analogous arguments hold for in- and out-of-the-money options. 'But suppose the call is in-the-money. Wouldn't you rather have the underlying, since the option might go back out-of-the-money? And shouldn't the option then be worth less than its intrinsic value?' The answer is, 'almost never'. To be precise:

- **A European call must be worth at least as much as the present value of the forward price minus the exercise price**.

This restriction states that no matter how high or low the underlying price is, an option is always worth at least its 'intrinsic present value'.

We can express this restriction algebraically. Denote by $C(X, t, T)$ the current (time t) market value of a European call with an exercise price X, expiring at time T. The proposition states that $C(X, t, T) \geqslant [1 + r_{t,T}(T - t)]^{-1}(F_{t,T} - X)$. In other words, the call must be worth at least its discounted 'forward intrinsic value'.

Let us prove this using a no-arbitrage argument. A no-arbitrage argument is based on the impossibility of a set of contracts that involve no cash outlay now and give you the possibility of a positive cash flow later with no possibility of a negative cash flow later. The set of contracts is

- Buy a European call on one dollar at a cost of $C(X, t, T)$.
- Finance the call purchase by borrowing.
- Sell one dollar forward at a rate $F_{t,T}$.

The option, the loan, and the forward all have the same maturity. The net cash flow now is zero. At expiry of the loan, option and forward, you have to repay $[1 + r_{t,T}(T - t)]C(X, t, T)$, the borrowed option price with interest. You deliver one dollar and receive $F_{t,T}$ to settle the forward contract. There are now two cases to examine:

Case (i): If the option expires in-the-money ($S_T > X$), exercise it to get the dollar to deliver into the forward contract. The dollar then costs K and your net proceeds from settling all the contracts at maturity are $F_{t,T} - X - [1 + r_{t,T}(T - t)]C(K, t, T)$.

Case (ii): If the option expires out-of-the-money ($S_T \leqslant X$), buy a dollar at the spot rate S_T to deliver into the forward contract. The dollar then costs S_T and your net proceeds from settling all the contracts at maturity is $F_{t,T} - S_T - [1 + r_{t,T}(T - t)]C(X, t, T)$.

For arbitrage to be impossible, these net proceeds must be non-positive, regardless of the value of S_T.

Case (i): If the option expires in-the-money, the impossibility of arbitrage implies $F_{t,T} - X - [1 + r_{t,T}(T - t)]C(X, t, T) \leqslant 0$.

Case (ii): If the option expires out-of-the-money, the impossibility of arbitrage implies $F_{t,T} - S_T - [1 + r_{t,T}(T - t)]C(X, t, T) \leqslant 0$,
which in turn implies $F_{t,T} - X - [1 + r_{t,T}(T - t)]C(X, t, T) \leqslant 0$.

This proves the restriction.

Time value

Time value is defined as the option value minus intrinsic value and is rarely negative, since option value is usually greater than intrinsic value. Time value is greatest for at-the-money-options and declines at a declining rate as the option goes in- or out-of-the-money.

The following restriction pertains to sets of American options which are identical in every respect – exercise prices, underlying asset – except their times to maturity.

- **A plain-vanilla American call or put option must be worth more than a similar option with a shorter time to maturity.**

This restriction does not necessarily hold for European options, but usually does.

Put-call parity

Calls can be combined with forwards or with positions in the underlying asset and the money market to construct synthetic puts *with the same exercise price* (and vice versa). In the special case of European at-the-money forward options:

- **The value of an at-the-money forward European call is equal to the value of an at-the-money forward European put.**

The reason is that, at maturity, the forward payoff equals the call payoff minus the put payoff. In other words, you can create a synthetic long forward by going long one ATM forward call and short one ATM forward put. The construction is illustrated in Figure 1.7.

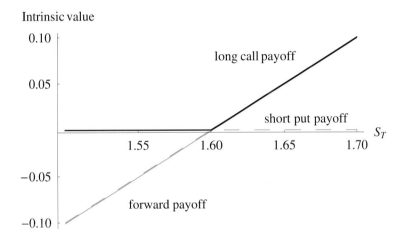

Figure 1.7 Put-call parity.

Option markets

Exchange-traded and over-the-counter options

Options are traded both on organized exchanges and over-the-counter. The two modes of trading are quite different and lead to important differences in market conventions. The over-the-counter currency and interest rate option markets have become much more liquid in recent years. Many option market participants prefer the over-the-counter markets because of the ease with which option contracts tailored to a particular need can be acquired. The exchanges attract market participants who prefer or are required to minimize the credit risk of derivatives transactions, or who are required to transact in markets with publicly posted prices.

Most money-center commercial banks and many securities firms quote over-the-counter currency, interest rate, equity and commodity option prices to customers. A smaller number participates in the interbank core of over-the-counter option trading, making two-way prices to one another. The Bank for International Settlements (BIS) compiles data on the size and liquidity of the derivatives markets from national surveys of dealers and exchanges. The most recent survey, for 1995, reveals that over-the-counter markets dominate trading in foreign exchange derivatives and a substantial portion of the interest rate, equity, and commodity derivatives markets.

We can summarize the key differences between exchange-traded and over-the-counter option contracts as follows:

- Exchange-traded options have standard contract sizes, while over-the-counter options may have any notional underlying amount.
- Most exchange-traded options are written on futures contracts traded on the same exchange. Their expiration dates do not necessarily coincide with those of the futures contracts, but are generally fixed dates, say, the third Wednesday of the month, so that prices on successive days pertain to options of decreasing maturity. Over-the-counter options, in contrast, may have any maturity date.
- Exchange-traded option contracts have fixed exercise prices. As the spot price changes, such an option contract may switch from out-of-the-money to in-the-money, or become deeper or less deep in- or out-of-the-money. It is rarely exactly at-the-money. Thus prices on succesive days pertain to options with different moneyness.
- Mostly American options are traded on the exchanges, while primarily European options, which are simpler to evaluate, are traded over-the-counter.

Prices of exchange traded options are expressed in currency units. The lumpiness of the tick size is not a major issue with futures prices, but can be quite important for option prices, particularly prices of deep out-of-the-money options with prices close to zero. The price of such an option, if rounded off to the nearest basis point or $\frac{1}{32}$ may be zero, close to half, or close to double its true market value. This in turn can violate no-arbitrage conditions on option prices. For example, if two options with adjacent exercise prices both have the same price, the convexity requirement is violated. It can also lead to absurdly high or low, or even undefined, implied volatilities and greeks.

In spite of their flexibility, there is a good deal of standardization of over-the-counter option contracts, particularly with respect to maturity and exercise prices:

- The typical maturities correspond to those of forwards: overnight, one week, one, two, three, six, and nine months, and one year. Interest rate options tend to have longer maturities, with five- or ten-year common. A fresh option for standard maturities can be purchased daily, so a series of prices on successive days of options of like maturity can be constructed.
- Many over-the-counter options are initiated **at-the-money forward**, meaning their exercise prices are set equal to the current forward rate, or have fixed deltas, so a series of prices on successive days of options of like moneyness can be constructed.

Fixed income options

The prices, payoffs, and exercise prices of interest rate options can be expressed in terms of bond prices or interest rates, and the convention differs for different instruments. The terms and conditions of all exchange-traded interest rate options and some over-the-counter interest rate options are expressed as prices rather than rates. The terms and conditions of certain types of over-the-counter interest rate options are expressed as rates. A call expressed in terms of interest rates is identical to a put expressed in terms of prices.

Caplets and **floorlets** are over-the-counter calls and puts on interbank deposit rates. The exercise price, called the **cap rate** or **floor rate**, is expressed as an interest rates rather than a security price. The payoff is thus a number of basis points rather than a currency amount.

- In the case of a caplet, the payoff is equal to the cap rate minus the prevailing rate on the maturity date of the caplet, or zero, which ever is larger. For example, a three-month caplet on six-month US dollar Libor with a cap rate of 5.00% has a payoff of 50 basis points if the six-month Libor rate six months hence ends up at 5.50%, and a payoff of zero if the six-month Libor rate ends up at 4.50%
- In the case of a floorlet, the payoff is equal to the prevailing rate on the maturity date of the cap minus the floor rate, or zero, which ever is larger. For example, a three-month floorlet on six-month US dollar Libor with a floor rate of 5.00% has a payoff of 50 basis points if the six-month Libor rate six months hence ends up at 4.50%, and a payoff of zero if the six-month Libor rate ends up at 5.50%

Figure 1.8 compares the payoffs of caplets and floorlets with that of a FRA.

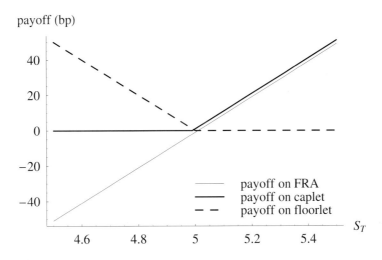

Figure 1.8 FRAs, caps and floors.

A caplet or a floorlet also specifies a notional principal amount. The obligation of the writer to the option owner is equal to the notional principal amount times the payoff times the term of the underlying interest rate. For example, for a caplet or floorlet on six-month Libor with a payoff of 50 basis points and a notional principal amount of USD 1 000 000, the obligation of the option writer to the owner is $USD\,0.0050 \cdot \frac{1}{2} \cdot 1\,000\,000 = 2500$.

To see the equivalence between a caplet and a put on a bond price, consider a caplet on six-month Libor struck at 5%. This is equivalent to a put option on a six-month zero coupon security with an exercise price of 97.50% of par. Similarly. A floor rate of 5% would be equivalent to a call on a six-month zero coupon security with an exercise price of 97.50.

A contract containing a series of caplets or floorlets with increasing maturities is called a **cap** or **floor**. A **collar** is a combination of a long cap and a short floor. It protects the owner against rising short-term rates at a lower cost than a cap, since the premium is reduced by approximately the value of the short floor, but limits the extent to which he benefits from falling short-term rates.

Swaptions are options on interest rate swaps. The exercise prices of swaptions, like those of caps and floors, are expressed as interest rates. Every swaption obliges the writer to enter into a swap at the initiative of the swaption owner. The owner will exercise the swaption by initiating the swap if the swap rate at the maturity of the swaption is in his favor. A **receiver swaption** gives the owner the right to initiate a swap in which he receives the fixed rate, while a **payer swaption** gives the owner the right to initiate a swap in which he pays the fixed rate.

There are two maturities involved in any fixed-income option, the maturity of the option and the maturity of the underlying instrument. To avoid confusion, traders in the cap, floor and swaption markets will describe, say, a six-month option on a two-year swap as a 'six-month into two year' swaption, since the six-month option is exercised 'into' a two-year swap (if exercised).

There are highly liquid over-the-counter and futures options on actively traded government bond and bond futures of industrialized countries. There are also liquid markets in over-the-counter options on Brady bonds.

Currency options

The exchange-traded currency option markets are concentrated on two US exchanges, the International Monetary Market (IMM) division of the Chicago Mercantile Exchange and the Philadelphia Stock Exchange (PHLX). Options on major currencies such as the German mark, Japanese yen, pound sterling and Swiss franc against the dollar, and on major cross rates such as sterling–mark and mark–yen are traded.

There are liquid over-the-counter markets in a much wider variety of currency pairs and maturities than on the exchanges.

Equity and commodities

There are small but significant markets for over-the-counter equity derivatives, many with option-like features. There are also old and well established, albeit small, markets in options on shares of individual companies.

Similarly, while most commodity options are on futures, there exists a parallel market in over-the-counter options, which are frequently components of highly structured transactions. The over-the-counter gold options market is also quite active and is structured in many ways like the foreign exchange options markets.

Option valuation

Black–Scholes model

In the previous section, we got an idea of the constraints on option prices imposed by ruling out the possibility of arbitrage. For more specific results on option prices, one needs either a market or a model. Options that trade actively are valued in the market; less actively traded options can be valued using a model. The most common option valuation model is the Black–Scholes model.

The language and concepts with which option traders do business are borrowed from the Black–Scholes model. Understanding how option markets work and how market participants' probability beliefs are expressed through option prices therefore requires some acquaintance with the model, even though neither traders nor academics believe in its literal truth. It is easiest to understand how asset prices actually behave, or how the markets believe they behave, through a comparison with this benchmark.

Like any model, the Black–Scholes model rests on assumptions. The most important is about how asset prices move over time: the model assumes that the asset price is a **geometric Brownian motion** or **diffusion** process, meaning that it behaves over time like a random walk with very tiny increments.

The Black–Scholes assumptions imply that a European call option can be replicated with a continuously adjusted trading strategy involving positions in the underlying asset and the risk-free bond. This, in turn, implies that the option can be valued using **risk-neutral valuation**, that is, by taking the mathematical expectation of the option payoff using the risk-neutral probability distribution.

The Black–Scholes model also assumes there are no taxes or transactions costs, and that markets are continuously in session. Together with the assumptions about the underlying asset price's behavior over time, this implies that a portfolio, called the **delta hedge**, containing the underlying asset and the risk-free bond can be constructed and continuously adjusted over time so as to exactly mimic the changes in value of a call option. Because the option can be perfectly and costlessly hedged, it can be priced by risk-neutral pricing, that is, as though the unobservable equilibrium expected return on the asset were equal to the observable forward premium.

These assumptions are collectively called the Black–Scholes model. The model results in formulas for pricing plain-vanilla European options, which we will discuss presently, and in a prescription for risk management, which we will address in more detail below. The formulas for both calls and puts have the same six inputs or arguments:

- The value of a call rises as the *spot price* of the underlying asset price rises (see Figure 1.9). The opposite holds for puts.

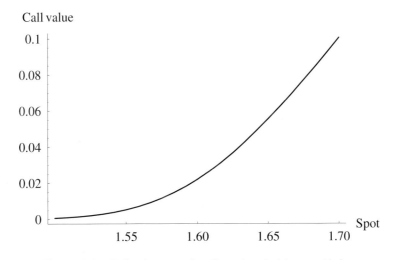

Figure 1.9 Call value as a function of underlying spot price.

- The value of a call falls as the *exercise price* rises (see Figure 1.10). The opposite holds for puts. For calls and puts, the effect of a rise in the exercise price is almost identical to that of a fall in the underlying price.

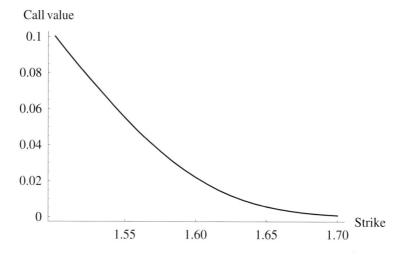

Figure 1.10   Call value as a function of exercise price.

- The value of a call rises as the call's *time to maturity* or *tenor* rises (see Figure 1.11).

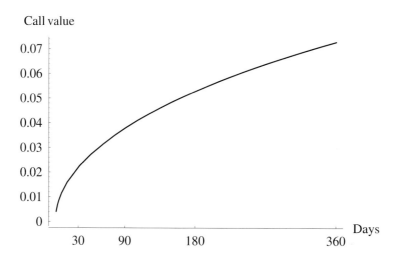

Figure 1.11   Call value as a function of time to maturity.

- Call and put values rise with *volatility*, the degree to which the asset price is expected to wander up or down from where it is now (see Figure 1.12).
- The call value rises with the *domestic interest rate*: since the call is a way to be long the asset, its value must be higher when the money market rate – the opportunity cost of being long the cash asset – rises. The opposite is true for put options, since they are an alternative method of being short an asset (see Figure 1.13).

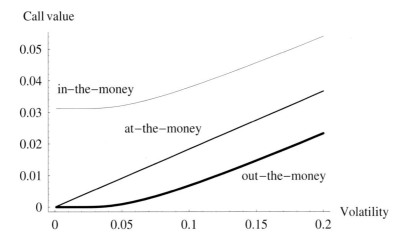

Figure 1.12 Call value as a function of volatility.

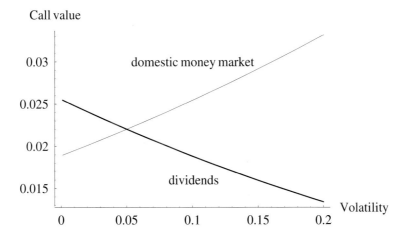

Figure 1.13 Call value as a function of interest and dividend rates.

- The call value falls with the *dividend yield* of the asset, e.g. the coupon rate on a bond, the dividend rate of an equity, or the foreign interest rate in the case of a currency (see Figure 1.13). The reason is that the call owner foregoes this cash income by being long the asset in the form of an option rather than the cash asset. This penalty rises with the dividend yield. The opposite is true for put options.

This summary describes the effect of variations in the inputs taken one at a time, that is, holding the other inputs constant. As the graphs indicate, it is important to keep in mind that there are important 'cross-variation' effects, that is, the effect of, say, a change in volatility when an option is in-the-money may be different from when it is out-of-the-money. Similarly, the effect of a declining time to maturity may be different when the interest rates are high from the effect when rates are low.

As a rough approximation, we can take the Black–Scholes formula as a reasonable approximation to the market prices of plain vanilla options. In other words, while we have undertaken to describe how the formula values change in response to the formula inputs, we have also sketched how market prices of options vary with changes in maturity and market conditions.

Implied volatility

Volatility is one of the six variables in the Black–Scholes option pricing formulas, but it is the only one which is not part of the contract or an observable market price. **Implied volatility** is the number obtained by solving one of the Black–Scholes formulas for the volatility, given the numerical values of the other variables. Let us look at implied volatility purely as a number for a moment, without worrying about its meaning.

Denote the Black–Scholes formula for the value of a call by $v(S_t, t, X, T, \sigma, r, r^*)$. Implied volatility is found from the equation $C(X, t, T) = v(S_t, t, X, T, \sigma, r, r^*)$, which sets the observed market price of an option on the left-hand side equal to the Black–Scholes value on the right-hand side. To calculate, one must find the 'root' σ of this equation. This is relatively straightforward in a spreadsheet program and there is a great deal of commercial software that performs this as well as other option-related calculations. Figure 1.14 shows that except for deep in- or out-of-the-money options with very low volatility, the Black–Scholes value of an option is strictly increasing in implied volatility.

There are several other types of volatility:

- **Historical volatility** is a measure of the standard deviation of changes in an asset price over some period in the past. Typically, it is the standard deviation of daily percent changes in the asset price over several months or years. Occasionally, historical volatility is calculated over very short intervals in the very recent past: the standard deviation of minute-to-minute or second-to-second changes over the course of a trading day is called **intraday volatility**.
- **Expected volatility**: an estimate or guess at the standard deviation of daily percent changes in the asset price for, say, the next year. Implied volatility is often interpreted as the market's expected volatility.

The interpretation of volatility is based on the Black–Scholes model assumption that the asset price follows a random walk. If the model holds true precisely, then implied volatility is the market's expected volatility over the life of the option from which it is calculated. If the model does not hold true precisely then implied volatility is closely related to expected volatility, but may differ from it somewhat.

Volatility, whether implied or historical, has several time dimensions that can be a source of confusion:

- Standard deviations of percent changes *over what time intervals*? Usually, close-over-close daily percent changes are squared and averaged to calculate the standard deviation, but minute-to-minute changes can also be used, for example, in measuring intraday volatility.
- Percent changes averaged *during what period*? This varies: it can be the past day, month, year or week.
- Volatility *at what per-period rate*? The units of both historical and implied volatility are generally percent per year. In risk management volatility may be scaled to the

one-day or ten-day horizon of a value-at-risk calculation. To convert an annual volatility to a volatility per some shorter period – a month or a day – multiply by the square root of the fraction of a year involved. This is called the **square-root-of-time rule**.

Price volatility and yield volatility

In fixed-income option markets, prices are often expressed as **yield volatilities** rather than the price volatilities on which we have focused. The choice between yield volatility and price volatility corresponds to the choice of considering the option as written on an interest rate or on a bond price.

By assuming that the interest rate the option is written on behaves as a random walk, the Black–Scholes model assumption, the Black–Scholes formulas can be applied with interest rates substituted for bond prices. The yield volatility of a fixed-income option, like the price volatility, is thus a Black–Scholes implied volatility. As is the case for other options quoted in volatility term, this practice does not imply that dealers believe in the Black–Scholes model. It means only that they find it convenient to use the formula to express prices.

There is a useful approximation that relates yield and price volatilities:

$$\text{Yield volatility} \cong \frac{\text{Price volatility}}{\text{Duration} \times \text{yield}}$$

To use the approximation, the yield must be expressed as a decimal. Note that when yields are low, yield volatility tends to be higher.

Option risk management

Option sensitivities and risks

Option sensitivities (also known as the 'greeks') describe how option values change when the variables and parameters change. We looked at this subject in discussing the variables that go into the Black–Scholes model. Now, we will discuss their application to option risk management.

We will begin by defining the key sensitivities, and then describe how they are employed in option risk management practice:

- **Delta** is the sensitivity of option value to changes in the underlying asset price.
- **Gamma** is the sensitivity of the option delta to changes in the underlying asset price.
- **Vega** is the sensitivity of the option delta to changes in the implied volatility of the underlying asset price.
- **Theta** is the sensitivity of the option delta to the declining maturity of the option as time passes.

Formally, all the option sensitivities can be described as mathematical partial derivatives with respect to the factors that determine option values. Thus, delta is the first derivative of the option's market price or fair value with respect to the price of the underlying, gamma is the second derivative with respect to the underlying price, vega is the derivative with respect to implied volatility, etc. The sensitivities are defined as partial derivatives, so each one assumes that the other factors are held constant.

Delta

Delta is important for two main reasons. First, delta is a widely used measure of the exposure of an option position to the underlying. Option dealers are guided by delta in determining option hedges. Second, delta is a widely used measure of the degree to which an option is in- or out-of-the-money.

The option delta is expressed in percent or as a decimal. Market parlance drops the word 'percent', and drops the minus sign on the put delta: a '25-delta put' is a put with a delta of -0.25 or minus 25%.

Delta is the part of a move in the underlying price that shows up in the price or value of the option. When a call option is deep in-the-money, its value increases almost one-for-one with the underlying asset price, so delta is close to unity. When a call option is deep out-of-the-money, its value is virtually unchanged when the underlying asset price changes, so delta is close to zero. Figure 1.14 illustrates the relationship between the call delta and the rate of change of the option value with respect to the underlying asset price.

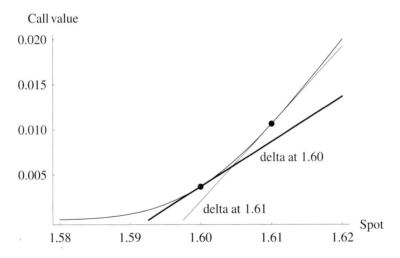

Figure 1.14   Delta as the slope of the call function.

The reader may find a summary of the technical properties of delta useful for reference. (Figure 1.15 displays the delta for a typical call option):

- The call option delta must be greater than 0 and less than or equal to the present value of one currency unit (slightly less than 1). For example, if the discount or risk-free rate is 5%, then the delta of a three-month call cannot exceed 1.0125^{-1} ($e^{-0.0125}$, to be exact).
- Similarly, the put option delta must be less than 0 and greater or equal to the negative of the present value of one currency unit. For example, if the discount or risk-free rate is 5%, then the delta of a three-month call cannot be less than -1.0125^{-1}.
- The put delta is equal to the call delta minus the present value of one currency unit.

- Put-call parity implies that puts and calls with the same exercise price must have identical implied volatilities. For example, the volatility of a 25-delta put equals the volatility of a 75-delta call.

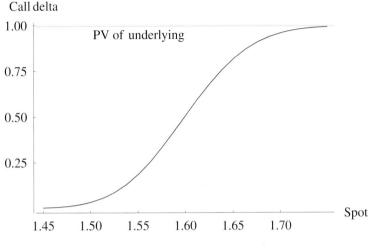

Figure 1.15 Call delta.

Gamma

Formally, gamma is the second partial derivative of the option price with respect to the underlying price. The units in which gamma is expressed depend on the units of the underlying. If the underlying is expressed in small units (Nikkei average), gamma will be a larger number. If the underlying is expressed in larger units (dollar–mark), gamma will be a smaller number.

Gamma is typically greatest for at-the-money options and for options that are close to expiry. Figure 1.16 displays the gamma for a typical call option.

Gamma is important because it is a guide to how readily delta will change if there is a small change in the underlying price. This tells dealers how susceptible their positions are to becoming unhedged if there is even a small change in the underlying price.

Vega

Vega is the exposure of an option position to changes in the implied volatility of the option. Formally, it is defined as the partial derivative of the option value with respect to the implied volatility of the option. Vega is measured in dollars or other base currency units. The change in implied volatility is measured in vols (one vol = 0.01). Figure 1.17 displays the vega of a typical European call option.

Implied volatility is a measure of the general level of option prices. As the name suggests, an implied volatility is linked to a particular option valuation model. In the context of the valuation model on which it is based, an implied volatility has an interpretation as the market-adjusted or risk neutral estimate of the standard deviation of returns on the underlying asset over the life of the option. The most common option valuation model is the Black–Scholes model. This model is now

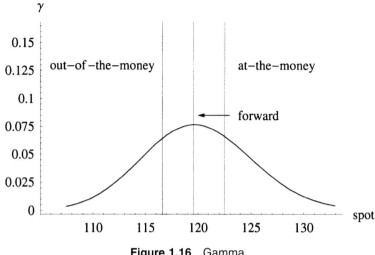

Figure 1.16 Gamma.

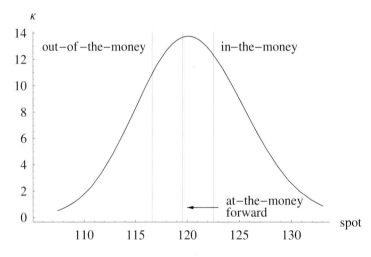

Figure 1.17 Vega.

familiar enough that in some over-the-counter markets, dealers quote prices in terms of the Black–Scholes implied volatility.

Vega risk can be thought of as the 'own' price risk of an option position. Since implied volatility can be used as a measure of option prices and has the interpretation as the market's perceived future volatility of returns, option markets can be viewed as markets for the 'commodity' asset price volatility: Exposures to volatility are traded and volatility price discovery occur in option markets.

Vega risk is unique to portfolios containing options. In her capacity as a pure market maker in options, an option dealer maintains a book, a portfolio of purchased and written options, and delta hedges the book. This leaves the dealer with risks that are unique to options: gamma and vega. The non-linearity of the option payoff with respect to the underlying price generates gamma risk. The sensitivity of the option book to the general price of options generates vega risk.

Because implied volatility is defined only in the context of a particular model, an option pricing model is required to measure vega. Vega is then defined as the partial derivative of the call or put pricing formula with respect to the implied volatility.

Theta

Theta is the exposure of an option position to changes in short-term interest rates, in particular, to the rate at which the option position is financed. Formally, it is defined as the partial derivative of the option value with respect to the interest rate. Like vega, theta is measured in dollars or other base currency units.

Theta, in a sense, is not a risk, since it not random. Rather, it is a cost of holding options and is similar to cost-of-carry in forward and futures markets. However, unlike cost-of-carry, theta is not a constant rate per unit time, but depends on other factors influencing option prices, particularly moneyness and implied volatility.

Delta hedging and gamma risk

Individuals and firms buy or write options in order to hedge or manage a risk to which they are already exposed. The option offsets the risk. The dealers who provide these long and short option positions to end-users take the opposite side of the option contracts and must manage the risks thus generated.

The standard procedure for hedging option risks is called **delta** or **dynamic hedging**. It ordains

- Buying or selling forward an amount of the underlying equal to the option delta when the option is entered into, and
- Adjusting that amount incrementally as the underlying price and other market prices change and the option nears maturity.

A dealer hedging, say, a short call, would run a long forward foreign exchange position consisting of delta units of the underlying currency. As the exchange rate and implied volatility changes and the option nears expiration, the delta changes, so the dealer would adjust the delta hedge incrementally by buying or selling currency.

The motivation for this hedging procedure is the fact that delta, as the first derivative of the option value, is the basis for a linear approximation to the option value in the vicinity of a specific point. For small moves in the exchange rate, the value of the hedge changes in an equal, but opposite, way to changes in the value of the option position.

The delta of the option or of a portfolio of options, multiplied by the underlying amounts of the options, is called the **delta exposure** of the options. A dealer may immediately delta hedge each option bought or sold, or hedge the net exposure of her entire portfolio at the end of the trading session.

In trades between currency dealers, the counterparties may exchange forward foreign exchange in the amount of the delta along with the option and option premium. The option and forward transactions then leave both dealers with no additional delta exposure. This practice is known as **crossing the delta**.

Delta hedging is a linear approximation of changes in the option's value. However, the option's value changes non-linearly with changes in the value of the underlying asset: the option's value is convex. This mismatch between the non-linearity of the option's value and the linearity of the hedge is called **gamma risk**.

If you are *long* a call or put, and you delta hedge the option, then a perturbation of the exchange rate in either direction will result in a gain on the hedged position. This is referred to as **good gamma**.

Good gamma is illustrated in Figure 1.18. The graph displays a long call position and its hedge. The option owner initially delta hedges the sterling call against the dollar at USD 1.60 by buying an amount of US dollars equal to the delta. The payoff on the hedge is the heavy negatively sloped line. If the pound falls one cent, the value of the call falls by an amount equal to line segment $\overline{bc}$, but the value of the hedge rises by $\overline{ab} > \overline{bc}$. If the pound rises one cent, the value of the hedge falls $\overline{ef}$, but the call rises by $\overline{de} > \overline{ef}$. Thus the hedged position gains regardless of whether sterling rises or falls.

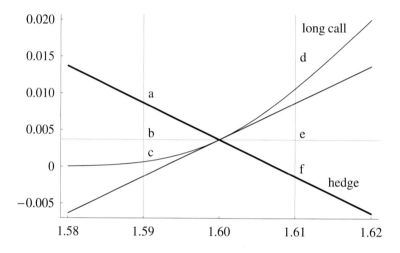

Figure 1.18   Good gamma.

If you are *short* a call or put, and you delta hedge the option, then a perturbation of the exchange rate in either direction will result in a loss on the hedged position. This is referred to as **bad gamma**.

Bad gamma is illustrated in Figure 1.19. The graph displays a short call position and its hedge. The option owner initially delta hedges the sterling call against the dollar at USD 1.60 by selling an amount of US dollars equal to the delta. The payoff on the hedge is the heavy positively sloped line. If the pound falls one cent, the value of the short call position rises by an amount equal to line segment $\overline{ab}$, but the value of the hedge falls by $\overline{bc} > \overline{ad}$. If the pound rises one cent, the value of the hedge rises $\overline{de}$, but the short call rises by $\overline{ef} > \overline{de}$. Thus the hedged position loses regardless of whether sterling rises or falls.

Why not hedge with both delta and gamma? The problem is, if you hedge only with the underlying asset, you cannot get a non-linear payoff on the hedge. To get a 'curvature' payoff, you must use a derivative. In effect, the only way to hedge gamma risk is to lay the option position off.

The volatility smile

The Black–Scholes model implies that all options on the same asset have identical implied volatilities, regardless of time to maturity and moneyness. However, there

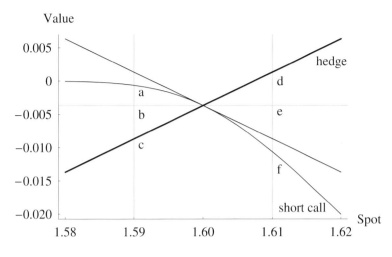

Figure 1.19 Bad gamma.

are systematic 'biases' in the implied volatilities of options on most assets. This is a convenient if somewhat misleading label, since the phenomena in question are biased only from the point of view of the Black–Scholes model, which neither dealers nor academics consider an exact description of reality:

- Implied volatility is not constant but changes constantly.
- Options with the same exercise price but different tenors often have different implied volatilities, giving rise to a **term structure of implied volatility** and indicating that market participants expect the implied volatility of short-dated options to change over time.
- Out-of-the money options often have higher implied volatilities than at-the-money options, indicating that the market perceives asset prices to be **kurtotic**, that is, the likelihood of large moves is greater than is consistent with the lognormal distribution.
- Out-of-the money call options often have implied volatilities which differ from those of equally out-of the money puts, indicating that the market perceives the distribution of asset prices to be **skewed**.

The latter two phenomena are known as the **volatility smile** because of the characteristic shape of the plot of implied volatilities of options of a given tenor against the delta or against the exercise price.

The term structure of implied volatility

A rising term structural volatility indicates that market participants expect short-term implied volatility to rise or that they are willing to pay more for protection against near-term asset price volatility. Figure 1.20 illustrates a plot of the implied volatilities of options on a 10-year US dollar swap (swaptions) with option maturities between one month and 5 years.

Typically, longer-term implied volatilities vary less over time than shorter-term volatilities on the same asset. Also typically, there are only small differences among the historical averages of implied volatilities of different maturities. Longer-term

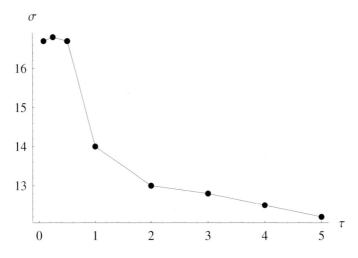

Figure 1.20   Term structure of volatility.

volatilities are therefore usually closer to the historical average of implied volatility than shorter-term implied volatilities.

Shorter-term implied volatilities may be below the longer-term volatilities, giving rise to an upward-sloping term structure, or above the longer-term volatilities, giving rise to a downward-sloping term structure. Downward-sloping term structures typically occur when shocks to the market have abruptly raised volatilities across the term structure. Short-term volatility responds most readily, since shocks are usually expected to abate over the course of a year.

The volatility smile

Option markets contain much information about market perceptions that asset returns are not normal. Earlier we discussed the differences between the actual behavior of asset returns and the random walk hypothesis which underlies the Black–Scholes option pricing model. The relationship between in- or out-of-the money option prices and those of at-the-money options contains a great deal of information about the market perception of the likelihood of large changes, or changes in a particular direction, in the cash price.

The two phenomena of curvature and skewness generally are both present in the volatility smile, as in the case depicted in Figure 1.21. The chart tells us that options which pay off if asset prices fall by a given amount are more highly valued than options which pay off if asset prices rise. That could be due to a strong market view that asset prices are more likely to fall than to rise; it could also be due in part to market participants seeking to protect themselves against losses from falling rates or losses in other markets associated with falling rates. The market is seeking to protect itself particularly against falling rather than rising rates. Also, the market is willing to pay a premium for option protection against large price changes in either direction.

Different asset classes have different characteristic volatility smiles. In some markets, the typical pattern is highly persistent. For example, the negatively sloping smile for S&P 500 futures options illustrated in Figure 1.22 has been a virtually

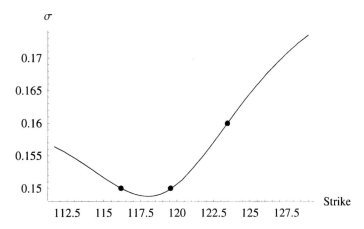

Figure 1.21　Volatility smile in the foreign exchange market.

permanent feature of US equity index options since October 1987, reflecting market eagerness to protect against a sharp decline in US equity prices. In contrast, the volatility smiles of many currency pairs such as dollar–mark have been skewed, depending on market conditions, against either the mark or the dollar.

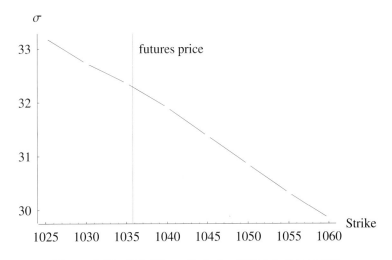

Figure 1.22　Volatility smile in the S&P futures market.

Over-the-counter option market conventions

Implied volatility as a price metric

One of the most important market conventions in the over-the-counter option markets is to express option prices in terms of the Black–Scholes implied volatility. This convention is employed in the over-the-counter markets for options on currencies, gold, caps, floors, and swaptions. The prices of over-the-counter options on bonds are generally expressed in bond price units, that is, percent of par. It is generally used only in price quotations and trades among interbank dealers, rather than trades between dealers and option end-users.

The unit of measure of option prices under this convention, is implied volatility at an annual percent rate. Dealers refer to the units as **vols**. If, for example, a customer inquires about dollar–mark calls, the dealer might reply that 'one-month at-the-money forward dollar calls are 12 at 12.5', meaning that the dealer buys the calls at an implied volatility of 12 vols and sells them at 12.5 vols. It is completely straight-forward to express options in terms of vols, since as Figure 1.12 makes clear, a price in currency units corresponds unambiguously to any price in vols. When a deal is struck between two traders in terms of vols, the appropriate Black–Scholes formula is used to translate into a price in currency units. This requires the counterparties to agree on the remaining market data inputs to the formula, such as the current forward price of the underlying and the money market rate.

Although the Black–Scholes pricing formulas are used to move back and forth between vols and currency units, this does not imply that dealers believe in the Black–Scholes model. The formulas, in this context, are divorced from the model and used only as a metric for price. Option dealers find this convenient because they are in the business of trading volatility, not the underlying. Imagine the dealer maintaining a chalkboard displaying his current price quotations for options with different under-lying assets, maturities and exercise prices. If the option prices are expressed in currency units, than as the prices of the underlying assets fluctuate in the course of the trading day, the dealer will be obliged to constantly revise the option prices. The price fluctuations in the underlying may, however, be transitory and random, related perhaps to the idiosyncrasies of order flow, and have no significance for future volatility. By expressing prices in vols, the dealer avoids the need to respond to these fluctuations.

Delta as a metric for moneyness

The moneyness of an option was defined earlier in terms of the difference between the underlying asset price and the exercise price. Dealers in the currency option markets often rely on a different metric for moneyness, the option delta, which we encountered earlier as an option sensitivity and risk management tool.

As shown in Figure 1.23, the call delta declines monotonically as exercise price rises – and the option goes further out-of-the-money – so dealers can readily find the unique exercise price corresponding to a given delta, and vice versa. The same holds for puts.

Recall that the delta of a put is equal to the delta of a call with the same exercise price, minus the present value of one currency unit (slightly less than one). Often, exercise prices are set to an exchange rate such that delta is equal to a round number like 25% or 75%. A useful consequence of put–call parity (discussed above) is that puts and calls with the same exercise price must have identical implied volatilities. The volatility of a 25-delta put is thus equal to the volatility of a 75-delta call.

Because delta varies as market conditions, including implied volatility, the exercise price corresponding to a given delta and the difference between that exercise price and the current forward rate vary over time. For example, at an implied volatility of 15%, the exercise prices of one-month 25-delta calls and puts are about 3% above and below the current forward price, while at an implied volatility of 5%, they are about 1% above and below.

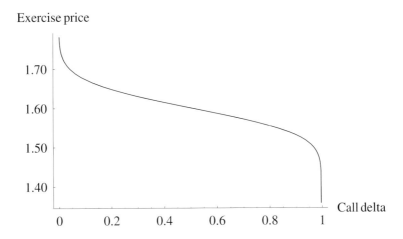

Figure 1.23 Exercise price as a function of delta.

The motivation for this convention is similar to that for using implied volatility: it obviates the need to revise price quotes in response to transitory fluctuations in the underlying asset price. In addition, delta can be taken as an approximation to the market's assessment of the probability that the option will be exercised. In some trading or hedging techniques involving options, the probability of exercise is more relevant than the percent difference between the cash and exercise prices. For example, a trader taking the view that large moves in the asset price are more likely than the market is assessing might go long a 10-delta strangle. He is likely to care only about the market view that there is a 20% chance one of the component options will expire in-the-money, and not about how large a move that is.

Risk reversals and strangles

A **combination** is an option portfolio containing both calls and puts. A **spread** is a portfolio containing only calls or only puts. Most over-the-counter currency option trading is in combinations. The most common in the interbank currency option markets is the **straddle**, a combination of an at-the-money forward call and an at-the-money forward put with the same maturity. Straddles are also quite common in other over-the-counter option markets. Figure 1.24 illustrates the payoff at maturity of a sterling–dollar straddle struck at USD 1.60.

Also common in the interbank currency market are combinations of out-of-the-money options, particularly the **strangle** and the **risk reversal**. These combinations both consist of an out-of-the-money call and out-of-the-money put. The exercise price of the call component is higher than the current forward exchange rate and the exercise price of the put is lower.

In a strangle, the dealer sells or buys both out-of-the-money options from the counterparty. Dealers usually quote strangle prices by stating the implied volatility at which they buy or sell both options. For example, the dealer might quote his selling price as 14.6 vols, meaning that he sells a 25-delta call and a 25-delta put at an implied volatility of 14.6 vols each. If market participants were convinced that exchange rates move as random walks, the out-of-the-money options would have the

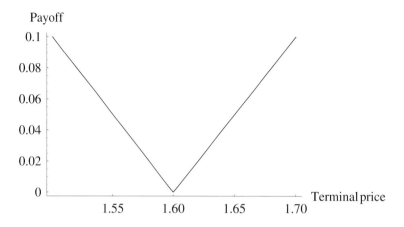

Figure 1.24 Straddle payoff.

same implied volatility as at-the-money options and strangle spreads would be zero. Strangles, then, indicate the degree of curvature of the volatility smile. Figure 1.25 illustrates the payoff at maturity of a 25-delta dollar–mark strangle.

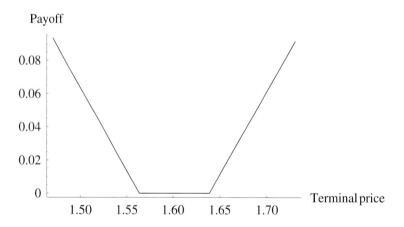

Figure 1.25 Strangle payoff.

In a risk reversal, the dealer exchanges one of the options for the other with the counterparty. Because the put and the call are generally not of equal value, the dealer pays or receives a premium for exchanging the options. This premium is expressed as the difference between the implied volatilities of the put and the call. The dealer quotes the implied volatility differential at which he is prepared to exchange a 25-delta call for a 25-delta put. For example, if dollar–mark is strongly expected to fall (dollar depreciation), an options dealer might quote dollar–mark risk reversals as follows: 'one-month 25-delta risk reversals are 0.8 at 1.2 mark calls over'. This means he stands ready to pay a net premium of 0.8 vols to buy a 25-delta mark call and sell a 25-delta mark put against the dollar, and charges a net premium of 1.2 vols to sell a 25-delta mark call and buy a 25-delta mark put. Figure 1.26 illustrates the payoff at maturity of a 25-delta dollar–mark risk reversal.

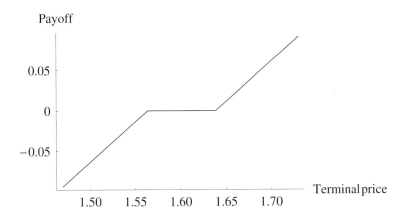

Figure 1.26   Risk reversal payoff.

Risk reversals are commonly used to hedge foreign exchange exposures at low cost. For example, a Japanese exporter might buy a dollar-bearish risk reversal consisting of a long 25-delta dollar put against the yen and short 25-delta dollar call. This would provide protection against a sharp depreciation of the dollar, and provide a limited zone – that between the two exercise prices – within which the position gains from a stronger dollar. However, losses can be incurred if the dollar strengthens sharply.

On average during the 1990s, a market participant desiring to put on such a position has paid the counterparty a net premium, typically amounting to a few tenths of a vol. This might be due to the general tendency for the dollar to weaken against the yen during the floating exchange rate period, or to the persistent US trade deficit with Japan.

2

Measuring volatility

KOSTAS GIANNOPOULOS

Introduction

The objective of this chapter is to examine the ARCH family of volatility models and its use in risk analysis and measurement. An overview of unconditional and conditional volatility models is provided. The former is based on constant volatilities while the latter uses all information available to produce current (or up-do-date) volatility estimates. Unconditional models are based on rigorous assumptions about the distributional properties of security returns while the conditional models are less rigorous and treat unconditional models as a special case. In order to simplify the VaR calculations unconditional models make strong assumptions about the distributional properties of financial time series. However, the convenience of these assumptions is offset by the overwhelming evidence found in the empirical distribution of security returns, e.g. fat tails and volatility clusters. VaR calculations based on assumptions that do not hold, underpredict uncommonly large (but possible) losses.

In this chapter we will argue that one particular type of conditional model (ARCH / GARCH family) provides more accurate measures of risk because it captures the volatility clusters present in the majority of security returns. A comprehensive review of the conditional heteroskedastic models is provided. This is followed by an application of the models for use in risk management. This shows how the use of historical returns of portfolio components and current portfolio weights can generate accurate estimates of current risk for a portfolio of traded securities. Finally, the properties of the GARCH family of models are treated rigorously in the Appendix.

Overview of historical volatility models

Historical volatility is a static measure of variability of security returns around their mean; they do not utilize current information to update their estimate. This implies that the mean, variance and covariance of the series are not allowed to vary over time in response to current information. This is based on the assumption that the returns series is stationary. That is, the series of returns (and, in general, any time series) has constant statistical moments over different periods. If the series is stationary then the historical mean and variance are well defined and there is no conceptual problem in computing them. However, unlike stationary time series, the mean of the sample may become a function of its length when the series is non-stationary. Non-stationarity, as this is referred to, implies that the historical means, variances and covariances estimates of security return are subject to error estimation. While sample variances and covariances can be computed, it is unlikely that it provides any information regarding the true unconditional second moments since the latter are not well defined. The stationarity of the first two moments in security return has been challenged for a long time and this has called into question the historical volatility models. This is highlighted in Figure 2.1 which shows the historical volatility of FTSE-100 Index returns over a 26- and 52-week interval.

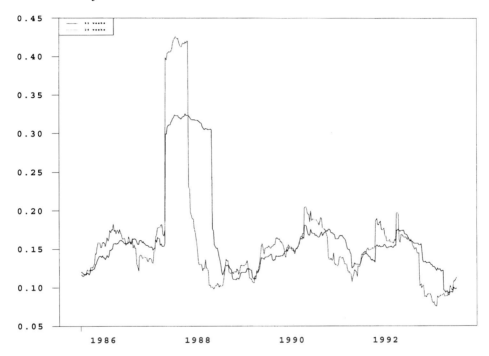

Figure 2.1 Historical volatility of FTSE-100 index.

Figure 2.1 shows that when historical volatilities are computed on overlapping samples and non-equal length time periods, they change over time. This is attributable to the time-varying nature of historical means, variances and covariances caused by sampling error.

Assumptions

VaR is estimated using the expression

$$\text{VaR} = P\sigma_p 2.33\sqrt{t} \qquad (2.1)$$

where $P\sigma_p 2.33$ is Daily-Earnings-at-Risk (DEaR), which describes the magnitude of the daily losses on the portfolio at a probability of 99%; σ_p is the daily volatility (standard deviation) of portfolio returns; t is the number of days, usually ten, over which the VaR is estimated; σ is usually estimated using the historical variance–covariance. In the historical variance–covariance approach, the variances are defined in

$$\sigma_t^2 = \frac{1}{T} \sum_{i=1}^{T} \varepsilon_{t-i}^2 \qquad (2.2)$$

where ε is the residual returns (defined as actual returns minus the mean). On the other hand, the ES approach is expressed as

$$\sigma_t^2 = \lambda \varepsilon_{t-1}^2 + (1 - \lambda) \sum_{i=1}^{\infty} \lambda^i \varepsilon_{t-i}^2 \tag{2.3}$$

where $0 \leqslant \lambda \leqslant 1$ and is defined as the decay factor that attaches different weights over the sample period of past squared residual returns. The ES approach attaches greater weight to more recent observations than observations well in the past. The implication of this is that recent shocks will have a greater impact on current volatility than earlier ones. However, both the variance–covariance and the ES approaches require strong assumptions regarding the distributional properties of security returns.

The above volatility estimates relies on strong assumptions on the distributional properties of security returns, i.e. they are independently and identically distributed (i.i.d. thereafter). The identically distributed assumption ensures that the mean and the variance of returns do not vary across time and conforms to a fixed probability assumption. The independence assumption ensures that speculative price changes are unrelated to each other at any point of time. These two conditions form the basis of the random walk model. Where security returns are i.i.d. and the mean and the variance of the distribution are known, inferences made regarding the potential portfolio losses will be accurate and remain unchanged over a period of time. In these circumstances, calculating portfolio VaR only requires one estimate, the standard deviation of the change in the value of the portfolio. Stationarity in the mean and variance implies that the likelihood of a specified loss will be the same for each day.

Hence, focusing on the distributional properties of security returns is of paramount importance to the measurement of risk. In the next section, we examine whether these assumptions are valid.

The independence assumption

Investigating the validity of the independence assumption has focused on testing for serial correlation in changes in price. The general conclusion reached by past investigations is that successive price changes are autocorrelated, but are too weak to be of economic importance. This observation has led most investigations to accept the random walk hypothesis. However, evidence has shown that a lack of autocorrelation does not imply the acceptance of the independence assumption. Some investigations has found that security returns are governed by non-linear processes that allow successive price changes to be linked through the variance. This phenomenon was observed in the pioneering investigations of the 1960s, where large price movements were followed by large price movements and vice versa. More convincing evidence is provided in later investigations in their more rigorous challenge to the identical and independence assumptions. In the late 1980s much attention was focused on using different time series data ranging from foreign exchange currencies to commodity prices to test the validity of the i.i.d. assumptions. Another development in those investigations is the employment of more sophisticated models such as the conditional heteroskedastic models (i.e. ARCH/GARCH) used to establish the extent to which the i.i.d. assumption is violated. These type of models will be examined below.

The form of the distribution

The assumption of normality aims to simplify the measurement of risk. If security returns are normally distributed with stable moments, then the two parameters, the mean and the variance, are sufficient to describe it. Stability implies that the probability of a specified portfolio loss is the same for each day.

These assumptions, however, are offset by the overwhelming evidence suggesting the contrary which is relevant to measuring risk, namely the existence of fat tails or leptokurtosis in the distribution that exceeds those of the normal. Leptokurtosis in the distribution of security returns was reported as early as the 1950s. This arises where the empirical distribution of daily changes in stock returns have more observations around the means and in the extreme tails than that of a normal distribution. Consequently, the non-normality in the distribution has led some studies to suggest that attaching alternative probability distributions may be more representative of the data and observed leptokurtosis. One such is the Paretian distribution, which has the characteristic exponent. This is a peakness parameter that measures the tail of the distribution. However, the problem with this distribution is that unlike normal distribution, the variance and higher moments are not defined except as a special case of the normal. Another distribution suggested is the Student t-distribution which has fatter tails than that of the normal, assuming that the degrees of freedom are less than unity. While investigations have found that t-distributions adequately describe weekly and monthly data, as the interval length in which the security returns are measured increases, the t-distribution tends to converge to a normal. Other investigations have suggested that security returns follow a mixture of distributions where the distribution is described as a combination of normal distributions that possess different variances and possible different means.

Non-stationarity in the distribution

The empirical evidence does not support the hypothesis of serial dependence (autocorrelation) in security returns. This has caused investigators to focus more directly on non-stationary nature of the two statistical moments, the mean and the variance, which arises when both moments vary over time. Changes in the means and variance of security returns is an alternative explanation to the existence of leptokurtosis in the distribution. Investigations that focus on the non-stationarity in the means have been found to be inconclusive in their findings. However, more concrete evidence is provided when focusing on non-stationarity with respect to the variance. It has been found that it is the conditional dependency in the variance that causes fatter tails in the unconditional distribution that is greater than that of the conditional one. Fatter tails and the non-stationarity in the distribution in the second moments are caused by volatility clustering in the data set. This occurs where rates of return are characterized by very volatile and tranquil periods. If the variances are not stationary then the formula $DEaR\sqrt{t}$ does not hold.[1]

Conditional volatility models

The time-varying nature of the variance may be captured using conditional time series models. Unlike historical volatility models, this class of statistical models make more effective use of the information set available at time t to estimate the means and variances as varying with time. One type of model that has been successful in capturing time-varying variances and covariances is a state space technique such as the Kalman filter. This is a form of time-varying parameter model which bases regression estimates on historical data up to and including the current time period. A useful attribute of this model lies in its ability to describe historical data that is generated from state variables. Hence the usefulness of Kalman filter in constructing volatility forecasts on the basis of historical data. Another type of model is the conditional heteroskedastic models such as the Autoregressive Conditional Heteroskedastic (ARCH) and the generalized ARCH (GARCH). These are designed to remove the systematically changing variance from the data which accounts for much of the leptokurtosis in the distribution of speculative price changes. Essentially, these models allow the distribution of the data to exhibit leptokurtosis and hence are better able to describe the empirical distribution of financial data.

ARCH models: a review

The ARCH(1)

The ARCH model is based on the principal that speculative price changes contain volatility clusters. Suppose that a security's returns Y_t can be modeled as:

$$Y_t = \xi_t \delta + \varepsilon_t \tag{2.4}$$

where ξ_t is a vector of variables with impact on the conditional mean of Y_t, and ε_t is the residual return with zero mean, $E_{t-1}(\varepsilon_t) = 0$, and variance $E_{t-1}(\varepsilon_t^2) = h_t$. The conditional mean are expected returns that changes in response to current information. The square of the residual return, often referred to as the squared error term, ε_t^2, can be modeled as an autoregressive process. It is this that forms the basis of the Autoregressive Conditional Heteroskedastic (ARCH) model. Hence the first-order ARCH can be written:

$$h_t = \omega + \alpha \varepsilon_{t-1}^2 \tag{2.5}$$

where $\omega > 0$ and $\alpha \geqslant 0$, and h_t denotes the time-varying conditional variance of Y_t. This is described as a first-order ARCH process because the squared error term ε_{t-1}^2 is lagged one period back. Thus, the conditional distribution of ε_t is normal but its conditional variance is a linear function of past squared errors.

ARCH models can validate scientifically a key characteristic of time series data that 'large changes tend to be followed by large changes – of either sign – and small changes tend to be followed by small changes'. This is often referred to as the clustering effect and, as discussed earlier, is one of the major explanations behind the violation of the i.i.d. assumptions. The usefulness of ARCH models relates to its ability to deal with this effect by using squared past forecast errors ε_{t-1}^2 to predict future variances. Hence, in the ARCH methodology the variance of Y_t is expressed as a (non-linear) function of past information, it validates earlier concerns about heteroskedastic stock returns and meets a necessary condition for modeling volatility as conditional on past information and as time varying.

Higher-order ARCH

The way in which equations (2.4) and (2.5) can be formulated is very flexible. For example, Y_t can be written as an autoregressive process, e.g. $Y_t = Y_{t-1} + \varepsilon_t$, and/or can include exogenous variables. More important is the way the conditional variance h_t can be expressed. The ARCH order of equation (2.5) can be increased to express today's conditional variance as a linear function of a greater amount of past information. Thus the ARCH(q) can be written as:

$$h_t = \omega + \alpha_1 \varepsilon_{t-1}^2 + \ldots + \alpha_q \varepsilon_{t-q}^2 \qquad (2.6)$$

Such a model specification is generally preferred to a first-order ARCH since now the conditional variance depends on a greater amount of information that goes as far as q periods in the past. With an ARCH(1) model the estimated h_t is highly unstable since single large (small) surprises are allowed to drive h_t to inadmissible extreme values. With the higher-order ARCH of equation (2.6), the memory of the process is spread over a larger number of past observations. As a result, the conditional variance changes more slowly, which seems more plausible.

Problems

As with the ARCH(1), for the variance to be computable, the sum of $\alpha_1, \ldots, \alpha_q$ in equation (2.6) must be less than one. Generally, this is not a problem with financial return series. However, a problem that often arises with the higher-order ARCH is that not every one of the $\alpha_1, \ldots, \alpha_q$ coefficients is positive, even if the conditional variance computed is positive at all times. This fact cannot be easily explained in economic terms, since it implies that a single large residual return could drive the conditional variance negative.

The model in equation (2.6) has an additional disadvantage. The number of parameters increases with the ARCH order and makes the estimation process formidable. One way of attempting to overcome this problem is to express past errors in an *ad hoc* linear declining way. Equation (2.6) can then be written as:

$$h_t = \omega + \alpha \sum w_k \varepsilon_{t-k}^2 \qquad (2.7)$$

where $w_k, k = 1, \ldots, q$ and $\Sigma w_k = 1$ are the constant linearly declining weights. While the conditional variance is expressed as a linear function of past information, this model attaches greater importance to more recent shocks in accounting for the most of the h_t changes. This model was adopted by Engle which has been found to give a good description of the conditional variance in his 1982 study and a later version published in 1983. The restrictions for the variance equation parameters remain as in ARCH(1).

GARCH

An alternative and more flexible lag structure of the ARCH(q) model is provided by the GARCH(p, q), or Generalized ARCH model:

$$h_t = \omega + \sum_{i=1}^{p} \alpha_i \varepsilon_{t-i}^2 + \sum_{j=1}^{q} \beta_j h_{t-j} \qquad (2.8)$$

with $i = 1, \ldots, p$ and $j = 1, \ldots, q$. In equation (2.8) the conditional variance h_t is a function of both past innovations and lagged values conditional variance, i.e.

$h_{t-1}, \ldots, h_{t-p}$. The lagged conditional variance is often referred to as old news because it is defined as

$$h_{t-j} = \omega + \sum_{i=1}^{p} \alpha \varepsilon_{t-i-1}^2 + \sum_{j=1}^{q} \beta_j h_{t-j-1} \qquad (2.9)$$

In other words, if $i, j = 1$, then h_{t-j} in equation (2.8) and formulated in equation (2.9) is explainable by past information and the conditional variance at time $t - 2$ or lagged two periods back. In order for a GARCH(p, q) model to make sense the next condition must be satisfied:

$$1 \geqslant \left(\sum \alpha_i + \sum \beta_j \right) > 0$$

In this situation the GARCH(p, q) corresponds to an infinite-order ARCH process with exponentially decaying weights for longer lags. Researchers have suggested that low-order GARCH(p, q) processes may have properties similar to high-order ARCH but with the advantage that they have significantly fewer parameters to estimate. Empirical evidence also exists that a low-order GARCH model fits as well or even better than a higher-order ARCH model with linearly declining weights. A large number of empirical studies has found that a GARCH(1, 1) is adequate for most financial time series.

GARCH versus exponential smoothing (ES)

In many respects the GARCH(1, 1) representation shares many features of the popular exponential smoothing to which can be added the interpretation that the level of current volatility is a function of the previous period's volatility and the square of the previous period's returns. These two models have many similarities, i.e. today's volatility is estimated conditionally upon the information set available at each period. Both the GARCH(1, 1) model in equation (2.8) and the (ES) model in equation (2.7) use the last period's returns to determine current levels of volatility. Subsequently, it follows that today's volatility is forecastable immediately after yesterday's market closure.[2] Since the latest available information set is used, it can be shown that both models will provide more accurate estimators of volatility than the use of historical volatility.

However, there are several differences in the operational characteristics of the two models. The GARCH model, for example, uses two independent coefficients to estimate the impact the variables have in determining current volatility, while the ES model uses only one coefficient and forces the variables e_{t-1}^2 and h_{t-1} to have a unit effect on current period volatility. Thus, a large shock will have longer lasting impact on volatility using the GARCH model of equation (2.8) than the ES model of (2.3)

The terms α and β in GARCH do not need to sum to unity and one parameter is not the complement of the other. Hence, it avoids the potential for simultaneity bias in the conditional variance. Their estimation is achieved by maximizing the likelihood function.[3] This is a very important point since the values of a and b are critical in determining the current levels of volatility. Incorrect selection of the parameter values will adversely affect the estimation of volatility. The assumption that a and b sum to unity is, however, very strong and presents an hypothesis that can be tested rather than a condition to be imposed. Acceptance of the hypothesis that a and b sum to unity indicates the existence of an Integrated GARCH process or I-GARCH. This is a specification that characterizes the conditional variance h_t as exhibiting a nonstationary component. The implication of this is that shocks in the lagged squared error term ε_{t-i}^2 will have a permanent effect on the conditional variance.

Furthermore, the GARCH model has an additional parameter, ω, that acts as a floor and prevents the volatility dropping to below that level. In the extreme case where α and $\beta = 0$, volatility is constant and equal to ω. The value of ω is estimated together with α and β using maximum likelihood estimation and the hypothesis $\omega = 0$ can be tested easily. The absence of the ω parameter in the ES model allows volatility, after a few quiet trading days, to drop to very low levels.

Forecasting with ARCH models

In view of the fact that ARCH models make better use of the available information set than standard time series methodology by allowing excess kurtosis in the distribution of the data, the resulting model fits the observed data set better. However, perhaps the strongest argument in favor of ARCH models lies in their ability to predict future variances.

The way the ARCH model is constructed it can 'predict' the next period's variance without uncertainty. Since the error term at time t, ε_t, is known we can rewrite equation (2.5) as

$$h_{t+1} = \omega + \alpha \varepsilon_t^2 \tag{2.10}$$

Thus, the next period's volatility is found recursively by updating the last observed error in the variance equation (2.5). For the GARCH type of models it is possible to deliver a multi-step-ahead forecast. For example, for the GARCH(1, 1) it is only necessary to update forecasts using:

$$E(h_{t+s}|\Phi_t) = \omega + (\alpha + \beta)E(h_{t+s-1}|\Phi_t) \tag{2.11}$$

where ω, α and β are GARCH(1, 1) parameters of equation (2.8) and are estimated using the data set available, until period t.

Of course, the long-run forecasting procedure must be formed on the basis that the variance equation has been parameterized. For example, the implied volatility at time t can enter as an exogenous variable in the variance equation:

$$E(h_{t+1}|\Phi_t) = \omega + \alpha \varepsilon_t^2 + \beta h_t + \delta \sigma_t^2 \qquad \text{if } s = 1 \tag{2.12a}$$

$$E(h_{t+s}|\Phi_t) = \omega + \delta \sigma_t^2 + (\alpha + \beta)E(h_{t+s-1}|\Phi_t) \qquad \text{if } s \geqslant 2 \tag{2.12b}$$

where the term σ_t^2 is the implied volatility of a traded option on the same underlying asset, Y.

ARCH-M (in mean)

The ARCH model can be extended to allow the mean of the series to be a function of its own variance. This parameterization is referred to as the ARCH-in-Mean (or ARCH-M) model and is formed by adding a risk-related component to the return equation, in other words, the conditional variance h_t. Hence, equation (2.4) can be rewritten as:

$$Y_t = \xi_t \delta + \lambda h_t + \varepsilon_t \tag{2.13}$$

Therefore the ARCH-M model allows the conditional variance to explain directly the dependent variable in the mean equation of (2.13). The estimation process consists of solving equations (2.13) and (2.5) recursively. The term λh_t has a time-varying impact on the conditional mean of the series. A positive λ implies that the conditional mean of Y increases as the conditional variance increases.

The (G)ARCH-M model specification is ideal for equity returns since it provides a unified framework to estimate jointly the volatility and the time-varying expected return (mean) of the series by the inclusion of the conditional variance in the mean equation. Unbiased estimates of assets risk and return are crucial to the mean variance utility approach and other related asset pricing theories. Finance theory states that rational investors should expect a higher return for riskier assets. The parameter λ in equation (2.13) can be interpreted as the coefficient of relative risk aversion of a representative investor and when recursively estimated, the same coefficient λh_t can be seen as the time-varying risk premium. Since, in the presence of ARCH, the variance of returns might increase over time, the agents will ask for greater compensation in order to hold the asset. A positive λ implies that the agent is compensated for any additional risk.

Thus, the introduction of h_t into the mean is another non-linear function of past information. Since the next period's variance, h_{t+1}, is known with certainty the next period's return forecast, $E(Y_{t+1})$, can be obtained recursively. Assuming that ξ_t is known we can rearrange equation (2.13) as

$$E[Y_{t+1}|I_t] \equiv m_{t+1} = \Phi_{t+1}\delta + \Theta h_{t+1} \tag{2.14}$$

Thus, the series' expectation at $t+1$ (i.e. one period ahead into the future) is equal to the series' conditional mean, m_{t+1}, at the same period. Unlike the unconditional mean, $\mu = E(Y)$, which is not a random variable, the conditional mean is a function of past volatility, and because it uses information for the period up to t, can generally be forecasted more accurately.

In contrast to the linear GARCH model, consistent estimation of the parameter estimates of an ARCH-M model are sensitive to the model specification. A model is said to be misspecified in the presence of simultaneity bias in the conditional mean equation as defined in equation (2.13). This arises because the estimates for the parameters in the conditional mean equation are not independent of the estimates of the parameters in the conditional variance. Therefore, it has been argued that a misspecification in the variance equation will lead to biased and inconsistent estimates for the conditional mean equation.

Using GARCH to measure correlation

Historical variance–covariance matrix: problems

In risk management, the monitoring of changes in the variance and covariance of the assets that comprises a portfolio is an extensive process of distinguishing shifts over a period of time. Overseeing changes in the variance (or risk) of each asset and the relationship between the assets in a portfolio through the variance is achieved using the variance–covariance matrix. For the variance and covariance estimates in the matrix to be reliable it is necessary that the joint distributions of security returns are multivariate normal and stationary. However, as discussed earlier, investigations have found that the distribution of speculative price changes are not normally distributed and exhibit fat tails. Consequently, if the distribution of return for individual series fails to satisfy the i.i.d. assumptions, it is inconceivable to expect the joint distribution to do so. Therefore, forecasts based on past extrapolations of historical estimates must be viewed with skepticism. Hence, the usefulness of conditional heteroskedastic models in multivariate setting to be discussed next.

The multivariate (G)ARCH model

All the models described earlier are univariate. However, risk analysis of speculative prices examines both an asset's return volatility and its co-movement with other securities in the market. Modeling the co-movement among assets in a portfolio is best archived using a multivariate conditional heteroskedastic model which accounts for the non-normality in the multivariate distribution of speculative price changes. Hence, the ARCH models can find more prominent use in empirical finance if they could describe risk in a multivariate context. There are several reasons for examining the variance parameter of a multivariate distribution of financial time series after modeling within the ARCH framework. For example, covariances and the beta coefficient which in finance theory is used as a measure of the risk could be represented and forecasted in the same way as variances.

The ARCH model has been extended to a multivariate case using different para-meterizations. The most popular is the diagonal one where each element of the conditional variance–covariance matrix $\mathbf{H}_t$ is restricted to depend only on its own lagged squared errors.[4]

Thus, a diagonal bivariate GARCH(1, 1) is written as:

$$Y_{1,t} = \Phi_{1,t}^T \delta_1 + \varepsilon_{1,t} \tag{2.15a}$$

$$Y_{2,t} = \Phi_{2,t}^T \delta_2 + \varepsilon_{2,t} \tag{2.15b}$$

with

$$\begin{vmatrix} \varepsilon_{1,t} \\ \varepsilon_{2,t} \end{vmatrix} \sim N(0, \mathbf{H}_t)$$

where $Y_{1,t}$, $Y_{2,t}$ is the return on the two assets over the period $(t-1, t)$. Conditional on the information available up to time $(t-1)$, the vector with the surprise errors ε_t is assumed to follow a bivariate normal distribution with zero mean and conditional variance–covariance matrix $\mathbf{H}_t$. Considering a two-asset portfolio, the variance–covariance matrix $\mathbf{H}_t$ can be decomposed as

$$h_{1,t} = \omega_1 + a_1 \varepsilon_{1,t-1}^2 + b_1 h_{1,t-1} \tag{2.16a}$$

$$h_{12,t} = \omega_{12} + a_{12} \varepsilon_{1,t-1} \varepsilon_{2,t-1} + b_{12} h_{12,t-1} \tag{2.16b}$$

$$h_{2,t} = \omega_2 + a_2 \varepsilon_{2,t-1}^2 + b_2 h_{2,t-1} \tag{2.16c}$$

Here $h_{1,t}$ and $h_{2,t}$ can be seen as the conditional variances of assets 1 and 2 respectively. These are expressed as past realizations of their own squared distur-bances denoted as $\varepsilon_{1,t-1}^2$. The covariance of the two return series, $h_{12,t}$, is a function of the cross-product between past disturbances in the two assets. The ratio $\sqrt{h_{1,t}h_{2,t}}/h_{12,t}$ forms the correlation between assets 1 and 2.

However, using the ARCH in a multivariate context is subject to limitations in modeling the variances and covariances in a matrix, most notably, the number of variances and covariances that are required to be estimated. For example, in a widely diversified portfolio containing 100 assets, there are 4950 conditional covariances and 100 variances to be estimated. Any model used to update the covariances must keep to the multivariate normal distribution otherwise the risk measure will be biased. Given the computationally intensive nature of the exercise, there is no guarantee that the multivariate distribution will hold.

Asymmetric ARCH models

The feature of capturing the volatility clustering in asset returns has made (G)ARCH models very popular in empirical studies. Nevertheless, these models are subject to limitations. Empirical studies have observed that stock returns are negatively related with changes in return volatility. Volatility tends to rise when prices are falling, and to fall when prices are rising. Hence, the existence of asymmetry in volatility, which is often referred to as the *leverage* effect. All the models described in the previous section assumed that only the magnitude and not the sign of past returns determines the characteristics of the conditional variance, h_t. In other words, the ARCH and GARCH models described earlier do not discriminate negative from positive shocks which has been shown to have differing impacts on the conditional variance.

Exponential ARCH (EGARCH)

To address some of the limitations an exponential ARCH parameterization or EGARCH has been proposed. The variance of the residual error term for the EGARCH(1, 1) is given by

$$\ln(h_t) = \omega + \beta \ln(h_{t-1}) + \gamma \psi_{t-1} + \phi(|\psi_{t-1}| - (2/\pi)^{1/2}) \qquad (2.17)$$

where $\psi_t = \varepsilon_t / h_t$ (standardized residual). Hence, the logarithm of the conditional variance $\ln(h_t)$ at period t is a function of the logarithm of the conditional period variance, lagged one period back $\ln(h_{t-1})$, the standarized value of the last residual error, ψ_{t-1}, and the deviation of the absolute value of ψ_{t-1} from the expected absolute value of the standardized normal variate, $(2/\pi)^{1/2}$. The parameter γ measures the impact 'asymmetries' on the last period's shocks have on current volatility. Thus, if $\gamma < 0$ then negative past errors have a greater impact on the conditional variance $\ln(h_t)$ than positive errors. The conditional variance h_t is expressed as a function of both the size and sign of lagged errors.

Asymmetric ARCH (AARCH)

An ARCH model with properties similar to those of EGARCH is the asymmetric ARCH (AARCH). In its simplest form the conditional variance h_t can be written as

$$h_t = \omega + \alpha(\varepsilon_{t-1} + \gamma)^2 + \beta h_{t-1} \qquad (2.18)$$

The conditional variance parameterization in equation (2.18) is a quadratic function of one-period-past error $(\varepsilon_{t-1} + \gamma)^2$. Since the model of equation (2.18) and higher-order versions of this model formulation still lie within the parametric ARCH, it can therefore, be interpreted as the quadratic projection of the squared series on the information set.

  The (G)AARCH has similar properties to the GARCH but unlike the latter, which explores only the magnitude of past errors, the (G)AARCH allows past errors to have an asymmetric effect on h_t. That is, because γ can take any value, a dynamic asymmetric effect of positive and negative lagged values of ε_t on h_t is permitted. If γ is negative the conditional variance will be higher when ε_{t-1} is negative than when it is positive. If $\gamma = 0$ the (G)AARCH reduces to a (G)ARCH model. Therefore, the (G)AARCH, like the EGARCH, can capture the leverage effect present in the stock market data. When the sum of α_i and β_j (where $i = 1, \ldots, p$ and $j = 1, \ldots, q$ are the orders of the (G)AARCH(p, q) process) is unity then analogously to the GARCH, the model is referred to as Integrated (G)AARCH.

As with the GARCH process, the autocorrelogram and partial autocorrelogram of the squares of ε, as obtained by an AR(1), can be used to identify the $\{p, q\}$ orders. In the case of the (G)AARCH(1, 1), the unconditional variance of the process is given by

$$\sigma^2 = (\omega + \gamma^2 \alpha) / (1 - \alpha - \beta) \tag{2.19}$$

Other asymmetric specifications

GJR or threshold:

$$h_t = \omega + \beta h_{t-1} + \alpha \varepsilon_{t-1}^2 + \gamma \bar{S}_{t-1} \varepsilon_{t-1}^2 \tag{2.20}$$

where $\bar{S}_t = 1$ if $\varepsilon_t < 0$, $\bar{S}_t = 0$ otherwise.

Non-linear asymmetric GARCH:

$$h_t = \omega + \beta h_{t-1} + \alpha (\varepsilon_{t-1} + \gamma \sqrt{h_{t-1}})^2 \tag{2.21}$$

VGARCH:

$$h_t = \omega + \beta h_{t-1} + \alpha (\varepsilon_{t-1} / \sqrt{h_{t-1}} + \gamma)^2 \tag{2.22}$$

If the coefficient γ is positive in the threshold model then negative values of ε_{t-1} have an additive impact on the conditional variance. This allows asymmetry on the conditional variance in the same way as EGARCH and AARCH. If $\gamma = 0$ the model reduces to a GARCH(1, 1). Similarly, as in the last two models, the coefficient γ measures the asymmetric effect where the negative errors have a greater impact on the variance when $\gamma < 0$.

Identification and diagnostic tests for ARCH

ARCH models are almost always estimated using the maximum likelihood method and with the use of computationally expensive techniques. Although linear GARCH fits well with a variety of data series and is less sensitive to misspecification, others like the ARCH-M requires that the full model be correctly specified. Thus identification tests for ARCH effects need to be carried out before, and misspecification tests after the estimation process are necessary for proper ARCH modeling.

Identification tests

One test proposed by Engle is based on the Lagrange Multiplier (LM) principle. To perform the test only estimates of the homoskedastic model are required. Assume that the AR(p) is a stationary process which generates the set of returns, Y_t, such that $\{\varepsilon\} \sim$ i.i.d. and $N(0, \sigma^2)$ and that $Y_{-p-1}, \ldots, Y_0$ is an initial fixed part of this series. Subsequent inference will be based on a conditional likelihood function. The least squares estimators of the parameters in the above process are denoted by $\hat{\mu}, \hat{a}_1, \hat{a}_2, \ldots, \hat{a}_p$, where $\hat{\sigma}^2$ is an estimator of σ^2, and setting $\hat{z}^2 = (-1, Y_{t-1}, \ldots, Y_{t-2}, \ldots, Y_{t-p})'$. When H_0 for homoskedasticity is tested against an ARCH(p) process then the LM statistic is asymptotically equivalent to nR^2 from the auxiliary regression

$$\hat{\varepsilon}_t^2 = \alpha + \Sigma \alpha \hat{\varepsilon}_{t-i}^2 + e_t \qquad \text{for } i = 1, \ldots, p$$

$$H_0 : \alpha_1 = \alpha_2 = \ldots = \alpha_p = 0 \tag{2.23}$$

$$H_1 : \alpha_i \neq 0$$

Under H_0 the $\text{LM} = nR^2$ has a chi-squared distribution denoted as $\chi^2(p)$, where p represents the number of lags. However, when the squared residuals are expressed as linearly declining weights of past squared errors the LM test for ARCH, which will follow a $\chi^2(1)$ distribution, will be

$$\hat{\varepsilon}_t^2 = \alpha + \alpha_1 \Sigma w_1 \hat{\varepsilon}_{t-1}^2 + e_t \tag{2.24}$$

where w_i are the weights which decline at a constant rate.

The above test has been extended to deal with the bivariate specification of the ARCH models. When the model is restricted to the diagonal representation, then $3N(R_1^2 + R_2^2 + R_{12}^2)$ is distributed as $\chi^2(3p)$, where R^2 is the coefficient of determination. The terms R_1^2, R_2^2 stand for the autoregression of squared residuals for each of the two assets, and R_{12}^2 denotes the autoregression of the covariance for the two series residuals.

Researchers also suggest that the autocorrelogram and partial autocorrelogram for $\hat{\varepsilon}_t^2$ can be used to specify the GARCH order $\{p, q\}$ in a similar way to that used to identify the order of a Box–Jenkins ARMA process. The Box–Pierce Q-statistic for the normalized squared residuals (i.e. $(\hat{\varepsilon}_t^2 / h_t)$) can be used as a diagnostic test against higher-order specifications for the variance equation.

If estimations are performed under both the null and alternative hypotheses, likelihood ratio (LR) tests can be obtained by

$$\text{LR} = -2(\text{ML}(\theta_0) - \text{ML}(\theta_\alpha)) \sim \chi^2(k)$$

where $\text{ML}(\theta_0)$ and $\text{ML}(\theta_\alpha)$ are the ML function evaluations and k is the number of restrictions in the parameters.

Diagnostic tests

Correct specification of h_t is very important. For example, because h_t relates future variances to current information, the accuracy of forecast depends on the selection of h_t. Therefore, diagnostic tests should be employed to test for model misspecification. Most of the tests dealing with misspecification examine the properties of the standardized residuals defined as $\hat{\varepsilon}_t^* = \hat{\varepsilon}_t \sqrt{h_t^{-1}}$ which is designed to make the residual returns conform to a normal distribution. If the model is correctly specified the standardized residuals should behave as a white noise series. That is because under the ARCH model

$$\hat{\varepsilon}_t^* = \hat{\varepsilon}_t \sqrt{h_t^{-1}} | \Phi_{t-1 \sim N(0,1)}$$

For example, the autocorrelation of squared residual returns, $\hat{\varepsilon}_t^2$, or normalized squared residuals $(\hat{\varepsilon}_2^*)^2$ may reveal a model failure. More advanced tests can also be used to detect non-linearities in $(\hat{\varepsilon}_2^*)^2$.

An intuitively appealing test has been suggested by Pagan and Schwert. They propose regressing $\hat{\varepsilon}_t^2$ against a constant and h_t, the estimates of the conditional variance, to test the null hypothesis that the coefficient β in equation (2.25) is equal to unity:

$$\hat{\varepsilon}_t^2 = \alpha + \beta h_t + v_t \tag{2.25}$$

If the forecasts are unbiased, $\alpha = 0$ and $\beta = 1$. A high R^2 in the above regression indicates that the model has high forecasting power for the variance.

An alternative test

A second test, based on the Ljung–Box Q-statistic, tests the standardized squared residuals (Y_1^2/σ^2) for normality and hence the acceptance of the i.i.d. assumptions. Large values of the Q-statistic could be regarded as evidence that the standardized residuals violate the i.i.d. assumption and hence normality, while low values of the Q-statistic would provide evidence that the standardized residuals are independent. In other words, when using this test failure to accept the maintained hypothesis of independence would indicate that the estimated variance has not removed all the clusters of volatility. This in turn would imply that the data still holds information that can be usefully translated into volatility.

An application of ARCH models in risk management

In this section, we provide an application of how to use GARCH techniques in a simplified approach to estimate a portfolio's VaR. We will show that the use of historical returns of portfolio components and current weights can produce accurate estimates of current risk for a portfolio of traded securities. Information on the time series properties of returns of the portfolio components is transformed into a conditional estimate of current portfolio volatility without needing to use complex time series procedures. Stress testing and correlation stability are discussed in this framework.

A simplified way to compute a portfolio's VaR

Traditional VaR models require risk estimates for the portfolio holdings, i.e. variance and correlations. Historical volatilities are ill-behaved measures of risk because they presume that the statistical moments of the security returns remain constant over different time periods. Conditional multivariate time series techniques are more appropriate since they use past information in a more efficient way to compute current variances and covariances. One such model which fits well with financial data is the multivariate GARCH. Its use, however, is restricted to few assets at a time.

A simple procedure to overcome the difficulties of inferring current portfolio volatility from past data, is to utilize the knowledge of current portfolio weights and historical returns of the portfolio components in order to construct a hypothetical series of the returns that the portfolio would have earned if its current weights had been kept constant in the past. Let $\mathbf{R}_t$ be the $N \times 1$ vector $(R_{1,t}, R_{2,t}, \ldots, R_{n,t})$ where $R_{i,t}$ is the return on the ith asset over the period $(t-1, t)$ and let W be the $N \times 1$ vector of the portfolio weights over the same period. The historical returns of our current portfolio holdings are given by:

$$Y_t = W^T R_t \qquad (2.26)$$

In investment management, if W represents actual investment holdings, the series Y can be seen as the historical path of the portfolio returns.[5] The portfolio's risk and return trade-off can be expressed in terms of the statistical moments of the multivariate distribution of the weighted investments as:

$$E(Y_t) = E(W^T R) = m \qquad (2.27a)$$

$$\mathrm{var}(Y_t) = W^T \Omega W = \sigma^2 \qquad (2.27b)$$

where Ω is the unconditional variance–covariance matrix of the returns of the N assets. A simplified way to find the portfolio's risk and return characteristics is by estimating the first two moments of Y:

$$E(Y) = m \qquad (2.28a)$$

$$\mathrm{var}(Y) = E[Y - E(Y)]^2 = \sigma^2 \qquad (2.28b)$$

Hence, if historical returns are known the portfolio's mean and variance can be found as in equation (2.28). This is easier than equation (2.27) and still yields identical results.

The method in (2.28b) can easily be deployed in risk management to compute the value at risk at any given time t. However, σ^2 will only characterize current conditional volatility if W has not changed. If positions are being modified, the series of past returns, Y, needs to be reconstructed and σ^2, the volatility of the new position, needs to be re-estimated as in equation (2.28b).

This approach has many advantages. It is simple, easy to compute and overcomes the dimensionality and bias problems that arise when the $N \times N$ covariance matrix is being estimated. On the other hand, the portfolio's past returns contain all the necessary information about the dynamics that govern aggregate current investment holdings. In this chapter we will use this approach to make the best use of this information.[6] For example, it might be possible to capture the time path of portfolio (conditional) volatility using conditional models such as GARCH.

An empirical investigation

In this example we selected closing daily price indices from thirteen national stock markets[7] over a period of 10 years, from the first trading day of 1986 (2 January) until the last trading day of 1995 (29 December). The thirteen markets have been selected in a way that matches the regional and individual market capitalization of the world index. Our data sample represents 93.3% of the Morgan Stanley International world index capitalization.[8] The *Morgan Stanley Capital International (MSCI) World Index* has been chosen as a proxy to the world portfolio. To illustrate how our methodology can be used to monitor portfolio risk we constructed a hypothetical portfolio, diversified across all thirteen national markets of our data sample. To form this hypothetical portfolio we weighted each national index in proportion to its

Table 2.1 Portfolio weights at December 1995

Country	Our portfolio	World index
Denmark	0.004854	0.004528
France	0.038444	0.035857
Germany	0.041905	0.039086
Hong Kong	0.018918	0.017645
Italy	0.013626	0.012709
Japan	0.250371	0.233527
Netherlands	0.024552	0.022900
Singapore	0.007147	0.006667
Spain	0.010993	0.010254
Sweden	0.012406	0.011571
Switzerland	0.036343	0.033898
UK	0.103207	0.096264
USA	0.437233	0.407818

capitalization in the world index as on December 1995. The portfolio weights are reported in Table 2.1.

The 10-year historical returns of the thirteen national indexes have been weighted according to the numbers in the table to form the returns of our hypothetical portfolio. Since portfolio losses need to be measured in one currency, we expressed all local returns in US dollars and then formed the portfolio's historical returns. Table 2.2 reports the portfolio's descriptive statistics together with the Jarque–Bera normality test. The last column is the probability that our portfolio returns are generated from a normal distribution.

Table 2.2 Descriptive statistics of the portfolio historical returns

Mean (p.a.)	Std dev. (p.a.)	Skewness	Kurtosis	JB test	*p*-value
10.92%	12.34%	− 2.828	62.362	3474.39	0.000

Notes: The test for normality is the Jarque–Bera test, $N((\sigma^3)^2/6 + (\sigma^4 - 3)^2/24)$. The last column is the significance level.

Modeling portfolio volatility

The excess kurtosis in this portfolio is likely to be caused by changes in its variance. We can capture these shifts in the variance by employing GARCH modeling. For a portfolio diversified across a wide range of assets, the non-constant volatility hypothesis is an open issue.[9] The LM test and the Ljung–Box statistic are employed to test this hypothesis. The test statistics with significance levels are reported in Table 2.3. Both tests are highly significant, indicating that the portfolio's volatility is not constant over different days and the squares of the portfolio returns are serially correlated.[10]

Table 2.3 Testing for ARCH

	LM test (6)	Ljung–Box (6)
Test statistic	352.84	640.64
p-value	(0.00)	(0.00)

One of the advantages that the model in (2.28) is that is simplifies econometric modeling on the portfolio variance. Because we have to model only a single series of returns we can select a conditional volatility model that bests fits the data. There are two families of models, the GARCH and SV (Stochastic Volatility), which are particularly suited to capturing changes in volatility of financial time series. To model the hypothetical portfolio volatility, we use GARCH modeling because it offers wide flexibility in the mean and variance specifications and its success in modeling conditional volatility has been well documented in the financial literature. We tested for a number of different GARCH parameterizations and found that an asymmetric GARCH(1, 1)-ARMA(0, 1) specification best fits[11] our hypothetical portfolio. This is defined as:

$$Y_t = \Phi\varepsilon_{t-1} + \varepsilon_t \qquad \varepsilon_t \sim NI(0, h_t) \qquad (2.29a)$$

$$h_t = \omega + \alpha(\varepsilon_{t-1} + \gamma)^2 + \beta h_{t-1} \qquad (2.29b)$$

The parameter estimates reported in Table 2.4 are all highly significant, confirming that portfolio volatility can be better modeled as conditionally heteroskedastic. The coefficient α that measures the impact of last period's squared innovation, ε, on today's variance is found to be positive and significant; in addition, $(\omega + \alpha\gamma^2)/(1 - \alpha - \beta) > 0$ indicating that the unconditional variance is constant.

Table 2.4   Parameter estimates of equation (2.30)

Series	Φ	ω	α	β	γ	Likelihood
Estimate	0.013	1.949	0.086	0.842	− 3.393	− 8339.79
t-statistic	(2.25)	(3.15)	(6.44)	(29.20)	(5.31)	

Moreover, the constant volatility model, which is the special case of $\alpha = \beta = 0$, can be rejected. The coefficient γ that captures any asymmetries in volatility that might exist is significant and negative, indicating that volatility tends to be higher when the portfolio's values are falling. Figure 2.2 shows our hypothetical portfolio's conditional volatility over the 10-year period. It is clear that the increase in portfolio volatility occurred during the 1987 crash and the 1990 Gulf War.

Diagnostics and stress analysis

Correct model specification requires that diagnostic tests be carried out on the fitted residual, $\hat{\varepsilon}$. Table 2.5 contains estimates of the regression:

$$\hat{\varepsilon}_t^2 = a + b_{h_t} \qquad (2.30)$$

with *t*-statistics given in parentheses.

Table 2.5   Diagnostics on the GARCH residuals

	a	b	R^2	Q(6) on $\hat{\varepsilon}_t$	Q(6) on $\hat{\varepsilon}_t^2$	JB
Statistic	− 7.054	1.224	0.373	3.72	10.13	468.89
Significance	(1.73)	(1.87)		(0.71)	(0.12)	(0.00)

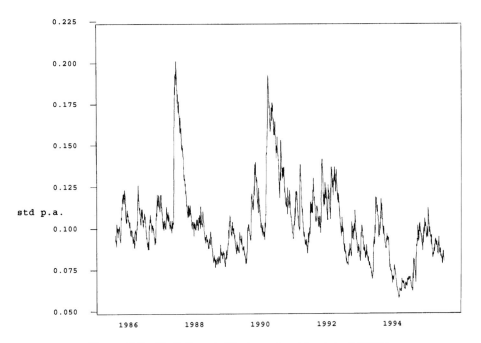

Figure 2.2 Portfolio volatility based on bivariate GARCH.

The hypotheses that $a = 0$ and $b = 1$ cannot be rejected at the 95% confidence level, indicating that our GARCH model produces a consistent estimator for the portfolio's time-varying variance. The uncentered coefficient of determination, R^2 in equation (2.30), measures the fraction of the total variation of everyday returns explained by the estimated conditional variance, and has a value 37.3%. Since the portfolio conditional variance uses the information set available from the previous day, the above result indicates that our model, on average, can predict more than one third of the next day's squared price movement. The next two columns in Table 2.5 contain the Ljung–Box statistic of order 6 for the residuals and squared residuals. Both null hypotheses, for serial correlation and further GARCH effect, cannot be rejected, indicating that our model has removed the volatility clusters from the portfolio returns and left white noise residuals. The last column contains the Jarque–Bera normality test on the standardized residuals. Although these residuals still deviate from the normal distribution, most of the excess kurtosis has been removed, indicating that our model describes the portfolio returns well.

Figure 2.3 illustrates the standardized empirical distribution of these portfolio returns which shows evidence of excess kurtosis in the distribution. The area under the continuous line represents the standardized empirical distribution of our hypothetical portfolio.[12] The dashed line shows the shape of the distribution if returns were normally distributed. The values on the horizontal axis are far above and below the $(3.0, -3.0)$ range, which is due to very large daily portfolio gains and losses.

In Figure 2.4 the standardized innovations of portfolio returns are shown. The upper and lower horizontal lines represent the 2.33 standard deviations (0.01 probability) threshold. We can see that returns are moving randomly net of any volatility clusters.

Figure 2.5 shows the Kernel distribution of these standardized innovations against

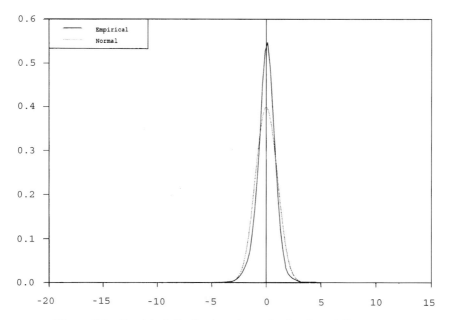

Figure 2.3   Empirical distribution of standardized portfolio returns.

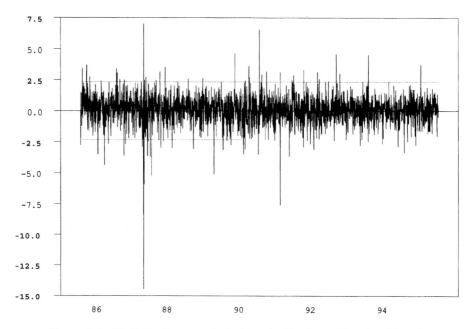

Figure 2.4   Portfolio stress analysis (standardized conditional residuals).

the normal distribution. It is apparent that the distribution of these scaled innovations is rather non-normal with values reaching up to fourteen standard deviations. However, when the outliers to the left (which reflect the large losses during the 1987 crash), are omitted, the empirical distribution of the portfolio residual returns matches that of a Gaussian.

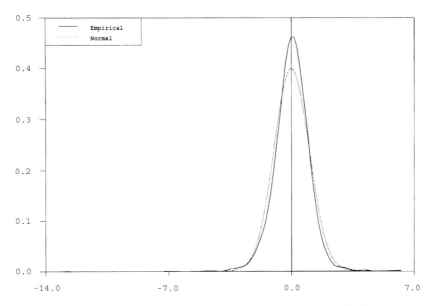

Figure 2.5 Empirical distribution of portfolio conditional distribution.

These results substantiate the credibility of the volatility model in equation (2.29) in monitoring portfolio risk. Our model captures all volatility clusters present in the portfolio returns, removes a large part of the excess kurtosis and leaves residuals approximately normal. Furthermore, our method for estimating portfolio volatility using only one series of past returns is much faster to compute than the variance–co-variance method and provides unbiased volatility estimates with higher explanatory power.

Correlation stability and diversification benefits

In a widely diversified portfolio, e.g. containing 100 assets, there are 4950 conditional covariances and 100 variances to be estimated. Furthermore, any model used to update the covariances must keep the multivariate features of the joint distribution. With a large matrix like that, it is unlikely to get unbiased estimates[13] for all 4950 covariances and at the same time guarantee that the joint multivariate distribution still holds. Obviously, errors in covariances as well as in variances will affect the accuracy of our portfolio's VaR estimate and will lead to wrong risk management decisions. Our approach estimates conditionally the volatility of only one univariate time series, the portfolio's historical returns, and so overcomes all the above problems. Furthermore, since it does not require the estimation of the variance–covariance matrix, it can be easily computed and can handle an unlimited number of assets. On the other hand it takes into account all changes in assets' variances and covariances.

Another appealing property of our approach is to disclose the impact that the overall changes in correlations have on portfolio volatility. It can tell us what proportion an increase/decrease in the portfolio's VaR is due to changes in asset variances or correlations. We will refer to this as *correlation stability*.

It is known that each correlation coefficient is subject to changes at any time.

Nevertheless, changes across the correlation matrix may not be correlated and their impact on the overall portfolio risk may be diminished. Our conditional VaR approach allows us to attribute any changes in the portfolio's conditional volatility to two main components: changes in asset volatilities and changes in asset correlations. If h_t is the portfolio's conditional variance, as estimated in equation (2.25), its time-varying volatility is $\sigma_t = \sqrt{h_t}$. This is the volatility estimate of a diversified portfolio at period t. By setting all pair-wise correlation coefficients in each period equal to 1.0, the portfolio's volatility becomes the weighted volatility of its asset components. Conditional volatilities of the individual asset components can be obtained by fitting a GARCH-type model for each return series. We denote the volatility of this undiversified portfolio as s_t. The quantity $1 - (\sigma_t / s_t)$ tells us what proportion of portfolio volatility has been diversified away because of imperfect correlations. If that quantity does not change significantly over time, then the weighted overall effect of time-varying correlations is invariant and we have *correlation stability*. The correlation stability shown in Figure 2.6 can be used to measure the risk manager's ability to diversify portfolio's risk. On a well-diversified (constantly weighted) portfolio, the quantity $1 - (\sigma_t / s_t)$ should be invariant over different periods. It has been shown that a portfolio invested only in bonds is subject to greater correlation risk than a portfolio containing commodities and equities because of the tendency of bonds to fall into step in the presence of large market moves.

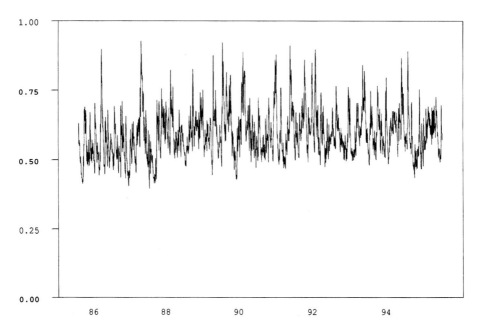

Figure 2.6   Portfolio correlation stability: volatility ratio (diversified versus non-diversified).

The 'weighted' effect of changes in correlations can also be shown by observing the diversified against the undiversified portfolio risk. Figure 2.7 illustrates how the daily annualized standard deviation of our hypothetical portfolio behaves over the tested period. The upper line shows the volatility of an undiversified portfolio; this is the volatility the same portfolio would have if all pair-wise correlation coefficients of the

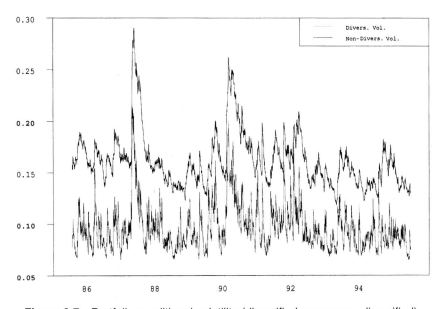

Figure 2.7   Portfolio conditional volatility (diversified versus non-diversified).

assets invested were 1.0 at all times. The undiversified portfolio's volatility is simply the weighted average of the conditional volatilities of each asset included in the portfolio. Risk managers who rely on average standard historical risk measures will be surprised by the extreme values of volatility a portfolio may produce in a crash. Our conditional volatility estimates provide early warnings about the risk increase and therefore are a useful supplement to existing risk management systems.

Descriptive statistics for diversified and undiversified portfolio risk are reported in Table 2.6. These range of volatility are those that would have been observed had the portfolio weights been effective over the whole sample period. Due to the diversification of risk, the portfolio's volatility is reduced by an average of 40%.[14] During the highly volatile period of the 1987 crash, the risk is reduced by a quarter.

Table 2.6   Portfolio risk statistic

Portfolio risk	Minimum	Maximum	Mean
Diversified	0.0644	0.2134	0.0962
Undiversified	0.01192	0.2978	0.1632

Portfolio VaR and 'worst case' scenario
Portfolio VaR

A major advantage that our methodology has is that it forecasts portfolio volatility recursively upon the previous day's volatility. Then it uses these volatility forecasts to calculate the VaR over the next few days. We discuss below how this method is implemented.

By substituting the last day's residual return and variance in equation (2.29b) we can estimate the portfolio's volatility for day $t+1$ and by taking the expectation, we can estimate recursively the forecast for longer periods. Hence, the portfolio volatility forecast over the next 10 days is

$$h_{t+i} = \omega + \alpha(\varepsilon_t + \gamma)^2 + \beta h_t \qquad \text{if } i = 1 \qquad (2.31\text{a})$$

$$h_{t+i/t} = \omega + \alpha\gamma^2(\alpha + \beta)h_{t+i-1/t} \qquad \text{if } i > 1 \qquad (2.31\text{b})$$

Therefore, when portfolio volatility is below average levels, the forecast values will be rising.[15] The portfolio VaR that will be calculated on these forecasts will be more realistic about possible future losses.

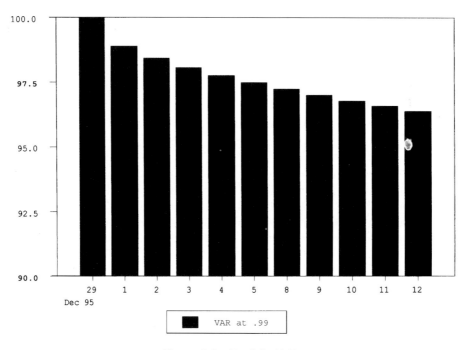

Figure 2.8   Portfolio VaR.

Figure 2.8 shows our hypothetical portfolio's VaR for 10 periods of length between one and 10 days. The portfolio VaR is estimated at the close of business on 29 December 1995. To estimate the VaR we obtain volatility forecasts for each of the next business days, as in equation (2.31). The DEaR is 1.104% while the 10-day VaR is 3.62%.

Worst-case scenario

VaR measures the market risk of a portfolio in terms of the frequency that a specific loss will be exceeded. In risk management, however, it is important to know the size of the loss rather than the number of times the losses will exceed a predefined threshold. The type of analysis which tells us the worst than can happen to a portfolio's value over a given period is known as the 'worst-case scenario' (WCS). Hence, the WCS is concerned with the prediction of uncommon events which, by definition, are bound to happen. The WCS will answer the question, how badly will it hit?

For a VaR model, the probability of exceeding a loss at the end of a short period is a function of the last day's volatility and the square root of time (assuming no serial correlation). Here, however, the issue of fat tails arises. It is unlikely that there exists a volatility model that predicts the likelihood and size of extreme price moves. For example, in this study we observed that the GARCH model removes most of the kurtosis but still leaves residuals equal to several standard deviations. Given that extreme events, such as the 1987 crash, have a realistic probability of occurring again at any time, any reliable risk management system must account for them.

The WCS is commonly calculated by using structured Monte Carlo simulation (SMC). This method aims to simulate the volatilities and correlations of all assets in the portfolio by using a series of random draws of the factor shocks (ε_{t+1}). At each simulation run, the value of the portfolio is projected over the VaR period. By repeating the process several thousand times, the portfolio returns density function is found and the WCS is calculated as the loss that corresponds to a very small probability under that area. There are three major weaknesses with this analysis. First, there is a dimensionality problem which also translates to computation time. To overcome this, RiskMetrics proposes to simplify the calculation of the correlation matrix by using a kind of factorization. Second, the SMC method relies on a (time-invariant) correlation structure of the data. But as we have seen, security covariances are changing over different periods and the betas tend to be higher during volatile periods like that of the 1987 crash. Hence, correlations in the extremes are higher and the WCS will underestimate the risk. Finally, the use of a correlation matrix requires returns in the Monte Carlo method to follow an arbitrary distribution. In practice the empirical histogram of returns is 'smoothed' to fit a known distribution. However, the WCS is highly dependent on a good prediction of uncommon events or catastrophic risk and the smoothing of the data leads to a cover-up of extreme events, thereby neutralizing the catastrophic risk.

Univariate Monte Carlo methods can be employed to simulate directly various sample paths of the value of the current portfolio holdings. Hence, once a stochastic process for the portfolio returns is specified, a set of random numbers, which conform to a known distribution that matches the empirical distribution of portfolio returns, is added to form various sample paths of portfolio return. The portfolio VaR is then estimated from the corresponding density function. Nevertheless, this method is still exposed to a major weakness. The probability density of portfolio residual returns is assumed to be known.[16]

In this application, to further the acceptance of the VaR methodology, we will assess its reliability under conditions likely to be uncorrelated in financial markets. The logical method to investigate this issue is through the use of historical simulation which relies on a uniform distribution to select innovations from the past.[17] These innovations are applied to current asset prices to simulate their future evolution. Once a sufficient number of different paths has been explored, it is possible to determine a portfolio VaR without making arbitrary distributional assumptions. This is especially useful in the presence of abnormally large portfolio returns.

To make historical simulation consistent with the clustering of large returns, we will employ the GARCH volatility estimates of equation (2.29) to scale randomly selected past portfolio residual returns. First, the past daily portfolio residual returns are divided by the corresponding GARCH volatility estimates to obtain standardized residuals. Hence, the residual returns used in the historical simulation are i.i.d., which ensures that the portfolio simulated returns will not be biased. A simulated portfolio return for tomorrow is obtained by multiplying randomly selected standardized residuals by the GARCH volatility to forecast the next day's volatility. This simulated return is then used to update the GARCH forecast for the following days, that is, it is multiplied by a newly selected standardized residual to simulate the return for the second day. This recursive procedure is repeated until the VaR horizon (i.e. 10 days) is reached, generating a sample path of portfolio volatilities and returns. A batch of 10 000 sample paths of portfolio returns is computed and a confidence band for the portfolio return is built by taking the first and the ninety-ninth percentile of the frequency distribution of returns at each time. The lower percentile identifies the VaR over the next 10 days.

To illustrate our methodology we use the standardized conditional residuals for our portfolio over the entire 1986–1995 period as shown in Figure 2.4. We then construct interactively the daily portfolio volatility that these returns imply according to equation (2.29). We use this volatility to rescale our returns. The resulting returns reflect current market conditions rather than historical conditions associated with the returns in Figure 2.3.

To obtain the distribution of our portfolio returns we replicated the above procedure 10 000 times. The resulting–normalized–distribution is shown in Figure 2.9. The normal distribution is shown in the same figure for comparison.

Not surprisingly, simulated returns on our well-diversified portfolio are almost

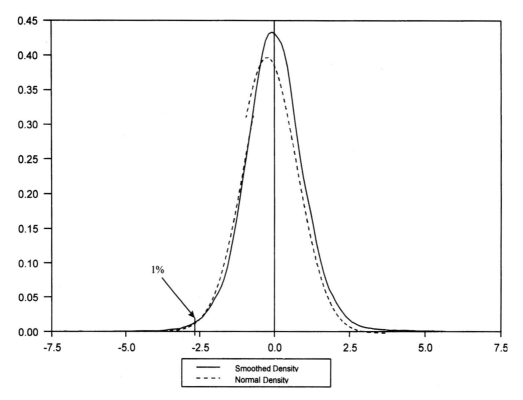

Figure 2.9 Normalized estimated distribution of returns in 10 days versus the normal density (10 000 simulations).

normal, except for their steeper peaking around zero and some clustering in the tails. The general shape of the distribution supports the validity of the usual measure of VaR for our portfolio. However, a closer examination of our simulation results shows how even our well-diversified portfolio may depart from normality under worst-case scenarios. There are in fact several occurrences of very large negative returns, reaching a maximum loss of 7.22%. Our empirical distribution implies (under the WCS) losses of at least 3.28% and 2.24% at confidence levels of 1% and 5% respectively.[18]

The reason for this departure is the changing portfolio volatility and thus portfolio VaR, shown in Figure 2.10. Portfolio VaR over the next 10 days depends on the random returns selected in each simulation run. Its pattern is skewed to the right, showing how large returns tend to cluster in time. These clusters provide realistic WCS consistent with historical experience. Of course, our methodology may produce more extreme departures from normality for less diversified portfolios.

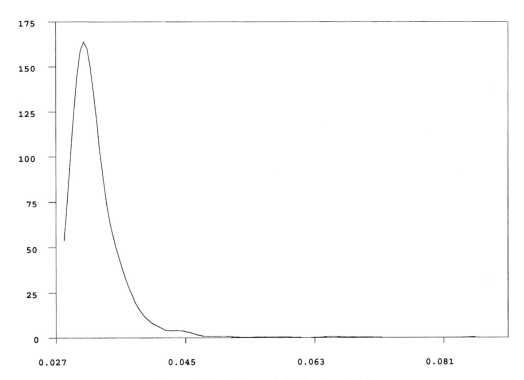

Figure 2.10 Estimated distribution of VaR.

Conclusions

While portfolio holdings aim at diversifying risk, this risk is subject to continuous changes. The GARCH methodology allows us to estimate past and current and predicted future risk levels of our current position. However, the correlation-based VaR, which employed GARCH variance and covariance estimates, failed the diagnostic tests badly. The VaR model used in this application is a combination of historical simulation and GARCH volatility. It relies only on historical data for securities prices but applies the most current portfolio positions to historical returns. The use of historical returns of portfolio components and current weights can produce accurate estimates of current risk for a portfolio of traded securities. Information on the time series properties of returns of the portfolio components is transformed into a conditional estimate of the current portfolio volatility with no need to use complex multivariate time series procedures. Our approach leads to a simple formulation of stress analysis and correlation risk.

There are three useful products of our methodology. The first is a simple and accurate measure of the volatility of the current portfolio from which an accurate assessment of current risk can be made. This is achieved without using computationally intensive multivariate methodologies. The second is the possibility of comparing a series of volatility patterns similar to Figure 2.7 with the historical volatility pattern of the actual portfolio with its changing weights. This comparison allows for an evaluation of the managers' ability to 'time' volatility. Timing volatility is an important component of performance, especially if expected security returns are not positively related to current volatility levels. Finally, the possibility of using the GARCH residuals on the current portfolio weights allows for the implementation of meaningful stress testing procedures. Stress testing and the evaluation of correlation risk are important criteria in risk management models.

To test our simplified approach to VaR we employed a hypothetical portfolio. We fitted an asymmetric GARCH on the portfolio returns and we forecasted portfolio volatility and VaR. The results indicate that this approach to estimating VaR is reliable. This is implied by the GARCH model yielding unbiased estimators for the portfolio conditional variance. Furthermore, this conditional variance estimate can now predict, on average, one third of the next day's square price movement.

We then applied the concept of correlation stability which we argue is a very useful tool in risk management in that it measures the proportion of an increase or decrease in the portfolio VaR caused by changes in asset correlations. In comparing the conditional volatility of our diversified and undiversified hypothetical portfolio, the effects of changes in correlations can be highlighted. While we found that the volatility of the diversified portfolio is lower than the undiversified portfolio, the use of correlation stability has the useful property of acting as an early warning to risk managers in relation to the effects of a negative shock, such as that of a stock market crash, on the riskiness of our portfolio. This is appealing to practitioners because it can be used to determine the ability of risk managers to diversify portfolio risk. Correlation stability is appealing to practitioners because it can be used, both in working with the portfolio selection and assessing the ability of risk managers to diversify portfolio risk.

Thereafter, we show how 'worst-case' scenarios (WCS) for stress analysis may be constructed by applying the largest outliers in the innovation series to the current GARCH parameters. While the VaR estimated previously considers the market risk of a portfolio in relation to the frequency that a specific loss will be exceeded, it does not determine the size of the loss. Our exercise simulates the effect of the largest historical shock on current market conditions and evaluates the likelihood of a given loss occurring over the VaR horizon.

In conclusion, our simulation methodology allows for a fast evaluation of VaR and WCS for large portfolios. It takes into account current market conditions and does not rely on the knowledge of the correlation matrix of security returns.

Appendix: ARCH(1) properties

The unconditional mean

The ARCH model specifies that $E(\varepsilon|\Phi_{t-1}) = 0$ for all realizations of Φ_{t-1}, the information set. Applying the law of iterated expectations we have

$$E(\varepsilon_t) = 0 = E[E(\varepsilon_t|\Phi_{t-1})] \tag{A1}$$

Because the ARCH model specifies that $E(\varepsilon_t|\Phi_{t-1}) = 0$ for all realizations of Φ_{t-1} this implies that $E(\varepsilon_t) = 0$ and so the ARCH process has unconditional mean zero. The set Φ_t contains all available information at time $t-1$ but usually includes past returns and variances only.

The unconditional variance

Similarly, the unconditional variance of the ARCH(1) process can be written as

$$E(\varepsilon_t^2) = E(\varepsilon_t^2|\Phi_{t-1}) = E(h_t) = \omega + \alpha E(\varepsilon_{t-1}^2) \tag{A2}$$

Assuming that the process began infinitely far in the past with finite initial variance, and by using the law of iterated expectations, it can be proved that the sequence of variances converge to a constant:

$$E(\varepsilon_t^2) = h_t = \sigma^2 = \frac{\omega}{(1 - \alpha)} \tag{A3}$$

The necessary and sufficient condition for the existence of the variance (the variance to be stationary) is $\omega > 0$ and $1 - \alpha > 0$. Equation (A3) implies that although the variance of ε_t conditional on Φ_{t-1} is allowed to change with the elements of the information set Φ, unconditionally the ARCH process is homoskedastic, hence $E(\varepsilon_t^2) = h_t = \sigma^2$, the historical variance.

After rearranging equation (A3) h_t can be written as

$$h_t - \sigma^2 = \alpha(\varepsilon_{t-1}^2 - \sigma^2) \tag{A4}$$

It follows then that the conditional variance will be greater than the unconditional variance σ^2, whenever the squared past error exceeds σ^2.

The skewness and kurtosis of the ARCH process

As ε_t is conditionally normal, it follows that for all odd integers m we have

$$E(\varepsilon_t^m|\Phi_{t-1}) = 0$$

Hence, the third moment of an ARCH process is always 0, and is equal to the unconditional moment.

However, an expression for the fourth moment, *kurtosis*, is available only for ARCH(1) and GARCH(1, 1) models. Using simple algebra we can write the kurtosis of an ARCH(1) as[19]

$$\frac{E(\varepsilon_t^4)}{\sigma_\varepsilon^4} = \frac{3(1 - \alpha^2)}{(1 - 3\alpha^2)} \tag{A5}$$

which is greater than 3, the kurtosis coefficient of the normal distribution. This allows the distribution of Y_t to exhibit fat tails without violating the normality assumption, and therefore to be symmetric.

Researchers have established that the distribution, of price changes or their logarithm, in a variety of financial series symmetric but with fatter tails than those of normal distribution, even if the assumption of normality for the distribution of Y_t is violated[20] the estimates of an ARCH (family) model will still be consistent, in a statistical sense. Other researchers have advanced the idea that any serial correlation present in conditional second moments of speculative prices could be attributed to the arrival of news within a serial correlated process.

We have seen so far that if $\alpha < 1$ and ε_t is conditionally normal, the ARCH model has one very appealing property. It allows the errors, ε_t, to be serially uncorrelated but not necessarily independent, since they can be related through their second moments (when $\alpha > 0$). Of course, if $\alpha = 0$ the process reduces to homoskedastic case.

Estimating the ARCH model

The efficient and popular method for computing an ARCH model is maximum likelihood. The likelihood function usually assumes that the conditional density is Gaussian, so the logarithmic likelihood of the sample is given by the sum of the individual normal conditional densities. For example, given a process $\{y_t\}$ with constant mean and variance and drawn from a normal distribution the log likelihood function is given by

$$\ln(\Theta) = -\left(\frac{T}{2}\right)\ln(2\pi) - \left(\frac{T}{2}\right)\ln\sigma^2 - \left(\frac{1}{2}\sigma^2\right)\sum_{t=1}^{T}(Y_t - \mu)^2 \qquad \text{(A6a)}$$

where $\ln(\Theta)$ is the natural logarithm of the likelihood function for $t = 1, \ldots, T$. The procedure in maximizing the above likelihood function stands to maximize $\ln(\Theta)$ for $t = 1, \ldots, T$. This involves finding the optimal values of the two parameters, σ^2 and μ. This is achieved by setting the first-order partial derivatives equal to zero and solving for the values of σ^2 and μ that yield the maximum value of $\ln(\Theta)$.

When the term μ is replaced with βX_t the likelihood function of the classical regression is derived. By replacing σ^2 with h_t and $Y_t - \mu$ with ε_t^2, the variance residual error at time t, the likelihood for the ARCH process is derived. Thus the likelihood function of an ARCM process is given as

$$\ln(\Theta) = -\frac{1}{2}\ln(2\pi) - \frac{1}{2}\sum_{t=1}^{T}\ln(h_t) - \frac{1}{2}\sum_{t=1}^{T}\frac{\varepsilon_t^2}{h_t} \qquad \text{(A6b)}$$

Unfortunately ARCH models are highly non-linear and so analytical derivatives cannot be used to calculate the appropriate sums in equation (A6b). However, numerical methods can be used to maximize the likelihood function and obtain the parameter vector Θ. The preferred approach for maximizing the likelihood function and obtaining the required results is an algorithm proposed by Berndt, Hall and Hausman in a paper published in 1974. Other standard algorithms are available to undertake this task, for example, Newton. These are not recommended since they require the evaluation of the Hessian matrix, and often fail to converge.

The strength of the maximum likelihood method to estimate an ARCH model lies in the fact that the conditional variance and mean can be estimated jointly, while exogenous variables can still have an impact in the return equation (A1), in the same way as in conventionally specified economic models.

However, because ML estimation is expensive to compute, a number of alternative econometric techniques have been proposed to estimate ARCH models. Among those is the generalized method of moments (GMM) and a two-stage least squares method (2SLS). The second is very simple and consists of regressing the squared residuals of an AR(1) against past squared residuals. Although this method provides a consistent estimator of the parameters, it is not efficient.

GARCH(1, 1) properties

Following the law of iterated expectations the unconditional variance for a GARCH(1, 1) can be written as

$$E(\varepsilon_t^2) = \sigma^2 = \omega/(1 - \alpha - \beta) \tag{A7}$$

which implies $(\alpha + \beta) < 1$ in order for h to be finite. An important property emerges from equation (A7). Shocks to volatility decay at a constant rate where the speed of the decay is measured by $\alpha + \beta$. The closer that $\alpha + \beta$ is to one, the higher will be the persistence of shocks to current volatility. Obviously if $\alpha + \beta = 1$ then shocks to volatility persist for ever, and the unconditional variance is not determined by the model. Such a process is known as 'Integrated GARCH', or IGARCH. It can be shown that ε_t^2 can be written as an ARMA(m, p) process with serially uncorrelated innovations V_t, where $V_t \equiv \varepsilon_t^2 - h_t$. The conditional variance of a GARCH(p, q) can be written as

$$\varepsilon_t^2 = \omega + \Sigma(\alpha_1 + \beta_1)\varepsilon_{t-1}^2 + \Sigma\beta_{jV_{t-1}} + V_t \tag{A8}$$

with $i = 1, \ldots, m$, $m = \max\{p, q\}$, $\alpha \equiv 0$ for $i > q$ and $\beta_i \equiv 0$ for $i > p$.

The autoregressive parameters are $\alpha(L) + \beta(L)$, the moving average ones are $-\beta(L)$, and V are the serially non-correlated innovations. The autocorrelogram and partial autocorrelogram for ε_t^2 can be used to identify the order $\{p, q\}$ of the GARCH model. Thus if $\alpha(L) + \beta(L)$ is close to one, the autocorrelation function will decline quite slowly, indicating a relatively slow-changing conditional variance.

An immediately recognized weakness of ARCH models is that a misspecification in the variance equation will lead to biased estimates for the parameters. Thus, estimates for the conditional variance and mean will no longer be valid in small samples but will be asymptotically consistent. However, GARCH models are not as sensitive to misspecification.

Exponential GARCH properties

Unlike the linear (G)ARCH models, the exponential ARCH always guarantees a positive h_t without imposing any restriction on the parameters in the variance equation (this is because logarithms are used). In addition, the parameters in the variance equation are always positive solving the problem of negative coefficients often faced in higher-order ARCH and GARCH models. It has been possible to overcome this problem by restricting the parameters to be positive or imposing a declining structure. Furthermore, unlike the GARCH models which frequently reveal that there is a *persistence* of shocks to the conditional variance, in exponential ARCH the $\ln(h_t)$ is strictly stationary and ergodic.

Notes

[1] ES techniques recognize that security returns are non-stationary (variances changes over time). However, they contradict themselves when used to calculate the VaR.

[2] The variance in Riskmetrics is using current period surprise (ε_t). Hence, they have superior information to the GARCH model.

[3] Maximization of the likelihood function is the computational price that is involved in using GARCH. The ES model involves only one parameter whose optimum value can be obtained by selecting that estimate which generates the minimum sum of squared residuals.

[4] Hence each of the two series of the conditional (GARCH) variance is restricted to depend on its own past values and the last period's residual errors to be denoted as surprises. Similarly, the conditional (GARCH) estimates for the covariance (which, among others, determine the sine of the cross-correlation coefficient) is modeled on its own last period's value and the cross-product of the errors of the two assets.

[5] When W represents an investment holding under consideration, Y describes the behavior of this hypothetical portfolio over the past.

[6] Markowitz incorporates equation (2.27b) in the objective function of his portfolio selection problem because his aim was to find the optimal vector of weights W. However, if W is known *a priori* then the portfolio's (unconditional) volatility can be computed more easily as in equation (2.28b).

[7] The terms 'local market', 'national market', 'domestic market', 'local portfolio', 'national portfolio' refer to the national indices and will be used interchangeably through this study.

[8] Due to investment restrictions for foreign investors in the emerging markets and other market misconceptions along with data non-availability, our study is restricted to the developed markets only.

[9] In a widely diversified portfolio, which may contain different types of assets, the null hypothesis of non-ARCH may not be rejected even if each asset follows a GARCH process itself.

[10] If the null hypothesis had not been rejected, then portfolio volatility could be estimated as a constant.

[11] A number of different GARCH parameterizations and lag orders have been tested. Among these conditional variance parameterizations are the GARCH, exponential GARCH, threshold GARCH and GARCH with t-distribution in the likelihood function. We used a number of diagnostic tests, i.e. serial correlation, no further GARCH effect, significant t-statistics. The final choice for the model in equation (2.29) is the unbiasedness in conditional variance estimates as tested by the Pagan–Ullah test which is expressed in equation (2.30) and absence of serial correlation in the residual returns. Non-parametric estimates of conditional mean functions, employed later, support this assumption.

[12] Throughout this chapter the term 'empirical distribution' refers to the Kernel estimators.

[13] The Pagan–Ullah test can also be applied to measure the goodness of fit of a conditional covariance model. This stands on regressing the cross product of the two residual series against a constant and the covariance estimates. The unbiasedness hypothesis requires the constant to be zero and the slope to be one. The uncentered coefficient of determination of the regression tells us the forecasting power of the model. Unfortunately, even with daily observations, for most financial time series the coefficient of determination tends to be very low, pointing to the great difficulty in obtaining good covariance estimates.

[14] That is, the average volatility of a diversified over the average of an undiversified portfolio.

[15] The forecast of the portfolio variance converges to a constant, $(\omega + \alpha\gamma^2)/(1 - \alpha - \beta)$, which is also the mean of the portfolio's conditional volatility.

[16] A second limitation arises if the (stochastic) model that describes portfolio returns restricts portfolio variance to be constant over time.

[17] Historical simulation is better known as 'bootstrapping' simulation.

[18] Note that the empirical distribution has asymmetric tails and is kurtotic. Our methodology ensures that the degree of asymmetry is consistent with the statistical properties of portfolio returns over time.

[19] The ARCH(1) case requires that $3\alpha^2 < 1$ for the fourth moment to exist.

[20] Thus, the assumption that the conditional density is normally distributed usually does not affect the parameter estimates of an ARCH model, even if it is false, see, for example, Engle and Gonzalez-Rivera (1991).

Further reading

Barone-Adesi, G., Bourgoin, F. and Giannopoulos, K. (1998) 'Don't look back', *Risk*, August.

Barone-Adesi, G., Giannopoulos, K. and Vosper, L. (1990) 'VaR without correlations for non-linear portfolios', *Journal of Futures Markets*, **19**, 583–602.

Berndt, E., Hall, B., Hall, R. and Hausman, J. (1974) 'Estimation and interference in non-linear structured models', *Annals of Economic and Social Measurement*, **3**, 653–65.

Black, M. (1968) 'Studies in stock price volatility changes', *Proceedings of the 1976 Business Meeting of the Business and Economic Statistics Section*, American Statistical Association, 177–81.

Bollerslev, T. (1986) 'Generalised autoregressive conditional heteroskedasticity', *Journal of Econometrics*, **31**, 307–28.

Bollerslev, T. (1988) 'On the correlation structure of the generalised autoregressive conditional heteroskedastic process', *Journal of Time Series Analysis*, **9**, 121–31.

Christie, A. (1982) 'The stochastic behaviour of common stock variance: value, leverage and interest rate effects', *Journal of Financial Economics*, **10**, 407–32.

Diebold, F. and Nerlove, M. (1989) 'The dynamics of exchange rate volatility: a multivariate latent factor ARCH model', *Journal of Applied Econometrics*, **4**, 1–21.

Engle, R. (1982) 'Autoregressive conditional heteroskedasticity with estimates of the variance in the UK inflation', *Econometrica*, **50**, 987–1008.

Engle, R. and Bollerslev, T. (1986) 'Modelling the persistence of conditional variances', *Econometric Reviews*, **5**, 1–50.

Engle, R. and Gonzalez-Rivera, G. (1991) 'Semiparametric ARCH models', *Journal of Business and Economic Statistics*, **9**, 345–59.

Engle, R., Granger, C. and Kraft, D. (1984) 'Combining competing forecasts of inflation using a bivariate ARCH model', *Journal of Economic Dynamics and Control*, **8**, 151–65.

Engle, R., Lilien, D. and Robins, R. (1987) 'Estimating the time varying risk premia in the term structure: the ARCH-M model', *Econometrica*, **55**, 391–407.

Engle, R. and Ng, V. (1991) 'Measuring and testing the impact of news on volatility', mimeo, University of California, San Diego.

Fama, E. (1965) 'The behaviour of stock market prices', *Journal of Business*, **38**, 34–105.

Glosten, L., Jagannathan, R. and Runkle, D. (1991) 'Relationship between the expected value and the volatility of the nominal excess return on stocks', mimeo, Northwestern University.

Joyce, J. and Vogel, R. (1970) 'The uncertainty in risk: is variance unambiguous?', *Journal of Finance*, **25**, 127–34.

Kroner, K., Kneafsey, K. and Classens, S. (1995) 'Forecasting volatility in commodity markets', *Journal of Forecasting*, **14**, 77–95.

LeBaron, B. (1988) 'Stock return nonlinearities: comparing tests and finding structure', mimeo, University of Wisconsin.

Mandelbrot, B. (1963) 'The variation of certain speculative prices', *Journal of Business*, **36,** 394–419.

Nelson, D. (1988) *The Time Series Behaviour of Stock Market Volatility Returns*, PhD thesis, MIT, Economics Department.

Nelson, D. (1990) 'Conditional heteroskedasticity in asset returns: a new approach', *Econometrica*, **59,** 347–70.

Nelson, D. (1992) 'Filtering and forecasting with misspecified ARCH models: getting the right variance with the wrong model', *Journal of Econometrics*, **52.**

Pagan, A. and Schwert, R. (1990) 'Alternative models for conditional stock volatility', *Journal of Econometrics*, **45,** 267–90.

Pagan, A. and Ullah, A. (1988) 'The econometric analysis of models with risk terms', *Journal of Applied Econometrics*, **3,** 87–105.

Rosenberg, B. (1985) 'Prediction of common stock betas', *Journal of Portfolio Management*, **11,** Winter, 5–14.

Scheinkman, J. and LeBaron, B. (1989) 'Non-linear dynamics and stock returns', *Journal of Business*, **62,** 311–37.

Zakoian, J.-M. (1990) 'Threshold heteroskedastic model', mimeo, INSEE, Paris.

3

The yield curve

P. K. SATISH

Introduction

Fundamental to any trading and risk management activity is the ability to value future cash flows of an asset. In modern finance the accepted approach to valuation is the discounted cash flows (DCF) methodology. If $C(t)$ is a cash flow occurring t years from today, according to the DCF model, the value of this cash flow today is

$$V_0 = C(t)Z(t)$$

where $Z(t)$ is the present value (PV) factor or discount factor. Therefore, to value any asset the necessary information is the cash flows, their payment dates, and the corresponding discount factors to PV these cash flows. The cash flows and their payment dates can be directly obtained from the contract specification but the discount factor requires the knowledge of the *yield curve*. In this chapter we will discuss the methodology for building the yield curve for the bond market and swap market from prices and rates quoted in the market.

The yield curve plays a central role in the pricing, trading and risk management activities of all financial products ranging from cash instruments to exotic structured derivative products. It is a result of the consensus economic views of the market participants. Since the yield curve reflects information about the microeconomic and macroeconomic variables such as liquidity, anticipated inflation rates, market risk premia and expectations on the overall state of the economy, it provides valuable information to all market participants. The rationale for many trades in the financial market are motivated by a trader's attempt to monetize their views about the future evolution of the yield curve when they differ from that of the market. In the interest rate derivative market, yield curve is important for calibrating interest rate models such as Black, Derman and Toy (1990), Hull and White (1990) and Heath, Jarrow and Morton (1992) and Brace, Gatarek and Musiela (1997) to market prices. The yield curve is built using liquid market instrument with reliable prices. Therefore, we can identify hedges by shocking the yield curve and evaluating the sensitivity of the position to changes in the yield curve. The time series data of yield curve can be fed into volatility estimation models such as GARCH to compute Value-at-Risk (VaR).

Strictly speaking, the yield curve describes the term structure of interest rates in any market, i.e. the relationship between the market yield and maturity of instruments with similar credit risk. The market yield curve can be described by a number of alternative but equivalent ways: discount curve, par-coupon curve, zero-coupon or spot curve and forward rate curve. Therefore, given the information on any one, any of the other curves can be derived with no additional information.

The discount curve reflects the discount factor applicable at different dates in the future and represents the information about the market in the most primitive fashion. This is the most primitive way to represent the yield curve and is primarily used for valuation of cash flows. An example of discount curve for the German bond market based on the closing prices on 29 October 1998 is shown in Figure 3.1. The par, spot, and forward curves that can be derived from the discount curve is useful for developing yield curve trading ideas.

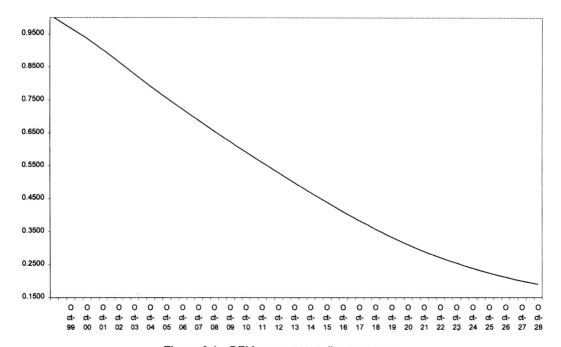

Figure 3.1   DEM government discount curve.

The par-coupon curve reflects the relationship between the yield on a bond issued at par and maturity of the bond. The zero curve or the spot curve, on the other hand, indicates the yield of a zero coupon bond for different maturity. Finally, we can also construct the forward par curve or the forward rate curve. Both these curves show the future evolution of the interest rates as seen from today's market yield curve. The forward rate curve shows the anticipated market interest rate for a specific tenor at different points in the future while the forward curve presents the evolution of the entire par curve at a future date. Figure 3.2 shows the par, spot, forward curves German government market on 29 October 1998. For example the data point (20y, 5.04) in the 6m forward par curve tell us that the 20-year par yield 6m from the spot is 5.04%. The data point (20y, 7.13) on the 6m forward rate curve indicates that the 6-month yield 20 years from the spot is 7.13%. For comparison, the 6-month yield and the 20-year par yield on spot date is 3.25% and 4.95% respectively.

Since discount factor curve forms the fundamental building block for pricing and trading in both the cash and derivative markets we will begin by focusing on the methodology for constructing the discount curve from market data. Armed with the

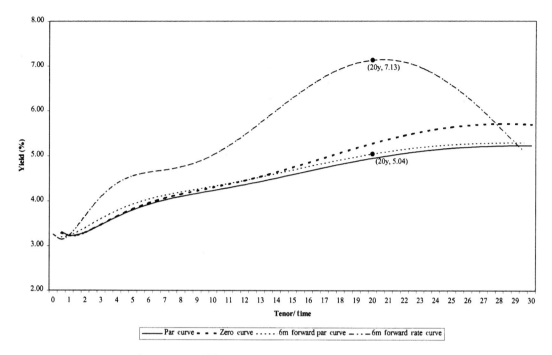

Figure 3.2   DEM par-, zero-, and forward yield curves.

knowledge of discount curve we will then devote our attention to developing other representation of market yield curve. The process for building the yield curve can be summarized in Figure 3.3.

Bootstrapping swap curve

Market participant also refers to the swap curve as the LIBOR curve. The swap market yield curve is built by splicing together the rates from market instruments that represent the most liquid instruments or dominant instruments in their tenors. At the very short end, the yield curve uses the cash deposit rates, where available the International Money Market (IMM) futures contracts are used for intermediate tenors and finally par swap rates are used for longer tenors. A methodology for building the yield curve from these market rates, referred to as *bootstrapping or zero coupon stripping*, that is widely used in the industry is discussed in this section.

The LIBOR curve can be built using the following combinations of market rates:

- Cash deposit + futures + swaps
- Cash deposit + swaps

The reason for the popularity of the bootstrapping approach is its ability to produce a no-arbitrage yield curve, meaning that the discount factor obtained from bootstrapping can recover market rates that has been used in their construction. The downside to this approach, as will be seen later, is the fact that the forward rate curve obtained from this process is not a smooth curve. While there exists methodologies to obtain smooth forward curves with the help of various fitting

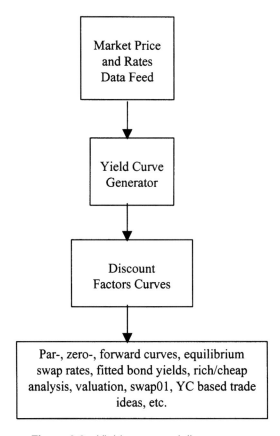

Figure 3.3   Yield curve modeling process.

algorithms they are not always preferred as they may violate the no-arbitrage constraint or have unacceptable behavior in risk calculations.

Notations

In describing the bootstrapping methodology we will adopt the following notations for convenience:

t_0 Spot date
$S(T)$:   Par swap rate quote for tenor T at spot date
$Z(T)$:   Zero coupon bond price or discount factor maturing on date T at spot date
$\alpha(t_1, t_2)$:   Accrual factor between date t_1 and t_2 in accordance to day count convention of the market (ACT/360, 30/360, 30E/360, ACT/ACT)
$F(T_1, T_2)$: Forward rate between date T_1 and T_2 as seen from the yield curve at spot date
$P(T_1, T_2)$: IMM futures contract price deliverable on date T_1 at spot date
$f(T_1, T_2)$: Futures rate, calculated as $100 - P(T_1, T_2)$ at spot date
$d(T)$:   Money market cash deposit rates for maturity T at spot date

Extracting discount factors from deposit rates

The first part of the yield curve is built using the cash deposit rates quoted in the market. The interest on the deposit rate accrue on a simple interest rate basis and as such is the simplest instrument to use in generating discount curve. It is calculated using the following fundamental relationship in finance:

Present value = future value × discount factor

The present value is the value of the deposit today and the future value is the amount that will be paid out at the maturity of the deposit. Using our notations we can rewrite this equation as

$$1 = (1 + d(T)\alpha(t_0, T) \times Z(T)$$

or equivalently,

$$Z(T) = \frac{1}{(1 + d(T)\alpha(t_0, T)} \tag{3.1}$$

The accrual factor, $\alpha(t_0, T)$, is calculated according to money market day count basis for the currency. In most currencies it is Actual/360 or Actual/365. For example, consider the deposit rate data for Germany in Table 3.1.

Table 3.1   DEM cash deposit rates data

Tenor	Bid	Accrual basis
O/N	3.35	
T/N	3.38	
T/N	3.38	
1M	3.45	
2M	3.56	Actual/360
3M	3.55	
6M	3.53	
9M	3.44	
12M	3.47	

The discount factor for 1W is

$$\frac{1}{\left(1 + 3.38\% \dfrac{7}{360}\right)} = 0.9993$$

Similarly, using expression (3.1) we can obtain the discount factor for all other dates as well. The results are shown in Table 3.2. These calculations should be performed after adjusting the maturity of cash rates for weekends and holidays where necessary.

In the above calculation the spot date is trade date plus two business days as per the convention for the DEM market and the discount factor for the spot date is defined to be 1. If instead of the spot date we define the discount factor for the trade date to be 1.0 then the above discount factor needs to be rebased using the overnight rate and tomorrow next rate. First, we can calculate the overnight discount factor as:

$$\frac{1}{\left(1 + 3.35\% \dfrac{7}{360}\right)} = 0.9999$$

Table 3.2 DEM cash deposit discount factor curve at spot date

Tenor	Maturity	Accrued days	Discount factor
Trade date	22-Oct-98		
Spot	26-Oct-98	0	1.0000
1W	02-Nov-98	7	0.9993
1M	26-Nov-98	31	0.9970
2M	28-Dec-98	63	0.9938
3M	26-Jan-99	92	0.9910
6M	26-Apr-99	182	0.9824
9M	26-Jul-99	273	0.9745
12M	26-Oct-99	365	0.9660

Next, we use the tomorrow next rate to calculate the discount factor for the spot date. The tomorrow next rate is a forward rate between trade day plus one business day to trade date plus two business day. Therefore, the discount factor for the spot date is:

$$0.9999 \times \frac{1}{\left(1 + 3.38\% \dfrac{3}{360}\right)} = 0.9996$$

The discount factors to trade date can be obtained by multiplying all the discount factors that has been previously calculated to spot date by 0.9996. This is shown in Table 3.3.

Table 3.3 DEM cash deposit discount curve at trade date

Tenor	Maturity	Accrued days	Discount factor
Trade Date	22-Oct-98	0	1.00000000
O/N	23-Oct-98	1	0.99990695
Spot	26-Oct-98	4	0.99962539
1W	02-Nov-98	11	0.99896885
1M	26-Nov-98	35	0.99666447
2M	28-Dec-98	67	0.99343628
3M	26-Jan-99	96	0.99063810
6M	26-Apr-99	186	0.98209875
9M	26-Jul-99	277	0.97421146
12M	26-Oct-99	369	0.96565188

Extracting discount factors from futures contracts

Next we consider the method for extracting the discount factor from the futures contract. The prices for IMM futures contract reflect the effective interest rate for lending or borrowing 3-month LIBOR for a specific time period in the future. The contracts are quoted on a price basis and are available for the months March, June, September and December. The settlement dates for the contracts vary from exchange to exchange. Typically these contracts settle on the third Wednesday of the month and their prices reflect the effective future interest rate for a 3-month period from the settlement date.

The relationship between the discount factor and the futures rate is given by the expression below.

$$Z(T_2) = Z(T_1) \frac{1}{[1 + f(T_1, T_2)\alpha(T_1, T_2)]} \qquad (3.2)$$

The futures rate is derived from the price of the futures contract as follows:

$$f(T_1, T_2) = \frac{100 - P(T_1, T_2)}{100}$$

Thus, with the knowledge of discount factor for date T_1 and the interest rate futures contract that spans time period (T_1, T_2) we can obtain the discount factor for date T_2.

If the next futures contract span (T_2, T_3) then we can reapply expression (3.2) and use for $Z(T_2)$ the discount factor calculated from the previous contract. In general,

$$Z(T_i) = Z(T_{i-1}) \frac{1}{(1 + f(T_{i-1}, T_i)\alpha(T_{i-1}, T_i))}$$

An issue that arises during implementation is that any two adjacent futures contract may not always adjoin perfectly. This results in gaps along the settlement dates of the futures contract making the direct application of expression (3.2) difficult. Fortunately, this problem can be overcome. A methodology for dealing with gaps in the futures contract is discussed later.

Building on the example earlier, consider the data in Table 3.4 for 3-month Euromark futures contract in LIFFE. The settlement date is the third Wednesday of the contract expiration month. We assume that the end date for the 3-month forward period is the settlement date of the next contract, i.e. ignore existence of any gaps.

Table 3.4 DEM futures price data

Contract	Price	Implied rate (A/360 basis)	Settle date	End date	Accrued days
DEC98	96.5100	3.4900%	16-Dec-98	17-Mar-99	91
MAR99	96.7150	3.2850%	17-Mar-99	16-Jun-99	91
JUN99	96.7500	3.2500%	16-Jun-99	15-Sep-99	91
SEP99	96.7450	3.2550%	15-Sep-99	15-Dec-99	91
DEC99	96.6200	3.3800%	15-Dec-99	15-Mar-00	91
MAR00	96.6600	3.3400%	15-Mar-00	21-Jun-00	91
JUN00	96.5600	3.4400%	21-Jun-00	20-Sep-00	91
SEP00	96.4400	3.5600%	20-Sep-00	20-Dec-00	91
DEC00	96.2350	3.7650%	20-Dec-00	21-Mar-01	91
MAR01	96.1700	3.8300%	21-Mar-01	20-Jun-01	91
JUN01	96.0800	3.9200%	20-Jun-01	19-Sep-01	91
SEP01	95.9750	4.0250%	19-Sep-01	19-Dec-01	91
DEC01	95.8350	4.1650%	19-Dec-01	20-Mar-02	91
MAR02	95.7750	4.2250%	20-Mar-02	19-Jun-02	91
JUN02	95.6950	4.3050%	19-Jun-02	18-Sep-02	91
SEP02	95.6100	4.3900%	18-Sep-02	18-Dec-02	91

The price DEC98 futures contract reflects the interest rate for the 91-day period from 16 December 1998 to 17 March 1999. This can be used to determine the discount factor for 17 March 1999 using expression (3.2). However, to apply expression (3.2) we need the discount factor for 16 December 1998. While there are several approaches to identify the missing discount factor we demonstrate this example by using linear interpolation of the 1-month (26 November 1998) and 2-month (28 December 1998) cash rate. This approach gives us a cash rate of 3.5188% and discount factor for 0.99504 with respect to the spot date. The discount factor for 17 March 1998 is

$$0.9950 \left(\frac{1}{1 + 3.49\% \frac{91}{360}} \right) = 0.9863$$

In the absence of any gaps in the futures contract the above discount factor together with the MAR99 contract can be used determine the discount factor for 16 June 1999 and so on until the last contract. The results from these computations are shown in Table 3.5.

Table 3.5   DEM discount curve from futures prices

Date	Discount factor	Method
26-Oct-98	1.00000	Spot
16-Dec-98	0.99504	Interpolated cash rate
17-Mar-99	0.98634	DEC98
16-Jun-99	0.97822	MAR99
15-Sep-99	0.97024	JUN99
15-Dec-99	0.96233	SEP99
15-Mar-00	0.95417	DEC99
21-Jun-00	0.94558	MAR00
20-Sep-00	0.93743	JUN00
20-Dec-00	0.92907	SEP00
21-Mar-01	0.92031	DEC00
20-Jun-01	0.91148	MAR01
19-Sep-01	0.90254	JUN01
19-Dec-01	0.89345	SEP01
20-Mar-02	0.88414	DEC01
19-Jun-02	0.87480	MAR02
18-Sep-02	0.86538	JUN02
18-Dec-02	0.85588	SEP02

Extracting discount factor from swap rates

As we go further away from the spot date we either run out of the futures contract or, as is more often the case, the futures contract become unsuitable due to lack of liquidity. Therefore to generate the yield curve we need to use the next most liquid instrument, i.e. the swap rate.

Consider a par swap rate $S(t_N)$ maturing on t_N with cash flow dates $\{t_1, t_2, \ldots t_N\}$.

The cash flow dates may have an annual, semi-annual or quarterly frequency. The relationship between the par swap rate and the discount factor is summarized in the following expression:

$$1 - Z(t_N) = S(t_N) \sum_{i=1}^{N} \alpha(t_{i-1}, t_i) Z(t_i) \tag{3.3}$$

The left side of the expression represents the PV of the floating payments and the right side the PV of the fixed rate swap payments. Since a par swap rate by definition has zero net present value, the PV of the fixed and floating cash flows must to be equal. This expression can be rearranged to calculate the discount factor associated with the last swap coupon payment:

$$Z(t_N) = \frac{1 - S(t_N) \sum_{i=1}^{N-1} \alpha(t_{i-1}, t_i) Z(t_i)}{1 + \alpha(t_{N-1}, t_N) S(t_N)} \tag{3.4}$$

To apply the above expression we need to know the swap rate and discount factor associated with all but the last payment date. If a swap rate is not available then it has to be interpolated. Similarly, if the discount factors on the swap payment dates are not available then they also have to be interpolated.

Let us continue with our example of the DEM LIBOR curve. The par swap rates are given in Table 3.6. In this example all swap rates are quoted in the same frequency and day count basis. However, note that this need not be the case; for example, the frequency of the 1–3y swap rate in Australia dollar is quarterly while the rest are semi-annual. First we combine our cash curve and futures curve as shown in Table 3.7. Notice that all cash discount factors beyond 16 December 1998 have been dropped. This is because we opted to build our yield curve using the first futures contract. Even though the cash discount factors are available beyond 16 December 1998 the futures takes precedence over the cash rates.

Since we have already generated discount factor until 18 December 2002 the first relevant swap rate is the 5y rate. Before applying expression (3.3) to bootstrap the

Table 3.6 DEM swap rate data

Tenor	Swap Rate	Maturity	Frequency/basis
2Y	3.4600%	26-Oct-00	Annual, 30E/360
3Y	3.6000%	26-Oct-01	Annual, 30E/360
4Y	3.7600%	28-Oct-02	Annual, 30E/360
5Y	3.9100%	27-Oct-03	Annual, 30E/360
6Y	4.0500%	26-Oct-04	Annual, 30E/360
7Y	4.1800%	26-Oct-05	Annual, 30E/360
8Y	4.2900%	26-Oct-06	Annual, 30E/360
9Y	4.4100%	26-Oct-07	Annual, 30E/360
10Y	4.4900%	27-Oct-08	Annual, 30E/360
12Y	4.6750%	26-Oct-10	Annual, 30E/360
15Y	4.8600%	28-Oct-13	Annual, 30E/360
20Y	5.0750%	26-Oct-18	Annual, 30E/360
30Y	5.2900%	26-Oct-28	Annual, 30E/360

Table 3.7   DEM cash plus futures discount factor curve

Date	Discount factor	Source
26-Oct-98	1.00000	Spot
27-Oct-98	0.99991	Cash
02-Nov-98	0.99934	Cash
26-Nov-98	0.99704	Cash
16-Dec-98	0.99504	Interpolated cash
17-Mar-99	0.98634	Futures
16-Jun-99	0.97822	Futures
15-Sep-99	0.97024	Futures
15-Dec-99	0.96233	Futures
15-Mar-00	0.95417	Futures
21-Jun-00	0.94558	Futures
20-Sep-00	0.93743	Futures
20-Dec-00	0.92907	Futures
21-Mar-01	0.92031	Futures
20-Jun-01	0.91148	Futures
19-Sep-01	0.90254	Futures
19-Dec-01	0.89345	Futures
20-Mar-02	0.88414	Futures
19-Jun-02	0.87480	Futures
18-Sep-02	0.86538	Futures
18-Dec-02	0.85588	Futures

discount factor for 27 October 2003 we have to interpolate the discount factor for all the prior payment dates from the 'cash plus futures' curve we have so far. This is shown in Table 3.8 using exponential interpolation for discount factors.

Table 3.8   DEM 5y swap payment date discount factor from exponential interpolation

Cash flow dates	Accrual factor	Discount factor	Method
26-Oct-99	1.0000	0.96665	Exponential
26-Oct-00	1.0000	0.93412	interpolation from
26-Oct-01	1.0000	0.89885	cash + futures
28-Oct-02	1.0056	0.86122	curve
27-Oct-03	0.9972	?	

Therefore, the discount factor for 27 October 2003 is

$$\frac{1 - 3.91\%(1.00 \times 0.9665 + 1.00 \times 0.93412 + 1.00 \times 0.89885 + 1.0056 \times 0.86122)}{1 + 3.91\% \times 0.9972}$$

$$= 0.82452$$

This procedure can be continued to derive all the discount factors. Each successive swap rate helps us identify the discount factor associated with the swap's terminal date using all discount factors we know up to that point. When a swap rate is not available, for example the 11y rate, it has to be interpolated from the other available swap rates. The results are shown in Table 3.9 below, where we apply linear interpolation method for unknown swap rates.

In many markets it may be that the most actively quoted swap rates are the annual tenor swaps. However, if these are semi-annual quotes then we may have more discount factors to bootstrap than available swap rates. For example, suppose that we have the six-month discount factor, the 1y semi-annual swap rate and 2y semi-annual swap rate. To bootstrap the 2y discount factor we need the 18 month discount factor which is unknown:

$$
\begin{array}{ccccc}
\text{Spot1} & \text{6m} & \text{1y} & \text{18y} & \text{2y} \\
Z_0 & Z_{6m} & Z_{1y} & Z_{18M} & Z_{2Y}
\end{array}
$$

A possible approach to proceed in building the yield curve is to first interpolate (possibly linear interpolation) the 18-month swap rate from the 1y and 2y swap rate. Next, use the interpolated 18-month swap rate to bootstrap the corresponding discount factor and continue onwards to bootstrap the 2y discount factor. Another alternative is to solve numerically for both the discount factors simultaneously. Let G be an interpolation function for discount factors that takes as inputs the dates and adjacent discount factors to return the discount factor for the interpolation date, that is,

$$Z_{18m} = G(T_{18m}, Z_{1y}, Z_{2y})$$

The 2y equilibrium swap is calculated as

$$S_{2y} = \frac{1 - Z_{2y}}{[\alpha_{spot,6m}Z_{6m} + \alpha_{6m,1y}Z_{1y} + \alpha_{1y,18y}Z_{18m} + \alpha_{18m,2y}Z_{2y}]}$$

where α's are the accrual factor according to the day count basis. Substituting the relationship for the 18m discount factor we get

$$S_{2y} = \frac{1 - Z_{2y}}{[\alpha_{spot,6m}Z_{6m} + \alpha_{6m,1y}Z_{1y} + \alpha_{1y,18y}G(T_{18m}, Z_{1y}, Z_{2y}) + \alpha_{18m,2y}Z_{2y}]}$$

The above expression for the 2y swap rate does not require the 18m discount factor as input. We can then use a numerical algorithm such as Newton–Raphson to determine the discount factor for 2y, Z_{2y}, that will ensure that the equilibrium 2y swap rate equals the market quote for the 2y swap rate.

Finally, putting it all together we have the LIBOR discount factor curve for DEM in Table 3.10. These discount factors can be used to generate the par swap curve, forward rate curve, forward swap rate curve or discount factors for pricing various structured products.

The forward rate between any two dates T_1 and T_2 as seen from the yield curve on spot date t_0 is

$$F(T_1, T_2) = \left(\frac{Z(T_1)}{Z(T_2)} - 1\right)\frac{1}{\alpha(T_1, T_2)}$$

Table 3.9 DEM discount factors from swap rates

Tenor	Maturity	Swap rate	Accrual factor	Discount factor
5y	27-Oct-03	3.9100%	0.9972	0.82452
6y	26-Oct-04	4.0500%	0.9972	0.78648
7y	26-Oct-05	4.1800%	1.0000	0.74834
8y	26-Oct-06	4.2900%	1.0000	0.71121
9y	26-Oct-07	4.4100%	1.0000	0.67343
10y	27-Oct-08	4.4900%	1.0028	0.63875
11y	26-Oct-09	4.5824%	0.9972	0.60373
12y	26-Oct-10	4.6750%	1.0000	0.56911
13y	26-Oct-11	4.7366%	1.0000	0.53796
14y	26-Oct-12	4.7981%	1.0000	0.50760
15y	28-Oct-13	4.8600%	1.0056	0.47789
16y	27-Oct-14	4.9029%	0.9972	0.45122
17y	26-Oct-15	4.9459%	0.9972	0.42543
18y	26-Oct-16	4.9889%	1.0000	0.40045
19y	26-Oct-17	5.0320%	1.0000	0.37634
20y	26-Oct-18	5.0750%	1.0000	0.35309
21y	28-Oct-19	5.0966%	1.0056	0.33325
22y	26-Oct-20	5.1180%	0.9944	0.31445
23y	26-Oct-21	5.1395%	1.0000	0.29634
24y	26-Oct-22	5.1610%	1.0000	0.27900
25y	26-Oct-23	5.1825%	1.0000	0.26240
26y	28-Oct-24	5.2041%	1.0056	0.24642
27y	27-Oct-25	5.2256%	0.9972	0.23127
28y	26-Oct-26	5.2470%	0.9972	0.21677
29y	26-Oct-27	5.2685%	1.0000	0.20287
30y	26-Oct-28	5.2900%	1.0000	0.18959

This can be calculated from the discount factor curve after applying suitable interpolation method to identify discount factors not already available. For example, using exponential interpolation we find that the discount factor for 26 April 1999 is 0.98271 and that for 26 October 1999 is 0.96665. The forward rate between 26 April 1999 and 26 October 1999 is

$$\left(\frac{0.98271}{0.96665} - 1\right)\frac{1}{\left(\frac{183}{360}\right)} = 3.27\%$$

The 6m forward rate curve for DEM is shown in Table 3.11. Forward rate curves are important for pricing and trading a range of products such as swaps, FRAs, Caps and Floors and a variety of structured notes.

Similarly, the equilibrium par swap rate and forward swap rates can be calculated from the discount from

$$S(t_s, t_{s+N}) = \frac{Z(t_s) - Z(t_{s+N})}{\sum_{i=1}^{N} \alpha(t_{s+i-1}, t_{s+i})Z(t_{s+i})}$$

Table 3.10 DEM swap or LIBOR bootstrapped discount factor curve

Cash		Futures		Swaps	
Date	Discount factor	Date	Discount factor	Date	Discount factor
26-Oct-98	1.00000	17-Mar-99	0.98634	27-Oct-03	0.82452
27-Oct-98	0.99991	16-Jun-99	0.97822	26-Oct-04	0.78648
02-Nov-98	0.99934	15-Sep-99	0.97024	26-Oct-05	0.74834
26-Nov-98	0.99704	15-Dec-99	0.96233	26-Oct-06	0.71121
16-Dec-98	0.99504	15-Mar-00	0.95417	26-Oct-07	0.67343
		21-Jun-00	0.94558	27-Oct-08	0.63875
		20-Sep-00	0.93743	26-Oct-09	0.60373
		20-Dec-00	0.92907	26-Oct-10	0.56911
		21-Mar-01	0.92031	26-Oct-11	0.53796
		20-Jun-01	0.91148	26-Oct-12	0.50760
		19-Sep-01	0.90254	28-Oct-13	0.47789
		19-Dec-01	0.89345	27-Oct-14	0.45122
		20-Mar-02	0.88414	26-Oct-15	0.42543
		19-Jun-02	0.87480	26-Oct-16	0.40045
		18-Sep-02	0.86538	26-Oct-17	0.37634
		18-Dec-02	0.85588	26-Oct-18	0.35309
				28-Oct-19	0.33325
				26-Oct-20	0.31445
				26-Oct-21	0.29634
				26-Oct-22	0.27900
				26-Oct-23	0.26240
				28-Oct-24	0.24642
				27-Oct-25	0.23127
				26-Oct-26	0.21677
				26-Oct-27	0.20287
				26-Oct-28	0.18959

$S(t_s, t_{s+N})$ is the equilibrium swap rate starting at time t_s and ending at time t_{s+N}. If we substitute zero for s in the above expression we get the equilibrium par swap rate. Table 3.12 shows the par swap rates and forward swap rates from our discount curve. For comparison we also provide the market swap rates. Notice that the market swap rate and the equilibrium swap rate computed from the bootstrapped does not match until the 5y swaps. This is due to the fact that we have used the futures contract to build our curve until 18 December 2002. The fact that the equilibrium swap rates are consistently higher than the market swap rates during the first 4 years is not surprising since we have used the futures contract without convexity adjustments (see below).

Curve stitching

Cash rates and futures contracts

In building the yield curve we need to switch from the use of cash deposit rates at the near end of the curve to the use of futures rates further along the curve. The choice of the splice date when cash deposit rate is dropped and futures rate is picked up is driven by the trader's preference, which in turn depends on the instruments

Table 3.11   DEM 6 month forward rates from discount factor curve

Date	Discount factor	Accrual factor	6m forward rate
26-Oct-98	1.00000		
26-Apr-99	0.98271	0.5083	3.27%
26-Oct-99	0.96665	0.5083	3.35%
26-Apr-00	0.95048	0.5083	3.44%
26-Oct-00	0.93412	0.5056	3.73%
26-Apr-01	0.91683	0.5083	3.93%
26-Oct-01	0.89885	0.5056	4.16%
26-Apr-02	0.88035	0.5083	4.32%
26-Oct-02	0.86142	0.5056	4.32%
26-Apr-03	0.84300	0.5083	4.38%
26-Oct-03	0.82463	0.5083	4.64%
26-Apr-04	0.80562	0.5083	4.79%
26-Oct-04	0.78648	0.5056	4.89%
26-Apr-05	0.76749	0.5083	5.03%
26-Oct-05	0.74834	0.5056	5.02%
26-Apr-06	0.72981	0.5083	5.14%
26-Oct-06	0.71121	0.5056	5.39%
26-Apr-07	0.69235	0.5083	5.52%
26-Oct-07	0.67343	0.5083	5.21%
26-Apr-08	0.65605	0.5083	5.30%
26-Oct-08	0.63884	0.5056	5.60%
26-Apr-09	0.62125		

Table 3.12   DEM equilibrium swap rates from discount factor curve

Tenor	Market swap rate	Equilibrium swap rate	6m forward start swap rate
2y	3.4600%	3.4658%	3.5282%
3y	3.6000%	3.6128%	3.7252%
4y	3.7600%	3.7861%	3.8917%
5y	3.9100%	3.9100%	4.0281%
6y	4.0500%	4.0500%	4.1678%
7y	4.1800%	4.1800%	4.2911%
8y	4.2900%	4.2900%	4.4088%
9y	4.4100%	4.4100%	4.5110%
10y	4.4900%	4.4900%	4.5970%

that will be used to hedge the position. However, for the methodology to work it is necessary that the settlement date of the first futures contract (referred to as a 'stub') lie before the maturity date of the last cash deposit rate. If both cash deposit rate and futures rates are available during any time period then the futures price takes precedence over cash deposit rates.

Once the futures contracts have been identified all discount factors until the last futures contract is calculated using the bootstrapping procedure. To bootstrap the curve using the futures contract, the discount factor corresponding to the first futures delivery date (or the 'stub') is necessary information. Clearly, the delivery date of the first futures contract selected may not exactly match the maturity date of one of the cash deposit rates used in the construction. Therefore, an important issue in the curve building is the method for identifying discount factor corresponding to the first futures contract or the stub rate.

The discount factor for all subsequent dates on the yield curve will be affected by the stub rate. Hence the choice of the method for interpolating the stub rate can have a significant impact on the final yield curve. There are many alternative approaches to tackle this problem, all of which involves either interpolation method or fitting algorithm. We will consider a few based on the example depicted in Figure 3.4.

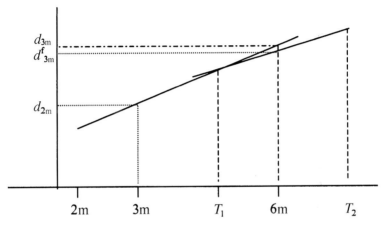

Figure 3.4   Cash-futures stitching.

The first futures contract settles on date T_1 and spans from T_1 to T_2. One alternative is to interpolate the discount factor for date T_1 with the 3m and 6m discount factor calculated from expression (3.1). The second alternative is to directly interpolate the 3m and 6m cash deposit rates to obtain the stub rate and use this rate to compute the discount factor using expression (3.1). The impact of applying different interpolation method on the stub is presented in Table 3.13.

Table 3.13   DEM stub rate from different interpolation methods

Data	Interpolation method	Discount factor	Cash rate (stub rate)
Spot date: 26-Oct-98	Linear cash rate	0.99504	3.5188%
1m (26-Nov-99): 3.45%	Exponential DF	0.99504	3.5187%
2m (28-Dec-98): 3.56%	Geometric DF	0.99502	3.5341%
Basis: Act/360	Linear DF	0.99502	3.5332%
Stub: 16-Dec-98			

The exponential interpolation of discount factor and linear interpolation of the cash rate provide similar results. This is not surprising since exponential interpolation of discount factor differs from the linear interpolation of rate in that it performs a linear interpolation on the equivalent continuously compounded yield.

To see the impact of the stitching method on the forward around the stub date we have shown the 1m forward rate surrounding the stub date in Figure 3.5 using different interpolation methods. Also, notice that the forward rate obtained from the bootstrapping approach is not smooth.

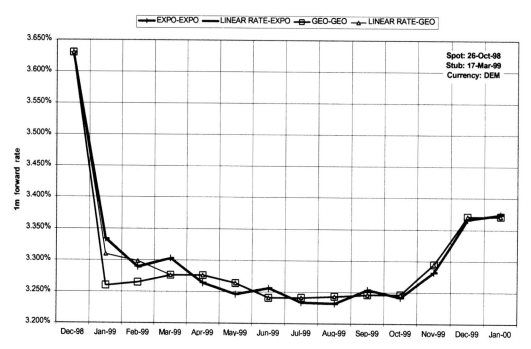

Figure 3.5 Six-month forward rate from different interpolation.

Going back to Figure 3.4, once the 3m and 6m rate has been used for interpolating the discount factor for T_1 all cash rates beyond the 3m is dropped. The yield curve point after the 3m is T_2 and all subsequent yield curve point follow the futures contract (i.e. 3 months apart). Since the 6m has been dropped, the 6m cash rate interpolated from the constructed yield curve may not match the 6m cash rate that was initially used.

This immediately raises two issues. First, what must be the procedure for discounting any cash flow that occurs between T_1 and 6m? Second, what is the implication of applying different methods of interpolation of the discount curve on the interpolated value of the 6m cash rate versus the market cash rate. Further, is it possible to ensure that the interpolated 6m cash rate match the market quoted 6m cash rate?

If recovering the correct cash rate from the yield curve points is an important criterion then the methodologies discussed earlier would not be appropriate. A possible way to handle this issue is to change the method for obtaining the stub rate by directly solving for it. We can solve for a stub rate such that 6m rate interpolated from the stub discount factor for T_1 and discount factor for T_2 match the market.

In some markets such as the USD the short-term swap dealers and active cash dealers openly quote the stub rate. If so then it is always preferable to use the market-quoted stub rate and avoid any interpolation.

Futures strip and swap rates

To extend the curve beyond the last futures contract we need the swap rates. The required swap rate may be available as input data or may need to be interpolated.

Consider the following illustration where the last futures contract ends on T_{LF}. If $S(T_2)$, the swap rate that follows the futures contract, is available as input then we can apply expression (3.3) to derive the discount factor for date T_2. This is a straightforward case that is likely to occur in currencies such as DEM with annual payment frequency:

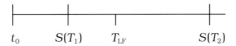

The discount factor corresponding to all payment dates except the last will need to be interpolated.

In the next scenario depicted below suppose that swap rate $S(T_2)$ is not available from the market:

We have two choices. Since we have market swap rate, $S(T_1)$ and $S(T_3)$, we could use these rates to interpolate $S(T_2)$. Alternatively, since we have discount factor until date T_{LF} we can use them to calculate a equilibrium swap rate, $S'(T_1)$, for tenor T_1. The equilibrium swap rate $S'(T_1)$ and market swap rate $S(T_3)$ can be used to interpolate the missing swap rate $S(T_2)$.

In some circumstances we may have to interpolate swap rates with a different basis and frequency from the market-quoted rates. In these cases we recommend that the market swap rates be adjusted to the same basis and frequency as the rate we are attempting to interpolate. For example, to get a 2.5y semi-annual, 30E/360 swap rate from the 2y and 3y annual, 30E/360 swap rate, the annual rates can be converted to an equivalent semi-annual rate as follows:

$$S_{\text{semi-annual}} = 2 \times [(1 + S_{\text{annual}})^{1/2} - 1]$$

Handling futures gaps and overlaps

In the construction of the discount factor using expression (3.2), we are implicitly assuming that all futures contract are contiguous with no gaps or overlaps. However, from time to time due to holidays it is possible that the contracts do not line up exactly.

Consider the illustration below:

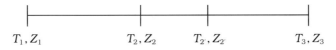

The first futures contract span from T_1 to T_2 while the next futures contract span from $T_{2'}$ to T_3 resulting in a gap. An approach to resolve this issue is as follows. Define $G(T, Z_a, Z_b)$ to be a function representing the interpolation method (e.g. exponential)

for discount factor. We can apply this to interpolate $Z_{2'}$ as follows:

$$Z_{2'} = G(T_{2'}, Z_2, Z_3) \tag{3.4}$$

From expression (3.2) we also know that

$$Z_3 = Z_{2'} \frac{1}{[1 + f(T_{2'}, T_3)\alpha(T_{2'}, T_3)]} \equiv \Psi(f, Z_{2'}) \tag{3.5}$$

Combining expressions (3.4) and (3.5) we have

$$Z_3 = \Psi(f, G(T_{2'}, Z_2, Z_3)) \tag{3.6}$$

All variables in expression (3.6) are known except Z_3. This procedure can be applied to find the discount factor Z_3 without the knowledge of $Z_{2'}$ caused by gaps in the futures contract.

For example, if we adopt exponential interpolation

$$Z_{2'} = G(T_{2'}, Z_2, Z_3) = Z_2^{\frac{(T_{2'} - t_0)}{(T_2 - t_0)}\lambda} Z^{\frac{(T_{2'} - t_0)}{(T_3 - t_0)}(1 - \lambda)}$$

and

$$\lambda = \frac{(T_3 - T_{2'})}{(T_3 - T_2)}$$

Therefore,

$$Z_3 = Z_2^{\frac{(T_{2'} - t_0)}{(T_2 - t_0)}\lambda} Z^{\frac{(T_{2'} - t_0)}{(T_3 - t_0)}(1 - \lambda)} \frac{1}{[1 + f(T_{2'}, T_3)\alpha(T_{2'}, T_3)]}$$

This can be solved analytically for Z_3. Specifically,

$$Z_3 = \mathrm{Exp}\left\{ \frac{\ln\left(Z_2^{\frac{(T_{2'} - t_0)}{(T_2 - t_0)}\lambda} \frac{1}{[1 + f(T_{2'}, T_3)\alpha(T_{2'}, T_3)]} \right)}{\left(1 - \frac{(T_{2'} - t_0)}{(T_3 - t_0)}(1 - \lambda) \right)} \right\} \tag{3.7}$$

As an example consider an extreme case where one of the futures price is entirely missing. Suppose that we know the discount factor for 16 June 1999 and the price of SEP99 futures contract. The JUN99 contract is missing. Normally we would have used the JUN99 contract to derive the discount factor for 15 September 1999 and then use the SEP99 contract to obtain the discount factor for 15 December 1999 (Table 3.14).

Table 3.14

Contract	Price	Implied rate (A/360 basis)	Settle date	End date	Discount factor
Spot				26-Oct-98 (t_0)	1.0000
				16-Jun-99 (T_2)	0.9782
JUN99	Missing	Missing	16-Jun-99	15-Sep-99 ($T_{2'}$)	N/A
SEP99	96.7450	3.2550%	15-Sep-99	15-Dec-99 (T_3)	?

In this example we can apply expression (3.7) to obtain the discount factor for 15 December 1999:

$$Z_{\text{15-Dec-99}} = \exp\left\{\frac{\ln\left(Z_2^{\frac{0.8877}{0.6384} \times 0.5} \frac{1}{[1 + 3.255\% \times 91/360]}\right)}{\left(1 - \left(\frac{0.8877}{1.1370}\right)(1 - 0.5)\right)}\right\}$$

$$= 0.96218$$

Earlier when we had the price for the JUN99 contract the discount factor for 15 December 1999 was found to be 0.96233.

Solution to overlaps are easier. If the futures contracts overlap (i.e. $T_{2'} < T_2$) then the interpolation method can be applied to identify the discount factor $Z_{2'}$ corresponding to the start of the next futures contract.

Futures convexity adjustment

Both futures and FRA are contracts written on the same underlying rate. At the expiration of the futures contract, the futures rate and the forward rate will both be equal to the then prevailing spot LIBOR rate. However, these two instruments differ fundamentally in the way they are settled. The futures contracts are settled daily whereas the FRAs are settled at maturity. As a result of this difference in the settlement procedure the daily changes in the value of a position in futures contract and that of a position in FRA to anticipated changes in the future LIBOR rate are not similar. The futures contract react linearly to changes in the future LIBOR rate while the FRA reacts non-linearly. This convexity effect creates an asymmetry in the gains / losses between being long or short in FRA and hedging them with futures contracts. To be more precise, there is an advantage to being consistently short FRA and hedging them with short futures contracts. This is recognized by the market and reflected in the market price of the futures contract. The convexity effect implies that the forward rate obtained from the futures price will be high. Since the futures rate and forward rate converge as we approach the maturity date, the futures rate must drift downwards. Hence while building the LIBOR yield curve it is important that the forward rates implied from the futures price be adjusted (downwards) by the drift.

In most markets the drift adjustments tend to be fairly small for futures contracts that expire within one year from the spot date, but can get progressively larger beyond a year. Consider an N futures contract for periods (t_i, t_{i+1}), $i = 1, 2, \ldots N$ and $(t_{i+1} - t_i) = \Delta t$. A simple method to calculate the drift adjustments for the kth futures contract is given below:[1]

$$\mu_k = \sum_{i=1}^{k} f(t_i, t_{i+1}) \rho_{fz} \sigma_{f(t_i, t_{i+1})} \sigma_{Z(t_{i+1})} \Delta t$$

where $f(t_i, t_{i+1})$ is the futures rate for the period t_i to t_{i+1}, $\sigma_{Z(t_{i+1})}$ is the volatility of the zero coupon bond maturing on t_{i+1}, $\sigma_{f(t_i, t_{i+1})}$ is the volatility of the forward rate for the corresponding period and ρ_{fz} is the correlation between the relevant forward rate and zero coupon bond price. The kth forward rate can be calculated from the futures contract as follows.

$$F(t_k, t_{k+1}) = f(t_k, t_{k+1}) + \mu_k$$

Since the correlation between the forward rate and the zero coupon price is expected to be negative the convexity adjustment would result in the futures rate being adjusted downwards.

We demonstrate the calculations for the convexity adjustment in the table below.

Table 3.15

Contract	Date	Futures rate (1)	Futures rate volatility (2)	Zero coupon volatility (3)	Correlation n (4)	Δt (5)	Drift (bp)=(1) $\times$ (2) $\times$ (3) $\times$ (4) $\times$ (5) (6)	Cumulative drift or convexity bias (bp) (7)	Convexity adjusted futures rate (8)=(1)+(7)
SPOT	26-Oct-98								
DEC98	16-Dec-98	3.49%	5%	0.25%	−0.99458	0.25	−0.0108	−0.01	3.49%
MAR99	17-Mar-99	3.29%	12%	0.75%	−0.98782	0.25	−0.0728	−0.08	3.28%
JUN99	16-Jun-99	3.25%	14%	1.25%	−0.97605	0.25	−0.1383	−0.22	3.25%
SEP99	15-Sep-99	3.26%	18%	1.50%	−0.96468	0.25	−0.2112	−0.43	3.25%
DEC99	15-Dec-99	3.38%	20%	2.00%	−0.95370	0.25	−0.3212	−0.75	3.37%
MAR99	15-Mar-00	3.34%	15%	2.25%	−0.94228	0.27	−0.2850	−1.04	3.33%
JUN00	21-Jun-00								

Typically the convexity bias is less that 1 basis point for contracts settling within a year from the spot. Between 1 year and 2 years the bias may range from 1 basis point to 4 basis point. For contracts settling beyond 2 years the bias may be as high as 20 basis point – an adjustment that can no longer be ignored.

Interpolation

The choice of interpolation algorithm plays a significant role in the process of building the yield curve for a number of reasons: First, since the rates for some of the tenors is not available due to lack of liquidity (for example, the 13-year swap rate) these missing rates need to be determined using some form of interpolation algorithm. Second, for the purposes of pricing and trading various instruments one needs the discount factor for any cash flow dates in the future. However, the bootstrapping methodology, by construction, produces the discount factor for specific maturity dates based on the tenor of the interest rates used in the construction process. Therefore, the discount factor for other dates in the future may need to be identified by adopting some interpolation algorithm. Finally, as discussed earlier, the discount factor corresponding to the stub will most of the time require application of interpolation algorithm. Similarly, the futures and swap rates may also need to be joined together with the help of interpolation algorithm.

The choice of the interpolation algorithm is driven by the requirement to balance the need to control artificial risk spillage (an important issue for hedging purposes) against the smoothness of the forward curve (an important issue in the pricing of exotic interest rate derivatives).

Discount factor interpolation

Consider the example described below:

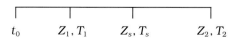

$t_0 \qquad Z_1, T_1 \qquad Z_s, T_s \qquad Z_2, T_2$

(a) Linear interpolation

The linear interpolation of discount factor for date T_s is obtained by fitting a straight line between the two adjacent dates T_1 and T_2. According to linear interpolation, the discount factor for date T_s is:

$$Z_s = Z_1 + \frac{Z_2 - Z_1}{T_2 - T_1}(T_s - T_1)$$

or

$$Z_s = \left(\frac{T_2 - T_s}{T_2 - T_1}\right)Z_1 + \left(\frac{T_s - T_1}{T_2 - T_1}\right)Z_2$$

Linear interpolation of the discount factor is almost never due to the non-linear shape of the discount curve, but the error from applying it is likely to be low in the short end where there are more points in the curve.

(b) Geometric (log-linear) Interpolation

The geometric or log linear interpolation of discount factor for date T_s is obtained by applying a natural logarithm transformation to the discount factor function and then performing a linear interpolation on the transformed function. To recover the interpolated discount factor we take the exponent of the interpolated value as shown below:

$$\ln(Z_s) = \left(\frac{T_2 - T_s}{T_2 - T_1}\right)\ln(Z_1) + \left(\frac{T_s - T_1}{T_2 - T_1}\right)\ln(Z_2)$$

or

$$Z_s = \exp\left(\left(\frac{T_2 - T_s}{T_2 - T_1}\right)\ln(Z_1) + \left(\frac{T_s - T_1}{T_2 - T_1}\right)\ln(Z_2)\right)$$

or

$$Z_s = Z_1^{\left(\frac{T_2 - T_s}{T_2 - T_1}\right)} Z_2^{\left(\frac{T_s - T_1}{T_2 - T_1}\right)}$$

(c) Exponential interpolation

The continuously compounded yield can be calculated from the discount factor as follows:

$$y_1 = -\frac{1}{(T_1 - t_0)}\ln(Z_1) \quad \text{and} \quad y_2 = -\frac{1}{(T_2 - t_0)}\ln(Z_2)$$

To calculate the exponential interpolated discount factor we first perform a linear interpolation of the continuously compounded yields as follows:

$$y_s = y_1\frac{(T_2 - T_s)}{(T_2 - T_1)} + y_2\frac{(T_s - T_1)}{(T_2 - T_1)}$$

Next we can substitute for yield y_1 and y_2 to obtain:

$$y_s = -\frac{1}{(T_1 - t_0)} \ln(Z_1)\lambda - \frac{1}{(T_2 - t_0)} \ln(Z_2)(1 - \lambda)$$

where

$$\lambda = \frac{(T_2 - T_s)}{(T_2 - T_1)}$$

The exponentially interpolated value for date T_s is

$$Z_s = \exp(-y_s(T_s - t_0))$$

or

$$Z_s = Z_1^{\frac{(T_s - t_0)}{(T_1 - t_0)}\lambda} Z_2^{\frac{(T_s - t_0)}{(T_2 - t_0)}(1 - \lambda)}$$

Interpolation example

Consider the problem of finding the discount factor for 26 February 1999 using the data in Table 3.16.

Table 3.16 Discount factor interpolation data

Date	Days to spot	Discount factor
26-Oct-98	0	1.00000
26-Jan-99	92	0.99101
26-Feb-99	123	?
26-Apr-99	182	0.98247

Linear interpolation:

$$Z_{26\text{-Feb-99}} = \left(\frac{182 - 123}{182 - 92}\right)0.99101 + \left(\frac{123 - 92}{182 - 92}\right)0.98247$$

$$= 0.98806$$

Geometric interpolation:

$$Z_{26\text{-Feb-99}} = 0.99101^{\left(\frac{182 - 123}{182 - 92}\right)}0.98247^{\left(\frac{123 - 92}{182 - 92}\right)}$$

$$= 0.98805$$

Exponential interpolation:

$$\lambda = \frac{(182 - 123)}{(182 - 92)}$$

$$= 0.6555$$

$$Z_s = 0.99101^{\frac{(123-0)}{(92-0)}0.6555} \, 0.98247^{\frac{(123-0)}{(182-0)}(1-0.6555)}$$

$$= 0.988039$$

(d) Cubic interpolation

Let $\{t = t_0, t_1, t_2, \ldots t_n = T\}$ be a vector of yield curve point dates and $Z = \{Z_0, Z_1, Z_2, \ldots Z_n\}$ be the corresponding discount factors obtained from the bootstrapping process. Define

$$Z_i = a_i + b_i t_i + c_i t_i^2 + d_i t_i^3$$

to be a cubic function defined over the interval $[t_i, t_{i+1}]$. A cubic spline function is a number of cubic functions joined together smoothly at a number of knot points. If the yield curve points $\{t, t_1, t_2, \ldots T\}$ are defined to be knot points, then coefficients of the cubic spline function defined over the interval $[t, T]$ can be obtained by imposing the following constraints:

$$
\begin{cases}
Z_i = a_i + b_i t_i + c_i t_i^2 + d_i t_i^3 & i = 0 \text{ to } n-1; \, n \text{ constraints} \\
Z_{i+1} = a_i + b_i t_{i+1} + c_i t_{i+1}^2 + d_i t_{i+1}^3 & i = 0 \text{ to } n-1; \, n \text{ constraints} \\
b_i + 2c_i t_i + 3d_i t_i^2 = b_{i+1} + 2c_{i+1} t_i + 3d_{i+1} t_i^2 & i = 0 \text{ to } n-2; \, n-2 \text{ constraints} \\
2c_i + 6d_i t_i = 2c_{i+1} + 6d_{i+1} t_i & i = 0 \text{ to } n-2; \, n-2 \text{ constraints}
\end{cases}
$$

The first sets of n constraints imply that the spline function fit the knot points exactly. The second sets of n constraints require that the spline function join perfectly at the knot point. The third and the fourth sets of constraints ensure that the first and second derivatives match at the knot point. We have a $4n$ coefficient to estimate and $4n$-2 equation so far. The two additional constraints are specified in the form of end point constraints. In the case of natural cubic spline these are that the second derivative equals zero at the two end points, i.e.

$$2c_i + 6d_i t_i = 0 \qquad i = 0 \text{ and } n$$

The spline function has the advantage of providing a very smooth curve.

In Figure 3.6 we present the discount factor and 3-month forward rate derived from exponential and cubic interpolation. Although the discount curves in both interpolation seem similar; comparison of the 3-month forward rate provides a clearer picture of the impact of interpolation technique. The cubic spline produces a smoother forward curve.

Swap rate interpolation

As in the discount curve interpolation, the swap rate for missing tenor can be interpolated using the methods discussed earlier for the discount factor. The exponential or geometric interpolation is not an appropriate choice for swap rate. Of the remaining methods linear interpolation is the most popular.

In Figure 3.7 we compare the swap rate interpolated from linear and cubic splines for GBP. The difference between the rate interpolated by linear and cubic spline ranges from $+0.15$ bp to -0.25 basis points. Compared to the swap rate from linear interpolation, the rate from cubic spline more often higher, particularly between 20y and 30y tenors. Unfortunately, the advantage of the smooth swap rate curve from the cubic spline is overshadowed by the high level of sensitivity exhibited by the

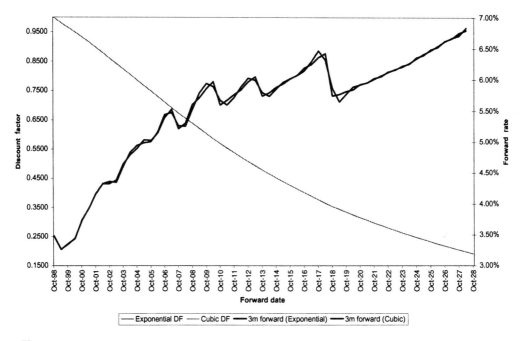

Figure 3.6   Forward rate and discount factor from cubic spline and exponential interpolation.

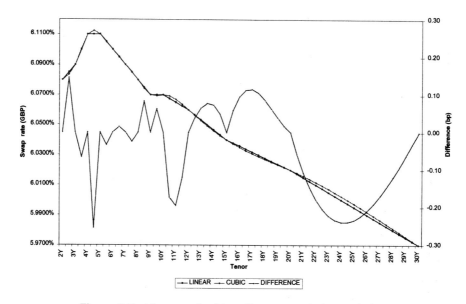

Figure 3.7   Linear and cubic spline swap rate interpolation.

method to knot point data. This can give rise to artificial volatility with significant implications for risk calculations.

Figure 3.8 shows the changes in the interpolated swap rate (DEM) for all tenors corresponding to a 1 basis point change in the one of the swap tenors. A 1 basis point change in one swap rate can change the interpolated swap rates for all tenors irrespective of their maturities! That is, all else being equal, the effects of a small change in one swap rate is not localized. For example, a 1 bp shift in the 2y swap rate results in a −0.07 bp shift in the 3.5y swap rate and a 1 bp shift in the 5y swap rate results in a −0.13 bp change in the 3.5y swap rate. This is an undesirable property of cubic spline interpolation, and therefore not preferred in the market.

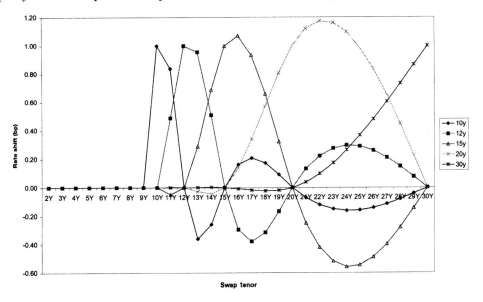

Figure 3.8 Sensitivity of cubic spline interpolation.

Figure 3.9 displays the implications of applying linear interpolation. The interpolation method, while not smooth like the cubic spline, does keep the impact of a small change in any swap rate localized. The effect on swap rates outside the relevant segment is always zero. This property is preferred for hedge calculations.

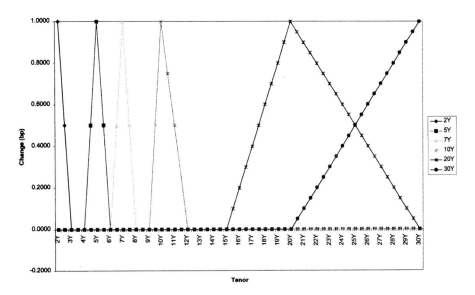

Figure 3.9 Sensitivity of linear interpolation.

Government Bond Curve

The bond market differs from the swap market in that the instruments vary widely in their coupon levels, payment dates and maturity. While in principle it is possible to follow the swap curve logic and bootstrap the discount factor, this approach is not recommended. Often the motivation for yield curve construction is to identify bonds that are trading rich or cheap by comparing them against the yield curve. Alternatively, one may be attempting to develop a time series data of yield curve for use in econometric modeling of interest rates. Market factors such as liquidity effect and coupon effect introduce noise that makes direct application of market yields unsuitable for empirical modeling. In either application the bootstrapping approach that is oriented towards guaranteeing the recovery of market prices will not satisfy our objective. Therefore the yield curve is built by applying statistical techniques to market data on bond price that obtains a smooth curve.

Yield curve models can be distinguished based on those that fit market yield and those that fit prices. Models that fit yields specify a functional form for the yield curve and estimate the coefficient of the functions using market data. The estimation procedure fits the functional form to market data so as to minimize the sum of squared errors between the observed yield and the fitted yield. Such an approach while easy to implement is not theoretically sound. The fundamental deficiency in this approach is that it does not constrain the cash flows occurring on the same date to be discounted at the same rate.

Models that fit prices approach the problem by specifying a functional form for the discount factor and estimate the coefficient using statistical methods. Among the models that fit prices there is also a class of models that treat forward rate as the fundamental variable and derive the implied discount function. This discount function is estimated using the market price data.

In this section we limit our discussion to the later approach that was pioneered by McCulloch (1971). This approach is well accepted, although there is no agreement among the practitioners on the choice of the functional form for discount factor. There is a large volume of financial literature that describes the many ways in which this can be implemented. The discussions have been limited to a few approaches to provide the reader with an intuition into the methodology. A more comprehensive discussion on this topic can be found in papers listed in the References.

Parametric approaches

The dirty price of a bond is simply the present value of its future cash flows. The dirty price of a bond with N coupon payments and no embedded options can be expressed as:

$$P(T_N) + A(T_N) = \sum_{i=1}^{N} c_N Z(T_i) + F_N Z(T_N) \tag{3.8}$$

where $P(T_N)$ is the clean price of a bond on spot date t_0 and maturing on T_N, $A(T_N)$ is its accrued interest, c_N is the coupon payment on date t, $Z(T_i)$ is the discount factor at date t and F_N is the face value or redemption payment of the bond. The process of building the yield curve hinges on identifying the discount factors corresponding to the payment dates. In the swap market we obtained this from bootstrapping the cash, futures and swap rates. In contrast, in the bond market we assume it to be one of the many functions available in our library of mathematical function and then estimate the function to fit the data.

While implementing this approach two factors must be kept in mind. First, the discount factor function selected to represent the present value factor at different dates in the future must be robust enough to fit any shape for the yield curve. Second, it must satisfy certain reasonable boundary conditions and characteristics. The discount curve must be positive monotonically non-increasing to avoid negative forward rates. Mathematically, we can state these conditions as

(a) $Z(0) = 1$
(b) $Z(\infty) = 0$
(c) $Z(T_i) > Z(T_{i-1})$

Conditions (a) and (b) are boundary conditions on present value factors based upon fundamental finance principles. Condition (c) ensures that the discount curve is strictly downward sloping and thus that the forward rates are positive.

A mathematically convenient choice is to represent the discount factor for any date in the future as a linear combination of k basis functions:

$$Z(T_i) = 1 + \sum_{j=1}^{k} a_i f_i(T_i)$$

where $f_j(t)$ is the jth basis function and a_j is the corresponding coefficient. The basis function can take a number of forms provided they produce sensible discount function. Substituting equation (3.9) into (3.8) we get

$$P(T_N) + A(T_N) = c_N \sum_{i=1}^{N} \left(1 + \sum_{j=1}^{k} a_j f(T_i) \right) + F_N \left(1 + \sum_{j=1}^{k} a_j f(T_N) \right) \tag{3.10}$$

This can be further simplified as

$$P(T_N) + A(T_N) - Nc_N - F_N = \sum_{j=1}^{k} a_j \left(c_N \sum_{i=1}^{N} f(T_i) = F_N f(T_N) \right) \tag{3.11}$$

Equivalently,

$$y_N = \sum_{j=1}^{k} a_j x_N \tag{3.12}$$

where

$$y_N = P(T_N) + A(T_N) - Nc_N - F_N \tag{3.13}$$

$$x_N = c_N \sum_{i=1}^{N} f(T_i) + F_N f(T_N) \tag{3.14}$$

If we have a sample of N bonds the coefficient of the basis function can be estimated using ordinary least squares regression. The estimated discount function can be used to generate the discount factors for various tenors and the yield curves.

McCulloch (1971) modeled the basis function as $f(T) = T^j$ for $j = 1, 2, \ldots k$. This results in the discount function being approximated as a kth degree polynomial. One of the problems with this approach is that it has uniform resolution power. This is not a problem if the observations are uniformly distributed across the maturities. Otherwise, it fits well wherever there is greatest concentration of observations and poorly elsewhere. Increasing the order of the polynomial while solving one problem can give rise to another problem of unstable parameters.

Another alternative suggested by McCulloch (1971) is to use splines. A polynomial spline is a number of polynomial functions joined together smoothly at a number of knot points. McCulloch (1971,1975) shows the results from applying quadratic spline and cubic spline functions. The basis functions are represented as a family of quadratic or cubic functions that are constrained to be smooth around the knot points. Schaefer (1981) suggested the use of Bernstein polynomial with the constraint that discount factor at time zero is 1. A major limitation of these methods is that the forwards rates derived from the estimated discount factors have undesirable properties at long maturity.

Vasicek and Fong (1982) model the discount function as an exponential function and describe an approach that produces asymptotically flat forward curve. This approach is in line with equilibrium interest rate models such as Vasicek (1977) and Hull and White (1990) that show that zero coupon bond price or the discount factor to have exponential form.

Rather than modeling the discount curve Nelson and Siegel (1987) directly model the forward rate. They suggest the following functional form for the forward rate:

$$F(t) = \beta_0 + \beta_1 \exp\left(-\frac{t}{\alpha_1}\right) + \beta_2 \left[\left(\frac{t}{\alpha_1}\right) \exp\left(-\frac{t}{\alpha_1}\right)\right] \tag{3.15}$$

This implies the following discount curve:

$$Z(t) = \exp\left\{-t\left[\beta_0 + (\beta_1 + \beta_2)\left(1 - \exp\left(-\frac{t}{\alpha_1}\right)\right)\frac{\alpha_1}{t} - \beta_2 \exp\left(-\frac{t}{\alpha_1}\right)\right]\right\} \tag{3.16}$$

Coleman, Fisher and Ibbotson (1992) also model the forward rates instead of the discount curve. They propose instantaneous forward rate to be a piecewise constant function. Partitioning the future dates into N segments, $\{t_0, t_1, t_2, \ldots t_N\}$, their model define the forward rate in any segment to be

$$F(t) = \lambda_i \qquad t_{i-1} < t \leqslant t_i \tag{3.17}$$

This model implies that the discount factor at date t between t_{k-1} and t_k is

$$Z(t) = \exp\left\{-\left[\lambda_1 t_1 + \sum_{i=2}^{k-1} \lambda_i(t_i - t_{i-1}) = \lambda_k(t - t_{k-1})\right]\right\} \tag{3.18}$$

The discount curve produced by this model will be continuous but the forward rate curve will not be smooth.

Chambers, Carleton and Waldman (1984) propose an exponential polynomial for the discount curve. The exponential polynomial function for discount factor can be written as

$$Z(t) = \exp\left\{-\sum_{j=1}^{k} a_j m^j\right\} \tag{3.19}$$

They recommend that a polynomial of degree 3 or 4 is sufficient to model the yield curve.

Finally, Wiseman (1994) model the forward curve as an exponential function

$$F(t) = \sum_{j=0}^{k} a_j e^{-k_j t} \tag{3.20}$$

Exponential model

To see how the statistical approaches can be implemented consider a simplified example where the discount curve is modeled as a linear combination of m basis functions. Each basis function is assumed to be an exponential function. More specifically, define the discount function to be:

$$Z(t) = \sum_{k=1}^{m} a_k (e^{-\beta t})^k \tag{3.21}$$

where α and β are unknown coefficients of the function that need to be estimated. Once these parameters are known we can obtain a theoretical discount factor at any future date. These discount factors can be used to determine the par, spot and forward curves.

Substituting the condition that discount factor must be 1 at time zero we obtain the following constraint on the α coefficients:

$$\sum_{k=1}^{m} \alpha_k = 1 \tag{3.22}$$

We can rearrange this as

$$\alpha_m = 1 - \sum_{k=1}^{m-1} \alpha_k \tag{3.23}$$

Suppose that we have a sample of N bonds. Let $P(T_i)$, $i = 1, 2, \ldots N$, be the market price of the ith bond maturing T_i years from today. If q_i is the time when the next coupon will be paid, according to this model the dirty price of this bond can be expressed as:

$$P(T_i) + A(T_i) = \sum_{t=q_i}^{T_i} c_j Z(t) + 100 Z(T_i) + \varepsilon_i$$

$$= \sum_{t=q_i}^{T_i} c_i \left(\sum_{k=1}^{m} a_k e^{-k\beta t} \right) + 100 \left(\sum_{k=1}^{m} \alpha_k e^{-k\beta T_i} \right) + \varepsilon_i \tag{3.24}$$

One reason for specifying the price in terms of discount factors is that price of a bond in linear in discount factor, while it is non-linear in either forward or spot rates. We can simplify equation (3.24) further and write it as:

$$P(T_i) + A(T_i) = \sum_{k=1}^{m-1} a_k \left(c_i \sum_{t=q_i}^{T_i} e^{-k\beta t} + 100 e^{-k\beta T_i} \right)$$

$$+ \left(1 - \sum_{k=1}^{m-1} \alpha_k \right) \left(c_i \sum_{t=q_i}^{T_i} e^{-m\beta t} + 100 e^{-m\beta T_i} \right) + \varepsilon_i \tag{3.25}$$

Rearranging, we get

$$
P(T_i) + A(T_i) - \left(c_i \sum_{t=q_i}^{T_i} e^{-m\beta t} + 100e^{-m\beta T_i} \right)
$$

$$
= \sum_{k=1}^{T_i} \alpha_k \left[\left(c_i \sum_{t=q_i}^{T_i} e^{-k\beta t} + 100e^{-k\beta T_i} \right) - \left(c_i \sum_{t=q_i}^{T_i} e^{-m\beta t} + 100e^{-m\beta T_i} \right) \right] + \varepsilon_i
$$

(3.26)

or

$$
y_i = \sum_{k=1}^{m-1} \alpha_k x_{i,k} + \varepsilon_i
$$

(3.27)

where

$$
z_{i,k} = \left(c_i \sum_{t=q_i}^{T_i} e^{-k\beta t} + 100e^{-k\beta T_i} \right)
$$

$$
y_i = P(T_i) + A(T_i) - z_{i,m}
$$

(3.28)

$$
x_{i,k} = z_{i,k} - z_{i,m}
$$

To empirically estimate the discount function we first calculate y_i and $x_{i,k}$ for each of the N bonds in our sample. The coefficient of the discount function must be selected such that they price the N bonds correctly or at least with minimum error. If we can set the β to be some sensible value then the α's can be estimated using the ordinary least squares regression.

$$
\begin{pmatrix} y_1 \\ y_2 \\ \cdot \\ y_N \end{pmatrix} = \begin{bmatrix} x_{1,1} & x_{1,2} & \cdot & x_{1,m} \\ x_{2,1} & \cdot & & \cdot \\ \cdot & \cdot & \cdot & \cdot \\ x_{N,1} & \cdot & \cdot & x_{N,m} \end{bmatrix} \begin{pmatrix} \hat{\alpha}_1 \\ \hat{\alpha}_2 \\ \cdot \\ \hat{\alpha}_m \end{pmatrix} + \begin{pmatrix} \varepsilon_1 \\ \varepsilon_2 \\ \cdot \\ \varepsilon_N \end{pmatrix}
$$

(3.29)

The $\hat{\alpha}$'s estimated from the ordinary least squares provide the best fit for the data by minimizing the sum of the square of the errors, $\sum_{i=1}^{N} \varepsilon_i^2$. The estimated values of $\hat{\alpha}$ and β can be substituted into (3.21) to determine the bond market yield curve.

The model is sensitive to the number of basis functions therefore it should be carefully selected so as not to over-fit the data. Also, most of the models discussed are very sensitive to the data. Therefore, it is important to implement screening procedures to identify bonds and exclude any bonds that are outliers. Typically one tends to exclude bonds with unreliable prices or bonds that due to liquidity, coupon or tax reasons is expected to have be unusually rich or cheap. A better fit can also be achieved by iterative least squares. The model can be extend in several ways to obtain a better fit to the market data such as imposing constraint to fit certain data point exactly or assuming that the model is homoscedastic in yields and applying generalized least squares.

Exponential model implementation

We now present the results from implementing the exponential model. The price data for a sample of German bond issues maturing less than 10 years and settling on 28 October 1998 is reported in Table 3.17.

Table 3.17 DEM government bond price data

	Issue	Price	Yield	Accrued	Coupon	Maturity (years)
1	TOBL5 12/98	100.21	3.3073	4.3194	5	0.1361
2	BKO3.75 3/99	100.13	3.3376	2.2813	3.75	0.3917
3	DBR7 4/99	101.68	3.3073	3.6556	7	0.4778
4	DBR7 10/99	103.41	3.3916	0.1556	7	0.9778
5	TOBL7 11/99	103.74	3.3907	6.4750	7	1.0750
6	BKO4.25 12/99	100.94	3.3851	3.6715	4.25	1.1361
7	BKO4 3/0	100.81	3.3802	2.4556	4	1.3861
8	DBR8.75 5/0	108.02	3.3840	3.7917	8.75	1.5667
9	BKO4 6/0	100.95	3.3825	1.4667	4	1.6333
10	DBR8.75 7/0	108.81	3.3963	2.3819	8.75	1.7278
11	DBR9 10/0	110.56	3.3881	0.2000	9	1.9778
12	OBL 118	104.05	3.3920	3.6021	5.25	2.3139
13	OBL 121	103.41	3.5530	4.4597	4.75	3.0611
14	OBL 122	102.80	3.5840	3.0750	4.5	3.3167
15	OBL 123	102.94	3.5977	2.0125	4.5	3.5528
16	OBL 124	103.06	3.6218	0.8625	4.5	3.8083
17	THA7.75 10/2	114.81	3.6309	0.5813	7.75	3.9250
18	OBL 125	104.99	3.6480	4.8056	5	4.0389
19	THA7.375 12/2	113.78	3.6846	6.6785	7.375	4.0944
20	OBL 126	103.35	3.6409	3.1250	4.5	4.3056
21	DBR6.75 7/4	114.74	3.8243	1.9313	6.75	5.7139
22	DBR6.5 10/5	114.85	4.0119	0.2528	6.5	6.9611
23	DBR6 1/6	111.75	4.0778	4.8833	6	7.1861
24	DBR6 2/6	111.91	4.0768	4.2000	6	7.3000
25	DBR6 1/7	112.05	4.2250	4.9000	6	8.1833
26	DBR6 7/7	112.43	4.2542	1.9000	6	8.6833
27	DBR5.25 1/8	107.96	4.1860	4.2875	5.25	9.1833
28	DBR4.75 7/8	104.81	4.1345	1.5042	4.75	9.6833

Suppose that we choose to model the discount factor with 5 basis functions and let β equal to the yield of DBR4.75 7/2008. The first step is to calculate the $z_{i,j}$, $i = 1$ to 28, $j = 1$ to 5. An example of the calculation for DBR6.75 7/4 is described below. This bond pays a coupon of 6.75%, matures in 5.139 years and the next coupon is payable in 0.7139 years from the settle date.

$$z_{21,2} = \left(6.75 \sum_{t=0}^{5} e^{-2 \times 0.0413 \times (t + 0.7139)} + 100 e^{-2 \times 0.0413 \times 5.7139} \right)$$

$$= 93.70$$

Similarly, we can calculate the $z_{i,j}$ for all the bonds in our sample and the results are shown in Table 3.18.

Next we apply equation (3.28) to obtain the data for the ordinary least square regression estimation. This is reported in Table 3.19.

Finally we estimate the α's using ordinary least square regression and use it in equation (3.20) to generate the discount factors and yield curves. The coefficient

Table 3.18   DEM government bond $z_{i,j}$ calculation results

Issue	$z_{i,1}$	$z_{i,2}$	$z_{i,3}$	$z_{i,4}$	$z_{i,5}$
TOBL5 12/98	104.41	103.82	103.24	102.66	102.09
BKO3.75 3/99	102.08	100.44	98.83	97.24	95.68
DBR7 4/99	104.91	102.86	100.84	98.87	96.94
DBR7 10/99	102.76	98.69	94.78	91.02	87.42
TOBL7 11/99	109.33	104.86	100.58	96.49	92.57
BKO4.25 12/99	103.69	99.10	94.73	90.55	86.56
BKO4 3/0	102.14	96.61	91.39	86.45	81.78
DBR8.75 5/0	110.48	103.89	97.70	91.89	86.45
BKO4 6/0	101.11	94.66	88.63	82.98	77.71
DBR8.75 7/0	109.74	102.51	95.77	89.48	83.61
DBR9 10/0	109.09	100.86	93.26	86.25	79.77
OBL 118	105.80	96.75	88.50	80.99	74.16
OBL 121	105.94	94.41	84.21	75.20	67.24
OBL 122	103.90	91.57	80.78	71.34	63.07
OBL 123	102.89	89.80	78.45	68.61	60.07
OBL 124	101.81	87.92	76.00	65.77	56.98
THA7.75 10/2	113.09	97.76	84.63	73.37	63.71
OBL 125	107.64	92.87	80.31	69.61	60.50
THA7.375 12/2	118.30	102.50	89.06	77.61	67.85
OBL 126	104.18	88.77	75.79	64.85	55.64
DBR6.75 7/4	114.51	93.70	77.03	63.63	52.85
DBR6.5 10/5	113.75	89.48	70.87	56.57	45.54
DBR6 1/6	115.70	91.23	72.64	58.47	47.64
DBR6 2/6	115.15	90.37	71.62	57.38	46.53
DBR6 1/7	116.98	89.92	70.05	55.40	44.54
DBR6 7/7	114.58	86.27	65.84	51.01	40.17
DBR5.25 1/8	111.97	83.45	63.28	48.92	38.62
DBR4.75 7/8	105.62	76.72	56.68	42.67	32.80

estimates and the resultant discount factor curve are reported in Tables 3.20 and 3.21, respectively.

The discount factor can be used for valuation, rich-cheap analysis or to generate the zero curve and the forward yield curves.

Model review

The discount factors produced by the yield curve models are used for marking-to-market of position and calculation of end-of-day gains/losses. Others bump the input cash and swap rates to the yield curve model to generate a new set of discount factors and revalue positions. This provides traders with an estimate of their exposure to different tenor and hedge ratios to manage risk of their positions. Models such as those of Heath, Jarrow and Morton (1992) and Brace, Gaterak and Musiela (1995) use the forward rates implied from the yield curve as a starting point to simulate the future evolution of the forward rate curve. Spot rate models such as those of Hull and White (1990), Black, Derman and Toy (1990) and Black and Karasinsky (1990) estimate parameters for the model by fitting it to the yield curve data. The model to

Table 3.19 DEM government bond $x_{i,j}$ regression data

Issue	y_i	$x_{i,1}$	$x_{i,2}$	$x_{i,3}$	$x_{i,4}$
TOBL5 12/98	2.4427	2.3240	1.7381	1.1555	0.5761
BKO3.75 3/99	6.7305	6.4027	4.7630	3.1495	1.5620
DBR7 4/99	8.3987	7.9702	5.9182	3.9064	1.9339
DBR7 10/99	16.1479	15.3430	11.2716	7.3615	3.6064
TOBL7 11/99	17.6444	16.7562	12.2852	8.0077	3.9153
BKO4.25 12/99	18.0511	17.1321	12.5442	8.1659	3.9876
BKO4 3/0	21.4836	20.3622	14.8299	9.6033	4.6653
DBR8.75 5/0	25.3652	24.0300	17.4390	11.2536	5.4485
BKO4 6/0	24.7094	23.3980	16.9496	10.9182	5.2768
DBR8.75 7/0	27.5772	26.1283	18.8960	12.1524	5.8641
DBR9 10/0	30.9865	29.3115	21.0826	13.4866	6.4741
OBL 118	33.4955	31.6457	22.5896	14.3445	6.8368
OBL 121	40.6304	38.7041	27.1683	16.9745	7.9648
OBL 122	42.8011	40.8274	28.4955	17.7065	8.2648
OBL 123	44.8833	42.8227	29.7297	18.3797	8.5376
OBL 124	46.9444	44.8324	30.9431	19.0232	8.7895
THA7.75 10/2	51.6844	49.3862	34.0537	20.9184	9.6586
OBL 125	49.2943	47.1380	32.3718	19.8071	9.1107
THA7.375 12/2	52.6131	50.4555	34.6570	21.2112	9.7599
OBL 126	50.8381	48.5455	33.1304	20.1514	9.2172
DBR6.75 7/4	63.8172	61.6541	40.8501	24.1722	10.7782
DBR6.5 10/5	69.5667	68.2133	43.9415	25.3377	11.0347
DBR6 1/6	68.9955	68.0584	43.5888	25.0013	10.8359
DBR6 2/6	69.5806	68.6234	43.8422	25.0908	10.8533
DBR6 1/7	72.4097	72.4375	45.3753	25.5126	10.8640
DBR6 7/7	74.1636	74.4180	46.1074	25.6739	10.8408
DBR5.25 1/8	73.6259	73.3496	44.8310	24.6579	10.2981
DBR4.75 7/8	73.5156	72.8177	43.9244	23.8769	9.8696

Table 3.20 DEM exponential model coefficient estimations

Coefficient	Estimate
β	4.13%
α_1	16.97
α_2	-77.59
α_3	139.55
α_4	-110.08
α_5	32.15

generate the yield curve model is not as complicated as some of the term structure models. However, any small error made while building the yield curve can have a progressively amplified impact on valuation and hedge ratios unless it has been reviewed carefully. We briefly outline some of the issues that must be kept in mind while validating them.

First, the yield curve model should be arbitrage free. A quick check for this would

Table 3.21   DEM government bond market discount factor curve

Time	Discount factor	Par coupon yield
0.00	1.0000	
1.00	0.9668	3.44%
2.00	0.9353	3.40%
3.00	0.9022	3.49%
4.00	0.8665	3.64%
5.00	0.8288	3.80%
6.00	0.7904	3.96%
7.00	0.7529	4.09%
8.00	0.7180	4.17%
9.00	0.6871	4.20%
10.00	0.6613	4.18%

be to verify if the discount factors generated by the yield curve model can produce the same cash and swap rates as those feed into the model. In addition there may be essentially four possible sources of errors – use of inappropriate market rates data, accrual factor calculations, interpolation algorithms, and curve-stitching.

The rates used to build the curve for the short-term product will not be the same as the rates used for pricing long-term products. The individual desk primarily determines this so any curve builder model should offer flexibility to the user in selecting the source and the nature of rate data. Simple as it may seem, another common source of error is incorrect holiday calendar and market conventions for day count to calculate the accrual factors. Fortunately the computation of accrual factors is easy to verify. Interpolation algorithms expose the yield curve model to numerical instability. As we have mentioned earlier, some interpolation methods such as the cubic spline may be capable of producing a very smooth curve but performs poorly during computation of the hedge ratio. A preferable attribute for the interpolation method is to have a local impact on yield curve to changes in specific input data rather than affecting the entire curve. There are many systems that offer users a menu when it comes to the interpolation method. While it is good to have such flexibility, in the hands of a user with little understanding of the implications this may be risky. It is best to ensure that the model provides sensible alternatives and eliminate choices that may be considered unsuitable after sufficient research.

In the absence of reasonable market data curve stitching can be achieved by interpolating either the stub rate or the discount factor. A linear interpolation can be applied for rates but not if it is a discount factor.

Summary

In this chapter we have discussed the methodology to build the market yield curve for the swap market and the bond market. The market yield curve is one of the most important pieces of information required by traders and risk managers to price, trade, mark-to-market and control risk exposure. The yield curve can be described as discount factor curves, par curves, forward curves or zero curves. Since the discount factors are the most rudimentary information for valuing any stream of cash flows it is the most natural place to start. Unfortunately discount factors are not directly observable in the market, rather they have to be derived from the market-quoted interest rates and prices of liquid financial instruments.

The swap market provides an abundance of par swap rates data for various tenors. This can be applied to extract the discount factors using the bootstrap method. The bootstrap approach produces a discount factor curve that is consistent with the market swap rates satisfying the condition of no-arbitrage condition. When a swap rate or discount factor for a specific date is not available then interpolation methods may need to be applied to determine the value. These methods must be carefully chosen since they can have significant impact on the resultant yield curve, valuations and risk exposure calculations. Linear interpolation for swap rates and exponential interpolation for discount factors is a recommended approach due to their simplicity and favorable performance attributes.

In the bond market due to non-uniform price data on various tenors, coupon effect and liquidity factors a statistical method has to be applied to derive the discount factor curves. The objective is not necessarily to derive discount factors that will price every bond to the market exactly. Instead we estimate the parameters of the model that will minimize the sum of squares of pricing errors for the sample of bonds used. In theory many statistical models can be prescribed to fit the discount curve function. We have reviewed a few and provided details on the implementation of the exponential model. An important criterion for these models is that they satisfy certain basic constraints such as discount factor function equal to one on spot date, converge to zero for extremely long tenors, and be a decreasing function with respect to tenors.

Note

[1] For an intuitive description of the futures convexity adjustment and calculations using this expression see Burghartt and Hoskins (1996). For other technical approaches to convexity adjustment see interest rate models such as Hull and White (1990) and Heath, Jarrow and Morton (1992).

References

Anderson, N., Breedon, F., Deacon, M. and Murphy, G. (1997) *Estimating and Interpreting the Yield Curve*, John Wiley.

Black, F., Derman, E. and Toy, W. (1990) 'A one-factor model of interest rates and its application to treasury bond options', *Financial Analyst Journal*, **46,** 33–39.

Black, F. and Karasinski, P. (1991) 'Bond and option pricing when short rates are lognormal', *Financial Analyst Journal*, **47,** 52–9.

Brace, A., Gatarek, D. and Musiela, M. (1997) 'The market model of interest-rate dynamics', *Mathematical Finance*, **7,** 127–54.

Burghartt, G. and Hoskins, B. (1996) 'The convexity bias in Eurodollar futures', in Konishi, A. and Dattatreya, R. (eds), *Handbook of Derivative Instruments*, Irwin Professional Publishing.

Chambers, D., Carleton, W. and Waldman, D. (1984) 'A new approach to estimation of the term structure of interest rates', *Journal of Financial and Quantitative Analysis*, **19,** 233–52.

Coleman, T., Fisher, L. and Ibbotson, R. (1992) 'Estimating the term structure of interest rates from data that include the prices of coupon bonds', *The Journal of Fixed Income*, 85–116.

Heath, D., Jarrow, R. and Morton, A. (1992) 'Bond pricing and the term structure of interest rates: a new methodology for contingent claim valuation', *Econometrica* **60,** 77–105.

Hull, J. and White, A. (1990) 'Pricing interest rate derivative securities', *Review of Financial Studies*, **3,** 573–92.

Jamshidian, F. (1997) 'LIBOR and swap market models and measures', *Finance & Stochastics*, **1,** 261–91.

McCulloch, J. H. (1971) 'Measuring the term structure of interest rates', *Journal of Finance*, **44,** 19–31.

McCulloch, J. H. (1975) 'The tax-adjusted yield curve', *Journal of Finance*, **30,** 811–30.

Nelson, C. R. and Siegel, A. F. (1987) 'Parsimonious modeling of yield curves', *Journal of Business*, **60,** 473–89.

Schaefer, S. M. (1981) 'Measuring a tax-specific term structure of interest rates in the market for British government securities', *The Economic Journal*, **91,** 415–38.

Shea, G. S. (1984) 'Pitfalls in smoothing interest rate term structure data: equilibrium models and spline approximation', *Journal of Financial and Quantitative Analysis*, **19,** 253–69.

Steeley, J. M. (1991) 'Estimating the gilt-edged term structure: basis splines and confidence interval', *Journal of Business, Finance and Accounting*, **18,** 512–29.

Vasicek, O. (1977) 'An equilibrium characterization of the term structure', *Journal of Financial Economics*, **5,** 177–88.

Vasicek, O. and Fong, H. (1982) 'Term structure modeling using exponential splines', *Journal of Finance*, **37,** 339–56.

Wiseman, J. (1994) *European Fixed Income Research*, 2nd edn, J. P. Morgan.

4

Choosing appropriate VaR model parameters and risk-measurement methods

IAN HAWKINS

Risk managers need a *quantitative* measure of market risk that can be applied to a single business, compared between multiple businesses, or aggregated across multiple businesses. The 'Value at Risk' or VaR of a business is a measure of how much money the business might lose over a period of time in the future. VaR has been widely adopted as the primary quantitative measure of market risk within banks and other financial service organizations.

This chapter describes how we define VaR; what the major market risks are and how we measure the market risks in a portfolio of transactions; how we use models of market behavior to add up the risks; and how we estimate the parameters of those models. A sensible goal for risk managers is to implement a measure of market risk that conforms to industry best practice, with the proviso that they do so at reasonable cost.

We will give two notes of caution. First, VaR is a necessary part of the firm-wide risk management framework, but not – on its own – sufficient to monitor market risk. VaR cannot replace the rich set of trading controls that most businesses accumulate over the years. These trading controls were either introduced to solve risk management problems in their own businesses or were implemented to respond to risk management problems that surfaced in other businesses. Over-reliance on VaR, or any other quantitative measure of risk, is simply an invitation for traders to build up large positions that fall outside the capabilities of the VaR implementation.

Second, as with any model, VaR is subject to model risk, implementation risk and information risk. Model risk is the risk that we choose an inappropriate model to describe the real world. The real world is much more complicated than any mathematical model of the real world that we could create to describe it. We can only try to capture the most important features of the real world, as they affect our particular problem – the measurement of market risk – and, as the world changes, try to change our model quickly enough for the model to remain accurate (see Chapter 14).

Implementation risk is the risk that we didn't correctly translate our mathematical model into a working computer program – so that even if we do feed in the right numbers, we don't get the answer from the program that we should. Finally, information risk is the risk that we don't feed the right numbers into our computer program. VaR calculation is in its infancy, and risk managers have to accept a considerable degree of all three of these risks in their VaR measurement solutions.

Choosing appropriate VaR model parameters

We will begin with a definition of VaR. Our VaR definition includes parameters, and we will go on to discuss how to choose each of those parameters in turn.

VaR definition

The VaR of a portfolio of transactions is usually defined as *the maximum loss, from an adverse market move, within a given level of confidence, for a given holding period.* This is just one definition of risk, albeit one that has gained wide acceptance. Other possibilities are *the maximum expected loss over a given holding period* (our definition above without the qualifier of a given level of confidence) or the *expected loss, over a specified confidence level, for a given holding period.* If we used these alternative definitions, we would find it harder to calculate VaR; however, the VaR number would have more relevance. The first alternative definition is what every risk manager really wants to know – 'How much could we lose tomorrow?' The second alternative definition is the theoretical cost of an insurance policy that would cover any excess loss, over the standard VaR definition. For now, most practitioners use the standard VaR definition, while the researchers work on alternative VaR definitions and how to calculate VaR when using them (Artzner *et al.*, 1997; Acar and Prieul, 1997; Embrechts *et al.*, 1998; McNeil, 1998).

To use our standard VaR definition, we have to choose values for the two parameters in the definition – confidence level and holding period.

Confidence level

Let's look at the picture of our VaR definition shown in Figure 4.1. On the horizontal axis, we have the range of possible changes in the value of our portfolio of transactions. On the vertical axis, we have the probability of those possible changes occurring. The confidence levels commonly used in VaR calculations are 95% or 99%. Suppose we want to use 95%. To find the VaR of the portfolio, we put our finger on the right-hand side of the figure and move the finger left, until 95% of the possible changes are to the right of our finger and 5% of the changes are to the left of it. The number on the horizontal axis, under our finger, is the VaR of the portfolio.

Using a 95% confidence interval means that, if our model is accurate, we expect to lose *more* than the VaR on only 5 days out of a 100[1] . The VaR does not tell how much we might *actually* lose on those 5 days. Using a 99% confidence interval means that we expect to lose *more* than the VaR on only 1 day out of a 100. Most organizations use a confidence level somewhere between 95% and 99% for their in-house risk management. The BIS (Bank for International Settlements) requirement for calculation of regulatory capital is a 99% confidence interval (Basel Committee on Banking Supervision, 1996). While the choice of a confidence level is a funda-

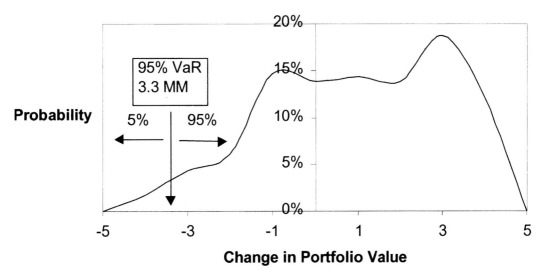

Figure 4.1   VaR definition.

mental risk management statement for the organization, there is one modeling issue to bear in mind. The closer that the confidence level we choose is to 100%, the rarer are the events that lie to the left of our VaR line. That implies that we will have seen those events fewer times in the past, and that it will be harder for us to make accurate predictions about those rare events in the future.

The standard VaR definition does not tell us much about the shape of the overall P/L distribution, other than the likelihood of a loss greater than the VaR. The distribution of portfolio change in value shown in Figure 4.2 results in the same VaR as the distribution in Figure 4.1, but obviously there is a greater chance of a loss of more than say, $4.5 million, in Figure 4.2 than in Figure 4.1.

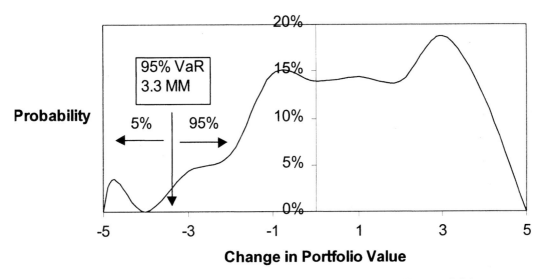

Figure 4.2   VaR definition (2) – same VaR as Figure 4.1, but different tail risk.

Holding period

The holding period is the length of time, from today, to the horizon date at which we attempt to model the loss of our portfolio of transactions. There is an implicit assumption in VaR calculation that the portfolio is not going to change over the holding period. The first factor in our choice of holding period is the frequency with which new transactions are executed and the impact of the new transactions on the market risk of the portfolio. If those new transactions have a large impact on the market risk of the portfolio, it doesn't make much sense to use a long holding period because it's likely that the market risk of the portfolio will change significantly before we even reach the horizon date, and therefore our VaR calculation will be extremely inaccurate.

The second factor in our choice of holding period is the frequency with which the data on the market risk of the portfolio can be assembled. We want to be able to look ahead at least to the next date on which we will have the data to create a new report. While banks are usually able to consolidate most of their portfolios at least once a day, for non-financial corporations, monthly or quarterly reporting is the norm.

The third factor in our choice of holding period is the length of time it would take to hedge the risk positions of the portfolio at tolerable cost. The faster we try to hedge a position, the more we will move the market bid or offer price against ourselves, and so there is a balance between hedging risk rapidly to avoid further losses, and the cost of hedging. It's unreasonable to try to estimate our maximum downside using a holding period that is significantly shorter than the time it would take to hedge the position. The ability to hedge a position is different for different instruments and different markets, and is affected by the size of the position. The larger the position is, in relation to the normal size of transactions traded in the market, the larger the impact that hedging that position will have on market prices. The impact of hedging on prices also changes over time.

We can account for this third factor in a different way – by setting aside P/L reserves against open market risk positions. For most institutions, reserves are a much more practical way of incorporating liquidity into VaR than actually modeling the liquidation process.

In banks, the most common choice of holding period for internal VaR calculations is 1 day. For bank regulatory capital calculations, the BIS specifies a 10-day holding period, but allows banks to calculate their 10-day VaR by multiplying their 1-day VaR by the square root of 10 (about 3.16). If, for example, a bank's 1-day VaR was $1.5 million, its 10-day VaR would be $4.74 million ($1.5 million *3.16). Using the square root of time to scale VaR from one time horizon to another is valid if market moves are independently distributed over time (i.e. market variables do not revert to the mean, or show autocorrelation). For the purpose of calculating VaR, this assumption is close enough to reality, though we know that most market variables do actually show mean reversion and autocorrelation.

Applicability of VaR

If all assets and liabilities are accounted for on a mark-to-market basis, for example financial instruments in a bank trading book or corporate Treasury, then we can use VaR directly. If assets and liabilities are *not* all marked to market, we can *either* estimate proxy market values of items that are accrual-accounted, and then use VaR, *or* use alternative measures of risk to VaR – that are derived from a more tradition ALM perspective. Some examples of alternative measures of performance to mark-to-market value are projected earnings, cash flow and cost of funds – giving rise to risk measures such as Earnings at Risk, Cash flow at Risk or Cost of Funds at Risk.

Uses of VaR

To place the remainder of the chapter in context, we will briefly discuss some of the uses of VaR measures.

Regulatory market risk capital

Much of the current interest in VaR has been driven by the desire of banks to align their regulatory capital with the bank's perception of economic capital employed in the trading book, and to minimize the amount of capital allocated to their trading books, by the use of internal VaR models rather than the 'BIS standardized approach' to calculation of regulatory capital.

Internal capital allocation

Given that VaR provides a metric for the economic capital that must be set aside to cover market risk, we can then use the VaR of a business to measure the returns of that business adjusted for the use of risk capital. There are many flavors of risk-adjusted returns, and depending on the intended use of the performance measure, we may wish to consider the VaR of the business on a stand-alone basis, or the incremental VaR of the business as part of the whole organization, taking into account any reduction in risk capital due to diversification.

Market risk limits

VaR can certainly be used as the basis of a limits system, so that risk-reducing actions are triggered when VaR exceeds a predefined level. In setting VaR limits, we must consider how a market loss typically arises. First we experience an adverse move and realize losses of the order of the VaR. Then over the next few days or weeks we experience more adverse moves and we lose more money. Then we review our position, the position's mark to market, and the model used to generate the mark to market. Then we implement changes, revising the mark to market by writing down the value of our position, and/or introducing a new model, and/or reducing our risk appetite and beginning the liquidation of our position.

We lose multiples of the VaR, then we rethink what we have been doing and take a further hit as we make changes and we pay to liquidate the position. The bill for the lot is more than the sum of the VaR and our liquidity reserves.

Risk measurement methods

This section describes what the sources of market risk are, and how we measure them for a portfolio of transactions. First, a definition of market risk: 'Market risk is the potential adverse change in the value of a portfolio of financial instruments due to changes in the levels, or changes in the volatilities of the levels, or changes in the correlations between the levels of market prices.'[2] Risk comes from the *combination* of uncertainty and exposure to that uncertainty. There is no risk in holding a stock if we are completely certain about the future path of the stock's market price, and even if we are uncertain about the future path of a stock's market price, there is no risk to us if we don't hold a position in the stock!

Market risk versus credit risk

It is difficult to cleanly differentiate market risk from credit risk. Credit risk is the risk of loss when our counterpart in a transaction defaults on (fails to perform) its contractual obligations, due to an inability to pay (as opposed to an unwillingness to pay). The risk of default in a loan with a counterpart will usually be classified as credit risk. The risk of default in holding a counterpart's bond, will also usually be classified as credit risk. However, the risk that the bond will change in price, because the market's view of the *likelihood* of default by the counterpart changes, will usually be classified as a market risk. In most banks, the amount of market risk underwritten by the bank is dwarfed in size by the amount of credit risk underwritten by the bank. While banks' trading losses attract a great deal of publicity, particularly if the losses involve derivatives, banks typically write off much larger amounts of money against credit losses from non-performing loans and financial guarantees.

General market risk versus specific risk.

When analyzing market risk, we break down the risk of a transaction into two components. The change in the transaction's value correlated with the behavior of the market *as a whole* is known as *systematic risk*, or *general market risk*. The change in the transaction's value not correlated with the behavior of the market as a whole is known as *idiosyncratic risk*, or *specific risk*.

The factors that contribute to *specific* risk are changes in the perception of the credit quality of the underlying issuer or counterpart to a transaction, as we discussed above, and supply and demand, which we will discuss below.

Consider two bonds, with the same issuer, and of similar maturities, say 9 years and 11 years. The bonds have similar systematic risk profiles, as they are both sensitive to interest rates of around 10 years maturity. However, they are not *fungible*, (can't be exchanged for each other). Therefore, supply and demand for each individual bond may cause the individual bond's *actual* price movements to be significantly different from that *expected* due to changes in the market as a whole. Suppose we sell the 9-year bond short, and buy the same notional amount of the 11-year bond. Overall, our portfolio of two transactions has small *net* general market risk, as the exposure of the short 9-year bond position to the general level of interest rates will be largely offset by the exposure of the long 11-year bond position to the general level of interest rates. Still, the portfolio has significant specific risk, as any divergence in the price changes of our two bonds from that expected for the market as a whole will cause significant unexpected changes in portfolio value. The only way to reduce the specific risk of a portfolio is to *diversify* the portfolio holdings across a large number of different instruments, so that the contribution to changes in portfolio value from each individual instrument are small relative to the total changes in portfolio value.

VaR typically only measures general market risk, while specific risk is captured in a separate risk measurement.

Sources of market risk

Now we will work through the sources of market uncertainty and how we quantify the exposure to that uncertainty.

Price level risk

The major sources of market risk are changes in the levels of foreign exchange rates, interest rates, commodity prices and equity prices. We will discuss each of these sources of market risk in turn.

FX rate risk

In the most general terms, we can describe the value of a portfolio as its expected future cash flows, discounted back to today. Whenever a portfolio contains cash flows denominated in, or indexed to, a currency other than the base currency of the business, the value of the portfolio is sensitive to changes in the level of foreign exchange rates. There are a number of different ways to represent the FX exposure of a portfolio.

Currency pairs

A natural way to represent a portfolio of foreign exchange transactions is to reduce the portfolio to a set of equivalent positions in currency *pairs*: so much EUR-USD at exchange rate 1, so much JPY-USD at exchange rate 2, so much EUR-JPY at exchange rate 3. As even this simple example shows, currency pairs require care in handling positions in *crosses* (currency pairs in which neither currency is the base currency).

Risk point method

We can let our portfolio management system do the work, and have the system revalue the portfolio for a defined change in each exchange rate used to mark the portfolio to market, and report the change in value of the portfolio for each change in exchange rate. This process is known as the Risk Point Method, or more informally as 'bump and grind' (bump the exchange rate and grind through the portfolio revaluation). As with currency pairs, we need to make sure that exposure in crosses is not double counted, or inconsistent with the treatment of the underlying currency pairs.

Cash flow mapping

A more atomic representation of foreign exchange exposure is to map each forward cash flow in the portfolio to an equivalent amount of spot cash flow in that currency: so many EUR, so many JPY, so many USD.

Reference (risk) currency versus base (accounting) currency

Global trading groups often denominate their results in US dollars (reference currency) and consider US dollars as the currency that has no foreign exchange risk.

When those trading groups belong to business whose base currency is not US dollars, some care is required to make sure that the group is not subject to the risk that a change in the US dollar exchange rate to the base currency will cause unexpected over- or under-performance relative to the budget set in the base currency.

Interest rate risk

It is fairly obvious that the level of interest rates affects fixed-income securities, but – as we have seen earlier in this book – the level of interest rates also affects the prices of all *futures* and *forward* contracts relative to spot prices. Buying a currency for delivery forward is equivalent to buying the currency spot and lending/borrowing the proceeds of the spot transaction. The interest rates at which the proceeds of the spot transaction are lent or borrowed determine the 'no-arbitrage' forward exchange rate relative to the spot exchange rate. Going back to our general statement that the value of a portfolio is the discounted value of its expected cash flows, it follows that a portfolio that has any future cash flows will be subject to some degree of interest rate risk. As with foreign exchange risk, there are several ways we can quantify interest rate exposure.

Cash flow mapping

We can map each cash flow in the portfolio to a standard set of maturities from today out to, say, 30-years. Each cash flow will lie between two standard maturities. The cash flow can be allocated between the two maturities according to some rule. For instance, we might want the present value of the cash flow, and the sensitivity of the cash flow to a parallel shift in the yield curve, to equal the present value and sensitivity of the two cash flows after the mapping.

Duration bucketing

Alternatively, we can take a portfolio of bonds and summarize its exposure to interest rates by bucketing the PV01 of each bond position according to the duration of each bond.

Risk point method

Finally, as with foreign exchange, one can let the portfolio system do the work, and revalue the portfolio for a defined change in each *interest rate*, rather than each foreign exchange rate.

Principal component analysis (PCA)

Given one of these measures of exposure we now have to measure the uncertainty in interest rates, so we can apply the uncertainty measure to the exposure measure and obtain a possible change in mark-to-market value. We know that the level and shape of the yield curve changes in a complicated fashion over time – we see the yield curve move up and down, and back and forth between its normal, upward-sloping, shape and flat or inverted (downward-sloping) shapes.

One way to capture this uncertainty is to measure the standard deviation of the changes in the yield at each maturity on the yield curve, and the correlation between the changes in the yields at each pair of maturities. Table 4.1 shows the results of analyzing CMT (Constant Maturity Treasury) data from the US Treasury's H.15 release over the period from 1982 to 1998. Reading down to the bottom of the

Table 4.1 CMT yield curve standard deviations and correlation matrix

Maturity in years	Standard deviation	Correlation									
		0.25	0.5	1	2	3	5	7	10	20	30
0.25	1.26%	100%									
0.5	1.25%	93%	100%								
1	1.26%	82%	96%	100%							
2	1.26%	73%	89%	97%	100%						
3	1.25%	67%	85%	94%	99%	100%					
5	1.19%	60%	79%	90%	97%	99%	100%				
7	1.14%	56%	75%	87%	94%	97%	99%	100%			
10	1.10%	54%	73%	84%	92%	95%	98%	99%	100%		
20	1.05%	52%	70%	80%	87%	91%	94%	96%	98%	100%	
30	0.99%	50%	67%	77%	85%	89%	92%	95%	97%	98%	100%

standard deviation column we can see that the 30-year CMT yield changes by about 99 bps (basis points) per annum. Moving across from the standard deviation of the 30-year CMT to the bottom-left entry of the correlation matrix, we see that the correlation between changes in the 30-year CMT yield and the 3-month CMT yield is about 50%.

For most of us, this table is a fairly unwieldy way of capturing the changes in the yield curve. If, as in this example, we use 10 maturity points on the yield curve in each currency that we have to model, then to model two curves, we will need a correlation matrix that has 400 (20 × 20) values. As we add currencies the size of the correlation matrix will grow very rapidly. For the G7 currencies we would require a correlation matrix with 4900 (70*70) values.

There is a standard statistical technique, called principal component analysis, which allows us to approximate the correlation matrix with a much smaller data set. Table 4.2 shows the results of applying a matrix operation called eigenvalue/ eigenvector decomposition to the product of the standard deviation vector and the correlation matrix. The decomposition allows us to extract common factors from the correlation matrix, which describe how the yield curve moves *as a whole*. Looking

Table 4.2 CMT yield curve factors

Proportion of variance	Factor shocks									
	0.25	0.5	1	2	3	5	7	10	20	30
86.8%	0.95%	1.13%	1.21%	1.25%	1.23%	1.16%	1.10%	1.04%	0.96%	0.89%
10.5%	−0.79%	−0.53%	−0.26%	−0.03%	0.10%	0.23%	0.30%	0.33%	0.34%	0.34%
1.8%	−0.23%	−0.01%	0.16%	0.19%	0.16%	0.08%	0.00%	−0.08%	−0.20%	−0.24%
0.4%	−0.11%	0.10%	0.11%	−0.01%	−0.07%	−0.08%	−0.04%	−0.01%	0.05%	0.05%
0.2%	0.01%	−0.06%	0.01%	0.05%	0.07%	−0.03%	−0.08%	−0.07%	0.01%	0.08%
0.1%	−0.01%	0.03%	−0.01%	−0.03%	0.01%	0.01%	0.00%	0.03%	−0.10%	0.07%
0.1%	0.02%	−0.06%	0.06%	−0.01%	−0.03%	−0.01%	0.03%	0.01%	−0.02%	0.00%
0.0%	0.00%	0.01%	−0.01%	0.00%	0.00%	0.00%	0.04%	−0.05%	0.00%	0.01%
0.0%	0.00%	0.00%	−0.02%	0.06%	−0.05%	0.01%	0.00%	0.00%	−0.01%	0.01%
0.0%	0.00%	0.00%	−0.02%	0.02%	0.02%	−0.06%	0.02%	0.02%	−0.01%	−0.01%

down the first column of the table, we see that the first three factors explain over 95% of the variance of interest rates! The first three factors have an intuitive interpretation as a shift movement, a tilt movement and a bend movement – we can see this more easily from Figure 4.3, which shows a plot of the yield curve movements by maturity for each factor.

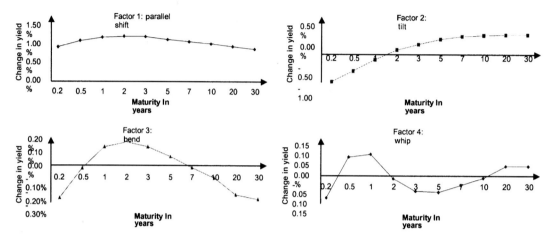

Figure 4.3 Yield curve factors.

In the shift movement, yields in all maturities change in the same direction, though not necessarily by the same amount: if the 3-month yield moves up by 95 bps, the 2-year yield moves up by 125 bps and the 30Y yield moves up by 89 bps. The sizes of the changes are annualized standard deviations. In the bend movement, the short and long maturities change in opposite directions: if the 3-month yield moves down by 79 bps, the 2-year yield moves down by 3 bps (i.e. it's almost unchanged) and the 30Y yield moves up by 34 bps. In the bend movement, yields in the short and long maturities change in the same direction, while yields in the intermediate maturities change in the opposite direction: if the 3-month yield moves down by 23 bps, the 2-year yield moves up by 19 bps and the 30Y yield moves down by 24 bps. As we move to higher factors, the sizes of the yield changes decrease, and the sign of the changes flips more often as we read across the maturities.

If we approximate the changes in the yield curve using just the first few factors we significantly reduce the dimensions of the correlation matrix, without giving up a great deal of modeling accuracy – and the factors are, by construction, uncorrelated with each other.

Commodity price risk

At first glance, commodity transactions look very much like foreign exchange transactions. However, unlike currencies, almost cost-less electronic 'book-entry' transfers of commodities are not the norm. Commodity contracts specify the form and location of the commodity that is to be delivered. For example, a contract to buy copper will specify the metal purity, bar size and shape, and acceptable warehouse locations that the copper may be sent to.

Transportation, storage and insurance are significant factors in the pricing of forward contracts. The basic arbitrage relationship for a commodity forward is that the cost of buying the spot commodity, borrowing the money, and paying the storage and insurance must be more than or equal to the forward price. The cost of borrowing a commodity is sometimes referred to as convenience yield. Having the spot commodity allows manufacturers to keep their plants running. The convenience yield may be more than the costs of borrowing money, storage and insurance.

Unlike in the foreign exchange markets, arbitrage of spot and forward prices in the commodity markets is not necessarily straightforward or even possible:

- Oil pipelines pump oil only in one direction. Oil refineries crack crude to produce gasoline, and other products, but can't be put into reverse and turn gasoline back into crude oil.
- Arbitrage of New York and London gold requires renting armored cars, a Jumbo jet and a gold refinery (to melt down 400 oz good delivery London bars and cast them into 100 oz good delivery Comex bars).
- Soft commodities spoil: you can't let sacks of coffee beans sit in a warehouse forever – they rot!

The impact on risk measurement of the constraints on arbitrage is that we have to be very careful about aggregating positions: whether across different time horizons, across different delivery locations or across different delivery grades. These mismatches are very significant sources of exposure in commodities, and risk managers should check, particularly if their risk measurement systems were developed for financial instruments, that commodity exposures are not understated by netting of longs and shorts across time, locations or deliverables that conceals significant risks.

Equity price risk

Creating a table of standard deviations and correlations is unwieldy for modeling yield curves that are made up of ten or so maturities in each currency. To model equity markets we have to consider hundreds or possibly even thousands of listed companies in each currency. Given that the correlation matrix for even a hundred equities would have 10 000 entries, it is not surprising that factor models are used extensively in modeling equity market returns and risk. We will give a brief overview of some of the modeling alternatives.[3]

Single-factor models and beta

Single-factor models relate the return on an equity to the return on a stock market index:

$\text{ReturnOnStock} = \alpha_i + \beta_i^* \, \text{ReturnOnIndex} + \varepsilon_i$

β_i is $\text{cov}(\text{ReturnOnStock}, \text{ReturnOnIndex}) / \text{var}(\text{ReturnOnIndex})$

ε_i is uncorrelated with the return on the index

The return on the stock is split into three components: a random general market return, measured as β multiplied by the market index return, which *can't* be diversified, (so you *do* get paid for assuming the risk); a random idiosyncratic return, ε, which can be diversified (so you *don't* get paid for assuming the risk); and an expected idiosyncratic return α.

This implies that all stocks move up and down together, differing only in the magnitude of their movements relative to the market index, the β, and the magnitude of an idiosyncratic return that is uncorrelated with either the market index return or the idiosyncratic return of any other equity. In practice many market participants use β as the primary measure of the market risk of an individual equity and their portfolio as a whole. While this is a very simple and attractive model, a single factor only explains about 35% of the variance of equity returns, compared to the single-factor yield curve model, which explained almost 90% of the yield curve variance.

Multi-factor models/APT

The low explanatory power of single-factor models has led researchers to use multi-factor models. One obvious approach is to follow the same steps we described for interest rates: calculate the correlation matrix, decompose the matrix into eigenvalues and eigenvectors, and select a subset of the factors to describe equity returns. More commonly, analysts use fundamental factors (such as *Price/Earnings ratio*, *Style*[Value, Growth, ...], *Market capitalization* and *Industry* [Banking, Transportation, eCommerce, ...]), or macro-economic factors (such as the *Oil price*, the *Yield curve slope*, *Inflation*, ...) to model equity returns.

Correlation and concentration risk

We can break equity risk management into two tasks: managing the overall market risk exposure to the factor(s) in our model, and managing the concentration of risk in individual equities. This is a lot easier than trying to use the whole variance–covariance matrix, and follows the same logic as using factor models for yield curve analysis.

Dividend and stock loan risk

As with any forward transaction, the forward price of an equity is determined by the cost of borrowing the two deliverables, in this case the cost of borrowing money, and the cost of borrowing stock. In addition, the forward equity price is affected by any known cash flows (such as expected dividend payments) that will be paid before the forward date. Relative to the repo market for US Treasuries, the stock loan market is considerably less liquid and less transparent.

Indexing benchmark risk

We are free to define 'risk'. While banks typically have absolute return on equity (ROE) targets and manage profit or loss relative to a fixed budget, in the asset management business, many participants have a return target that is variable, and related to the return on an index. In the simplest case, the asset manager's risk is of a shortfall relative to the index the manager tracks, such as the S&P500. In effect this transforms the VaR analysis to a different 'currency' – that of the index, and we look at the price risk of a portfolio in units of, say, S&P500s, rather than dollars.

Price volatility risk

One obvious effect of a change in price volatility is that it changes the VaR! Option products, and more generally instruments that have convexity in their value with respect to the level of prices, are affected by the volatility of prices. We can handle exposure to the *volatility* of prices in the same way as exposure to prices. We measure the exposure (or vega, or kappa[4]) of the portfolio to a change in volatility, we measure the uncertainty in volatility, and we bring the two together in a VaR calculation. In much the same way as the price *level* changes over time, price *volatility* also changes over time, so we measure the volatility of volatility to capture this uncertainty.

Price correlation risk

In the early 1990s there was an explosion in market appetite for structured notes, many of which contained option products whose payoffs depended on more than one underlying price. Enthusiasm for structured notes and more exotic options has cooled, at least in part due to the well-publicized problems of some US corporations and money market investors, the subsequent tightening of corporate risk management standards, and the subsequent tightening of the list of allowable investment products for money market funds. However, there are still many actively traded options that depend on two or more prices – some from the older generation of exotic products, such as options on baskets of currencies or other assets, and some that were developed for the structured note market, such as 'diff swaps' and 'quantos'. Options whose payoffs depend on two or more prices have exposure to the volatility of each of the underlying prices and the correlation between each pair of prices.

Pre-payment variance risk

Mortgage-backed-securities (MBS) and Asset-backed-securities (ABS) are similar to callable bonds. The investor in the bond has sold the borrower (ultimately a homeowner with a mortgage, or a consumer with credit card or other debt) the option to pay off their debt early. Like callable debt, the value of the prepayment option depends directly on the level and shape of the yield curve, and the level and shape of the volatility curve. For instance, when rates fall, homeowners refinance and the MBS prepays principal back to the investor that the MBS investor has to reinvest at a lower rate than the MBS coupon. MBS prepayment risk can be hedged at a macro level by buying receivers swaptions or CMT floors, struck below the money: the rise in the value of the option offsets the fall in the MBS price.

Unlike callable debt, the value of the prepayment option is also indirectly affected by the yield curve, and by other factors, which may not be present in the yield curve data. First, people move!

Mortgages (except GNMA mortgages) are not usually assumable by the new buyer. Therefore to move, the homeowner may pay down a mortgage even if it is uneconomic to do so. The housing market is seasonal – most people contract to buy their houses in spring and close in summer.

The overall state of the economy is also important: in a downturn, people lose their jobs. Rather than submit to a new credit check, a homeowner may not refinance, even if it would be economic to do so.

So, in addition to the yield curve factors, a prepayment model will include an econometric model of the impact of the factors that analysts believe determine prepayment speeds: pool coupon relative to market mortgage rates, pool size, pool seasoning/burn-out: past yield curve and prepayment history, geographic composition of the pool, and seasonality. A quick comparison of Street models on the Bloomberg shows a wide range of projected speeds for any given pool! Predicting future prepayments is still as much an art as a science.

The MBS market is both large and mature. Figure 4.4 shows the relative risk and return of the plain vanilla pass-through securities, and two types of derived securities that assign the cash flows of a pass-through security in different ways – stable

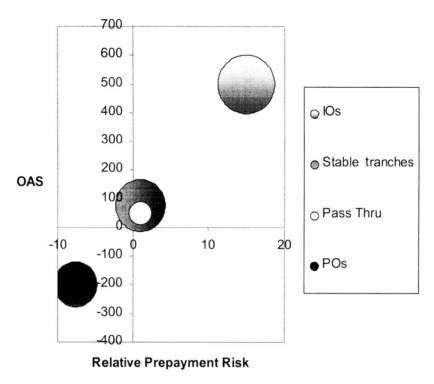

Figure 4.4 Relative risk of different types of MBS (after Cheyette, *Journal of Portfolio Management*, Fall 1996).

tranches, which provide some degree of protection from prepayment risk to some tranche holders at the expense of increased prepayment risk for other tranche holders, and IOs/POs which separate the principal and interest payments of a pass-through security.

Under the general heading of prepayment risk we should also mention that there are other contracts that may suffer prepayment or early termination due to external factors other than market prices. Once prepayment or early termination occurs, the contracts may lose value. For example, synthetic guaranteed investment contracts ('GIC wraps'), which provide for the return of principal on a pension plan investment, have a legal maturity date, but typically also have provisions for compensation of the plan sponsor if a significant number of employees withdraw from the pension plan early, and their investments have lost money. Exogenous events that are difficult to hedge against may trigger withdrawals from the plan: layoffs following a merger or acquisition, declining prospects for the particular company causing employees to move on, and so on.

Portfolio response to market changes

Following our brief catalogue of market risks, we now look at how the portfolio changes in value in response to changes in market prices, and how we can summarize those changes in value.

Linear versus non-linear change in value

Suppose we draw a graph of the change in value of the portfolio for a change in a market variable. If it's a straight line, the change in value is *linear* in that variable. If it's curved, the change in value is *non-linear* in that variable. Figure 4.5 shows a linear risk on the left and a non-linear risk on the right.

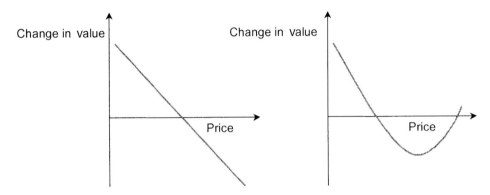

Figure 4.5 Linear versus non-linear change in value.

If change in value of the portfolio is completely linear in a price, we can summarize the change in value with a single number, the *delta*, or first derivative of the change in value with respect to the price. If the change in value is not a straight line, we can use higher derivatives to summarize the change in value. The second derivative is known as the *gamma* of the portfolio. There is no standard terminology for the third derivative on. In practice, if the change in value of the portfolio can't be captured accurately with one or two derivatives then we simply store a table of the change in value for the range of the price we are considering!

Using two or more derivatives to approximate the change in value of a variable is known as a *Taylor series expansion* of the value of the variable. In our case, if we wanted to estimate the change in portfolio value given the delta and gamma, we would use the following formula:

$$\text{Change in portfolio value} = \text{DELTA} * (\text{change in price}) + 1/2\,\text{GAMMA} * (\text{change in price})^2$$

If the formula looks familiar, it may be because one common application of a Taylor series expansion in finance is the use of *modified duration* and *convexity* to estimate the change in value of a bond for a change in yield. If that doesn't ring a bell, then perhaps the equation for a parabola ($y = ax + bx^2$), from your high school math class, does.

Discontinuous change in value

Both the graphs in Figure 4.5 could be drawn with a smooth line. Some products, such as digital options, give risk to jumps, or discontinuities, in the graph of portfolio change in value, as we show in Figure 4.6. Discontinuous changes in value are difficult to capture accurately with Taylor series.

Path-dependent change in value

Risk has a time dimension. We measure the change in the value of the portfolio *over time*. The potential change in value, estimated today, between today and a future

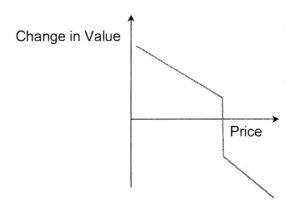

Figure 4.6 Discontinuous change in value.

date, may depend on what happens in the intervening period of time, not just on the state of the world at the future date. This can be because of the payoff of the product (for example, a barrier option) or the actions of the trader (for example, a stop loss order). Let's take the case of a stop loss order. Suppose a trader buys an equity for 100 USD. The trader enters a stop loss order to sell at 90 USD. Suppose at the end of the time period we are considering the equity is trading at 115 USD. Before we can determine the value of the trader's portfolio, we must first find out whether the equity traded at 90 USD or below after the trader bought it. If so, the trader would have been stopped out, selling the position at 90 USD (more probably a little below 90 USD); would have lost 10 USD on the trade and would currently have no position. If not, the trader would have a mark-to-market gain on the position of 15 USD, and would still be long. Taylor series don't help us at all with this type of behavior.

When is a Taylor series inaccurate?

- *Large moves*: if the portfolio change in value is not accurately captured by one or two derivatives,[5] then the larger the change in price over which we estimate the change in value, the larger the slippage between the Taylor series estimate and the true portfolio change in value. For a *large* change in price, we have to change the inputs to our valuation model, recalculate the portfolio value, and take the difference from the initial value.
- *Significant cross-partials*: our Taylor series example assumed that the changes in value of the portfolio for each different risk factor that affects the value of the portfolio are independent. If not, then we have to add terms to the Taylor series expansion to capture these *cross-partial* sensitivities. For example, if our vega changes with the level of market prices, then we need to add the derivative of vega with respect to prices to our Taylor series expansion to make accurate estimates of the change in portfolio value.

Risk reports

Risk managers spend a great deal of time surveying risk reports. It is important that risk managers understand exactly what the numbers they are looking at mean. As we have discussed above, exposures are usually captured by a measure of the derivative of the change in value of a portfolio to a given price or other risk factor.

The derivative may be calculated as a true derivative, obtained by differentiating the valuation formula with respect to the risk factor, or as a numerical derivative, calculated by changing the value of the risk factor and rerunning the valuation to see how much the value changes. Numerical derivatives can be calculated by just moving the risk factor one way from the initial value (a one-sided difference), or preferably, by moving the risk factor up and down (a central difference). In some cases, the differences between true, one-sided numerical, and central numerical derivatives are significant.

Bucket reports versus factor reports

A *bucket report* takes a property of the trade (say, notional amount), or the output of a valuation model (say, delta), and allocates the property to one or two buckets according to a trade parameter, such as maturity. For example, the sensitivity of a bond to a parallel shift in the yield curve of 1 bp, might be bucketed by the maturity of the bond.

A *factor report* bumps model inputs and shows the change in the present value of the portfolio for each change in the model input. For example, the sensitivity of a portfolio of FRAs and swaps to a 1 bp change in each input to the swap curve (money market rates, Eurodollar futures prices, US Treasuries and swap spreads).

Both types of report are useful, but risk managers need to be certain what they are looking at! When tracking down the sources of an exposure, we often work from a factor report (say, sensitivity of an options portfolio to changes in the volatility smile) to a bucket report (say, option notional by strike and maturity) to a transaction list (transactions by strike and maturity).

Hidden exposures

The exposures that are not captured at all by the risk-monitoring systems are the ones that are most likely to lose risk managers their jobs. Part of the art of risk management is deciding what exposures to monitor and aggregate through the organization, and what exposures to omit from this process.

Risk managers must establish criteria to determine when exposures must be included in the monitoring process, and must establish a regular review to monitor whether exposures meet the criteria. We will point out a few exposures, which are often not monitored, but may in fact be significant:

- *Swaps portfolios*: the basis between Eurodollar money market rates, and the rates implied by Eurodollar futures; and the basis between 3M Libor and other floating rate frequencies (1M Libor, 6M Libor and 12M Libor).
- *Options portfolios*: the volatility smile.
- *Long-dated option portfolios*: interest rates, and borrowing costs for the underlying (i.e. repo rates for bond options, dividend and stock loan rates for equity options, metal borrowing rates for bullion options, ...)

Positions that are not entered in the risk monitoring systems at all are a major source of problems. Typically, new products are first valued and risk managed in spreadsheets, before inclusion in the production systems. One approach is to require that even spreadsheet systems adhere to a firm-wide risk-reporting interface and that spreadsheet systems hand off the exposures of the positions they contain to the production systems. A second alternative is to limit the maximum exposure that may be assumed while the positions are managed in spreadsheets. Risk managers have to balance the potential for loss due to inadequate monitoring with the potential loss of revenue from turning away transactions simply because the transactions would have to be managed in spreadsheets (or some other non-production system).

In general, trading portfolios have gross exposures that are much larger than the net exposures. Risk managers have to take a hard look at the process by which exposures are netted against each other, to ensure that significant risks are not being masked by the netting process.

Market parameter estimation

As we will see below, risk-aggregation methods rely on assumptions about the distributions of market prices and estimates of the volatility and correlation of market prices. These assumptions quantify the uncertainty in market prices.

When we attempt to model the market, we are modeling human not physical behavior (because market prices are set by the interaction of traders). Human behavior isn't always rational, or consistent, and changes over time. While we can apply techniques from the physical sciences to modeling the market, we have to remember that our calculations may be made completely inaccurate by changes in human behavior. The good news is that we are not trying to build valuation models for all the products in our portfolio, we are just trying to get some measure of the risk of those products over a relatively short time horizon. The bad news is that we are trying to model rare events – what happens in the tails of the probability distribution. By definition, we have a lot less information about past rare events than about past common events.

Choice of distribution

To begin, we have to choose a probability distribution for changes in market prices – usually either the normal or the log-normal distribution. We also usually assume that the changes in one period are *independent* of the changes in the previous period, and finally we assume that the properties of the probability distribution are constant over time. There is a large body of research on non-parametric estimation of the distributions of market prices. Non-parametric methods are techniques for extracting the real-world probability distribution from large quantities of observed data, without making many assumptions about the actual distribution beforehand. The research typically shows that market prices are best described by complex mixtures of many different distributions that have changing properties over time (Ait-Sahalia, 1996, 1997; Wilmot *et al.*, 1995).

That said, we use the normal distribution, *not* because it's a great fit to the data or the market, but because we can scale variance over time easily (which means we can translate VaR to a different time horizon easily), because we can calculate the variance of linear sums of normal variables easily (which means we can add risks easily), and because we can calculate the moments of functions of normal variables easily (which means we can *approximate* the behavior of some other distributions easily)!

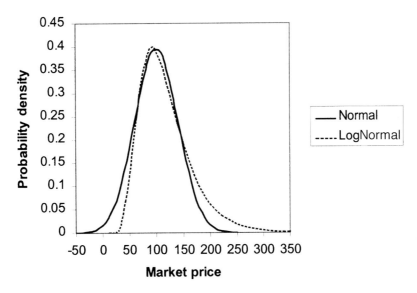

Figure 4.7 Normally and log-normally distributed variables.

As its name suggests, the log-normal distribution is closely related to the normal distribution. Figure 4.7 shows the familiar 'bell curve' shape of the probability density of a *normally* distributed variable with a mean of 100 and a standard deviation of 40. When we use the normal distribution to describe prices, we assume that up-and-down moves of a certain absolute size are equally likely. If the moves are large enough, the price can become negative, which is unrealistic if we are describing a stock price or a bond price. To avoid this problem, we can use the log-normal distribution. The log-normal distribution assumes that *proportional* moves in the stock price are equally likely.[6] Looking at Figure 4.7 we see that, compared to the normal distribution, for the log-normal distribution the range of lower prices is compressed, and the range of higher prices is enlarged. In the middle of the price range the two distributions are very similar. One other note about the log-normal distribution – market participants usually refer to the standard deviation of a log-normal variable as the variable's *volatility*. Volatility is typically quoted as a percentage change per annum.

To investigate the *actual* distribution of rates we can use standardized variables. To standardize a variable we take each of the original values in turn, subtracting the average value of the whole data set and dividing through by the standard deviation of the whole data set:

Standard variable value = (original variable value – average of original variable)/ standard deviation of original variable

After standardization the mean of the standard variable is 0, and the standard deviation of the new variable is 1. If we want to compare different data sets, it is much easier to see the differences between the data sets if they all have the same mean and standard deviation to start with. We can do the comparisons by looking at probability density plots.

Figure 4.8 shows the frequency of observations of market changes for four years

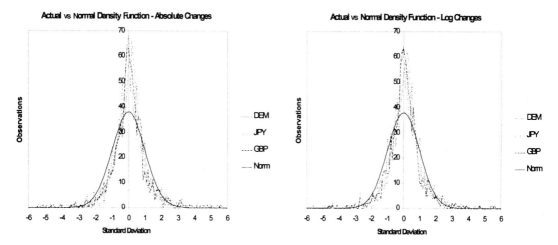

Figure 4.8 Empirical FX data compared with the normal and log-normal distributions.

of actual foreign exchange rate data (DEM–USD, JPY–USD and GBP–USD), overlaid on the normal distribution. On the left-hand side of the figure the absolute rate changes are plotted, while on the right-hand side the changes in the logarithms of the rate are plotted. If foreign exchange rates were *normally* distributed, the colored points on the left-hand side of the figure would plot on top of the smooth black line representing the normal distribution. If foreign exchange rates were *log-normally* distributed, the colored points in the right-hand side of the figure would plot on top of the normal distribution.

In fact, it's quite hard to tell the difference between the two figures: neither the normal nor the log-normal distribution does a great job of matching the actual data. Both distributions fail to predict the frequency of large moves in the actual data – the 'fat tails' or leptokurtosis of most financial variables. For our purposes, either distribution assumption will do. We recommend using whatever distribution makes the calculations easiest, or is most politically acceptable to the organization!

We could use other alternatives to capture the 'fat tails' in the actual data: such as the *T*-distribution; the distribution implied from the option volatility smile; or a mixture of two normal distributions (one regular, one fat). These alternatives are almost certainly not worth the additional effort required to implement them, compared to the simpler approach of using the results from the normal or log-normal distribution and scaling them (i.e. multiplying them by a fudge factor so the results fit the tails of the actual data better). Remember that we are really only concerned with accurately modeling the tails of the distribution at our chosen level of confidence, not the whole distribution.

Volatility and correlation estimation

Having chosen a distribution, we have to estimate the parameters of the distribution. In modeling the uncertainty of market prices, we usually focus on estimating the standard deviations (or volatilities) of market prices, and the correlations of pairs of market prices. We assume the first moment of the distribution is zero (which is reasonable in most cases for a short time horizon), and we ignore higher moments than the second moment, the standard deviation. One consequence of using standard deviation as a measure of uncertainty is that we don't take into account asymmetry in the distribution of market variables. Skewness in the price distribution may increase or decrease risk depending on the sign of the skewness and whether our exposure is long or short. Later, when we discuss risk aggregation methods, we'll see that some of the methods do account for the higher moments of the price distribution.

Historical estimates

One obvious starting point is to estimate the parameters of the distribution from historical market data, and then apply those parameters to a forward-looking analysis of VaR (i.e. we assume that past market behavior can tell us something about the future).

Observation period and weighting

First, we have to decide how much of the historical market data we wish to consider for our estimate of the parameters of the distribution. Let's suppose we want to use 2 months' of daily data. One way to achieve this is to plug 2 months' data into a standard deviation calculation. Implicitly, what we are doing is giving equal weight to the recent data and the data from two months ago. Alternatively, we may choose to give recent observations more weight in the standard deviation calculation than data from the past. If recent observations include larger moves than most of the data, then the standard deviation estimate will be higher, and if recent observations include smaller moves than most of the data, the standard deviation estimate will be lower. These effects on our standard deviation estimate have some intuitive appeal.

If we use 2 months of equally weighted data, the weighted-average maturity of the data is 1 month. To maintain the same average maturity while giving more weight to more recent data, we have to sample data from more than 2 months. We can demonstrate this with a concrete example using the *exponential* weighting scheme. In exponential weighting, the weight of each value in the data, working back from today, is equal to the previous value's weight multiplied by a decay factor. So if the decay factor is 0.97, the weight for today's value in the standard deviation calculation is $0.97^0 = 1$, the weight of yesterday's value in the standard deviation is $0.97^1 = 0.97$, the weight of previous day's value in the standard deviation is $0.97^2 = 0.9409$, and so on. Figure 4.9 shows a graph of the cumulative weight of n days, values, working back from today, and Table 4.3 shows the value of n for cumulative weights of 25%, 50%, 75% and 99%.

Twenty-two business days (about 1 calendar month) contribute 50% of the weight of the data, so the weighted-average maturity of the data is 1 month. In contrast to the equally weighted data, where we needed 2 months of data, now we need 151 business days or over 7 months of data to calculate our standard deviation, given that we are prepared to cut off data that would contribute less than 1% to the total weight. Exponential weighting schemes are very popular, but while they use *more* data for the standard deviation calculation than unweighted schemes, it's important to note that they *effectively* sample much *less* data – a quarter of the weight is contributed by the first nine observations, and half the weight by 22 observations. Our decay factor of 0.97 is towards the high end of the range of values used, and lower decay factors sample even less data.

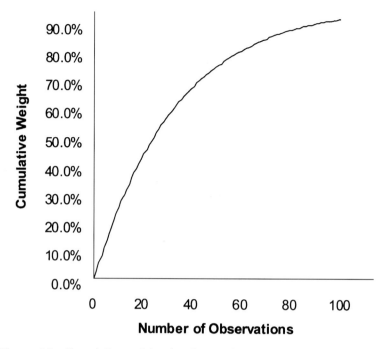

Figure 4.9   Cumulative weight of *n* observations for a decay factor of 0.97.

Table 4.3   Cumulative weight for a given number of observations.

Weight	Observations
25%	9
50%	22
75%	45
99%	151

GARCH estimates

GARCH (Generalized Auto Regressive Conditional Heteroscedasticity) models of standard deviation can be thought of as a more complicated version of the weighting schemes described above, where the weighting factor is determined by the data itself. In a GARCH model the standard deviation today depends on the standard deviation yesterday, and the size of the change in market prices yesterday. The model tells us how a large move in prices today affects the likelihood of there being another large move in prices tomorrow.

Estimates implied from market prices

Readers familiar with option valuation will know that the formulae used to value options take the uncertainty in market prices as input. Conversely, given the price of an option, we can *imply* the uncertainty in market prices that the trader used to value the option. If we believe that option traders are better at predicting future uncertainty in prices than estimates from historical data, we can use parameters implied from the market prices of options in our VaR models. One drawback of this approach is that factors other than trader's volatility estimates, such as market liquidity and the balance of market supply and demand, may be reflected in market prices for options.

Research on different estimation procedures

Hendricks (1996) studies the performance of equally and exponentially weighted estimators of volatility for a number of different sample sizes in two different VaR methods. His results indicate that there is very little to choose between the different estimators. Boudoukh *et al.* (1997) study the efficiency of several different weighting schemes for volatility estimation. The 'winner' is non-parametric multivariate density estimation (MDE). MDE puts high weight on observations that occur under conditions similar to the current date. Naturally this requires an appropriate choice of state variables to describe the market conditions. The authors use yield curve level and slope when studying Treasury bill yield volatility. MDE does not seem to represent a huge forecasting improvement given the increased complexity of the estimation method but it is interesting that we can formalize the concept of using only representative data for parameter estimation.

Naive use of a delta normal approach requires estimating and handling very large covariance matrices. Alexander and Leigh (1997) advocate a divide-and-conquer strategy to volatility and correlation estimation: break down the risk factors into a sets of highly correlated factors; then perform principal components analysis to create a set of orthogonal risk factors; then estimate variances of the orthogonal factors and covariances of the principal components. Alexander and Leigh also conclude from backtesting that there is little to choose between the regulatory-year equally weighted model and GARCH(1,1), while the RiskMetrics™ exponentially weighted estimator performs less well.

BIS quantitative requirements

The BIS requires a minimum weighted average maturity of the historical data used to estimate volatility of 6 months, which corresponds to a historical observation period of at least 1 year for equally weighted data. The volatility data must be updated at least quarterly: and more often if market conditions warrant it.

Much of the literature on volatility estimation recommends much shorter observation periods[7] but these are probably more appropriate for volatility traders (i.e. option book runners) than risk managers. When we use a short observation period, a couple of weeks of quiet markets will significantly reduce our volatility estimate. It is hard to see that the market has really become a less risky place, just because it's been quiet for a while. Another advantage of using a relatively long observation period, and revising volatilities infrequently, is that the units of risk don't change from day to day – just the position. This makes it easier for traders and risk managers to understand why their VaR has changed.

Beta estimation

Looking back at our equation for the return on a stock, we see that it is the equation of a straight line, where β represents the slope of the line we would plot through the scatter graph of stock returns plotted on the y-axis, against market returns plotted on the x-axis.

Most of the literature on beta estimation comes from investment analysis, where regression analysis of stock returns on market returns is performed using estimation periods that are extremely long (decades) compared to our risk analysis horizon. While betas show a tendency to revert to towards 1, the impact of such reversion over the risk analysis horizon is probably negligible.

One criticism of historical estimates of beta is that they do not respond quickly to changes in the operating environment – or capital structure – of the firm. One alternative is for the risk manager to estimate beta from regression of stock returns on accounting measures such as earnings variability, leverage, and dividend payout, or to monitor these accounting measures as an 'early-warning system' for changes, not yet reflected in historical prices, that may impact the stock's beta in the future.

Yield curve estimation

We discussed yield curve construction and interpolation in Chapter 3. Risk managers must have detailed knowledge of yield curve construction and interpolation to assess model risk in the portfolio mark to market, to understand the information in exposure reports and to be able to test the information's integrity. However, for risk aggregation, the construction and interpolation methods are of secondary importance, as is the choice of whether risk exposures are reported for cash yields, zero coupon yields or forward yields.

As we will emphasize later, VaR measurement is not very accurate, so we shouldn't spend huge resources trying to make the VaR very precise. Suppose we collect risk exposures by perturbing cash instrument yields, but we have estimated market uncertainty analysing zero coupon yields. It's acceptable for us to use the two somewhat inconsistent sets of information together in a VaR calculation – as long as we understand what we have done, and have estimated the error introduced by what we have done.

Risk-aggregation methods

We have described how we measure our exposure to market uncertainty and how we estimate the uncertainty itself, and now we will describe the different ways we calculate the risks and add up the risks to get a VaR number.

Factor push VaR

As its name implies, in this method we simply push each market price in the direction that produces the maximum adverse impact on the portfolio for that market price. The desired confidence level and horizon determine the amount the price is pushed.

Confidence level and standard deviations

Let's assume we are using the 99% confidence level mandated by the BIS. We need to translate that confidence level into a number of standard deviations by which we will push our risk factor.

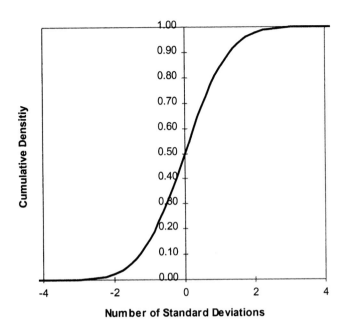

Figure 4.10 Cumulative normal probability density.

Figure 4.10 shows the cumulative probability density for the normal distribution as a function of the number of standard deviations. The graph was plotted in Microsoft® Excel™, using the cumulative probability density function, NORMSDIST (NumberOfStandardDeviations). Using this function, or reading from the graph, we can see that one standard deviation corresponds to a confidence level of 84.1%, and two standard deviations correspond to a confidence level of 97.7%. Working back the other way, we can use the Excel™ NORMSINV(ConfidenceLevel) function to tell us how many standard deviations correspond to a particular confidence level. For example, a 95% confidence level corresponds to 1.64 standard deviations, and a 99% confidence level to 2.33 standard deviations.

Growth of uncertainty over time

Now we know that for a 99% confidence interval, we have to push the risk factor 2.33 standard deviations. However, we also have to scale our standard deviation to the appropriate horizon period for the VaR measurement. Let's assume we are using a 1-day horizon.

For a normally distributed variable, uncertainty grows with the square root of time. Figure 4.11 shows the growth in uncertainty over time of an interest rate with a standard deviation of 100 bps per annum,[8] for three different confidence levels (84.1% or one standard deviation, 95% or 1.64 standard deviations, 99% or 2.33 standard deviations). Table 4.4 shows a table of the same information.

Standard deviations are usually quoted on an annual basis. We usually assume that all the changes in market prices occur on business days – the days when all the markets and exchanges are open and trading can occur. There are approximately 250 business days in the year.[9] To convert an annual (250-day) standard deviation to a 1-day standard deviation we multiply by $\sqrt{(1/250)}$, which is approximately 1/16.

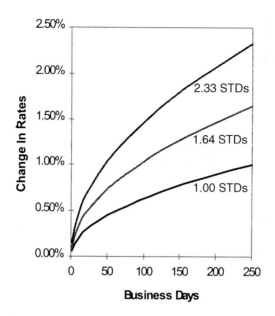

Figure 4.11   Growth in uncertainty over time.

Table 4.4   Growth of uncertainty over time (annual standard deviation 1%)

Horizon		Confidence	84.10%	95.00%	99.00%
Tenor	Days	STDs	1.00	1.64	2.33
1D	1		0.06%	0.10%	0.15%
2W	10		0.20%	0.33%	0.47%
1M	21		0.29%	0.48%	0.67%
3M	62.5		0.50%	0.82%	1.16%
6M	125		0.71%	1.16%	1.64%
9M	187.5		0.87%	1.42%	2.01%
1Y	250		1.00%	1.64%	2.33%

So, if we wanted to convert an interest rate standard deviation of about 100 bps per annum to a daily basis, we would divide 100 by 16 and get about 6 bps per day. So, we can calculate our interest rate factor push as a standard deviation of 6 bps per day, multiplied by the number of standard deviations for a 99% confidence interval of 2.33, to get a factor push of around 14 bps.

Once we know how to calculate the size of the push, we can push each market variable to its worst value, calculate the impact on the portfolio value, and add each of the individual results for each factor up to obtain our VaR:

FactorPushVaR = Sum of ABS(SingleFactorVaR) for all risk factors, where
SingleFactorVaR = Exposure*MaximumLikelyAdverseMove
MaximumLikelyAdverseMove = NumberOfStandardDeviations*StandardDeviation* $\sqrt{}$Horizon, and
ABS(x) means the absolute value of x

The drawback of this approach is that it does not take into account the correlations between different risk factors. Factor push will usually overestimate VaR[10] because it does not take into account any diversification of risk. In the real world, risk factors are not all perfectly correlated, so they will not *all* move, at the same time, in the worst possible direction, by the same number of standard deviations.

FX example

Suppose that we bought 1 million DEM and sold 73.6 million JPY for spot settlement. Suppose that the daily standard deviations of the absolute exchange rates are 0.00417 for USD–DEM and 0.0000729 for USD–JPY (note that both the standard deviations were calculated on the exchange rate expressed as USD per unit of foreign currency). Then the 95% confidence interval, 1-day single factor VaRs are:

$$1\,000\,000 * 1.64 * 0.00417 * \sqrt{1} = 6863 \text{ USD for the DEM position}$$
$$-73\,594,191 * 1.64 * 0.0000729 * \sqrt{1} = -8821 \text{ USD for the JPY position}$$

The total VaR using the Factor Push methodology is the sum of the absolute values of the single factor VaRs, or 6863 USD plus 8821 USD, which equals 15 683 USD. As we mentioned previously, this total VaR takes no account of the fact that USD–DEM and USD–JPY foreign exchange rates are correlated, and so a long position in one currency and a short position in the other currency will have much less risk than the sum of the two exposures.

Bond example

Suppose on 22 May 1998 we have a liability equivalent in duration terms to $100 million of the current 10-year US Treasury notes. Rather than simply buying 10-year notes to match our liability, we see value in the 2-year note and 30-year bond, and so we buy an amount of 2-year notes and 30-year bonds that costs the same amount to purchase as, and matches the exposure of, the 10-year notes. Table 4.5 shows the portfolio holdings and duration, while Table 4.6 shows the exposure to each yield curve factor, using the data from Table 4.2 for the annualized change in yield at each maturity, for each factor.

Table 4.5 Example bond portfolio's holdings and duration

	Holding (millions)	Coupon	Maturity	Price	Yield	Modified duration	v01
Liability: 10-year note	100	5 5/8	5/15/08	99-29	5.641	7.56	75 483
Assets: 2-year note	44	5 5/8	4/30/00	100-01	5.605	1.81	7 948
30-year bond	54.25	6 1/8	11/15/18	103-00	5.909	13.79	77 060
						Total	85 008

To convert the net exposure numbers in each factor to 95% confidence level, 1-day VaRs, we multiply by 1.64 standard deviations to get a move corresponding to 95% confidence and divide by 16 to convert the *annual* yield curve changes to *daily* changes. Note that the net exposure to the first factor is essentially zero. This is

Table 4.6   Example bond portfolio's factor sensitivity

	Holding (millions)	Yield curve change (basis points)			Change in market value		
		Factor 1 Shift	Factor 2 Tilt	Factor 3 Bend	Factor 1 Shift	Factor 2 Tilt	Factor 3 Bend
Liability: 10-year note	100	104	33	−8	(7 850 242)	(2 490 942)	603 865
Assets: 2-year note	44	125	−3	19	(933 497)	23 844	(151 012)
30-year bond	54.25	89	34	−24	(6 858 310)	(2 620 028)	1 849 432
				Total	(7 851 807)	(2 596 184)	1 698 420
Net exposure					1 565	105 242	(1 094 556)
Single factor VaR					162	10 916	(113 530)

because we choose the amounts of the 2-year note and 30-year bond to make this so.[11] Our total factor push VaR is simply the sum of the absolute values of the single factor VaRs: $162 + 10\,916 + 113\,530 = 124\,608$ USD.

Covariance approach

Now we can move on to VaR methods that *do*, either explicitly or implicitly, take into account the correlation between risk factors.

Delta-normal VaR

The standard RiskMetrics™ methodology measures positions by reducing all transactions to cash flow maps. The volatility of the *returns* of these cash flows is assumed to be normal, i.e. the cash flows each follow a log-normal random walk. The change in the value of the cash flow is then approximated as the product of the cash flow and the return (i.e. using the first term of a Taylor series expansion of the change in value of a log-normal random variable, e^x).

Cash flow mapping can be quite laborious and does not extend to other risks beyond price and interest rate sensitivities. The Delta-normal methodology is a slightly more general flavor of the standard RiskMetrics methodology, which considers *risk factors* rather than *cash flow maps* as a measure of exposure. The risk factors usually correspond to standard trading system sensitivity outputs (price risk, vega risk, yield curve risk), are assumed to follow a multivariate normal distribution and are all first derivatives. Therefore, the portfolio change in value is linear in the risk factors and the position in each factor and the math for VaR calculation looks identical to that for the RiskMetrics approach, even though the assumptions are rather different.

Single risk factor delta-normal VaR

Delta-normal VaR for a single risk factor is calculated the same way as for the factor push method.

Multiple risk factor delta-normal VaR

How do we add multiple single factor VaRs, taking correlation into account? For the two risk factor case:

$$\text{VaR}_{\text{Total}} = \sqrt{(\text{VaR}_1^2 + \text{VaR}_2^2 + 2*\rho_{12}*\text{VaR}_1*\text{VaR}_2)},$$
where ρ_{12} is the correlation between the first and second risk factors.

For the three risk factor case:

$$\text{VaR}_{\text{Total}} = \sqrt{(\text{VaR}_1^2 + \text{VaR}_2^2 + \text{VaR}_3^2 + 2*\rho_{12}*\text{VaR}_1*\text{VaR}_2 + 2*\rho_{13}*\text{VaR}_1*\text{VaR}_3 + 2*\rho_{32}*}$$
$$\text{VaR}_3*\text{VaR}_2)},$$

For n risk factors:

$$\text{VaR}_{\text{Total}} = \sqrt{(\Sigma_i \Sigma_j \rho_{ij}*\text{VaR}_i*\text{VaR}_j)}^{12}$$

As the number of risk factors increases, the long hand calculation gets cumbersome, so we switch to using matrix notation. In matrix form, the calculation is much more compact:

$$\text{VaR}_{\text{Total}} = \sqrt{(V*C*V^{\text{T}})}$$

where:
V is the row matrix of n single-factor VaRs, one for each risk factor
C is the n by n correlation matrix between each risk factor and
T denotes the matrix Transpose operation

Excel™ has the MMULT() formula for matrix multiplication, and the TRANSPOSE() formula to transpose a matrix, so – given the input data – we can calculate VaR in a single cell, using the formula above.[13] The essence of what we are doing when we use this formula is adding two or more quantities that have a *magnitude* and a *direction*, i.e. adding *vectors*.

Suppose we have two exposures, one with a VaR of 300 USD, and one with a VaR of 400 USD. Figure 4.12 illustrates adding the two VaRs for three different correlation coefficients. A correlation coefficient of 1 (perfect correlation of the risk factors) implies that the VaR vectors point in the same direction, and that we can just perform simple addition to get the total VaR of $300 + 400 = 700$ USD. A correlation coefficient of 0 (no correlation of the risk factors) implies that the VaR vectors point at right

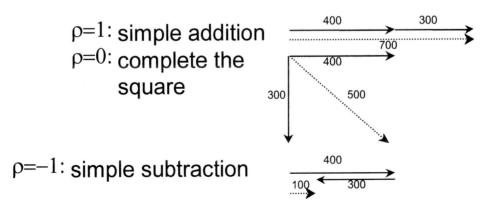

Figure 4.12 VaR calculation as vector addition.

angles to each other, and that we can use Pythagoras's theorem to calculate the length of the hypotenuse, which corresponds to our total VaR. The total VaR is the square root of the sum of the squares of 300 and 400, which gives a total VaR of $\sqrt{(300^2 + 400^2)} = 500$ USD. A correlation coefficient of -1 (perfect inverse correlation of the risk factors) implies that the VaR vectors point in the opposite direction, and we can just perform simple subtraction to get the total VaR of $300 - 400 = -100$ USD.

We can repeat the same exercise, of adding two VaRs for three different correlation coefficients, using the matrix math that we introduced on the previous page. Equations (4.1)– (4.3) show the results of working through the matrix math in each case.

Perfectly correlated risk factors

$$VaR = \sqrt{(300 \quad 400) \begin{pmatrix} 1 & 1 \\ 1 & 1 \end{pmatrix} \begin{pmatrix} 300 \\ 400 \end{pmatrix}}$$

$$= \sqrt{(300.1 + 400.1 \quad 300.1 + 400.1) \begin{pmatrix} 300 \\ 400 \end{pmatrix}}$$

$$= \sqrt{(700.300 + 700.400)} \tag{4.1}$$

$$= \sqrt{(210\,000 + 280\,000)}$$

$$= \sqrt{(490\,000)}$$

$$= 700$$

Completely uncorrelated risk factors

$$VaR = \sqrt{(300 \quad 400) \begin{pmatrix} 1 & 0 \\ 0 & 1 \end{pmatrix} \begin{pmatrix} 300 \\ 400 \end{pmatrix}}$$

$$= \sqrt{(300.1 + 400.0 \quad 300.0 + 400.1) \begin{pmatrix} 300 \\ 400 \end{pmatrix}}$$

$$= \sqrt{(300.300 + 400.400)} \tag{4.2}$$

$$= \sqrt{(90\,000 + 160\,000)}$$

$$= \sqrt{(250\,000)}$$

$$= 500$$

Perfectly inversely correlated risk factors

$$VaR = \sqrt{(300 \quad 400) \begin{pmatrix} 1 & -1 \\ -1 & 1 \end{pmatrix} \begin{pmatrix} 300 \\ 400 \end{pmatrix}}$$

$$= \sqrt{(300.1 + 400. - 1 \quad 300. - 1 + 400.1)\begin{pmatrix} 300 \\ 400 \end{pmatrix}}$$

$$= \sqrt{(-100.300 + 100.400)} \tag{4.3}$$

$$= \sqrt{(-30\,000 + 40\,000)}$$

$$= \sqrt{(10\,000)}$$

$$= 100$$

Naturally in real examples the correlations will not be 1,0 or -1, but the calculations flow through the matrix mathematics in exactly the same way. Now we can recalculate the total VaR for our FX and bond examples, this time using the delta-normal approach to incorporate the impact of correlation.

FX example

The correlation between USD–DEM and USD–JPY for our sample data is 0.063. Equation (4.4) shows that the total VaR for the delta-normal approach is 7235 USD – more than the single-factor VaR for the DEM exposure but actually *less* than the single-factor VaR for the JPY exposure, and about *half* the factor push VaR.

$$\text{VaR} = \sqrt{(6863 \quad -8821)\begin{pmatrix} 1 & 0.603 \\ 0.603 & 1 \end{pmatrix}\begin{pmatrix} 6863 \\ -8821 \end{pmatrix}}$$

$$= \sqrt{(6863.1 + -8821.0.603 \quad 6863.0.603 + -8821.1)\begin{pmatrix} 6863 \\ -8821 \end{pmatrix}}$$

$$= \sqrt{(1543.6863 + -4682. - 8921)} \tag{4.4}$$

$$= \sqrt{(10\,589\,609 + 41\,768\,122)}$$

$$= \sqrt{52\,357\,731)}$$

$$= 7235$$

Bond example

By construction, our yield curve factors are completely uncorrelated. Equation (4.5) shows that the total VaR for the delta-normal approach is $114\,053$ USD – more than any of the single-factor VaRs, and *less* than total factor push VaR.

$$\text{VaR} = \sqrt{(162 \quad 10\,916 \quad -113\,530)\begin{pmatrix} 1 & 0 & 0 \\ 0 & 1 & 0 \\ 0 & 0 & 1 \end{pmatrix}\begin{pmatrix} 162 \\ 10\,916 \\ -113\,530 \end{pmatrix}}$$

$$= \sqrt{(162.1 + 10\,916.0 + -113\,530.0 \quad 162.0 + 10\,916.1 + -113\,530.0}$$

$$162.0 + 10\,916.0 + -113\,530.1) \begin{pmatrix} 162 \\ 10\,916 \\ -113\,530 \end{pmatrix}$$

$$= \sqrt{(162.162 + 10\,916.10\,916 + -113\,530. -113\,530)} \tag{4.5}$$

$$= \sqrt{(26\,244 + 119\,159\,056 + 12\,889\,060\,900)}$$

$$= \sqrt{(13\,008\,246\,200)}$$

$$= 114\,053$$

The bond example shows that there are indirect benefits from the infrastructure that we used to calculate our VaR. Using yield curve factors for our exposure analysis also helps identify the yield curve views implied by the hedge strategy, namely that we have a significant exposure to a bend in the yield curve. In general, a VaR system can be programmed to calculate the implied views of a portfolio, and the best hedge for a portfolio.

Assuming that the exposure of a position can be captured entirely by first derivatives is inappropriate for portfolios containing significant quantities of options. The following sections describe various ways to improve on this assumption.

Delta-gamma VaR

There are two different VaR methodologies that are called 'delta-gamma VaR'. In both cases, the portfolio sensitivity is described by first *and* second derivatives with respect to risk factors.

Tom Wilson (1996) works directly with normally distributed risk factors and a second-order Taylor series expansion of the portfolio's change in value. He proposes three different solution techniques to calculate VaR, two of which require numerical searches. The third method is an analytic solution that is relatively straightforward, and which we will describe here. The gamma of a set of N risk factors can be represented by an $N \times N$ matrix, known as the *Hessian*. The matrix diagonal is composed of second derivatives – what most people understand by gamma. The off-diagonal or cross-terms describe the sensitivities of the portfolio to joint changes in a pair of risk factors. For example, a yield curve moves together with a change in volatility. Wilson transforms the risk factors to orthogonal risk factors. The transformed gamma matrix has no cross-terms – the impact of the transformed risk factors on the portfolio change in value is independent – so the sum of the worst-case change in value for each transformed risk factor will also be the worst-case risk for the portfolio. Wilson then calculates an adjusted delta that gives the same worst-case change in value for the market move corresponding to the confidence level as the original delta and the original gamma.

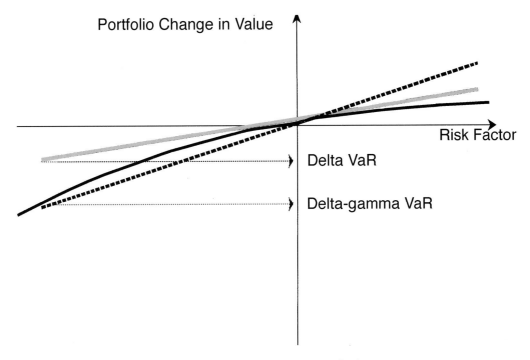

Figure 4.13 Delta-gamma method.

Figure 4.13 shows the portfolio change in value for a single transformed risk factor as a black line. The delta of the portfolio is the grey line, the tangent to the black line at the origin of the figure, which can be projected out to the appropriate number of standard deviations to calculate a delta-normal VaR. The adjusted delta of the portfolio is the dotted line, which can be used to calculate the delta-gamma VaR. The adjusted delta is a straight line from the origin to the worst-case change in value for the appropriate number of standard deviations,[14] where the straight line crosses the curve representing the actual portfolio change in value. Given this picture, we can infer that the delta-gamma VaR is correct only for a specified confidence interval and cannot be rescaled to a different confidence interval like a delta-normal VaR number. The adjusted delta will typically be *different* for a long and a short position in the same object.

An *ad-hoc* version of this approach can be applied to untransformed risk factors – provided the cross-terms in the gamma matrix are small. To make things even simpler, we can require the systems generating delta information for risk measurement to do so by perturbing market rates by an amount close to the move implied by the confidence interval and then feed this number into our delta-normal VaR calculation.

RiskMetrics[15] takes a very different approach to extending the delta-normal framework. The risk factor delta and gamma are used to calculate the first four moments of the portfolio's return distribution. A function of the normal distribution is chosen to match these moments. The percentile for the normal distribution can then be transformed to the percentile for the actual return distribution. If this sounds very complicated, think of the way we calculate the impact of a 99th percentile/2.33 standard deviation move in a log-normally distributed variable. We multiply the volatility by 2.33 to get the change in the normal variable, and then multiply the spot price by e^{change} to get the up move and divide by e^{change} to get the down move. This is essentially the same process. (Hull and White (1998) propose using the same approach for a slightly different problem.)

Now let's see how we can improve on the risk factor distribution and portfolio change in value assumptions we have used in delta-normal and delta-gamma VaR.

Historical simulation VaR

So far we have assumed our risk factors are either normally or log-normally distributed. As we saw in our plots of foreign exchange rates, the distribution of real market data is not that close to either a normal or a log-normal distribution. In fact, some market data (electricity prices are a good example) has a distribution that is completely unlike either a normal or log-normal distribution. Suppose that instead of modeling the market data, we just 'replayed the tape' of past market moves? This process is called *historical simulation.*

While the problems of modeling and estimating parameters for the risk factors are eliminated by historical simulation, we are obviously sensitive to whether the historic time series data we use is representative of the market, and captures the features we want – whether the features are fat tails, skewness, non-stationary volatilities or the presence of extreme events.

We can break historical simulation down into three steps: generating a set of historical changes in our risk factors, calculating the change in portfolio value for each historical change, and calculating the VaR.

Let's assume that we are going to measure the changes in the risk factors over the same period as our VaR horizon – typically 1 day. While we said that we were eliminating modeling, we do have to decide whether to store the changes as absolute or percentage changes. If the overall level of a risk factor has changed significantly over the period sampled for the simulation, then we will have some sensitivity to the choice.[16] Naturally, the absence of a historical time series for a risk factor you want to include in your analysis is a problem! For instance, volatility time series for OTC (over-the-counter) options are difficult to obtain (we usually have to go cap in hand to our option brokers) and entry into a new market for an instrument that has not been traded for long requires some method of 'back-filling' the missing data for the period prior to the start of trading.

Next, we have to calculate the change in portfolio value. Starting from today's market data, we apply one period's historical changes to get new values for all our market data. We can then calculate the change in portfolio value by completely revaluing the whole portfolio, by using the sensitivities to each risk factor (delta, gamma, vega, . . .) in a Taylor series or by interpolating into precalculated sensitivity tables (a half-way house between full revaluation and risk factors). We then repeat the process applying the next period's changes to today's market data. Full revaluation addresses the problem of using only local measures of risk, but requires a *huge* calculation resource relative to using factor sensitivities.[17] The space required for storing all the historical data may also be significant, but note that the time series takes up less data than the covariance matrix if the number of risk factors is more than twice the number of observations in the sample (Benson and Zangari, 1997).

Finally, we have to calculate the VaR. One attractive feature of historical simulation is that we have the whole distribution of the portfolio's change in value. We can either just look up the required percentile in the table of the simulation results, or we can model the distribution of the portfolio change and infer the change in value at the appropriate confidence interval from the distribution's properties (Zangari, 1997; Butler and Schachter, 1996). Using the whole distribution uses information from all the observations to make inference about the tails, which may be an advantage for a small sample, and also allows us to project the behavior of the portfolio for changes that are larger than any changes that have been seen in our historic data.

FX example

Suppose we repeat the VaR calculation for our DEM–JPY position, this time using the actual changes in FX rates and their impact on the portfolio value. For each day, and each currency, we multiply the change in FX rate by the cash flow in the currency. Then, we look up the nth smallest or largest change in value, using the Excel™ SMALL() and LARGE() functions, where n is the total number of observations multiplied by (1-confidence interval).

Table 4.7 FX example of historical simulation VaR versus analytic VaR

Confidence	Method	DEM	JPY	DEM–JPY
95%	AnalyticVaR	6 863	(8 821)	7 196
	SimulationVaR	6 740	(8 736)	(7 162)
	SimulationVaR/AnalyticVaR	98.2%	99.0%	99.5%
99%	AnalyticVaR	9 706	(12 476)	10 178
	SimulationVaR	12 696	(16 077)	(12 186)
	SimulationVaR/AnalyticVaR	130.8%	128.9%	119.7%

Table 4.7 shows the results of the analytic and historical simulation calculations. The simulation VaR is *less* than the analytic VaR for 95% confidence and below, and *greater* than the analytic VaR for 99% confidence and above. If we had shown results for long and short positions, they would not be equal.[18]

Monte Carlo simulation VaR

Monte Carlo VaR replaces the first step of historical simulation VaR: generating a set of historic changes in our risk factors. Monte Carlo VaR uses a model, fed by a set of random variables, to generate complete paths for all risk factor changes from today to the VaR horizon date. Each simulation path provides all the market data required for revaluing the whole portfolio. For a barrier FX option, each simulation path would provide the final foreign exchange rate, the final foreign exchange rate volatility, and the path of exchange rates and interest rates. We could then determine whether the option had been 'knocked-out' at its barrier between today and the horizon date, and the value of the option at the horizon date if it survived. The portfolio values (one for each path) can then be used to infer the VaR as described for historical simulation.

Creating a model for the joint evolution of all the risk factors that affect a bank's portfolio is a massive undertaking that is almost certainly a hopeless task for any institution that does not already have similar technology tried and tested in the front office for portfolio valuation and risk analysis.[19] This approach is also at least as computationally intensive as historical simulation with full revaluation, if not more so. Both Monte Carlo simulation and historical simulation suffer from the fact that the VaR requires a large number of simulations or paths before the value converges towards a single number. The potential errors in VaR due to convergence decrease with the square of the number of Monte Carlo paths – so we have to run four times as many paths to cut the size of the error by a factor of 2.

While, in principle, Monte Carlo simulation can address both the simplifying assumptions we had to make for other methods in modeling the market and in representing the portfolio, it is naive to expect that most implementations will actually achieve these goals. Monte Carlo is used much more frequently as a research tool than as part of the production platform in financial applications, except possibly for mortgage-backed securities (MBS).

Current practice

We have already discussed the assumptions behind VaR. As with any model, we must understand the sensitivity of our VaR model to the quality of its inputs. In a perfect world we would also have implemented more than one model and have reconciled the difference between the models' results. In practice, this usually only happens as we refine our current model and try to understand the impact of each round of changes from old to new. Beder (1995) shows a range of VaR calculations of 14 times for the same portfolio using a range of models – although the example is a little artificial as it includes calculations based on two different time horizons. In a more recent regulatory survey of Australian banks, Gizycki and Hereford (1998) report an even larger range (more than 21 times) of VaR values, though they note that 'crude, but conservative' assumptions cause outliers at the high end of the range. Gizycki and Hereford also report the frequency with which the various approaches are being used: 12 Delta-Normal Variance–Covariance, 5 Historical Simulation, 3 Monte Carlo, 1 Delta-Normal Variance–Covariance and Historical Simulation. The current best practice in the industry is historical simulation, using factor sensitivities, while participants are moving towards historical simulation, using full revaluation, or Monte Carlo.

Note that most implementations study the *terminal probabilities* of events, not *barrier probabilities*. Consider the possibility of the loss event happening at *any* time over the next 24 hours rather than the probability of the event happening when observed at a single time, after 24 hours have passed. Naturally, the probability of exceeding a certain loss level at any time over the next 24 hours is higher than the probability of exceeding a certain loss level at the end of 24 hours. This problem in handling time is similar to the problem of using a small number of terms in the Taylor series expansion of a portfolio's P/L function. Both have the effect of masking large potential losses inside the measurement boundaries.

The BIS regulatory multiplier (Stahl, 1997; Hendricks and Hirtle, 1998) takes the VaR number we first calculated and multiplies it by at least three – and more if the regulator deems necessary – to arrive at the required regulatory capital. Even though this goes a long way to addressing the modeling uncertainties in VaR, we would still not recommend VaR as a measure of downside on its own. Best practice requires that we establish market risk reserves (Group of Thirty, 1993) and model risk reserves (Beder, 1995). Model risk reserves should include coverage for potential losses that relate to risk factors that are not captured by the modeling process and/or the VaR process. Whether such reserves should be included in VaR is open to debate.[20]

Robust VaR

Just how robust is VaR? In most financial applications we choose fairly simple models and then abuse the input data *outside* the model to fit the market. We also build a set of rules about when the model output is likely to be invalid. VaR is no different. As an example, consider the Black–Scholes–Merton (BSM) option pricing model: one way we abuse the model is by varying the volatility according to the strike. We then add a rule not to sell very low delta options at the model value because even with a steep volatility smile we just can't get the model to charge enough to make it worth our while to sell these options. A second BSM analogy is the modeling of stochastic volatility by averaging two BSM values, one calculated using market volatility plus a perturbation, and one using market volatility minus a perturbation, rather than building a more complicated model which allows volatility to change from its initial value over time.

Given the uncertainties in the input parameters (with respect to position, liquidation strategy, time horizon and market model) and the potential mis-specification of the model itself, we can estimate the uncertainty in the VaR. This can either be done formally, to be quoted on our risk reports whenever the VaR value is quoted, or informally, to determine when we should flag the VaR value because it is extremely sensitive to the input parameters or to the model itself.

Here is a simple analysis of errors for single risk factor VaR. Single Risk factor VaR is given by Exposure*NumberOfStandardDeviations*StandardDeviation*$\sqrt{\text{Horizon}}$. If the exposure is off by 15% and the standard deviation is off by 10% then relative error of VaR is $15 + 10 = 25\%$! Note that this error estimate excludes the problems of the model itself. The size of the error estimate does not indicate that VaR is meaningless – just that we should exercise some caution in interpreting the values that our models produce.

Specific risk

The concept of specific risk is fairly simple. For any instrument or portfolio of instruments for which we have modeled the general market risk, we can determine a residual risk that is the difference between the actual change in value and that explained by our model of general market risk. Incorporating specific risk in VaR is a current industry focus, but in practice, most participants use the BIS regulatory framework to calculate specific risk, and that is what we describe below.

Interest rate specific risk model

The BIS specific risk charge is intended to 'protect against adverse movement in the price of an individual security owing to factors relating to the individual issuer'. The charge is applied to the *gross* positions in trading book instruments – banks can only offset matched positions in the *identical issue* – weighted by the factors in Table 4.8.

Table 4.8 BIS specific risk charges

Issuer category	Weighting factor	Capital charge
Government	0%	0%
Qualifying issuers: e.g. public sector entities, multilateral development banks and OECD banks	3.125%	0.25% residual term to final maturity < 6M
	12.5%	1.0% residual term to final maturity 6–24M
	20%	1.6% residual term to final maturity 24M +
Other	100%	8%

Interest rate and currency swaps, FRAs, forward foreign exchange contracts and interest rate futures are not subject to a specific risk charge. Futures contracts where the underlying is a debt security, are subject to charge according to the credit risk of the issuer.

Equity-specific risk model

The BIS specific risk charge for equities is 8% of *gross* equity positions, unless the portfolio is 'liquid and well-diversified' according to the criteria of the national authorities, in which case the charge is 4%. The charge for equity *index* futures, forwards and options is 2%.

Concentration risk

Diversification is one of the cornerstones of risk management. Just as professional gamblers limit their stakes on any one hand to a small fraction of their net worth, so they will not be ruined by a run of bad luck, so professional risk-taking enterprises must limit the concentration of their exposures to prevent any one event having a significant impact on their capital base. Concentrations may arise in a particular market, industry, region, tenor or trading strategy.

Unfortunately, there is a natural tension between pursuit of an institution's core competencies and comparative advantages into profitable market segments or niches, which produces concentration, and the desire for diversification of revenues and exposures.

Conclusion

We can easily criticize the flaws in the VaR models implemented at our institutions, but the simplicity of the assumptions behind our VaR implementations is actually an *asset* that facilitates education of both senior and junior personnel in the organization, and helps us retain intuition about the models and their outputs. In fact, VaR models perform surprisingly well, given their simplicity. Creating the modeling, data, systems and intellectual infrastructure for firm-wide quantitative risk management is a huge undertaking. Successful implementation of even a simple VaR model is a considerable achievement and an ongoing challenge in the face of continually changing markets and products.

Acknowledgements

Thanks to Lev Borodovsky, Randi Hawkins, Yong Li, Marc Lore, Christophe Rouvinez, Rob Samuel and Paul Vogt for encouragement, helpful suggestions and/or reviewing earlier drafts. The remaining mistakes are mine. Please email any questions or comments to IanHawkins@aol.com This chapter represents my personal opinions, and is supplied without any warranty of any kind.

Notes

[1] Rather than saying '*lose*', we should really say '*see a change in value below the expected change of*'.

[2] Here, and throughout this chapter, when we use *price* in this general sense, we take price to mean a price, or an interest rate or an index.

[3] The classic reference on this topic is Elton and Gruber (1995).

[4] Option traders like using Greek letters for exposure measures. *Vega* isn't a Greek letter, but is does begin with a 'V', which is easy to remember for a measure of *v*olatility exposure. Classically trained option traders use *Kappa* instead.

[5] For instance, when the portfolio contains significant positions in options that are about to expire, or significant positions in exotic options.

[6] Stricly speaking, changes in the *logarithm* of the price are normally distributed.

[7] The Riskmetrics Group recommends a estimator based on daily observations with a decay factor of 0.94, and also provides a regulatory data set with monthly observations and a decay factor of 0.97 to meet the BIS requirements. Their data is updated daily.

[8] To keep the examples simple, we have used absolute standard deviations for market variables throughout the examples. A percentage volatility can be converted to an absolute standard deviation by multiplying the volatility by the level of the market variable. For example, if interest rates are 5%, or 500 bps, and volatility is 20% per year, then the absolute standard deviation of interest rates is $500*0.2 = 100$ bps per year.

[9] Take 365 calendar days, multiply by 5/7 to eliminate the weekends, and subtract 10 or so public holidays to get about 250 business days.

[10] However, in some cases, factor push can underestimate VaR.

[11] Note also that, because our factor model tells us that notes and bonds of different maturities experience yield curve changes of different amounts, the 2-year note and 30-year bond assets do not have the same duration and dollar sensitivity to an 01 bp shift (v01) as the 10-year liability. Duration and v01 measure sensitivity to a *parallel* shift in the yield curve.

[12] As a reference for the standard deviation of functions of random variables see Hogg and Craig (1978).

[13] This is not intended to be an (unpaid!) advertisement for Excel™. Excel™ simply happens to be the spreadsheet used by the authors, and we thought it would be helpful to provide some specific guidance on how to implement these calculations.

[14] The worst-case change in value may occur for an up or a down move in the risk factor – in this case it's for a down move.

[15] RiskMetrics Technical Document, 4th edition, pp. 130–133 at http://www.riskmetrics.com/rm/pubs/techdoc.html

[16] Consider the extreme case of a stock that has declined in price from $200 per share to $20 per share. If we chose to store absolute price changes, then we might have to try to apply a large decline from early in the time series, say $30, that is larger than today's starting price for the stock!

[17] In late 1998, most businesses could quite happily run programs to calculate their delta-normal VaR, delta-gamma VaR or historical simulation VaR using risk factor exposures on a single personal computer in under an hour. Historical simulation VaR using full revaluation would require many processors (more than 10, less than 100) working together (whether over a network or in a single multi-processor computer), to calculate historical simulation VaR using full revaluation within one night. In dollar terms, the PC hardware costs on the order of 5000 USD, while the multi-processor hardware costs on the order of 500 000 USD.

[18] Assuming the antithetic variable variance reduction technique was not used.

[19] The aphorism that springs to mind is 'beautiful, but useless'.

[20] Remember that VaR measures *uncertainty* in the portfolio P/L, and reserves are there to cover *potential* losses. *Certain* changes in the P/L or actual losses, even if not captured by the models used for revaluation, should be included in the mark to market of the portfolio as adjustments to P/L.

References

Acar, E. and Prieve, D. (1927) 'Expected minimum loss of financial returns', *Derivatives Week*, 22 September.

Ait-Sahalia, Y. (1996) 'Testing continuous time models of the spot rate', *Review of Financial Studies*, **2**, No. 9, 385–426.

Ait-Sahalia, Y. (1997) 'Do interest rates really follow continuous-time Markov diffusions?' Working Paper, Graduate School of Business, University of Chicago.

Alexander, C. (1997) 'Splicing methods for VaR', *Derivatives Week*, June.

Alexander, C. and Leigh, J. (1997) 'On the covariance matrices used in VaR models', *Journal of Derivatives*, Spring, 50–62.

Artzner, P. *et al.* (1997) 'Thinking coherently', *Risk*, **10**, No. 11.

Basel Committee on Banking Supervision (1996) *Amendment to the Capital Accord to incorporate market risks*, January. http://www.bis.org/publ/bcbs24.pdf

Beder, T. S. (1995) 'VaR: seductive but dangerous', *Financial Analysts Journal*, **51**, No. 5, 12–24, September/October or at http://www.cmra.com/ (registration required).

Beder, T. S. (1995) *Derivatives: The Realities of Marking to Model*, Capital Market Risk Advisors at http://www.cmra.com/

Benson, P. and Zangari, P. (1997) 'A general approach to calculating VaR without volatilities and correlations', *RiskMetrics Monitor*, Second Quarter.

Boudoukh, J., Richardson, M. and Whitelaw, R. (1997) 'Investigation of a class of volatility estimators', *Journal of Derivatives*, Spring.

Butler, J. and Schachter, B. (1996) 'Improving Value-at-Risk estimates by combining kernel estimation with historic simulation', *OCC Report*, May.

Elton, E. J. and Gruber, M. J. (1995) *Modern Portfolio Theory and Investment Analysis*, Wiley, New York.

Embrechs, P. *et al.* (1998) 'Living on the edge', *Risk*, January.

Gizycki, M. and Hereford, N. (1998) 'Differences of opinion', *Asia Risk*, 42–7, August.

Group of Thirty (1993) *Derivatives: Practices and Principles*, Recommendations 2 and 3, Global Derivatives Study Group, Washington, DC.

Hendricks, D. (1996) 'Evaluation of VaR models using historical data', *Federal Reserve Bank of New York Economic Policy Review*, April, or http://www.ny.frb.org/rmaghome/econ_pol/496end.pdf

Hendricks, D. and Hirtle, B. (1998) 'Market risk capital', *Derivatives Week*, 6 April.

Hogg, R. and Craig, A. (1978) *Introduction to Mathematical Statistics*, Macmillan, New York.

Hull, J. and White, A. (1998) 'Value-at-Risk when daily changes in market variables are not normally distributed', *Journal of Derivatives*, Spring.

McNeil, A. (1998) 'History repeating', *Risk*, January.

Stahl, G. (1997) 'Three cheers', *Risk*, May.

Wilmot, P. *et al.* (1995) 'Spot-on modelling', *Risk*, November.

Wilson, T. (1996) 'Calculating risk capital', in Alexander, C. (ed.), *The Handbok of Risk Management*, Wiley, New York.

Zangari, P. (1997) 'Streamlining the market risk measurement process', *RiskMetrics Monitor*, First Quarter.

Part 2

Market risk, credit risk and operational risk

5

Yield curve risk factors: domestic and global contexts

WESLEY PHOA

Introduction: handling multiple risk factors

Methodological introduction

Traditional interest rate risk management focuses on duration and duration management. In other words, it assumes that only parallel yield curve shifts are important. In practice, of course, non-parallel shifts in the yield curve often occur, and represent a significant source of risk. What is the most efficient way to manage non-parallel interest rate risk?

This chapter is mainly devoted to an exposition of *principal component analysis*, a statistical technique that attempts to provide a foundation for measuring non-parallel yield curve risk, by identifying the 'most important' kinds of yield curve shift that occur empirically. The analysis turns out to be remarkably successful. It gives a clear justification for the use of duration as the primary measure of interest rate risk, and it also suggests how one may design 'optimal' measures of non-parallel risk.

Principal component analysis is a popular tool, not only in theoretical studies but also in practical risk management applications. We discuss such applications at the end of the chapter. However, it is first important to understand that principal component analysis has limitations, and should not be applied blindly. In particular, it is important to distinguish between results that are economically meaningful and those that are statistical artefacts without economic significance.

There are two ways to determine whether the results of a statistical analysis are meaningful. The first is to see whether they are consistent with theoretical results; the Appendix gives a sketch of this approach. The second is simply to carry out as much exploratory data analysis as possible, with different data sets and different historical time periods, to screen out those findings which are really robust. This chapter contains many examples.

In presenting the results, our exposition will rely mainly on graphs rather than tables and statistics. This is not because rigorous statistical criteria are unnecessary – in fact, they are very important. However, in the exploratory phase of any empirical study it is critical to get a good feel for the results first, since statistics can easily mislead. The initial goal is to gain insight; and visual presentation of the results can convey the important findings most clearly, in a non-technical form.

It is strongly suggested that, after finishing this chapter, readers should experiment with the data themselves. Extensive hands-on experience is the only way to avoid the pitfalls inherent in any empirical analysis.

Non-parallel risk, duration bucketing and partial durations

Before discussing principal component analysis, we briefly review some more primitive approaches to measuring non-parallel risk. These have by no means been superseded: later in the chapter we will discuss precisely what role they continue to play in risk management.

The easiest approach is to *group securities into maturity buckets*. This is a very simple way of estimating exposure to movements at the short, medium and long ends of the yield curve. But it is not very accurate: for example, it ignores the fact that a bond with a higher coupon intuitively has more exposure to movements in the short end of the curve than a lower coupon bond with the same maturity.

Next, one could *group securities into duration buckets*. This approach is somewhat more accurate because, for example, it distinguishes properly between bonds with different coupons. But it is still not entirely accurate because it does not recognize that the different individual cash flows of a single security are affected in different ways by a non-parallel yield curve shift.

Next, one could *group security cash flows into duration buckets*. That is, one uses a finer-grained unit of analysis: the cash flow, rather than the security. This makes the results much more precise. However, bucketed duration exposures have no direct interpretation in terms of changes in some reference set of yields (i.e. a shift in some reference yield curve), and can thus be tricky to interpret. More seriously, as individual cash flows shorten they will move across bucket duration boundaries, causing discontinuous changes in bucket exposures which can make risk management awkward.

Alternatively, one could *measure partial durations*. That is, one directly measures how the value of a portfolio changes when a single reference yield is shifted, leaving the other reference yields unchanged; note that doing this at the security level and at the cashflow level gives the same results. There are many different ways to define partial durations: one can use different varieties of reference yield (e.g. par, zero coupon, forward rate), one can choose different sets of reference maturities, one can specify the size of the perturbation, and one can adopt different methods of interpolating the perturbed yield curve between the reference maturities.

The most popular partial durations are the *key rate durations* defined in Ho (1992). Fixing a set of reference maturities, these are defined as follows: for a given reference maturity T, the T-year key rate duration of a portfolio is the percentage change in its value when one shifts the T-year zero coupon yield by 100 bp, leaving the other reference zero coupon yields fixed, and linearly interpolating the perturbed zero coupon curve between adjacent reference maturities (often referred to as a 'tent' shift). Figure 5.1 shows some examples of key rate durations.

All the above approaches must be used with caution when dealing with option-embedded securities such as callable bonds or mortgage pools, whose cashflow timing will vary with the level of interest rates. Option-embedded bonds are discussed in detail elsewhere in this book.

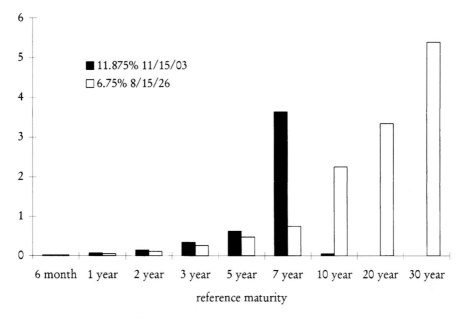

Figure 5.1 Key rate durations of non-callable Treasury bonds.

Limitations of key rate duration analysis

Key rate durations are a popular and powerful tool for managing non-parallel risk, so it is important to understand their shortcomings.

First, key rate durations can be unintuitive. This is partly because 'tent' shifts do not occur in isolation, and in fact have no economic meaning in themselves. Thus, using key rate durations requires some experience and familiarization.

Second, correlations between shifts at different reference maturities are ignored. That is, the analysis treats shifts at different points in the yield curve as independent, whereas different yield curve points tend to move in correlated ways. It is clearly important to take these correlations into account when measuring risk, but the key rate duration methodology does not suggest a way to do so.

Third, the key rate duration computation is based on perturbing a theoretical zero coupon curve rather than observed yields on coupon bonds, and is therefore sensitive to the precise method used to strip (e.g.) a par yield curve. This introduces some arbitrariness into the results, and more significantly makes them hard to interpret in terms of observed yield curve shifts. Thus swap dealers (for example) often look at partial durations computed by directly perturbing the swap curve (a par curve) rather than perturbing a zero coupon curve.

Fourth, key rate durations for mortgage-backed securities must be interpreted with special care. Key rate durations closely associated with specific reference maturities which drive the prepayment model can appear anomalous; for example, if the mortgage refinancing rate is estimated using a projected 10-year Treasury yield, 10-year key rate durations on MBS will frequently be negative. This is correct according to the definition, but in this situation one must be careful in constructing MBS hedging strategies using key rate durations.

Fifth, key rate durations are unwieldy. There are too many separate interest rate risk measures. This leads to practical difficulties in monitoring risk, and inefficiencies in hedging risk. One would rather focus mainly on what is 'most important'.

To summarize: while key rate durations are a powerful risk management tool, it is worth looking for a more sophisticated approach to analyzing non-parallel risk that will yield deeper insights, and that will provide a basis for more efficient risk management methodologies.

Principal component analysis

Definition and examples from US Treasury market

As often occurs in finance, an analogy with physical systems suggests an approach. Observed shifts in the yield curve may seem complex and somewhat chaotic. In principle, it might seem that any point on the yield curve can move independently in a random fashion. However, it turns out that most of the observed fluctuation in yields can be explained by more systematic yield shifts: that is, bond yields moving 'together', in a correlated fashion, but perhaps in several different ways. Thus, one should not focus on fluctuations at individual points on the yield curve, but on shifts that apply to the yield curve as a whole. It is possible to identify these systematic shifts by an appropriate statistical analysis; as often occurs in finance, one can apply techniques inspired by the study of physical systems.

The following concrete example, taken from Jennings and McKeown (1992), may be helpful. Consider a plank with one end fixed to a wall. Whenever the plank is knocked, it will vibrate. Furthermore, when it vibrates it does not deform in a completely random way, but has only a few 'vibration modes' corresponding to its natural frequencies. These vibration modes have different degrees of importance, with one mode – a simple back-and-forth motion – dominating the others: see Figure 5.2.

One can derive these vibration modes mathematically, if one knows the precise physical characteristics of the plank. But one should also be able to determine them empirically by observing the plank. To do this, one attaches motion sensors at different points on the plank, to track the motion of these points through time. One will find that the observed disturbances at each point are correlated. It is possible to extract the vibration modes, and their relative importance, from the correlation matrix. In fact, the vibration modes correspond to the eigenvalues of the matrix: in other words, the eigenvectors, plotted in graphical form, will turn out to look exactly as in Figure 5.2. The relative importance of each vibration mode is measured by the size of the corresponding eigenvectors.

Let us recall the definitions. Let $\mathbf{A}$ be a matrix. We say that $\mathbf{v}$ is an *eigenvector* of $\mathbf{A}$, with corresponding *eigenvalue* λ, if $\mathbf{A} \cdot \mathbf{v} = \lambda \mathbf{v}$. The eigenvalues of a matrix must be mutually orthogonal, i.e. 'independent'. Note that eigenvectors are only defined up to a scalar multiple, but that eigenvalues are uniquely defined.

Suppose $\mathbf{A}$ is a correlation matrix, e.g. derived from some time series of data; then it must be *symmetric* and also *positive definite* (i.e. $\mathbf{v} \cdot \mathbf{A} \cdot \mathbf{v} > 0$ for all vectors $\mathbf{v}$). One can show that all the eigenvalues of such a matrix must be real and positive. In this case it makes sense to compare their relative sizes, and to regard them as 'weights' which measure the importance of the corresponding eigenvectors.

For a physical system such as the cantilever, the interpretation is as follows. The

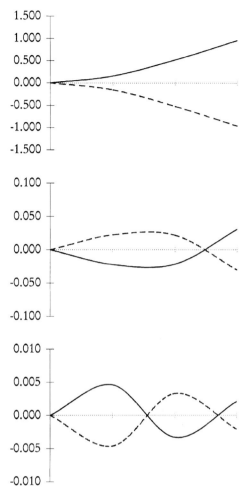

Figure 5.2 Vibration modes of the cantilever.

eigenvectors describe the independent vibration modes: each eigenvector has one component for each sensor, and the component is a (positive or negative) real number which describes the relative displacement of that sensor under the given vibration mode. The corresponding eigenvalue measures how much of the observed motion of the plank can be attributed to that specific vibration mode.

This suggests that we can analyze yield curve shifts analogously, as follows. Fix a set of reference maturities for which reasonably long time series of, say, daily yields are available: each reference maturity on the yield curve is the analog of a motion sensor on the plank. Construct the time series of daily changes in yield at each reference maturity, and compute the correlation matrix. Next, compute the eigenvectors and eigenvalues of this matrix. The eigenvectors can then be interpreted as independent 'fundamental yield curve shifts', analogous to vibration modes; in other words, the actual change in the yield curve on any particular day may be regarded as a combination of different, independent, fundamental yield curve shifts. The relative sizes of the eigenvalues tells us which fundamental yield curve shifts tend to dominate.

Table 5.1   Principal component analysis of a sample financial dataset

Daily changes

1	1	1	1
0	1	2	3
−2	−2	−2	−2
5	4	3	2
0	0	1	0

Correlation matrix

1.00	0.97	0.83	0.59
0.97	1.00	0.92	0.77
0.83	0.92	1.00	0.90
0.59	0.77	0.90	1.00

Eigenvalues and eigenvectors

[A]	0.000 (0%)	0.607	−0.762	0.000	0.225
[B]	0.037 (1%)	−0.155	−0.263	0.827	−0.471
[C]	0.462 (11%)	−0.610	−0.274	0.207	0.715
[D]	3.501 (88%)	0.486	0.524	0.522	0.465

For a toy example, see Table 5.1. The imaginary data set consists of five days of observed daily yield changes at four unnamed reference maturities; for example, on days 1 and 3 a perfectly parallel shift occurred. The correlation matrix shows that yield shifts at different maturity points are quite correlated. Inspecting the eigenvalues and eigenvectors shows that, at least according to principal component analysis, there is a dominant yield curve shift, eigenvector (D), which represents an almost parallel shift: each maturity point moves by about 0.5. The second most important eigenvector (C) seems to represent a slope shift or 'yield curve tilt'. The third eigenvector (B) seems to appear because of the inclusion of day 5 in the data set.

Note that the results might not perfectly reflect one's intuition. First, the dominant shift (D) is not perfectly parallel, even though two perfectly parallel shifts were included in the data set. Second, the shift that occurred on day 2 is regarded as a combination of a parallel shift (D) and a slope shift (C), not a slope shift alone; shift (C) has almost the same shape as the observed shift on day 2, but it has been 'translated' so that shifts of type (C) are uncorrelated with shifts of type (D). Third, eigenvector (A) seems to have no interpretation. Finally, the weight attached to (D) seems very high – this is because the actual shifts on all five days are regarded as having a parallel component, as we just noted.

A technical point: in theory, one could use the covariance matrix rather than the correlation matrix in the analysis. However using the correlation matrix is preferable when observed correlations are more stable than observed covariances – which is usually the case in financial data where volatilities are quite unstable. (For further discussion, see Buhler and Zimmermann, 1996.) In the example of Table 5.1, very similar results are obtained using the covariance matrix.

Table 5.2 shows the result of a principal component analysis carried out on actual US Treasury bond yield data from 1993 to 1998. In this case the dominant shift is a virtually parallel shift, which explains over 90% of observed fluctuations in bond yields. The second most important shift is a slope shift or tilt in which short yields fall and long yields rise (or vice versa). The third shift is a kind of curvature shift, in

Table 5.2 Principal component analysis of US Treasury yields, 1993–8

	1 year	2 year	3 year	5 year	7 year	10 year	20 year	30 year
0.3%	0.00	0.05	−0.20	0.31	−0.63	0.50	0.32	−0.35
0.3%	0.00	−0.08	0.49	−0.69	0.06	0.27	0.30	−0.34
0.2%	0.01	−0.05	−0.10	0.25	0.30	−0.52	0.59	−0.48
0.4%	−0.05	−0.37	0.65	0.27	−0.45	−0.34	0.08	0.22
0.6%	0.21	−0.71	0.03	0.28	0.35	0.34	−0.27	−0.26
1.1%	0.70	−0.30	−0.32	−0.30	−0.19	−0.12	0.28	0.32
5.5%	−0.59	−0.37	−0.23	−0.06	0.14	0.20	0.44	0.45
91.7%	0.33	0.35	0.36	0.36	0.36	0.36	0.35	0.35

Historical bond yield data provided by the Federal Reserve Board.

which short and long yields rise while mid-range yields fall (or vice versa); the remaining eigenvectors have no meaningful interpretation and are statistically insignificant.

Note that meaningful results will only be obtained if a consistent set of yields is used: in this case, constant maturity Treasury yields regarded as a proxy for a Treasury par yield curve. Yields on physical bonds should not be used, since the population of bonds both ages and changes composition over time. The analysis here has been carried out using CMT yields reported by the US Federal Reserve Bank.

An alternative is to use a dataset consisting of historical swap rates, which are par yields by definition. The results of the analysis turn out to be very similar.

Meaningfulness of factors: dependence on dataset

It is extremely tempting to conclude that (a) the analysis has determined that there are exactly three important kinds of yield curve shift, (b) that it has identified them precisely, and (c) that it has precisely quantified their relative importance.

But we should not draw these conclusions without looking more carefully at the data. This means exploring datasets drawn from different historical time periods, from different sets of maturities, and from different countries. *Risk management should only rely on those results which turn out to be robust.*

Figure 5.3 shows a positive finding. Analyzing other 5-year historical periods, going back to 1963, we see that the overall results are quite consistent. In each case the major yield curve shifts turn out to be parallel, slope and curvature shifts; and estimates of the relative importance of each kind of shift are reasonably stable over time, although parallel shifts appear to have become more dominant since the late 1970s.

Figures 5.4(a) and (b) show that some of the results remain consistent when examined in more detail: the estimated form of both the parallel shift and the slope shift are very similar in different historical periods. Note that in illustrating each kind of yield curve shift, we have carried out some normalization to make comparisons easier: for example, estimated slope shifts are normalized so that the 10-year yield moves 100 bp relative to the 1-year yield, which remains fixed. See below for further discussion of this point.

However, Figure 5.4(c) does tentatively indicate that the form of the curvature shift has varied over time – a first piece of evidence that results on the curvature shift may be less robust than those on the parallel and slope shifts.

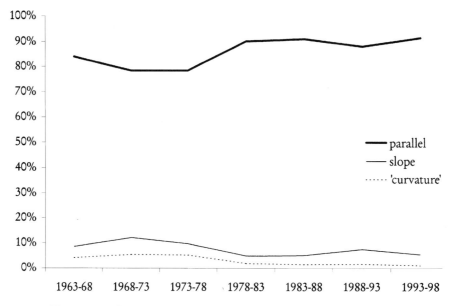

Figure 5.3   Relative importance of principal components, 1963–98.

Figure 5.5 shows the effect of including 3- and 6-month Treasury bill yields in the 1993–8 dataset. The major yield curve shifts are still identified as parallel, slope and curvature shifts. However, an analysis based on the dataset including T-bills attaches somewhat less importance to parallel shifts, and somewhat more importance to slope and curvature shifts. Thus, while the estimates of relative importance remain qualitatively significant, they should not be regarded as quantitatively precise.

Figures 5.6(a) and (b) show that the inclusion of T-bill yields in the dataset makes almost no difference to the estimated form of both the parallel and slope shifts. However, Figure 5.6(c) shows that the form of the curvature shift is totally different. Omitting T-bills, the change in curvature occurs at the 3–5-year part of the curve; including T-bills, it occurs at the 1-year part of the curve. There seem to be some additional dynamics associated with yields on short term instruments, which become clear once parallel and slope shifts are factored out; this matter is discussed further in Phoa (1998a,b).

The overall conclusions are that parallel and slope shifts are unambiguously the most important kinds of yield curve shift that occur, with parallel shifts being dominant; that the forms of these parallel and slope shifts can be estimated fairly precisely and quite robustly; but that the existence and form of a third, 'curvature' shift are more problematic, with the results being very dependent on the dataset used in the analysis. Since the very form of a curvature shift is uncertain, and specifying it precisely requires making a subjective judgment about which dataset is 'most relevant', the curvature shift is of more limited use in risk management.

The low weight attached to the curvature factor also suggests that it may be less important than other (conjectural) phenomena which might somehow have been missed by the analysis. The possibility that the analysis has failed to detect some important yield curve risk factors, which potentially outweigh curvature risk, is discussed further below.

International bond yield data are analyzed in the next section. The results are

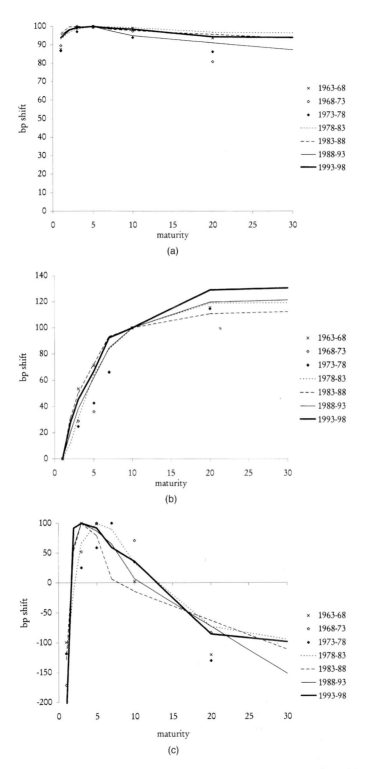

Figure 5.4 Shapes of (a) 'parallel' shift, 1963–98, (b) 'slope' shift, 1963–98, (c) 'curvature' shift, 1963–98.

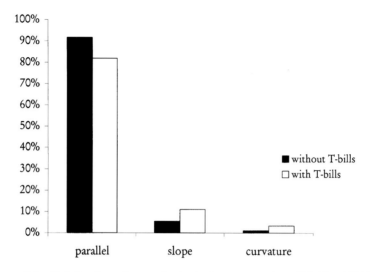

Figure 5.5 Relative importance of principal components, with/without T-bills.

broadly consistent, but also provide further grounds for caution. The Appendix provides some theoretical corroboration for the positive findings.

We have glossed over one slightly awkward point. The fundamental yield curve shifts estimated by a principal component analysis – in particular, the first two principal components representing parallel and slope shifts – are, by definition, uncorrelated. But normalizing a 'slope shift' so that the 1-year yield remains fixed introduces a possible correlation. This kind of normalization is convenient both for data analysis, as above, and for practical applications; but it does mean that one then has to estimate the correlation between parallel shifts and normalized slope shifts. This is not difficult in principle, but, as shown in Phoa (1998a,b), this correlation is time-varying and indeed exhibits secular drift. This corresponds to the fact that, while the estimated (non-normalized) slope shifts for different historical periods have almost identical shapes, they have different 'pivot points'. The issue of correlation risk is discussed further below.

Correlation structure and other limitations of the approach

It is now tempting to concentrate entirely on parallel and slope shifts. This approach forms the basis of most useful two factor interest rate models: see Brown and Schaefer (1995). However, it is important to understand what is being lost when one focuses only on two kinds of yield curve shift.

First, there is the question of *whether empirical correlations are respected*. Figure 5.7(a) shows, graphically, the empirical correlations between daily Treasury yield shifts at different maturity points. It indicates that, as one moves to adjacent maturities, the correlations fall away rather sharply. In other words, even adjacent yields quite often shift in uncorrelated ways.

Figure 5.7(b) shows the correlations which would have been observed if only parallel and slope shifts had taken place. These slope away much more gently as one moves to adjacent maturities: uncorrelated shifts in adjacent yields do not occur. This observation is due to Rebonato and Cooper (1996), who prove that the correlation structure implied by a two-factor model must always take this form.

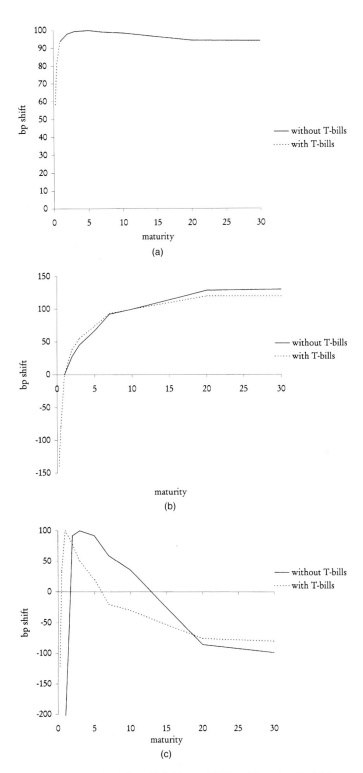

Figure 5.6 (a) Estimated 'parallel' shift, with/without T-bills, (b) estimated 'slope' shift, with/without T-bills, (c) estimated 'curvature' shift, with/without T-bills.

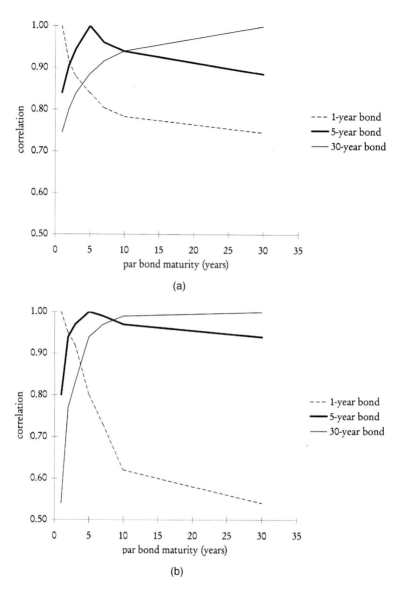

Figure 5.7 (a) Empirical Treasury yield correlations, (b) theoretical Treasury yield correlations, two-factor model.

What this shows is that, even though the weights attached to the 'other' eigen-vectors seemed very small, discarding these other eigenvectors radically changes the correlation structure. Whether or not this matters in practice will depend on the specific application.

Second, there is the related question of *the time horizon of risk*. Unexplained yield shifts at specific maturities may be unimportant if they quickly 'correct'; but this will clearly depend on the investor's time horizon. If some idiosyncratic yield shift occurs, which has not been anticipated by one's risk methodology, this may be disastrous for a hedge fund running a highly leveraged trading book with a time horizon of hours or days; but an investment manager with a time horizon of months or quarters, who is confident that the phenomenon is transitory and who can afford to wait for it to reverse itself, might not care as much.

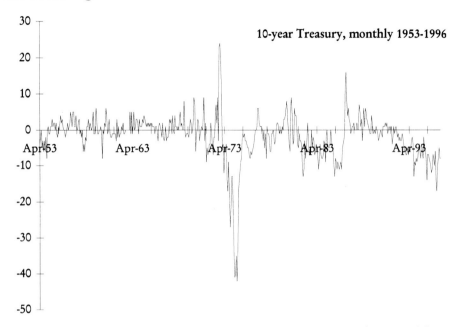

Figure 5.8 Actual Treasury yield versus yield predicted by two-factor model.

This is illustrated in Figure 5.8. It compares the observed 10-year Treasury yield from 1953 to 1996 to the yield which would have been predicted by a model in which parallel and slope risk fully determine (via arbitrage pricing theory) the yields of all Treasury bonds. The actual yield often deviates significantly from the theoretical yield, as yield changes unrelated to parallel and slope shifts frequently occurred. But deviations appear to mean revert to zero over periods of around a few months to a year; this can be justified more rigorously by an analysis of autocorrelations. Thus, these deviations matter over short time frames, but perhaps not over long time frames. See Phoa (1998a,b) for further details.

Third, there is the question of *effects due to market inhomogeneity*. In identifying patterns of yield shifts by maturity, principal component analysis implicitly assumes that the only relevant difference between different reference yields is maturity, and that the market is homogeneous in every other way. If it is not – for example, if there are differences in liquidity between different instruments which, in some circumstances, lead to fluctuations in relative yields – then this assumption may not be sound.

The US Treasury market in 1998 provided a very vivid example. Yields of on-the-run Treasuries exhibited sharp fluctuations relative to off-the-run yields, with 'liquidity spreads' varying from 5 bp to 25 bp. Furthermore, different on-the-run issues were affected in different ways in different times. A principal component analysis based on constant maturity Treasury yields would have missed this source of risk entirely; and in fact, even given yield data on the entire population of Treasury bonds, it would have been extremely difficult to design a similar analysis which would have been capable of identifying and measuring some systematic 'liquidity spread shift'. In this case, risk management for a Treasury book based on principal component analysis needs to be supplemented with other methods.

Fourth, there is the possibility that *an important risk factor has been ignored*. For example, suppose there is an additional kind of fundamental yield curve shift, in which 30- to 100-year bond yields move relative to shorter bond yields. This would not be identified by a principal component analysis, for the simple reason that this maturity range is represented by only one point in the set of reference maturities. Even if the 30-year yield displayed idiosyncratic movements – which it arguably does – the analysis would not identify these as statistically significant. The conjectured 'long end' risk factor would only emerge if data on other longer maturities were included; but no such data exists for Treasury bonds.

An additional kind of 'yield curve risk', which could not be detected at all by an analysis of CMT yields, is the varying yield spread between liquid and illiquid issues as mentioned above. This was a major factor in the US Treasury market in 1998; in fact, from an empirical point of view, fluctuations at the long end of the curve and fluctuations in the spread between on- and off-the-run Treasuries were, in that market, more important sources of risk than curvature shifts – and different methods were required to measure and control the risk arising from these sources.

To summarize, a great deal more care is required when using principal component analysis in a financial, rather than physical, setting. One should always remember that the rigorous justifications provided by the differential equations of physics are missing in financial markets, and that seemingly analogous arguments such as those presented in the Appendix are much more heuristic. The proper comparison is with biology or social science rather than physics or engineering.

International bonds

Principal component analysis for international markets

All our analysis so far has used US data. Are the results applicable to international markets? To answer this question, we analyze daily historical bond yield data for a range of developed countries, drawn from the historical period 1986–96.

In broad terms, the results carry over. In almost every case, the fundamental yield curve shifts identified by the analysis are a parallel shift, a slope shift and some kind of curvature shift. Moreover, as shown in Figure 5.9, the relative importance of these different yield curve shifts is very similar in different countries – although there is some evidence that parallel shifts are slightly less dominant, and slope shifts are slightly more important, in Europe and Japan than in USD bloc countries.

It is slightly worrying that Switzerland appears to be an exception: the previous results simply do not hold, at least for the dataset used. This proves that one cannot simply take the results for granted; they must be verified for each individual country. For example, one should not assume that yield curve risk measures developed for use in the US bond market are equally applicable to some emerging market.

Figure 5.10(a) shows the estimated form of a parallel shift in different countries. Apart from Switzerland, the results are extremely similar. In other words, duration is an equally valid risk measure in different countries.

Figure 5.10(b) shows the estimated form of a slope shift in different countries; in this case, estimated slope shifts have been normalized so that the 3-year yield

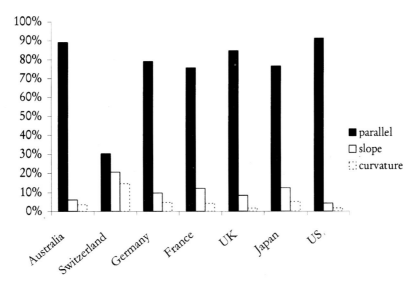

Figure 5.9 Relative importance of principal components in various countries. (Historical bond yield data provided by Deutsche Bank Securities).

remains fixed and the 10-year yield moves by 100 bp. Unlike the parallel shift, there is some evidence that the slope shift takes different forms in different countries; this is consistent with the findings reported in Brown and Schaefer (1995). For risk management applications it is thus prudent to estimate the form of the slope shift separately for each country rather than, for example, simply using the US slope shift. Note that parallel/slope correlation also varies between countries, as well as over time.

Estimated curvature shifts are not shown, but they are quite different for different countries. Also, breaking the data into subperiods, the form of the curvature shift typically varies over time as it did with the US data. This is further evidence that there is no stable 'curvature shift' which can reliably be used to define an additional measure of non-parallel risk.

Co-movements in international bond yields

So far we have only used principal component analysis to look at *data within a single country*, to identify patterns of co-movement between yields at different maturities. We derived the very useful result that two major kinds of co-movement explain most variations in bond yields.

It is also possible to analyze data *across countries*, to identify patterns of co-movements between bond yields in different countries. For example, one could carry out a principal component analysis of daily changes in 10-year bond yields for various countries. Can any useful conclusions be drawn?

The answer is yes, but the results are significantly weaker. Figure 5.9 shows the dominant principal component identified from three separate datasets: 1970–79, 1980–89 and 1990–98. As one might hope, this dominant shift is a kind of 'parallel shift', i.e. a simultaneous shift in bond yields, with the same direction and magnitude, in each country. In other words, the notion of 'global duration' seems to make sense:

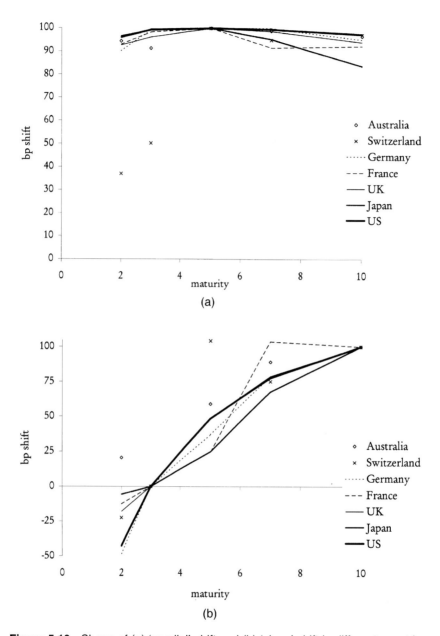

Figure 5.10 Shape of (a) 'parallel' shift and (b) 'slope' shift in different countries.

the aggregate duration of a global bond portfolio is a meaningful risk measure, which measures the portfolio's sensitivity to an empirically identifiable global risk factor.

However, there are three important caveats. First, the 'global parallel shift' is not as dominant as the term structure parallel shift identified earlier. In the 1990s, it explained only 54% of variation in global bond yields; in the 1970s, it explained only 29%. In other words, while duration captures most of the interest rate risk of a domestic bond portfolio, 'global duration' captures only half, or less, of the interest rate risk of a global bond portfolio: see Figure 5.11.

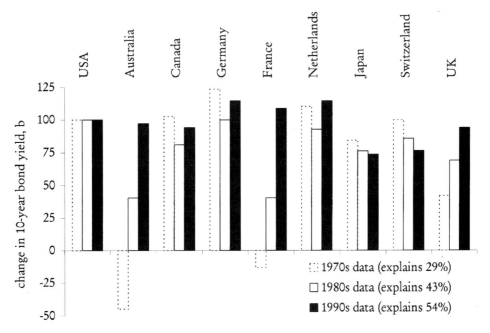

Figure 5.11 Dominant principal component, global 10-year bond yields.

Second, the shift in bond yields is not perfectly equal in different countries. It seems to be lower for countries like Japan and Switzerland, perhaps because bond yields have tended to be lower in those countries.

Third, the 'global parallel shift' is not universal: not every country need be included. For example, it seems as if Australian and French bond yields did not move in step with other countries' bond yields in the 1970s, and did so only partially in the 1980s. Thus, the relevance of a global parallel shift to each specific country has to be assessed separately.

Apart from the global parallel shift, the other eigenvectors are not consistently meaningful. For example, there is some evidence of a 'USD bloc shift' in which US, Canadian, Australian and NZ bond yields move while other bond yields remain fixed, but this result is far from robust.

To summarize, principal component analysis provides some guidelines for global interest rate risk management, but it does not simplify matters as much as it did for yield curve risk. The presence of currency risk is a further complication; we return to this topic below.

Correlations: between markets, between yield and volatility

Recall that principal component analysis uses a single correlation matrix to identify dominant patterns of yield shifts. The results imply something about the correlations themselves: for instance, the existence of a global parallel shift that explains around 50% of variance in global bond yields suggests that correlations should, on average, be positive.

However, in global markets, correlations are notoriously time-varying: see Figure 5.12. In fact, short-term correlations between 10-year bond yields in different coun-

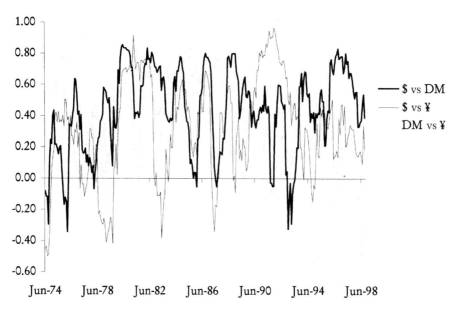

Figure 5.12   Historical 12-month correlations between 10-year bond yields.

tries are significantly less stable than correlations between yields at different maturities within a single country. This means that, at least for short time horizons, one must be especially cautious in using the results of principal component analysis to manage a global bond position.

We now discuss a somewhat unrelated issue: the relationship between yield and volatility, which has been missing from our analysis so far. Principal component analysis estimates the form of the dominant yield curve shifts, namely parallel and slope shifts. It says nothing useful about the size of these shifts, i.e. about parallel and slope volatility. These can be estimated instantaneously, using historical or implied volatilities. But for stress testing and scenario analysis, one needs an additional piece of information: whether there is a relationship between volatility and (say) the outright level of the yield curve. For example, when stress testing a trading book under a + 100 bp scenario, should one also change one's volatility assumption?

It is difficult to answer this question either theoretically or empirically. For example, most common term structure models assume that basis point (parallel) volatility is either independent of the yield level, or proportional to the yield level; but these assumptions are made for technical convenience, rather that being driven by the data.

Here are some empirical results. Figures 5.13(a)–(c) plot 12-month historical volatilities, expressed as a percentage of the absolute yield level, against the average yield level itself. If basis point volatility were always proportional to the yield level, these graphs would be horizontal lines; if basis point volatility were constant, these graphs would be hyperbolic.

Neither seems to be the case. The Japanese dataset suggests that when yields are under around 6–7%, the graph is hyperbolic. All three datasets suggest that when yields are in the 7–10% range, the graph is horizontal. And the US dataset suggests that when yields are over 10%, the graph actually slopes upward: when yields rise,

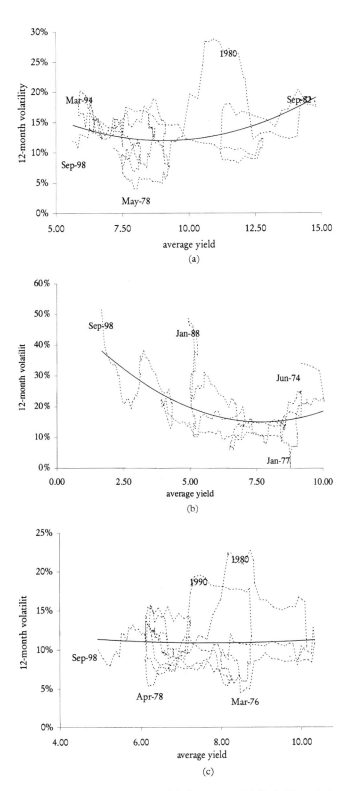

Figure 5.13 (a) US, (b) Japan and (c) Germany yield/volatility relationships.

volatility rises more than proportionately. But in every case, the results are confused by the presence of volatility spikes.

The conclusion is that, when stress testing a portfolio, it is safest to assume that when yields fall, basis point volatility need not fall; but when yields rise, basis point volatility will also rise. Better yet, one should run different volatility scenarios as well as interest rate scenarios.

Practical implications

Risk management for a leveraged trading desk

This section draws some practical conclusions from the above analysis, and briefly sketches some suggestions about risk measurement and risk management policy; more detailed proposals may be found elsewhere in this book.

Since parallel and slope shifts are the dominant yield curve risk factors, it makes sense to focus on measures of parallel and slope risk; to structure limits in terms of maximum parallel and slope risk rather than more rigid limits for each point of the yield curve; and to design flexible hedging strategies based on matching parallel and slope risk. If the desk as a whole takes proprietary interest rate risk positions, it is most efficient to specify these in terms of target exposures to parallel and slope risk, and leave it to individual traders to structure their exposures using specific instruments.

Rapid stress testing and Value-at-Risk estimates may be computed under the simplifying assumption that only parallel and slope risk exist. This approach is not meant to replace a standard VaR calculation using a covariance matrix for a whole set of reference maturities, but to supplement it.

A simplified example of such a VaR calculation appears in Table 5.3, which summarizes both the procedure and the results. It compares the Value-at-Risk of three positions, each with a net market value of $100 million: a *long portfolio* consisting of a single position in a 10-year par bond; a *steepener portfolio* consisting of a long position in a 2-year bond and a short position in a 10-year bond with offsetting durations, i.e. offsetting exposures to parallel risk; and a *butterfly portfolio* consisting of long/short positions in cash and 2-, 5- and 10-year bonds with zero net exposure to both parallel and slope risk. For simplicity, the analysis assumes a 'total volatility' of bond yields of about 100 bp p.a., which is broadly realistic for the US market.

The long portfolio is extremely risky compared to the other two portfolios; this reflects the fact that most of the observed variance in bond yields comes from parallel shifts, to which the other two portfolios are immunized. Also, the butterfly portfolio appears to have almost negligible risk: by this calculation, hedging both parallel and slope risk removes over 99% of the risk. However, it must be remembered that the procedure assumes that the first three principal components are the only sources of risk.

This calculation was oversimplified in several ways: for example, in practice the volatilities would be estimated more carefully, and risk computations would probably be carried out on a cash flow-by-cash flow basis. But the basic idea remains straightforward. Because the calculation can be carried out rapidly, it is easy to vary assumptions about volatility/yield relationships and about correlations, giving additional insight into the risk profile of the portfolio. Of course, the calculation is

Table 5.3 Simplified Value-at-Risk calculation using principal components

Definitions

d_i	'duration' relative to factor i	$\propto$ duration . (factor i shift)
v_i	variance of factor i	$\propto$ factor weight
σ_i	bp volatility of factor i	$= v_i^{1/2}$
VaR$_i$	Value-at-Risk due to factor i	$\propto \sigma_i . d_i . \sqrt{T}$
VaR	aggregate Value-at-Risk	$= \left(\sum_i \text{VaR}_i^2 \right)^{1/2}$

Long portfolio	$100m	10-year par bond
Steepener portfolio	$131m	2-year par bond
	$-$31m	10-year par bond
Butterfly portfolio	$64m	cash
	$100m	2-year par bond
	$-$93m	5-year par bond
	$29m	10-year par bond

Calculations

Assume 100 bp p.a. 'total volatility', factors and factor weights as in Table 5.2. Ignore all but the first three factors (those shown in Figure 5.4).

		Parallel	Slope	Curvature	1 s.d. risk	Daily VaR
Long	10yr durn	7.79	1.50	-0.92		
	Total durn	7.79	1.50	-0.92		
	Risk (VaR)	5.75%	0.27%	-0.07%	5.95%	$376 030
Steepener	2yr durn	2.39	-0.87	-0.72		
	10yr durn	-2.39	-0.46	0.28		
	Total durn	0.00	-1.33	-0.44		
	Risk (VaR)	0.00	-0.24	-0.04	0.28%	$17 485
Butterfly	Cash durn	0.00	0.00	0.00		
	2yr durn	1.83	-0.67	-0.55		
	5yr durn	-4.08	0.24	1.20		
	10yr durn	2.25	0.43	-0.26		
	Total durn	0.00	0.00	0.38		
	Risk (VaR)	0.00%	0.00%	0.03%	0.03%	$1 954

approximate, and in practice large exposures at specific maturities should not be ignored. That would tend to understate the risk of butterfly trades, for example.

However, it is important to recognize that a naive approach to measuring risk, which ignores the information about co-movements revealed by a principal component analysis, will tend to overstate the risk of a butterfly position; in fact, in some circumstances a butterfly position is no riskier than, say, an exposure to the spread between on- and off-the-run Treasuries. In other words, the analysis helps risk managers gain some sense of perspective when comparing the relative importance of different sources of risk.

Risk management for a global bond book is harder. The results of the analysis are mainly negative: they suggest that the most prudent course is to manage each country exposure separately. For Value-at-Risk calculations, the existence of a 'global parallel shift' suggests an alternative way to estimate risk, by breaking it into two components: (a) risk arising from a global shift in bond yields, and (b) country-specific risk relative to the global component.

This approach has some important advantages over the standard calculation, which uses a covariance matrix indexed by country. First, the results are less sensitive to the covariances, which are far from stable. Second, it is easier to add new countries to the analysis. Third, it is easier to incorporate an assumption that changes in yields have a heavy-tailed (non-Gaussian) distribution, which is particularly useful when dealing with emerging markets. Again, the method is not proposed as a replacement for standard VaR calculations, but as a supplement.

Total return management and benchmark choice

For an unleveraged total return manager, many of the proposals are similar. It is again efficient to focus mainly on parallel and slope risk when setting interest rate risk limits, implementing an interest rate view, or designing hedging strategies. This greatly simplifies interest rate risk management, freeing up the portfolio manager's time to focus on monitoring other forms of risk, on assessing relative value, and on carrying out more detailed scenario analysis.

Many analytics software vendors, such as CMS, provide measures of slope risk. Investment managers should ensure that such a measure satisfies two basic criteria. First, it should be consistent with the results of a principal component analysis: a measure of slope risk based on an unrealistic slope shift is meaningless. Second, it should be easy to run, and the results should be easy to interpret: otherwise, it will rarely be used, and slope risk will not be monitored effectively.

The above comments on risk management of global bond positions apply equally well in the present context. However, there is an additional complication. Global bond investors tend to have some performance benchmark, but it is most unclear how an 'optimal' benchmark should be constructed, and how risk should be measured against it. For example, some US investors simply use a US domestic index as a benchmark; many use a currency unhedged global benchmark. (Incidentally, the weights of a global benchmark are typically determined by issuance volumes. This is somewhat arbitrary: it means that a country's weight in the index depends on its fiscal policy and on the precise way public sector borrowing is funded. Mason has suggested using GDP weights; this tends to lower the risk of the benchmark.)

Figures 5.14(a)–(c) may be helpful. They show the risk/return profile, in USD terms, of a US domestic bond index; currency unhedged and hedged global indexes; and the full range of *post hoc* efficient currency unhedged and hedged portfolios. Results are displayed separately for the 1970s, 1980s and 1990s datasets. The first observation is that the US domestic index has a completely different (and inferior) risk/return profile to any of the global portfolios. It is not an appropriate benchmark.

The second observation is that hedged and unhedged portfolios behave in completely different ways. In the 1970s, hedged portfolios were unambiguously superior; in the 1980s, hedged and unhedged portfolios behaved almost like two different asset types; and in the 1990s, hedged and unhedged portfolios seemed to lie on a continuous risk/return scale, with hedged portfolios at the less risky end. If a benchmark is intended to be conservative, a currency hedged benchmark is clearly appropriate.

What, then, is a suitable global benchmark? None of the *post hoc* efficient portfolios will do, since the composition of efficient portfolios is extremely unstable over time – essentially because both returns and covariances are unstable. The most plausible

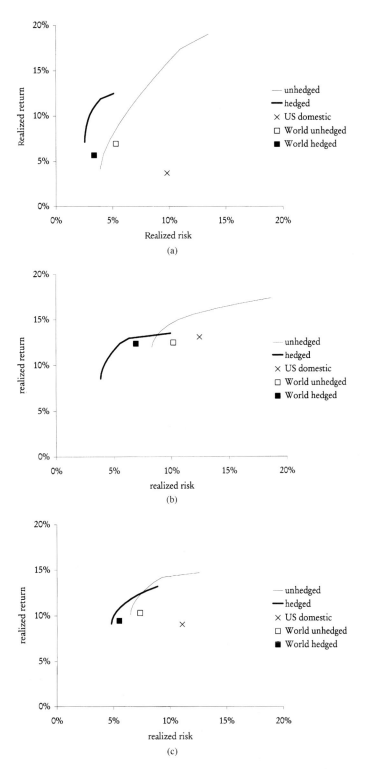

Figure 5.14 Global bond efficient frontier and hedged index: (a) 1970s, (b) 1980s and (c) 1990s. (Historical bond and FX data provided by Deutsche Bank Securities).

candidate is the currency hedged global index. It has a stable composition, has relatively low risk, and is consistently close to the efficient frontier.

Once a benchmark is selected, principal component analysis may be applied as follows. First, it identifies countries which may be regarded as particularly risk relative to the benchmark; in the 1970s and 1980s this would have included Australia and France (see Figure 5.11). Note that this kind of result is more easily read off from the analysis than by direct inspection of the correlations.

Second, it helps managers translate country-specific views into strategies. That it, by estimating the proportion of yield shifts attributable to a global parallel shift (around 50% in the 1990s) it allows managers will a bullish or bearish view on a specific country to determine an appropriate degree of overweighting.

Third, it assists managers who choose to maintain open currency risk. A more extensive analysis can be used to identify 'currency blocs' (whose membership may vary over time) and to estimate co-movements between exchange rates and bond yields. However, all such results must be used with great caution.

Asset/liability management and the use of risk buckets

For asset/liability managers, the recommendations are again quite similar. One should focus on immunizing parallel risk (duration) and slope risk. If these two risk factors are well matched, then from an economic point of view the assets are an effective hedge for the liabilities. Key rate durations are a useful way to measure exposure to individual points on the yield curve; but it is probably unnecessary to match all the key rate durations of assets and liabilities precisely. However, one does need to treat both the short and the very long end of the yield curve separately.

Regarding the long end of the yield curve, it is necessary to ensure that really long-dated liabilities are matched by similarly long-dated assets. For example, one does not want to be hedging 30-year liabilities with 10-year assets, which would be permitted if one focused only on parallel and slope risk. Thus, it is desirable to ensure that 10-year to 30-year key rate durations are reasonably well matched.

Regarding the short end of the yield curve, two problems arise. First, for maturities less than about 18–24 months – roughly coinciding with the liquid part of the Eurodollar futures strip – idiosyncratic fluctuations at the short end of the curve introduce risks additional to parallel and slope risk. It is safest to identify and hedge these separately, either using duration bucketing or partial durations.

Second, for maturities less than about 12 months, it is desirably to match actual cashflows and not just risks. That is, one needs to generate detailed cashflow forecasts rather than simply matching interest rate risk measures.

To summarize, an efficient asset/liability management policy might be described as follows: *from 0–12 months, match cash flows in detail; from 12–24 months, match partial durations or duration buckets in detail; from 2–15 years, match parallel and slope risk only; beyond 15 years, ensure that partial durations are roughly matched too.*

Finally, one must not forget optionality. If the assets have very different option characteristics from the liabilities – which may easily occur when callable bonds or mortgage-backed securities are held – then it is not sufficient to match interest rate exposure in the current yield curve environment. One must also ensure that risks are matched under different interest rate and volatility scenarios. Optionality is treated in detail elsewhere in this book.

In conclusion: principal component analysis suggests a simple and attractive solution to the problem of efficiently managing non-parallel yield curve risk. It is easy to understand, fairly easy to implement, and various off-the-shelf implementations are available. However, there are quite a few subtleties and pitfalls involved. Therefore, risk managers should not rush to implement policies, or to adopt vendor systems, without first deepening their own insight through experimentation and reflection.

Appendix: Economic factors driving the curve

Macroeconomic explanation of parallel and slope risk

This appendix presents some theoretical explanations for why (a) parallel and slope shifts are the dominant kinds of yield curve shift that occur, (b) curvature shifts are observed but tend to be both transitory and inconsistent in form, and (c) the behavior of the short end of the yield curve is quite idiosyncratic. The theoretical analysis helps to ascertain which empirical findings are really robust and can be relied upon: that is, an empirical result is regarded as reliable if it has a reasonable theoretical explanation. For reasons of space, the arguments are merely sketched.

We first explain why parallel and slope shifts emerge naturally from a macro-economic analysis of interest rate expectations. For simplicity, we use an entirely standard linear macroeconomic model, shown in Table 5A.1; see Frankel (1995) for details.

Table 5A.1 A macroeconomic model of interest rate expectations

Model definitions:

i	short-term nominal interest rate
π^e	expected long-term inflation rate
r^e	expected long-term real interest rate
y	log of output
$\bar{y}$	log of normal or potential output
m	log of the money supply
p	log of the price level
$\gamma, \phi, \lambda, \rho$	constant model parameters (elasticities)

Model assumptions:

The output gap is related to the current real interest rate through investment demand:

$$y - \bar{y} = -\gamma(i - \pi^e - r^e)$$

Real money demand depends positively on income and negatively on the interest rate:

$$m - p = \phi y - \lambda i$$

Price changes are determined by excess demand and expected long-term inflation:

$$\frac{dp}{dt} = \rho(y - \bar{y}) + \pi^e$$

Theorem (Frankel, 1995): The expected rate of change of the interest rate is given by:

$$\frac{di}{dt} = -\delta(i - \pi^e - r^e), \text{ where } \delta = \frac{\rho\gamma}{\phi\gamma + \lambda}$$

The model is used in the following way. Bond yields are determined by market participants' expectations about future short-term interest rates. These in turn are determined by their expectations about the future path of the economy: output, prices and the money supply. It is assumed that market participants form these expectations in a manner consistent with the macroeconomic model. Now, the model implies that the short-term interest rate must evolve in a certain fixed way; thus, market expectations must, 'in equilibrium', take a very simple form.

To be precise, it follows from the theorem stated in Table 5A.1 that if i_0 is the current short-term nominal interest rate, i_t is the currently expected future interest rate at some future time t, and i_∞ is the long-term expected future interest rate, then rational interest rate expectations must take the following form in equilibrium:

$$i_t = i_\infty + (i_0 - i_\infty)e^{-\delta t}$$

In this context, a slope shift corresponds to a change in either i_∞ or i_0, while a parallel shift corresponds to a simultaneous change in both. Figure 5A.1 shows, schematically, the structure of interest rate expectations as determined by the model. The expected future interest rate at some future time is equal to the expected future rate of inflation, plus the expected future real rate. (At the short end, some distortion is possible, of which more below.)

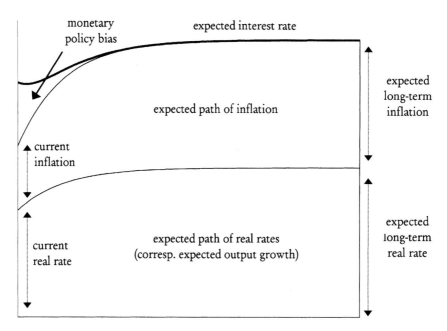

Figure 5A.1 Schematic breakdown of interest rate expectations.

In this setting, yield curve shifts occur when market participants revise their expectations about future interest rates – that is, about future inflation and output growth. A *parallel shift* occurs when both short- and long-term expectations change at once, by the same amount. A *slope shift* occurs when short-term expectations change but long-term expectations remain the same, or vice versa.

Why are parallel shifts so dominant? The model allows us to formalize the following simple explanation: in financial markets, changes in long-term expectations are primarily driven by short-term events, which, of course, also drive changes in short-term expectations. For a detailed discussion of this point, see Keynes (1936).

Why is the form of a slope shift relatively stable over time, but somewhat different in different countries? In this setting, the shape taken by a slope shift is determined by δ, and thus by the elasticity parameters γ, ϕ λ, ρ of the model. These parameters depend in turn on the flexibility of the economy and its institutional framework – which may vary from country to country – but not on the economic cycle, or on the current values of economic variables. So δ should be reasonably stable.

Finally, observe that there is nothing in the model which ensures that parallel and slope shifts should be uncorrelated. In fact, using the most natural definition of 'slope shift', there will almost certainly be a correlation – but the value of the correlation coefficient is determined by how short-term events affect market estimates of the different model variables, not by anything in the underlying model itself. So the model does not give us much insight into correlation risk.

Volatility shocks and curvature risk

We have seen that, while principal component analysis seems to identify curvature shifts as a source of non-parallel risk, on closer inspection the results are somewhat inconsistent. That is, unlike parallel and slope shifts, curvature shifts do not seem to take a consistent form, making it difficult to design a corresponding risk measure.

The main reason for this is that 'curvature shifts' can occur for a variety of quite different reasons. A change in mid-range yields can occur because (a) market volatility expectations have changed, (b) the 'term premium' for interest rate risk has changed, (c) market segmentation has caused a temporary supply/demand imbalance at specific maturities, or (d) a change in the structure of the economy has caused a change in the value δ above. We briefly discuss each of these reasons, but readers will need to consult the References for further details.

Regarding (a): The yield curve is determined by forward short-term interest rates, but these are not completely determined by expected future short-term interest rates; forward rates have two additional components. First, forward rates display a downward 'convexity bias', which varies with the square of maturity. Second, forward rates display an upward 'term premium', or risk premium for interest rate risk, which (empirically) rises at most linearly with maturity. The size of both components obviously depends on expected volatility as well as maturity.

A change in the market's expectations about future interest rate volatility causes a curvature shift for the following reason. A rise in expected volatility will not affect short maturity yields since both the convexity bias and the term premium are negligible. Yields at intermediate maturities will rise, since the term premium dominates the convexity bias at these maturities; but yields at sufficiently long maturities will fall, since the convexity bias eventually dominates. The situation is illustrated in Figure 5A.2. The precise form taken by the curvature shift will depend on the empirical forms of the convexity bias and the term premium, neither of which are especially stable.

Regarding (b): The term premium itself, as a function of maturity, may change. In theory, if market participants expect interest rates to follow a random walk, the term premium should be a linear function of maturity; if they expect interest rates to range trade, or mean revert, the term premium should be sub-linear (this seems to be observed in practice). Thus, curvature shifts might occur when market participants revise their expectations about the nature of the dynamics of interest rates,

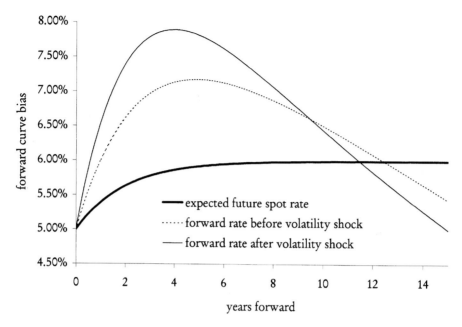

Figure 5A.2 Curvature shift arising from changing volatility expectations.

perhaps because of a shift in the monetary policy regime. Unfortunately, effects like this are nearly impossible to measure precisely.

Regarding (c): Such manifestations of market ineffiency do occur, even in the US market. They do not assume a consistent form, but can occur anywhere on the yield curve. Note that, while a yield curve distortion caused by a short-term supply/ demand imbalance may have a big impact on a leveraged trading book, it might not matter so much to a typical mutual fund or asset/liability manager.

Regarding (d): It is highly unlikely that short-term changes in δ occur, although it is plausible that this parameter may drift over a secular time scale. There is little justification for using 'sensitivity to changes in δ' as a measure of curvature risk.

Curvature risk is clearly a complex issue, and it may be dangerous to attempt to summarize it using a single stylized 'curvature shift'. It is more appropriate to use detailed risk measures such as key rate durations to manage exposure to specific sections of the yield curve.

The short end and monetary policy distortions

The dynamics of short maturity money market yields is more complex and idiosyncratic than that of longer maturity bond yields. We have already seen a hint of this in Figure 5.6(c), which shows that including T-bill yields in the dataset radically changes the results of a principal component analysis; the third eigenvector represents, not a 'curvature shift' affecting 3–5 year maturities, but a 'hump shift' affecting maturities around 1 year. This is confirmed by more careful studies.

As with curvature shifts, hump shifts might be caused by changes in the term premium. But there is also an economic explanation for this kind of yield curve shift: it is based on the observation that market expectations about the path of interest rates in the near future can be much more complex than longer term expectations.

For example, market participants may believe that monetary policy is 'too tight' and can make detailed forecasts about when it may be eased. Near-term expected future interest rates will not assume the simple form predicted by the macroeconomic model of Figure 5.4 if investors believe that monetary policy is 'out of equilibrium'. This kind of bias in expectations can create a hump or bowl at the short end of the yield curve, and is illustrated schematically in Figure 5A.1.

One would not expect a 'hump factor' to take a stable form, since the precise form of expectations, and hence of changes in expectations, will depend both on how monetary policy is currently being run and on specific circumstances. Thus, one should not feed money market yields to a principal component analysis and expect it to derive a reliable 'hump shift' for use in risk management.

For further discussion and analysis, see Phoa (1998a,b). The overall conclusion is that when managing interest rate risk at the short end of the yield curve, measures of parallel and slope risk must be supplemented by more detailed exposure measures. Similarly, reliable hedging strategies cannot be based simply on matching parallel and slope risk, but must make use of a wider range of instruments such as a whole strip of Eurodollar futures contracts.

Acknowledgements

The research reported here was carried out while the author was employed at Capital Management Sciences. The author has attempted to incorporate several useful suggestions provided by an anonymous reviewer.

References

The following brief list of references is provided merely as a starting point for further reading, which might be structured as follows. For general background on matrix algebra and matrix computations, both Jennings and McKeown (1992) and the classic Press *et al.* (1992) are useful, though there are a multitude of alternatives. On principal components analysis, Litterman and Scheinkman (1991) and Garbade (1996) are still well worth reading, perhaps supplemented by Phoa (1998a,b) which contain further practical discussion. This should be followed with Buhler and Zimmermann (1996) and Hiraki *et al.* (1996) which make use of additional statistical techniques not discussed in the present chapter.

However, at this point it is probably more important to gain hands-on experience with the techniques and, especially, the data. Published results should not be accepted unquestioningly, even those reported here! For numerical experimentation, a package such as Numerical Python or MATLAB™ is recommended; attempting to write one's own routines for computing eigenvectors is emphatically *not* recommended. Finally, historical bond data for various countries may be obtained from central banking authorities, often via the World Wide Web.[1]

Brown, R. and Schaefer, S. (1995) 'Interest rate volatility and the shape of the term structure', in Howison, S., Kelly, F. and Wilmott, P. (eds), *Mathematical Models in Finance*, Chapman and Hall.

Buhler, A. and Zimmermann, H. (1996) 'A statistical analysis of the term structure of interest rates in Switzerland and Germany', *Journal of Fixed Income*, December.

Frankel, J. (1995) *Financial Markets and Monetary Policy*, MIT Press.

Garbade, K. (1996) *Fixed Income Analytics*, MIT Press.

Hiraki, T., Shiraishi, N. and Takezawa, N. (1996) 'Cointegration, common factors and the term structure of Yen offshore interest rates', *Journal of Fixed Income*, December.

Ho, T. (1992) 'Key rate durations: measures of interest rate risk', *Journal of Fixed Income*, September.

Jennings, A. and McKeown, J. (1992) *Matrix Computation* (2nd edn), Wiley.

Keynes, J. M. (1936) *The General Theory of Employment, Interest and Money*, Macmillan.

Litterman, R. and Scheinkman, J. (1991) 'Common factors affecting bond returns', *Journal Fixed Income*, June.

Phoa, W. (1998a) *Advanced Fixed Income Analytics*, Frank J. Fabozzi Associates.

Phoa, W. (1998b) *Foundations of Bond Market Mathematics*, CMS Research Report.

Press, W., Teukolsky, S., Vetterling, W. and Flannery, B. (1992) *Numerical Recipes in C: The Art of Scientific Computing* (2nd edn), Cambridge University Press.

Rebonato, R., and Cooper, I. (1996) 'The limitations of simple two-factor interest rate models', *Journal Financial Engineering*, March.

Note

[1] The International datasets used here were provided by Sean Carmody and Richard Mason of Deutsche Bank Securities. The author would also like to thank them for many useful discussions.

6

Implementation of a Value-at-Risk system

ALVIN KURUC

Introduction

In this chapter, we discuss the implementation of a value-at-risk (VaR) system. The focus will be on the practical nuts and bolts of implementing a VaR system in software, as opposed to a critical review of the financial methodology. We have therefore taken as our primary example a relatively simple financial methodology, a first-order variance/covariance approach. The prototype of this methodology is the basic RiskMetrics[TM] methodology developed by J. P. Morgan [MR96].[1]

Perhaps the main challenge in implementing a VaR system is in coming up with a systematic way to express the risk of a bewilderingly diverse set of financial instruments in terms of a relatively small set of risk factors. This is both a financial-engineering and a system-implementation challenge. The body of this chapter will focus on some of the system-implementation issues. Some of the financial-engineering issues are discussed in the appendices.

Overview of VaR methodologies

VaR is distinguished from other risk-management techniques in that it attempts to provide an explicit probabilistic description of future changes in portfolio value. It requires that we estimate the probability distribution of the value of a financial portfolio at some specific date in the future, termed the **target date**. VaR at the $1 - \alpha$ confidence level is determined by the α percentile of this probability distribution. Obviously, this estimate must be based on information that is known today, which we term the **anchor date**.

Most procedures for estimating VaR are based on the concept that a given financial portfolio can be valued in terms of a relatively small of factors, which we term **risk factors**. These can be prices of traded instruments that are directly observed in the market or derived quantities that are computed from such prices. One then constructs a probabilistic model for the risk factors and derives the probability distribution of the portfolio value as a consequence.

To establish a VaR methodology along these lines, we need to

1   Define the risk factors.
2   Establish a probabilistic model for the evolution of these risk factors.

3 Determine the parameters of the model from statistical data on the risk factors.
4 Establish computational procedures for obtaining the distribution of the portfolio value from the distribution of the risk factors.

For example, the RiskMetrics methodology fits into this framework as follows:

1 The risk factors consist of FX rates, zero-coupon discount factors for specific maturities, spot and forward commodity prices, and equity indices.
2 Returns on the risk factors are modeled as being jointly normal with zero means.
3 The probability distribution of the risk factors is characterized by a covariance matrix, which is estimated from historical time series and provided in the Risk-Metrics datasets.
4 The portfolio value is approximated by its first-order Taylor-series expansion in the risk factors. Under this approximation, the portfolio value is normally distributed under the assumed model for the risk factors.

Defining the risk factors

The risk factors should contain all market factors for which one wishes to assess risk. This will depend upon the nature of one's portfolio and what data is available. Important variables are typically foreign-exchange (FX) and interest rates, commodity and equity prices, and implied volatilities for the above. In many cases, the market factors will consist of derived quantities, e.g. fixed maturity points on the yield curve and implied volatilities, rather than directly observed market prices. Implied volatilities for interest rates are somewhat problematic since a number of different mathematical models are used and these models can be inconsistent with one another. It should be noted that the risk factors for risk management might differ from those used for pricing. For example, an off-the-run Treasury bond might be marked to market based on a market-quoted price, but be valued for risk-management purposes from a curve built from on-the-run bonds in order to reduce the number of risk factors that need to be modeled.

A key requirement is that it should be possible to value one's portfolio in terms of the risk factors, at least approximately. More precisely, it should be possible to assess the change in value of the portfolio that corresponds to a given change in the risk factors. For example, one may capture the general interest-rate sensitivity of a corporate bond, but not model the changes in value due to changes in the credit-worthiness of the issuer.

Another consideration is analytical and computational convenience. For example, suppose one has a portfolio of interest-rate derivatives. Then the risk factors must include variables that describe the term structure of interest rates. However, the term structure of interest rates can be described in numerous equivalent ways, e.g. par rates, zero-coupon discount rates, zero-coupon discount factors, etc. The choice will be dictated by the ease with which the variables can be realistically modeled and further computations can be supported.

Probabilistic model for risk factors

The basic dichotomy here is between parametric and non-parametric models. In parametric models, the probability distribution of the risk factors is assumed to be of a specific functional form, e.g. jointly normal, with *parameters* estimated from historical time series. In non-parametric models, the probability distribution of changes in the risk factors is taken to be precisely the distribution that was observed empirically over some interval of time in the past. The non-parametric approach is what is generally known as **historical VaR**.

Parametric models have the following advantages:

1   The relevant information from historical time series is encapsulated in a relatively small number of parameters, facilitating its storage and transmission.
2   Since the distribution of the market data is assumed to be of a specific functional form, it may be possible to derive an analytic form for the distribution of the value of the portfolio. An analytic solution can significantly reduce computation time.
3   It is possible to get good estimates of the parameters even if the individual time series have gaps, due to holidays, technical problems, etc.
4   In the case of RiskMetrics, the necessary data is available for free.

Parametric models have the following disadvantages:

1   Real market data is, at best, imperfectly described by the commonly used approximating distributions. For example, empirical distributions of log returns have skewed fat tails and it is intuitively implausible to model volatilities as being jointly normal with their underlyings.
2   Since one does not have to worry about model assumptions, non-parametric models are more flexible, i.e. it is easy to add new variables.
3   In the opinion of some, non-parametric models are more intuitive.

Data for probabilistic model

For non-parametric models, the data consists of historical time-series of risk factors. For parametric models, the parameters are usually estimated from historical time series of these variables, e.g. by computing a sample covariance matrix. Collection, cleaning, and processing of historical time-series can be an expensive proposition. The opportunity to avoid this task has fueled the popularity of the RiskMetrics datasets.

Computing the distribution of the portfolio value

If the risk factors are modeled non-parametrically, i.e. for historical VaR, the time series of changes in the risk factors are applied one by one to the current values of the risk factors and the portfolio revalued under each scenario. The distribution of portfolio values is given simply by the resulting histogram. A similar approach can be used for parametric models, replacing the historical perturbations by pseudo-random ones drawn from the parametric model. This is termed **Monte Carlo VaR**. Alternatively, if one makes certain simplifying assumptions, one can compute the distribution of portfolio values analytically. For example, this is done in the Risk-Metrics methodology. The benefit of analytic methodologies is that their computational burden is much lower. In addition, analytic methods may be extended to give additional insight into the risk profile of a portfolio.

Variance/covariance methodology for VaR

We will take as our primary example the variance/covariance methodology, specifically RiskMetrics. In this section, we provide a brief overview of this methodology.

Fundamental assets

For the purposes of this exposition, it will be convenient to take certain asset prices as risk factors. We will term these **fundamental assets**. In what follows, we will see that this choice leads to an elegant formalism for the subsequent problem of estimating the distribution of portfolio value.

We propose using three types of fundamental assets:

1 *Spot foreign-exchange* (*FX*) *rates*. We fix a base currency. All other currencies will be termed foreign currencies. We express spot prices of foreign currencies as the value of one unit of foreign currency in units of base currency. For example, if the base currency were USD, the value of JPY would be in the neighborhood of USD 0.008.
2 *Spot asset prices*. These prices are expressed in the currency unit that is most natural and convenient, with that currency unit being specified as part of the price. We term this currency the **native currency** for the asset. For example, shares in Toyota would be expressed in JPY. Commodity prices would generally be expressed in USD, but could be expressed in other currencies if more convenient.
3 *Discount factors*. Discount factors for a given asset, maturity, and credit quality are simply defined as the ratio of the value of that asset for forward delivery at the given maturity by a counterparty of a given credit quality to the value of that asset for spot delivery. The most common example is discount factors for currencies, but similar discount factors may be defined for other assets such as commodities and equities. Thus, for example, we express the value of copper for forward delivery as the spot price of copper times a discount factor relative to spot delivery.

In the abstract, there is no essential difference between FX rates and asset prices. However, we distinguish between them for two reasons. First, while at any given time we work with a fixed base currency, we need to be able to change this base currency and FX rates need to be treated specially during a change of base currency. Second, it is useful to separate out the FX and asset price components of an asset that is denominated in a foreign currency.

Statistical model for fundamental assets

Single fundamental assets

The essential assumption behind RiskMetrics is that short-term, e.g. daily, changes in market prices of the fundamental assets can be approximated by a zero-mean normal distribution. Let $v_i(t)$ denote the present market value of the ith fundamental asset at time t. Define the **relative return** on this asset over the time interval Δt by $r_i(t) \equiv [v_i(t + \Delta t) - v_i(t)]/v_i(t)$. The relative return is modeled by a zero-mean normal distribution. We will term the standard deviation of this distribution the **volatility**, and denote it by $\xi_i(t)$. Under this model, the **absolute return** $v_i(t + \Delta t) - v_i(t)$ is normally distributed with zero mean and standard deviation $\sigma_i(t) = v_i(t)\xi_i(t)$.

Multiple fundamental assets

The power of the RiskMetrics approach comes from modeling the changes in the prices of the fundamental assets by a *joint* normal distribution which takes into account the *correlations* of the asset prices as well as their volatilities. This makes it possible to quantify the risk-reduction effect of portfolio diversification.

Suppose there are m fundamental assets and define the relative-return vector $\mathbf{r} \equiv [r_1, r_2, \ldots, r_m]^T$ (T here denotes vector transpose). The relative-return vector is modeled as having a zero-mean multivariate normal distribution with covariance matrix Ξ.

Statistical data

The covariance matrix is usually constructed from historical volatility and correlation data. In the particular case of the RiskMetrics methodology, the data needed to construct the covariance matrix is provided in the RiskMetrics datasets, which are published over the Internet free of charge. RiskMetrics datasets provide a volatility vector $\xi(t)$ and a correlation matrix $\mathbf{R}$ to describe the distribution of $\mathbf{r}$. The covariance matrix is given in terms of the volatility vector and correlation matrix by

$$\Xi = \xi \xi^T * \mathbf{R}$$

where $*$ denotes element-by-element matrix multiplication.

Distribution of portfolio value

Primary assets

The fundamental assets are spot positions in FX relative to base currency, spot positions in base- and foreign-currency-denominated assets, and forward positions in base currency. We define a **primary asset** as a spot or forward position in FX or in another base- or foreign-currency-denominated asset *expressed in base currency*. We will approximate the sensitivity of any primary asset to changes in the fundamental assets by constructing an approximating portfolio of fundamental assets. The process of going from a given position to the approximating portfolio is termed **mapping**.

The rules are simple. A primary asset with present value v has the following exposures in fundamental assets:

1 Spot and forward positions in non-currency assets have an exposure to the corresponding spot asset price numerically equal to its present value.
2 Forward positions have an exposure to the discount factor for the currency that the position is denominated in numerically equal to its present value.
3 Foreign-currency positions and positions in assets denominated in foreign currencies have a sensitivity to FX rates for that foreign currency numerically equal to its present value.

Example
Suppose the base currency is USD. A USD-denominated zero-coupon bond paying USD 1 000 000 in one year that is worth USD 950 000 today has an exposure of USD 950 000 to the 1-year USD discount factor. A GBP-denominated zero-coupon bond paying GBP 1 000 000 in one year that is worth USD 1 500 000 today has an exposure of USD 1 500 000 to both the 1-year GBP discount factor and the GBP/USD exchange rate. A position in the FTSE 100 that is worth USD 2 000 000 today has an exposure of USD 2 000 000 to both the FTSE 100 index and the GBP/USD exchange rate.

Example
Suppose the current discount factor for the 1-year USD-denominated zero-coupon

bond is 0.95, and the current daily volatility of this discount factor is 0.01. Then the present value of the bond with face value USD 1 000 000 is USD 950 000 and the standard deviation of the change in its value is USD 9500.

Portfolios of primary assets

Gathering together the sum of the portfolio exposures into a total exposure vector $\mathbf{v} \equiv [v_i, v_2, \ldots, v_m]^T$, the model assumed for the fundamental assets implies that the absolute return of the portfolio, i.e.

$$\sum_{i=1}^{m} v_i(t + \Delta_t) - v_i(t) = \sum_{i=1}^{m} v_i(t) r_i(t)$$

has a zero-mean normal distribution. The distribution is completely characterized by its variance, $\sigma^2 = \mathbf{v}^T \Xi \mathbf{v}$.

Example

Consider a portfolio consisting of fixed cashflows in amounts USD 1 000 000 and USD 2 000 000 arriving in 1 and 2 years, respectively. Suppose the present value of 1 dollar paid 1 and 2 years from now is 0.95 and 0.89, respectively. The present-value vector is then

$$\mathbf{v} = [950\,000 \quad 1\,780\,000]^T$$

Suppose the standard deviations of daily relative returns in 1- and 2-year discount factors are 0.01 and 0.0125, respectively, and the correlation of these returns is 0.8. The covariance matrix of the relative returns is then given by

$$\Xi = \begin{pmatrix} 0.01^2 & 0.8 \cdot 0.01 \cdot 0.00125 \\ 0.8 \cdot 0.01 \cdot 0.00125 & 0.0125^2 \end{pmatrix}$$

$$= \begin{pmatrix} 0.0001 & 0.0001 \\ 0.0001 & 0.00015625 \end{pmatrix}$$

The variance of the valuation function is given by

$$\sigma = [950\,000 \quad 1\,780\,000] \begin{pmatrix} 0.0001 & 0.0001 \\ 0.0001 & 0.00015625 \end{pmatrix} \begin{pmatrix} 950\,000 \\ 1\,780\,000 \end{pmatrix}$$

$$= 0.9025 \times 10^8 + 3.3820 \times 10^8 + 4.9506 \times 10^8$$

$$= 9.2351 \times 10^8$$

and the standard deviation of the portfolio is USD 30 389.

Value at risk

Given that the change in portfolio value is modeled as a zero-mean normal distribution with standard deviation σ, we can easily compute the probability of sustaining a loss of any given size. The probability that the return is less than the α percentile point of this distribution is, by definition, α. For example, the 5th percentile of the normal distribution is $\approx -\$1.645\sigma$, so the probability of sustaining a loss of greater than 1.645σ is 5%. In other words, at the 95% confidence level, the VaR is 1.645σ.

The 95% confidence level is, of course, arbitrary and can be modified by the user to fit the requirements of a particular application. For example, VaR at the 99% confidence level is $\approx 2.326\sigma$.

Example
The 1-year zero-coupon bond from the above examples has a daily standard deviation of USD 9500. Its daily VaR at the 95% and 99% confidence levels is thus USD 15 627.50 and USD 22 097.00, respectively.

Asset-flow mapping

Interpolation of maturity points

Earlier we outlined the VaR calculation for assets whose prices could be expressed in terms of fundamental asset prices. Practical considerations limit the number of fundamental assets that can be included as risk factors. In particular, it is not feasible to include discount factors for every possible maturity. In this section, we look at approximating assets not included in the set of fundamental assets by linear combinations of fundamental assets. As a concrete example, consider the mapping of future cashflows. The fundamental asset set will contain discount factors for a limited number of maturities. For example, RiskMetrics datasets cover zero-coupon bond prices for bonds maturing at 2, 3, 4, 5, 7, 9, 10, 15, 20, and 30 years. To compute VaR for a real coupon-bearing bond, it is necessary to express the principal and coupon payments maturities in terms of these vertices. An obvious approach is to apportion exposures summing to the present value of each cashflow to the nearest maturity or maturities in the fundamental asset set. For example, a payment of USD 1 000 000 occurring in 6 years might have a present value of USD 700 000. This exposure might be apportioned to exposures to the 5- and 7-year discount factors totaling USD 700 000.

In the example given in the preceding paragraph, the condition that the exposures at the 5- and 7-year points sum to 700 000 is obviously insufficient to determine these exposures. An obvious approach would be to divide these exposures based on a simple linear interpolation. RiskMetrics suggests a more elaborate approach in which, for example, the *volatility* of the 6-year discount factor would be estimated by linear interpolation of the volatilities of the 5- and 7-year discount factors. Exposures to the 5- and 7-year factors would then be apportioned such that the volatility obtained from the VaR calculation agreed with the interpolated 6-year volatility. We refer the interested reader to Morgan and Reuters (1996) for details.

Summary of mapping procedure

At this point, it will be useful to summarize the mapping procedure for asset flows in a systematic way. We want to map a spot or forward position in an asset. This position is characterized by an asset identifier, a credit quality, and a maturity. The first step is to compute the present value (PV) of the position. To do so, we need the following information:

1 The **current market price** of the asset in its native currency.

2   If the native currency of the asset is not the base currency, we need the **current FX rate** for the native currency.

3   If the asset is for forward delivery, we need the **current discount factor** for the asset for delivery at the given maturity by a counterparty of the given credit quality.

To perform the PV calculation in a systemic manner, we require the following data structures:

1   We need a table, which we term the **asset-price table**, which maps the identifying string for each asset to a current price in terms of a native currency and amount. An example is given in Table 6.1.

Table 6.1   Example of an asset-price table

Asset	Currency	Price
Copper	USD	0.64
British Airways	GBP	4.60

2   We need a table, which we term the **FX table**, which maps the identifying string for each currency to its value in base currency. An example is given in Table 6.2.

Table 6.2   Example of an FX table with USD as base currency

Currency	Value
USD	1.0
GBP	1.6
JPY	0.008

3   We need an object, which we term a **discounting term structure** (DTS), that expresses the value of assets for forward delivery in terms of their value for spot delivery. DTS are specified by an asset-credit quality pair, e.g. USD-Treasury or Copper-Comex. The essential function of the DTS is to provide a discount factor for any given maturity. A simple implementation of a DTS could be based on an ordered list of maturities and discount factors. Discount factors for dates not on the list would be computed by log-linear interpolation. An example is given in Table 6.3.

Table 6.3   Example DTS for Copper-Comex

Maturity (years)	Discount factor
0.0	1.0
0.25	0.98
0.50	0.96

The steps in the PV calculation are then as follows:

1 Based on the asset identifier, look up the asset price in the asset price table.
2 If the price in the asset price table is denominated in a foreign currency, convert the asset price to base currency using the FX rate stored in the FX table.
3 If the asset is for forward delivery, discount its price according to its maturity using the DTS for the asset and credit quality.

Example
Consider a long 3-month-forward position of 100 000 lb of copper with a base currency of USD. From Table 6.1, the spot value of this amount of copper is USD 64 000. From Table 6.2, the equivalent value in base currency is USD 64 000. From Table 6.3, we see that this value should be discounted by a factor of 0.98 for forward delivery, giving a PV of USD 62 720.

Having computed the PV, the next step is to assign exposures to the fundamental assets. We term the result an **exposure vector**. To facilitate this calculation, it is useful to introduce another object, the **volatility term structure** (VTS). The data for this object is an ordered, with respect to maturity, sequence of volatilities for discount factors for a given asset and credit quality. Thus, for example, we might have a VTS for USD-Treasury or GBP-LIBOR. The most common example is discount factors for currencies, but similar discount factors may be defined for other assets such as commodities and equities. An example is given in Table 6.4.

Table 6.4 Example VTS for Copper-Comex

Term (years)	Volatility
0.0	0.0
0.25	0.01
0.5	0.0125

The steps to compute the exposure vector from the PV are as follows:

1 If the asset is not a currency, add an exposure in the amount of the PV to the asset price.
2 If the asset is denominated in a foreign currency, add an exposure in the amount of the PV to the native FX rate.
3 If the asset is for forward delivery, have the VTS add an exposure in the amount of the PV to its discount factor. If the maturity of the asset is between the maturities represented in the fundamental asset set, the VTS will apportion this exposure to the one or two adjacent maturity points.

Example
Continuing our copper example from above, we get exposures of USD 62 720 to the spot price of copper and the 3-month discount factor for copper.

A good example of the utility of the VTS abstraction is given by the specific problem of implementing the RiskMetrics methodology. RiskMetrics datasets supply volatilities for three types of fixed-income assets: money market, swaps, and government bonds. Money-market volatilities are supplied for maturities out to one year, swap-rate volatilities are supplied for maturities from 2 up to 10 years, and government bond rate volatilities are supplied for maturities from 2 out to 30 years. In a software implementation, it is desirable to isolate the mapping process from these specifics. One might thus construct two VTS from these data, a Treasury VTS from the money market and government-bond points and a LIBOR VTS from the money-market and swap rates, followed by government-bond points past the available swap rates. The mapping process would only deal with the VTS abstraction and has no knowledge of where the underlying data came from.

Mapping derivatives

At this point, we have seen how to map primary assets. In particular, in the previous section we have seen how to map asset flows at arbitrary maturity points to maturity points contained within fundamental asset set. In this section, we shall see how to map assets that are derivatives of primary assets contained within the set of risk factors. We do this by approximating the derivative by primary asset flows.

Primary asset values

The key to our approach is expressing the value of derivatives in terms of the values of primary asset flows. We will do this by developing expressions for the value of derivatives in terms of basic variables that represent the *value* of primary asset flows. We shall term these variables **primary asset values** (PAVs). An example of such a variable would be the value at time t of a US dollar to be delivered at (absolute) time T by the US government. We use the notation $USD_T^{\text{Treasury}}(t)$ for this variable. We interpret these variables as equivalent ways of expressing value. Thus, just as one might express length equivalently in centimeters, inches, or cubits, one can express value equivalently in units of spot USD or forward GBP for delivery at time T by a counterparty of LIBOR credit quality.

Just as we can assign a numerical value to the relative size of two units of length, we can compare any two of our units of value. For example, the spot FX rate GBP/USD at time t, $X_{\text{GBP/USD}}(t)$, can be expressed as

$$X_{\text{GBP/USD}}(t) = GBP_t(t) / USD_t(t)^2$$

Since both $USD_t(t)$ and $GBP_t(t)$ are units of value, the ratio $X_{\text{GBP/USD}}(t)$ is a pure unitless number. The physical analogy is

$$\text{inch} / \text{cm} = 2.54$$

which makes sense since both inches and centimeters are units of the same physical quantity, length. The main conceptual difference between our units of value and the usual units of length is that the relative sizes of our units of value change with time. The zero-coupon discount factor at time t for a USD cashflow with maturity $\tau = T - t$, $D_\tau^{\text{USD}}(t)$, can be expressed as

$$D_\tau^{\text{USD}}(t) = USD_T(t) / USD_t(t)$$

(We use upper case D here just to distinguish it typographically from other uses of d below.)

Thus, the key idea is to consider different currencies as completely fungible units for expressing value rather than as incommensurable units. While it is meaningful to assign a number to the relative value of two currency units, an expression like

$USD_t(t)$ is a pure unit of value and has no number attached to it; the value of $USD_t(t)$ is like the length of a centimeter.

Example
The PV as of $t_0 = 30$ September 1999 of a zero-coupon bond paying USD 1 000 000 at time $T = 29$ September 2000 by a counterparty of LIBOR credit quality would normally be written as

$$v = USD\, 1\, 000\, 000\, D_\tau^{\text{USD-LIBOR}}(t_0)$$

where $D_\tau^{\text{USD-LIBOR}}(t_0)$ denotes the zero-coupon discount factor (ZCDF) for USD by a counterparty of LIBOR credit quality for a maturity of $\tau = T - t_0$ years at time t_0. Using the identity

$$D_\tau^{\text{USD-LIBOR}}(t_0) = USD_T^{\text{LIBOR}}(t_0) / USD_t^{\text{LIBOR}}(t_0)$$

we can rewrite this expression in terms of PAVs by

$$v = USD_{t_0}^{\text{LIBOR}}(t_0)\, 1\, 000\, 000\, USD_T^{\text{LIBOR}}(t_0) / USD_{t_0}^{\text{LIBOR}}(t_0)$$

$$= 1\, 000\, 000\, USD_T^{\text{LIBOR}}(t_0)$$

Example
The PV as of time t of a forward FX contract to pay USD 1 600 000 in exchange for GBP 1 000 000 at time $T = 29$ September 2000, is given by

$$v = 1\, 000\, 000\, GBP_T(t) - 1\, 600\, 000\, USD_T(t)$$

Example
The Black–Scholes value for the PV on 30 September 1999 of a GBP call/USD put option with notional principal USD 1 600 000, strike 1.60 USD/GBP, expiration 29 September 2000, and volatility 20% can be expressed in terms of PAVs as

$$v = 1\, 000\, 000[GBP_T(t)\Phi(d_1) - 1.60\, USD_T(t)\Phi(d_2)]$$

with

$$d_{1,2} = \frac{\ln[GBP_T(t) / 1.60\, USD_T(t)] \pm 0.02}{0.20}$$

where Φ denotes the standard cumulative normal distribution.

Delta-equivalent asset flows

Once we have expressed the value of a derivative in terms of PAVs, we obtain approximating positions in primary assets by taking a first-order Taylor-series expansions in the PAVs. The Taylor-series expansion in terms of PAVs provides a first-order proxy in terms of primary asset flows. We term these fixed asset flows the **delta-equivalent asset flows** (DEAFs) of the instrument.

Example
Expanding the valuation function from the first example in the previous subsection in a Taylor series in the PAVs, we get

$$dv(t) = 1\, 000\, 000\, dUSD_T(t)$$

This says that the delta-equivalent position is a *T*-forward position in USD of size 1 000 000. This example is a trivial one since the valuation function is linear in PAVs. But it illustrates the interpretation of the coefficients of the first-order Taylor-series expansion as DEAFs.

Primary assets have the nice property of being linear in PAVs. More interesting is the fact that many derivatives are linear in PAVs as well.

Example

Expanding the valuation function from the second example in the previous subsection in a Taylor series in the PAVs, we get

$$dv(t) = 1\,000\,000\,dGBP_T(t) - 1\,600\,000\,dUSD_T(t)$$

This says that the delta-equivalent positions are a long *T*-forward position in GBP of size 1 000 000 and a short *T*-forward position in USD of size 1 600 000. Of course, options will generally be non-linear in PAVs.

Example

If the option is at the money, the DEAFs from the third example in the previous subsection are (details are given later in the chapter)

$$dv(t) = 539\,828\,dGBP_T(t) - 863\,725\,dUSD_T(t)$$

This says that the delta-equivalent positions are *T*-forward positions in amounts GBP 539 828 and USD − 863 725.

Gathering portfolio information from source systems

Thus far, we have taken a bottom-up approach to the mapping problem; starting with the fundamental assets, we have been progressively expanding the range of assets that can be incorporated into the VaR calculation. At this point, we switch to a more top-down approach, which is closer to the point of view that is needed in implementation. Mathematically speaking, the VaR calculation, at least in the form presented here, is relatively trivial. However, gathering the data that is needed for this calculation can be enormously challenging. In particular, gathering the portfolio information required for the mapping process can present formidable problems. Information on the positions of a financial institution is typically held in a variety of heterogeneous systems and it is very difficult to gather this information together in a consistent way.

We recommend the following approach. Each source system should be responsible for providing a description of its positions in terms of DEAFs. The VaR calculator is then responsible for converting DEAFs to exposure vectors for the fundamental assets. The advantage of this approach is that the DEAFs provide a well-defined, simple, and stable interface between the source systems and the VaR computational engine. DEAFs provide an unambiguous financial specification for the information that source systems must provide about financial instruments. They are specified in terms of basic financial-engineering abstractions rather than system-specific concepts, thus facilitating their implementation in a heterogeneous source-system environment. This specification is effectively independent of the particular selections made for the fundamental assets. Since the latter is likely to change over time, it is highly desirable to decouple the source–system interface from the internals of the risk system. Changes in the source–system interface definitions are expensive to implement, as they require analysis and changes in all of the source systems. It is therefore important that this interface is as stable as possible.

In the presence of heterogeneous source systems, one reasonable approach to gathering the necessary information is to use a relational database. In the following two subsections, we outline a simple two-table design for this information.

The FinancialPosition table

The rows in this table correspond to financial positions. These positions should be at the lowest level of granularity that is desired for reporting. One use of the table is as an index to the DEAFs, which are stored in the LinearSensitivities table described in the following subsection. For this purpose, the FinancialPosition table will need columns such as:

mnemonicDescription   A mnemonic identifier for the position.

positionID   This is the primary key for the table. It binds this table to the LinearSensitivities table entries.

A second use of the FinancialPosition table is to support the selection of subportfolios. For example, it will generally be desirable to support limit setting and reporting for institutional subunits. For this purpose, one might include columns such as:

book   A string used to identify subportfolios within an institution.

counterparty   Counterparty institution for the position. For bonds, this will be the issuer. For exchange-traded instruments, this will be the exchange.

currency   The ISO code for currency in which presentValue is denominated, e.g. 'USD' or 'GBP'.

dealStatus   An integer flag that describes that execution status of the position. Typically statuses might include analysis, executed, confirmed, etc.

entity   The legal entity within an institution that is party to the position, i.e. the internal counterpart of counterparty.

instrumentType   The type of instrument (e.g. swap, bond option, etc.).

notional   The notional value of the position. The currency units are determined by the contents of the currency column (above).

Third, the FinancialPosition table would likely be used for operational purposes. Entries for such purpose might include:

linearity   An integer flag that describes qualitatively 'how linear' the position is. A simple example is described in Table 6.5. Such information might be useful in updating the table. The DEAFs for non-linear instruments will change with market conditions and therefore need to be updated frequently. The DEAFs for linear

Table 6.5   Interpretation of linearity flag

Value	Accuracy
0	Linear sensitivities give 'almost exact' pricing.
1	Linear sensitivities are not exact due to convexity.
2	Linear sensitivities are not exact due to optionality.

instruments remain constant between instrument lifecycle events such as resets and settlements.

lastUpdated   Date and time at which the FinancialPosition and LinearSensitivities table entries for this position were last updated.

presentValue   The present value (PV) of the position (as of the last update). The currency units for presentValue are determined by the contents of the currency column (above).

source   Indicates the source system for the position.

unwindingPeriod   An estimate of the unwinding period for the instrument in business days. (The unwinding period is the number of days it would take to complete that sale of the instrument after the decision to sell has been made.) A discussion of the use of this field is given later in this chapter.

validUntil   The corresponding entries in the LinearSensitivities table (as of the most recent update) remain valid on or before this date. This data could be used to support as-needed processing for LinearSensitivities table updates. An abbreviated example is shown in Table 6.6.

Table 6.6   Example of a FinancialPosition table

positionID	instrumentType	currency	notional	presentValue
1344	FRA	USD	5 000 000	67 000
1378	Swap	USD	10 000 000	−36 000

The LinearSensitivities table

This table is used to store DEAFs. Each row of the LinearSensitivities table describes a DEAF for one of the positions in the FinancialPosition table. This table might be designed as follows:

amount   The amount of the DEAF. For fixed cashflows, this is just the undiscounted amount of the cashflow.

asset   For DEAFs that correspond to currency assets, this is the ISO code for the currency, e.g. 'USD' or 'GBP'. For commodities and equities, it is an analogous identifier.

date   The date of the DEAF.

positionID   This column indicates the entry in the FinancialPosition table that the DEAF corresponds to.

termStructure   For cash flows, this generally indicates credit quality or debt type, e.g. 'LIBOR' or 'Treasury'. An example is given in Table 6.7.

Table 6.7   Example of a LinearSensitivity table

positionID	Asset	termStructure	Date	Amount
1344	USD	LIBOR	15 Nov. 1999	−5 000 000
1344	USD	LIBOR	15 Nov. 2000	5 000 000
1378	USD	LIBOR	18 Oct. 1999	−35 000

Translation tables

The essential information that the source systems supply to the VaR system is DEAFs. As discussed in the previous section, it is desirable to decouple the generation of DEAFs from the specific choice of fundamental assets in the VaR system. A convenient means of achieving this decoupling is through the use of a 'translation table'. This is used to tie the character strings used as asset and quality-credit identifiers in the source system to the strings used as fundamental-asset identifiers in the VaR system at run time.

For example, suppose the base currency is USD and the asset in question is a corporate bond that pays in GBP. The source system might provide DEAFs in currency GBP and credit quality XYZ_Ltd. The first step in the calculation of the exposure vector for these DEAFs is to compute their PVs. To compute the PV, we need to associate the DEAF key GBP-XYZ_Ltd with an appropriate FX rate and discounting term structure (DTS). The translation table might specify that DEAFs with this key are assigned to the FX rate GBP and the DTS GBP-AA. The second step in the calculation of the exposure vector is assignment to appropriate volatility factors. The translation table might specify that DEAFs with this key are assigned to the FX volatility for GBP and the VTS GBP-LIBOR.

The translation table might be stored in a relational database table laid out in the following way:

externalPrimaryKey This key would generally be used to identify the asset in question. For example, for a currency one might use a standard currency code, e.g. USD or GBP. Similarly, one might identify an equity position by its symbol, and so forth.

externalSecondaryKey This key would generally be used to specify discounting for forward delivery. For example, currency assets could be specified to be discounted according to government bond, LIBOR, and so forth.

DTSPrimaryKey This key is used to identify asset prices in the asset price table as well as part of the key for the DTS.

DTSSecondaryKey Secondary key for DTS.

VTSPrimaryKey This key is used to identify asset volatilities in the asset price volatility table as well as part of the key for the VTS.

VTSSecondaryKey Secondary key for VTS.

A timely example for the need of the translation table comes with the recent introduction of the Euro. During the transition, many institutions will have deals denominated in Euros as well as DEM, FRF, and so on. While it may be convenient to use DEM pricing and discounting, it will generally be desirable to maintain just a Euro VTS. Thus, for example, it might be desirable to map a deal described as DEM-LIBOR in a source system, to a DEM-Euribor DTS and a Euro-Euribor VTS. This would result in the table entries shown in Table 6.8.

At this point, it may be worthwhile to point out that available discounting data will generally be richer than available volatility data. Thus, for example, we might have a AA discounting curve available, but rely on the RiskMetrics dataset for volatility information, which covers, at most, two credit-quality ratings.

Table 6.8 Sample row in a translation table

externalPrimaryKey	DEM
externalSecondaryKey	LIBOR
DTSPrimaryKey	DEM
DTSSecondaryKey	LIBOR
VTSPrimaryKey	EUR
VTSSecondaryKey	Euribor

Design strategy summary

There is no escaping the need to understand the semantics of instrument valuation. The challenge of doing this in a consistent manner across heterogeneous systems is probably the biggest single issue in building a VaR system. In large part, the design presented here has been driven by the requirement to make this as easy as possible. To summarize, the following analysis has to be made for each of the source systems:

1 For each instrument, write down a formula that expresses the present value in terms of PAVs.
2 Compute the sensitivities of the present value with respect to each of the PAVs.
3 If the Taylor-series expansion of the present value function in PAVs has coefficient c_i with respect to the ith PAV, its first-order sensitivity to changes in the PAVs is the same as that of a position in amount c_i in the asset corresponding to the PAV. Thus the sensitivities with respect to PAVs may be interpreted as DEAFs.

In addition, we need to map the risk factors keys in each source system to appropriate discounting and volatility keys in the VaR system.

Covariance data

Construction of volatility and correlation estimates

At the heart of the variance/covariance methodology for computing VaR is a covariance matrix for the relative returns. This is generally computed from historical time series. For example, if $r_i(t_j), j = 1, \ldots, n$, are the relative returns of the ith asset over $n + 1$ consecutive days, then the variance of relative returns can be estimated by the sample variance

$$\xi_i^2 = \sum_{j=1}^{n} r_j^2(t_j)/n$$

In this expression, we assume that relative returns have zero means. The rationale for this is that sample errors for estimating the mean will often be as large as the mean itself (see Morgan and Reuters, 1996). Volatility estimates provided in the RiskMetrics data sets use a modification of this formula in which more recent data are weighted more heavily. This is intended to make the estimates more responsive to changes in volatility regimes. These estimates are updated daily.

   Estimation of volatilities and correlations for financial time series is a complex subject, which will not be treated in detail here. We will content ourselves with pointing out that the production of good covariance estimates is a laborious task.

First, the raw data needs to be collected and cleaned. Second, since many of the risk factors are not directly observed, financial abstractions, such as zero-coupon discount factor curves, need to be constructed. Third, one needs to deal with a number of thorny practical issues such as missing data due to holidays and proper treatment of time-series data from different time zones. The trouble and expense of computing good covariance matrices has made it attractive to resort to outside data providers, such as RiskMetrics.

Time horizon

Ideally, the time interval between the data points used to compute the covariance matrix should agree with the time horizon used in the VaR calculation. However, this is often impractical, particularly for longer time horizons. An alternative approach involves scaling the covariance matrix obtained for daily time intervals. Assuming relative returns are statistically stationary, the standard deviation of changes in portfolio value over n days is $\sqrt{n}$ times that over 1 day.

The choice of time horizon depends on both the nature of the portfolio under consideration and the perspective of the user. To obtain a realistic estimate of potential losses in a portfolio, the time horizon should be at least on the order of the unwinding period of the portfolio. The time horizon of interest in an investment environment is generally longer than that in a trading environment.

Heterogeneous unwinding periods and liquidity risk

As mentioned in the previous subsection a realistic risk assessment needs to incorporate the various unwinding periods present in a portfolio. If a position takes 5 days to liquidate, then the 1-day VaR does not fully reflect the potential loss associated with the position. One approach to incorporating liquidity effects into the VaR calculation involves associating an unwinding period with each instrument. Assuming that changes in the portfolio's value over non-overlapping time intervals are statistically independent, the variance of the change in the portfolio's value over the total time horizon is equal to the sum of the variances for each time-horizon interval. In this way, the VaR computation can be extended to incorporate liquidity risk.

Example
Consider a portfolio consisting of three securities, A, B, and C, with unwinding periods of 1, 2, and 5 days, respectively. The total variance estimate is obtained by adding a 1-day variance estimate for a portfolio containing all three securities, a 1-day variance estimate for a portfolio consisting of securities B and C, and a 3-day variance estimate for a portfolio consisting only of security C.

The above procedure is, of course, a rather crude characterization of liquidity risk and does not capture the risk of a sudden loss of liquidity. Nonetheless, it may be better than nothing at all. It might be used, for example, to express a preference for instrument generally regarded as liquid for the purpose of setting limits.

Change of base currency

With the system design that we have described, a change of base currency is relatively simple. First of all, since the DEAFs are defined independently of base currency, these remain unchanged. The only aspect of the fundamental assets that needs to be changed is the FX rates. The FX rate for the new base currency is removed from the set of risk factors and replaced by the FX rate for the old base currency. In addition, the definition of all FX rates used in the system need to be changed so that they are relative to the new base currency. Thus the rates in the FX table need to be recomputed. In addition, the volatilities of the FX rates and the correlations of FX rates with all other risk factors need to be recomputed. Fortunately, no new information is required, the necessary volatilities and correlations can be computed from the previously ones. The justification for this statement is given later in this chapter.

Information access

It is useful to provide convenient access to the various pieces of information going into the VaR calculation as well as the intermediate and final results.

Input information

Input information falls into three broad categories, portfolio data, current market data, and historical market data.

Portfolio data

In the design outline presented here, the essential portfolio data are the DEAF proxies stored in the FinancialPosition and LinearSensitivities tables.

Current market data

This will generally consist of spot prices and DTSs. It is convenient to have a graphical display available for the DTS, both in the form of zero-coupon discount factors as well as in the form of zero-coupon discount rates.

Historical market data

Generally speaking, this will consist of the historical covariance matrix. It may be more convenient to display this as a volatility vector and a correlation matrix. Since the volatility vector and correlation matrix will be quite large, some thought needs to be given as to how to display them in a reasonable manner. For example, reasonable size portions of the correlation matrix may be specified by limiting each axis to factors relevant to a single currency. In addition, it will be desirable to provide convenient access to the VTS, in order to resolve questions that may arise about the mapping of DEAFs.

Intermediate results – exposure vectors

It is desirable to display the mapped exposure vectors. In the particular case of RiskMetrics, we have found it convenient to display mapped exposure vectors in the form of a matrix. The rows of this matrix correspond to asset class and maturity identifiers in the RiskMetrics data sets and the columns of this matrix correspond to currency codes in the RiskMetrics data set.

VaR results

In addition to total VaR estimates, it is useful to provide VaR estimate for individual asset classes (interest, equities, and FX) as well as for individual currencies.

Portfolio selection and reporting

The VaR system must provide flexible and powerful facilities to select deals and portfolios for analysis. This is conveniently done using relational database technology. This allows the users to 'slice and dice' the portfolio across a number of different axes, e.g. by trader, currency, etc. It will be convenient to have persistent storage of the database queries that define these portfolios. Many institutions will want to produce a daily report of VaR broken out by sub-portfolios.

Appendix 1: Mathematical description of VaR methodologies

One of the keys to the successful implementation of a VaR system is a precise financial-engineering design. There is a temptation to specify the design by providing simple examples and leave the details of the treatment of system details to the implementers. The result of this will often be inconsistencies and confusing behavior. To avoid this, it is necessary to provide an almost 'axiomatic' specification that provides an exact rule to handle the various contingencies that can come up. This will typically require an iterative approach, amending the specification as the implementers uncover situations that are not clearly specified. Thus, while the descriptions that follow may appear at first unnecessarily formal, experience suggests that a high level of precision in the specification pays off in the long run.

The fundamental problem of VaR, based on information known at the anchor time, t_0, is to estimate the probability distribution of the value of one's financial position at the target date, T. In principle, one could do this in a straightforward way by coming up with a comprehensive probabilistic model of the world. In practice, it is necessary to make heroic assumptions and simplifications, the various ways in which these assumptions and simplifications are made lead to the various VaR methodologies.

There is a key abstraction that is fundamental to almost all of the various VaR methodologies that have been proposed. This is that one restricts oneself to estimating the profit and loss of a given trading strategy that is due to changes in the value of a relatively small set of underlying variables termed risk factors. This assumption can be formalized by taking the risk factors to be the elements of a m-dimensional vector $\mathbf{m}_t$ that describes the 'instantaneous state' of the market as it evolves over time. One then assumes that the value of one's trading strategy at the target date expressed in base currency is given by a function $v_{t_0,T}: \Re^m \times [t_0, T] \to \Re$ of the trajectory of $\mathbf{m}_t$ for $t \in [t_0, T]$. We term a valuation function of this form a **future valuation function** since it gives the value of the portfolio in the future as a function of the evolution of the risk factors between the anchor and target date.[3] Note that $v_{t_0,T}$ is defined so that any dependence on market variables prior to the anchor date t_0, e.g. due to resets, is assumed to be known and embedded in the valuation function $v_{t_0,T}$.

The same is true for market variables that are not captured in $\mathbf{m}_t$. For example, the value of a trading strategy may depend on credit spreads or implied volatilities that are not included in the set of risk factors. These may be embedded in the valuation function $v_{t_0, T}$, but are then treated as known, i.e. deterministic, quantities.

To compute VaR, one postulates the existence of a probability distribution μ_T on the evolution of $\mathbf{m}_t$ in the interval $[t_0, T]$. Defining $M_{[t_0, T]} \equiv \{\mathbf{m}_t : t \in [t_0, T]\}$, the quantity $v_{t_0, T}(M_{[t_0, T]})$, where $M_{[t_0, T]}$ is distributed according to μ_T, is then a real-valued random variable. VaR for the time horizon $T - t_0$ at the $1 - \alpha$ confidence level is defined to be the α percentile of this random variable. More generally, one would like to characterize the entire distribution of $v_{t_0, T}(M_{[t_0, T]})$.

The problem of computing VaR thus comes down to computing the probability distribution of the random variable $v_{t_0, T}(M_{[t_0, T]})$. To establish a VaR methodology, we need to

1 Define the market-state vector $\mathbf{m}_t$.
2 Establish a probabilistic model for $M_{[t_0, T]}$.
3 Determine the parameters of the model for $M_{[t_0, T]}$ based on statistical data.
4 Establish computational procedures for obtaining the distribution of $v_{t_0, T}(M_{[t_0, T]})$.

In fact, most existing procedures for computing VaR have in common a stronger set of simplifying assumptions. Instead of explicitly treating a trading strategy whose positions may evolve between the anchor and target date, they simply consider the existing position as of the anchor date. We denote the valuation function as of the anchor date as a function of the risk factors by $v_{t_0} : \mathfrak{R}^m \to \mathfrak{R}$. We term a valuation function of this form a **spot valuation function**. Changes in the risk factors, which we term perturbations, are then modeled as being statistically stationary. The VaR procedure then amounts to computing the probability distribution of $v_{t_0}(\mathbf{m}_{t_0} + \Delta\mathbf{m})$, where $\Delta\mathbf{m}$ is a stochastic perturbation.

Appendix 2: Variance/covariance methodologies

In this appendix, we formalize a version of the RiskMetrics variance/covariance methodology. The RiskMetrics Technical Document sketches a number of methodological choices by example rather than a single rigid methodology. This has the advantage that the user can tailor the methodology somewhat to meet particular circumstances. When it comes time for software implementation, however, it is advantageous to formalize a precise approach. One source of potential confusion is in the description of the statistical model for portfolio value. In some places, it is modeled as normally distributed (see Morgan and Reuters, 1996, §1.2). In other places it is modeled as log-normally distributed (Morgan and Reuters, 1996, §1.1). The explanation for this apparent inconsistency is that RiskMetrics depends on an essential approximation. The most natural statistical model for changes in what we earlier termed fundamental asset prices is a log-normal model. An additional attractive feature of the log-normal model for changes in fundamental asset prices is that it implies that primary asset prices are log-normal as well. However, the difficulty with the log-normal model is that the distribution of a portfolio containing more than one asset is analytically intractable. To get around this difficulty, the RiskMetrics methodology uses an approximation in which relative changes in the primary assets are equated to changes in the log prices of these assets. Since relative returns over a short period of time tend to be small, the approximation is a reasonable one. For example, for a relative change of 1%,

$$\ln 1.01 - \ln 1.0 = \ln(1.01)$$

$$\approx 0.00995.$$

Perhaps the main danger is the possibility of conceptual confusion, the approximation means that a primary asset has a different statistical model when viewed as a market variable than when viewed as a financial position. In this appendix, we provide a formalization of these ideas that provides a consistent approach to multiple-asset portfolios.

Risk factors

While in the body of this chapter we loosely referred to the fundamental assets as the risk factors, we now more precisely take the risk factors to be the *logarithms* of the fundamental asset prices. We denote the log price of the ith fundamental asset at time t by $l_i(t)$ for $i = 1, \ldots, m$.

Statistical model for risk factors

Changes in the log asset prices between the anchor and target dates are assumed to have a jointly normal distribution with zero means. We denote the covariance matrix of this distribution by Ξ. When Δt is small, e.g. on the order of one day, the mean of this distribution is small and is approximated as being equal to zero.

Distribution of portfolio value

We assume that we can write the valuation function of the portfolio as a function of the risk-factor vector $\mathbf{l} \equiv [l_1, \ldots, l_m]^T$. Our procedure for computing the distribution of the portfolio is then defined by approximating the valuation function by its first-order linear approximation in $\mathbf{l}$. Thus, the first-order approximation to the change in the valuation function is given by

$$dv \approx \frac{\partial v}{\partial \mathbf{l}} d\mathbf{l}$$

where

$$\frac{\partial v}{\partial \mathbf{l}} \equiv \left(\frac{\partial v}{\partial \mathbf{l}_2} \quad \cdots \quad \frac{\partial v}{\partial l_m} \right)$$

We thus formalize what we termed an exposure to the ith risk factor as the partial derivative of the valuation function with respect to l_i. Under this approximation, it follows that dv is normally distributed with mean zero and variance

$$\sigma^2 = \frac{\partial v}{\partial \mathbf{l}} \Xi \frac{\partial v^T}{\partial \mathbf{l}}$$

Mapping of primary assets

We now show that the above definitions agree with the mapping procedure for primary assets given in the body of this chapter. To begin with, consider, for example, a fundamental asset such as a zero-coupon bond in the base currency USD with face value N and maturity τ. The valuation function for this bond is given by

$$v_{t_0} = \text{USD } N D_{\tau}^{\text{USD}}(t_0)$$

We have

$$\frac{\partial v_{t_0}}{\partial \ln D_{\tau}^{\text{USD}}(t_0)} = D_{\tau}^{\text{USD}}(t_0)\frac{\partial v_{t_0}}{\partial D_{\tau}^{\text{USD}}(t_0)}$$

$$= v_{t_0}$$

We thus see that the required exposure to the discount factor is the present value of the bond.

As another example, consider a primary asset such as a zero-coupon bond in a foreign currency with face value GBP N and maturity τ. The valuation function for this bond from a USD perspective is given by

$$v_{t_0} = \text{USD } N X_{\text{GBP/USD}}(t_0) D_{\tau}^{\text{GBP}}(t_0)$$

where $X(t_0)$ is the FX rate for the foreign currency. A calculation similar to the one in the preceding paragraph shows that

$$\frac{\partial v_{t_0}}{\partial \ln D_{\tau}^{\text{GBP}}(t_0)} = \frac{\partial v_{t_0}}{\partial \ln X_{\text{GBP/USD}}(t_0)} = v_{t_0}$$

We thus see that the required exposure to the discount factor and the FX rate are both equal to the present value of the bond in the base currency.

In summary, we can express the value of any primary asset for spot or forward delivery as a product of fundamental asset prices. It follows that a primary asset has an exposure to the fundamental asset prices affecting its value equal to the present value of the primary asset. This is the mathematical justification for the mapping rule presented in the body of this chapter.

Mapping of arbitrary instruments

Arbitrary instruments, in particular derivatives, are treated by approximating them by positions in primary instruments. The procedure is to express the valuation function of the instrument in terms of PAVs. The approximating positions in primary instruments are then given by the coefficients of the first-order Taylor series expansion of the valuation function in the PAVs. To see this, suppose the valuation function v for a given derivative depends on m PAVs, which we denote $PAV_j, i = 1, \ldots, m$. We write out the first-order expansion in PAVs:

$$dv = \sum_{i=1}^{m} \frac{\partial v}{\partial PAV_i} dPAV_i$$

Now consider a portfolio consisting of positions in amounts $\partial v / \partial PAV_i$ of the primary asset corresponding to the ith PAV. It is clear that the sensitivity of this portfolio to the PAVs is given by the right-hand side of the above equation. To summarize, the Taylor-series expansion in PAVs provides a first-order proxy in terms of primary asset flows. We term these fixed asset flows the **delta-equivalent asset flows** (DEAFs) of the instrument.

One of the attractive features of expressing valuation functions in terms of PAVs is the base-currency independence of the resulting expressions. Consider, for example, the PV at time t of a GBP-denominated zero-coupon bond, paying amount N at time T. The expression in PAVs is given by

$$v_t = N\,GBP_T(t)$$

regardless of the base currency. In order to appreciate the base-currency independence of this expression, start from a USD perspective:

$$v_t = USD_t(t)NX_{\text{GBP/USD}}(t)D_\tau^{\text{GBP}}(t)$$

$$= USD_t(t)N\frac{GBP_t(t)GBP_T(t)}{USD_t(t)GBP_t(t)}$$

$$= N\,GBP_T(t)$$

As an example of a non-trivial DEAF calculation, we consider an FX option. The Black–Scholes value for the PV at time t of a GBP call/USD put option with strike $\bar{X}_{\text{GBP/USD}}$ with time $\tau = T - t$ to expiry is given by

$$v_t = USD_t(t)[X_{\text{GBP/USD}}(t)D_\tau^{\text{GBP}}(t)\Phi(d_1) - \bar{X}_{\text{GBP/USD}}D_\tau^{\text{USD}}(t)\Phi(d_2)]$$

where $\bar{X}_{\text{GBP/USD}}$ is the strike, Φ denotes the cumulative probability distribution function for a standard normal distribution, and

$$d_{1,2} = \frac{\ln(X_{\text{GBP/USD}}/\bar{X}_{\text{GBP/USD}}) + \ln(D_\tau^{\text{GBP}}/D_\tau^{\text{USD}}) \pm \sigma^2\tau/2}{\sigma\tau}$$

where σ is the volatility of the FX rate (Hull, 1997). Making use of the identities

$$X_{\text{GBP/USD}}(t) = GBP_t(t)/USD_t(t)$$

$$D_\tau^{\text{GBP}}(t)GBP_t(t) = GBP_T(t)$$

and

$$D_\tau^{\text{USD}}(t)USD_t(t) = USD_T(t)$$

the equivalent expression in terms of PAVs is given by

$$v_t = GBP_T\Phi(d_1) - \bar{X}_{\text{GBP/USD}}USD_T\Phi(d_2)$$

with

$$d_{1,2} = \frac{\ln[GBP_T(t)/USD_T(t)] - \ln(\bar{X}_{\text{GBP/USD}}) \pm \sigma^2\tau/2}{\sigma\tau}$$

Some calculation then gives the first-order Taylor-series expansion

$$dv_t = \Phi(d_1)dGBP_T(t) - \bar{X}_{\text{GBP/USD}}\Phi(d_2)dUSD_T(t)$$

This says that the delta-equivalent positions are T-forward positions in amounts $GBP\,\Phi(d_1)$ and $USD\,\bar{X}_{\text{GBP/USD}}\Phi(d_1)$.

Change of base currency

A key and remarkable fact is that the log-normal model for FX risk factors is *invariant* under a change of base currency. That is, if one models the FX rates relative to a given base currency as jointly log normal, the FX rates relative to any other currency induced by arbitrage relations are jointly log normal as well. Moreover, the covariance matrix for rates relative to a new base currency is determined from the covariance matrix for the old base currency. These two facts make a change of base currency a painless operation.

These nice properties hinge on the choice of log FX rates as risk factors. For example, suppose the original base currency is USD so that the FX risk factors consist of log FX rates relative to USD. The statistical model for risk factors is that changes in log asset prices have a joint normal distribution. If we were to change base currency to, say GBP, then the new risk factors would be log FX rates relative to GBP. Thus, for example, we would have to change from a risk factor of $\ln X_{\text{GBP/USD}}$ to $\ln X_{\text{USD/GBP}}$. But, using the PAV notation introduced earlier,

$$\ln X_{\text{USD/GBP}} = \ln \frac{USD}{GBP}$$

$$= -\ln \frac{GBP}{USD}$$

$$= -\ln X_{\text{GBP/USD}}$$

Thus the risk factor from a GBP respective is just a scalar multiple of the risk factor from a USD perspective. For a third currency, say JPY, we have

$$\ln X_{\text{JPY/GBP}} = \ln \frac{JPY}{GBP}$$

$$= \ln \frac{JPY}{USD} - \ln \frac{GBP}{USD}$$

$$= \ln X_{\text{JPY/USD}} - \ln X_{\text{GBP/USD}}$$

Thus the log FX rate for JPY relative to GBP is a linear combination of the log FX rates for JPY and GBP relative to USD. We see that the risk factors with GBP as base currency are just linear combinations of the risk factors with USD as base currency. Standard results for the multivariate normal distribution show that linear combination of zero-mean jointly normal random variables are also zero-mean and jointly normal. Moreover, the covariance matrix for the new variables can be expressed in terms of the covariance matrix for the old variables. We refer the reader to Morgan and Reuters (1996, §8.4) for the details of these calculations.

Appendix 3: Remarks on RiskMetrics

The methodology that we described in this chapter agrees quite closely with that presented in RiskMetrics, although we deviate from it on some points of details. In this appendix, we discuss the motivations for some of these deviations.

Mapping of non-linear instruments

In the previous appendix we described a general approach to treating instruments whose value depends non-linearly on the primary assets. This approach involved computing a first-order Taylor series expansion in what we termed PAVs. The coefficients of this expansion gave positions in primary assets that comprised a first-order proxy portfolio to the instrument in question. The RiskMetrics Technical Document (Morgan and Reuters, 1996) describes a similar approach to mapping non-linear FX and/or interest-rate derivatives. The main difference is that the first-order Taylor series expansion of the PV function is taken with respect to FX rates and zero-coupon discount factors (ZCDF). Using this expansion, it is possible to construct a portfolio of proxy instruments whose risk is, to first order, equivalent. This approach, termed the delta approximation, is illustrated by a number of relatively simple examples in Morgan and Reuters (1996).

While the approach described in Morgan and Reuters (1996) is workable, it has a number of significant drawbacks relative to the DEAF approach:

1 As will be seen below, the proxy instrument constructed to reflect risk with respect to ZCDFs in foreign currencies does not correspond to a commonly traded asset; it is effectively a zero-coupon bond in a foreign currency whose FX risk has been removed. In contrast, the proxy instrument for the DEAF approach, a fixed cashflow, is both simple and natural.
2 Different proxy types are used for FX and interest-rate risk. In contrast, the DEAF approach captures both FX and interest-rate risk with a single proxy type.
3 The value of some primary instruments is non-linear in the base variables, with the proxy-position depending on current market data. This means they need to be recomputed whenever the market data changes. In contrast, primary instruments are linear in the DEAF approach, so the proxy positions are independent of current market data.
4 The expansion is base-currency dependent, and thus needs to be recomputed every time the base currency is changed. In contrast, proxies in the DEAF approach are base-currency independent.

In general, when an example of first-order deal proxies is given in Morgan and Reuters (1996), the basic variable is taken to be the market *price*. This is stated in Morgan and Reuters (1996, table 6.3), where the underlying market variables are stated to be FX rates, bond prices, and stock prices. For example, in Morgan and Reuters (1996, §1.2.2.1), the return on a DEM put is written as $\delta_{\text{DEM/USD}}$, where $r_{\text{DEM/USD}}$ is the return on the DEM/USD exchange rate and δ is the delta for the option.[4]

Consider the case of a GBP-denominated zero-coupon bond with a maturity of τ years. For a USD-based investor, the PV of this bond is given by

$$v_{t_0} = \text{USD} \, N X_{\text{GBP/USD}}(t_0) D_\tau^{\text{GBP}}(t_0)$$

where $X_{\text{GBP/USD}}$ is the (unitless) GBP/USD exchange rate, $D_\tau^{\text{GBP}}(t_0)$ denotes the τ-year ZCDF for GBP, and N is the principal amount of the bond. We see that the PV is a *non-linear* function of the GBP/USD exchange rate and the ZCDF for GBP. (While the valuation function is a linear function of the risk factors *individually*, it is quadratic in the set of risk factors as a whole.) Expanding the valuation function in a first-order Taylor series in these variables, we get

$$\mathrm{d}v_t = \frac{\partial v}{\partial D_\tau^{\text{GBP}}} \mathrm{d}D_\tau^{\text{GBP}} + \frac{\partial v}{\partial X_{\text{GBP/USD}}} \mathrm{d}X_{\text{GBP/USD}}$$

$$= \text{USD} \, N(X_{\text{GBP/USD}} \mathrm{d}D_\tau^{\text{GBP}} + D_\tau^{\text{GBP}} \mathrm{d}X_{\text{GBP/USD}})$$

This says that the delta-equivalent position is a spot GBP position of ND_T^{GBP} and a τ-year GBP N ZCDF position with an exchange rate locked at $X_{GBP/USD}$. Note that these positions are precisely what one would obtain by following the standard mapping procedure for foreign cashflows in RiskMetrics (see example 2 in Morgan and Reuters, 1996). This non-linearity contrasts with the DEAF formulation, where we have seen that the value of this instrument is a linear function of the PAV $GBP_T(T)$ and the delta-equivalent position is just a fixed cashflow of GBP N at time T.

Commodity prices

Our treatment of commodities is somewhat different from the standard RiskMetrics approach, although it should generally give similar results. The reason for this is that the standard RiskMetrics approach is essentially 'dollar-centric', the RiskMetrics data sets give volatilities for forward commodities in forward dollars. The problem with this is that it conflates the commodity term structure with the dollar term structure. For example, to express the value of a forward copper position in JPY, we convert price in forward dollars to a price in spot dollars, using the USD yield curve, and then to JPY, based on the JPY/USD spot rate. As a result, a simple forward position becomes enmeshed with USD interest rates without good reason.

To carry out our program of treating commodities in the same way as foreign currencies, we need to convert the volatility and correlation data for commodities in the RiskMetrics data sets so that they reflect future commodity prices expressed in terms of spot commodity instead of future dollars. Fortunately, the volatilities and correlations for the commodity discount factors can be derived from those provided in the RiskMetrics data sets. The flavor of the calculations is similar to that for the change of base currency described in the previous appendix. This transformation would be done when the RiskMetrics files are read in.

Appendix 4: Valuation-date issues

We noted above that most VaR methodologies do not explicitly deal with the entire evolution of the risk factors and the valuation function between the anchor date and target date. Rather they just evaluate the valuation function as of the anchor date at perturbed values of the risk factors for the anchor date. This simplification, while done for strong practical reasons, can lead to surprising results.

Need for future valuation functions

Consider, for example, a cashflow in amount USD N in the base currency payable one year after the anchor date. We would write the valuation function with respect to the USD base currency in terms of our risk factors as

$$v_{t_0} = \text{USD } ND_1(t_0)$$

where $D_1(t_0)$ denotes the 1-year discount factor at time t_0. This equation was the starting point for the analysis in the example on page 191, where we calculated VaR for a 1-day time horizon. Scaling this example to a 1-year time horizon, as discussed on page 201 would give a VaR approximately 16 times as large.

But this is crazy! The value of the bond in one year is N, so there is no risk at all and VaR should be equal to zero. What went wrong? The problem is that we based our calculation on the valuation function as of the anchor date. But at the target date, the valuation function is given simply by

$$v_T = ND_0(T)$$

$$= N$$

Thus the formula that gives the value of the instrument in terms of risk factors changes over time. This is due to the fact that our risk factors are fixed-maturity assets. (Changing to risk factors with fixed-date assets is not a good solution to this problem as these assets will not be statistically stationary, indeed they will drift to a known value.)

The first idea that comes to mind to fix this problem is to use the spot valuation function as of the target date instead of the anchor date. While this would fix the problem for our 1-year cashflow, it causes other problems. For example, consider an FRA that resets between the anchor and target dates and pays after the target date. The value of this instrument as of the target date will depend on the risk-factor vector between the anchor and target date and this dependence will not be captured by the spot valuation function at the target date. For another example, consider a 6-month cashflow. In most systems, advancing the valuation date by a year and computing the value of this cashflow would simply return zero. It therefore appears that in order to properly handle these cases, the entire trajectory of the risk factors and the portfolio valuation function needs to be taken into account, i.e. we need to work with future valuation functions are described in Appendix 1.

Path dependency

In some instances, the future valuation function will only depend on the market-state vector at the target time T. When we can write the future valuation function as a function of $\mathbf{m}_T$ alone, we say that the future valuation function is **path-independent**. For example, consider a zero-coupon bond maturing after time T. The value of the bond at time T will depend solely on the term structure as of time T and is thus path independent. It should be recognized that many instruments that are not commonly thought of as being path dependent *are* path dependent in the context of future valuation. For example, consider a standard reset-up-front, pay-in-arrears swap that resets at time t_r and pays at time t_p, with $t_0 < t_r < T < t_p$. To perform future valuation at time T, we need to know the term-structure at time T, to discount the cashflow, as well as the term-structure as of time t_r, to fix the reset. Thus, we see that the swap is path dependent. Similar reasoning shows that an option expiring at time t_e and paying at time t_p, with $t_0 < t_e < T < t_p$, is, possibly strongly, path dependent.

Portfolio evolution

Portfolios evolve over time. There is a natural evolution of the portfolio due to events such as coupon and principal payments and the expiration and settlement of forward and option contracts. To accurately characterize the economic value of a portfolio at the target date, it is necessary to track cashflows that are received between the anchor and target dates and to make some reasonable assumptions as to how these received cashflows are reinvested.

Probably the most expedient approach to dealing with the effects of received cashflows is to incorporate a reinvestment assumption into the VaR methodology.

There are two obvious choices; a cashflow is reinvested in a cash account at the risk-free short rate or the coupon is reinvested in a zero-coupon bond maturing at time T, with the former choice being more natural since it is independent of the time horizon. If we make the latter choice, we need to know the term structure at time t_p; if we make the former choice, we need to know the short rate over the interval $[t_p, T]$.

Implementation considerations

Path-dependence and received cashflows in the context of future valuation can create difficulties in the implementation of VaR systems. The reason is that most instrument implementations simply do not support future valuation in the sense described above, distinguishing between anchor and target dates. Rather, all that is supported is a spot valuation function, with dependence on past market data, e.g. resets, embedded in the valuation function through a separate process. Thus the usual practice is to generate samples of the instantaneous market data vector as of time T, $\mathbf{m}_T$, and evaluate the instantaneous valuation function at time t_0 or T, i.e. $v_{t_0}(\mathbf{m}_T)$ or $v_T(\mathbf{m}_T)$. It is easy to think of cases where this practice gives seriously erroneous results. An obvious problem with using $v_{t_0}(\mathbf{m}_T)$ as a proxy for a future valuation function is that it will erroneously show market risk for a fixed cashflow payable at time T. A better choice is probably $v_T(\mathbf{m}_T)$, but this will return a PV of zero for a cashflow payable between t_0 and T. In addition, one needs to be careful about resets. For example, suppose there is a reset occurring at time t_r with $t_0 < t_r < T$. Since the spot valuation function only has market data as of time T available to it, it cannot determine the correct value of the reset, as it depends on past market data when viewed from time T. (In normal operation, the value of this reset would have been previously set by a separate process.) How the valuation function treats this missing reset is, of course, implementation dependent. For example, it may throw an error message, which would be the desired behavior in a trading environment or during a revaluation process, but is not very helpful in a simulation. Even worse, it might just fail silently, setting the missing reset to 0 or some other arbitrary value. To solve this problem completely, instrument implementations would have to support future valuation function with distinct anchor and target dates. Such a function would potentially need to access market-data values for times between the anchor and target date. As of today, valuation functions supporting these semantics are not generally available. Even if they were, a rigorous extension of even the parametric VaR methodology that would properly account for the intermediate evolutions of variables would be quite involved.

   We can, however, recommend a reasonably simple approximation that will at least capture the gross effects. We will just sketch the idea at a conceptual level. First of all, we construct DEAF proxies for all instruments based on the spot valuation function as of the anchor date. We then modify the mapping procedure as follows:

1   Exposures are numerically equal to the forward value of the asset at the target date rather than the present value at the anchor date. Forward values of assets for delivery prior to the target date are computed by assuming that the asset is reinvested until the target date at the forward price as of the anchor date.
2   Asset flows between the anchor and target dates do not result in discount-factor risk. Asset flows after the target date are mapped to discount factors with maturities equal to the difference between the delivery and target date.

Glossary of terms

Absolute Return: The change in value of an instrument or portfolio over the time horizon.

Analytic VaR: Any VaR methodology in which the distribution of portfolio value is approximated by an analytic expression. Variance/covariance VaR is a special case.

Anchor Date: Roughly speaking, 'today'. More formally, the date up until which market conditions are known.

DEAFs: Delta-equivalent asset flows. Primary asset flows that serve as proxies for derivative instruments in a VaR calculation.

DTS: Discounting term structure. Data structure used for discounting of future asset flows relative to their value today.

Exposure: The present value of the equivalent position in a fundamental asset.

Fundamental Asset: A fundamental market factor in the form of the market price for a traded asset.

Future Valuation Function: A function that gives the value of a financial instrument at the target date in terms of the evolution of the risk factors between the anchor and target date.

FX: Foreign exchange.

Historical VaR: A value-at-risk methodology in which the statistical model for the risk factors is directly tied to the historical time series of changes in these variables.

Maturity: The interval of time between the anchor date and the delivery of a given cashflow, option expiration, or other instrument lifecycle event.

Monte Carlo VaR: A value-at-risk methodology in which the distribution of portfolio values is estimated by drawing samples from the probabilistic model for the risk factors and constructing a histogram of the resulting portfolio values.

Native Currency: The usual currency in which the price of a given asset is quoted.

PAV: Primary asset value. A variable that denotes the value of an asset flow for spot or future delivery by a counterparty of a given credit quality.

PV: Present value. The value of a given asset as of the anchor date.

Relative Return: The change in value of an asset over the time horizon divided by its value at the anchor date.

Risk Factors: A set of market variables that determine the value of a financial portfolio. In most VaR methodologies, the starting point is a probabilistic model for the evolution of these factors.

Spot Valuation Function: A function that gives the value of a financial instrument at a given date in terms of the evolution of the risk factor vector for that date.

Target Date Date in the future on which we are assessing possible changes in portfolio value.

Time Horizon: The interval of time between the anchor and target dates.

VaR: Value at risk. A given percentile point in the profit and loss distribution between the anchor and target date.

Variance/Covariance VaR: A value-at-risk methodology in which the risk factors are modeled as jointly normal and the portfolio value is modeled as a linear combination of the risk factors and hence is normally distributed.

VTS: Volatility term structure. Data structure used for assigning spot and future asset flows to exposure vectors.

ZCDF: Zero-coupon discount factor. The ratio of the value of a given asset for future delivery with a given maturity by a counterparty of a given credit quality to the spot value of the asset.

Acknowledgments

This chapter largely reflects experience gained in building the Opus Value at Risk system at Renaissance Software and many of the ideas described therein are due to the leader of that project, Jim Lewis. The author would like to thank Oleg Zakharov and the editors of this book for their helpful comments on preliminary drafts of this chapter.

Notes

[1] RiskMetrics is a registered trademark of J. P. Morgan.

[2] We use the term spot rate to mean for exchange as of today. Quoted spot rates typically reflect a settlement lag, e.g. for exchange two days from today. There is a small adjustment between the two to account for differences in the short-term interest rates in the two currencies.

[3] Our initial impulse was to use the term **forward valuation function**, but this has an established and different meaning. The forward value of a portfolio, i.e. the value of the portfolio for forward delivery in terms of forward currency, is a deterministic quantity that is determined by an arbitrage relationship. In contrast, the future value is a stochastic quantity viewed from time t_0.

[4] The RiskMetrics Technical Document generally uses the notation r to indicate *log* returns. However, the words in Morgan and Reuters (1996, §1.2.2.1) seem to indicate that the variables are the prices themselves, not log prices.

References

Hull, J. C. (1997) *Options, Futures, and other Derivatives*, Prentice-Hall, Englewood Cliffs, NJ, third edition.

Morgan, J. P. and Reuters (1996) *RiskMetrics™-Technical Document*, Morgan Guaranty Trust Company, New York, fourth edition.

7

Additional risks in fixed-income markets

TERI L. GESKE

Introduction

Over the past ten years, risk management and valuation techniques in fixed-income markets have evolved from the use of static, somewhat naïve concepts such as Macaulay's duration and nominal spreads to option-adjusted values such as effective duration, effective convexity, partial or 'key rate' durations and option-adjusted spreads (OAS). This reflects both the increased familiarity with these more sophisticated measures and the now widespread availability of the analytical tools required to compute them, including option models and Monte Carlo analyses for securities with path-dependent options (such as mortgage-backed securities with embedded prepayment options).

However, although these option-adjusted measures are more robust, they focus exclusively on a security's or portfolio's *interest rate* sensitivity. While an adverse change in interest rates is the dominant risk factor in this market, there are other sources of risk which can have a material impact on the value of fixed-income securities. Those securities that offer a premium above risk-free Treasury rates do so as compensation either for some type of credit risk (i.e. that the issuer will be downgraded or actually default), or 'model risk' (i.e. the risk that valuations may vary because future cash flows change in ways that models cannot predict). We have seen that gains from a favorable interest rate move can be more than offset by a change in credit spreads and revised prepayment estimates can significantly alter previous estimates of a mortgage portfolio's interest rate sensitivity. The presence of these additional risks highlights the need for measures that explain and quantify a bond's or portfolio's sensitivity to changes in these variables.

This chapter discusses two such measures: spread duration and prepayment uncertainty. We describe how these measures may be computed, provide some historical perspective on changes in these risk factors, and compare spread duration and prepayment uncertainty to interest rate risk measures for different security types. A risk manager can use these measures to evaluate the firm's exposure to changes in credit spreads and uncertainty associated with prepayments in the mortgage-backed securities market. Since spread duration and prepayment uncertainty may be calculated both for individual securities and at the portfolio level, they may be used to establish limits with respect to both individual positions and the firm's overall exposure to these important sources of risk. Both measures are summarized below:

- **Spread Duration** – A measure of a bond's (or portfolio's) credit spread risk, i.e. its sensitivity to a change in the premium over risk-free Treasury rates demanded by investors in a particular segment of the market, where the premium is expressed in terms of an option-adjusted spread (OAS). The impact of a change in spreads is an important source of risk for all dollar-denominated fixed-income securities other than US Treasuries, and will become increasingly important in European debt markets if the corporate bond market grows as anticipated as a result of EMU. To calculate spread duration, a bond's OAS (as implied by its current price) is increased and decreased by a specified amount; two new prices are computed based on these new OASs, holding the current term structure of interest rates and volatilities constant. The bond's spread duration is the average percentage change in its price, relative to its current price, given the higher and lower OASs (scaled to a 100 bp shift in OAS).

  Spread duration allows risk managers to quantify and differentiate a portfolio's sensitivity to changes in the risk premia demanded across market segments such as investment grade and high yield corporates, commercial mortgage-backed and asset-backed securities and so on.

- **Prepayment Uncertainty** – A measure of the sensitivity of a security's price to a change in the forecasted rate of future prepayments. This concept is primarily applicable to mortgage-backed securities,[1] where homeowner prepayments due to refinancing incentives and other conditions are difficult to predict. To calculate this measure, alternative sets of future cash flows for a security are generated by adjusting the current prepayment forecast upward and downward by some percentage, e.g. 10% (for mortgage-backed securities, prepayment rates may be expressed using the 'PSA' convention, or as SMMs, single monthly mortality rates, or in terms of CPR, conditional/constant prepayment rates). Holding all other things constant (including the initial term structure of interest rates, volatility inputs and the security's OAS), two new prices are computed using the slower and faster versions of the base case prepayment forecasts. The average percentage change in price resulting from the alternative prepayment forecasts versus the current price is the measure of prepayment uncertainty; the more variable a security's cash flows under the alternative prepay speeds versus the current forecast, the greater its prepayment uncertainty and therefore its 'model' risk.

  An alternative approach to deriving a prepayment uncertainty measure is to evaluate the sensitivity of *effective duration* to a change in prepayment forecasts. This approach provides additional information to the risk manager and may be used in place of or to complement the 'price sensitivity' form of prepayment uncertainty. Either method helps to focus awareness on the fact that while mortgage-backed security valuations capture the impact of prepayment variations under different interest rate scenarios (typically via some type of Monte Carlo simulation), these valuations are subject to error because of the uncertainty of any prepayment forecast.

We now discuss these risk measures in detail, beginning with spread duration.

Spread duration

As summarized above, spread duration describes the sensitivity of a bond's price to a change in its option-adjusted spread (OAS). For those who may be unfamiliar with the concept of option-adjusted spreads, we give a brief definition here. In a nutshell, OAS is the constant spread (in basis points) which, when layered onto the Treasury spot curve, equates the present value of a fixed-income security's expected future cash flows *adjusted to reflect the exercise of any embedded options* (calls, prepayments, interest rate caps and so on) to its market price (see Figure 7.1).

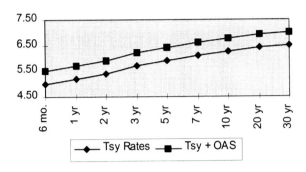

Figure 7.1   Treasury curve and OAS.

To solve for a security's OAS, we invoke the appropriate option model (e.g. a binomial or trinomial tree or finite difference algorithm for callable/puttable corporate bonds, or some type of Monte Carlo-simulation for mortgage-backed and other path-dependent securities) to generate expected future cash flows under interest rate uncertainty and iteratively search for the constant spread which, when layered onto the Treasury spot rates, causes the present value of those option-adjusted cash flows, discounted at the Treasury spot rates plus the OAS, to equal the market price of the security.

OAS versus nominal spread

For bonds with embedded options (e.g. call options, prepayments, embedded rate caps, and so on), the difference between the option-adjusted spread and nominal spread (the difference between the bond's yield-to-maturity or yield-to-call and the yield on a specific Treasury) can be substantial. Compared to nominal spread, OAS is a superior measure of a security's risk premium for a number of reasons:

- OAS analysis incorporates the potential variation in the present value of a bond's expected future cash flows due to option exercise or changes in prepayment speeds. Nominal spread is based on a single cash flow forecast and therefore cannot accommodate the impact of interest rate uncertainty on expected future cash flows.
- OAS is measured relative to the entire spot curve, whereas nominal spread is measured relative to a single point on the Treasury curve. Even for option-free securities, this is a misleading indication of expected return relative to a portfolio of risk-free Treasuries offering the same cash flows, particularly in a steep yield curve environment.
- Nominal spread is a comparison to a single average life-matched Treasury, but if a security's average life is uncertain its nominal spread can change dramatically (especially if the yield curve is steeply sloped) if a small change in the Treasury curve causes the bond to 'cross over' and trade to its final maturity date instead

of a call date, or vice versa. OAS is computed relative to the entire set of Treasury spot rates and uses expected cash flows which may fluctuate as interest rates change, thus taking into account the fact that a security's average life can change when interest rates shift and a call option is exercised or prepayments speed up or slow down.

- Nominal spread assumes all cash flows are discounted at a single yield, which ultimately implies that cash flows from different risk-free securities which are paid in the same period (e.g. Year 1 or Year 2) will be discounted at different rates, simply because the securities have different *final* maturities, and so on.

Although OAS is clearly superior to nominal spread in determining relative value, there are a number of problems associated with using OAS. For example, OAS calculations can vary from one model to another due to differences in volatility parameters, prepayment forecasts, etc. Nonetheless, OAS is now a commonly accepted valuation tool, particularly when comparing the relative value of fixed-income securities across different markets.

Spread risk – a 'real-world' lesson

In the Fall of 1998, fixed-income securities markets experienced unprecedented volatility in response to the liquidity crisis (real or perceived) and 'flight to quality' that resulted from the turmoil in Russian and Brazilian debt markets and from problems associated with the 'meltdown' of the Long Term Capital Management hedge fund. As Treasury prices rallied, sending yields to historic lows, spreads on corporate bonds, mortgage-backed securities and asset-backed securities all widened in the course of a few days by more than the sum of spread changes that would normally occur over a number of months or even years. Many 'post-mortem' analyses described the magnitude of the change as a '5 standard deviation move', and one market participant noted that 'spreads widened more than anyone's risk models predicted and meeting margin calls sucked up liquidity' (*Bond Week*, 1998). Spreads on commercial mortgage-backed securities widened to the point where liquidity disappeared completely and no price quotes could be obtained. While there are undoubtedly many lessons to be learned from this experience, certainly one is that while a firm's interest rate risk may be adequately hedged, spread risk can overwhelm interest rate risk when markets are in turmoil.

Spread Duration/Spread Risk

Since investors demand a risk premium to hold securities other than risk-free (i.e. free of credit risk, liquidity risk, prepayment model risk, etc.) debt, and that risk premium is not constant over time, spread duration is an important measure to include in the risk management process. Spreads can change in response to beliefs about the general health of the domestic economy, to forecasts about particular sectors (e.g. if interest rates rise, spreads in the finance sector may increase due to concerns about the profitability of the banking industry), to political events (particularly in emerging markets) that affect liquidity, and so on. Often, investors are just as concerned with the magnitude and direction of changes in spreads as with changes in interest rates, and spread duration allows the risk manager to quantify the impact of changes in option-adjusted sector spreads across a variety of fixed-income investment alternatives.

Computing spread duration

To calculate spread duration, we increase and decrease a security's OAS by some amount and, holding Treasury (spot) rates and volatilities at current levels, compute two new prices based on these new spreads:

$$\frac{P_{\text{OAS}-100\,\text{bps}} - P_{\text{OAS}+100\,\text{bps}}}{2 \times P_{\text{Base case OAS}}} \times 100$$

Spread duration is the average percentage change in the security's price given the lower and higher OASs. It allows us to quickly translate a basis point change in spreads to a percentage change in price, and by extension, a dollar value change in a position. For example, the impact of a 20 bp shift in OAS on the price of a bond with a spread duration of 4.37 is estimated by $(0.20 \times 4.37) = 0.874\%$. Therefore, a $50 million position in this security would decline by \$43.7K ($50 million $\times$ 0.874) if spreads widened by 20 bps.

Spread changes – historical data

Since the correlation between changes in credit spreads and changes in interest rates is unstable (the correlation even changes sign over time), it is important to measure a portfolio's or an institution's exposure to spread risk independent of an assessment of interest rate risk. For example, a portfolio of Treasuries with an effective duration of 5.0 has no spread risk, but does have interest rate risk. A portfolio of corporate bonds with an effective duration of 3.0 has less interest rate risk than the Treasury portfolio, but if adverse moves in interest rates and spreads occur simultaneously, the corporate portfolio may be a greater source of risk than the Treasury portfolio. Spread risk affects corporate bonds, mortgage-backed securities, asset-backed securities, municipal bonds and so on, and a change in spreads in one segment of the market may not carry over to other areas, as the fundamentals and technicals that affect each of these markets are typically unrelated. Nonetheless, we have seen that in times of extreme uncertainty, correlations across markets can converge rapidly to $+1.0$, eliminating the benefits that might otherwise be gained by diversifying spread risk across different market sectors.

What magnitude of spread changes can one reasonably expect over a given period? Table 7.1 shows the average and standard deviations of option-adjusted spreads for various sectors over the six-year period, August 1992 to July 1998. In parentheses, we show the standard deviations computed for a slightly different six-year period, November 1992 to October 1998 (note: statistics were computed from weekly observations). The reason the two standard deviations are so different is that the values in parentheses include October 1998 data and therefore reflect the spread volatility experienced during the market crisis discussed above. Of course, six years is a long time and statistics can change significantly depending upon the observations used to compute them, so we also show the average and standard deviation of option-adjusted spreads measured over a one-year period, August 1997 to July 1998, with the standard deviation computed over the one year period November 1997 to October 1998 shown in parentheses.

When evaluating the importance of spread risk, it is important to stress-test a portfolio under scenarios that reflect possible market conditions. Although the October 1998 experience may certainly be viewed as a rare event, if we use the one-year data set *excluding* October 1998 to forecast future spread changes (based on

Table 7.1   Average and standard deviations of option-adjusted spreads

Sector/quality	Option-Adjusted Spread (OAS) six years of data		Option-Adjusted Spread (OAS) one year of data	
	8/92–7/98 Average	(11/92–10/98) Standard dev.	8/97–7/98 Average	(11/97–10/98) Standard dev.
Industrial – AA	47	6.2 (8.8)	49	4.4 (13.8)
Industrial – A	67	8.4 (11.8)	68	5.5 (18.2)
Industrial – BAA	111	21.2 (22.7)	93	5.8 (26.9)
Utility – AA	48	5.4 (8.1)	47	2.9 (15.0)
Utility – A	72	14.8 (14.4)	63	5.1 (15.2)
Utility – BAA	95	15.1 (15.7)	87	5.4 (17.8)
Finance – AA	56	6.5 (11.6)	59	4.7 (21.3)
Finance – A	74	11.1 (16.1)	72	5.1 (27.2)
Finance – BAA	99	16.1 (19.7)	96	9.1 (28.9)
Mortgage pass-throughs (30-yr FNMA)	73	16.4 (17.1)	54	11.2 (25.2)
	Average:	12.1 (14.6)	Average:	5.9 (20.9)

Note: OASs for corporate sectors are based on securities with an effective duration of approximately 5.0.

standard deviation), we could potentially underestimate a portfolio's spread risk by more than threefold (the average standard deviation based on one year of data including October 1998 is 3.5 times the average standard deviation based on one year of data excluding October 1998). When stress-testing a portfolio, it would be a good idea to combine spread changes with interest rate shocks – for example, what would happen if interest rates rise by X bps while corporate spreads widen by Y bps and mortgage spreads widen by Z bps? If we have computed the portfolio's effective duration and the spread duration of the corporate and mortgage components of the portfolio, we can easily estimate the impact of this scenario: [(Effective duration$_{\text{Overall}}$ × X) + (Spread duration$_{\text{Corporates}}$ × Y) + (Spread duration$_{\text{Mortgages}}$ × Z)].

Spread risk versus interest rate risk

How, if at all, does spread duration relate to the more familiar effective duration value that describes a bond's or portfolio's sensitivity to changes in interest rates? In this section, we attempt to provide some intuition for how spread risk compares to interest rate risk for different types of securities. In attempting to understand spread duration, it is necessary to think about how a change in spreads affects both the present value of a security's future cash flows and the amount and timing of the cash flows themselves. In this respect, an interesting contrast between corporate bonds and mortgage-backed securities may be observed when analyzing spread duration.

Corporate bonds

A change in the OAS of a callable (or puttable) corporate bond directly affects the cash flows an investor expects to receive, since the corporate issuer (who is long the call option) will decide whether or not to call the bond on the basis of its price in the secondary market. If a security's OAS narrows sufficiently, its market price will rise above its call price, causing the issuer to exercise the call option. Likewise, the investor who holds a puttable bond will choose to exercise the put option if secondary market spreads widen sufficiently to cause the bond's price to drop below the put price (typically par).

Since changing the bond's OAS by X basis points has the same impact on its price as shifting the underlying Treasury yields by an equal number of basis points, the spread duration for a fixed rate corporate bond is actually equal to its effective duration.[2] Therefore, either spread duration or effective duration can be used to estimate the impact of a change in OAS on a corporate bond's price. The same applies to a portfolio of corporate bonds, so if a risk management system captures the effective (option-adjusted) duration of a corporate bond inventory, there is no need to separately compute the spread duration of these holdings. (Note that Macaulay's, a.k.a. 'Modified', duration is *not* an acceptable proxy for the spread risk of corporate bonds with embedded options, for the same reasons it fails to adequately describe the interest rate sensitivity of these securities.)

Floating rate securities

Although we can see that for fixed rate corporate bonds, spread duration and effective duration are the same, for floating rate notes (FRNs), this is not the case. The effective duration of an (uncapped) FRN is roughly equal to the amount of time to its next reset date. For example, an FRN with a monthly reset would have an effective duration of approximately 0.08, indicating the security has very little interest rate sensitivity. However, since a change in secondary spreads does not cause the FRN's coupon rate to change; a FRN can have substantial spread risk. This is due to the impact of a change in secondary spreads on the value of the remaining coupon payments – if spreads widen, the FRN's coupon will be below the level now demanded by investors, so the present value of the remaining coupon payments will decline. The greater the time to maturity, the longer the series of below-market coupon payments paid to the investor and the greater the decline in the value of the FRN. Therefore, the spread duration of an FRN is related to its time to maturity; e.g. an FRN maturing in two years has a lower spread duration than an FRN maturing in ten years.

Mortgage passthroughs

The spread duration of a mortgage-backed security is less predictable than for a corporate bond and is not necessarily related to its effective duration. We observed that for corporate bonds, a change in secondary market spreads affects the cash flows to the bondholder because of the effect on the exercise of a call or put option. Can we make the same claim for mortgage-backed securities? In other words, can we predict whether or not a change in secondary market mortgage spreads will affect a homeowner's prepayment behavior, thereby altering the expected future cash flows to the holder of a mortgage-backed security? What implications does this have for the spread risk involved in holding these securities?

Let us consider two separate possibilities, i.e. that homeowners' prepayment decisions are *not* affected by changes in secondary spreads for MBS, and conversely, that spread changes *do* affect homeowners' prepayments. If we assume that a homeowner's incentive to refinance is not affected by changes in spreads, we would expect the spread duration of a mortgage passthrough to resemble its Macaulay's duration, with good reason. Recall that Macaulay's duration tells us the percentage change in a bond's price given a change in yield, assuming no change in cash flows. Spread duration is calculated by discounting a security's projected cash flows using a new OAS, which is roughly analogous to changing its yield. Therefore, if we assume that a change in spreads has no effect on a mortgage-backed security's expected cash flows, its spread duration should be close to its Macaulay's duration.[3]

However, it may be more appropriate to assume that a change in OAS affects not only the discount rate used to compute the present value of expected future cash flows from a mortgage pool, but also the refinancing incentive faced by homeowners, thereby changing the amount and timing of the cash flows themselves. As discussed in the next section on prepayment uncertainty, the refinancing incentive is a key factor in prepayment modeling that can have a significant affect on the valuation and assessment of risk of mortgage-backed securities. If we assume that changes in spreads do affect refinancings, the spread duration of a mortgage passthrough would be unrelated to its Macaulay's duration, and unrelated to its effective (option-adjusted) duration as well.

Adjustable rate mortgage pools (ARMs) are similar to FRNs in that changes in spreads, unlike interest rate shifts, do not affect the calculation of the ARM's coupon rate and thus would not impact the likelihood of encountering any embedded reset or lifetime caps. Therefore, an ARM's spread duration may bear little resemblance to its effective duration, which reflects the interest rate risk of the security that is largely due to the embedded rate caps.

CMOs and other structured securities

The spread duration of a CMO depends upon the deal structure and the tranche's payment seniority within the deal. If we assume that a widening (narrowing) of spreads causes prepayments to decline (increase), a CMO with extension (contraction) risk could have substantial spread risk. Also, it is important to remember that as interest rates change, changes in CMO spreads may be different than changes collateral spreads. For example, when interest rates fall, spreads on well-protected PACs may tighten as spreads on 'cuspy' collateral widen, if investors trade out of the more prepayment-sensitive passthroughs into structured securities with less contraction risk. Therefore, when stress-testing a portfolio of mortgage-backed securities, it is important to include simulation scenarios that combine changes in interest rates with changes in spreads that differentiate by collateral type (premium versus discount) and by CMO tranche type (e.g. stable PACs and VADMs versus inverse floaters, IOs and so on).

PSA-linked index-amortizing notes (IANs) have enjoyed some degree of popularity among some portfolio managers as a way to obtain MBS-like yields without actually increasing exposure to mortgage-backed securities. Since the principal amortization rate on these securities is linked to the prepayment speed on a reference pool of mortgage collateral, one might think that the spread duration of an IAN would be similar to the spread duration of the collateral pool. However, it is possible that spreads on these structured notes could widen for reasons that do not affect the market for mortgage-backed securities (such as increased regulatory scrutiny of the structured note market). Therefore, when stress-testing a portfolio that includes both mortgage-backed securities and IANs, it would be appropriate to simulate different changes in spreads across these asset types.

To summarize, spread risk for corporate bonds is analogous to interest rate risk, as a change in OAS produces the same change in price as a change in interest rates.

Spread duration for mortgage-backed securities reflects the fact that a change in OAS affects the present value of expected future cash flows, but whether or not the cash flows themselves are affected by the change in the OAS is a function of assumptions made by the prepayment model used in the analysis. The spread duration of a diversified portfolio measures the overall sensitivity to a change in OASs across all security types, giving the portfolio manager important information about a portfolio's risk profile which no other risk measure provides.

Prepayment uncertainty

Now we turn to the another important source of risk in fixed-income markets, prepayment uncertainty. Prepayment modeling is one of the most critical variables in the mortgage-backed securities (MBS) market, as a prepayment forecast determines a security's value and its perceived 'riskiness' (where 'risky' is defined as having a large degree of interest rate sensitivity, described by a large effective duration and/or negative convexity). For those who may be unfamiliar with CMOs, certain types of these securities (such as principal-only tranches, and inverse floaters) can have effective durations that are two or three times greater than the duration of the underlying mortgage collateral, while interest-only (IO) tranches typically have negative durations, and many CMOs have substantial negative convexity. Changes in prepayment expectations can have a considerable impact on the value of mortgage-backed and asset-backed securities and therefore represents an important source of risk.

Let's briefly review how mortgage prepayment modeling affects the valuation of mortgage-backed securities. To determine the expected future cash flows of a security, a prepayment model must predict the impact of a change in interest rates on a homeowner's incentive to prepay (refinance) a mortgage; as rates decline, prepayments typically increase, and vice versa. Prepayment models take into account the age or 'seasoning' of the collateral, as a homeowner whose mortgage is relatively new is less likely to refinance in the near-term than a homeowner who has not recently refinanced. Prepayment models also typically incorporate 'burnout', a term that reflects the fact that mortgage pools will contain a certain percentage of homeowners who, despite a number of opportunities over the years, simply cannot or will not refinance their mortgages. Many models also reflect the fact that prepayments tend to peak in the summer months (a phenomenon referred to as 'seasonality'), as homeowners will often postpone moving until the school year is over to ease their children's transition to a new neighborhood. Prepayment models attempt to predict the impact of these and other factors on the level of prepayments received from a given pool of mortgages over the life of the collateral.

Earlier, we alluded to the fact that mortgage valuation is a path-dependent problem. This is because the path that interest rates follow will determine the extent to which a given collateral pool is 'burned out' when a new refinancing opportunity arises. For example, consider a mortgage pool consisting of fairly new 7.00% mortgages, and two interest rate paths generated by a Monte Carlo simulation. For simplicity, we make the following assumptions:

- Treasury rates are at 5.25% across the term structure
- Mortgage lending rates are set at 150 bps over Treasuries
- Homeowners require at least a 75 bp incentive to refinance their mortgages.

Given this scenario, homeowners with a 7.00% mortgage do not currently have sufficient incentive to trigger a wave of refinancings. Now, imagine that along the first interest rate path Treasury rates rise to 6.00% over the first two years, then decline to 4.75% at the end of year 3; therefore, mortgage lending rates at the end of year 3 are at 6.25%, presenting homeowners with sufficient incentive to refinance at a lower rate for the first time in three years. Along this path, we would expect a significant amount of prepayments at the end of year 3. On the second path, imagine that rates decline to 4.75% by the end of the first year and remain there. This gives homeowners an opportunity to refinance their 7.00% mortgages for two full years before a similar incentive exists on the first path. Consequently, by the end of year 3 we would expect that most homeowners who wish to refinance have already done so, and the cash flows forecasted for the end of year 3 would differ markedly compared to the first path, even though interest rates are the same on both paths at that point in time.

Therefore, we cannot forecast the prepayments to be received at a given point in time simply by observing the current level of interest rate; we must know the path that rates followed prior to that point. In valuing mortgage-backed securities, this is addressed by using some type of Monte Carlo simulation to generate a sufficient number of different interest rate paths which provide the basis for a prepayment model to predict cash flows from the collateral pool under a variety of possible paths, based upon the history of interest rates experienced along each path.

Differences in prepayment models

Prepayment speed forecasts in the mortgage-backed securities market often differ considerably across various reliable dealers. Table 7.2 shows the median prepayment estimates provided to the Bond Market Association by ten dealer firms for different types of mortgage collateral, along with the high and low estimates that contributed to the median. Note that in many cases, the highest dealer prepayment forecast is more than twice as fast as the lowest estimate for the same collateral type.

To illustrate the degree to which differences in prepayment model forecasts can affect one's estimate of a portfolio's characteristics, we created a portfolio consisting

Table 7.2 Conventional 30-year fixed-rate mortgages as of 15 October 1998

Collateral type		Dealer prepay (PSA%) forecast			High versus low differences	
Coupon	Issue year	Median	Low	High	Absolute	Percent
6.0	1998	170	152	286	134 PSA	188%
6.0	1996	176	150	256	156 PSA	171%
6.0	1993	173	137	243	106 PSA	177%
6.5	1998	226	175	365	190 PSA	209%
6.5	1996	234	176	320	144 PSA	182%
6.5	1993	215	151	326	175 PSA	216%
7.0	1998	314	213	726	513 PSA	341%
7.0	1996	334	235	585	350 PSA	249%
7.0	1993	300	219	483	264 PSA	221%
7.5	1997	472	344	907	563 PSA	264%
7.5	1993	391	311	721	410 PSA	232%

of the different mortgage collateral shown in Table 7.2, with equal par amounts of eleven collateral pools with various coupons and maturities, using the 'Low' (slowest) PSA% and the 'High' (fastest) PSA% for each collateral type. Using the 'Low' speed, the portfolio had an average life of 6.85 years, with a duration of 4.73; using the 'High' speeds, the same portfolio had an average life of 3.67 years and a duration of 2.69. Clearly, the uncertainty in prepayment modeling can have a large impact on one's assessment of a portfolio's risk profile.

There are a number of reasons why no two prepayment models will produce the same forecast, even with the same information about the interest rate environment and the characteristics of the mortgage collateral of interest. For example, different firms' prepayment models may be calibrated to different historical data sets – some use five or even ten years of data, others may use data from only the past few years; some models attach greater weight to more recent data, others attach equal weight to all time periods; the variables used to explain and forecast prepayment behavior differ across models, and so on. Therefore, differences in prepayment modeling across well-respected providers is to be expected.[4]

In addition to differences in the way models are calibrated and specified, there is some likelihood that the historical data used to fit the model no longer reflects current prepayment behavior. When new prepayment data indicates that current homeowner behavior is not adequately described by existing prepayment models, prepayment forecasts will change as dealers and other market participants revise their models in light of the new empirical evidence For example, in recent years mortgage lenders have become more aggressive in offering low-cost or no-cost refinancing. As a result, a smaller decline in interest rates is now sufficient to entice homeowners to refinance their mortgages compared to five years ago (the required 'refinance incentive' has changed). Further developments in the marketplace (e.g. the ability to easily compare lending rates and refinance a mortgage over the Internet) will undoubtedly affect future prepayment patterns in ways that the historical data used to fit today's prepayment models does not reflect.

As mentioned previously, in the Fall of 1998 a combination of events wreaked havoc in fixed-income markets. Traditional liquidity sources dried up in the MBS market, which forced a number of private mortgage lenders to file for bankruptcy over the course of a few days. At the same time, Treasury prices rose markedly as investors sought the safe haven of US Treasuries in the wake of the uncertainties in other markets. As a rule, when Treasury yields decline mortgage prepayments are expected to increase, because mortgage lenders are expected to reduce borrowing rates in response to the lower interest rate environment. This time, however, mortgage lenders actually *raised* their rates, because the significant widening of spreads in the secondary market meant that loans originated at more typical (narrower) spreads over Treasury rates were no longer worth as much in the secondary market, and many lenders rely on loan sales to the secondary market as their primary source of funds. (Note that this episode is directly relevant to the earlier discussion of spread duration for mortgage-backed securities.)

These conditions caused considerable uncertainty in prepayment forecasting. Long-standing assumptions about the impact of a change in Treasury rates on refinancing activity did not hold up but it was uncertain as to whether or not this would be a short-lived phenomenon. Therefore, it was unclear whether prepayment models should be revised to reflect the new environment or whether this was a short-term aberration that did not warrant a permanent change to key modeling parameters. During this time, the reported durations of well-known benchmark mortgage indices, such as the Lehman Mortgage Index and Salomon Mortgage Index, swung wildly (one benchmark index's duration more than doubled over the course of a week), indicating extreme uncertainty in risk assessments among leading MBS dealers. In other words, there was little agreement as to prepayment expectations for, and therefore the value of, mortgage-backed securities.

Therefore we must accept the fact that a prepayment model can only provide a forecast, or an 'educated guess' about actual future prepayments. We also know that the market consensus about expected future prepayments can change quickly, affecting the valuation and risk measures (such as duration and convexity) that are being used to manage a portfolio of these securities. Therefore, the effect of revised prepayment expectations on the valuation of mortgage-backed securities constitutes an additional source of risk for firms that trade and/or invest in these assets. This risk, which we may call prepayment uncertainty risk, may be thought of as a 'model risk' since it derives from the inherent uncertainty of all prepayment models.

For an investment manager who is charged with managing a portfolio's exposure to mortgages relative to a benchmark, or for a risk manager who must evaluate a firm's interest rate risk including its exposure to mortgage-backed securities, this episode clearly illustrates the importance of understanding the sensitivity of a valuation or risk model's output to a change in a key modeling assumption. We do this by computing a 'prepayment uncertainty' measure that tests the 'stability' of a model's output given a change in prepayment forecasts.

Defining a measure of prepayment uncertainty

While standard definitions for effective duration and convexity have gained universal acceptance as measures of interest rate risk,[5] no standard set of prepayment uncertainty measures yet exists. Some proposed measures have been called 'prepayment durations' or 'prepayment sensitivities' (Sparks and Sung, 1995; Patruno, 1994). Here, we describe three measures that are readily understood and capture the major dimensions of prepayment uncertainty. These measures are labeled overall prepayment uncertainty, refinancing ('refi') partial prepayment uncertainty, and relocation ('relo') partial payment uncertainty.

To derive an overall prepayment uncertainty measure, the 'base case' prepayment speeds predicted by a model are decreased by 10%, then increased by 10%, and two new prices are derived under the slower and faster versions of the model (holding the term structure of interest rates, volatilities and security's option-adjusted spread constant):[6]

$$\frac{P_{SMM-10\%} - P_{SMM+10\%}}{2 \times P_{\text{Base case } SMM}} \times 100$$

where P = price and SMM = single monthly mortality rate (prepayment speed expressed as a series of monthly rates).

Computed this way, securities backed by discount collateral tend to show a negative prepayment uncertainty. This makes intuitive sense, as a slowdown in prepayment speeds means the investor must wait longer to be repaid at par. Conversely, securities backed by premium collateral tend to show a positive prepayment uncertainty, because faster prepayments decrease the amount of future income expected from the high-coupon mortgage pool compared to the base case forecast.

Note that for CMOs, a tranche may be priced at a premium to par even though the underlying collateral is at a discount, and vice versa. Therefore, one should not assume that the prepayment uncertainty of a CMO is positive or negative simply by noting whether the security is priced below or above par.

Refinance and relocation uncertainty

One of the most important variables in a prepayment model is the minimum level or 'threshold' incentive it assumes a homeowner requires to go to the trouble of refinancing a mortgage. The amount of the required incentive has certainly declined over the past decade; in the early days of prepayment modeling, it was not unusual to assume that new mortgage rates had to be at least 150 bps lower than a homeowner's mortgage rate before refinancings would occur. Today, a prepayment model may assume that only a 75 bp incentive or less is necessary to trigger a wave of refinancings. Therefore, we may wish to examine the amount of risk associated with a mis-estimate in the minimum incentive the model assumes homeowners will require before refinancing their mortgages.

To do so, we separate the total prepayment uncertainty measure into two components: refinancing uncertainty and relocation uncertainty. The 'refi' measure describes the sensitivity of a valuation to changes in the above-mentioned refinancing incentive, and the 'relo' measure shows the sensitivity to a change in the level of prepayments that are independent of the level of interest rates (i.e. due to demographic factors such as a change in job status or location, birth of children, divorce, retirement, and so on). Table 7.3 shows the overall and partial ('refi' and 'relo' prepayment uncertainties) for selected 30-year passthroughs.

Table 7.3 Prepayment uncertainty – 30-year mortgage collateral as of August 1998

Coupon	Collateral seasoning*	Price	Prepayment uncertainty (%)			Effective duration
			Total	Refi	Relo	
6.50%	New	99.43	−0.042	0.036	−0.080	3.70
7.50%	New	102.70	0.169	0.155	0.014	1.93
8.50%	New	103.69	0.300	0.245	0.055	1.42
6.50%	Moderate	99.60	−0.024	0.036	−0.060	3.37
7.50%	Moderate	102.51	0.191	0.161	0.031	1.92
8.50%	Moderate	104.38	0.341	0.257	0.083	1.87
6.50%	Seasoned	99.66	−0.014	0.038	−0.050	3.31
7.50%	Seasoned	102.58	0.206	0.163	0.042	1.94
8.50%	Seasoned	104.48	0.363	0.258	0.105	1.83

*Note: 'Seasoning' refers to the amount of time since the mortgages were originated; 'new' refers to loans originated within the past 24 months, 'moderate' applies to loans between 25 and 60 months old, fully 'seasoned' loans are more than 60 months old.

At first glance, these prepayment uncertainty values appear to be rather small. For example, we can see that a 10% increase or decrease in expected prepayments would produce a 0.191% change in the value of a moderately seasoned 7.50% mortgage pool. However, it is important to note that a 10% change in prepayment expectations is a rather modest 'stress test' to impose on a model. Recall the earlier discussion of differences in prepayment forecasts among Wall Street mortgage-backed securities dealers, where the high versus low estimates for various collateral types differed by more than 200%. Therefore, it is reasonable to multiply the prepayment uncertainty percentages derived from a 10% change in a model by a factor of 2 or 3, or even more.

It is interesting that there appears to be a negative correlation between total prepayment uncertainty and effective duration; in other words, as prepayment uncertainty increases, interest rate sensitivity decreases. Why would this be so? Consider the 'New 6.50%' collateral with a slightly negative total prepay uncertainty measure (-0.042). This collateral is currently priced at a slight discount to par, so a slowdown in prepayments would cause the price to decline as the investor would receive a somewhat below-market coupon longer than originally expected. Both the 'refi' and 'relo' components of this collateral's total uncertainty measure are relatively small, partly because these are new mortgages and we do not expect many homeowners who have just recently taken out a new mortgage to relocate or even to refinance in the near future, and partly because the collateral is priced slightly below but close to par. Since the collateral is priced below par, even a noticeable increase in the rate of response to a refinancing incentive would not have much impact on homeowners in this mortgage pool so the 'refi' component is negligible. Also, since the price of the collateral is so close to par it means the coupon rate on the security is roughly equal to the currently demanded market rate of interest. An increase or decrease in prepayments without any change in interest rates simply means the investor will earn an at-market interest rate for a shorter or longer period of time; the investor is be indifferent as to whether the principal is prepaid sooner or later under these circumstances as there are reinvestment opportunities at the same interest rate that is currently being earned.

In contrast, the effective duration is relatively large at 3.70 precisely because the collateral is new and is priced close to par. Since the collateral is new, the remaining cash flows extend further into the future than for older (seasoned) collateral pools and a change in interest rates would have a large impact on the present value of those cash flows. Also, since the price is so close to par a small decline in interest rates could cause a substantial increase in prepayments as homeowners would have a new-found incentive to refinance (in other words, the prepayment option is close to at-the-money).

This highlights a subtle but important difference between the impact of a change in refinance incentive due to a change in interest rates, which effective duration reflects, and the impact of a prepayment model misestimate of refinancing activity *absent any change in interest rates*. We should also note that since prepayment uncertainty is positive for some types of collateral and negative for others, it is possible to construct a portfolio with a prepayment uncertainty of close to zero by diversifying across collateral types.

Prepayment uncertainty – CMOs

For certain CMO tranche types, such as IO (interest-only), PO (principal only), inverse floaters and various 'support' tranches, and mortgage strips, the prepayment uncertainty measures can attain much greater magnitude, both positive and negative, than for passthroughs. By the same token, well-protected PACs will exhibit a lesser degree of prepayment uncertainty than the underlying pass-through collateral. At times, the prepayment uncertainty values for CMOs may seem counterintuitive; in other words, tranches that one would expect to be highly vulnerable to a small change in prepayment forecasts have fairly low prepayment uncertainties, and vice versa. This surprising result is a good reminder of the complexity of these securities. Consider the examples in Table 7.4.

Table 7.4 Prepayment uncertainties for CMOs

Tranche Type	IO	PO	PAC #1	PAC #2
Total prepay. uncertainty	7.638	−2.731	0.315	0.049
'Refi' uncertainty	5.601	−2.202	0.220	0.039
'Relo' uncertainty	2.037	−0.529	0.095	0.010
Collateral prepay. uncertainty	0.190	(re-remic)	0.115	0.177

Here we see an IO tranche with an overall prepayment uncertainty value of 7.638; in other words, the tranche's value would increase (decrease) by more than 7.5% if prepayments were expected to be 10% slower (faster) than originally forecasted. This is not surprising, given the volatile nature of IO tranches. If prepayment forecasts are revised to be faster than originally expected, it means that the (notional) principal balance upon which the IO's cash flows are based is expected to pay down more quickly, thus reducing the total interest payments to the IO holder. In contrast, the prepayment uncertainty of the collateral pool underlying the IO tranche is a modest 0.19 – a 10% change in expected prepayment speeds would produce only a small change in the value of the collateral.

One would expect PO tranches to exhibit fairly large prepayment uncertainty measures as well, as POs are priced at a substantial discount to par (they are zero coupon instruments) and a change in prepayment forecasts means the tranche holder expects to recoup that discount either sooner or later than originally estimated. The total prepayment uncertainty for this particular PO is –2.731; note that the underlying collateral of this PO is a 're-remic' – in other words, the collateral is a combination of CMO tranches from other deals, which may be backed by various types of collateral. In a re-remic, the underlying collateral may be a combination of highly seasoned, premium mortgages of various 'vintages' so it is virtually impossible to estimate the tranche's sensitivity to prepayment model risk simply by noting that it is a PO. The exercise of computing a prepayment uncertainty measure for CMOs reminds us that these are complicated securities whose sensitivities to changing market conditions bears monitoring.

Measuring prepayment uncertainty – a different approach

An alternative way of looking at prepayment uncertainty is to consider the effect of a change in prepayment speed estimates on the effective duration of a mortgage or portfolio of mortgage-backed securities. Since many firms hedge their mortgage positions by shorting Treasuries with similar durations, it is important to note that that the duration of a mortgage portfolio is uncertain and can be something of a moving target.

These tables show the impact of a ± 10% change in prepayment speeds on the average life, effective duration and convexity of different types of mortgage collateral. We can see that a small change in prepayment expectations could significantly

Table 7.5   Average life, effective duration and convexity – base case and prepay speeds ±10%

Coupon*	Base case				PSA% +10%				PSA% −10%			
	Avg life	Dur.	Conv	PSA%	Avg life	Dur	Conv	PSA%	Avg life	Dur	Conv	PSA%
30 year collateral												
6.50	3.8	3.9	−1.2	470	3.6	3.7	−1.2	517	4.2	4.1	−1.1	423
6.50	3.0	3.6	−1.0	467	2.7	3.4	−1.0	514	3.3	3.8	−1.0	420
6.50	2.7	3.3	−0.9	511	2.4	3.1	−1.0	562	3.0	3.6	−0.9	460
7.00	3.0	2.8	−1.1	631	2.8	2.6	−1.1	694	3.3	3.1	−1.0	568
7.00	2.3	2.7	−0.8	572	2.1	2.4	−0.8	629	2.7	3.0	−0.8	515
7.00	2.2	2.5	−0.7	609	1.9	2.3	−0.7	669	2.4	2.8	−0.7	549
7.50	3.3	3.0	−0.6	577	3.0	3.0	−0.7	635	3.6	3.4	−0.7	519
7.50	2.5	2.1	−0.2	536	2.3	2.0	−0.3	590	2.9	2.7	−0.4	482
7.50	2.3	2.1	−0.3	594	2.0	1.9	−0.3	663	2.6	2.5	−0.4	535
8.00	2.3	1.9	−0.1	618	2.2	1.7	−0.1	680	2.7	2.2	−0.2	556
8.00	2.4	2.0	−0.1	562	2.2	1.9	−0.1	618	2.8	2.4	−0.2	506
15 year collateral												
6.50	3.3	2.3	−1.1	493	3.1	2.1	−1.1	542	3.5	2.42	−1.0	444
6.50	2.6	2.0	−0.9	457	2.4	1.8	−0.9	503	2.8	2.18	−0.8	411
7.00	2.0	1.4	−0.7	599	1.8	1.2	−0.6	659	2.3	1.66	−0.7	537

Change in average life, effective duration and convexity versus base case prepay estimates

Coupon*	Avg absolute chg ±10%			Avg percent chg ±10%		
	Avg life	Eff dur	Conv	Avg life	Eff dur	Conv
30 year collateral						
6.50	0.29	**0.22**	0.02	7.62	**5.54**	−2.03
6.50	0.33	**0.23**	0.02	11.11	**6.30**	−2.07
6.50	0.29	**0.21**	0.01	10.92	**6.34**	−1.48
7.00	0.25	**0.22**	0.01	8.33	**7.80**	−0.45
7.00	0.29	**0.28**	−0.02	12.52	**10.34**	2.53
7.00	0.25	**0.25**	−0.02	11.52	**9.96**	2.90
7.50	0.29	**0.23**	−0.01	8.97	**7.40**	1.02
7.50	0.29	**0.33**	−0.07	11.67	**15.70**	29.55
7.50	0.29	**0.32**	−0.06	12.96	**14.79**	18.18
8.00	0.25	**0.29**	−0.08	10.73	**15.24**	61.54
8.00	0.29	**0.29**	−0.07	12.05	**14.18**	59.09
15 year collateral						
6.50	0.21	**0.16**	0.02	6.26	**6.86**	−1.32
6.50	0.21	**0.18**	0.01	8.07	**8.79**	−1.11
7.00	0.21	**0.21**	−0.02	10.42	**14.79**	2.11

*Note: The same coupon rate may appear multiple times, representing New, Moderately Seasoned and Fully seasoned collateral.

change the computed interest rate sensitivity of a portfolio of mortgage-backed securities. For example, a 10% change in our prepayment forecast for 30-year, 7.0% collateral changes our effective duration (i.e. our estimated interest rate risk) by an average of 9.37% (across new, moderately seasoned and fully seasoned pools with a coupon rate, net WAC, of 7.0%). Since a small change in prepayment speeds can cause us to revise our estimated duration by close to 10% (or more), this means that an assessment of an MBS portfolio's interest rate risk is clearly uncertain.

With these two approaches to measuring prepayment uncertainty, i.e. the change in *price* or change in *effective duration* given a change in prepayment forecasts, a risk manager can monitor the portfolio's sensitivity to prepayment model risk in terms of both market value and/or the portfolio's interest rate sensitivity. For example, the 'change in market value' form of prepayment uncertainty might be used to adjust the results of a VAR calculation, while the 'change in effective duration' version could be used to analyze a hedging strategy to understand how a hedge against interest rate risk for a position in MBS would have to be adjusted if prepayment expectations shifted. The prepayment uncertainty measures presented here can also assist with trading decisions on a single-security basis, as differences in prepayment uncertainty may explain why two securities with seemingly very similar characteristics trade at different OASs.

Summary

Risk management for fixed-income securities has traditionally focused on interest rate risk, relying on effective duration and other measures to quantify a security's or portfolio's sensitivity to changes in interest rates. Spread duration and prepayment uncertainty are measures that extend that risk management and investment analysis beyond interest rate risk to examine other sources of risk which impact fixed-income markets. At the individual security level these concepts can assist with trading and investment decisions, helping to explain why two securities with seemingly similar characteristics have different OASs and offer different risk/return profiles. At the portfolio level, these measures allow a manager to quantify and manage exposure to these sources of risk; trading off one type of exposure for another, depending upon expectations and risk tolerances. Examining the effect of interest rate moves combined with spread changes and shifts in prepayment modeling parameters can provide a greater understanding of a firm's potential exposure to the various risks in fixed-income markets.

Notes

[1] The term 'mortgage-backed security' refers to both fixed and adjustable rate mortgage pass-throughs as well as CMOs.

[2] Assuming effective duration is calculated using the same basis point shift used to calculate spread duration.

[3] The two durations still would not be exactly equal, as spread duration is derived from a Monte Carlo simulation that involves an average of the expected prepayments along a number of possible interest rate paths, whereas Macaulay's duration is computed using only a single set of cash flows generated by a specified lifetime PSA% speed.

[4] For a discussion of how to assess the accuracy of a prepayment model, see Phoa and Nercessian. *Evaluating a Fixed Rate Payment Model* – White Paper available from Capital Management Sciences.

[5] Although convexity may be *expressed* as either a 'duration drift' term or a 'contribution to return' measure (the former is approximately twice the latter), its *definition* is generally accepted by fixed-income practitioners.

[6] Our methodology assumes that a Monte Carlo process is used to compute OASs for mortgage-backed securities.

References

Bond Week (1998) **XVIII,** No. 42, 19 October.

Patruno, G. N. (1994) 'Mortgage prepayments: a new model for a new era', *Journal of Fixed Income*, March, 7–11.

Phoa, W. and Nercessian, T. *Evaluating a Fixed Rate Prepayment Model*, White Paper available from Capital Management Sciences, Los Angeles, CA.

Sparks, A. and Sung, F. F. (1995) 'Prepayment convexity and duration', *Journal of Fixed Income*, December, 42–56.

8

Stress testing

PHILIP BEST

Does VaR measure risk?

If you think this is a rhetorical question then consider another: What is the purpose of risk management? Perhaps the most important answer to this question is to prevent an institution suffering unacceptable loss. 'Unacceptable' needs to be defined and quantified, the quantification must wait until later in this chapter. A simple definition, however, can be introduced straight away:

An unacceptable loss is one which either causes an institution to fail or materially damages its competitive position.

Armed with a key objective and definition we can now return to the question of whether VaR measures risk. The answer is, at best, inconclusive. Clearly if we limit the VaR of a trading operation then we will be constraining the size of positions that can be run. Unfortunately this is not enough. Limiting VaR does not mean that we have prevented an unacceptable loss. We have not even identified the scenarios, which might cause such a loss, nor have we quantified the exceptional loss.

VaR normally represents potential losses that may occur fairly regularly – on average, one day in twenty for VaR with a 95% confidence level. The major benefit of VaR is the ability to apply it consistently across almost any trading activity. It is enormously useful to have a comparative measure of risk that can be applied consistently across different trading units. It allows the board to manage the risk and return of different businesses across the bank and to allocate capital accordingly. VaR, however, does not help a bank prevent unacceptable losses.

Using the *Titanic* as an analogy, the captain does not care about the flotsam and jetsam that the ship will bump into on a fairly regular basis, but does care about avoiding icebergs. If VaR tells you about the size of the flotsam and jetsam, then it falls to stress testing to warn the chief executive of the damage that would be caused by hitting an iceberg.

As all markets are vulnerable to extreme price moves (the fat tails in financial asset return distributions) stress testing is required in all markets. However, it is perhaps in the emerging markets where stress testing really comes into its own. Consideration of an old and then a more recent crisis will illustrate the importance of stress testing.

Figure 8.1 shows the Mexican peso versus US dollar exchange rate during the crisis of 1995. The figure shows the classic characteristics of a sudden crisis, i.e. no prior warning from the behavior of the exchange rate. In addition there is very low volatility prior to the crisis, as a result VaR would indicate that positions in this currency represented very low risk.[1] Emerging markets often show very low volatility

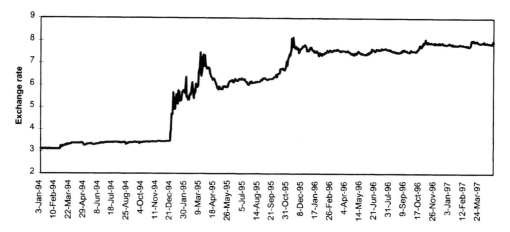

Figure 8.1   Mexican peso versus USD.

during normal market conditions, the lack of volatility results, in part, from the low trading volumes in these markets – rather than the lack of risk. It is not uncommon to see the exchange rate unchanged from one trading day to the next.

Figure 8.2 shows the VaR 'envelope' superimposed on daily exchange rate changes (percent). To give VaR the best chance of coping with the radical shift in behavior the exponentially weighted moving average (EWMA) volatility model has been used (with a decay factor of 0.94 – giving an effective observation period of approximately 30 days). As can be seen, a cluster of VaR exceptions that make a mockery of the VaR measured before the crisis heralds the start of crisis. The VaR envelope widens rapidly in response to the extreme exchange rate changes. But it is too late – being after the event! If management had been relying on VaR as a measure of the riskiness of positions in the Mexican peso they would have been sadly misled. The start of the crisis sees nine exchange rate changes of greater than 20 standard deviations,[2] including one change of 122 standard deviations!

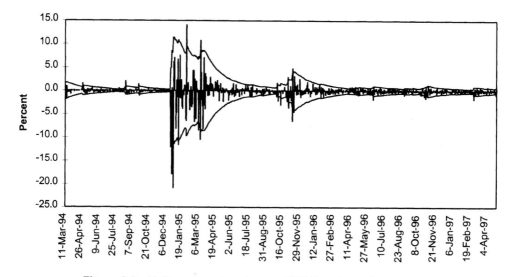

Figure 8.2   VaR versus price change: EWMA – decay factor: 0.94.

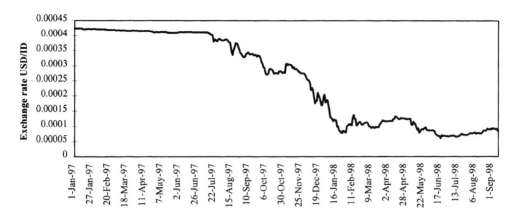

Figure 8.3 USD/IDR exchange rate (January 1997 to August 1998).

Figure 8.3 shows the Indonesian rupiah during the 1997 tumult in the Asian economies. Note the very stable exchange rate until the shift into the classic exponential curve of a market in a developing crisis. Figure 8.4 shows the overlay of VaR on daily exchange rate changes.

There are several points to note from Figure 8.4. First, note that the VaR envelope prior to the crisis indicated a very low volatility and, by implication, therefore a low risk. VaR reflects the recent history of exchange rate changes and does not take account of changes in the economic environment until such changes show up in the asset's price behavior. Second, although the total number of exceptions is within reasonable statistical bounds (6.2% VaR excesses over the two years[3]), VaR does not say anything about how large the excesses will be. In the two years of history examined for the Indonesian rupiah there were 12 daily changes in the exchange rate of greater than twice the 95% confidence VaR – and one change of 19 standard deviations.

Consideration of one-day price changes, however, is not enough. One-day shocks are probably less important than the changes that happen over a number of days.

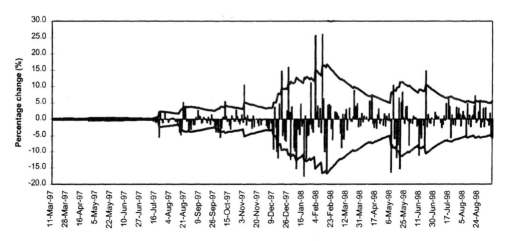

Figure 8.4 IDR/USD–VaR versus rate change: EWMA – decay factor: 0.94.

Examining Figures 8.3 and 8.4 shows that the largest one-day change in the Indonesian rupiah exchange rate was 18%, bad enough you might think, but this is only one third the 57% drop during January 1998. Against this, the 95% confidence VaR at the beginning of January was ranging between 9% and 11.5%. Most people would agree that stress testing is required to manage 'outliers'[4] it is perhaps slightly less widely understood that what you really need to manage are strong directional movements over a more extended period of time.

Stress testing – central to risk control

By now it should be clear that VaR is inadequate as a measure of risk by itself. Risk management must provide a way of identifying and quantifying the effects of extreme price changes on a bank's portfolio. A more appropriate risk measurement methodology for dealing with the effect of extreme price changes is a class of methods known as stress testing. The essential idea behind stress testing is to take a large price change or, more normally, a combination of price changes and apply them to a portfolio and quantify the potential profit or loss that would result. There are a number of ways of arriving at the price changes to be used, this chapter describes and discusses the main methods of generating price changes and undertaking stress testing:

- **Scenario analysis**: Creation and use of potential future economic scenarios to measure their profit and loss impact on a portfolio
- **Historical simulation**: The application of actual past events to the present portfolio. The past events used can be either a price shock that occurred on a single day, or over a more extended period of time.
- **Stressing VaR**: The parameters, which drive VaR, are 'shocked', i.e. changed and the resultant change in the VaR number produced. Stressing VaR will involve changing volatilities and correlations, in various combinations.
- **Systematic stress testing**: The creation of a comprehensive series of scenarios that stress all major risk factors within a portfolio, singly and in combination. As with the first two methods, the desired end result is the potential profit and loss impact on the portfolio. The difference with this method is the comprehensive nature of the stress tests used. The idea is to identify all major scenarios that could cause a significant loss, rather than to test the impact of a small number scenarios, as in the first two methods above.

One of the primary objectives of risk management is to protect against bankruptcy. Risk management cannot guarantee bankruptcy will never happen (otherwise all banks would have triple A credit ratings) but it must identify the market events that would cause a severe financial embarrassment. Note that 'event' should be defined as an extreme price move that occurs over a period of time ranging from one day to 60 days. Once an event is identified the bank's management can then compare the loss implied by the event against the available capital and the promised return from the business unit.

The probability of an extreme event occurring and the subsequent assessment of whether the risk is acceptable in prevailing market conditions has until now been partly subjective and partly based on a simple inspection of historic return series. Now, however, a branch of statistics known as extreme value theory (EVT) holds out the possibility of deriving the probability of extreme events consistently across different asset classes. EVT has long been used in the insurance industry but is now being applied to the banking industry. An introduction to EVT can be found below.

Given the low probabilities of extreme shocks the judgement as to whether the loss event identified is an acceptable risk will always be subjective. This is an important point, particularly as risk management has become based increasingly on statistical estimation. Good risk management is still and always will be based first and foremost on good risk managers, assisted by statistical analysis.

Stress testing must be part of the bank's daily risk management process, rather than an occasional investigation. To ensure full integration into the bank's risk management process, stress test limits must be defined from the bank's appetite for extreme loss. The use of stress testing and its integration into the bank's risk management framework is discussed in the final part of this chapter.

Extreme value theory – an introduction

Value at risk generally assumes that returns are normally or log-normally distributed and largely ignores the fat tails of financial return series. The assumption of normality works well enough when markets are themselves behaving normally. As already pointed out above, however, risk managers care far more about extreme events than about the 1.645 or 2.33 standard deviation price changes (95% or 99% confidence) given by standard VaR.

If measuring VaR with 99% confidence it is clear that, on average, a portfolio value change will be experienced one day in every hundred that will exceed VaR. By how much, is the key question. Clearly, the bank must have enough capital available to cover extreme events – how much does it need?

Extreme value theory (EVT) is a branch of statistics that deals with the analysis and interpretation of extreme events – i.e. fat tails. EVT has been used in engineering to help assess whether a particular construction will be able to withstand extremes (e.g. a hurricane hitting a bridge) and has also been used in the insurance industry to investigate the risk of extreme claims, i.e. their size and frequency. The idea of using EVT in finance and specifically risk management is a recent development which holds out the promise of a better understanding of extreme market events and how to ensure a bank can survive them.

EVT risk measures

There are two key measures of risk that EVT helps quantify:

- **The magnitude of an 'X' year return.** Assume that senior management in a bank had defined its extreme appetite for risk as the loss that could be suffered from an event that occurs only once in twenty years – i.e. a twenty-year return. EVT allows the size of the twenty-year return to be estimated, based on an analysis of past extreme returns. We can express the quantity of the X year return, R_X, where:

$$P(r > R_X) = 1 - F(R_X)$$

Or in words; the probability that a return will exceed R_X can be drawn from the distribution function, F. Unfortunately F is not known and must be estimated by fitting a fat-tailed distribution function to the extreme values of the series. Typical distribution functions used in EVT are discussed below. For a twenty-year return $P(r > R_X)$ is the probability that an event, r, occurring that is greater than R_X will only happen, on average, once in twenty years.

- **The excess loss given VaR.** This is an estimate of the size of loss that may be suffered given that the return exceeds VaR. As with VaR this measure comes with a confidence interval – which can be very wide, depending on the distribution of the extreme values. The excess loss given VaR is sometimes called 'Beyond VaR', *B-VaR*, and can be expressed as:

$$B - VaR = E\langle r - VaR \,|\, r > VaR \rangle$$

In words; Beyond VaR is the expected loss (mean loss) over and above VaR given (i.e. conditional on the fact) that VaR has been exceeded. Again a distribution function of the excess losses is required.

EVT distribution functions

EVT uses a particular class of distributions to model fat tails:

$$F(X) = \exp\left\{ -\left(1 + \xi \frac{x - \mu}{\psi}\right)^{-1/\xi}_+ \right\}$$

where ξ, μ and ψ are parameters which define the distribution, μ is the location parameter (analogous to the mean), ψ is the scale parameter and ξ, the most important, is the shape parameter. The shape parameter defines the specific distribution to be used. $\xi = 0$ is called the Gumbel distribution, $\xi < 0$ is known as the Weibull and finally and most importantly for finance, $\xi > 0$ is referred to as the Frechet distribution. Most applications of EVT to finance use the Fréchet distribution.

From Figure 8.5 the fat-tailed behavior of the Fréchet distribution is clear. Also notice that the distribution has unbounded support to the right. For a more formal exposition of the theory of EVT see the appendix at the end of this chapter.

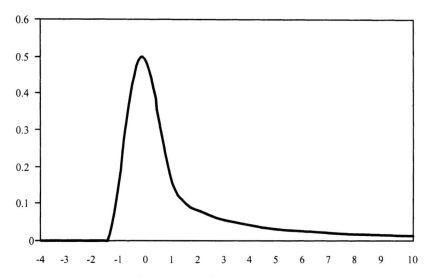

Figure 8.5   Fréchet distribution.

The use and limitations of EVT

At present EVT is really only practically applicable to single assets. There is no easy to implement multivariate application available at the time of writing. Given the amount of academic effort going into this subject and some early indications of progress it is likely that a tractable multivariate solution will evolve in the near future. It is, of course, possible to model the whole portfolio as a single composite 'asset' but this approach would mean refitting the distribution every time the portfolio changed, i.e. daily.

For single assets and indices EVT is a powerful tool. For significant exposures to single-asset classes the results of EVT analysis are well worth the effort. Alexander McNeil (1998) gives an example of the potential of EVT. McNeil cites the hypothetical case of a risk analyst fitting a Fréchet distribution to annual maxima of the S&P 500 index since 1960. The analyst uses the distribution to determine the 50-year return level. His analysis indicates that the confidence interval for the 50-year return lies between 4.9% and 24%. Wishing to give a conservative estimate the analyst reports the maximum potential loss to his boss as a 24% drop. His boss is sceptical. Of course the date of this hypothetical analysis is the day before the 1987 crash – on which date the S&P 500 dropped 20.4%. A powerful demonstration of how EVT can be used on single assets.

Scenario analysis

When banks first started stress testing it was often referred to as Scenario Analysis. This seeks to investigate the effect, i.e. the change in value of a portfolio, of a particular event in the financial markets. Scenarios were typically taken from past, or potential future, economic or natural phenomena, such as a war in the Middle East. This may have a dramatic impact on many financial markets:

- Oil price up 50%, which may cause
- Drop in the US dollar of 20%, which in turn leads to
- A rise in US interest rates of 1%

These primary market changes would have significant knock-on effects to most of the world's financial markets. Other political phenomena that could be investigated include the unexpected death of a head of state, a sudden collapse of a government or a crisis in the Euro exchange rate. In all cases it is the unexpected or sudden nature of the news that causes an extreme price move. Natural disasters can also cause extreme price moves, for example the Japanese earthquake in 1995. Financial markets very quickly take account of news and rumour. A failed harvest is unlikely to cause a sudden price shock, as there is likely to be plenty of prior warning, unless the final figures are much worse than the markets were expecting. However, a well-reported harvest failure could cause the financial markets to substantially revalue the commodity, thereby causing a sustained price increase. A strong directional trend in a market can have an equally devastating effect on portfolio value and should be included in scenario analyses.

Stress testing with historical simulation

Another way of scenario testing is to recreate actual past events and investigate their impact on today's portfolio. The historical simulation method of calculating VaR lends itself particularly well to this type of stress testing as historical simulation uses actual asset price histories for the calculation of VaR.

Scenario testing with historical simulation simply involves identifying past days on which the price changes would have created a large change in the value of today's portfolio. Note that a large change in the portfolio value is sought, rather than large price changes in individual assets. Taking a simple portfolio as an example: $3 million Sterling, $2 million gold and $1 million Rand, Figure 8.6 below shows 100 days of value changes for this portfolio.

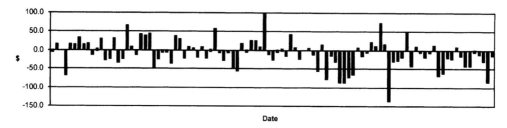

Figure 8.6   Portfolio value change.

It is easy to see the day on which the worst loss would have occurred. The size of the loss is in itself an interesting result: $135000, compared to the VaR for the portfolio of $43000. Historical simulation allows easy identification of exactly what price changes caused this extreme loss (see Table 8.1).

Table 8.1   Asset price change (%)

Asset	% change
Sterling	−2.5
Gold	−5.6
Rand	−0.2
Total (weighted)	−2.3

This is useful information, a bank would be able to discuss these results in the context of its business strategy, or intended market positioning. It may also suggest that further analysis of large price changes in gold are indicated to see whether they have a higher correlation with large price changes in sterling and rand. Identifying the number of extreme price moves, for any given asset, is straightforward. Historical simulation enables you to go a step further, and identify which assets typically move together in times of market stress. Table 8.2 shows the price changes that caused the biggest ten losses in five years of price history for the example portfolio above.

It can be seen from Table 8.2 that the two currencies in the portfolio seem to move together during market shocks. This is suggesting that in times of market stress the currencies have a higher correlation than they do usually. If this was shown to be the case with a larger number of significant portfolio value changes then it is extremely important information and should be used when constructing stress tests for a portfolio and the corresponding risk limits for the portfolio.

In fact, for the example portfolio, when all changes in portfolio value of more than 1% were examined it was found that approximately 60% of them arose as a result of large price moves (greater than 0.5%) in both of the currencies. This is particularly

Table 8.2 Top ten portfolio losses

Percentage change			Change in portfolio value
Gold	Rand	Sterling	
−1.41	−13.31	−0.05	−162 956
−0.17	−5.62	−2.53	−135 453
−3.30	−1.77	−0.67	−103 728
0.06	−3.72	−1.77	−89 260
−0.29	−0.71	−2.54	−89 167
−0.33	−3.12	−1.66	−87 448
0.88	−0.79	−3.23	−87 222
0.03	−2.62	−1.98	−85 157
−0.60	−2.14	−1.72	−85 009
−0.60	1.44	−2.68	−77 970

interesting as the correlation between rand and sterling over the 5-year period examined is very close to zero. In times of market stress the correlation between sterling and rand increases significantly, to above 0.5.

Assessing the effect of a bear market

Another form of scenario testing that can be performed with historical simulation is to measure the effect on a portfolio of an adverse run of price moves, no one price move of which would cause any concern by itself. The benefit of using historical simulation is that it enables a specific real life scenario to be tested against the current portfolio. Figure 8.7 shows how a particular period of time can be selected and used to perform a scenario test. The example portfolio value would have lost $517 000 over the two-week period shown, far greater than the largest daily move during the five years of history examined and 12 times greater than the calculated 95% VaR.

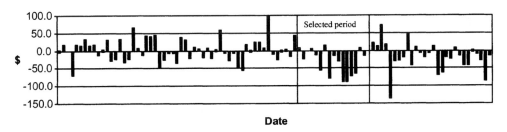

Figure 8.7 Portfolio value change.

A bank must be able to survive an extended period of losses as well as extreme market moves over one day. The potential loss over a more extended period is known as 'maximum drawdown' in the hedge-fund industry. Clearly it is easier to manage a period of losses than it is to manage a sudden one-day move, as there will be more opportunities to change the structure of the portfolio, or even to liquidate the portfolio.

Although in theory it is possible to neutralize most positions in a relatively short period of time this is not always the case. Liquidity can become a real issue in times of market stress. In 1994 there was a sudden downturn in the bond markets. The first reversal was followed by a period of two weeks in which liquidity was much reduced. During that period, it was extremely difficult to liquidate Eurobond positions. These could be hedged with government bonds but that still left banks exposed to a widening of the spreads between government and Eurobonds. This example illustrates why examining the impact of a prolonged period of market stress is a worthwhile part of any stress-testing regime. One of the characteristics of financial markets is that economic shocks are nearly always accompanied by a liquidity crunch.

There remains the interesting question of how to choose the extended period over which to examine a downturn in the market. To take an extreme; it would not make sense to examine a prolonged bear market over a period of several months or years. In such prolonged bear markets liquidity returns and positions can be traded out of in a relatively normal manner. Thus the question of the appropriate length of an extended period is strongly related to liquidity and the ability to liquidate a position – which in turn is dependent on the size of the position.

Market crises, in which liquidity is severely reduced, generally do not extend for very long. In mature and deep markets the maximum period of severely restricted liquidity is unlikely to last beyond a month, though in emerging markets reduced liquidity may continue for some time. The Far Eastern and Russian crises did see liquidity severely reduced for periods of up to two months, after which bargain hunters returned and generated new liquidity – though at much lower prices. As a rule of thumb, it would not make sense to use extended periods of greater than one month in the developed markets and two months in the emerging markets. These guidelines assume the position to be liquidated is much greater than the normally traded market size.

In summary, historical simulation is a very useful tool for investigating the impact of past events on today's portfolio. Therein also lies its limitation. If a bank's stress testing regime relied solely on historical simulation it would be assuming that past events will recur in the same way as before. This is extremely unlikely to be the case. In practice, as the dynamics of the world's financial markets change, the impact of a shock in one part of the world or on one asset class will be accompanied by a new combination of other asset/country shocks – unlike anything seen before. The other limitation is, of course, that historical simulation can only give rise to a relatively small number of market shock scenarios. This is simply not a sufficiently rigorous way of undertaking stress testing. It is necessary to stress test shocks to all combinations of significant risk factors to which the bank is exposed.

Stressing VaR – covariance and Monte Carlo simulation methods

The adoption of VaR as a new standard for measuring risk has given rise to a new class of scenario tests, which can be undertaken with any of the three main VaR calculation methods: covariance, historical simulation and Monte Carlo simulation (see Best, 1998). The use of historical simulation for scenario testing was discussed in the preceding section. With the covariance and Monte Carlo simulation methods the basic VaR inputs can be stressed to produce a new hypothetical VaR.

Scenario testing using either covariance or Monte Carlo simulation is essentially the same, as volatilities and correlations are the key inputs for both the VaR methods.

Before describing the stress testing of VaR it is worth considering what the results of such a stress test will mean. At the beginning of this chapter stress testing was defined as the quantification of potential significant portfolio losses as a result of changes in the prices of assets making up the portfolio. It was also suggested that stress tests should be used to ascertain whether the bank's portfolio represents a level of risk that is within the bank's appetite for risk. Scenario and stress testing have been implicitly defined so far as investigating the portfolio impact of a large change in market prices. Stress testing VaR is not an appropriate way to undertake such an investigation, as it is simpler to apply price changes directly to a portfolio. The stressing of volatility and correlation is asking how the bank's operating, or day-to-day, level of risk would change if volatilities or correlations changed. This is a fundamentally different question than is answered by stress testing proper.

Nonetheless it is a valid to ask whether the bank would be happy with the level of risk implied by different volatilities and correlations. Given that changes in volatilities and correlations are not instantaneous they do not pose the same threat to a trading institution as a market shock or adjustment.

Stressing volatility

When stressing volatility in a VaR calculation it is important to be clear as to what is being changed with respect to the real world. Often, when volatility is stressed in a VaR calculation it is intended to imitate the effect of a market shock. If this is the intention, then it is better to apply the price move implied by the stressed volatility directly to the portfolio and measure its effect. Given that volatilities are calculated as some form of weighted average price change over a period of time it is clear that stressing volatility is an inappropriate way to simulate the effect of an extreme price movement. Therefore, we should conclude that the change in VaR given by stressing volatilities is answering the question 'what would my day-to-day level of risk be if volatilities changes to X ?'

Stressing correlations

Similar arguments apply to correlations as for volatilities. Stressing correlations is equivalent to undertaking a stress test directly on a portfolio. Consider a portfolio of Eurobonds hedged with government bonds. Under normal market conditions these two assets are highly correlated, with correlations typically lying between 0.8 and 0.95. A VaR stress test might involve stressing the correlation between these two asset classes, by setting the correlations to zero. A more direct way of undertaking this stress test is to change the price of one of the assets whilst holding the price of the second asset constant. Again, the question that must be asked is; what is intended by stressing correlations?

Applying scenarios to VaR input parameters may give some useful insights and an interesting perspective on where the sources of risk are in a portfolio and equally, where the sources of diversification are in a portfolio. Nonetheless, stressing a VaR calculation, by altering volatilities and correlations, is not the most effective or efficient way of performing stress tests.

Stressing volatilities and correlations in a VaR calculation will establish what the underlying risk in a portfolio would become if volatilities and correlations were to change to the levels input. Bank management can then be asked whether they would be happy with regular losses of the level given by the new VaR.

The problem with scenario analysis

The three methods described above are all types of scenario analysis, i.e. they involve applying a particular scenario to a portfolio and quantifying its impact. The main problem with scenario testing, however it is performed, is that it only reveals a very small part of the whole picture of potential market disturbances. As shown below, in the discussion on systematic testing, there are an extremely large number of possible scenarios. Scenario analysis will only identify a tiny number of the scenarios that would cause significant losses.

A second problem with scenario analysis is that the next crisis will be different. Market stress scenarios rarely if ever repeat themselves in the same way. For any individual asset over a period of time there will be several significant market shocks, which in terms of a one-day price move will look fairly similar to each other. What is unlikely to be the same is the way in which a price shock for one asset combines with price shocks for other assets. A quick examination of Table 8.2 above shows this to be true.

'All right, so next time will be different. We will use our economists to predict the next economic shock for us.' Wrong! Although this may be an interesting exercise it is unlikely to identify how price shocks will combine during the next shock. This is simply because the world's financial system is extremely complex and trying to predict what will happen next is a bit like trying to predict the weather. The only model complex enough to guarantee a forecast is the weather system itself. An examination of fund management performance shows that human beings are not very good at predicting market trends, let alone sudden moves. Very few fund managers beat the stock indices on a consistent basis and if they do, then only by a small percentage. What is needed is a more thorough way of examining all price shock combinations.

Are simulation techniques appropriate?

One way of generating a large number of market outcomes is to use simulation techniques, such as the Monte Carlo technique. Simulation techniques produce a random set of price outcomes *based on the market characteristics assumed*. Two points should be made here. One of the key market characteristics usually assumed is that price changes are normally distributed. The second point to note is that modelling extreme moves across a portfolio is not a practical proposition at present. Standard Monte Carlo simulation models will only produce as many extreme price moves as dictated by a normal distribution. For stress testing we are interested in price moves of greater than three standard deviations, as well as market moves covered by a normal distribution. Therefore, although simulation may appear to provide a good method of producing stress test events, in practice it is unlikely to be an efficient approach.

Systematic testing

From the previous section, it should be clear that a more comprehensive method of stress testing is required. The methods so far discussed provide useful ways to investigate the impact of specific past or potential future scenarios. This provides valuable information but is simply not sufficient. There is no guarantee that all significant risk factors have been shocked, or that all meaningful combinations have been stressed. In fact it is necessary to impose systematically (deterministically) a large number of different combinations of asset price shocks on a portfolio to produce a series of different stress test outcomes. In this way scenarios that would cause the bank significant financial loss can be identified.

Stress testing is often only thought about in the context of market risk, though it is clearly also just as applicable to credit risk. Stress tests for market and credit risk do differ as the nature and number of risk factors are very different in the two disciplines. Market risk stress testing involves a far greater number of risk factors than are present for credit risk. Having said this it is clear that credit risk *exposure* for traded products is driven by market risk factors. This relationship is discussed further in the section on credit risk stress testing.

Market risk stress tests

As noted above, the dominant issue in stress testing for market risk is the number of risk factors involved and the very large number of different ways in which they can combine. Systematic stress testing for market risk should include the following elements:

- Non-linear price functions (gamma risk)
- Asymmetries
- Correlation breakdowns
- Stressing different combinations of asset classes together and separately
- appropriate size shocks

This section looks at ways of constructing stress tests that satisfy the elements listed above, subsequent sections look at how to determine the stress tests required and the size of the shocks to be used. Table 8.3 shows a matrix of different stress tests for an interest rate portfolio that includes options. The table is an example of a matrix of systematic stress tests.

Table 8.3 Stress test matrix for an interest rate portfolio containing options – profit and loss impact on the portfolio

(£000s) Vol. multipliers	Parallel interest rates shifts (%)									
	−2	−1	−0.5	−0.1	Null	0.1	0.5	1	2	4
× 0.6	1145	435	34	−119	−102	−102	−188	−220	37	−130
× 0.8	1148	447	78	−60	−48	−52	−145	−200	−10	−165
× 0.9	1150	456	100	−33	−24	−29	−125	−189	−12	−164
Null	1153	466	122	−8	0	−6	−103	−173	2	−151
× 1.1	1157	478	144	18	25	18	−77	−151	32	−126
× 1.2	1162	490	167	46	52	45	−46	−119	80	−90
× 1.4	1174	522	222	113	118	114	37	−25	223	21

The columns represent different parallel shifts in the yield curve and the rows represent different multiples of volatility. It should be noted that it is not normally sufficient to stress only parallel shifts to the yield curve. Where interest rate trading forms a substantial part of an operation it would be normal to also devise stress test matrices that shock the short and long end of the yield and volatility curves.

The stress test matrix in Table 8.3 is dealing with gamma risk (i.e. a non-linear price function) by stressing the portfolio with a series of parallel shifts in the yield curve. The non-linear nature of option pricing means that systematic stress testing must include a number of different shifts at various intervals, rather than the single shift that would suffice for a portfolio of linear instruments (for example, equities). Also note that the matrix deals with the potential for an asymmetric loss profile by using both upward and downward shifts of both interest rates and implied volatility.

The first thing to note is that the worst-case loss is not coincident with the largest price move applied. In fact had only extreme moves been used then the worst-case loss would have been missed altogether. In this example the worst-case loss occurs with small moves in rates. This is easier to see graphically, as in Figure 8.8.

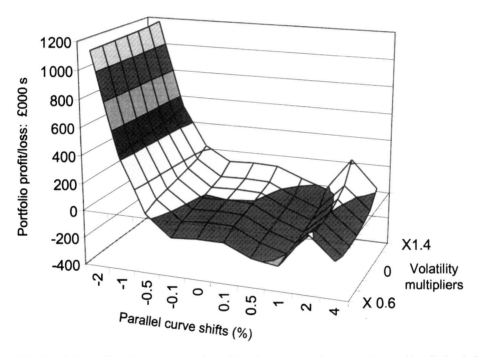

Figure 8.8   Portfolio profit and loss impact of combined stresses to interest rates and implied volatilities.

Stress test matrices are often presented graphically as well as numerically as the graphical representation facilitates an instant comprehension of the 'shape' of the portfolio – giving a much better feel for risks being run than can be obtained from a table of numbers.

Table 8.3 shows a set of stress tests on a complete portfolio where price changes are applied to all products in the portfolio at the same time. This is only one of a number of sets of stress tests that should be used. In Table 8.3 there are a total of 69 individual scenarios. In theory, to get the total number of stress test combinations, the number of different price shocks must be applied to each asset in turn and to all combinations of assets. If the price shocks shown in Table 8.3 were applied to a portfolio of 10 assets (or risk factors), there would be a possible $70\,587^{6}$ stress tests. With a typical bank's portfolio the number of possible stress tests would render comprehensive stress testing impractical. In practice a little thought can reduce the number of stress tests required.

Table 8.3 is an example of a stress test matrix within a single asset class: interest rates. As a bank's portfolio will normally contain significant exposures to several asset classes (interest rates, equities, currencies and commodities), it makes sense to devise stress tests that cover more than one asset class. Table 8.4 shows a stress test matrix that investigates different combinations of shocks to a bank's equity and interest rate portfolios.

Table 8.4 Cross-asset class stress test for equities and interest rates – profit and loss impact on the portfolio (£000s)

Index (% change)	Parallel interest rate shift (basis points)						
	−200	−100	−50	0	50	100	200
−50%	50	−250	−370	−500	−625	−700	−890
−30%	250	−50	−170	−300	−425	−500	−690
−10%	450	150	30	−100	−225	−300	−490
0	550	250	130	0	−125	−200	−390
10%	650	350	230	100	−25	−100	−290
30%	850	550	430	300	175	100	−90
50%	1050	750	630	500	375	300	110

As in the previous example, the columns represent different parallel shifts in the yield curve; the rows represent different shocks to an equity index. It should be noted that this stress test could be applied to a single market, i.e. one yield curve and the corresponding index, to a group of markets, or to the whole portfolio, with all yield curves and indices being shocked together.

Again, it can be helpful to view the results graphically. Figure 8.9 instantly proves its worth, as it shows that the portfolio is behaving in a linear fashion, i.e. that there is no significant optionality present in the portfolio.

In normal circumstances equity and interest rate markets are negatively correlated, i.e. if interest rates rise then equity markets often fall. One of the important things a stress test matrix allows a risk manager to do is to investigate the impact of changing the correlation assumptions that prevail in normal markets. The 'normal' market assumption of an inverse correlation between equities and interest rates is in effect given in the bottom right-hand quarter of Table 8.4. In a severe market shock one might expect equity and interest rate markets to crash together i.e. to be highly correlated. This scenario can be investigated in the upper right-hand quarter of the stress test matrix.

Credit risk stress testing

There is, of course, no reason why stress testing should be constrained to market risk factors. In fact, it makes sense to stress all risk factors to which the bank is exposed and credit risk is, in many cases, the largest risk factor. It would seem natural having identified a potentially damaging market risk scenario to want to know what impact that same scenario would have on the bank's credit exposure. Table 8.5 shows a series of market scenarios applied to trading credit risk exposures.

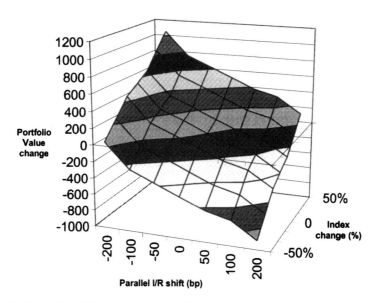

Figure 8.9 Portfolio profit and loss impact of combined stresses to interest rates and an equity index.

Table 8.5 A combined market and credit risk stress test (£000s)

| | | Market risk scenario | | | |
Credit scenarios	Now	A	B	C	D
Portfolio portfolio value	10 000	9 000	8 000	6 000	4 000
Portfolio unrealized profit and loss	0	−1 000	−2 000	−4 000	−6 000
Counterparty A exposure	5 000	1 740	−720	−4 320	−7 040
Counterparty B exposure	5 000	7 260	8 720	10 320	11 040
Collateral value	5 000	3 750	2 950	2 400	1 375
Loss given default; collateral agreement works	0	−3 510	−5 770	−7 920	−9 665
Loss given default; collateral agreement failure	−5 000	−7 260	−8 720	−10 320	−11 040
Total portfolio loss – default of counterparty B	−5 000	−8 260	−10 720	−14 320	−17 040

In general, a bank's loan portfolio is considered to be relatively immune to market scenarios. This is not strictly true, as the value of a loan will change dependent on the level of the relevant yield curve; also, many commercial loans contain optionality (which is often ignored for valuation purposes). Recently there has been a lot of discussion about the application of traded product valuation techniques to loan books and the desirability of treating the loan and trading portfolio on the same basis for credit risk. This makes eminent sense and will become standard practice over the next few years. However, it is clear that the value of traded products, such as swaps, are far more sensitive to changes in market prices than loans.

Table 8.5 shows a portfolio containing two counterparties (customers) the value of their exposure is equal at the present time (£5 million). Four different market risk scenarios have been applied to the portfolio to investigate the potential changes in the value of the counterparty exposure. The four scenarios applied to the portfolio can be taken to be a series of increasing parallel yield curve shifts. It is not really important, however, it may be the case that the counterparty portfolios contain mainly interest rate instruments, such as interest rate swaps, and that the counterparty portfolios are the opposite way round from each other (one is receiving fixed rates whilst the other is paying fixed rates).

The thought process behind this series of stress could be that the systematic stress testing carried out on the market risk portfolio has enabled the managers to identify market risk scenarios that concern them. Perhaps they result from stressing exposure to a particular country. Risk managers then remember that there are two counterparties in that country that they are also concerned about from a purely credit perspective, i.e. they believe there is a reasonable probability of downgrade or default. They decide to run the same market risk scenarios against the counterparties and to investigate the resultant exposure and potential losses given default. Of course, multiple credit risk stress tests could be run with different counterparties going into default, either singly or in groups.

Table 8.5 shows that exposure to counterparty A becomes increasingly negative as the scenarios progress. Taking scenario D as an example, the exposure to counterparty A would be − £7.04 million. In the case of default, the profit and loss for the total portfolio (unrealized plus realized profit and loss) would not change. Prior to default, the negative exposure would be part of the unrealized profit and loss on the portfolio. After default, the loss would become realized profit and loss.[7] As the net effect on the portfolio value is zero, counterparties with negative exposure are normally treated as a zero credit risk.

More worrying is the rapid increase in the positive value of exposure to counterparty B, this warrants further analysis. Table 8.5 gives further analysis of the credit risk stress test for counterparty B in the grey shaded area. The line after the exposure shows the value of collateral placed by counterparty B with the bank. At the current time, the exposure to counterparty B is fully covered by the value of collateral placed with the bank. It can be seen that this situation is very different, dependent on the size of the market shock experienced. In the case of scenario D the value of the collateral has dropped to £1.375 million – against an exposure of £11.04 million, i.e. the collateral would only cover 12.5% of the exposure! This may seem unrealistic but is actually based on market shocks that took place in the emerging markets in 1997 and 1998.

The next part of the analysis is to assume default and calculate the loss that would be experienced. This is shown in the next two lines in Table 8.5. The first line assumes the collateral agreement is enforceable. The worst-case loss scenario is that the collateral agreement is found to be unenforceable. Again this may sound unrealistic but more than one banker has been heard to remark after the Asian crises that 'collateral is a fair-weather friend'. The degree of legal certainty surrounding collateral agreements – particularly in emerging markets is not all that would be wished for.

Note that the credit risk stress test does not involve the probability of default or the expected recovery rate. Both of these statistics are common in credit risk models but do not help in the quantification of loss in case of an actual default. The recovery rate says what you may expect to get back *on average* (i.e. over a large number of defaults with a similar creditor rating) and does not include the time delay. In case of default, the total loss is written off, less any enforceable collateral held, no account is taken of the expected recovery rate. After all, it may be some years before the counterparty's assets are liquidated and distributed to creditors.

The final piece of analysis to undertake is to examine the impact the default has on the total portfolio value. For a real portfolio this would need to be done by stripping out all the trades for the counterparties that are assumed to be in default and recalculating the portfolio values under each of the market scenarios under investigation. In the very simple portfolio described in Table 8.5, we can see what the impact would be. It has already been noted that the impact of counterparty A defaulting would be neutral for the portfolio value, as an unrealized loss would just be changed into a realized loss.

In the case of counterparty B, it is not quite so obvious. Once a credit loss has occurred, the portfolio value is reduced by the amount of the loss (becoming a realised loss). The final line in Table 8.5 shows the total portfolio loss as a combination of the market scenario and the default of counterparty B. This is actually the result of a combined market and credit risk stress test.

Which stress test combinations do I need?

The approach to determining which stress tests to perform is best described by considering a simple portfolio. Consider a portfolio of two assets, a 5-year Eurobond hedged with a 10-year government bond. The portfolio is hedged to be delta neutral, or in bond terminology, has a modified duration of zero. In other words the value of the portfolio will not change if the par yield curve moves up (or down) in parallel, by small amounts. If the stress test matrix shown in Table 8.3 were performed on the delta neutral bond portfolio the results would be close to zero (there would be some small losses shown due to the different convexity[8] of the bonds). The value of this simple portfolio will behave in a linear manner and there is therefore no need to have multiple parallel shifts. However, even with the large number of shifts applied in Table 8.3, not all the risks present in the portfolio have been picked up.

Being delta neutral does not mean the portfolio is risk free. In particular this portfolio is subject to spread risk; i.e. the risk that the prices of Euro and government bonds do not move in line with each other. It is speculated that this is the risk that sunk LTCM; it was purportedly betting on spreads narrowing and remaining highly correlated. The knock-on effect of the Asian crisis was that spreads widened dramatically in the US market. The other risk that the portfolio is subject to is curve risk; i.e. the risk that yield curve moves are not parallel. Stress tests must be designed that capture these risks. Curve risk can be investigated by applying curve tilts to the yield curve, rather than the parallel moves used in Table 8.3. Spread risk can be investigated by applying price shocks to one side of a pair of hedged asset classes. In this example a price shock could be applied to the Eurobonds only.

This example serves to illustrate the approach for identifying the stress tests that need to be performed. A bank's portfolio must be examined to identify the different types of risk that the portfolio is subject to. Stress tests should be designed that test the portfolio against price shocks for all the significant risks identified.

There are typically fewer significant risks than there are assets in a portfolio and stress tests can be tailored to the products present in the portfolio. A portfolio without options does not need as many separate yield curve shocks as shown in Table 8.3, as the price function of such a portfolio will behave approximately linearly. From this example it can be seen that the actual number of stress tests that need to be performed, whilst still significant, is much smaller than the theoretical number of combinations.

The stress tests illustrated by Table 8.3 in the previous section did not specify whether it is for a single market or group of markets. It is well known that the world's interest rates are quite highly correlated and that a shock to one of the major markets, such as America, is likely to cause shocks in many of the world's other markets. When designing a framework of systematic stress test such relationships must be taken into account. A framework of systematic stress test should include:

- Stressing individual markets to which there is significant exposure
- Stressing regional groups, or economic blocks; such as the Far East (it may also make sense to define a block whose economic fortunes are closely linked to Japan, The Euro block (with and without non-Euro countries) and a block of countries whose economies are linked to that of the USA[9]
- Stressing the whole portfolio together – i.e. the bank's total exposure across all markets and locations

stressing exposure in each trading location (regardless of the magnitude of the trading activity – Singapore was a minor operation for Barings). Stress tests in individual trading locations should mirror those done centrally but should be extended to separately stress any risk factors that are specific to the location.

Which price shocks should be used?

The other basic question that needs to be answered is what magnitude of price shocks to use. A basic approach will entail undertaking research for each risk factor to be stressed to identify the largest ever move and also the largest move in the last ten years. Judgement must then be used to choose price shocks from the results of the research. The size of the price shocks used may be adjusted over time as asset return behavior changes. At the time of writing the world was in a period of high volatility. In such an environment it may make sense to increase the magnitude of price shocks. The price shocks used will not need to change often but should be reviewed once a year or as dictated by market behavior and changes in portfolio composition.

A more sophisticated approach, for individual assets, would involve the use of extreme value theory (EVT). There are two approaches to designing stress tests with EVT:

- Find the magnitude of price change that will be exceeded only, on average, once during a specified period of time. The period of time is a subjective decision and must be determined by the risk manager, typical periods to be considered may be 10, 20 or 50 years. If 20 years were chosen, the price change identified that would not be exceeded on average more than once in 20 years is called the '20-year return level'.
- The second approach is merely the inverse of the first. Given that a bank will have identified its risk appetite (see below) in terms of the maximum loss it is prepared to suffer, then EVT can be used to determine the likelihood of such a loss. If the probability were considered to be too great (i.e. would occur more often than the bank can tolerate) then the risk appetite must be revisited.

Determining risk appetite and stress test limits

The primary objective of stress testing is to identify the scenarios that would cause the bank a significant loss. The bank can then make a judgement as to whether it is happy with the level of risk represented by the current portfolios in the present market.

Stress testing and capital

In order to determine whether a potential loss identified by stress testing is acceptable, it must be related to the bank's available capital. The available capital in this case will not be the 'risk capital', or shareholder-capital-at-risk allocated to the trading area (i.e. the capital used in risk-adjusted performance measures such as RAROC) but the bank's actual shareholder capital.

Shareholder-capital-at-risk is often based on VaR (as well as measures of risk for credit and operational risk). VaR will represent the amount of capital needed to cover losses due to market risk on a day-to-day basis. If, however, an extreme period of market stress is encountered then the bank may lose more than the allocated shareholder-capital-at-risk. This will also be the case if a downturn is experienced over a period of time. Clearly institutions must be able to survive such events, hence the need for the actual capital to be much larger than the shareholder-capital-at-risk typically calculated for RAROC. As with shareholder-capital-at-risk, the question of allocation arises. It is not possible to use stress testing for the allocation of actual shareholder capital until it is practical to measure the probability of extreme events consistently across markets and portfolios. Therefore it continues to make sense for shareholder-capital-at-risk to be used for capital allocation purposes.

Determining risk appetite

A bank must limit the amount it is prepared to lose under extreme market circumstances; this can be done using stress test limits. As with all limit setting, the process should start with the identification of the bank's risk appetite.

If we start with the premise that a bank's risk appetite is expressed as a monetary amount, let us say $10 million, then a natural question follows. Are you prepared to lose $10 million every day, once per month, or how often? The regularity with which a loss of a given magnitude can be tolerated is the key qualification of risk appetite. Figure 8.10 shows how a bank's risk appetite could be defined. Several different losses are identified, along with the frequency with which each loss can be tolerated.

The amount a bank is prepared to lose on a regular basis is defined as the 95%

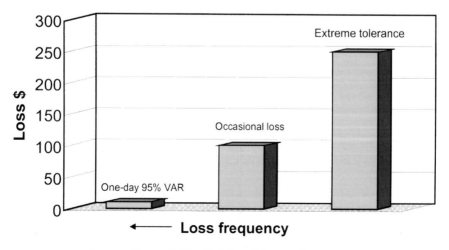

Figure 8.10   Defining risk appetite.

confidence VaR (with a one-day holding period). The daily VaR limit should be set after consideration of the bank's, or trading unit's profit target. There would be little point in having a daily VaR limit that is larger than the annual profit target, otherwise there would be a reasonable probability that the budgeted annual profit would be lost during the year.

The second figure is the most important in terms of controlling risk. An institution's management will find it difficult to discuss the third figure – the extreme tolerance number. This is because it is unlikely that any of the senior management team have ever experienced a loss of that magnitude. To facilitate a meaningful discussion the extreme loss figure to be used to control risk must be of a magnitude that is believed possible, even if improbable.

The second figure is the amount the bank is prepared to lose on an infrequent basis, perhaps once every two or three years. This amount should be set after consideration of the available or allocated capital. This magnitude of loss would arise from an extreme event in the financial markets and will therefore not be predicted by VaR. Either historic price changes or extreme value theory could be used to predict the magnitude. The bank's actual capital must more than cover this figure. Stress tests should be used to identify scenarios that would give rise to losses of this magnitude or more.

Once the scenarios have been identified, management's subjective judgement must be used, in conjunction with statistical analysis, to judge the likelihood of such an event in prevailing market conditions. Those with vested interests should not be allowed to dominate this process. The judgement will be subjective, as the probabilities of extreme events are not meaningful over the short horizon associated with trading decisions. In other words the occurrence of extreme price shocks is so rare that a consideration of the probability of an extreme event would lead managers to ignore such events. EVT could be used in conjunction with management's subjective judgement of the likelihood of such an event, given present or predicted economic circumstance.

The loss labelled 'extreme tolerance' does not have an associated frequency, as it is the maximum the bank is prepared to lose – ever. This amount, depending on the degree of leverage, is likely to be between 10% and 20% of a bank's equity capital and perhaps equates to a 1 in 50-year return level. Losses greater than this would severely impact the bank's ability to operate effectively. Again stress tests should be used to identify scenarios and position sizes that would give rise to a loss of this magnitude. When possible (i.e. for single assets or indices) EVT should then be used to estimate the probability of such an event.

Stress test limits

A bank must limit the amount it is prepared to lose due to extreme market moves, this is best achieved by stress test limits. As VaR only controls day-to-day risk, stress test limits are required in addition to VaR limits. Stress test limits are entirely separate from VaR limits and can be used in a variety of ways (see below). However they are used, it is essential to ensure that stress test limits are consistent with the bank's VaR risk management limits, i.e. the stress test limits should not be out of proportion with the VaR limits. Stress test limits should be set at a magnitude that is consistent with the 'occasional loss' figure from Figure 8.10, above. However, significantly larger price shocks should also be tested to ensure that the 'extreme tolerance number is not breached'.

Stress test limits are especially useful for certain classes of products, particularly options. Traditional limits for options were based around the greeks; delta, gamma, vega, rho and theta. A single matrix of stress tests can replace the first three greeks. The advantage of stress tests over the greeks is that stress tests quantify the loss on a portfolio in a given market scenario. The greeks, particularly, gamma, can provide misleading figures. When options are at-the-money and close to expiry gamma can become almost infinitely large. This has nothing to do with potential losses and everything to do with the option pricing function (Black–Scholes). Figure 8.11 gives an example of stress limits for an interest rate option portfolio. This example of stress test limits could be used for the matrix of stress tests given above in Table 8.3.

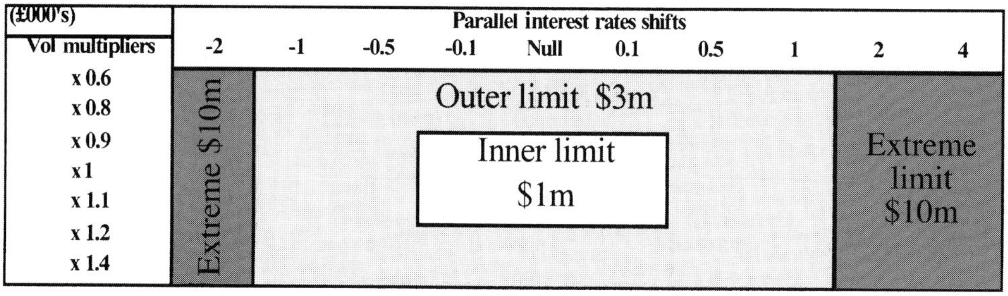

(£000's)	Parallel interest rates shifts									
Vol multipliers	-2	-1	-0.5	-0.1	Null	0.1	0.5	1	2	4
x 0.6 x 0.8 x 0.9 x 1 x 1.1 x 1.2 x 1.4	Extreme $10m		Outer limit $3m — Inner limit $1m						Extreme limit $10m	

Figure 8.11 Stress test limits for an interest option portfolio.

Figure 8.11 shows three stress test limits, which increase in magnitude with the size of the shift in interest rates and the change in volatility. Stress tests limits like this make it easy for trading management to see that losses due to specified ranges of market shifts are limited to a given figure. Using the greeks, the loss caused by specific market shifts is not specified (except for the tiny shifts used by the greeks).

Stress test limits can be used as are standard VaR, or other, risk limits, i.e. when a stress test identifies that a portfolio could give rise to a loss greater than specified by the stress test limit, then exposure cannot be increased and must be decreased. This approach establishes stress test limits as 'hard' limits and therefore, along with standard risk limits, as absolute constraints on positions and exposures that can be created.

Another approach is to set stress test limits but use them as 'trigger points' for discussion. Such limits need to be well within the bank's absolute tolerance of loss. When a stress test indicates that the bank's portfolio could give rise to a specified loss, the circumstances that would cause such a loss are distributed to senior management, along with details of the position or portfolio. An informed discussion can then take place as to whether the bank is happy to run with such a risk. Although EVT and statistics can help, the judgement will be largely subjective and will be based on the experience of the management making the decision.

Conclusion

Due to the extreme price shocks experienced regularly in the world's financial markets VaR is not an adequate measure of risk. Stress testing must be used to complement VaR. The primary objective of stress testing is to identify the scenarios that would cause a significant loss and to put a limit on risk exposures that would cause such losses.

Stress testing must be undertaken in a systematic way. *Ad-hoc* scenario tests may produce interesting results but are unlikely to identify the worst-case loss a bank could suffer. Care must be taken to identify the stress tests required by examining the types of risk in the bank's portfolio. Stress tests should be run daily as a bank's portfolio can change significantly over a 24-hour period.

A bank's risk appetite should be set with reference to VaR and to the worst-case loss a bank is prepared to countenance under extreme market conditions. This is best done with reference to the frequency with which a certain loss can be tolerated. Stress test limits can then be established to ensure that the bank does not create positions that could give rise, in severe market circumstances, to a loss greater than the bank's absolute tolerance of loss. Stress testing should be an integral part of a bank's risk management framework and stress test limits should be used along side other risk limits, such as VaR limits.

Appendix: The theory of extreme value theory – an introduction
© Con Keating

In 1900 Bachelier introduced the normal distribution to financial analysis (see also Cootner, 1964); today most students of the subject would be able to offer a critique of the shortcomings of this most basic (but useful) model. Most would point immediately to the 'fat tails' evident in the distributions of many financial time series.

Benoit Mandelbrot (1997), now better known for his work on *fractals*, and his doctoral student Eugene Fama published extensive studies of the empirical properties of the distributions of a wide range of financial series in the 1960s and 1970s which convincingly demonstrate this non-normality. Over the past twenty years, both academia and the finance profession have developed a variety of new techniques, such as the ARCH family, to simulate the observed oddities of actual series. The majority fall short of delivering an entirely satisfactory result.

At first sight the presence of skewness or kurtosis in the distributions suggests that of a central limit theorem failing but, of course, the central limit theorem should only be expected to apply strongly to the central region, the kernel of the distribution. Now this presents problems for the risk manager who naturally is concerned with the more unusual (or extreme) behavior of markets, i.e. the probability and magnitudes of the events forming the tails of the distributions.

There is also a common misunderstanding that the central limit theorem implies that any mixture of distributions or samplings from a distribution will result in a normal distribution, but a further condition exists, which often passes ignored, that these samplings should be independent.

Extreme value theory (EVT) is precisely concerned with the analysis of tail behaviour. It has its roots in the work of Fisher and Tippett first published in 1928 and a long tradition of application in the fields of hydrology and insurance. EVT considers the asymptotic (limiting) behavior of series and, subject to the assumptions listed below, states

$$\lim_{n \to \infty} P\left\{ \left(\frac{1}{a_n} \right) (X_n - b_n) \leqslant x \right\} = \lim_{n \to \infty} F^n(a_n x + b_n) = H(x) \qquad \text{(A1)}$$

which implies that:

$$F \in MDA(H_\xi(x)) \quad \text{for some } \xi \tag{A2}$$

which is read as: F is a realization in the maximum domain of attraction of H.

To illustrate the concept of a maximum domain of attraction, consider a fairground game: tossing ping-pong balls into a collection of funnels. Once inside a funnel, the ball would descend to its tip – a point attractor. The domain of attraction is the region within a particular funnel and the maximum domain of attraction is any trajectory for a ping-pong ball which results in its coming to rest in a particular funnel. This concept of a stable, limiting, equilibrium organization to which dynamic systems are attracted is actually widespread in economics and financial analysis.

The assumptions are that b_n and $a_n > 0$ (location and scaling parameters) exist such that the financial time series, X, demonstrates regular limiting behavior and that the distribution is not degenerate. These are mathematical technicalities necessary to ensure that we do not descend inadvertently into paradox and logical nonsenses. ξ is referred to as a shape parameter. There is (in the derivation of equation (A1)) an inherent assumption that the realisations of X, $x_0, x_1, \ldots, x_n$ are independently and identically distributed. If this assumption were relaxed, the result, for serially dependent data, would be slower convergence to the asymptotic limit.

The distribution $H_\xi(x)$ is defined as the generalized extreme value distribution (GEV) and has the functional form:

$$H_\xi(x) = \begin{cases} \exp(-(1 + \xi x)^{-1/\xi}) \\ \exp(-e^{-x}) \end{cases} \quad \text{for } \xi \neq 0, \, \xi = 0 \text{ respectively} \tag{A3}$$

The distributions where the value of the tail index, ξ, is greater than zero, equal to zero or less than zero are known, correspondingly, as Fréchet, Gumbel and Weibull distributions. The Fréchet class includes Student's T, Pareto and many other distributions occasionally used in financial analysis; all these distributions have heavy tails. The normal distribution is a particular instance of the Gumbel class where ξ is zero.

This constitutes the theory underlying the application of EVT techniques but it should be noted that this exposition was limited to univariate data.[10] Extensions of EVT to multivariate data are considerably more intricate involving measure theory, the theory of regular variations and more advanced probability theory. Though much of the multivariate theory does not yet exist, some methods based upon the use of copulas (bivariate distributions whose marginal distributions are uniform on the unit interval) seem promising.

Before addressing questions of practical implementation, a major question needs to be considered. At what point (which quantile) should it be considered that the asymptotic arguments or the maximum domain of attraction applies? Many studies have used the 95th percentile as the point beyond which the tail is estimated. It is far from clear that the arguments do apply in this still broad range and as yet there are no simulation studies of the significance of the implicit approximation of this choice.

The first decision when attempting an implementation is whether to use simply the ordered extreme values of the entire sample set, or to use maxima or minima in defined time periods (blocks) of, say, one month or one year. The decision trade-off is the number of data points available for the estimation and fitting of the curve parameters versus the nearness to the i.i.d. assumption. Block maxima or minima should be expected to approximate an i.i.d. series more closely than the peaks over a threshold of the whole series but at the cost of losing many data-points and enlarging parameter estimation uncertainty. This point is evident from examination of the following block maxima and peaks over threshold diagrams.

Implementation based upon the whole data series, usually known as peaks over threshold (POT), uses the value of the realization (returns, in most financial applications) beyond some (arbitrarily chosen) level or threshold. Anyone involved in the insurance industry will recognize this as the liability profile of an unlimited excess of loss policy. Figures 8A.1 and 8A.2 illustrate these two approaches:

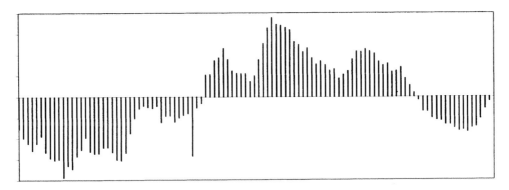

Figure 8A.1   25-Day block minima.

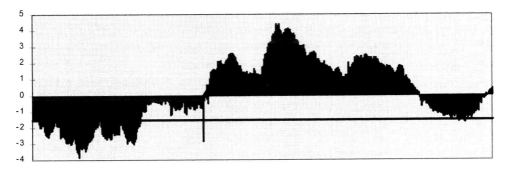

Figure 8A.2   Peaks over thresholds.

Figure 8A.1 shows the minimum values in each 25-day period and may be compared with the whole series data-set below. It should be noted that both series are highly autocorrelated and therefore convergence to the asymptotic limit should be expected to be slow.

Figure 8A.2 shows the entire data-set and the peaks under an arbitrary value (1.5). In this instance, this value has clearly been chosen too close to the mean of the distribution – approximately one standard deviation. In a recent paper, Danielsson and De Vries (1997) develop a bootstrap method for the automatic choice of this cut-off point but as yet, there is inadequate knowledge of the performance of small sample estimators. Descriptive statistics of the two (EVT) series are given in Table 8A.1.

Table 8A.1

	Pot	Minima
No. of observations	604	108
Minimum	−2.38	−3.88
Maximum	−0.00203	3.7675
Mean	−0.87826	−0.15054
Standard deviation	0.511257	1.954465
1st quartile	−1.25063	−1.6482
Median	−0.885	−0.47813
3rd quartile	−0.42	1.509511
Kurtosis	−0.8293	−1.12775
Skewness	−0.11603	0.052863

Notice that the data-set for estimation in the case of block minima has declined to just 108 observations and further that neither series possesses 'fat tails' (positive kurtosis). Figure 8A.3 presents these series.

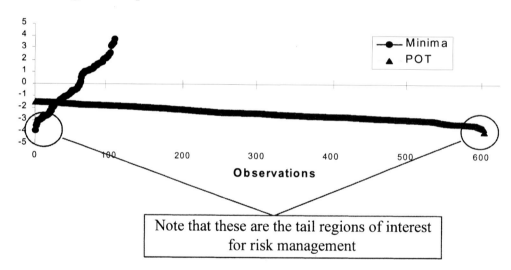

Figure 8A.3   Ordered 25-day block minima and peaks over (1.5) threshold.

The process of implementing EVT is first to decide which approach, then the level of the tail boundary and only then to fit a parametric model of the GEV class to the processed data. This parametric model is used to generate values for particular VaR quantiles. It is standard practice to fit generalized Pareto distributions (GPD) to POT data:

$$
GPD_{\xi, \beta}(x) = \begin{cases} 1 - (1 + \xi x/\beta)^{-1/\xi} & \text{for } \xi \neq 0 \\ 1 - \exp(-x/\beta) & \text{for } \xi = 0 \end{cases} \tag{A4}
$$

where $\beta > 0$ is a scaling parameter.

There is actually a wide range of methods, which may be used to estimate the parameter values. For the peaks over threshold approach it can be shown that the tail estimator is:

$$\hat{F}(x) = 1 - \frac{n_u}{N} \left(1 + \hat{\xi} \frac{x-u}{\hat{\beta}} \right)^{-1/\hat{\xi}}$$ (A5)

where n is the number of observations in the tail, u is the value of the threshold observation and the 'hatted' parameters β, ξ are the estimated values. These latter are usually derived using maximum likelihood (MLE) from the log likelihood function, which can be shown to be:

$$L^n(\xi, \beta) = -n \ln(\beta) + \sum_{i=1}^{n} \ln \left(1 + \xi \frac{x-u}{\beta} \right)^{-1/\xi} - \ln \left(1 + \xi \frac{x-u}{\beta} \right)$$ (A6)

omitting the u and x subscripts. The numerical MLE solution should not prove problematic provided $\xi > -\frac{1}{2}$ which should prove the case for most financial data. A quotation from R. L. Smith is appropriate: 'The big advantage of maximum likelihood procedures is that they can be generalized, with very little change in the basic methodology, to much more complicated models in which trends or other effects may be present.' Estimation of the parameters may also be achieved by either linear (see, for example, Kearns and Pagan, 1997) or non-linear regression after suitable algebraic manipulation of the distribution function.

It should be immediately obvious that there is one potential significant danger for the risk manager in using EVT; that the estimates of the parameters introduce error non-linearly into the estimate of the VaR quantile. However, by using profile likelihood, it should be possible to produce confidence intervals for these estimates, even if the confidence interval is often unbounded.

Perhaps the final point to make is that it becomes trivial to estimate the mean expected loss beyond VaR in this framework; that is, we can estimate the expected loss given a violation of the VaR limit – an event which can cause changes in management behavior and cost jobs.

This brief appendix has attempted to give a broad overview of the subject. Of necessity, it has omitted some of the classical approaches such as Pickand's and Hill's estimators. An interested reader would find the introductory texts[10] listed far more comprehensive.

There has been much hyperbole surrounding extreme value theory and its application to financial time series. The reality is that more structure (ARCH, for example) needs to be introduced into the data-generating processes before it can be said that the method offers significant advantages over conventional methods. Applications, however, do seem most likely in the context of stress tests of portfolios.

Acknowledgements

Certain sections of this chapter were drawn from *Implementing Value at Risk*, by Philip Best, John Wiley, 1998. John Wiley's permission to reproduce these sections is kindly acknowledged.

The author would also like to thank Con Keating for his invaluable assistance in reviewing this chapter and for writing the appendix on Extreme Value Theory. This chapter also benefited from the comments of Gurpreet Dehal and Patricia Ladkin.

Notes

[1] Note that observing other market parameters, such as the volatility of short-term interest rates, might have warned the risk manager that a currency devaluation was possible. Observed by a central risk management function in a different country, however, the chances of spotting the danger are much reduced.

[2] That is, twenty times the return volatility prior to the crisis.

[3] Z score of binomial distribution of exceptions: 1.072, i.e. the VaR model would not be rejected by a Type I error test.

[4] Extreme price changes that have an almost infinitesimally small probability in a normal distribution but which we know occur with far greater regularity in financial markets.

[5] For a more comprehensive coverage of EVT see Embrechs *et al.* (1997).

[6] This is the number of ways of selecting n assets from a set of 10, all multiplied by the number of scenarios – 69 for this example.

[7] Counterparty A's liquidators would expect the bank to perform on the contracts, thus their value at the time of default would have to be written off. Once written off, of course, there is no potential for future beneficial market moves to improve the situation.

[8] Bond price curvature – the slight non-linearity of bond prices for a given change in yield.

[9] Note that this is not the same as the group of countries who have chosen to 'peg' their currencies to the US dollar.

[10] For a more formal and complete introduction to EVT see Embrechs *et al.* (1997), Reiss and Thomas (1997) and Beirlant *et al.* (1996). Readers interested in either the rapidly developing multivariate theory or available software should contact the author.

References

Bachelier, L. (1900) 'Theorie de la speculation', *Annales Scientifique de l'Ecole Normale Superieur*, 21–86, 111–17.

Beirlant, J., Teugels, J. and Vynckier, P. (1996) *Practical Analysis of Extreme Values*, Leuven University Press.

Best, P. (1998) *Implementing Value at Risk*, John Wiley.

Cootner, E. (ed.) (1964) *The Random Character of Stock Market Prices*, MIT Press.

Danielsson, J. and de Vries, C. (1997) *Beyond the Sample: Extreme Quantile and Probability Estimation*, Tinbergen Institute.

Embrechs, P., Kluppelberg, C. and Mikosch, T. (1997) *Modelling Extremal Events for Insurance and Finance*, Springer-Verlag.

Fisher, R. and Tippett, L. (1928) 'Limiting forms of the frequency distribution of the largest and smallest member of a sample', *Proceedings of the Cambridge Philosophical Society*, **24**, 180–90.

Kearns, P. and Pagan, A. (1997) 'Estimating the tail density index for financial time series', *Review of Economics and Statistics*, **79**, 171–5.

Mandelbrot, B. (1997) *Fractals and Scaling in Finance: Discontinuity, Concentration, Risk*, Springer-Verlag.

McNeil, A. (1998) *Risk*, January, 96–100.

Reiss, R. and Thomas, M. (1997) *Statistical Analysis of Extreme Values*, Birhausen.

9

Backtesting

MARK DEANS

The aim of backtesting is to test the effectiveness of market risk measurement by comparing market risk figures with the volatility of actual trading results. Banks must carry out backtesting if they are to meet the requirements laid down by the Basel Committee on Banking Supervision in the *Amendment to the Capital Accord to incorporate market risks* (1996a). If the results of the backtesting exercise are unsatisfactory, the local regulator may impose higher capital requirements on a bank. Further, when performed at a business line or trading desk level, backtesting is a useful tool to evaluate risk measurement methods.

Introduction

Backtesting is a requirement for banks that want to use internal models to calculate their regulatory capital requirements for market risk. The process consists of comparing daily profit and loss (P&L) figures with corresponding market risk figures over a period of time. Depending on the confidence interval used for the market risk measurement, a certain proportion of the P&L figures are expected to show a loss greater than the market risk amount. The result of the backtest is the number of losses greater than their corresponding market risk figures: the 'number of exceptions'. According to this number, the regulators will decide on the multiplier used for determining the regulatory capital requirement.

Regulations require that backtesting is done at the whole bank level. Regulators may also require testing to be broken down by trading desk (Figure 9.1). When there is an exception, this breakdown allows the source of the loss to be analysed in more detail. For instance, the loss might come from one trading desk, or from the sum of losses across a number of different business areas.

In addition to the regulatory requirements, backtesting is a useful tool for evaluating market risk measurement and aggregation methods within a bank. At the whole bank level, the comparison between risk and P&L gives only a broad overall picture of the effectiveness of the chosen risk measurement methods. Satisfactory backtesting results at the aggregate level could hide poor risk measurement methods at a lower level. For instance, risks may be overestimated for equity trading, but underestimated for fixed income trading. Coincidentally, the total risk measured could be approximately correct. Alternatively, risks could be underestimated for each broad risk category (interest rate, equity, FX, and commodity risk), but this fact could be hidden by a very conservative simple sum aggregation method.

Backtesting at the portfolio level, rather than just for the whole bank, allows

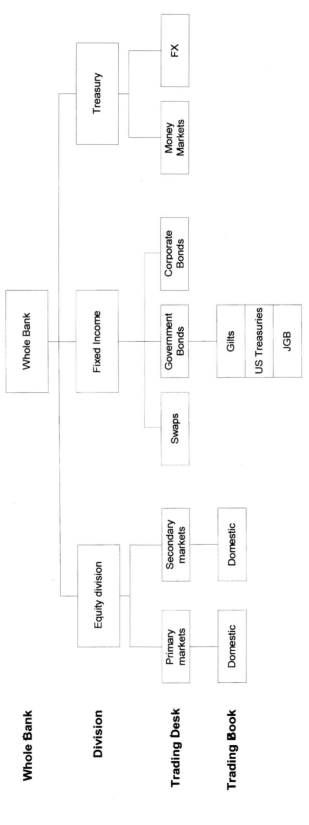

Figure 9.1 Hierarchy of trading divisions and desks at a typical investment bank.

individual market risk measurement models to be tested in practice. The lower the level at which backtesting is applied, the more information becomes available about the risk measurement methods used. This allows areas to be identified where market risk is not measured accurately enough, or where risks are being taken that are not detected by the risk measurement system.

Backtesting is usually carried out within the risk management department of a bank where risk data is relatively easily obtained. However, P&L figures, often calculated by a business unit control or accounting department, are equally important for backtesting. The requirements of these departments when calculating P&L are different from those of the risk management department. The accounting principle of prudence means that it is important not to overstate the value of the portfolio, so where there is uncertainty about the value of positions, a conservative valuation will be taken. When backtesting, the volatility of the P&L is most important, so capturing daily changes in value of the portfolio is more important than having a conservative or prudent valuation. This difference in aims means that P&L as usually calculated for accounting purposes is often not ideal for backtesting. It may include unwanted contributions from provisions or intraday trading. Also, the bank's breakdown of P&L by business line may not be the same as the breakdown used for risk management.

To achieve effective backtesting, the risk and P&L data must be brought together in a single system. This system should be able to identify exceptions, and produce suitable reports. The data must be processed in a timely manner, as some regulators (e.g. the FSA) require an exception to be reported to them not more than one business day after it occurs.

In the last few years, investment banks have been providing an increasing amount of information about their risk management activities in their annual reports. The final part of this chapter reviews the backtesting information given in the annual reports of some major banks.

Comparing risk measurements and P&L

Holding period

For regulatory purposes, the maximum loss over a 10-business-day period at the 99% confidence level must be calculated. This measurement assumes a static portfolio over the holding period. In a realistic trading environment, however, portfolios usually change significantly over 10 days, so a comparison of 10-day P&L with market risk would be of questionable value. A confidence level of 99% and a holding period of 10 days means that one exception would be expected in 1000 business days (about 4 years). If exceptions are so infrequent, a very long run of data has to be observed to obtain a statistically significant conclusion about the risk measurement model. Because of this, regulators require a holding period of one day to be used for backtesting. This gives an expected 2.5 events per year where actual loss exceeds the market risk figure. Figure 9.2 shows simulated backtesting results. Even with this number of expected events, the simple number of exceptions in one year has only limited power to distinguish between an accurate risk measurement model and an inaccurate one.

As noted above, risk figures are often calculated for a holding period of 10 days. For backtesting, risks should ideally be recalculated using a 1-day holding period.

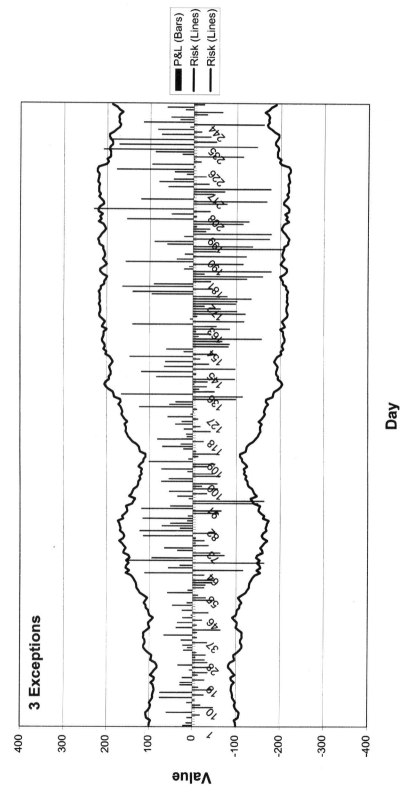

Figure 9.2 Backtesting graph.

For the most accurate possible calculation, this would use extreme moves of risk factors and correlations based on 1-day historical moves rather than 10-day moves. Then the risk figures would be recalculated. The simplest possible approach is simply to scale risk figures by the square root of 10. The effectiveness of a simple scaling approach depends on whether the values of the portfolios in question depend almost linearly on the underlying risk factors. For instance, portfolios of bonds or equities depend almost linearly on interest rates or equity prices respectively. If the portfolio has a significant non-linear component (significant gamma risk), the scaling would be inaccurate. For example, the value of a portfolio of equity index options would typically not depend linearly on the value of the underlying equity index. Also, if the underlying risk factors are strongly mean reverting (e.g. spreads between prices of two grades of crude oil, or natural gas prices), 10-day moves and 1-day moves would not be related by the square root of time. In practice, the simple scaling approach is often used. At the whole bank level, this is likely to be reasonably accurate, as typically the majority of the risk of a whole bank is not in options portfolios. Clearly, this would not be so for specialist businesses such as derivative product subsidiaries, or banks with extensive derivative portfolios.

Comparison process

Risk reports are based on end-of-day positions. This means that the risk figures give the loss at the chosen confidence interval over the holding period for the portfolio that is held at the end of that business day. With a 1-day holding period, the risk figure should be compared with the P&L from the following business day. The P&L, if unwanted components are removed, gives the change in value from market movements of the portfolio the risk was measured for. Therefore, the risk figures and P&L figures used for comparison must be skewed by 1 business day for meaningful backtesting.

Profit and loss calculation for backtesting

When market risk is calculated, it gives the loss in value of a portfolio over a given holding period with a given confidence level. This calculation assumes that the composition of the portfolio does not change during the holding period. In practice, in a trading portfolio, new trades will be carried out. Fees will be paid and received, securities bought and sold at spreads below or above the mid-price, and provisions may be made against possible losses. This means that P&L figures may include several different contributions other than those related to market risk measurement.

To compare P&L with market risk in a meaningful way, there are two possibilities. Actual P&L can be broken down so that (as near as possible) only contributions from holding a position from one day to the next remain. This is known as cleaning the P&L. Alternatively, the trading positions from one day can be revalued using prices from the following day. This produces *synthetic* or *hypothetical P&L*. Regulators recognize both these methods. If the P&L cleaning is effective, the clean figure should be almost the same as the synthetic figure. The components of typical P&L figures, and how to clean them, or calculate synthetic P&L are now discussed.

Dirty or raw P&L

As noted above, P&L calculated daily by the business unit control or accounting department usually includes a number of separate contributions.

Fees and commissions

When a trade is carried out, a fee may be payable to a broker, or a spread may be paid relative to the mid-market price of the security or contract in question. Typically, in a market making operation, fees will be received, and spreads will result in a profit. For a proprietary trading desk, in contrast, fees would usually be paid, and spreads would be a cost. In some cases, fees and commissions are explicitly stated on trade tickets. This makes it possible to separate them from other sources of profit or loss. Spreads, however, are more difficult to deal with. If an instrument is bought at a spread over the mid-price, this is not generally obvious. The price paid and the time of the trade are recorded, but the current mid-price at the time of the trade is not usually available. The P&L from the spread would become part of intraday P&L, which would not impact clean P&L. To calculate the spread P&L separately, the mid-price would have to be recorded with the trade, or it would have to be calculated afterwards from tick-by-tick security price data. Either option may be too onerous to be practical.

Fluctuations in fee income relate to changes in the volume of trading, rather than to changes in market prices. Market risk measures give no information about risk from changes in fee income, therefore fees and commissions should be excluded from P&L figures used for backtesting.

Provisions

When a provision is taken, an amount is set aside to cover a possible future loss. For banking book positions that are not marked to market (e.g. loans), provisioning is a key part of the portfolio valuation process. Trading positions are marked to market, though, so it might seem that provisioning is not necessary. There are several situations, however, where provisions are made against possible losses.

- The portfolio may be marked to market at mid-prices and rates. If the portfolio had to be sold, the bank would only receive the bid prices. A provision of the mid–bid spread may be taken to allow for this.
- For illiquid instruments, market spreads may widen if an attempt is made to sell a large position. Liquidity provisions may be taken to cover this possibility.
- High yield bonds pay a substantial spread over risk-free interest rates, reflecting the possibility that the issuer may default. A portfolio of a small number of such bonds will typically show steady profits from this spread with occasional large losses from defaults. Provisions may be taken to cover losses from such defaults.

When an explicit provision is taken to cover one of these situations, it appears as a loss. For backtesting, such provisions should be removed from the P&L figures. Sometimes, provisions may be taken by marking the instrument to the bid price or rate, or to an even more conservative price or rate. The price of the instrument may not be marked to market daily. Price testing controls verify that the instrument is priced conservatively, and therefore, there may be no requirement to price the instrument except to make sure it is not overvalued. From an accounting point of view, there is no problem with this approach. However, for backtesting, it is difficult to separate out provisions taken in this way, and recover the mid-market value of the portfolio. Such implicit provisions smooth out fluctuations in portfolio value, and lead to sudden jumps in value when provisions are reevaluated. These jumps may lead to backtesting exceptions despite an accurate risk measurement method. This is illustrated in Figure 9.9 (on p. 281).

Funding

When a trading desk buys a security, it requires funding. Often, funding is provided by the bank's treasury desk. In this case, it is usually not possible to match up funding positions to trading positions or even identify which funding positions belong to each trading desk. Sometimes, funding costs are not calculated daily, but a monthly average cost of funding is given. In this case, daily P&L is biased upwards if the trading desk overall requires funds, and this is corrected by a charge for funding at the month end. For backtesting, daily funding costs should be included with daily P&L figures. The monthly funding charge could be distributed retrospectively. However, this would not give an accurate picture of when funding was actually required. Also, it would lead to a delay in reporting backtesting exceptions that would be unacceptable to some regulators.

Intraday trading

Some trading areas (e.g. FX trading) make a high proportion of their profits and losses by trading during the day. Daily risk reports only report the risk from end of day positions being held to the following trading day. For these types of trading, daily risk reporting does not give an accurate picture of the risks of the business. Backtesting is based on daily risk figures and a 1-day holding period. It should use P&L with contributions from intra-day trading removed. The Appendix gives a detailed definition of intra- and interday P&L with some examples.

It may be difficult to separate intraday P&L from the general P&L figures reported. For trading desks where intraday P&L is most important, however, it may be possible to calculate synthetic P&L relatively easily. Synthetic P&L is based on revaluing positions from the end of the previous day with the prices at the end of the current day (see below for a full discussion). Desks where intraday P&L is most important are FX trading and market-making desks. For these desks, there are often positions in a limited number of instruments that can be revalued relatively easily. In these cases, calculating synthetic P&L may be a more practical alternative than trying to calculate intraday P&L based on all trades during the day, and then subtracting it from the reported total P&L figure.

Realized and unrealized P&L

P&L is usually also separated into realized and unrealized P&L. In its current form, backtesting only compares changes in value of the portfolio with value at risk. For this comparison, the distinction between realized and unrealized P&L is not important. If backtesting were extended to compare cash-flow fluctuations with a cash-flow at risk measure, this distinction would be relevant.

Clean P&L

Clean P&L for backtesting purposes is calculated by removing unwanted components from the dirty P&L and adding any missing elements. This is done to the greatest possible extent given the information available. Ideally, the clean P&L should not include:

- Fees and commissions
- Profits or losses from bid–mid–offer spreads
- Provisions
- Income from intraday trading

The clean P&L should include:

- Interday P&L
- Daily funding costs

Synthetic or hypothetical P&L

Instead of cleaning the existing P&L figures, P&L can be calculated separately for backtesting purposes. Synthetic P&L is the P&L that would occur if the portfolio was held constant during a trading day. It is calculated by taking the positions from the close of one trading day (exactly the positions for which risk was calculated), and revaluing these using prices and rates at the close of the following trading day. Funding positions should be included. This gives a synthetic P&L figure that is directly comparable to the risk measurement. This could be written:

$$\text{Synthetic P\&L} = P_0(t_1) - P_0(t_0)$$

where

$P_0(t_0)$ is the value of the portfolio held at time 0 valued with the market prices as of time 0

$P_0(t_1)$ is the value of the portfolio held at time 0 valued with the market prices as of time 1

The main problem with calculating synthetic P&L is valuing the portfolio with prices from the following day. Some instruments in the portfolio may have been sold, so to calculate synthetic P&L, market prices must be obtained not just for the instruments in the portfolio but for any that were in the portfolio at the end of the previous trading day. This can mean extra work for traders and business unit control or accounting staff. The definition of synthetic P&L is the same as that of interday P&L given in the Appendix.

Further P&L analysis for option books

P&L analysis (or P&L attribution) breaks down P&L into components arising from different sources. The above breakdown removes unwanted components of P&L so that a clean P&L figure can be calculated for backtesting. Studying these other components can reveal useful information about the trading operation. For instance, on a market-making desk, does most of the income come from fees and commissions and spreads as expected, or is it from positions held from one day to the next? A change in the balance of P&L from different sources could be used to trigger a further investigation into the risks of a trading desk.

The further breakdown of interday P&L is now considered. In many cases, the P&L analysis would be into the same factors as are used for measuring risk. For instance, P&L from a corporate bond portfolio could be broken down into contributions from treasury interest rates, movements in the general level of spreads, and the movements of specific spreads of individual bonds in the portfolio. An equity portfolio could have P&L broken down into one component from moves in the equity index, and another from movement of individual stock prices relative to the index. This type of breakdown allows components of P&L to be compared to general market risk and specific risk separately. More detailed backtesting can then be done to demonstrate the adequacy of specific risk measurement methods.

P&L for options can be attributed to delta, gamma, vega, rho, theta, and residual terms. The option price will change from one day to the next, and according to the change in the price of the underlying and the volatility input to the model, this change can be broken down. The breakdown for a single option can be written as follows:

$$\Delta c = \frac{\partial c}{\partial S}\Delta S + \frac{1}{2}\frac{\partial^2 c}{\partial S^2}(\Delta S)^2 + \frac{\partial c}{\partial \sigma}\Delta \sigma + \frac{\partial c}{\partial r}\Delta r + \frac{\partial c}{\partial t}\Delta t + \text{Residual}$$

This formula can also be applied to a portfolio of options on one underlying. For a more general option portfolio, the greeks relative to each underlying would be required. If most of the variation of the price of the portfolio is explained by the greeks, then a risk measurement approach based on sensitivities is likely to be effective. If the residual term is large, however, a full repricing approach would be more appropriate. The breakdown of P&L allows more detailed backtesting to validate risk measurement methods by risk factor, rather than just at an aggregate level.

When it is possible to see what types of exposure lead to profits and losses, problems can be identified. For instance, an equity options desk may make profits on equity movements, but losses on interest rate movements.

Regulatory requirements

The Basel Committee on Banking Supervision sets out its requirements for backtesting in the document *Supervisory framework for the use of 'backtesting' in conjunction with the internal models approach to market risk capital requirements* (1996b). The key points of the requirements can be summarized as follows:

- Risk figures for backtesting are based on a 1-day holding period and a 99% confidence interval.
- A 1-year observation period is used for counting the number of exceptions.
- The number of exceptions is formally tested quarterly.

The committee also urges banks to develop the ability to use synthetic P&L as well as dirty P&L for backtesting.

The result of the backtesting exercise is a number of exceptions. This number is used to adjust the multiplier used for calculating the bank's capital requirement for market risk. The multiplier is the factor by which the market risk measurement is multiplied to arrive at a capital requirement figure. The multiplier can have a minimum value of 3, but under unsatisfactory backtesting results can have a value up to 4. Note that the value of the multiplier set by a bank's local regulator may also be increased for other reasons. Table 9.1 (Table 2 from Basel Committee on Banking Supervision (1996b)) provides guidelines for setting the multiplier.

The numbers of exceptions are grouped into zones. A result in the green zone is taken to indicate that the backtesting result shows no problems in the risk measurement method. A result in the yellow zone is taken to show possible problems. The bank is asked to provide explanations for each exception, the multiplier will probably be increased, and risk measurement methods kept under review. A result in the red zone is taken to mean that there are severe problems with the bank's risk measurement model or system. Under some circumstances, the local regulator may decide

Table 9.1   Guidelines for setting the multiplier

Zone	Number of exceptions	Increase in multiplier	Cumulative probability %
Green	0	0.00	8.11
Green	1	0.00	28.58
Green	2	0.00	54.32
Green	3	0.00	75.81
Green	4	0.00	89.22
Yellow	5	0.40	95.88
Yellow	6	0.50	98.63
Yellow	7	0.65	99.60
Yellow	8	0.75	99.89
Yellow	9	0.85	99.97
Red	10 or more	1.00	99.99

The cumulative probability column shows the probability of recording at least the number of exceptions shown if the risk measurement method is accurate, and assuming normally distributed P&L figures.

that there is an acceptable reason for an exception (e.g. a sudden increase in market volatilities). Some exceptions may then be disregarded, as they do not indicate problems with risk measurement.

Local regulations are based on the international regulations given in Basel Committee on Banking Supervision (1996b) but may be more strict in some areas.

FSA regulations

The Financial Services Authority (FSA) is the UK banking regulator. Its requirements for backtesting are given in section 10 of the document *Use of Internal Models to Measure Market Risks* (1998). The key points of these regulations that clarify or go beyond the requirements of the Basel Committee are now discussed.

- When a bank is first seeking model recognition (i.e. approval to use its internal market risk measurement model to set its market risk capital requirement), it must supply 3 months of backtesting data.
- When an exception occurs, the bank must notify its supervisor orally by close of business two working days after the loss is incurred.
- The bank must supply a written explanation of exceptions monthly.
- A result in the red zone may lead to an increase in the multiplication factor greater than 1, and may lead to withdrawal of model recognition.

The FSA also explains in detail how exceptions may be allowed to be deemed 'unrecorded' when they do not result from deficiencies in the risk measurement model. The main cases when this may be allowed are:

- Final P&L figures show that the exception did not actually occur.
- A sudden increase in market volatility led to exceptions that nearly all models would fail to predict.
- The exception resulted from a risk that is not captured within the model, but for which regulatory capital is already held.

Other capabilities that the bank 'should' rather than 'must' have are the ability to analyse P&L (e.g. by option greeks), and to split down backtesting to the trading book level. The bank should also be able to do backtesting based on hypothetical P&L (although not necessarily on a daily basis), and should use clean P&L for its daily backtesting.

EBK regulations

The Eidgenössische Bankenkommission, the Swiss regulator, gives its requirements in the document *Richtlinien zur Eigenmittelunterlegung von Marktrisiken* (Regulations for Determining Market Risk Capital) (1997). The requirements are generally closely in line with the Basel Committee requirements. Reporting of exceptions is on a quarterly basis unless the number of exceptions is greater than 4, in which case, the regulator must be informed immediately. The bank is free to choose whether dirty, clean, or synthetic P&L are used for backtesting. The chosen P&L, however, must be free from components that systematically distort the backtesting results.

Backtesting to support specific risk measurement

In September 1997, the Basel Committee on Banking Supervision released a modi-fication (1997a,b) to the *Amendment to the Capital Accord to include market risks* (1996) to allow banks to use their internal models to measure specific risk for capital requirements calculation. This document specified additional backtesting requirements to validate specific risk models. The main points were:

- Backtesting must be done at the portfolio level on portfolios containing significant specific risk.
- Exceptions must be analysed. If the number of exceptions falls in the red zone for any portfolio, immediate action must be taken to correct the model. The bank must demonstrate that it is setting aside sufficient capital to cover extra risk not captured by the model.

FSA and EBK regulations on the backtesting requirements to support specific risk measurement follow the Basel Committee paper very closely.

Benefits of backtesting beyond regulatory compliance

Displaying backtesting data

Stating a number of exceptions over a given period gives limited insight into the reliability of risk and P&L figures. How big were the exceptions? Were they closely spaced in time, or separated by several weeks or months? A useful way of displaying backtesting data is the backtesting graph (see Figure 9.2). The two lines represent the 1-day 99% risk figure, while the columns show the P&L for each day. The P&L is shifted in time relative to the risk so that the risk figure for a particular day is compared with the P&L for the following trading day. Such a graph shows not only how many exceptions there were, but also their timing and magnitude. In addition, missing data, or unchanging data can be easily identified.

Many banks show a histogram of P&L in their annual report. This does not directly compare P&L fluctuations with risk, but gives a good overall picture of how P&L was distributed over the year. Figure 9.3 shows a P&L histogram that corresponds to the backtesting graph in Figure 9.2.

Analysis of backtesting graphs

Backtesting graphs prepared at a trading desk level as well as a whole bank level can make certain problems very clear. A series of examples shows how backtesting graphs can help check risk and P&L figures in practice, and reveal problems that may not be easily seen by looking at separate risk and P&L reports. Most of the examples below have been generated synthetically using normally distributed P&L, and varying risk figures. Figure 9.5 uses the S&P 500 index returns and risk of an index position.

Risk measured is too low

When there are many exceptions, the risk being measured is too low (Figures 9.4 and 9.5).

Possible causes

There may be risk factors that are not included when risk is measured. For instance, a government bond position hedged by a swap may be considered riskless, when there is actually swap spread risk. Some positions in foreign currency-denominated bonds may be assumed to be FX hedged. If this is not so, FX fluctuations are an extra source of risk.

Especially if the problem only shows up on a recent part of the backtesting graph, the reason may be that volatilities have increased. Extreme moves used to calculate risk are estimates of the maximum moves at the 99% confidence level of the underlying market prices or rates. Regulatory requirements specify a long observation period for extreme move calculation (at least one year). This means that a sharp increase in volatility may not affect the size of extreme moves used for risk measurement much even if these are recalculated. A few weeks of high volatility may have a relatively small effect on extreme moves calculated from a two-year observation period. Figure 9.5 shows the risk and return on a position in the S&P 500 index. The risk figure is calculated using two years of historical data, and is updated quarterly. The period shown is October 1997 to October 1998. Volatility in the equity markets increased dramatically in September and October 1998. The right-hand side of the graph shows several exceptions as a result of this increase in volatility.

The mapping of business units for P&L reporting may be different from that used for risk reporting. If extra positions are included in the P&L calculation that are missing from the risk calculation, this could give a risk figure that is too low to explain P&L fluctuations. This is much more likely to happen at a trading desk level than at the whole bank level. This problem is most likely to occur for trading desks that hold a mixture of trading book and banking book positions. Risk calculations may be done only for the trading book, but P&L may be calculated for both trading and banking book positions.

Solutions

To identify missing risk factors, the risk measurement method should be compared with the positions held by the trading desk in question. It is often helpful to discuss sources of risk with traders, as they often have a good idea of where the main risks

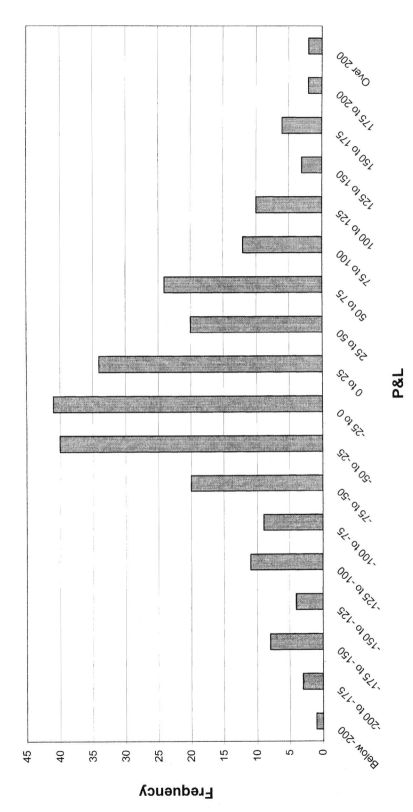

P&L

Figure 9.3 P&L distribution histogram.

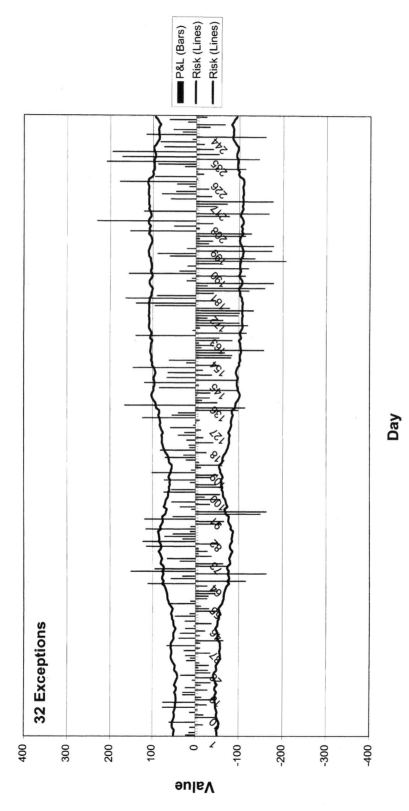

Figure 9.4   Backtesting graph – risk too low.

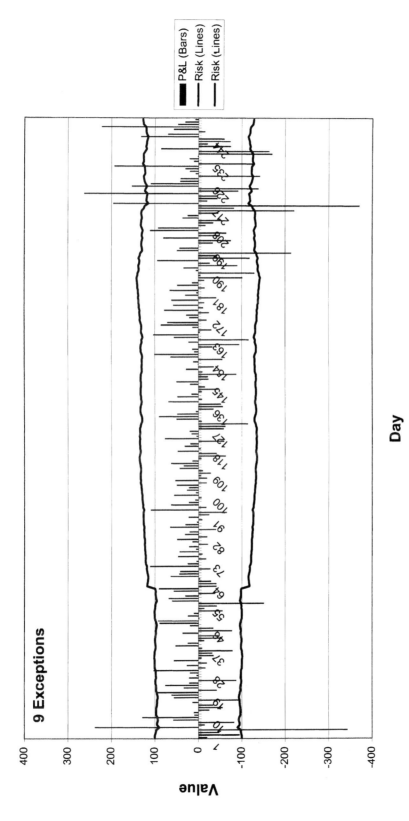

Figure 9.5 Backtesting graph – volatility increase.

of their positions lie. A risk factor could be missed if instruments' prices depend on a factor outside the four broad risk categories usually considered (e.g. prices of mortgage backed securities depend on real estate values). Also, positions may be taken that depend on spreads between two factors that the risk measurement system does not distinguish between (e.g. a long and a short bond position both fall in the same time bucket, and appear to hedge each other perfectly).

When volatility increases suddenly, a short observation period could be substituted for the longer observation period usually used for calculating extreme moves. Most regulators allow this if the overall risk figure increases as a result.

Mapping of business units for P&L and risk calculation should be the same. When this is a problem with banking and trading book positions held for the same trading desk, P&L should be broken down so that P&L arising from trading book positions can be isolated.

Risk measured is too high

There are no exceptions, and the P&L figures never even get near the risk figures (Figure 9.6).

Possible causes

It is often difficult to aggregate risk across risk factors and broad risk categories in a consistent way. Choosing too conservative a method for aggregation can give risk figures that are much too high. An example would be using a simple sum across delta, gamma, and vega risks, then also using a simple sum between interest rate, FX, and equity risk. In practice, losses in these markets would probably not be perfectly correlated, so the risk figure calculated in this way would be too high.

A similar cause is that figures received for global aggregation may consist of sensitivities from some business units, but risk figures from others. Offsetting and diversification benefits between business units that report only total risk figures cannot be measured, so the final risk figure is too high.

Solutions

Aggregation across risk factors and broad risk categories can be done in a number of ways. None of these is perfect, and this article will not discuss the merits of each in detail. Possibilities include:

- Historical simulation
- Constructing a large correlation matrix including all risk factors
- Assuming zero correlation between broad risk categories (regulators would require quantitative evidence justifying this assumption)
- Assuming some worst-case correlation (between 1 and 0) that could be applied to the risks (rather than the sensitivities) no matter whether long or short positions were held in each broad risk category.

To gain full offsetting and diversification benefits at a global level, sensitivities must be collected from all business units. If total risks are reported instead, there is no practical way of assessing the level of diversification or offsetting present.

P&L has a positive bias

There may be exceptions on the positive but not the negative side. Even without exceptions, the P&L bars are much more often positive than negative (Figure 9.7).

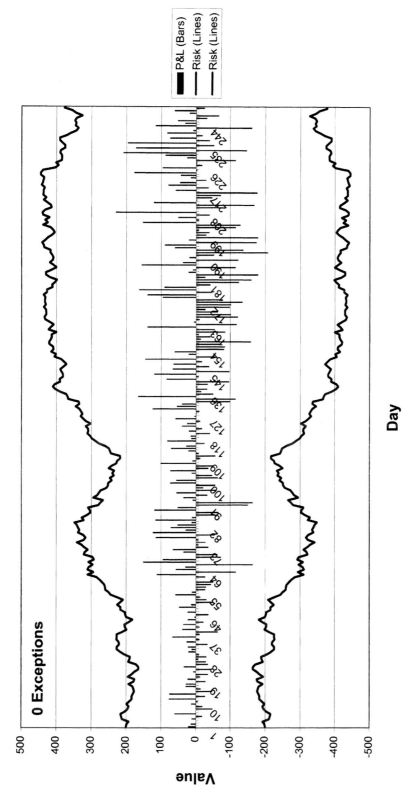

Figure 9.6 Backtesting graph – risk too high.

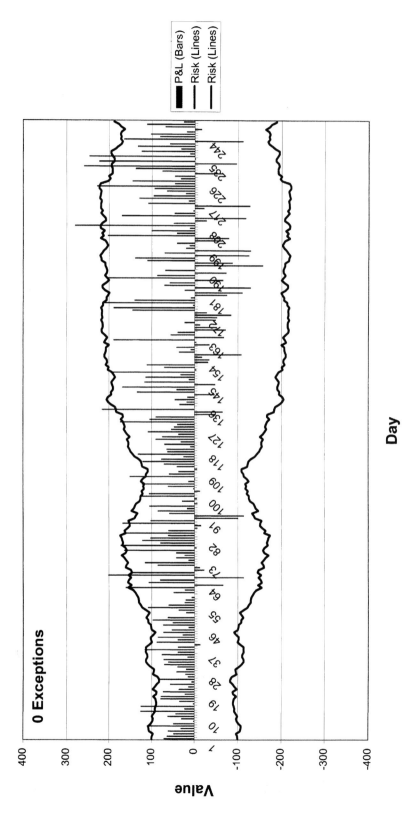

Figure 9.7 Backtesting graph – positive P&L bias.

Possible causes

A successful trading desk makes a profit during the year, so unless the positive bias is very strong, the graph could be showing good trading results, rather than identifying a problem.

The P&L figures may be missing funding costs or including a large contribution from fees and commissions. A positive bias is especially likely for a market making desk, or one that handles a lot of customer business where profits from this are not separated from P&L arising from holding nostro positions.

Solutions

P&L should include daily funding costs, and exclude income from fees and commissions.

Risk figures are not being recalculated daily

The risk lines on the backtesting graph show flat areas (Figure 9.8).

Possible causes

Almost flat areas indicating no change in risk over a number of days could occur for a proprietary trading desk that trades only occasionally, specialising in holding positions over a period of time. However, even in such a situation, small changes in risk would usually be expected due to change in market prices and rates related to the instruments held.

Backtesting is often done centrally by a global risk management group. Sometimes risk figures from remote sites may be sent repeatedly without being updated, or if figures are not available, the previous day's figures may be used. On a backtesting graph the unchanging risk shows up clearly as a flat area.

Solutions

First it is necessary to determine if the flat areas on the graph are from identical risk figures, or just ones that are approximately equal. Risk figures that are identical from one day to the next almost always indicate a data problem. The solution is for daily risk figures to be calculated for all trading desks.

Instruments are not being marked to market daily

P&L is close to zero most of the time, but shows occasional large values (Figure 9.9).

Possible causes

The portfolio may include illiquid instruments for which daily market prices are not available. Examples of securities that are often illiquid are corporate bonds, emerging market corporate bonds and equities, and municipal bonds. Dynamically changing provisions may be included in the P&L figures. This can smooth out fluctuations in P&L, and mean that a loss is only shown when the provisions have been used up. Including provisions can also lead to a loss being shown when a large position is taken on, and a corresponding provision is taken.

In securitization, the assets being securitized may not be marked to market. P&L may be booked only when realized, or only when all asset backed securities have been sold.

If the bank invests in external funds, these may not be marked to market daily.

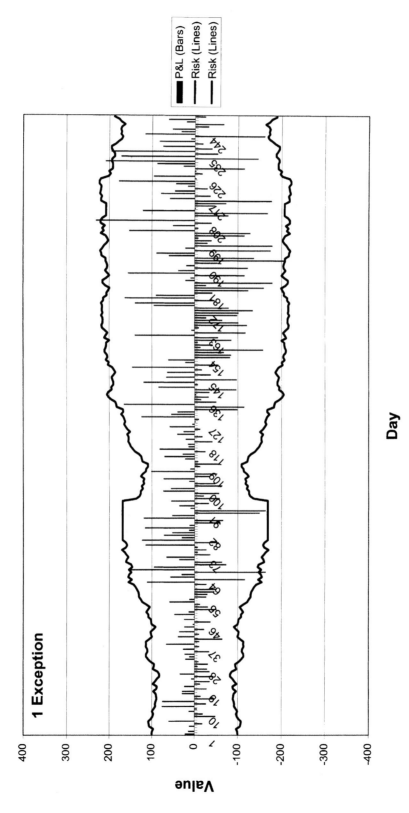

Figure 9.8   Backtesting graph – risk values not updated.

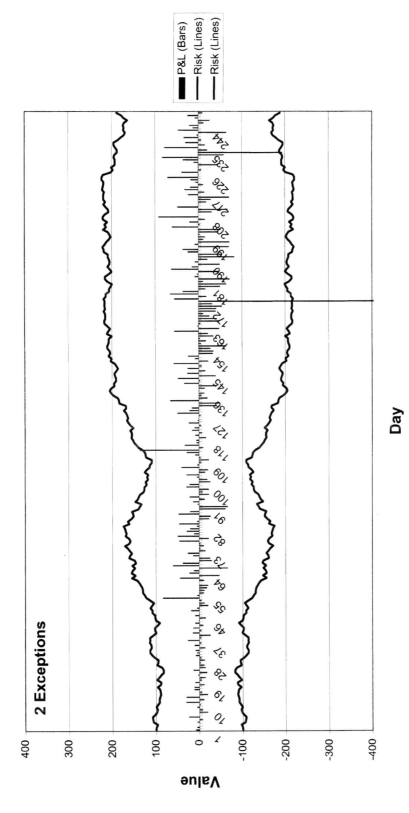

Figure 9.9 Backtesting graph – smooth P&L due to provisioning or infrequent valuation.

However, such investments would not normally form part of the trading book. It is not usually possible to measure market risk in any meaningful way for such funds, because as an external investor, details of the funds' positions would not be available.

Solutions

Illiquid instruments should be priced using a model where possible. For example, an illiquid corporate bond could be priced using a spread from the treasury yield curve for the appropriate currency. If the spread of another bond from the same issuer was available, this could be used as a proxy spread to price the illiquid bond. A similar approach could be used for emerging market corporate bonds. Emerging market equities could be assigned a price using a beta estimate, and the appropriate equity index. These last two methods would only give a very rough estimate of the values of the illiquid securities. However, such estimates would work better in a backtesting context than an infrequently updated price. Where possible, provisions should be excluded from P&L used for backtesting.

Risk measurement methods were changed

When risk measurement methods are changed, the backtesting graph may have a step in it where the method changes (Figure 9.10). This is not a problem in itself. For example, if a simple sum aggregation method was being used across some risk factors, this might prove too conservative. A correlation matrix may be introduced to make the risk measurement more accurate. The backtesting graph would then show a step change in risk due to the change in method. It is useful to be able to go back and recalculate the risk using the new method for old figures. Then a backtesting graph could be produced for the new method. Backtesting like this is valuable for checking and gaining regulatory approval for a new risk measurement method.

Note that a step change in risk is also likely when extreme moves are updated infrequently (e.g. quarterly). This effect can be seen clearly in Figure 9.5, where the extreme move used is based on the historical volatility of the S&P 500 index.

P&L histograms

Backtesting graphs clearly show the number of exceptions, but it is difficult to see the shape of the distribution of P&L outcomes. A P&L histogram (Figure 9.3) makes it easier to see if the distribution of P&L is approximately normal, skewed, fat-tailed, or if it has other particular features. Such a histogram can give additional help in diagnosing why backtesting exceptions occurred.

The weakness of such histograms is that they show the distribution of P&L arising from a portfolio that changes with time. Even if the underlying risk factors were normally distributed, and the prices of securities depended linearly on those risk factors, the changing composition of the portfolio would result in a fat-tailed distribution.

A histogram showing the P&L divided by the risk figure gives similar information to a backtesting graph. However, it is easier to see the shape of the distribution, rather than just the number of exceptions. Figure 9.11 shows an example. This graph can be useful in detecting a fat-tailed distribution that causes more exceptions than expected.

Systems requirements

A backtesting system must store P&L and risk data, and be able to process it into a suitable form. It is useful to be able to produce backtesting graphs, and exception

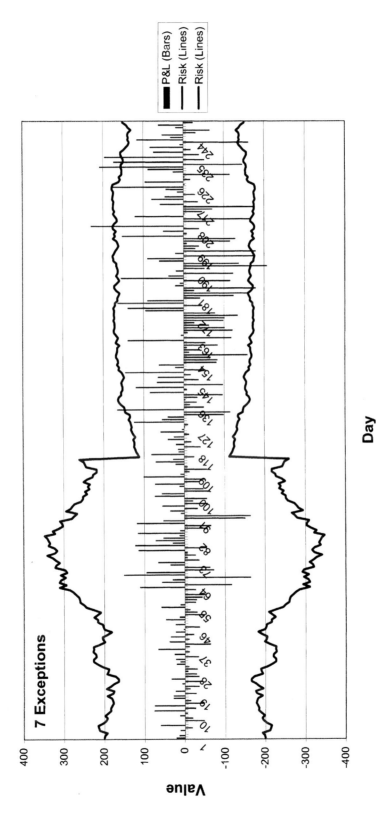

Figure 9.10 Backtesting graph – risk measurement methods changed.

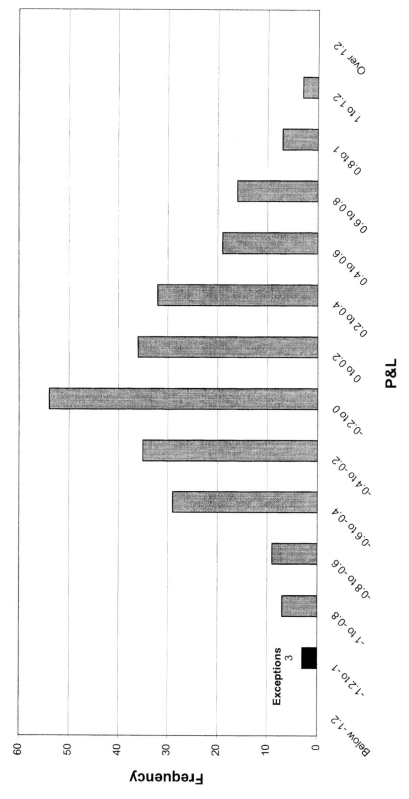

Figure 9.11   P&L/risk distribution histogram.

statistics. The following data should be stored:

- P&L figures broken down by:
  - Business unit (trading desk, trading book)
  - Source of P&L (fees and commissions, provisions, intraday trading, interday trading)
- Risk figures broken down by:
  - Business unit

The backtesting system should be able at a minimum to produce backtesting graphs, and numbers of exceptions at each level of the business unit hierarchy. The system should be able to process information in a timely way. Data must be stored so that at least 1 year's history is available.

Review of backtesting results in annual reports

Risk management has become a focus of attention in investment banking over the last few years. Most annual reports of major banks now have a section on risk management covering credit and market risk. Many of these now include graphs showing the volatility of P&L figures for the bank, and some show backtesting graphs. Table 9.2 shows a summary of what backtesting information is present in annual reports from a selection of banks.

Table 9.2 Backtesting information in annual reports

Company	Date	Risk management section	P&L graph	Backtesting graph
Dresdner Bank	1997	Yes	No	No
Merrill Lynch	1997	Yes	Yes[a]	No
Deutsche Bank	1997	Yes	No	No[b]
J. P. Morgan	1997	Yes	Yes	No[c]
Lehman Brothers	1997	Yes	Yes[d]	No
ING Group	1997	Yes	No	No
ABN AMRO Holding	1997	Yes	No	No
Credit Suisse Group	1997	Yes	Yes	Yes
Sanwa Bank	1998	Yes	No[e]	Yes

[a] Merrill Lynch's P&L graph is of weekly results. It shows 3 years' results year by year for comparison.
[b] Deutsche Bank show a graph of daily value at risk
[c] J. P. Morgan gives a graph of Daily Earnings at Risk (1-day holding period, 95% confidence interval) for two years. The P&L histogram shows average DEaR for 1997, rebased to the mean daily profit.
[d] Lehman Brothers graph is of weekly results.
[e] Sanwa Bank also show a scatter plot with risk on one axis and P&L on the other. A diagonal line indicates the confidence interval below which a point would be an exception.

Of the banks that compare risk to P&L, J. P. Morgan showed a number of exceptions (12 at the 95% level) that was consistent with expectations. They interpret their Daily Earnings at Risk (DEaR) figure in terms of volatility of earnings, and place the confidence interval around the mean daily earnings figure of $12.5 million. The shift of the P&L base for backtesting obviously increases the number of exceptions. It compensates for earnings that carry no market risk such as fees and commissions, but also overstates the number of exceptions that would be obtained from a clean P&L figure by subtracting the average profit from that figure. Comparing to the average DEaR could over or understate the number of exceptions relative to a comparison of each day's P&L with the previous day's risk figure.

Credit Suisse Group show a backtesting graph for their investment bank, Credit Suisse First Boston. This graph plots the 1-day, 99% confidence interval risk figure against P&L (this is consistent with requirements for regulatory reporting). The graph shows no exceptions, and only one loss that even reaches close to half the 1-day, 99% risk figure. The Credit Suisse First Boston annual review for 1997 also shows a backtesting graph for Credit Suisse Financial Products, Credit Suisse First Boston's derivative products subsidiary. This graph also shows no exceptions, and has only two losses that are around half of the 1-day, 99% risk figure. Such graphs show that the risk figure measured is overestimating the volatility of earnings. However, the graph shows daily trading revenue, not clean or hypothetical P&L prepared specially for backtesting. In a financial report, it may make more sense to show actual trading revenues than a specially prepared P&L figure that would be more difficult to explain.

Sanwa Bank show a backtesting graph comparing 1-day, 99% confidence interval risk figures with actual P&L (this is consistent with requirements for regulatory reporting). Separate graphs are shown for the trading and banking accounts. The trading account graph shows only one loss greater than half the risk figure, while the banking account graph shows one exception. The trading account graph shows an overestimate of risk relative to volatility of earnings, while the banking account graph is consistent with statistical expectations

The backtesting graphs presented by Credit Suisse Group and Sanwa Bank indicate a conservative approach to risk measurement. There are several good reasons for this:

- It is more prudent to overestimate, rather than underestimate risk. This is especially so as market risk measurement systems in general do not have several years of proven performance.
- From a regulatory point of view, overestimating risk is acceptable, whereas an underestimate is not.
- Risk measurement methods may include a margin for extreme events and crises. Backtesting graphs for 1998 will probably show some exceptions.

This review of annual reports shows that all banks reviewed have risk management sections in their annual reports. Backtesting information was only given in a few cases, but some information on volatility of P&L was given in over half the reports surveyed.

Conclusion

This chapter has reviewed the backtesting process, giving practical details on how to perform backtesting. The often difficult task of obtaining useful profit and loss figures has been discussed in detail with suggestions on how to clean available P&L figures for backtesting purposes. Regulatory requirements have been reviewed, with specific discussion of the Basel Committee regulations, and the UK (FSA) and Swiss (EBK) regulations. Examples were given of how backtesting graphs can be used to pinpoint problems in P&L and risk calculation. The chapter concluded with a brief overview of backtesting information available in the annual reports of some investment banks.

Appendix: Intra- and interday P&L

For the purposes of backtesting, P&L from positions held from one day to the next must be separated from P&L due to trading during the day. This is because market risk measures only measure risk arising from the fluctuations of market prices and rates with a static portfolio. To make a meaningful comparison of P&L with risk, the P&L in question should likewise be the change in value of a static portfolio from close of trading one day to close of trading the next. This P&L will be called interday P&L. Contributions from trades during the day will be classified as intraday P&L. This appendix aims to give unambiguous definitions for inter- and intraday P&L, and show how they could be calculated for a portfolio. The basic information required for this calculation is as follows:

- Prices of all instruments in the portfolio at the close of the previous business day. This includes the prices of all OTC instruments, and the price and number held of all securities or exchange traded contracts.
- Prices of all instruments in the portfolio at the close of the current business day. This also includes the prices of all OTC instruments, and the price and number held of all securities or exchange traded contracts.
- Prices of all OTC contracts entered into during the day. Price and amount of security traded for all securities trades (including exchange traded contract trades).

The definitions shown are for single-security positions. They can easily be extended by summing together P&L for each security to form values for a whole portfolio. OTC contracts can be treated similarly to securities, except that they only have one intraday event. This is the difference between the value when the contract is entered into and its value at the end of that business day.

Inter- and intraday P&L for a single-security position can be defined as follows:

$$\text{Interday P\&L} = N(t_0)(P(t_1) - P(t_0))$$

where

$N(t)$ = number of units of security held at time t
$P(t)$ = Price of security at time t
t_0 = Close of yesterday
t_1 = Close of today

This is also the definition of synthetic P&L.

Intraday P&L is the total value of the day's transactions marked to market at the end of the day. For a position in one security, this could be written:

$$\text{Intraday P\&L} = (N(t_1) - N(t_0))P(t_1)) - \sum_{i=1}^{\text{No. of trades}} \Delta N_i P_i$$

where

ΔN_i = number of units of security bought in trade i
P_i = price paid per unit of security in trade i

The first term is the value of net amount of the security bought during the day valued at the end of the day. The second term can be interpreted as the cost of purchase of this net amount, plus any profit or loss made on trades during the day which result in no net increase or decrease in the amount of the security held. For a portfolio of securities, the intra- and interday P&L figures are just the sum of those for the individual securities.

Examples

1. Hold the same position for one day

Size of position	$N(t_0)$ and $N(t_1)$	1000 units
Price at close of yesterday	$P(t_0)$	$100.00
Price at close of today	$P(t_1)$	$100.15
Intraday P&L		0
Interday P&L	$N(t_0)(P(t_1) - P(t_0))$	$150

With no trades during the day, there is no intraday P&L.

2. Sell off part of position

Size of position at close of yesterday	$N(t_0)$	1000 units
Price at close of yesterday	$P(t_0)$	$100.00
Size of position at close of today	$N(t_1)$	500 units
Price at close of today	$P(t_1)$	$100.15
Trade 1, sell 500 units at $100.10	ΔN_1	−500 units
	P_1	$100.10
Intraday P&L	$(N(t_1) - N(t_0)) P(t_1) - \Delta N_1 P_1$	−$25
Interday P&L	$N(t_0)(P(t_1) - P(t_0))$	$150
Total P&L	Intraday P&L + interday P&L	$125

The intraday P&L shows a loss of $25 from selling out the position 'too soon'.

3. Buy more: increase position

Size of position at close of yesterday	$N(t_0)$	1000 units
Price at close of yesterday	$P(t_0)$	$100.00
Size of position at close of today	$N(t_1)$	1500 units
Price at close of today	$P(t_1)$	$100.15
Trade 1, sell 500 units at $100.05	ΔN_1	500 units
	P_1	$100.05
Intraday P&L	$(N(t_1) - N(t_0)) P(t_1) - \Delta N_1 P_1$	$50
Interday P&L	$N(t_0)(P(t_1) - P(t_0))$	$150
Total P&L	Intraday P&L + interday P&L	$200

Extra profit was generated by increasing the position as the price increased.

4. Buy then sell

Size of position at close of yesterday	$N(t_0)$	1000 units
Price at close of yesterday	$P(t_0)$	$100.00
Size of position at close of today	$N(t_1)$	500 units
Price at close of today	$P(t_1)$	$100.15

Trade 1, sell 500 units at $100.05	ΔN_1	500 units
	P_1	$100.05
Trade 2, sell 1000 units at $100.10	ΔN_2	-1000 units
	P_2	$100.10
Intraday P&L	$(N(t_1) - N(t_0))P(t_1) - \Delta N_1 P_1 - \Delta N_2 P_2$	$0
Interday P&L	$N(t_0)(P(t_1) - P(t_0))$	$150
Total P&L	Intraday P&L + interday P&L	$150

The profit from buying 500 units as the price increased was cancelled by the loss from selling 1000 too soon, giving a total intraday P&L of zero.

References

Basel Committee on Banking Supervision (1996a) *Amendment to the Capital Accord to incorporate market risks*, January.

Basel Committee on Banking Supervision (1996b) *Supervisory framework for the use of 'backtesting' in conjunction with the internal models approach to market risk capital requirements.*

Financial Services Authority (1998) *Use of Internal Models to measure Market Risks*, September.

Eidgenössische Bankenkommission (1997) *Richtlinien zur Eigenmittelunterlegung von Marktrisiken.*

Basel Committee on Banking Supervision (1997a) *Modifications to the market risk amendment: Textual changes to the Amendment to the Basel Capital Accord of January 1996*, September.

Basel Committee on Banking Supervision (1997b) *Explanatory Note: Modification of the Basel Accord of July 1988, as amended in January 1996*, September.

10

Credit risk management models

RICHARD K. SKORA

Introduction

Financial institutions are just beginning to realize the benefits of credit risk management models. These models are designed to help the risk manager project risk, measure profitability, and reveal new business opportunities.

This chapter surveys the current state of the art in credit risk management models. It provides the reader with the tools to understand and evaluate alternative approaches to modeling. The chapter describes what a credit risk management model should do, and it analyses some of the popular models. We take a high-level approach to analysing models and do not spend time on the technical difficulties of their implementation and application.[1]

We conclude that the success of credit risk management models depends on sound design, intelligent implementation, and responsible application of the model. While there has been significant progress in credit risk management models, the industry must continue to advance the state of the art. So far the most successful models have been custom designed to solve the specific problems of particular institutions.

As a point of reference we refer to several credit risk management models which have been promoted in the industry press. The reader should not interpret this as either an endorsement of these models or as a criticism of models that are not cited here, including this author's models. Interested readers should pursue their own investigation and can begin with the many references cited below.

Motivation

Banks are expanding their operation around the world; they are entering new markets; they are trading new asset types; and they are structuring exotic products. These changes have created new opportunities along with new risks. While banking is always evolving, the current fast rate of change is making it a challenge to respond to all the new opportunities.

Changes in banking have brought both good and bad news. The bad news includes the very frequent and extreme banking debacles. In addition, there has been a divergence between international and domestic regulation as well as between regulatory capital and economic capital. More subtly, banks have wasted many valuable resources correcting problems and repairing outdated models and methodologies. The good news is that the banks which are responding to the changes have been rewarded with a competitive advantage. One response is the investment in risk management. While risk management is not new, not even in banking, the current rendition of risk management is new.

Risk management takes a firmwide view of the institution's risks, profits, and opportunities so that it may ensure optimal operation of the various business units. The risk manager has the advantage of knowing all the firm's risks extending across accounting books, business units, product types, and counterparties. By aggregating the risks, the risk manager is in the unique position of ensuring that the firm may benefit from diversification. Risk management is a complicated, multifaceted profession requiring diverse experience and problem-solving skills (see Bessis, 1998).

The risk manager is constantly taking on new challenges. Whereas yesterday a risk manager may have been satisfied with being able to report the risk and return characteristics of his firm's various business units, today he or she is using that information to improve his firm's business opportunities.

Credit risk is traditionally the main risk of banks. Banks are in the business of taking credit risk in exchange for a certain return above the riskless rate. As one would expect, banks deal in the greatest number of markets and types of products. Banks above all other institutions, including corporations, insurance companies, and asset managers, face the greatest challenge in managing their credit risk. One of the credit risk managers' tools is the credit risk management model.

Functionality of a good credit risk management model

A credit risk management model tells the credit risk manager how to allocate scarce credit risk capital to various businesses so as to optimize the risk and return characteristics of the firm. It is important to understand that optimize does not mean minimize risk otherwise every firm would simply invest its capital in riskless assets. Optimize means for any given target return, minimize the risk.

A credit risk management model works by comparing the risk and return characteristics between individual assets or businesses. One function is to quantify the diversification of risks. Being well-diversified means that the firm has no concentrations of risk to, say, one geographical location or one counterparty.

Figure 10.1 depicts the various outputs from a credit risk management model. The output depicted by credit risk is the probability distribution of losses due to credit risk. This reports for each capital number the probability that the firm may lose that amount of capital or more. For a greater capital number, the probability is less. Of course, a complete report would also describe where and how those losses might occur so that the credit risk manager can take the necessary prudent action.

The marginal statistics explain the affect of adding or subtracting one asset to the portfolio. It reports the new risks and profits. In particular, it helps the firm decide whether it likes that new asset or what price it should pay for it.

The last output, optimal portfolio, goes beyond the previous two outputs in that it tells the credit risk manager the optimal mix of investments and/or business ventures. The calculation of such an output would build on the data and calculation of the previous outputs.

Of course, Figure 10.1 is a wish lists of outputs. Actual models may only produce

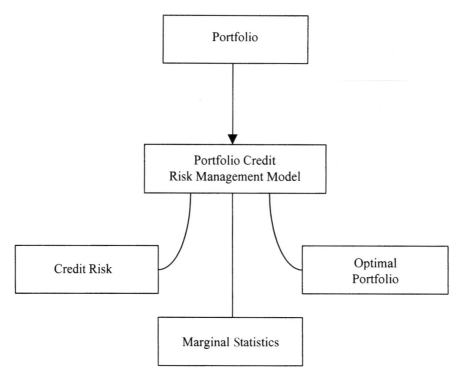

Figure 10.1   Various outputs of a portfolio credit risk management model.

some of the outputs for a limited number of products and asset classes. For example, present technology only allows one to calculate the optimal portfolio in special situations with severe assumptions. In reality, firms attain or try to attain the optimal portfolio through a series of iterations involving models, intuition, and experience. Nevertheless, Figure 10.1 will provide the framework for our discussion.

Models, in most general terms, are used to explain and/or predict. A credit risk management model is not a predictive model. It does not tell the credit risk manger which business ventures will succeed and which will fail. Models that claim predictive powers should be used by the firm's various business units and applied to individual assets. If these models work and the associated business unit consistently exceeds its profit targets, then the business unit would be rewarded with large bonuses and/or increased capital. Regular success within a business unit will show up at the credit risk management level. So it is not a contradiction that the business unit may use one model while the risk management uses another.

Credit risk management models, in the sense that they are defined here, are used to explain rather than predict. Credit risk management models are often criticized for their failure to predict (see Shirreff, 1998). But this is an unfair criticism. One cannot expect these models to predict credit events such as credit rating changes or even defaults. Credit risk management models can predict neither individual credit events nor collective credit events. For example, no model exists for predicting an increase in the general level of defaults.

While this author is an advocate of credit risk management models and he has seen many banks realize the benefits of models, one must be cautioned that there are risks associated with developing models. At present many institutions are rushing to lay claim to the best and only credit risk management model. Such ambitions may actually undermine the risk management function for the following reasons.

First, when improperly used, models are a distraction from the other responsibilities of risk management. In the bigger picture the model is simply a single component, though an important one, of risk management. Second, a model may undermine risk management if it leads to a complacent, mechanical reliance on the model. And more subtly it can stifle competition. The risk manager should have the incentive to innovate just like any other employee.

Review of Markowitz's portfolio selection theory

Harry Markowitz (1952, 1959) developed the first and most famous portfolio selection model which showed how to build a portfolio of assets with the optimal risk and return characteristics.

Markowitz's model starts with a collection of assets for which it is assumed one knows the expected returns and risks as well as all the pair-wise correlation of the returns. Here risk is defined as the standard deviation of return.

It is a fairly strong assumption to assume that these statistics are known. The model further assumes that the asset returns are modeled as a standard multivariate normal distribution, so, in particular, each asset's return is a standard normal distribution.

Thus the assets are completely described by their expected return and their pair-wise covariances of returns

$$E[r_i] \text{ and}$$

$$\text{Covariance}(r_i, r_j) = E[r_i r_j] - E[r_i]E[r_j]$$

respectively, where r_i is the random variable of return for the ith asset. Under these assumptions Markowitz shows for a target expected return how to calculate the exact proportion to hold of each asset so as to minimize risk, or equivalently, how to minimize the standard deviation of return. Figure 10.2 depicts the theoretical workings of the Markowitz model. Two different portfolios of assets held by two different institutions have different risk and return characteristics.

While one may slightly relax the assumptions in Markowitz's theory, the assumptions are still fairly strong. Moreover, the results are sensitive to the inputs; two users of the theory who disagree on the expected returns and covariance of returns may calculate widely different portfolios. In addition, the definition of risk as the standard deviation of returns is only reasonable when returns are a multi-normal distribution. Standard deviation is a very poor measure of risk. So far there is no consensus on the right probability distribution when returns are not a multi-normal distribution.

Nevertheless, Markowitz's theory survives because it was the first portfolio theory to quantify risk and return. Moreover, it showed that mathematical modeling could vastly improve portfolio theory techniques. Other portfolio selection models are described in Elton and Gruber (1991).

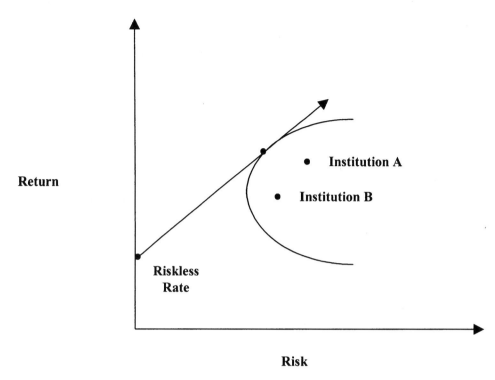

Figure 10.2 Space of possible portfolios.

Adapting portfolio selection theory to credit risk management

Risk management distinguishes between market risk and credit risk. *Market risk* is the risk of price movement due either directly or indirectly to changes in the prices of equity, foreign currency, and US Treasury bonds. *Credit risk* is the risk of price movement due to credit events. A credit event is a change in credit rating or perceived credit rating, which includes default. Corporate, municipal, and certain sovereign bond contain credit risk.

In fact, it is sometimes difficult to distinguish between market risk and credit risk. This has led to debate over whether the two risks should be managed together, but this question will not be debated here. Most people are in agreement that the risks are different, and risk managers and their models must account for the differences. As will be seen below, our framework for a credit risk management model contains a market risk component.

There are several reasons why Markowitz's portfolio selection model is most easily applied to equity assets. First, the model is what is called a *single-period portfolio model* that tells one how to optimize a portfolio over a single period, say, a single day. This means the model tells one how to select the portfolio at the beginning of the period and then one holds the portfolio without changes until the end of the period.

This is not a disadvantage when the underlying market is liquid. In this case, one just reapplies the model over successive periods to determine how to manage the portfolio over time. Since transaction costs are relatively small in the equity markets, it is possible to frequently rebalance an equity portfolio.

A second reason the model works well in the equity markets is that their returns seem to be nearly normal distributions. While much research on equity assets shows that their returns are not perfectly normal, many people still successfully apply Markowitz's model to equity assets.

Finally, the equity markets are very liquid and deep. As such there is a lot of data from which to deduce expected returns and covariances of returns.

These three conditions of the equity markets do not apply to the credit markets. Credit events tend to be sudden and result in large price movements. In addition, the credit markets are sometimes illiquid and have large transaction costs. As a result many of the beautiful theories of market risk models do not apply to the credit markets. Since credit markets are illiquid and transactions costs are high, an appropriate single period can be much longer that a single day. It can be as long as a year. In fact, a reasonable holding period for various instruments will differ from a day to many years.

The assumption of normality in Markowitz portfolio model helps in another way. It is obvious how to compare two normal distributions, namely, less risk is better than more risk. In the case of, say, credit risk, when distributions are not normal, it is not obvious how to compare two distributions. For example, suppose two assets have probability distribution of losses with the same mean but standard deviations of $8 and $10, respectively. In addition, suppose they have maximum potential losses of $50 and $20, respectively. Which is less risky? It is difficult to answer and depends on an *economic utility function* for measuring. The theory of utility functions is another field of study and we will not discuss it further. Any good portfolio theory for credit risk must allow for the differences between market and credit risk.

A framework for credit risk management models

This section provides a framework in which to understand and evaluate credit risk management models. We will describe all the components of a complete (or nearly complete) credit risk model. Figure 10.3 labels the major components of a credit risk model.

While at present there is no model that can do everything in Figure 10.3, this description will be a useful reference by which to evaluate all models. As will be seen below, portfolio models have a small subset of the components depicted in Figure 10.3. Sometimes by limiting itself to particular products or particular applications, a model is able to either ignore a component or greatly simplify it. Some models simply settle for an approximately correct answer. More detailed descriptions and comparisons of some of these models may be found in Gordy (1998), Koyluglu and Hickman (1998), Lopez and Saidenber (1998), Lentino and Pirzada (1998), Locke (1998), and Crouhy and Mark (1998).

The general consensus seems to be that we stand to learn much more about credit risk. We have yet to even scratch the surface in bringing high-powered, mathematical techniques to bear on these complicated problems. It would be a mistake to settle for the existing state of the art and believe we cannot improve. Current discussions should promote original, customized solutions and thereby encourage active credit risk management.

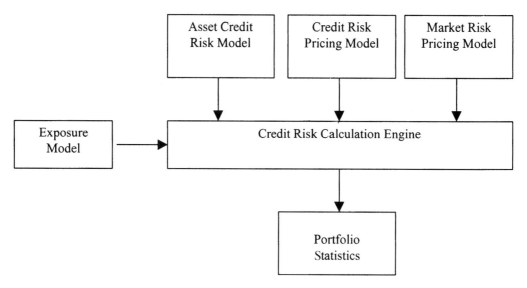

Figure 10.3 Portfolio credit risk model.

Value-at-Risk

Before going into more detail about credit risk management models, it would be instructive to say a few words about Value-at-Risk. The credit risk management modeling framework shares many features with this other modeling framework called Value-at-Risk. This has resulted in some confusions and mistakes in the industry, so it is worth-while explaining the relationship between the two frameworks.

Notice we were careful to write *framework* because Value-at-Risk (VaR) is a framework. There are many different implementations of VaR and each of these implementations may be used differently.

Since about 1994 bankers and regulators have been using VaR as part of their risk management practices. Specifically, it has been applied to market risk management. The motivation was to compute a regulatory capital number for market risk. Given a portfolio of assets, Value-at-Risk is defined to be a single monetary capital number which, for a high degree of confidence, is an upper bound on the amount of gains or losses to the portfolio due to market risk. Of course, the degree of confidence must be specified and the higher that degree of confidence, the higher the capital number. Notice that if one calculates the capital number for every degree of confidence then one has actually calculated the entire probability distribution of gains or losses (see Best, 1998).

Specific implementation of VaR can vary. This includes the assumptions, the model, the input parameters, and the calculation methodology. For example, one implementation may calibrate to historical data and another to econometric data. Both implementations are still VaR models, but one may be more accurate and useful than the other may. For a good debate on the utility of VaR models see Kolman, 1997.

In practice, VaR is associated with certain assumptions. For example, most VaR implementations assume that market prices are normally distributed or losses are independent. This assumption is based more on convenience than on empirical evidence. Normal distributions are easy to work with.

Value-at-Risk has a corresponding definition for credit risk. Given a portfolio of assets, *Credit Value-at-Risk* is defined to be a single monetary capital number which, for a high degree of confidence, is an upper bound on the amount of gains or losses to the portfolio due to credit risk.

One should immediately notice that both the credit VaR model and the credit risk management model compute a probability distribution of gains or losses. For this reason many risk managers and regulators do not distinguish between the two. However, there is a difference between the two models. Though the difference may be more of one of the mind-frame of the users, it is important.

The difference is that VaR models put too much emphasis on distilling one number from the aggregate risks of a portfolio. First, according to our definition, a credit risk management model also computes the marginal affect of a single asset and it computes optimal portfolios which assist in making business decisions. Second, a credit risk management model is a tool designed to assist credit risk managers in a broad range of dynamic credit risk management decisions.

This difference between the models is significant. Indeed, some VaR proponents have been so driven to produce that single, correct capital number that it has been at the expense of ignoring more important risk management issues. This is why we have stated that the model, its implementation, and their applications are important.

Both bankers and regulators are currently investigating the possibility of using the VaR framework for credit risk management. Lopez and Saidenberg (1998) propose a methodology for generating credit events for the purpose of testing and comparing VaR models for calculating regulatory credit capital.

Asset credit risk model

The first component is the *asset credit risk model* that contains two main subcomponents: the credit rating model and the dynamic credit rating model. The credit rating model calculates the credit riskiness of an asset today while the dynamic credit rating model calculates how that riskiness may evolve over time. This is depicted in more detail in Figure 10.4. For example, if the asset is a corporate bond, then the credit riskiness of the asset is derived from the credit riskiness of the issuer. The credit riskiness may be in the form of a probably of default or in the form of a credit rating. The credit rating may correspond to one of the international credit rating services or the institution's own internal rating system.

An interesting point is that the credit riskiness of an asset can depend on the particular structure of the asset. For example, the credit riskiness of a bond depends on its seniority as well as its maturity. (Short- and long-term debt of the same issuer may have different credit ratings.) The credit risk does not necessarily need to be calculated. It may be inputted from various sources or modeled from fundamentals. If it is inputted it may come from any of the credit rating agencies or the institution's own internal credit rating system. For a good discussion of banks' internal credit rating models see Treacy and Carey (1998).

If the credit rating is modeled, then there are numerous choices – after all, credit risk assessment is as old as banking itself. Two examples of credit rating models are the Zeta model, which is described in Altman, Haldeman, and Narayanan (1977), and the Lambda Index, which is described in Emery and Lyons (1991). Both models are based on the entity's financial statements.

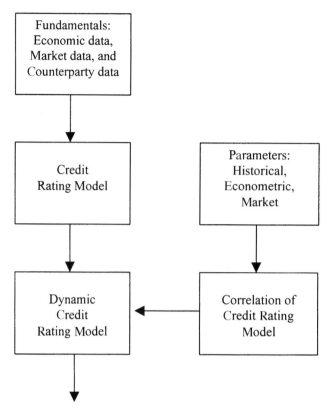

Figure 10.4 Asset credit risk model.

Another well-publicized credit rating model is the EDF Calculator. The EDF model is based on Robert Merton's (1974) observation that a firm's assets are the sum of its equity and debt, so the firm defaults when the assets fall below the face value of the debt. It follows that debt may be thought of as a short option position on the firm's assets, so one may apply the Black–Scholes option theory.

Of course, real bankruptcy is much more complicated and the EDF Calculator accounts for some of these complications. The model's strength is that it is calibrated to a large database of firm data including firm default data. The EDF Calculator actually produces a probability of default, which if one likes, can be mapped to discrete credit ratings. Since the EDF model is proprietary there is no public information on it. The interested reader may consult Crosbie (1997) to get a rough description of its workings. Nickell, Perraudin, and Varotto (1998) compare various credit rating models including EDF.

To accurately measure the credit risk it is essential to know both the credit riskiness today as well as how that credit riskiness may evolve over time. As was stated above, the dynamic credit rating model calculates how an asset's credit riskiness may evolve over time. How this component is implemented depends very much on the assets in the portfolio and the length of the time period for which risk is being calculated. But if the asset's credit riskiness is not being modeled explicitly, it is at least implicitly being modeled somewhere else in the portfolio model, for example in a pricing model – changes in the credit riskiness of an asset are reflected in the price of that asset.

Of course, changes in credit riskiness of various assets are related. So Figure 10.4 also depicts a component for the correlation of credit rating which may be driven by any number of variables including historical, econometric, or market variables.

The oldest dynamic credit rating model is the Markov model for credit rating migration. The appeal of this model is its simplicity. In particular, it is easy to incorporate non-independence of two different firm's credit rating changes.

The portfolio model CreditMetrics (J.P. Morgan, 1997) uses this Markov model. The basic assumption of the Markov model is that a firm's credit rating migrates at random up or down like a Markov process. In particular, the migration over one time period is independent of the migration over the previous period. Credit risk management models based on a Markov process are implemented by Monte Carlo simulation.

Unfortunately, there has been recent research showing that the Markov process is a poor approximation to the credit rating process. The main reason is that the credit rating is influenced by the economy that moves through business cycles. Thus the probability of downgrade and, thus, default is greater during a recession. Kolman (1998) gives a non-technical explanation of this fact. Also Altman, and Kao (1991) mention the shortcomings of the Markov process and propose two alternative processes. Nickell, Perraudin, and Varotto (1998a,b) give a more thorough criticism of Markov processes by using historical data. In addition, the credit rating agencies have published insightful information on their credit rating and how they evolve over time. For example, see Brand, Rabbia and Bahar (1997) or Carty (1997).

Another credit risk management model, CreditRisk+, models only two states: non-default and default (CSFP, 1997). But this is only a heuristic simplification. Rolfes and Broeker (1998) have shown how to enhance CreditRisk+ to model a finite number of credit rating states. The main advantage of the CreditRisk+ model is that it was designed with the goal of allowing for an analytical implementation as opposed to Monte Carlo.

The last model we mention is Portfolio View (McKinsey, 1998). This model is based on econometric models and looks for relationships between the general level of default and economic variables. Of course, predicting any economic variable, including the general level of defaults, is one of the highest goals of research economics. Risk managers should proceed with caution when they start believing they can predict risk factors.

As mentioned above, it is the extreme events that most affect the risk of a portfolio of credit risky assets. Thus it would make sense that a model which more accurately measures the extreme event would be a better one. Wilmott (1998) devised such a model called CrashMetrics. This model is based on the theory that the correlation between events is different from times of calm to times of crisis, so it tries to model the correlation during times of crisis. This theory shows great promise. See Davidson (1997) for another discussion of the various credit risk models.

Credit risk pricing model

The next major component of the model is the credit risk pricing model, which is depicted in detail in Figure 10.5. This portion of the model together with the market

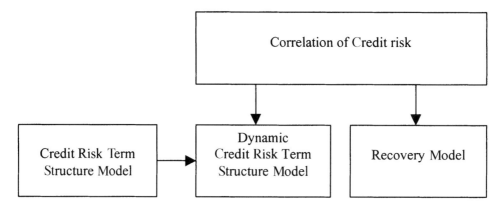

Figure 10.5 Credit risk pricing model.

risk model will allow the credit risk management model to calculate the relevant return statistics.

The credit risk pricing model is necessary because the price of credit risk has two components. One is the credit rating that was handled by the previous component, the other is the spread over the riskless rate. The spread is the price that the market charges for a particular credit risk. This spread can change without the underlying credit risk changing and is affected by supply and demand.

The credit risk pricing model can be based on econometric models or any of the popular risk-neutral pricing models which are used for pricing credit derivatives. Most risk-neutral credit pricing models are transplants of risk-neutral interest rate pricing models and do not adequately account for the differences between credit risk and interest rate risk. Nevertheless, these risk-neutral models seem to be popular. See Skora (1998a,b) for a description of the various risk-neutral credit risk pricing models.

Roughly speaking, static models are sufficient for pricing derivatives which do not have an option component and dynamic models are necessary for pricing derivatives which do have an option component. As far as credit risk management models are concerned, they all need a dynamic credit risk term structure model. The reason is that the credit risk management model needs both the expected return of each asset as well as the covariance matrix of returns. So even if one had both the present price of the asset and the forward price, one would still need to calculate the probability distribution of returns.

So the credit risk model calculates the credit risky term structure, that is, the yield curve for the various credit risky assets. It also calculates the corresponding term structure for the end of the time period as well as the distribution of the term structure. One way to accomplish this is by generating a sample of what the term structure may look like at the end of the period. Then by pricing the credit risky assets off these various term structures, one obtains a sample of what the price of the assets may be.

Since credit spreads do not move independently of one another, the credit risk pricing model, like the asset credit risk model, also has a correlation component. Again depending on the assets in the portfolio, it may be possible to economize and combine this component with the previous one.

Finally, the choice of inputs can be historical, econometric or market data. The choice depends on how the portfolio selection model is to be used. If one expects to invest in a portfolio and divest at the end of the time period, then one needs to calculate actual market prices. In this case the model must be calibrated to market data. At the other extreme, if one were using the portfolio model to simply calculate a portfolio's risk or the marginal risk created by purchasing an additional asset, then the model may be calibrated to historical, econometric, or market data – the choice is the risk manager's.

Market risk pricing model

The market risk pricing model is analogous to the credit risk pricing model, except that it is limited to assets without credit risk. This component models the change in the market rates such as credit-riskless, US Treasury interest rates. To price all the credit risky assets completely and accurately it is necessary to have both a market risk pricing model and credit risk pricing model.

Most models, including CreditMetrics, CreditRisk+, Portfolio Manager, and Portfolio View, have a dynamic credit rating model but lack a credit risk pricing model and market risk pricing model. While the lack of these components partially cripples some models, it does not completely disable them. As such, these models are best suited to products such as loans that are most sensitive to major credit events like credit rating migration including defaults. Two such models for loans only are discussed in Spinner (1998) and Belkin *et al.* (1998).

Exposure model

The exposure model is depicted in Figure 10.6. This portion of the model aggregates the portfolio of assets across business lines and legal entities and any other appropriate category. In particular, netting across a counterparty would take into account the relevant jurisdiction and its netting laws. Without fully aggregating, the model cannot accurately take into account diversification or the lack of diversification.

Only after the portfolio is fully aggregated and netted can it be correctly priced. At this point the market risk pricing model and credit risk pricing model can actually price all the credit risky assets.

The exposure model also calculates for each asset the appropriate time period, which roughly corresponds to the amount of time it would take to liquidate the asset. Having a different time period for each asset not only increases the complexity of the model, it also raises some theoretical questions. Should the time period corresponding to an asset be the length of time it takes to liquidate only that asset? To liquidate all the assets in the portfolio? Or to liquidate all the assets in the portfolio in a time of financial crisis? The answer is difficult. Most models simply use the same time period, usually one year, for all exposures. One year is considered an appropriate amount of time for reacting to a credit loss whether that be liquidating a position or raising more capital. There is an excellent discussion of this issue in Jones and Mingo (1998). Another responsibility of the exposure model is to report the portfolio's various concentrations.

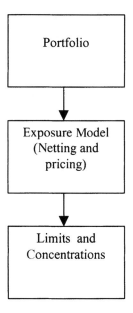

Figure 10.6 Exposure model and some statistics.

Risk calculation engine

The last component is the risk calculation engine which actually calculates the expected returns and multivariate distributions that are then used to calculate the associated risks and the optimal portfolio. Since the distributions are not normal, this portion of the portfolio model requires some ingenuity.

One method of calculation is Monte Carlo simulation. This is exemplified in many of the above-mentioned models. Another method of calculating the probability distribution is numerical. One starts by approximating the probability distribution of losses for each asset by a discrete probability distribution. This is a reasonable simplification because one is mainly interested in large, collective losses – not individual firm losses.

Once the individual probability distributions have been discretized, there is a well-known computation called convolution for computing the aggregate probability distribution. This numerical method is easiest when the probability distributions are independent – which in this case they are not. There are tricks and enhancements to the convolution technique to make it work for nonindependent distributions.

The risk calculation engine of CreditRisk+ uses the convolution. It models the nonindependence of defaults with a factor model. It assumes that there is a finite number of factors which describe nonindependence. Such factors would come from the firm's country, geographical location, industry, and specific characteristics.

Capital and regulation

Regulators ensure that our financial system is safe while at the same time that it prospers. To ensure that safety, regulators insist that a bank holds sufficient capital

Table 10.1 Model checklist

Component	Subcomponent	Question
Counterparty credit risk model	Fundamental data	Accepts fundamental counterparty, market, or economic data?
	Credit rating	Computes credit rating?
	Credit rating model	Models evolution of credit rating?
	Correlation model	Changes in credit rating are non-independent?
Credit risk model	Credit risk term structure	Accurately constructs credit risk term structure?
	Dynamic credit risk term structure	Robust model of changes in credit risk term structure?
	Recovery model	Recovery is static or dynamic?
	Correlation model	Changes in credit risk term structure non-independent?
Market risk model	Interest rate model	Robust model of changes in riskless interest rate term structure?
	Foreign exchange rate model	Robust model of changes in exchange rates?
	Correlation	Market risk and credit risk non-independent?
Products	Loans	Accepts loans?
	Bonds	Accepts bonds?
	Derivatives	Accepts derivatives?
	Structured products	Accepts credit derivatives, credit-linked notes, etc.?
	Collateral	Accepts collateral?
	Risk reduction	Models covenants, downgrade triggers, etc.?
	Liquidity	Accounts for differences in liquidity?
	Concentration	Calculates limits?
Aggregation	Legal	Nets according to legal jurisdiction?
	Products	Aggregate across products?
	Counterparty	Aggregate across counterparty?
	Business	Aggregate across business lines?
	Books	Aggregate across bank books?
Output	Probability distribution	Computes cumulative probability distribution of losses?
	Capital	Computes economic capital?
	Marginal statistics	Computes marginal statistics for one asset?
	Optimization	Computes optimal portfolio?
Other	Stress	Performs stress tests?
	Scenario	Performs scenario tests?

to absorb losses. This includes losses due to market, credit, and all other risks. The proper amount of capital raises interesting theoretical and practical questions. (See, for example, Matten, 1996 or Pratt, 1998.) Losses due to market or credit risk show up as losses to the bank's assets. A bank should have sufficient capital to absorb not only losses during normal times but also losses during stressful times.

In the hope of protecting our financial system and standardizing requirements around the world the 1988 Basel Capital Accord set minimum requirements for calculating bank capital. It was also the intent of regulators to make the rules simple. The Capital Accord specified that regulatory capital is 8% of risk-weighted assets. The risk weights were 100%, 50%, 20%, or 0% depending on the asset. For example, a loan to an OECD bank would have a risk weighting of 20%. Even at the time the regulators knew there were shortcomings in the regulation, but it had the advantage of being simple.

The changes in banking since 1988 have proved the Capital Accord to be very inadequate – Jones and Mingo (1998) discuss the problems in detail. Banks use exotic products to change their regulatory capital requirements independent of their actual risk. They are arbitraging the regulation. Now there is arbitrage across banking, trading, and counterparty bank books as well as within individual books (see Irving, 1997).

One of the proposals from the industry is to allow banks to use their own internal models to compute regulatory credit risk capital similar to the way they use VaR models to compute add-ons to regulatory market risk capital. Some of the pros and cons of internal models are discussed in Irving (1997). The International Swaps and Derivatives Association (1998) has proposed a model. Their main point is that regulators should embrace models as soon as possible and they should allow the models to evolve over time.

Regulators are examining ways to correct the problems in existing capital regulation. It is a very positive development that the models, and their implementation, will be scrutinized before making a new decision on regulation.

The biggest mistake the industry could make would be to adopt a one-size-fits all policy. Arbitrarily adopting any of these models would certainly stifle creativity. More importantly, it could undermine responsibility and authority of those most capable of carrying out credit risk management.

Conclusion

The rapid proliferation of credit risk models, including credit risk management models, has resulted in sophisticated models which provide crucial information to credit risk managers (see Table 10.1). In addition, many of these models have focused attention on the inadequacy of current credit risk management practices. Firms should continue to improve these models but keep in mind that models are only one tool of credit risk management. While many banks have already successfully implemented these models, we are a long way from having a 'universal' credit risk management model that handles all the firm's credit risky assets.

Author's note

This paper is an extension of Richard K. Skora, 'Modern credit risk modeling', presented at the meeting of the Global Association of Risk Professionals. 19 October 1998.

Note

[1] Of course implementing and applying a model is a crucial step in realizing the benefits of modeling. Indeed, there is a feedback effect, the practicalities of implementation and application affect many decisions in the modeling process.

References

Altman, E., Haldeman, R. G. and Narayanan, P. (1997) 'ZETA analysis: A new model to identify bankruptcy risk of corporations', *J. Banking and Finance*, **1**, 29–54.

Altman, E. I. and Kao, D. L. (1991) 'Examining and modeling corporate bond rating drift', working paper, New York University Salomon Center (New York, NY).

Belkin, B., Forest, L., Aguais, S. and Suchower, S. (1998) 'Expect the unexpected', CreditRisk – a Risk special report, *Risk*, **11**, No. 11, 34–39.

Bessis, J. (1998) *Risk Management in Banking*, Wiley, Chichester.

Best, P. (1998) *Implementing Value at Risk*, Wiley, Chichester.

Brand, L., Rabbia, J. and Bahar, R. (1997) *Rating Performance 1996: Stability and Transition, Standard & Poor's*.

Carty, L. V. (1997) *Moody's Rating Migration and Credit Quality Correlation, 1920–1996*, Moody's.

Crosbie, P. (1997) *Modeling Default Risk*, KMV Corporation.

Crouhy, M. and Mark, R. (1998) 'A comparative analysis of current credit risk models', Credit Risk Modelling and Regulatory Implications, organized by The Bank of England and Financial Services Authority, 21–22 September.

Davidson, C. (1997) 'A credit to the system', CreditRisk – supplement to *Risk*, **10**, No. 7, July, 61–4.

Credit Suisse Financial Products (1997) *CreditRisk+*.

Dowd, K. (1998) *Beyond Value at Risk*, Wiley, Chichester.

Elton, E. J. and Gruber, M. J. (1991) *Modern Portfolio Theory and Investment Analysis*, fourth edition, Wiley, New York.

Emery, G. W. and Lyons, R. G. (1991) 'The Lambda Index: beyond the current ration', *Business Credit*, November/December, 22–3.

Gordy, M. B. (1998) 'A comparative anatomy of credit risk models', Finance and economics discussion series, Federal Reserve Board, Washington DC.

Irving, R. (1997) 'The internal question', Credit Risk – supplement to *Risk*, **10**, No. 7, July, 36–8.

International Swaps and Derivatives Association (1998) *Credit Risk and Regulatory Capital*, March.

Jones, D. and Mingo, J. (1998) 'Industry practices in credit risk modeling and internal capital allocations: implications for a models-based regulatory standard', in *Financial Services at the Crossroads: Capital Regulation in the Twenty First Century*, Federal Reserve Bank of New York, February.

Jorion, P. (1997) *Value at Risk*, McGraw-Hill, New York.

Kolman, J. (1997) 'Roundtable on the limits of VAR', *Derivatives Strategy*, **3**, No. 4, April, 14–22.

Kolman, J. (1998) 'The world according to Edward Altman', *Derivatives Strategy*, **3**, No. 12, 47–51 supports the statement that the models do not try to match reality.

Koyluoglu, H. V. and Hickman, A. (1998) 'Reconcilable differences', *Risk*, **11**, No. 10, October, 56–62.

Lentino, J. V. and Pirzada, H. (1998) 'Issues to consider in comparing credit risk management models', *J. Lending & Credit Risk Management*, **81**, No. 4, December, 16–22.

Locke, J. (1998) 'Off-the-peg, off the mark?' CreditRisk – a *Risk* special report, *Risk*, **11**, No. 11, November, 22–7.

Lopez, J. A. and Saidenberg, M. R. (1998) 'Evaluating credit risk models', Credit Risk

Modelling and Regulatory Implications, organized by The Bank of England and Financial Services Authority, 21–22 September.

Markowitz, H. (1952) 'Portfolio selection', *J. of Finance*, March, 77–91.

Markowitz, H. (1959) *Portfolio Selection*, Wiley, New York.

Matten, C. (1996) *Managing Bank Capital*, Wiley, Chichester.

Merton, R. C. (1974) 'On the pricing of corporate debt: the risk structure of interest rates', *Journal of Finance*, **29**, 449–70.

J. P. Morgan (1997) *CreditMetrics*.

McKinsey & Company, Inc. (1998) *A Credit Portfolio Risk Measurement & Management Approach*.

Pratt, S. P. (1998) *Cost of Capital*, Wiley, New York.

Rhode, W. (1998a) 'McDonough unveils Basel review', *Risk*, **11**, No. 9, September.

Nickell, P., Perraudin, W. and Varotto, S. (1998a) 'Stability of rating transitions', Credit Risk Modelling and Regulatory Implications, organized by The Bank of England and Financial Services Authority, 21–22 September.

Nickell, P., Perraudin, W. and Varotto, S. (1998b) 'Ratings-versus equity-based risk modelling', Credit Risk Modelling and Regulatory Implications, organized by The Bank of England and Financial Services Authority, 21–22 September.

Rolfes, B. and Broeker, F. (1998) 'Good migrations', *Risk*, **11**, No. 11, November, 72–5.

Shirreff, D. (1998) 'Models get a thrashing', *Euromoney Magazine*, October.

Skora, R. K. (1998a) 'Modern credit risk modeling', presented at the meeting of the Global Association of Risk Professionals, 19 October.

Skora, R. K. (1998b) Rational modelling of credit risk and credit derivatives', in *Credit Derivatives – Applications for Risk Management, Investment and Portfolio Optimization*, Risk Books, London.

Spinner, K. (1998) 'Managing bank loan risk', *Derivatives Strategy*, **3**, No. 1, January, 14–22.

Treacy, W. and Carey, M. (1998) 'Internal credit risk rating systems at large U.S. banks', Credit Risk Modelling and Regulatory Implications, organized by The Bank of England and Financial Services Authority, 21–22 September.

Wilmott, P. (1998) *CrashMetrics*, Wilmott Associates, March.

11

Risk management of credit derivatives

KURT S. WILHELM

Introduction

Credit risk is the largest single risk in banking. To enhance credit risk management, banks actively evaluate strategies to identify, measure, and control credit concentrations. Credit derivatives, a market that has grown from virtually zero in 1993 to an estimated $350 billion at year end 1998,[1] have emerged as an increasingly popular tool. Initially, banks used credit derivatives to generate revenue; more recently, bank usage has evolved to using them as a capital and credit risk management tool. This chapter discusses the types of credit derivative products, market growth, and risks. It also highlights risk management practices that market participants should adopt to ensure that they use credit derivatives in a safe and sound manner. It concludes with a discussion of a portfolio approach to credit risk management.

Credit derivatives can allow banks to manage credit risk more effectively and improve portfolio diversification. Banks can use credit derivatives to reduce undesired risk concentrations, which historically have proven to be a major source of bank financial problems. Similarly, banks can assume risk, in a diversification context, by targeting exposures having a low correlation with existing portfolio risks. Credit derivatives allow institutions to customize credit exposures, creating risk profiles unavailable in the cash markets. They also enable creditors to take risk-reducing actions without adversely impacting the underlying credit relationship.

Users of credit derivatives must recognize and manage a number of associated risks. The market is new and therefore largely untested. Participants will undoubtedly discover unanticipated risks as the market evolves. Legal risks, in particular, can be much higher than in other derivative products. Similar to poorly developed lending strategies, the improper use of credit derivatives can result in an imprudent credit risk profile. Institutions should avoid material participation in the nascent credit derivatives market until they have fully explored, and developed a comfort level with, the risks involved. Originally developed for trading opportunities, these instruments recently have begun to serve as credit risk management tools. This chapter primarily deals with the credit risk management aspects of banks' use of credit derivatives.

Credit derivatives have become a common element in two emerging trends in how banks assess their large corporate credit portfolios. First, larger banks increasingly devote human and capital resources to measure and model credit portfolio risks more *quantitatively*, embracing the tenets of modern portfolio theory (MPT). Banks have pursued these efforts to increase the efficiency of their credit portfolios and look to increase returns for a given level of risk or, conversely, to reduce risks for a given level of returns. Institutions adopting more advanced credit portfolio measurement techniques expect that increased portfolio diversification and greater insight into portfolio risks will result in superior relative performance over the economic cycle.

The second trend involves tactical bank efforts to reduce regulatory capital requirements on high-quality corporate credit exposures. The current Basel Committee on Bank Supervision Accord ('Basel') requirements of 8% for all corporate credits, regardless of underlying quality, reduce banks' incentives to make higher quality loans. Banks have used various securitization alternatives to reconcile regulatory and economic capital requirements for large corporate exposures. Initially, these securitizations took the form of collateralized loan obligations (CLOs). More recently, however, banks have explored ways to reduce the high costs of CLOs, and have begun to consider synthetic securitization structures.

The synthetic securitization structures banks employ to reduce regulatory capital requirements for higher-grade loan exposures use credit derivatives to purchase credit protection against a pool of credit exposures. As credit risk modeling efforts evolve, and banks increasingly embrace a MPT approach to credit risk management, banks increasingly may use credit derivatives to adjust portfolio risk profiles.

Size of the credit derivatives market and impediments to growth

The first credit derivative transactions occurred in the early 1990s, as large derivative dealers searched for ways to transfer risk exposures on financial derivatives. Their objective was to be able to increase derivatives business with their largest counterparties. The market grew slowly at first. More recently, growth has accelerated as banks have begun to use credit derivatives to make portfolio adjustments and to reduce risk-based capital requirements.

As discussed in greater detail below, there are four credit derivative products: credit default swaps (CDS), total return swaps (TRS), credit-linked notes (CLNs) and credit spread options. Default swaps, total return swaps and credit spread options are over-the-counter transactions, while credit-linked notes are cash market securities.

Market participants estimate the current global market for credit derivatives will reach $740 billion by the year 2000.[2] Bank supervisors in the USA began collecting credit derivative information in Call Reports as of 31 March 1997. Table 11.1 tracks the quarterly growth in credit derivatives for both insured US banks, and all institutions filing Call Reports (which includes uninsured US offices of foreign branches). The table's data reflect substantial growth in credit derivatives. Over the two years US bank supervisors have collected the data, the compounded annual growth rate of notional credit derivatives for US insured banks, and all reporting entities (including foreign branches and agencies), were 216.2% and 137.2% respectively.

Call Report data understates the size of the credit derivatives market. First, it includes only transactions for banks domiciled in the USA. It does not include the activities of banks domiciled outside the USA, or any non-commercial banks, such as investment firms. Second, the data includes activity only for off-balance sheet transactions; therefore, it completely excludes CLNs.

Table 11.1 US credit derivatives market quarterly growth (billions)

	31-3-97	30-6-97	30-9-97	31-12-97	31-3-98	30-6-98	30-9-98	31-12-98	31-3-99
Insured US banks	$19.1	$25.6	$38.9	$54.7	$91.4	$129.2	$161.8	$144.1	$191.0
US banks, foreign branches and agencies	$40.7	$69.0	$72.9	$97.1	$148.3	$208.9	$217.1	$198.7	$229.1

Source: Call Reports

Activity in credit derivatives has grown rapidly over the past two years. Nevertheless, the number of institutions participating in the market remains small. Like financial derivatives, credit derivatives activity in the US banking system is concentrated in a small group of dealers and end-users. As of 31 March 1999, only 24 insured banking institutions, and 38 uninsured US offices (branches and agencies) of foreign banks reported credit derivatives contracts outstanding. Factors that account for the narrow institutional participation include:

1 Difficulty of measuring credit risk
2 Application of risk-based capital rules
3 Credit risk complacency and hedging costs
4 Limited ability to hedge illiquid exposures and
5 Legal and cultural issues.

An evaluation of these factors helps to set the stage for a discussion of credit derivative products and risk management issues, which are addressed in subsequent sections.

Difficulty of measuring credit risk

Measuring credit risk on a portfolio basis is difficult. Banks traditionally measure credit exposures by obligor and industry. They have only recently attempted to define risk quantitatively in a portfolio context, e.g. a Value-at-Risk (VaR) framework.[3] Although banks have begun to develop internally, or purchase, systems that measure VaR for credit, bank managements do not yet have confidence in the risk measures the systems produce. In particular, measured risk levels depend heavily on underlying assumptions (default correlations, amount outstanding at time of default, recovery rates upon default, etc.), and risk managers often do not have great confidence in those parameters. Since credit derivatives exist principally to allow for the effective transfer of credit risk, the difficulty in measuring credit risk and the absence of confidence in the results of risk measurement have appropriately made banks cautious about using credit derivatives. Such difficulties have also made bank supervisors cautious about the use of banks' internal credit risk models for regulatory capital purposes.

Measurement difficulties explain why banks have not, until very recently, tried to implement measures to calculate Value-at-Risk (VaR) for credit. The VaR concept, used extensively for market risk, has become so well accepted that bank supervisors allow such measures to determine capital requirements for trading portfolios.[4] The models created to measure credit risk are new, and have yet to face the test of an economic downturn. Results of different credit risk models, using the same data, can vary widely. Until banks have greater confidence in parameter inputs used to measure the credit risk in their portfolios, they will, and should, exercise caution in using credit derivatives to manage risk on a portfolio basis. Such models can only complement, but not replace, the sound judgment of seasoned credit risk managers.

Application of risk-based capital rules

Regulators have not yet settled on the most appropriate application of risk-based capital rules for credit derivatives, and banks trying to use them to reduce credit risk may find that current regulatory interpretations serve as disincentives.[5] Generally, the current rules do not require capital based upon economic risk. For example, capital rules neither differentiate between high- and low-quality assets nor do they recognize diversification efforts. Transactions that pose the same economic risk may involve quite different regulatory capital requirements. While the Basel Committee has made the review of capital requirements for credit derivatives a priority, the current uncertainty of the application of capital requirements has made it difficult for banks to measure fully the costs of hedging credit risk.[6]

Credit risk complacency and hedging costs

The absence of material domestic loan losses in recent years, the current strength of the US economy, and competitive pressures have led not only to a slippage in underwriting standards but also in some cases to complacency regarding asset quality and the need to reduce credit concentrations. Figure 11.1 illustrates the 'lumpy' nature of credit losses on commercial credits over the past 15 years. It plots charge-offs of commercial and industrial loans as a percentage of such loans.

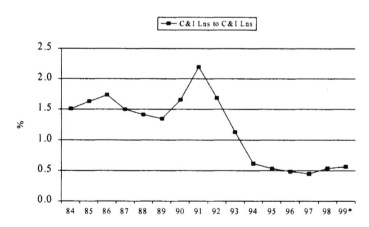

Figure 11.1 Charge-offs: all commercial banks. *99Q1 has been annualized. (*Data source:* Bank Call Reports)

Over the past few years, banks have experienced very small losses on commercial credits. However, it is also clear that when the economy weakens, credit losses can become a major concern. The threat of large losses, which can occur because of credit concentrations, has led many larger banks to attempt to measure their credit risks on a more quantitative, 'portfolio', basis.

Until recently, credit spreads on lower-rated, non-investment grade credits had contracted sharply. Creditors believe lower credit spreads indicate reduced credit risk, and therefore less need to hedge.

Even when economic considerations indicate a bank should hedge a credit exposure, creditors often choose not to buy credit protection when the hedge cost exceeds the return from carrying the exposure. In addition, competitive factors and a desire to maintain customer relationships often cause banks to originate credit (funded or unfunded) at returns that are lower than the cost of hedging such exposures in the derivatives market. Many banks continue to have a book value, as opposed to an economic value, focus.

Limited ability to hedge illiquid exposures

Credit derivatives can effectively hedge credit exposures when an underlying borrower has publicly traded debt (loans or bonds) outstanding that can serve as a reference asset. However, most banks have virtually all their exposures to firms that do not have public debt outstanding. Because banks lend to a large number of firms without public debt, they currently find it difficult to use credit derivatives to hedge these illiquid exposures. As a practical matter, banks are able to hedge exposures only for their largest borrowers. Therefore, the potential benefits of credit derivatives largely remain at this time beyond the reach of community banks, where credit concentrations tend to be largest.

Legal and cultural issues

Unlike most financial derivatives, credit derivative transactions require extensive legal review. Banks that engage in credit derivatives face a variety of legal issues, such as:

1 Interpreting the meaning of terms not clearly defined in contracts and confirmations when unanticipated situations arise
2 The capacity of counterparties to contract and
3 Risks that reviewing courts will not uphold contractual arrangements.

Although contracts have become more standardized, market participants continue to report that transactions often require extensive legal review, and that many situations require negotiation and amendments to the standardized documents.

Until recently, very few default swap contracts were triggered because of the relative absence of default events. The recent increase in defaults has led to more credit events, and protection sellers generally have met their obligations without threat of litigation. Nevertheless, because the possibility for litigation remains a significant concern, legal risks and costs associated with legal transactional review remain obstacles to greater participation and market growth.

Cultural issues also have constrained the use of credit derivatives. The traditional separation within banks between the credit and treasury functions has made it difficult for many banks to evaluate credit derivatives as a strategic risk management tool. Credit officers in many institutions are skeptical that the use of a portfolio model, which attempts to identify risk concentrations, can lead to more effective risk/reward decision making. Many resist credit derivatives because of a negative view of derivatives generally.

Over time, bank treasury and credit functions likely will become more integrated, with each function contributing its comparative advantages to more effective risk management decisions. As more banks use credit portfolio models and credit derivatives, credit portfolio management may become more 'equity-like'. As portfolio managers buy and sell credit risk in a portfolio context, to increase diversification and to make the portfolio more efficient, however, banks increasingly may originate exposure without maintaining direct borrower relationships. As portfolio management evolves toward this model, banks will face significant cultural challenges. Most banks report at least some friction between credit portfolio managers and line lenders, particularly with respect to loan pricing. Credit portfolio managers face an important challenge. They will attempt to capture the diversification and efficiency benefits offered by the use of more quantitative techniques and credit derivatives. At the same time, these risk managers will try to avoid diminution in their qualitative understanding of portfolio risks, which less direct contact with obligors may imply.

What are credit derivatives?

Credit derivatives permit the transfer of credit exposure between parties, in isolation from other forms of risk. Banks can use credit derivatives both to assume or reduce (hedge) credit risk. Market participants refer to credit hedgers as protection purchasers, and to providers of credit protection (i.e. the party who assumes credit risk) as protection sellers.

There are a number of reasons market participants have found credit derivatives attractive. First, credit derivatives allow banks to customize the credit exposure desired, without having a direct relationship with a particular client, or that client having a current funding need. Consider a bank that would like to acquire a two-year exposure to a company in the steel industry. The company has corporate debt outstanding, but its maturity exceeds two years. The bank can simply sell protection for two years, creating an exposure that does not exist in the cash market. However, the flexibility to customize credit terms also bears an associated cost. The credit derivative is less liquid than an originated, directly negotiated, cash market exposure. Additionally, a protection seller may use only publicly available information in determining whether to sell protection. In contrast, banks extending credit directly to a borrower typically have some access to the entity's nonpublic financial information.

Credit derivatives allow a bank to transfer credit risk without adversely impacting the customer relationship. The ability to sell the risk, but not the asset itself, allows banks to separate the origination and portfolio decisions. Credit derivatives therefore permit banks to hedge the concentrated credit exposures that large corporate relationships, or industry concentrations created because of market niches, can often present. For example, banks may hedge existing exposures in order to provide capacity to extend additional credit without breaching internal, in-house limits.

There are three principal types of credit derivative products: credit default swaps, total return swaps, and credit-linked notes. A fourth product, credit spread options, is not a significant product in the US bank market.

Credit default swaps

In a credit default swap (CDS), the protection seller, the provider of credit protection, receives a payment in return for the obligation to make a payment that is contingent on the occurrence of a credit event for a reference entity. The size of the payment reflects the decline in value of a reference asset issued by the reference entity. A credit event is normally a payment default, bankruptcy or insolvency, failure to pay, or receivership. It can also include a restructuring or a ratings downgrade. A reference asset can be a loan, security, or any asset upon which a 'dealer price' can be established. A dealer price is important because it allows both participants to a transaction to observe the degree of loss in a credit instrument. In the absence of a credit event, there is no obligation for the protection seller to make any payment, and the seller collects what amounts to an option premium. Credit hedgers will receive a payment only if a credit event occurs; they do not have any protection against market value declines of the reference asset that occur without a credit event. Figure 11.2 shows the obligations of the two parties in a CDS.

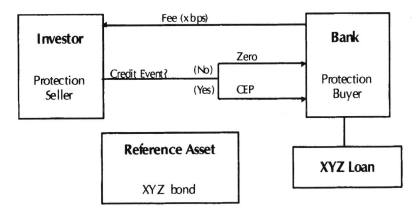

Investor (which could also be a bank) sells credit protection to the bank with a reference asset of XYZ bond. The bank pays a fee of x basis points. Under the terms of the contract, if a credit event with respect to XYZ Corp. occurs, the investor will pay the bank the Credit Event Payment (CEP). If no credit event occurs, the contract will expire at maturity with no payment from the investor. The bank may or may not own XYZ Loan.

Figure 11.2 Credit default swap.

In the figure the protection buyer looks to reduce risk of exposure to XYZ. For example, it may have a portfolio model that indicates that the exposure contributes excessively to overall portfolio risk. It is important to understand, in a portfolio context, that the XYZ exposure may well be a high-quality asset. A concentration in any credit risky asset, regardless of quality, can pose unacceptable portfolio risk. Hedging such exposures may represent a prudent strategy to reduce aggregate portfolio risk.

The protection seller, on the other hand, may find the XYZ exposure helpful in diversifying its own portfolio risks. Though each counterparty may have the same qualitative view of the credit, their own aggregate exposure profiles may dictate contrary actions.

If a credit event occurs, the protection seller must pay an amount as provided in the underlying contract. There are two methods of settlement following a credit event: (1) cash settlement; and (2) physical delivery of the reference asset at par value. The reference asset typically represents a marketable obligation that participants in a credit derivatives contract can observe to determine the loss suffered in the event of default. For example, a default swap in which a bank hedges a loan exposure to a company may designate a corporate bond from that same entity as the reference asset. Upon default, the decline in value of the corporate bond should approximate the loss in the value of the loan, if the protection buyer has carefully selected the reference asset.

Cash-settled transactions involve a credit event payment (CEP) from the protection seller to the protection buyer, and can work in two different ways. The terms of the contract may call for a fixed dollar amount (i.e. a 'binary' payment). For example, the contract may specify a credit event payment of 50% upon default; this figure is negotiated and may, or may not, correspond to the expected recovery amount on the asset. More commonly, however, a calculation agent determines the CEP. If the two parties do not agree with the CEP determined by the calculation agent, then a dealer poll determines the payment. The dealer poll is an auction process in which dealers 'bid' on the reference asset. Contract terms may call for five independent dealers to bid, over a three-day period, 14 days after the credit event. The average price that the dealers bid will reflect the market expectation of a recovery rate on the reference asset. The protection seller then pays par value less the recovery rate. This amount represents the estimate of loss on assuming exposure to the reference asset. In both cases, binary payment or dealer poll, the obligation is cash-settled because the protection seller pays cash to settle its obligation.

In the second method of settlement, a physical settlement, the protection buyer may deliver the reference asset, or other asset specified in the contract, to the protection seller at par value. Since the buyer collects the par value for the defaulted asset, if it delivers its underlying exposure, it suffers no credit loss.

CDSs allow the protection seller to gain exposure to a reference obligor, but absent a credit event, do not involve a funding requirement. In this respect, CDSs resemble and are economically similar to standby letters of credit, a traditional bank credit product.

Credit default swaps may contain a materiality threshold. The purpose of this is to avoid credit event payments for technical defaults that do not have a significant market impact. They specify that the protection seller make a credit event payment to the protection buyer, if a credit event has occurred **and** the price of the reference asset has fallen by some specified amount. Thus, a payment is conditional upon a specified level of value impairment, as well as a default event. Given a default, a payment occurs only if the value change satisfies the threshold condition.

A basket default swap is a special type of CDS. In a basket default swap, the protection seller receives a fee for agreeing to make a payment upon the occurrence of the first credit event to occur among several reference assets in a basket. The protection buyer, in contrast, secures protection against only the *first* default among the specified reference assets. Because the protection seller pays out on one default, of any of the names (i.e. reference obligors), a basket swap represents a more leveraged transaction than other credit derivatives, with correspondingly higher fees. Basket swaps represent complicated risk positions due to the necessity to understand the correlation of the assets in the basket. Because a protection seller can lose on only one name, it would prefer the names in the basket to be as highly correlated as possible. The greater the number of names in the basket and the lower the correlation among the names, the greater the likelihood that the protection seller will have to make a payment.

The credit exposure in a CDS generally goes in one direction. Upon default, the protection buyer will receive a payment from, and thus is exposed to, the protection seller. The protection buyer in a CDS will suffer a default-related credit loss only if both the reference asset and the protection seller default simultaneously. A default by either party alone should not result in a credit loss. If the reference entity defaults, the protection seller must make a payment. If the protection seller defaults, but the reference asset does not, the protection purchaser has no payment due. In this event, however, the protection purchaser no longer has a credit hedge, and may incur higher costs to replace the protection if it still desires a hedge. The protection seller's only exposure to the protection buyer is for periodic payments of the protection fee. Dealers in credit derivatives, who may have a large volume of transactions with other dealers, should monitor this 'receivables' exposure.

Total return swaps

In a total return swap (TRS), the protection buyer ('synthetic short') pays out cash flow received on an asset, plus any capital appreciation earned on that asset. It receives a floating rate of interest (usually LIBOR plus a spread), *plus* any depreciation on the asset. The protection seller ('synthetic long') has the opposite profile; it receives cash flows on the reference asset, plus any appreciation. It pays any depreciation to the protection buying counterparty, plus a floating interest rate. This profile establishes a TRS as a synthetic sale of the underlying asset by the protection buyer and a synthetic purchase by the protection seller. Figure 11.3 illustrates TRS cash flows.

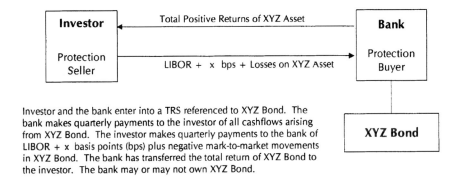

Investor and the bank enter into a TRS referenced to XYZ Bond. The bank makes quarterly payments to the investor of all cashflows arising from XYZ Bond. The investor makes quarterly payments to the bank of LIBOR + x basis points (bps) plus negative mark-to-market movements in XYZ Bond. The bank has transferred the total return of XYZ Bond to the investor. The bank may or may not own XYZ Bond.

Figure 11.3 Total return swap.

TRSs enable banks to create synthetic long or short positions in assets. A long position in a TRS is economically equivalent to the financed purchase of the asset. However, the holder of a long position in a TRS (protection seller) does not actually purchase the asset. Instead, the protection seller realizes all the economic benefits of ownership of the bond, but uses the protection buyer's balance sheet to fund that 'purchase'.

TRSs enable banks to take short positions in corporate credit more easily than is possible in the cash markets. It is difficult to sell short a corporate bond (i.e. sell a bond and hope to repurchase, subsequently, the same security at a lower price), because the seller must deliver a specific bond to the buyer. To create a synthetic short in a corporate exposure with a TRS, an investor agrees to pay total return on an issue and receive a floating rate, usually LIBOR (plus a spread) plus any depreciation on the asset. Investors have found TRSs an effective means of creating short positions in emerging market assets.

A TRS offers more complete protection to a credit hedger than does a CDS, because a TRS provides protection for market value deterioration short of an outright default.

A credit default swap, in contrast, provides the equivalent of catastrophic insurance; it pays out only upon the occurrence of a credit event, in which case the default swap terminates. A TRS may or may not terminate upon default of the reference asset. Most importantly, unlike the one-way credit exposure of a CDS, the credit exposure in a TRS goes both ways. A protection buyer assumes credit exposure of the protection seller when the reference asset depreciates; in this case, the protection seller must make a payment to the protection buyer. A protection seller assumes credit exposure of the protection buyer, who must pay any appreciation on the asset to the protection seller. A protection buyer will suffer a loss only if the value of the reference asset has declined and simultaneously the protection seller defaults. A protection seller can suffer a credit loss if the protection buyer defaults and the value of the reference asset has increased.

In practice, banks that buy protection use CDSs to hedge credit relationships, particularly unfunded commitments, typically with the objective to reduce risk-based capital requirements. Banks that sell protection seek to earn the premiums, while taking credit risks they would take in the normal course of business. Banks typically use TRSs to provide financing to investment managers and securities dealers. TRSs thus often represent a means of extending secured credit rather than a credit hedging activity. In such cases, the protection seller 'rents' the protection buyer's balance sheet. The seller receives the total return of the asset that the buyer holds on its balance sheet as collateral for the loan. The spread over LIBOR paid by the seller compensates the buyer for its funding and capital costs.

Credit derivative dealers also use TRSs to create structured, and leveraged, investment products. As an example, the dealer acquires $100 in high-yield loans and then passes the risk through to a special-purpose vehicle (SPV) by paying the SPV the total return on a swap. The SPV then issues $20 in investor notes. The yield, and thus the risk, of the $100 portfolio of loans is thus concentrated into $20 in securities, permitting the securities to offer very high yields.[7]

Credit-linked Notes

A credit-linked note (CLN) is a cash market-structured note with a credit derivative, typically a CDS, embedded in the structure. The investor in the CLN sells credit protection. Should the reference asset underlying the CLN default, the investor (i.e. protection seller) will suffer a credit loss. The CLN issuer is a protection buyer. Its obligation to repay the par value of the security at maturity is contingent upon the *absence* of a credit event on the underlying reference asset. Figure 11.4 shows the cash flows of a CLN with an embedded CDS.

A bank can use the CLN as a funded solution to hedging a company's credit risk because issuing the note provides cash to the issuing bank. It resembles a loan participation but, as with other credit derivatives, the loan remains on the bank's books.

The investor in the CLN has sold credit protection and will suffer a loss if XYZ defaults, as the issuer bank would redeem the CLN at less than par to compensate it for its credit loss. For example, a bank may issue a CLN embedded with a fixed payout (binary) default swap that provides for a payment to investors of 75 cents on the dollar in the event a designated reference asset (XYZ) defaults on a specified obligation. The bank might issue such a CLN if it wished to hedge a credit exposure to XYZ. As with other credit derivatives, however, a bank can take a short position if

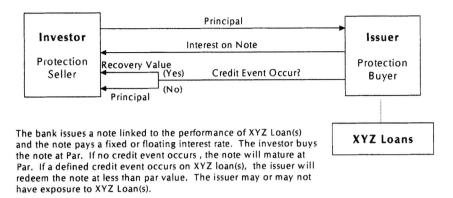

The bank issues a note linked to the performance of XYZ Loan(s) and the note pays a fixed or floating interest rate. The investor buys the note at Par. If no credit event occurs, the note will mature at Par. If a defined credit event occurs on XYZ loan(s), the issuer will redeem the note at less than par value. The issuer may or may not have exposure to XYZ Loan(s).

Figure 11.4 A credit-linked note.

it has no exposure to XYZ, but issues a CLN using XYZ as the reference asset. Like the structured notes of the early 1990s, CLNs provide a cash market alternative to investors unable to purchase off-balance sheet derivatives, most often due to legal restrictions.

CLNs are frequently issued through special-purpose vehicles (SPV), which use the sale proceeds from the notes to buy collateral assets, e.g. Treasury securities or money market assets. In these transactions, the hedging institution purchases default protection from the SPV. The SPV pledges the assets as collateral to secure any payments due to the credit hedger on the credit default swap, through which the sponsor of the SPV hedges its credit risk on a particular obligor. Interest on the collateral assets, plus fees on the default swap paid to the SPV by the hedger, generate cash flow for investors. When issued through an SPV, the investor assumes credit risk of both the reference entity and the collateral. When issued directly, the investor assumes two-name credit risk; it is exposed to both the reference entity and the issuer.

Credit hedgers may choose to issue a CLN, as opposed to executing a default swap, in order to reduce counterparty credit risk. As the CLN investor pays cash to the issuer, the protection buying issuer eliminates credit exposure to the protection seller that would occur in a CDS.

Dealers may use CLNs to hedge exposures they acquire by writing protection on default swaps. For example, a dealer may write protection on a default swap, with XYZ as the reference entity, and collect 25 basis points. The dealer may be able to hedge that exposure by issuing a CLN, perhaps paying LIBOR + 10 basis points, that references XYZ. The dealer therefore originates the exposure in one market and hedges it in another, arbitraging the difference between the spreads in the two markets.

Credit spread options

Credit spread options allow investors to trade or hedge changes in credit quality. With a credit spread option, a protection seller takes the risk that the spread on a reference asset breaches a specified level. The protection purchaser buys the right to sell a security if the reference obligor's credit spread exceeds a given 'strike' level.

For example, assume a bank has placed a loan yielding LIBOR plus 15 basis points in its trading account. The bank may purchase an option on the borrower's spread to hedge against trading losses should the borrower's credit deteriorate. The bank may purchase an option, with a strike spread of 30 basis points, allowing it to sell the asset should the borrower's current market spread rise to 30 basis points (or more) over the floating rate over the next month. If the borrower's spread rises to 50 basis points, the bank would sell the asset to its counterparty, at a price corresponding to LIBOR plus 30 basis points. While the bank is exposed to the first 15 basis point movement in the spread, it does have market value (and thus default) protection on the credit after absorbing the first 15 basis points of spread widening. The seller of the option might be motivated by the view that a spread of LIBOR plus 30 basis points is an attractive price for originating the credit exposure.

Unlike other credit derivative products, the US market for credit spread options currently is not significant; most activity in this product is in Europe. Until recently, current market spreads had been so narrow in the USA that investors appeared reluctant to sell protection against widening. Moreover, for dealers, hedging exposure on credit spread options is difficult, because rebalancing costs can be very high. Table 11.2 summarizes some of the key points discussed for the four credit derivative products.

Table 11.2 The four credit derivative products

Product	Market	Credit coverage for protection buyer	Principal bank uses
Credit default swaps	OTC	Default only; no payment for MTM losses unless a 'credit event' occurs and exceeds a materiality threshold	Protection buyers seek to: (1) reduce regulatory capital requirements on high-grade exposures; (2) make portfolio adjustments; (3) hedge credit exposure. Protection sellers seek to book income or acquire targeted exposures
Total return swaps	OTC	Protection buyer has MTM coverage	(1) Alternative to secured lending, typically to highly leveraged investors; (2) used to pass-through risk on high yield loans in structured (leveraged) investment transactions
Credit-linked notes	Cash	Typically default only	Hedge exposures: (1) owned in the banking book; or (2) acquired by a dealer selling protection on a CDS
Credit spread options	OTC	MTM coverage beyond a 'strike' level	Infrequently used in the USA

Risks of credit derivatives

When used properly, credit derivatives can help diversify credit risk, improve earnings, and lower the risk profile of an institution. Conversely, the improper use of credit derivatives, as in poor lending practices, can result in an imprudent credit risk profile.

Credit derivatives expose participants to the familiar risks in commercial banking; i.e. credit, liquidity, price, legal (compliance), foreign exchange, strategic, and reputation risks. This section highlights these risks and discusses risk management practices that can help to manage and control the risk profile effectively.

Credit Risk

The most obvious risk credit derivatives participants face is credit risk. Credit risk is the risk to earnings or capital of an obligor's failure to meet the terms of any contract with the bank or otherwise to perform as agreed. For both purchasers and sellers of protection, credit derivatives should be fully incorporated within credit risk management processes. Bank management should integrate credit derivative activity in their credit underwriting and administration policies, and their exposure measurement, limit setting, and risk rating/classification processes. They should also consider credit derivative activity in their assessment of the adequacy of the allowance for loan and lease losses (ALLL) and their evaluation of concentrations of credit.

There are a number of credit risks for both sellers and buyers of credit protection, each of which raises separate risk management issues. For banks selling credit protection (i.e. buying risk), the primary source of credit risk is the reference asset or entity. Table 11.3 highlights the credit protection seller's exposures in the three principal types of credit derivative products seen in the USA.

Table 11.3 Credit protection seller – credit risks

Product	Reference asset risk	Counterparty risk
Credit default swaps (CDS)	If a 'credit event' occurs, the seller is required to make a payment based on the reference asset's fall in value. The seller has *contingent* exposure based on the performance of the reference asset. The seller may receive physical delivery of the reference asset	Minimal exposure. Exposure represents the amount of deferred payments (fees) due from counterparty (risk protection buyer)
Total return swaps (TRS)	If the value of the reference asset falls, the seller must make a payment equal to the value change. The seller 'synthetically' owns and is exposed to the performance of the reference asset	If the value of the reference asset increases, the seller bank will have a payment due from the counterparty. The seller is exposed to the counterparty for the amount of the payment
Credit linked notes (CLN)	If the reference asset defaults, the seller (i.e. the bond investor) will not collect par value on the bond	If the issuer defaults, the investor may not collect par value. The seller is exposed to **both** the reference asset and the issuer (i.e. 'two-name risk'). Many CLNs are issued through trusts, which buy collateral assets to pledge to investors. This changes the investor's risk from issuer nonperformance to the credit risk of the collateral

Note: In CLNs the seller of credit protection actually buys a cash market security from the buyer of credit protection.

As noted in Table 11.3, the protection seller's credit exposure will vary depending on the type of credit derivative used. In a CDS, the seller makes a payment only if a predefined credit event occurs. When investors sell protection through total rate-of-return swaps (i.e. receive total return), they are exposed to deterioration of the reference asset and to their counterparty for the amount of any *increases* in value of the reference asset. In CLN transactions, the investor (seller of credit protection) is exposed to default of the reference asset. Directly issued CLNs (i.e. those not issued through a trust) expose the investor to both the reference asset and the issuer.

When banks buy credit protection, they also are exposed to counterparty credit risk as in other derivative products. Table 11.4 highlights the credit protection buyer's exposures in the three principal types of credit derivative products.

Table 11.4 Credit protection buyer – credit risks

Product	Reference asset risk	Counterparty risk
Credit default swaps (CDS)	The buyer has hedged default risk on reference asset exposure if it has an underlying exposure. The extent of hedge protection may vary depending on the terms of the contract. Mismatched maturities result in forward credit exposures. If the terms and conditions of the reference asset differ from the underlying exposure, the buyer assumes residual or 'basis' risk. A CDS provides default protection only; the buyer retains market risk short of default.	If a credit event occurs, the counterparty will owe the buyer an amount normally determined by the amount of decline in the reference asset's value.
Total return swaps (TRS): pay total return	The buyer has 'synthetically' sold the asset. If the asset value increases, the buyer owes on the TRS but is covered by owning the asset.	The buyer has credit exposure of the counterparty if the reference asset declines in value.
Credit-linked notes (CLN)	The protection buyer has obtained cash by issuing CLNs. The buyer may assume basis risk, depending upon the terms of the CLN.	Not applicable. The protection buyer in these transactions receives cash in exchange for the securities.

As noted in Table 11.4, the protection buyer's credit exposure also varies depending on the type of credit derivative. In a CDS, the buyer will receive a payment from the seller of protection when a default event occurs. This payment normally will equal the value decline of the CDS reference asset. In some transactions, however, the parties fix the amount in advance (binary). Absent legal issues, or a fixed payment that is less than the loss on the underlying exposure, the protection buyer incurs a credit loss only if both the underlying borrower (reference asset) and the protection seller **simultaneously** default.

In a CDS transaction with a cash settlement feature, the hedging bank (protection buyer) receives a payment upon default, but remains exposed to the original balance-sheet obligation. Such a bank can assure itself of complete protection against this residual credit risk by physically delivering the asset to the credit protection seller upon occurrence of a credit event. The physical delivery form of settlement has become more popular as the market has evolved. Absent a credit event, the protection buyer has no coverage against market value deterioration.

If the term of the credit protection is less than the maturity of the exposure, the hedging bank will again become exposed to the obligation when the credit derivative matures. In that case, the bank has a forward credit risk.

In a TRS, the protection buyer is exposed to its counterparty, who must make a payment when the value of the reference asset declines. Absent legal issues, a buyer will not incur a credit loss on the reference asset unless both the reference asset declines in value **and** the protection seller defaults.

A bank that purchases credit protection by issuing a credit-linked note receives cash and thus has no counterparty exposure; it has simply sold bonds. It may have residual credit exposure to the underlying borrower if the recovery rate as determined by a bidding process is different than the value at which it can sell the underlying exposure. This differential is called 'basis risk'.

Managing credit risk: underwriting and administration

For banks selling credit protection (buying risk) through a credit derivative, management should complete a financial analysis of both reference obligor(s) and the counterparty (in both default swaps and TRSs), establish separate credit limits for each, and assign appropriate risk ratings. The analysis of the reference obligor should include the same level of scrutiny that a traditional commercial borrower would receive. Documentation in the credit file should support the purpose of the transaction and creditworthiness of the reference obligor. Documentation should be sufficient to support the reference obligor's risk rating. It is especially important for banks to use rigorous due diligence procedures in originating credit exposure via credit derivatives. Banks should not allow the ease with which they can originate credit exposure in the capital markets via derivatives to lead to lax underwriting standards, or to assume exposures indirectly that they would not originate directly.

For banks purchasing credit protection through a credit derivative, management should review the creditworthiness of the counterparty, establish a credit limit, and assign a risk rating. The credit analysis of the counterparty should be consistent with that conducted for other borrowers or trading counterparties. Management should continue to monitor the credit quality of the **underlying credits** hedged. Although the credit derivative may provide default protection, in many instances (e.g. contracts involving cash settlement) the bank will retain the underlying credit(s) after settlement or maturity of the credit derivative. In the event the credit quality deteriorates, as legal owner of the asset, management must take actions necessary to improve the credit.

Banks should measure credit exposures arising from credit derivative transactions and aggregate with other credit exposures to reference entities and counterparties. These transactions can create highly customized exposures and the level of risk/ protection can vary significantly between transactions. Management should document and support their exposure measurement methodology and underlying assumptions.

Managing basis risk

The purchase of credit protection through credit derivatives may not completely eliminate the credit risk associated with holding a loan because the reference asset may not have the same terms and conditions as the balance sheet exposure. This residual exposure is known as basis risk. For example, upon a default, the reference asset (often a publicly traded bond) might lose 25% of its value, whereas the underlying loan could lose 30% of its value. Should the value of the loan decline more than that of the reference asset, the protection buyer will receive a smaller payment on the credit default swap (derivative) than it loses on the underlying loan (cash transaction). Bonds historically have tended to lose more value, in default situations, than loans. Therefore, a bank hedging a loan exposure using a bond as a reference asset could benefit from the basis risk. The cost of protection, however, should reflect the possibility of benefiting from this basis risk. More generally, unless all the terms of the credit derivative match those of the underlying exposure, some basis risk will exist, creating an exposure for the protection buyer. Credit hedgers should carefully evaluate the terms and conditions of protection agreements to ensure that the contract provides the protection desired, and that the hedger has identified sources of basis risk.

Managing maturity mismatches

A bank purchasing credit protection is exposed to credit risk if the maturity of the credit derivative is less than the term of the exposure. In such cases, the bank would face a *forward credit exposure* at the maturity of the derivative, as it would no longer have protection. Hedging banks should carefully assess their contract maturities to assure that they do not inadvertently create a maturity mismatch by ignoring material features of the loan. For example, if the loan has a 15-day grace period in which the borrower can cure a payment default, a formal default can not occur until 15 days after the loan maturity. A bank that has hedged the exposure only to the maturity date of the loan could find itself without protection if it failed to consider this grace period.

In addition, many credit-hedging transactions do not cover the full term of the credit exposure. Banks often do not hedge to the maturity of the underlying exposure because of cost considerations, as well as the desire to avoid short positions that would occur if the underlying obligor paid off the bank's exposure. In such cases, the bank would continue to have an obligation to make fee payments on the default swap, but it would no longer have an underlying exposure.

Evaluating counterparty risk

A protection buyer can suffer a credit loss on a default swap only if the underlying obligor and the protection seller simultaneously default, an event whose probability is technically referred to as their 'joint probability of default'.

To limit risk, credit-hedging institutions should carefully evaluate the correlation between the underlying obligor and the protection seller. Hedgers should seek protection seller counterparties that have the lowest possible default correlation with the underlying exposure. Low default correlations imply that if one party defaults, only a small chance exists that the second party would also default. For example, a bank seeking to hedge against the default of a private sector borrower in an emerging market ordinarily would not buy protection from a counterparty in that same emerging market. Since the two companies may have a high default correlation, a default by one would imply a strong likelihood of default by the other. In practice, some credit hedging banks often fail to incorporate into the cost of the hedge the additional risk posed by higher default correlations. The lowest nominal fee offered by a protection seller may not represent the most effective hedge, given default correlation concerns. Banks that hedge through counterparties that are highly correlated with the underlying exposure should do so only with the full knowledge of the risks involved, and after giving full consideration to valuing the correlation costs.

Evaluating credit protection

Determining the amount of protection provided by a credit derivative is subjective, as the terms of the contract will allow for varying degrees of loss protection. Management should complete a full analysis of the reference obligor(s), the counterparty, and the terms of the underlying credit derivative contract and document its assessment of the degree of protection. Table 11.5 highlights items to consider.

Table 11.5 Evaluating credit protection

Factor	Issues
Reference asset	Is the reference asset an effective hedge for the underlying asset(s)? Same legal entity? Same level of seniority in bankruptcy? Same currency?
Default triggers	Do the 'triggers' in credit derivative match the default definition in the underlying assets (i.e. the cross-default provisions)?
Maturity mismatches	Does the maturity of the credit derivative match the maturity of the underlying asset(s)? Does the underlying asset have a grace period that would require the protection period to equal the maturity plus the grace period to achieve an effective maturity match? If a maturity mismatch exists, does the protection period extend beyond 'critical' payment/rollover points in the borrower's debt structure? (As the difference between the protection period and the underlying asset maturity increases, the protection provided by the credit derivative decreases.)
Counterparty	Is there a willingness and ability to pay? Is there a concentration of credit exposure with the counterparty?
Settlement issues	Can the protection buyer deliver the underlying asset at its option? Must the buyer obtain permission of the borrower to physically deliver the asset? Are there any restrictions that preclude physical delivery of the asset? If the asset is required to be cash settled, how does the contract establish the payment amount? Dealer poll? Fixed payment? When does the protection-buying bank receive the credit derivative payment? (The longer the payment is deferred, the less valuable the protection.)
Materiality thresholds	Are thresholds low enough to effectively transfer all risk or must the price fall so far that the bank effectively has a deeply subordinated (large first loss) position in the credit?
Legal issues	Is the contract legally enforceable? Is the contract fully documented? Are there disputes over contract terms (e.g. definition of restructuring)? What events constitute a restructuring? How is accrued interest treated?

Banks **selling** credit protection assume reference asset credit risk and must identify the potential for loss, they should risk rate the exposure based on the financial condition and resources of the reference obligor.

Banks face a number of less obvious credit risks when using credit derivatives. They include leverage, speculation, and pricing risks.

Managing leverage considerations

Most credit derivatives, like financial derivatives, involve leverage. If a bank selling credit protection does not fully understand the leverage aspects of some credit derivative structures, it may fail to receive an appropriate level of compensation for the risks assumed.

A fixed payout (or binary) default swap can embed leverage into a credit transaction. In an extreme case, the contract may call for a 100% payment from the protection seller to the protection buyer in the event of default. This amount is independent of the actual amount of loss the protection buyer (lender) may suffer on its underlying exposure. Fixed payout swaps can allow the protection buyer to 'over-hedge', and achieve a 'short' position in the credit. By contracting to receive a greater credit-event payment than its expected losses on its underlying transaction, the protection buyer actually benefits from a default. Protection sellers receive higher fees for assuming fixed payment obligations that exceed expected credit losses and should always evaluate and manage those exposures prudently.

For a protection seller, a basket swap also represents an especially leveraged credit transaction, since it suffers a loss if **any** one of the basket names defaults. The greater the number of names, the greater the chance of default. The credit quality of the transaction will ordinarily be less than that of the lowest rated name. For example, a basket of 10 names, all rated 'A' by a national rating agency, may not qualify for an investment grade rating, especially if the names are not highly correlated. Banks can earn larger fees for providing such protection, but increasing the number of exposures increases the risk that they will have to make a payment to a counterparty.

Conceptually, protection sellers in basket swaps assume credit exposure to the weakest credit in the basket. Simultaneously, they write an option to the protection buyer, allowing that party to substitute another name in the basket should it become weaker than the originally identified weakest credit. Protection buyers in such transactions may seek to capitalize upon a protection seller's inability to quantify the true risk of a default basket. When assuming these kinds of credit exposures, protection-selling banks should carefully consider their risk tolerance, and determine whether the leverage of the transaction represents a prudent risk/reward opportunity.

Speculation

Credit derivatives allow banks, for the first time, to sell credit risk short. In a short sale, a speculator benefits from a decline in the price of an asset. Banks can short credit risk by purchasing default protection in a swap, paying the total return on a TRS, or issuing a CLN, in each case without having an underlying exposure to the reference asset. Any protection payments the bank receives under these derivatives would not offset a balance sheet exposure, because none exists.

Short positions inherently represent trading transactions. For example, a bank may pay 25 basis points per year to buy protection on a company to which it has no exposure. If credit spreads widen, the bank could then sell protection at the new market level; e.g. 40 basis points. The bank would earn a net trading profit of 15 basis points.

The use of short positions as a credit portfolio strategy raises concerns that banks may improperly speculate on credit risk. Such speculation could cause banks to lose the focus and discipline needed to manage traditional credit risk exposures. Credit policies should specifically address the institution's willingness to implement short credit risk positions, and also specify appropriate controls over the activity.

Pricing

Credit trades at different spread levels in different product sectors. The spread in the corporate bond market may differ from the loan market, and each may differ from the spread available in the credit derivatives market. Indeed, credit derivatives allow institutions to arbitrage the different sectors of the credit market, allowing for a more complete market.

With an asset swap, an investor can synthetically transform a fixed-rate security into a floating rate security, or vice versa. For example, if a corporate bond trades at a fixed yield of 6%, an investor can pay a fixed rate on an interest rate swap (and receive LIBOR), to create a synthetic floater. If the swap fixed rate is 5.80%, the floater yields LIBOR plus 20 basis points. The spread over LIBOR on the synthetic floater is often compared to the market price for a default swap as an indicator of value. If the fee on the default swap exceeds, in this example, 20 basis points, the default swap is 'cheap' to the asset swap, thereby representing value.

While benchmark indicators are convenient, they do not consider all the factors a bank should evaluate when selling protection. For example, when comparing credit derivative and cash market pricing levels, banks should consider the liquidity disadvantage of credit derivatives, their higher legal risks, and the lower information quality generally available when compared to a direct credit relationship.

Using asset swap levels to determine appropriate compensation for selling credit protection also considers the exposure in isolation, for it ignores how the new exposure impacts aggregate portfolio risk, a far more important consideration. The protection seller should consider whether the addition of the exposure increases the diversification of the protection seller's portfolio, or exacerbates an existing concern about concentration. Depending on the impact of the additional credit exposure on its overall portfolio risk, a protection seller may find that the benchmark pricing guide; i.e. asset swaps, fails to provide sufficient reward for the incremental risk taken. Banks face this same issue when extending traditional credit directly to a borrower. The increasing desire to measure the portfolio impacts of credit decisions has led to the development of models to quantify how incremental exposures could impact aggregate portfolio risk.

Liquidity risk

Market participants measure liquidity risk in two different ways. For dealers, liquidity refers to the spread between bid and offer prices. The narrower the spread, the greater the liquidity. For end-users and dealers, liquidity risk refers to an institution's ability to meet its cash obligations as they come due.

As an emerging derivative product, credit derivatives have higher bid/offer spreads than other derivatives, and therefore lower liquidity. The wider spreads available in credit derivatives offer dealers profit opportunities which have largely been competed away in financial derivatives. These larger profit opportunities in credit derivatives explain why a number of institutions currently are, or plan to become, dealers. Nevertheless, the credit derivatives market, like many cash credit instruments, has limited depth, creating exposure to liquidity risks. Dealers need access to markets to hedge their portfolio of exposures, especially in situations in which a counterparty that provides an offset for an existing position defaults. The counterparty's default could suddenly give rise to an unhedged exposure which, because of poor liquidity, the dealer may not be able to offset in a cost-effective manner. Like financial derivatives, credit and market risks are interconnected; credit risks becomes market risk, and vice versa.

Both dealers and end-users of credit derivatives should incorporate the impact of these scenarios into regular liquidity planning and monitoring systems. Cash flow projections should consider all significant sources and uses of cash and collateral. A contingency funding plan should address the impact of any early termination agreements or collateral/margin arrangements.

Price risk

Price risk refers to the changes in earnings due to changes in the value of portfolios of financial instruments; it is therefore a critical risk for dealers. The absence of historical data on defaults, and on correlations between default events, complicates the precise measurement of price risk and makes the contingent exposures of credit derivatives more difficult to forecast and fully hedge than a financial derivatives book. As a result, many dealers try to match, or perfectly offset, transaction exposures. Other dealers seek a competitive advantage by not running a matched book. For example, they might hedge a total return swap with a default swap, or hedge a senior exposure with a junior exposure. A dealer could also hedge exposure on one company with a contract referencing another company in the same industry (i.e. a proxy hedge). As dealers manage their exposures more on a portfolio basis, significant basis and correlation risk issues can arise, underscoring the importance of stress testing the portfolio.

Investors seeking exposure to emerging markets often acquire exposures denominated in currencies different from their own reporting currency. The goal in many of these transactions is to bet against currency movements implied by interest rate differentials. When investors do not hedge the currency exposure, they clearly assume foreign exchange risk. Other investors try to eliminate the currency risk and execute forward transactions. To offset correlation risk which can arise, an investor should seek counterparties on the forward foreign exchange transaction who are not strongly correlated with the emerging market whose currency risk the investor is trying to hedge.

Legal (compliance) risks

Compliance risk is the risk to earnings or capital arising from violations, or nonconformance with, laws, rules, regulations, prescribed practices, or ethical standards. The risk also arises when laws or rules governing certain bank products or activities of the bank's clients may be ambiguous or untested. Compliance risk exposes the institution to fines, civil money penalties, payment of damages, and the voiding of contracts. Compliance risk can lead to a diminished reputation, reduced franchise value, limited business opportunities, lessened expansion potential, and an inability to enforce contracts.

Since credit derivatives are new and largely untested credit risk management products, legal risks associated with them can be high. To offset such risks, it is critical for each party to agree to all terms prior to execution of the contract. Discovering that contracts have not been signed, or key terms have not been clearly defined, can jeopardize the protection that a credit risk hedger believes it has obtained. Banks acting in this capacity should consult legal counsel as necessary to ensure credit derivative contracts are appropriately drafted and documented.

The Russian default on GKO debt in 1998 underscores the importance of understanding the terms of the contract and its key definitions. Most default swap contracts in which investors purchased protection on Russian debt referenced external debt obligations, e.g. Eurobond debt. When Russia defaulted on its internal GKO obligations, many protection purchasers were surprised to discover, after reviewing their contracts, that an internal default did not constitute a 'credit event'. As of July 1999, Russia has continued to pay its Eurobond debt. Although investors in Russia's Eurobonds suffered significant mark-to-market losses when Russia defaulted on its internal debt, protection purchasers could not collect on the default swap contracts. Credit hedgers must assess the circumstances under which they desire protection, and then negotiate the terms of the contract accordingly.

Although no standardized format currently exists for all credit derivatives, transactions are normally completed with a detailed confirmation under an ISDA Master Agreement. These documents will generally include the following transaction information:

- trade date
- maturity date
- business day convention
- reference price
- key definitions (credit events, etc.)
- conditions to payment
- materiality requirements
- notice requirements
- dispute resolution mechanisms
- reps and warranties designed to reduce legal risk
- credit enhancement terms or reference to an ISDA master credit annex
- effective date
- identification of counterparties
- reference entity
- reference obligation(s)
- payment dates
- payout valuation method
- settlement method (physical or cash)
- payment details

Documentation should also address, as applicable, the rights to obtain financial information on the reference asset or counterparty, restructuring or merger of the reference asset, method by which recovery values are determined (and any fallback procedures if a dealer poll fails to establish a recovery value), rights in receivership or bankruptcy, recourse to the borrower, and early termination rights.

Moral hazards

To date, no clear legal precedent governs the number of possible moral hazards that may arise in credit derivatives. The following examples illustrate potentially troubling issues that could pose legal risks for banks entering into credit derivative transactions.

Access to material, nonpublic information

Based on their knowledge of material, nonpublic information, creditors may attempt to buy credit protection and unfairly transfer their risk to credit protection sellers. Most dealers acknowledge this risk, but see it as little different from that faced in loan and corporate bond trading. These dealers generally try to protect themselves against the risk of information asymmetries by exercising greater caution about intermediating protection as the rating of the reference asset declines. They also may want to consider requiring protection purchasers to retain a portion of the exposure when buying protection so that the risk hedger demonstrates a financial commitment in the asset. Bank dealers also should adopt strict guidelines when intermediating risk from their bank's own credit portfolios, for they can ill afford for market participants to suspect that the bank is taking advantage of nonpublic information when sourcing credit from its own portfolio. Implementation of firewalls between the public and nonpublic sides of the institution is an essential control.

When the underlying instrument in a credit derivatives transaction is a security (as defined in the federal securities laws), credit protection sellers may have recourse against counterparties that trade on inside information and fail to disclose that information to their counterparties. Such transactions generally are prohibited as a form of securities fraud. Should the underlying instrument in a credit derivatives transaction not be a security and a credit protection seller suspects that its counterparty possessed and traded on the basis of material, nonpublic information, the seller would have to base a claim for redress on state law antifraud statutes and common law.

Inadequate credit administration

The existence of credit protection may provide an incentive for protection purchasers to administer the underlying borrower relationship improperly. For example, consider technical covenant violations in a loan agreement a bank may ordinarily waive. A bank with credit protection may be tempted to enforce the covenants and declare a default so that the timing of the default occurs during the period covered by the credit protection. It is unclear whether the protection seller has a cause of action against such a bank by charging that it acted improperly to benefit from the credit derivative.

Another potential problem could involve the definition of a default event, which typically includes a credit restructuring. A creditor that has purchased protection on an exposure can simply restructure the terms of a transaction, and through its actions alone, declare a credit event. Most contracts require a restructuring to involve a material adverse change for the holder of the debt, but the legal definition of a material adverse change is subject to judgment and interpretation. All participants in credit derivative transactions need to understand clearly the operative definition of restructuring.

In practice, credit derivative transactions currently involve reference obligors with large amounts of debt outstanding, in which numerous banks participate as creditors. As a result, any one creditor's ability to take an action that could provide it with a benefit because of credit derivative protection is limited, because other participant creditors would have to affirm the actions. As the market expands, however, and a greater number of transactions with a single lender occur, these issues will assume increasing importance. Protection sellers may consider demanding voting rights in such cases.

Optionality

Credit derivative contracts often provide options to the protection purchaser with respect to which instruments it can deliver upon a default event. For example, the purchaser may deliver any instrument that ranks *pari passu* with the reference asset. Though two instruments may rank *pari passu*, they may not have the same value upon default. For example, longer maturities may trade at lower dollar prices. Protection purchasers can thus create greater losses for protection sellers by exploiting the value of these options, and deliver, from among all potentially deliverable assets, the one that maximizes losses for the protection seller. Protection sellers must carefully assess the potential that the terms of the contract could provide uncompensated, yet valuable, options to their counterparties. This form of legal risk results when one party to the contract and its legal counsel have greater expertise in credit derivatives than the counterparty and its counsel. This is particularly likely to be the case in transactions between a dealer and an end-user, underscoring the importance of end-users transacting with reputable dealer counterparties.

These issues highlight the critical need for participants in credit derivatives to involve competent legal counsel in transaction formulation, structure, and terms.

Reputation Risk

Banks serving as dealers in credit derivatives face a number of reputation risks. For example, the use of leveraged credit derivative transactions, such as basket default swaps and binary swaps, raises significant risks if the counterparty does not have the requisite sophistication to evaluate a transaction properly. As with leveraged financial derivatives, banks should have policies that call for heightened internal supervisory review of such transactions.

A mismatched maturity occurs when the maturity of the credit derivative is shorter than the maturity of the underlying exposure the protection buyer desires to hedge. Some observers have noted that protection sellers on mismatched maturity transactions can face an awkward situation when they recognize a credit event may occur shortly, triggering a payment obligation. The protection seller might evaluate whether short-term credit extended to the reference obligor may delay a default long enough to permit the credit derivative to mature. Thinly veiled attempts to avoid a payment obligation on a credit derivative could have adverse reputation consequences.

The desire many dealers have to build credit derivatives volume, and thus distinguish themselves in the marketplace as a leader, can easily lead to transactions of questionable merit and/or which may be inappropriate for client counterparties. Reputation risks are very difficult to measure and thus are difficult to manage.

Strategic Risk

Strategic risk is the risk to earnings or capital from poorly conceived business plans and/or weak implementation of strategic initiatives. Before achieving material participation in the credit derivatives market, management should assess the impact on the bank's risk profile and ensure that adequate internal controls have been established for the conduct of all trading and end-user activities. For example, management should assess:

- The adequacy of personnel expertise, risk management systems, and operational capacity to support the activity.
- Whether credit derivative activity is consistent with the bank's overall business strategy.
- The level and type of credit derivative activity in which the bank plans to engage (e.g. dealer versus end-user).

- The types and credit quality of underlying reference assets and counterparties.
- The structures and maturities of transactions.
- Whether the bank has completed a risk/return analysis and established performance benchmarks.

Banks should consider the above issues as part of a new product approval process. The new product approval process should include approval from all relevant bank offices or departments such as risk control, operations, accounting, legal, audit, and line management. Depending on the magnitude of the new product or activity and its impact on the bank's risk profile, senior management, and in some cases the board, should provide the final approval.

Regulatory capital issues

The Basel Capital Accord generally does not recognize differences in the credit quality of bank assets for purposes of allocating risk-based capital requirements. Instead, the Accord's risk weights consider the type of obligation, or its issuer. Under current capital rules, a 'Aaa' corporate loan and a 'B' rated corporate loan have the same risk weight, thereby requiring banks to allocate the same amount of regulatory capital for these instruments. This differentiation between regulatory capital requirements and the perceived economic risk of a transaction has caused some banks to engage in 'regulatory capital arbitrage' (RCA) strategies to reduce their risk-based capital requirements. Though these strategies can reduce regulatory capital allocations, they often do not materially reduce economic risks.

To illustrate the incentives banks have to engage in RCA, Table 11.6 summarizes the Accord's risk weights for on-balance sheet assets and credit commitments.

Table 11.6 Risk-based-capital risk weights for on-balance-sheet assets and commitments

Exposure	Risk weight
Claims on US government; OECD central governments; credit commitments less than one year	0%
Claims on depository institutions incorporated in OECD countries; US government agency obligations	20%
First mortgages on residential properties; loans to builders for 1–4 family residential properties; credit commitments greater than one year	50%
All other private sector obligations	100%

Risk weighted assets (RWA) are derived by assigning assets to one of the four categories above. For example, a $100 commitment has no risk-based capital requirement if it matures in less than one year, and a $4 capital charge ($100 × 50% × 8%) if greater than one year. If a bank makes a $100 loan to a private sector borrower with a 100% risk weight, the capital requirement is $8 ($100 × 8%).

Under current capital rules, a bank incurs five times the capital requirement for a 'Aaa' rated corporate exposure (100% risk weight) than it does for a sub-investment grade exposure to an OECD government (20% risk weight). Moreover, within the 100% risk weight category, regulatory capital requirements are independent of asset quality. A sub-investment grade exposure and an investment grade exposure require the same regulatory capital.

The current rules provide a regulatory incentive for banks to acquire exposure to lower-rated borrowers, since the greater spreads available on such assets provide a greater return on regulatory capital. When adjusted for risk, however, and after providing the capital to support that risk, banks may not economically benefit from acquiring lower quality exposures. Similarly, because of the low risk of high-quality assets, risk-adjusted returns on these assets may be attractive. Consequently, returns on regulatory and 'economic' capital can appear very different. Transactions attractive under one approach may not be attractive under the other.

Banks should develop capital allocation models to assign capital based upon *economic* risks incurred. Economic capital allocation models attempt to ensure that a bank has sufficient capital to support its true risk profile, as opposed to the necessarily simplistic Basel paradigm. Larger banks have implemented capital allocation models, and generally try to manage their business based upon the economic consequences of transactions. While such models generally measure risks more accurately than the Basel paradigm, banks implementing the models often assign an additional capital charge for transactions that incur regulatory capital charges which exceed capital requirements based upon measured economic risk. These additional charges reflect the reality of the cost imposed by higher regulatory capital requirements.

Credit Derivatives[8]

Under current interpretations of the Basel Accord, a bank may substitute the risk weight of the protection-selling counterparty for the weight of its underlying exposure. To illustrate this treatment, consider a $50 million, one year bullet loan to XYZ, a high-quality borrower. The loan is subject to a 100% risk-weight, and the bank must allocate regulatory capital for this commitment of $4 million ($50 million × 100% × 8%). If the bank earns a spread over its funding costs of 25 basis points, it will net $125 000 on the transaction ($50 million × 0.0025). The bank earns a 3.125% return on regulatory capital (125 000/4 000 000).

Because of regulatory capital constraints, the bank may decide to purchase protection on the exposure, via a default swap costing 15 basis points, from an OECD bank. The bank now earns a net spread of 10 basis points, or $50 000 per year. However, it can substitute the risk weight of its counterparty, which is 20%, for that of XYZ, which is 100%. The regulatory capital for the transaction becomes $800 000 ($50 million × 20% × 8%), and the return on regulatory capital doubles to 6.25% (50 000/800 000).[9]

The transaction clearly improves the return on regulatory capital. Because of the credit strength of the borrower, however, the bank in all likelihood does not attribute much economic capital to the exposure. The default swap premium may reduce the return on the loan by more than the economic capital declines by virtue of the enhanced credit position. Therefore, as noted earlier, a transaction that increases the return on regulatory capital may simultaneously reduce the return on economic capital.

As discussed previously, many credit derivative transactions do not cover the full maturity of the underlying exposure. The international supervisory community has concerns about mismatches because of the forward capital call that results if banks reduced the risk weight during the protection period. Consequently, some countries do not permit banks to substitute the risk weight of the protection provider for that of the underlying exposure when a mismatch exists. Recognizing that a failure to provide capital relief can create disincentives to hedge credit risk, the mismatch issue remains an area of active deliberation within the Basel Committee.

Securitization

In an effort to reduce their regulatory capital costs, banks also use various special-purpose vehicles (SPVs) and securitization techniques to unbundle and repackage risks to achieve more favorable capital treatment. Initially, for corporate exposures, these securitizations have taken the form of collateralized loan obligations (CLOs). More recently, however, banks have explored ways to reduce the high costs of CLOs, and have begun to consider synthetic securitization structures.

Asset securitization allows banks to sell their assets and use low-level recourse rules to reduce RWA. Figure 11.5 illustrates a simple asset securitization, in which the bank retains a $50 'first loss' equity piece, and transfers the remaining risk to bond investors. The result of the securitization of commercial credit is to convert numerous individual loans and/or bonds into a single security. Under low-level recourse rules,[10] the bank's capital requirements cannot exceed the level of its risk, which in this case is $50. Therefore, the capital requirement falls from $80 ($1000 × 8%) to $50, or 37.5%.

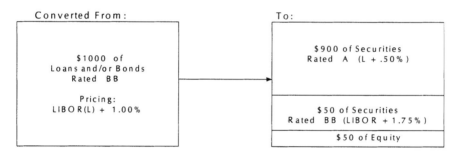

Figure 11.5 CLO/BBO asset conversions.

The originating bank in a securitization such as a CLO retains the equity (first loss) piece. The size of this equity piece will vary; it will depend primarily on the quality and diversification of the underlying credits and the desired rating of the senior and junior securities. For example, to obtain the same credit rating, a CLO collateralized by a diversified portfolio of loans with strong credit ratings will require a smaller equity piece than a structure backed by lower quality assets that are more concentrated. The size of the equity piece typically will cover some multiple of the pool's expected losses. Statistically, the equity piece absorbs, within a certain confidence interval, the entire amount of credit risk. Therefore, a CLO transfers only catastrophic credit risk.[11] The retained equity piece bears the expected losses. In this sense, the bank has not changed its economic risks, even though it has reduced its capital requirements.

To reduce the cost of CLO issues, banks recently have explored new, lower-cost, 'synthetic' vehicles using credit derivatives. The objective of the synthetic structures is to preserve the regulatory capital benefits provided by CLOs, while at the same time lowering funding costs. In these structures, a bank attempting to reduce capital requirements tries to eliminate selling the full amount of securities corresponding to the credit exposures. It seeks to avoid paying the credit spread on senior tranches that makes traditional CLOs so expensive.

In synthetic transactions seen to date, the bank sponsor retains a first loss position, similar to a traditional CLO. The bank sponsor then creates a trust that sells securities against a small portion of the total exposure, in sharp contrast to the traditional CLO, for which the sponsor sells securities covering the entire pool. Sponsors typically have sold securities against approximately 8% of the underlying collateral pool, an amount that matches the Basel capital requirement for credit exposure. The bank sponsor purchases credit protection from an OECD bank to reduce the risk weight on the top piece to 20%, subject to maturity mismatch limitations imposed by national supervisors. The purpose of these transactions is to bring risk-based capital requirements more in line with the economic capital required to support the risks. Given that banks securitize their highest quality exposures, management should consider whether their institutions have an adequate amount of capital to cover the risks of the remaining, higher-risk, portfolio.

A portfolio approach to credit risk management

Since the 1980s, banks have successfully applied modern portfolio theory (MPT) to market risk. Many banks are now using earnings at risk (EaR) and Value-at-Risk (VaR)[12] models to manage their interest rate and market risk exposures. Unfortunately, however, even through credit risk remains the largest risk facing most banks, the practical application of MPT to credit risk has lagged.

The slow development toward a portfolio approach for credit risk results from the following factors:

- The traditional view of loans as hold-to-maturity assets.
- The absence of tools enabling the efficient transfer of credit risk to investors while continuing to maintain bank customer relationships.
- The lack of effective methodologies to measure portfolio credit risk.
- Data problems.

Banks recognize how credit concentrations can adversely impact financial performance. As a result, a number of sophisticated institutions are actively pursuing quantitative approaches to credit risk measurement. While data problems remain an obstacle, these industry practitioners are making significant progress toward developing tools that measure credit risk in a portfolio context. They are also using credit derivatives to transfer risk efficiently while preserving customer relationships. The combination of these two developments has precipitated vastly accelerated progress in managing credit risk in a portfolio context over the past several years.

Asset-by-asset approach

Traditionally, banks have taken an asset-by-asset approach to credit risk management. While each bank's method varies, in general this approach involves periodically evaluating the credit quality of loans and other credit exposures, applying a credit risk rating, and aggregating the results of this analysis to identify a portfolio's expected losses.

The foundation of the asset-by-asset approach is a sound loan review and internal credit risk rating system. A loan review and credit risk rating system enables management to identify changes in individual credits, or portfolio trends, in a timely manner. Based on the results of its problem loan identification, loan review, and credit risk rating system, management can make necessary modifications to portfolio strategies or increase the supervision of credits in a timely manner.

Banks must determine the appropriate level of the Allowance for Loan and Lease Losses (ALLL) on a quarterly basis. On large problem credits, they assess ranges of expected losses based on their evaluation of a number of factors, such as economic conditions and collateral. On smaller problem credits and on 'pass' credits, banks commonly assess the default probability from historical migration analysis. Combining the results of the evaluation of individual large problem credits and historical migration analysis, banks estimate expected losses for the portfolio and determine provision requirements for the ALLL.

Migration analysis techniques vary widely between banks, but generally track the loss experience on a fixed or rolling population of loans over a period of years. The purpose of the migration analysis is to determine, based on a bank's experience over a historical analysis period, the likelihood that credits of a certain risk rating will transition to another risk rating.

Table 11.7 illustrates a one-year historical migration matrix for publicly rated corporate bonds. Notice that significant differences in risk exist between the various credit risk rating grades. For example, the transition matrix in Table 11.7 indicates the one-year historical transition of an AAA-rated credit to default is 0.0%, while for a B-rated credit the one-year transition to default is 6.81%. The large differences in default probabilities between high and low grade credits, given a constant 8% capital requirement, has led banks to explore vehicles to reduce the capital cost of higher quality assets, as previously discussed.

Table 11.7 Moody's investor service: one-year transition matrix

Initial rating	Aaa	Aa	A	Baa	Ba	B	Caa	Default
Aaa	93.40	5.94	0.64	0.00	0.02	0.00	0.00	**0.00**
Aa	1.61	90.55	7.46	0.26	0.09	0.01	0.00	0.02
a	0.07	2.28	92.44	4.63	0.45	0.12	0.01	0.00
Baa	0.05	0.26	5.51	88.48	4.76	0.71	0.08	0.15
Ba	0.02	0.05	0.42	5.16	86.91	5.91	0.24	1.29
B	0.00	0.04	0.13	0.54	6.35	84.22	1.91	**6.81**
Caa	0.00	0.00	0.00	0.62	2.05	2.05	69.20	24.06

Source: Lea Carty, Moody's Investor Service from CreditMetrics – Technical Document

Default probabilities do not, however, indicate loss severity; i.e. how much the bank will lose if a credit defaults. A credit may default, yet expose a bank to a minimal loss risk if the loan is well secured. On the other hand, a default might result in a complete loss. Therefore, banks currently use historical migration matrices with information on recovery rates in default situations to assess the expected loss potential in their portfolios.

Portfolio approach

While the asset-by-asset approach is a critical component to managing credit risk, it does not provide a complete view of portfolio credit risk, where the term 'risk' refers to the possibility that actual losses exceed expected losses. Therefore, to gain greater insights into credit risk, banks increasingly look to complement the asset-by-asset approach with a quantitative portfolio review using a credit model.

A primary problem with the asset-by-asset approach is that it does not identify or quantify the probability and severity of unexpected losses. Historical migration analysis and problem loan allocations are two different methods of measuring the same variable; i.e. expected losses. The ALLL absorbs expected losses. However, the nature of credit risk is that there is a small probability of very large losses. Figure 11.6 illustrates this fundamental difference between market and credit portfolios. Market risk returns follow a normal distribution, while credit risk returns exhibit a skewed distribution.

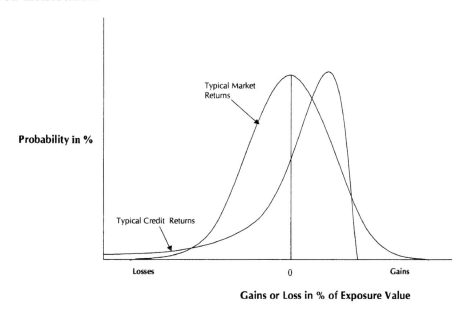

Figure 11.6 Comparison of distribution of credit returns and market returns. (*Source:* J. P. Morgan)

The practical consequence of these two return distributions is that, while the mean and variance fully describe (i.e. they define all the relevant characteristics of) the distributions of market returns, they do not fully describe the distribution of credit risk returns. For a normal distribution, one can say that the portfolio with the larger variance has greater risk. With a credit risk portfolio, a portfolio with a larger variance need not automatically have greater risk than one with a smaller variance, because the skewed distribution of credit returns does not allow the mean and variance to describe the distribution fully. Credit returns are skewed to the left and exhibit 'fat tails'; i.e. a probability, albeit very small, of very large losses. While banks extending credit face a high probability of a small gain (payment of interest and return of principal), they face a very low probability of large losses. Depending upon risk tolerance, an investor may consider a credit portfolio with a larger variance less risky than one with a smaller variance, if the smaller variance portfolio has some probability of an unacceptably large loss.

Credit risk, in a statistical sense, refers to deviations from expected losses, or unexpected losses. Capital covers unexpected losses, regardless of the source; therefore, the measurement of unexpected losses is an important concern.

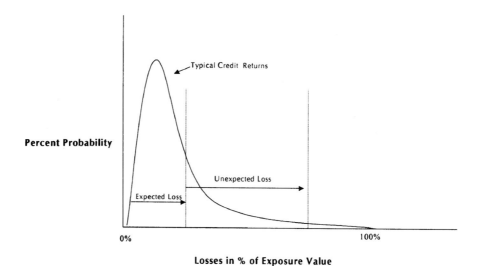

Figure 11.7 Probability of distribution of loss.

Figure 11.7 shows a small probability of very large losses. Banks hold capital to cover 'unexpected' loss scenarios consistent with their desired debt rating.[13] While the probability of very large losses is small, such scenarios do occur, usually due to excessive credit concentrations, and can create significant problems in the banking system.

Banks increasingly attempt to address the inability of the asset-by-asset approach to measure unexpected losses sufficiently by pursuing a 'portfolio' approach. One weakness with the asset-by-asset approach is that it has difficulty identifying and measuring concentration risk. Concentration risk refers to additional portfolio risk resulting from increased exposure to a borrower, or to a group of correlated borrowers. For example, the high correlation between energy and real estate prices precipitated a large number of failures of banks that had credit concentrations in those sectors in the mid-1980s.

Traditionally, banks have relied upon arbitrary concentration limits to manage concentration risk. For example, banks often set limits on credit exposure to a given industry, or to a geographic area. A portfolio approach helps frame concentration risk in a quantitative context, by considering correlations. Even though two credit exposures may not come from the same industry, they could be highly correlated because of dependence upon common economic factors. An arbitrary industry limit may not be sufficient to protect a bank from unwarranted risk, given these correlations. A model can help portfolio managers set limits in a more risk-focused manner, allocate capital more effectively, and price credit consistent with the portfolio risks entailed.[14]

It is important to understand what diversification can and cannot do for a portfolio. The goal of diversification in a credit portfolio is to shorten the 'tail' of the loss distribution; i.e. to reduce the probability of large, unexpected, credit losses. Diversification cannot transform a portfolio of poor quality assets, with a high level of expected losses, into a higher quality portfolio. Diversification efforts can reduce the uncertainty of losses around the expectation (i.e. credit 'risk'), but it cannot change the level of expected loss, which is a function of the quality of the constituent assets.

A low-quality portfolio will have higher expected losses than a high quality portfolio. Because all credit risky assets have exposure to macro-economic conditions, it is impossible to diversify a portfolio completely. Diversification efforts focus on eliminating the issuer specific, or 'unsystematic', risk of the portfolio. Credit managers attempt to do this by spreading the risk out over a large number of obligors, with cross correlations as small as possible.

Figure 11.8 illustrates how the goal of diversification is to reduce risk to its 'systematic' component; i.e. the risks that a manager cannot diversify away because of the dependence of the obligors on the macro economy.

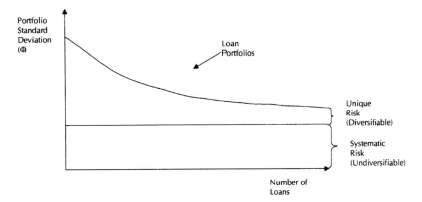

Figure 11.8 Diversification benefits. (*Source:* CIBC World Markets)

While the portfolio management of credit risk has intuitive appeal, its implementation in practice is difficult because of the absence of historical data and measurement problems (e.g. correlations). Currently, while most large banks have initiatives to measure credit risk more quantitatively, few currently manage credit risk based upon the results of such measurements. Fundamental differences between credit and market risks make application of MPT problematic when applied to credit portfolios.

Two important assumptions of portfolio credit risk models are: (1) the holding period or planning horizon over which losses are predicted (e.g. one year) and (2) how credit losses will be reported by the model. Models generally report either a default or market value distribution. If a model reports a default distribution, then the model would report no loss unless a default is predicted. If the model uses a market value distribution, then a decline in the market value of the asset would be reflected even if a default did not occur.[15]

To employ a portfolio model successfully the bank must have a reliable credit risk rating system. Within most credit risk models, the internal risk rating is a critical statistic for summarizing a facility's probability of defaulting within the planning horizon. The models use the credit risk rating to predict the probability of default by comparing this data against: (1) publicly available historical default rates of similarly rated corporate bonds; (2) the bank's own historical internal default data; and (3) default data experienced by other banks. A sufficiently stratified ('granular') credit risk rating system is also important to credit risk modeling. The more stratified the system, the more precise the model's predictive capability can be. Moreover, greater granularity in risk ratings assists banks in risk-based pricing and can offer a competitive advantage.

The objective of credit risk modeling is to identify exposures that create an unacceptable risk/reward profile, such as might arise from credit concentrations. Credit risk management seeks to reduce the unsystematic risk of a portfolio by diversifying risks. As banks gain greater confidence in their portfolio modeling capabilities, it is likely that credit derivatives will become a more significant vehicle to manage portfolio credit risk. While some banks currently use credit derivatives to hedge undesired exposures, much of that activity only involves a desire to reduce regulatory capital requirements, particularly for higher-grade corporate exposures that incur a high regulatory capital tax. But as credit derivatives are used to allow banks to customize their risk exposures, and separate the customer relationship and exposure functions, banks will increasingly find them helpful in applying MPT.

Overreliance on statistical models

The asymmetric distribution of credit returns makes it more difficult to measure credit risk than market risk. While banks' efforts to measure credit risk in a portfolio context can represent an improvement over existing measurement practices, portfolio managers must guard against over-reliance on model results. Portfolio models can complement, but not replace, the seasoned judgment that professional credit personnel provide.

Model results depend heavily on the validity of assumptions. Banks must not become complacent as they increase their use of portfolio models, and cease looking critically at model assumptions. Because of their importance in model output, credit correlations in particular deserve close scrutiny. Risk managers must estimate credit correlations since they cannot observe them from historical data. Portfolio models use different approaches to estimating correlations, which can lead to very different estimated loss distributions for the same portfolio.

Correlations are not only difficult to determine but can change significantly over time. In times of stress, correlations among assets increase, raising the portfolio's risk profile because the systematic risk, which is undiversifiable, increases. Credit portfolio managers may believe they have constructed a diversified portfolio, with desired risk and return characteristics. However, changes in economic conditions may cause changes to default correlations. For example, when energy and Texas real estate prices became highly correlated, those correlation changes exposed banks to significant unanticipated losses. It remains to be seen whether portfolio models can identify changes in default correlation early enough to allow risk managers to take appropriate risk-reducing actions.

In recent years, there have been widely publicized incidents in which inaccurate price risk measurement models have led to poor trading decisions and unanticipated losses. To identify potential weaknesses in their price risk models, most banks use a combination of independent validation, calibration, and backtesting. However, the same data limitations that make credit risk measurement difficult in the first place also make implementation of these important risk controls problematic. The absence of credit default data and the long planning horizon makes it difficult to determine, in a statistical sense, the accuracy of a credit risk model. Unlike market risk models, for which many data observations exist, and for which the holding period is usually only one day, credit risk models are based on infrequent default observations and a much longer holding period. Backtesting, in particular, is problematic and would involve an impractical number of years of analysis to reach statistically valid conclusions. In view of these problems, banks must use other means, such as assessing model coverage, verifying the accuracy of mathematical algorithms, and comparing the model against peer group models to determine its accuracy. Stress testing, in particular, is important because models use specified confidence intervals. The essence of risk management is to understand the exposures that lie outside a model's confidence interval.

Future of credit risk management

Credit risk management has two basic processes: transaction oversight and portfolio management. Through transaction oversight, banks make credit decisions on individual transactions. Transaction oversight addresses credit analysis, deal structuring, pricing, borrower limit setting, and account administration. Portfolio management, on the other hand, seeks to identify, measure, and control risks. It focuses on measuring a portfolio's expected and unexpected losses, and making the portfolio more efficient. Figure 11.9 illustrates the efficient frontier, which represents those portfolios having the maximum return, for any given level of risk, or, for any given level of return, the minimum risk. For example, Portfolio A is inefficient because, given the level of risk it has taken, it should generate an expected return of $E(R_{EF})$. However, its actual return is only $E(R_A)$.

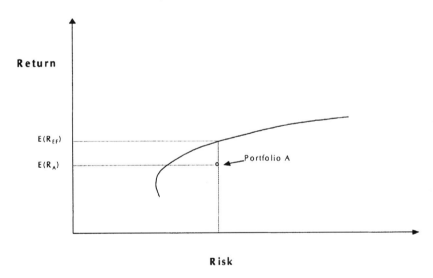

Figure 11.9 The efficient frontier.

Credit portfolio managers actively seek to move their portfolios to the efficient frontier. In practice, they find their portfolios lie inside the frontier. Such portfolios are 'inefficient' because there is some combination of the constituent assets that either would increase returns given risk constraints, or reduce risk given return requirements. Consequently, they seek to make portfolio adjustments that enable the portfolio to move closer toward the efficient frontier. Such adjustments include eliminating (or hedging) risk positions that do not, in a portfolio context, exhibit a satisfactory risk/reward trade-off, or changing the size (i.e. the weights) of the exposures. It is in this context that credit derivatives are useful, as they can allow banks to shed unwanted credit risk, or acquire more risk (without having to originate a loan) in an efficient manner. Not surprisingly, banks that have the most advanced portfolio modeling efforts tend to be the most active end-users of credit derivatives.

As banks increasingly manage credit on a portfolio basis, one can expect credit portfolios to show more market-like characteristics; e.g. less direct borrower contact, fewer credit covenants, and less nonpublic information. The challenge for bank portfolio managers will be to obtain the benefits of diversification and use of more sophisticated risk management techniques, while preserving the positive aspects of more traditional credit management techniques.

Author's note

Kurt Wilhelm is a national bank examiner in the Treasury & Market Risk unit of the Office of the Comptroller of the Currency (OCC). The views expressed in this chapter are those of the author and do not necessarily reflect official positions of either the OCC or the US Department of the Treasury. The author acknowledges valuable contributions from Denise Dittrich, Donald Lamson, Ron Pasch and P. C. Venkatesh.

Notes

[1] 1997/1998 British Bankers Association Credit Derivatives Survey.

[2] Source: 1997/1998 British Bankers Association Credit Derivatives Survey.

[3] For a discussion of the range of practice in the conceptual approaches to modeling credit risk, see the Basel Committee on Banking Supervision's 21 April 1999 report. It discusses the choice of time horizon, the definition of credit loss, the various approaches to aggregating credits and measuring the connection between default events.

[4] Banks may use VaR models to determine the capital requirements for market risk provided that such models/systems meet certain qualitative and quantitative standards.

[5] Banks generally should not, however, base their business decisions solely on regulatory capital ramifications. If hedging credit risk makes economic sense, regulatory capital considerations should represent a secondary consideration.

[6] On 3 June 1999, the Basel Committee issued a consultative paper proposing a new capital adequacy framework to replace the previous Capital Accord, issued in 1988. The proposal acknowledges that 'the 1988 Accord does not provide the proper incentives for credit risk mitigation techniques'. Moreover, 'the Accord's structure may not have favoured the development of specific forms of credit risk mitigation by placing restrictions on both the type of hedges acceptable for achieving capital reduction and the amount of capital relief'. The Committee proposes to expand the scope for eligible collateral, guarantees, and on-balance sheet netting.

[7] In this example, the dealer has exposure to credit losses exceeding the $20 cushion supplied by investors, and must implement procedures to closely monitor the value of the loans and take risk-reducing actions if losses approach $20.

[8] This section describes capital requirements for end-users. Dealers use the market risk rule to determine capital requirements. Some institutions may achieve regulatory capital reduction by transferring loans from the banking book to the trading book, if they meet the quantitative and qualitative requirements of the market risk rule.

[9] Note that this transaction has no impact on leverage capital (i.e. capital/assets ratio). A

credit derivative hedge does not improve the leverage ratio because the asset remains on the books.

[10] Low-level recourse rules are only applicable to US banks.

[11] CLO transactions typically carry early amortization triggers that protect investors against rapid credit deterioration in the pool. Such triggers ensure that the security amortizes more quickly and, as a practical matter, shield investors from exposure to credit losses.

[12] EAR and VaR represents an estimate of the maximum losses in a portfolio, over a specified horizon, with a given probability. One might say the VaR of a credit portfolio is $50 million over the next year, with 99% confidence, i.e. there is a 1% probability that losses will exceed $50 million in the next 12 months.

[13] Banks do not hold capital against outcomes worse than required by their desired debt ratings, as measured by VaR. These scenarios are so extreme that a bank could not hold enough capital against them and compete effectively.

[14] For a discussion of setting credit risk limits within a portfolio context see *CreditMetrics-Technical document*.

[15] For an excellent discussion of credit risk modeling techniques, see *Credit Risk Models at Major US Banking Institutions: Current State of the Art and Implications for Assessments of Capital Adequacy*, Federal Reserve Systems Task Force on Internal Models, May 1998.

12

Operational risk

MICHEL CROUHY, DAN GALAI and BOB MARK

Introduction

Operational risk (OR) has not been a well-defined concept. It refers to various potential failures in the operation of the firm, unrelated to uncertainties with regard to the demand function for the products and services of the firm. These failures can stem from a computer breakdown, a bug in a major computer software, an error of a decision maker in special situations, etc. The academic literature generally relates operational risk to operational leverage (i.e. to the shape of the production cost function) and in particular to the relationship between fixed and variable cost.

OR is a fuzzy concept since it is often hard to make a clear-cut distinction between OR and 'normal' uncertainties faced by the organization in its daily operations. For example, if a client failed to pay back a loan, is it then due to 'normal' credit risk, or to a human error of the loan officers that should have known better all the information concerning the client and should have declined to approve the loan? Usually all credit-related uncertainties are classified as part of business risk. However, if the loan officer approved a loan against the bank's guidelines, and maybe he was even given a bribe, this will be classified as an OR.

Therefore the management of a bank should first define what is included in OR. In other words, the typology of OR must be clearly articulated and codified. A key problem lies in quantifying operational risk. For example, how can one quantify the risk of a computer breakdown? The risk is a product of the probability and the cost of a computer breakdown. Often OR is in the form of discrete events that don't occur frequently. Therefore, a computer breakdown today (e.g. a network related failure) is different in both probability and the size of the damage from a computer breakdown 10 years ago. How can we quantify the damage of a computer failure? What historical event can we use in order to make a rational assessment?

The problems in assessing OR does not imply that they should be ignored and neglected. On the contrary, management should pay a lot of attention to understanding OR and its potential sources in the organization precisely because it is hard to quantify OR. Possible events or scenarios leading to OR should be analyzed. In the next section we define OR and discuss its typology. In some cases OR can be insured or hedged. For example, computer hardware problems can be insured or the bank can have a backup system. Given the price of insurance or the cost of hedging risks, a question arises concerning the economic rationale of removing the risks. There is the economic issue of assessing the potential loss against the certain insurance cost for each OR event.

Regulators require a minimum amount of regulatory capital for price risk in the trading book (BIS 98) and credit risk in the banking book (BIS 88), but there are currently no formal capital requirements against operational risk. Nevertheless, the 1999 Basel conceptual paper on a comprehensive framework for arriving at the minimum required regulatory capital includes a requirement for capital to be allocated against operational risk. Previous chapters of the book are devoted to the challenges associated with capital allocation for credit and market risk. This chapter examines the challenges associated with the allocation of capital for OR.

In this chapter we look at how to meet these present and future challenges by constructing a framework for operational risk control. After explaining what we think of as a key underlying rule – the control functions of a bank need to be carefully harmonized – we examine the typology of operational risk. We describe four key steps in implementing bank operational risk, and highlight some means of risk reduction. Finally, we look at how a bank can extract value from enhanced operational risk management by improving its capital attribution methodologies.

Failure to identify an operational risk, or to defuse it in a timely manner, can translate into a huge loss. Most notoriously, the actions of a single trader at Barings Bank (who was able to take extremely risky positions in a market without authority or detection) led to losses ($1.5 billion) that brought about the liquidation of the bank.

The Bank of England report on Barings revealed some lessons about operational risk. First, management teams have the duty to understand *fully* the businesses they manage. Second, responsibility for each business activity has to be *clearly* established and communicated. Third, relevant internal controls, including independent risk management, *must* be established for all business activities. Fourth, top management and the Audit Committee must ensure that significant weaknesses are resolved *quickly*.

Looking to the future, banks are becoming aware that technology is a double-edged sword. The increasing complexity of instruments and information systems increase the potential for operational risk. Unfamiliarity with instruments may lead to their misuse, and raise the chances of mispricing and wrong hedging; errors in data feeds may also distort the bank's assessment of its risks. At the same time, advanced analytical techniques combined with sophisticated computer technology create new ways to add value to operational risk management.

The British Bankers' Association (BBA) and Coopers & Lybrand conducted a survey among the BBA's members during February and March 1997. The results reflect the views of risk directors and managers and senior bank management in 45 of the BBA's members (covering a broad spectrum of the banking industry in the UK). The survey gives a good picture of how banks are currently managing operational risk and how they are responding to it. Section I of the report indicated that many banks have some way to go to formalize their approach in terms of policies and generally accepted definitions. They pointed out that it is difficult for banks to manage operational risk on a consistent basis without an appropriate framework in place. Section II of the report indicated that experience shows that it is all too easy for different parts of a bank inadvertently to duplicate their efforts in tackling operational risk or for such risks to fall through gaps because no one has been made responsible for them. Section III of the report revealed that modeling operational risk generates the most interest of all operational risk topic areas. However, the survey results suggest that banks have not managed to progress very far in terms of arriving at generally accepted models for operations risk. The report emphasized that this may well be because they do not have the relevant data. The survey also revealed that data collection is an area that banks will be focusing on. Section IV revealed that more than 67% of banks thought that operational risk was as (or more) significant as either market or credit risk and that 24% of banks had experienced losses of more than £1 million in the last 3 years. Section VI revealed that the percentage of banks that use internal audit recommendations as the basis of their response to operational risk may appear high, but we suspect this is only in relation to operational risk identified by internal audit rather than all operational risks. Section VII revealed that almost half the banks were satisfied with their present approach to operational risk. However, the report pointed out that there is no complacency among the banks. Further, a majority of them expect to make changes in their approach in the next 2 years.

For reasons that we discuss towards the end of the chapter, it is important that the financial industry develop a consistent approach to operational risk. We believe that our approach is in line with the findings of a recent working group of the Basel committee in autumn 1998 as well as with the 20 best-practice recommendations on derivative risk management put forward in the seminal Group of Thirty (G30) report in 1993 (see Appendix 1).

Typology of operational risks

What is operational risk?

Operational risk is the risk associated with operating the business. One can subdivide operational risk into two components: operational failure risk and operational strategic risk.

Operational failure risk arises from the potential for failure in the course of operating the business. A firm uses *people, process, and technology* to achieve business plans, and any one of these factors may experience a failure of some kind. Accordingly, operational failure risk is the risk that exists *within* the business unit caused by the failure of people, process or technology. A certain level of the failures may be anticipated and should be built into the business plan. It is the unanticipated and therefore uncertain failures that give rise to risk. These failures can be expected to occur periodically, although both their impact and their frequency may be uncertain. The impact or the financial loss can be divided into the expected amount, the severe unexpected amount and the catastrophic unexpected amount. The firm may provide for the losses that arise from the expected component of these failures by charging revenues with a sufficient amount of reserve. The firm should set aside sufficient economic capital to cover the severe unexpected component.

Operational strategic risk arises from environmental factors such as a new competitor that changes the business paradigm, a major political and regulatory regime change, earthquakes and other factors that are generally outside the control of the firm. It also arises from a major new strategic initiative, such as getting into a new line of business or redoing how current business is to be done in the future. All businesses also rely on people, processes and technology **outside** their business unit, and the same potential for failure exists there. This type of risk will be referred to as external dependencies.

In summary, operational failure risk can arise due to the failure of people, process or technology and external dependencies (just as market risk can be due to unexpected changes in interest rates, foreign exchange rates, equity prices and commodity prices).

In short, operational failure risk and operational strategic risk, as illustrated in Figure 12.1, are the two main categories of operational risks. They can also be defined as 'internal' and 'external' operational risks.

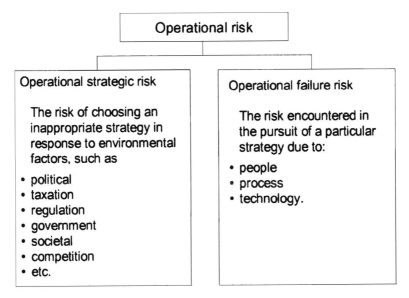

Figure 12.1 Two broad categories of operational risk.

This chapter focuses on operational failure risk, i.e. on the internal factors that can and should be controlled by management. However, one should observe that a failure to address a strategic risk issue could translate into an operational failure risk. For example, a change in the tax laws is an operational failure risk. Furthermore, from a business unit perspective it might be argued that external dependencies include support groups *within* the bank, such as information technology. In other words, the two types of operational risk are interrelated and tend to overlap.

Beginning to End

Operational risk is often thought to be limited to losses that can occur in operations or processing centers (i.e. where transaction processing errors can occur). This type of operational risk, sometimes referred to as operations risk, is an important component but by no means all of the operational risks facing the firm.

Operational risk can arise before, during and after a transaction is processed. Risks exist before processing, while the potential transaction is being designed, during negotiation with the client, regardless whether the negotiation is a lengthy structuring exercise or a routine electronic negotiation, and continues after the negotiation through various continual servicing of the original transaction.

A complete picture of operational risk can only be obtained if the activity is analyzed from beginning to end. Take the example of a derivatives sales desk shown in Figure 12.2. Before a transaction can be negotiated several things have to be in place, and each exposes the firm to risk. First, sales may be highly dependent on a valued relationship between a particular sales person and the client. Second, sales are usually dependent on the highly specialized skills of the product designer to come up with both a structure and a price that the client finds more attractive than all the other competing offers. These expose the institution to key people risks. The risk arises from the uncertainty as to whether these key people continue to be available. In addition, do they have the capacity to deal with an increase in client needs or are they at full capacity dealing with too many clients to be able to handle increases in client needs? Also do the people have the capability to respond to evolving and perhaps more complex client needs?

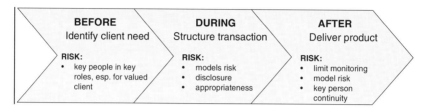

Figure 12.2   Where operational risk occurs.

The firm is exposed to several risks during the processing of the transaction. First, the sales person may either willingly or unwillingly not fully disclose the full range of the risk of the transaction to a client. This may be a particular high risk during periods of intense pressure to meet profit and therefore bonus targets for the desk. Related to this is the risk that the sales person persuades the client to engage in a transaction that is totally inappropriate for the client, exposing the firm to potential lawsuits and regulatory sanctions. This is an example of people risk. Second, the sales person may rely on sophisticated financial models to price the transaction, which creates what is commonly, called model risk. The risk arises because the model may be used outside its domain of applicability, or the wrong inputs may be used. Once the transaction is negotiated and a ticket is written, several errors may occur as the transaction is recorded in the various systems or reports. For example, an error may result in delayed settlement giving rise to late penalties, it may be misclassified in the risk reports, understating the exposure and lead to other transactions that would otherwise not have been performed. These are examples of process risk. The system which records the transaction may not be capable of handling the transaction or it may not have the capacity to handle such transactions, or it may not be available (i.e. it may be down). If any one of the steps is outsourced, such as phone transmission, then external dependency risk arises.

The list of what can go wrong before, during, and after the transaction, is endless. However, each type of risk can be broadly captured as a people, a process, a technology risk, or an external dependency risk and in turn each can be analyzed in terms of capacity, capability or availability

Who manages operational risk?

We believe that a partnership between business, infrastructure, internal audit and risk management is the key to success. How can this partnership be constituted? In particular, what is the nature of the relationship between operational risk managers and the bank audit function?

The essentials of proper risk management require that (a) appropriate policies be in place that limit the amount of risk taken and (b) authority be provided to change the risk profile, to those who can take action, and (c) that timely and effective monitoring of the risk is in place. No one group can be responsible for setting policies, taking action, and monitoring the risk taken, for to do so would give rise to all sorts of conflict of interest Policy setting remains the responsibility of **senior management**, even though the development of those policies may be delegated, and submitted to the board of directors for approval (see Figure 12.3).

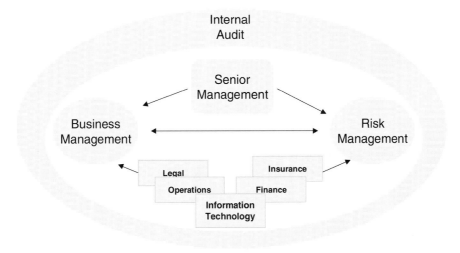

Figure 12.3   Managing operational risk.

The authority to take action rests with **business management**, who are responsible for controlling the amount of operational risk taken within their business. Business management often relies on expert areas such as information technology, operations, legal, etc. to supply it with services required to operate the business. These infrastructure and governance groups share with business management the responsibility for managing operational risk.

The responsibility for the development of the methodology for measuring operational risk resides with **risk management**. Risk management also needs to make risks transparent through monitoring and reporting. Risk management should also portfolio manage the firm's operational risk. Risk management can actively manage residual risk through using tools such as insurance. Portfolio management adds value by ensuring that operational risk is adequately capitalized as well as analyzed for operational risk concentration. Risk management is also responsible for providing a regular review of trends, and needs to ensure that proper operational risk reward analysis is performed in the review of existing business as well as before the introduction of new initiatives and products. In this regard risk management works very closely but is independent of the business infrastructure, and the other governance groups.

Operational risk is often managed on an *ad hoc* basis. and banks can suffer from a lack of coordination among functions such as risk management, internal audit, and business management. Most often there are no common bank-wide policies, methodologies or infrastructure. As a result there is also often no consistent reporting on the extent of operational risk within the bank as a whole. Furthermore, most bank-wide capital attribution models rarely incorporate sophisticated measures of operational risk.

Senior management needs to know if the delegated responsibilities are actually being followed and if the resulting processes are effective. **Internal audit** is charged with this responsibility. Audit determines the effectiveness and integrity of the controls that business management puts in place to keep risk within tolerable levels.

At regular intervals the internal audit function needs to ensure that the operational risk management process has integrity, and is indeed being implemented along with the appropriate controls. In other words, auditors analyze the degree to which businesses are in compliance with the designated operational risk management process. They also offer an independent assessment of the underlying design of the operational risk management process. This includes examining the process surrounding the building of operational risk measurement models, the adequacy and reliability of the operations risk management systems and compliance with external regulatory guidelines, etc. Audit thus provides an overall assurance on the adequacy of operational risk management.

A key audit objective is to evaluate the design and conceptual soundness of the operational value-at-risk (VaR) measure, including any methodologies associated with stress testing, and the reliability of the reporting framework. Audit should also evaluate the operational risks that affect all types of risk management information systems – whether they are used to assess market, credit or operational risk itself – such as the processes used for coding and implementation of the internal models. This includes examining controls concerning the capture of data about market positions, the accuracy and completeness of this data, as well as controls over the parameter estimation processes. Audit would typically also review the adequacy and effectiveness of the processes for monitoring risk. and the documentation relating to compliance with the qualitative/quantitative criteria outlined in any regulatory guidelines.

Regulatory guidelines typically also call for auditors to examine the approval process for vetting risk management models and valuation models used by front- and back-office personnel (for reasons made clear in Appendix 2). Auditors also need to examine any significant change in the risk measurement process. Audit should verify the consistency, timeliness and reliability of data sources used to run internal models, including the independence of such data sources. A key role is to examine the accuracy and appropriateness of volatility and correlation assumptions as well as the accuracy of the valuation and risk transformation calculations. Finally, auditors should examine the verification of the model's accuracy through an examination of the backtesting process.

The key to implementing bank-wide operational risk management

In our experience, eight key elements (Figure 12.4) are necessary to successfully implement such a bank-wide operational risk management framework. They involve setting policy and establishing a common language of risk identification. One would need to construct business process maps as well as to build a best-practice measurement methodology One would also need to provide exposure management as well as to allocate a timely reporting capability Finally, one wouyld need to perform risk analysis (inclusive of stress testing) as well as to allocate economic capital. Let's look at these in more detail.

Figure 12.4 Eight key elements to achieve best practice operational risk management.

1 *Develop well-defined operational risk policies.* This includes articulating explicitly the desired standards for risk measurement. One also needs to establish clear guidelines for practices that may contribute to a reduction of operational risks. For example, the bank needs to establish policies on model vetting, off-hour trading, off-premises trading, legal document vetting, etc.

2 *Establish a common language of risk identification.* For example, people risk would include a failure to deploy skilled staff. Process risk would include execution errors. Technology risk would include system failures, etc.

3 *Develop business process maps of each business.* For example, one should map the business process associated with the bank's dealing with a broker so that it becomes transparent to management and auditors. One should create an 'operational risk catalogue' as illustrated in Table 12.1 which categorizes and defines the various operational risks arising from each organizational unit This includes analyzing the products and services that each organizational unit offers, and the action one needs to take to manage operational risk. This catalogue should be a tool to help with operational risk identification and assessment. Again, the catalogue should be based on common definitions and language (as Reference Appendix 3).

4 *Develop a comprehensible set of operational risk metrics.* Operational risk assessment is a complex process and needs to be performed on a firm-wide basis at regular intervals using standard metrics. In the early days, as illustrated in Figure 12.5, business and infrastructure groups performed their own self-assessment of operational risk. Today, self-assessment has been discredited – the self-assessment of operational risk at Barings Bank contributed to the build-up of market risk at that institution – and is no longer an acceptable approach. Sophisticated financial institutions are trying to develop objective measures of operational risk that build significantly more reliability into the quantification of operational risk. To this end, operational risk assessment needs to include a review of the *likelihood* of a particular operational risk occurring as well as the *severity* or magnitude of

Table 12.1 Types of operational failure risks

1 **People risk**:	Incompetency
	Fraud
	etc.
2 **Process risk**:	Mark-to-model error
A Model risk (see Appendix 2)	Model/methodology error
	etc.
B Transaction risk	Execution error
	Product complexity
	Booking error
	Settlement error
	Documentation/contract risk
	etc.
C Operational control risk	Exceeding limits
	Security risks
	Volume risk
	etc.
3 **Technology risk**:	System failure
	Programming error
	Information risk (see
	Appendix 4)
	Telecommunication failure
	etc.

the impact that the operational risk will have on business objectives. This is no easy task. It can be challenging to assess the probability of a computer failure (or of a programming bug in a valuation model) and to assign a potential loss to any such event. We will examine this challenge in more detail in the next section of this chapter.

5 *Decide how one will manage operational risk exposure and take appropriate action to hedge the risks.* For example, a bank should address the economic question of the cost–benefit of insuring a given risk for those operational risks that can he insured.

6 *Decide on how one will report exposure.* For example, an illustrative summary report for the Tokyo equity arbitrage business is shown in Table 12.2.

7 *Develop tools for risk analysis and procedures for when these tools should be deployed.* For example, risk analysis is typically performed as part of a new product process, periodic business reviews, etc. Stress testing should be a standard part of the risk analyst process. The frequency of risk assessment should be a function of the degree to which operational risks are expected to change over time as businesses undertake new initiatives, or as business circumstances evolve. A bank should update its risk assessment more frequently (say, semiannually) following the initial assessment of operational risk. Further, one should reassess the operational risk whenever the operational risk profile changes significantly (e.g. implementation of a new system, entering a new service, etc).

8 *Develop techniques to translate the calculation of operational risk into a required amount of economic capital.* Tools and procedures should be developed to enable one to make decisions about operational risk based on incorporating operational

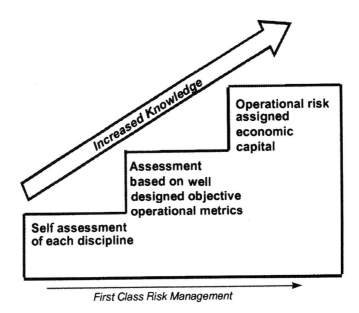

Figure 12.5 The process of implementing operational risk management.

risk capital into the risk reward analyses, as we discuss in more detail later in the chapter.

Clear guiding principles for the operational risk process should be set to ensure that it provides an appropriate measure of operational risk across all business units throughout the bank. These principles are illustrated in Figure 12.6. Objectivity refers to the principle that operational risk should be measured using standard objective criteria. 'Consistency' refers to ensuring that similar operational risk profiles in different business units result in similar reported operational risks. Relevance refers to the idea that risk should be reported in a way that makes it easier to take action to address the operational risk. 'Transparency' refers to ensuring that all material operational risks are reported and assessed in a way that makes the risk transparent to senior managers. 'Bank-wide' refers to the principle that operational risk measures should be designed so that the results can be aggregated across the entire organization. Finally, 'completeness' refers to ensuring that *all* material operational risks are identified and captured.

A four-step measurement process for operational risk

As pointed out earlier, one can assess the amount of operational risk in terms of the likelihood of operational failure (net of mitigating controls) and the severity of potential financial loss (given that a failure occurs). This suggests that one should measure operational risk using the four-step operational risk process illustrated in Figure 12.7. We discuss each step below.

Input (step 1)

The first step in the operational risk measurement process is to gather the information needed to perform a complete assessment of all significant operational risks. A key

Table 12.2   Operational risk reporting worksheet

The overall operational risk of the Tokyo Equity Arbitrage
Trading desk is Low

	Risk profile
1. **People risk**	
Incompetency	Low
Fraud	Low
2. **Process risk**	
A. **Model risk**	
Mark-to-model error	Low
Model/methodology error	Low
B. **Transaction risk**:	
Execution error	Low
Product complexity	Low
Booking error	Low
Settlement error	Low
Documentation/contract risk	Medium
C. **Operational control risk**	
Exceeding limits	Low
Security risk	Low
Volume risk	Low/medium
3. **Technology risk**	
System failure	Low
Programming error	Low
Information risk	Low
Telecommunication failure	Low
Total operational failure risk measurement	Low
Strategic risk	
Political risk	Low
Taxation risk	Low
Regulatory risk	Low/medium
Total strategic risk measurement	Low

source of this information is often the finished products of other groups. For example. a unit that supports a business group often publishes reports or documents that may provide an excellent starting point for the operational risk assessment.

Relevant and useful reports (e.g. Table 12.3) include audit reports, regulatory reports, etc. The degree to which one can rely on existing documents for control assessment varies. For example, if one is relying on audit documents as an indication of the degree of control, then one needs to ask if the audit assessment is current and sufficient. Have there been any significant changes made since the last audit assessment? Did the audit scope include the area of operational risk that is of concern to the present risk assessment?

Gaps in information are filled through discussion with the relevant managers. Information from primary sources needs to be validated, and updated as necessary. Particular attention should be paid to any changes in the business or operating environment since the information was first produced.

Typically, sufficient reliable historical data is not available to project the likelihood

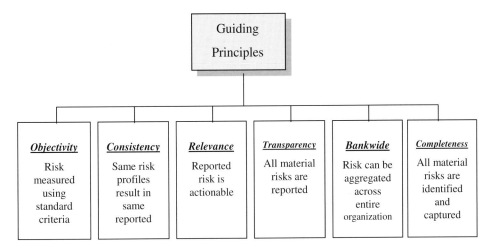

Figure 12.6 Guiding principles for the operational risk measurement.

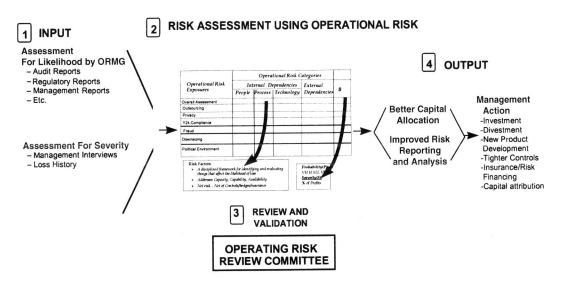

Figure 12.7 The operational risk measurement process.

or severity of operational losses with confidence. One often needs to rely on the expertise of business management. The centralized operational risk management group (ORMG) will need to validate any such self-assessment by a business unit in a disciplined way. Often this amounts to a 'reasonableness' check that makes use of historical information on operational losses within the business and within the industry as a whole.

The time frame employed for all aspects of the assessment process is typically one year. The one-year time horizon is usually selected to align with the business planning cycle of the bank. Nevertheless, while some serious potential operational failures may not occur until after the one-year time horizon, they should be part of the current risk assessment. For example, in 1998 one may have had key employees

Table 12.3 Sources of information in the measurement process of operational risk – the input

Assessment for:	
Likelihood of occurrence	*Severity*
• Audit reports • Regulatory reports • Management reports • Expert opinion • BRP (Business Recovery Plan) • Y2K (year 2000) reports • Business plans • Budget plans • Operations plans • etc.	• Management interviews • Loss history • etc.

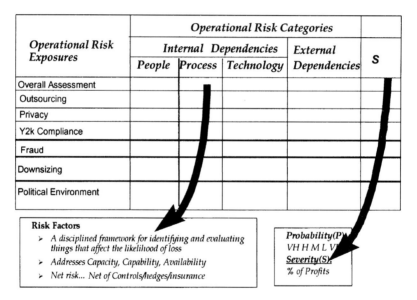

Figure 12.8 Second step in the measurement process of operational risk: risk assessment framework. VH: very high, H: high, M: medium, L: low, VL: very low.

under contract working on the year 2000 problem – the risk that systems will fail on 1 January 2000. These personnel may be employed under contracts that terminate more than 12 months into the future. However, while the risk event may only occur beyond the end of the current one-year review period, current activity directed at mitigating the risk of that future potential failure should be reviewed for the likelihood of failure as part of the *current* risk assessment.

Risk assessment framework (step 2)

The 'input' information gathered in step 1 needs to be analyzed and processed through the risk assessment framework sketched in Figure 12.8. The risk of unexpected operational failure, as well as the adequacy of management processes and controls to manage this risk, needs to be identified and assessed. This assessment leads to a measure of the net operational risk, in terms of likelihood and severity.

Risk categories

We mentioned earlier that operational risk can be broken down into four headline *risk categories* (representing the risk of unexpected loss) due to operational failures in people, process and technology deployed within the business – collectively the *internal dependencies* and *external dependencies*.

Internal dependencies should each be reviewed according to a common set of factors. Assume, for illustrative purposes, that the common set of factors consist of three key components of capacity, capability and availability. For example, if we examine operational risk arising from the people risk category then one can ask:

- Does the business have enough people (capacity) to accomplish its business plan?
- Do the people have the right skills (capability)?
- Are the people going to be there when needed (availability)?

External dependencies are also analyzed in terms of the specific type of external interaction. For example, one would look at clients (external to the bank, or an internal function that is external to the business unit under analysis).

Net operational risk

Operational risks should be evaluated net of risk mitigants. For example, if one has insurance to cover a potential fraud then one needs to adjust the degree of fraud risk by the amount of insurance. We expect over time that insurance products will play an increasingly larger role in the area of mitigating operational risk.

Connectivity and interdependencies

The headline risk categories cannot be viewed in isolation from one another. Figure 12.9 illustrates the idea that one needs to examine the degree of interconnected risk exposure across the headline operational risk categories in order to understand the full impact of any risk. For example, assume that a business unit is introducing a new computer technology. The implementation of that new technology may generate

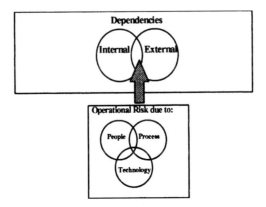

Figure 12.9 Connectivity of operational risk exposure.

a set of interconnected risks across people, process and technology. For example, have the people who are to work with the new technology been given sufficient training and support? All this suggests that the overall risk may be higher than that accounted for by each of the component risks considered individually.

Change, complexity, complacency

One should also examine the sources that drive the headline categories of operational risk. For example, one may view the drivers as falling broadly under the categories of change, complexity, and complacency.

Change refers to such items as introducing new technology or new products, a merger or acquisition, or moving from internal supply to outsourcing, etc. *Complexity* refers to such items as complexity in products, process or technology. *Complacency* refers to ineffective management of the business, particularly in key operational risk areas such as fraud, unauthorized trading, privacy and confidentiality, payment and settlement, model use, etc. Figure 12.10 illustrates how these underlying sources of a risk connect to the headline operational risk categories.

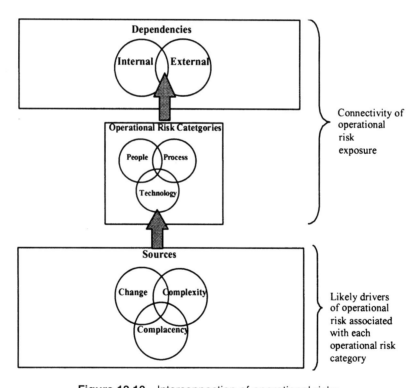

Figure 12.10 Interconnection of operational risks.

Net likelihood assessment

The likelihood that an operational failure may occur within the next year should be assessed (net of risk mitigants such as insurance) for each identified risk exposure and for each of the four headline risk categories (i.e. people, process and technology, and external dependencies). This assessment can be expressed as a rating along a five-point likelihood continuum from very low (VL) to very high (VH) as set out in Table 12.4.

Table 12.4 Five-point likelihood continuum

Likelihood that an operational failure will occur within the next year	
VL	Very low (very unlikely to happen: less than 2%)
L	Low (unlikely: 2-5%)
M	Medium (may happen: 5–10%)
H	High (likely to happen: 10–20%)
VH	Very high (very likely: greater than 20%)

Severity assessment

Severity describes the potential loss to the bank given that an operational failure has occurred. Typically, this will be expressed as a range of dollars (e.g. $50–$100 million), as exact measurements will not usually be possible. Severity should be assessed for each identified risk exposure. As we mentioned above, in practice the operational risk management group is likely to rely on the expertise of business management to recommend appropriate severity amounts.

Combining likelihood and severity into an overall operational risk assessment

Operational risk measures are not exact in that there is usually no easy way to combine the individual likelihood of loss and severity assessments into an overall measure of operational risk within a business unit. To do so, the likelihood of loss would need to be expressed in numerical terms – e.g. a medium risk represents a 5–10% probability of occurrence. This cannot be accomplished without statistically significant historical data on operational losses.

The financial industry for the moment measures operational risk using a combination of both quantitative and qualitative points of view. To be sure, one should strive to take a quantitative approach based on statistical data. However, where the data is unavailable or unreliable – and this is the case for many risk sources – a qualitative approach can be used to generate a risk rating. Neither approach on its own tells the whole story: the quantitative approach is often too rigid, while the qualitative approach is often too vague. The hybrid approach requires a numerical assignment of the amount at risk based on both quantitative and qualitative data.

Ideally, one would also calculate the correlation between the various risk exposures and incorporate this into the overall measure of business or firm-wide risk. Given the difficulty of doing this, for the time being risk managers are more likely to simply aggregate individual seventies assessed for each operational risk exposure.

Defining cause and effect

One should analyze cause and effect of an operational loss. For example, failure to have an independent group vet all mathematical models is a cause, and a loss event arising from using erroneous models is the effect (see Table 12.5).

Loss or effect data is easier to collect than the causes of loss data. There may be many causes to one loss. The relationship can be highly subjective and the importance of each cause difficult to assess. Most banks start by collecting the losses and then try to fit the causes to them. The methodology is typically developed later, after

Table 12.5 Risk categories: causes, effects and source

Risk category	The cause	The effect
People (human resource)	• Loss of key staff due to defection of key staff to competitor	Variance in revenues/profits (e.g. cost of recruiting replacements, costs of training, disruption to existing staff)
Process	• Declining productivity as volume grows	Variance in process costs from predicted levels (excluding process malfunctions)
Technology	• Year 2000 upgrade expenditure • Application development	Variance in technology running costs from predicted levels

Source: Extracted from a table by Duncan Wilson, Risk Management Consulting, IBM Global Financial Markets

the data has been collected. One needs to develop a variety of empirical analyses to test the link between cause and effect.

Sample risk assessment report

What does this approach lead to when put into practice? Assume we have examined Business Unit A and have determined that the sources of operational risk are related to:

- outsourcing
- privacy
- compliance
- fraud
- downsizing and
- the political environment.

The sample report, as illustrated in Table 12.6, shows that the business has an overall 'low' likelihood of operational loss within the next 12 months. Observe that the assessment has led to an overall estimate of the severity as ranging from $150 to $300 million. One typically could display for each business unit a graph showing the relationship between severity and likelihood across each operational risk type (see Appendix 4).

The summary report typically contains details of the factors considered in making a likelihood assessment for each operational risk exposure (broken down by people, process, technology and external dependencies) given an operational failure.

Review and validation (step 3)

What happens after such a report has been generated? First. the centralized operational risk management group (ORMG) reviews the assessment results with senior business unit management and key officers in order to finalize the proposed operational risk rating. Key officers include those with responsibility for the management and control of operational activities (such as internal audit, compliance, IT, human resources, etc.). Second, ORMG can present its recommended rating to an operational risk rating review committee – a process similar that followed by credit rating agencies

Table 12.6 Example of a risk assessment report for Business Unit A

Operational risk scenarios	Likelihood of event (in 12 months)					Severity ($million)
	Internal dependencies			External dependencies	Overall assessment	
	People	Process	Technology			
Outsourcing	L	VL	VL	M	M	50–100
Privacy	L	M	VL	L	L	50–100
Compliance	L	VI	VL	VL	L	35–70
Fraud	L	L	VL	VL	L	5–10
Downsizing	I	VL	VL	L	L	5–10
Political environment	VL	M	VL	VL	L	5–10
Overall assessment	L	M	VL	L	L	150–300

such as Standard & Poors. The operational risk committee comments on the ratings prior to publication. ORMG may clarify or amend its original assessment based on feedback from the committee.

The perational risk committee reviews the individual risk assessments to ensure that the framework has been consistently applied across businesses. The committee should have representation from business management, audit, functional areas, and chaired by risk management. Risk management retains the right to veto.

Output (step 4)

The final assessment of operational risk should be formally reported to business management, the centralized Raroc group, and the partners in corporate governance (such as internal audit. compliance, etc.). As illustrated in Figure 12.11, the output of the assessment process has two main uses. First, the assessment provides better operational risk information to management for use in improving risk management decisions. Second, the assessment improves the allocation of economic capital to better reflect the extent of operational risk being taken by a business unit (a topic we discuss in more detail below). Overall, operational risk assessment guides management action – for example, in deciding whether to purchase insurance to mitigate some of the risks.

Figure 12.11 Fourth step in the measurement process of operational risk: output.

The overall assessment of the likelihood of operational risk and severity of loss for a business unit can be plotted to provide relative information on operational risk exposures across the bank (or a segment of the bank) as shown in Figure 12.12 (see

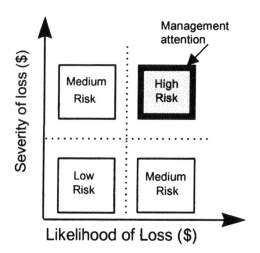

Figure 12.12   Summary risk reporting.

also Appendix 4). Of course, Figure 12.12 is a very simplified way of representing risk, but presenting a full probability distribution for many operational risks is too complex to be justified – and may even be misleading given the lack of historical evidence. In Figure 12.12, one can see very clearly that if a business unit falls in the upper right-hand quadrant then the business unit has a high likelihood of operational risk and a high severity of loss (if failure occurs). These units would be the focus of management's attention.

A business unit may address its operational risks in several ways. First, one can avoid the risk by withdrawing from a business activity. Second, one can transfer the risk to another party (e.g. through more insurance or outsourcing). Third, one can accept and manage the risk, say, through more effective management. Fourth, one can put appropriate fallback plans in place in order to reduce the impact should an operational failure occur. For example, management can ask several insurance companies to submit proposals for insuring key risks. Of course, not all operational risks are insurable, and in the case of those that are insurable the required premium may be prohibitive.

Capital attribution for operational risks

One should make sure that businesses that take on operational risk incur a transparent capital charge. The methodology for translating operational risk into capital is typically developed by the Raroc group in partnership with the operational risk management group.

Operational risks can be divided into those losses that are expected and those that are unexpected. Management, in the ordinary course of business, knows that certain operational activities will fail. There will be a 'normal' amount of operational loss that the business is willing to absorb as a cost of doing business (such as error correction, fraud, etc.). These failures are explicitly or implicitly budgeted for in the annual business plan and are covered by the pricing of the product or service.

The focus of this chapter, as illustrated in Figure 12.13, has been on *unexpected*

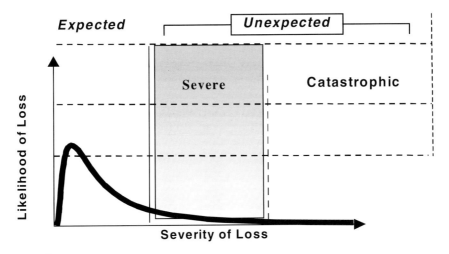

Figure 12.13   Distribution of operational losses.

failures, and the associated amount of economic capital that should be attributed to business units to absorb the losses related to the unexpected operational failures. However, as the figure suggests, unexpected failures can themselves be further subdivided:

- *Severe but not catastrophic losses.* Unexpected severe operational failures, as illustrated in Table 12.7, should be covered by an appropriate allocation of operational risk capital These kinds of losses will tend to be covered by the measurement processes described in the sections above.

Table 12.7   Distribution of operational losses

Operational losses	Expected event (high probability, low losses)	Unexpected event (low probability, high losses)	
		Severe financial impact	Catastrophic financial impact
Covered by	Business plan	Operational risk capital	Insurable (risk transfer) or 'risk financing'

- *Catastrophic losses.* These are the most extreme but also the rarest forms of operational risk events – the kind that might destroy the bank entirely. Value-at-Risk (VaR) and Raroc models are not meant to capture catastrophic risk, since potential losses are calculated up to a certain confidence level and catastrophic risks are by their very nature extremely rare. Banks will attempt to find insurance coverage to hedge catastrophic risk since capital will not protect a bank from these risks.

Although VaR/Raroc models may not capture catastrophic loss, banks can use these approaches to assist their thought process about insurance. For example, it might be argued that one should retain the risk if the cost of capital to support the asset is less than the cost of insuring it. This sort of risk/reward approach can bring discipline to an insurance program that has evolved over time into a rather *ad hoc* set of policies – often where one type of risk is insured while another is not, with very little underlying rationale.

Banks have now begun to develop databases of historical operational risk events in an effort to quantify unexpected risks of various types. They are hoping to use the databases to develop statistically defined 'worst case' estimates that may be applicable to a select subset of a bank's businesses – in the same way that many banks already use historical loss data to drive credit risk measurement.

A bank's internal loss database will most likely be extremely small relative to the major losses in certain other banks. Hence, the database should also reflect the experience of others. Blending internal and external data requires a heavy dose of management judgement. This is a new and evolving area of risk measurement.

Some banks are moving to an integrated or concentric approach to the 'financing' of operational risks. This financing can be achieved via a combination of external insurance programs (e.g. with floors and caps), capital market tools and self-insurance. If the risk is self-insured, then the risk should be allocated economic capital.

How will the increasing emphasis on operational risk and changes in the financial sector affect the overall capital attributions in banking institutions? In the very broadest terms, we would guess that the typical capital attributions in banks now stand at around 20% for operational risk, 10% for market risk, and 70% for credit risk (Figure 12.14). We would expect that both operational risk and market risk might evolve in the future to around 30% each – although, of course, much depends on the nature of the institution. The likely growth in the weighting of operational risk can be attributed to the growing risks associated with people, process, technology and external dependencies. For example, it seems inevitable that financial institutions will experience higher worker mobility, growing product sophistication, increases in business volume, rapid introduction of new technology and increased merger/acquisitions activity – all of which generate operational risk.

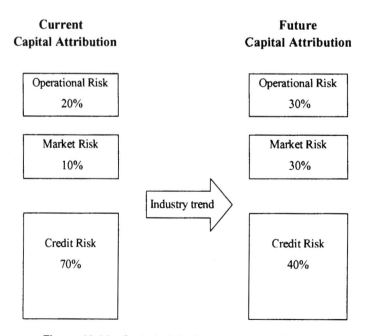

Figure 12.14 Capital attribution: present and future.

Self-assessment versus risk management assessment

Some would argue that the enormity of the operational risk task implies that the only way to achieve success in terms of managing operational risk without creating an army of risk managers is to have business management self-assess the risks. However, this approach is not likely to elicit the kind of necessary information to effectively control operational risk. It is unlikely that a Nick Leeson would have self-assessed his operational risk accurately.

In idealized circumstances senior management aligns, through the use of appropriate incentives, the short- and perhaps long-term interest of the business manager with those of the corporation as a whole. If we assume this idealized alignment then business management is encouraged to share their view of both the opportunities and the risk with senior management. Self-assessment in this idealized environment perhaps would produce an accurate picture of the risk. However, a business manager in difficult situations (that is, when the risks are high) may view high risk as temporary and therefore may not always be motivated towards an accurate self-assessment. In other words, precisely when an accurate measurement of the operational risk would be most useful is when self-assessment would give the most inaccurate measurement. Risk management should do the gathering and processing of this data to ensure objectivity, consistency and transparency.

So how is this to be done without the army of risk management personnel? First, as described earlier, a reasonable view of the operational risk can be constructed from the analysis of available information, business management interviews, etc. This can be accomplished over a reasonable timeframe with a small group of knowledgeable risk managers. Risk managers (who have been trained to look for risk and have been made accountable for obtaining an accurate view of the risk at a reasonable cost) must manage this trade-off between accuracy, granularity and timeliness. Second, risk managers must be in the flow of all relevant business management information. This can be accomplished by having risk managers sit in the various regular business management meetings, involved in the new product approval process, and be the regular recipient of selected management reports, etc. This is the same as how either a credit risk manager or a market risk manager keeps a timely and a current view of their respective risks.

A second argument often used in favor of self-assessment is that an operational risk manager cannot possibly know as much about the business as the business manager, and therefore a risk assessment by a risk manager will be incomplete or inaccurate. This, however, confuses their respective roles and responsibilities. The business manager should know more about the business than the risk manager, otherwise that itself creates an operational risk and perhaps the risk manager should be running the business. The risk manager is trained in evaluating risk, much like a life insurance risk manager is trained to interpret the risk from a medical report and certain statistics. The risk manager is neither expected to be a medical expert nor even to be able to produce the medical report, only to interpret and extract risk information. This, by the way, is the same with a credit risk manager. A credit risk manager is expected to observe, analyze, interpret information about a company so as to evaluate the credit risk of a company, not be able to manage that company. To demand more from an operational risk manager would be to force that risk manager to lose focus and therefore reduce their value added. Operational risk can be mitigated by training personnel on how to use the tools associated with best practice risk management. (see Appendix 5.)

Integrated operational risk

At present, most financial institutions have one set of rules to measure market risk, a second set of rules to measure credit risk, and are just beginning to develop a third set of rules to measure operational risk. It seems likely that the leading banks will work to integrate these methodologies (Figure 12.15). For example, they might attempt to first integrate market risk VaR and credit risk VaR and subsequently work to integrate an operational risk VaR measure.

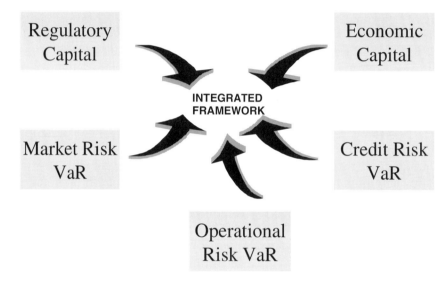

Figure 12.15   Integrated risk models.

Developing an integrated risk measurement model will have important implications from both a risk transparency and a regulatory capital perspective. For example, if one simply added a market risk VaR plus an operational risk VaR plus a credit risk VaR to obtain a total VaR (rather than developing an integrated model) then one would overstate the amount of risk. The summing ignores the interaction or correlation between market risk, credit risk and operational risk.

The Bank for International Settlement (1988) rules for capital adequacy are generally recognized to be quite flawed. We would expect that in time regulators will allow banks to use their own internal models to calculate a credit risk VaR to replace the BIS (1988) rules, in the same way that the BIS 1998 Accord allowed banks to adopt an internal models approach for determining the minimum required regulatory capital for trading market risk. For example, we would expect in the near term that BIS would allow banks to use their own internal risk-grading system for purposes of arriving at the minimum required regulatory capital for credit risk.

The banking industry, rather than the regulators, sponsored the original market VaR methodology. (In particular, J. P. Morgan's release of its RiskMetrics product.) Industry has also sponsored the new wave of credit VaR methodologies such as the

J. P. Morgan CreditMetrics offering, and CreditRisk+ from Credit Suisse Financial Products. Similarly, vendor-led credit VaR packages include a package developed by KMV (which is now in use at 60 financial institutions). The KMV model is based on an expanded version of the Merton model to allow for an empirically accurate approximation in lieu of a theoretically precise approach. All this suggests that, in time the banking industry will sponsor some form of operational risk VaR methodology.

We can push the parallel a little further. The financial community, with the advent of products such as credit derivatives, is increasingly moving towards valuing loan products on a mark-to-model basis. Similarly, with the advent of insurance products we will see increased price discovery for operational risk. Moreover, just as we have seen an increasing trend toward applying market-risk-style quantification techniques to measure the credit VaR, we can also expect to see such techniques applied to develop an operational risk VaR. Accounting firms (such as Arthur Anderson) are encouraging the development of a common taxonomy of risk (see Appendix 6). Consulting firms (such as Net Risk) are facilitating access to operational risk data (see Appendix 7).

A major challenge for banks is to produce comprehensible and practical approaches to operational risk that will prove acceptable to the regulatory community. Ideally, the integrated risk model of the future will align the regulatory capital approach to operational risk with the economic capital approach.

Conclusions

An integrated goal-congruent risk management process that puts all the elements together, as illustrated in Figure 12.16, will open the door to optimal firm-wide management of risk. 'Integrated' refers to the need to avoid a fragmented approach to risk management – risk management is only as strong as the weakest link. 'Goal-congruent' refers to the need to ensure that policies and methodologies are consistent with each other. Infrastructure includes having the right people, operations technology and data to appropriately control risk.

One goal is to have an 'apple-to-apple' risk measurement scheme so that one can compare risk across all products and aggregate risk at any level. The end product is a best-practice management of risk that is also consistent with business strategies. This is a 'one firm, one view' approach that also recognizes the complexity of each business within the firm.

In this chapter we have stressed that operational risk should be managed as a partnership among business units, infrastructure groups, corporate governance units, internal audit and risk management. We should also mention the importance of establishing a risk-aware business culture. Senior managers play a critical role in establishing a corporate environment in which best-practice operational risk management can flourish. Personnel will ultimately behave in a manner dependent on how senior management rewards them.

Indeed, arguably the key single challenge for senior management is to harmonize the behavior patterns of business units, infrastructure units, corporate governance units, internal audit and risk management and create an environment in which all sides 'sink or swim' together in terms of managing operational risk.

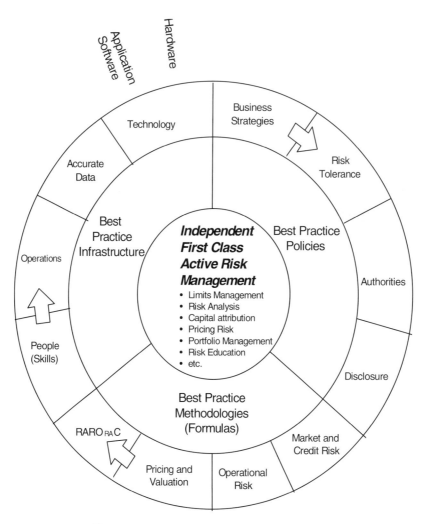

Figure 12.16   Best practice risk management.

Appendix 1: Group of Thirty recommendations

Derivatives and operational risk

In 1993 the Group of Thirty (G30) provided 20 best-practice risk management recommendations for dealers and end-users of derivatives. These have proved seminal for many banks structuring their derivatives risk management functions, and here we offer a personal selection of some key findings for operational risk managers in institutions who may be less familiar with the report.

The G30 working group was composed of a diverse cross-section of end-users, dealers, academics, accountants, and lawyers involved in derivatives. Input also came from a detailed survey of industry practice among 80 dealers and 72 end-users worldwide, involving both questionnaires and in-depth interviews. In addition, the G30 provides four recommendations for legislators, regulators, and supervisors.

The G30 report noted that the credit, market and legal risks of derivatives capture most of the attention in public discussion. Nevertheless, the G30 emphasized that the successful implementation of systems operations, and controls is equally important for the management of derivatives activities. The G30 stressed that the complexity and diversity of derivatives activities make the measurement and control of those risks more difficult. This difficulty increases the importance of sophisticated risk management systems and sound management and operating practices These are vital to a firm's ability to execute, record, and monitor derivatives transactions, and to provide the information needed by management to manage the risks associated with these activities.

Similarly, the G30 report stressed the importance of hiring skilled professionals: Recommendation 16 states that one should 'ensure that derivatives activities are undertaken by professionals in sufficient number and with the appropriate experience, skill levels, and degrees of specialization'. The G30 also stressed the importance of building best-practice systems. According to Recommendation 17, one should 'ensure that adequate systems for data capture, processing, settlement, and management reporting are in place so that derivatives transactions are conducted in an orderly and efficient manner in compliance with management policies'. Furthermore, 'one should have risk management systems that measure the risks incurred in their derivatives activities based on their nature, size and complexity'.

Recommendation 19 emphasized that accounting practices should highlight the risks being taken. For example, the G30 pointed out that one 'should account for derivatives transactions used to manage risks so as to achieve a consistency of income recognition treatment between those instruments and the risks being managed'.

People

The survey of industry practices examined the involvement in the derivatives activity of people at all levels of the organization and indicated a need for further development of staff involved in back-office administration, accounts, and audit functions, etc. Respondents believed that a new breed of specialist, qualified operational staff, was required. It pointed out that dealers (large and small) and end-users face a common challenge of developing the right control culture for their derivatives activity.

The survey highlighted the importance of the ability of people to work in cross functional teams. The survey pointed out that many issues require input from a number of disciplines (e.g. trading, legal and accounting) and demand an integrated approach.

Systems

The survey confirmed the view that dealing in derivatives can demand integrated systems to ensure adequate information and operational control. It indicated that dealers were moving toward more integrated systems, between front- and back-office (across types of transactions).

The industry has made a huge investment in systems, and almost all large dealers are extensive users of advanced technology. Many derivative groups have their own research and technology teams that develop the mathematical algorithms and systems necessary to price new transactions and to monitor their derivatives portfolios. Many dealers consider their ability to manage the development of systems capabilities an important source of competitive strength.

For large dealers there is a requirement that one develop systems that minimize manual intervention as well as enhance operating efficiency and reliability, the volume of activity, customization of transactions, number of calculations to be performed, and overall complexity.

Systems that integrate the various tasks to be performed for derivatives are complex Because of the rapid development of the business, even the most sophisticated dealers and users often rely on a variety of systems, which may be difficult to integrate in a satisfactory manner. While this situation is inevitable in many organizations, it is not ideal and requires careful monitoring to ensure sufficient consistency to allow reconciliation of results and aggregation of risks where required.

The survey results indicated that the largest dealers, recognizing the control risks that separate systems pose and the expense of substantial daily reconciliations, are making extensive investments to integrate back-office systems for derivatives with front-office systems to derivatives as well as other management information.

Operations

The role of the back-office is to perform a variety of functions in a timely fashion. This includes recording transactions, issuing and monitoring confirmations, ensuring legal documentation for transactions is completed, settling transactions, producing information for management and control purposes. This information includes reports of positions against trading and counterparty limits, reports on profitability, and reports on exceptions.

There has been significant evolution in the competence of staff and the adequacy of procedures and systems in the back office. Derivatives businesses, like other credit or securities businesses, give the back-office the principal function of recording, documenting, and confirming the actions of the dealers. The wide range of volume and complexity that exists among dealers and end-users has led to a range of acceptable solutions

The long timescales between the trade date and the settlement date, which is a feature of some products, means that errors not detected by the confirmation process may not be discovered for some time. While it is necessary to ensure that the systems are adequate for the organization's volume and the complexity of derivatives activities, there can be no single prescriptive solution to the management challenges that derivatives pose to the back office. This reflects the diversity in activity between different market participants.

Controls

Derivative activities, by their very nature, cross many boundaries of traditional financial activity. Therefore the control function must be necessarily broad, covering all aspects of activity. The primary element of control lies in the organization itself. Allocation of responsibilities for derivatives activities, with segregation of authority where appropriate, should be reflected in job descriptions and organization charts.

Authority to commit the institution to transactions is normally defined by level or position. It is the role of management to ensure that the conduct of activity is consistent with delegated authority. There is no substitute for internal controls; however, dealers and end-users should communicate information that clearly indicates which individuals within the organization have the authority to make commitments. At the same time, all participants should fully recognize that the legal doctrine of 'apparent authority' may govern the transactions to which individuals within their organization commit.

Definition of authority within an organization should also address issues of suitability of use of derivatives. End-users of derivatives transactions are usually institutional borrowers and investors and as such should possess the capability to understand and quantify risks inherent in their business. Institutional investors may also be buyers of structured securities exhibiting features of derivatives. While the exposures to derivatives will normally be similar to those on institutional balance sheets, it is possible that in some cases the complexity of such derivatives used might exceed the ability of an entity to understand fully the associated risks. The recommendations provide guidelines for management practice and give any firm considering the appropriate use of derivatives a useful framework for assessing suitability and developing policy consistent with its over-all risk management and capital policies. Organizational controls can then be established to ensure activities are consistent with a firm's needs and objectives.

Audit

The G30 pointed out that internal audit plays an important role in the procedures and control framework by providing an independent, internal assessment of the effectiveness of this framework. The principal challenge for management is to ensure that internal audit staff has sufficient expertise to carry out work in both the front and back office. Able individuals with the appropriate financial and systems skills are required to carry out the specialist aspects of the work. Considerable investment in training is needed to ensure that staff understand the nature and characteristics of the instruments being transacted and the models that are used to price them.

Although not part of the formal control framework of the organization, external auditors and regulatory examiners provide a check on procedures and controls. They also face the challenge of developing and maintaining the appropriate degree of expertise in this area.

Appendix 2: Model risk

Model risk relates to the risks involved in the erroneous use of models to value and hedge securities and is typically defined as a component of operational risk. It may seem to be insignificant for simple instruments (such as stocks and straight bonds) but can become a major operational risk for institutions that trade sophisticated OTC derivative products and execute complex arbitrage strategies.

The market price is (on average) the best indicator of an asset's value in liquid (and more or less efficient) securities markets. However, in the absence of such a price discovery mechanism, theoretical valuation models are required to 'mark-to-model' the position. In these circumstances the trader and the risk manager are like the pilot and co-pilot of a plane which flies under Instrument Flight Rules (IFR), relying only on sophisticated instruments to land the aircraft. An error in the electronics on board can be fatal to the plane.

Pace of model development

The pace of model development over the past several years has accelerated to support the rapid growth of financial innovations such as caps, floors, swaptions, spread options and other exotic derivatives. These innovations were made possible by developments in financial theory that allow one to efficiently capture the many facets of financial risk. At the same time these models could never have been implemented on the trading floor had the growth in computing power not accelerated so dramatically.

In March 1995, Alan Greenspan commented, 'The technology that is available has increased substantially the potential for creating losses'. Financial innovations, model development and computing power are engaged in a sort of leapfrog, whereby financial innovations call for more model development, which in turn requires more computing power, which in turn results in more complex models. The more sophisticated the instrument, the larger the profit margin – and the greater the incentive to innovate.

If the risk management function does not have the authority to approve (vet) new models, then this dynamic process can create significant operational risk. Models need to be used with caution. In many instances, too great a faith in models has led institutions to make unwitting bets on the key model parameters – such as volatilities or correlations – which are difficult to predict and often prove unstable over time.

The difficulty of controlling model risk is further aggravated by errors in implementing the theoretical models, and by inexplicable differences between market prices and theoretical values. For example, we still have no satisfactory explanation as to why investors in convertible bonds do not exercise their conversion option in a way that is consistent with the predictions of models.

Different types of model risk

Model risk, as illustrated in Figure 12A.1, has a number of sources:

- The data input can be wrong
- One may wrongly estimate a key parameter of the model
- The model may be flawed or incorrect
- Models may give rise to significant hedging risk.

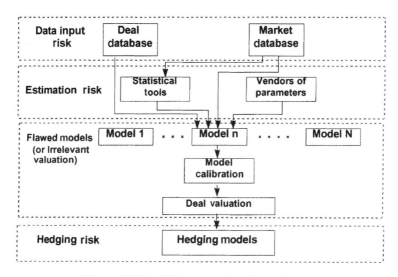

Figure 12A.1 Various levels of model risks.

In fact, when most people talk about model risk they are referring to the risk of flawed or incorrect models. Modern traders often rely heavily on the use of mathematical models that involve complex equations and advanced mathematics. Flaws may be caused by mistakes in the setting of equations, or wrong assumptions may have been made about the underlying asset price process. For example, a model may be based on a flat and fixed term structure, while the actual term structure of interest rates is steep and unstable.

Appendix 3: Types of operational risk losses

Operational risk is multifaceted. The type of loss can take many different forms such as damage to physical assets, unauthorized activity, unexpected taxation, etc. These various operational risk types need to be tightly defined. For example, an illustrative table of definitions such as illustrated in Table 12A.1 should be developed. This list is not meant to be exhaustive. It is critical that operational risk management groups are clear when they communicate with line management (in one direction) and senior managers (in the other).

Appendix 4: Operational risk assessment

The process of operational risk assessment needs to include a review of the likelihood (or frequency) of a particular operational risk occurring as well as the magnitude (or severity) of the effect that the operational risk will have on the business. The assessment should include the options available to manage and take appropriate action to reduce operational risk. One should regularly publish graphs as shown in Figure 12A.2 displaying the relationship between the potential severity and frequency for each operational risk.

Appendix 5: Training and risk education

One major source of operational risk is people – the human factor. Undoubtedly, operational risk due to people can be mitigated through better educated and trained staff. First-class risk education is a key component of any optimal firm-wide risk management program. Staff should be aware of why they may have to change the way they do things. Staff are more comfortable if they know new risk procedures exist for a good business reason. Staff need to clearly understand more than basic limit monitoring techniques (i.e. the lowest level of knowledge illustrated in Figure 12A.3). Managers need to be provided with the necessary training to understand the mathematics behind risk analysis.

Business units, infrastructure units, corporate governance units and internal audit should also be educated on how risk can be used as the basis for allocating economic capital. Staff should also learn how to utilize measures of risk as a basis for pricing transactions. Finally, as illustrated in the upper-right corner of the figure, one should educate business managers and risk managers on how to utilize the risk measurement tools to enhance their portfolio management skills.

Table 12A.1   Illustrative definitions of operational risk loss

Nature of loss	Definition
Asset loss or damage	• Risk of either an uninsured or irrecoverable loss or damage to bank assets caused by fire, flooding, power supply, weather, natural disaster, physical accident, etc. • Risk of having to use bank assets to compensate clients for uninsured or irrecoverable loss or damage to client assets under bank custody Note: Excludes loss or damage due to either theft, fraud or malicious damage (see below for separate category)
Cost management	• Risk of projects or other initiatives costing more than budgeted
Credit losses due to operational failures	• Risk of operational failure (failure of people, process, technology, external dependencies) resulting in credit losses • This is an internal failure unrelated to the creditworthiness of the borrower or guarantor e.g. inexperienced credit adjudicator assigns higher than appropriate risk rating – loan priced incorrectly and not monitored as it should be for the risk that it is, with greater risk of credit loss than should have been
Customer satisfaction	• Risk of losing current customers and being unable to attract new customers, with a consequent loss of revenue. This definition would include reputation risk as it applies to clients
Disputes	• Risk of having to make payments to settle disputes either through lawsuit or negotiated settlement (includes disputes with clients, employees, suppliers, competitors, etc.)
Market losses due to operational failures	• Risk of operational failure (failure of people, process, technology, external dependencies) resulting in market losses • This is an internal failure unrelated to market movements – e.g. incomplete or inaccurate data used in calculating VaR – true exposures not known and decisions made based on inaccurate VaR, with greater risk of market loss than should have been
Model risk (see Appendix 2)	• Models used for risk measurement and valuation are wrong • Risk of inaccurate reporting of positions and results. If the true numbers were understood, then action could have been taken to stem losses or otherwise improve results. Risk of potential losses where model not programmed correctly or inappropriate or incorrect inputs to the model, or inappropriate use of model results, etc.
Regulatory/ compliance	• Risk of regulatory fines, penalties, client restitution payments or other financial cost to be paid • Risk of regulatory sanctions (such as restricting or removal of one's license, increased capital requirements, etc.) resulting in reduced ability to generate revenue or achieve targeted profitability
Taxation	• Risk of incurring greater tax liabilities than anticipated
Theft/fraud/ malicious damage	• Risk of uninsured and irrecoverable loss of bank assets due to either theft, fraud or malicious damage. The loss may be caused by either internal or external persons. • Risk of having to use bank assets to compensate clients for either uninsured or irrecoverable loss of their assets under bank custody due to either theft, fraud or malicious damage Note: Excludes rogue trading (see below for separate category)
Transaction processing, errors and omissions	• Risk of loss to the bank where unable to process transactions. This includes cost of correcting the problem which prevented transactions from being processed • Risk of a cost to the bank to correct errors made in processing transactions, or in failing to complete a transaction. This includes cost of making client whole for transactions which were processed incorrectly (e.g. restitution payments)
Unauthorized activity (e.g. rogue trading)	• Risk of a loss of or Increased expenses as a result of unauthorized activity. For example, this includes the risk of trading loss caused by unauthorized or rogue trading activities

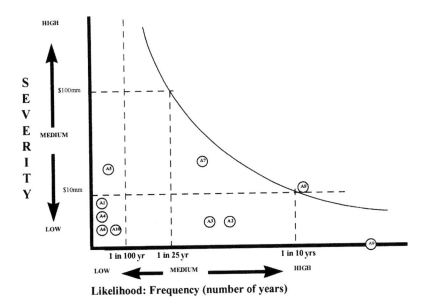

Figure 12A.2 Severity versus frequency. A1–A10 are symbolic of 10 key risks.

Figure 12A.3 Increased operational risk knowledge required.

Appendix 6: Taxonomy for risk

Arthur Anderson has developed a useful taxonomy for risk. Anderson divides risk into 'environmental risk', 'process risk', and 'information for decision making risk' (Figure 12A.4). These three broad categories of risk are further divided. For example, process risk is divided into operations risk, empowerment risk, information processing/technology risk, integrity risk and financial risk. Each of these risks are further subdivided. For example, financial risk is further subdivided into price, liquidity and credit risk.

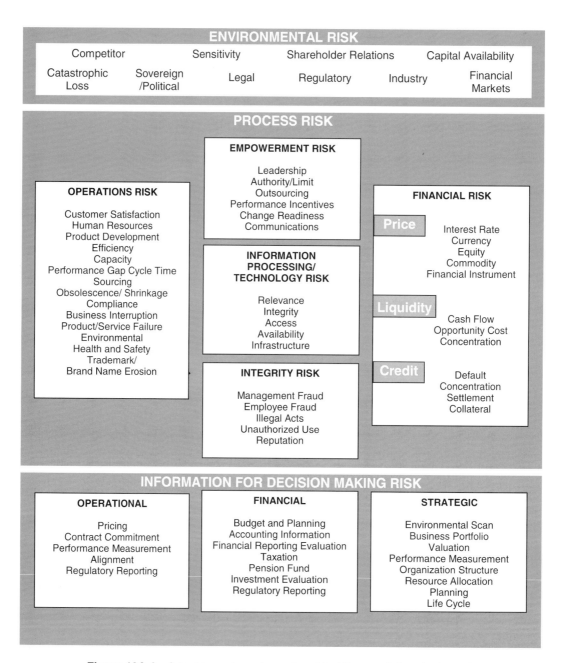

Figure 12A.4 A taxonomy for cataloguing risk. (*Source:* Arthur Anderson)

Appendix 7: Identifying and quantifying operational risk

Consulting firms are providing value added operational risk services. For example, Net Risk has developed a tool which allows the user to identify operational risk causes and quantify them (Figure 12A.5). For example, the RiskOps product offered by Net Risk enables the user to utilize a 'cause hierarchy' to arrive at a pie chart of loss amount by cause as well as a frequency histogram of loss amounts. The RiskOps product also provides a description of specific losses. For example, as shown on the bottom of Figure 12A.5, RiskOps indicates that Prudential settled a class action suit for $2 million arising from improper sales techniques. Further, as shown in the middle of Figure 12A.6, one can see under the 'personnel cause' screen that Prudential had six different operational risk incidents ranging from firing an employee who reported improper sales practices to failure to supervise the operations of its retail CMO trading desk.

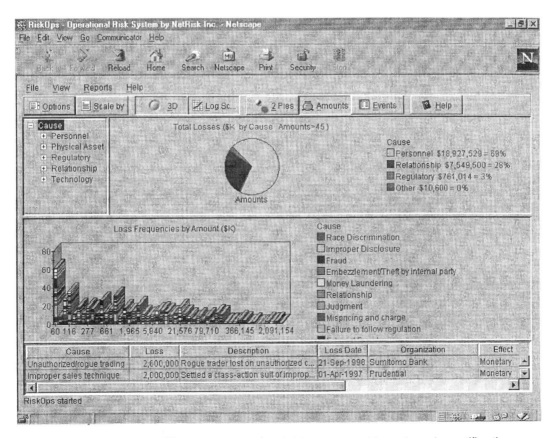

Figure 12A.5 RiskOps™ identifies operational risk causes and impacts and quantifies them.

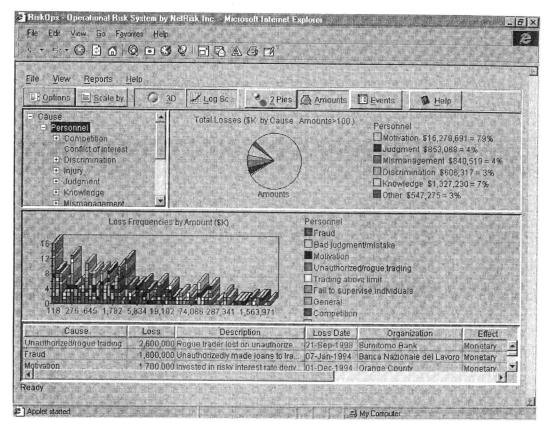

Figure 12A.6.

13

Operational risk

DUNCAN WILSON

Introduction

The purpose of this chapter is initially to identify and explain the reasons why banks are focusing on operational risk management in relation to the following key issues:

- Why invest in operational risk management?
- Defining operational risk
- Measuring operational risk
- Technology risk
- What is best practice?
- Regulatory guidance
- Operational risk systems

The main objective of the chapter is to highlight the pros and cons of some of the alternative approaches taken by financial institutions to address the issues and to recommend the most practical route to take in addressing them.

Why invest in operational risk management?

This section will explain the reason why operational risk has become such an important issue. Over the past five years there have been a series of financial losses in financial institutions which have caused them to rethink their approach to the management of operational risk. It has been argued that mainstream methods such as control self-assessment and internal audit have failed to provide management with the tools necessary to manage operational risk.

It is useful to note *The Economist's* comments in their 17 October 1998 issue on Long Term Capital Management which caused some banks to provide for over US$1billion each due to credit losses:

> The fund, it now appears, did not borrow more than a typical investment bank. Nor was it especially risky. What went wrong was the firm's risk-management model – which is similar to those used by the best and brightest bank.

The Economist states further that 'Regulators have criticized LTCM and banks for not stress-testing risk models against extreme market movements'.

This confusing mixture of market risks, credit risks and liquidity risks is not assisted by many banks insistence to 'silo' the management of these three risks into different departments (market risk management, credit risk management and treasury). This silo mentality results in many banks arguing about who is to blame about the credit losses suffered because of their exposures to LTCM. Within LTCM itself the main risk appears to be operational according to *The Economist*: lack of stress-testing the risk models. This lack of a key control is exactly the issue being addressed by regulators in their thinking about operational risks.

Although much of the recent focus has been on improving internal controls this is still associated with internal audit and control self-assessment. Perhaps internal controls are the best place to start in managing operational risk because of this emphasis. The Basel Committee in January 1998 published *Internal Controls* and this has been welcomed by most of the banking industry, as its objective was to try to provide a regulatory framework for regulators of banks. Many regulators are now reviewing and updating their own supervisory approaches to operational risk. Some banking associations such as the British Bankers Association have conducted surveys to assess what the industry consider to be sound practice.

The benefits (and therefore the goals) of investing in an improved operational risk framework are:

- Avoidance of large unexpected losses
- Avoidance of a large number of small losses
- Improved operational efficiency
- Improved return on capital
- Reduced earnings volatility
- Better capital allocation
- Improved customer satisfaction
- Improved awareness of operational risk within management
- Better management of the knowledge and intellectual capital within the firm
- Assurance to senior management and the shareholders that risks are properly being addressed.

Avoidance of unexpected loss is one of the most common justifications of investing in operational risk management. Such losses are the high-impact low-frequency losses like those caused by rogue traders. In order to bring attention to senior management and better manage a firm's exposure to such losses it is now becoming best practice to quantify the potential for such events. The difficulty and one of the greatest challenges for firms is to assess the magnitude and likelihood of a wide variety of such events. This has led some banks to investigate the more quantitative aspects of operational risk management. This will be addressed below.

The regulators in different regions of the world have also started to scrutinize the approach of banks to operational risk management. The papers on Operational Risk and Internal Control from the Basel Committee on Banking Supervision are instructive and this new focus on operational risk implies that regulatory guidance or rules will have to be complied within the next year or two.

This interest by the regulators and in the industry as a whole has caused many banks to worry about their current approach to operational risk. One of the first problems that banks are unfortunately encountering is in relation to the definition of this risk.

Defining operational risk

The problem of defining operational risk is perplexing financial institutions. Many banks have adopted the approach of listing categories of risk, analyzing what they are and deciding whether they should be reporting and controlling them as a separate risk 'silo' within their risk management framework as many of them have done for market and credit risk. It is also important to note that operational risk is not confined to financial institutions and useful examples of approaches to defining and measuring operational risk can be gained from the nuclear, oil, gas, construction and other industries.

Not surprisingly, operational risk is already being managed locally within each business area with the support of functions such as legal, compliance and internal audit. It is at the group level where the confusion is taking place on defining operational risk. Therefore a good place to start is to internally survey 'local' practice within each business unit. Such surveys will invariably result in a risk sub-categorisation of operational risk as follows:

- Control risk
- Process risk
- Reputational risk
- Human resources risk
- Legal risk
- Takeover risk
- Marketing risk
- Systems outages
- Aging technology
- Tax changes
- Regulatory changes
- Business capacity
- Legal risk
- Project risk
- Security
- Supplier management

The above may be described in the following ways:

Control risk

This is the risk that an unexpected loss occurs due to both the lack of an appropriate control or the effectiveness of an appropriate control and may be split into two main categories:

- **Inherent risk** is the risk of a particular business activity, irrespective of related internal controls. Complex business areas only understood by a few key people contain higher inherent risk such as exotic derivatives trading.
- **Control risk** is the risk that a financial loss or misstatement would not be prevented or detected and corrected on a timely basis by the internal control framework.

Inherent risk and control risk are mixed together in many banks but it useful to make the distinction because it enables an operational risk manager to assess the degree of investment required in the internal control systems. This assessment of the relative operational risk of two different business may result in one being more inherently risky than the other and may require a higher level of internal control.

Optimal control means that unexpected losses can happen but their frequency and severity are significantly reduced.

Process risk

This is the risk that the business process is inefficient and causes unexpected losses. Process risk is closely related to internal control as internal control itself, according to COSO, should be seen as a process. It is differentiated from internal control clearly when a process is seen as a continuing activity such as risk management but the internal controls within the risk management process are depicted as 'control points'.

Reputational risk

This is the risk of an unexpected loss in share price or revenue due to the impact upon the reputation of the firm. Such a loss in reputation could occur due to mis-selling of derivatives for example. A good 'control' for or mitigating action for reputational risk is strong ethical values and integrity of the firm's employees and a good public relations machine when things do go wrong.

Human resources risk

Human resources risk is not just the activities of the human resources department although they do contribute to controlling the risk. However, there are particular conditions which reside within the control of the business areas themselves which the operational risk manager should be aware or when making an assessment. For example, the firm's performance may hinge on a small number of key teams or people or the age of the teams may be skewed to young or old without an appropriate mix of skills and experience to satisfy the business objectives which have been set.

Given the rogue trader problems which some banks have suffered it is also important that the operational risk manager checks that the human resources department has sufficient controls in relation to personnel security. Key items the manager should assess on personnel security are as follows:

Hiring procedures:
- references and work credentials
- existing/ongoing security training and awareness program
- job descriptions defining security roles and responsibilities

Termination procedures:
- the extent of the termination debriefing: reaffirm non-competition and non-disclosure agreements,
- ensure revocation of physical access: cards, keys, system access authority, IDs, timescales

Human Resources can help mitigate these risks by setting corporate standards and establishing an infrastructure such as 'knowledge management' databases and appropriate training and career progression. However, higher than average staff turnover or the ratio of temporary contractors to permanent staff is one indication that things are not working. Another indication of human resources risk is evidence of clashing management styles or poor morale.

Legal risk

Legal risk can be split into four areas:

- The risk of suffering legal claims due to product liability or employee actions
- The risk that a legal opinion on a matter of law turns out to be incorrect in a court of law. This latter risk is applicable to netting or new products such as credit derivatives where the enforceability of the agreements may not be proven in particular countries
- Where the legal agreement covering the transaction is so complicated that the cash flows cannot be incorporated into the accounting or settlement systems of the company
- Ability to enforce the decision in one jurisdiction in a different jurisdiction.

Takeover risk

Takeover risk is highly strategic but can be controllable by making it uneconomic for a predator to take over the firm. This could be done by attaching 'golden parachutes' to the directors' contracts which push up the price of the firm.

Marketing risk

Marketing risk can occur in the following circumstances:

- The benefits claimed about a products are misrepresented in the marketing material or
- The product fails due to the wrong marketing strategy.

Marketing risk is therefore at the heart of business strategy as are many of the risk subcategories.

Technology risk

Systems risk in the wide definition will include all systems risks including external pressure such as the risk of not keeping up with the progress of changing technology when a company insists on developing risk management applications in-house. Technology risk is at the heart of a business such as investment banking.

Tax changes

If tax changes occur, particularly retrospectively, they may make a business immediately unprofitable. A good example of this are changes in the deductibility of expenses such as depreciation of fixed assets. Normally the business should address the possibility of tax changes by making the customer pay. However, it normally comes down to a business decision of whether the firm or the customer takes the risk.

Regulatory changes

Changes in regulations need to be monitored closely by firms. The effect on a business can be extremely important and the risk of volatility of returns high. A good example of this is the imminent changes in risk weighted asset percentages to be implemented.

Business capacity

If the processes, people and IT infrastructure cannot support a growing business the risks of major systems failure is high.

Project risk

Project failure is one of the biggest causes for concern in most firms, particularly with the impact of some of the current project (year 2000 testing on the business).

Security

The firms assets need to be secure from both internal and external theft. Such assets include not just the firm's money or other securities/loans but also customer assets and the firm's intellectual property.

Supplier management risk

If your business is exposed to the performance of third parties you are exposed to this risk.

Natural catastrophe risk

Natural catastrophes are one of the main causes of financial loss. The operational risk manager should asses whether the building is likely to be affected by: major landslide/mudslide, snow storm/blizzard, subsidence faulting, thunder/electrical storm, seasonal/local/tidal flooding, volcano, geomorphic erosion (landslip), or be located in an earthquake zone. Past history is normally used to assess such risks.

Man-made catastrophe risks

There may also be man-made catastrophes such as those caused by activities inherently risky located nearby such as a prison, airport, transportation route (rail, road), chemical works, landfill site, nuclear plant, military base, defence plant, foreign embassy, petrol station, terrorist target, tube/rail station, exclusion zone. There may be other factors which need to be taken into account based on historical experience such as whether the area is likely to be affected by: epidemic, radioactive/toxic contamination, gas, bomb threat, arson, act of war, political/union/religious/activism, a high incidence of criminal activity.

The questions above are similar to those that would be asked by any insurer of the buildings against the events described.

Other approaches

Dr Jack King of Algorithmics has developed a general operational risk approach and proposes the following definition and criteria for operational risk: 'Operational risk is the uncertainty of loss due to the failure in processing of the firms goods and services.' For a full discussion of the rationale and consequences of adopting this definition, see his article in the January 1999 edition of the *Algorithmics Research Quarterly*.

Peter Slater, Head of Operations Risk of Warburg Dillon Read, recently spoke at the IBC conference on Operational risk in London (December 1998). At that conference Peter explained that his bank split risks into the following categories:

- Credit and Settlement
- Market
- Operations
- Funding
- Legal
- IT
- Tax
- Physical and crime
- Compliance

He defined operations risk narrowly to be the risk of a unexpected losses due to deficiencies in internal controls or information systems caused by human error, system failures and controls. The scope of operations risk in Warburg Dillon Read is confined to the risks in their definition applied to the back office. The advantage of this approach is that it allows the back office management of the bank to focus on the critical areas of operational risk applicable to their department. The disadvantage is that other operational risks may not be managed in the other categories and unexpected losses may occur without being captured by the other risk management or business activities.

Many banks are now differentiating between controllable and uncontrollable risks. Controllable risks are those where bank actions can influence the outcome so the risks can be mitigated without (normally) resorting to the involvement of a third party. Uncontrollable risks are those that cannot normally be 'internally controlled' by the firm. Common risk mitigation techniques for uncontrollable risks are:

- Insurance for earthquakes, floods or other natural disasters
- Allocating the risks to a captive insurance company
- Outsourcing to a third party.

The alternative approaches

There seem to be three schools of thought in relation to the alternative approaches to defining operational risk. The first takes a very broadbrush approach and assumes that operational risk is everything except for market and credit risk. I will call this the 'wide definition'. The problem with this approach is that it becomes increasingly difficult to manage and measure all the risks identified. However, the big advantage is that it captures everything that is left. The second school of thought argues that operational risk is only the risk associated with the operations department of the financial institution. I will call this the 'narrow definition'. There is a third school of thought the approach of which differentiates those events over which we have control from those which we do not due to the influence of external entities such as regulators or competitors. An institution's exposure to controllable events is operational risk whereas the 'beyond our control' events are part of what some institutions are calling 'strategic' and or 'business' risk.

There is also a fourth approach to defining operational risk steeped in political compromise. This takes the existing departments of the bank and splits the various subcategories of operational risks in accordance with that organization. If any department objects to being considered as a subcategory of the operational risk framework they are excluded.

The problem that a lot of today's operational risk managers are finding is that if they adopt the wide definition they step on many toes throughout the organization. That is why a number of banks are now adopting the third school of thought as it allows for some political expediency by providing a convenient place to put those risks which are deemed wholly contentious for the operational risk manager to be involved with. Some good examples are the risks of:

- being taken over
- poor product packaging
- bad marketing
- poor public relations/reputation
- being uncompetitive due to pricing, customer service or poor relationship management
- change in the tax laws, regulations or a change in a regulator's interpretation of existing rules.

This split between wide, narrow and strategic is shown in Table 13.1.

Table 13.1

Operational risk subcategories	Wide definition	Narrow definition	Strategic risk
Control risk	✓	✓	
Process risk	✓	✓	
Reputational risk	✓		✓
Human resources risk	✓	✓	
Legal risk	✓		✓
Takeover risk	✓		✓
Marketing risk	✓		✓
Systems outages	✓	✓	
Aging technology	✓		✓
Tax changes	✓		✓
Regulatory changes	✓		✓
Business capacity	✓		✓
Legal risk	✓		✓
Project risk	✓		✓
Security	✓	✓	✓
Supplier management	✓		✓

IBM (UK) Ltd established the first Operational Risk Forum, an industry thought leadership forum on 21 May 1998. At the first meeting an interesting and pragmatic view was presented to a group of leading banks. The approach outlined was to satisfy the following objectives:

- economic capital to reflect operational risk
- transparent calculation
- enable management to influence the amount of capital required through their activities.

A number of activities had to be performed:

- develop methodology for Operational Event Risk measurements
- develop reporting infrastructure and exposure/risk calculations
- integrate Operational Event Risk in Economic Capital Reporting

The approach was to fit the definition of operational risk to what was achievable in the timescales allowed by management. This approach is likely to produce early deliverables but may not address all aspects of operational risk. The resulting definition presented at the Operational Risk Forum was as follows:

> Operational Risk is any risk or exposure associated with: customers, inadequately defined controls, control/system failure, and unmanageable events.

It is interesting to note that 'unmanageable events', effectively those which are not controllable, have been included from the perspective of managing the security of the event. It could be argued that a firm needs to go further and address the risk of inadequately *designed* controls.

The participants at the Operational Risk Forum agreed that the definition of operational risk was the first step in addressing issues such as setting up dedicated operational risk management groups, identifying risk types and exposures, financial modeling, data collection, assessing regulatory requirements and addressing resource, planning and reporting needs.

Before we attempt to offer a definition of operational risk it is worth reviewing some of the sources of sound practice. The British Bankers' Association/Coopers & Lybrand survey on operational risk (March 1997) concentrated on a lack of adequate internal controls. The more common examples of operational risk used by banks in the survey included: system failure/error; transaction processing/control error; business interruption; internal/external criminal act including breach of security; and personnel risks. The Basel definition referred to by many of the Operational Risk Forum's participants also concentrates on losses caused by omissions of controls, inadequacies in systems and lack of management information. The Forum agreed that these definitions were very useful as they recognized the importance of banks' internal control frameworks, systems and reporting mechanisms in mitigating operational risk. However, as highlighted by many participants in the Operational Risk Forum, the Basel definition is meant to address the minimum standard across all banks rather than define best practice. Therefore to satisfy the more complex issues faced by banks, who on average may have a wider business mix, products geographies as well as a larger size it was recognized that a wider definition could be made.

Wide or narrow definition?

The Operational Risk Forum appeared to arrive at two main definitions: a narrow and a wide definition:

- **Narrow definition**: some banks view the risk as residing in the departments called 'Operations' and have defined it as those errors and omissions of controls, systems and processes which may lead to potential losses. Other risks such as reputation, legal, compliance human resources may either be managed by an 'all risks' committee which considers the exposure of the bank to all risks or operational risk is the responsibility of individual department managers. Some banks therefore do not see the need for a separate operational risk function.

- **Wide definition**: other banks have adopted a wide definition of operational risk. Some have defined it as all risks not covered by market or credit risk. The rationale for this is to consider all potential impacts on the profit and loss account not measured by the risk measures employed to address market and credit risks. This definition has, however, caused problems as many banks feel that this should be limited to what we can (relatively) easily measure. For example, in relation to a system failure, the loss may be quantified as the amount of revenue lost and extra cost incurred during the time when the system was not operational. For an event like a transaction error, such as late settlement, the loss can be quantified as the sum of the penalty charges, interest costs and labour costs of remedial action. The problem with this approach is that it may leave an unidentified residue which could impact the profit and loss statement materially and undermine the wide definition approach. Other banks have analyzed a fourth risk category: business, external or strategic risk. This may be defined as the risk of external events or trends which impact the profit and loss account such as loss of market share due to competitor pressure or changes in laws or regulations. This has been stripped out of the risk universe as a separate category as it is normally addressed by the strategy department in conjunction with the business units as part of the normal planning process.

In conclusion

In order to accommodate both the wide and narrow definitions, the Operational Risk Forum formulated the following definition:

> Operational Risk is the exposure to potential financial losses. Such losses may be caused by internal or external events, trends and changes which were not captured and prevented by the corporate governance and internal control framework, systems, policies, organisation, ethical standards or other key controls and standards of the firm. Such losses exclude those already captured by other risk categories such as market, credit or strategic/business risk.

This definition seems to have been adopted by many banks since this meeting.

Measuring operational risk

This section will investigate the various methods of measuring operational risk including risk ranking, checklists, and the balanced scorecard approach. It will also put forward ideas updated since the author's first paper on applying Value at Risk techniques to operational risk published in *Risk* (December 1995). The section will review the latest techniques applied to a practical example such as the costs of late payments due to operational failures.

The Basel Committee on Banking Supervision in their report of September 1998 interviewed thirty major banks on the key issues in operational risk. In relation to operational risk measurement their report states:

> Many banks have identified significant conceptual issues and data needs, which would need to be addressed in order to develop general measures of operational risk. Unlike market and perhaps credit risk, risk factors are largely internal to the bank and a clear mathematical or statistical link between risk factors and the likelihood and size of

operational loss does not exist. Experience with large losses is infrequent and many banks lack a time series of historical data on their own operational losses and their causes. While the industry is far from converging on a set of standard models, such as are increasingly available for market and credit risk measurement, the banks that have developed or are developing models rely on a surprisingly similar set of risk factors. Those factors include internal audit ratings or internal control self-assessments, operational indicators such as volume, turnover or rate of errors, loss experience, and income volatility.

Therefore the key tasks to be addressed by any measurement method are the:

- identification of an approach to clearly describe operational exposures, risk factors and potential losses
- establishment of a relationship between exposures, risk factors, and potential losses
- treatment of high-frequency low-impact events and low-frequency high-impact events
- incorporation of the resulting model and reports into the key business and management processes of the firm.

When analyzing market or credit risk many institutions take a 'step-wise' approach as follows:

- Define risk
- Identify risk factors
- Measure exposures to those risk factors
- Calculate risk (dependent on a number of assumptions such as: the particular application of the risk factors to exposure, time exposed to them and confidence level assumed)

Table 13.2 takes the step-wise approaches to analyzing market and credit risk and compares this to a similar approach for operational risk.

Unfortunately, as we can see from the table, the comparison is not an easy one to make because market risk Value at Risk quantification techniques have been accepted for many years as best practice. Credit VaR methods are only just being piloted in only a handful of banks for the first time. These new methods are not accepted as best practice but by the end of 2000 or 2001 we should see some regulatory flexibility in using internal credit VaR models for calculating regulatory capital. This will then lead to Credit VaR being *the* benchmark in credit risk measurement.

Where, you may ask, does this comparison leave operational risk? There is little alternative but to implement quantitative or semi-quantitiative methods of measuring operational risk. However, there are a number of methods available and currently no consensus on which is best practice.

Another approach to measuring operational risk is to analyze the volatility of earnings, take out the earnings related to market and credit risk. The residual risk may be considered to be operational risk. This approach has the advantage that you are able to relate operational risk to the earnings of the company. Unfortunately it is impossible to measure the individual operational risk factors which cause residual earnings to be volatile without implementing some form of causal model earnings volatility or operational risk losses. It is also not easy to segregate volatility of earnings due to market, credit and strategic business risks.

Table 13.2   Step-wise approaches to analyzing market and credit risk

	Market risk	Credit risk	Operational risk
Define risk types	Interest rate risk Equity risk Commodity risk Foreign exchange risk	Counterparty default risk Concentration risk Credit deterioration risk Sovereign risk	Control risk Process risk Human resources risk
Identify risk factors	Basis point values and curve volatility by time bucket	Credit rating migration matrix, default rates and recovery rates	Incorrect trade details Wrong incoming message Aging technology Fraud/collusion Staff sickness/turnover Morale Culture
Measure exposure to risk factors	Net cash flows by time bucket	Mark to market, potential exposure	Volume of trades IT capacity utilization Level of mismatched confirms Unreconciled items Failed settlements Degree of segregation of duties
Calculate risk	Parametric VaR method Exposures, risk factors and their correlation	Credit VaR method, exposure multiplied by default less recovery and their correlation	Operational risk VaR method: exposures multiplied by probability. Generate loss distribution and to a specifed confidence interval measure unexpected loss
Calculate profit and loss and explain sources	Change in risk factors/exposures intraday transactions explain daily variation in profit and loss	Change in risk factors explain monthly variation in value of credit portfolios	Volatility in residual earnings after stripping out the effect of market credit and strategic business risk
Compare risk against return	Parametric VaR method Exposures, risk factors and their correlation	Credit VaR method, exposure multiplied by default less recovery and their correlation	Calculation of the incremental effect

Qualitative approaches to measuring operational risk

Most approaches to operational risk and internal control have been qualitative in that the identification of operational risk has been measured in words rather than numbers. A common approach has been to perform a review of the way a business manages operational risk and then to perform a risk assessment based upon the 'objective' judgement of an experienced reviewer. Much of this type of review work has, in the past, been performed by internal audit during the fulfillment of their normal duties. In most banks, until recently, there were no other departments involved in operational risk assessment except for internal audit and the businesses.

Many auditors have argued that they have been measuring operational risk for as long as audit has existed (centuries). Their approach to operational risk can be summarized by referring to various standards and guidelines on auditing.

In America, in September 1992, the Committee of Sponsoring Organizations of the Treadway Commission produced 'Internal Control – Integrated Framework' for all firms, not only financial institutions. All the key concepts of this document have been incorporated into American Statements of Auditing Standards. SAS 55 states that internal control is a process – effected by an entity's board of directors, management, and other personnel – designed to provide reasonable assurance regarding the achievement of objectives in the following categories:

- reliability of financial reporting
- effectiveness and efficiency of operations and
- compliance with applicable laws and regulations.

COSO pointed out that internal control is a *process* and that it is 'a series of actions which permeate an entity's activities'.

COSO contained the following five components of the internal control framework:

1 Control Environment
2 Risk Assessment
3 Control Activities
4 Information and Communication
5 Monitoring

- **Control Environment** – this provides the foundation on which people conduct their activities and carry out their control activities. It includes the integrity and ethical values of the firm.
- **Risk Assessment** – the firm must be aware of the risks it faces, including operational risks. It must set business objectives, integrated with the sales, production and marketing, financial and other activities so that the organization is operating with consistency across the different business units. The firm must establish mechanisms to identify, analyze and manage the related risks.
- **Control Activities** – control policies and procedures must be established and executed to help ensure that the actions identified by management as necessary to address risks to the achievement of the entity's objectives are effectively carried out.
- **Information and Communication** – Surrounding these activities are information and communication systems. These enable the entity's people to capture and exchange the information needed to conduct, manage and control its operations.
- **Monitoring** – the entire process must be monitored, and modifications made as necessary. In this way, the system can react dynamically, changing as conditions warrant.

COSO identified a methodology of operational risk management before the current trend. The five components support the three objectives mentioned above of:

- Financial reporting
- Compliance
- Operations.

It is with operations that we will deal with to illustrate how qualitative operational risk measurement can be achieved using the COSO framework. We will do this by considering the way in which COSO recommends that the 'Effectiveness' of the internal control system is measured. In relation to operations the five components must be working effectively. The test is whether the board of directors are able to form a view about the extent to which the entity's operations objectives are being met. COSO believes that the effectiveness test is a subjective assessment of whether the five components are present and operating.

The method employed by most firms to address internal control is to employ Control Self-assessment, normally through interactive workshops with the business to set the framework followed up by a checklist of key controls based around the five components highlighted above. The risks (or internal control weaknesses) can be ranked in order of priority and resources allocated to address them. The ranking is meant to take account of the magnitude and likelihood of loss. However, this is extremely subjective and relies on the experience of the auditor, business manager or operational risk manager. A better approach is to quantify the operational risk.

Quantitative approaches to measuring operational risk

One of the first proponents of allocating risk capital to operational risk was Duncan Wilson in *Risk* magazine in December 1995, 'VaR in Operation'. The argument put forward was that operational risk could be modeled by using Value at Risk (VaR) techniques in the same way as market and credit risks. The idea put forward in the article was to build a database of operational loss event data from both internal and external sources and fit a distribution to the data points. By taking a certain confidence interval such as 95% a firm could then calculate the operational risk VaR.

Wilson's conclusions were, however, that any quantitative methods are only as good as the the application of VaR to market risk and stress testing and scenario analysis were still required. The use of 'gut-feel' was still relevent and the article advocated a 'blended'approach' of quantitative and qualitative methods. It argues for a strong 'subjective overlay' of any quantitative methods so that relative risk ranking and the application of a 'panel of experts' approach is combined with modeling based on loss event databases.

One of the first banks to describe how they allocated capital to Operational Risk was Bankers Trust. Douglas Hoffman and Marta Johnson in *Risk* magazine October 1996 published an article entitled 'Operating Procedures'.

> At Bankers Trust, we view business operational risk as encompassing all dimensions of the firm's decentralized resources – client relationships, personnel, the physical plant, property and assets for which we are responsible, and technology resources. We also capture certain external areas such as regulatory risk and fraud risk.

It is well known that Bankers Trust is one of the few banks who have successfully implemented a Risk Adjusted Return on Capital methodology and it was natural for them to wish to take account of operational risk in that methodology. Their approach was to develop a database of loss events so that they could produce distributions of losses to calculate the risk capital. Bankers use a 99% confidence interval to ensure consistency with their market and credit risk RAROC figures.

The reasons Bankers Trust give for allocating capital to operational risk are as follows:

- To help in strategic business/investment decisions (what is the *total* risk exposure of this decision?)

- Manage efforts to finance risk more effectively (not just insurance but also alternative risk transfer within the firm)
- To assist in managing business risk

In *Risk* magazine Bankers Trust describes the following steps to calculating operational risk capital using external and internal databases of information:

- Identify centralized information (from centralized departments such as human resources) which predicts control risk across the whole firm (e.g. staff turnover)
- Categorize which risks the information falls under (e.g. human resources risk)
- Compare new centralized information to internal and external loss events database
- Match risk categories where the reasons for losses in the using external and internal databases are the same as the centralized data predictors

To attribute the risk capital Bankers Trust split risk into three risk factors:

- Inherent risk factors which are those created by the nature of the business such as product complexity (exotic derivatives would have a higher operational risk than spot foreign exchange)
- Control risk factors which highlight existing and potential control weaknesses (age of technology)
- Actual losses suffered by each business division

Each of these factors were scored for each division and controllable risks were weighted higher than non-controllable (inherent) and 'the core capital figure was attributed proportionally across the divisions, based upon their total, weighted score for overall operational risk'.

The parametric approach to quantifying operational risk

One of the most common ways of starting to analyze operational risk from a quantitative perspective is to look at losses arising from the day-to-day operations of the bank. Caban Thantanamatoo, of Manchester Business School, published a paper on quantifying mishanding losses which arise in the Operations Department. He decided to look at mishandling losses as they were quantifiable and there was a significant amount of data available within the bank and defined a mishandling loss is a loss arising from a control failure/uncontrolled process. This failure will result in one of the following:

- Compensation being paid to a counterparty for any loss incurred by them
- Charges being levied by corresponding banks to cover amendments or cancellations (usually dependent on the amount and period involved)
- Overdraft costs on 'nostro accounts'
- Funding loss – where an account is overdrawn due to incorrect funding and the overdraft rate is higher than the funding (lending) rate
- Penalty fees charged by corresponding banks/central banks for late payments, amendments/cancellations, late/no preadvice or FNR (Funds Not Received costs
- Opportunity loss – where no actual loss is made, but funds are out of the bank and an opportunity to invest funds at a higher rate was missed. The concept also applies if an account is left with a long balance which a firm is unable to use in the market.

A typical *frequency versus severity of losses* relationship for a given department/

subsidiary is given in Figure 13.1. The figure shows that the frequency of mishandling losses is inversely proportional to the severity of the payment. This is to be expected since, on average, the low-penalty cases outnumber the high-penalty cases. Assume the figure at t0 relates to the current mishandling loss risk distribution, the curve at t1 is an acceptable risk distribution and that the curve at t2, the minimum Mishandling Loss distribution that the bank can tolerate. Then a risk management effort should aim towards shifting the curve at least from t0 to t1 and ideally to t2. Possible implementation could involve investment projects in IT and personnel or in personnel only.

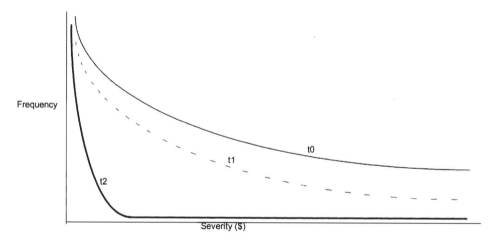

Figure 13.1 Typical graphs for mishandling losses.

The approaches described in this study have evolved since it was published. For further explanation see Mark Laycock's excellent chapter 'Quantifying Mishandling Losses' in *Risk* publication *Operational Risk in Financial Institutions*.

For a number of banks, such as Bankers Trust and Deutsche Bank, the implementation of Raroc has been one of the driving forces behind the allocation of capital for operational risk. It may therefore be an existing commitment to firm-wide capital allocation and Raroc that causes banks to venture down the operational risk capital allocation route. However, given the difficulty of quantifying aspects of operational risk, the reliance on a single number may itself be an operational risk!

Many banks are concerned about the benefits of trying quantifying operational risk. Quite a number are looking for an approach which combines both a quantitative and a qualitative approach. Some banks think they have found the solution using a causal model approach.

The causal model approach to quantifying operational risk

I have developed the 'causal model' approach based upon my previous experiences with operational risk management projects, operations management, pricing project risk and outsourcing. The methodology consists of the following steps:

- Define operational risk
- Document and collect data
- Build a prototype of the system

- Refine data collection
- Finalize prototype and roll out firm-wide

Defining operational risk

Above we discussed defining operational risk so we will not duplicate the various ways of defining it. IBM prefers the wide definition but the methodology can accommodate any definition.

When defining operational risk it is also important to differentiate between risk and exposure. Exposure to operational risk occurs in all operations/activities all the time. The size of the unexpected loss can, however, be mitigated by strong internal controls. A measure of exposure might be the number of transactions or people. The operational risk is the magnitude and likelihood of a loss as measured by the value and probability of a loss on the transactions being processed. Exposure can only be eliminated if no business is done. Risk can be limited by investing in process, people and technology.

Document and collect data

It is essential to observe causes as well as effects (losses) otherwise you will end up with a database of useless information. A lack of internal controls such as segregation of duties is a cause. A loss event such as fraud is the effect.

In order to identify the causes and effects of operational risk it is essential to take the approach advocated above of splitting operational risk into 'risk sub-categories', e.g.:

- Tied into departments/divisions
- Tied into the existing internal control framework and processes

However, a better approach is to start with a 'blank-page' and brainstorm a long list of categories with their causes and effects with the business concerned (bottom-up approach) or at a corporate level (top-down).

The advantage of the top-down approach is that the results can be used to comply with regulation/audit guidelines such as COSO. Bottom-up (perhaps using a modified version of Control Self-assessment) is advantageous as it obtains the buy-in of the business. For a number of different risk categories we have analyzed the potential losses and possible causes shown in Table 13.3.

It is much easier to collect loss or effect data than to collect than the causes of loss data. Most banks start by collecting the losses and then try to fit the causes to them, developing a methodology later. A number of insurers have large databases of causes such as earthquakes and separate databases of loss/claims made. They have developed techniques to fit causes to effects. However, it is a major problem as there may be many causes to one loss or probability driver. The relationship can be highly subjective and the importance of each cause on the effect difficult to assess. Sources of loss data are contained in Table 13.4.

After loss and cause data has been collected, empirical analysis may be used to assess the link between the causes and effects. It is essential to group similar losses together in order to measure the frequency of the different causes. A distribution of causes can be made with the most frequent being the main cause. This will then enable remedial management action to be taken on a prioritized basis. However, there may be dependencies between causes in which case the use of root-cause analysis may be appropriate to find the start of the chain.

Table 13.3 Potential losses and possible causes of risk

Risk category	The effect/potential loss	The causes of the loss
Process risks	Variance in process costs from predicted levels (excluding process malfunctions)	Declining productivity as volume grows
Control risks	Variance in costs as a result of control failures (e.g. write-offs due to failure to bill/collect monies owed on a timely basis)	Process malfunction, control failure, fraud
Project risks	Project cost overruns/failures	Poor planning, project management, scope creep, poor budgeting
Technology risks	Variance in technology running costs from predicted levels	Year 2000 upgrade expenditure required Application development
Human resource risks	Variance in revenues/profits (e.g. cost of recruiting replacements, costs of training, disruption to existing staff)	Loss of key staff due to defection of key staff to competitor
Client service risks	Variance in revenues/profits as a result of customers lost	Inappropriate derivative sale followed by litigation to poor ethical reputation Poor client service (e.g. incorrect statements)
Supplier management risks	Variance in costs of inputs (purchases of resources or services)	Increases in consulting fees over budget due to poorly negotiated contract
Regulatory risk	Reputational damage, fines levied by regulators	Failure to follow regulatory procedures

Some banks split losses between high-frequency low-impact and high-impact low-frequency events. The high-impact events are usually the catastrophic ones. Few banks have much internal data on the latter loss (or they would be out of business). Therefore there is a need to use external as well as internal data. High-frequency low-impact events lend themselves to statistical modeling. The treatment of high-impact low-frequency events, particularly if the data is about an event in another bank, is more open.

The types of data collected can be divided into four main sources:

- Historical variances/loss events (past settlement losses from the back office)
- Supplier/vendor estimates
- Industry benchmarking (competitors' average failure rate on trades per 1000)
- Delphic techniques based upon business assessment.

The last technique is the preferred method of the causal model, particularly when there is a general lack of data from the other three methods. The delphic oracle was the priestess who was able to predict the future based upon her superior knowledge and forsight. The delphic technique involves gathering a panel of experts together in the bank and forcing them to look forward in time, usually for the next financial year and getting them to generate scenarios of what can go wrong in terms of causes,

Table 13.4 Sources of loss data

Type	Sources of probabability and magnitude of loss data
Process risks	Historical variances Supplier/vendor estimates Industry benchmarking
Control risks	Historical variances Industry and non-industry benchmarking Delphic techniques based on business assessment
Project risks	Historical variances Industry and non-industry benchmarking
Technology risks	Historical variances Supplier/vendor estimates Industry benchmarking
Human resource risks	Delphic techniques based on business assessment
Client service risks	Delphic techniques based on business assessment
Supplier management risks	Historical variances Supplier/vendor estimates Industry benchmarking

effects, magnitude and likelihood. By forcing the senior executives to place a value on the scenarios the link is made between the qualitative and quantitative methods of measuring operational risk. The results of the delphic workshops can be calibrated against internal and external databases at a later date but this method results in a quick implementation of a quasi-quantitative method of measuring operational risk and gets the essential buy-in of the business.

Build prototype

Once we have enough data we can build a prototype. The causal model approach models the cause/effect data and analyzes the relationship between them. If the relationship has been determined in a delphic workshop it is input directly. The incorporation of balanced scorecarding may also be necessary if the firm are keen on this approach. This is where the competitor or industry benchmark data will be found useful.

An example of balanced scorecarding could be in a dealing room where the firm could set standards for each unit:

- 'No more than 5 settlement fails per 1000 trades'
- If exceed score, allocate extra capital and charge them for it

A charge for allocated capital, that affects the profit and loss account, certainly focuses the mind.

The use of risk visualization can also be incorporated into the prototype using exception reporting of a 'red, amber, green' nature where the exceptions are against quality control standards. A frequency distribution of high-frequency low-impact events should be modeled and a distribution (a non-normal one) fitted. (This is a non-trivial exercise as causes may be a Poisson distribution with losses a Weibull one. After setting an appropriate confidence interval (say, 95%) the firm can measure the unexpected loss and then be able to allocate risk capital for operational risk.

Technology risk

Technology risk can arise from maintenance contracts for existing IT infrastructure and application software through to complete outsourcing of projects or the whole IT service. The risks involved in this type of business are operational. The issues most firms face in managing technology risks can be illustrated by considering the various risk factors through a series of structured 'control questions'. This technique was advocated above.

So often, a firm, particularly in the trading/investment banking/securities businesses, has a spaghetti soup of systems, some old some very new with the resultant problem of old and new technologies which both need to be supported to make the business run smoothly. Many trading divisions have their own dedicated IT professionals who perform Rapid Application Development (RAD) to keep up with the traders. This increases operational risk as some firms then have poorly documented systems and rely on a few key IT personnel. The traders in many firms will still prefer their spreadsheets for their flexibility and speed. Such reliance will lead to increased operational risk as spreadsheets are rarely secure and can easily be corrupted. In addition, only the author really understands his or her spreadsheet.

Many firms have multiple IT projects being carried out at the same time and this inevitably leads to problems such as:

- Lack of security requirements developed and agreed before IT development commences
- Lack of capacity planning and resource utilization

Many of the project failures on risk management projects I have observed before I was called in to rescue the projects have been due to issues such as:

- Scope creep
- Poor design not complying with best practice
- Poor performance of the risk engine compared to spreadsheet models
- Lack of early deliverables
- No agreement on the acceptance criteria
- Lack of suitable testing carried out for new systems
- No change control implemented and
- Business process owners resisted the changes required to use the new system.

In addition to the specific problems of working in a trading environment the firm will be exposed across all business areas to general technology risk. The operational risk manager should assess general technology risks by reviewing a firm's compliance with the typical technology controls. Such controls would be designed to protect the IT facility against: human error (operations, maintenance, users, programmers); data theft; voice equipment failure; other failures (media, central computer equipment, purchased software, undetected and ancillary equipment); to minimize exposure to fire, heat, water, smoke, corrosive fumes. Protection against these risk factors can be divided into three types:

- Physical protection
- Functional protection
- Data protection

Physical protection

Physical protection is extremely important and often firms underinvest in the controls above which then lead to increased operational risks. However, physical protection is not enough ensure that a firm is protected against all operational risks contained in 'technology risk'. Functional protection is also essential.

Functional protection

The operational risk manager should ask the following control questions for assessing the functional protection the firm has against technology risk:

- Is the back-up strategy sufficient?
- Is it centrally managed (including distribution systems)?
- Is any critical data held on C drives?
- Are backups taken off-site?

In my experience few firms can positively answer the questions above. With negative responses the operational risk manager needs to assess the impact and likelihood of an unexpected loss.

Data protection

The final part of protection necessary against technology risks is data protection. The operational risk manager should ask the following key control questions for assessing the data protection the firm has against technology risk:

- What are the data retention policies? Is there any legislation that must be followed?
- What is the data classification system (levels of physical access, restriction, classified, data sensitivity, review procedure, periodic verification of classified data)?

Computer security

Many of the frauds that have been perpetrated in the financial sector could not have been achieved without a breach of computer security. It is essential that the operational risk manager ensures that adequate computer security controls are in place. Computer security is more than just passwords. Some of the key questions the operational risk might ask in assessing computer security are as follows:

- Is there an information security policy? How definitive is it?
- Is it documented?
- Are responsibilities for security processes clearly allocated?

Although I initially suggested that computer security is more than just passwords there are some important factors which will undermine the password security unless implemented correctly as follows:

- Are passwords required to sign on?
- What are the rules of password generation?
- Is there an alert to indicate when a sign-on has failed more than three times?

The operational risk manager should try to gather data about computer failures or security breaches in order to assess the likelihood and impact of operational risks recurring. However, if the firm does not have adequate records of past events and a method for 'learning from past mistakes' it could be argued that this is a key operational weakness in itself!

The operational risk manager should ask the following key questions to ensure incident management is performed correctly:

- What is the security incident reporting procedure? Is there a focal point?
- Are suspected security weaknesses reported?
- Are software malfunctions reported?
- Is there a disciplinary process for dealing with security breaches?

The data collected by strong incident management will be very useful in building up a database of past operational failures when the operational risk manager starts to measure operational risk.

Power

Many of the problems technology failures IBM have observed in the past have been due simply to inadequate power supply controls. The key questions the operational risk manager should ask are:

- Is there UPS or CPS? What does it support (CPU, tape drives, printers, communication front ends, DASD, LAN servers) and for how long?
- Is there a standby generator?
- Is there emergency lighting in the computer room?
- Where does the power supply enter the building, a single source?
- Is there a past history of any power problems? Quantify.
- Are there in-line power distribution units to suppress surges or spikes?

Risk mitigation

Inevitably, particularly in the trading/investment banking business, the reliance on technology can become so great that a firm would like to mitigate its risks. Risk mitigation can take the form of

- Insurance
- Allocating the risks to a captive insurance company
- Outsourcing to a third party.

When insuring technology it is essential to review the coverage. Examples of items normally covered are as follows:

- Hardware
- Loss of software
- Reinstatement of data
- Consequential business or financial loss
- Fidelity bonding

- Cost of emergency standby facilities
- Cost of software failure

Apart from coverage it is also essential to check that what is included and what exceptions are stated, e.g. normal wear and tear, telecommunications failure, war/terrorist damage.

All firms should have a plan which tries to ensure business continuity in the event of a disaster. In relation to firms totally reliant on technology this is even more important.

Off-site facility

Many firms have off-site storage facilities. Some have whole dealing rooms in out-of-town locations where the traders can go in the event of a business interruption. However, there are still operational risks involved with having an off-site facility. Some key questions the operational risk manager should ask are:

- Where is the location of off site facility versus customer location: far enough?
- What type of disaster is likely to affect both locations? Is that type of disaster a possibility?
- What is the physical security of the off-site storage vendor?

Suppliers/service providers risk

In the definition of operational risk above, supplier management risk was listed as a key operational risk. Technology suppliers pose very difficult operational risks due to the reliance firms have on technology as a whole. Key questions to ask are:

- Does the third party have a security policy?
- Does the policy describe organizational measures to safeguard the security of information and service provision on behalf of its clients)?
- Do suppliers have business recovery plans?
- Are there any service level agreements (SLAs) in place?

Some lessons can also be learnt in relation to questions often asked of risk management systems suppliers during the process of evaluation:

- Do you support all versions of your software or only the current and previous version?
- How many people do you employ?
- What are your growth plans in terms of headcount over the next three years?
- How reliant are you on the performance of third-party suppliers?

The last question is never-ending in reality as you could ask how reliant the third-party is on third parties.

Best practice

It is currently unclear what best practice actually consists of because of the embryonic nature of the operational risk function. This section will put forward an up-to-date view of best practice reviewing older studies such as survey by the British

Bankers' Association on operational risk (March 1997) and whether any significant changes are being made.

The Basel Committee on Banking Supervision published a paper in September 1998 entitled 'Operational Risk Management' which explained the scope of some recent research on operational risk management. The committee formed a working group which interviewed thirty major banks with a view to understanding the current industry issues prior to making any recommendations for regulation or supervision. The report states:

> The most important types of operational risk involve breakdowns in internal controls and corporate governance. Such breakdowns can lead to financial losses through error, fraud, or failure to perform in a timely manner or cause the interests of the bank to be compromised in some other way, for example, by its dealers, lending officers or other staff exceeding their authority or conducting business in an unethical or risky manner. Other aspects of operational risk include major failure of information technology systems or events such as major fires or other disasters.

In common with existing regulatory guidance the committee sees the important aspects of operational risk as relatively narrow as breakdowns in internal controls and corporate governance. This is probably because these two things are reasonably clear and can be assessed with relative ease by the regulators.

The working group also reported that:

> Awareness of operational risk among bank boards and senior management is increasing. Virtually all banks assign primary responsibility for managing operational risk to the business line head. Those banks that are developing measurement systems for operational risk often are also attempting to build some form of incentive for sound operational risk management practice by business line managers. This incentive could take the form of capital allocation for operational risk, inclusion of operational risk measurement into the performance evaluation process, or requiring business line management to present operational loss details and resultant corrective action directly to the bank's highest levels of management.

It is interesting to note the assignment of responsibility for managing operational risk to the business line head. This recognition by banks of direct business responsibility has both positive and negative aspects. On the positive side is the immediate buy-in obtained of the business lines by recognizing their direct responsibility. On the negative side is the potential for non-uniformity of approaches throughout the bank. There is also a risk of omitting an approach to 'corporate-level' operational risk such as reputational risk, lack of effective communication of key management information, or simply poor management.

A test is whether a bank has a plan to adopt a uniform approach to operational risk throughout the business lines and at the corporate level to review the scope and objectives of the operational risk manager. If a bank does not have an operational risk manager in place independent of the business line management (half the banks on the working group's study) this suggests that little has changed in the firm. The firms who adopt this approach tend to define operational risk as 'operations risk' and repackage the mix of existing activities such as internal and external audit, control self-assessment of internal controls and key operational performance indicators. However, the banks who are adopting this status quo approach are not considered by many to be falling below best practice. It is useful to describe three key issues of operational risk and profile what the authors consider to be best practice (see Table 13.5)

At a recent ISDA meeting on Operational Risk in London (February 1999) Fred Bell and Colin Plenderleith described the approach to operational risk management at the Royal Bank of Scotland plc. The Royal Bank of Scotland is a diversified group, active in UK banking and insurance. They offer services to personal customers that include bank and savings accounts, credit cards and mortgages, life assurance and innovative investment products, motor and home insurance. Their business customers range from small businesses to large corporates. As well as lending, leasing, structured finance and development capital, they offer money market, foreign exchange and derivative products. They are active in telephone and electronic banking – all the business of Direct Line is conducted by telephone. Outside the UK their US subsidiary, Citizens Financial Group, is a leading bank in New England.

The bank sees the following as the key benefits to the business of investing in operational risk management:

- Raised awareness of the need for better operational risk management
- Clearer identification of business unit risk profiles
- Better resource allocation
- More accurate product pricing
- A means of optimizing capital allocation
- Ultimately, improving shareholder value

To address operational risk a Head of Group Operational Risk reports to the Director, Group Risk alongside the Head of Group Credit Risk and Head of Group Market Risk. RBS categorizes operational risk as follows:

- Process; e.g. error, fraud, complexity, capacity, MIS
- People; e.g. integrity, competence, management
- Systems; e.g. integrity, confidentiality, availability
- Business environment; e.g. regulation, legal, natural disaster
- Business strategy; e.g. change management, projects

The RBS operational risk framework is solidly based upon the following:

- Setting corporate standards
- Communication of those standards
- A clearly defined organizational structure
- Analysis and monitoring of operational risks
- Application of technology to facilitate operational risk management
- Supply of tools and techniques to the business units which will add value to their management of operational risks

In the opinion of the author, the Royal Bank of Scotland are, among a small number of banks, setting standards of best practice in their approach to managing operational risk for both UK banks in particular and generally for 'universal' banks across the world. The main advantage of their approach is that it is easily understood by the businesses and links corporate governance 'top-down' standard setting to 'bottom-up' operational issue resolution within each business by supplying tools and techniques to facilitate the better management of risk. However, the approach currently taken by RBS is to adopt a 'qualitative approach' by using measures of risk

Table 13.5 Three key issues of operational risk

Issue	Retail bank (mortgages, credit cards and deposits)	Universal bank (commercial, retail, asset management, insurance and treasury divisions)	Investment bank (proprietary trading of all money and capital markets products, merger and acquisitions and corporate finance)
Organization	Independent Operational Risk Manager within Group Risk function. No independent operational risk managers within operations/business areas	Independent Operational Risk Manager within Group Risk function and independent operational risk managers within operations/ business areas, sometimes referred to as control units or process QA	Independent Operational Risk Manager within Risk Management but business line operations areas also manage what they refer to as 'Operations Risk'. No independent business line management
Definition	As the products have been homogenized and processes reengineered (e.g. call centres) operational risk is well understood and managed through scorecards and algorithms (e.g. Fraud detection on loan applications	For a bank with such diversified activities the definition of operational risk is causing difficulty. Each division is just starting to define its own view of operational risk and usually takes a narrow view based upon key controls in its operations divisions. This is currently at odds with the Group Risk department who have adopted a broader definition	The definition of operational risk split in investment banks between the operations departments who define it very narrowly as 'operations risk' and the Risk Management function which includes the whole universe of controllable and uncontrollable risks. The reason for this is that they are also responsible for insuring, internally or externally, uncontrollable risks
Measurement	Key performance indicators are commonly used. A number of retail banks have as part of their reengineering process implemented total quality management (TQM) which has a number of operational performance measures such as customer satisfaction, employee morale. However, the measurement is qualitative except for items such as level of complaints and staff absences, turnover	As the definitions of operational risk vary by division so does the level of sophistication of measurement. Most universal banks are currently assessing the feasibility of operational risk measurement but there are two views emerging: Group Risk are adopting a 'top-down' capital allocation approach based upon a simple measure such as residual earnings volatility (after market and credit risk have been stripped out) while the business lines are adopting a 'bottom-up approach' based upon process mapping and expense volatility	The two definitions are also giving rise to at least two approaches The contrasts with other banks are that many risk management functions within investment banks are applying their quantitative skills gained through their work in market and credit risk to operational risk Therefore best practice in an investment bank or securities house is to calculate and allocate capital to operational risk in the same way as it has been done to market and credit risk as part of an ongoing RAROC program

which they call 'Key Risk Indicators', KRIs. The further step of quantifying the potential for unexpected loss in relation to these KRIs has, so far, not been taken.

Dr Jack King of Algorithmics believes that the following are the success criteria for a successful operational risk framework:

- Includes provision for the calculation of a relevant capital requirement for operations
- Provides incentives for increased operational efficiency
- Supports decision-making process for operations using scenarios
- Assures avoidance of major losses due to operations
- Generates a measure that is compatible with market and credit risk
- Can be validated through methods such as back testing
- Includes sufficient reporting for proper management and regulation.

It is difficult to satisfy these success criteria without taking a more quantitative approach to operational risk management. Qualitative measures such as volumes, number of customer complaints, nostro breaks, need to be translated to financial losses to enable this to take place. However, once the 'operational risk management process' has been implemented adopting the RBS approach quantitative modeling can be used to calibrate the decisions made under a qualitative framework.

Regulatory guidance

As a minimum all companies must adhere to regulatory requirements. However, there are few countries where specifically drafted requirements cover operational risk management. The Bank of International Settlements (BIS) have just published a set of requirements on internal control which contain guidance in operational risk management. It is expected that regulators in each country will incorporate these into their own regimes. However, some regulators would claim that they already have a robust approach to operational risk.

Different countries have different approaches to operational risk. In the United Kingdom the Bank of England has since the Banking Act 1987 asked banks to appoint reporting accountants to review under Section 39 of that Act the internal control environments and to report on their adequacy for the risks to which each firm is exposed. The Bank of England published a Guidance Note on *Reporting Accountants' Reports on Internal Controls and other Control Systems* which provides a description of key controls and their expectations about their adequacy. In the next year the author expects further regulatory guidance on operational risk.

Various countries already have the elements of operational risk regulatory frameworks:

- RATE process in the UK
- CAMEL process in the USA
- BAK Minimum Requirements for Trading Institutions in Germany

The challenge for the regulators is to build an approach on the solid foundations already established in many countries.

Operational risk systems/solutions

There are a small number of software suppliers who are now attempting to address operational risk. However, because of the wide range of requirements from each company it is difficult to see a generic solution emerging in terms of a 'risk-engine'. However diverse the requirements, the data collection problem remains and this section will consider the steps required to provide a working solution in the shortest possible time. It will discuss the need for a cross-industry and industry/activity-specific database of operational risk measures.

There are many new entrants to the operational risk systems market and a number of different levels in the operational risk hierarchy are addressed. For example, two particular levels are:

- Enterprise-wide operational risk
- Operations department/processing

The basic components of the solutions are based upon the following key requirements:

- Operational risk engine
- Data collection
- Management reporting

Operational risk engine

The operational risk engine requirements are varied depending on the particular firm but can include:

- Calculates the risk capital to be allocated to operational risk
- Runs scenarios against the exposures
- Fits statistical distributions to loss data
- Links cause and effect
- Conducts fault tree analysis
- Qualitative risk ranking
- Balanced Scorecards

Data collection

As we saw above, the system may need to collect vast amounts of data such as:

- Transactions
- Events
- Interfaces
- Exceptions
- Variances
- Control checklists
- Balanced scorecards
- Benchmarks
- Process maps
- Self-Assessment/Delphic techniques

Management reporting

This can vary from providing day-to-day tools for operations management such as information on broken interfaces, incomplete trades and unmatched confirmations, through to enterprise-wide tools for group risk/operational risk management such as:

- Risk capital
- Correlation/trends across the organization
- Corporate governance.

It is essential to identify whether the management information is day-to-day operations management or firm-wide as the engine and data collected could be severely undermined and fail to provide the users with useful deliverables.

What the vendors are doing

Meridien Research Inc. published a research paper in 1998, 'Operational Risk Management Technologies': and divided the vendors into three types:

- Internal Data Collection and Monitoring Solutions
- External Operational Risk Databases
- Risk Quantification and Analysis Solutions

In the author's opinion a fourth type needs to be highlighted:

- Operations management solutions

Internal data collection and monitoring solutions

These are simple tools based on the collection of internal control data. They are built for auditors by auditors and are of limited use in a comprehensive firm-wide operational risk management process. They are largely checklist based but do have some advantages:

- Good for interviewing business units
- Good for control self-assessment

The solutions are generally qualitative not quantitative in nature so do not satisfy the requirement for capital allocation.

External operational risk databases

These consist of large databases of external event data which provide potential users with the ability to develop their own quantitative analytics. An example of such a database is NetRisk's OpCam.

Risk quantification and analysis solutions

These products address the issue of risk capital quantification for operational risk. Some take account of risk-adjusted performance measurement. Examples of such products include:

- Algorithmics, Jack King (see below)
- NetRisk, RiskOps
- 'Causal Model'

Operations management solution

These assist the day-to-day management of operations within the operations department. This type of product sits as a 'temperature gauge' above the operations systems and by comparing data about the same process can highlight broken interfaces to external and internal systems, breaks in reconciliations and other data. Traffic light reporting (red, amber green) can be incorporated in order to assist senior management. A good example of this is Pacemetrics' Pacemaker product.

Peter Slater at Warburg Dillon Read has also developed an in-house solution incorporating traffic light reporting.

Algorithmics' solution

Algorithmics methodology is based on a powerful method of causal modeling. They represent causes and events in a graphical modeling tool that is populated with conditional probabilities and distributions. This tool is used to generate event frequency distributions and loss distributions based on empirical data, built-in standard parametric distributions, and subjective evaluations. Interactive scenario-based modeling and full Monte Carlo simulation are integrated into the modeling tool, which forms the heart of our enterprise-wide operational risk management system. After building models based on actual losses, key indicators, and assessments, the modeling tool is embedded in an advanced three-tier architecture to become part of a powerful integrated solution.

Example: Investment banking

Algorithmics have taken a pragmatic approach to modeling the processes in operations and measuring and modeling the exposures and expected losses associated with processing the transactions in a financial firm (Figure 13.2). This provides a consistent, relevant, and meaningful measure for day-to-day operations and executive decision making. The explanation of the rationale behind capital allocation, loss

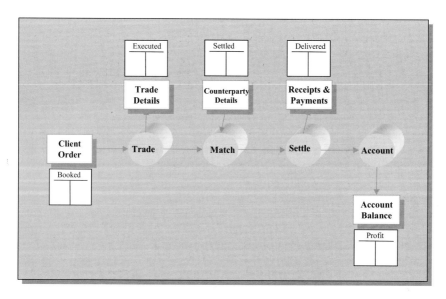

Figure 13.2   Process model with control point accounts.

avoidance measures, and loss-mitigation measures using this methodology will benefit from its sound theoretical base. Subjective models and *ad hoc* rare events can be added, subject to the individual client's specification.

Example: Measuring operational risk exposure

Algorithmics consider the primary areas of operational risk exposure in an investment banking example to be measured due to transactions. These areas include reconciliation, valuation, settlement, compliance, and limits. Algorithmics considers each of these areas in detail and provide exposure to loss using the value of the transaction that is unreconciled, the difference in a transaction's value and an independent valuation, the value of a transaction that is not in compliance, the cost of carry for a transaction, and the amount of limit violation a transaction causes. Each of these areas results in an exposure in home currency of potential loss due to operations. Expected loss is modeled for each of the areas and used to provide estimates such as value at loss and loss under scenario (Figure 13.3).

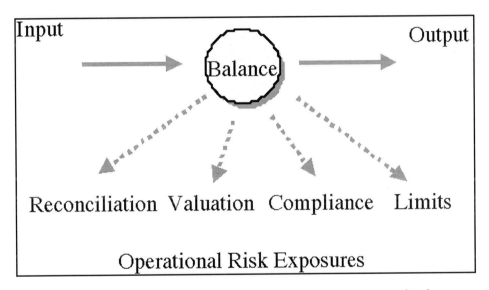

Figure 13.3 Operational risk exposure calculations on a process level.

Exposures are calculated by transaction for each process and a statistical sequence of exposures over a time period is generated. The measurement of operational risk is a statistic on this sequence that includes variability of exposure. These measurements are used to generate quality control charts and provide the input to the monitoring for goal-based monitoring (target versus actual) and exception monitoring.

Modeling losses and rare events

Several techniques have been proposed for operational risk models. Unfortunately there has not been a clear distinction between measuring operational risk and modeling operational risk. The actuarial approach of measuring rare events across the industry has led some to adopt the approach for a particular investment bank. While this approach may be appropriate for industry-wide statistics it should be used with care when applying it to a specific financial institution's operations. A systematic method of modeling losses and rare events may include specific models for individual firms. An outline of the approach for the investment banking example is as follows:

- **Model the processes and key control points.** Algorithmics begins with the process model for investment banking. Using this model they define the data requirements at control points in order to determine the operational risk exposures due to valuation, compliance, reconciliation, settlement, limits, and systems. For each of the processes and associated control points, the risk variables that will be included in the model are identified. This is the major business analytical effort required.

- **Parameterize the model using actual data.** Transactions are used to determine the probabilities to be attached at each process and control point that relate the processing to the data available in the transactions. Using these parameters, the model is trained so that outliers and anomalies can be detected and dealt with on a day-to-day basis.

- **Measure exposures due to transactions in processes.** For each process, the exposures based on values of the transactions for each of the operational risk factors described above are calculated. Each process includes a balance for each of the exposures as a sequence generated from the transactions going through the process. Statistical control for the process is established by generating statistics from this sequence of balances for the risk factor exposures.

- **Model expected loss.** For each exposure, an expected loss model is developed. This includes a time horizon, probability of loss, and loss function to calculate the amount of loss, given an exposure. These expected losses form a loss distribution for the process and contain a component for each risk factor.

- **Add models for rare events.** Rare events are then modeled as probabilities of loss and an associated loss model is attached. These models can be actuarial, *ad hoc*, or reliability models for elements of the processes. The primary event models to date are system failure models using mean time between failure and mean time to repair. The primary rare event models are assessment models based on questionnaires or workshops.

- **Simulate overall expected losses for value at operational risk.** Using Monte Carlo simulation (or historical simulation) Algorithmics then generates a large sample space and calculate the value at operational risk for a particular confidence level. This figure is compatible with VaR and can be combined with it or used separately for capital allocation.

- **Simulate scenarios for loss under operational risk scenario.** Setting individual variables in the model to specific values, scenarios are simulated for operations and calculate loss is calculated under operational scenario to support decision-making and perform stress testing.

Algorithmics Operational Risk provides a clear, effective system for managing operational risk through measuring, and modeling the transaction processing at key control points. Using advanced visualization and reporting techniques, it can deliver the relevant information accurately and timely. The benefits of such an approach means that a firm can:

- Reduce operational costs through more effective information delivery.
- Improve compliance checking capability.

- Improve market conformity verification capability.
- Reduce potential loss due to operational failure.
- Improve capability of detecting anomalies in operational processes.
- Measure value at operational risk for capital allocation.
- Measure potential loss under rare event scenarios.
- Measure potential loss under system failure scenarios.

Dr King's causal modelling approach and solution to operational risk represents *the* future for operational risk modeling and systems in all firms.

PaceMetrics Group

The PaceMetrics Group have recently launched a product, PaceMaker, which is best described as a *transaction flow monitor*. PaceMaker is a solution to one of the key issues for many banks, i.e. too many systems, as a result of which:

- Operational costs are too high
- There is no end-to-end view of the lifecycle of trades
- There are too many points of failure
- Too many staff are involved in non-productive activities
- Fire-fighting and internal reconciliation
- Providing efficient and satisfactory global customer service is difficult
- Data is dispersed and inconsistent
- Operational risk management is a big challenge.

Figure 13.4 illustrates the problem of potential data inconsistency between the

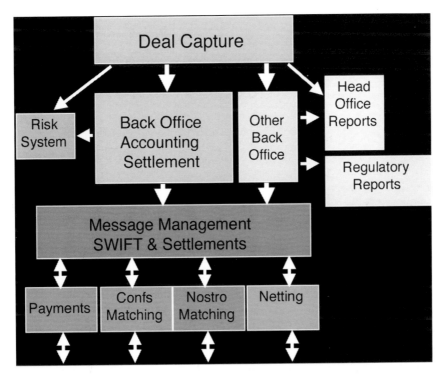

Figure 13.4 Potential data inconsistency between systems.

different systems of the bank. This problem may be even more complex when we consider differerent geographical locations. This is particularly a problem in banks where the architectures and applications differ by location for the same activities. PaceMakers' proposed solution to the above problem is:

- Follow end-to-end life-cycles of all trades as they pass from system to system
- Automatically reconcile the trade data contained in one system to the 'same' data in another
- Present users with a single view of the whole operation in real-time
- Dissassociate operational staff from the underlying infrastructre.

As you can see from Figure 13.5, PaceMaker sits on the side of a bank's infrastructure and does not try to change it. This 'passive' approach is beneficial as the product will be accepted more easily by personnel if there is no (immediate) threat to existing operational systems.

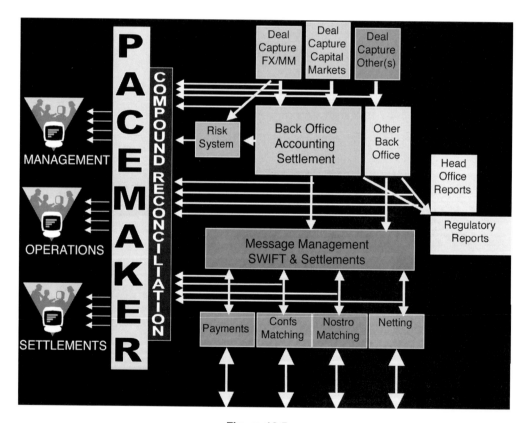

Figure 13.5

The system captures the flow of data between a bank's various systems and reconstitutes consolidated and reconciled deal details in full. PaceMaker provides a unique graphical view of the whole business operation end-to-end, delivered to management and staff through web-based technology: locally, remotely, at home, or overseas using standard browsers. The technology disassociates the operation from the underlying infrastructure in terms of location and platform. It enables banks to manage their operation wherever they may be: investigations, exception management and customer service all benefit immensely.

Figure 13.6 illustrates the top-level view of the trade lifecycle monitor. Note that the left side of the diagram contains the event description which occurs throughout the life of the transaction and the event status indicates whether the event has significant problems through the use of 'traffic-light reporting'.

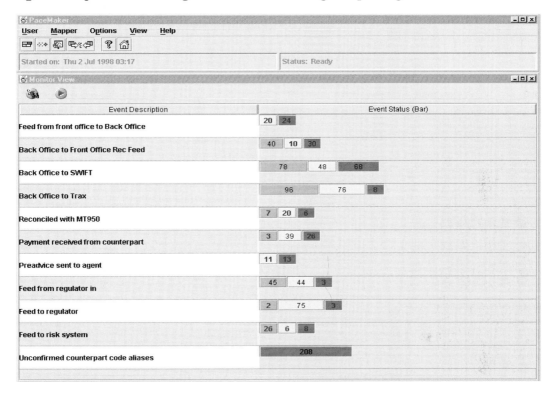

Figure 13.6   The trade lifecycle monitor.

It is interesting to note that in deploying PaceMaker, PaceMetrics don't attempt to reengineer any legacy systems, since they are mission-critical. Nor do they believe in up-front big bang, expensive process reengineering. Their approach is different and is based on incremental deployment and rapid investment.

Figure 13.7 represents an example of a 'best of breed' component solution to operational risk:

- Enterprise Wide Risk Assessment using Ernst & Young's web-enabled tool HORIZON (www.horizoncsa.com).
- IBM's MQ Integrator as the data collection tool
- Pacemetrics Pacemaker as the day-to-day Operations Management's 'traffic light reporting system
- Operational Risk engine and events database such as that available from Algorithmics, NetRisk (RiskOps) or Ernst & Young's agent-based simulation tool
- Infinity's forex dealing system is an example of a source system of trades.

There will be other architectures and components driven by a firm's particular requirements but the above represents a way to link operations with firm-wide risk.

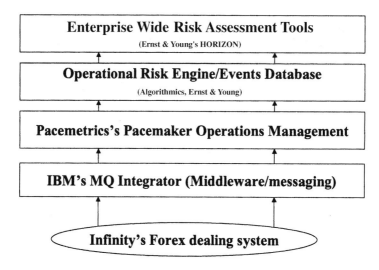

Figure 13.7   Best of breed solutions to operational risk.

Conclusion

This chapter looks forward and postulates what the future development of operational risk holds. Many banks are still struggling with data collection without really understanding what they will do with it once they have it. The future will be determined by the extent to which banks allocate capital to market, credit and strategic business risk. If Raroc and capital allocation becomes more common in banks then all banks will have to quantify operational risk. The regulators may also force capital to be allocated to operational risk and if this happens the whole industry will change.

Some areas of research currently at the feasibility study stage within Ernst & Young are the application of the following to operational risk:

- Knowledge management
- Artificial intelligence and knowledge-based systems
- Fuzzy logic in relation to cause and effect

The future is anybody's guess (probably using a delphic technique).

Author's Note

This chapter represents Duncan Wilson's personal views and should not in any way be interpreted as the views of any part of Ernst & Young.

Part 3

Additional risk types

14

Coping with model risk

FRANÇOIS-SERGE LHABITANT

Introduction

The collapse of the Bretton Woods Agreement, the resulting dollar devaluation and shift from floating to fixed currency exchange rates, the world oil price crisis and the explosive increase in interest rates volatility in the late 1970s and early 1980s, the successive crashes of the stock markets in 1973/4, 1987, 1997 and 1998, the crash of the bond markets in 1994 – all these events have produced a progressive revolution in the art and science of risk management and have contributed to the development of a vast array of financial instruments and quantitative models for eliminating exposure to risk. These instruments and models have become central to a large number of practitioners, financial institutions and markets around the world. Indeed, risk management is certainly the central topic for the management of financial institutions in the 1990s.

Sophisticated mathematical models and a strong influence on practice were not always hallmark of finance theory. Finance has long remained a rather descriptive discipline, based on rules of thumb and experience. The original Bachelier (1900) work on option pricing remained forgotten for a long time.

The major strides in mathematical modeling came in the area of investments and capital markets with the Markowitz (1952) portfolio selection model and the Sharpe (1963) capital asset pricing model. Sharpe's and Markowitz's models began a shift away from the traditional *ad-hoc* selection of the 'best' stock for an investor towards the concept of a quantified trade-off between risk and return. Both authors were awarded by the Nobel Prize in Economics in 1990.

The most important development in terms of impact on practice was the publication of the Black and Scholes (1973) and Merton (1973) model for option pricing just a month after the Chicago Board Options Exchange started trading the first listed options in the United States. The simplicity of the model, its analytical tractability as well as its ease of understanding rapidly seduced practitioners.[1] They adopted it. A new era of mathematical modeling was born.

The extraordinary flow of financial innovations stimulated the further development of mathematical models. The increasing technical sophistication in financial markets and the explosion of exotic and over-the-counter instruments induced a concomitant need for models and, consequently, for analysis and computation. Inexorably, they led to an escalation in the level of mathematics, including probability theory, statistics, programming, partial differential equations and numerical analysis. The application of mathematics to important problems related to derivatives pricing, hedging, or risk management has expanded rapidly over the past few years, yielding a proliferation of models.

In the early 1970s, the major problem for financial institutions was the lack of models. Thirty years later, the problem is now the excessive number of them. Therefore, a new kind of risk must be considered: model risk. This includes all the dangers of accepting models without carefully questioning them.

Model risk: towards a definition

Most economic and financial models fall into one of the following categories:

- Macro-economic models typically attempt to forecast macro-economic data such as interest rates, inflation, unemployment rate, etc. Their complexity ranges from naive single-equation models to models with several hundred equations and thousands of variables.
- Micro-economic models attempt to explain relationships in a given market, such as the link between savings and past returns, or between interest rates and consumption. They are generally simple, not necessarily true, but provide a useful picture and an understanding of reality.
- Valuation models are typically used by investors to select their portfolios, by traders to price financial instruments and by banks to determine their investment strategy and asset-allocation mix. They range from very simple models based on discounting and compounding cashflows to more elaborate ones, typically those used for exotic options or complex swaps pricing.
- Risk models attempt to estimate how the value of a given position will change due to a particular change in its environment. This change can find its source in a general market change (interest rates, stock market, commodity prices, etc.) or from a position-specific characteristic (credit risk, operational risk, etc.). Typical examples of risk models are hedging strategies and Value-at-Risk calculations.

In the following, we will focus mainly on models belonging to the third and fourth categories, but we could easily extend our framework to include macro- and micro-economic models.

Model risk results from the use of an inappropriately specified model, or the use of an appropriate model but in an inadequate framework or for the wrong purpose. Uncertainty in a financial model arises from four sources. First, there is an inherent uncertainty due to the stochastic nature of a given model. By definition, market moves are not totally predictable, which means that any financial model is subject to this uncertainty. Next, there is the uncertainty about the applying a model in a specific situation, given the model structure and its parameter estimation. Can we use the model extensively? Is it restricted to specific situations, financial assets or markets? One should carefully examine these points before the use of any model. Third, there is an uncertainty in the values of the parameters in a given model. Statistical estimates (particularly for non-observable quantities such as volatility or correlation) are subject to errors, and can therefore lead to errors when they serve as an input. Finally, there is the specification error, that is, the uncertainty of the model structure itself. Did we really specify the right model? Even after the most diligent model selection process, we cannot be sure that we have adopted the true model, if any.

Generally, only the first source of uncertainty receives rigorous attention. The others are simply ignored. The values of the parameters and the underlying model are generally assumed to be the true ones. At best, a limited sensitivity analysis is performed with respect to the parameters.

Nevertheless, analysing model risk is crucial, whatever the market risk, credit risk or operational risk approach is employed for the institution. Table 14.1 lists some of the stunning losses that were due entirely to model risk. Additional cases could easily be added to the list. Disasters such as Metallgesellschaft, Procter & Gamble, Orange County, Kashima Oil, Nippon Steel, Gibson Greetings, Bankers Trust, Cargill, Sumitomo and others resulted from inadequate mark-to-market (in fact, as we will see, mark-to-model), improper hedging techniques (use of a wrong model or instrument), unexpected market moves (market moves not considered by the model), incorrect model feeding (in terms of data) or omission of real-world frictions modeling (such as liquidity reduction or margin calls). In a sense, all these are consequences of model risk.

Table 14.1   Official losses due to model risk

Year	Company	Loss (millions)	Market and causes
1970	Merrill Lynch	USD 70	Use of an incorrect yield curve to price stripped government bonds
1987	Merrill Lynch	USD 350	Incorrect pricing model for stripped mortgage-backed securities
1992	J.P. Morgan	USD 200	Inadequate model for the prepayments in the mortgage-backed securities market
1997	NatWest Markets	GBP 90	Improper volatility estimation for GBP interest rate options
1997	Bank of Tokyo-Mitsubishi	USD 83	Inadequate pricing model, which led to systematic overvaluation of a position in US interest rate derivatives
1997	UBS AG	CHF 120	Inadequate pricing model for structured equity derivatives
1998	LTCM	Unknown	Inadequate models for arbitrage between US and European interest rates, and excessive leverage

How do we create model risk?

Unlike market risk, model risk does not come solely from unexpected or unpredicted market movements. Each individual step, each decision, each action during a model-building process is a potential source of model risk.

Selecting or building a model

We can divide the model-building process into five steps: the environment characterization, the identification of the factor(s) driving the model, the specification of their behaviour, the estimation of the model parameters, and the implementation issues.

Step 1 Characterize the theoretical environment

The first step in the model-building process is characterization of the theoretical environment in which the model is going to be used. The model can be a normative one (which describes how the things should be) or a positive one (which describes how they are). In both cases, the goal is to build an abstraction close enough to reality. What does the world look like? Does trading take place continuously or at selected time intervals? Are all prices and information observable, or is there some form of asymmetric information? Is the market free of frictions, or do we face transaction costs or differential taxes? Is the market for the instruments considered always liquid enough, or should we also consider the possibility of excess demand or supply? Are borrowing and short selling allowed without restriction? Do investors' actions have an effect on prices? Are all required hedging instruments available to ensure market completeness? The answers to all these questions will result in a set of hypotheses that are fundamental for the model to be developed.

In any case, understanding and being comfortable with the model's assumptions is essential. Challenging them is recommended. In fact, most of the main strands of theoretical work in finance are concerned with the relaxation of assumptions in existing models. However, this should not be considered as a sport, as it results in an abundant profusion of similar models. We must always remember that a theory should not be judged by the restrictiveness of its assumptions, but rather by the contribution of its conclusions to improve our understanding of the real world and the robustness of these conclusions. Important objections were already raised with the original Markowitz (1952) model; despite this, even the attacks on Markowitz have triggered new concepts and new applications that might have never come about without his innovative contributions.

Table 14.2 The Black and Scholes (1973) environment

Environment

A1   There are no market frictions, such as bid/ask spreads, transaction costs or taxes.
A2   Trading can take place continuously.
A3   Short selling is permitted.
A4   The assets are perfectly divisible.
A5   The risk-free rate is constant (and known) over the life of the option.
A6   The underlying asset pays no dividend during the life of the option.
A7   There are no arbitrage opportunities.
A8   There is no default risk.

Factors driving the model

A9   The only uncertainty in the model is the stock price future evolution.

Factor dynamics specification

A10   The asset price follows a geometric Brownian motion (that is, the asset price at the option maturity is log-normally distributed).
A11   The underlying asset volatility is constant (and known) over the life of the option.

As an illustration, Table 14.2 lists the set of idealizing assumptions that characterize the original Black and Scholes (1973) world. All of them are necessary to the further development of the model. Of course, one may criticize or reject some of them, and argue that they are highly unrealistic with respect to the real world. This is often a subjective point of view. For instance:

- Assumptions A1 (no market frictions) and A3 (short selling) are highly unrealistic for the individual investor; they may hold as a first approximation for large market participants, at least in normal market conditions. What are considered as 'normal' conditions remain to be defined. In the recent collapse of the Long Term Capital Management hedge fund, the partners (including Robert Merton and Myron Scholes) looked for fancy mathematical models, but they failed to appreciate the liquidity of investments and the ability to execute their trades. After the Russian debacle, markets lost confidence and liquidity dried up. There were no more buyers, no more sellers, and therefore no trades. This is a typical violation of the Black and Scholes necessary hypotheses.
- Assumption A8 (no default risk) is also acceptable for futures and options that trade in organized exchanges, where a clearinghouse acts as a counterpart for both sides of the contracts; it is subject to caution when pricing over-the-counter derivatives.

Assumptions can also be visionary. Consider, for instance, assumption A2 (continuous time). In the 1970s, this was a fiction, justified by saying that if the length of time between successive market quotes is relatively small, the continuous-time solution given by the model will be a reasonable approximation to the discrete-time solution. But with electronic stock exchanges, continuous time trading has now become a reality. As Merton initially noticed, 'reality will eventually imitate theory'.

Step 2 Identify and select a set of relevant risk factors

Once the environment has been carefully and entirely characterized, the next step in the model-building process is the identification and selection of a set of relevant risk factors. Two distinct lines of inquiry can be followed.

The factors can be specified exogenously, as a result of experience, intuition, or arbitrary decision. Such risk factors are typically fundamental or macro-economic factors. For instance, when one attempts to build a model to explain stock returns, factors such as the return on the stock market index, the market capitalization, the dividend yield, the growth rate in industrial production, the return on default-free securities, the oil price variations or the expected change in inflation should *a priori* be considered good candidates.

The factors can also be determined endogenously by the use of statistical techniques such as principal components and/or factor analysis. Typically, a succession of models with an increasing number of factors is fitted to the data. Each factor is not constructed according to any economic meaning, but statistically, according to its incremental explanatory power with respect to the previous model. The goodness of fit is monitored, with the idea that a strong increase in its value implies that the last factor added is significant. The process stops when additional factors do not measurably increase the goodness of fit of the model.

Each of the two methods has its own advantages and shortcomings. In the exogenous specification, the resulting model is economically very tractable and is expressed easily in a language with which most senior managers, brokers and financial analysts are familiar. But omitting factors is frequent, as it is usually easier to catalogue which risk factors are present rather than which are missing. With the endogenous specification, the model includes the factors with the highest explanatory power, but the next difficulty is to identify these statistical factors as relevant economic variables. Of course, both techniques can be used simultaneously to complement and validate their results.

As an example, on the equity side, the capital asset pricing model of Sharpe (1963) has remained for a long time the unique model to explain expected returns. It is nothing more than a single-factor model, with the market return taken as the only explanatory variable. Although empirical evidence suggested the multidimensionality of risk, it is only with the arbitrage pricing theory of Ross (1976) that multi-factor models started to gain popularity. A significant enhancement was the three-factor pricing model of Fama and French (1992), showing that adding size and book to market value of equity as explanatory variables significantly improved the results of the CAPM.

Another interesting example is the field of interest rate contingent claims. In this case, the underlying variable is the entire interest rate term structure, that is, the set of all yields for all maturities. How many factors should we consider to price interest rate contingent claims, or equivalently, to explain yield curve variations? The answers generally differ across models. Most empirical studies using principal component analysis have decomposed the motion of the interest rate term structure into three independent and non-correlated factors: the first is a shift of the term structure, i.e. a parallel movement of all the rates. It usually accounts for up to 80–90% of the total variance (the exact number depends on the market and on the period of observation); the second one is a twist, i.e. a situation in which long rates and short-term rates move in opposite directions. It usually accounts for an additional 5–10% of the total variance. The third factor is called a butterfly (the intermediate rate moves in the opposite direction of the short- and long-term rate). Its influence is generally small (between 1% and 2% of the total variance).

Since the first statistical component has a high explanatory power, it may be tempting to model the yield curve variations by a one-factor model. It must be stressed at this point that this does not necessarily imply that the whole term structure is forced to move in parallel, as this was the case in all duration-based models commonly employed since the 1970s and still used by many asset and liability managers. It simply implies that one single source of uncertainty is sufficient to explain the movements of the term structure or the price of a particular interest rate contingent claim. Most early interest rate models – such as Merton (1973), Vasicek (1977), or Cox, Ingersoll and Ross (1985) – are single-factor models, and they assume the instantaneous spot rate to be the single state variable.

One the one hand, single-factor models are generally adequate for securities which are sensible to the level of the term structure of interest rates, such as short-term bonds and their contingent claims. On the other, some securities such as swaptions are sensible to the shape of the term structure (or to other aspects such as the volatility term structure deformations) and not only to its level. They will require at least a two-factor model. This explains why a second state variable, such as the long-term interest rate, a spread or the rate of inflation was added in subsequent models, even if it is cumbersome to handle (see Table 14.3).

Step 3 Model the future evolution of the risk factors

Once the numbers of factors and their identities have been chosen, the rules regulating their behaviour must be specified. The finance literature has considered different models for describing risk factor dynamics in a financial market. The most common assumption is the trajectory of a stochastic process, that is, a probability distribution for the value of each factor over future time.[2]

The choice of a particular stochastic process is also the consequence of a long list

Table 14.3 Examples of various two and three factor models for interest rates

Authors	Factors driving the term structure
Richard (1978)	Real short-term rate, expected instantaneous inflation rate
Brennan and Schwartz (1979)	Short-term rate, long-term rate
Schaefer and Schwartz (1984)	Long-term rate, spread between the long- and short-term rates
Cox, Ingersoll and Ross (1985)	Short-term rate, inflation
Schaefer and Schwartz (1987)	Short-term rate, spread between the long- and short- term rates
Longstaff and Schwartz (1992)	Short-term rate, short-term rate volatility
Das and Foresi (1996)	Short-term rate, mean of the short-term rate
Chen (1996)	Short-term rate, mean and volatility of the short-term rate

of questions. Let us quote some of them: Should the specification be made in a discrete or in a continuous-time framework? Should we allow for jumps in the risk factors or restrict ourselves to diffusion processes?[3] Should we allow for time-varying parameters in the stochastic process, or remain with constant ones? Should we have restrictions placed on the drift coefficient, such as linearity or mean-reversion? Should the stochastic process be Markovian?[4] Can we allow for negative values for the risk factor, if it has a low probability? Carefully answering every question is essential, as this will determine the quality and future success of a model.

The adoption of a particular stochastic process to model a financial variable is generally a trade-off between two contradictory goals. On the one hand, the process should account for various empirical regularities such as normality, fat tails,[5] mean reversion, absorption at zero, etc. On the other, the model should provide a simple procedure for its application. Accounting for more empirical observations generally increases the complexity of the model and loses analytical tractability, which is an undesirable feature.

As an example, let us consider stochastic processes for the stock price. The arithmetic Bachelier Brownian motion model, despite its simplicity and tractability, was not really adopted by the financial community as it had the unfortunate implications of allowing negative stock prices. On the other hand, the Black and Scholes geometric Brownian motion was widely adopted in the early days of option pricing; it assumes that log-returns are normally distributed with a constant volatility, which precludes negative prices and results also in a simple closed-form expression for the option price. Later, most of the generalizations of the Black–Scholes option pricing model focused on asset price dynamics, as the geometric Brownian motion fails to account for excess kurtosis and skewness which are often empirically observed in most asset return distributions (see Table 14.4). Some authors, including Merton (1976a,b), Hull and White (1987), Scott (1987), Wiggins (1987), Bates (1996a,b), have answered by modeling asset prices by a different process, typically adding a jump component to the original model or considering that the stock price and the volatility level were following separate correlated stochastic processes. The resulting models provide a better fit to the empirical data, but lose their analytical tractability and ease of implementation. This explains why practitioners were very reluctant to adopt them.

More recently, instead of assuming an exogenous stochastic process for the volatility, researchers have assumed an empirical distribution of the ARCH/GARCH type that is much easier to estimate and better fits the data. Then, they have derived

Table 14.4   Some option pricing models and their price dynamics specification

Authors	Stock price dynamics specification
Bachelier (1900)	Asset prices follow an arithmetic Brownian motion (prices are normally distributed)
Black and Scholes (1973) Merton (1973)	Asset prices follow a geometric Brownian motion (prices are log-normally distributed)
Merton (1976a,b)	Asset prices follow a geometric Brownian motion with a jump component
Hull and White (1987)	Volatility follows a geometric Brownian motion
Scott (1987)	Volatility follows a mean-reverting process
Wiggins (1987)	General Wiener process
Stein and Stein (1991)	General Wiener process
Bates (1996a,b)	Combines both jumps and volatility diffusion

consistent option pricing models (see for instance Duan, 1995). Alternatively, the empirical stock return distribution can be implied from the smile and the term structure of volatility, and a modified binomial model (with a distorted tree) is derived to price standard or exotic options. This second approach was explored by Derman and Kani (1994), Dupire (1994) and Rubinstein (1994). All these new models are simply pragmatic approaches to cope with model risk. They do not attempt to build a better economic model; they simply adapt an existing one in order to fit market data better.

For bond prices, the route was quite different. Bond prices cannot follow geo-metrical Brownian motions, since the prices and returns are subject to strong constraints: typically, zero-coupon bond prices cannot exceed their face value; close to maturity, the bond price should be close to its face value and the volatility of the bond returns must be very small. However, a large variety of stochastic processes is available for choice, and this has also led to a profusion of models.[6]

We should note here that many authors justified the adoption of a particular stochastic process for interest rates by its analytical tractability rather than by its economic significance. For instance, many models assume normally distributed interest rates, allowing for the possibility of negative values for nominal rates. Assuming log-normality would solve the problem, but at the cost of losing analytical tractability. Furthermore, portfolios of assets with log-normal returns are not log-normal. Therefore, what was an essential problem for stocks is simply ignored for fixed income assets.

Step 4 Estimate the parameters of the model

Finally, once the model is theoretically fully specified, we reach the estimation procedure. Model risk is often confused with estimation risk. This confusion is easily explainable: if poor estimates of the parameters are used, the model's results will be misleading. In addition, the problem of reconciling imperfect theory with reality is often transformed into that of determining the most probable parameter values for a specified stochastic model so that the output of the model is as close as possible to the observations.

Several econometric techniques can be found in the literature to estimate the observable parameters of a model from empirical data. The most popular are max-imum likelihood estimation (MLE), the generalized method of moments (GMM), and the estimation of a state space model with a Kalman filter.[7] These techniques proceed under the possibly false presumption of a correct model specification. Furthermore, they are not always well suited for the estimation of some particular stochastic processes parameters. For instance, using maximum likelihood estimation with jump-diffusion models–such as Merton's (1976a,b) option pricing model–is inconsistent.[8] Despite this, it is often encountered in the financial literature.

For unobservable parameters, matters are slightly more complicated. For instance, in applying option pricing models a systematic difficulty is the estimation of the volatility of the underlying variable, which is not directly observable. A first guess may be to assume that the past is a good indicator of volatility in the future, and to use historical volatility, which is defined as the annualized standard deviation of the natural logarithms of the price relatives. But there are strong critiques against the use of the simple historical volatility. First, recent data should be given more weight than more distant data, as it conveys more information. A solution may be exponential smoothing, that is, to give progressively less weight to the more distant prices. Second, the more information, the better the model. Therefore, why don't we use the information available in the intradaily high and low values in addition to closing prices? Finally, in the case of time-varying volatility, the considerable literature on ARCH and GARCH models explicitly addresses the issue of optimally estimating conditional volatility.

An additional problem is the choice of the data period to estimate model parameters. Statistically, using more data will provide better estimates. Financially, using more data will often include outdated situations.

To avoid using an inappropriate time frame, good market practice is to use current market data to compute an implied volatility. The procedure requires the use of an explicit analytical pricing formula, that is, of a model and its hypothesis. And it is not unusual to see the implied volatility calculated using the Black and Scholes (1973) model plugged into an alternative model! We are back to the problem of model risk . . .

The estimation problem is not restricted to the volatility. On the fixed-income side, a very similar observation applies to the 'short-term rate', which plays an essential part in most interest rate models. The 'short-term rate' is in fact an instantaneous rate of return, which is, in general, unobservable. Therefore, if the estimation of its parameters is based on a pure time-series approach, it is necessary to approximate the spot rate with the yield on a bond with non-zero maturity. The proxy is typically an overnight, a weekly or a monthly rate. But authors do not really agree on a common proxy for their tests. For instance, Stanton (1997) uses the yield on a 3-month Treasury-bill; Chan *et al.* (1992) use the one-month Treasury-bill yield; Ait-Sahalia (1996a,b) uses the one-week Eurodollar rate; Conley *et al.* (1997) use the Federal Funds rate. All these rates are rather different and subject to important microstructure effects. This can bias the estimated parameters for the spot rate, leading to important model risk effects. Let us recall that in the mid-1970s, Merrill Lynch lost more than US\$70 million in a stripping operation of 30-year government bonds just because they used a yield curve calculated from inadequate instruments to price their product.

Step 5 Implementation issues

The implementation issues are the final sources of model risk in the model-building process. Let us provide some examples.

First, data problems. Which data source should be used? Datastream, Reuters, Telekurs, Bloomberg, Telerate, Internet and others often provide different quotations for closing prices, depending on their providers. At what time of the day should the data be pulled into the model? And in the presence of multiple currencies or multiple time zones, other problems arise. For instance, should the CHF/USD exchange rate be taken at New York or at Zurich closing time? In a global book, at what time should the mark-to-market be performed? Can the data be verified on an independent basis?

Second, continuous time problems. Despite its limitations, the concept of delta hedging is a cornerstone of modern financial risk management. In theory, the constructed hedge requires continuous rebalancing to reflect the changing market conditions. In practice, only discrete rebalancing is possible. The painful experiences of the 1987 and 1998 crashes or the European currency crisis of 1992 have shown the problems and risks of implementing delta-hedging strategies in discrete time.

Third, oversimplifying assumptions. For instance, an important model risk source is risk mapping. When calculating the Value-at-Risk for a portfolio using the variance–covariance method, it is common practice to take the actual instruments and map them into a set of simpler standardized positions or instruments. This step is necessary because the covariance matrix of changes in the value of the standardized positions can be computed from the covariance matrix of changes in the basic risk factors. Typically, an option on a stock will be mapped into its delta equivalent position, which is itself related to the volatility and correlation of a given stock market index. This suffers from important drawbacks. First, the dependence of the option on other risk factors – such as interest rates – will often be omitted, because the delta equivalent position does not depend on them. Second, the computation of the delta requires a pricing model, which may differ from the general risk model. Third, the resulting mapping becomes rapidly unrealistic if the market moves, as the delta of the position changes very rapidly.

While the concept of Value-at-Risk is straightforward, its implementation is not. For the same portfolio, as evidenced by Beder (1995) or Hendricks (1996), there is a variety of models that will produce very different estimates of risk. Surprisingly, for the same model, there are also a large number of implementations that produce also very different estimates of risk. For instance, Marshal and Siegel (1997) assess the variance in Value-at-Risk estimates produced by different implementations[9] of the RiskMetrics™ parametric model. For a linear portfolio, the Value-at-Risk estimates range from US$2.9 million to US$5.4 million around a mean of US$4.2 million. For a portfolio with options, they obtain a range from US$0.75 to US$2.1 million around a mean of US$1.1 million. With the increasing optionality and complexity of the new products, the divergence of answers produced by the various models should increase in the future.

What should be the properties of a 'good' model?

Several approaches to the model-building process have been reviewed in the previous section. This brief survey is, by necessity, far from complete. However, a general comment should have emerged from the presentation: in each step, we have reached very quickly the limits of traditional modeling. Most financial models built using such a framework are primarily motivated by their mathematical tractability or by their statistical fit rather than by their ability to describe the data. Many choices are made in the places where the trade-off between the reduction in mathematical complexity and the losses in generality appears to be favourable. One should always remember that the first goal of a model should not be to improve its statistical fit, but to provide a reasonable approximation of reality. Therefore, it is important to think more carefully about the actual physical or behavioural relationships connecting a given model to reality.

What should be the properties of an ideal model? First, it should be theoretically consistent, both internally and with the widely accepted theories in the field. Unless it is a path-finder, a model that contradicts every existing model in its field should be considered suspect and must prove its superiority. An ideal model should also be flexible, simple, realistic, and well specified, in the sense that its inputs should be observable and easily estimable, and should afford a direct economic or financial interpretation. It should provide a good fit of the existing market data (if any), but not necessarily an exact one. One should not forget that liquidity effects, tax effects, bid–ask spreads and other market imperfections can often lead to 'errors' in the quotations.[10] Arbitrageurs exploit these errors, and including them in a perfectly fitted model would result in a model with built-in arbitrage opportunities! Finally, it should allow for an efficient and tractable pricing and hedging of financial instruments. Of course, analytical methods are preferred, but numerical algorithms are also acceptable if they do not lead to a computational burden.

Unfortunately, in practice, all these conditions are rarely met, and a trade-off has to be made (see Figure 14.1). If we take the example of fixed-income derivatives, single-factor time-invariant models do not fit the term structure well, do not explain some humped yield curves, do not allow for particular volatility structures and

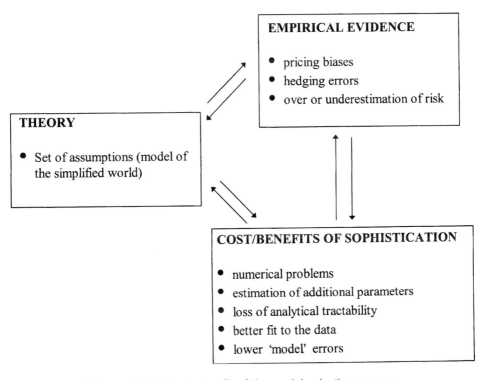

Figure 14.1 The trade-offs of the model-selection process.

cannot match at the same time cap and swaption prices.[11] But they provide simple analytical solutions for bonds and bond options pricing and hedging. In fact, the answer to model choice will depend on the specific use of the model. For interest rates, the important questions are: What is the main goal of the model? How many factors do we really need? Which factors? Is the model incremental complexity justified in light of their pricing and risk management effectiveness?

Very often, the best model will also vary across time. An interesting study related to this is Hegi and Mujynya (1996). The authors attempted to select the 'best' model to explain the behaviour of the one-month Euro–Swiss franc rate across a range of popular one-factor models. The set of potential candidates included the Merton (1973), Vasicek (1977), Cox, Ingersoll and Ross (1985) square root process, the Dothan (1978) the geometric Brownian motion, the Brennan and Schwartz (1980), Cox, Ingersoll and Ross (1980) variable rate, and the Cox (1975) constant elasticity of variance. The parameters were estimated each month from weekly data on a moving period of five or ten years. The results (see Figure 14.2) clearly show the supremacy of the Vasicek (1977) and constant elasticity of variance models. But they also evidence that the best model depends crucially on the time period considered and on the length of the historical data used for estimation. Clearly, historical data can include unique episodes that may not repeat in the future.

Consequences of model risk

What are the major consequences of model risk? As an illustration, we will examine the situation for three fields of application for financial models: pricing, hedging, and calculating risk capital charge.

Pricing

For listed and standardized products, the first visible consequence of model risk is a price discrepancy: theoretical prices diverge from effectively quoted prices. Such behaviour is rapidly detected for standard liquid instruments, but not for over-the-counter or structured products, since similar assets are generally not available on the market. Sometimes, for a particular product, the firm's trading desk itself is even 'the' market!

Despite a bewildering large set of models, relatively little work has been done to examine how these models compare in terms of their ability to capture the behaviour of the true world. Because of a lack of a common framework, most studies have focused on testing a specific model rather than on a comparison across models. Noticeable exceptions are the studies of Bates (1995), Bakshi, Cao, and Chen (1997) and Buhler *et al.* (1998), where prices resulting from the application of different models and different input parameters estimations are compared to quoted market prices in order to determine which model is the 'best' in terms of market price calibration.

It is worth noting that the pricing bias is not necessarily captured by the price, but by an alternative parameter such as the implied volatility. For instance, it is now well documented by various academics and practitioners that using the Black and Scholes model to price options results in several biases:

- A bias related to the degree of moneyness of the option. This moneyness bias is

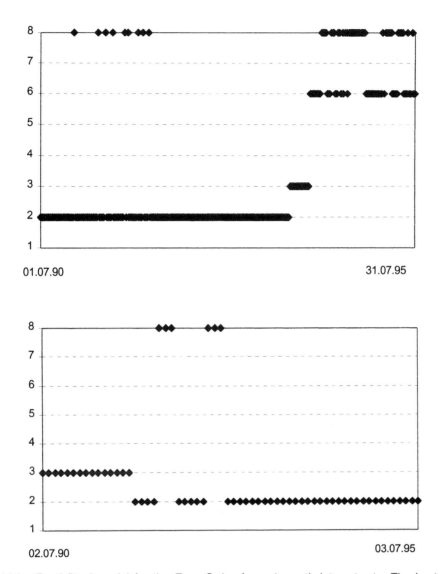

Figure 14.2 'Best' fitted model for the Euro–Swiss franc 1-month interest rate. The best model is estimated every month from weekly data on a moving window of five (top) or ten (bottom) years. The competing models are the following: 1: Merton, 2: Vasicek, 3: CIR_SR, 4: Dothan, 5: GBM, 6: Brennan and Schwartz, 7: CIR_VR, 8: Constant elasticity of variance. This figure is reproduced by courtesy of Hegi and Mujynya (1996).

often referred to as the 'smile', the 'smirk' or the 'skew', depending on its shape. Typically, since the October 1987 crash, out-of-the-money puts trade at a higher implied volatility than out-of-the-money calls. For options on dollar prices of major currencies, the most common pattern is a smile, with an implied volatility at-the-money lower than the implied volatility in- or out-of-the-money.
- A 'volatility term structure' effect, that is, biases related to the time to expiration of the options of at-the-money options. Generally, for currency options, one can observe a lower implied volatility for at-the-money short-maturity options. These variations are small, but they are nevertheless a recurring phenomenon.

- A 'volatility' bias, where typically the Black and Scholes model over-estimates options on stocks with high historic volatility and under-estimates options on stocks with low historic volatility.

These volatility smiles and other patterns are often attributed to departure from normality in the logarithm of the price of the underlying asset or to market frictions. To 'live with the smile', most practitioners have adopted a rather pragmatic approach and use an 'implied volatility matrix' or an 'implied volatility surface'. Depending on the time to maturity and the moneyness of the option, the volatility level is different. This contradicts one of the fundamental assumptions of the model, namely, the constant level of the volatility. It is nothing else than a rule of thumb to cope with an inadequate model.

Hedging

It is amusing to note that the academic literature essentially focuses on pricing models, while what most practitioners need are effective hedging models. Many people see model risk as the risk that a theoretical value produced by a model differs from the value obtained in the market. But model risk is the potential loss that can arise from the use of a particular model, and hedging is also a field that relies heavily on mathematical models.

For hedging contingent claims, accurate forecasts of the volatility and correlation parameters are the key issues. Such estimates are generally obtained by statistical analysis of historical data or the use of implied volatility. In any case, the result is an estimate or a confidence interval for the required parameter, and not its precise value. The sampling variations of parameter estimates will induce sampling variation in the estimated contingent-claims about their true values, and therefore, about the hedging parameters. When there is uncertainty in the parameters, a model must be viewed as a prediction model. **Given the parameter's estimates**, it provides an answer.

Indeed, the effects of engaging in a hedging strategy using an incorrect value of the volatility can be severe. As a simple example, the scatterplot of Figure 14.3 illustrates what happens when a trader sells an at-the-money one-year call option on a stock and engages in a daily hedging strategy to cover his position. The realized volatility is 20%, while the hedger uses 10% in his own model. Each point corresponds to one path out of the 1000 Monte Carlo simulations. It is very clear that the result of a hedging strategy is a loss, whatever the terminal price of the stock.

Therefore, it may be tempting to resume the model risk in hedging to two numbers, namely, the vega of the position and the expected volatility. For an option, we would say, for instance, that the risk is larger for the short-term at-the-money option, where the impact of volatility is very high. One has to remember that calculating the vega of an option requires a pricing model, and that the calculation of volatility requires another model – that is, two potential sources of model risk.

Very often, model risk is only examined in pricing, and hedging is considered as a direct application of the pricing model. This is not necessarily true. Some decisions may not affect pricing, but will have an impact on hedging. For instance, what matters in the Black and Scholes model is in fact the 'cumulative variance'. If we carefully examine the pricing equation, we can see that everywhere it appears, the variance (σ^2) is multiplied by the time to maturity $(T-t)$. Therefore, as evidenced by Merton (1973), if the volatility is not constant, but is a deterministic function of time $(\sigma = \sigma(t))$, we can still use the Black and Scholes formula to price a European option.

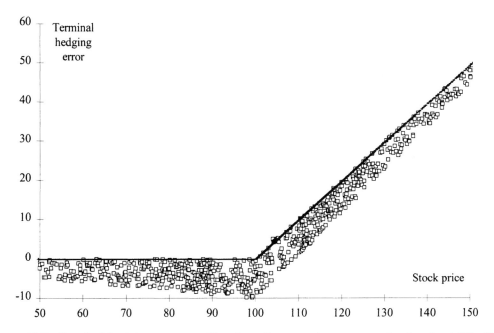

Figure 14.3 Terminal hedging error resulting from the use of a wrong estimate of volatility (10% versus 20%) to hedge a short at-the-money one-year call position.

We just have to replace the volatility parameter (σ) by its average ($\bar{\sigma}$) over the remaining life of the option (see Figure 14.4). A similar argument holds for the interest rate level parameter. Replacing the variance or the interest rate level by its average over the remaining life of the option does not affect the option value. But it impacts substantially the hedge ratios when the option position is rebalanced periodically. There will be no model risk in pricing, but an important model risk for hedging.

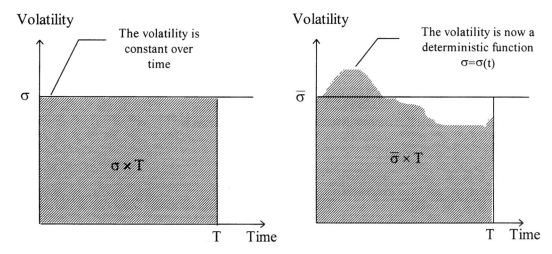

Figure 14.4 Replacing the deterministic volatility $\sigma(t)$ by the average volatility $\bar{\sigma}$ in the Black and Scholes (1973) equation.

Capital charge determination

One of the most important developments in financial risk management over the last few years has been the development of the risk capital measurement such as Bankers Trust's Capital-at-Risk (CaR) or J.P. Morgan's Value-at-Risk (VaR) and daily earnings at risk (DEaR). The calculation of risk capital is essential for financial institutions for consistent risk comparability across diverse positions, for the determinants of capital adequacy, and for the performance measurement and evaluation of business units or strategies on a risk-adjusted basis. It is now regarded as 'best practice' for market risk measurement by financial institutions. However, one should remember that Value-at-Risk is only a useful quick and dirty snapshot risk measure. Believing that it is possible to collapse the multiple dimensions of financial risk into one single number (or even just a few) is itself an example of model risk.

First, there is a large set of basic approaches to measure the VaR, such as historical simulation, delta-normal (also called analytic or variance–covariance, later extended to delta–gamma for non-linear instruments), and Monte Carlo. All these methods were extended for trade-offs between speed of computation and accuracy. They all assume liquid markets and constant portfolios over a given holding period. They involve statistical assumptions, approximations, estimates, and are subject to a strong implementation risk from a software point of view. As evidenced by Mahoney (1995) and Hendricks (1996), the results of different methods for computing Value-at-Risk can differ in a dramatic way, even if they use the same methodology and rely on the same dataset! However, this should not reduce the value of the information they provide.

Second, from an ideal point of view, the Holy Grail for any bank or financial institution is to have a single model covering all its assets and liabilities across the world. In practice, the goal of such a universal model is rarely achieved. Each business, each country, each trading desk has a local model that fits its needs and makes very simplified assumptions for (apparently) secondary issues. For instance, an equity derivative trader may use a sophisticated multi-factor equity model, while a bond trader will rather focus on a multi-factor yield curve model. Both models will perform well in their respective tasks, but as we move across businesses, for instance to assess the Value-at-Risk of the entire firm, these models have to be integrated. When a set of disparate and inconsistent models is used conjointly, the result is generally inconsistent. Therefore, analysing model risk is crucial, whatever market risk approach is used.

Evidently, the tail behaviour of the distribution of asset returns plays a central role in estimating Value-at-Risk. Mathematically, the problem is complicated. First, it is very difficult to estimate the tail of a distribution from (by definition) a limited number of points. Second, violations of statistical assumptions may not impact the average behaviour of a model, but will result in non-robust results in extreme conditions. And the use of the law of large numbers and the central limit theorem to justify normality are generally dangerously deceptive, as they result in an under-estimation of the Value-at-Risk on moving further into the tails.

In addition, existing capital risk models are subject to important critiques. Local approximations (such as Taylor series extensions and truncations) and the use of local sensitivity measures (such as the greeks) make most models inconsistent with large market events. Reliance on pricing models and distribution assumptions[12] is heavy. The parameters' stability over time is a crucial assumption. However, all these models provide very valuable information in spite of their limitations. Many of their adverse trade-offs can be mitigated through the design of adequate risk management procedures.

Within certain limits, banks are now allowed to build their own Value-at-Risk models to complement other existing models, such as the regulator's building-block approach, the covariance method with a normal portfolio, the delta-normal method, the delta–gamma methods, or simulation-based models. An increasing challenge for risk managers is to protect their institution's capital against the realities of marking to model versus marking to market. Although institutions begin with the same generic definition, the calculation methods and results differ widely.

Facing the increasing complexity of products and the diversity of models, regulators themselves have adopted a very pragmatic approach. Banks may calculate their ten-days-ahead Value-at-Risk using their own internal models. To ensure that banks use adequate internal models, regulators have introduced the idea of exceptions, backtesting and multipliers. An exception occurs when the effective loss exceeds the model calculated Value-at-Risk. The market risk capital charge is computed using the bank's own estimate of the Value-at-Risk, times a multiplier that depends on the number of exceptions over the last 250 days. As noted by the Basel Committee on Banking Supervision (1996), the multiplier varies between 3 and 4, depending on the magnitude and the number of exceptions (which must remain below a threshold; otherwise, the bank's model is declared inaccurate).

Whatever these penalties or Value-at-Risk adjustments, they result generally in an over-estimation of the capital charge and are nothing else than simple *ad-hoc* safety procedures to account for the impact of model risk. A bank might use an inadequate or inappropriate model, but the resulting impact will be mitigated by adjusting the capital charge.

Model risk management

Model risk management can be divided into two steps: first, the detection of model risk; second, its control, quantification and effective management.

How can you detect model risk?

Unfortunately, we have to admit that there is no unique method to detect model risk. The essential problem is that the model-building process is a multi-step procedure, whereas model risk is generally assessed at the end of the chain. The result is an amalgamation of conceptually distinct discrepancy terms. All successive errors in the model-building process are aggregated into a single real-valued variable, typically the average difference between some empirically observed value (for instance, an option price) and the result of the model. This makes it difficult to detect which aspects of the model, if any, are seriously misspecified.

However, some signals should be carefully monitored, as they are good early indicators of model risk. For instance, a model with a poor performance out of the sample while its performance was excellent in the sample, or time-varying parameters that vary too much should arise suspicion. Using all the degrees of freedom in a model to fit the data often results in an over-parametrization. If we need, say, two degrees of freedom and we have three or more available, we can simply use the third degree to capture the model errors as a time-varying component.

It is now widely known that models with time-varying parameters have an excellent in-sample performance, particularly for pricing and hedging purposes. But all the model risk is concentrated into the time-varying parameters. This is particularly true if the parameter is not observable, such as a mean-reversion for interest rate, a risk-aversion parameter for a given investor, or a risk premium or a given source of risk. In a sense, these models are built specifically to fit an arbitrary exogenous set of data.

How can you manage and control model risk?

Managing and controlling model risk is a difficult task, which should be performed on a case-by-case basis. Therefore, the following should not be considered as a set of recipes, but rather as the beginning of a checklist for model risk management and control. Surprisingly, we have to say that the process depends crucially on the personal judgement and experience of the model builder.

Define clearly your 'model risk' metric and a benchmark

The first step to assess model risk is the definition of a complete model risk metric. What are the criteria used to qualify a model as 'good' or 'bad'? Which goal should a model pursue? The answer can vary widely across applications. For pricing purposes, one might consider minimizing the difference between the results of a model and market prices or a given benchmark. The latter is not always possible: for instance, for stock options, the Black and Scholes (1973) model appears to be relatively robust and is widely accepted as a benchmark, while for interest rate options, there are many different models of the term structure of interest rates, but little agreement on any natural benchmark. For hedging purposes, one may want to minimize the terminal profit and loss of a hedged position, its average daily variation or its volatility. But others will also focus only on the maximum possible loss, on the drawdown or on the probability of losing money. And for regulatory capital, some institutions will prefer minimizing the required capital, while others will prefer to be safe and reduce the number or probability of exceptions.

Whenever possible, prefer simple models

The power of any model – at least in finance – is directly proportional to its simplicity. Obscurity is the first sign of something being amiss, and a lack of clarity at least invites scepticism. Remember that more sophisticated models are not necessarily better than simpler ones. A simple model may be perfectly adequate for a specific job. Someone driving from, say, Paris to Monte Carlo will not be delayed much if he ignores the earth's curvature. The conclusion might be different for a plane or a satellite. It is the same in the risk management industry. There is a fundamental difference between being approximately right and precisely wrong.

Check your data accuracy and integrity

The qualities of a model's results depend heavily on the quality of the data feed. Garbage in, garbage out (GIGO) is the law in risk management. Therefore, all data inputs to a model should always be checked and validated carefully. Typically, should you use a bid, an ask, or a mid-price? To discount, should you build a zero-coupon curve, a swap curve, or a government bond curve? The difference can be quite substantial on illiquid securities, and can impact all the subsequent computations.

Data sources should also be reduced to a minimum. For instance, on a liquid market such as US Treasuries, the end of the day pricing can differ by up to 5 basis points across sources. Added to a little leverage, this can result in a 2% valuation error for a simple 10-year position. Another important problem is data synchronicity, particularly if you are dealing with multiple currency or different time zone portfolios. Where should you get the US dollar–Swiss franc exchange rate? In New York or in Zurich at the close? Using non-simultaneous price input can lead to wrong pricing, or create artificial arbitrage opportunities.

Know your model

Users should always understand the ideas behind a model. Treating a model as a black box is definitely a wrong approach. Devices that mysteriously come out with an answer are potential sources of model risk. Generally, the persons that have built the black box are no longer in contact with it, which makes things even worse.

Of course, many senior managers do not understand sophisticated mathematical models. But the key is not there. The key is to understand the risks associated with a model and its limits. Essential questions are: 'Are you comfortable with the model results? Which variables have a high likelihood of change? Where and why does a small change in a variable cause a large variation in the results? What is the model's acceptance in the marketplace?'

Use a model for what it is made

Most models were initially created for one specific purpose. Things start breaking down when a model is used outside its range of usefulness. Applying an existing model to a new field, a new product, or a new market should not be considered as a straightforward operation, but must be performed as cautiously as the development of a new model from scratch.

Many model risk issues happen when dealers extend an existing business or enter a new one. They also attempt to recycle the models and tools with which they are familiar. Unfortunately, a model can be good in one area and bad in another. As an example, compare a pricing model versus a Value-at-Risk model. Pricing errors are not translated in the Value-at-Risk estimates, since these focus only on price variations and not on price levels. Therefore, a good model for Value-at-Risk will not necessarily be a good pricing model!

Revise and update the model regularly

Outdated models can also originate model risk. Once implemented and accepted, a model should not be considered as a finished manufactured good, but should be revised and updated on a regular basis. Would you buy risk management software if the vendor does not update it regularly? So why not do this as well with your models? A related issue is the update of input parameters: the environment is changing. Therefore, the input parameters should be revised and updated as frequently as necessary.

Here again, a good signal is the acceptance of a model in the marketplace. If the majority of the market uses similar data inputs and assumptions for comparable activities, this is a good signal that the model is still up to date.

Stress test the model

Before using a model, one should perform a set of scenario analysis to investigate the effect of extreme market conditions on a case-by-case analysis. The G30 states that dealers 'regularly perform simulations to determine how their portfolio would perform under stress conditions'. Stress tests should 'measure the impact of market conditions, however improbable, that might cause market gaps, volatility swings, or disruption of major relationships, or might reduce liquidity in the face of unfavourable market linkages, concentrated market making, or credit exhaustion'.

Scenario analysis is appealing for its simplicity and wide applicability. Its major drawback is the strong dependence on the ability to select the appropriate extreme scenarios. These are often based on historical events (Gulf War, 1987 crash, European currency crisis, Mexican peso devaluation, Russian default, etc.) during an arbitrarily chosen time period. Unfortunately, on the one hand, history may not repeat itself in the future; on the other, for complex derivatives, extreme scenarios may be difficult to identify.[13] Of course, increasing the number of scenarios to capture more possible market conditions is always a solution, but at the expense of computational time.

In addition, stress testing should not only focus on extreme market events. It should also test the impact of violations of the model hypothesis, and how sensitive are the model's answers to its assumptions. What happens if prices jump, correlations behave differently, or liquidity evaporates? Model stress testing is as important as market stress testing. If the effects are unacceptable, the model needs to be revised.

Unfortunately, the danger is that one does not really suspect a model until something dramatic happens. Furthermore, there is no standard way of carrying out stress model risk testing, and no standard set of scenarios to be considered. Rather, the process depends crucially on the qualitative judgement and experience of the model builder.

Use non-parametric techniques to validate the model

A statistician once said that parametric statistics finds exact solutions to 'approximate problems', while non-parametric statistics finds approximate solutions to 'exact problems'. Non-parametric tests make very few assumptions, and are generally much more powerful and easier to understand than parametric tests. In addition, non-parametric statistics often involve less computational work and are easier to apply than other statistical techniques. Therefore, they should be used whenever possible to validate or invalidate the parametric assumptions.

Their results may sometimes be surprising. For instance, Ait-Sahalia (1996a,b) estimates the diffusion coefficient of the US short-term interest rate non-parametrically by comparing the marginal density implied by a set of models with the one implied by the data, given a linear specification for the drift. His conclusions are that the fit is extremely poor. Indeed, the non-parametric tests reject 'every parametric model of the spot rate previously proposed in the literature', that is, all linear-drift short-term interest rate models!

Whenever possible, mark to market

Marking to market is the process of regularly evaluating a portfolio on the basis of its prevailing market price or liquidation value. Even if you use hedge accounting, a person separate from the dealer using quotes from multiple dealers should perform it on a regular basis, and immediately report increasing divergences between market and theoretical results. Unfortunately, mark to market is often transformed in mark to model, since illiquid or complex assets are only priced accordingly to proprietary in-house models.

When mark to market is impossible (typically when the trading room is the unique or leading market for an instrument), one should identify the sources of the majority of risk and reserve a cushion between the mark to model value and those of other models.

Aggregate carefully

A financial institution may use different models for different purposes. Analytical tractability, ease of understanding, and simplicity in monitoring transactions can favour the use of distinct models for separate tasks. However, mixing or aggregating the results of different models is risky. For instance, with respect to market prices, an asset might appear as overvalued using one model and undervalued using an alternative one. In such a case, the two arbitrage opportunities are just model-induced illusions.

The problem of model risk in the aggregation process is crucial for derivatives, which are often decomposed into a set of simpler building blocks for pricing or hedging purposes. The pieces together may not behave as the combined whole, as was shown by some recent losses in the interest rates derivatives and the mortgage back securities sectors.

Be aware of operational risk consequences

One should also be aware of possible operational risk consequences on model risk. Several banks use very sophisticated market or credit risk models, but they do not protect their systems from an incorrect data input for some 'unobservable' parameters, such as volatility or correlation. For instance, in the NatWest case, the major problem was that the bank was using a single volatility number for all GBP/DEM options, whatever the exercise price and maturity. This wiped off the smile effect, which was very important for out-of-the-money deals.

The problem can also happen with multiple yield curve products. In 1970s, Merrill Lynch had to book a US$70 million loss because it underpriced the interest component and overpriced the principal component of a 30-year strip issue.[14] The problem was simply that the par-yield curve used to price the components was different from the annuity and the zero yield curves.

Many model risk problems also occur in the calibration of the model in use. This is particularly true for interest rate derivatives, where complex models fail to capture deeply out-of-the money behaviour.

To reduce the impact of operational matters on model risk, and particularly the problem of inaccurate data, it is essential to implement as much as possible a central automatic capture of data, with a regular data validation by mid-office, in agreement with traders and dealers.

Identify responsibilities and set key controls for model risk

Of course, a strong and independent risk oversight group is the first step towards fighting model risk. Given the range of models, assumptions and data used in any bank, such a group has a substantial role to play. But risk managers often lack the time and resources to effectively accomplish a comprehensive and extensive model review, audit and test. It is therefore extremely important to define relevant roles and responsibilities, and to establish a written policy on model adoption and use. The policy should typically define who is able to implement, test, and validate a model, and who is in charge of keeping careful track of all the models that are used, knowing who uses them, what they are used for, who has written the mathematics and/or the code, who is allowed to modify them, and who will be impacted by a change. It should also set rules to ensure that any change is verified and implemented on a consistent basis across all appropriate existing models within the institution. Without this, installing new software or performing a software upgrade may have dramatic consequences on the firm's capital market activities.

A new trend: uncertain parameter models

Finally, we will say a few words on a new trend that has been recently introduced in academic research that could help in assessing model risk for a given position: the uncertain volatility models. Work in the area was pioneered by Avellaneda, Levy, and Paras (1995) for stocks and by Lhabitant, Martini, and Reghai (1998) for interest rate contingent claims.

The new idea here is to build pricing and hedging models that work regardless of the true world's underlying model. As an example, should we consider the volatility as constant, deterministic, or stochastic? This is difficult to answer, since the volatility itself is a non-observable quantity! Rather than using a specific and probably misspecified model, the uncertain volatility models take a very pragmatic view: if you are able to bound the volatility between two arbitrary values, they will provide you with valid prices and hedging parameters, whatever the underlying model. Rather than specifying the behaviour of the volatility, you just specify a confidence interval for its value. The volatility may evolve freely between these two bounds[15]. The resulting pricing and hedging models are therefore much more robust than the traditional ones, as they do not assume any particular stochastic process or require going through an estimation procedure.

Conclusions

The application of mathematics to important problems related to financial derivatives and risk management has expanded rapidly over the past few years. The increasing complexity of the financial products coupled with the vast quantity of available financial data explains why both practitioners and academics have found that the language of mathematics is extremely powerful in modeling the returns and risks in the application of risk management techniques. The result from this global trend is a profusion of highly technical mathematical models, rather confusing for the financial community. Which model to adopt? The past decade is full of examples where undue reliance on inadequate models led to losses. The collapse of Long Term Capital Management, which relied heavily on mathematical models for its investment strategy, has raised some important concerns among model users. The mathematics in a model may be precise, but they are useless if the model itself is inadequate or wrong. Over-reliance on the security of mathematical models is simply an invitation for traders to build up large and directional positions!

The most dangerous risks are where we do not even think about them. And they tend to be there when we least expect them. Model risk is one of those. Furthermore, it now appears to be present everywhere, and that we have to live with it. Virtually all market participants are exposed to model risk and must learn to deal with it. Regulators are also aware of it. Proposition 6 of the Basel Committee Proposal (1997) is directly in line: 'It is essential that banks have interest rate risk measurement systems that capture all material sources of interest rate risk and that assess the effect of interest rates changes in ways which are consistent with the scope of their activities. The assumptions underlying the system should be clearly understood by risk managers and bank management.' Similar recommendations apply to any other market.

However, uncertainty about the appropriate model should not necessarily reduce the willingness of financial institutions to take risk. It should simply add one star in the galaxy of risks because this risk is only an additional one, which can be priced, hedged, and managed.

Author's note

The content of this chapter is the personal opinion of the author and does not necessarily represent the views or practice of any of the firms or organizations to which he belongs. Any comment is welcome. Contact: lhabitant@attglobal.net

Notes

[1] Myron Scholes and Robert Merton were awarded the Nobel Prize in Economics in 1997.

[2] This probabilistic approach was in fact initiated by Bachelier (1900) in his doctoral thesis, where he used the Brownian motion (i.e. normally distributed stock prices) as a model for price fluctuations on the Paris stock market.

[3] A diffusion process is characterized by smooth variations as opposed to jumps. Jump-diffusion processes allow for a mix of both.

[4] A stochastic process is Markovian if it has the property that knowledge about past behaviour does not increase the probabilistic knowledge about behaviour at some time in the future. For instance, given a current stock price, knowledge about yesterday's closing price will not give any additional information regarding tomorrow's price.

[5] The fat tails phenomenon (also called excess kurtosis) occurs when some extreme events have a higher probability in the empirical distribution than in the theoretical one.

[6] See Gibson *et al.* (1998) for a comprehensive survey of existing interest rate models.

[7] The maximum likelihood (ML) deals with the probability of moving from one value to another. The parameters are calibrated on a path to ensure that this path is the most probable one. The general method of moments (GMM) relies upon finding different functions (called 'moments') which should be zero if the model is valid. Then it attempts to set them to zero to find correct values of model parameters. The Kahlman filter is an algorithm to update sequentially the information on parameters for dynamic systems.

[8] The reason is that in jump diffusion models, the log-return is equivalent to an infinite mixture of normally distributed variables, and the likelihood function is unbounded. See Honoré (1998) for a discussion.

[9] The models tested were Algorithmic, Brady, C-ATS Software, Dow Jones/Telerate, Financial Engineering Associates, Infinity, Price Waterhouse, Renaissance, Softek, True Risk and Wall Street Systems.

[10] Following a classification recently introduced by Jacquier and Jarrow (1995), we have only in mind 'model errors' (no model can perfectly explain prices) and not 'market errors' (market mispricing). While the latter can be the source of an arbitrage strategy, model errors cannot.

[11] A cap is a portfolio of independent options, while a swaption is an option on portfolio of rates and therefore depends on the imperfect correlation between them. As single-factor models assume perfect instantaneous correlation between all rates, they can account for all the cap prices, but not for any swaption simultaneously. But two-factor models do not do much better: they can match all cap prices, plus one swaption.

[12] Commonly found principal assumptions are that market returns are normally and independently distributed, and that the distribution of returns is stationary (i.e. as one moves through time, the mean and the variance of the distribution remain constant).

[13] Sometimes stability of markets is the worst-case scenario.

[14] In a strip issue, a bond is stripped into its regular coupon annuity payment ('interest only') and principal repayment ('principal only').

[15] This interval may be the range of past historical or implied volatility, or encompass both of these. It may also be a confidence interval in the statistical sense, or the extremes of the smile.

References

Ait-Sahalia, Y. (1996a) 'Testing continuous-time models of the spot interest rate', *Review of Financial Studies*, **9,** 385–426.

Ait-Sahalia, Y. (1996b) 'Non-parametric pricing of interest rate derivative securities', *Econometrica*, **64,** 527–560.

Avellaneda, M., Levy, A. and Paras, A. (1995) 'Pricing and hedging derivative securities in markets with uncertain volatilities', *Applied Mathematical Finance*, **2,** 73–88.

Bachelier, L. (1900) 'Théorie de la spéculation', in Cootner, P. H. (ed.) (1960) *The Random Character of Stock Market Prices*, MIT Press, Cambridge, MA, pp. 17–78.

Bakshi, G., Cao, C. and Chen, Z. (1997) 'Empirical performance of alternative options pricing models', *Journal of Finance*, **52,** 2003–2049.

Bates, D. S. (1995) 'Testing option pricing models', NBER Working Paper No. 5129.

Bates, D. S. (1996a) 'Dollar jump fears, 1984–1992: distributional abnormalities implied in currency futures options', *Journal of International Money and Finance*, **15,** 65–93.

Bates, D. S. (1996b) 'Jumps and stochastic volatility: exchange rate processes implicit in PHLX Deutschemark options', *Review of Financial Studies*, **9,** 69–107.

Beder, T. S. (1995) 'VaR: seductive, but dangerous', *Financial Analysts Journal*, September–October.

Black, F. and Scholes, M. (1973) 'The pricing of options and corporate liabilities', *Journal of Political Economy*, **81,** 637–659.

Bollerslev, T. (1986) 'Generalised autoregressive conditional heteroskedasticity', *Journal of Econometrics*, **31,** 307–327.

Bossy, M., Gibson, R., Lhabitant, F. S., Pistre, N. and Talay, D. (1998) 'Model risk analysis for discount bond options', Working paper, HEC–University of Lausanne.

Brennan, M. J. and Schwartz, E. S. (1979) 'A continuous-time approach to the pricing of bonds', *Journal of Banking and Finance*, **3,** 135–155.

Buhler, W., Uhrig-Homburg, M., Walter, U. and Weber, T. (1998) 'An empirical comparison of forward and spot rate models for valuing interest rate options', *Journal of Finance*, **54,** 269–305.

Chan, K. C., Karolyi, A., Longstaff, F. and Sanders, A. (1992) 'An empirical comparison of alternative models of the short term interest rate', *Journal of Finance*, **47,** 1209–1227.

Chapman, D. A., Long, J. B. and Pearson, N. (1998) 'Using proxies for the short rate. When are three months like an instant?' Working paper, University of Texas.

Chen, L. (1996) 'Interest rate dynamics, derivatives pricing and risk management', *Lecture Notes in Economics and Mathematical Systems*, Vol. 435, Springer.

Chen, N. F., Roll, R. and Ross, S. (1986) 'Economic forces and the stock market', *Journal of Business*, **59.**

Conley, T. G., Hanson, L. P., Luttmer, E. G. J. and Scheinkman, J. A. (1997) 'Short-term interest rates as subordinated diffusions', *Review of Financial Studies*, **10,** 525–577.

Cox, J. C. (1975) 'Notes on option pricing I: constant elasticity of variance diffusions', Stanford University Working Paper.

Cox, J. C., Ingersoll, J. E. and Ross, S. A. (1985) 'A theory of the term structure of interest rates', *Econometrica*, **53,** 385–407.

Das, S. R. and Foresi, S. (1996) 'Exact solution for bond and option prices with systematic jump risk', *Review of Derivatives Research*, **1,** 7–24.

Derman, E. and Kani, I. (1994) 'Riding on the smile', *RISK*, **7,** 32–39.

Dothan, U. L. (1978) 'On the term structure of interest rates', *Journal of Financial Economics*, **6,** 59–69.

Duan, J. (1995 'The GARCH option pricing model', *Mathematical Finance*, **5,** 13–32.

Dupire, B. (1994) 'Pricing with a smile', *RISK*, **7,** 18–20.

Engle, R. (1982) 'Autoregressive Conditional Heteroskedasticity with estimates of the variance of U.K. inflation', *Econometrica*, **50,** 987–1008.

Fama, E. and French, K. (1992) 'The cross-section of expected stock returns', *Journal of Finance*, **47,** 427–465.

Gibson, R., Lhabitant, F. S., Pistre, N. and Talay, D. (1998) 'Modeling the term structure of interest rates: a survey of the literature', Working paper, HEC–University of Lausanne.

Gibson, R., Lhabitant, F. S., Pistre, N. and Talay, D. (1999) 'Model risk: an overview', to appear in *Journal of Risk.*

Hegi, S. and Mujynya, M. (1996) 'Valuation and hedging of interest rate term structure contingent claims for the Swiss market', Working Paper, HEC–University of Lausanne.

Hendricks, D. (1996) 'Evaluation of Value-at-Risk models using historical data', *Federal Reserve Bank of New York Economic Policy Review*, April.

Honoré, B. (1998) *Five essays on financial econometrics in continuous-time models*, unpublished PhD thesis, Aarhus School of Business, Denmark.

Hull, J. and White, A. (1987) 'The pricing of options on assets with stochastic volatilities', *The Journal of Finance*, **XLII,** 282–300.

Jacquier, E. and Jarrow, R. (1996) 'Model error in contingent claim models dynamic evaluation', Cirano Working Paper 96s-12.

Lhabitant, F., Martini, C. and Reghai, A. (1998) 'Volatility risk for options on a zero-coupon bond', Working paper, HEC–University of Lausanne.

Longstaff, F. and Schwartz, E. S. (1992) 'Interest rate volatility and the term structure: a two factor general equilibrium model', *Journal of Finance*, **47,** 1259–1282.

Mahoney, J. M. (1995) 'Correlation products and risk management issues', Federal Reserve Bank of New-York Economic Policy Review, October, 7–20.

Markowitz, H. M. (1952) 'Portfolio selection', *Journal of Finance*, **7,** 77–91.

Marshall, C. and Siegel, M. (1997) 'Implementing a risk measurement standard', *The Journal of Derivatives*, Spring, 91–111.

Merton, R. C. (1973) 'Theory of rational option pricing', *Bell Journal of Economics and Management Science*, **4,** 141–183.

Merton, R. C. (1976a) 'Option pricing when underlying stock returns are discontinuous', *Journal of Financial Economics*, **3,** 125–144.

Merton, R. C. (1976b) 'The impact on option pricing of specification error in the underlying stock price returns', *Journal of Finance*, **31**, 333–350.

Richard, S. (1978) 'An arbitrage model of the term structure of interest rates', *Journal of Financial Economics*, **6**, 33–57.

Ross, S. (1976) 'The arbitrage theory of capital asset pricing', *Journal of Economic Theory*, **13**, 341-360.

Rubinstein, M. (1994) 'Implied binomial trees', *Journal of Finance*, **69,** 771–818.

Schaefer, S. M. and Schwartz, E. S. (1984) 'A two factor model of the term structure: an approximate analytical solution', *Journal of Financial and Quantitative Analysis*, **19**, 413–424.

Schaefer, S. M. and Schwartz, E. S. (1987) 'Time-dependant variance and the pricing of bond options', *Journal of Finance*, **42**, 1113–1128.

Scott, L. O. (1987) 'Option pricing when the variance changes randomly: theory, estimation and an application', *Journal of Financial and Quantitative Analysis*, **22,** 419–438.

Sharpe, W. (1963) 'A simplified model of portfolio analysis', *Management Science*, **9,** 277–293.

Stanton, R. (1997) 'A non parametric model of term structure dynamics and the market price of interest rate risk", Working paper, U.C.L.A.

Stein, E. and Stein, J. E. (1991) 'Stock price distribution with stochastic volatility', *Review of Financial Studies*, **4**, 727–752.

Vasicek, O. (1977) 'An equilibrium characterization of the term structure', *Journal of Financial Economics*, **5**, 177–188.

Wiggins, J. B. (1987) 'Option values understochastic volatility. Theory and empirical estimates', *Journal of Financial Economics*, **19,** 351–372.

15

Liquidity risk

ROBERT E. FIEDLER

Notation

cob: Close of Business

$B_{\text{model}}(deal, date1, date2)$:   Balance of a model 'model' for deal 'deal' forecasted on day '*date1*' for day '*date2*'

$C_{\text{model}}(deal, date1, date2)$:   Cash flow of a model 'model' for deal '*deal*' forecasted on day '*date1*' for day '*date2*'

$\Delta B_{\text{model1,model2}}(deal, date1, date2): = B_{\text{model1}}(deal,date1,date2) - B_{\text{model2}}(deal,date1,date2)$
Balance difference between two models or reality and model, for example if *model1 = real*

Simplification:
$CF(d,k): = C_{\text{real}}(d, k,k)$ the real cash flow for deal d on the day k.

$CF_{\text{pos}}(d,k): = CF(d,k)$; if $CF(d,k) > 0$
$CF_{\text{neg}}(d,k): = CF(d,k)$; if $CF(d,k) \leqslant 0$

$CF_{\text{var}}(d,k)$:   the variable part of $CF(d,k)$
$CF_{\text{fix}}(d,k)$:   the fix part of $CF(d,k)$

rc: counterparty risk
rf: delivery failure risk
rp: prepayment risk

$CF_{\text{rc}}(d, k)$:   cash flow only out of the counterparty risk for deal d on day k
$CF_{\text{rf}}(d, k)$:   cash flow only out of the delivery failure risk for deal d on day k
$CF_{\text{rp}}(d, k)$:   cash flow only out of the prepayment risk for deal d on day k

d: deal
D: portfolio, containing deals d_i, $i = 1, \ldots, n$
d_i: single deal out of the portfolio D.

$\Sigma_i CF(d_i, k)$:   sum over all cash flows of the deals d_i on the fix day k analogues: $\Sigma_i CF_{\text{pos}}(d_i, k)$
$\Sigma_i CF_{\text{neg}}(d_i, k)$

$cumCF(d, m): = \Sigma_{i=1 \text{ to } m} F(d, i)$ cumulative cash flows: for day m, that means all cash flows before are summed up to day m.

l_k: the lowest expected value for a cash flow $CF(d, k)$ on a day k due to a given quantile α
h_k: the highest expected value for a cash flow $CF(d, k)$ on a day k due to a given quantile β

$cum\,L_i$: cumulative lowest cash flow at day i.
$cum\,H_i$: cumulative highest cash flow at day i

q: quantile
Q: chooses the quantile of a function

$^{(m)}CF(D,k)$: kth cash flow of deal D in currency m.

First approach

Introduction: different types of liquidity

The concept of liquidity is used in two quite different ways. It is used in one way to describe financial instruments and their markets. A liquid market is one made up of liquid assets; normal transactions can be easily executed – the US treasury market for on-the-run bonds is an especially good example. Liquidity is also used in the sense of the solvency of a company. A business is liquid if it can make payments from its income stream, either from the return on its assets or by borrowing the funds from the financial markets.

The liquidity risk we consider here is about this second kind of liquidity. Financial institutions are particularly at risk from a liquidity shortfall, potentially ending in insolvency, simply due to the size of their balance sheets relative to their capital. However, a financial institution with sufficient holdings of liquid assets (liquid in the sense of the first type) may well be able sell or lend such assets quickly enough to generate cash to avoid insolvency.

The management of liquidity risk is about the measurement and understanding of the liquidity position of the organization as a whole. It also involves understanding the different ways that a shortfall can arise, and what can be done about it. These ideas will be explored in more depth in the following sections.

Liquidity of financial markets and instruments

It would seem straightforward to define the concept of market liquidity and the liquidity of financial instruments.

A financial market is liquid *if the instruments in this market are liquid,* **a financial instrument is liquid** *if it can be traded at the 'market price' at all times in normal or near-normal market amounts.*

However, we shall see that this is a fairly general definition.

Consider market liquidity from the perspective of a bond trader. The yield of a bond can be considered as:

$$Y_{Bond} = Y_{Interest} + Y_{Credit} + Y_{Option} + Y_{Residual}$$

where:
$Y_{Interest}$ is the yield corresponding to a risk-free bond with the same coupon and maturity
Y_{Credit} is the credit spread
Y_{Option} is the spread reflecting the value of any imbedded optionality in the bond
$Y_{Residual}$ is everything that is left over.

$$\text{Does } Y_{Residual} = Y_{Liquidity}?$$

This definition has the disadvantage of every 'residual' definition: it is only a description of the effects a phenomenon creates in certain environment rather than describing the effect itself.[1]

Apart from this ontological drawback and the naive use of notation (there is no risk-free bond) it remains unclear if the above equations are equations in a mathematical sense, thus allowing the known algebraic operations. In any case this definition, while it may not be mathematically explicit, provides a starting point, at the very least a guide to intuition. We expect that the market liquidity of a tradable asset will be reflected in its price.

Example: Different prices of liquidity in different situations

If we have a look at the spread of a 29Y versus 30Y US Treasury Bond, we see it rising from 5 bp to 25 bp in 2 Mths (Oct.–Dec. 98). Credit and option characteristics of both bonds are the same (those spreads are zero for our bond trader). The difference between the interest components can be neglected or at least do not explain the large difference. A possible answer is that the 'relative liquidity relation' (the one we meant intuitively to capture with this approach) between both bonds can be assumed constant during this period. Nevertheless the 'spot price' of liquidity has changed dramatically during this period – quite understandably, given the general situation in the markets with highlights as emerging markets in Asia, LTCM, the MBS business of American investment banks and others.

Another naive measure for liquidity is the concept of tradability of bonds. A relatively small amount of bonds from an issue which are held for trading purposes (assuming the rest are blocked in longer-term investment portfolios) will tend towards higher liquidity premiums.

But does the liquidity premium depict the amount of 'tradable' bonds in the market? It can be observed that bonds with a high liquidity margin are traded heavily – in contrast to the theory. The explanation is that traders do not determine the 'right' price for a financial object; they try to 'determine' whether the spot price is higher or lower than a future price; buy low – sell high. The same is true for liquidity spreads. A high spread is not necessarily downsizing the amount of trades: if the spread is anticipated to be stable or even to widen, it can even spur trading. All in all we have to deal with the term *structure of liquidity spreads*. Unfortunately such a curve does not exist, the main reason being that loan and deposit markets are complementary markets from a bank's point of view and, moreover, segregated into different classes of credit risk.[2]

Liquidity of financial institutions

In the context of a FI liquidity can have different meanings. It can describe

- Funds (central bank money held with the central bank directly or with other institutions)
- The ability of the FI itself to attract such funds
- The status of the central bank account of the FI in a certain moment in the payment process (i.e. to have enough funds).

We will concentrate on the latter and refine the description by introducing the concept of solvency.

Liquidity as measure of solvency

Solvency

> Annual income twenty pounds, annual expenditure nineteen nineteen six, result happiness. Annual income twenty pounds, annual expenditure twenty pounds ought and six, result misery. (Charles Dickens, *David Copperfield*)

A financial institution is defined as being **solvent** *if it is able to meet its (payment) obligations*; consequently it is **insolvent** if it is not able to meet them. Insolvency 'in the first degree' basically means 'not having enough money' but even if the liquid assets seem to properly cover the liabilities, insolvency can stem from various technical reasons:

- *Insolvency in time* – incoming payments on central bank accounts do not arrive in time, so there is not enough coverage to initiate outgoing payments
- *Insolvency in a particular currency* – this can occur by simple FX cash mismanagement: the institution is unexpectedly long in one currency and short in another; but it could also be the result of an inability to buy the short currency, due to exchange restrictions etc.
- *Insolvency in a payment system* – even if there is enough central bank money in one payment system to cover the shortage in another payment system (in the same currency) both may not necessarily be netted.

In practice, of course, it makes a big difference if a FI is insolvent in the first degree or 'only' technically. 'Friendly' institutions will have good economic reasons to 'help out' with funds; or central banks might act as lenders of last resort and thus bring back the FI into the status of solvency. Nevertheless it is very hard to differentiate consistently between those grades of insolvency. Concentrating on the end of a payment day makes things clear: the FI is either solvent or not (by whatever means and transactions), *tertium non datur*. In such a digital system it does not make sense to distinguish between 'very' and 'just' solvent, a differentiation we want to make for grades of liquidity.

Being only 'generally liquid' could mean having the required funds available later, in another currency or another place or payment system or nostro account. In any case, they are not available where and when they are required – a third party is needed to help out.

Liquidity

In this context let us define the **liquidity** *of a FI as the probability of staying solvent.* More precisely, let $CF_+(D, k)$ and $CF_-(D, k)$ be the sum of all incoming and outgoing cash flows respectively (*inflows* and *outflows*) of one currency, in one payment system at the 'normal' end of the trading day k for a portfolio D (a positive balance at the central bank account is regarded as inflow). The FI stays *solvent* as long as

$$CF_+(D, k) + CF_-(D, k) + CF_L(D, k) > 0 \tag{15.1}$$

holds, where $CF_L(D, k)$ is the possible sum of all inflows the FI is able to initiate in the above settings in the very last payment round. We can now define

$$\text{Liquidity} = \text{Probability } (CF_+(D, k) + CF_-(D, k) + CF_L(D, k) > 0) \tag{15.2}$$

It has to be clear that this is only a quasi-mathematical definition, but it illustrates the approach we want to take. Before we clarify the above further, some additional comments are required.

P/L non-neutrality

It is intuitively clear that it is the task of every liquidity manager to minimize the risk of being insolvent for his or her institution. He achieves this by accomplishing the highest possible liquidity for his institution. So far so good, but as always there is a trade-off: liquidity is not free. Maximizing CF_+ as well as minimizing CF_- puts restrictions on the businesses that normally result in smaller profits or even losses. Ensuring CF_- does not fall below a certain threshold triggers direct costs in general.[3] As a consequence, liquidity management turns out to be the task of maximizing the liquidity of the bank under the constraint of minimizing costs.

How does insolvency occur?

In general, accounts with a central bank cannot be 'overdrawn'. The status of insolvency is finally reached if a contractual payment cannot be executed by any means because not enough central bank funds are available. In any case, insolvency might exist with a hidden or undetected status if such contractual payments are not initiated (and therefore their failure cannot be detected by the central bank) but nevertheless constitute a severe breach of terms, leaving the other institution unclear whether it was only an operational problem leading to a lack of inflow or something more problematic.

Lack of central bank money (CBM)

A temporary lack of CBM does not necessarily mean upcoming insolvency, the relation between the shortage and the capacity to attract external funds is crucial. Nevertheless is it a necessary condition to be insolvent: if the central bank account is long, there is no necessity to act immediately. Again, this does not mean the institution will be solvent in the future. We have to investigate further into the term *structure of solvency*. There are intrinsic, specific and systematic reasons to become insolvent and they are decreasingly manageable for a FI.

Intrinsic: the forward payment structure is unbalanced

Let $CF_+(D, k)$ and $CF_-(D, k)$ be the in-/outflows at a day k in the future. The cumulated sum of incoming and outgoing cash flows $cumCF(D, k)$ is defined as:

$$cumCF(D, k) := \sum_{i=1}^{k} [CF_+(d, i) + CF_-(d, i)] \tag{15.3}$$

Ex ante $cumCF(D, k)$ can be negative for a day k, but in reality the central bank account cannot be short. In order to ensure that, we make the assumption that temporary shortages $cumCF(D, j) < 0$ on a day j will be covered by an amount greater or equal to $cumCF(D, j)$, flowing back out the next business day, say $j + 1$.[4] On the other hand, long positions will be held at the central bank account and will be available next day again; then treated as symbolic inflows.

The cash flow vector $(cumCF(D, 1), cumCF(D, 2), \ldots, cumCF(D, K))$ will be called the **forward payment structure (FPS)** of the institution. A negative forward payment structure is not bad *per se*, it only bears a problem together with a weak ability to rebalance it.

Example: forward payment structure of a bond

Assume a FI buys a straight government bond. The components in time are as shown in Table 15.1.

Table 15.1 Components in time

Cash flow			Action	FPS		
$CF(\text{Bond},1)$	$=$	0	Purchase of the bond but no cash action	cum$CF(\text{Bond},1)$	$=$	0
$CF(\text{Bond},2)$	$=$	-100	Exchange of cash against security	cum$CF(\text{Bond},2)$	$=$	-100
$CF(\text{Bond},3)$	$=$	$+8$	Coupon	cum$CF(\text{Bond},3)$	$=$	-92
...						
$CF(\text{Bond},11)$	$=$	$+8$	Coupon	cum$CF(\text{Bond},11)$	$=$	-28
$CF(\text{Bond},12)$	$=$	$+100$ $+8$	Last coupon plus redemption	cum$CF(\text{Bond},12)$	$=$	$+80$

If the interest rate level at the purchase date is, say, 5% this transaction makes sense and is of overall positive impact on the FI; nevertheless the FPS bears liquidity risk.

The above-considered imbalances of the FPS are intrinsic: they are only due to the fact that they were initiated by the institution itself. No 'unexpected events' such as failure of counterparties were considered.

Specific: unexpected loss of funds caused by counterparties

A FI might have expected inflows actually not coming in (a counterparty becomes insolvent) thus causing an unexpected shortage of funds. On the other hand, unexpected outflow might be caused by the decision of counterparty to subtract funds (withdrawal of savings deposits during a run on a bank). Those factors are out of control of the FI when they happen, nevertheless there is a certain possibility of steering them in advance by selecting customers.

Systemic: the payment process is disturbed

These events are even more out of the control of the FI. Counterparties pay as scheduled but the payments simply do not get through. Reasons might be technical problems as well as the unwillingness of the central bank to fix them. The problem is truly systemic.

Insufficient counterbalancing capacity

The FI is not able to raise enough funds to balance its central bank account. There are a variety of possible reasons for that. Again they can be ordered intrinsic, specific and systematic, reflecting the decreasing ability of the FI to manage them.

Intrinsic reasons

The FI is not able to raise enough funds because:

- Too much money was raised in the past by means of unsecured borrowing (other FIs' credit lines are not large enough)
- Liquid asset are not available in the right time and place, with the appropriate legal framework.

Specific reasons

There are various reasons leading to an insufficient ability of the FI to rebalance its shortages:

- Its rating could be downgraded. If sufficient collateral is available in time the FI could switch from unsecured to secured borrowing.
- There may be rumours about its solvency. The ability to attract funds from other liquid market participants is weakened. Liquid assets that can be sold or repoed instantly could restore the confidence of the market.
- Even with undoubted standing it could be hard to raise cash: the limits other institutions hold for the FI could be utilized.

Some of those reasons are hardly under the control of the FI. Others like the building up of collateral and liquid asset holdings are at least controllable if handled *ex ante*.

Systemic reasons

The systemic reasons are contrary to the specific reasons as they are totally out of control of the FI. There could be:

- *A lack of CBM* in the system itself. This is quite unlikely, but it happened in Germany after the Herstatt crisis when the Bundesbank steered the central bank money so short that many banks were unable to hold the required minimum reserves. Nevertheless this could be categorised as well as
- *A failure* in the mutual exchange mechanism of central bank money: Although the central bank allots sufficient money into the market, some market participants hold bigger balances than they need. The reason could be an adversity to credit risk hindering their lending out of surplus funds or it could lie in the anticipation of upcoming market shortages that are forward covered.
- *A technical problem*: Payments systems fail to distribute the money properly as planned by the market participants thus leaving them with unintended positions and/or fulfilled payment obligations.

Measurement of insolvency risk

Measuring insolvency risk falls apart into three tasks:

- Evaluating the forward payment structure of the FI to gain a first forecast of the FI's exposure to a critical lack of funds,
- Assessing the correctness of this projection in order to come to an understanding of the nature and magnitude of possible departure from reality in the forecast, and finally
- Analysing the structure of assets of the FI to estimate its counterbalancing capacity.

Evaluation of the forward payment structure (FPS)

The first step is to collect all cash flows likely to arise from deals already existing. That means we have to treat only business that is on the balance sheet. Alterations of existing deals such as a partial early repayment of a loan will be treated as new business.

Existing deals

Although the business is completely described, the anticipated cash flows have different grades of certainty (we do not treat credit and operational risks here). There are:

- *Known CF*, which are known in time and amount. Example: a straight bond; we do not consider selling the bond, this would be changing business.
- *Contingent CF*, which are unknown either in time and/or amount.
  Example A: *A future rate agreement (FRA)*.
  The forward CF is dependent on the yet unknown market rates of the underlying on the fixing date – nevertheless the payment date is known.
  Example B: *A European option sold*.
  As above with the difference that the counterparty has to decide if he or she wants to execute the option (if certain market circumstances prevail).
  Example C: *An American option*.
  As above with the difference that the payment date is not known.

New deals

Up to now the FPS predicts cash flows that happen in the future if no new business arises. In order to predict the future cash flows that will actually happen we have to include new deals. Some can be forecasted with high probability (especially those initiated by ourselves), others might be harder to tackle. We differentiate between

- *Renewal of existing deals*. Example: Customers tend to renew some percentage of their term deposits. Hopefully a relation between the existing deal and the new deal can be detected.
- *Totally new deals*. This could be a new customer placing a deposit or trying to trade a new instrument as well as a new business starting.

Assessment of the quality of the FPS

Nobody would expect a FPS to be totally correct and in fact this never happens in reality. 'How correct is the FPS?' is the crucial question. The answer has to be given *ex ante*. Therefore we have to:

- Estimate errors due to shortcomings in data (incorrect/incomplete reporting) and
- Evaluate the uncertainty arising from our incorrect/incomplete assumptions (no credit and operational risk) as well as deviations stemming from unpredictable developments.

The above will lead us to a distribution of the FPS. From that we will be able to deduce expectations for the most probable FPS and upper and lower limits of the FPS.

Analysis of the liquifiability of assets

If the FPS has provided us with a good understanding of potential future liquidity gaps we then have to investigate in our ability to generate cash. The natural way is to increase our liabilities: we have to measure our ability to generate cash by means of secured or unsecured borrowing in time. On the other hand, we have to classify all assets in respect to our ability to generate cash by selling or repoing them and the speed with which this can be done.

Conclusions

The approach to characterize liquidity as the probability of being solvent is straight-forward. Nevertheless it is incomplete in two senses:

1   After having quantified a potential future lack of funds we have not clarified how large is the risk triggered by this shortage for the FI. Analysing the FI's counterbalancing capacities could give a solution: the probability that the lack exceeds the ability to raise funds can be detected. In a VaR-like approach we would try to determine the maximal forward deficit of funds in order not to exceed the existing counterbalancing capacities – within a predefined probability.

2   Once we have gathered this knowledge, we are still left with the problem of its economic impacts. One way to transform the information into a policy could be to establish limits to restrict the business, another would be to increase the counterbalancing capacity. Both approaches are costly, but more than that we have to compare actual expenses against the potential loss at least of the equity capital if the FI ends its existence by becoming insolvent.

A solution will be developed in the next section,

Re-approaching the problem

The following conceives a methodology to consistently measure, evaluate and manage liquidity risk. Although it is tailored for a bank, it can quite easily be adapted for other kinds of FIs.

Lack and excess of liquidity: symmetric approach

The idea here is to move from a *simply illiquidity orientated view* on liquidity risk to a view on both *insufficient as well as exceeding liquidity*. Both cases could lead to situations where we have to bear economic losses in respect to rates relatively to the market. We might be only able to attract funds at 'high' rates as well as only being able to place excess funds at sub-market rates.[5] Another very good reason to consider 'over-liquidity' is the fact that excess funds have to be loaned out and thus create credit risk if not collaterized.

Cash flow liquidity risk: redefinition

We regard cash inflows (i.e. paid in favour of our central bank account) as being positive and cash outflows as negative. Deals between the bank's entities that are not executed via third parties (internal deals) are treated like regular transactions. As they match out, it has to be ensured that such deals are completely reported (by both parties).

Definition:
Cash liquidity risk *is the risk of economic losses resulting from the fact the sum of all inflows and outflows of a day* t *plus the central bank account's balance* B_{t-1} *of the previous day are not equal to a certain anticipated (desired) amount.*

This definition aims at manifestations of cash liquidity risk such as:

1 Only being able to
   - Raise funds at rates higher than or
   - Place funds at rates lower than (credit ranking adjusted) market rates (*opportunity costs*)
2 Illiquidity: not being able to raise enough funds to meet contractual obligations (as a limit case of the latter, funding rates rise to infinity)
3 Having correctly anticipated a market development but ending up with a 'wrong' position.

Regardless if cash liquidity risk is manifested gradually as in 1 or absolute as in 2 – where 2 can be seen as an 'infinite limit' of 1 – the probability of the occurrence of 2 can be developed as a continuously monotonous function out of 1.

In addition to analysing our liquidity position relative to the market, we need to estimate our projected liquidity position and the degree of its uncertainty for predictable periods of market fluctuations (see Figure 15.1).

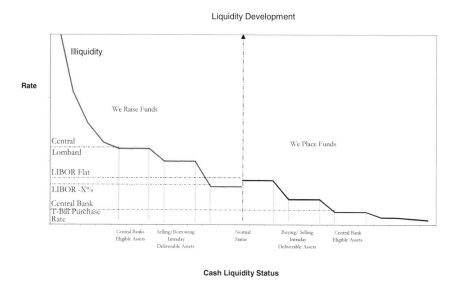

Figure 15.1 Cash liquidity status.

Simplifying the problem

In order to find a starting point, we reduce the complexity of the situation by treating the (theoretical) situation where we have to deal only with:

- One currency
- One payment system
- One legal entity
- No internal deals
- Only existing business (no new business)
- *K* days into the future

Later we will expand the problem again.

Clean/dirty cash flows

We try to formally dissect cash flows in the parts which can be analytically described (not necessarily estimated) and diverse 'distorting' risk factors.

Definition:
Let d denote a deal, and let us assume that we already know its vector $(CF(d, 1), CF(d, 2), \dots, CF(d, K))$ of cash flows. A single cash flow element

$$CF(d, k) = CF_{fix}(d, k) + CF_{var}(d, k) \qquad (15.4)$$

at a certain day k $(k \in \{1, \dots, K\})$ of a deal d may be of pure fixed $(CF_{var}(d, k) = 0)$, pure variable $(CF_{fix}(d, k) = 0)$ type, or a mixture of the two.

$CF(d, k)$ will be called *clean expected cash flow* on day k. We regard in addition:

rc: counterparty risk
rf: delivery failure risk and
rp: prepayment risk,

and refine the above definition of $CF(d, k)$ by redefining:

$$\tilde{C}F(d, k) = CF(d, k) + CF_{rc}(d, k) + CF_{rf}(d, k) + CF_{rp}(d, k) \qquad (15.5)$$

whereby

$$CF_{rc}(d, k), CF_{rf}(d, k), CF_{rp}(d, k)$$

designates cash flow functions which produces out of the risk values rc, rf, and rp a cash flow due to day k.

$\tilde{C}F(d, k)$ will be called **dirty expected cash flow** on day k.

In general $CF_{rc}(d, k), CF_{rf}(d, k)$ will be negative (for inflows), whereas $CF_{rp}(d, k)$ is positive. When does $\tilde{C}F(d, k)$ occur?

Counterparty-specific reasons:

- Default
- Hidden default
- Delivery versus payment failure
- Human errors
- System failure
- Our failure
- Delivery versus payment failure
- Human errors

For simplicity we will only treat clean cash flows and thereby omit all other risks, reflected in the dirty cash flows. Clearly, this is an over-simplification but it may be an acceptable way to gain an insight into such a complicated matter.

Probabilistic measurement of liquidity – Concepts

The following attempts to find a way to forecast the forward payment structure (FPS) practically. Moreover, we will apply *ex ante* bounds on the difference between forecast and reality by stochastically modeling the prediction.

Getting started: expansion to portfolios

Expected cash flows of a portfolio are seen as sums of the cash flows of the single deals. Looking at deals on an aggregated (portfolio) level, for the following set of deals:

$$\{d_1, \ldots, d_N\}$$

we separate for each date k the positive $CF_+(d_n, k)$ from the negative cash flow elements $CF_-(d_n, k)$ (with $n \in \{1, \ldots, N\}$). These components are now added up to the sum of all expected inflows on day k:

$$\Sigma_i CF_+(d_i, k) = CF_+(d_1, k) + \ldots + CF_+(d_N, k) \qquad (15.6)$$

as well as the sum of all expected outflows on day k:

$$\Sigma_i CF_-(d_i, k) = CF_-(d_1, k) + \ldots + CF_-(d_N, k) \qquad (15.7)$$

for that portfolio. Obviously,

$$CF_+(d_n, k) + CF_-(d_n, k) = CF(d_n, k) \qquad \forall k \in \{1, \ldots, K\}, \forall n \in \{1, \ldots, N\} \qquad (15.8)$$

Cash liquidity

When we talk about incoming and outgoing cash flows, we need a representation of the liquidity status, which can be understood intuitively. As in cumulative interest gap analysis for interest-bearing cash flows we define a liquidity maturity ladder. It will be called static as it includes only contractual data.

If we add all known outflows (negative) and inflows (positive) for a given portfolio D: $CF_+(D, k) + CF_-(D, k) = CF(D, k)$ will give the liquidity status of that day.

The contractual known cash liquidity ladder is now constructed as follows:

$$\text{NetFlow: } CF(D, k) = CF_-(D, k) + CF_+(D, k), \qquad \forall k \in \{1, \ldots, K\} \qquad (15.9)$$

$$\text{CumFlow: } cumCF(D, k) = \sum_{i=1}^{k} CF(D, i) \qquad \forall k \in \{1, \ldots, K\} \qquad (15.10)$$

CCL: contractual known cash liquidity

Contractual known cash liquidity is the anticipated FPS based on all existing business, counting deterministic cash flows only. All cash flows where amount and time of occurrence in the future are unequivocally determined by contractual specifications are taken and cumulated (still under all assumptions about non-existence of credit, operational and untimely payment risk).

That is, we collect all deterministically known cash flows and cumulate them. Contractually fixed but *ex ante* unknown (in time and/or amount) cash flows will be by definition set to zero. Clearly this is dependent on the relative amount of non-deterministic (contingent) cash flows, generally a very poor forecast. In particular the fact that cash flows known in amount but not in time are simply suppressed is unsatisfactory (see Figure 15.2):

$$\text{CCL} = \text{deterministic CF} \qquad (15.11)$$

ECL: expected cash liquidity

Expected cash liquidity is the anticipated FPS based on all existing business, including deterministic cash flows as well as stochastically estimating non-deterministic cash flows.

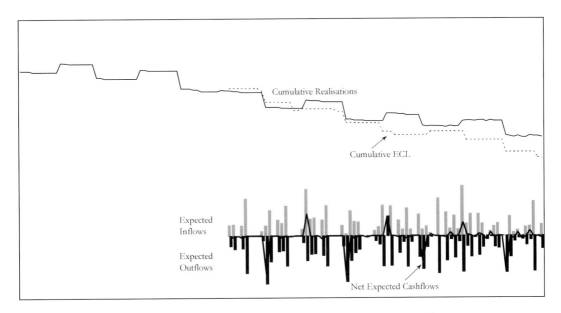

Figure 15.2 Cash flow distinction (for explanation see text).

We calculate the expected cash flows of all deals. Deterministic deals can be regarded as single-point-distributed (the vector of the expected cash flows equals the vector of the deterministic cash flows). Therefore (and by definition), the ECL cash flows contain the CCL cash flows:

$$ECL = CCL + \text{stochastic CF} \qquad (15.12)$$

ELaR: expected liquidity at risk

Expected liquidity at risk quantifies the uncertainty in ECL. ECL as a forecast for FPS will naturally differ from any realization of FPS. Unfortunately we will only be able to quantify this dispersion *ex post*. *Ex ante* we are only able to estimate the dispersion stochastically. As such, ELaR is a concept similar to that of Value-at-Risk (VaR). We produce an envelope encompassing the forward ECL. The extremes of the envelope are defined as quantiles of the underlying distribution. As the CCL part of ECL is deterministic, we only have to treat the residuum ECL − CCL in order to determine the dispersion:

$$ELaR = \text{dispersion (ECL)} = \text{dispersion (ECL − CCL)} \qquad (15.13)$$

DCL: dynamic cash liquidity

Dynamic cash liquidity – in contrast to CCL, ECL and ELaR – not only incorporates deals that are already in the portfolio but estimates new deals as well. That means DCL includes ECL (and thus CCL) and adds all 'unexpected' cash flows, be they totally new or simply alterations of already existing deals such as:

- New deals opening payments
- Regular payments of new deals
- Unexpected cancellation or alterations of existing deals

- Prepayments or variable interest payments
- Failure of a contractual payment, etc

CCL, ECL and ELaR can be treated on a single-deal basis as well as on a portfolio level. DCL can only be treated at a portfolio level, since it does not make much sense to predict new business on an individual transaction basis. This scopes beyond the basic measurement of CCL for the earliest likely return of outstanding positions and its extension to expected value of cash flows. Making a forecast for new business and combining this with ECL gives a measure of the dynamic cash liquidity (DCL) of a portfolio. That is:

$$DCL = ECL + \text{dynamic CF} \tag{15.14}$$

DyLaR: dynamic liquidity at risk

The transition from ECL to DCL leads to the same question we already had to ask ourselves after having moved from CCL to ECL: What do we know *ex ante* about the quality of our estimation? We extend our concept of ELaR to the **dynamic liquidity at risk (DyLaR)**. As with ELaR, DyLaR measures the dispersion of our anticipated DCL (see Figure 15.3).

$$DyLaR = \text{dispersion (DCL)} = \text{dispersion (DCL} - \text{CCL)} \tag{15.15}$$

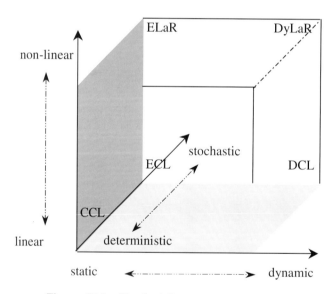

Figure 15.3 The liquidity measurement cube.

Example: FRA portfolio

Example for CCL, ECL and DCL

After introducing the terms CCL, ECL, DCL, ELaR and DyLaR, it helps to have an example, which shows what these terms mean for a given case.

Given a portfolio containing FRAs, the time point from which the forecast is being made will be *cob*. If the portfolio is considered in *cob*, a cash flow forecast for the next two days *cob* + 1 and *cob* + 2 is made. For all existing deals, within the portfolio, the cash flow is known for $cob + 1$ and $cob + 2$ since the rates have already been fixed for cob and $cob - 1$ respectively. This type of cash liquidity is therefore CCL (since amount and point in time for the cash flows are already well known at cob).

It is not possible to know exactly the cash flows of existing deals for days after day $cob + 2$. On the one hand, since the content of the portfolio is known, the point of time of these cash flows is also known. On the other hand, the amount is unknown. This then falls under the definition ECL. If the portfolio is not only a buy and hold portfolio but a dynamic one, new deals are entered and old deals are cancelled on a daily basis.

All cash liquidity figures CCL, ECL, DCL consider only the most likely cash flow for a given date. In order to consider the values which could happen with a given likelihood we look at the defined ELaR and DyLaR as an envelope around the ECL and DCL curve (Figure 15.4).

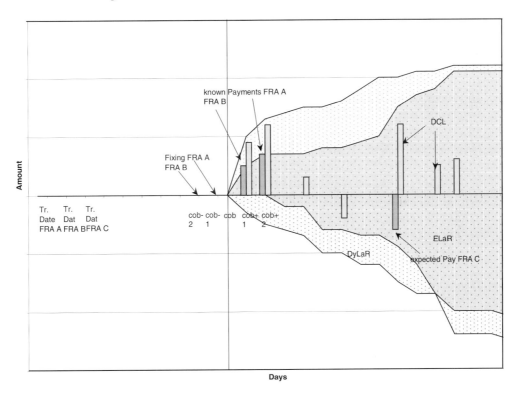

Figure 15.4 The simple FRA-portfolio.

Probabilistic measurement of liquidity – Methods

Expected cash flows: quantitative methods

After the introduction of CCL, ECL and DCL and their relationships to each other, it is necessary to give a little more substance to these definitions. The question must be: 'How do we compute expected cash liquidity'?

Currently a distinction of the models into two groups can be made:

Probabilistic models

- Monte Carlo simulation
- Term structure model

Behavioral models

- Trend model
- Periodic model
- Correlation related models
- Blend model

Monte Carlo simulation

A Monte Carlo simulation can be used in liquidity risk to simulate a variety of different scenarios for the portfolio cash flow for a target date (in the future). The basic concept of a Monte Carlo simulation is to simulate repeatedly a random process for a financial variable (e.g. interest rates, volatilities etc.) in a given value range of this variable. Using enough repetitions the result is a distribution of possible cash flows on the target date.

In order to get a simulation running it is necessary to find a particular stochastic model which describes the behavior of the cash flows of the underlying position, by using any or all of the above-mentioned financial variables.

In general the Monte Carlo approach for ECL, we suggest here, is much the same as that used in the VaR concept. Instead of the consideration of the PV, the focus is now on the cash flow simulation itself.

Having reached this point it is crucial to find a suitable stochastic model which:

- Describes the cash flow behavior of the underlying instrument
- Describes the cash flow development of new business (necessary for DCL)
- Is not using that many parameters to make computation still efficient

Based on the distribution generated by the Monte Carlo run the following becomes clear:

- The mean of the distribution is a forecast for ECL or DCL
- The tails which fulfil a given confidence level (e.g. the 99% quantile in which 99% of the upcoming cash flows are floating in, the 1% quantile respectively) define the two limits for the envelope encompassing expected future cash flows.

Using term structure models for interest rates

Another approach, which is especially relevant for commercial business, is to look for correlations of the balance to interest rates. If a significant correlation between the deposit balances and the short rate (O/N or 3M-deposit rate) exists, it is possible to build a simple regression model based on this rate. It is also feasible to build more sophisticated regression models using past balances, a time trend and changes in interest rates.

The crucial point is now the following. As soon as we have defined such a model, based on the short rate, one of the now classic term structure models for interest rates as proposed by Cox, Ingersoll and Ross or Heath, Jarrow and Morton can be used to forecast the future demand deposit behavior. One can then calculate the sensitivity of the demand deposits to bumps in the yield curve. These sensitivities can then be used to assign probabilities of duration for different levels of the demand deposits.

Behavioral model

The analysis of an existing time series for the construction of a forward projection is a means of determining the 'behavior' of the series. This is the investigation of historical data for the existence of trends, periodicity or frequencies of specific events, the correlation to other time series and the autocorrelation to itself. We can look at any portfolio of non-maturing assets and liabilities as such a series. The balance of customer sight deposits is an appropriate example, as neither payment dates nor amounts are known in advance and the correlation to existing interest rate curves is negligible.

The general tendency of the data can be used not only to interpolate between data points but also to extrapolate beyond the data sequence. Essentially, this is the construction of a projected forecast or 'behavioral model' of the series itself.

An understanding of the trends in a broad sense is an answer to 'What is the behavior of the time series?' The investigation as to 'why' it is the behavior leads to an understanding of other stochastic processes driving the evolution of the series itself and is the logical progression towards ELaR/DyLaR.

Example 'future'

No free lunch: arbitrage freedom

Considering a simple future as an example for what the ECL could be, we get the following result: Using the cash flow notation introduced above, every clean cash flow on day k can be written as: $CF(d, k) = CF_{fix}(d, k) + CF_{var}(d, k)$ with $CF_{fix}(d, k) = 0$. (We are not considering the initial margin in this example for the sake of simplicity.)

When we are looking for the ECL we try to determine the value of the $CF(d, k)$. Assuming that we are trying to make a forecast for a special day k in the future, we have in general the possibilities:

either $CF_{var}(d, k) > 0$

or $CF_{var}(d, k) = 0$

or $CF_{var}(d, k) < 0$

Assume there is no arbitrage possible in this market and $CF_{var}(d, k) > 0$. As the future price is its own forward, one could enter into this instrument at a zero price and generate a risk-free profit by simply selling it at $CF_{var}(d, k) > 0$. For the complementary reason the cash flow cannot be $CF_{var}(d, k) < 0$. That means $CF_{var}(d, k) = 0$ must be the ECL for a future cash flow (i.e. it is the most likely value of a forward 'future' cash flow).

Does this reflect 'the risk we meant'?

The reality tells us that it is of course possible to have huge positive or negative cash flows on a future margin account. So is our ECL forecast $CF(d, k) = 0$ of any use to compute the risk? Is this zero cash flow really the risk we meant?

What we are able to forecast with ECL is the most likely cash flow for this date, but it does not tell us anything about the actual risk that *can* happen with the cash flow in a worse case in both directions. Before making any statements about actual liquidity risk, it is necessary to give an estimation of the likelihood of special events; e.g. how likely is it that a cash flow will be over/under a defined amount? Or given a specified quantile, what is the biggest/smallest cash flow we can expect?

From ECL to ELaR

Expected values of cash flows, unfortunately do not always bear the anticipated amount of risk. For example, a deposit future has expected future values equal to zero assuming that we clear the margin accounts daily. This is in contrast to observations of high-margin cash flows that do occur. To look at the 'worst outflow' would simplify the situation for the lack of liquidity risk. However, at the same time, it could hide the risk of a heavy cash surplus position, which might lead to interest rate losses. These losses result from the placement of surplus liquidity at less than present market rates.

Therefore, the risk needs to be made visible in an additional instrument, which will give an indication of the nature and magnitude of the uncertainty. In a concept similar to that of VaR we can introduce **expected liquidity at risk (ELaR).** Its design is a compensation for the shortcomings of ECL as a forecast and a means to measure how the realizations scatter around this expected value.

If we look at a single cash flow $CF(d, k)$ of a deal d, realizations $C_{real}(d, k, k)$ of this cash flow will fluctuate around expected cash flows $C_{expect}(d, cob, k)$ seen from cob. We now look at the tails of a general distribution of $CF(d, k)$.

For a given **level of significance**, α and β, define l_k, h_k such that:

1 l_k is the maximum value so that the probability of a realization $C_{real}(d, k, k)$ less than l_k is α:

$$P(C_{real}(d, k, k) < l_k) = \alpha.$$

2 h_k is the minimum value so that the probability of a realization $C_{real}(d, k, k)$ higher than h_k is β.

$$P(C_{real}(d, k, k) > h_k) = \beta.$$

l_k can be regarded as the *lowest* and h_k as the *highest expected* value of $CF(d, k)$ for a given confidence level α and β. This may be written as:

$$l_k = C_{expect}(d, cob, k) - \alpha \text{quantile} P(C_{expect}(d, cob, k))$$
$$h_k = C_{expect}(d, cob, k) + \beta \text{quantile} P(C_{expect}(d, cob, k))$$

(15.16)

Consequently, the desired level of significance for α and β will have to be set by the business entities in coordination with the risk department.

Whether on an individual deal or on a portfolio basis, l_k and h_k are derived from descriptional statistics or directly deduced from the underlying statistical assumptions that the risk department has set for a certain product. The construction of the distributions is obviously the critical point of any analysis.

In fact we are interested in estimating the lowest and highest cash flows l_k and h_k of a portfolio of deals. In its present form, it is not possible to extend the use of the above quantiles α and β per individual deal to the entire portfolio of deals D directly by simply calculating and summing it for its elements $CF(d, k)$. They are not independent, nor can the dependency between the different deals be ignored. Establishing an expansion to the cumulative sum of expected cash flows (ECL) allows us to continue with the concept of ELaR. With this in mind, consider a portfolio of deals as above:

$$\{d_1, \ldots, d_N\}$$

Let L_k denote the lowest and H_k the highest expected value of $C_{\text{expected}}(D, cob, k)$.

Note: For the sake of simplicity we use $CF(D, k)$ instead of $C_{\text{expected}}(D, cob, k)$ whenever it is clear that we are considering expected cash flow predictions for day k as seen from *cob*.

The forward envelope encompassing the cumulative ECL value is obviously the sum of the lowest L_k and highest flows H_k for days $i = 1$ to k is:

$$cumL_k = \sum_{i=1}^{k} L_i \tag{15.17}$$

$$cumH_k = \sum_{i=1}^{k} H_i \tag{15.18}$$

where $L_k \leqslant CF(D, k) \leqslant H_k$ holds true. Therefore: $cumL_k \leqslant cumCF(D, k) \leqslant cumH_k$.

While increasing k, the two curves diverge considerably from the cumulative ECL. For ELaR in its pure form both $cumL_k$ and $cumH_k$ imply extreme scenarios that remain throughout the period described. Under these circumstances the preceding methodology yields a limited analysis of possible, yet very unlikely extreme situations and does not help us in describing the liquidity risk at hand.

Alternatively, one could concentrate on the possible fluctuations of the daily in- and outflows. By adding the cumulative net expected cash flows to L_k and to H_k the result should not be far from the $cumCF(D, k)$ itself. That is:

$$c\bar{u}mL_k = \sum_{i=1}^{k} CF(D, i) + L_k \tag{15.19}$$

$$c\bar{u}mH_k = \sum_{i=1}^{k} CF(D, i) + H_k \tag{15.20}$$

However, this situation presents itself in contrast to the cumulative lowest L_k and highest flows H_k (Figure 15.5) as being too conservative. Over any extended forecast period the cumulative drift of the expected cash flows away from the actual realizations could result in potentially large discrepancies and the undesired situation of the cumulative realizations lying outside the constructed envelopes for prolonged periods of time.

The options are to use an appropriate scaling-down factor for our approximations of $cumL_k / cumH_k$ (equations (15.17) and (15.18)), a scaling-up factor for equations (15.19) and (15.20) or to develop an independent approach which lies between the two extremes. The scaling factors may be a choice of a lower level of confidence in α and β or a statistically based shift of the envelopes.

Having defined the extremes, an attempt to approach an appropriately conservative but equally meaningful estimate could be along the following lines. Adding the cumulative expected outflows to L_k and the cumulative expected inflows to H_k would

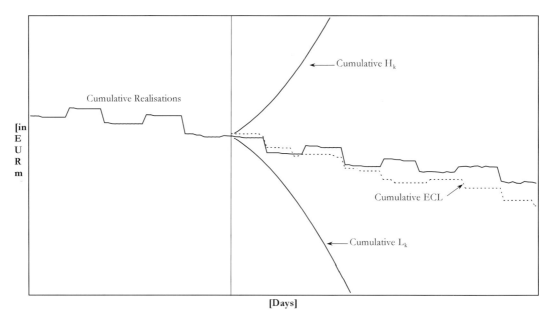

Figure 15.5 Cumulative H_k and L_k.

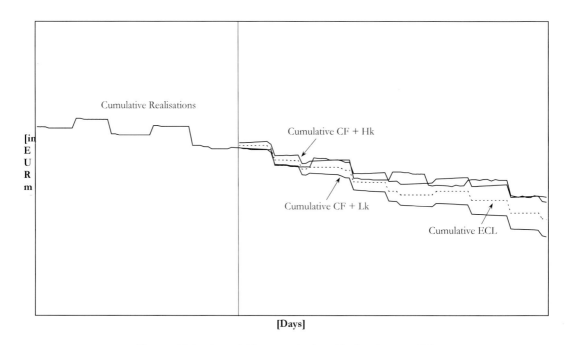

Figure 15.6 L_k and H_k respectively added to the *cumCF*.

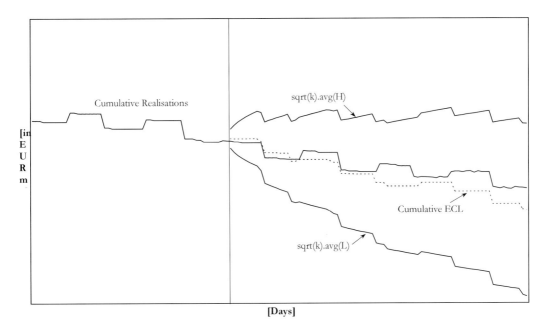

Figure 15.7 sqrt(day) times average of the L_k and H_k.

lie between the previously constructed ELaR envelope (Figure 15.7). That is:

$$c\tilde{u}mL_k = \sum_{i=1}^{k} CF_-(D, i) + L_k \qquad (15.21)$$

$$c\tilde{u}mH_k = \sum_{i=1}^{k} CF_+(D, i) + H_k \qquad (15.22)$$

where $L_k \leqslant CF_-(D, k) \leqslant CF_+(D, k) \leqslant H_k$. Therefore: $cumL_k \leqslant cumCF_-(D, k) \leqslant cumCF(D, k) \leqslant cumCF_+(D, k) \leqslant cumH_k$.

Alternatively, in a similar approach to that adopted by VaR, L_k and H_k increasing as a function of days k in the future may be considered:

$$c\tilde{\tilde{u}}mL_k = \sqrt{k} \cdot avg_{i=1}^{K} L_i + \sum_{i=1}^{k} CF(D, i) \qquad (15.23)$$

$$c\tilde{\tilde{u}}mH_k = \sqrt{k} \cdot avg_{i=1}^{K} H_i + \sum_{i=1}^{k} CF(D, i) \qquad (15.24)$$

The resulting envelope then tends to lie outside the cumulative expected cash flows added L_k and H_k (15.19) and (15.20) and within the cumulative values of L_k and H_k (15.17) and (15.18).

Behavioral ELaR

If at this point we return to the basics of what ELaR is trying to achieve we come to a fourth possibility for the construction of a meaningful distribution. Fundamentally, ELaR has been designed to compensate for the discrepancies of ECL as a forecast of the future realizations. This clearly gives us a means of determining the accuracy of ECL as it allows us to see historically the error between it and the actual realizations.

We wish to look at the 'behavior' of a sufficiently long series in relation to past forecasts made on that series. The constructed distributions can be based upon the fluctuations of the historical expected cash flows about the realizations $C_{\text{real}}(d, k, k)$. The creation of the general distribution for a given level of significance is separated by the positive or negative differences of $C_{\text{expect}}(d, cob, k)$ to reality such that:

1 An expected cash flow for day k as projected from day m in the past $C_{\text{expect}}(d, m, k)$ (where $m + k \leqslant cob$), less than $C_{\text{real}}(d, k, k)$ results in:

$$\Delta l_k = C_{\text{expect}}(d, m, k) - C_{\text{real}}(d, k, k) \; (\text{if} < 0) \tag{15.25}$$

2 An expected cash flow for day k as projected from day m in the past $C_{\text{expect}}(d, m, k)$ (where $m + k \leqslant cob$), greater than $C_{\text{real}}(d, k, k)$ results in:

$$\Delta h_k = C_{\text{expect}}(d, m, k) - C_{\text{real}}(d, k, k) \; (\text{if} > 0) \tag{15.26}$$

where Δl_k and Δh_k are the lowest and highest differences between the expected and realized cash flows. Since we can fix k for every day in the desired historical past and run in m, we obtain a series of values for Δl_k and Δh_k from which a distribution (possibly non-normal due to the nature of the process) can be constructed.

As for determining l_k and h_k, the upper and lower ranges of ELaR result from the consideration of a specified level of significance of $\Delta l_k, \Delta h_k$. In brief, defining the construction of the desired envelope encompassing the forward-expected cash flows leads to a calculation of the lowest and highest cash flows, such that:

$$l_k = C_{\text{expect}}(d, cob, k) + \text{quantile}\Delta \, l_k$$
$$h_k = C_{\text{expect}}(d, cob, k) + \text{quantile}\Delta \, h_k \tag{15.27}$$

At this point it is important to remember that behavioral ELaR considers the distribution of the differences of the cash flows to reality, in order to approximate lowest and highest cash flows l_k and h_k. On the other hand, ELaR in its pure sense considers only the distributions of the cash flows to determine l_k and h_k. The cumulative envelopes of the portfolio aggregated l_k and h_k are handled in an identical manner to that of L_k and H_k in equations (15.19) and (15.20), that is:

$$BehELaR\_L_k = L_k + \sum_{i=1}^{k} CF(D, i)$$
$$BehELaR\_H_k = H_k + \sum_{i=1}^{k} CF(D, i) \tag{15.28}$$

The advantage of constructing distributions in this way is that they require the application of no further scaling functions since they are, in reality, only the measure of maximum historical errors.

The construction of meaningful distributions of expected cash flows, L_k and H_k in all methodologies discussed to date is more than a visual means of displaying ELaR, it is essential for maintaining the integrity of the approach. In our deposit future example, the possible margin payment for any day in the future may be small. However, the aggregation of a series of one-sided margin payments leads to the possibility of an undesirable liquidity position.

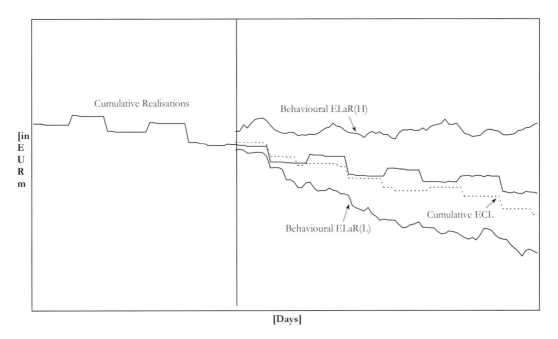

[Days]

Figure 15.8 Behavioral ElaR.

In the case of Metallgesellschaft, a series of rolling forward short-term futures contracts combined with falling oil prices resulted in margin calls of over 1 billion USD. The outcome was almost insolvency despite the certain future cash inflow awaiting at maturity of the fixed-price long-term contracts. Correct reporting of cash flows is a measure of the absolute portfolio position for any day k in the future.

Example: VaR as ELaR for a deposit future

Returning to the deposit future example previously considered, we saw that the expected cash flows for any day in the future are zero. To investigate the possible development of the future margin payments and to obtain an understanding of the magnitude of deviation of maximum payments that *could occur* is a measure of VaR.

We can use available market data in a Monte Carlo type simulation to measure the possible outcome of the cumulative payments for a given day k in the future. This would result in a normal distribution with the most likely cumulative cash flow being zero. As we are concerned predominantly with the forecast of outgoing payments, we look to the right-hand tail of the distribution. The maximal forward deficit of funds within a predefined probability is chosen by setting the desired quantile.

Knowing that VaR is actually a forecast for the loss in PV for a given confidence level, we come to the obvious conclusion that the cumulative liquidity at risk for day 1 is in fact VaR for day 1. That is:

$$ELaR_1 = VaR_1$$

$ELaR_2$, however, is not VaR_2, instead it is the progression of VaR_1 to VaR_2: or:

$$ELaR_2 = VaR_2 - VaR_1$$
$$\cdots$$
$$ELaR_k = VaR_k - VaR_{k-1} \tag{15.29}$$

As often in VaR reporting procedures, this can be represented as:

$$ELaR_k = \alpha(\sqrt{k} - \sqrt{k-1}) \quad \text{with } \alpha := ELaR_1 \tag{15.30}$$

Dynamic modeling of liquidity

Behavioral modeling: DCL

The construction of a behavioral model is the progression from an understanding of movements within the historical data to a quantitative projection forward of *cob* based on this knowledge. Ideally the link between any financial series and existing market parameters (e.g. LIBOR, PIBOR etc.) will be strong enough to construct a robust forecast. As is often the case for non maturing assets and liabilities, the correlation to other series is often small. The alternative, therefore, is an analysis of the account balances or cash flows themselves.

Basis of trend analysis

The initial analysis of a time series is to look at the trends that exist within the data itself. Following this logic, it seems intuitively reasonable to construct a curve (surface) through a portion of the existing data so that deviations from it are minimized in some way. This curve can then be projected forward from *cob* as a forecast of the expected future tendency of the series.

Having agreed upon the characteristics of the desired trend line, its construction can be simply defined as the requirement to reduce historically the standard deviation of the errors between the behavioral function and the mean of the real values. That is:

$$\sigma^2 = \sum_{i=1}^{n} \frac{1}{n}(P_i - \mu)^2 \tag{15.31}$$

is a minimum! where:

σ = standard deviation of the defined error
μ = historical mean of real values
P_i = projected value of the behavioral function for day i $(i = 1, \ldots, n)$

In some situations it may be deemed that part of the historical series is unreliable. In such cases, preprocessing of the raw data for the removal of erroneous points, smoothing of data or the filling of undesired gaps may be necessary before investigating the behavioral patterns of the series.

Basis of periodicity and frequency analysis

For systems incorporating or aggregating payment structures, which are often based on market parameters, cash flows occurring at regular intervals in time would be expected. Armed with this knowledge and depending upon the nature of the periodicity, the expected value of such a series can be projected with a greater degree of confidence for either specific points in the forecast window or for the entire forecast period as a whole.

At this stage, a series containing regular payments (e.g. mortgages, personal and company loans, and sight deposit balance sheet movements) can be addressed and quantified for projection purposes. The construction of a periodic model for a calendar-based time series would logically consider dates on a weekly, monthly, quarterly, half-yearly and yearly basis. It would also incorporate a corrective feature for the often-occurring situation of due payments falling on weekends or public holidays. In its simplest form, the concept of a monthly periodic model is the average of historical values from a selected time window for the creation of a forward forecast. That is:

$$CF(d, k) = \sum_{i=1}^{x} \frac{1}{x} \cdot Value_{k-1} \qquad (15.32)$$

where
$CF(p, k)$ = projected value for any date k (forward of *cob*)
$Value_{k-1}$ = historical value for the day $k - i$ for $i = 1$ to x months

and where the conditional of a payment roll forward, backward or averaging needs to be defined for those payments occurring on weekends or public holidays.

Direct frequency analysis

Partitioning a significantly large historical time series into components according to the duration or length of the intervals within the series is one approach to spectral or frequency analysis. By considering the series to be the sum of many simple sinusoids with differing amplitudes, wavelengths and starting points, allows for the combination of a number of the fundamentals to construct an approximating forecasting function. The Fourier transform uses the knowledge that if an infinite series of sinusoids are calculated so that they are orthogonal or statistically independent of one another, the sum will be equal to the original time series itself. The expression for frequency function $F(n)$ obtained from the time function $f(t)$ is represented as:

$$F(n) = \int_{-\infty}^{\infty} f(t) \cos 2\pi nt \, dt - i \int_{-\infty}^{\infty} f(t) \sin 2\pi nt \, dt \qquad (15.33)$$

The downside of such an approach for practical usage is that the combination of a limited number of sin functions results in a relatively smooth curve. Periodicity in financial markets will more than likely be a spike function of payments made and not a gradual and uniform inflow/outflow.

In addition, a Fourier transform functions optimally on a metrically based time series. The calendar is not a metric series and even when weekends and holidays are removed in an attempt to normalize the series, the length of the business month remains variable. The result is that any Fourier function will have a phase distortion over longer periods of time if a temporal correction or time stretching/shrinking component is not implemented. However, as a means of determining the fundamental frequencies of a series, the Fourier transform is still a valuable tool, which can be used for periodicity analysis and as a basis for the construction of a periodic model.

Use of further behavioral information

Regardless as to the robustness and strength of any forecast, without the addition of new information a limit of model accuracy will always be reached. A study of the behavior of a series can in many cases be broken down to 'grass roots' levels.

Below the analysis of a total or accumulated position could, for instance, be strong underlying counterparty trends. Their behavior could be of the nature of having regular, payment structures, transaction openings or of a trend in the portfolio itself. In line with this is the study of any correlation existing between more than one time series. The detection of one or both of these behavioral features leads to the logical progression of the modeling procedure.

The blending of behaviors

The weakness of any model designed to measure a specific trend is that it stands independently alone. Each model until this point addresses only one aspect of the time series. In reality, the data will more than likely have other faces. Realizing that each series is dependent upon different variables and that no one model can be consistently used to achieve the desired 'exactness' needed, a method of blending behaviors can be constructed. Working on the proviso that all models have the potential to produce a forecast of future realities with varying degrees of accuracy a blend approach weighting the working models may be written as:

$$\text{Blend model}_k = \alpha \cdot BM1_k + \beta \cdot BM2_k + \gamma \cdot BM3_k \qquad \text{for } k \text{ days in the future}$$

where $BM1$, $BM2$, $BM3$ are the predefined behavioral models and α, β, γ are the optimized weightings that historically give the fit of least error as defined in 'basis of trend analysis.' By the nature of the base models it is then valid to presume that, to some extent, $\alpha + \beta + \gamma \approx 1$.

From ELaR to DyLaR

Extending from our ELaR platform for predicting cash flows into the future we arrive at the point of needing to consider new business, such business being classified as all activities forward of *cob* as previously defined. In looking at the dynamic component, we are now based at a portfolio level, since it is not possible to predict new business on an individual transaction basis. Previously we saw that:

$$\text{DCL} = \text{ECL} + \text{dynamic cash flows} \qquad (15.34)$$

At this stage we encounter the same problem as before, the forecast value of cash flows, which now incorporates new business as well as existing, has an uncertain path. The inescapable reality is that all models based on financial markets operate in an often chaotic manner. That is, small parameter movements can lead to previously unrecognized paths. Allowing for this is a development of our concept of ELaR to bring us to *Dynamic Liquidity at Risk* (*DyLaR*).

In a broad sense, the behavioral model is one possible representation of DCL. In which case DCL hasn't been analysed by its individual components (ECL and new business) as it would be ideally. Instead it is treated as an ongoing whole based on the trends and periodicity of a given portfolio.

DyLaR and behavioral DyLaR

Looking at the cash flow value for a dynamic portfolio of deals d, we proceed with a behavioral DyLaR approach similar to that adopted for ELaR. For the purpose of demonstration, the general distribution is again created by measuring the fluctuations of historical forecasts $C_{\text{expected}}(D, k)$ about the realizations $C_{\text{real}}(D, k)$:

1. A forecast cash flow for day k as projected from day m in the past $C_{\text{expected}}(D, m, k)$ (where $m + k \leqslant cob$), less than $C_{\text{real}}(D, k, k)$ results in:

$$\Delta L_k = C_{\text{expected}}(D, m, k) - C_{\text{real}}(D, k, k) \text{ (if} < 0) \qquad (15.35)$$

2. A forecast cash flow for day k as projected from day m in the past $C_{\text{expected}}(D, m, k)$ (where $m + k \leqslant cob$), greater than $C_{\text{real}}(D, k, k)$ results in:

$$\Delta H_k = C_{\text{expected}}(D, m, k) - C_{\text{real}}(D, k, k) \text{ (if} > 0) \qquad (15.36)$$

where ΔL_k and ΔH_k are the lowest and highest *differences* between the forecast and realized cash flows. As before, we can fix k and run in m to obtain a series of values for ΔL_k and ΔH_k from which the distribution is constructed.

Having defined the distribution (behavioral in this situation, but it could be any statistically suitable distribution), the upper and lower ranges of DyLaR at the desired level of significance encompassing the forward projection (DCL) is defined as:

$$L_k = C_{\text{real}}(D, k, k) + \text{quantile } \Delta L_k$$
$$H_k = C_{\text{real}}(D, k, k) + \text{quantile } \Delta H_k \qquad (15.37)$$

What is true for the cash flows of one day is also true for the cumulative cash flows:

$$cumL_k \leqslant C_{\text{real}}(D, k, k) \leqslant cumH_k$$

Goodness of fit

The goodness of fit of any model-based forecast will be seen from the extent of divergence of the envelope/wings $cumL_k$ and $cumH_k$ from the projected forecast $C_{\text{expected}}(D, \cdot, k)$.

That is, for the behavioral model approach, as

$$C_{\text{expected}}(D, m, k) - C_{\text{real}}(D, k, k) \to |\min| \text{ (theoretically: } \to 0)$$

then

$$L_k \text{ and } H_k \to 0$$

therefore

$$cumL_k \text{ and } cumH_k \to C_{\text{expected}}(D, m, k)$$

Quantile selection and ELaR/DyLaR correction

The preferred level of confidence for behavioral DyLaR can be determined from the analysis of past projections over the desired period of 6, 12 or 24 months. For methodological purposes the adoption of the 12-month period or 250 working days would be in line with current methods of VaR analysis. Periodically the projected upper and lower DyLaR values will lie outside of the desired L_k and H_k envelope, as should be the case for any quantile selection of less than 100%. This leads to the requirement of a self-correcting mechanism for any forecast of behavioral DyLaR.

Under these circumstances, the previously maximum quantile value ΔH_k is self-repairing, since for $cob + 1$ the maximum value for $\Delta H_k = C_{\text{expected}}(D, m, k) - C_{\text{real}}(D, k, k)$ is replaced by the ΔH_k calculated for $cob - 1$. Should a significant change occur in the cash flows of any portfolio the result will be a spreading of the $cumL_k/cumH_k$ envelope leading to a more cautious estimate.

Forecast bias

Forecast bias or the tendency of our model to consistently over- or underestimate the realizations is a concern of distributions addressed by the separation of upper and lower quantiles. For a forecast which consistently overestimates the realizations to a greater extent than to underestimate them, then:

$$|H_k| > |L_k| \text{ for all } k$$

and similarly, for a forecast which consistently underestimates the realizations to a greater extent than to underestimate them, then:

$$|L_k| > |H_k| \text{ for all } k$$

Visually, the forecast DCL value would have the appearance of lying more closely to one edge of the $cumL_k/cumH_k$ envelope. This would probably be a good indicator that the model parameters need some form of adjustment depending on the extent of bias present in order to rebalance future forecasts.

Liquidity portfolios

Treasury units of financial institutions often hold special portfolios in order to be able to generate liquidity for different maturities quickly and at low costs. Depending on the credit rating of the FI the liquidity portfolio can have positive, negative or no carry.

'Real' currency of liquidity portfolios

As financial institutions usually trade in many different currencies, they also have to manage their liquidity risk in many different currencies. Nevertheless, they usually do not hold liquidity portfolios in all these currencies for reasons of cost. Therefore, the question arises, which currencies and locations are optimal for liquidity portfolios? In practice the liquidity portfolios are located in the regional head offices and are denominated in the main currencies (USD, EUR, JPY).

Liquidity of liquidity portfolios

The liquidity portfolio is a part of the liquidity reserve of FI, therefore it should contain securities, which will

- Be pledgeable/repoable by the central bank or other counterparties
- Have a large issue volume
- Have an effective market
- Have no credit risk
- Be issued by international well-known issuers

These characteristics normally enable the FI to get liquidity quickly and at relatively low cost from the central bank or other counterparties.

Availability

Depending how quickly liquidity is requested the inventory of the portfolio should be split and held with different custodians. For example:

- The credit line with the Bundesbank is dependent on the volume of pledgeable securities held in the depot with the Bundesbank.
- If a repo is done with the market one part of the inventory should be held with a national or an international custodian to ensure settlement.
- For settlement purposes the securities should be deliverable easily in national settlement systems and in/between international depositary systems.

Volume

The volume of the liquidity portfolio should cover a potential liquidity gap for the period of an occurring liquidity gap.

Funding

The use of the liquidity portfolio as a liquidity reserve is based on the assumption that the cash equivalent for that portfolio can be funded by the normal credit line based upon a good credit standing. As a result existing inventory will be free for funding purposes. Based on a normal yield curve the inventory will be funded for shorter periods producing a return on the spread difference. The funding period will be rolled every 3–6 months.

If additional funding is needed the inventory can be used as collateral to acquire additional liquidity from other counterparties. Normally funds are received at a lower interest rate because the credit risk is reduced to that of the issuer, which is in most cases better than the FI's own credit risk. In the best case one will receive the mark to market value without a haircut (sell-buy-back trade). In the case of repo trades there will be a haircut (trades with the central bank).

The worst case would occur if funds are borrowed in one transaction and upon the rollover date a 'temporary illiquidity' occurs. In the meantime the credit rating of the FI may have deteriorated. For all future fundings with this FI, counterparties will demand both collateral and a haircut. This means that if 10 units of cash are required for clearing and 100 units for the liquidity funding the FI will receive 90 units against every 100 units of collateral. The result is that due to the increased funding of the liquidity portfolio, the original liquidity gap of 10 units increased by an additional 10 units to 20. As such, the liquidity portfolio failed to fulfil its purpose of supplying additional necessary reserves. In the case of a rise in interest rates, the price of the liquidity portfolio will also fall and may, for example, result in the FI receiving only 80 units; the total additional funding gap for the portfolio would now be 20 units and total difference 30 (see Figure 15.9).

If the funding of the liquidity portfolio is carried out incorrectly it can lead to an increase of the liquidity gap. Therefore, it would be beneficial to structure the funding into several parts. These would be funded in different periods and with different counterparts. One part should be covered by 'own capital' and the market risk should be hedged.

Term structure of liquidity

One of the main scopes in A/L management is the classification of balance sheet items according to their maturities. The reason for this is twofold and has con-

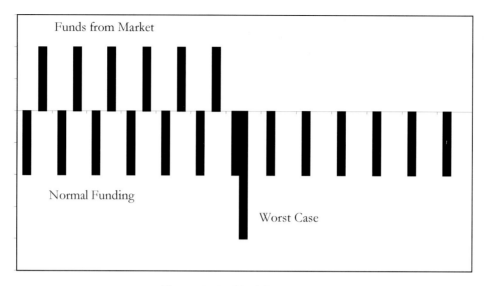

Figure 15.9 Liquidity request.

sequences on the concept of 'maturity'. The first reason is the management of interest rate risk and the second is the management of liquidity risk. For liquidity risk management purposes classical gap analysis is misleading as the term structure of interest rates and liquidity will differ considerably for many financial instruments. We give an example to clarify this.

Example: Plain vanilla interest rate swap

For interest rate risk measurement the variable leg of an interest rate swap would 'end' at the next fixing date of the variable interest rate. For interest rate considerations the notional amount could be exchanged at that date. For liquidity risk measurement, the variable leg of a swap matures at the end of the lifetime of the swap. The payments can be estimated using the forward rates.

In order to optimize their liquidity management, the treasury function of a FI is faced with the problem of determining the term structure of liquidity for their assets and liabilities. For many investment banking products, such as derivatives and fixed-income products this is a straightforward task as payment dates are often known in advance and the estimated amounts can be derived from the pricing formulae. An exception is obviously the money market and repo business. A more challenging task (and more important in terms of liquidity) is the term structure of liquidity for the classic commercial banking products, such as transaction accounts, demand deposits, credit card loans or mortgages (prepayments) as these products have no determined maturity.

Example: Demand deposits

In order to determine the term structure of liquidity for demand deposits one has to create a model for the deposit balance. The approach we propose here is in the spirit of the techniques as described in the sections above. In order to estimate the proportion of the demand deposits that can be used over given time horizons, one has to answer questions like: 'What is the lowest possible balance in the next K days with a p% probability?' One way to attack the problem is to calculate the p quantiles of the distribution of the K day balance returns. An alternative consists of looking for the minimal balance in the last K days. The minimum of this balance and the actual balance can then be lent out for K days

This method has the advantage of being applicable also to balance sheet items which are uncorrelated to interest rate changes but it has the same weaknesses as all historic simulations. These weaknesses are very well known for the estimation of volatility or the calculation VaR and can be summed up by the wise saying that: 'The past is not the future.'

Transfer pricing of liquidity

Here we want to highlight the question of what price for liquidity the treasury unit of a financial institution should quote to the different entities of the bank. This question is closely related to the role of the treasury in the bank. If it is merely a servicing unit, which provides liquidity to the different business lines for the best price or if it is a trading unit, which is entitled to take active positions on the yield curve. The following example should highlight the ideas.

Example: Transaction accounts
The treasury is offered money from transaction accounts by the commercial bank department. What should the treasury pay for this money? The ideas we have in mind are all more or less inspired by time series analysis.

1 Calculate the standard deviation or another quantile of a certain time period of past balances. The proportion of today's balance, which corresponds to this quantile, could be lent to the treasury at the O/N rate. The remaining part of the balance could be lent out at the O/N rate plus a spread. The determination of the quantile and the spread is a business decision.
2 The term structure of liquidity for demand deposits as described above can be used for transfer pricing in the following sense. The proportion of the balance, which can invested at a given term, is determined by the term structure. The used interest rate is taken from the yield curve at that term plus or minus a spread. Again, the spread is a business decision.
3 Instead of taking quantiles as in 2, it is also possible to use the minimum balances in this period.
4 The next approach uses a segmentation hypothesis of the customers which contribute to the balance. Customers who do not receive any or do receive only very low interest on their accounts are likely to be insensitive to interest rate changes. Changes in market interest rates do not have to be passed through to those customers. On the other hand, customers who receive interest rates close to the market will be very interest sensitive. Now it is obvious that the non-interest-sensitive accounts will be worth more to the bank than the interest-sensitive ones. The business has then to make a decision as to what price should be paid to the portions of the balance, which have different interest rate sensitivities. The transfer price of the clearing balance can then be calculated as the weighted average of the single rates.

Notes

[1] 'Illusion, daß etwas erkannt sei, wo wir eine mathematische Formel für das Geschehene haben: es ist nur *bezeichnet, beschrieben*: nichts mehr' (Friedrich Nietzsche) seems to anticipate the situation perfectly.

[2] In terms of a possible transfer pricing of liquidity this bears the inability to come up with a mid-price curve that reflects the mean price between bid and offer prices. The current approach of defining the mid-curve in, say swaps pricing, as $LIMEAN := (LIBID + LIBOR)/2$ only works under the unexpressed hypothesis that the bid is, on average, as far away from the 'true' price as the offer.

[3] The fact that some liquidity portfolios generate profit (expressed as a certain spread over LIBOR or funding levels) instead of cost seems to be contradictory, but it is not: the spread never meets the required profit per capital employed as it is requested by investors normally.

[4] For the sake of simplicity long positions on the central bank account held in order to satisfy minimum reserve requirements are formally treated as overnight loans to the central bank.

[5] One could argue that the rate at which a deal is done defines what is regarded as the market rate. On the other hand, it can be perceived that at virtually the same time identical deals with different prices are done. This contravenes the concept of one market price but does not necessarily lead to liquidity as a unique explanation. This brings us back to the price effect of liquidity for financial instruments.

16

Accounting risk

RICHARD SAGE

Definition

Accounting risk is the risk that inappropriate accounting information causes sub-optimal decisions to be made and may be due to inappropriate policy, faulty interpretation of policy, or plain error. We can distinguish accounting risk from fraud, which is deliberate manipulation of reported numbers, although the faulty interpretation of policy in a computer system can facilitate fraud, as would appear to have happened at Kidder Peabody in 1994.

Salomon Brothers recorded a USD250 million hit as due to accounting errors in 1994, but most errors which are discovered are wrapped up in other results for the same reasons that frauds are unless they are really enormous – management judges the costs from loss to reputation to be too high. Merger provisions are an obvious dumping ground. Most of the problems discussed in this chapter are unresolved at many institutions today due to lack of understanding.

Dealing with accounting risk is not something that concerns only the financial reporting function – decisions which need to be made on accounting matters affect valuation and risk-reporting systems, interbook dealing mechanisms, and the relationship of Treasury to trading businesses. Senior management needs to understand the issues and make consistent decisions.

There is continual tension in most trading organizations between traders and trading management who want to show profits as high as possible, and the risk, control, and accounting departments, who are charged by senior management with ensuring that what is reported is 'true'.

Most risk information is concerned with looking at what may happen in the future. Accounting is showing what has already happened. While traders are typically focused purely on the future, the past does matter. One has to judge performance based on what has already happened, rather than just on what is promised for the future. Anything other than the net profit number is generally more relevant for management and the control functions than for traders.

Direct losses from accounting risk typically happen when a large profit is reported for a business and significant bonuses are paid out to the personnel involved before it is discovered that the actual result was a much smaller profit or even a loss. In addition, extra capital and resources may be diverted to an area which is apparently highly profitable with the aim of increasing the business's overall return on capital. However, if the profitability is not real, the extra costs incurred can decrease the business's overall profit. As these losses are dispersed across an organization they do not receive the same publicity as trading mistakes. Such risks are magnified where the instruments traded have long lives, so that several years' bonuses may have been paid before any losses are recognized. The risk of profits being understated is generally much lower, because those responsible for generating them will be keen to show that they have done a good job, and will investigate with great diligence any problems with the accounting producing unflattering numbers.

Indirect losses from the discovery and disclosure of accounting errors arise only for those rare mistakes which are too large to hide. The additional losses come from the associated poor publicity which may cause a downgrade in reputation. This can result in increased costs for debt and for personnel. Regulators may require expensive modification to systems and procedures to reduce what they see as the risk of repetition. In addition, announcements of such failings can lead to the loss of jobs for multiple levels of management.

In many large trading organizations the daily and monthly accounting functions have become extremely fragmented, and it is very difficult to see a complete picture of all the assets and liabilities of the organization. Especially in organizations which have merged, or expanded into areas of business removed from their original areas, there is often inconsistency of approach, which may result in substantial distortion of the overall results. There is often a tendency for individual business lines within an organization to paint the best possible picture of their own activities. Considerable discipline is required from head office to ensure that the overall accounts are valid.

In many trading organizations the accounting function is held in low regard. As a result, many of the people who are best at understanding the policy complications which arise in accounting find that they are better rewarded in other functions. These individuals may therefore act in an economically rational manner and move to another function. The resulting shortage of thinkers in the accounting function can increase the risk of problems arising.

Many non-accountants find it astonishing that there could be more than one answer to the question 'How much profit have we made?'. This is a very reasonable attitude. This chapter seeks to explain some examples of where accountants commonly tangle themselves, sometimes unnecessarily.

The main focus in this chapter is on the risks that arise from choice and interpretation of policy in accounting performed for internal reporting in organizations for whom the provision or use of financial instruments is the main business. These are the organizations which knowingly take on risk, either making a margin while matching with an offsetting risk, or gaining an excess return by holding the risk. This is the main area which affects risk managers and is illustrated by several common areas in which problems arise. FX, funding, and internal consistency are areas where many accountants in banks will be well used to seeing multiple arguments. We then briefly consider external reporting by such organizations, and the additional complexities for internal and external reporting by 'end-users' – the organizations which use financial instruments to reduce their risks.

Accounting for market-makers

Internal reporting

Many accountants need to unlearn some rules they have picked up in 'normal', accounting. The differences are greater for the Japanese and continental European methods of accounting than for the Anglo-Saxon methods. It is unfortunate that while many of the rules of historical-cost accounting are not applicable to trading businesses, many organizations have thrown the baby out with the bathwater by also abandoning for their daily reporting the double-entry record-keeping invented by Pacioli in Italy in 1497. Double-entry provides a welcome discipline which is valid whatever accounting conventions are used.

All serious players use mark-to-market accounting (where the value of assets and liabilities is recalculated daily based on market parameters) for most of their trading business, although this may require exceptions (see discussion of arbitrage businesses below). The remaining trading entities which may still be using accrual accounting (where a profit is calculated at the time of trade, and recognized over the lifetime of the position, while losses are recognized as soon as they occur) are those which are subsidiary businesses of organizations whose main business is other than trading.

Uses

The purpose of accounting is to be able to list the assets and liabilities of the organization. This is the balance sheet. The increase in the net assets in a period (plus any amounts paid out as dividends) is the amount by which wealth has increased. This is the profit for the period. This simple paradigm should be constantly remembered in the following discussion. Those concerned with setting accounting standards for historical-cost accounting spend many hours defining what is an asset or a liability, and how their values should be measured. For mark-to-market accounting these definitions are much simpler:

- An asset is something that has value to the holder and its market value is the amount of cash which a rational independent third party would pay now to acquire it.
- A liability is an obligation to another party and its market value is the amount of cash which a rational independent third party would accept now in exchange for taking on the obligation.

Traders and management care about the reported profit figures because they determine their bonuses. Most traders are not interested in the balance sheet, instead preferring to judge their exposures from the 'greeks', the sensitivities. Regulators and senior management are more likely to consider what information the balance sheet can give regarding exposures, and about adherence to capital requirements. Balance sheet information and profit numbers are used together to calculate returns on capital. These numbers are often important to senior management in determining where to shrink or expand business activities.

Regulatory capital requirements typically apply at the level of individual legal entities, as well as of groups. Trading businesses frequently consist of many legal entities and so it is important that the balance sheet can be accurately split by legal entity. This may sound simple, but most decision-making systems and any daily ledgers support only an individual business line. Combined with the fact that traders care little for legal-entity split, it can be a major challenge to obtain and consolidate this information on a timely basis.

On the other hand, some of the calculations of capital are often only implemented in systems owned by the financial reporting department, which tend to be more focused on the split between legal entities than on the split between business lines.

Thus while in many more advanced organizations there is a wish to charge the usage of capital to the business lines which use it, the information required to do so may not be available. As a result, such capital charges may be calculated on a somewhat *ad-hoc* basis, leading to inaccuracies and disputes which distract staff time from earning money for the business.

Any profit calculation that does not involve subtracting two balance sheets carries an increased risk of being erroneous. Unfortunately it is all too common to find that daily profits are reported based on spreadsheets which may not capture all the assets and liabilities. When the financial reporting department attempts to add up the net assets at the end of the month, there are numerous differences which nobody ever has time to fully clear.

The solution to these problems is to prepare the daily profits from trading ledgers which use the double-entry discipline, and have all information split by legal entity and business line. If these trading ledgers feed the general ledger at the end of the month then reconciliation issues become vastly more manageable. The importance of keeping the ledgers split by transaction currency and of reconciling internal positions on a daily basis is explained in the following subsections.

A separate risk is that trading lines attempt to 'smooth' their profit, since senior management asks them awkward questions if profits go up and down. In some cases swings are indeed due to inaccurate accounting, often because of inadequate systems, and so an assumption may arise that all such swings are errors. In fact many well-hedged positions will show volatility of earnings, and users of the accounting reports should be educated not to panic at such moves.

FX

Potential pitfalls

Accounting for the fact that business is carried out in different currencies should not be difficult, but it is probably the greatest single cause of accounting faults causing unwanted risk in trading houses today. This may be because it is an area where mark-to-market accounting involves a very different approach from typical historical-cost accounting and most accountants find it very difficult to ignore the distorting rules they have learnt in their training for incorporating the results of foreign-currency subsidiaries into published group accounts.

The worked examples which follow are deliberately simple and extreme, since this is the easiest way to see the effect of different treatments. Some of the complications which arise when considering interaction between groups of assets and liabilities are considered in later subsections, but in this subsection we deliberately isolate individual assets. As mentioned above, any implementation should be in a double entry system, but it is easier to read the simpler presentation below. Many people's responses to these sorts of examples is 'Of course I would never follow the incorrect route', but they fail to see that in real life these situations are clouded by all sorts of other complications, and that such mistakes are being made underneath.

We start a period with 9oz of gold when the gold price is USD300/oz, and as a result of buying and selling gold for other things end with 10 oz of gold when the gold price is USD250/oz (for the purposes of this example assume that cash balances at beginning and end are both zero). Few people would compute the profit as anything other than:

	oz	USD/oz	USD
Final position	10	250	2500
(less) starting position	(9)	300	(2700)
Profit (loss)			(200)

The fact that we have 1oz extra of gold does not mean that we have made a profit.

However, consider the following example where we have effectively the same numbers.

	GBP	CHF.GBP	CHF
Final position	1000	2.50	2500
(less) starting position	(900)	3.00	(2700)
Profit (loss)	100		(200)

Trading is carried on in GBP, but reported in CHF. The effect of the trading activity on the wealth of the organization is to have decreased it by CHF200. This approach has tracked the net assets of the business and is referred to in the following sections as the 'net assets method'.

The classic accounting for a subsidiary would take the profit in the transaction currency and multiply by the average exchange rate to the reporting currency – in this case giving a profit of:

$$(100 * (2.50 + 3.00)/2) = CHF275$$

The difference between $+275$ and -200 would be taken to reserves – i.e. the balance sheet would recognize that the shareholders are CHF200 worse off, but management and traders would be congratulated (and rewarded) on a profit of CHF275. At a published accounts level, this was one of the problems with Polly Peck International which went into administration in 1990. At a more common level, this sort of translation happens all the time in major trading houses today, even when the lines being combined are within one legal entity.

More unpredictable is the profit which would be reported if ledger entries are converted to the base currency as they are made. In this case the trading profit number would depend not only on the start and end position, but also on the route taken between them. One sequence of events might be:

	GBP	CHF.GBP	CHF	CHF
Starting position	900	3.00		2700
Entry 1	600	3.50	2100	
Entry 2	(500)	2.00	(1000)	
Trading profit			1100	1100
FX profit (balancing number)				(1300)
Retranslate	1000	2.50		2500

However, if the exchange rate had moved in the opposite direction first we might have:

	GBP	CHF.GBP	CHF	CHF
Starting position	900	3.00		2700
Entry 1	600	2.00	1200	
Entry 2	(500)	3.50	(1750)	
Trading profit			(550)	(550)
FX profit (balancing number)				350
Retranslate	1000	2.50		2500

The FX profit line tends to be lost in central overheads, at least if it is a loss, so in the first case management and traders might be rewarded on a trading profit of CHF 1100 while in the second case they would probably persuade the accountants to pull together a spreadsheet showing that they had not really lost CHF 550.

Only one of these last two scenarios would arise in any one period. Let us assume the former was the case. We are faced with the situation that the different numbers for trading profit of CHF −200, +275, or +1100 could all be reported from systems which their vendors would proudly proclaim to be 'multi-currency'.

There are other candidates for the trading profit number which must be considered. One is the GBP profit * the closing exchange rate, i.e. 100*3=CHF 300. Another possibility is that head office had earlier entered into a forward FX transaction to sell the expected GBP profit for CHF. If the rate in question for the particular month was 3.3 then we can consider reporting 100*3.3=CHF 330.

Which number should be reported? The methods of average rate and immediate conversion, here giving results of CHF +275 and CHF +1100 are not justifiable. The use of a forward rate (sometimes communicated as a budgeted rate) is only justified if the amount sold forward by head office is exactly the same as the profit actually made, in other words that head office is deemed to have perfect knowledge of future profits. This is unlikely, and so the CHF +330 figure can be discarded. This leaves us with a choice of CHF −200, calculated using the net assets method, and CHF +300, converting GBP profit to CHF at the closing FX rate. The decision on which to report depends on a high-level policy choice.

The importance of policy

Senior management needs to decide on a policy for profit remittance by each business line. Too often this policy is not clearly communicated, even if it is made. It is important that remuneration of traders is based on numbers which are aligned with the interests of the shareholders. If the businesses do not have any requirement to pay over their profits to head office at the end of each period then the net assets method, which gave a result of −200, is the only correct approach. If the businesses do have a requirement to pay over their exact profits (and receive their losses) at the end of each month (or day or year) then the use of the closing exchange rate appears appropriate. In fact, if properly implemented, the two methods would give much closer answers because if the profits have to be paid over at the end of each period, there would never have been an opening balance of GBP900. Indeed, if the policy is that the profits are paid over in the currency in which they arise, then the two methods will give exactly the same answer. Paying over the profit in the reporting currency is a policy that may be easier for everybody to understand. If the amount required is obtained by the business line selling exactly all its profit in the transaction currency then the closing exchange-rate method gives exactly the same answer as the net asset approach. If the business line does not make its FX position totally flat at the end of each period, then there will be an exposure which does affect the wealth of the organization, and the closing-rate method will miss this. Thus all the transactions related to profit remittance should be reflected in the cash accounts in the ledger system and the net assets method used.

Profit remittance policies are often less than clear because they are embedded in systems calculations. This is particularly true of any policy which involves a daily remittance. The logic will have been perfectly clear to the founding sponsor of the system, but even if the programmers understood it and implemented in correctly, later users may never have really understood the motivation behind the numbers which the computer spews out. Such embedding is a good example of system logic risk. Such risk is usually thought of in conjunction with complicated valuation models, but we see here that it can also apply to accounting systems, which are generally considered to be simple.

Policies which say that all FX risk is transferred to the FX desk are effectively policies of daily remittance in transaction currency. It is important that whatever policy is chosen is clearly understood by all trading personnel, otherwise avoidable FX risks may be hedged out, or even unnecessarily introduced. Policies which do not involve daily remittance need to specify the exact timing of remittances, and the treatment of any FX gains or losses which arise between the end of the month/year and the date of payment.

Cross-currency products

A ledger which maintains all entries in the transaction currency can handle all the pitfalls mentioned above and can give the FX exposures of the business line so long as all the instruments are mono-currency. The exposures are simply the balances on the profit accounts.

However, there are some products which involve more than one currency. Forward FX trades are the simplest and the population includes currency swaps as well as the more exotic instruments often referred to as quantos. Terminology is not standardized in this area, but an example of such an instrument would be an option which paid out USD1000 * $\max((S_t - S_0), 0)$ where S_t and S_0 are the final and strike values of a stock quoted in a currency other than USD.

Currency exposure reporting is not easy for systems with such cross-currency instruments. If FX delta is to be calculated by the risk system performing recalculation then the risk system must have cash balances in it (including those related to the profit remittances discussed above) which is not often the case. Performing recalculation on the market instruments while ignoring cash balances can give very misleading reports of exposure resulting in mishedging. The best approach for FX delta is therefore to have such instruments valued in component currencies, so that the ledger will indeed show the correct exposure. FX gamma can only be obtained by recalculation within the valuations system (the FX gamma on a cash balance is zero).

Note that not every product which pays out in a currency different from that of the underlying is a true cross-currency instrument. For example, if the payout is (Any function of the underlying alone) * (Spot rate on expiry) then there is no actual FX risk for the seller, since one can execute an FX spot trade at the spot rate on expiry, effectively on behalf of the client. This is an example where complexity is sometimes seen where it does not exist, in what has been called 'phantom FX'.

Funding

While the definition of cash is fairly obvious for most businesses, this is less so for a bank. The money-market business line of a bank has both deposits and obligations with other banks and other market participants, of various maturities yielding various rates. Other business lines deal in other instruments which are settled in what they view as cash. Clarity is much improved by having a treasury desk with which all other business lines have accounts which they regard as their 'bank accounts'. The treasury desk then functions as the in-house bank, charging interest to those business lines that have borrowed from it, and crediting interest to those which have deposited funds with it. Because of the fine margins in many trading businesses this interest charge is usually a very material proportion of the profit/ loss of many business lines, and so its accuracy is extremely important.

The treasury desk will usually charge a spread to its internal customers, reflecting the fact that there is a spread between the borrowing and lending rates in the market, and will make a profit even if it charges no larger spread than the market as we see from the following example:

	Balance	Rate	Interest	Effective.rate
Trading Line A	1000	10%	100	
Trading Line B	(400)	11%	(44)	
Total	600		56	9.33%
Net	600	10%	60	10.00%
Gain to Treasury			4	

If each trading desk went independently to the money-market the effective rate of interest received would be 9.33%, but by netting before going to the market the bank can achieve10%. The treasury desk takes the difference as profit.

One could argue that since the bank as a whole deposits at 10%, Trading LineB should only be charged 10% rather than 11%, but with rational traders this would merely lead to an unstable game of cat and mouse to be continually on the minority side, which is best avoided. While other trading desks should be encouraged to use the in-house treasury rather than outside banks, there is danger if this is a fixed rule that treasury will widen its spreads to make extra profit at the expense of the other trading desks. It is therefore usual to leave trading desks the right to go outside. The threat is usually sufficient to make treasury's rates reasonable and so the right is never exercised.

Some trading houses have no internal cash accounts, but use other data for calculating funding costs. This makes it virtually impossible to perform accurate and transparent calculations of the amount that each business line should be charged/ credited, and as such is a significant risk. As we saw above, segregated cash accounts are also needed for calculating FX exposure and the effect on profit of FX rate movements.

If a trading desk knows, or at least expects, that it will have a long or short cash position for some time, then it will usually be able to obtain a better rate for a term loan/deposit rather than continually rolling over the overnight position. Such positions will usually also be taken with the in-house treasury desk.

While bond-trading and money-market desks tend to be very aware of the effect on values and profits of the different ways of calculating and paying interest, and the movement in market rates, such sophistication does not often extend to systems used for internal cash accounts. Thus accrual accounting is common in these systems.

This can cause mismatch problems. Say a trading desk buys an instrument which is effectively an annuity, and values it by discounting the expected future cash flows. The trading desk takes out a term loan from the treasury desk to make the purchase. If nothing else happens other than that interest rates fall, then the value calculated for the instrument will rise, but the value of the term loan from treasury will not. In order to get accurate profit numbers it is necessary to value all instruments in all books using market rates, including internal term loans and deposits. Once again, systems need to reflect the policies adapted.

Internal consistency

As with funding costs, the effects discussed in this subsection are usually very small compared to the gross positions involved, but due to margins being very thin, can be very large in comparison to the net profits of trading.

Consistency with trading strategy

Valuation and accounting policies are intimately linked. Many of the examples below may seem rather detailed but they can lead to big swings in reported profits and have often taken up many hours which could be used for other work.

There are some businesses where the rule that all instruments should be valued using market rates causes complications. For example, arbitrage businesses would never show any profit until the market moved back into line or the instruments expired. Given the history of supposedly arbitraged trading strategies resulting in large losses, this may not be regarded by senior management as a particular problem, but the theory is worth thinking through.

If exactly the same instrument can be bought in one situation for a price lower than it can be sold in another, then the rational action is to buy it at the lower price and sell at the higher. As the instrument is exactly the same, the net position will be zero, and there will be a positive cash balance representing the profit.

If the two instruments are very similar, and react in the same way to changes in underlying prices, but are not quite identical then it still makes sense to buy at the lower price and sell at the higher one. However, this time the instrument positions will not net off and if prices have not moved, the difference between the values of the positions will be exactly the opposite of the cash received, so the net profit will be reported as zero. Eventually the market prices of the two instruments will become closer, or they will turn into identical offsetting amounts of cash (or the strategy will be shown not to be a perfect arbitrage!) and the profit will be recognized. Indeed in the time before expiry it is possible that the prices will move further apart from equality and a loss will be reported. This is not popular with traders who want to be able to report that they have locked in a 'risk-free' profit with their trading at inception.

A theoretical example of such a situation would be where an OTC instrument is identical to the sum of two or more listed instruments. The listed instruments can be valued at market prices. If the OTC valuation model uses inputs such as implied volatility derived from other listed instruments and the market prices of the various listed instruments are inconsistent, then we will end up with a profit/loss being reported when it is certain that none will be eventually realized. This is a good illustration that markets are not always perfect, and that accounts based on marking to market may also not be perfect. It is easy to suggest that human judgement should be left to identify and correct such situations, but once one introduces the potential for judgement to override policy, there is a danger that its application becomes too common, thus reducing the objectivity of reports.

Such considerations often lead to trading desks seeking to ensure that their positions are valued using a basis which is internally consistent to reduce 'noise' in the reported profit. However, for different trading desks to value the same instrument differently causes great problems for central accounting functions which may be faced with values which are supposed to net off, but do not do so. The benefit of smoothing within a trading desk is usually obtained at the cost of introducing inconsistency for group reporting.

A particular case where instruments may be valued differently without either trading desk even seeing that there might be a problem is in options on interest rate instruments. In some situations the underlying may be regarded as the price of a bond, while in others it may be the yield on a bond. Most option valuation methodologies require the assumption that the distribution of the underlying is log-normal. As price and yield are more or less reciprocal, it is not possible for both of them to be log-normal, and indeed different values will be obtained from two such systems for the same instrument.

Valuing all the listed instruments involved using market prices rather than theoretical prices is the correct approach. The reason why this can be said to have accounting risk is that the reporting of the loss may lead senior management to order a liquidation of the positions, which will definitely crystalize that loss, when holding the instruments to maturity would have resulted in a profit. While there is much dispute in the academic and business community, this is arguably at least part of what happened at Metallgesellschaft in 1993.

The bid–offer spread

The standard prudent accounting methodology is to value long positions at bid, and short positions at offer. However, what about positions between two trading desks, which clearly have no overall profit effect, but will show a loss under the standard policy? Then there are trades between two books within one trading desk, which may have been entered merely to neaten up books but will cause a loss to be reported until the positions expire. The obvious approach is to price all positions at mid-market, which has justification if the organization is a market-maker. However, it is unlikely that the organization is a market-maker in all the instruments on its books. The answer to this is to price at mid-market with provisions for the spread. When there are offsetting positions within the organization no such provisions are made.

The method of implementation of this policy has implications for accountability. If the provisions are made at a level above the books then there is the problem that the sum of the profits of the books will be greater than the total, which is a sure way to arguments over bonuses. If the provisions are made at book level, then the profit in a given book can vary due purely to whether another book closed out its offsetting position.

A related point concerns volatility. As volatility is an input parameter for OTC option-pricing models, for valuation purposes it should be derived as far as possible from prices for traded instruments. However, there will be a bid–offer spread on the implied volatility. Should the volatility parameter be the bid–offer or mid implied volatility? As with absolute prices the recommended approach is to use mid-market with provisions for the fact that one cannot usually close out at mid. However, with volatility, not only are the bid–offer spreads typically very wide, but there are the extra complexities that the market is frequently one-sided and the volatility parameter also affects the hedge ratios calculated by the models.

Non-simultaneous market closes

A particular hazard regarding certain instruments is the definition of closing price. If distinct but related instruments (e.g. the underlying stocks, and the future on the index consisting of those stocks) are traded on markets which close at different times then a genuinely arbitraged position between the two markets will show noise in the reported profit which may well be material.

While this is easy enough for one trading desk to allow for, by taking prices on the later-closing exchange at the time of the earlier close, or by using theoretical prices for instruments on the earlier-closing exchange derived from prices on the later close, such an approach will again cause matching problems unless applied consistently across an organization. Adopting one approach for daily reporting and a different approach for month-end or year-end is not a good idea since it leads to everyone having less confidence in any of the numbers.

Intragroup timing

Counterintuitively, it may *add* distortion to price the same instrument at the same price in all businesses in all time zones. This is most disturbing for most accountants who learn early in their training that internal balances must always net out on consolidation.

We consider the extreme example that there is a position between the offices in Tokyo and New York which is exactly matched by positions with the outside world at each end. If Tokyo positions are valued at the end of the trading day in Tokyo, and New York positions at the end of the trading day in New York, we would see:

	Tokyo	New York	Total
Position with external counterparty in Tokyo	87		
Back-to-back with New York office	(87)		
Back-to-back with Tokyo office		85	
Position with external counterparty in New York		(85)	
Net assets	0	0	0

This correctly shows the net assets, and therefore profit, as zero in both locations. However, forcing the internal asset in Tokyo to have the same value as in New York gives:

	Tokyo	New York	Total
Position held with external counterparty in Tokyo	87		
Back-to-back with New York office	(85)		
Back-to-back with Tokyo office		85	
Position held with external counterparty in New York		(85)	
Net assets	2	0	2

showing a profit of 2 which is wrong. In practice the situation would never be that obvious, but it holds with equal force whatever the positions are with the external counterparties, if they have been valued using the parameters at different closing times. One could value every position at New York close, but by that time Tokyo is almost ready to start trading again, and so the time required for overnight batch processes, which may take several hours to run, even on today's computers, is not available. The correct approach is therefore to accept that the same instrument may have different values depending on its location, and to educate senior management and auditors that this does not lead to distortion of profits.

Netting (for balance sheet)

All the above complications concerning internal consistency are most evident to the accounting function which puts together all the assets and liabilities reported by the separate trading desks to produce the group, or legal entity, balance sheets on which regulatory capital is based. This is difficult when, as is common, information for different trading desks is stored on separate systems. The resultant information may lack accuracy especially if the trading function cares little for the result, and so is not helpful.

The greatest lack of accuracy in practice concerns determining which assets and liabilities can be netted. As capital charges are based on netted assets, and trading organizations are usually short of capital, it is the interest of the organization to net as much as possible, but this puts great requirements on systems.

While traders rarely care about the accounting function in its preparation of the balance sheets, that changes when trading desks are charged for their use of capital since the capital charge will generally be based on numbers calculated by the accounting function. Thus introducing charging for capital may result in the trading function being more helpful to the accountants so reducing the accounting risk. Such behavioural aspects of risk management are important, and should not be neglected in the pursuit of mathematical measures of risk.

External reporting

The discussion above has shown that even with freedom to choose policies there are plenty of ways in which reported accounting information can be misleading. For external reporting there are the additional restrictions of legal regulations and accounting standards, as well as the complications of separate legal entities. A given trading desk frequently trades in several legal entities, the entity for each individual trade being chosen based on where it is most tax-efficient.

While the paradigm of current-cost accounting for published accounts was investigated in some detail during the inflation of the 1970s, it has sunk with very little trace and virtually all published sets of accounts are prepared on a historic cost basis. However, that would present a most misleading picture for most trading houses. Treatments vary between countries, e.g. in the UK, banks therefore use the 'true and fair' override, in other words breaking the accounting rules laid down by the law to use more appropriate methods. The particular, more appropriate, method used is marking the trading assets and liabilities to market prices. In Switzerland the individual entity statutory accounts are prepared on a historic cost basis and so are of little use to understanding profitability, but group accounts are published using International Accounting Standards which do permit marking to market.

This is not the place for a discussion of the meaning of published accounts, but if one assumes that they are for the benefit of current and potential investors, who in a commonsense way define profit as being the amount by which the net assets of the group have grown, then all the earlier discussion about FX seems unnecessary here since the net assets approach will give the answer that they seek. However, there is one important difference which is that published consolidated profits of groups of companies are generally performed based on the accounts of the individual entities rather than looking at the whole list of assets and liabilities. Thus a profit made in GBP in a Swiss subsidiary of an American bank may be converted first to CHF and then to USD. This raises the likelihood that at least one of the conversions will be done using the average rate method as discredited above. If so, then the reported profit can depend on which entity a given transaction is booked in, which is not sensible.

As a worked example, let us take the situation discussed above and extend it by saying that the other side of the trade was in a Sydney subsidiary of the same organization so we might obtain:

Zurich	GBP	CHF.GBP	CHF	USD.CHF	USD
Final position	1000	2.50	2500	0.70	1750
(less) starting position	(900)	3.00	(2700)	0.60	(1620)
Profit (loss)	100		(200)		130

Sydney	GBP	AUD.GBP	AUD	USD.AUD	USD
Final position	(1000)	2.40	(2400)	0.73	(1750)
(less) starting position	(900)	2.30	(2070)	0.78	(1620)
Profit (loss)	(100)		(330)		(130)
Total	0				0

We see that the position correctly shows no profit if we view both sides in any one currency, here USD are shown as well as GBP. However, if one had to produce a profit number using just the Zurich reported loss of CHF200 and the Sydney reported loss of AUD330 (both of which are correctly calculated) it is difficult to see how one would ever come up with 0!

Management accounting is generally indifferent to whether an instrument is off-balance sheet. The significance is higher concerning published accounts, and the effect can be seen in the following example, which compares the effect of a futures position with that of a 'cash' position in the underlying, and also of a marginned 'cash' position. As can be seen, the numbers appearing on the balance sheet are much smaller for the off-balance-sheet futures position.

Purchase price of underlying	100
Day 1 closing price	96
Day 2 closing price	103
Quantity	50
Initial futures margin	10%
Initial 'cash' margin	15%

	'Cash'	'Cash' on margin	Futures
Initial margin		(750)	(500)
Variation margin re day 1 paid day 2		(200)	(200)
		(950)	(700)
Variation margin re day 2 to pay day 3		350	350
Initially owing to broker		(4250)	
Variation margin paid		200	
		(4050)	
Cost of underlying			(5000)
Value of underlying			5150
Margin paid to broker			700
			850

End of day 2	**'Cash'**	**'Cash' on margin**	**Futures**
Asset on register	5150	5150	
Owed by broker/exchange			850
Owing to broker		(4050)	
Cash	(5000)	(950)	(700)
Net assets	150	150	150

Readers of accounts have no way of knowing how many such instruments are held from the balance sheets. The notes to the accounts give some information about notional values, but often at a fairly aggregated level which is often difficult to interpret.

Trading groups also have other assets, of which the most material is often property. These are generally not marked to market. Integrated finance houses which have significant income from say asset management or corporate finance activities will generally report those activities using a historical cost method. The resultant mixing of historical-cost and market values makes the published accounts very hard to interpret.

Accounting for end-users

End-users are different because financial instruments are only part of the business. While financial instruments can easily be marked to market since the assets are fungible and there are more or less liquid two-way markets, this does not apply to assets such as factories or work in progress. Thus such entities use historical cost accounting as a default. However, they may use accrual accounting or mark to market for their trading assets.

Internal reporting

Historical cost versus market to market

To clarify the difference between the different methods of accounting let us present a simple example:

			USD/bbl	(13.00)
Buy oil spot				
Sell oil forward 6 months			USD/bbl	15.00
Quantity			bbl	1000
Storage costs payable in arrears			USD/bbl/year	(2.00)
6-month USD borrowing cost payable in arrears				6.00%

	Historic cost	Accrual	Mark to market at inception	Mark to market at delivery
	USD	USD	USD	USD
Cost of oil purchased	(13 000)	(13 000)	(13 000)	(13 000)
Receivable for oil when delivered	15 000	15 000		15 000
Forward value of sold oil			14 563	
Storage costs payable in arrears	(1 000)	(1 000)		(1 000)
Forward value of storage costs			(971)	
Interest costs		(390)		(390)
Profit recognized at end of six months	1 000			
Profit recognized over six months		610		610
Profit recognized on day of deal			592	
Profit recognition per month 1	0	102	592	
2	0	102	4	
3	0	102	4	
4	0	102	4	
5	0	102	3	
6	1 000	102	3	
	1 000	610	610	

The pure historical cost method does not recognize the cost of borrowing in the trading accounts because that is included with all the other borrowing costs for the organization, and delays recognizing the profit until the sales invoice is due. The accrual method includes all the costs, but at their final cash value, and spreads the profit over the period of the deal. The mark to market method calculates the net present value of all income and costs, but recognizes the gain immediately. As the spot and forward prices of oil move over the following six months, the mark to market method would recognize any net differences each day, but with such a cleanly hedged position the effect would be unlikely to be much different from the smooth drip shown which represents the interest on the net profit (592*6%/2 = 18).

Profit is recognized earlier in the mark to market method. Losses are recognized at the same time under all methods, since the historical cost and accrual methods are not symmetrical, because they embrace the concept of prudency. Applying such lack of uniformity requires more human judgement. This illustrates the higher risk associated with longer-term trades, where the acceleration in the recognition of profit is most marked.

Hedge accounting

For management decision-making all relevant instruments should be marked to market. For the financial instruments this is conceptually straightforward, although all but the largest end-users lack the critical mass of banks in terms of modelling expertise and market price knowledge so for OTC instruments may rely on the provider of the instrument. OTC instruments also suffer from a lack of liquidity, but *per se* this should not affect their value, since most end-users intend to hold their instrument until maturity.

The more difficult aspect can be in identifying the movements in value of the assets or liabilities against which the financial transactions were entered into as hedges. If an interest-rate swap is entered into as a hedge to fix the rate of a floating rate debenture then it is easy to value the debenture using a market yield curve and show how effective the hedge is. Such matching is similarly easy if a specific oil cargo in transit is sold forward, or put options representing the same volume of oil as in the cargo are purchased, since the physical commodity can be separately identified and valued at the spot price.

Things become less clear-cut when considering the situation faced by an oil refinery which has sold a three-month crack spread future. The volume sold may be chosen to approximate the physical capacity of the refinery for the third month, but operational realities may result in a slightly different actual throughput. The mix of refined products that will be produced is not known exactly in advance, and hopefully will depend on which provide the greatest profit at the time of sale. Should all the firm purchases and sales for the third month, for the next three months, or for all time, also be marked to market?

One way to make the decisions easier as to what to include in the mark-to-market model is to transact trades in the underlying commodities between the operational department and the treasury department. With this approach the operational department treats treasury like any other customer, and mark-to-market accounting is restricted to the treasury department. This certainly places a clear understandable boundary around market operations. It has the disadvantage that the same position may be valued differently in two departments within the one entity, but such a mismatch has to happen somewhere in an entity using two methods of accounting. In the case of a flexible refinery there is also the mismatch between the product mix sold to treasury and that produced in fact.

Treating treasury as an external customer has implications for culture, and possible choice of personnel, which need to be addressed. There is a danger that operational department will feel exposed to treasury, and therefore recruit what is effectively a subsidiary treasury function themselves, thus duplicating effort and increasing costs unnecessarily. To prevent this it is necessary to have an overall firm culture (with matching appraisal and bonus policies) which stresses cooperation.

We can also consider the case of the ice-cream manufacturer which has sold heating degree days in a weather swap on the basis that the hotter the weather, the more ice cream it will sell and thus the higher will be the gross margin. The swap could be valued based only on actuals with historic averages for the future, or including latest forecast. Which is considered most appropriate would depend on whether the manufacturer sold direct to the public, in which case sales would only be recognized on the day of consumption, or to wholesalers who might buy greater quantities as soon as they saw more warm weather coming.

The fact that the profit or loss on the derivative transaction can be accurately and precisely defined, while the hopefully opposite result which it is hedging is often more difficult to measure, may result in treasury being unfairly criticized for losses on hedges. One would expect hedges to lose money half the time – the benefit is that the volatility of overall earnings should be lower and the risk of bankruptcy lower.

A particular situation which occurs frequently is FX transactions entered into to hedge the results of the operations of foreign-currency subsidiaries. For end-users the average-rate translation of profits is standard, and management may well have entered into the hedge with the first priority being to protect the operating profits line appearing in the published accounts rather than net assets. This is a clear case of an inappropriate policy, in this case an accounting standard, leading to suboptimal economic decisions. In such a situation it makes sense for management reports to show the hedge marked to market, together with the effect of rate movements on the projected profit of the foreign subsidiary.

It is clear that this is a field where there are few definitive answers, and judgement is required by management to define what they want to gain from the information they receive. Unless there is a move to full current cost accounting, any mark to market information in an end-user environment will only ever be indicative information.

Discount rate

Non-banks need to consider the discount rate they use, but there is no simple answer. Banks blithely reach for LIBOR in nearly any situation because that is the rate at which they can lend and borrow in the market (unless they are beset by rumours of impending bankruptcy). A non-bank may well face a rather higher rate for loans, although it should be able to obtain a rate very similar to the banks for deposits. Thus if an industrial organization is short of cash it might consider valuing future predicted cashflow streams at its cost of borrowing.

Otherwise if LIBOR is used, a trader would appear to make profits on inception for loans to counterparties at rates above LIBOR but below the organization's cost of borrowing, although this profit would leak away as the real cost of funding was recognized over time. However, it does not seem sensible for such an organization valuing options using the Black–Scholes model to use anything other than LIBOR as the input parameter. This is an area where consensus has not yet been reached.

External reporting

The external reporting of the effect of financial instruments by end-users is the area which attracts most of the commentary in the press on accounting for derivatives, but as discussed in the previous section, neat answers will never be obtainable while historical cost accounting is standard for these entities. The impossibility of coming up with a neat answer is probably the explanation for the great amount of discussion, although considerable effort has gone into trying to define tightly the scope of hedge accounting. As discussed above, that is almost by definition a very subjective area.

Given that the primary financial statements (balance sheet and profit and loss account) cannot currently be changed from historical cost, the various accounting standards promulgated by various standard-setters concentrate on requiring extra disclosures in the annual accounts. The usefulness of these is debatable, and as accounts are hardly ever published until at least 60 days after the end of the year, when positions can be changed with a five-minute phone call they cannot be any more than an indication to investors of possible questions for management.

The most obvious sticking point is any fixed rate debt used for funding the company. Unless this is revalued using the market yield curve, does it really make sense to revalue the interest rate swap that converts some floating rate debt to fixed? If the company is considered a poor credit risk and so its debt is trading at a significant discount, should the accounts value it at the amount that it would actually cost to buy it back? It seems intuitively wrong to record a gain just because the company is considered more likely to go bankrupt! There are no easy answers to such questions, and so the risk of accounting treatments leading to inappropriate decisions is higher when dealing with investment decisions based on published accounts than with management accounts.

As the published accounts may not reflect the full economic mark to market position, there may be situations where management has to choose between hedging the economic position and hedging the published numbers. Such a conflict of objectives can be reduced by providing extra information in the accounts, and educating the analysts who use it.

Conclusion

While the accounting function may seem simple until accountants start talking, we have shown in this chapter some examples of how a clear and coherent policy is essential to avoid the various traps which can cause accounting data to encourage suboptimal decisions. It is important that policy on all such issues is clearly set out at a senior and knowledgeable level on such matters as profit remittance which has implications for both FX and interest allocation. Such policy needs to be implemented in the systems and procedures throughout the organization, and monitored by Control departments or Internal Audit. Inaccuracies are less likely to arise if senior management does not fret at some 'noise' in the reported profits.

17

External reporting: compliance and documentation risk

THOMAS DONAHOE

Introduction

Billions of dollars have been lost in the financial services industry due to compliance violations and documentation errors. The misuse or misapplication of derivative instruments has been a major factor in many of these losses. The actual violations have ranged from inadequate disclosure to clients, unlicensed sales personnel, improper corporate governance, *ultra vires* transactions, and inadequate or error-prone documentation. The root causes have been primarily insufficient or outdated controls or failure to enforce controls. The media focus on these major losses due to lax internal controls or violations of external regulatory requirements has become a permanent blotch on the reputation of the industry.

While Value-at-Risk and stress scenarios can help optimize the use of risk capital and improve returns, large equity losses are often the result not of market risk but rather of compliance failures. Often it is a trusted or highly regarded employee (often long standing) who causes the damage. Typically, the loss is not triggered by a single event but occurs over time. A recent example occurred in Chicago in late 1998, where a futures brokerage was being sold. Just prior to the scheduled closing, the CFO of Griffin Trading Co. revealed that he had lost millions by trading stock options with the firm's money. The unauthorized trading went undetected for more than a year and the company became another compliance casualty (see Ewing and Bailey, 1999).

While compliance and documentation risks can never be eliminated, they can be contained. This chapter is intended as a broad overview of compliance risk and highlights the major issues confronting manager of derivatives sales staffs. It focuses on practical methods to ensure compliance that will survive the continuing consolidation of financial service companies and changes in regulatory oversight. This chapter is divided into four main parts:

- Structuring a compliance unit
- Creating enforceable policies
- Implementing compliance policies
- Reporting and documentation controls.

There will be reference throughout the chapter to actual losses that have occurred to emphasize the critical importance of appropriate controls. The goal is not to detect actual problems. Rather it is to discover ineffective, omitted, or outdated controls that could lead to actual losses. The reader should have an overview of why compliance controls are critical and how they can be used to limit business risk.

A compliance unit should play an active role in a firm's business strategy. It enables business lines to optimize revenues by limiting non-market risks such as credit, operations, and reputational risk. In many firms, however, compliance is viewed as an add-on expense and an impediment to performance. It is perceived to drain valuable resources and time and to serve as an adversary to achieving business goals. This chapter reflects the view that compliance is necessary and beneficial. Complying with external regulations and internal policies will insure greater consistency of performance and will in the long run, reduce capital needed to fund incidences of operational failure and fraud.

Defining compliance risk

Compliance risk can be defined as 'the risk to earnings or capital from violations, or nonconformance with laws, rules, regulations, prescribed practices, or ethical standards' (*OCC Comptroller's Handbook*, 1997). Compliance programs typically originate to satisfy external laws and regulations. As programs become more developed, they start to include monitoring of adherence to internal guidelines and management directives. One stumbling block is that compliance risk is often not subject to sufficient scrutiny. Instead, 'compliance risk is often overlooked as it blends into operational risk and transaction processing.'[1]

Focusing exclusively on satisfying external compliance is a necessary but perhaps not a sufficient standard. The derivatives markets continue to outpace the regulators and oversight often lags behind the creation of new products and markets. The 'crazy quilt' structure of derivatives' regulations tends to compound these compliance risks since oversight gaps occur. Given the overlapping and sometime conflicting framework of oversight, this can be a real challenge. (See the Appendix for an outline of US and UK regulatory schemes.) Compliance controls remain a front-line defense and the proper goals should be to help insure against large losses as well as prevent regulatory violations.

The typical reaction to compliance standards is that one needs only to maintain minimal standards. Cooperation from the business staff is often limited. Compliance is not a particularly popular topic among traders and salespeople since they focus on business targets leading directly to higher compensation. Only grudgingly will employees focus on this type of risk and often, the focus is on the negative duties of compliance. The reality is that compliance can 'empower people'. These controls enable people to accomplish goals and ensure closure. 'It is only when procedures are neglected or abused that they become an impediment.'[2]

The other extreme may occur where compliance controls represent a virtual straitjacket. In some organizations, compliance standards to satisfy regulatory requirements are set so high that they become obstacles to daily business. Typically this occurs when a company has suffered a major loss and attempts to 'overcompensate' for past errors.[3] A companion danger is when internal controls are so rigid, an exception must be made for normal, large-sized transactions. The automatic granting of exceptions can easily undermine controls or foster an attitude that all standards can be negotiated.

The dramatic growth and widespread usage of derivative instruments as well as the diversity of market participants have provided fertile ground for disputes. Given the large sums of money involved and the relatively small amount of initial cash outlays (i.e. leverage), compliance failures have been costly. This has been a major risk in the derivatives world since the Hammersmith and Fulham case in the 1980s, through the Procter & Gamble fiasco of 1994–5, to today where companies in Asia are attempting to renege on losing derivatives contracts.

Hammersmith and Fulham was a municipal UK entity that engaged in swap transactions. The English courts determined that the transactions were outside the scope of the municipality's charter (i.e. *ultra vires*) and the municipality was not required to pay accumulated losses of several hundred million pounds. A more thorough legal review of the counterparty's 'capacity to contract' would likely have limited the losses suffered by the counterparty banks.

Procter & Gamble was able to avoiding paying much of its swap losses due to the failure of the counterparty bank to provide accurate valuations and full disclosure as to transaction risks. A stricter control oversight of client communications and of periodic valuations sent to the client would likely have limited these losses by the counterparty bank. The current litigation involving Asian companies centers again around similar issues of disclosure and fiduciary duties, if any, that exist between the swap counterparties. In today's litigious environment, compliance errors often have expensive consequences.

Structuring a compliance unit

This section focuses on properly structuring a compliance unit. It details the duties of senior management, describes how to align compliance with business lines, and describes a range of compliance activities. The section ends with a review of common compliance errors.

Delegation by board of directors

Compliance controls, like any core business strategy, emanate from the top. The board of directors oversees the control culture and corporate personality of a firm. The board should promulgate a mission statement that highlights the importance of compliance and evidences the board's full support for compliance efforts. The head of compliance should likely report to the head of the law department or the CFO. As regards derivatives, the board has several key responsibilities including:

- Understanding the broad risks of derivatives
- Setting clear objectives
- Making informed decisions
- Identifying specifically who can authorize risk taking
- Ensuring adequate controls are in place
- Ensuring that senior management hires qualified personnel
- Complying with external regulations and with company's stated compliance and investment policies
- Overseeing public disclosures

The board must understand the fundamental risks of derivatives. They must be conversant with concepts ranging from liquidity, volatility and market share to option fundamentals. Risk measurements such as the broad outlines of Value-at-Risk must be a familiar subject.

The board must set clear objectives as to risk appetite, permitted instruments, and maturity limits that are measurable and enforceable. Notional amounts often are too crude a measure since they do not adequately account for leverage and imbedded options. A credit equivalent exposure may be more appropriate.

The board must review proposed transactions/programs and ratify completed transactions, ensuring full disclosure of risks and volatility of returns. Where information is inadequate, the board must be sufficiently knowledgeable to know the proper questions to ask.

The control of which individuals can take risk is perhaps the most significant preventative measure that a board retains and should ensure this oversight is strictly enforced. The board should be especially alert to those who have actual authority as well as those with apparent authority. A periodic update sent to counterparty dealers indicating changes in authorized employees is a useful control.

The board must put in place a structure that will ensure controls adequate to the proposed uses of derivatives. Compliance risk is a key consideration in managing the business risks of a firm. A compliance officer should be linked to each major business stream. Many compliance losses result generally from a pattern of conduct as opposed to a single event. Having compliance personnel 'rubbing elbows' with the business side is an essential safeguard.

Compliance officers should exercise independence of the line of business, otherwise there is a fundamental flaw in the compliance structure itself. A common mistake is that the compliance process is designed around employees rather than job functions. Another potential flaw is when turnover of staff allows business employees to 'drift into' compliance-related functions. This frequently happens when the compliance staff lacks a thorough understanding of the business processes.

Senior management must ensure that qualified personnel staff the critical compliance functions. The staff should be experienced, sufficiently trained, and provided with sufficient resources and tools to remain current. This means adequate technology support, seminars, publications and access to internal/external counsel. There is no implication that the board of directors follow every nuance in derivatives activity. Rather they can and do rely on the representations of senior managers and audit professionals. They must review derivatives reports and information and activity for consistency, accuracy, and conformity to company goals and delegated authority. Not only must there be a sufficient control environment, the Board must actively verify the effectiveness of these controls.

Senior managers often view exposures in economic terms and do not focus on legal or disclosure requirements. Management may lose sight of the fact that legal liabilities related to compliance errors often dwarf business risks. Products need to be sold, customers need to be served, and profits need to be made. The full impact of which legal entity is used for booking a non-standard deal is often an afterthought. The deal may run foul of compliance and legal requirements despite the best of intentions. The demands of immediate economic performance should not be a rationalization for sloppy controls.

A companion concern is when a company has so many large businesses that the ramifications of a smaller segment of a business seems unimportant. Management focus is often on dollar volume or profit margins and less focus is given to products having lower profiles. Another issue is that given the increased complexity of the business, compliance and audit staffs may be understaffed or insufficiently trained. Control activities are most effective when they are viewed by management and other personnel as integral part of, rather than an addition to, the daily operations of the company [bank] (Basel Committee on Banking Supervision, 1998).

Public disclosures are generally the responsibility of the controller's unit and it is often the audit committee of the board, with some help from the law department, that oversees these activities. Problems in this area tend to occur infrequently but often have major impact. There has been increasing SEC focus on this area and inadequate or inaccurate disclosure has enabled the SEC to pursue an enforcement action that might otherwise have been doubtful. In the Gibson Greeting case, the deliberate misvaluations of derivatives provided by the counterparty bank led to Gibson releasing inaccurate financial statements. This led to SEC charges against the bank as well as against officers of Gibson Greetings itself.[4]

Division of labor

The term 'derivative' covers a wide range of instruments that could be construed alternatively as a security, a futures contract, a hybrid, or have an uncertain status. For the purposes of this chapter, we eliminate all discussion of derivative securities such as Mortgage Backed Securities (MBS). Instead the focus is primarily on over-the counter (OTC) derivative contracts: swaps, caps, floors, etc. with some discussion of exchange traded instruments.

There is no single, proper compliance structure given the wide range of business structures using derivatives. Instead, a *proper* infrastructure reflecting the specific needs of each organization is the goal. Ideally, the compliance framework should be structured along business and functional lines. The key departments are likely to be divisional compliance units, possibly a central compliance department (for a large firm) and the law department.

Divisional compliance units should be independent of the business stream but would likely report to a business head as well as to central compliance. Divisional compliance personnel should be on-site providing immediate access to the business people. This facilitates daily interaction and allows compliance to be familiar with customer flows, market changes, and problems as they occur. In addition, they can provide an immediate response to business people. This encourages an informal exchange of information as well as facilitating business processes. This informality allows information to be placed in context and enables compliance to observe the behavior and attitude of the business people. This proximity should function as a 'safety net' or early-warning system. Relying exclusively on formalized reports and scripted encounters ensures that compliance can only detect, they cannot prevent. Whistleblowers are also more likely to alert compliance to activities which merit further review in an informal environment.

A central compliance unit can focus on regulations applying across an entire legal entity. These macro concerns would include regulatory inquiries, Chinese wall issues, employee licensing, compliance training, business conduct issues, and employees' personal trading accounts and the coordinating of regulatory reporting (with controllers being primarily responsible).

The law department properly focuses on approving the ISDA, IFEMA[5] templates, regulatory disclosures and filings, and certifying reports to the board of directors. The law department also confirms the range of activities permitted by each legal entity, approves press releases, and oversees contacts with the media. The department would also work with a company's governmental affairs unit as relevant legislation is proposed.

Many large institutions tend to have several attorneys involved in the compliance area and given the typical complexity of derivatives oversight, this is often a preferred approach. In a large institution, there is frequently an imprecise allocation of compliance responsibilities that sometimes results in an overlap or gap of responsibilities. Depending on the corporate structure, if the compliance attorneys are placed in competition with attorneys from the law department there may be an effectiveness concern. Compliance personnel will be closer to the market but the law department may have more time for additional analysis. Without a clear hierarchy, one may have a situation where compliance could handle matters in a manner independent from and without the knowledge of the law department. As a result, the business people may simply choose the lowest compliance hurdle. In a similar vein, if the head of a compliance unit does not strictly enforce requirements, then it will difficult for the subordinates to get full cooperation from the business people.

It is difficult to determine how many compliance people are required for an institution since it depends heavily on the nature of the products sold, the complexity of line of business or products, type of legal entity, and the nature of the customer base. A simple adequacy test is whether or not delays occur in sending out marketing materials because compliance is not able to review the disclosure language. Serious mistakes can occur equally from insufficient staffing or from an overworked staff. If expansion of the compliance staff is needed, it should not be allowed to lead to a diminution of quality. At a minimum, it is recommended that management review the adequacy of training and knowledge base of the compliance officers on an annual basis.

Staffing the compliance unit

Compliance officers typically have experience in operations, audit, legal, or trading. Within a divisional staff, one needs compliance specialists especially for exchange traded contracts or equity derivatives. The expertise need will vary by the complexity of the product and of the regulatory scheme. It may be helpful if the compliance staff is licensed to the same degree as the sales staff since compliance personnel may in some circumstances need to talk to a client directly.

The compliance staff should also be cross-trained in a different discipline so that the firm has a 'deeper bench' and so the compliance staff has a better understanding of activities across the firm. This keeps the staff fresh and rotation allows a new set of eyes to review the processes. This cross-pollination may also expose areas where the compliance guidelines have not kept pace with market activities. To increase their usefulness, a compliance officer should develop a solid knowledge of the economics of the products being sold as well as an intimate understanding of the applicable regulations.

Some turnover is not necessarily bad within the compliance function. A new employee may well discover items that have been overlooked. Alternatively, the new employee may help identify short-cuts or bad habits that have been allowed to creep into the compliance process.

Typical compliance issues

The following are examples of compliance issues that can often lead to significant problems (ignoring the obvious example of insider trading):

- Lack of notification
- Focusing exclusively on a transaction and not the aggregate effects
- Miscommunication internally
- Unwillingness to admit error
- Lack of planning
- Fragmented internal oversight
- Failure to segregate customer and proprietary trading
- Failure to enforce basic rules
- Failure to follow market changes
- Failure to link system reports
- Multi-tasking of compliance
- Failure to track competitor activities

Lack of notification may lead a firm to be unaware that a compliance event has occurred. Businesses typically focus on sales volumes or profits. What many in a large corporate family overlook is that positions and actions are often aggregated across related companies for regulatory purposes. A related affiliate may be active with the same customer or use the same futures contract. These positions might need to be aggregated for purposes of complying with contract reporting or contract position limits. Alternatively, special regulatory filings may be triggered unless regulatory exemptions can be obtained.

Business people often focus on transaction specifics and may overlook the marginal impact on existing portfolio(s). The purchase of a specific bond may be entirely prudent. However, the regulations or internal policies and procedures might have credit concentration limits or country basket limits. There might well be enough room under the credit line for the particular obligor but the transaction runs foul of various macro limits. If the deals are not properly coded in inventory systems then country limits or currency limits may be unknowingly breached.

Miscommunication often occurs when people lapse into jargon. In one company, managers using futures have confused reporting limits with position limits. As a result, they used a less appropriate futures contract to hedge an exposure since they mistakenly thought they were nearing a position limit for a specific futures contract. This can result in an economic cost of executing a suboptimal hedging strategy. In a related occurrence, an external auditor disallowed favorable accounting treatment for short positions in futures. Short hedges were not utilized by the company until the external auditor later corrected the restriction so it would be applied properly only to naked 'short sales'.

Business people are often unwilling to say 'I don't know' or 'I made a mistake'. A trader might err when trading a position with a broker. In order to hide the error, he arranges with the broker to 'correct' the price. In turn, the trader directs new business to the broker to pay for the favor. Several large derivatives losses have occurred as a result of a trader speculating in the market to hide a previous error. In the late 1980s, ABN's New York branch had a FX options trader that executed sales instead of buying FX call options. The trader attempted to 'trade out' of the mistake and eventually lost more than $50 million.[6]

Simply not planning ahead with compliance can trigger problems. Traders often focus strictly on the economics of a transaction to the exclusion of regulatory requirements. They may wait until the last minute to consult with compliance. In the heat of battle during a trading day, traders may not inquire about the rules since there is time only for reflex action and not for reflection. A preventable violation may ensue and corrective action must then be undertaken.

Compliance areas sometimes exercise fragmented oversight and there is a danger that compliance staff becomes too specialized. They may be focused strictly on the requirements of securities law or commodities law and fail to see the full range of other regulations that may apply (e.g. pension money typically invokes ERISA regulations). There may be filing or disclosure documents that are triggered. Simply focusing on product-related compliance does not ensure success in satisfying complex entitywide regulatory requirements or customer disclosure requirements.

Failure to segregate customer and proprietary trading leads to the abusive practice of front running, i.e. knowing a customer's order and trading in the market ahead of the customer's trade. It is an ethical violation as well as violation of the fiduciary relationship that is created when a firm acts on behalf of its customer. An equally insidious practice is when a trader can execute for both a firm's account and customer accounts. Unless there is strict compliance control, losing trades have a tendency to wind up in the account that best suits the trader's compensation scheme. A trader of Canadian Governments at a New York money center bank had trading authority on a proprietary book as well as on clients' behalf. The bond clearing was done in Canada, the accounting in the UK, and trading in New York. The trader hid losses in customer accounts and eventually cost the bank more than $50 million in unauthorized trading losses. The division of controls in three geographic locations certainly played a role as well.

Failure to enforce simple rules and deadlines tends to lead to larger violations. Non-cooperation on the part of the business people with compliance is a frequent experience. If the business people are not required to abide by filing or reporting requirements, they may be enticed by gaps in oversight to violate more significant compliance guidelines.

As products and markets change, the type and range of compliance requirements will change as well. Frequently, business people will rely on documents that were negotiated and signed years before. Market practices could well have changed and the document no longer reflects best practices or current market conventions.

Failure to link systems reporting to all functional areas leads to gaps in oversight. Incompatible systems where manual reentry of data occurs is a companion issue. One large derivative dealer started to trade credit derivatives and the transactions were reported to all departments except the risk department. The risk unit was caught by surprise since the risk module report had not been linked-in. The risk unit knew that the product had been approved but were never notified that trading had actually started until a small portfolio had already been created.

When compliance units are charged with other duties, compliance may lose its focus. Production duties tend to get priority since they typically have pressing closing schedules. Frequently a compliance area may be doing a review just prior to the deadline. This tends to result either in an incomplete or hurried review which creates the opportunity for more errors to occur.

When a competitor makes a high-profile error, the regulators will often focus on the same issues in their next review Given the public awareness of the type of error made, regulators will often apply a higher standard of evaluation if they encounter a similar problem in the organization. This may occur even if no updated legislation or regulations have been enacted. Regulators typically can discover large compliance problems in a variety of ways: newspaper story, trade journal comments, competitor, disgruntled employee, aggrieved customer, private litigant, or auditor contact.

Creating enforceable policies

This section details the purpose and content of compliance policies. It examines in detail a suggested policies format and focuses on the challenges of overseeing a dealer's sales staff. This section ends with a review of compliance controls suited for money managers.

Purpose of policies

To be usable, Polices and Procedures (P&Ps) must stand in the context of a complete control environment. As a stand-alone document, they have limited usefulness unless they shape and reinforce corporate policies. P&Ps should provide a context for determining what rules apply, who has oversight, and what compliance documentation is appropriate. In order to be effective, the compliance manuals should be explanatory documents and not simply a listing of requirements. The front office must adhere closely to these permitted activities. Moreover, the back office must understand the business strategy so they can help identify bottlenecks and danger areas. An action may appear valid on the surface but has an unintended consequence which may breach a limit or cause a change in status. Dangers are often hidden from plain view and the players are simply caught looking the other way.

P&P exposure limits should reflect true exposure such as leverage or market replacement cost. Notional limits invite violations since they are a crude measure of risk. Escalation procedures should be in the document itself and having a bubble-up process is likely to be more reliable than a static 'break glass in case of emergency'. One should specifically designate that if the P&Ps are silent then they *do not* enable. Policies should also not be engulfed in such minute detail that they are applicable to a few desks or for a limited time only.

As one writes derivatives compliance policies, one should build on existing best practices as exemplified in industry and regulatory guidance.[7] Today, there are good resources and materials available on the Internet so that keeping pace with the changes and communicating them can be more easily effected. Industry groups, lobbyists and outside counsel are also good resources.

Desk procedure manuals and guides are required for the micro level of activity. They should describe the interfaces and responsibilities between and within departments. A typical compliance manual is often a stand-alone document, a chapter within an operations manual or woven into an omnibus document. It is often structured as follows. It commences with a description of the overall compliance goals and importance of the those goals. It then moves to a classification of derivatives by category: fixed income, equity, commodity, or credit and describes which products belong in the appropriate categories. Then a hierarchy of compliance requirements is laid out. Often there is an accompanying workflow chart that indicates which department or unit handles each specific step and it outlines the proper sequence of events. It will provide key questions to ask and answer as well as identify specific pitfalls to avoid.

The compliance manual will also direct the reader where to seek additional direction and how to determine whether any of the procedures have been updated or changed. A typical compliance manual may also become outdated rather quickly. Frequently, regulations change or the business mix changes and a business outgrows its controls. Updates must be sent as needed and on a timely basis. Some banks even distribute single-sheet risk placemats that can be kept at each trading or sales station so that compliance essentials are available for immediate reference.

A planning and coordination process should occur, so that you have a comprehensive and logical approach to compliance control that mimics your business processes. The problem often exists that the compliance process at many large institutions is the result of *ad-hoc*, incremental changes and not part of a coherent strategy. This almost ensures that gaps occur in the oversight process.

A prudent compliance and business strategy is to maintain the same level of control for unregulated OTC derivative sales as would be sufficient to meet the quality of SEC/CFTC oversight for exchange traded derivatives. There is always a danger that at a later date or during the course of litigation a transaction or relationship may be reclassified and a *post-facto* application of a different (higher) standard will be invoked. An aggrieved party might also attempt to invoke the fraud or disclosure provisions of securities law or commodities law in hopes of bolstering a cause of action.

Format of policies

The typical content of derivatives policies can be organized in the following way:

- Introduction
- Objectives
- Organization and responsibilities
- Permitted instruments/strategies
- Pre-transaction approval
- Post-transaction reporting
- Program approvals
- Counterparty guidelines
- Discipline/sanctions
- Policy review and modification

The introduction should outline the source of authorization and invoke underlying law and/or regulations and corporate authorization. The reader of the policies should be able to understand the reasoning and importance of fulfilling regulatory requirements and of conforming to internal control measures. There can be minimum standards but there should also be preferred standards that may provide the firm with an additional layer of protection. The information should be distilled down to the essentials. The business staff rarely embraces compliance requirements willingly but if they follow compliance rules then the intended goals are achieved.

The objectives section should delineate what are the appropriate uses for derivatives. They should be specific as to what type of risk-reduction is permitted and whether trading is contemplated or permitted. Issues such as leverage, holding period, and return measures should be specified.

The organization section should trace the delgation of authority from the board to senior managers. It should alert the reader to the chain of responsibility within the company. In addition, the escalation triggers and procedures should be outlined.

Permitted instruments should address which items are approved and for what customer/which purposes. It should indicate what is excluded as well. It might be prudent to mention the specific types of risk being hedged in addition to simply naming the instruments. There appears to be a whole cottage industry devoted to 'regulatory arbitrage' where instrument name does not always provide a true description of the instrument. The name serves mainly to fit it within regulatory reporting requirements or authorizations. This section should also address limits as to positions and credit exposure in notional terms (if applicable) but more likely in terms of actual and potential market and credit exposure terms. Duration measures and replacements costs are likely needed as additional measures of reference. This section would likely also address issues such as use of collateral, margin, and limits.

Pre-transaction approval should delineate the process of approval to be followed. It should specify with particulars, who is permitted to approve a transaction. An appendix, listing authorized employees, is appropriate and should be updated as needed. One could also provide a copy of a sample trade authorization form, numbering system methodology, and which departments are notified electronically of transactions.

Post-transaction reporting is especially important since this is often where problems are first detected. The more intractable problems with derivatives tend to be with non-standardized products. Initial cash flows often occur 3 or 6 months into the future so problems can remain hidden or undiscovered for some time and the market can move significantly in that time period.

Program approvals are especially important in order to expedite business. It makes no sense to revisit a specific type of transaction if each deal is a carbon copy of a previous one. One must ensure that the transactions are indeed standardized and not just similar. It would be prudent to spot test these types of transactions in order to verify/ensure that they are being recorded accurately.

Counterparty approval is especially important since credit risk typically represents one of the biggest risks taken by most institutions. The approval process should be specified and what resources need to be checked, e.g. the specific credit monitoring system. The counterparty section should also address the use of affiliates or related entities of approved counterparties. There should be a strong focus on the appropriateness of intercompany, arm's-length transactions and ensure safeguards that normal industry practices are adhered to. It is important to be alert for trades done at off-market prices or 'rolled into' a new reporting period.

Discipline and treatment of violations should be consistent, clear, and timely. Enforcing discipline will give 'teeth' to the guidelines and encourage active efforts at compliance. Problems corrected early are generally less costly and regulators tend to react less aggressively if a company can mend itself.

Providing an established routine for policy modification is paramount. You can rarely anticipate every situation and markets are dynamic enough that an annual review to policies and procedures, while a prudent choice, may not always be sufficient. With an escalation process in place, you will not find yourself locked into having to go to the board for marginal changes. Within certain constraints board ratification, as opposed to preapproval, may be a process that provides sufficient flexibility.

The ideal situation is to have compliance requirements that dovetail with sales, business, and investment practices. It eases the compliance process and enables employees to fold compliance into the normal business activity routine. You want to avoid too high hurdles, overly conservative compliance, and, even worse, redundant controls and reporting. If the reports ever become perfunctory, it may lead to problems that will remain under the radar. You will then have the most insidious of all situations, where there is an appearance of control where none in fact exists.

Compliance should be done on a formalized basis not *ad hoc*. The purpose, procedures, and protocol should be set out clearly so that employees know what is required. If everyone is responsible then no one is likely performing the necessary function. When specific individuals are not charged with oversight, gaps often occur. An analogy from the credit world is when a security is fully collateralized no one is responsible for monitoring the credit risk of the bond.

Sell side versus buy side

The compliance structure tends to be highly formalized on the sell side but less so on the buy side. Generally, the buy side has a single location and may not support a full-time derivatives team. Indeed the derivatives person might be charged with other duties as well. Control is more informal and subject to periodic oversight and periodic audit inquiries.

The buy side should generally have an easier time in ensuring compliance. Often they are not as heavily regulated an entity as a broker dealer. The number of individuals involved is typically small. Since derivative products are often used solely for risk-reducing purposes there is significantly less latitude for engaging in derivative activities. The debate continues as to whether highly formalized controls are needed by end-users. One industry study advises that 'it is crucial to rely on established reports and procedures, rather than culture or single individuals to sound the alarm' (Risk Standards Working Group, 1996).

The danger is that the people on staff understand the product but the audit function does not. Volumes are low and so the derivatives profile may be relatively low. The cost–benefit of doing a compliance audit is not deemed worth while. The obvious danger of this is shown by the off-site foreign affiliates of major banks that have lost great sums using derivatives or securities. The speculation using Treasury securities and forwards by Daiwa's New York office is a classic example of the difficulties faced in policing a remote office. Here a trader hid losses on US government bond trades over a 10-year period which totaled over several billion dollars.

The sell side given its enormous size and multi-site locations tends to have extensive formalized controls. Given that some of the trading sites are located in foreign money centers, it frequently occurs that compliance is controlled initially by on-site staff in each geographical location. Appropriate regional safeguards should be in place and enforced and head office should be kept informed. Head office should make periodic, comprehensive compliance reviews. The failure is often twofold– regional oversight fails and head office fails to follow up. The classic case was Nick Leeson who single-handedly bankrupted Barings plc. There the trader controlled trading as well as funds disbursement for the Singapore office of a UK merchant bank. Moreover, audit recommendations pointed out control lapses and recommended corrective measures. These audit recommendations were never enacted and within year, the firm was sold for a $1 to ING. A similar example with far fewer losses is now unfolding for Merrill Lynch in 1999. Its Singapore office finds itself embroiled in a scandal where a single private banker circumvented 'Merrill's accounting, compliance, and auditing operations' to engage in unauthorized trading using client funds (McDermott and Webb, 1999). The regional director knew that something was amiss but apparently did not pursue the issue.

Sales function checklist

Looking specifically at a dealer's sales force, the following is a generalized checklist of problem areas encountered:

- Market information
- Sales materials
- Term sheets
- Transactions
- Confirmations
- Valuations
- Warranties and representations
- Business conduct

Dealer salespeople should endeavor to ensure market information disseminated to clients is obtained from sources believed reliable. Appropriate written disclaimers should be employed. Salespeople should refrain from casting competitors in an unfavorable light. Competitor comments should be limited to our credit department has/has not changed its credit outlook on that name. As to derivatives transactions activity, other customers' names and activities should not be directly revealed and any trade information should be shrouded sufficiently so that other clients' confidentiality is preserved.

Derivatives sales materials should provide reasonable illustrations of the product. The pricing over various scenarios should represent a valid range of scenarios and assumptions should be clearly stated. Disclosure should provide all the relevant information that is needed to enable a comprehensive analysis. The more standardized the product, the more likely that standardized disclosure language may be sufficient.

Term sheets should be accurate and disclose appropriate risks to consider. Pricing and liquidity issues are especially important to mention. If the term sheet is being sent out to multiple clients, it should be proofed carefully to remove any mention of a specific company. The law department should approve standardized disclosures and should be consulted for the one-off situations where a customized product is involved. A legal department approval number with expiry date should be included.

For non-standard trades, it is often wise to do a 'dry run' if feasible and involve the operations unit. Frequently there is a clearing issue or documentation issue or details of the trade that turn out not to have been considered/finalized in advance. It's a preferred time to resolve these omissions before trade time. The completed transaction should reflect the term sheet. 'Bidding to miss' (where a dealer makes only a semi-interested bid for business) should be avoided since it hurts all parties involved. The customer does not receive a true market price comparison, the bidder may develop a bad reputation, and the winner does not get an accurate 'cover'.

The following are items that should be clarified prior to time of trade:

- Exact legal name of the counterparty

- Verify credit availability
- End-user company has power to transact
- End-user employee has specific authority to transact
- Derivative is suitable given client's size, sophistication, and risk profile
- End-user has analyzed or has the capacity to analyze the deal(s)
- Dealer is not acting as a fiduciary

Most large corporations have a large number of affiliates, partnerships, or joint ventures. It is imperative that the dealer establishes who is the exact, legal counter-party on a transaction. It will help determine the dealer's legal rights in the event of breach/non-performance. It is critically important to determine whether the end-user is dealing in the name of its holding company, operating company, or other corporate affiliate.

Credit availability should be obtained from a listing that is current. Some firms rely on a printout from the previous day and do not have on-line capabilities to know the full, current exposure. If credit approval is not preset, then salespeople need to obtain current financials from client for the credit approval department. Even when a dealer sells an option to an end-user, due diligence dictates that the dealer obtain end-user financials as part of the 'know your customer' requirements.

Most corporate end-users are empowered by their charter to do almost anything. Highly regulated industries like insurance companies and municipalities have significant restrictions. The law department of the dealer should be comfortable with the end-user's power to contract or alternatively the dealer must ask for an amendment to the charter or board approval or alternatively for a legal opinion from the end-user's counsel indicating that the contemplated transaction is permitted.

An end-user may have actual or apparent authority. The dealer should rely on actual authority and the dealer should ask for a listing of approved traders. After the trade, it may be prudent to ask for a certificate of incumbency of the end-user employee/officer who signs the derivative confirmation.

Suitability does not simply mean that the end-user can use derivatives. Rather it is a higher standard. Given the size, skill, and sophistication of the end-user (coupled with its outside advisers if any) and in view of its risk appetite, past activity, etc. is the deal appropriate? It is advisable to look inside the customer and establish that the customer meets this suitability threshold.

One needs to 'know the customer'. One should examine closely the economic purposes for using derivatives. Some end-users in the past have used the swap market to mask loans. A bank would make an upfront payment (or during the first year) and the recipient would then repay the loan amount as part of the coupon payments scheduled over the remaining life of the swap. In a similar vein, Merrill Lynch currently is engaged in a lawsuit filed by the CFTC. Merrill is charged with 'aiding and abetting' Sumitomo to corner the copper market by providing a trading account and more than a half billion dollars' worth of financing and letters of credit. The regulator charges that Merrill employees knew of the illegal conspiracy to corner the copper market (Peteren, 1999).

The salesperson must be properly licensed and communication with the client should be monitored periodically. Term sheets must be vetted to ensure sufficient disclosures and disclaimer. It is important to note that adequacy of disclosure may well vary with the complexity and risk of the product being sold. Although futures contracts lend themselves to standardized disclosure, the OTC derivatives market does not. Proper safeguards should be in place so that no side guarantees are being made to the customer. Beware salespeople who are CPAs or JDs, since they may cross the line and provide professional advice. One of the biggest sources of litigation in the past has been the failure to adequately supervise the sales staff.

Confirmations should be timely and accurate. Typically in a large dealer, the salesman, trader, and compliance/legal will review a confirmation before it is sent out to the client. If a dealer is not able to send out a confirmation on a timely basis, it should send out a preliminary confirmation. This would contain the name of the product and a description of the transaction included essential information such as notional amount, index, start and end date, and with the disclaimer that it is a preliminary confirmation to be superseded by a formal confirmation. In times of market turmoil, it sometimes occurs that confirmations are delayed. Given the lack of written confirmation and fast moving markets, there exists the moral hazard where a losing party denies the existence or terms of a deal. This can be combated most effectively by securing a written confirmation.

Valuations sent to customers should always be written and qualified as whether it is a firm price or an estimate. Whenever possible, it should also contain a reference interest rate and/or volatility level along with date and time so that customer can place the pricing in context.

Business conduct policy

Employees need a roadmap to guide them and a typical conduct policy would address the following issues:

- No insider trading
- No acceptance of gifts over a certain value
- No interested transactions with the company
- Whistleblower protection
- Salespersons shall not own stock of companies covered
- Traders shall not trade the same instrument for personal accounts that they trade on the job
- Competitor contact parameters
- Comments to media
- Software development
- Client entertainment
- Confidential information

Policies are often too broad or simply written poorly. It is typically helpful to provide examples when there is any likelihood of any misunderstanding or confusion. pwdAlternatively, one may want to use an example to emphasize the significance of a particular rule.

No employee should trade based on non-public information of information obtained due to his or her unique relationship with a company. Even the appearance of impropriety should be avoided. Salespersons cannot own customer stock simply to ensure that there are no trades that can 'tainted' by possible access to confidential information. In the same spirit, a trader cannot trade the same product for the company that he or she trades for their own personal account. This discourages moral hazard and the temptation to focus on personal positions to the detriment of the company's position. Competitors can be contacted as long as it is on a professional basis and no laws are violated such as price fixing, collusion, etc. or the meetings can be construed as creating a buying cartel.

Media comments and training tapes are two areas of special caution. Publicity is generally good but you want to ensure that it is controlled and that there is no inadvertent release of information. Moreover, there may be strategic initiatives that are occurring unknown to the person providing media comments and those comments may be misconstrued in retrospect. Training tapes are often given to hyperbole and when taken out of context, may present a distorted view of company policies.

Client entertainment should be appropriate to the overall client–dealer relationship. For clients similarly situated, the frequency and expense should be in a comparable range. It is a preferred practice to accompany a client rather than send a client to an event.

Salespersons may become privy to confidential information about a client. They should be especially careful not to divulge the information especially if it is material, non-public information. Conversely, compliance should ensure that spreadsheets and dealers' proprietary information are not being sent out to a customer via facsimile, e-mail or other means without proper authorization. Any non-standard information that does not fit into a prespecified template should be approved by divisional compliance. There are two main cautions. The customer might rely on a spreadsheet or adjust it for purposes/transactions for which it was not intended. In addition, if there are any dealer trade secrets or protected information, it may lose its protected status if it is widely or indiscriminately disseminated.

In the documentation of a transaction, a dealer should establish non-reliance on the part of the end-user. Moreover, the dealer is not a financial advisor and each party to the trade is acting independently and the end-user should determine that transaction is an appropriate one. No guarantees or assurances as to the results of the transaction should be made. Each party should have the authority to enter into the transaction and take on the risks entailed in the specific transaction.

Outside money managers

An outside money manager can do an excellent investment job. The problems are that they are typically off-site, have a different investment strategy, are not your company employees, and their credit analysis and standards may be different from those of your company.

The investment agreement and policies and procedures for the use of derivatives must be carefully crafted. The policies must be comprehensible, focused, comprehensive and enforceable. We are a contract-based society. It must be clear about what has been delegated to other institutions and what fiduciary responsibilities we have assumed (Erikson, 1996).

As we have reviewed, compliance policies developed and implemented within an organization should be internally consistent and provide sufficient controls. When funds are transferred for management to a partnership, affiliate, or outside money manager, control becomes significantly more difficult. These legal divisions must be respected and limited partners should be cautious not to direct the business and infringe upon the rights of the general partner and so jeopardize tax and legal benefits of the structure.

With any investment approach, there are typically multiple objectives and these should be ranked by priority to ensure that the manager will follow guidelines. It is prudent to evaluate how a hedging strategy will be viewed under various market scenarios and whether end of year results or interim mark to market pricing has priority. An equity collar to protect a stock position, will look poorly if the equity market rises sharply. Although collars may be a prudent strategy, performance could be several percentage points behind an unhedged equity position on an interim mark-to-market basis.

To maintain independence, an investor cannot control a manager's credit selections as they are made. Rather one must set up a process that reflects desired parameters. A common predicament is when an asset is sold by the investor and yet the outside manager may buy it as attractive. How do you reconcile that to your board? If you sell assets and incur a tax loss, one must wait the requisite period of time before repurchasing them or else 'wash sale' rules may be invoked. What happens if an outside manager buys those same assets in the market prior to the time limit? It may jeopardize your tax strategy.

In order to avoid 'delegating in the dark', the proper controls must be communicated. After all, your controls' effectiveness will always be reviewed *post facto*. Reports may not be available until days or weeks after the end of the reporting time period. If reports arrive by fax and have to be reentered into your systems, it's a process rife with error.

With money managers, the following topics are especially important to focus upon:

- Clearly document fiduciary relationship
- Explicitly outline investment policy
- Summarize derivatives policy
- Agree on methodology for tracking performance
- Specify credit standards
- Select permitted counterparties
- Collateral usage
- Repo activity/leverage
- Types of reports and frequency

The investment manager contract should be clear and crisply written. The fee schedule should be clearly agreed upon. Any 'buzzwords' should be defined. Proxy hedges should be limited to specific circumstances. Leveraging should be prohibited or controlled as deemed appropriate. If the outside manager uses futures contracts, the activity may impact the treatment/status of the investor. The futures position may need to be aggregated for reporting purposes.

The derivatives policy should be clearly summarized. Note that separate investment guidelines and derivatives guidelines are commonly prepared for external managers. Also the external manger should provide the client with a derivatives strategy statement citing types of derivative to be used and for what purpose(s). The strategy statement should be signed by the board of directors or its designate. The derivatives products allowed should be clearly stated. Some firms categorize derivatives by level of risk and depth of market. These categories are not permanent classification since markets may become more developed over time, e.g. credit derivatives. In one classification schema, 'A' derivatives are liquid and standardized products, 'B' are semi-liquid and customized, and 'C' are leveraged or exotic products and so off limits. There is room for the 'B' and 'C' products to migrate over time to a higher status. Limitations of hedging to transaction specific as opposed to macro hedges should also be enumerated.

The methodology for tracking performance should be explicit. What is the benchmark/performance objective and how frequently can the portfolio rebalance? What are investment guidelines, asset selection methodology, and portfolio composition/allocation ranges? Define duration and spread parameters. What are the gain/loss constraints? Tax guidelines? How will income be reinvested? It takes time to invest sufficient amounts of money to achieve diversification. When do the standards as to diversification kick in? Are you monitoring all purchases or the aggregate impact on the portfolio?

Credit parameters are a common area of dispute. Is subordinated or junior paper permitted? Is the credit test simply at inception or is it a maintenance test? Quality ratings for individual securities and total portfolio? How are split ratings handled? If a downgrade occurs, is there an automatic sale provision or is each investment considered separately? Permitted counterparties are a companion issue. Must they be from the same approved list of the investor or can the investment manager make his or her own determination?

Collateral usage brings with it all the issues of monitoring, valuation, custody, and rehypothecation. As the investor, you are one step removed from the investment process already and this adds another layer of complexity to the outside manager. Repo activity, leverage, and the writing of covered calls are all methods of enhancing income. Depending on the risk tolerance of the investor and how restrictive the fiduciary guidelines that the investor must follow, these may be avenues open for pursuit.

Implementing compliance policies

This section covers the proper implementation of policies and motivating employees to implement these policies. It addresses the differing challenges of offering new products to old and new customers as well as managing existing business and details the training needed for employees.

Gaining acceptance

The full cooperation of business lines is needed to meet compliance goals. It is an ongoing struggle to generate assistance and cooperation from the business side since compliance is viewed as a fixed cost drag on profits. No matter now skilled the compliance people nor how detailed the reports, there are business subtleties and nuances that are known best by the business people. In the case of a money manager, compliance may be focused on satisfying external regulations and overlook 'fairness issues' relating to equal treatment for all investors.

You will obtain more cooperation from business line employees by making it convenient to comply. Staff the compliance function adequately, give them cellular phones and beepers. Ensure that you have an early and late shift, if necessary, to cover the full trading day. Business people are notorious for making one feeble attempt at compliance and not following up. Help ensure that they connect with compliance the first time.

The derivatives industry is too dynamic for permanent organizational charts. Never believe that having formal lines of communication will ever be sufficient by themselves. Informal contact should supplement control measures and will allow greater insight into risks being taken. When a potential error is spotted or an error made repeatedly, it may be time to update the procedures and communicate those changes. Some errors are correctable with certain efforts and there may not be a need to elevate an error to a violation level if it is easily corrected or controlled.

You must ask proactive questions. Is the trader using derivatives in an authorized fashion? Is he or she reducing risk the market has created or creating certain exposures that force him to use derivatives to bring his exposure back into line? One should closely monitor credit downgrades and mark-to-market changes. Will the cheapest to deliver change dramatically for a specific futures contract or when it is rolled to a new contract month?

Employees should be conditioned to report on possible problems or positions that are deteriorating. Given some lead time, it may be possible to address pending compliance issues if actions can be taken in advance of the possible violation. If a transaction has just occurred, it may be possible to rectify the damage or ask that deal be booked elsewhere with the consent of the client. To obtain full disclosure, you need to maintain an open environment. They need to come to you with their mistakes and problems. Be careful that unclear wording as to trading parameters may enable traders to take unwanted liberties. One should also monitor the behavior of traders. Measuring changes are an important control measure and one should focus on new trends and new counterparties.

Some compliance issues are well known and can be planned for via compliance calendars, e.g. periodic audits, regulatory reports, etc. There are often prealerted situations, e.g. we are sending a new term sheet to five clients, and can you review it first thing tomorrow morning? Others do not present themselves until a transaction evolves into its final form. You want to prevent short cuts like an informal, unreviewed term sheet being sent out and then followed by a full, properly completed term sheet. Odds are that the informal term sheet will be the one retained by the client since the major analysis may be done on the basis of the preliminary term sheet.

You want the compliance efforts to be systematic and comprehensive. You want it done right every time. It is paramount to obtain full disclosure the first time. Compliance often has to ferret out problems since there is an innate tendency by business people to bend the rules. Business staff have to be encouraged to provide information. At the same time, the compliance staff should have the expertise to know what they should be looking for. The business people should not have to 'spoonfeed' the compliance staff: it is a recipe for a later, unhappy surprise.

The markets have a propensity to outpace existing regulations and internal guidelines. Certainly, no one should presume that a control structure designed for plain vanilla swaps will adequately adjust to leveraged or exotic swaps. Similarly, a credit monitoring system geared to corporate exposure might not work as well for monitoring hedge fund exposure since most investment-grade corporations borrow without posting collateral and are generally not highly leveraged.

It is an innate human tendency to look for short cuts or rules of thumb in order to simplify things. As elaborate or logical as a compliance system may be, people will still finds ways to make it perfunctory or use less time, probably at a cost of stripping away some of the safeguards. Sloppiness and inattention are culprits as well as a general casual attitude.

The team environment is fostered with clearly written policies, which itemize the requirements and explain the need for compliance. The compliance staff can alert business staff to potential problems and steps to be taken to avoid problems. The compliance staff, by responding quickly, authoritatively, and accurately, can help foster this cooperation.

The compliance staff can also alert the business side to the costs of non-compliance. With violations such as lack of supervision or non-disclosure, each occurrence may be considered a separate violation. If there is a systematic flaw in the operations process or sales process in an institution, they will be making the same mistake many times. If each violation is serious enough the individual penalties could add up.

Proper compliance means digging into the details of each transaction to be reviewed. If the salesperson represents that a deal is just like a previous transaction, do not accept that representation at face value. Buying a foreign pay security along with a cross-currency swap back to US dollars is one thing. Buying all the shares of a company whose only asset is the foreign pay security is another. Economically the contractual cash flows are identical and the swap provides a valid hedge. In the former case it is simply an interest payment, in the latter it may be construed as a dividend payment and may cause withholding taxes to be paid in the foreign jurisdiction.

Ensuring trained sales staff

During the applicant process and before a salesperson starts employment, the central compliance/human resources should perform a due diligence check on the potential employee. This review includes a background check including credit history and verification of past employment and education.

Once hired, central compliance will oversee the license application requirements and sponsor the employee for testing. Once the appropriate tests (typically Series 7 and Series 63) are passed, the employee will be approved for contact with customers. Given the variety of disciplines involved in creating and selling derivatives it is a prudent precaution that all individuals involved in packaging or assembling are appropriately licensed. In some companies, anyone on the trading floor must be licensed in order to avoid any inadvertent lapses. In light of employee turnover due to mergers and market changes, some employees may arrive pretrained and prelicensed. Special attention should be given to ensuring that these experienced employees are trained in how your firm focuses on compliance and what standard is required. These employees may have learned various short cuts or expedited processes and you want to ensure these processes fall within your requirements. As a business person is licensed, there is also a need to train them in the internal policies and practices of the firm.

There should be a compliance manual disseminated by e-mail or resident in a database. In addition, a hard-copy manual should be retained for reference within the employee's immediate work area. Updates to compliance procedures should be prominently noted, numbered, dated, and sent by e-mail and hard copy. The manual should contain an appendix with an organizational chart indicating clearly who has the supervisory role and both the employee and supervisor should confirm that relationship in writing on an annual basis. Formalized checklists should be provided to help guide the salespeople and traders to operate within the guidance provided. It is best to have a continuously updated distribution list so that those who need to know, get the message.

The compliance information should be standardized to ensure that the same requirements are disseminated and known throughout the firm. It should be perceived as being part of the job, part of normal, required activities. Because things are getting done should not end the inquiry. It may be due to the Herculean efforts by a few that the job is accomplished or perhaps it is being done informally without proper documentation.

Existing business

Compliance cannot realistically control every transaction nor all activities. The focus of resources must be driven by a cost/benefit analysis of where the highest probability of risk and loss might occur. Table 17.1 indicates the situations where one may likely have a greater risk than normal. Well-established clients using standard products for true risk-reducing purposes is probably not a problem area. Other variations appear to have a greater likelihood of problems.

Table 17.1 Analysis of risks

Derivative	Customer	Oversight
Plain vanilla swap	New	Medium
	Established	Low
	Government entity	High
Swaption/options sold to client	New	Low
	Established	Low
	Government entity	High
Swaption/options purchased from client	New	High
	Established	Medium
	Government entity	High
Semi-liquid/new instrument type	New	High
	Established	High
	Government entity	High

One should monitor credit exposure and documentation aging schedules. Specific attention should be paid that documents are appropriately signed (certificate of incumbency) and not altered and or simply initialed. Option expiry/exercise notices also merit a 'tickler system'. The pricing methodologies of some options may make it difficult to value but one should be at least alerted to the possibility of exercise.

New product review

A product risk committee will likely include representatives from the following disciplines: sales, trading, systems, credit, funding, documentation, legal, risk management, audit, tax, accounting, compliance, and operations areas. New products are especially fraught with compliance risk. Many disciplines are involved and it's not just the nature of the risk but who buys it and how it's sold. The targeted client bases might not be the ones who ultimately buy the product. Assuming it is, however, in what manner will they use it and what economic and liquidity risks need to be disclosed? Will the sale of this product curtail the sale of other products or alternatively spur more sales? Distribution channels are important. Will the sales be direct or will a broker or third party represent the firm?

Trading must present how they intend to hedge the product and review and track correlation analysis using historic data. These correlation assumptions and backtesting must be performed over a sufficiently long time horizon to ensure that the results provide a high level of confidence.

Systems are typically a weak link and may be inadequate for the new task at hand. A trade may be jerry-rigged into existing systems and entered in several pieces in order to capture the position (e.g. LIBOR in arrears originally had to be entered by section into most systems). Systems must specify how the trade will be captured and what reports can be created and whether it can be included in the master reports. Over time, this 'band aid' approach may falter. Accurate exposure numbers may not be available if the system is weak. Additionally, people are often not alert to a changing product mix or get distracted by other priorities.

Credit should review the expected counterparty exposure and advise whether the exposure can be netted or treated separately. Compliance will review sales material and term sheets to ensure conformity with external regulations and internal guidelines. There may be a need to amend existing general authorizations of the company in order to market the product.

The funding unit will need to determine how much capital will be used or allocated for the product. Will the money be needed at inception or over the life of the trade? Credit exposure may grow gradually or immediately. It may be concentrated in specific industries and the bank may find itself with an over-concentration of risk. A related issue is the operations unit's ability to process the transaction and monitor it on a regular basis. If market share is concentrated in a few hands, it may be difficult to competitive pricings.

Documentation staff must determine whether they will be able to use an ISDA Master Agreement or whether there will be a need for more tailored documentation. The law department needs to determine that it is a permitted product and how it should be sold. Compliance must determine how they will they track the new product. Risk management must determine how they will measure the new risk. One big hurdle is where to obtain reference prices. If it is a new product, there may be few players making a market. Typically there are not insignificant liquidity problems encountered with the introduction of new products.

Enforcing sanctions

One of the worst sins by management is to not 'rap knuckles' when violations occur or to treat malefactors unequally. Management should prioritize what compliance goals are sacrosanct and which are less significant. Violation of a credit limit is less culpable typically if it occurs due to a movement in the market as opposed to the act of booking a deal that violates the credit limit. (Note that passive credit violations can be a problem, however, when the underlying instrument is illiquid.) If a salesperson makes an inadvertent representation that does not go to the heart of the deal (risk, liquidity, etc.) but rather who he or she actually believed was active in the market, that is likely not culpable.

Regulators will often look favorably on a situation where a firm brings them the violation and make an effort to rectify the error(s) and/or make the counterparty financially whole. You must be able to document that there was no inordinate delay between the time of the discovery and the time when steps were taken to address the issue. Taking the opposite tack of hiding violations is a recipe for disaster. In the Salomon bid-rigging scandal of the early 1990s, the penalties were especially severe since the Treasury Department alleged that a senior Salomon officer had denied auction violations directly while visiting Treasury officials in DC. More recently, the Credit Suisse Group in 1999 'has apologized to Japanese regulators for [previously] obstructing an investigation'. The inquiry 'focuses on allegations' that Credit Suisse aided Japanese clients to hide losses from investments (Singer, 1999).

Compliance review must be formalized and easy to implement. One should always ask the open-ended question, is there anything else I should know or anything else that would be useful to know? The onus should be on the line of business to 'come clean'. If sanctions are never or rarely imposed for violations then the day-to-day and annual compliance sign-off becomes a sham. The attitude of the business people becomes simply 'don't get caught'.

Transactions can appear to fall within the standard guidelines yet are special animals. One should be alert for special items like off-market derivatives where the premium or discount functions as a borrowing or deposit by the counterparty. If the salesperson does not alert or volunteer this type of information, the sanctions should be severe for this type of 'bending the rules'.

Reporting and documentation controls

This section outlines a full range of compliance and document reports that are typically needed. It focuses on building from existing information sources and how to automate some of the processes. The section ends with a review of how to perform periodic evaluations as to effectiveness.

Purpose and range of reports

Reports serve as the lifeblood of any organization. Their purpose is to inform management and staff as to past activity, current positions and profitability and to measure performance versus budget. In addition, the reports provide a basis for guidance and planning future activity. Market and credit risk are likely two of the largest risks that an institution faces and these risks are often analyzed from a patchwork of reports. Reports are focused primarily on providing an accurate reflection of current positions and providing mark-to-market valuations and exposures. The reports often provide static, snapshots of positions as of a cut-off time. Those focusing specifically on compliance needs are generally less available.

Reports should provide aggregate numbers certainly, but they should be accompanied with supporting trend analysis. There should be sufficient detail to enable management to determine if the composition of the business is changing. This can have a significant impact on future business plans as well as alerting compliance to refocus some of its resources. It is axiomatic that the reports generated for management originate from departments independent of the trading activity.

Regulators have an evolving focus today. Since management has specific informational needs, the reporting is primarily geared to business requirements. There is a realization among regulators now that there is a benefit to be achieved by focusing more on management's own reports rather than creating entirely new reports for the regulatory agencies.

In addition, regulators are more open to the concept of sharing information among themselves (to the extent legally possible) and in some cases even relying on the expertise and analysis of another regulator, especially a foreign one. Although the regulators are cognizant of the cost of providing special reports to regulators, they have little choice in times of financial crisis but to request *ad-hoc* reports. This occurred with the hedge funds being scrutinized closely during the Long Term Capital Management crisis in 1998. Regulators asked for special reports keyed to counterparty concentrations as well as exposures to specific markets from hedge funds and counterparty banks.

To this end, an essential listing of documents and reports needed by divisional compliance would be as follows:

- Organizational chart of business unit and divisional groups
- Work processes mapped out
- Current compliance manuals
- Compliance databases
- Copies of applicable regulations
- Copies of corporate authorizations
- List of authorized traders
- List of permitted products
- Approved counterparty list
- List of signed ISDA/IFEMA agreements
- Listing of available reports (e.g. credit line usage, exception reports)
- List of brokers used
- List of bank accounts
- List of custodians
- List of safety deposit boxes
- List of repo agreements signed
- Document aging list

The central compliance unit is typically focused on more firmwide issues. The unit would likely work closely with the law department on setting policies for implementation by the divisional compliance units. Central compliance typically focuses on the following:

- Outside money managers
- List of approved signatories (internal)
- Certificates of incumbency
- Filings required for regulatory agencies
- Disaster recovery plans/business resumption plans
- Coordination of internal audit recommendations

The law department's focus would include some of the following issues:

- Software contracts
- Data vendor contracts
- Insurance coverage
- Bonding

The lists of documents and reports represent the initial step of the compliance review. Using an ISDA master agreement as an example, the law department should create a template as to the preferred language and range of alternative language permitted. It is advisable that there be a large degree of standardization as to the ISDA contracts that are signed. Whenever there are omissions or variations in language, they may expose the company to additional legal risk. Legal planning becomes more difficult since outcomes may be less certain if contracts need to be enforced and there is no uniformity of terms among the agreements that one institution has negotiated. As the credit derivatives market experienced in 1998, lack of uniformity of interpretation by signatories to a contract is another impediment to limiting risk. Whether certain sovereigns experienced a default remains a matter in dispute.

The legal agreement is not the end point. The organization must have a strong operations team to monitor the implementation of the terms of the contract. Let's use, as an example, an agreement to post collateral. Some derivatives contracts have springing collateral language. Operations has to verify receipt of collateral, often by trustee if it is a tripartite agreement. They must determine that it is acceptable collateral, value it, and they may need to perfect an interest in the collateral as well. The analysis should not end with the question, has collateral been posted?

With posting of collateral or mark-to-market triggers, it may be preferable not to key them to counterparty credit grades. If a major dealer were to get downgraded then everyone's collateral or termination trigger might be invoked at the same time. It may be more prudent to require language that calls for an automatic posting of collateral if exposure rises above a preset limit. If it is simply a right to be exercised, a 'tickler system' might not catch the change. With a mandatory posting of collateral, your firm is less susceptible to the moral suasion of a senior officer of the other company calling and requesting that the demand to post collateral be waived. You can always decline to exercise your right but you should avoid having the situation of needing to assert a right that is not clear-cut or that could forseeably force the counterparty into bankruptcy.

Tracking the aging and disposition of unsigned documents is an important preventative control. Deals may be fully negotiated but the contract memorializing the terms may remain unsigned. Alternatively, ISDAs could be signed but a term might be unilaterally initialed and so not fully agreed upon. Some firms require the counterparty to sign a one-page acknowledgement agreeing to all terms of the confirmation. This approach precludes a counterparty from initialing a change on page 2 or 3 in the confirmation and faxing it back and the change being overlooked. Months or years later, the initialed contract term might become a source of contention and no final agreement would be documented for that contract term. A fully signed contract should provide each party with a clearer legal position in the event of a breach.

Another problem area exists when there is no signed ISDA in place between counterparties or where the terms of the swap confirmation are made to supercede the terms of the ISDA master agreement. It may be appropriate but you want to ensure that the desired results occur. The law department should review the master agreement and the swap supplement language. If an unsigned deal confirmation remains outstanding for a long period of time, an overly efficient officer may just sign them to reduce the backlog. Some end-users simply sign off on master agreements without examining or understanding all the ramifications of various terms agreed. They may even agree to netting across entities in same corporate family without evaluating the appropriateness of such action.

Build on existing reports

A major challenge is simply to track changes and rejig reports and information to accommodate changing regulatory needs and senior management requests. Given the likelihood of unanticipated situations in the future, reports must be built to be flexible with a variety of key fields or sorting methodologies. Query tools should make reporting quite flexible. The range of reports frequently requested are market or credit exposure by instrument, by counterparty, by industry, by country, by maturity, etc. Depending on where the latest 'crisis' occurs, requests will change accordingly.

In most companies there are official board reports that are prepared for use by the board of directors. Generally the law department will review them to certify that all transactions were done in compliance with applicable law and in compliance with internal policies and authorizations. When a compliance problem occurs, the board needs to know the nature and scope of the problem. A major pitfall is that board meetings tend to be heavily scripted and have full agendas and focus on compliance, other than audit reviews, may not be given high priority.

In order to ensure compliance success, the staff needs to inventory those items and processes to be monitored. The need here is to cast as wide a net as is appropriate. To monitor properly, one needs to know who the players are, what instruments do they use, and how the work is organized. The following is a sample listing of the types of reports that would be needed:

1   Aggregate volume and profitability numbers
2   Itemized information on all trades
3   VaR and scenarios results
4   Limits violation reports
5   New customer listing
6   Turnover in staff (front and back office)
7   Systems failure reports
8   UOR unusual occurrence reports (catchall)
9   Trend analysis
10 Sample term sheets used

Other relevant reports are error logs, limit violations and revenue reports. Unsigned document aging reports are also important. These monitoring reports should be viewed in the context of how they enable the proper timing of regulatory review and reporting. Given the ease of renaming products for regulatory purposes, compliance staff are well advised to request risk reports as well. Measurement of economic exposure in the risk reports might shed more light on the true nature of some derivative instruments.

Centralized data gathering

Compliance casts a wide net but there are events and occurrences that can slip through the interstices. A major pitfall of centralized data gathering is the wide variety of derivatives products offered and the need to standardize the data. This aggregation process can come at a cost of accuracy in the details of individual transactions. The derivatives business has evolved dramatically and controls and compliance efforts may fail to keep pace.

Business and technical support often falls into strict control units or divisions and there is little overlap with other units. The systems requirements are often developed devoid of ensuring compatibility within the entire organization. Since the same salesperson can often sell products on behalf of a number of legal entities, effective control becomes more problematic. Data fields, reports, etc. can mean different things or be used for different purposes within different parts of an organization. Information is often aggregated for risk management or accounting purposes and it becomes difficult to isolate all the details of individual transactions. A related problem occurs when holding are managed by an outside manager and the numbers need to be manually 'rolled into' total holdings reports.

With specially tailored transactions, there may be special provisions or options that cannot be recorded in the existing systems. As a result they may not appear on a regular report. For simplicity, information may be ordered by stated maturity date and not include other pertinent data. A major challenge is that report cutoff times are often different and a good deal of time is spent on needless reconciliation. There may be classification overlaps as well. Trusts, partnerships and affiliates and custody agents may all figure in the equation and one may not readily obtain a complete listing of all positions held.

To ensure that all data is being collected, one should obtain process flow diagrams covering all product and customer flows. Lists of reports and samples of each reports should be obtained to ensure completeness. Special attention should be paid to reports whose formats or scope change over time since this may trigger unintended omissions or other unhappy consequences.

Typical problem signs occur when you sometimes have the original trade documents and sometimes copies. This indicates a lack of consistency or control. All transactions should be serial numbered or time stamped in order to enable cross-checking with market levels and credit limits. Files that contain only part of the required documents or inconsistency in contents and storage locations of the files should also cause concern. One should be especially alert for backdated approvals.

One should also obtain a document-aging list. A signed document gives protection against breaches since it provides the written terms of the deal and often the four corners of the document may be the exclusive basis for determining the terms and condition of the contract. If unsigned documents are outstanding longer than 60 days, you may want to reconsider doing another deal with the same counterparty.

Automating processes

Automating processes for the benefit of compliance is a difficult sell in most organizations. It costs money and compliance is not a revenue area. Compliance often finds itself looking to risk management reports generated for different purposes in order to track activities and transactions. Information may indeed be available but the focus of the data architects was on different goals. A common hurdle is that reconciliation are done manually to end reports and not to source input. This causes the similar reconciliation to be preformed periodically and sometimes previous corrections are omitted in later reports and have to be redone.

Risk management reports may utilize different standards of accuracy since those reports are focused more on economic exposure as opposed to legal risks and documentation risks. The reports will likely focus on end-of-day or reporting period rather than providing equal focus with intraday trades and closed-out positions. Obviously any computer report will not provide the reader with the context for the decision nor whether sufficient disclosure occurred nor what suitability checks were performed.

Given the variety of systems and derivative instruments available, there may not be a ready ability to perform an electronic file transfer. The alternative is to work with existing reports and often a rekeying the data into a spreadsheet format. If the number of transactions are too cumbersome then a possible approach is to sample typical transactions and test the thoroughness and timeliness of the supporting documentation.

With the proliferation of databases, these are useful tools to help standardize documentation and disclosure. A database can provide a sample of standardized disclosures and consistent templates for term sheets. One should require that all term sheets sent out be copied and retained by a compliance unit.

When compliance standards and controls are set too high, it can engender resistance, avoidance, or a hesitation to do something profitable and in the best interests of the shareholders. The following are several examples of processes or procedures that were counterproductive.

An end-user established an elaborate approval process for the approval of foreign exchange forwards. Only a couple of senior managers could authorize transactions. Given the difficulty of getting a time slot to see the senior people and the elaborate form, the employee simply waited until the forward exposure became a spot transaction. He then executed in the market and avoided the approval process. The trader was not held accountable for gains or losses on unhedged positions and so expediency ruled.

In another case, a company allowed only its CEO to authorize the use of the company's guarantee. Given the inability to schedule time with the CEO and the smaller relative size of the transaction that need a guarantee, the profitable opportunity was allowed to be passed by.

In another situation, the SVP level in a company could approve expenditures up to a limited dollar amount on IT systems, otherwise it went to the board for approval. A derivatives monitoring system was needed. So the need was split into different budget cycles. The result was two systems that did not provide a consistent valuation and monitoring capabilities to the derivatives holdings.

In another case, an end-user in a highly regulated industry wanted to buy receiver swaptions in order to hedge MBS prepayment risk in the event of lower rates. There was no specific authorization or prohibition in the law as to the use of swaptions. The in-house legal department refrained from going for regulatory approval since derivatives were considered to have too high a profile and the company wanted to avoid additional oversight requirements. So no hedges were ever done.

The highest comfort level possible is obtained by performing a compliance audit. Although onerous and time-consuming, it's the best approach. If practical, randomly select several days a month where you review each transaction that occurred and 'track through' the process to ensure that all procedures were adequately followed.

Look more closely than simply verifying that all documents were signed. How many revisions occurred (were they material), was there a delay in the sign-off confirmations? Were intraday or overnight position limits breached? Did the market trigger the violation or was it an active breach? How long did the breach languish? Was the breach properly escalated? Did management reports contain all the required information? Were exceptions properly noted? Is there a compliance calendar? Were regulatory reports filed on time?

Each salesperson should be able to provide a listing of active clients and deactivate old customers. Old authorizations or documentation that becomes stale should be reviewed automatically. On an annual basis, a compliance staffer should review the documentation file to ensure that it remains adequate and there are no omissions. Companies are rarely blindsided by regulatory change, rather it is the failure to adequately prepare to accommodate the change that is the problem.

Consistency in approach and effort is a critical standard for effective compliance oversight. It is inconsistent controls that create the opportunity for problems to occur, fester, and multiply. Critical to success is a good personal and working relationship between the business side and compliance 'crew'. If personality conflicts occur or egos clash, then the each side may work at cross-purposes or simply revert to a 'help only if asked' approach. Effectiveness only occurs with consistent teamwork and trust.

Special issues

There should be frequent interaction between the risk managers and the and compliance unit. Risk managers can alert compliance to risk concentrations as well as large risk changes. Conversely, compliance violations may serve as an early warning for the risk managers that analysis or operations controls may be insufficient.

Both internal and external auditors provide a fresh perspective on compliance and documentation controls. Regulators frequently refer to external auditors' work papers. Since work papers may be accessed by the regulators, it is important to review problem areas or challenges cited in these reports. On a cautionary note, one should not always rely on the conclusions of external auditors. Often they are not tough enough, especially if they have been reviewing the same firm for many years. They may become complacent. Alternatively, in a merger situation, there is the moral hazard risk that the auditors may be less confrontational if they fear losing the company's business. Audits typically occur on an annual basis but rarely more frequently. One should ensure that the day-to-day gets done properly and a year between recommendations of changes and the next audit may be too long a time.

The required implementation of FAS 133, delayed until after June 2000, will necessitate extensive new documentation requirements for individual companies. The exact contours of these requirements are still being worked out by a FAS working group and interested parties. Each derivatives hedge will need to be classified, e.g. as a fair value or cash flow hedge and each hedge will need to be tested periodically for effectiveness. The economic performance of the hedge will be divided into ineffective and effective components, assuming it is not a perfect offset. New subledger accounts need to be created to record these entries and income and/or equity volatility is likely occur due to these changes. High-volume users will need to integrate FAS 133 classification directly into the reporting systems. An ironic result of FAS 133 is that the accounting hurdles to qualify for hedge accounting may well be more stringent that legal requirements authorizing the use of derivatives for some end-users. Since the new changes are so fundamental, it is likely that a new accounting policy manual will need to be written to incorporate all the contemplated changes. Ensuring consistent usage and treatments across portfolios will create new compliance hurdles.

Y2K preparations have received endless attention in the popular media and industry meetings. Business resumption plans and back-up systems are an integral part of theses efforts. Special issues to be addressed include the need to maintain ready (manual) access to trade confirmations, ISDA master agreements, cash forecast reports, credit line availability, etc. The prompt receipt of and sending of trade confirmations is a crucial control to establishing contractual rights.

Summary

Compliance and documentation controls are rarely popular topics. In the area of derivatives, controls are complicated by overlapping or inconsistent regulatory oversight. One senior attorney termed the complicated US regulatory system as a 'bifurcated mess' (Russo, 1994). Compliance extends beyond addressing regulators' guidance or adherence to internal polices; other agencies can exercise oversight. Witness First Union Corp.'s problems for violating US Treasury auction rules. These violations were against restrictions prohibiting the prior resale of Treasuries bought via no-competitive bids at government auction. Although the US Treasury did not have regulatory oversight and was not on the 'radar screen', it still was able to enforce sanctions against First Union (Vames, 1999).

Compliance serves an especially valuable role in safeguarding the reputation of a firm and ensuring that there are no nasty surprises. There is a variety of compliance infrastructures and the most workable ones have the flexibility to respond to market and regulatory changes. Large compliance problems do not typically result as the result of a single transaction but of a pattern of action that develops over time. On-site monitoring helps discourage these patterns of behavior. The support of business lines should be sought and they should be involved in the writing of the compliance policies. Compliance controls should be on-site, comprehensive, linked to the business, and coordinated by a central compliance unit. Effective controls can help reduce capital needed for the business.

Compliance must examine the microlevel transactions as well as the macrolevel (e.g. credit concentrations.) Partnerships, joint ventures, and third-party sales forces are especially troublesome since a firm's money and reputation are on the line and the firm may have limited oversight of compliance controls.

Compliance management can be costly and may absorb valuable resources, and regulators are cognizant of this. In the future, regulators will likely rely more on internal business reports and function more as supervisors than regulators. This oversight should allow examination to be more streamlined and to focus on existing and emerging problem areas (Wixted, 1987). Regulators will ask for special exposure reports as new crises emerge and a firm's data systems must be able to run these special queries.

The goal of compliance is not to achieve a minimum passing grade. Rather it is to ensure that regulations are being followed, internal policies and procedures are being adhered to, effective controls are in place, and that timely and accurate information is being provided to senior management and ultimately to the board. If a company performs its compliance duties well, the controls will be professional and unobtrusive, and enable senior management to focus on other business concerns. The best compliance efforts are those that will keep pace with the ever-expanding derivatives markets.

Notes

[1] OCC, release 96.2, occ.treas.gov

[2] Enterprise Risk Management, Glyn Holton, p. 7, contingencyanalysis.com

[3] Several large US life insurers have implemented enhanced compliance policies due to the sales practices scandal of the early 1990s. (Salesforces often view them as quite burdensome since every new sale is checked as opposed to a spot-checking process.) Several companies received large fines from state regulators due to the manner in which policies were sold to the public. Although derivatives were not involved, the lack of disclosure is analogous to derivative sales problems.

[4] Charges were based on the 'books and records' provision of the Securities Exchange Act of 1934.

[5] ISDA stands for International Swaps and Derivatives Association, Inc. and IFEMA for International Foreign Exchange Master Agreement. Standard contract forms created by these industry groups are used as the basis for documenting the rights and duties of parties to over-the-counter derivatives contracts.

[6] ABN's New York office discovered the misvaluations of foreign currency call options held by a FX options trader. In the news stories published, it was indicated that the implied volatilities of options held were overstated in order to hide losses.

[7] There is a wealth of guidance in the area of derivative risk control. Several regulatory organizations as well as private industry groups have produced excellent suggestions and guidelines for writing risk policies. Most prominent are Group of 30, the Federal Reserve, the OCC, and others as well as the Risk Standards Working Group (focusing on money managers).

[8] By David E. Aron, an associate in the futures and derivatives practice at Dechert Price & Rhoads in Washington, DC, and Jeremy Bassil, an associate in the Financial Services Department at Titmuss Sainer Dechert in London.

Appendix: US and UK regulatory schemes

Table A1 Major US regulatory oversight

Commercial bank (depending on charter)
    Federal Reserve Board and local Fed OCC (depending on charter)
    State Banking Department (depending on charter)
    FDIC

Insurance company (pension fund monies trigger ERISA laws)
    State Insurance Department
    NAIC
    SEC
    NASD

Investment bank
    SEC
    State securities (blue sky) laws
    NASD
    Exchanges and their clearing corporations (e.g. NYSE)
    Banking Regulator (if bank sub)
    CFTC and commodities exchanges

Table A2 Current major UK regulatory oversight[8]

Commercial or investment bank[a]
Bank of England (BoE)[b]
Financial Services Authority (FSA)[c]
Insurance company[d]
Her Majesty's Treasury (HMT)[e]
Pesonal investment authority (PIA)[f]
Retail brokerage
SFA[g]
PIA

[a] Insofar as commercial or investment banks (or other entities in this table) conduct certain activities, they may also be regulated by the Investment Management Regulatory Organization (investment management) or Securities and Futures Authority (SFA) (e.g. corporate finance).
[b] Has only general market protection authority – regulates the banking system, the money supply and payment systems.
[c] Regulates authorization and supervision.
[d] Lloyd's and other commercial insurers are generally unregulated.
[e] Responsible fo prudential and related regulation.
[f] Regulates intermediaries marking investment products to retail customers and regulates the product providers themselves.
[g] Regulates broker-dealers.

Table A3 UK regulatory oversight upon enactment of the Financial services and Markets Bill[a,8]

Commercial or investment bank
BoE
FSA
Insurance company
FSA[b]
Retail brokerage
FSA[c]

[a] The Financial Services and Markets Bill is expected to be enacted by early 2000.
[b] Will assume current authority of HMT and PIA; regulation of Lloyd's and other commercial insurers is being considered.
[c] Will assume current authority of SFA and PIA.

References

Basel Committee on Banking Supervision (1998) *Framework for the evaluation of internal control systems*, Basel, January, p. 15.

Erikson, J. O. (1996) 'Lessons for policymakers and private practitioners in risk management', Derivatives and Public Policy Conference, frbchi.org, p. 54.

Ewing, T. and Bailey, J. (1999) 'Dashed futures: how a trading firm's founders were blindsided by a bombshell', *Wall Street Journal*, 18 February, C1.

McDermott, D. and Webb, S. (1999) 'How Merrill wished upon a star banker and wound up in a Singapore sling', *Wall Street Journal*, 21 May, C1.

OCC Comptroller's Handbook (1997) 'Risk management of financial derivatives', Washington, DC, January. occ.treas.gov, p. 64.

Peteren, M. (1999) 'Merrill charged with 2d firms in copper case', *New York Times*, 21 May, d7.

Risk Standards Working Group (1996) *Risk Standards for Institutional Investment Managers and Institutional Investors*, p. 19, cmra.com.

Russo, T. A. (1996) Address to Futures Industry Association, 4 March.

Singer, J. (1999) 'Credit Suisse apologizes for blocking Japan probe', Bloomberg News Service, 21 May.

Vames, S. (1999) 'Some public penance is payment in full for breaking rules', *Wall Street Journal*, 20 May, C20.

Wixted, J. J., Jr (1987) 'The future of bank regulation', Federal Reserve Bank of Chicago, 18 July, address to the Iowa Independent Bankers Annual Meeting and Convention, frbchi.org, p. 8.

18

Energy risk management

GRANT THAIN

Introduction

This chapter focuses on the challenges facing a risk manager overseeing an energy portfolio. It sets out a general overview of the markets as they relate to risk management and the risk quantification and control issues implicit in an energy portfolio.

The energy markets are extremely intricate, rich in multiple markets, liquidity problems, extreme volatility issues, non-normal distributions, 'real' option pricing problems, mark-to-model problems, operational difficulties and data management nightmares. The market, to use the academic understatement, is complex and challenging but most of all it is extremely interesting. In particular, this chapter will focus on the challenges in the electricity market, which is by far the largest market within energy[1] and exhibits most of the problems faced by energy risk managers, whether in power or not.

Background

Risk management has always been at the forefront of those within the energy industry and indeed those within government and other regulatory bodies setting energy policy. From OPEC to nationalized generation and distribution companies, the risks associated with movements in energy prices have been keenly debated by both politicians and industry observers. As such, assessing the risks associated with the energy markets is not a new phenomenon. However, the recent global trend to shift the risk management of the gas and power markets from regulated to open markets is radically changing the approach and tools necessary to operate in these markets.

Energy price hedging in oil can be traced back to the introduction of the first heating oil contracts on NYMEX in 1978 and the development of oil derivative products in the mid-1980s, in particular with the introduction of the 'Wall Street Refiners' including the likes of J. Aron and Morgan Stanley who developed derivative products such as 'crack' spreads which reflected the underlying economics of refineries. While the traditional risk management techniques of oil companies changed radically in the 1970s and 1980s the traditional model for managing gas and power risk remained one of pass through to a captive customer group well into the 1990s.

In gas and electricity, regionalized regulated utility monopolies have traditionally bought long-term contracts from producers and passed the costs onto their retail base. The focus was on what the correct costs to pass through were and what 'regulatory pact' should be struck between regulators and the utilities. Starting with a politically driven trend away from government ownership in the 1980s and early 1990s, this traditional model is now changing rapidly in the USA, Europe, Australia, Japan and many other parts of the world.

Apart from the underlying shift in economic philosophy, the primary driver behind the change in approach has been the dramatic price uncertainty in the energy markets. Large price movements in the only unregulated major energy market, oil, left utilities with increasing uncertainty in their planning and thus an increasing financial cost of making incorrect decisions. For instance, the worldwide move by utilities towards nuclear power investments as a means to diversify away from the high oil prices in the 1970s led to significant 'above market' or stranded costs for many utilities.

Development of alternative approaches to risk in the energy markets

In response to this market price uncertainty, many oil companies modified traditional investment analysis approaches to include scenario analysis rather than forecasting analysis as well as starting to lever off their hedging and trading operations. The use of a scenario approach in investment decisions was an early indication that even oil majors accepted that they could not predict future price movements with any certainty.

Meanwhile the financial engineers on Wall Street were solving the same issue from another direction, notably the development and refinement of the derivative pricing models using quantitative approaches. Option pricing models through the 1980s began by stripping out the observable forward markets from market uncertainty. Although relatively straightforward in nature, these models facilitated a key move away from a fundamental analysis approach and allowed the application of some proven statistical concepts to the markets, most notably the measure of market uncertainty through the use of volatility estimators.

With the exception of a small group of specialized oil traders, the energy markets were much slower than the financial markets in embracing these quantitative approaches. The reasons for this are many and begin to signal many of the risk management issues associated with energy, notably: ... energy markets are immature and often still partly regulated, complex in their interrelationships (both between products and regional delivery points), constrained by lack of storage, subject to large seasonal swings, mean reversion, subject to large investment cycle issues, delivered products tend to be very complex in nature ... and the list goes on. On a continuum the complexity increases exponentially as we move from the money markets to the oil market to the gas market to the electricity markets.

In the last few years an increasing number of practitioners and academics have began to take on the challenge of developing and modifying quantitative approaches for the energy markets. The reason for this is simple: while the complexity is much higher in these markets, the underlying assumption in the quantitative models that the future is essentially random rather than predictable in nature is particularly relevant to an increasingly commoditized energy sector. The quantitative approach is also particularly useful when aggregating a diverse book like an energy portfolio. For instance, Value-at-Risk (VaR) allows us to aggregate separate oil, gas and power books daily on a consistent basis. It is difficult to do this without applying a statistical approach.

The development of risk management professionals within the energy sector has also accelerated as energy companies have developed their commodity trading experience and embraced the middle-office concept. An independent middle office is particularly important in the energy sector given the complexity of the markets. A combination of market knowledge, a healthy dose of skepticism and a control culture focused on quantifying the risks provides an essential balance in developing markets with little historical information and extreme volatility.

Each of the three principal risk management areas – market risk, counterparty credit risk and operational risk – are relevant to an energy business. There is not enough space in one chapter to describe the markets themselves in any detail so I shall focus primarily on those parts of the markets that impinge on the role of the risk manager. In addition, the examples used will relate primarily to the power markets, in particular in the USA. This is not to imply that this is the most important market or the most developed, but quite simply because it provides useful examples of most of the quantitative problems that need to be addressed by risk management professionals within energy companies, whether based in Houston, London or Sydney.

The energy forward curve

Energy forward curves generally exhibit certain common characteristics; notably, forward curves in the USA are based upon a wheel and spoke design. A small number of strong trading hubs exist that, relative to the remaining parts of the market, are very liquid. In addition, liquidity has been enhanced by the formation of exchange-based contracts (in particular NYMEX and the IPE) as well as OTC (over-the-counter) trading.

The currently developed trading hubs do not represent a product that all the buyers and sellers want, but a particular quality and delivery point that can set a transparent and 'unbiased' benchmark that the industry can price around. Trading away from these hubs are normally done on 'basis'. In other words, premiums or discounts are paid depending on the differential value of the product compared to the hub product. This differential may reflect a higher or lower transport cost, quality or locational supply/demand conditions.

The oil market

Crude oil can come from almost any part of the world and the oil market, unlike gas and power, can be described as a truly global market. The principal production regions can be generally grouped into the following: North Sea (the most notable grade being Brent), West Africa, Mediterranean, Persian Gulf (notably Dubai), Asia, USA (notably WTI), Canada and Latin America. Each region will have a number of quality grades and specifications within it, in particular, depending on their API gravity[2] and sulfur content.

In Europe the benchmark crude product is North Sea Brent while in the USA it is often quoted as WTI. WTI is the principal product meeting the NYMEX sweet crude specifications for delivery at Cushing (a number of other qualities can also be deliverable, although many non-US crudes receive a discount to the quoted settlement price). The other major crude product is Dubai, representing the product shipped from the Persian Gulf.

Each of these three products will trade in close relation to each other, generally reflecting their slightly different qualities and the transport cost from end-user markets, all three markets reflecting the overall real or perceived supply/demand balance in the world market. Other crude specifications and delivery points will then trade some 'basis' from these benchmark prices.

As well as the three crude products noted above, the oil market encompasses the refined products from crude oil. While thousands of different qualities and delivery points world-wide will ultimately result in hundreds of thousands of different prices, in Europe and North America these can generally be linked back to a number of relatively strong trading hubs that exist, notably:

Product type	*Principal hubs*
Crude	Brent/Cushing/Dubai
Unleaded	NWE[3]/New York/Gulf Coast
Gas Oil/No. 2 Oil	NWE/New York Harbor
Heavy Fuel Oil/No. 6 Oil	NWE/New York Harbor/Far East

In addition, the rest of the barrel, propane, butane, naphtha and kerosene trade actively, but are more limited in terms of their relevance to the energy complex.

Within the various product ranges prices are quoted for particular standard grades. For instance, No. 6 oil (also known as HFO or residual oil) can be segmented to 1%, 2.2%, 3% and 3.5% sulfur specifications. Each have their own forward curves and active trading occurs both on the individual product and between the products. The market has developed to the point where NYMEX lists not only option prices but also Crack Spread Options (the option on the spread between the products).[4]

Like its other energy counterparts most of the trading is done in the OTC 'brokered' market that supports most of the commonly traded options, swaps and other derivative structures seen in the financial markets. Derivatives are particularly useful in oil compared to other energy products given the international nature of the product and the relationship between the overall oil complex. For instance, if we take an airline company, this needs a jet fuel hedge that reflects the weighted average cost of its physical spot fuel price purchases in different parts of the world. At the same time it would like to avoid any competitive loss it might experience from hedging out at high prices. This would be complex (and unnecessary) to achieve physically, but relatively straightforward to hedge using a combination of different swaps and average price options, which can be easily linked to currency hedges.

Another common swap is the front-to-back spread, or synthetic storage. This allows the current spot price to be swapped for a specified forward month. It should be noted that this relationship may be positive or negative, depending on market expectations. Locational swaps are also very common, providing a synthetic transport cost. Such swap providers in this market (and all energy markets), however, need to be very aware of both the physical logistics and the spot market volatility.

Crack spreads and Crack spread options are used to create synthetic refineries.

The 3:2:1 crack spread that is traded in NYMEX is a standard example of this linking the prices of crude, heating oil and gasoline.

In oil, the majority of swap transactions are carried out against Platt's indices that cover most products and locations, although a number of other credible indices exist in different locations. For instance, CFD's (Contracts for Differences) are commonly traded against 'dated' Brent, the price for physical cargoes loading shortly and a forward Brent price approximately three months away.

While such derivatives are easy to construct and transact against the liquid hubs they have their dangers when using them to hedge physical product at a specific delivery point. Specific supply/demand factors can cause spreads between locations and the hubs to change dramatically for short periods of time before they move back into equilibrium. For example, extreme weather conditions can lead to significant shortages in specific locations where imports are not possible leading to a complete breakdown of the correlation between the physical product and the index being used to hedge. In other words you lose your hedge exactly when you need it. A risk manager must look carefully at the spreads during such events and the impact on the correlations used in VaR and Stress tests. They should also understand the underlying supply/demand conditions and how they could react during such extreme events.

It should also be noted that oil products are often heavily taxed and regulated on a state and national basis which can lead to a number of legal, settlement and logistical complexities. Going hand in hand with this is the environmental risks associated with storage and delivery, where insurance costs can be very substantial.

Ever-changing refinery economics, storage and transportation costs associated with the physical delivery of oil are thus a significant factor in pricing which results in the forward curve dynamics being more complex than those seen in the financial markets. As a result the term structure is unpredictable in nature and can vary significantly over time. Both backwardation[5] and contago[6] structures are seen within the curve, as is a mean reversion component. Two components are commonly used to describe the term structure of the oil forward curve: the price term structure, notably the cost of financing and carry until the maturity date, and the convenience yield. The convenience yield can be described as the 'fudge factor' capturing the market expectations of future prices that are not captured in the arbitrage models. This would include seasonal and trend factors.

Given the convenience yield captures the 'unpredictable' component of the curve, much of the modeling of oil prices has focused on describing this convenience yield which is significantly more complex than those seen in the financial markets. For instance, under normal conditions (if there is such a thing), given the benefit of having the physical commodity rather than a paper hedge, the convenience yield is often higher than the cost of carry driving the market towards backwardation.

Fitting a complex array of price data to a consistent forward curve is a major challenge and most energy companies have developed proprietary models based on approaches such as HJM to solve this problem. Such models require underlying assumptions on the shape of the curve fitting discrete data points and rigorous testing of these assumptions is required on an ongoing basis.

Assumptions about the shape of the forward market can be very dangerous as MG discovered. In their case they provided long-term hedges to customers and hedged them using a rolling program of short-term future positions. As such they were exposed to the spread or basis risk of the differential between the front end of the market (approximately three-month hedges) and the long-term sales (up to ten years). When oil prices in 1993 fell dramatically they had to pay out almost a billion dollars or margin calls in their short-term positions but saw no offsetting benefit from their long-term sales. In total they were reported to have lost a total of $1.3 billion by misunderstanding the volatility of this spread.

Particularly in the case of heating oil, significant seasonality can exists. Given the variation in demand throughout the year and storage economics, the convenience yield will vary with these future demand expectations. This has the characteristic of pronounced trends, high in winter when heating oil is used, low in summer and a large random element given the underlying randomness of weather conditions.

The oil market also exhibits mean reversion characteristics. This makes sense, since production economics show a relatively flat cost curve (on a worldwide basis the market can respond to over- and under-supply and that weather conditions (and thus the demand parameters) will return to normal after some period.

In addition, expected supply conditions will vary unpredictably from time to time. Examples of this include the OPEC and Gulf War impacts on perceived supply risks. Such events severely disrupt the pricing at any point leading to a 'jump' among the random elements and disrupting both the spot prices and the entire dynamics of the convenience yield. I will return to the problem of 'jumps' and 'spikes' later in this chapter.

Gas forward curve

Price discovery in gas is not as transparent as in the oil market. The transport and storage capabilities of the gas market is relatively inflexible compared to the oil market. The market is also more regional[7] than the oil market, with international trade being restricted by pipeline costs and LNG (liquefied natural gas) processing and transport costs.

The US gas trading market (although probably the most developed in the world) is much more fragmented than in the oil market with a large number of small producers, particularly at the production end. Given the inability to hedge through vertical integration or diversity this has resulted in a significant demand for risk management products. The market after the deregulation in the 1980s and early 1990s has been characterized by the development of a very significant short-term market. This sets prices for a thirty-day period during what is known as 'bid week'.[8] The prices generated during this 'bid week' create an important benchmark[9] against which much of the trading market is based.

The futures contracts in gas have been designed to correspond with the timing of bid week, the largest and most developed contract being known as Henry Hub. This has been quoted on NYMEX since 1990, supports a strong options market and extends out three years on a relatively liquid basis. Basis relationships between Henry Hub and the major gas-consuming regions within the USA are well established and, in the short term, fairly stable. The OTC market supports most basis locations and a reasonable option market can be found for standard products. It is worth noting that, credit aside, in energy the value of the futures market and the OTC forward market is the same, albeit the delivery mechanisms are different. This is true because there is no direct correlation to interest rates and the EFP (Exchange for Physical) option imbedded in the futures contract.

In gas, storage costs play a critical role in determining the shape of the forward curve. A variety of storage is employed from line pack (literally packing more gas molecules into the pipe) to salt caverns and reservoirs (gas can be injected and extracted with limited losses) and the pricing and flexibility of the different storage options varies significantly.

As a general rule, the gas market stores (injects) during seven or eight 'summer' months and extracts during the winter months. Significant short-run price movements occur when this swing usage is out of balance. In these circumstances gas traders will spend much of the time trying to predict storage usage against their demand estimations it order to determine what type of storage will be used during the peak season and thus help set the future marginal price.

Like the oil market, the gas markets exhibit mean reversion, and are subject to occasional jumps due to particular 'events' such as hurricanes shutting down supplies. But most importantly, despite this storage, gas remains significantly more seasonal in nature than most of the oil market (see Figure 18.1).

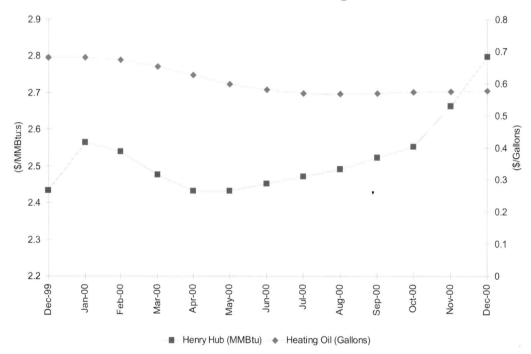

Figure 18.1   The seasonality of the gas market. (*Source:* Citizens Power)

Basis trading from Henry Hub plays a vital part in the market with differentials to the major consumption zones being actively traded in the OTC market. These basis prices are less stable than those seen in the oil market given the more constrained transport infrastructure and volatility in demand. As a result, the monitoring of these basis relationships under normal and extreme conditions becomes critical.

Risk managers should be very wary of basis traders or regional traders marking their books against a contract in a different region such as Henry Hub who are seen to have large 'book' profits based on future positions. There have been a number of instances where such regional traders have had their positions wiped out overnight when the correlations have broken down under extreme market conditions. In other words, you need to ensure that the higher volatility or 'spike potential' in less liquid regional markets compared to a large liquid hub has been reflected in the pricing.

Historical 'basis' positions may also fundamentally change as the pipeline positions change. For instance, the increasing infrastructure to bring Canadian gas to the Chicago and North US markets could significantly change the traditional basis 'premium' seen in these markets compared to Henry Hub.

While most trades up to three years are transacted as forward or future positions an active swap market also exists, particularly for longer-term deals where the counter-parties do not want to take on the potential risks associated with physical delivery. These index trades are generally against the published Inside FERC Gas Market Report Indices although Gas Daily and other publications are also used regularly. It is necessary to be aware that indices at less liquid points may not be based on actual transaction prices at all times, but may be based on a more informal survey of where players think the market is. This may lead to indices being unrepresentative of the true market.

Electricity/power

The electricity market (often described in the USA as the power market) is very different for one fundamental reason: both storage and transportation are incredibly expensive.[10] Let us briefly describe the nature of the power market from a trading and risk management perspective.

First, like many products, electricity demand varies significantly throughout the day, week and year. However, electricity has the same properties as a highly perishable product in that not only must supply meet demand, but production must meet demand minute by minute. The result of this unique attribute is that the market must keep a significant amount of idle capacity in place for start-up when the demand is there and shut-down when demand recedes. In some cases, this is a generation station that is already running, ready to meet anticipated customer demand. In other cases it is plant that may only be asked to start up once every few years. Typically a local market (or grid system) will keep 15–20% more plant capacity than it expects to use on the highest hour of demand during a normal year. This will often represent over double the average demand.

This, coupled with the physical challenges of transporting electricity,[11] leads to a general position of over-supply combined with short periods when the normally idle plant needs to run. At such peak times, when all the capacity on the system is needed, spot market prices[12] will rise dramatically as plant owners will need to recover not only their higher cost of running but also their capital costs in a relatively short period of time. This is exacerbated by the fact that electricity generation is one of the most capital-intensive industries in the world.

The forward market will, of course, smooth this by assigning probabilities to the likelihood of the high prices. Higher probabilities are obviously assigned during the periods when demand is likely to be at a peak and this will generally only occur during two or three months of the year. In the USA this is generally in the summer. Thus unless there is a huge over-supply the summer prices will be significantly higher than the rest of the year. When there is a potential shortage prices will be dramatically higher, as was seen in the Cinergy market in late June 1998 where daily prices that trade most of the year at $30/MWh increased to $7000/MWh.

It is these important market characteristics that lead to the extreme seasonality, jumps, spikes and mean reversion that will be discussed below in the section on Market Risk. Given the extreme nature of these factors trying to capture them on one term structure or convenience yield is extremely difficult.

Despite this price uncertainty, a forward market for electricity has developed along a standard commodity structure. In fact seven exchange contracts, reflecting the regional nature of power, currently exist at Palo Verde, California/Oregon Border (COB), Entergy, Cinergy (NYMEX), TVA, ComEd (CBOT) and Twin Cities (M. Grain Exchange) and PJM. The forward curves for Cinergy is shown in Figure 18.2 compared to the Henry Hub gas curve.

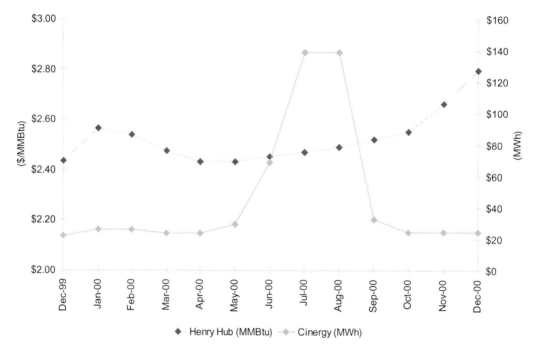

Figure 18.2 Forward curves for Cinergy compared to the Henry Hub gas curve. (*Source:* Citizens Power, June 1999)

Some standard options are traded at the most liquid hubs. These tend to be 'strips' of daily European calls based on monthly blocks. However, the bid/ask on such products are often wide and the depth of liquidity very limited.

Forward curve price discovery – the problems with power

Let us focus on two major differences in power:

- *Storage* First, you have virtually no stack and roll storage arbitrage. In other words, since you cannot keep today's power for tomorrow there is no primary 'arbitrage' linkage between today's price and tomorrow's. There are, of course, many secondary links. The underlying drivers are likely to be similar – demand, plant availability, fuel costs, traders' expectations and general market environment. But as you move forward in time, secondary links break down quickly and so does the price relationship. Figure 18.3 shows the forward correlation between an April contract and the rest of the year. As you can see, almost no relationship

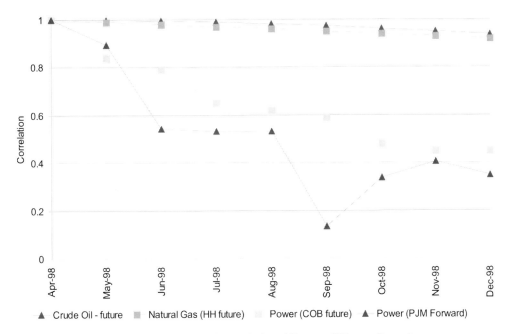

Figure 18.3 Forward correlation. (*Source:* Citizens Power)

exists between April and October and most of the relationship has evaporated once you are beyond one month. In other words, the October Cinergy contract has no more relationship with the April contract than, say, an oil, gas or even interest rate market.

- *Transportation* Second, you have limited 'hub basis' arbitrage. Since there are numerous logistical limitations on moving electricity it is difficult to arbitrage between many of the power markets within the USA (never mind internationally). Even hubs that are relatively close show large variations in the spread between prices. Figure 18.4 shows some of the correlations between major power hubs in the USA. Rather than thinking of them as one market, it is more accurate to view the power market as at least twelve (the final number of hubs is still being determined by the marketplace) independent markets with some but often little relationship.

Once you put all these factors together you see a picture similar to the one a global risk managers in a big bank will have experienced, a huge number of independent products that need to be combined for risk purposes. Instead of having one forward curve for US Power, we have up to eighteen independent months for twelve independent markets, in other words 216 products. This brings both the curse of lack of liquidity and data integrity for each product and, on the positive side from a risk perspective, diversity.

Forward curves up to 24 months are traditionally built using daily trader/broker marks for monthly peak/off-peak prices, with the breakdown, where necessary, into smaller time periods (down to an hourly profile) using historical prices adjusted for normal weather conditions. Prices beyond two years are significantly less liquid and where information is available bid/ask spreads can increase significantly. Forward

	Cob	Mid C	PV	Four Corners	TVA	Entergy	Ercot	PJM	Cinergy
Cob	1	0.77	0.70	0.60	0.08	0.11	0.13	0.09	0.16
Mid C		1	0.61	0.50	0.07	0.06	0.11	0.11	(0.04)
PV			1	0.59	0.00	0.03	0.05	0.06	(0.04)
Four Corners				1	(0.01)	0.04	0.08	(0.02)	0.12
TVA					1	0.92	0.22	0.72	0.31
Entergy						1	0.29	0.65	0.26
Ercot							1	0.23	0.11
PJM								1	0.31
Cinergy									1

Figure 18.4 Correlations between major power hubs in the USA. (*Source:* Citizens Power)

price curves (and volatility curves) beyond 24 months thus need to be created through more of a mark to model rather than mark to market process. As noted above, using a model to connect price quotes inevitably involved a number of assumptions about how the market behaves. In power, this involves not just fitting a serious of different price quotes together, but also filling in the gaps where price quotes are not available.

The price structure will have to make certain model assumptions based on historical observation about seasonality and the year-to-year transition process. Models can be bought (such as the SAVA forward curve builder) or, more often, built in-house. However, given the developing nature of the market this still tends to be a relatively manual process to ensure all the relevant market information can be input into the curve and minimize the error terms.

It needs to be remembered that in making assumptions about the structure of the curve in this process to estimate the fair value of a transaction that the forward curve, while objective, unbiased and arbitrage-free, may be unreliable given the incomplete data sets. Throughout the process it is thus necessary to estimate the impact of such assumptions and modeling or prudency reserves are likely to need to be applied against the fair value under these circumstances. The collection of market data with an illiquid market also becomes a major operational issue with a need to continuously verify and search for independent data.

Coal

Coal is often seen as the poor relation in the energy market and the emergence of a liquid commodity trading market in coal has been very sluggish. One reason for this is that the market has traditionally sold bespoke long-term contracts to utilities.

These were very specific with respect to quality since many power station boilers were designed to take particular quality specifications. This was more than just sulfur and calorific differences, but would also include specifications for chlorine, ash content, hardness (grindability), sodium, ash fusion temperature, volatile matter, moisture and others.

Another issue rests with the transport of coal. Coal is an expensive energy product to transport. For instance, although the cost of mine-mouth coal from an open-cast area can be as low as $3/tonnes FOB, the delivered cost of that coal could be closer to $30/tonne. While there is a competitive shipping market for seaborne trade, railroads are often oligopolistic in nature.

Finally, the market has been traditionally oversupplied by a large number of fragmented producers. This has led to extreme price competition and a market traditionally seeing a backwardated forward market. As a result, annualized historical volatility in this market is very low (10–15%). In addition, the lack of liquidity in standard products means clear forward curves cannot be easily found.

The coal market is, however, slowly changing. Faced with the challenges of deregulation and environmental constraints, utilities are moving to buying shorter-term, more standard coal qualities. These forces have led to some industry and the development of a coal trading market that is still in its infancy.

A reasonable international trading market exists and this is being complemented by standardized contracts in the USA. 'Hubs' are developing in Powder River Basin, Appalachia, Illinois Basin, Colorado-Utah and Pittsburgh Seam. Evidencing this trend, NYMEX has proposed launching a coal contract based on the Big Sandy River (Appalachia) in 1999.

Some early option and swap trading has taken place with indices being priced off publications such as Coal Daily in the USA. However, liquidity in these products has been very limited and, to date, they have not proved to be useful hedging mechanisms for major producers or consumers.

Other energy-related products – emissions and weather

Two other trading markets have been recently developing that complement energy trading in the USA: emissions and weather derivatives. Emissions trading become possible with the introduction of tradable tickets for Sulfur Dioxide (SO_2) on a national basis and Nitrous Oxide (NO_x) on a regional basis. Producers must have enough allowances to cover production of SO_2 and NO_x (a by-product from fossil fuel-burning stations, particularly oil and coal stations) and can sell excess allowances to those requiring additional allowances. The value of such allowances now represents a significant proportion of production costs and as such have a direct impact on the pricing in the fuel oil and coal markets. The emissions market is relatively active through a brokered OTC market and a small number of options have been traded.

Weather derivatives also play an interesting role in the energy markets that are particularly weather sensitive. A utility's revenue is obviously dependent on its unit sales, which are sensitive to the weather. Given this risk, weather derivatives are now being used by a number of utilities to hedge their exposure to temperature and other weather-related factors. In particular, swaps against heating degree-days are now becoming common, and options against, snow fall, snow pack (a price driver for hydro-based systems), river flow and other weather-related factors have been seen. A number of energy traders now actively buy and sell weather derivatives which are also of interest to insurance companies and have obvious applicability beyond energy players.

To date, the market is still at the early stages both in the USA and Europe and contracts have tended to have a limited payoff structure (a limit on the maximum payout).

Estimating market risk

Before we jump into the issues surrounding the difficulties of estimating risk within the energy sector it is worth putting the different products into some framework with respect to liquidity. Let us compare the volume, open interest and the term of the forward contracts in the products traded on the NYMEX (see Table 18.1).

Table 18.1   Products traded on the NYMEX (as of 14 June 1999)

	Daily volume (contracts)	Open interest (contracts)	Latest forward contract
Crude oil – WTI	51 456	120 068	Dec-05
Heating oil – NY Harbor	15 228	38 815	Dec-00
Gasoline – NY Harbor	15 623	41 230	Jun-00
Natural gas – Henry Hub	23 931	67 860	May-02
Electricity – Palo Verde	121	989	Dec-00
Electricity – COB	144	1 177	Sep-00
Electricity – Cinergy	98	527	Aug-00
Electricity – Entergy	12	343	Feb-00
Electricity – PJM	9	23	Oct-99
Electricity – TVA	0	0	Sep-99
Electricity – ComEd	0	0	Sep-99

Note: The electricity contracts are relatively new: the last contract was only launched in March 1999. It is unlikely that all the contracts will survive.
Source: NYMEX, CBOT

Given the infancy of the market, only limited liquidity exists in some of the power products, even where the OTC market has been robust enough to launch a futures contract. Any price data that is used must therefore be checked closely before conclusions can be drawn. This is particularly important when looking back at a significant period of time – many of the electricity markets simply did not exist more than a year or so ago.

Scenario analysis

As stated at the beginning of this chapter, many observers have been assessing energy market risk for a significant time. In addition, large numbers of consultantcy firms who specialize in the forecasting of energy prices to aid companies make investment or other business planning decisions. In addition, large energy companies will spend significant amounts of time and money determining their own views of the world.

Most will provide a range of possible scenarios recognizing the difficulty of providing an accurate forecast and a business can estimate the impact of both positive and not so positive scenarios. In other words a risk assessment of adverse price movements is made on a heuristic 'scenario'-based approach using some form of economic model. Where no discernible forward curves can be established this is still the most common form of market risk assessment. One advantage of this approach is that it can link into known market indicators. For instance, it can take a gas and oil forward curve and help 'translate' it into a power curve. As such, the models can be used as tools to provide a number of different types of forecasts, and to estimate:

- A pure arbitrage model
- A new entrant model (assuming 'potential' new entrants set forward prices)
- A macro model incorporating political, environmental, regulatory and economic model (e.g. a 'game theory' model)
- A micro 'dispatch' optimization model

The advantage of such an approach is that it can incorporate the important regulatory or market power issues that can dominate many regional energy markets. For instance, models that allow for the gradual deregulation of the local distribution companies and the transition away from cost plus pricing can provide useful insights into future price movements.

The important aspect of scenario analysis is consistency in the 'story' being told and 'buy-in' from senior management early in the process. As such, you need to establish that the scenarios are plausible, cover the key market risks to the business and then go through the painstaking process to ensure internal consistency.

The quantitative/statistical approach

As many have learned the hard way, forecasts, regardless of how sophisticated, are always wrong.[13] So it is not surprising that when the financial markets offered up an alternative approach it was readily embraced by the energy market players. In other words rather than try to estimate what the market might do and the implications of such a move, take the market's best guess at where future prices are going and then focus on estimating how wrong it is likely to be.

The two principal components used for this have been the forward curve price discovery and volatility estimation.

Volatility estimation – models

As discussed above, energy commodity prices show both high and variable volatility. This characteristic poses particular difficulty for the standard volatility models. The starting point for estimation of volatility is the standard constant volatility models as applied within the Black and Scholes model (1973). This allows us to incorporate the standard Brownian motion assumptions[14] in and expand them over a continuous time period using the square-root (uncorrelated) assumption.[15]

Many simplistic models have taken this assumption to estimate volatility in the energy markets. Given the lack of implied volatility estimates, the most common have taken simple average volatility (for instance, the average of the last six months' spot data) and projected it forward to create an annualized number which can be later converted for option pricing models or holding period for Value-at-Risk estimation (Figure 18.5).

A slight improvement to is to use a weighted average approach that weights the more recent events more heavily. This approach will undoubtedly improve the events but will not take account of the 'events' problem in energy (such as seasonality) or mean reversion. In other words the constant forward volatility assumption does not hold.

As can be seen from Figure 18.6 and as confirmed by the statistical tests, significant clustering occurs around the seasons and particular events. So while the basic

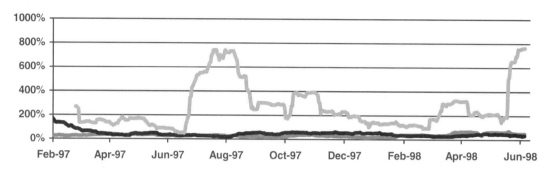

Figure 18.5   Volatility of commodities. (*Source:* Citizens Power)

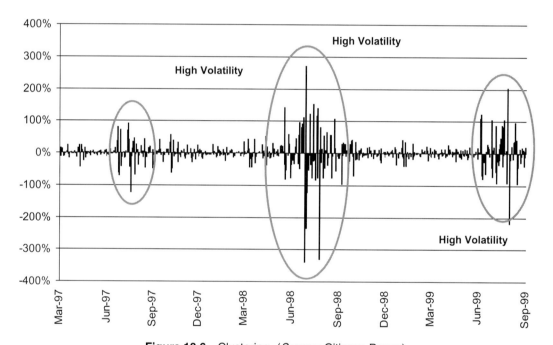

Figure 18.6   Clustering. (*Source:* Citizens Power)

stochastic 'random' toolkit with constant volatility provides a useful starting point it is not helpful in estimating the volatility parameters in energy. In fact, a number of issues need to be overcome before the quantitative models can be used effectively in the energy markets. These are addressed below.

Why energy is different – spot versus term markets

An important aspect of many commodity prices and energy in particular is the significant increase in volatility as a contract nears expiry. In many ways the nature of spot price movement is very different from those seen in the forward markets.

Spot prices are driven by observable short-run market price signals including actual supply and demand conditions. In power this will include plant availability and weather forecasts that provide a good proxy for electricity demand. Prices at this stage are likely to reduce to 'floor' levels or increase rapidly if supply conditions look like they are going to be particularly tight. This will occur whether you have a managed spot market, such as an electricity pool, or a pure OTC spot market. Given these movements away from the 'expected value' in the forwards volatility will rise dramatically as you move from the prompt month to the spot month. Figure 18.7 shows movement of volatilities as you move towards contact expiry, ending with extremely high volatility compared to other markets.

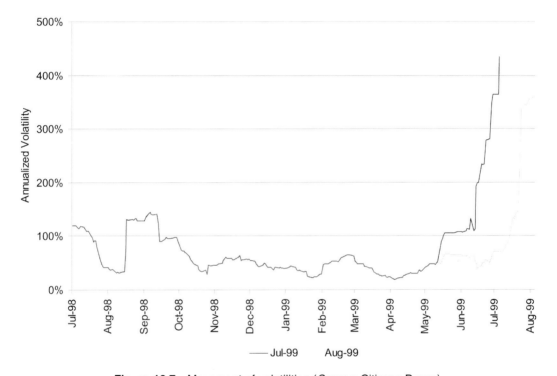

Figure 18.7   Movement of volatilities (*Source:* Citizens Power).

One consequence of this price movement characteristic is that VaR estimates will increase rapidly for any contracts that are taken to expiration. This means that risk managers need to both understand the trading strategy being employed and ensure that contracts that are not easily trading prior to expiration (such as some option structures) are treated very carefully.

Mean reversion

We discussed earlier that energy prices tend to mean revert, i.e. to move back to some mean over time. A number of models have been developed to adjust for mean reversion. The crucial components that are needed to adjust in mean reversion models are the mean itself and the speed of reversion. Two basic forms of mean reversion occur: short run and long run.

Short-run mean reversion occurs when the particular events that have 'knocked' prices away from their mean recede. In power, this seems to occur between three to five days after the event, which is generally weather driven. Long-run mean reversion is driven more by the economics of the industry. For instance, the ability to bring additional production on line or shut down uneconomic production will tend to put caps and floors on prices over longer-term periods. However, such supply/demand mismatches can last for periods of up to two or three years.

Additionally, given the extreme market movements in the power markets up- and down-volatilities are not symmetric. Down-volatilities will be high when prices are high and up-volatilities will be high when prices are low. This will have a material impact on the pricing models. The impact on VaR will, however, depend on the holding period being used. We have generally observed reversion taking five days or longer, resulting in a minimal impact on a 5-day or less holding period VaR.

Seasonality

As we discussed earlier, energy markets are inherently seasonal in nature. There are a number of ways to deal with this from fitting a sin/cosin curve to 'normalization' factors. The challenge is that no year is 'normal', which means that last year will be very different from next year. At least 10–20 years' data is needed to see any normal trend. Unfortunately, in most cases, the power markets are not mature enough to provide adequate pricing data.

Given this lack of data, the alternative is to try to model spot price volatility as a function of weather data, which can then be cast into a normal year. Such models can be useful providing the underlying production costs are similar in the study years. Unfortunately this is seldom the case.

Seasonality can present itself in a number of forms.

- An increase in the volatility of the entire curve during certain times of the year
- An increase in a segment of the curve during certain times
- Parts of the curve always being more volatile.

Unfortunately, in power, we see all three effects.

Two approaches can provide useful outcomes. First, adjusting volatility for monthly seasonal factors can provide useful results in most of the oil and gas markets. This deals with the fact that the entire curve tends to be more volatile at certain times of the year. Second, treating each month as an independent price variable can provide more useful results in the power market, and to a lesser extent, in gas. This allows for the fact that, say, summer is generally more volatile than spring and that their volatilities are normally independent.

This latter approach abandons the use of a single forward curve for the actively traded forward markets (up to 24 months), given the lack of storage and therefore correlation linkage between forward months (or quarters). The linkages between the months can then be rebuilt through a correlation matrix in the same way as linkages are drawn between different products. This brings with it significant data and sizing issues. Solving these seasonality issues is key to effective volatility estimation in energy.

Non-normal distributions

One of the keys to successfully applying volatility estimation and the stochastic process is some form of normal (or log-normal) distribution. We cannot assume this in the energy spot markets. Figure 18.8 shows a typical distribution of spot power prices. As you can observe prices are leptokurtic rather than normal in nature. This

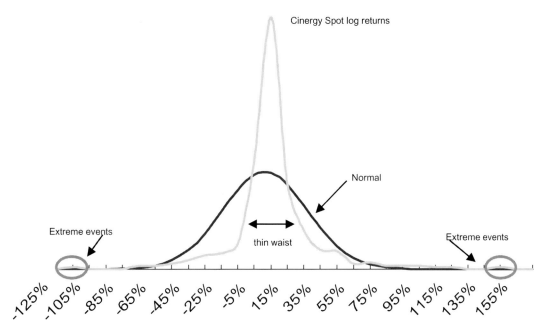

Figure 18.8 Distribution of spot power prices. (*Source:* Citizens Power)

causes major problems for most of the closed-form models. It is thus necessary to test continuously for normality assumptions within the energy markets.

The solutions to this are more problematical and are likely to lead to using historic or 'adjusted' historic data within a Monte Carlo simulation model to obtain realistic representations. Luckily most of the forward markets in energy are much more 'normal' in nature than their spot counterparts and are much easier to correct.

Price Spikes

Price spikes occur because ultimately the demand for most energy products and power in particular is inelastic. This means that once supply becomes scarce, prices potentially need to rise to astronomical levels before there is a demand response. In many cases consumers never see such price signals, meaning that prices could rise to any level and they would continue consuming.

A major issue in the power market (and to a lesser extent in the other energy markets) is that of price spikes within the spot market. These are of particular concern for risk managers since they will blow through previously realistic Value-at-Risk limits extremely quickly.

The 'jump diffusion' process provides some structure to capture this within a quantitative structure. This requires three factors to estimate the impacts of spikes: number, height and the duration. Traditionally, the three factors would be taken from historical information, but risk managers may well want to change the factors based on other fundamental analysis. For instance, simulation models can provide an estimate of the likelihood of spikes based on the likelihood of supply shortages.

The duration of spikes can be problematical. Generally, spikes mean revert very quickly. However, when prices go to extremely high levels liquidity and 'shock' factors can see a significant widening of bid/ask spreads and leave prices 'stranded' at high levels for some considerable time. Stress testing for different durations of spikes is thus advisable when considering the maximum potential exposures.

An interesting affect of spikes is that you get very pronounced smile effects in energy volatility. This is due to the fact that once prices rise above the normal levels there may be no limit to the ultimate level. To take an example, say prices normally range between \$15/MWh and \$40/MWh, occasionally moving up to \$150/MWh. When prices rise above \$150/MWh you are beyond the 'normal' supply/demand conditions. Given the inelastic demand, the probability of prices spiking to \$5000/MWh is similar to the probability of prices spiking to \$500/MWh. Thus, while the extrinsic value of a \$100 call will be significantly lower than a \$40 call; the extrinsic value of \$500 and \$1000 calls may be very similar. When translating these back into implied volatilities the result is very pronounced smile effects.

Historical versus implied volatilities

A simple answer to many of the above problems is to use implied rather than historical volatilities. This provides a particularly useful solution for monitoring option positions in liquid markets. However, they are less useful for the less liquid positions for applying VaR in energy.

The principal reason for this is the level of liquidity in the option market. Without a full-volatility 'smile' (i.e. the volatilities across a range of in- and out-of-the-money strike prices) and option pricing for a range of contract terms it is difficult to see fully how the market perceives volatility. For instance, you would want to break out the volatility most consistent with your VaR confidence interval for each forward contact. While this is possible in very liquid products such as crude oil it is difficult in gas and impossible in power.

The other problem is ensuring a consistency when using volatilities within models such as covariance matrices. Unless all your volatilities are calculated on a consistent basis, cross-correlations will not be consistent.

Given the option liquidity problems it is generally easier to use historical volatilities and 'test them' against the implied numbers that are available from the market. From this you can recalibrate the volatility models to the market numbers rather than fit to historical numbers, probably as a stress test.

Volatility models and model risk

Given the large number of specialist volatility models available to use and the numerous issues set out above it is impossible to review those that are most appropriate to the energy markets without becoming immersed in the technical details that are best left to the specialist academics and financial engineers. It is worth stating that, to date, the modeling challenges associated with the power markets have not been fully resolved and as such no model is fully adequate. The important factor given the dynamic nature of the energy markets is to have a model that can be continually updated from historical data and flexible enough to add in manual adjustments as necessary. The challenge is to find the model that closest meets your needs and which does the least amount of harm.

GARCH

The GARCH structures appear to be the most flexible and appropriate framework providing they are developed to adjust for the factors outlined above. These tend to hold up well under normal conditions with the energy markets placing particularly strong weighting to the most recent data. Where appropriate these models can be developed to capture the mean reversion and seasonality characteristics (although calibration is a more difficult problem).

However, the non-normal distribution issue is more difficult to solve. The principal approach being used by many parties to date is through the use of historical distributions in Monte Carlo, primarily as a stress test.

Correlations

Few, if any, energy companies trade single products at the same delivery point. The cross-correlation between energy products this becomes crucial in estimating the overall value and risk profile for a particular position.

As stated above, oil correlations are actively traded as crack spreads, locational spreads and time spreads. Similarly, 'spark spreads' between gas and power are commonly traded and these create a synthetic gas-fired power station. The higher the correlation between the input gas costs and output electricity prices, the easier it is to hedge power prices with gas prices and thus reduce the overall risk. In other words a high correlation will reduce the risk associated with a spark spread option, as well as reducing the potential upside.

US power markets create particularly complex correlations between power delivered at different points. There are between twelve and fifteen actively traded hubs in the USA that show a wide range of correlations, depending on the ability to transfer power between the regions and similarity of weather conditions. For instance, there is little or no correlation between COB (California / Oregon border) and Cinergy (near Cincinnati), while a relatively close correlation is seen between COB and Palo Verde (in southern California). A matrix of correlations for power was shown in Figure 18.4.

The inherent problem of relying on correlations to hedge risk is that they are prone to break down particularly during significant market events. For instance, when prices rose in Cinergy in June 1998 many participants wanted to transport power from the PJM region to cover their positions. This proved impossible given PJM's high demand conditions and the correlations between PJM and Cinergy broke down, leaving some players with significant losses despite their 'hedged' position. Even under 'normal' market conditions correlations can vary significantly over time and risk managers need to be very careful of traders leveraging what seem to be stable correlations.

As stated above, it is also common within the power sector to treat different forward months as individual products. If this approach is taken it is necessary to link the contracts by their estimated correlations. While this solves one problem, it creates another computational one given the resultant matrix and computation necessary to keep the correlations up to date.

Energy options – financial and 'real' options

Many energy contracts have significant optionality built into them at both the producer and consumer ends. This can range from standard traded options to complex embedded options in long-term contracts. Unfortunately, one of the most complex options to price is a power station.

In the gas market, in both the USA and Europe, many of the annual or longer-dated contacts have some degree of flexibility or 'swing' built into them reflecting the production flexibility and/or storage capabilities of the supplier. These allow buyers to amend their daily or monthly takes provided they meet overall volume requirements. This flexibility from the buyer may be offset by the ability of the seller to interrupt the contract, for instance if there are production problems.

Such a situation leads to a complex option pricing model where it is easy to mis-specify the parameters unless the quantitative analyst is very familiar with the model restrictions, the nature of the pricing volatility and the contract structure. Complex contract structures should not be finalized before these problems can be solved.

Many sellers of such options will link the structure back to actual capabilities of the underlying asset and given the developments of hedge accounting rules (for instance, FASB 133 in the USA) this is likely to become more pronounced. If this is a gas field, only limited flexibility will exist to increase or decrease production and different storage techniques will be able to respond to market prices at different speeds. Given these operational constraints and the sale of European- or American-style options based on single-period clearing, prices need to be handled very carefully since the 'real option' may not be available or able to respond to that particular price signal. This is particularly true when pricing against illiquid and volatile prices that may take some time to find their equilibrium rates.

Another concern is the ability to effectively delta hedge positions given that standard 'lot' sizes in the power OTC markets is relatively large, transaction costs relatively high and liquidity often sporadic. It is important to evaluate the practicality of the delta hedging strategy in assessing the value of such a position. It is also important to distinguish between pseudo-random and commercial optionality. Force majeure, such as pipeline failures, can be priced like a call option but the likelihood of the call is part random, part correlated with higher prices. This will be significantly less expensive than commercial options that are driven purely by price. They are, however, seldom as neutral as many like to assume, i.e. the assumption that if it was purely random it would be costless in optionality over some time period.

Given the popularity of spreads in energy to create synthetic transport, power stations, refineries and storage it is not surprising that spread options are also popular. Similarly, the underlying assets need to be valued on a consistent basis with their financial counterparts leading many (if not most) energy players to value asset positions against their real option value.

For instance, a power station is a particularly complex 'real' spread option. Given the right contract structure, it allows you to arbitrage between two energy markets, say gas and power at a given cost. Their value will thus be driven not only by their expected arbitrage value but also by the volatility and correlation between the markets (high volatility/low correlation leading to high values). Some power stations (such as a large nuclear plant) are deep in the money on the power side, increasing their intrinsic value but reducing their option value. Others (such as an open-cycle gas turbine which has a high energy cost, low capital cost) may be out of the money maintaining significant option value but little intrinsic value.

The ability of a power station to take advantage of the optionality will depend on its availability and flexibility. Power stations are not like contracts: as one electricity executive once said, 'contracts do not have tube leaks'. They also don't have to obey the laws of physics in starting up, which for some plant can take several hours or even days. A plant that takes a long time and is expensive to start up will be significantly less valuable from an option/arbitrage viewpoint.

Finally, some power stations can arbitrage between several markets. They may be able to run on more than one fuel source and trade into the 'ancillary service'[16] markets.

Like many real options, these unique characteristics make it extremely difficult to model a power station in standard models. Unless you are intent on solving the intellectual challenge of the generalized closed-form solution for power stations I would suggest that a Monte Carlo simulation package is a much more effective tool. A number of companies have been developing these for years and if combined with a quantitative understanding of the price volatility can provide an effective pricing tool set.

It is also important to consider who will buy the option value. Many consumers of power and gas must buy on a daily basis since they have no storage capability and with the underlying daily volatility of these markets will be looking for firm-average price options to hedge their physical consumption. Unfortunately this won't match with the production assets, leaving a complex basis position.

Model risk

Many of the issues outlined above primarily exist or are exaggerated in the spot markets where many quantitative estimation tools are less effective and the resultant model risk becomes very significant. One of the major reasons for hedging into forward markets should be to avoid this model risk.

Model risk can come from a number of sources, but are principally driven from forward curve models (particularly the volatility forward curve) and pricing models (option, simulation and optimization models). It is generally recommended that traders and risk managers have a preset (and audited) library of pricing tools to work from, but in many cases longer-term contracts will require the correct building blocks to correctly price a particular offering. One example of where such pricing can go wrong is taking account of correlations between different components of a deal in hedging a variable retail load.

It is common in both the gas and power markets to offer retail hedges where the volume sold is linked to actual consumption of a customer group. In these circumstances there is a positive correlation between the volume being hedged and market clearing prices (the customer group's consumption itself being part of the demand driver in prices). This correlation changes at different consumption levels following a generally exponential curve.

A simplistic approach could make a mistake on two fronts. If you ignore the extent of the positive (non-linear) correlation between price and demand you could significantly under-price the hedge. Above certain overall market demand levels, prices will rise exponentially, which will occur exactly as the volume requirement of the hedge increases. While most models will take account of the cost of increased demand at high prices, they often do not simulate the non-linear relationship, thus under-pricing the option.

A number of early power deals reportedly made this mistake when taking on such positions. They hedged full requirement positions (supply all the load a group of customers take) at expected volumes. With increasing volatility in the marketplace and a positive correlation between prices and the customer's consumption they then found themselves long at lower than expected prices and short at higher than expected prices, resulting in a significant overall loss compared to the hedged position.

The alternative problem is to ignore the fact that the call option is not being optimized against high prices (customers use energy when they need it, not when it has most value in the market) and it is a positive but by no means perfect correlation. If the customer's 'call option' to increase their volume is priced, ignoring this the option will be significantly over-priced. A diverse portfolio of different customer types dissipates much of this call risk.

As well as the problem associated with volume uncertainty, energy contracts abound with complexity reflecting the immaturity of the market (many older contracts still in force reflect the realities of a regulated utility world) and physical realities of the market price. Combinations of average price options, look-back index options, knock-out features, swing contracts and time spread options are common. In addition, it is not uncommon to see contracts against terms such as 'average market prices' rather than a specific published index, making the translation from contract to model more complex (as well as opening up a number of other pricing issues).

To minimize model risk, an extensive testing program needs to be put in place to ensure this is quantified on an on-going basis. The backtesting of model estimates should be used to estimate potential model errors and incorporated into the hedging strategy. In particular the assumptions surrounding mean reversion in the volatility curve (which significantly reduces the volatility over time) need to be carefully tested against actual marks wherever possible given the lack of implied curves that can be derived. Market illiquidity will make this process difficult, often resulting in arbitrary allocations between liquidity and modeling risk allocations. A risk manager needs to be very careful of such allocations to ensure consistency across different products and markets.

Value-at-Risk for energy

As in many markets, VaR has been accepted as the most common way of communicating risk parameters within the energy sector. A detailed description of VaR itself is addressed elsewhere in this book.

VaR is driven by four principal factors: volatility, correlations, holding period and confidence interval. Given the first two parameters VaR models are going to be susceptible to many of the problems outlined above. However, the holding period and confidence interval assumptions have mixed effects. A holding period of ten days or less is common in the actively traded energy markets. This allows for a relative lack of liquidity compared to financial markets and the 'communication delay' – it may take 24 hours to identify a problem, another 24 to agree on the way forward.

A five-day holding period will tend to avoid much of the mean reversion and seasonality issues, provided the volatilities have been estimated correctly. You can thus give a reasonable five-day estimate of VaR despite many of the issues outlined above. The concern is that it gives a very incomplete picture of your risk profile. In particular, the chairman and CEO is often more concerned about potential major losses. In other words they will be more worried about the 5% rather than the 95%. While a VaR can give some clues to the maximum loss, with significant spikes the losses may be many multiples of the VaR estimation.

Also, many of the traded products cannot be hedged within 10 days (many cannot be hedged at all). In this case the holding periods need to be re-assessed in light of the particular product. The overall VaR associated will then be affected by the time to maturity, ability to find partial hedges and mean reversion of volatility.

Also, as we discussed above, optionality is pervasive in energy and the more traditional VaR needs to be expanded and complemented to take account of the full range of option risks. It other words, delta, gamma, vega and theta risks need to be quantified and added to the VaR calculation. Where significant optionality exists a simulation approach is likely to be most effective, although this may be at the cost of timely information.

Stress testing

Some of the solutions outlined above fall into the category of 'stress testing', which is vital in all markets and energy is certainly no exception. Stress testing can take many forms, the most common being historical tests. Others will include model tests and extreme event forecasting. A sample set of tests would include:

- Apply the highest observed volatility
- Apply the highest observed prices
- Combination of high prices and volatility
- Zero correlation
- Adverse correlations
- Six sigma event
- Price shock (i.e. price times ten , or divided by ten)
- Different price shapes (i.e. ratio summer/winter; weekday/weekend)
- Alternative distribution shapes
- Clustering extreme events
- Assuming particular positions cannot be hedged before expiry

While many of the tests should be automated and produced on a regular basis (daily or weekly) stress tests need to be designed around the particular portfolio and should be an iterative process to find particular weaknesses in the portfolio. They are also likely to be a key part in the overall portfolio analysis that will drive the trading and hedging strategy.

Stress tests play a vital role in setting overall liquidity and reserve requirements of the business as well as a vital communication tool to senior management. The single biggest danger with VaR is complacency because the portfolio has not been appropriately stressed.

Stress testing should also encompass all the correlated risks within the business that may not otherwise be combined. The most obvious is the combination of credit and market risks under alternative 'market crisis' scenarios defaults, leading to additional volatility, leading to more defaults.

Pricing issues

The lack of liquidity and the complexity of market, means that many positions cannot be easily hedged. In this case, the risk-free pricing models may over-estimate the value of deals since such deals will carry significant market risk that should be factored into the price.

It is thus important to assess the profit and risk impact the deal will make on the overall portfolio. In turn, this may require a re-optimization of portfolio using all available hedges, which can be a complex process, creating additional model and operational risk in the assessment of complex deals.

Credit risk – why 3000% plus volatility matters

Credit risk can be defined in a number of ways, but will consist of the following:

- Unpaid bills (current and aged debt)
- Delivered but unbilled (realized)
- Replacement cost of future commitments (unrealized) – mark to market exposure
- Potential adverse movements or replacement costs – CVaR (Credit Value-at-Risk) and potential exposure (maximum exposure given potential movements in prices and volatilities over the life of the contract)

The volatility of energy prices, particularly power, makes the challenge of managing credit risk particularly interesting as exposure is potentially unlimited.

The challenges of Utility Y

Let us take the example of a Cinergy Power trade by Utility Y. Utility Y is very prudent, they like to have a fully hedged position and severely limit purchases from small players.

Initiated in November 1997 for July 1998. Y buys a 50 MW contract from a small counterparty for $35/MWh at a total cost $560 000, and with annualized volatility running around 20%. Given they are buying, they see no receivable exposure, no mark to market exposure, and estimate the potential market exposure to be $112 000.

By February the price is $50/MWh and a mark to market value is $240 000. Volatility is now 30%, so potential exposure (receivables plus mark to market plus potential market exposure) is equal to $313 600. Although the counterparty is a small player they are still well within Y's 'prudent' limit of $1 million set for this particular counterparty.

In June 1998 the market price has risen to $350/MWh (annualized volatility is now over 1000%) and Y's counterparty defaults by telling them they will not deliver the power under the contract. The replacement power they need to buy to meet their customer's requirements cost $5.6 million, a net loss of over $5 million, five times the limit they thought. This could have been a true story for anyone trading the US power market industry in the summer of 1998.

Given such volatility in these markets and their early stages of development, it is not surprising to see some casualties. This tends to occur during major market movements and can provide additional impetus to the market movement that started it. The defaults of Federal Energy and Power Company of America were both caused by and caused the extreme volatility experienced in the Cinergy spot market (it reached x000% on an annualized, historical basis).[17]

It is an important point to note that the biggest risk facing many companies at this stage was the non-delivery of power rather than the non-payment of delivered power. As such credit managers switched their attention away from the traditional accounts receivable approach to focusing on counterparty mark to market and credit VaR approaches. This reinforced the need to focus on the total exposure to a counterparty default and the potential for domino effects within a particular sector. We will set out below a number of 'must-haves' in assessing credit risk within the energy sector within an overall credit process.

Credit breaks down into two distinct areas: the initial credit evaluation process and the on-going monitoring of exposures. Credit evaluation includes the evaluation of a particular counterparty, taking account of the market they are in (country and sector) as well as the current financial strength and track record of the company. Counterparty credit limits are then based on your own risk appetite and strategic importance of that counter-party.[18]

Exposure monitoring includes the identification and measurement of exposures as well as the operational reporting and control process. This should be done at a counterparty and portfolio level.

Counterparty evaluation: some challenges

Unfortunately, the standard assessment measures employed by credit rating services such as Moody's, Standard & Poor's, Fitch Investors or Dunn & Bradstreet, while useful, often provide insufficient detail when evaluating an energy trading businesses. Rating agencies rarely address in detail the controls within the business and the potential for major losses. Coupled with this is the lack of financial information on subsidiary trading businesses. The result is that risk professionals who rely solely on the rating agencies can miss potential problems or set an overly prudent approach.[19]

Companies that want to quantify adequately the creditworthiness of a counterparty will need to develop their own internal scoring methodologies to complement the rating agencies and develop their own specialist ratings. The internal scoring system should take account of qualitative as well as quantitative factors such as the ownership and control of the entity, track record and diversification. This need for an internal scoring system is reinforced by the fact that many trading organizations are not rated by the agencies and that their financial strength can change very rapidly. Second, as evidenced in the above Utility Y scenario, the significance of the replacement cost of electricity becomes particularly important.

The legal issues around default can also be complex. In the US power market the legal framework was initially created through 'enabling' agreements which have not fully addressed the problem of credit risk appropriately. Failure to deliver may not result in either default or damages. The enforceability of netting or set-off agreements can also be problematical, as can the implementation of credit enhancement or 'further assurances' clauses that are intended to improve your position when a counterparty's creditworthiness is called into doubt.

One area that is still being clarified is whether electricity constitutes a good or a commodity. As the market becomes more 'commodity-like' it moves more into line with the protection given to commodities under the relevant bankruptcy codes and allows the default process set out within ISDA documentation to be used. This development in the legal framework surrounding electricity and gas contracts is one that is likely to repeat itself throughout the world.

Thus, ensuring the master agreements reflect appropriate termination and netting provisions is an important first step to mitigate credit exposure. Understanding the interactions between utility tariffs, master agreements for different products, guarantees and additional agreements (such as separate netting agreements) is an essential but unfortunately major exercise, as is ensuring you understand the corporate structure of the counterparty with whom you are dealing. With this structure in place you can set an exposure limit for each counterparty.

Setting limits

Setting appropriate limits by counterparty will depend on both your risk tolerance and the evaluation of the counterparty. For example, a reasonable approach employed by many is to set the limits based on a percentage of their net tangible equity or net asset value. Depending on your appetite for risk, you may want to set a limit of, say, 3% of any one party's equity position. A similar percentage limit could be set off your own liquid asset or equity position which would set the maximum exposure you would want to any counterparty, however strong. These percentages would be adjusted for the creditworthiness of the counterparty in question.

Once you have the credit evaluation structure in place the use of Credit-Value-at-Risk (CVaR) is one way of estimating the potential credit exposure using a probability distribution of price movements in the same way VaR is calculated for market risk. This has particular relevance given the volatilities in power. Estimating this requires the same fundamental information as VaR itself, including the current market price for the contract, a price distribution, the magnitude of unpredictable price movements (volatility and confidence interval) and the appropriate time it would take to rehedge the position (holding period). The three latter components have distinctive traits in the case of default since the event itself will be closely correlated with price movements.

A key issue is the determination of what volatility and time frame to apply. If we take the example of Utility Y above, the trade was hedging an existing exposure six months out and as such that hedge must remain for the entire period to minimize the market risk. In addition, the magnitude of this event and the time it takes to unwind positions will also depend on the market share of the defaulting party. The immediate question that needs to be addressed is that if VaR is driven by the assumption of normal market conditions, surely a default (being an abnormal market event) makes it meaningless.

A starting point in solving this issue is to significantly lengthen the holding period. A thirty-day holding period may be more appropriate in the instance of default rather than the shorted period of, say, five days used of VaR itself. A credit risk manager also needs to look at the potential movement of CVaR into the future as a way of managing credit risk. In other words limits should be set on 'potential exposures' as well as on CVaR itself. Graphing the predicted movements of exposure including CVaR movements over the future duration of the portfolio provides a useful warning of potential risks on the horizon, particularly given the seasonal nature of the volatility outlined above. It is important to note that CVaR does not define your credit risk (how likely you are to lose money) but it is a useful construct which will quantify the likely exposure in the case of default.

The next step is to combine these risks with the probability of default and the likelihood of multiple defaults (unfortunately all too common). This would allow you to estimate the total portfolio credit risk to combine with the market risks within the book.

We can thus quantify two principal control points in setting credit policy – at the individual level, the maximum potential exposure per counterparty, and at the macro level, the credit risk within the book or portfolio. Both are fundamental to running a well-managed energy trading book, although unfortunately while they provide strong markers to how much risk is in the book they cannot accurately predict actual losses in the case of default.

Timing is everything

The important factor all credit risk managers need in energy is timely and accurate information. This is far from simple, especially since most utilities are more used to monthly or even multiple-month turnarounds. Getting an up-to-date list of counterparty exposures and their associated lists was traditionally seen an initiative that sometimes happened after a major event.

Unfortunately credit managers need to work within these constraints and balance between what is desirable versus what is feasible. As such their ability to get timely exposure reports and lists of potential counterparties is often hampered by antiquated accounting systems and a bemused sales force and management. In some cases the credit managers are still divorced from the trading team and housed with the corporate finance and treasury function.

Given the potential for extreme volatility, isolation of credit from market risk is extremely dangerous in energy. With prices moving dramatically credit exposures become significant in hours rather than days or weeks, and problems often need to be dealt with before the next day. Energy has neither the luxury of the institutionalized nature of the finance markets nor the ability to take the more blasé approach of a traditional utility who has experienced few historical defaults. As such, the credit manager and risk manager need to be side by side on the trading floor as should the most important person on the energy trade floor, the operational risk manager.

Operational risk

Operational risk management can be defined as ensuring:

- The limits and controls are unambiguous and appropriate for the on-going business
- The day-to-day mark to market and corresponding risk reports are correct
- Limits are monitored and breaches alerted in line with predefined procedures
- Data and system integrity (including trade input errors)

Operational Risk area is both the most important area under the remit of risk management but is often given least attention outside the periodic audit review.

Within energy it is virtually impossible to quantify the value of operational risks. It is often seen as a pure audit or control function adding little value to the enterprise beyond the 'let's keep the auditors happy' once a year. The operational risk manager often has thus a 'no-win' role of unnecessary bureaucrat in the good times and fall guy when things go wrong. The role also sits awkwardly between the market/credit risk functions, the operational accounting functions, the internal audit functions, the IS department and any front-office operations. As such it is the least well defined and least emphasized area of risk management.

However, the majority of the big trading losses within the energy business, as well as other trading businesses, can be traced back to inadequate controls or reporting. Extreme volatility and a developing market make operational risk management all the more important.

Overall framework, policies and procedures

Most risk managers will start from the G30 recommendations and other derivative market control frameworks to set their 'best practice' standards for middle-office controls. However, once you are beyond setting up an independent reporting line they fall short of specific advice on detailed procedures and controls.

The starting point in defining the framework is a consistent Scheme of Authority and Trading Compliance Guidelines. These will draw upon the existing corporate scheme, but need to be radically expanded for the energy trading business. Perhaps more important is to develop a process to ensure traders and risk managers alike are aware of the controls and how they impact on their day-to-day work. Once the high-level control environment has been established the difficult problem of product authorization should start.

Deals versus trades

As is evident from the above, the underlying characteristics of energy products are extremely complex. Electricity customers want to switch on a light and get instantaneous power from a product that has extremely expensive storage; millions of customers are doing this by a varying amount minute by minute throughout the year. Many of the transactions in electricity are designed to back this type of delivery and are non-standard and complex. On the other hand, the US power marketers are churning millions of MWhs of standard 5×16 blocks of power. A similar dichotomy exists in gas and oil.

The energy company risk manager has to be conversant with the two different 'products' equally efficiently. The standard product must be able to churn a high transaction rate without creating significant transaction risk, while the 'bespoke' contracts need to be broken down into their risk buckets and assessed individually.

The control process needs to make this distinction early. Standard products or trades should be closely defined under pre-agreed master agreements, which lead to 'deals' failing the authorization tests and thus falling into the deal process. Figure 18.9 sets out a standard trade authorization process for power.

It is important to note that with energy trading it is very easy to put general product authorizations in place that could be interpreted very widely. For instance, one description could be US Eastern Interconnect Electricity, but does that include the sale or ancillary services on the hourly or even minute-by-minute market? Does it allow knock-out options linked to a foreign currency? Many traders will answer yes, while the board could answer no.

Product authorizations is an area that is fraught with potential problems as portfolio authorization becomes more complex. The risk manager has to make sure everyone has a common understanding of their authorizations and that trader understanding remains a subset of the board members.

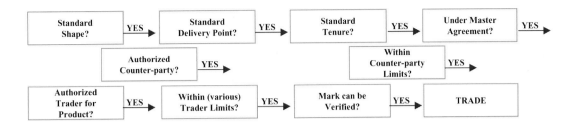

Figure 18.9 A standard trade authorization process for power. (*Source:* Citizens Power)

Once you have the product definitions and corresponding legal agreements you can build a highly efficient trade processing system. The standardization allows for efficient hand-offs which can give you a much higher degree of specialization in the business, almost to the point where separate individuals are looking at the different parts of the chain set out above. To make this work you need to be very specific in defining the physical product definition (including quality specs), delivery point, tenure and contract specification. Once it is in place and working you can automate it and let the IT and IS systems take the strain as transaction volumes increase.

The reporting controls at this stage begin to focus on trade input errors, changed trades and delivery (or book out) issues. As mentioned above, anything falling outside this needs to fall into deal analysis. This is identical to trade analysis but many of the components can occur concurrently, often by a specific deal team that has cross-functional skills.

The risk manager's job with the 'deal' is to break it down to the appropriate risk components, the so-called risk bucketing or risk mapping which becomes key within energy. This is normally done working closely with the structured products or marketing desks and will encompass operational, market and credit issues.

With respect to all these issues the operational risk manager is very dependent on the information systems supporting the trade capture and reporting system. Extremely close links are needed with the IS department who need to meet the challenge of developing error-free systems within a rapid application environment. This is only possible where the IS, operations and trading staff each have a good appreciation of the requirements and limitations of each other. Again communication becomes the vital link which is aided by a corporate structure that encourages common goals and a floor plan that keeps these key individuals within reasonable proximity of each other.

Price data collection

Operational risk managers are dependent on and often responsible to price data collection and verification. Constructing good forward curves on a daily basis was briefly discussed above, but one of the biggest difficulties is ensuring that accurate price data is being used.

Particularly in power, it cannot be assumed that price quotes are reflective of where people would be willing and able to transact. Liquidity is often extremely limited and brokers may well estimate the market prices giving an appearance of liquidity that does not exist. This is also true of NYMEX prices in power where estimates need to be made for margining previous transactions but actual transactions may not have occurred at these levels. In these circumstances, it is not unknown to see a significant divergence between NYMEX and OTC prices for the same product for a limited period of time.

It is thus necessary to check price data using a number of information sources, notably trader's marks, a range of broker quotes, spread prices (using actual or historical spreads to relate closely traded markets), implied volatility from options and derivative prices. Standard techniques for fitting average or strip prices should be used and resultant errors monitored on an on-going basis.

The overall control framework

We have not discussed the most important piece a risk manager needs – the overall risk framework. With a highly volatile commodity like power this needs to be multi-layered, with a strong linkage down to a variety of control points.

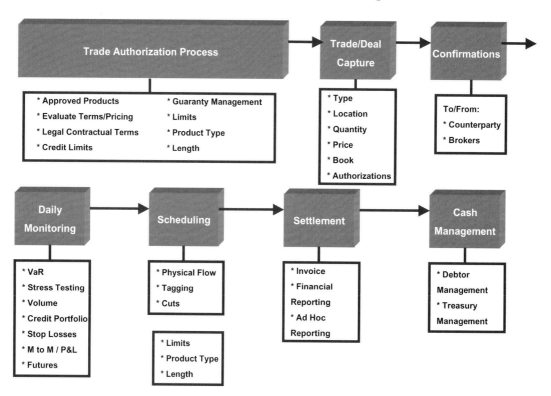

Figure 18.10 Quantifiable limits set by an organization's control structure. (*Source:* Citizens Power)

Figure 18.10 sets out some of the most important quantifiable limits that can be set and how they relate to each other. This control structure links many parts of the organization. As well as monitoring for trade input error, significant emphasis needs to be placed on verifying counterparty and broker confirmations to the trade capture systems. Conformations can often be slow and inconsistent depending on the counterparty, which combined with the potential volatility in the market makes for a dangerous mix. We have seen players lose several million dollars based on trading input errors that never got picked up by the confirmation process.

Summary

Energy markets are probably the most challenging commodity markets a risk manager will face in terms of level of complexity, volatility and quantification. Many of the issues raised and approaches outlined in this chapter are a reflection of the developing nature of the markets. In addition, some fundamental risk management issues still need to be adequately addressed.

As the developing energy markets continue to evolve, the tools used by risk managers to measure, monitor and control market, credit and operational risk will also continue to develop. These developments will impact energy markets on a worldwide basis. I suspect many of today's models will be rendered obsolete in the very near future.[20]

However, the establishment of VaR, CVaR and associated quantitative processes being modified and developed for the energy market provides a strong framework to effectively communicate and control risk as well as providing a useful process to isolate the component risks within the overall company. The use of these quantitative approaches needs to be complemented by an appropriate stress testing and model testing environment that challenges both the assumptions made by traders and the risk management department itself.

One of the most useful aspects of the quantitative approach is that it can be easily encompassed within an overall risk framework for setting risk/reward ratios, internal capital allocation, liquidity and reserve requirements. This puts the role of risk management as a key element in any business organization, truly bridging the gap between the financial accounting and 'commercial' departments.

The risk management strategy, allocating risk and investing in control and analytical systems needs to be an integral part of the overall business and enterprise risk framework. This chapter has not sought to recommend how such allocations should be made since they are a function of individual business environments. Rather, we would stress that as risk managers are faced with such decisions and organizations are being restructured it important for the risk manager not to lose sight of the fact that there is no substitute for common sense.

Acknowledgements

Many thanks to Mark Williams and Karin Hjalmers for their comments and additions.

Notes

[1] The retail US electricity market is estimated to be at least $200 billion.
[2] A measure of the density of the oil.
[3] North West Europe.
[4] This has been likened to creating a virtual oil refinery.

[5] Backwardation describes the situation where prices are highest in the nearest date periods and lower in forward delivery dates.

[6] Contango describes the situation where prices are progressively higher as you move from near-dated to far-dated forward contracts.

[7] Spurred by deregulation, the recent pipeline developments in Europe and the USA are consolidating and expanding the size of the regional markets at a rapid pace.

[8] The fourth week of the month when gas orders are placed.

[9] The best-known index generated from this is from the Inside FERC Gas Market Report.

[10] Storage is so difficult that most will characterize electricity as having no storage potential.

[11] The complexity of electricity transmission is immense. At a simple level you need to remember that electricity doesn't travel huge distances easily. It's like a good car, given a good road (an EHV transmission line) it can travel remarkably far. On a bad road (an LV line) it will go nowhere fast, and expend a lot of energy getting there. Without huge expense and remarkable civil engineering it can rarely get across major water expanses or mountain ranges.

[12] Within the next thirty days or less.

[13] My favorite old proverb is 'those that claim to forecast are liars, even if they are later proved to be correct'.

[14] The changes in price have a normal distribution.

[15] Using the square root of time factor implies that the return increases linearly with time and that the variance increases linearly with the square root of time.

[16] I won't begin to describe these here given their technical complexity and specialized nature. However, if you trade electricity they cannot be ignored.

[17] See *Wall Street Journal* article, July 1998.

[18] I always hesitate to use the word 'strategic': in this case it means the overall risk/reward balance may increase even if the credit risk decreases.

[19] While many with accounting backgrounds are keen on prudence, it may lead to an inappropriate use of your risk capital.

[20] Potentially rendering chapters like this out of date before they are published!

Further reading

Fusaro, P. C. (1998) *Energy Risk Management*.

Hull, J. C. (1993) *Options, Futures and Other Derivative Securities*, 2nd edition.

Myerson, A. (1998) 'A 20,000% bounce: now that's volatility: deregulation adds to perils of trading', *The New York Times*, 23 August.

Neftçi, S. N. (1996) *An Introduction to the Mathematics of Financial Derivatives*.

Pilipović, D. (1997) *Energy Risk*.

Schimko, D. and St Germain, J.-P. (1998) 'Substandard deviations', *Risk*, February.

From the Editors of *Derivatives Week Learning Curves*, Volume IV.

19

Implementation of price testing

ANDREW FISHMAN

Overview

The purpose of this chapter is to provide the risk practitioner with an overview of the key goals and challenges of designing and implementing a price testing strategy for an organization. It identifies the users of price testing reporting from both a minimum required control and added value perspectives.

Price testing and provisioning are sometimes spoken of in the same context and sometimes viewed as separate exercises. In some organizations these responsibilities are sometimes performed by separate functions at different points in time or upon separate cycles. Regardless of the organizational structure and timing, the chapter is written to cover the key concepts of price testing and to be fungible across organizational structures.

An overview of the design of the document is:

- Objectives and defining the control framework – setting the game plan for the location or organization that lead to developing the strategy, implementation and performance benchmarks
- Implementing the strategy – decision time is required when the theoretical approach of how price testing is to be performed meets with the reality of actually performing the task with incomplete data and balancing this with other responsibilities.
- Managing the price testing process – challenges in getting the most coverage with the best sources of data within the agreed deliverable time
- Reporting – with price testing, don't drop the ball before the goal line. Reporting for basic control purposes is a requirement. With a little more effort and identifying target audiences, added value can be obtained to support decisions on trading strategies and booking.

Layout of each section

One process flow chart drives the entire document and the reader can use it to reference where each section is in the transaction process (Figure 19.1).

Each section will begin with a decision box and will contain a section that highlights the key topics and decisions that are needed to be defined or addressed in the section. An example from the second section of this chapter is as follows:

Topic	Decision point or challenge
1 Defining the price testing objectives for the organization	Agree the *objectives* of price testing control function within the organization.
	Define the overall target objectives

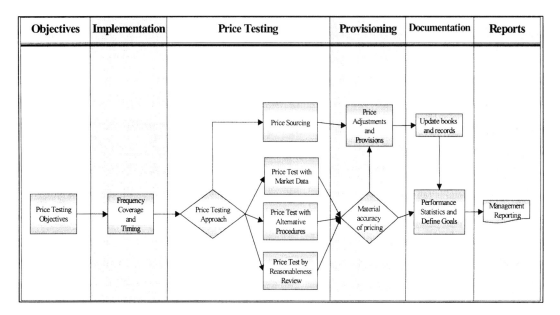

Figure 19.1 The highlighted flow diagram.

Examples are included to provide perspectives on the narrative and theory. Real-world situations are not black and white binary answers. These examples are meant to highlight considerations in the decision process rather than provide absolute examples. The examples are aids in the following order:

Objectives and defining the control framework
Example 1 Banking versus trading books
Large losses remain hidden on the balance sheet in the banking book. The markets have moved significantly against a position which has become a real dog. To avoid having to show the loss, the position is moved to the banking book at cost and accounted for on an accrual basis.

Implementing the Strategy
Example 2 Handling of illiquid positions
Positions are illiquid and not valued. As prices are not readily available, traders assure the control practitioner that prices are used to mark to market the positions are fair and reasonable.

Example 3   Timing of end of day prices

Clear specification is required to automate market data grabs. Not specifying the details can result in the wrong information.

Example 4   Making the call on an illiquid bond valuation

The challenges on determining a market to market valuation when the market data appear inconsistent.

Example 5   Making the call on a valuation when a trader strategy is guaranteed

Valuation and strategy collide

Managing the price testing process

Example 6   Don't worry, price testing is being done

Performance measures to be sure that cultural differences do not get in the way of obtaining comparable analysis.

Objectives and defining the control framework

Table 19.1   Decision box

Topic	Decision point or challenge
• Defining the price testing objectives for the oganization	Agree the *objectives* of price testing control function within the organization. Define the overall target objectives
• Timing of testing cycle	Define the frequency and reporting cycles of price testing in the portfolio Timing of capturing the market data
• Targeting and prioritizing books that are to be included in price testing – trading and banking books	Determine the handling of the price testing of the banking book is to be included in the price testing cycle Determine a manner in which it can be price tested and not affect the core processing and accounting records that maintain it on a mark to market basis

Objectives

It is the responsibility of the risk control functions within a firm to ensure that positions are prudently marked to fair valuation on the books and records and that the risks are properly calculated and reported. Both the calculation of the PnL and the risks for the positions of the firm are typically generated on the same end of day positions.

1   The *fair valuation of products* is the easier of the two to digest and see the impact. The valuations of the positions are marked to the prudent market value that is represented both in the financial statements and in the management reporting process. This is a fairly straightforward concept to visualize when considering liquid exchange traded products. Pick up the newspaper, see the valuation and make sure the end of day position is marked to it. The challenges of implementing this are not difficult to visualize. However, the concept becomes challenging when one considers simultaneously testing a series of global portfolios composed of liquid and illiquid exchange traded and OTC products.

2   The *fair valuation risks* related to positions are represented in terms of sensitivities ('Greeks'). These risk sensitivity positions are based on system-generated calculations that are less transparent. To the end user these calculations are generally less intuitive and less transparent. These calculations are sometimes assumed to be black box processes that are not easily understood. With a bit of effort, this presumption is not quite true.

Defining objectives, measuring performance and determining what is need to achieve objectives are all part of managing a process. The price testing objective sets out the framework in which to operate and to judge performance. The objective should include:

- Timing of positions to be tested
- Minimum frequency
- Goals on coverage
- Timeliness of reporting
- Self-assessment of price testing performance

An example of a price testing objective

We have established an objective of performing price testing the portfolios to *end of day marks at least twice a month*, at the each month end and around the middle of the month. Our goal is to test *100 per cent* of the population for month end with vigour and have the results summarized and reported *within 5 business day of the test date*. Self-assessment will identify, document and address issues.

Timing of testing

The purpose of price testing is to validate the valuation of positions and risks at a specific point in time. The challenge is to perform the price testing function frequently enough to provide reasonable assurance that positions are materially marked. The price testing priority is clearly the trading book, rather than the banking book, as it is required to be marked to market.

A generalized best practice that seems to be developing for market-making institutions is to price test the trading books at least twice a month. The benefits and expense of performing this function needs to be balanced with the risks and nature of the positions.

- Once at month end to validate the financial statements.
- The second price testing is usually performed on a variable date basis some time in the middle of the month. It provides an added control function as the traders cannot predict the date of testing. The mid-month test also defines that the maximum length of the misstatement of financial statements and risks that can occur to about two weeks before being picked up. One of the nice attributes of the variable second price testing is that it provides the manager of this control process with flexibility to schedule it as best suits the workload of the team (i.e. projects, system implementations, vacation schedules).

It is important to understand who are the users of the PnL and position information within the firm. The users of the information are beyond financial reporting. As can be seen in Figure 19.2, the users cover regulatory reporting, risk management, front office and the senior management who are required to understand both the PnL and risks of a firm on a daily basis. Much of the downstream processing (i.e. PnL and risk valuations) is dependent upon the accuracy of the priced positions. The timing

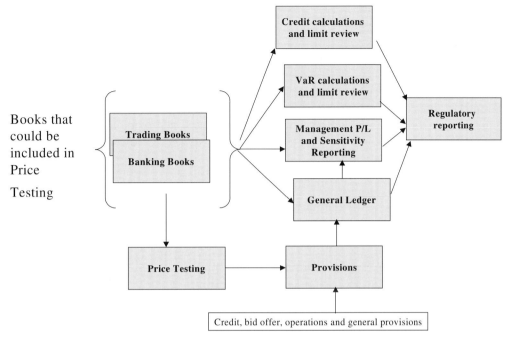

Figure 19.2 Downstream flow of reported PnL and risk positions.

of the tests and delivery of the reported results should be designed with consideration of the downstream users and routine meetings where the information will be a discussion topic.

Timing of data capture

The timing of when prices will be obtained for price testing needs to be specified by the organization. The question the organization needs to address is to define the timing and market data sources that are to be used. One consideration is to determine if it is necessary to have the same end of day price available on a global basis for price testing and end of day marking (i.e. all prices as of 4.15 p.m. London time). Timing is more of an issue in larger institutions when the same instrument may be booked at several locations.

Trading personnel generally prefer the end of day marks from each of the exchange close as it provides better risk numbers at the end of day for portfolio hedging. It also allows the Flash PnL and accounting (T + 1) PnL to be more accurately validated. However, obtaining all prices 'as of' a certain point in time is preferred from a financial viewpoint. It is usually preferred from a system implementation viewpoint as well as it is generally easier to implement prices as of one point in time for simpler logic and exception reporting and tighter batch processing frames. Usually practical implementation issues decide the decision.

Regardless of the timing chosen, the organization should define and document the timing. Audit personnel generally do not feel comfortable with different prices being used for end price testing and end of day marks without it being thought through, communicated to management and documented.

Price testing target priorities and options – trading and banking books

The trading assets and liabilities of a firm are maintained in a book that is defined as a trading book or as a banking book. The distinction between the two is quite important for regulatory reporting requirements and accounting treatment. The trading books should be marked to market allowing regulatory capital calculations to be based more on market risks. The banking book is based on accrual accounting and capital calculations are based more on counterparty credit risk.

- *Trading books* contain short-term assets, customer and bank trades and the securities portfolio for trading, hedging and resale. The trading book typically contains marketable assets that are required to be marked to market or marked to model. The key risks in the trading book are market events and are addressed by the Market Risk Amendment. Profits from the assets maintained in the trading book are expected to be generated from the difference between the buying and selling prices. Regulatory capital is based mostly on market factors.
- *Banking books* generally include the deposits, loans and the investment portfolio. These assets are usually considered to be held to term and the main component of risk is due to default or credit risk for the counterparty. They typically contain mortgages, personal loans and a portfolio of proprietary securities in stocks and bonds. As these assets are not expected to be sold in the short term, it is thought that the PnL derived from the marked to market or marked to model of these assets does not present a clear picture of the actual PnL and risks reflected by the strategies. These assets are typically maintained using accrual accounting practices and are not marked to market or marked to model. Regulatory capital is based on default risk, that is, counterparty credit risk.

Price testing the banking books may be viewed as a 'nice to have' compared to the absolute requirements of the trading books. As the banking book is not marked to market, and positions may not be actively managed for changes in market conditions, then one may question the purpose of price testing these books, which is for control and management reporting. Price testing the banking book makes sure that there are no large landmine losses hidden in the accrual-based banking book. Management should be aware of the value of positions that are maintained on these books that have significantly changed since they were booked. This can be due to market movements or to changes in counterparty credit profiles. Additional challenges in the banking book arise as it is the place where illiquid positions are booked and it may be extremely difficult to obtain valid prices for these. However, quantifying and reporting the number of these positions does have added value in an organization and lends itself to best practices.

Example 1 Price test the banking book

The banking book has not been looked at in depth and turnover of trading personnel raised the issue of unknown trading losses lurking in the banking book. Price testing of the positions forced the risk practitioner to review the positions and relevant hedges in the books. In developing techniques to assess the less liquid positions, the risk practitioner became more familiar with the number and type of transactions on the banking book and identified liquid positions that were in the banking report as hedges.

Table 19.2   Decision to price test the banking book

+ + Pluses + +	− − Minuses − −
Quantify mark to market valuation compared to accrued valuation and identify potential hidden losses so they can be managed effectively	Additional work. Lower priority relative to the coverage and timing requirements of the trading books. It may be as a 'nice to have' and have limited control value
Identity positions that belong on the trading book for proper accounting and regulatory reporting treatment	The ability to automate the price testing function may have additional challenges due to infrastructure limitations (i.e. cannot source market data)
Keeping the banking positions intuitively close	Introduces new product valuation challenges that may be difficult

When reviewing the valuation between marked to market and accrual valuation, the practitioner is able to assure management that there are no unexpected surprises hidden in the banking books and proper accounting treatment is being followed.

Level of policy in the organization

Regardless of the size of the organization, it is recommended that it develop and implements a written price testing policy. A policy, if written at a high enough level, is flexible for local challenges and eliminates the need for multiple policy developments. This is more challenging the larger and the more global an organization becomes.

The purpose is to impose consistency across trading desks and products that have separate challenges. The policies will foster consistency to the approach and considerations made while developing procedures and the level of documentation maintained.

In large organizations that are typically product aligned, such a policy provides consistency across product lines and locations. This supports both business line and regional reporting requirements. In smaller organizations, or those with fewer diverse product offerings, the policy should be able to address products without additional revision.

Implementing the strategy

Knowing your portfolios

When determining the price testing strategy it is important to understand the composition of the portfolios in terms of materiality, concentration and liquidity. The key task is to validate the material and risk positions of the firm, and the practitioner should have a sense of both the portfolio compositions and the availability of information available. In addition to the material risks, the practitioner will consider the sensitive issues and changes in specific positions. This understanding along with the changes in the markets allow the practitioner to position the discretionary elements of price testing.

The test coverage should be designed to feature the most material elements of the

Table 19.3 Decision box

Topic	Decision point or challenge
• Availability of market prices	Assess the sources of market data and the degree of automation that is practical and feasible for the team to implement
• Method of price testing each product group	Decision points on approach to price testing each product group
• Acceptable ranges	Define the acceptable price variances from mid-market for derivatives

portfolio and certain control elements. For example, the information on unusual volatility in a market along with the sensitivities of the firm's positions may be included in the price testing report. This information should be obtained during the price testing process. Targeting the featured area can be included with little additional effort if the strategy is defined at the beginning of the price testing cycle. Users of the price testing reports can be asked for their thoughts on featured areas.

Methods of obtaining market data for price testing

The cost and speed of obtaining quality prices to make a business statement on the controls and accuracy is the business of running the control function. The goal is obtain the maximum amount of quality market data in the shortest amount of time. This can be obtained when the control team is focused on analysis rather than data gathering, which can be time consuming, frustrating and disruptive. The disruptive nature and the actual amount of time to implement some of the manual processes is frequently significantly underestimated in terms of costs and speed of delivery.

The sources of market data are placed into the following categories:

- Automated market data extract – prices are available by market data providers or broker pages in a form that can be downloaded directly into a spreadsheet or database. Automated market data extract with parsing – prices are available by market data providers or broker pages but need to be in a test string data format. The data needs to be 'parsed' to obtain prices in a numeric comparable state.
- Manual broker pages – automated data available entered manually in a spreadsheet or in work papers
- Newspaper – price data available in various financial papers. Note that the risk controller should make sure that the firm is not the market data provider to the newspaper, otherwise you will be testing like to like.
- Calling brokers – to obtain market data, sometimes required for OTC derivatives or illiquid bonds.

Note on market data solutions: When implementing electronic market data solutions it is always necessary to consider the quality of data with regard to the contributors of the data and the time of day when the information will be updated and closed. Spending time upfront in the design of automating market data and corresponding controls and understanding the nuances of market data is a very good long-term investment.

Table 19.4 Matrix describing the methods and attributes of price testing methods

Priority	When to use method	Cost leverage	Speed	Accuracy/ efficiency	Managing the process
Automated market data extract	Available market data and available technology	High. Cheap after implementation sunk costs	Fastest	Good	Requirement to build a staff with market data and data handling skills
Market data extract – parsing	Available market data and available technology	Highly leveraged	Fastest	Good	Data parsing adds more complexity and documentation to the process
Manual broker pages	Available technology and skilled staff	Low	Moderate	Moderate	Can be the stepping stone to the above methods
Newspaper	Limited technology or a staff skill issue	Low	Slow	Moderate	Can be used for a very limited portfolio that is static
Calling brokers	Prices not available in an electronic form	Lowest	Slow	Mixed	May be necessary for less liquid or unavailable price data. Worst method to perform and bulkiest to document
Alternative procedure	Illiquid and exotic transactions	Low Expensive method to implement	Slow	Mixed	Modelling tools or procedures are used to validate the value or model parameters. May require advanced quantitative or system skills. May include implementation risks and estimation errors

Table 19.4 contains some of the key elements and examples of choosing one method over another will be covered in the next section.

Contacting brokers

Calling brokers for prices is extremely helpful for developing junior staff and allows them to feel much more confident with specifying market parameters such as volatility, bid offer spreads, etc. This confidence is part of the overall on the job training regime and helps overall confidence of the markets and products. Note that once the rapport is developed with target brokers over the phone, this method can be more efficiently implemented, first by email and then by fax.

Due to the nature of the broker network it is important to consider rotating brokers and to average several quotes is best practice. However, the practical nature and justification must be considered. When calling a broker for a quote, the broker will ask which firm you are from. When specifying the firm there are two risks. The first is that you are giving the position of the firm to the market. This is an issue in less liquid markets. For volatilities it can slightly disguised by asking for a range of strikes. The second risk is that the broker has a relationship with your firm. Due to the nature of the market, the price that comes back can be informally from the brokers of the firm. More brokers called can reduce this risk at the trade off cost of giving away the position to more players in the market.

Example 2   Price testing of illiquid positions via broker quotes

Prices for illiquid bonds are not available by way of market data providers and calling brokers for quotes is the only method of obtaining prices. Traders indicate that they are becoming concerned with the frequency of price testing and are beginning to complain to management that they are being overly controlled. When sitting down with the traders it becomes apparent that the traders are concerned with the market knowing the less liquid positions just prior to accumulating or selling a position. The risk practitioner agrees with the traders a policy that if there are sensitive positions that are not to be included in price testing they obtain approval from the head of trading. This note is included in the price testing report and is to be discussed at the risk committee meeting.

Decisions of sourcing and timing of market data

A key decision should be agreed and documented regarding the approach to ensuring the *quality* of market data and the *time frames* that will be used to obtain it. It is common to see that several booking locations contain the same instruments, particularly hedge instruments such as futures. Depending how the firm is structured, it is not uncommon that different locations use different sources of market data and capturing market data at different points in time for end of day processing and price testing. A decision should be made to define organizationally the boundaries of acceptable practice. For larger institutions, in some instances, it may be agreed that the sourcing of market data may come from one desk, such as a market-making desk, and all other desks should use their marks. In other cases it may be deemed acceptable that different desks have slightly different prices depending on the time of capture and the trading strategy (i.e. arbitrage desk). In the case of sharing data, a certain amount of time is required for the coordination of control teams, particularly in large institutions.

Example 3   Timing of end of day prices

A London-based firm is trading in Europe, Asia and the Americas in exchange traded futures. For end of day price testing the organization must determine if they will use closing price for each of the exchanges or take the price of each of the exchanges at a certain point in time. Some exchanges close to generate an 'official exchange closing price' and then reopen for late hours changing (i.e. LIFFE and DTB). In this global environment and end of day batch processing cycles standard pricing policies are required.

The risk practitioner chose to implement the price of all of the exchanges at a specific point in time for financial reporting purposes. This was weighed with the trade-off of not having the official close in the Americas, after 9 p.m. in London. The procedure was documented and agreed with front office, systems Financial and Operations teams. At a granular implementation level, this means specifying .LAST on the market data screen rather than .CLOSE (that would provide the previous days' close in the Americas).

Methods of price testing

If the goal of price testing is to compare the current prices of the books and records to the market we seemingly have a relatively straightforward exercise. It is really only a question of:

Generally, five approaches are useful in describing the degree of price testing and comfort level of this process and the categories outlined below are in the order of degree of control (see Figure 19.3 and Table 19.5). Previously these approaches were described in the efficiency of implementation. The manager of the price testing process needs to consider the best way to apply these methods in light of the portfolio composition, staff skill sets, available technology and timing of reporting:

1   Obtaining prices/parameters via automated market data/newspapers sources that are compared directly with systems values
2   Calling brokers for quotes and comparing to system values or input into models for valuation
3   Alternative market-based valuation procedures
4   Review of prices/parameters for reasonableness to determine if they are in a reasonably expected range – without going to the market. Making sure that absurd values are not included in the valuation. This technique can also be used as a reasonableness review when there is not sufficient time to perform a comprehensive review of available liquid market data.
5   Independent price sourcing – the independent control function provides prices that cannot be modified by the front office marketing and trading teams. These prices do not need to be price tested
X   Not reviewed – the products not reviewed need to be quantified in terms of materiality for reporting and performance measures

Sourcing – an alternative to price testing

Sourcing prices is the process of independently providing end of day instrument and parameter marks to the production valuation, market risk and credit risk systems. It is preferable to price testing as it occurs more frequently and remarks positions independently. When sourcing of prices and parameters is performed independently and with proper data quality controls, it replaces the need for providing price testing as a separate control event. Price sourcing is considered preferable as it provides more objective pricing and mitigates the potential of price and PnL manipulation. When price sourcing is utilized, an assessment needs to be taken whether additional quotes should be obtained to validate the data quality and to identify data blips.

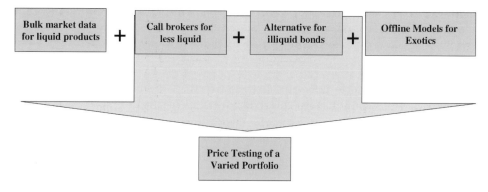

Figure 19.3

Table 19.5

Quality of market data	Price testing technique	Examples of products implemented	The bigger provisions taken for bid/offer or liquidity
Available market data Most available prices – most liquid	Obtaining prices/parameters via automated market data / newspapers sources that are compared directly with systems values	Liquid stocks, bonds, treasury and governments, exchange traded commodities, ATM swaps, GC repos	Tight bid/offer provisions
	Calling brokers for quotes and comparing to system values or input into models for valuation	Equity derivative volatility Illiquid bonds OTM/ITM interest rate derivatives	
	Alternative valuation techniques	Way out of the money or long-dated volatilities Like prices for bonds	
Not available Unavailable market data	Review of pricing parameters for reasonableness	Illiquid option volatilities and correlations	Wider bid/offer provisions with consideration of liquidity provisions

There is a preference for independent price *sourcing* (i.e. direct market feeds into a valuation system). General guidelines are to consider price sourcing when quotes are readily available; automation of process to obtain quotes is possible, and controls have been developed to ensure that data are clean.

Automated controls for sourced data

It is surprising to recognize the amount of market data that is required to be validated and the extent of data handling. The timing and efficiencies are necessary as these prices are needed for end of day processing. There generally is too much data to do this exception checking manually. Therefore the requirements are to identify and resolve any material differences in a timely manner.

Automating the controls around trader sourced and market sourced data are conceptually similar and require similar skills – downloading end of day firm prices and comparing them to market prices for the first case and downloading multiple sources of market data to verify the quality of market data sourcing for the second. Both require that market data be brought down into a system or control spreadsheet for exception reporting.

If prices/parameters are directly sourced into the valuation systems, it is the Risk Management Team group's responsibility to ensure the validity, accuracy and continued maintenance of the data feeds. Graphing and exception reporting are the two ways to see market data errors easily.

Validating market data quality

The spreadsheet in Figure 19.4 is used to validate the market data used to generate the official daily yield curve for the firm. The yield curve is made up of OTC and exchange traded instruments and automatically sources data from a variety of sources. The spreadsheet performs two key controls. First, it validates the accuracy of the automated market data feeds by comparing Telerate data to Bloomberg market data. Second, it ensures that automated market feed to the in-house system is in line with the automated market data, highlighting differences. Time is saved by highlighting exceptions that require manual intervention and decisions and research. A number is changed to bold (below) when the difference in market data between market data sources is greater than an absolute number of basis points, and turns the cell grey when the value is greater than the bid/offer spread.

Graphing is clearly more fun to look at but is also applicable to surfaces. Figure 19.5 has a similar concept and purpose except when applied to swaption volatilties. This spreadsheet shows a way of highlighting exceptions over a three-dimensional surface with the specific volatilities on the left. This market data is less available and highlights a data biip (bad market data) of a market data provider. It may be overlooked during a time-pressured end of day process and can be quickly identified in the graph.

Verifying trader sourced volatilities

If traders are providing (sourcing) end of day prices, price testing of all the prices is a consideration. Traders' sourcing prices are more likely for certain derivatives products where market data is less likely to be available and the quality of some market data is questionable. In this graph technique, the trader-supplied price and bid offer spread is compared to that of the market. This graph is useful to determine the overall reasonableness of less liquid/available data. This technique highlighted differences prior to discussion with the trader – allowing time for research. In this example, the difference was the use of forward versus flat volatilities. This difference was caused by mis-communication and would have a substantial valuation impact.

Testing to mid-market

Price testing for derivatives is usually performed by comparing transaction valuations to mid-market prices with the bid/offer spreads calculated and reported separately as provisions. Mid-market pricing provides consistency in less liquid markets where the middle is sometimes the best estimate of where the true market is. For exchange traded products the exchange close is taken as the end of the day price. Provisions

ANALYSIS CLEAR	SUMMARY CONNECT	GOTO USD		GOTO JPY		GOTO EURB		GOTO GBP		GOTO CHF		GOTO AUD	
LOAD INFINITY FOR THE DATE	10/03/1999	Telerate to InHouse	Telerate to Bloomberg	Telerate to InHouse	Telerate to Bloomberg	Telerate to InHouse	Telerate to Bloomberg	Telerate to InHouse	Telerate to Bloomberg	Telerate to InHouse	Telerate to Bloomberg	Telerate to InHouse	Telerate to Bloomberg
Money Market	1d	0.00	-5.00	0.00	0.50	0.00	8.00	0.00	18.50	0.00	no bb data	0.00	no bb data
	2d	0.00	6.00	0.00	3.44	0.00	9.00	0.00	0.00	0.00	no bb data	0.00	no bb data
	1w	0.00	-1.00	0.00	5.50	0.00	3.00	0.00	2.88	0.00	no bb data	0.00	no bb data
	1m	0.00	-1.00	0.00	-8.50	0.00	-2.50	0.00	8.12	0.00	4.87	0.00	-13.00
	2m	0.00	-2.00	0.00	-1.31	0.00	-2.50	0.00	46.66	0.00	2.81	0.00	-13.00
	3m	0.00	0.00	0.00	-1.94	0.00	-1.50	0.00	3.00	0.00	-1.81	0.00	-13.00
Futures	1	0.00	0.00	0.00	0.00	0.00	0.00	0.00	0.00	0.00	0.00	0.00	1.00
	2	0.00	0.50	0.00	0.00	0.00	0.00	0.00	0.00	0.00	0.00	0.00	3.00
	3	-0.50	0.00	0.00	0.00	0.00	0.00	0.00	0.00	0.00	0.00	0.00	3.00
	4	0.00	0.00	0.00	0.00	0.00	0.00	0.00	0.00	0.00	0.00	0.00	0.00
	5	0.00	0.00			0.00	0.00	0.00	0.00	0.00	0.00		
	6	0.00	0.00			0.00	0.00	0.00	0.00	0.00	0.00		
	7	-0.50	0.00			0.00	0.00	0.00	0.00	0.00	0.00		
	8	0.50	0.50			0.00	0.00	0.00	0.00	0.00	0.00		
	9	0.00	0.00			0.00	0.00	0.00	0.00	0.00	0.00		
	10	0.00	-2.00			0.00	0.00	0.00	0.00				
	11	0.00	0.00			0.00	0.00	0.00	0.00				
	12	3.00	3.00			0.00	0.00	0.00	0.00				
	13	0.00	0.00										
	14	0.00	0.00										
	15	0.00	0.00										
	16	0.00	0.00										
	17	0.00	0.00										
	18	0.00	0.00										
	19	0.00	0.00										
	20	0.00	0.00										
Swaps	2y			0.00	1.50							0.00	-5.00
	3y			0.00	0.50					0.00	-0.50	0.00	-1.50
	4y			0.00	1.50	0.00	0.30	0.00	1.00	0.00	0.50	0.00	3.00
	5y			0.00	1.50	0.00	0.00	0.00	-1.00	0.00	0.50	0.00	4.50
	6y	0.00	3.50	0.00	1.50	0.00	0.00	0.00	-1.00	0.00	1.00	no tr data	no tr data
	7y	0.00	2.50	0.00	1.50	0.00	-0.50	0.00	0.00	0.00	0.50	0.00	3.25
	8y	0.00	3.50	0.00	0.50	0.00	-1.50	0.00	2.00	0.00	0.00	no tr data	no tr data
	9y	0.00	4.00	0.00	1.50	0.00	-2.00	0.00	2.50	0.00	0.00	no tr data	no tr data
	10y	0.00	3.50	0.00	1.50	0.00	-0.90	0.00	3.00	0.00	0.00	0.00	3.75
	15y	0.00	2.50	0.00	-0.50	0.00	-2.65	0.00	-0.50	0.00	-0.50	no tr data	no tr data
	20y	0.00	1.50	0.00	-1.50	0.00	-2.10	0.00	no bb data	0.00	-1.50	no tr data	no tr data
	25y	0.00	no bb data	0.00	no bb data	0.00	-2.00	0.00	no bb data				
	30y	0.00	1.50	0.00	no bb data	0.00	-2.20	0.00	no bb data				

Figure 19.4   Ensuring all market data points are captured by graphing.

USD Swaption Volatility								
	1Y	2Y	3Y	4Y	5Y	10Y	12Y	15Y
1 Month	12.5	15.2	15.3	15.4	15.5	15.7	15.2	14.4
3 Month	12.5	15.2	15.3	15.4	15.5	15.7	15.2	14.4
6 Month	14.0	15.2	15.3	15.4	15.5	15.7	15.2	14.4
1 Year	16.7	16.4	16.2	16.0	15.9	15.7	14.8	14.2
2 Year	17.7	16.8	16.5	16.3	16.2	15.8	14.9	14.3
3 Year	17.7	16.8	16.5	16.2	16.1	15.7	14.7	14.1
4 Year	17.5	16.6	16.3	16.0	15.9	15.2	14.5	13.5
5 Year	17.3	16.4	16.1	15.8	15.4	14.4	13.7	12.7
7 Year	15.8	15.3	14.6	(41.0)	13.8	13.0	12.3	11.7
10 Year	13.9	13.3	12.7	12.2	11.9	10.9	10.3	9.8

The outlier

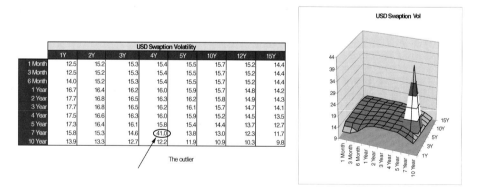

USD Swaption Vol

Figure 19.5   Example of graphing market data to quickly highlight a data exception (in this example caused by the broker typing 41.0 rather than 14.0).

on the financial statements should be a separate line item. Cash products are usually marked to the conservative bid or offer.

Comparing automated and brokers' quotes from several sources

Once price sources have been obtained, the prices are reviewed for reasonableness and overall consistency. For derivatives, the first step is to verify the quality of the

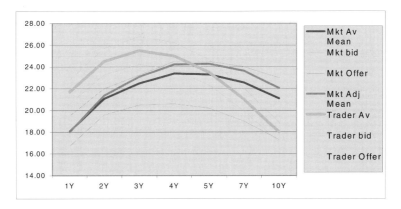

Figure 19.6 Example of graphing range of bid/offer quotes supplied by a trader versus the market data to quickly highlight a data exception (in this example caused by the trader's views not being in line with the market).

prices and to remove obvious outliers. In the best cases, there are five or more quotes, the outliers are removed and the midmarket price is calculated and compared to the prices on the books and records of the firm. If the prices are within the agreed tolerance range, no adjustment is necessary. In some firms, risk management has the responsibility to update the prices without discussion with the front office, in other firms a discussion is required. Then later a more lengthy process and stronger conviction is required. For cash products, the valuation is to the bid or offer of the exchange close.

Regardless of the manner of making adjustments, a view of the materiality must be considered. The risk practitioner should view each price adjustment with an administrative cost (including system processing, capture and documentation and communication). This quickly leads one to establish a materiality level required to be exceeded prior to making a price adjustment.

Example 4   Making the call on illiquid bond valuation

Due to market turmoil the liquidity of certain bonds dried up and the pricing became less clear. The practitioner could not get a price for the bond using automated market providers as in the past. Calling brokers provided indicative prices quoted in terms of Libor spreads. The quotes were Libor + 30, Libor + 120 and Libor + 300. Converting the booked price to a Libor spread, revealed a Libor spread of Libor + 150. The current market data is unclear, without consistency, and the booked price appears within the wide range of the market. The position will be reviewed closer during the next price testing cycle by using alternative price testing procedures, looking at spreads of bonds of similar credit rated firms, in the same industry, in the same country with similar bond terms.

Alternative valuation techniques

These are where the risk practitioner can demonstrate an understanding of products, markets and valuation techniques. Such techniques calculate or estimate a valuation based on market information and principles. As an assessor of real estate is in the business of providing a valuation of a unique product, so must a risk practitioner develop techniques to evaluate the appropriateness of the financial products. Some of the techniques used are:

- Like products – in terms of the previous example, like bonds are probably the best approach if one can find a similar rated instrument in the same sector, geographic region and matching tenor and yield
- Perform a theoretical calculation of each of the components
- Historical data – history is not a good predictor of the future but it is useful when no better technique is available
- Discussion with product or quantitative experts in another trading area of the firm
- Off-line models – track the performance of the model by reviewing the PnL and risk changes when positions using the model for valuation were recently sold. The best indicator of model performance is when a position is sold and marked to market rather than being marked to model.

Note on OTCs – ATM and the Smile/Long dated challenges

One of the more difficult problems for the risk practitioner is that market data for OTC derivatives is not readily available. Having to mark these transactions to model presents challenges for the practitioner.

When multiple market data points are available for the more liquid OTC instruments, an interpolation method can be used as the best approximation (a quantitative input is required to validate the interpolation technique that best suits the product). When quotes are not available, or are not available for the tenor, the risk practitioner needs to obtain a consensus on the valuation. Some choose to calculate and extend the volatility surface or interest rate curves with quantitative techniques. Some choose to keep it flat. Extending the surfaces flat or as a straight line is usually not advisable without discussion and documenting the approach in the policy.

Either way, when one is moving towards long dated and further Out of The Money and further In The Money, a wider range of bid/offer provisions should provide some cushion for availability of the market data. It also moves the practitioner towards the areas of reasonableness reviews when tools or market data are not available.

Note on off-line products and spreadsheets

Off-line valuations warrant a special category only because they are problematic and time consuming. Price testing off-line products that are maintained in spreadsheets is troublesome. This involves the validation of the pricing models and sometimes parameters that are required for input to the models that are not available in the marketplace. This presents additional challenges of coordaining the availability of quantitative resources and acceptable variance of the model performance. Price testing spreadsheets is a necessary evil to contend with because they:

- Lack access controls
- Lack version controls
- Are expensive to use, document and cross train – errors in maintaining market data are correlated to personnel turnover
- Require risk management to perform model reviews and take a stand as to when the spreadsheet population is growing beyond supportable means

- Create additional challenges of calculating and populating sensitivities into the daily process (i.e. VaR calculation)
- Maintain a model inventory and communication of new or modifications of models may not be a high priority for the developers or the front office.

Managing the price testing process

Table 19.6 Decision box

Topic	Decision point or challenge
• Balancing quality and delivery targets	Monitoring the price testing process and resolving issues as they arise to ensure the price testing deliverable meets the target date
• Responding to business needs for market data and positions	Extending price testing coverage and tweaking the deliverable report to support the needs of the business

Keeping an eye on the clock

The balance of managing multiple responsibilities, unexpected technical glitches and changes in the market and portfolios all present challenges to the risk practitioner. There is a tendency to trade-off with the timing of the deliverable. The person close to the process has a tendency to perform more testing, more sources to obtain the coveted 100 per cent of market coverage. The quality of the deliverable quickly depreciates as a business tool as time progresses. It is helpful if the objectives are stated at the beginning of the cycle and these include:

- Materiality of positions – the larger the position, the more frequently price testing should be performed. Think of it in terms of materiality (general ledger and off balance sheet) and in potential exposure terms
- The materiality of risk – the larger the risk, the more frequently the price testing should be performed. Think of it in portfolio management and hedging terms
- Changes in portfolio composition
- Market events – if there is a crisis in certain markets or if a specific event that may affect the portfolio, additional rigor is required. The risk management team should be closely following market conditions and having discussions with the traders to determine whether any change in the frequency of testing is warranted.
- Hot spots and follow-up – open items and areas where there has been ambiguity in the previous cycle. The control function should strive to address the open issue. If there is still confusion on the status of the valuation the control function should consider market events, alternative sources and trends of relevant data to establish a position of the data or to make prudent provision.
- Strategy on how the price testing will be performed (price sourced, automated testing, alternative procedures) and valuation type – instruments such as bond prices and parameters such as volatility.

Taking a position with the front office

Some view the discussion of price testing differences as a confrontational experience with the front office. With the goal of validating the fair valuation of the books and records of the firm the exercise should be a meaningful discussion with a minimal amount of stress. As was evidenced in the past by some of the front page derivative losses, any disagreement in terms of valuation should be raised and documented in a formal report. Follow-up actions should be agreed and followed through. For those that have done proper background work and can consider definitively the market data available, it is an opportunity to discuss market perspectives and product views with the trading experts. It also positions the work to be presented and discussed with senior trading management with conviction as to the fair valuation, necessary adjustments and agreed next steps. When sufficient work has not been performed, discussion with the front office can lead to a conflict of opinion and overall disagreement with the valuation results (see Figure 19.7).

Price Testing Strategy Cycle

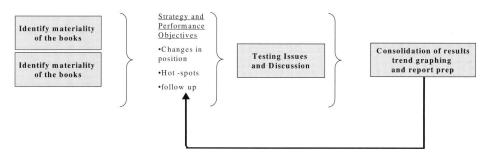

Figure 19.7   Price testing strategy cycle.

Example 5   Making the call on a valuation when a trader strategy is guaranteed to be certain

The portfolio contains a bond of a BBB US company which has been rumoured in the press to be bought out by a much higher rated European firm. The trader strategy is to build the position, as the current price does not fully reflect the expected announcement. The effect of the announcement would be that the BBB bond would now be rated more highly, increasing the value. The available market pricing on the BBB bond is reasonable. The trader requested that the bond be rated for the expected market event. The risk practitioner has identified this as a price testing issue.

The risk practitioner should take a strong stand and the position should be left marked to market as the position is liquid, and the market will factor the value of the rumor into the market rumor and publicly available information should have been factored into the price.

Reporting

Table 19.7   Decision box

Topic	Decision point or challenge
• Consistency of reporting	Determining the need for consistent price testing reporting – defining the categories for making global statements
• Performance management	Using the reports to monitor the performance of the price testing report

Knowing the users

The price testing responsibility works hand in hand with other key controls such as ensuring positions have been captured and calculated correctly, market data sourcing and INPV checking. The users of the information are:

- Front office – price testing results, underlying data source and time frames, volatility surfaces, sources of risk
- Financial for accuracy of financial reporting
- Downstream users such as financial, risk (VaR) and, regulatory reporting
- Control function – internal audit, external audit and regulatory supervisors particularly for CAD application

Key areas covered in the price testing report are:

1 Overall opinion on the mark of the books
2 Statement on coverage by product, business, book or region (see example at the end of this section)
3 Trends and issues including the number and materiality of remarks
4 Provisions taken by book, product desk – this will drive comparability and highlight approach differences and system calculation issues
5 Added value information (for example, new trades, changes in interest rate curves, changes in volatility surfaces, off-line inventory and model reviews)

Global reporting and performance targets

Global reporting of price testing should be consistent and comparable (see Figure 19.8). The price testing typically needs to reported on a common denominator to address the needs of:

- The head of the global product line
- A legal entity basis
- A location basis for local management responsibilities.

Depending upon the size and organizational structure, users in each location may include:

- Front office personnel
- Financial personnel
- Control functions – internal and external auditing

Financial statement users

Financial statement users of price testing are driven by the timing and demands of the financial statement reporting cycle. These users are usually interested in the overall material correctness of the portfolio rather than a specific position. During the financial reporting cycle, the timing and reporting requirements on the financial personnel are very demanding. Users are frequently looking for a binary answer: are the positions correct – if not by how much? This is the key information that they need to determine if the overall differences in the price testing results are material in terms of financial statement impact.

A key timing for financial users is assurance that the positions are materially correct. The 'as of date' in priority order is:

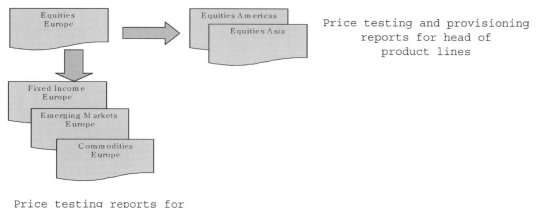

Figure 19.8 Consolidating global reporting.

- Financial year end – for the preparation and reporting of the firm's financial results
- Quarter end
- Month end and regulatory reporting

Example 6 Don't worry, price testing is being done

A global product is price tested at each of the three global booking locations. The global head of risk control keeps in touch with price testing issues by conference calls to the local risk managers. The global head is assured that everything is OK and is given a false sense of security due to cultural and language differences of what OK means to each individual. One location performs in depth testing of half the book, another a 100 per cent reasonableness check and a third has various approaches and coverage depending on the product.

By instituting and documenting global standards and analytical reporting of results, the global head of risk control has a tool to make a comparative analysis. This has important feedback on statements on the quality of controls of the firm and business and the internal management information with regards to performance, resourcing and skill sets.

Figure 19.9 is a graphical representation of price testing results that can lead to a quick comparison of coverage in terms of material and in quality terms – by product and region. The user of this report can quickly compare the instruments in terms of materiality. Price testing coverage can be compared in relation to the market data availability and effort by the risk control team. For example, one would expect futures to be price tested to an exchange close rather than reviewed for reasonableness (i.e. 'reviewed only'). By using the same format in larger organizations, products and region comparisons can be made and used to assess performance and the investment required.

Documentation

The Risk Management Team should document a price testing approach, price testing coverage, price testing results and provisioning in a specified manner to allow

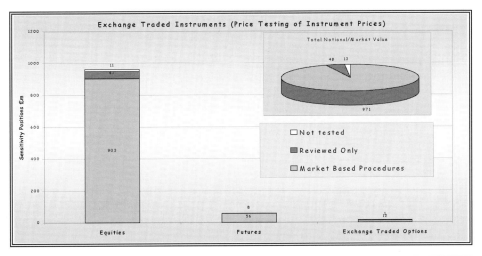

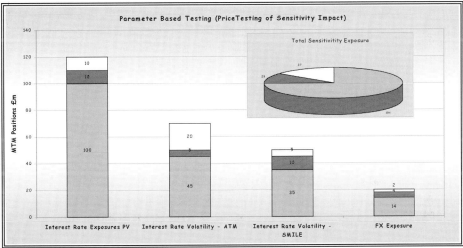

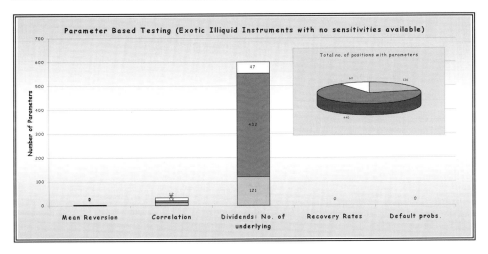

Figure 19.9 Price testing results.

performance measures to be computed. These will also be used as a tool to communicate the status of the control environment to management and to define the goals of the team.

Evidence of price testing sources and completeness checking should be maintained in an orderly fashion for audit purposes. The team needs to determine the minimum documentation that is needed for price testing. Once this is done, audit surprises will be less frequent when you can prove what and how you performed a process and the thought process behind such decisions.

Conclusion

Price testing provides a base line control as well as an assessment of booked values that are fundamental to reporting business results and are input to credit, capital and risk calculations. When implementing a price testing strategy it is sometimes initially surprising to identify the amount of market data that is not available. The investment to implement the strategy, staffing, technology and infrastructure varies with complexity and amount of product mix and materiality. The trade-off on automating certain procedures is usually driven by the trading strategy and expected volume of trading. Skill sets to automate the testing process usually requires PC desktop spreadsheet or database coding and text string handling. In complex trading environments, the requirement may also include access to front office tools and market data.

Communication of price testing results is good practice for management control purposes. It also ensures that the risk control personnel do not get too far from looking at positions in books and drifting too far from an intuitive feel of the positions and liquidity of portfolios. The deliverable can be linked to risk management or with financial reporting results. The comparability of price testing results stems from having common objectives and performance measures. Once this is done added value results and deliverables across the organization can be provided in a more meaningful manner.

Part 4

Capital management, technology and regulation

20

Implementing a firm-wide risk management framework

SHYAM VENKAT

Introduction

In recent years the need for improved risk management in business has become increasingly clear. Widely publicized losses and market-induced volatility in the earning streams of banks, securities houses and other financial and non-financial institutions have raised the risk management concerns of boards of directors, senior management, investors, analysts and regulators. While there continues to be debate on whether the losses could have been avoided altogether, there is collective agreement on the need to develop a framework that introduces greater transparency around an institution's risk profile through consistent and comprehensive risk measurement, aggregation and management.

In examining the causes of these losses, it appears that the main contributing factors have been inadequate management controls, over-reliance on imperfect analytical methods, and absence of risk awareness and governance at senior management levels. Since the groundbreaking report on risk management for derivatives issued by the Group of Thirty (G30) in 1993 there has been a succession of further recommendations on risk management put forth by industry self-governance groups, consulting firms (e.g. Coopers & Lybrand, 1996) and a succession of individual practitioners. Many of these recommendations have focused on strengthening the organizational environment through segregation of duties, instituting operational controls, implementing statistical risk measurement methodologies, analyzing portfolio-level risk, and more.

The regulatory guidance on risk management practices has also taken on much of the same flavor. In the United States, both the Office of the Comptroller of the Currency (1993) and the Federal Reserve Board (1993), among others, have published comprehensive guidelines on the standards they expect of the institutions under their supervisory oversight. The regulatory viewpoint has been shaped largely by the doctrine of safety and soundness – ensure the avoidance of bank failures and the consequent potential systemic risks posed to the global financial system. Therefore, the regulatory focus has primarily been on the controls required to prevent large, unexpected losses.

The collective result of these related initiatives has resulted in a set of 'best practices' for risk management and has increased the overall awareness of financial market participants with regard to this discipline. Yet, while many institutions have adopted several of these best practices, the list of companies that have suffered large, unanticipated financial losses continues to grow. The heightened volatility in the world financial markets has served to emphasize the interconnectedness of these markets. It has also underscored an equally important fact – the uncertainty in earnings streams, coupled with potential or realized losses, has caused many global banks that have large capital markets-related trading activities to under-perform broader market indices for much of the latter half of the 1990s. This is illustrated in part in Figure 20.1, which depicts total shareholder returns of US money-center banks relative to other segments in the financial services sector and the S&P 500 index.

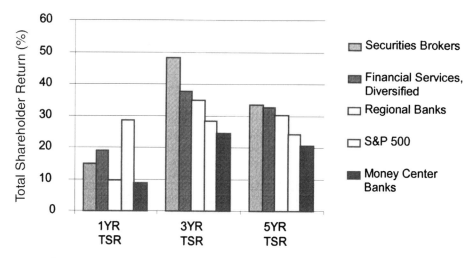

Figure 20.1 Comparative total shareholder return. (Total Shareholder Returns weighted by market capitalization and calculated for periods ending 31 December 1998). (*Source*: Shareholder scoreboard, *The Wall Street Journal*, Supplement, 25 February 1999)

Why is this the case, given all the advancements in risk management thinking, practices and tools? One can only surmise that although firms have adopted many of the recommendations surrounding risk management practices, they may not be achieving the overall intent and benefits of this. Financial markets, by their very nature, are volatile. To succeed in this arena, institutions must not only measure risks and control them well; they must also actively incorporate all other necessary aspects of an effective risk management framework.

An effective firm-wide risk management frame work is built on the premise that the overriding objective of any firm-wide risk management approach should be to enhance shareholder value. This objective reflects a marked departure from the earlier, more established and commonly subscribed viewpoint that risk management consists of compliance procedures, management controls and hedging techniques to prevent the firm from incurring losses. This shift in thinking comes at a time when companies are renewing their focus on revenue-generation opportunities after having spent much of the last decade on cost-cutting and re-engineering initiatives. Institutions are beginning to recognize that creating shareholder value over the long term requires both risk assessment – comprehending the potential upside and downside of business decisions – as well as risk management – increasing the likelihood of success, reducing the probability of failure, and limiting the uncertainty of overall financial performance.

This evolution of risk management has resulted in combining its historically defensive posture with a new, strategic orientation targeted towards explicitly optimizing the risk/return tradeoffs across the firm's portfolio of risk-taking activities. Under this approach, all elements of traditional risk management remain important and necessary. However, strategic risk management takes these elements and builds on them to improve decision making. This entails linking analytical risk measurement tools to strategy, portfolio structuring, limit setting, cost and operational controls, and performance measurement and compensation. Firmwide risk management, when undertaken in a thoughtful, proactive manner, enables an institution to maximize its risk-adjusted returns by undertaking more productive risk-taking activities and by making more informed decisions regarding business direction and capital allocation. This ultimately has a direct bearing on the key determinants of shareholder value, such as return (earnings), growth, and risk (volatility, quality and sustainability of earnings).

Understanding the risk management landscape

Historically, financial firms, whether domestic or international in nature, typically adopted a geographic orientation to managing their businesses. Risktaking and risk management activities were organized along regional lines or on a legal entity basis. Risks were measured, aggregated, and managed within the confines of local markets and/or according to product classifications. Although several international banks and securities firms were engaged in cross-border transactions that exposed them to currency, political, and other cross-market risks, the primary responsibility for managing these risks was still assigned to the local, country or regional transacting office and its resident risk control infrastructure.

This philosophy of decentralized risk management caused financial services companies to end up with fragmented risk management approaches. In many instances, the same types of risks within an institution were assessed and controlled very differently depending on the particular approach adopted by regional management. Different management approaches led to separate, inconsistent, and sometimes conflicting policies, procedures, methodologies, models and risk systems. Segregated risk management activities resulted in varying levels of risk definition and risk tolerance and thus prevented a consistent and comparable analysis of organizationwide risks across different business lines. Furthermore, there was little or no recognition of the interrelationships across different risk types. However, all this began to change with the evolving business profiles of financial institutions.

The changing nature of the international financial markets since the late 1980s highlighted the difficulties of running businesses according to organizational silos defined by regional or legal entity orientation. As the world markets grew closer to one another and as corporate clients began to look to intermediaries to service them around the globe, the organization structures of financial firms became more functionally defined and globally directed. This gave rise to matrix organization structures wherein the vertical business model was combined with aspects of the old regional management model. The different functional or business lines, such as investment banking, corporate finance, capital markets, treasury, and the like, were run as global business units while country or regional managers were responsible for coordinating the firm's different activities as they related to local markets, clients, regulators, and the like. Risk management activities became more closely aligned with the lines of business.

Since the mid-1990s, several significant trends and developments have caused firms to expand their risk management focus beyond this line-of-business orientation:

- *Continuing globalization of world financial markets* with around-the-clock trading has resulted in many institutions becoming increasingly international in focus and taking on more exposure to different markets. This heightens the need to view risks across the firm. For example, two traders in different locations may have exposures that offset each other, or conversely, may be increasing the overall risk of the institution to undesirable levels. Institutions with international presence and exposures need to manage their risks on an integrated rather than a regional basis.
- *Increasing volatility and interconnectivity of global markets* has created a situation where market events in one country or region can have adverse effects on markets in other parts of the world. In the late 1990s, market turmoil in South-East Asia affected both the US and European markets even though individual country economies in these sectors continued to grow and remain healthy. The so-called 'Asian contagion' sped across the globe with startling speed causing market volatility in different countries to rise dramatically for short periods of time. The ever-growing interdependencies across financial markets makes it necessary for firms to be able to assess the risk impact of interrelated market movements on their own portfolios of exposures.
- *Accelerating product innovation and risk transformation*, as reflected by the growth in derivatives, structured products and securitization activities, exposes financial institutions to all manner of new risks. Furthermore, the risks themselves can change rapidly and take on different dimensions in disconcerting fashion. Market risk can turn into credit risk and credit risk into market risk – witness the sequence of events experienced during the summer of 1999–the Russian debt crisis, widening of bond spreads in the USA, the credit crunch felt by US-based hedge funds, etc. Taking effective advantage of financial innovation and seizing new market opportunities, without exposing the enterprise to unintended or undesirable risks, requires firms to adopt more rigorous and dynamic risk management practices on a firm-wide basis.
- *Intensifying competition* within the financial services industry continues to erode profit margins. The explosive growth of financial flows into different, often short-lived, market opportunities requires profits to be quickly captured through streamlined risk-taking and risk management processes. With capital in the banking system under ever-increasing pressure to safely maximize returns, only those companies that can provide superior execution, generate superior risk-adjusted returns, and allocate capital to more efficient uses will succeed.
- *Ongoing consolidation and diversification* allow companies strengthen their positions in existing markets and create new opportunities to enter new businesses. Witness the mega-mergers in the financial services sector towards the end of the 1990s – Union Bank of Switzerland and Swiss Bank Corporation, Citibank and

Travelers Group, NationsBank and Bank of America, Deutsche Bank and Bankers Trust, to name but a few. With the enormous breadth and depth of risk-taking activities that characterize this scale of financial enterprise, the need for firm-wide risk management becomes paramount and critical to managing these behemoths effectively.

- *Advancing technologies* are also helping institutions to transform themselves from the vertical product-oriented organization to a horizontal, risk-type driven, customer-oriented environment. Risk management technology is becoming more powerful at reduced costs and more capable of handling different types of data, housing different analytic engines, and providing pricing, valuation and risk measurement functionality for both normal conditions as well as user-defined market scenarios. This is enabling leading financial institutions to obtain a more comprehensive picture of their financial risks across their businesses.

- *Increasing scrutiny by regulators and rating agencies* is also driving the need of firm-wide risk management. The regulators want to ensure that banks can measure and understand the risks being taken, and that these risks can be supported by the enterprise's available capital. Rating agencies are also influencing the process. They want to be sure that firms that take risks can properly control them and avoid situations that could negatively impact credit rating.

This rapid evolution of financial markets, financial intermediaries, and other market participants, over the last two decades, has expanded the scope of risk management today to take a firm-wide view across different business activities and to encompass a plethora of different risks.

Establishing the scope for firm-wide risk management

The first step in developing any approach to risk management is to understand the nature of risk. In the commonly used sense of the term, risk is the potential for loss underlying the value of an investment. This concept of risk connotes an adverse outcome – one that is to be avoided whenever possible.

For businesses, however, the notion of risk takes on more ambiguous and complex connotations. When business managers talk about risk, they may refer to competitive risk, financial market risk, operational risk, technology risk, environmental risk, regulatory risk, legislative risk, legal risk, sovereign risk, and so on. Yet, in many instances, there is lack of clarity surrounding what exactly is meant by risk.

Puschaver and Eccles (1996) provide some interesting discussion on the subject of risk. At one end of the spectrum is the view of *risk as opportunity*; this first view implicitly acknowledges the relationship between risk and return. The greater the risk, the greater the potential for return and, consequently, the greater the potential for loss. At the other end of the spectrum is the concept of *risk as hazard*; this notion of risk is often what most business managers in the world mean when they talk about risk. It is perceived as a negative event, one that can produce a financial loss. A third definition of risk falls somewhere in the middle of the spectrum and takes on the more academic view of risk as an *uncertainty*.

Most business managers would agree that it is neither possible nor desirable to completely eliminate risk from the business proposition. In business, offensive tactics as well as defensive measures are required for winning. Focusing entirely on defense may help to prevent risks completely, but in so doing, eliminates returns as well. Instead, what is required is an understanding of all the risks that arise from a particular business and then managing these risks effectively. In this context, risk management is a discipline consisting of three distinct dimensions:

- *Upside management* – Creating and capitalizing on opportunities where an institution has distinct advantages to achieve positive gains with improved chances of success
- *Downside management* – Instituting controls and counter-measures to prevent or mitigate losses as a result of the constraints posed by the organization's operating environment
- *Uncertainty management* – Applying methods and techniques to reduce the variance between anticipated financial outcomes and actual results.

Risk management is not a new discipline for financial intermediaries; indeed, one might argue that such firms have always been in the business of risk management given that risk is inextricably linked with intermediating financial flows. Many elements of a risk management framework have been present in financial institutions for several years. In banks, where credit risk has historically been the most significant risk, substantial investments were, and continue to be, made in developing credit policies, procedures and processes. The chief credit officer of a bank was an important member of the senior management team who was responsible for presenting credit-related issues to the institution's board of directors. The compliance and legal departments at securities firms provided the necessary risk controls and oversight to ensure that regulatory and compliance requirements were met. Risk management was generally aimed at managing credit risk and overall asset/liability mismatch risk. Very little consideration, if any, was given to identifying, quantifying and managing other types of risks.

The state of risk management today, while tracing its roots to the types of risk management functions described earlier, has evolved well beyond traditional compliance and controls for a limited set of risks. Today's firm-wide risk manager must contend with what some have characterized as the galaxy of risks depicted in Figure 20.2.

Figure 20.2 The galaxy of risks.

While each of these risks can be defined in individually descriptive terms, they broadly break down into four categories. While more detailed descriptions of the various risks are to be found elsewhere in this book, a brief definition of these high-level risk categories is useful since they provide context for establishing the scope of the firm-wide risk management function:

- *Market risk* – The risk of loss due to adverse changes in financial markets.
- *Credit risk* – The risk of loss arising from the failure of a counterparty to perform on a financial obligation.
- *Insurance risk* – The risk of loss due to claims experience or expenses exceeding expected levels reflected in premiums.
- *Operational risk* – The risk of loss resulting from human acts (intentional and unintentional), technology failure, breakdown in internal controls, disaster, or the impact of external factors.

To effectively manage the galaxy of risks, firm-wide risk management entails identifying, rationalizing, measuring, managing and reaffirming the risks that arise from both internal and external sources, not only within business units but also at the consolidated corporate level.

The remainder of this chapter is devoted to addressing two fundamental questions:

- *What do we mean by a firm-wide risk management framework?* The bulk of this chapter will be devoted to providing a basic definition of a firm-wide risk management framework and a description of its different components. Since this book is being written from a practitioner's viewpoint the different aspects of a risk management framework will be explored in some detail in order to provide implementation guidance.
- *How do we go about implementing a firm-wide risk management framework?* This discussion will address the key factors and building blocks for successfully implementing an effective firm-wide risk management framework.

Defining a firm-wide risk management framework

A firm-wide risk management framework may be defined as an amalgam of strategy, process, infrastructure and environment which helps companies make intelligent risk-taking decisions prior to committing limited resources and then helps them monitor the outcomes of these decisions. The establishment of an integrated risk management framework ensures the identification and awareness of all significant risks faced by an organization. It permits the development of consistent risk measures and proper management controls. An integrated risk management framework incorporates leading industry practices and ensures optimal management throughout the organization.

An effective risk management framework balances the infrastructure aspects of risk management, such as roles, responsibilities, accountabilities, policies, methodologies, controls, and information tools, with the more qualitative aspects of risk management such as philosophy, culture, training, awareness, and appropriate behavioral reinforcement. Driving all this is the linkage between an institution's overall goals and strategies and the permissible types, levels and returns of risk-taking activities required for achieving those business objectives.

Figure 20.3 depicts a firm-wide risk management framework that has four dimen-

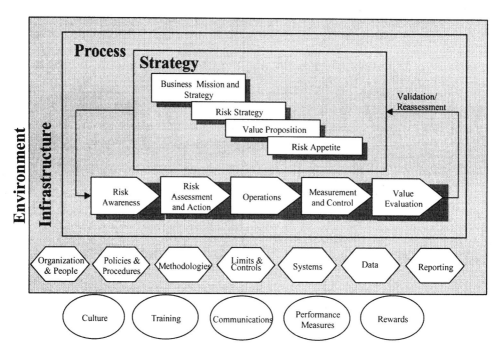

Figure 20.3   Firm-wide risk management framework. (*Source*: PricewaterhouseCoopers LLP)

sions: Strategy, Process, Infrastructure, and Environment. Many leading financial and non-financial companies around the world have successfully implemented this model of a financial risk management framework. The robustness of this model springs from its simplicity and its top-down approach to meeting the following risk management objectives:

- Link the business strategy to the risk management strategy to ensure consistency with the enterprise's competitive advantages to assume, distribute and retain risks
- Institute a risk governance process that is well understood within the organization and proactively supports the execution of business strategy
- Enhance risk management conduct through proper alignment of personnel, organizational guidance, and support infrastructure with risk-taking activities
- Establish rational and dynamic boundaries across all risk types in a manner that reflects the business strategy and the external market environment
- Institute a risk and performance measurement framework that aligns individual behaviors with business strategies and risk management objectives by being transparent, credible, timely and actionable
- Create heightened organizational awareness and focus on improving quality and sustainability of earnings, enhancing risk-taking efficiency, meeting customer needs and increasing shareholder value.

Each of the dimensions and their components are discussed in greater detail in the remainder of this section.

Strategy

Prudent firm-wide risk management begins with a clear articulation of the business mission, objectives and strategies. The corporate strategies should, in turn, be supported by a business proposition that is founded on some aspect of competitive or comparative advantage that allows the enterprise to provide value to its customers and shareholders. All strategies must have a clear identification of the risks to be taken, the levels of risk-taking, and the expected risk-adjusted returns.

Linking business strategy to risk management strategy and the value proposition

Institutions can enhance the overall effectiveness of risk management by closely linking it to business strategy formulation. This can be accomplished by proactively acknowledging and incorporating risk management considerations into business decisions regarding new ventures, products, trading strategies, and customer initiatives. Risk managers can provide objective input to evaluating new business opportunities and highlight risk management issues proactively rather than reactively where business alternatives may be more limited. To the extent that the risks present in different business opportunities may not be inherently aligned with the firm's risk management, operational or business competencies, it becomes necessary to frequently reexamine the links between business purpose, risk-taking capacity and risk management practices. Business decisions taken in this fashion regarding the assumption, intermediation, retention and distribution of risks will, in the long run, help the institution deliver earnings of superior quality and sustainability and ultimately increase shareholder value.

For this approach to be successful, both business line managers as well as risk managers must be involved in the formulation, evaluation and implementation of business and risk management strategies. The relationship between the two constituencies must be one of a partnering and team-oriented nature rather than the more typical adversarial interaction that is to be found within some firms. It is important to note that this approach is not intended to suggest that risk managers should second-guess the business units. Rather, risk managers should support the business units by increasing risk awareness and ensuring that all risk aspects of the proposed venture have been carefully considered in the context of broader corporatewide objectives. Risk management strategy balances the opportunity for revenue generation against the possibility that losses will occur and offers alternatives for mitigating the impact of these potential losses.

The better opportunities for revenue generation spring from a meaningful *value proposition* that the enterprise brings to the marketplace for both itself and its customers. This is central to assessing the appropriateness of the risk-taking activities. This can be best conveyed through the use of the following example.

Illustrative example: A mini-case study in risk taking and the value proposition

Consider the case of a financial institution that occupied a niche position in the equity derivatives market involving structured equity derivative transactions for corporate stock hedging and buyback programs in which the institution purchased single-stock volatility from corporate issuers. While this institution enjoyed very strong competitive positioning in the corporate segment, it had very little penetration in the institutional investor segment and no presence in the cash equity markets. The firm's inability to offer the full range of capital markets relative to its competition limited its opportunities to seek natural offsets to its customer-driven equity derivatives business, thereby forcing it to hedge its long single-stock volatility positions by selling index volatility. The structural risk mismatch in the equity derivatives portfolio manifested itself in the form of large basis volatility risk arising from potential breakdown in correlation between single-stock and index volatilities. When this breakdown did occur during the equity market events of October 1997, this particular institution did suffer large losses. A compelling value proposition for the equity derivatives business just did not exist for this institution.

Setting risk appetite

Linking business strategy to risk management strategy and the value proposition then allows an institution to establish its risk appetite. The risk appetite dictates the nature and level of risks that are acceptable to the firm and its various business units. Unambiguous and measurable risk tolerances need to be clearly established and communicated within the organization's policies and procedures. Linking the firm's risk appetite to its business strategies facilitates a clearer assessment of the corporate and business unit performance through limit monitoring and risk–return analysis.

Best practices observed among leading global financial institutions suggest that establishing risk appetite involves answering the following questions:

- In business, what risks are we to take and what risks are we not to take?
- What is our desired mix of risk taking?
- Are we comfortable with the amount of risks each of our business takes?
- Are these risk levels consistent with our strategy, business objectives, profitability targets and capital levels?
- Where should we reduce our risks?
- Are there business opportunities that we are not capitalizing on as a result of being too risk averse? What additional risks can then be taken to avail ourselves of these opportunities?
- How much capital can appropriately be put at risk by taking a particular course of action?

The leading financial firms seek answers to these questions by employing a variety of decision frameworks that include several external and internal factors. One such decision framework is described in Figure 20.4. Many leading institutions include strategic considerations, capital levels and internal constraints either formally or informally into the risk appetite-setting process.

When determining risk appetite, key strategic considerations that must be evaluated include the competitive or comparative advantages enjoyed in terms of market presence, business/product mix, customer base, and execution capabilities that might justify risk-taking intent. Investor considerations with respect to how this will be perceived by the marketplace based on past institutional performance also need to be factored into the equation. Commencing in the late 1980s and early 1990s, many US banks shifted their businesses from traditional, relatively predictable, wholesale banking to heavy reliance on more risky capital market activities. However, these same institutions were slow to recognize and to apply risk management effectively to contain the earnings volatility of these businesses. As a result, the unforgiving discipline of the stock market caused many such bank stocks to languish or under-perform other market sectors, resulting in substandard shareholder value creation.

Companies also have an obligation to disclose to their shareholders the risks they are in business of taking and how they are managing these risks. The investment community may favor a particular financial stock if it understands the rationale

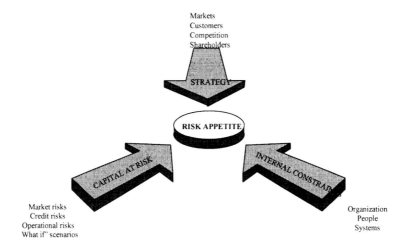

Markets
Customers
Competition
Shareholders

STRATEGY

RISK APPETITE

CAPITAL AT RISK

INTERNAL CONSTRAINT

Market risks
Credit risks
Operational risks
What if' scenarios

Organization
People
Systems

Figure 20.4 Decision framework for setting risk appetite. (*Source*: PricewaterhouseCoopers LLP)

underlying the aggregate and component risk profiles of the company, and is confident that management has undertaken the necessary steps to produce the required quality and sustainability of earnings over the long term. In any case, the firm should make sure that the level of risk taken is consistent with investors' return expectations and tolerance for risk. For instance, when contemplating entering a new type of activity or significantly increasing the risk exposure of a specific business, senior management should measure the impact of this new venture on earnings volatility. Senior management should gauge whether shareholders are willing to take higher risks in order to potentially achieve higher returns or whether their risk aversion may incline them to desire reduced risk exposure even if it means giving up some potential returns.

Having defined the amount of risk an institution is willing to take, it should then determine how much risk it can actually take. The firm's risk appetite, given the competitive landscape and shareholder expectations, should correspond to the amount of risk it would theoretically need to take to achieve its business objectives. But what is the maximum risk a firm can actually tolerate? To define its 'acceptable risk appetite' an institution should consider how much risk it can both afford and manage.

By definition, the maximum amount of risk a firm can take is limited by the capital it is required to hold both for regulatory and rating agency purposes as well as that established under an economic capital attribution scheme. Regulatory and rating agency thresholds for capital are driven by considerations of safety, soundness, balance sheet health and debt service capabilities. These thresholds serve as constraints on the extent of permissible risk taking. If an institution's risk profile becomes exacerbated relative to its regulatory and rating agency capital, this can adversely impact its ability to effectively transact business. In instances such as these, the risk/reward equation must be weighed against the potential reduction in business prospects arising from increased regulatory scrutiny or rating downgrades.

Economic capital levels set by an institution's internal capital attribution methodologies also play a role in defining risk appetite. Economic capital represents the level of equity capital required to withstand unexpected losses for given levels of confidence. Such capital is computed by defining and measuring all relevant risk factors at both the individual business unit levels as well as at the corporate level and will take into account any correlations that may exist between and across risk factors and businesses. The higher the risk appetite and the resultant risk taking, the higher the level of internal capital and capital charges that will be set by the firm's internal capital attribution program. This, in turn, will raise the level of risk-adjusted returns that the business will be required to earn to compensate for the increased level of risk taking. Embedding the capital attribution into *ex-ante* strategic planning process as well as into *ex-post* performance measurement is a best practice that should employed when determining risk appetite.

Finally, when establishing risk appetite, the firm should only take those risks its organization, people and system can handle. This is a truism that is ignored all too often as business units make 'compelling' cases for pursuing certain revenue opportunities without pragmatically considering whether they are internally equipped to handle the resultant risks. The acceptable risk appetite should depend upon whether the firm has the appropriate organizational structure to establish, monitor and control risk-taking activities. In addition, risk appetite should be consistent with the level of risk awareness and risk culture within the enterprise, as well as the company's management's skills and experience. The company should therefore make sure that the organizational model reinforces risk culture and that risk management infrastructure and resources are commensurate with the types, complexity and extent of risks that are taken.

Process

As financial institutions come under increasing pressure to improve shareholder value, they need to consider a business and risk management model that goes beyond merely measuring, monitoring and reporting of risks – one that links business mission and strategies to execution and to the elements of the risk management infrastructure. An integrated approach to managing risks ensures full identification and awareness of significant risks, consistent risk measures across asset classes and businesses, and proper management controls. Furthermore, it links risk-taking activities to capital consumption and performance evaluation at the business unit and the firm-wide levels.

Risk management process is the structured cycle of control activities that provide management with assurance that all risks within the institution are being effectively managed. Whether for an individual transaction or an aggregated portfolio, risks are identified, captured, assessed, measured, and reported. A comprehensive risk management process includes not only elements of risk control but also additional steps that logically permit effective business performance monitoring. The results of risk-taking activities are continuously evaluated, validated, and assessed relative to the organization's stated business goals and objectives. This validation and reassessment is often the missing link in many organizations that precludes risk management from assuming a strategic role that proactively helps the businesses to accomplish unit-specific goals in a manner consistent with corporate-wide mission and strategies.

Risk awareness

This represents an important, but often overlooked, qualitative attribute of the risk management process. Risk awareness comes from demonstrating a top-down commitment to risk management that acknowledges the exposure and risk impact of each business initiative on the overall risk profile of the firm. Risk awareness is reinforced through communicating risks, sharing lessons learned, and implementing industry best practices.

Risk assessment

Through risk assessment, the organization is able to determine whether a specific transaction, portfolio or business is appropriate from a risk-return perspective. The process of identifying, quantifying, and analyzing inherent risks and expected returns must be performed prior to the approval or execution of any transaction, new products or business activities. By assessing the sources of revenues and risks associated with a transaction or business activity, management is able to assess both desired as well as unhealthy concentrations of risk within portfolios or businesses. Within risk assessment, firm management needs to define clearly and consistently the role and authority of risk management with respect to establishing clear policies and criteria for approving new products or business ventures.

Operations

Operations consists of the front-, middle- and back-office functions that are involved in executing, capturing, recording, processing and settling all relevant aspects of the business transaction. While the operational aspects of execution can either be centralized or specific to products, geographies, or business units, it is imperative that appropriate procedures are in place to ensure that all aspects of business execution are undertaken in a controlled fashion. In this regard, ensuring the integrity and accessibility of data is critical for meaningful risk management.

Measurement and control

Measurement and control are fundamental attributes of risk management. Measurement entails quantifying risks in a consistent, corporatewide manner to determine that the types and extent of risk being assumed are in line with the expressed risk appetite. A variety of risk measurement approaches may be used depending on the business need and the appropriate level of sophistication. Risk measurement then serves as a basis for control mechanisms such as the setting of limits or other constraints to prevent undue levels or concentrations of risk.

Evaluation

Evaluation entails an examination of different risk-taking activities to ensure that there is adequate differentiation of businesses or products according to those that create value from those that destroy value. This aspect of the risk management process allows the firm to actively allocate and balance different types of risks. When doing so, due consideration must be accorded to the impact of regulatory capital and rating agency constraints as well as economic capital considerations. Success evaluation requires that internal performance measures and compensation practices are closely focused on the creation of shareholder value. This will ultimately help to ensure that the business proposition has supported the firm strategy and has generated value to both clients and shareholders in a way that is commensurate with the risks assumed.

Infrastructure

The risk management infrastructure forms the foundation for the risk management framework. It provides the organizational, analytic, operational and system(s) support for effectively executing the risk management process. It consists of:

- A central and independent risk management unit with clearly defined roles and participation in the strategic decision-making processes
- Formalized policies and procedures that clearly define and communicate the risk management process
- Consistent methodologies for risk measurement that capture the potential for losses, foregone opportunities and risk diversification effects across different risk categories
- Limit structures that set maximum tolerances in relation to capital and the firm's risk-taking philosophy
- Comprehensive management reports that communicate risk on periodic basis
- Information technology to satisfy risk information needs throughout the organization.

Organization

The organization model for firm-wide risk management sets the tone for the appropriate culture and processes required to make risk management a shareholder value-enhancing activity. This function requires a broad range of knowledge and experience because of the diverse nature of risks faced by today's financial enterprise. The inevitable realities of corporate politics combined with the need to coordinate risk management activities across virtually the entire institution makes firm-wide risk management a very challenging exercise.

The risk management organization communicates the firm's stance on risk taking, the goals of risk management, and senior management's endorsement of the risk management process. The risk management organization also provides the oversight structure necessary to establish the appropriate checks and balances. The oversight of risk management begins and ends with an institution's board of directors which 'is ultimately accountable for risk assumed by the firm' (Government Accounting Office, 1994).

The board of directors is responsible for clearly understanding at a high level the risks inherent in the enterprise's business activities and defining guidelines for governing those risks. It is responsible for ensuring that management has defined and implemented the necessary risk management policies, controls and systems and for asking the necessary questions to ensure that they are consistent with the firm's overall business strategies, expertise, and risk appetite. The board needs to regularly evaluate the risk policies and procedures particularly with respect to defining and evaluating risk tolerances. It must also ensure that the company's risk management policies are communicated and strictly enforced, and periodic reviews of risk policies are conducted. The board must also be aware of the organization's risk exposure and the effects that adverse market movements will have on its balance sheet and income statement.

While the board is ultimately responsible for risk management, it delegates its authority in this area to the firm's risk management function within the institution which actually carries out the tasks for managing and controlling risks.

Organizing principles for establishing a firm-wide risk management function

The specific organizational model chosen by an institution is as unique as the institution itself. The 'correct' model should be customized to fit the company's strategic objectives, culture and personnel. In establishing the firm-wide risk management function, institutions typically need to address the following questions, among others:

- Does the institution currently have a firm-wide risk management framework that sets the stage for overseeing different risks across the organization?
- What are the mission, objectives and accountabilities for firm-wide risk management?
- Are the firm-wide risk management mission, objectives and accountabilities communicated and accepted throughout the organization?
- Does the firm have a culture of information sharing and interdepartmental cooperation that is core to the success of a firm-wide risk management function?
- Who should be responsible for assessing, authorizing, taking, and controlling each type of risk?
- Who is responsible for measuring and monitoring risk-adjusted performance?
- What level of empowerment should be vested with firm-wide risk management as it relates to performing an advisory role versus being a control-oriented function that has real authority to mandate and/or execute risk reduction?
- What authority does/should the firm-wide risk manager have *vis-à-vis* policy and limit setting, and approving exceptions thereto?
- What are the reporting lines into, above, and around the firm-wide risk manager?
- What other corporate mechanisms, such as various committees, exist for different aspects of risk management and how effective are these?
- What level of financial and human resources can/should be allocated to firm-wide risk management for developing and implementing appropriate risk management initiatives and carrying through on assigned responsibilities?

Roles and responsibilities of the firm-wide risk management function

Firmwide risk management attempts to bring the responsibility for market, credit and operational risks under the oversight of one organizational unit. While sometimes done separately for market and credit risks, or through various committees, the firm-wide risk manager and his or her staff represent the corporate management function with responsibility for the identification, measurement, monitoring and management of all risks under an integrated risk management framework.

Although firm-wide risk management is different at each institution, the following represents an initial list of the responsibilities of the firm-wide risk manager:

- Participate in target market and business strategy formulation
- Create an increased awareness of different types of risks across the firm
- Review risk-taking strategies adopted by business units
- Create or recommend enterprisewide risk policies and procedures
- Identify existing and potential market, credit and operational risks along with potential interrelationships across these risks
- Develop, update and implement methodologies (Value-at-Risk, risk-adjusted return on capital, etc.) for measuring risks across the institution in a consistent and uniform manner
- Develop risk-related performance measures and indicators

- Communicate policies and methodologies across the firm
- Set or recommend limits and diversification strategies
- Ensure compliance with the firm's risk policies, limit structures and diversification strategies
- Monitor overall exposures and risks and report on these to RFC senior management on a frequent periodic basis
- Develop and maintain risk measurement models and validate valuation models
- Perform enterprisewide stress testing
- Develop capital measurement methodologies and participate in capital-allocation decisions
- Assist the business units in achieving stability of earnings, improved risk-adjusted returns, and enhanced shareholder value contributions through better risk measurement and informed risk taking.

In comparing the generic organizational approaches, the differences between them can be attributed primarily to the authorities ascribed to the different models. Some of the key differences in organizational approaches arise from the manner in which each institution has addressed the following issues:

- Is risk management centralized or distributed? What functions and authorities are retained at the corporate center versus those that are distributed to business units and/or locations outside the corporate center?
- Does risk management perform valuation and develop risk measures? It is commonly a policy-setting and evaluation function, but the day-to-day risk measurement and reporting function is often placed under risk management, back office or finance.
- Who approves credit? Is credit approval (i.e. the chief credit officer) included in the chief risk officer role?
- Who can approve temporary market or credit risk limit excesses?
- Is there clear responsibility for operational risk? While operational risks are always incurred throughout the organization and managed by respective specialists, is there one person responsible for pulling together exposures and assessing risk across risk types and organizational units?
- What are the direct versus dotted-line reporting relationships? Audit, control and support groups (e.g. internal audit, risk review, insurance, security, compliance) all have a role in risk management. Which of these groups fall directly under the supervision of firm-wide risk manager?

As illustrated by the different risk management organization models discussed in the remainder of this subsection, the actual roles and authorities associated with firm-wide risk management differ across firms, but the objectives are similar.

The 'traditional' risk management organization model

Prior to increased awareness surrounding the concept of firm-wide risk management, most financial institutions employed what can be called the 'traditional' risk management model, where different organizations are responsible for various risks. There is typically a chief credit officer who sets policy and approves exposures, a market risk executive who also sets policy and measures and reports risk limits, and various organizations that are involved in managing operational and other risks. This model is illustrated in Figure 20.5 (see Haubenstock, 1999).

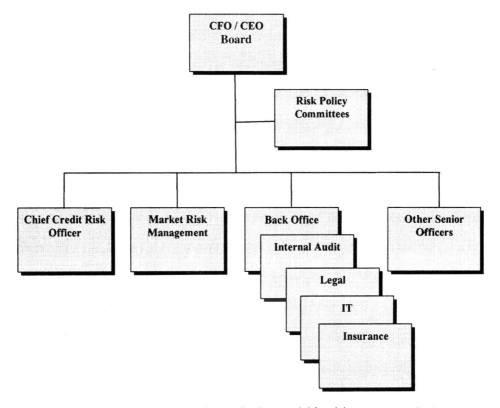

Figure 20.5 Traditional organization model for risk management.

Under this scenario, there is clear responsibility for market and credit risks, but operational risks have a fragmented approach. While all major risks are managed, the institution would be performing firm-wide functions at a committee level and could have more difficulty in achieving uniformity in methodology, measurements and policy.

Other corporatewide committees involved in risk management generally include the heads of related risk disciplines such as finance, compliance, internal audit, legal and selected business unit heads. Although each institution is different, one or more committees are typically responsible for credit risk, market risk, asset/liability management, liquidity risk, and operating risk. These committees meet on a regular basis to discuss the risk condition of the institution. The question faced by institutions with such a model is who really is in charge of the agenda and consequently has direct accountability for firm-wide risk.

The 'financial' risk management organizational model

Several firms have implemented an enterprisewide risk management framework with clear integration of market and credit risk. Responsibility for operational risk remains split among various organizational units or may be addressed by a separate committee. Under this approach, market and credit risks are better integrated and receive heightened awareness at the senior management levels but operational risk management remains fragmented and lack clear accountability. Figure 20.6 illustrates this type of organization model (see Haubenstock, 1999).

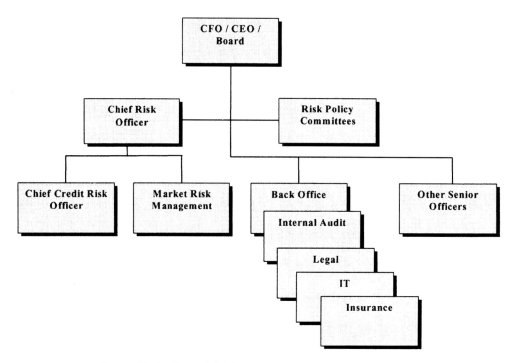

Figure 20.6   Financial risk management organization model.

For example, at one money center bank, market and credit risk management departments have a common director. This director heads a risk management group responsible for developing, communicating and implementing the firm's view and process for managing credit and market risks. This group seeks ways to optimize the firm's risk-based return on capital. The group is also responsible for maintaining a common risk management framework; establishing and controlling market risk limits and credit risk concentrations; reviewing significant risk concentrations; and overseeing the allocation of balance sheet capacity and adherence to capital targets. The director chairs the risk management committee, which is an oversight body for all market and credit risks. In addition, there are various other committees, including the operating risk committee, liquidity risk committee, capital committee and investment committee. Each of these committees is responsible for setting the firm's strategies and monitoring the risks within its own area of expertise.

A proposed model for firm-wide risk management

Figure 20.7 represents an example of a firm-wide risk management organizational structure that takes into account an integration of risks and allows a chief risk officer (CRO) to have considerable influence over the firm's risk philosophy and strategy. While there is no one approach for all institutions, this model can be a starting point for organizational design. The CRO has close reporting ties to the chief executive officer, the chief financial officer, and/or the board, enabling him or her to provide input to risk-related decisions. The CRO may also chair or be a member of various risk governance and approval committees within the corporation (e.g. market risk committee, credit risk committee, operational risk committee, asset/liability committee, etc.) (see Haubenstock, 1999).

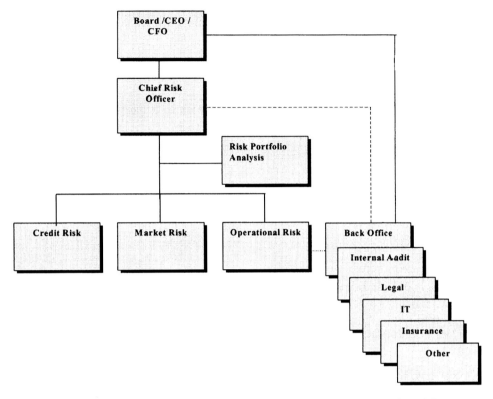

Figure 20.7   Proposed firm-wide risk management organizational model.

The heads of the various risk management disciplines (credit, market and operational) have direct reporting lines to the CRO. A portfolio analysis group is included to help the staff clearly examine cross-risk issues. These could include integration of market and credit risk, capital allocation, risk-adjusted performance measurement or new product/acquisition analysis. In addition, senior managers from the information technology department and control functions such as finance, internal audit and legal have coordination roles (usually indirect) to the CRO in order to promote a multi-disciplinary approach. Finally, cooperation from the various business units within the organization is critical. In order for the CRO to be effective, he or she must disseminate a risk culture throughout the organization so each employee is, in essence, a 'risk manager' who can balance risk and return considerations in the course of day-to-day business.

Policies and procedures

Risk management policies and procedures must be developed using a top-down approach to ensure that they are consistent with one another and appropriately reflect the strategic objectives and the overall risk appetite of the institution. This means that corporate risk management policies and procedures must be endorsed by senior management who should actively work towards infusing them into the culture of the organization.

Risk management policies and procedures provide detailed guidance on an organization's risk management approach. They should clearly communicate how the risk management infrastructure will work on a day-to-day basis and the roles, responsibilities and accountabilities of different personnel with respect to risk management. Given the importance of policies and procedures, it is critical that different constituencies within the firm work collaboratively to develop them to ensure that they encompass all aspects of risk management. This is particularly important from the standpoint of securing business unit buy-in with respect to wider acceptance, understanding and adherence. Securing the participation of the business units in policy formulation also helps to ensure that they are proactively tailored to the specifics of the markets, products, customers, transactions and risks they are intended to address.

Methodologies

Risk measurement in many institutions, both financial and non-financial, has become increasingly sophisticated and driven by various quantitative approaches. A robust risk management framework must bring together these different methodological components in a cohesive, interlinked fashion. Not only must these methodologies capture the underlying risks appropriately but they must also support various levels of risk aggregation and decomposition within and across various hierarchies such as product type, geography, risk type, etc. While overall business risks such as competition, new regulation, evolving market structure, macroeconomic changes, etc. are addressed in the course of setting and executing overall corporate strategy, the infrastructure for firm-wide risk management typically includes different quantification methodologies for market risk, credit risk and operational risk. Methodologies for quantifying insurance risk are not addressed in this chapter since they are more appropriately addressed within the realm of actuarial science.

Market risk

Market risk comprises the risks of adverse changes in interest rates, foreign exchange rates, equity prices, commodity prices and real estate prices. Until the mid-1980s, most financial institutions typically employed an asset-liability management (ALM) approach to measuring the market risk exposures on their balances. Maturity gap, duration gap, simulation of net interest income and market value of portfolio equity were the primary risk measures that were employed to measure the risks arising from mismatches in on-balance sheet assets and liabilities. These ALM techniques were complemented by notional or volume-based measures that were used to reflect the exposures from trading on-balance sheet financial instruments. As many of the large global institutions began to move away from an 'accrual' framework to a mark-to-market basis, these measures quickly proved themselves to be ineffective at reflecting the 'true' level of market risk faced by institutions. These approaches also did not allow for comprehensive risk aggregations and comparisons within and across portfolios. This became particularly evident as institutions began to derive an increasing portion of their revenues from trading activities both on- and off-balance sheet in different domestic and geographic markets.

With this marked shift away from traditional commercial and investment banking towards capital market trading and securities activities, the mark-to-market framework employed by a firm came under increasing scrutiny. Since risk arises from the likelihood and magnitude of adverse changes in earnings and value, a critical element of market risk measurement is the soundness of the mark-to-market framework that is applied to the institutions' traded assets and liabilities. This requires that mark-to-market calculations be subject to independent price verification to ensure the appropriateness of resultant earnings and portfolio values. An absence or breakdown of this basic control has been the root cause of many well-known losses suffered by various companies over the years.

In addition to volume-driven risk measures and sound mark-to-market principles, a comprehensive, well-designed suite of risk measurement techniques must also include sensitivities to individual market risk factors as well as provide aggregate risk measures like earnings-at-risk (EaR) and value-at-risk (VaR). The latter two measures represent portfolio-level risk measurement methods that consider volatilities and correlations across portfolios of instruments, positions, risk factors and geographies. In addition, while some of the above-mentioned ALM approaches continue to be valid for non-trading or 'accrual' books, they are also being refined with the application of the mean-variance approach that underlie EaR/VaR.

VaR-type measures are well suited to risk quantification under normal, statistically expected market movements. However, in times of extreme market stress, the relationships between different market risk factors often break down, thereby rendering the volatilities and correlations used in VaR calculations quite meaningless. Therefore, best practices to market risk measurement typically include stress testing of specific market factors such as interest rates, exchange rates and other prices to gauge the impact of outsized market movements in these variables. Liquidity risk measures are also used to assess the impact of market events that may make it difficult for an institution to either access funds readily and/or unwind its positions at reasonable price levels. In addition, user-defined scenario analyses are used to determine the impact of different market scenarios that may affect the firm's entire portfolio through different combinations of various risk factors–market, credit and operational. Given the breadth, depth and complexity of the portfolios that are present on some institutions' balance sheets, it is critical that the scenarios are constructed in a thoughtful and meaningful manner. Equally important is the communication of the results of the scenario analyses to senior management that can then apply these outcomes as a basis for decision making concerning the firm's overall risk profile.

Given that firm-wide risk management is becoming increasingly reliant on the output of quantitative models, a key element of a firm's risk measurement methodologies is its process for calibrating both valuation and risk models. In many instances, in the absence of observable market prices, the outputs of valuation models represent the only source for estimating the value of instruments and positions. Therefore, it is very important to periodically reaffirm the continued validity of the assumptions underlying these models as well as to gauge the sensitivity of the models' results to changes in specific assumptions or market inputs. Comparing model results with actual market prices and realized cash flows, as well as validating models with the assistance of credentialed, independent experts, also reflect best practices.

Finally, many models, particularly the trading and valuation models, can be a real source of market advantage in pricing, execution and overall risk management and represent a firm's intellectual capital. For this reason, prudent risk management practice suggests that they must be appropriately inventoried, evaluated, documented, and duly approved for use on an ongoing basis.

Credit risk

Credit risk is the risk of loss due to adverse changes in a borrower or counterparty's creditworthiness as a result of diminished ability or willingness to meet its financial obligations under the terms and conditions of a financial contract. Credit risk can be further subdivided into issuer risk, default risk, sovereign risk, settlement risk, etc., all of which stem from the basic lack of performance under a binding financial contract. In the case of traditional credit products such as loans, the maximum credit exposure is usually limited to the principal or notional amount of the transaction. However, over time, the measurement of credit exposure, particularly for trading books involving derivative products, has evolved from notional amounts to static credit factors applied against notional amounts to more dynamic measures that include both current exposure (i.e. mark-to-market amounts) as well as potential exposures. The state-of-the-art approaches to credit risk now include portfolio models that apply a VaR approach to measuring credit risk after considering the impact of credit quality migrations, defaults and correlations.

Credit risk poses several challenges from an analytical and a measurement standpoint relative to market risk. Apart from issues related to the availability and integrity of credit data, credit risk that is embedded in positions is not always explicitly apparent. In such instances, the specific contractual provisions of each transaction can become critical for valid credit analysis and modeling. Furthermore, internal credit rating schemes need to be periodically calibrated against externally published ratings and different credit data sets provided by other vendors. The considerable processing requirements for credit risk also need to be addressed to prevent the overloading of credit risk information systems. Along with collateral and netting provisions, data pertaining to obligor relationships, obligor domiciles, rating migrations, defaults, recoveries and portfolio correlations must also be incorporated into calculating credit exposure. Finally, all of these aspects must be supported by sound, fundamental credit underwriting practices and fair provisioning methods.

Operational risk

Operational risk is broadly defined as the risk of unexpected loss resulting from human acts (intentional and unintentional), technology failure, disaster or the impact of the external environment. Operational risk typically encompasses all risks other than the traditionally quantifiable market (including liquidity), credit, and insurance risks. Operational risk can result in actual realized losses and cause legal liability, damage to a firm's reputation, and loss of revenues and even market share.

In many institutions, operational risk can be the most prevalent and significant risk present. In fact, several of the major losses that have made the headlines over the last decade have been caused as a result of operational breakdowns. Historically, most attempts to measure operational risk have been hampered by the lack of appropriate methodologies and data that can be applied to a meaningful quantification framework. Consequently, most institutions that attempted to measure this type of risk (usually in the context of economic capital attribution for risk-adjusted performance measurement) did so by using revenue volatility measures or some factor applied to an expense base.

Today, certain financial institutions and consulting firms have invested significant research and development effort in developing innovative methodologies to quantify this type of risk. These approaches typically apply a combination of actuarial science and VaR techniques to comprehensive databases of historical operational loss events.

Some of these models also incorporate the unique attributes of specific businesses such as size, nature of business, level of controls, insurance coverage, etc., thereby providing broad applicability to any institution. Because these models are based on similar principles as market and credit risk measurement models, they can be consistently applied within a comprehensive economic capital attribution framework. In addition, they also provide cost/benefit analysis related to risk avoidance and risk transfer strategies such as internal controls and insurance programs.

Transfer pricing, capital allocation and risk-based pricing

The above methodologies for market, credit and operational risks can be leveraged to develop three other important risk-based decision support mechanisms: transfer pricing, economic capital attribution and risk-based pricing. Discussion of these topics is limited to a brief introduction since these concepts have been dealt with more exhaustively elsewhere in this book and in other literature.

Transfer pricing can be applied to ensure that various business units are appropriately compensated or charged for the funds they source or consume as well as for the risks they retain or hedge internally within the institution. Transfer pricing techniques are used to insulate business units from risks that are non-core to their activities. At the same time, they can also prove effective in helping realize economies of scale by allowing specific risks to be hedged by the respective centers of excellence within the firm.

Table 20.1 illustrates some applications for different types of transfer pricing. Transfer pricing helps to ensure that economic revenues are appropriately recognized both at the corporate center and within the business units consistently and in a fashion that precludes internal arbitrage between the units and aligns actions with the goal of increasing overall shareholder value.

Table 20.1 Transfer pricing applications

Risk types	Transfer pricing applications
Franchise risk	• Charge branch for use of brand name • Charge transactors for use of brand name
Market risk • Funding risk • Interest rate risk • Foreign exchange risk	• Charge business units for funding costs incurred by funding desks • Charge marketers for market risk hedging costs • Charge trading desks for centrilized currency risk hedging limits
Credit risk • Settlement risk • Counterparty risk	• Charge by credfit derivatives desk to transactors for credit risk hedging costs
Cross-border risk	• Charge transactors for the usage of scarce cross-border limits • Charge transactors for increased potential losses arising from cross-border exposure

Economic capital attribution frameworks are used to determine the level of capital-at-risk or equity that is required to cushion an institution against unexpected market, credit and operational risks based on some specified confidence level. Economic capital attribution is the cornerstone of a risk-adjusted performance measurement framework and represents a marked improvement over the book equity levels that have been used in return on equity calculations traditionally used to measure business unit results. Such a capital allocation framework introduces consistency and comparability into the evaluation of business unit performance and can be used as an important input for strategic decision making.

Risk-based pricing can be used to calculate the required net revenue on a financial product. Table 20.2 illustrates an example of how to derive required revenue in basis points of the notional value of a mortgage loan. The net cost of capital is the residual of the gross cost of capital, or the firm's cost of equity capital, less the marginal yield required on financial assets. Capital-at-risk is assumed to range from 4 to 14 basis points, depending on the loan type. Capital-at-risk is multiplied by the net capital cost to derive required net income. The marginal tax rate is assumed to be 40%. Required revenue is calculated by adding expenses, credit costs, and funding/hedging costs to the required pretax income. As shown in Table 20.2, required revenue ranges from 3.13 basis points for a fixed 15-year mortgage to 4.92 for a 30-year nonconforming mortgage loan.

Table 20.2   Illustrative example – risk-based pricing for mortgages

Notional amount	200,000			
Net capital cost	6.50%			
(BP of notional)	CF-30	NCF-30	FIX 15	Balloon 7
Capital-at-risk	10.00	14.00	4.00	6.00
Required net income	0.65	0.91	0.26	0.39
Tax	0.43	0.61	0.17	0.26
Required pretax income	1.08	1.52	0.43	0.65
Expenses	1.50	2.00	2.00	3.00
Credit provision	0.30	0.40	0.20	0.20
Funding/hedging costs	0.50	1.00	0.50	0.70
Required revenue	3.38	4.92	3.13	4.55

Limits and controls

Limits and controls represent the mechanism by which a firm's risk appetite is articulated and communicated to different constituencies – senior management, business line management, traders and other risk takers, risk managers and operations personnel. Each limit represents a threshold or acceptable boundary within which permissible risk-taking activities may be pursued. Therefore, a firm's limit structure should be consistent with its overall business strategies and reflect the different types of risk-taking activities that are engaged in to execute those strategies.

As shown in Figure 20.8, limit setting in many institutions begins with a bottom-up requisition for limits that are defined in the context of revenue and net income budgets that are drawn up by or set for each business unit. These limit requests are then evaluated and aggregated at the overall corporate level, usually by the firm-wide risk management function, and presented by senior management to the board of directors for approval. The board-approved or delegated limits are then parceled back to the various business units. Within the business units, limits are usually allocated to specific desks or traders at the discretion of the respective business unit heads.

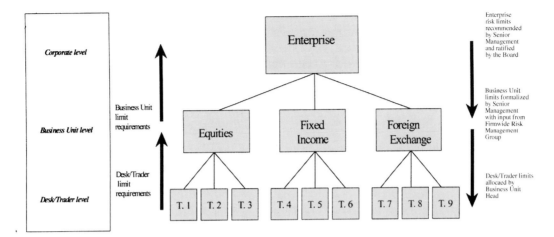

Figure 20.8 Best practices to limit-setting process.

An institution's limit framework should include a combination of volume limits, risk sensitivity limits, portfolio-level VaR limits, and stop-loss/advisory limits.

Volume or notional limits

Notional limits represent the original type of limits that institutions used to manage their risk-taking activities. These limits are intended to put some constraints around the overall magnitude of the portfolios that an institution can accumulate either on- or off-balance sheet. However, because the amount of risk may be quite different from overall portfolio volume, these limits are not particularly useful for reflecting the 'true' extent of risk taking within and across portfolios. Nevertheless, these type of limits are useful for controlling exposure concentrations after giving due consideration to overall market size, depth, liquidity, etc. Such limits can be expressed in a number of ways: the maximum permissible currency value of transactions; the maximum percentage share in relation to overall total volume or specific issue; the maximum net position (after offsetting long and short positions); or the maximum concentration of specific groupings of counterparties, industries, types of instruments, etc.

Risk sensitivity limits

Risk sensitivity limits are aimed at containing the sensitivity of positions to changes in specific risk factors at the portfolio, business unit or other organization level. Such limits are useful for putting boundaries around the extent of allowable changes in portfolio values as a result of shifts in market factors such as interest rates, currency exchange rates, prices, etc. Complying with limits denominated in this fashion becomes more intuitive to traders since they use sensitivity measures to hedge their positions against various risk factors. These measures are particularly relevant for option portfolios that contain non-linear risk profiles. For such books, best practices approaches usually include limits on the various 'greeks'; i.e. delta, gamma, vega, theta, rho, lambda, etc.

Value-at-Risk limits

VaR limits can be set at the desk, business unit, division and enterprise level. These limits are useful for monitoring overall risk levels under normal market conditions after giving due consideration to volatilities and correlations of different risk factors. VaR limits can also be set for major asset class such as interest rates, foreign exchange, equities, commodities, real estate, etc. Many institutions monitor and report trends in actual VaR against corresponding limits to periodically validate the appropriateness of these limits.

Stop loss/advisory limits

Best practices to limit setting suggest that stop loss limits are an integral aspect of a well-defined system of limits. While stop loss limits may not necessarily require the liquidation of positions in events involving market stress (in which case they are *advisory* in nature), they are often used as management triggers for reevaluating the wisdom of continuing to hold certain positions before they suffer some predefined maximum threshold level of losses. Stop loss/advisory limits are usually set in the context of acceptable cumulative losses within a defined period or in relation to some specified level of capital.

Stress/scenario limits

In addition to the above limits, institutions have also implemented stress/scenario testing to monitor portfolio risk levels under extreme market conditions. However, most institutions do not place specific limits on the results of specific stress tests or scenario analyses that are applied to their portfolios.

Data and information systems

Accurate, timely and comprehensive data along with robust, integrated information systems are an integral part of an effective risk management program. The firm's risk management systems must have the ability to capture and measure key risks in a globally integrated manner. This implies that transaction and position data, counterparty information, real-time market data, and modeling assumptions are appropriately captured in the system. Unfortunately, many institutions today are faced with the legacy of fragmented risk management systems that preclude an effective corporatewide view of portfolio risks.

This is because spending on enterprise risk management systems has historically been only a small component of the total expenditures on trading technology. As shown in Figure 20.9, risk technology investment has historically centered on front- and middle-office systems as the majority of efforts related to risk capture and measurement take place within the trading or trade support functions.

Measuring risk management technology spending requires certain assumptions as most banks measure their investments differently and may be in different phases of the implementation life cycle. The spending estimates for firm-wide risk technology, as provided by global banks, varies considerably because of the nature of the risk management function and its overlap with other technology initiatives within the institution. For example, considerable spending occurs when integrating different front- and back-office systems within the bank. Although the middleware used may also contribute to supporting the enterprise risk applications, its cost may not be appropriately reflected in total enterprisewide risk technology expenditures. Certain other factors also contribute to the assessment of total spending on risk management technology:

• Whether the technology is developed internally or acquired from external vendors

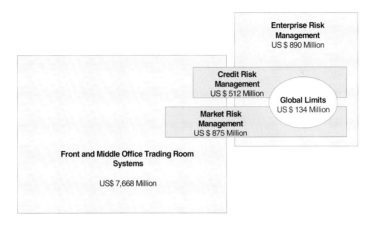

Figure 20.9 Breakdown of firmwide risk technology spending. (*Source*: Meridien Research, 1998)

- Whether the technology is being implemented, updated or in a maintenance phase
- Diversity of businesses, financial instruments and locations supported by the technology base.

Most research estimates are consistent in suggesting that spending on enterprisewide risk management technology is increasing at most global banking institutions. However, industry research shows that global banks will be investing more on enterprisewide risk technology (23% compound annual growth) than on desk-level risk management (8% compound annual growth) over the next five years. As shown in Table 20.3, within the USA and Canada, the top 21 banks averaged approximately $4 million in 1997 in enterprisewide risk management technology expenditures with annual growth of 16% expected through the year 2002. The top five banks within this group account for a disproportionate share of this spending.

Table 20.3 Enterprise risk spending at global bank institutions (US$ millions)

	Number of firms	1997	2002	Compound annual growth %
Americas	21	80	167	16
Asia	51	62	301	37
Europe	78	206	505	20
Subtotal	150	$348	$973	23

Source: Meridien Research, 1997

As shown in Figure 20.10, firm-wide risk management systems contain several different elements: data models and repositories; interfaces to legacy systems; valuation models, risk calculation engines and analytics; and data extraction and information reporting capabilities. These can exist within and across the front, middle and back offices in an institution.

Data models and repositories are required to capture transactional, position and cash flow data in consistent fashion for different and changing asset classes, products and instruments. In addition, different organizational hierarchies, financial entities, and risk factors (e.g. prices, rates, volatilities, indices, etc.) also need to be appro-

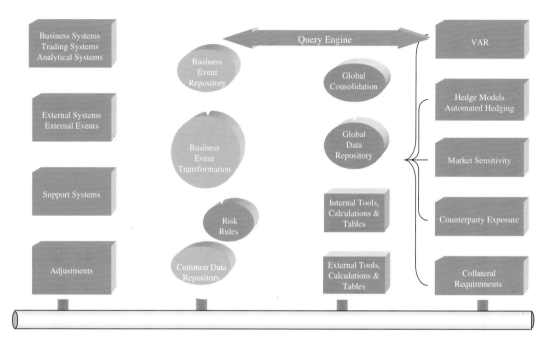

Figure 20.10   Firm-wide risk management systems architecture. (*Source*: PricewaterhouseCooper LLP)

priately represented in static, dynamic and time series forms. Although most vendor systems will probably not capture all required data elements, package data repositories provide a departure point for further development and, therefore, possess the critical advantage of time. Vendor-developed data models also provide the benefits that come from ongoing enhancements that are likely to leverage broader customer bases and be spurred by competitive market pressures.

Since most risk management systems in place today are deployed at institutions with existing application systems, interfaces to these legacy processing systems are required. Some of these interfaces may operate in a real-time mode with continuous updating of positions as transactions are captured in the front-end systems. Other interfaces may exist in an intra-day or end-of-day batch mode. In all instances, to the extent possible, these interfaces must be designed such that future changes can be made easily with minimum of programming effort and impact on other areas of the risk management system. Data loaders, translaters, enhancers and editors help to effect this by serving as a middleware layer or 'bus' that establishes interconnectivity between various systems and repositories.

Valuation models and financial analytics run against the data stored in the repositories to produce yield curves and other valuation benchmarks, mark-to-market values, sensitivities, accruals and 'greeks'. Other risk calculation engines provide aggregate, portfolio-level risk measures such as EaR/VaR, current and potential exposures for credit risk, and the results of stress tests and scenario analysis. Additional limit monitoring functionality is also a common feature of many risk management information systems that are available today, although on-line limit tracking is typically restricted to high-volume generic instruments such as foreign exchange and equities. The flexibility to augment existing libraries of financial models and or add new functionality without requiring changes to base application systems is a key attribute that must be considered in developing a robust risk management systems architecture.

Once risk data has been transformed into meaningful risk management information, it must be delivered to different users in a fast, flexible, efficient and friendly manner. Speed of delivery is critical to monitor the firm's risk positions under fast-changing market conditions. Flexibility is key to allow users to vary their views of data with respect to scope, content, frequency, and format. Efficiency is necessary to minimize the drain on system and user resources. Finally, user friendliness of risk management systems is extremely important if end-users are to feel empowered to extract, evaluate and act upon risk information.

Risk reporting

A key objective of firm-wide risk management is to articulate clearly the nature of an institution's business including its major risks, its risk-reward relationships as reflected in the profitability of its risk-taking activities in relation to economic capital, and the impact of current and future market and internal factors. However, while risk management departments in most institutions produce reams of paper containing position- and risk-related data, this is usually not transformed into meaningful risk management information that can help to support, evaluate and execute business decisions.

An effective risk reporting framework focuses on the generation of risk management information that meets the objectives and needs of different target audiences including business, trading and risk managers; senior management; executive management; and other potential users such as financial controllers, middle and back office operations and auditors and regulators. Figure 20.11 depicts an example of a risk-reporting framework that can be delivered to different target audiences.

To enhance the delivery of this reporting framework, data-visualization techniques are increasingly being used to transform raw data into information that supports business and risk management objectives. This becomes possible as visualization allows large amounts of complex data to be condensed by using advanced graphical presentation to convey relevant information. This increases the capability of the information recipient to process patterns and trends, discern relationships between variables, detect significant deviations and outliers, identify major sources of risk, and develop new insights and hypotheses.

A word of caution, however, when taking the best-practices approach to implementing a risk reporting framework as described above – this requires striking a medium between a firm's ultimate risk measurement and reporting goals and its current capabilities. Thus, a pragmatic first step would entail developing initial reports that appropriately capture the risk profiles of different businesses. A next step would be to design risk reports that balance 'ideal' information content with current data availability and report generation capabilities. This, in turn, will highlight gaps in the current risk reporting environment with respect to risk management information and serve as the basis for developing an action plan to address these gaps.

Environment

There are several environmental or 'softer' aspects that accompany the successful implementation of a firm-wide risk management framework. While the different

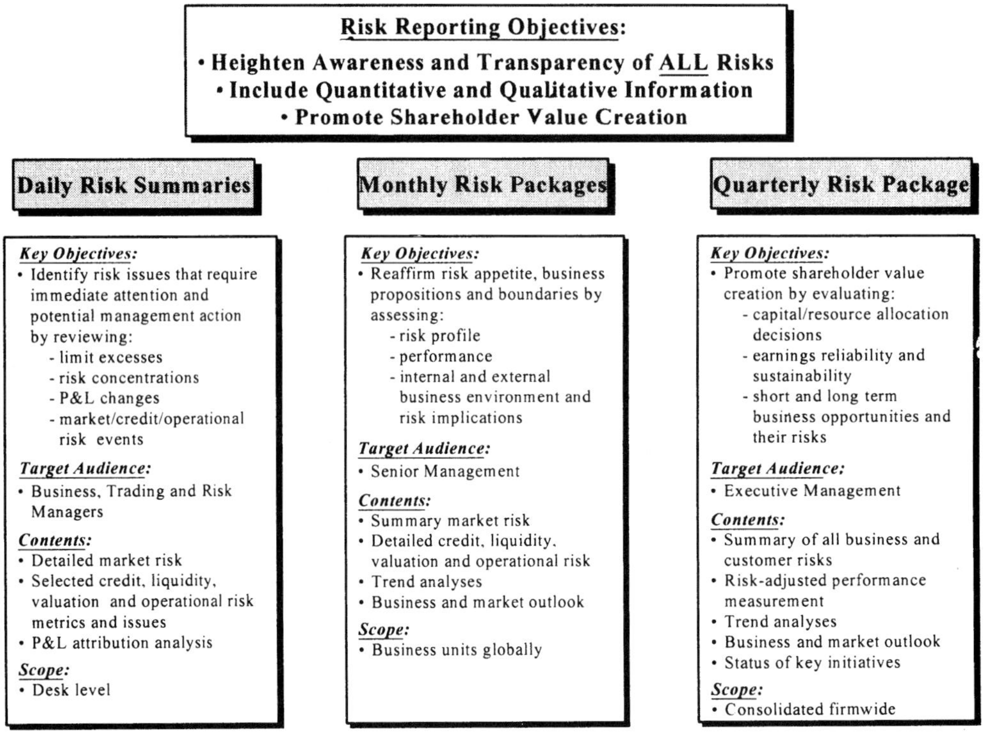

```
┌─────────────────────────────────────────────────────────────┐
│                    Risk Reporting Objectives:                │
│      • Heighten Awareness and Transparency of ALL Risks      │
│        • Include Quantitative and Qualitative Information     │
│              • Promote Shareholder Value Creation            │
└─────────────────────────────────────────────────────────────┘
```

Daily Risk Summaries

Key Objectives:
• Identify risk issues that require
  immediate attention and
  potential management action
  by reviewing:
    - limit excesses
    - risk concentrations
    - P&L changes
    - market/credit/operational
      risk events

Target Audience:
• Business, Trading and Risk
  Managers

Contents:
• Detailed market risk
• Selected credit, liquidity,
  valuation and operational risk
  metrics and issues
• P&L attribution analysis

Scope:
• Desk level

Monthly Risk Packages

Key Objectives:
• Reaffirm risk appetite, business
  propositions and boundaries by
  assessing:
    - risk profile
    - performance
    - internal and external
      business environment and
      risk implications

Target Audience:
• Senior Management

Contents:
• Summary market risk
• Detailed credit, liquidity,
  valuation and operational risk
• Trend analyses
• Business and market outlook

Scope:
• Business units globally

Quarterly Risk Package

Key Objectives:
• Promote shareholder value
  creation by evaluating:
    - capital/resource allocation
      decisions
    - earnings reliability and
      sustainability
    - short and long term
      business opportunities and
      their risks

Target Audience:
• Executive Management

Contents:
• Summary of all business and
  customer risks
• Risk-adjusted performance
  measurement
• Trend analyses
• Business and market outlook
• Status of key initiatives

Scope:
• Consolidated firmwide

Figure 20.11 Firm-wide risk reporting framework. (*Source*: PricewaterhouseCoopers LLP)

infrastructure aspects represent the various tools for risk management, the surrounding environment provides the credibility for risk management to take on a meaningful value-added role within the organization. These are discussed briefly below.

Culture

Firm-wide risk management in many institutions is limited to a risk measurement and risk monitoring function – often it has been one that can be displayed to appease regulators and auditors. Obviously, the treatment as we have described it in this chapter makes it a far more compelling and vital management discipline. The extent to which firm-wide risk management pervades the value system of an organization and the authority and respect accorded to this discipline greatly influence the likelihood of success in getting risk management effectively implemented. To a large extent, the behavior and attitude of a firm's leaders define organizational culture. The 'tone at the top' must take risk management seriously, set strong accountability for sound risk management principles and conduct, and allocate the necessary resources to carry out risk management. Only then will this culture manifest its benefits in the breadth and depth of risk management contributions made by firm personnel – risk takers, risk managers and other constituencies – to ultimately enhance corporate value.

Training and communications

Ongoing training and communications are integral aspects for effective risk management. There are many industry developments and new applications that continually take place within each of the infrastructural elements of risk management described earlier. Risk management personnel must remain abreast of these advances so that risk management continues to evolve and improve over time. In addition, it is equally important for senior management, business unit management and risk takers to be educated on the benefits of firm-wide risk management. Obtaining appropriate understanding of various measurement methodologies and other aspects of risk management also enables these different constituencies to correctly interpret risk analysis, raise intelligent questions about other risk issues that may not yet have been considered, and incorporate risk management into broader business decisions. Clear, open communications are also critical to ensuring that there is corporatewide awareness of the roles and responsibilities of the firm-wide risk management group and the various initiatives under implementation. This sets appropriate expectations on the part of different elements of the organization and helps to preserve healthy tension and balance between the objectives of senior management, line management, risk takers, and risk managers.

Performance measurement and compensation

Linking the results of risk-taking activities to performance measurement and compensation ultimately brings home the importance and discipline of risk management to where it matters most – our individual bottom lines. A risk-conscious performance measurement and compensation structure considers risk-adjusted returns on economic capital rather than conventional accounting-based profit and loss calculations. In measuring the performance of different business units, many institutions continue to focus only on revenues or trading profit and loss without explicitly introducing risk into the assessment. This impedes any meaningful evaluation and comparison of economic results within and across business units both on a single period basis as well as over time. It also sets up incentives that may not necessarily align individual behavior with the broader corporate objective of maximizing shareholder value.

By considering risk-adjusted return on economic capital, it is possible to compensate managers and risk takers for minimizing risk and maximizing performance. The example in Table 20.4 illustrates this point.

Table 20.4 Illustrative example – risk based incentive compensation

	Business A	Business B
Notional amount ($ million)	10 000	10 000
Average tenor	10	1
Inception and trading revenues	$10	$2
Bonus @ 20% revenue	$2.00	$0.40
Economic risk capital	1000	20
Return on risk capital	0.10%	10.0%

In the example, we show that risk-based incentive schemes can alter the incentives to encourage a business to maximize risk-adjusted returns, rather than revenues. Assume that the traders can transact structured basket-type options (Business A) or plain vanilla options (Business B). Inception revenues vary greatly depending on the strategy employed by the business. Typically, a bonus pool for a business is some fraction of gross revenues. Such a scheme in this example gives incentives to traders to transact long-tenor, structured deals that may be difficult to hedge. Business A generates higher revenues, but lower risk-adjusted returns. The firm may be better off following strategy B and linking performance to risk-adjusted returns and long-term risk-adjusted performance. Alternatively, the analysis may demonstrate to management that neither strategy presents a viable proposition because of insufficient risk-adjusted returns over the long run.

Risk-adjusted performance measurement and risk-based compensation give 'teeth' to risk management and encourage longer-term decision making to improve overall corporate value rather than focusing on short-term profits.

Conclusion

Firmwide risk management is a discipline that is rapidly gaining ground within financial institutions and other non-financial services firms. There is an increasing trend in today's marketplace to address the potential interrelationships among market, credit and operational risks and to manage these risks in a consistent, balanced and integrated manner. This approach to risk management enables a firm to maximize risk-adjusted returns by undertaking more productive risk-taking activities, and to make better-informed decisions regarding business direction and capital allocation. Above all, firm-wide risk management undertaken in a thoughtful, proactive manner can allow an institution to enhance overall shareholder value. This can be accomplished by:

- Instituting a common risk management framework and risk policy
- Developing a strong corporatewide risk management-oriented culture
- Establishing a focal point of coordination for risk management initiatives for market, credit and operational risks
- Defining and implementing consistent risk measurement, capital allocation and risk-adjusted performance measurement methodologies
- Leveraging risk-related analytical efforts particularly where market and credit risks overlap for many instruments
- Balancing quantitative risk measurement techniques with qualitative, 'common sense' approaches to examining risk
- Understanding better the interrelationships across risks and proactively addressing potential and prospective exposures and risks
- Making better cost/benefit decisions on risk mitigation, risk management and risk optimization efforts.

Acknowlegements

The ideas expressed in this chapter have been greatly influenced by and draw heavily on the body of risk management knowledge developed by the Financial Risk Management Practice at PricewaterhouseCoopers LLP. I would like to especially acknowledge contributions to this chapter from the following individuals: Brenda Boultwood, Mike Haubenstock and Richard Reynolds. However, any errors or omissions are entirely my own.

References

Coopers & Lybrand (1996) *Generally Accepted Risk Principles*, January.

Federal Reserve Board (1993) *Examination Memo on Risk Management and Internal Control for Trading Activities of Banking Organizations*, December.

Government Accounting Office (1994) *Report on Financial Derivatives*, May.

Group of Thirty (1993) *Derivatives: Practices and Principles*, Global Derivatives Study Group, Washington, DC, July.

Haubenstock, M. (1999) Organizing a financial institution to deliver enterprise-wide risk management', *The Journal of Lending & Credit Risk Management*, February.

Office of the Comptroller of the Currency (1993) *Circular on Risk Management for Financial Derivatives (BC-277)*, November; Q&A Supplement, May 1994.

Puschaver, L. and Eccles, R. G. (1996) 'In pursuit of the upside: the new opportunity in risk management', *PW Review*, December.

21

Selecting and implementing enterprise risk management technologies

DEBORAH L. WILLIAMS

Introduction: enterprise risk management, a system implementation like no other

As we close out the twentieth century, we are entering the era of enterprise technology. Large-scale computerized automation was first introduced to the financial services industry in the 1960s. Accounting systems were joined by check reader sorters and other core systems technologies. In the 1980s, the advent of personal computers brought technology to the end user. Line managers gained access to powerful decision-support systems in increasing numbers throughout the 1990s. The creation of hundreds of business solutions throughout the institutions, however, has had the unintended effect of creating pockets of data that cannot be leveraged by the institution as a whole. The ability of individual business lines to implement specialized solutions has created computing silos. Institution-wide data at many institutions cannot be aggregated anywhere except the general ledger, by which time it has been converted into debits and credits in such a way as to render it useless for anything but accounting.

Risk management was one of the first business requirements to create a need for technology that could draw on information from all over the institution. Since the early 1990s when enterprise risk was born, other enterprise solutions have been created, including customer management, profitability analysis, resource planning, etc. For most financial institutions, however, risk management was the first attempt at enterprise-wide analysis. The challenges of planning, building and implementing a system to span the entire institution are immense. They can be broken into five major categories: scope, complexity, definition, ownership and management. Most of these issues were new and are unique to the implementation of enterprise technology. The last five years have taught us some valuable lessons on how to use this type of technology.

The challenges

There are five major challenges to implementing enterprise risk systems.

- Scope
- Complexity
- Definition
- Ownership
- Management

Some of these challenges can be overcome once, while others require a more constant vigilance. Each is likely to occur at one point or another during the selection or implementation process. Identifying these issues in advance are creating a plan to deal with them as they occur will benefit an institution greatly.

Scope

There is no unit at a financial institution that is not impacted by the new risk management culture. Virtually every department takes some form of risk in its everyday operations, even if it is only operational risk itself. In addition, there are risks that are not inherent to any individual unit but exist at the enterprise level, such as reputation risk. The technology that supports such broad requirements must also have wide-ranging tentacles. Data related to risk is in virtually all the individual operating systems, including (but by no means limited to) deposit systems, trading systems, payments systems and loan-origination systems. The difficulty is that it is impossible to build and implement an enterprise risk system that encompasses the hundreds of products and operating units of an institution all at once.

Monster IT projects that never end are doomed to failure, but only after the institution has spent far too much time and money. Enterprise risk projects, especially, are susceptible to scope creep, or the constant enlargement of project goals. The reason is simple. There are many potential users for such a system and it is very difficult to make one user's needs a priority over another's unless there is clear direction from senior levels and a strong project lead to keep the team focused. It is very typical for these projects to continue to grow until the list of requirements makes them impossible to complete. Regular and predictable deliverables that add value to the users are mandatory for an enterprise risk system project. Goals must be realistic and bite-sized so that they can be achieved in installments, yet still provide recognizable value to the institution.

Complexity

There are two levels of complexity. The first is the complexity caused by the enormous list of products and services that must be included in an all-encompassing risk system. Any large financial institution will have hundreds of different types, each of which must be defined and assessed for its inherent risks. In addition to the number of products, they vary dramatically. Enterprise risk systems must be able to assess very simple products, such as fixed rate time deposits, and very complex products, such as index amortizing swaps. To add further to the challenge, new products are introduced constantly, as are variations in the existing offerings. To assess risk accurately, the technology must be able-to adapt to these changes as they occur. A second level of complexity is added by the technologies that already exist to process these products. These systems were introduced, at different times and rely on different operating systems, different databases and different hardware platforms. They operate in different time frames, some real-time, some batch. They also have a variety of assumptions and definitions built into them, different customer identifiers, different rate assumptions, different product definitions. Any enterprise technology that needs data from a variety of systems must somehow translate all the different sources into a single coherent and consistent data set in order to use it for analysis.

To cope with these various complexities, an enterprise risk system must embody two opposing forces, both vital to its success. It must create a level of standardization upon which it may depend; standard definitions of products and customers, standard data structures, a standard time line for processing. These standards may not be reflected in the processing systems around the institution, but they must be well defined and understood centrally so that data obtained from those systems can be translated consistently. At the same time as the process creates standardization, the technology infrastructure must remain flexible and able to reflect all the myriad changes that occur in the surrounding internal and external environments. This can be done in many ways, the most common of which is to create a multi-tiered system where data, analysis, reporting, etc. are integrated but not interdependent. This involves each system component running separately, often on different computer hardware, such that the individual processes can be run (and changed) independent of each other. In some cases, creating this flexibility may take more time and cost more in the short run, but the ability of the infrastructure to grow and change with the discipline of risk management will be more than worth the investment in the long term.

Flexibility

Not only do internal business practices change, risk management methodologies and practices are also rapidly evolving. Value at risk may have been unheard of two or three years ago, but today virtually all financial institutions calculate VaR for some part of their portfolios. Today, risk management is still poorly defined. There are few industry standards and the state of the art is changing constantly. There is no telling what risk concept may come into common use in the future, even in the next 12–18 months. Technology has to be able to adapt to these external industry changes. Because industry standards don't really exist, each institution creates their own definition of risk measurements and controls. Even relatively common risk practices vary considerably in their application from institution to institution. This creates challenges in using commercial packages for risk. No two institutions have a common underlying technology architecture, nor will they have a common definition of how risk should be managed.

The real solution to this issue will require more than one institution's efforts, and will likely only come over time. To cope with this problem, however, institutions should create very clear definitions of their risk management goals and practices and then work to embed these definitions into their risk technology. In addition, each institution should continue to explore new risk ideas and stay abreast of new theories and their application at peer institutions. Risk technology should constantly be updated as changes in practice occur. External changes should always be considered in terms of the technology ramifications. Too often industry groups create new risk ideals and define new practices without considering how they might be implemented in reality and whether technology infrastructures in place will be able to meet the new demands.

Ownership

The issue of ownership has many layers. The question is who owns and is responsible for the enterprise risk infrastructure, especially if multiple business lines, in addition to the enterprise risk group, use the analysis tools or databases. Each user will have their own set of requirements and priorities. None may wish to shoulder the cost or responsibility of any functionality not used directly by his or her own group. This extends from the initial system definition and cost of implementation through to maintenance and definition of system changes and updates. Who decides what gets done and what doesn't? Each business line may own a portion of the system, in which case, who is responsible for the whole? It is very dangerous to have components defined by different people without someone looking out for the integrity of the infrastructure as a whole. Enterprise infrastructures are owned by everyone, and no one.

The answer to this issue is to identify individual sponsors within each organizational unit intending to make use of the system. Initially this may be a small number of individuals. Over time, as the users grow, the ability to identify the person responsible for coordinating the needs of each unit will be very important. The sponsors are responsible both for their own users as well as for the data contributed to the enterprise systems. They are the ones who will articulate the needs of their organizations and provide information to the central coordinator on data availability and underlying systems architectures in their units. When necessary they can come together to discuss issues of universal importance. The central group is free to concentrate on matters related to the system as a whole. They coordinate needs of other users as well as defining their own. They take responsibility for the integrity of the whole, buy may not be responsible for each individual component. It is imperative to maintain the connection to the individual business lines. The further away from the business lines, the greater the likelihood that the system will, in the end, benefit no one.

Management

There are multiple management issues that are unique to an enterprise risk technology implementation. As discussed above, the project is likely to be larger and more complex than most implementations ever attempted. A larger than average price tag also comes with the effort. Because of the systems use primarily as a management tool, it can be nearly impossible to justify the investment on the basis of a typical return on investment (ROI) calculation. The cost of the investment is likely to look far out of touch with any real, measurable financial return on the investment. Given that normal measures of how much should be spent are not applicable, it can be difficult to determine how much is the right amount to spend on enterprise risk. The complexity of the solution and its somewhat distributed nature means that it can also be difficult to track and account for spending as well.

Another factor contributing both to the difficulty in predicting and managing costs as well as the overall management challenges is the lack of a complete vendor-provided solution. Although there is more choice in vendor components than ever before, it is still likely that an enterprise risk project will end up with a minimum of half a dozen vendor relationships to be managed. Recent growth in consulting groups and database expertise within risk application software firms may help to reduce the number somewhat. There is still no such thing as one-stop shopping for enterprise risk. No single vendor provides all the required components. Even within the individual component areas, the products are often immature enough to make it difficult to compare vendor systems to each other. After the selection is done, the implementation is likely to run over 12–18 months. Coordinating between the various internal and external development groups is a full-time job. Worse yet, failing to do so guarantees extra cost and time spent and may doom the project completely.

Combating these management issues requires effort on two fronts. Senior management must both believe in and openly support the project. They must be apprised of progress constantly and must see results to continue their support, adding another burden to the project. The level of cost in time and effort (and cash) will make it an easy target if this is not done. Clear and concise communication on deliverables to supporters, who should include the CEO, CIO and COO as well as board members, is imperative. Business line managers should be kept in the loop whenever possible as well, especially if they are early end users of the systems. The key to this and many of the solutions described above is extremely good project management. A good project manager will foster communication, keep the project focused and coordinate the many internal and external players in the project.

If done correctly, the technology infrastructure created for enterprise risk will serve the institutions for many years. It will be the platform upon which the institution will grow its risk management practices, as well as the businesses that depend upon them. It can also serve as a model for other enterprise technology projects to follow. Understanding the issues and being prepared with adequate resources to cope with each as they occur is critical. Without adequate planning and management, enterprise risk has the very real potential to be a very costly and embarrassing disaster.

The solution components

Despite the fact that each risk management technology implementation is unique it is possible to extrapolate the individual industry solutions into an overall framework for risk architecture. This architecture is useful in planning to be sure that all components have been considered before final decisions on technology are made. Typically, most institutions will chose analysis tools before determining the other components. Although important, analysis is far from the most costly or time-consuming part of the solution. Moreover, it is the most likely to be replaced or altered in the short term. To maintain the flexibility required for the evolution of the risk systems, it is imperative to consider all the components in system design.

The four major elements of an enterprise level risk solution are Analysis, Integration, Data Storage and Reporting. The core underlying technologies used may differ (e.g. applications for analysis may run on Unix or Windows NT) from institution to

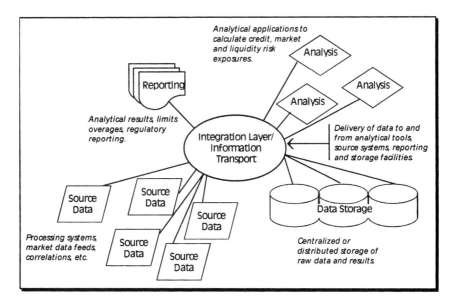

Figure 21.1 The evolving risk management architecture. (*Source:* Meridien Research)

institution, but the fundamental purpose and functionality required is common to all risk implementations (see Figure 21.1).

Analysis

The analysis component of an enterprise risk solution is typically an application that enables risk management staff to calculate current and likely future risk exposures and compare them to the risk appetite of the institution. Popular component calculations include value at risk (VaR), stress testing, risk adjusted return on capital (Raroc), regulatory capital ratios, and counterparty credit exposures. Though these measures are widely used throughout the industry, they are far from standard calculations. There are at least three major variations on VaR, each of which requires distinct data inputs. Every institution must perform stress testing according to the makeup of their exposures. And finally, regulatory calculations differ greatly from the risk calculations used to manage the institution on a daily basis.

At a minimum, analysis applications must include the following functionality to compete:

- An easy-to-use graphical user interface for defining methodologies and parameters for calculation
- Calculation engines for market risk, including value at risk (historical, Monte Carlo and variance/covariance methods), stress testing, the ability to create and combine multiple scenario analyses, and backtesting capabilities
- Basic instrument definitions and the ability to define new instruments or new valuation models for previously defined instruments, as well as the ability to define multiple valuation methods for an instrument type
- Flexible portfolio definition and aggregation and
- Drill-down capabilities to provide further detail as needed on the source or composition of exposures.

In addition, institutions are now requiring the ability to manage credit exposures and global limit setting and tracking. These credit risk functions will be integrated with the market risk systems that have been deployed throughout the industry, and will not be entirely separate systems. Several vendors are actively working on or have developed counterparty credit functionality but there are currently no commercially available comprehensive credit exposure calculators that are truly able to include all of the institutions products (including traded and non-traded products).

The analysis application segment of the risk solutions market is the most competitive. Often analysis packages are bundled with some integration capability, some reporting and a tailored data solution. However, the industry is still frustrated by the level of support and sophistication offered by analysis systems vendors outside of their core competency. There is still a trade-off between the sophistication of the analytical tools provided for valuation and exposure calculations and the level of completeness of the solution. Most of the solution vendors in this area compete on their knowledge of modeling financial instruments. Those that do not keep up with the latest theoretical developments quickly fall out of favor with the leading financial institutions. Since that is where the majority of the spending has been, this could spell disaster for a vendor. Therefore, most have invested heavily in financial engineering resources and academic liaisons to bolster their reputations and their access to emerging theory. This often leaves them with little time or R&D budget left for investing in data management or reporting, both of which are critical to the success of the system. This is gradually changing due to industry consolidation and the entrance of new vendors from outside of the trading systems arena.

Integration

The integration component of the overall solution goes by many names. Sometimes called 'integrationware' or 'middleware', it provides the glue that holds the pieces of the solution together. This component, which provides data transport from source system to analysis tool or data warehouse application, was traditionally provided by the application vendors or custom built for each application individually. Within the last decade, third-party tools have been developed for easier creation and management of data extracts.

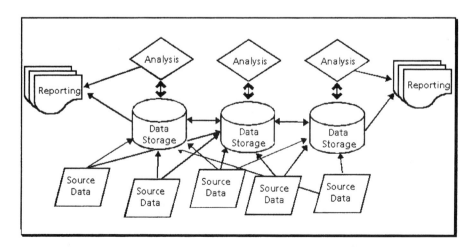

Figure 21.2 Integration the old way. (*Source:* Meridien Research)

Most enterprise risk implementations still look something like Figure 21.2, with analysis tools, databases, source data and reporting forced to coexist through custom extracts, multiple reformatting and manual intervention. Building extract upon extract has put an unwieldy burden on already taxed legacy systems and slowed down the risk management process. In addition, the manual movement of data into new databases and new formats has made data ownership and accountability nearly impossible. The scalability of this kind of solution is also problematic.

An entirely new class of software has evolved, however, which will make enterprise risk implementations less painful. These applications provide a standard interface, communication between systems and the ability to prevent systems failures for as many source and destination systems as needed. Intelligence built into the integration layer can even determine, based on the content of the message, how it should be formatted and where it should be directed.

This new software, which includes such technologies as object request brokers (ORBs) and publish and subscribe methodologies, is likely to be the single most important development for enterprise level risk management in this decade. It is through this common layer that multinational financial institutions will be able to standardize and consolidate data so that it can be used to feed analysis tools in a timely and accurate manner. Furthermore, the level of auditability in these tools will provide fault tolerance and security even when implementations are distributed around the world.

Common functionality provided by this new breed of software includes:

- Queuing and messaging
- Guaranteed delivery
- Rules-based routing
- Formatting
- Management and control
- Events and triggers
- Data(base) replication and
- Workflow management.

Data

Data has always been the biggest and most underrated challenge of an enterprise risk solution. Volumes, disparity in sources and locations, and the need for accuracy and speed have all contributed to compromise after compromise by global risk managers. Every institution with a risk implementation underway has struggled with the trade-off between comprehensiveness and speed, detailed and summarized information, and local and centralized analyses. Relational databases have replaced most of the flat file, hierarchical databases on which financial services institutions once relied. This shift should have represented advances in the data solutions for risk. However, building the relationships between data elements and optimizing those relationships for both speed and accuracy have proven challenging, especially given the diversity of products and their related needs for raw data. Relational databases can often be quite slow if not optimized for a specific type of use. This makes design and careful implementation of the data infrastructure critical.

An enterprise risk data solution handles both the data inputs to the analysis and the results of the analysis. It can be either centralized in one physical location or distributed across local or wide area networks. Often the data solution provides for both centralized risk data and distributed risk data. Most implementations have a data model at their center, though many lack well-defined relationships between data entities.

Commercially available data models have helped some institutions to create their data solutions, but by and large, the results of these efforts have been disappointing. The value of the data model is in its ability to reflect an institution's specific business needs and customization efforts are often long and tedious. Vendor-built data models are often provided by the analysis tool vendors. They are often too closely tied to the analysis tools of the provider and do not establish a common solution for multiple analyses. These data models can, in fact, be absolutely useless beyond their ability to feed a specific vendor's analysis tool. This can leave a financial institution with a well-designed data solution, but one that doesn't really have the ability to grow with the needs of the institution. Although it is impossible to know in advance what the data requirements of future analysis tools will be, it is essential that data solutions be chosen with an eye toward extendibility and data definitions which are general enough to be usable for other future applications. When buying a vendor solution, it is important to spend as much time performing due diligence on the data solution as on the analysis tool.

Reporting

Reporting is the segment of the solution that formats information for the user and then makes it available either on paper or by electronic means such as e-mail or via an intranet. Reporting is certainly not the most critical of the solution components of the enterprise risk solution and it is probably for this reason that it has been largely ignored. Nearly every analysis tool vendor includes some standard reports in its application, but these reporting capabilities are not very flexible and generally do not meet the needs of the users.

The reporting challenge is growing in complexity. Getting a high-level report that describes the institution's exposures is good, unless those exposures do not match expectations in some way. If there are issues, problems or questions, it is necessary to drill down into the data to get more detailed information explaining the anomaly. This *ad hoc* reporting requirement is still being met largely through the use of MS Excel or other general-purpose data manipulation tools. This is a highly manual, and often very time-consuming, process.

A further problem, which has recently surfaced, is information overload. As risk reports proliferate, standard reports do not actually need to be viewed every day by everyone involved. Graphical representation of information can speed up the comprehension of risk information and promote the use of risk information in a way that rows of numbers cannot. Just as paper reports used to stack up on desktops, electronic reports, often in the form of e-mail, now clog up networks and computer desktops. To solve this problem, many institutions have begun to develop intranet-based risk reporting databases. Reports can be posted to the site and viewed by users on an as-needed basis. There is still relatively little effort put into the reporting component of the risk solution, and this is not expected to change much until after the other components have become more stable. As more regulators put pressure on financial institutions for increased risk reporting, it is likely to increase attention on the reporting component of the solution, at least for regulatory purposes. Since a majority of the users of risk information, however, never see the system itself, the reporting that these systems generate is very much equivalent to the value of the system for most of the beneficiaries. More attention needs to be paid to presenting data is a useful manner in order to maximize the usefulness of the technology beyond the skilled few that run the systems.

Enterprise risk technology market segments

The number and kind of vendors selling risk solutions vary greatly depending on the market solution subsegment. Some segments have a relatively large number of well-entrenched providers, while others have almost none. We have broken down the solution components individually in order to describe the type of providers in each area and the dynamics of each market subsegment. Buyers should understand the depth and breadth of providers for each part of the solution in order to better understand what is available to be bought rather than built.

It is important to note here, once again, the distinction we have drawn between the integration function that is responsible for data cleaning, mapping and transportation, and the storage of data once it has been transformed. During the past five years, the responsibility for the acquisition and accuracy of data has moved steadily away from the group responsible for the overall maintenance of the database itself. These changes are highlighted by the existence of new specialty vendors in the area of integration.

Spending on enterprise risk solutions can be broken into the components shown in Figure 21.3. A vast majority of the time, effort and expense (approximately 65%) is devoted to the integration of source data and risk analysis tools. The second largest component of the solution cost is the data storage solution (about 18% of the total capital expenditure). Finally, the analysis and the reporting components together make up the remainder of the solution cost, with most of the expense devoted to the analysis solution.

On an individual basis, large financial firms are likely to invest in risk technology over a number of years. Average annual spending on the solution components described above is about $12 million. The average, however, can be misleading since the range of spending levels is quite wide. Even for institutions of equivalent size, there can be a great disparity of investment. Spending is typically in proportion to the complexity of the business mix within the organization (see Table 21.1). For example, market makers are more likely to understand, and actively make use of, risk information to create and manage new and existing products.

Table 21.1 Expenditures on enterprise risk IT

(US$ million)	Average annual ERM spending (per institution)	Average total cost of implementation (per institution)	Range of total cost (per institution)
Large institutions *(assets greater than US$100 billion)*	$7	$12	$7.5–$100
Mid-sized institutions	$0.75	$1.5	$0.5–$5

Source: Meridien Research

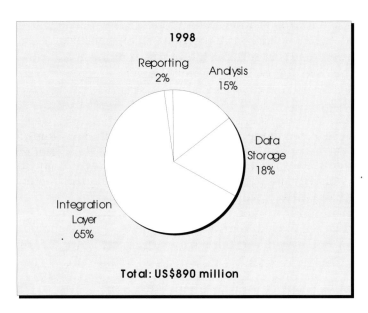

Figure 21.3   Relative expenditures on solution components. (Source: Meridien Research)

Commercially available analysis tools

The analysis tools market subsegment is the best developed and most mature of the market segments. (By most standards, this market segment is still rather immature, but for enterprise risk, this is as stable as the market has become in any area.) There are at least a dozen providers of analytical software packages. This space is very competitive in terms of new functionality offered. A few very high-end firms consistently compete at having the most sophisticated modeling and exposure calculations available. Yet, despite the relatively high number of vendor offerings in this area, at least a third of the spending on analysis tools is devoted to in-house proprietary development of technology. Much of this is by top-tier financial institutions that consider risk management a strategic competitive advantage and refuse to rely on outside firms to supply software to support such a sensitive business area.

Since most of the high-end vendors have been small, relatively new organizations, relying on outside vendors has been especially disturbing for the large financial institutions. As the vendor community has consolidated, this issue has been somewhat put to rest, but the absence of customized functionality still prevents most of the largest global financial institutions from buying packaged software and there are few institutions today that rely entirely on in-house developed software.

Another large portion of this market subsegment is the custom development firms, such as the consulting practices of the Big Five accounting firms, which build proprietary solutions for financial institutions that do not have the internal resources to do so themselves. Spending has already begun to shift from in-house development and consulting firms to application vendors, perhaps increasing their share of the market to closer to 70% of total spending within the next few years. Much of this shift is taking place as an increasingly large number of smaller financial services institutions begin to invest in enterprise risk. They cannot afford to build their own, nor will they be able to pay the fees associated with a consulting firm's efforts. They will rely almost entirely on vendor-provided analysis tools.

Until then, vendor consolidation will continue. In a subsegment which used to be characterized by small, smart, entrepreneurial organizations, the analysis tools vendors have increasingly been the targets of mergers and acquisitions as bigger firms look for a way to buy into the lucrative enterprise risk market. These mergers are necessary before analysis tools can be made available to smaller financial institutions. The economics of small, entrepreneurial software vendors do not allow for the enormous, multinational support and maintenance operations that will be needed to supply the large number of middle- and bottom-tier institutions. Furthermore, as the focus shifts from risk for sophisticated and leading edge financial engineering to risk for more standardized products for internal management and regulatory purposes, the ability to provide seamless integration, standard features and low cost will become paramount.

There are few independent software vendors remaining in the market. Firms like Algorithmics have already begun to cede the majority of the overall market to larger firms with international sales, marketing and support arms like SunGard and Midas Kapiti. There will still be a market for sophisticated analysis at top-tier institutions globally, but it is small and highly competitive. New market entrants (such as SAP and SAS) are not the small entrepreneurial software shops of a few years ago. They represent a new type of risk vendor; large, well established and global, whose focus is on infrastructure rather than sophisticated analysis. We do not believe that the financial services companies themselves are likely to make any noticeable impact on this market. Despite the media coverage of J. P. Morgan's RiskMetrics and Bankers Trust's RAROC 2020, neither has found much of a market among other financial institutions. We believe those products will stay in the corporate market, which is what they were designed for in the first place. The global *Fortune 100* is likely to be next high-growth risk management market. Already financial firms, like State Street with their recent purchase of risk vendor Askari, are positioning themselves to sell risk information and solutions, to their corporate customers. This trend will continue.

The market for data storage solutions

The data storage market subsegment is more complex than the analysis subsegment in some ways. Although the relational database core of the solution has been reduced to a race between Sybase and Oracle, the data model and database management tools available still do not meet industry needs.

Only a few vendors offer risk data models as separately packaged solution components. Most analysis software providers offer a data model of some kind, but these are typically embedded in the software. They are not necessarily extensible beyond the analysis for which they were originally intended. Other than these two options, which account for only about 11% of this market subsegment, the options are similar to those offered for analysis software: build with internal resources or build with vendor-provided resources. Overall, the consulting firms and the systems integrators together dominate this segment, taking about 73% of expenditures in this area. The 5% or so of spending dedicated to in-house efforts is predominately data model development. Every risk implementation today will use some form of commercial database application and management tools.

The consulting firm revenue associated with this market subsegment will erode significantly over the next three to five years. The value of the data model is in its ability to accurately reflect and, to a certain extent, predict future business needs.

No one will understand the business needs better than the business and IT group that supports them on a regular basis. To the extent that those business needs are encapsulated in a vendor's analysis solution, the vendor's data model can be used, but this is not likely to represent a majority of needs except at smaller institutions. Financial institutions increasingly recognize the value of starting with a data model that provides a core that can be easily extended. For this reason, we believe that the share of market held by the application vendors will continue to increase steadily, until it is nearly even with that of the consulting firms and systems integrators. The database vendors are unlikely to increase their market share much more in this area. They do not understand the business well enough to create a data model for risk purposes and they have already sold the core relational database software to nearly everybody.

The market for integration solutions

There are massive changes occurring in this market subsegment. The 'brute force' method of integration required enormous person-hours to build each individual extract and massage the data to meet requirements. This led to institutions relying heavily on consulting firms and systems integrators to provide the low value-added manpower to write the extract code. These firms still have dominant positions in the market, accounting for over 50% of the expenditures in this subsegment. Another third of the market represents the internal efforts of financial service institutions. Many with large IT organizations do at least part of the integration work internally. In addition, these kinds of implementations require ongoing work to maintain the extracts and often there is a great deal of manual intervention required to make the data transfers happen. This cost is included under in-house development as well.

Application vendors, primarily the companies that supply the analysis tools bundled with a data storage solution, also provide some data extract and data management capabilities. Most of the functionality here is tailored to the needs of the individual application. It is not designed to provide a generalized integration layer for all risk management.

Finally, the most exciting entrants into this market subsegment are firms that specialize in integration. These firms have learned to apply some of the advanced technologies of middleware to the risk management marketplace. This is still a very new area of product offerings. It is an idea, however, that the leading financial institutions have already explored. Some firms, such as Credit Suisse First Boston, decided not to wait for a proven commercially available product and have built their own integration layer. The integration layer in an enterprise risk solution will more typically be purchased from a vendor. This is likely to be a vendor that specializes in integration software, not one that specializes in risk management. Consulting firms and systems integrators will still play a role in this process, but they will be moved to more value-added positions, defining what data is needed and where to source it, rather than building extract after extract.

There will be a dramatic shift in market share away from consulting firms and systems integrators toward specialized providers of integration software. We estimate these firms will responsible for up to a quarter of the market within a couple of years.

The market for reporting solutions

The reporting subsegment of the market is the least well developed and the solutions used to satisfy reporting needs are extremely diverse. Often more than one provider will be used. Most reporting needs are still met on an *ad hoc* basis, primarily with spreadsheets, e-mail and other general-purpose business software packages. We estimate that about 50% of this subsegment is provided by these unspecialized applications. An additional 15% of the reporting market is held by application vendors, typically the vendors of analysis tools that also include some reporting capabilities. Increasingly, vendors are bundling reporting packages, such as Crystal Reports or Business Objects with the software rather than building reporting functionality themselves. These reports are typically augmented by spreadsheets, or a custom-developed reporting system. In-house development accounts for about 10% of the total market.

Very little attention has been paid to reporting. There are vendors that specialize in reporting systems, such as Crystal Reports, but these are not industry-specific, nor are they specific to risk management. It is likely that these are the most powerful of the reporting solutions available, though they require set-up and are not as familiar to most users as a spreadsheet package.

We do not anticipate major changes in this market subsegment, despite the current inefficiencies. Market share will probably shift increasingly to the specialized reporting tools, but it will be a slow and steady movement.

Different sources for different pieces: whom to ask for what?

The world of enterprise risk solution providers is extremely complex. No two solutions are alike and the type and priority of user needs varies in the extreme from one implementation to another. These factors make it very difficult to generalize about a vendor's capabilities. Nonetheless, there are ways to distinguish among the providers and risk management technology offerings. There are varying degrees of skill in the implementation of the four components discussed above and the focus, even within a subsegment like analysis, is different from vendor to vendor.

Software vendors

Within the broad category 'software vendors' there are at least three types of providers:

- Risk software vendors
- Integration software vendors and
- Financial services institutions.

Each of these providers comes at the enterprise risk solution with a different perspective, different goals and different skill sets.

Risk software vendors

This kind of provider is focused on risk analysis. There are a few that lead the market in high-end functionality tailored to the needs of very sophisticated market makers (Algorithmics, C*ATS, Infinity). These vendors have all made their names in the area of derivative valuation. Some started out as front-office solutions and grew into the middle-office and risk management areas.

Beyond this group of leaders, there are a few up-and-coming software vendors as well as some that seem to be stalled and in danger of elimination. Fringe players each typically have a specialty product group and/or geography. Some focus on a specific geographic market. Some focus on a specific aspect of risk management, e.g. regulatory reporting. The success or failure of these companies depends on their ability to differentiate themselves from the increasingly bundled approach of larger vendors, many of whom are marketing their software globally.

Integration software vendors

This remains a very small, specialized group. Newer players like NEON compete with established providers such as IBM and TIBCO (which is owned by Reuters). Increasingly, middleware solutions are being combined to create best of breed solutions. One may be employed for messaging while another is used for its intelligent routing. These vendors have entered the risk market by partnering with software vendors to offer predefined mappings from the software into the middleware layer. Tools from the database vendors (such as Sybase and Oracle) also compete to a certain extent with these vendors.

Financial services institutions

Given the risk technology investment and experience levels within financial services institutions, it is not surprising that an increasing number are looking to become technology providers themselves. Three banks, Bankers Trust, CIBC and J. P. Morgan, began openly marketing software. Some others, including Goldman Sachs, began developing risk software to be sold to their clients. Over the last year, all these efforts have failed to develop. Bankers Trust and J. P. Morgan both spun off their risk software efforts into separate subsidiaries, preferring to have them outside the bank. CIBC's efforts, which involved a partnership with HP, have not resulted in any sales and Goldman Sachs decided not to pursue its own project.

Does this mean that financial institutions will not find a way to capitalize on their risk expertise? We don't think so. These efforts, however, are likely to take a different shape. Financial institutions will provide risk information as a service to their clients (for which they will charge annual or other periodic fees). They are unlikely to sell software (which they would have to support) to these companies. They are also unlikely to sell anything to other banks. Nearly every major financial services firm in the world also has a risk advisory group today. These groups provide help with valuation and deal structuring, as well as financial products to hedge away unwanted exposures. It seems that financial institutions have learned to stick with what they know best and leave the software to the software vendors.

Data storage vendors

The database vendors do not really play a critical role in defining enterprise risk solutions. Though they are an integral part of the solution, the database has largely become a commodity and the database vendors find it increasingly difficult to differentiate themselves from their competitors. In an interesting twist, all the major database vendors now have consulting practices that focus exclusively on risk management. Typically headquartered in New York City, these groups so far seem geared at supporting sales efforts and managing partner relationships in this market subsegment more than at providing actual technology or risk consulting.

Ultimately the data storage component chosen is of little consequence to the overall solution, however, as long as it is standard and easily integrated. Furthermore, the decision which database to use is likely to be made based on the data warehousing strategy of the institution or on the software partnerships that exist, rather than on the individual merits of one database versus another at any given point in time. The issues for an enterprise risk solution have been scalability, data integrity and integration but are moving closer to on-demand data distribution and information synchronization.

Integrators and consultants

The most important outside party in any enterprise risk implementation will be the integrator or consultant chosen to help the institution define its needs and select a solution. There is a vast array of organizations to chose from, everything from very small, virtually unknown, risk specialists to huge, multinational corporations. Each has its specialty and is competing to take as large a portion of the spending on integration as possible.

The largest providers in the risk management integration subsegment are the Big Five accounting firms. These provide business strategy and planning in addition to technology strategy and implementation. The best one for the job will depend on the focus of the project. Typical projects at any of these firms are over US$1 million in fees and probably average closer to US$3–4 million.

In addition to the consulting firms above, hardware and software providers have also devoted consulting resources to risk management and have grown into a considerable presence in enterprise risk integration. This type of consulting firm clearly approaches the solution from a technology perspective. They have leading-edge internally developed technology as well as solution sets often formed through partnerships with other component vendors. Despite their clear preference for their own solutions, some hardware and software firms have the integration and technical skills that are required for enterprise risk. The hardware firms, especially, have a global presence and pockets deep enough to propel their own solutions. These players are likely to continue to be major providers of integration and technology consulting services.

Among the firms that specialize in systems integration, most have now completed some projects related to risk management. Though they are not long on risk expertise, they are some of the most experienced systems integration groups in the industry. They do not provide the one-stop-shopping of a Big Five (since they lack the business knowledge), nor do they have the hardware or networking expertise of the hardware vendors, but they do systems integration well and do not come with a Big Five price tag. These firms are not likely to be innovators but they play an important role globally in the pure integration part of the enterprise risk solution.

The selection process

There are five distinct stages in the decision-making process as it exists at most institutions investing in enterprise risk management technologies. This is an important process to understand for two reasons. Because it is a long and involved process, the decision itself may come some time after the initial request for information. Second, we believe there are differences in the weighting of individual decision criteria based on the stage of the process. For example, some issues seem more important in the initial RFP than they actually turn out to be in the final decision.

Request for information (RFI)

Typically, the first step undertaken is a request for materials describing the product or solution that is sent to an average of six to eight different vendors. The responses to the RFI are not tailored to the requestor's needs and contain little information that would determine whether the solutions should be pursued. Despite this, they are often used to eliminate solutions which do not appear to meet the general goals of the institution (e.g. stated goal is credit risk management but the vendor materials describe the solution as a market risk solution).

In addition to sometimes eliminating vendors, the initial round of RFIs is often insufficient and leaves out appropriate vendors, which may be discovered later in the process. In our opinion this stage rarely results in much. The firm requesting the information has typically not completed user specifications and probably does not completely understand the scope of their needs at this point. This stage may be initiated a year or more before the actual decision takes place.

Request for proposal (RFP)

Most institutions do take considerable time and effort in constructing their RFPs for risk solutions. A typical RFP would include a description of the needed functionality, type and number of users, and any technical requirements (e.g. maximum calculation time). It might also provide a description of the requestor's business including the number and type of transactions, the risk methodologies used, and underlying systems architecture.

These RFP responses form the core of information used to make the final decision. They are augmented by the presentations and Q&A process that follows, but the information contained in them is critical in determining whether the requesting firm will pursue the solution at all, and the final decision itself. Despite this fact, most RFP responses are poorly prepared and frequently do not respond to information requested by the RFPs. This can therefore be a very frustrating process for the requestor and one that can influence how the firm feels about the vendor even before entering into a discussion about the pros and cons of the solution. The RFP process will probably be started six to eight months or more before the final decision. The vendors are often provided with four to six weeks to respond (although not always) and those responses must then be evaluated. This stage can take three or four months to complete.

Presentations

The presentation stage of the process is usually the first opportunity for face-to-face meetings between the vendor and the decision maker(s). Of the six to eight RFP responses, the institution might request presentations from three or four finalists. This is very typically the most important part of the overall process that can be influenced by the vendor.

Vendors that are good at these presentations, that provide knowledgeable staff with polished answers to respond to questions, and attractive demonstrations of their products can come away from the presentation stage well ahead of solutions that are actually more appropriate to the firm's needs. On the other hand, strong solutions that are not presented well can find themselves out of contention before the final decision takes place. This is not to say that a strong presentation is all that counts, but it is a critical step in the process. The scheduling of presentations is not very time consuming. Depending on scheduling, they may be set up within a month or six weeks of the receipt of the RFP responses and are typically scheduled during a single week or two consecutive weeks. The first presentations can precede the final decision by a couple of months or more.

Questions and clarification

After the presenters depart, the committee working toward a decision invariably finds a list of questions for which they do not have answers. This is often due to the fact that comparable data on all the solutions is still missing. It can also be issues raised by a later presenter that were not addressed by early presenters. Whatever the cause, there is typically a series of faxes and phone calls that take place after the presentation to answer odd questions, confirm information obtained during the presentation and fill in any blank spots in their comparison to other solutions.

Final decision

The final step in the process is the actual decision. Most institutions have a committee that is responsible for making the final recommendation. This committee can be made up of any combination of end users, management, technology staff and external consultants. The most influential people on the committee are usually the end users. They may not be responsible for making the decision, but management depends on them to determine which system would best meet their needs. The recommendations of this committee are typically presented to senior management due to the size and importance of the project. Scheduling can delay this presentation and the resulting decision. The senior management is usually presented with a single or possibly two options. They may ask for further clarification, which can send the whole process back to the previous stage. The item most likely to result in a rejection of the proposed solution is cost. This is typically the only item that cannot be addressed by further clarification or consultation with the vendor. If the cost is far higher than anticipated, the solution may well be rejected and the process may be left with an indeterminate result. The decision that results from this stage may not result in an immediate contract. It may take several more months after the internal decision, including possibly a pilot project, before a contract for the complete solution is signed.

These stages may be compressed or drawn out even further depending on the size of the institution, the sophistication of risk management practices and organizational structure. Some institutions skip the RFI stage or don't send out formal RFPs. The process is very much the same, however, regardless of the formality of the steps.

Key issues in launching a successful implementation

There are several aspects of implementing risk management technologies that are challenging. Of these, there are three that bear closer attention.

User specifications

One of the more difficult aspects of managing risk technology selection and implementation is determining user requirements. In many cases, the risk process is not well defined. Even where it is, the discipline of risk management is evolving rapidly enough that user requirements are often a moving target. It is important to define the primary user of the system and to create a user specification that is not allowed to change until after it is fully implemented. The users should also determine prioritization of functionality. As the project progresses, new users are usually added, as are new functional requirements. However, because of the delays these changes inevitable introduce, it is preferable to start defining a 'Stage 2' implementation, rather than delaying the initial implementation. These projects are very expensive and are often very high profile. Delays in a high-profile IT project can be deadly. Maintaining control over the system's functional requirements and setting realistic goals for the first implementation deadlines is the key to overcoming 'scope creep' problems.

Project management

All enterprise risk projects, and most risk technology projects of any kind, should have the support of a senior management sponsor. Typically this person reports directly to the CEO or board of directors. This is because of the financial and human resources invested in the project. This senior sponsor does not have to have risk management responsibilities but they must understand the significance of the decisions involved and must be willing to stand up for the project at board level discussions. Without this senior ombudsman, risk projects can die of lack of funding or inconsistencies caused by the need to satisfy the concerns of the multiple business lines required to support the size of the effort. In addition to senior level support (and because of the dangers of high-cost, unending projects with little to show for the effort), we recommend that projects of this size have major deliverables at a maximum of six months apart. This provides proof to all around of the value of the project, as well as giving early warnings if there are problems. It is also important that project management carefully monitor scope (as noted above) and that they clearly communicate to all participants what will and will not be included in the project's various stages. This can be very difficult to do and may require an advanced degree in diplomacy to achieve, but it is critical in ensuring the success of the project.

Budgeting

The biggest problem in most risk IT budgets is a lack of a thorough understanding of the costs and their proportions. It is very clear that the institution will be spending money on system licenses and server hardware. What is often not so clear is that there will be costs beyond these two that are likely to make up 80–85% of the project. These, often left out, items include systems integration and consulting services, data cleansing and extract building, and database construction. These costs are typically not included in responses to RFPs and often are not fully understood until after the project is well underway. Budgeting for risk systems implementations should comprise both internal and external expenses and should be sure to include all expenses required to get the system up and running. An analysis tool that is fully installed will not produce results unless it is fed with the correct data. This data may be hard to find, or may not exist at all. It will probably be in the wrong format. It will likely be difficult to extract, and there may be not one around who understands its current location and format well enough to do the work that needs to be done. All these things must be assessed before it will be possible to come up with an accurate idea of the complete cost of a risk system implementation.

Conclusions

Some institutions have begun implementation of second- and even third-generation enterprise risk solutions. Over the years the systems have grown beyond the market risk for traded products into market and credit risk for traded products. Most still have a long way to go before reaching market, credit, and operational risk for all products globally. Some institutions are building their first enterprise risk systems now. Over the years, it has become increasingly clear that the completion of the current, or most recent, enterprise risk system implementation does not mark the completion of a firm's investment in enterprise risk IT. For many firms, it is just the beginning. Even for those who have been working on enterprise risk IT for three or four years, there is no way to predict when the discipline will settle down enough to be able to stop investing at the current rate. Therefore, it is extremely important to take the lessons learned in each implementation and study them for the future:

- *Enterprise risk is the first of many enterprise technology solutions.* The first decade of the twenty-first century is likely to be the era of the enterprise solution. If risk management is truly just the beginning of this trend than solving the technology issues associated with risk will truly be one of the better investments of time and money that a financial institution could make.
- *Technology is only one piece of the puzzle.* Institutions that invest in technology without investing an equal amount of time and effort in organization and procedural issues are very likely to find their technology investments wasted. Technology alone will not impact the way the institution does business. If risk management practices cannot be integrated back into each of the business lines, the enterprise risk technology will, in the end, have had no value to the business.
- *Risk management is not a fad.* In a time when buzzwords come and go, risk management is here to stay. Although much of the hype may be passing, risk management has been incorporated into too many of the regulatory and accounting standards to go away any time soon. For institutions that thought they could ignore the risk revolution and wait for it to go away, it is time to wake up and create a game plan.
- *The technology exists to implement enterprise risk.* Although there have been many well-publicized failures, careful planning and attention can aid in the creation of a technology architecture that can calculate firm-wide exposures and make them meaningful to the business units and to senior management. The perfect system does not yet exist, but we are rapidly approaching the ideal.

The challenges ahead are to extend risk management beyond the trading room, to integrate traditional credit concepts with newer ideas on exposures, and to build in a feedback loop from business line to enterprise risk back to the business line. Risk is no longer just market risk. The industry's focus has move fully to credit risk. Operational risk will be the next major category for automation. Beyond that, there are probably several other categories of risk to be uncovered. Technology architectures for balance sheet management, profitability and financial planning and enterprise risk are converging rapidly. This convergence will be another major technology challenge toward the end of the next decade.

An institution's ability to manage risk is competitive advantage. Since this ability is so highly dependent on technology, an institution's ability to plan, create, implement and maintain risk IT will also be a required core competency in the future.

22

Establishing a capital-based limit structure

MICHAEL HANRAHAN

Introduction

One of the primary functions of any risk management department is to protect the capital of the shareholders of the bank, while at the same time ensuring that the bank can take on the risk required to generate a reasonable return on equity. There are many ways in which a risk management department performs this function, ranging from detailed calculations on the potential losses of positions to establishing sophisticated RAROC monitoring systems. However, by far the most important way in which we can protect the capital of the bank is by putting absolute limits on the levels of risk that the bank can undertake.

In this chapter we will outline a system of tiered limits that are designed to allow a bank to protect its capital while producing adequate returns. We will also demonstrate that when used effectively limits can assist in optimizing capital usage, and therefore profits within the firm.

There are two overriding considerations that go into the creation of any limit structure – the limits are reactive to changes in the economic environment and also directly linked to the capital base of the bank. These two principles underpin the methodology that are outlined below, and while many of the ideas may seem common sense, it is nevertheless necessary to stress their importance.

As a starting point we should look at the limits-setting process form start to finish. The basic outline in Figure 22.1 will be discussed thoroughly in this chapter.

This may seem quite intuitive, but it is surprising how many banks fail to follow this structure, as very often they are too caught up in the minutia of day-to-day risk management to properly protect the bank's capital in a transparent fashion (failing to see the wood for the trees).

Purpose of limits

There are three main methods for managing the risk of a firm, namely authorization, control and limit setting. Authorization is the process whereby the firm decides which products it will trade and control determines the processes and procedures of executing the actual trades. Both of these are of little use, however, unless there is some limit over the size of transactions. Limit setting has emerged as the prevalent

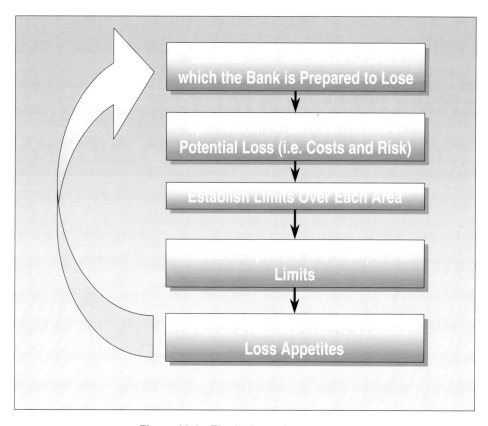

Figure 22.1   The limits-setting process.

means of providing an effective method to manage risk. Traditionally, however, limits have been under-utilized as a purely inert technique for ensuring diversified exposure. This has failed to capture the concept that limits can be used, in conjunction with economic capital, as a means of determining expected levels of revenue.

Managing economic capital

As will be described below, we can allocate a certain proportion of our total capital to economic capital, which is a measure of the amount of capital that the firm is willing to put at risk. Obviously the more capital that is put at risk, the higher the expected or potential returns. The capital that is allocated has to be distributed between the various desks of the firm, effectively telling the desks how much risk they are allowed to take. The risk that each desk exposes itself to can be divided into five distinct sections: market, credit, specific, operational and event risk.

In order to ensure that each desk does not exceed their quota of economic capital it is necessary to limit the amount of risk taken. These limits necessarily have to take a number of different forms, depending on the type of risk we are trying to limit. We say necessarily, as a single limit on the economic capital used by a desk would be of little practical use for management purposes. If, for example, we are limiting the market risk component of economic capital we would most likely institute a system of VaR[1] limits.

The return of each desk will be a function of the size of their various limits, as for an increased amount of risk we would expect an increased return. Therefore by altering the limit structure we can affect the projected return of the business. By monitoring returns and risk over time we can adjust limits to ensure that the firm's capital is allocated to where it will generate the highest risk return ratio, thus increasing overall returns of the firm. This process can be integrated with the budgeting and cost allocation processes to improve capital management. This is discussed in greater detail in the next section.

Ensuring diversity of exposure

The traditional use of limits is to foster diversity in the portfolio of the firm and a properly implemented limit system can be extremely effective in achieving this. It is necessary to ensure that the resources of the firm are not concentrated in any one particular area. The reasons for this are obvious in that diversification will stop losses from any one area or event being excessive. Limits that foster diversification are known as concentration limits, the main ones of which are country and counterparty limits. Diversification is necessary both in the portfolio and in the funding of the portfolio, so that we have funding/cash flow limits to complement portfolio limits. Naturally ensuring diversity will also protect the capital of the bank.

Maintaining tight management control

The monitoring of limits is a particularly potent method by which a senior manager can assess the activity of a desk or trader. If limits are monitored consistently management will quickly pick up significant changes in the level of usage. Limits are an ideal management tool to automate and monitor through exception reporting. Computers can easily assess limit breaches and generate reports for management should they occur.

For example, limits can be set which trigger an action once they have been breached. This action might involve alerting senior management or forcing a trader to close out his positions. Management alert limits (MALs) are the primary limits that assist in the management function. MALs are generally revenue-based limits which when breached require the attention of senior management. An excessive loss over a certain time period would be an example of something that requires management attention.

Limits placed at a desk level on the various risks (market, credit, etc.) can ensure that a desk exposes itself only to those risks that have been approved by management (e.g. a credit trading desk would have a zero market risk limit). This also assists in management control.

Economic capital

We have stated already that the basis for any limit should be the capital of the bank. This capital has to be expressed not in terms of the absolute shareholders equity, but rather that portion of the equity that will be used to generate revenue. It is important to distinguish between these two ideas, as if the limits are based on shareholders equity, rather than the working portion of the equity, then inevitably the limits will be set at too high a level. We can define that portion of the equity that is used to generate revenue as the economic capital.

Therefore, before building a limit structure centred on the capital of the bank it is important to establish the capital base, or economic capital, that is being used as the foundation for the limits. The first step is to establish the firm level economic capital. This figure is composed of two distinct elements, both of which are equally important for the functioning of the operations of the bank. The first of these is risk capital, which quite simply is the amount of capital that the board is prepared to risk (i.e. potentially lose) in any one period. The second element is cost capital, which is the amount of capital that is required to generate the revenue (and additionally, capital that could be lost in the event that the business fails). If the board sets their risk appetite they have to be also prepared to support a cost base sufficient to utilize that risk capital. These ideas are explored further below (see Figure 22.2).

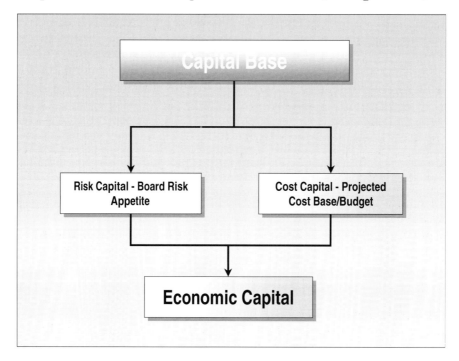

Figure 22.2   The elements of a firm's capital base.

We should note that a high risk capital will drive a high cost capital, as a sophisticated infrastructure will usually be required to monitor and control a high level of risk. The converse is not necessarily true, as costs can generate revenues from sources other than risk-related activities (e.g. fees, commissions).

Across banking institutions the ratio of cost capital to risk capital will vary depending on the type of business being operated. If the business is low risk or fee based then we would expect the cost capital element to make up the most of the economic capital. If, on the other hand, there is a lot of proprietary trading then the bulk of the economic capital will consist of risk capital. Within a bank, changes in the ratio of risk capital to cost capital, when combined with revenues, can be a powerful tool in measuring desk performance. This idea is explored further in the chapter.

Cost capital

Every business requires a certain level of capital to cover its cost base in the event that revenues cease (most likely in the event that a decision is taken to stop trading). Although not traditionally considered as a factor in the larger scheme of capital management within banking we cannot afford to ignore this important element. Therefore a portion of the capital base has to be set aside to cover these *potential* closeout costs.

The question then arises as to what portion of the capital is to be set aside for cost capital. To answer this we need to look at the time frame over which we could reasonably run down the costs associated with the business (or what outlay would be required to completely close the business). A conservative estimate would be 6 months' ordinary running costs. While this may seem a long time we should consider that redundancies, exiting lease agreements, etc. could very easily represent 6 months' normal operating costs. If the business can estimate closeout costs with reasonable certainty then this figure should be used. This can be a difficult exercise, however, as the circumstances under which you would have to close the business are most likely very different from the normal operating circumstances.

Therefore the cost capital for a business is simply calculated as the closeout cost, which for simplicity and prudence sake we take to be 6 months' costs (or whatever time period we estimate we can shut down). This figure should be constantly reassessed in the light of budget variances or changes in the nature of the business.

When allocating cost capital to particular businesses we simply allocate on the basis of costs budgeted for each business (of which closeout costs are a function). The level of costs is generally set by senior management and is a solid indicator of how much they want to invest in the business. This investment translates into a portion of equity capital for that business by calculating closeout costs for that particular business.

For the purposes of performance assessment it is normal to calculate two measures of economic capital, equating to the utilized resources of a desk and the available resources of a desk. In terms of cost capital the utilized resources are the actual incurred costs of the desk, while the available resources are the budgeted or approved costs for a desk.

The cost capital therefore represents both the maximum loss that will be incurred by the failure of the business and also the level of investment in the business. For this reason we should put limits on the level of cost capital and its utilization so that we can also assess performance on the return on cost capital. We do not do this, however, until the cost capital has been combined with risk capital to form the total firm economic capital.

Risk capital

The risk capital of the firm is the amount of capital that the shareholders of the firm are willing to put at risk. As with cost capital, risk capital can be divided into utilized and allocated/available. The utilized risk capital is equal to the risk taken by the desks, as calculated by the risk management department using VaR and other methods. The available risk capital of a desk is equal to the risk capital that has been allocated by senior management (who should represent the shareholders' risk appetite).

Risk capital is expressed as a percentage of equity capital. This level should be set by the board of directors taking into account the risk appetite of the bank and the required return. A figure of 33% would be consistent with the risk appetite of most major banks, but ultimately it is left to the discretion of the board. Once we have decided on the level of risk capital we should break it down into its various components that are detailed below. When we have identified the components we can use them to assist in setting limits.

Components

Risk capital is required to cover the risks of the bank. Therefore we have to examine the risk profile of the bank, from which we can draw a clearer picture of the elements of our risk capital. We do this by aggregating various risk measures, the sum of which is equal to the risk capital utilized. This can then be used as a pretty good guide as to the risk profile of the bank.

The risk measures can be calculated from various internal/external models and should cover all significant trading risks including market risk, credit risk, specific risk, event risk, and other financial risks:

Total risk capital = market risk capital + credit risk capital + specific risk capital + event risk capital + operational risk capital

Market risk capital

Market risk capital is the amount of capital necessary to cover the potential loss (99/95% confidence level) due to adverse market conditions over some predefined holding period. Market risk capital will cover the risks relating to yield curve risk, FX risk, commodity risk, equity risk and all non-linear market risk. The market risk relating to equities is the risk that can be explained by beta. The risk that cannot be explained by beta is considered specific risk and will be covered by the capital apportioned to credit/specific risk capital. The measure of market risk capital is most commonly market VaR.

Credit risk capital

Credit risk capital covers the potential loss (95/99% confidence level) that could arise from changes in credit spreads. In the case of credit instruments such as eurobonds, corporates, asset-backed securities, or floating rate notes the risk capital would cover the potential loss due to changes in the credit spread of the issuer. The issuer-specific risk capital amount can also be calculated using a VaR technique, which utilizes volatilities of spreads.

Specific risk capital

The specific risk capital is intended to cover potential losses that arise from a change in specific spread. This can be measured using a VaR calculation similar to that for market risk capital.

Event risk capital

Event risk capital is used to cover potential losses resulting from a sudden and unexpected event not covered by market risk or issuer-specific risk capital. Such events would include a default event or a deal break-up for example. Defaults events cover both counterparty risk and issuer default.

It is important to recognize that the nature of event risk is different from market-

and issuer-specific in that an event is usually binary, i.e. it occurs or it does not, whereas market and credit movements are generally more continuous. For event risk it is not easy to hedge the position. Therefore, it is more appropriate to calculate potential loss assuming a one-year time horizon and a 99% confidence level. A one-year time horizon has intuitive appeal since budgets, profits and bonuses are viewed on an annual cycle. In addition, rating agencies usually quote default rates on a per annum basis.

Operational risk capital

Operational risk capital should cover non-financial risks such as operational control risk, legal risk, tax risk, systems risk, etc. It should protect against potential losses arising from unauthorized trading activities, fraudulent practices, miscalculation of trading losses, inadequate legal documentation, the inability of systems to handle complex trading products, etc. Since this risk is often difficult to quantify the amount of capital allocated to cover these risks will be subjective in nature.

If we calculate the various risks to which the bank is exposed over a period of time we can get a good idea of the risk profile. This can be used to split the economic capital into its various components, or alternatively if management were unhappy with the current risk profile, they could change the components of economic capital, which, as we will see, should change the risk profile of the bank. We will see later how the above breakdown of risk capital can be used to assist in limit setting.

Desk level risk capital

Once the board has set the amount of risk capital at a firm level it then has to be allocated among the various trading desks, so that they know how much risk they can take, expressed in the form of allocated risk capital. Basically the process has two distinct parts, in which the risk capital is split between an amount required for covering costs and an amount to be allocated where the best return is achieved.

The element allocated to cover costs should be small in relation to the total risk capital, but should be sufficient to cover the costs given a reasonable return on risk. This should not be confused with cost capital, which is capital required to pay any close down costs of a business. The second allocation should form the bulk of the risk capital.

Cost coverage

The first allocation of risk capital determines the level of trading that a particular desk should undertake. This is taken to be a function of direct costs, as if a desk is incurring costs then presumably it should have a certain level of trading. Therefore to cover the costs the desks will need risk capital to fund their trading activities. The higher the direct cost base of a desk then presumably the higher the absolute level of revenue will be generated, e.g. if a trader is making a high salary he or she should be relied on to take greater calculated risks, and thus produce more profit. If a high portion of absolute revenue is required then more risk capital will be allocated.

Naturally this calculation will be tempered by other factors such as that proportion of the desks' revenues that arise from non-risk-taking activities. Ideally, we should have a breakdown of desk revenue between risk and non-risk. The direct costs can then be divided into this ratio to determine the risk capital required to cover the risk costs. This process is based on the assumption that each desk will achieve a certain level of return from the risk capital allocated. We all know, of course, that this is not the case, which is where is the second allocation of risk capital is undertaken.

Risk return

If the firm's businesses were perfectly correlated then the total risk capital allocation process would be simple. However, due to diversification benefits the sum of the risk capital required for each desk will be greater then the sum of the risk capital required at the firm level. The extent of the diversification effect will depend on the correlation of the profits of each trading desk. When there is less then perfect correlation it will allow for one business to do well while another business performs poorly. In effect, the businesses of the bank co-insure one another via a common pool of capital.

The second allocation of the risk capital therefore involves allocating the capital to where it is anticipated the best return will be achieved, while accounting for the diversification benefit. This is done effectively using portfolio optimization theory, where the correlations between desk returns are taken into account. Due to the fact that the returns on desks are correlated we can allocate to the individual desks a risk capital amount that is greater than the limit set by the board (as set out in Figure 22.3). At a practical level some desks may only be able to absorb a certain amount of risk capital, in which case the capital will be allocated with reference to the capacity of each desk. This may result in unallocated capital, which can be used to explore other business opportunities.

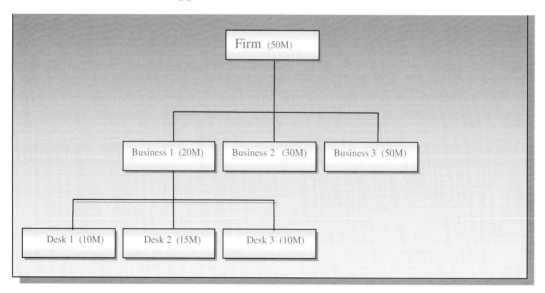

Figure 22.3 Risk capital allocation.

We can get a good idea of the diversification benefit of the desks by calculating risk at an individual desk level (i.e. each desk is a separate portfolio) and at a firm level (all positions are in the same portfolio). The ratio between the sum of the desk risk figures and firm figure represents the diversification benefit. If this is done over a period of time and using different combinations of desks we can get a very good estimation of what each desk contributes to the diversification benefit. This information, along with returns on risk capital, is required to implement portfolio optimization to the process of allocating risk capital.

Portfolio optimization theory takes into account correlation benefit between desks, so that if, for example, a desk produced little P&L, but added a large risk diversification benefit to the firm as a whole, then that desk would receive a large portion of risk capital. This ensures that a desk gets credit for 'allowing' other desks to take risks that generate profit. This correlation/diversification effect would have to be taken into account when assessing a desk's performance.

Risk capital allocation, therefore, is the process by which risk capital is allocated to the individual businesses and trading desks. The amount of risk capital to be allocated to each business will be a function of:

- The individual budget of the business
- The value added by the business (in terms of risk return and correlation with other desks)
- The amount of risk diversification added by the business.

Value added by the business

Certain businesses in the firm may contribute considerable value to the firm without themselves making any profit. An example is where it may be necessary to trade with particular counterparties in order to maintain a client relationship. A business should not be penalized if they incur additional risk from their trading that is essential to the firm as a whole. In addition to necessary trades, businesses may generate value without generating risk (fees etc.). Obviously we would not allocate any risk capital to this type of activity.

Budgeting

As can be seen above, the process of calculating the economic capital and assigning it to desks requires virtually the same information as that required for the budgeting process. Ideally these two processes should be done in conjunction with each other.

The cost element of budgeting is relatively straightforward. We can use last year's costs as a guide, or if the nature of the business is changing we can estimate a new cost structure. In either event the economic capital and the allocation of economic capital to desks will be a function of these costs. The revenue side of the budgeting process can also be directly calculated from the economic capital. We know the historical returns on risk that a particular desk has achieved and we know how much risk we want them to take, and therefore we can calculate the expected revenues. If there is a new desk, or change in risk profile of an existing desk, we can still set expected revenues based on the risk we want the desk to take and estimating a return on risk capital.

Regulatory capital

When setting the level of economic capital we have to remember that an important constraint is regulatory capital which is essentially an expression of the amount of risk that regulatory bodies will allow a bank to take. If we set the level of economic capital too high then we are bound to reach our regulatory capital limit before our economic capital limit. If this is the case then we should reassess the risk element of economic capital basically to scale it down to regulatory capital level.

When doing this we will have to reduce our limits and reassess the current allocation of these limits. In the process described above we looked at return on risk capital when deciding where to place the economic capital. However, if regulatory capital is the constraint, rather than the risk appetite of the board, then we have to examine returns on regulatory capital. We also have to look at the diversification benefit that each desk adds to the overall regulatory capital figure. Essentially therefore we are rerunning our portfolio optimization program and replacing risk returns with regulatory capital returns and VaR diversification benefit with regulatory capital diversification benefit.

Economic capital summary

In summary, therefore, we will calculate two economic capital figures for all desks. The first is for utilized economic capital and consists of the sum of utilized cost capital and utilized risk capital (based on costs incurred and risk taken). The second economic capital figure is for allocated economic capital and consists of available cost capital plus available risk capital (set by the board through the budgeting process). The reason we look at the calculation of economic capital in such detail is that this figure will form the basis for all the limits that are subsequently set. The one additional constraint is regulatory capital, which should replace risk capital in our calculations if it is likely to be the overall constraining factor.

Types of limit

We have described above how the firm calculates its economic capital. The next step in the process is to set limits in order to ensure that the capital utilized is not in excess of the capital allocated. This process has to be achieved at various levels of the bank. The primary level is naturally the firm level, and from there we drill down to the desk and trader level. The question then arises as to what measurable and controllable factors we have to limit in order to effectively cap the economic capital used in the bank.

   These measurable factors generally fall into three categories. The first is statistically measurable risk and the limits that cover this are called VaR limits. These limits essentially cap the amount of market, credit and specific risk that the firm can take. These limits are most closely related to the economic capital of the bank and can be derived directly from it. They are also ideal for imposing at various levels in the bank (e.g. trader, desk). The second measurable factor is absolute exposure. The limits over this are known as concentration limits and ensure diversity of exposure. These limits should also be a function of the capital base or economic capital. The final set of limits is a catch-all, which can contain any limits that would be used for general management of the business. It is not so easy to relate these directly to the economic capital, but we should get a feel for the general level of these limits from knowing the risk appetite of the bank, as expressed in the economic capital.

   Figure 22.4 details the various limits that a firm should consider. As described in the previous section, the limits have a number of functions, particularly the VaR limits which help foster diversification while also managing the capital of the firm.

Value-at-Risk limits

VaR limits are limits that restrict the amount of risk to which a trader can be exposed. Basically it calculates the amount of unexpected loss with 95/99% confid-

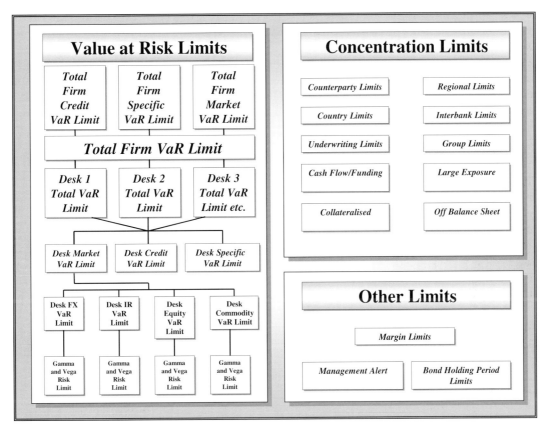

Figure 22.4 The limits for a firm.

ence over one day. On the assumption of greater risks equals greater returns, it is expected that traders would try to ensure that the VaR on the positions would be close to the VaR limit whenever possible. The VaR limit is derived from the amount of economic capital that has been allocated to the desk.

The first stage in calculating the VaR limit is to establish the economic capital of the desk. We have described above how we calculate the firm economic capital. Essentially the process of calculating firm economic capital will tell us how much capital to allocate to each desk. This is because in assessing our firm economic capital and risk appetite we have to look at how each desk currently contributes to risk and return. We also have to account for the return correlation and risk diversification factors. The outcome of this assessment will define the amount of economic capital that is to be allocated to each desk.

Having allocated the economic capital to the desks we will have to further divide it into sections for market, credit, specific, event and operational risks. Not every desk will have every type of risk so the economic capital allocated to each desk will only be divided into those risks to which the desk is subject. Event and operational risks are binary in nature and do not lend themselves to one-day VaR calculations and as such will not have a VaR limit. Market, credit and specific risks, however, can be calculated over a short time horizon and will have VaR limits. Therefore we allocate a portion of the economic capital of the desk to market, credit and specific risk and leave a remaining balance to cover operational and event risks (we will see how later how concentration limits derived from capital enable us to link economic capital to event risk).

The third and final stage in linking the capital directly to the VaR limits is to translate the economic capital directly into limits. Once we have the economic capital allocated to each type of risk on each desk we can set the limit as a function of this figure. The first step in this function is to limit the economic capital by some arbitrary figure (regulatory bodies would suggest a factor of 3) due to the shortcomings of the VaR methodology. These shortcomings are detailed below. The limit will be equal to the reduced economic capital for that risk divided by average holding period for the risks on that particular desk. Therefore the limit will be expressed in terms of one-day VaR and can be compared to the daily VaR figures. The reason we divide by the holding period is that the original economic capital was calculated by examining average risk, whereas the limit has to be a one-day figure for it to be of practical use.

Once we do this we will have a desk one-day VaR limit for each of the three types of risk; market, credit and specific. These can be aggregated across the bank to give a firm overall VaR limit for each risk type. This aggregation process must take account of correlation effects between each desk. This process can be seen in Figure 22.4.

Market VaR sub-limits

The market VaR can be further divided into sub-limits for interest rate, FX, equity and commodity risk. Within interest rate and equity risk we will also have gamma and vega risk and these will also have to be limited. The split between the market risk sub-limits will be based on the type of product traded at each particular desk.

Advantages of VaR limits

There are a number of major advantages to the use of VaR limits as a risk-monitoring tool. These are what have made the VaR methodology the prevalent risk measurement technique, despite some serious drawbacks.

The primary advantage of VaR limits is that they are very flexible in terms of the type of risk to which we can expose ourselves. As mentioned above, the economic capital is divided into portions for market, credit and specific risk. However, on the whole we should not care to which risk we are exposed, as long as the total economic capital used by the desk does not exceed our overall limit. This concept is best explained by means of an example.

Suppose we have a trading desk that has been allocated £5.25 million economic capital, has an average holding period of 5 days and an even split between market, credit and specific risk. We would calculate the one-day VaR limit as £1 050 000 (being £5.25 million divided by 5). We initially would allocate £350 000 to each of market, credit and specific risk. However, if a desk is using its full allocation of market risk and only a fraction of the other two limits then there is no reason why we cannot allocate the unutilized portion of credit and specific risk limits to the market risk limit. Essentially therefore we should be indifferent as to how we split the limit, unless there was a specific reason we wanted to curtail the types of risk to which a desk was exposed.

Another major advantage of VaR limits is that the exposure is relatively easily calculated and we can aggregate exposure across different desk and currencies. This means that we can have various levels of granularity (down to, for example, the VaR in individual currencies to which a particular trader is exposed) and assign limits to each level. With modern computing power the calculations required to achieve this should not be prohibitive.

Shortcomings of VaR limits

There are a number of problems with trying to limit risk on positions purely through the implementation of VaR limits. The main drawbacks are:

1 The actual movement of market prices often has patterns that are different from those used in the statistical simplifications used in the VaR modeling process (i.e. we assume a normal distribution).
2 The past is not always necessarily a good indication of the future. VaR modeling relies on historical data of volatilities to calculate the risk amounts.
3 VaR calculations are generally performed on end-of-day positions and as such may not capture the full risk associated with intraday trading.
4 There are a significant number of simplifying assumptions in the VaR model, particularly in relation to the calculation of risk on options.

We can see therefore that VaR calculations may not always capture the true possible losses on a position. We do not adjust the VaR limit directly to account for this, but rather we limit the economic capital allocation to approximately one third or one quarter of the total capital. This in turn reduces the VaR limits, ensuring that the firm cannot suffer catastrophic losses. In addition, we limit our exposure through other limits which force diversification in the portfolio.

Concentration limits

Concentration limits are the main means of ensuring diversification in the portfolio of the firm. They basically put a cap on the size of positions that can be taken within various categories. The limits are set by reference to the three basic parameters of capital base, size of position and risk (expressed normally as a credit rating). Naturally the capital base is the most important of the constraints as this will determine the level of risk to which the firm can expose itself. The concentration limits can be split into the following categories:

- Country limits
- Counterparty limits
- Regional limits
- Large exposure limits (and related limits)
- Underwriting limits
- Cash flow/funding limits
- Long/short position limits
- Banking trading limits

The limits are designed to be flexible and to incorporate various types of products and sub-limits. The country and regional limits are particularly important because historically there has been a certain correlation of default within regions. The use of limits therefore will ensure diversification and reduce risk. Unlike VaR, which naturally can incorporate products of different types, we have to establish a consistent method of measuring exposure to particular counterparties, regions, etc. The way we do this is to translate everything into loan equivalent amounts.

Loan equivalent amounts

Different types of products have different types and levels of risk attached to them. Therefore it may often be necessary to have different limits for each counterparty corresponding to different types of risk. This can lead quite quickly to an unwieldy and unnecessarily large system of limits. To avoid this we can express all exposures to countries, counterparties, issuers, etc. in terms of loan equivalency and have only one limit per counterparty or country. Loan equivalency basically tries to translate the exposure to what it would be if expressed in terms of a simple loan. This means that it is possible to only have one limit for each country and counterparty for all positions, be they equities or fixed rate notes, so that all positions can be simply aggregated to determine the level of exposure to a particular counterparty, country or region. To calculate the loan equivalent figure we take the mark to market value and add on an amount to represent potential loss over the period. This ensures that each product can be aggregated by simple summing of the loan equivalent amount. The basic products are outlined below.

Bonds/loans

The loan equivalent amount is basically equal to the mark to market value of the bond or loan.

Off-balance sheet positions

The loan equivalent amount for off-balance sheet positions is calculated as the mark to market plus an add-on for potential loss. This add-on can be calculated by any number of methods, but should take into account the rating of the counterparty, the type of position and the maturity of the position. Most regulatory attempts at calculating exposures use some simple system of add-on.

Repos

To calculate the loan equivalent amount for repos we take the difference between the loan amount and the collateral amount and add on an amount for potential loss.

Equities

Financial difficulties with a counterparty have a much greater effect on the equity value of the counterparty than on any bonds or loans they may have issued. Therefore for equity positions we calculate the loan equivalent amount as being twice the mark to market value. We are effectively saying therefore that we would be indifferent to having £1 worth of equity or £2 worth of bonds with a particular counterparty. Obviously you can use whatever factor you think is appropriate, but a factor of two would seem prudent.

DVP

The loan equivalent for DVP exposure is equal to the DVP value plus an add-on for potential loss.

Therefore using the above criteria we can calculate an exposure for each counterparty, from which we can derive industry, country, etc. exposures. The point of using loan equivalent amounts is that we can treat all counterparties on an equivalent basis, irrespective of the type of exposure.

Calculation of concentration limits

Country limits

These basically ensure that a bank does not overly expose itself to a particular country. We cannot rely on VaR limits to ensure this because VaR limits only reflect the 99th percentile loss, whereas the country limit will account for the entire amount of possible losses.

Calculating the limit

The purpose of the limit structure is to limit risk relative to the size of the bank. Therefore we have to account for the capital base when determining the level of the limits. The other factors that should determine the limits are the size of the country and its rating. We need to incorporate these three factors into a simple formula that will calculate the limits.

The individual limits are determined therefore by reference to the capital base, the rating of the country and the size of the country expressed in terms of GDP. Two countries of equal size would have a limit that is directly proportional to their probability of default, as denoted by their credit rating, the idea being that we can attempt to achieve maximum diversification by equating expected loss for all positions. Two countries with the same rating will have a limit that is related to their size, as determined by a simple function that basically says that as the country size becomes larger the difference in limit becomes smaller (and the difference is thus then determined by rating).

A simple and effective way to relate the limits to capital size is to select a base country (or basket of countries) and set its limit as a percentage of the capital base (that percentage being equal to whatever level you would feel comfortable with). The limits of the other countries will follow naturally from this initial starting point based on their size and rating.

Calculating each exposure's contribution to the limit

An individual counterparty's contribution to the country limit is calculated by using the total loan equivalent amount exposure and scaling it to account for the difference in rating between the counterparty and the country. For example, if we had exposure to General Electric (Aaa) and General Motors (A3), both of which are in America (Aaa sovereign), the individual risk weighted country exposures for these two counterparties would be as follows. GE which has the same rating as the country (both Aaa) would have a risk weighted exposure equal to that of its total exposure. GM, on the other hand, would contribute $10.0 \times$ its nominal exposure to the country exposure. The idea is to prevent traders from trading in securities that are of very poor quality in the same country, which is not picked up if we were to simply look at the nominal exposures. Table 22.1 shows the multiples that we will apply to each counterparty's nominal exposure to determine their contribution to the country risk weighted exposure. These multiples are based entirely on the probability of default between the various ratings. As no counterparty's rating is higher than the rating of the country in which it is resident, the lowest factor in the table is 1.

Industry limits

Calculating the limits

The industry limits are also calculated as a percentage of the capital base. We do not need to be as exacting as for country limits and could set limits, for example, of

Table 22.1 Country and counterparty ratings

Counter-party rating	Country rating														
	Aaa	Aa1	Aa2	Aa3	A1	A2	A3	Baa1	Baa2	Baa3	Ba1	Ba2	Ba3	B1	B2	B3
Aaa	1.0															
Aa1	1.7	1.0														
Aa2	2.4	1.5	1.0													
Aa3	3.9	2.3	1.6	1.0												
A1	5.6	3.3	2.3	1.4	1.0											
A2	6.7	4.0	2.7	1.7	1.2	1.0										
A3	10.0	6.0	4.1	2.6	1.8	1.5	1.0									
Baa1	14.4	8.7	5.9	3.7	2.6	2.2	1.4	1.0								
Baa2	17.8	10.7	7.3	4.6	3.2	2.7	1.8	1.2	1.0							
Baa3	77.8	46.7	31.8	20.0	14.0	11.7	7.8	5.4	4.4	1.0						
Ba1	138.9	83.3	56.8	35.7	25.0	20.8	13.9	9.6	7.8	1.8	1.0					
Ba2	198.9	119.3	81.4	51.1	35.8	29.8	19.9	13.8	11.2	2.6	1.4	1.0				
Ba3	440.0	264.0	180.0	113.1	79.2	66.0	44.0	30.5	24.8	5.7	3.2	2.2	1.0			
B1	682.2	409.3	279.1	175.4	122.8	102.3	68.2	47.2	38.4	8.8	4.9	3.4	1.6	1.0		
B2	923.3	554.0	377.7	237.4	166.2	138.5	92.3	63.9	51.9	11.9	6.6	4.6	2.1	1.4	1.0	
B3	1675.6	1005.3	685.5	430.9	301.6	251.3	167.6	116.0	94.3	21.5	12.1	8.4	3.8	2.5	1.8	1.0
Caa1	2217.8	1330.7	907.3	570.3	399.2	332.7	221.8	153.5	124.8	28.5	16.0	11.2	5.0	3.3	2.4	1.3

300% (of capital) for sovereigns, 200% for banking sector and 150% for all other industries.

Calculating each exposure's contribution to the limit

As with country limits we should look at exposure on a risk weighted basis. To do this we have to pick a base rating and scale other exposures in relation to that base. In the example below we have selected 'A3' as our base rate. The other multipliers then follow from the ratio probability of default between 'A3' and the rating. The multipliers by which exposures are scaled are detailed in the table below. A counterparty that is B1 rated will contribute $68.2 \times$ its loan equivalent amount exposure to its industry exposure.

Rating	Aaa	Aa1	Aa2	Aa3	A1	A2	A3	Baa1	Baa2	Baa3	Ba1	Ba2	Ba3	B1	B2	B3
Factor	0.10	0.17	0.24	0.39	0.56	0.67	1.0	1.4	1.8	7.8	13.9	19.9	44.0	68.2	92.3	167.6

Counterparty limits

We will describe counterparty sub-limits later, but before we do we should note that the counterparty limit will place a ceiling on the aggregate of all the sublimits. The counterparty limits are set in the same manner as the country limits, with all the limits being a function of the capital base and the counterparty's size and rating. As with the country limits, a simple function is used that tapers the effect of counterparty size as the sizes get bigger, at which point the probability of default (as determined by the rating) will totally determine the difference between the limits. This function is shown in Figure 22.5.

The size of the counterparties is determined by their market capitalization, while

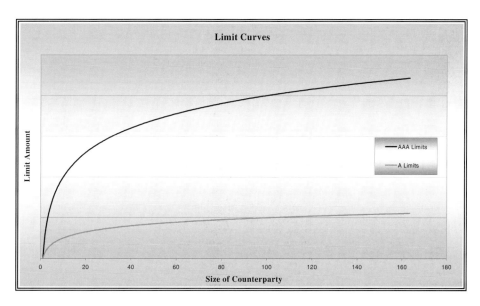

Figure 22.5 Limit curves.

the rating can be taken from any rating agency (although prudence would dictate using the lowest rating found). As with the country limit, we need to select a base point for our curve from which all other limits will flow. To set the base limit we should select a small, medium and large counterparty and give them limits (expressed as a percentage of capital) with which we would be comfortable. The weighted average of this limit will then form the base point for all other counterparty limits. Under this structure as either the capital base of the bank changes or the rating or size of the counterparty changes, the limit will change.

Table 22.2 gives a list of examples of the size of limit (in £ millions) that would apply to a counterparty depending on the credit rating and the size of the company. For all listed counterparties, market capitalization is used as an indicator of size. For non-listed counterparties, market capitalization should be estimated using a multiple of net asset value, a ratio of price to earnings or the market capitalization of a similar size listed company. These will depend on the type of industry, profitability trend, etc. Where a counterparty is unrated, risk management should assign an internal rating commensurate with rated companies similar in size and other fundamental characteristics to the unrated counterparty.

Country and counterparty limits, and all limits based around these, are calculated by reference to the firm's capital base and the credit rating and size of the counterparty. The capital base effectively tells us the maximum we can put at risk. The size and rating will determine how much risk we are prepared to accept with individual counterparties or countries. Obviously, with large, high-rated countries the limit calculated will be irrelevant as it will be of a size that would be impossible to reach. With countries such as these other limits (primarily VaR) would be reached prior to the concentration limit being reached.

Sub-limits

In addition to a counterparty limit we also need some sub-limits to manage the business practically. It can be difficult to link these directly to capital, but a process

Table 22.2 Limits applying to counterparties

Market capitalization/ size of counterparty	Counterparty rating														
	Aaa	Aa1	Aa2	Aa3	A1	A2	A3	Baa1	Baa2	Baa3	Ba1	Ba2	Ba3	B1	B2	B3
100	11.2	7.1	5.1	3.4	2.5	2.1	1.5	1.1	0.9	0.3	0.2	0.1	0.1	0.1	0.0	0.0
200	21.4	13.6	9.7	6.4	4.7	4.0	2.8	2.1	1.7	0.5	0.3	0.2	0.1	0.1	0.1	0.1
500	47.5	30.2	21.5	14.3	10.5	9.0	6.3	4.6	3.9	1.1	0.7	0.6	0.3	0.2	0.2	0.1
1 000	81.3	51.6	36.8	24.5	17.9	15.3	10.8	7.9	6.6	2.0	1.2	0.9	0.5	0.4	0.3	0.2
2 000	128.8	81.8	58.3	38.8	28.4	24.3	17.1	12.5	10.5	3.1	2.0	1.5	0.8	0.6	0.5	0.4
5 000	210.1	133.4	95.1	63.2	46.4	39.6	27.9	20.4	17.1	5.1	3.2	2.4	1.4	1.0	0.9	0.6
10 000	281.2	178.5	127.2	84.6	62.0	53.0	37.3	27.3	22.9	6.8	4.3	3.3	1.8	1.4	1.1	0.8
50 000	461.1	292.7	208.6	138.8	101.7	86.8	61.2	44.7	37.5	11.1	7.1	5.4	3.0	2.3	1.9	1.4
100 000	541.2	343.5	244.9	162.9	119.4	101.9	71.9	52.5	44.0	13.1	8.3	6.3	3.5	2.6	2.2	1.6
200 000	621.9	394.8	281.4	187.2	137.2	117.1	82.6	60.4	50.6	15.0	9.5	7.2	4.1	3.0	2.5	1.8

similar to that described above for country and counterparty limits could be employed if so desired. In any event the counterparty limit, which is linked to capital, will ultimately cap the sub-limits. Some of the normal sub-limits and their treatment under a capital-based limit structure are detailed below.

Regional limits

In addition to country limits we also have regional limits to ensure that our exposure to each region is not excessive. The regional limit will be calculated in the same manner as the country limit. The size of the region will be the sum of the individual GDPs and the rating will be the weighted average of the country ratings. The limit size will then be determined by the ratio of default rates

DVP limits

There will not be individual Delivery versus Payment (DVP) limits, but rather the risk from DVP will be converted into a loan equivalent amount (as described previously) and aggregated with other exposures to form part of the overall counterparty risk.

Management alert limit

In addition to risk/concentration limits we also have management alert limits (MALs). MALs are a control on daily, monthly and overall trading risks, as they specifically focus management attention on preset loss levels. Once a particular loss amount has been reached it will be necessary to inform senior management, who can decide on the required course of action. The management alert limits are set by reference to VaR and budget (i.e. they should be some multiple of VaR or allocated economic capital). By setting the MAL limits in this way they will be ultimately linked to the capital of the firm.

Margin limits

In order to ensure that we use our capital effectively it is essential that we do not place too much money with brokers for the purpose of margin. To prevent this we simply put a limit on the margin we can place. Naturally, this limit should have some bearing on the capital base of the bank.

Cash flow/funding limits

Managing cash flow is a very important part of the treasury strategy of any bank. It is vital to monitor a bank's ability to repay total outstanding borrowings across various maturity bands. To do this it is essential to ensure that different funding sources are available and that maturity of treasury funding is diverse. This can be achieved by placing limits on funding activities. These limits could take the form of caps on the term of funding (e.g. overnight, TOMnext) or caps on the amount of funding from particular counterparties (this would force diversity of funding sources, which may be necessary in time of crisis).

Cost limits

In addition to the above-described limits, which arise primarily from the risk capital, we should also limit the cost capital. We have described above the calculation of cost capital and the amount of the cost capital is essentially the limit. Costs can be easily attributed to desks and that represents the desk limit.

Costs are an area that are and have always been closely monitored. There is no subjective element in relation to the monitoring or measuring of costs, particularly at a firm level. Strict accounting rules, well-established accounting practices and strong systems will generally ensure that a bank keeps close tabs on its cost base. For this reason we do not need implicit limits on costs and the usage of cost capital, as it is controlled sufficiently well from other sources. We can think of the budgeted costs as the cost limits. Should there be a breach it will be quickly picked up and explained. Also, unlike risk, we generally know in advance if there is going to be additional costs.

Where we can improve our cost monitoring in the banking sector is by fully examining what is driving our costs. It is all very well to monitor the direct costs of a trading desk and say that they are performing well, but if that desk is generating large back- or middle-office costs then this should be reflected in the cost capital allocated (and hence the cost limit). To improve this process we can apply a technique that is used in industry, namely activity-based costing, quite easily to the banking sector.

Activity-based costing

When looking at the returns of a desk we cannot ignore the costs that have been generated by that desk. It would also be very short-sighted of us only to examine the direct costs of each desk, as obviously each desk also contributes to back-office costs. On the premise that without the trading desks there would be no other costs we can validly allocate all of a bank's costs to the revenue-generating centres.

This allocation can be achieved by examining what drives the costs of each department and applying those drivers to the front-office desks. Naturally a portion of back-office costs will be allocated to other back-office cost centers. Where this is the case we can reallocated the costs over and over until such time as all costs are allocated to the front office.

This process should be part of the economic capital calculation as outlined at the start of this chapter, so that we can say with reasonable certainty that we have properly estimated the costs that would be incurred in the event of a business failure. Aside from gaining confidence about the level of costs there are many other advantages of activity-based costing, which are outside the scope of this chapter.

Monitoring of capital-based limits

Without efficient monitoring of the limits described above there is little point in implementing such a system. With the current wealth of technology available to most banks it should be an easy task to monitor all limits as soon as there is any change in exposure. The difficult part is setting the limits and calculating the related exposures. Once this has been achieved we should be able to compare the two quite simply.

Monitoring utilization

Many institutions have a very black and white method of monitoring limit utilization, whereby a limit breach triggers a report or action. This, however, fails to utilize the full management potential that is offered by limits. If we take the limit to be a benchmark against which we monitor changes over time we can garner a lot of information about the business. The most potent area where this applies is in VaR limits. If we look at trends of limit usage over time we can get a good sense of changing risk profiles. This has the advantage over absolute VaR monitoring of stripping out changes in the profile that may occur due to changes in the size or nature of the business. If, for example, we expect a desk to take more risk and allocate a bigger VaR limit we would like to know if this limit is being utilized to the same percentage as before. This, in other words, will tell us if the relative increase in risk was what we expected.

Generally the best method of utilization monitoring is to represent utilization of limits graphically. This may be impractical if there are large numbers of limits to monitor (such as counterparty limits), but it should be done wherever possible. The reasons for this are obvious as graphical representations can generally impart a lot more data in a quicker time frame than a page of figures. Needless to say, all the normal control processes should be in place over any limit system to ensure integrity and completeness of data.

Monitoring level of limits

When monitoring limits we should constantly reassess the appropriateness of the level of the limits. The system of limit setting should be as flexible as possible, while still maintaining control of the business. There are enough constraints on business from various sources other than internal limits and we should be mindful of this when looking at the level and number of limits.

As described in the preceding sections, the limits are based on and generally derived from the capital base of the bank. Therefore this is the first element that should be constantly monitored. If a bank takes a big loss during the year then its capital base is necessarily reduced. The risk appetite of the firm should reduce if the capital base reduces, which should be reflected in a reduction of the limits.

After examining the capital base, the other elements that go into calculating the various limits (e.g. rating, interdesk correlation) should be examined individually. A practical viewpoint should then be taken as to when to adjust the limits. Obviously if limits are changing constantly it becomes difficult for traders and managers alike to keep track of the level of the limits. A good approach would be to recalculate the limits constantly, but to only change the actual limit when the recalculated limit differs from the current limit by a certain percentage (say, 10%). This ensures that all material changes in the underlying elements on which the limits are based are actually reflected in the limits without resulting in constant changes and updates.

Summary

The process of limit setting is one of the most important risk management techniques, assisting, as it does, in the process of managing economic capital, diversifying exposure and helping maintain tight management control. We have all heard stories of the catastrophic consequences of not having an effective system of limits in place. These can range from unknown exposure to a particular counterparty party to over-exposure to a particular type of risk. If we fail to limit exposures and things turn against us then naturally large losses will ensue.

The question then arises as to what constitutes an effective limit system. We would contend that the most important element of any limit is to link it to the level of exposure with which the institution is comfortable. This can only happen if we realize that our risk profile should be a function of the size of the bank, and therefore a function of the capital base of the bank.

How we calculate the capital to use as a gauge of setting limits is a very important process, which can yield additional benefits such as:

- Assisting in the budgeting process
- Adding value to an activity-based costing system
- Ensuring that we assess returns on risk from each desk
- Providing a way to acknowledge and quantify the value that a desk may add to the business through a diversification benefit

The capital figure that is calculated should take account of costs incurred, returns on risk, diversification of a portfolio and naturally the capital of the bank. This 'capital' constraint should also be tempered by any additional constraints arising from regulatory bodies.

The next essential element of an effective limit system is to ensure that it is as granular as possible. This means setting limits at a trader level if possible. The granularity element should also assist in making the limits flexible. If we see that a particular type of risk is under-utilized in one area we can transfer any excess limit to another area. This becomes easier as limits become more granular.

The types of limits to which we can apply these concepts of capital related and granularity include risk related limits such as VaR limits and concentration limits such as counterparty and country limits. All these limits should be directly related to the capital base of the bank and change when the capital base changes. The process of changing limits brings us to the next important part of any effective limits system, and that is limit monitoring.

When monitoring limits we have to look not just at whether there has been a breach, but also at the level of limit usage over a period of time. It is important to know whether there are unused limits so that they can be transferred to areas of the business that could use them to generate revenue. We can also learn a lot of information about businesses by looking at their limit utilization over a period of time. Any change in this can alert us to changing risk profiles in a desk. The level of limits is also something that needs to be monitored. If the capital base changes then limits should be adjusted accordingly. This also applies to any other quantity of which the limits are a function. This process should be done in such a way that limits are not constantly changing, but yet reflect the economic position of the bank.

We hope to have demonstrated a practical method for linking limits to the capital base of the bank. Unfortunately to go into the minutiae of calculating these limits is not practical in the context of this book, but a broad understanding of the various methods is an ideal springboard to implement a comprehensive limit system tailored to the needs of each institution. If one bears in mind the concepts of always linking limits to capital and ensuring flexibility and adequate monitoring then the resultant limits are bound to go a long way to meeting the objectives of management capital and diversifying exposure.

Note

[1] VaR is a widely used statistical method for estimating the risk that is generated by a portfolio or single asset. It is based on the idea that movement in factors that affect the valuation of an asset can be predicted within a certain confidence level. VaR calculates the possible loss (or risk exposure) by assessing the maximum adverse move (within a certain confidence level) in the underlying factors that affect price (e.g. interest rates, credit spreads). VaR takes into account correlation effects and is more fully explained in other chapters in this book.

23

A framework for attributing economic capital and enhancing shareholder value

MICHAEL HAUBENSTOCK and FRANK MORISANO

Introduction

Financial institutions engage in diverse activities with varying risk characteristics. These different types of risk arise out of transactions or business decisions for which there is uncertainty concerning a possible outcome. Because each transaction includes some level of uncertainty, virtually every transaction contributes to the overall level of risk the financial institution faces. Some examples of the uncertainties financial institutions encounter are:

- Will a counterparty to a loan be able to repay it according to the terms and conditions?
- How will interest rates fluctuate in the near future?
- How strong will demand be for a new product next year?

All uncertainties eventually lead to fluctuations in a financial institution's profitability. For this reason, it is important to identify the different types of risk as precisely as possible, quantify those risks, and understand how they affect profitability. With a more accurate understanding of the risk–return relationship, management can measure the profitability of its capital investments.

The amount of capital that a financial institution holds should be directly proportional to the risks it faces on a regular basis. Theoretically, a financial institution that takes no risk, and has completely certain streams of revenue and expense, would have no need for capital. Conversely, a financial institution that experiences significant fluctuations in its revenues, expenses, or losses would need significant levels of capital.

In recent years, financial institutions have begun to use risk-adjusted capital methodologies to manage their capital investments. This chapter focuses on risk-adjusted methodologies for computing capital requirements and describing a uniform methodology for computing *economic capital* (capital-at-risk.) The authors explain how this measurement technique provides the following advantages over a regulatory or book capital framework:

- Profitability can represent the true economics and risks incurred
- Improved decision making for capital allocation and strategic planning
- A clear link between business performance and shareholder value creation and
- Consistent information on pricing.

They also present examples showing how the application of this dynamic measurement technique – even on a rudimentary basis – can increase shareholder value in financial institutions.

Capital-at-risk or economic capital

For more than two decades, financial institutions have been developing return on common equity (ROE) and risk-adjusted profitability measurement (RAPM[1]) methodologies. Return on common equity, the simplest form of profitability measurement, is calculated by dividing net income by common equity. This is an accounting measure that – unlike risk-adjusted profitability measurement – fails to include risk. Risk-adjusted profitability measurement, on the other hand, includes risk in its generic model: Return (Revenues – Costs – Expected losses) divided by capital-at-risk.

With the promulgation of the Basel Accord in 1988,[2] the passage of FDICIA (Federal Deposit Insurance Corporation Improvement Act) of 1991, and the OCC (Office of the Comptroller of the Currency) Staff Study on Capital Allocation in 1996 (Marvin, 1996), risk-adjusted profitability measurement methodologies have gained general acceptance as reliable, indeed optimal, tools for attributing capital and measuring performance for subsidiaries, lines of business, products, and/or projects.

Risk-adjusted profitability measurement methodologies have their intellectual roots in the Nobel prize-winning work of Harry Markowitz (1959) and William Sharpe (1970). The basic concept of risk-adjusted profitability measurement is that, to justify the taking of risks, there should be a return or profit in excess of the cost of funding the investment. The purpose of risk-adjusted profitability measurement is to provide financial institution management with a more reliable way of selecting the best investments.

The *economic capital* a financial institution requires is different from both the book capital and the regulatory capital (capital required by regulators.) Book capital can easily be observed from the balance sheet. It is computed by subtracting liabilities from the financial institution's assets and is an accounting measure of how much capital a financial institution has, rather than how much it should have. In calculating regulatory capital, regulators limit the maximum level of a financial institution's 'risk assets' and off-balance sheet commitments to a fixed multiple of its capital. Although regulatory capital attempts to provide an ideal measure of capital requirements, it is hampered by simplicity.

We are suggesting that capital-at-risk be expressed as economic capital. *Economic capital is defined as the aggregate amount of equity capital that is required as a cushion for a company's unexpected losses due to all its credit, market, and operational risks.* The losses that are expected to occur are a normal cost of doing business and are usually priced into the products and services. When economic capital is calculated and attributed correctly, it is an ideal measure of the capital level that is required, given the risks inherent in the activities of a financial institution.

Economic capital is calculated by defining and measuring all risks as precisely as possible on a component and on an aggregated basis. An institution determines what level of equity capital is necessary to guard against its risks on the basis of a desired level of confidence or comfort. (The *level of confidence* is a statistical term that describes the proportion of all possible future outcomes that will be within the specified volatility range.) The more capital a firm has, the higher the level of confidence and the safer it will be. A firm wishing to be perceived by rating agencies, industry analysts, and regulators as extremely secure, therefore, needs an especially large amount of capital in proportion to the risk it undertakes.

Calculating economic capital supports a better understanding of how much value a business unit creates. The Office of the Comptroller of the Currency advocates using economic capital allocation processes that can 'provide bank managers and directors with valuable information for decision making and strategic planning' (Marvin, 1996). In its 1996 study of the capital allocation practices at ten large US banks, the Office of the Comptroller of the Currency found that while the specific objectives and methodologies were vastly different among these leading institutions, there were several common themes:

- Capital allocation is part of a disciplined management process (i.e. it is wholly integrated into management processes such as strategic planning, risk governance and/or management, budgeting, and performance measurement)
- The focus is on the maximization of shareholder value
- There is consistency between the capital allocation systems and the banks' corporate risk governance frameworks
- Capital allocation is comprehensive (i.e. it includes all risks and activities)
- Both quantitative and qualitative analyses are applied
- Capital allocation is well understood throughout the institutions and is effectively controlled and communicated and
- The banks believe that even if it is less than perfect, capital allocation is a credible tool for decision making.

A methodology for computing economic capital

Within financial institutions, any attempt to measure absolute return (revenue less the cost of funding) on a transaction without considering risk would be incomplete. To have a meaningful comparative measure of return, financial institutions must measure that return in relation to the value that was exposed to risk. Thus, the concept of return on risk is fundamental.

This section outlines the elements of an economic capital framework – describing the common risks that financial institutions measure and the basics for quantifying those risks in terms of economic capital.

Common risks

To assess economic capital for performance measurement purposes, it is necessary to distinguish the risks that are associated with each financial transaction, product, or customer relationship in question. These are the risks on which a financial institution earns the majority of its revenue. Developing an economic capital methodology involves identifying all risks by qualitative research through a series of detailed interviews with both business line management and support personnel such as legal, human resources, and internal audit. The common risks for a financial institution are generally classified as three major categories: market risk, credit risk, or operational risk.

Market risk

Market risk is the potential earnings loss due to adverse movements in market prices or rates, as well as changes in such financial market conditions as interest rates, currency trading, equity and options markets, and commodity trading. For financial institutions, balance sheet risk can be viewed as a special type of market risk, since interest rate risk affects the earnings volatility of the total balance sheet by virtue of the movements in interest rates that arise out of the mismatch between assets and liabilities. In addition, a financial institution can consider funding liquidity risk as the assurance that there are funds available to meet financial obligations.

Credit risk

Credit risk is the risk that financial loss will result from the failure of a counterparty to a financial transaction to perform according to the terms and conditions of a contract. Credit risk has two major components: the risk of loss in asset values due to changes in the credit quality of a counterparty; and the severity of the loss, which varies with the distinctive characteristics of a specific product or transaction. The risk of default or deterioration in a counterparty's credit quality encompasses several more specific risk types, such as borrower risk; issuer risk; trading counterparty risk; concentration of the risk by customer, industry, or geographic region; underwriting risk; and settlement risk. The second component of credit risk – severity – is relevant only in the event of default. When default occurs, several factors, including seniority, guarantees, collateral, and replacement value determine the magnitude of the loss.

Operational risks

Operational risks are the deviation from an expected or planned level of loss due to risks that cannot be defined as credit risk or market risk. They can be split into two categories – business risk and event risks.

- *Business risk* is the risk arising from changes in business conditions (including product obsolescence, product substitution, and price competition) and competitor and/or management actions (including changes in the financial institutions reputation.) Business risk also encompasses strategic failures, such as the loss of key personnel and business closures.
- *Event risks* includes surprises to earnings due to human activities (malicious errors as well as errors in judgement), process problems, business interruption, technology failures, or external events (losses due to natural and unnatural disasters affecting physical plant, property, and computer equipment.) Also included as event risks are compliance, taxation, regulatory, and political changes.

Fundamentals of an economic capital framework

After all risks are classified, the next step is to quantify the economic capital required for the common risks as part of a framework. In an economic capital framework, consistency of approach is very important in the computation of economic capital. The measurement of all risks should be treated in the same way throughout the institution.[3] The foundation for developing all economic capital frameworks consists of estimates of the following:

- The confidence interval for the institution
- The specific time horizon for measuring risks and returns
- The exposure for the common risks (market, credit, and operational risks) and
- The hurdle rate.

Together, these fundamentals of an economic capital framework make it possible to measure the risk/return relationship.

Confidence interval

The underpinning for all economic capital methodologies begin with estimates of the financial institution's risk tolerance or probability of default. This is achieved by determining the economic capital that is required to ensure that the probability that unexpected losses could exhaust the economic capital is less than some target risk-coverage level. Of course, there is no particular level of confidence that is the best (for example, 97.5%, 99%, or 99.9%.) However, within a given level of confidence, the more capital a firm holds, the safer it will be – the higher its debt rating and the lower its probability of insolvency.

In an economic capital model, a charge is usually included in the income statement for expected losses and capital to cover unexpected earnings fluctuations. The sum of the cumulative expected losses and capital should be sufficient to cover losses to a desired confidence level (see Figure 23.1). It is worth noting that throughout the year, financial institutions usually build up a cushion of earnings that can become a cushion (the 'first loss' position) for unexpected losses. The amount of this cushion will depend upon the institution's dividend structure and procedures for adding to retained earnings throughout the year.

The senior management should choose the level of confidence for the financial

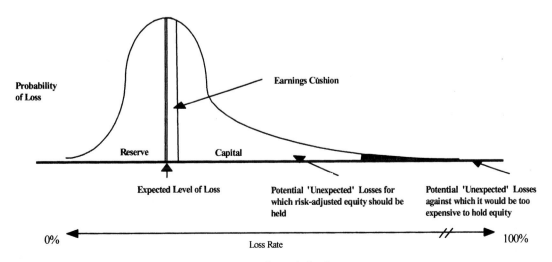

Figure 23.1 Cumulative losses.

institution. Consider the example of a financial institution that wishes to be seen by analysts and bond rating agencies as an A-rated company. The risk and default rates would be assessed by performing an analysis of publicly traded debt over a specific time horizon.[4] For example, the outcome of the analysis might indicate to the financial institution that a 99.9% coverage level for all risks would assist them in achieving the A rating. By providing capital coverage for all but one out of 1000 unexpected events, the institution is holding significantly more capital than an institution that holds only 99% (capital coverage for all but 1 out of 100 unexpected events.) Capitalization at the 99.9% level limits the possibility of default and bankruptcy to only extreme unexpected losses.

Table 23.1 is based on peer analysis of financial institution and their bond ratings. It depicts the appropriate level of confidence senior management can choose based on the desired debt rating.

Table 23.1 Target rating confidence levels

Debt rating	Confidence level	Rate of occurrence
AAA	99.98	1 out of 5000
AA	99.95	1 out of 2000
A	99.90	1 out of 1000
BBB	99.75	1 out of 400

The financial institution's economic capital will be calculated based upon the chosen level of confidence. Once it is selected, the institution's level of confidence should be used consistently for all the common risks (market, credit and operational.) In calculating the desired level of confidence, the percentile or fractal level should be used rather than a standard deviation multiplier.[5] (This is because the underlying statistical distribution may be different from the normal distribution.)

Time horizon

The key to developing a functioning and reliable economic capital model to measure performance, profitability, or pricing is the correct matching of revenues, costs, and risks within a defined time horizon. Since no amount of capital would be sufficient to absorb unexpected losses forever, financial institution management must establish a time horizon to facilitate the attribution of capital. There are numerous issues to be addressed in choosing a time horizon to measure revenue, costs, and risks.

First, there is the need for financial institution management to decide whether a year or other period should be used to measure revenue for businesses, products, and / or traders. For performance measurement, an annual period is most common, less for mid-year reporting. For pricing purposes, one would typically use the term of the transaction or some shorter liquidation period for trading transactions. For instance, actual maturities can be an alternative to annual periods.

Second, there is the need to match overhead costs to revenues. Financial institutions typically employ transfer-pricing mechanisms to match the cost of funding with overhead and revenue. However, in most processes, the overhead costs are attributable for the present time period and not for future time periods. Thus, the matching of revenues and overhead costs for the duration of a transaction needs to be estimated.

Third, there is the need to select a consistent, relevant accounting basis for asset valuation. Many financial institutions still use historical costs as their accounting basis, and historical costs can be inaccurate for trading instruments. Mark-to-market accounting is typically used only for trading businesses and provides a more relevant measure of an asset's value. In some instances, financial institutions mix and match mark-to-market valuation of the assets with accrual accounting for the liability funding of those assets.

Finally, there is the need to select the appropriate time horizon for measuring the common risks undertaken by the financial institution. While there is no one best practice or accepted financial theory, the common alternatives are:

- *Time-to-close* – The time-to-close a risk position is defined as the number of days it would take to eliminate an exposure by selling it in an illiquid market or fully hedging it – plus a time horizon to take into account management's reaction time. For example, this time period may be one day[6] if the position is a very liquid tradable instrument, or the time period may be final maturity for illiquid loan positions that are not readily marketable.

- *One-year (annual) time horizon* – An annual time horizon is linked to the normal revenue measurement period and therefore the term of capital matches the measurement period of risk adjusted returns. An annual time horizon is a realistic time that it would take to recapitalize the financial institution as a result of an unexpected loss, or the time it would take to raise additional equity.

- *Term of transaction* – The term of transaction is the remaining number of days left on a risk position. This is very similar to time-to-close, but it excludes a senior management decision period. For example, a 5-year loan would carry capital for five years' unexpected losses.

- *Regulatory guidelines* – Many economic capital initiatives are developed to overcome the limitations of regulatory guidelines however, in some instances (e.g. market risk[7]), the regulatory rules are an acceptable alternative. Following market risk guidelines eliminates one source of difference between economic and regulatory capital, however, it may result in an inconsistent economic capital framework.

- *Combination* – A combination plan exists when an institution uses different time horizon alternatives for different risks. Another type of combination is calculating capital for a liquidation period (e.g. one month) and then using a lower level of capital to extend the term to one year, recognizing that even after a major loss, the bank will likely continue in business, albeit at a reduced risk level.

Most financial institutions typically select a one-year time horizon and construct their economic capital frameworks to gear revenues, costs, and risks to that common time horizon.

Measuring exposure

To effectively attribute economic capital, it is necessary to have an accurate measure of the financial institution's true exposure. This is the task of exposure measurement. While the balance sheet shows the amount a financial institution has in assets, liabilities, and equity at a point in time, the institution's exposure is another matter.

Credit risk

For credit risk of traded transactions, mark-to-market accounting tries to overcome the limitations of the traditional balance sheet by valuing a position at a point in time. However, mark-to-market exposures do not reflect the potential change in exposure that could occur between now and the time when a default occurs. Techniques to measure potential exposure, netting and portfolio effects make estimates of these changes to get a better picture of credit exposure.

In lending, exposure starts with the outstanding loan amount that is on the balance sheet. However, to properly measure lending exposure, a financial institution should also include accrued interest and unused commitments – since the worst-case assumption is that a borrower draws down the full loan committed amount before going bankrupt. For example, products such as commercial loans, lines of credit, and credit cards, customers will likely use up available lines when they are close to default.

Market risk

In trading businesses, a financial institution exposure is the current open position, measured on a mark-to-market basis. Some firms add a capital charge for unused position limits, but this needs to be done carefully or the charge could induce traders to take excessive risks to recover the charge.

Operational risks

For operational risks, there is no position or exact. For example, what is the maximum exposure due to inefficiencies in the operating environment? Or what is the maximum exposure due to inadequate monitoring and control of operational functions or inadequate or insufficient systems (i.e. software bugs and limitation, technical snafus)? Or what is the maximum exposure due to human error or management failures? Identifying these exposures often requires estimating the potential size of the loss or using a comprehensive history of incurred losses that permits estimation of the 'expected loss' for operational risk management. (See the section on quantifying operational risk capital.)

Hurdle rates

The *hurdle rate* is the rate management has determined as the minimum acceptable return from a business activity. The most common method of calculating risk-based hurdle rates is by using the Capital Asset Pricing Model (CAPM),[8] yet another concept from the pages of financial theory.

The Capital Asset Pricing Model derives the cost of equity as the risk-free rate plus a premium for the risk that a share has beyond that of a risk-free security. The premium (known as the *market premium*) is determined as a proportion of the difference between the market return and the risk-free rate. For a long time the market risk premium $(R_m - R_f)$ was assumed to be approximately between 6% and 8%.[9] However, historically, market risk premiums have been very sensitive to the time period that the institution selects for the analysis. Recently, for example, the general consensus of the analyst community is that this premium has fallen to between 3% and 5%.

The beta factor component in the Capital Asset Pricing Model formula measures the systematic risk (the risk inherent in the stock itself) taken on when an investor buys a share of a company, expressed in terms of how closely a company's performance corresponds to that of the market (see Figure 23.2). Thus, a beta factor of 1.0 indicates that the company's performance should be the same as the market's performance. This measurement is important because, while investors can offset

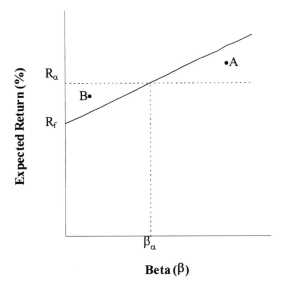

Figure 23.2   Expected return versus beta.

specific risks associated with individual shares by holding diversified portfolios, they remain exposed to the systematic risks associated with the market as a whole, and diversifying cannot mitigate these systematic risks. Just as a company's performance, as a whole, can be related to that of the market, so can the performance of an individual business unit. Usually, individual business units have their own pattern of performance relative to the market, resulting in a beta factor that is unique to the business unit and separate from the company's overall beta. This pattern of performance can be a result of different geographic locations, unique product line offerings, or customer mix.

Product-line betas can be calculated by using regression analysis, in which the company betas become the dependent variable against the percentage of business revenue attributed to each product line (independent variables.) If the product lines in the regression do not exactly match a company's business units, the calculation can be based on a weighted average of the betas for the product lines that best represent each of the company's business units.

Measuring economic capital

Some losses are either so remote or so routinely small they have only minor consequences for the financial institution. At the other extreme of the spectrum lurk risks with sufficient probability and severity to adversely impact the earnings of the financial institution. These are the losses that give rise to managerial concern.

With statistical inference, one can estimate the distribution of future loss probabilities on the basis of historical data. The alternative approaches include volatility and simulation measurement. Volatility captures both upside and downside variations about the average (variance.) Measuring the volatility of an asset requires a financial institution to estimate the magnitude of losses for each common risk the institution faces. The most obvious source of data from which to estimate a future loss is the past loss experience of the financial institution and other institutions engaged in similar activities.

Simulation permits modeling of the behavior of an asset under a restricted set of assumptions. Simulation mimics actual loss experience on the basis of randomly selected estimates of the loss-frequency and loss-severity distributions. Replicating this process many times, each with different random loss numbers, will give a distribution of possible results that can be summarized by their mean (average) and variance.

Non-statistical sources of data include a firm's subjective judgement about how probable a specific event is, and when it occurs, the probable economic consequences of such an event. Other potential sources of data include industry associations, industry surveys, and the sharing of information among firms. The issue of how relevant the information is depends on whether the individual firm is representative of the industry.

Market risk and economic capital

In recent years, financial institutions and their regulators have placed much emphasis on market risk, responding to the growth of global financial markets and the continuous introduction of new and increasingly complex instruments. Financial institutions that are active in trading have established a comprehensive market risk management environment.[10] This comprehensive environment institutionalizes the risk management philosophies and processes in a manner that effectively supports the institutions' stated business objectives and strategies. Such a strong culture of market risk management promotes an institution-wide awareness and understanding of the risks resulting from business transactions. These institutions have also refined their risk measurement methodologies, using leading-edge financial and statistical techniques to quantify risk.

The best measure of market risk is Value-at-Risk[11] (VaR). Value-at-Risk is a statistical estimate of the maximum potential loss in value for a financial transaction or a portfolio of transactions, within a specified level of confidence over a given time horizon for a given loss distribution assumption. It provides a consistent measure of risk across diverse financial instruments and markets.

Essentially, two approaches are used to calculate Value-at-Risk: a parametric and a non-parametric approach. Parametric approaches assume that returns on assets conform to a statistical distribution that is either normal or lognormal. The parametric category includes analytic models such as variance–covariance, delta normal, and RiskMetrics™.[12] Non-parametric approaches do not make statistical assumptions about an expected return on assets. This category includes three approaches: historical, historical simulation, and Monte Carlo simulation.

Quantifying market risk capital.

Value-at-Risk estimates the potential economic loss an institution faces. It answers the question 'How much could be lost in closing down a position or a portfolio, with a given degree of confidence and term?'

VaR is the most common method for calculating market risk capital, and also the method used by the regulators.[13] However, there are adjustments needed to transform Value-at-Risk to economic capital. The first change is to assure the level of confidence is consistent with that chosen for capital (the number used for limits and risk reporting is frequently less). The second is selection of the appropriate time horizon.

As we have noted in an earlier section, there are various alternatives (e.g. one-year, time-to-close) to adjust for time horizon. While liquid positions should carry less capital than illiquid ones, they can have lower volatility and therefore liquidity is to some respect factored in the VaR calculation. Regardless of the time horizon chosen, the VaR calculation needs to be modified.

Other adjustments may be made. For example, in some trading businesses, it is common to take significant intraday positions (and therefore risks) but to bring down the position at the end of the day. Consequently the average risk is not reflected in an end-of-day VaR calculation. An adjustment made by some financial institutions is to calculate VaR based on a portion of the intraday limits, rely on an intraday VaR calculation, or use a behavior model based on earnings volatility instead of positions. Another adjustment that has been gaining popularity is the quantification of intraday volatility using Extreme Value Theory (see Christoffersen *et al.*, 1998), which focuses on forecasting extreme events whether across time or intraday.

Quantifying balance sheet risk capital.

As we have noted, interest rate risk in a financial institution is a special case of market risk. A standard measure of a financial institution's interest rate exposure is interest rate in the gap. This measure addresses the earnings volatility that results from the mismatch between assets and liabilities. Institutions commonly use their Asset Liability Management (ALM) systems as a basis for analysis. In simplest terms, balance sheet risks are interest rate, currency, and liquidity risks that arise when a bank funds its assets with liabilities of different interest rate repricing characteristics, different currencies, and different lengths of maturity.

The economic capital for interest rate risk is estimated from the volatility and the time it takes to close the gap between borrowing and lending rates. Considerable attention has to be paid to the time it takes to close the gap because it tends to be longer than the time horizon used for trading positions. One should consider the following components:

- The size of the gap and the time that is required to close the gap
- The volume of hedging activities that can be completed, particularly in illiquid markets
- An estimate of the worst-case losses that can occur over the time that is needed to close the gap and
- Time to restructure the balance sheet.

The economic capital for interest rate risk represents risk capital for the financial institution, not the interest rate risk for a business line or an individual product. Therefore, the financial institutions senior management must decide whether to pro rata the attributed capital to the business lines or leave it in the Asset Liability organization.

Quantifying liquidity risk capital.

The management of liquidity[14] is always considered important, yet good measurement approaches have evaded the financial industry. Capital is necessary but not sufficient to maintain liquidity.

Given the good credit rating of most financial institutions and the alternate funding sources available to them, quantification of liquidity risk as part of an economic capital process is usually considered a low priority, or an event beyond the confidence level of the capital assumptions. It is common for most financial institutions to ignore it.

Credit risk and economic capital

In measuring credit risk, it is important to understand the underlying default distribution and to test the sensitivity of the underlying models to predicting losses. The distribution of such losses can be used to estimate the probability of future loss. From a theoretical perspective, the simplest probability distribution to explain and justify is the normal distribution (used by Value-at-Risk.) However, in lending portfolios, it is rarely correct to assume that losses will occur according to the normal distribution. To quantify the economic capital for credit risk, it is necessary to calculate its two major constituents: loss frequency (expected and unexpected) and the severity of the loss:

- *Expected loss* is an estimate of the average probability of default. All financial institutions reserve for expected losses, either through specific provisions for potential losses or through statistical provisioning. Statistical provisioning involves performing analyses on the portfolio to determine the statistical mean of the distribution. This statistical mean is otherwise known as *the expected or average loss.*
- *Unexpected loss* is an estimate of the 'worst-case' probability of default over and above *the expected or average loss.* This product- or transaction-specific risk is represented by an estimate of the severity of the possible loss in the event of default – calculated as an estimate of the entire possible loss, net of any recovery of principal and/or interest, expressed as a percentage of the credit exposure.
- *Loss severity* estimates the potential cost of recovery from the loss of an asset. Loss severity depends on the nature of the assets, and provisions that mitigate the loss in event of default, such as guarantees and loan covenants. However, loss severity is also affected by inflation, the legal and workout costs of recovering the assets, and lost opportunity costs due to the unavailability of the cash.

Loss frequency and loss severity may be combined using statistical processes.

Quantifying credit risk capital

Several methodologies can be used to quantify the capital requirements for credit risk (see Figure 23.3). These range from the simple attribution of factors by asset class to the highly sophisticated measurement of the portfolio Value-at-Risk. They take into account the fluctuations of asset values in the market, diversification of assets, and correlation among assets.

Each institution that seeks to quantify credit risk capital must make a decision regarding the level of complexity and precision that is necessary given its current business activities and the availability of data upon which to base the necessary calculations and analyses. For instance, businesses with relatively homogeneous pools of assets, such as credit card businesses and mortgage lending businesses, may choose to develop factors based solely on asset class. Businesses such as commercial lending, which involve credit scoring of transactions and whose products have various tenors, may find that they need to develop capital factors for each rating and/or tenor category. If a portfolio's assets all tend to have similar recovery rates, a standard severity of loss factor may be used. However, if the expected loss tends to

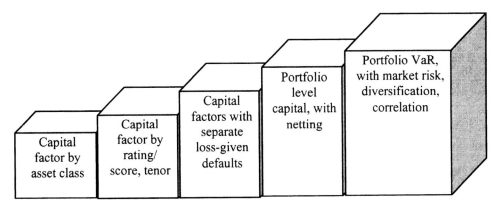

Figure 23.3 Alternative methodologies for quantifying credit.

vary by transaction or by product, the institution may need to develop severity factors as well as a factor for default.

Statistical analysis techniques – such as cohort analysis, migration, and simulation – can be used to derive capital factors by selected asset groupings. Cohort analysis evaluates historical loss experience by building a statistical distribution of the losses. The distribution can then be used to estimate the probability of losses within the portfolio at a specified level of confidence and to appropriately allocate capital to cover these losses. Migration analysis estimates the likelihood of a credit upgrade or downgrade, including default that is based upon historical movements in credit scores. Simulations (e.g. Monte Carlo) may also be performed to estimate a distribution of losses for a specific asset class, risk grading, and / or tenor.

It is important to note that the results of any statistical analysis are highly dependent upon the depth, breadth, and accuracy of the data available. As most institutions do not have sufficient data internally, it may be necessary to supplement the institution's own data with external data sources. However, if external data is used, it is important to perform an analysis regarding the applicability of the data and to make any necessary adjustments to ensure that it is compatible.

For those institutions that deal in highly liquid instruments, it may be worth-while to consider taking the next step, which is using a Value-at-Risk methodology. Value-at-Risk not only takes into account the potential losses resulting from default, but it also recognizes changes in the market value of assets due to changes in credit quality. Credit tools such as CreditMonitor,[15] CreditMetrics[TM][16] and CreditRisk+[TM][17] can be used to calculate credit Value-at-Risk. However, institutions that use these and similar tools should note that they are highly dependent upon data inputs and should ensure that the data that is used is applicable to and compatible with their own business activities.

The methodology or methodologies that are used to calculate credit risk capital requirements are highly dependent upon the institution's data and personnel resources. In addition, each institution needs to choose the methodologies that are appropriate for its lines of business. For instance, it does not make sense for a small middle-market lender that holds all its loans to maturity to use Value-at-Risk. At the same time, a single capital factor for each asset class may too simple for a commercial bank with both investment grade and non-investment grade customers. The types of business activities in which an institution is involved and the types of credit risk that it encounters will determine the proper course of action.

Once economic capital requirements are calculated by transaction or by asset class, the next step is to aggregate the capital requirements at the portfolio level. It is possible to calculate the total credit risk capital that is necessary for the portfolio by simply summing up the capital requirements for each asset in the portfolio. However, the simple sum is not quite accurate. Diversification and correlation can play a major role in calculating required capital and are discussed later.

Operational risks and economic capital

Financial institutions are striving to develop a sound measurement methodology for operational risks. The reasons for measuring operational risk include:

- The need to complement the more established capital methodologies already being used for market and credit risk
- Institutions must minimize operational losses – an organization needs a process that will enable its staff to identify, evaluate, and manage the attendant risks effectively, a process that will promote a culture of risk awareness and
- Knowing how much operational risk exposure a type of business has, permits cost–benefit analyses and enables management to make critical and informed decisions on individual transactions or investment decisions.

The major issue is how to measure operational risk, and many financial institution believe it to be infeasible. Measuring operational risk requires estimating both the probability of an operational loss and the potential size of the loss. This task is formable since most financial institutions simply do not have comprehensive internal loss data that can be analysed and/or modeled.

Quantifying operational risk capital.

There are a number of approaches used for both operational risk management and the capital quantification experts that put operational risk on the same comparable terms as market and credit risk. There are fundamentally two basic approaches to quantify operational risk capital: top-down and bottom-up. The top-down alternatives include earnings volatility analysis, peer or surrogate comparisons, and the determination and allocation of total capital. The most common top-down approach is earnings volatility analysis. Volatility estimates are developed for each business line, based on extensive financial analysis of historical returns. These estimates are converted to capital at the selected time horizon and level of confidence. If feasible, the financial history could be cleaned to eliminate volatility due to market or credit risk. The key assumption in this approach is that the earnings history contains incidents, which reflect the frequency and severity of operational losses. Given the low frequency and potentially high severity of events, this is a big assumption.

The peer or surrogate comparison approach involves assembling a group of financial and non-financial companies to match each of the company's operations. Equity levels are quantified, and all credit and market risks are deducted from the company's overall equity capital to isolate operational risk. For consistency, the level of confidence, and consequently the equity capital, for each peer must be adjusted to match the risk coverage level that the institution has chosen. The economic capital arising from this exercise is then allocated to the appropriate business units. On the basis of these capital factors, the institution can estimate the required equity capital for operational risk.

The determination and allocation method requires a financial institution to decide on the institution's total economic capital requirement, using one of many financial techniques (e.g. CAPM, operational leverage, valuation, or available capital to allocate.) All credit and market risks are deducted from the company's overall equity capital to isolate operational risk (if applicable). The capital arising from this exercise is then applied to the appropriate business units. A common base for allocation is the non-interest expense base.

One advantage of top-down approaches is that they are relatively easy to implement and business line management easily understands them. They also can be designed to induce desired behavioral change by incorporating risk-related factors that business units can control. For example, a common input is audit report ratings or business self-assessment processes. Good ratings can reduce capital by some arbitrary percentage, weak ratings generate a penalty. Another advantage of top-down models is that they do not require comprehensive loss data.

Top-down approaches also have obvious limitations. Their credibility and relevance are open to challenge. For example, capital calculated as a percentage of expenses can misrepresent low-cost, high-risk businesses, as well as the effect of overly aggressive cost-reduction programs. They can also discourage risk-reducing investments such as major systems, which could increase the expense base. In addition, they are not based on the underlying risk exposures or experience of the firm. The lack of a statistical basis, consistent with the methodologies for market and credit risk lead to questions on credibility. Lastly, the top-down nature of these approaches combines all sources of risk into one number. While they could function as a capital measure, they do not reinforce operational risk management as a discipline since there is no analysis by type of risk, nor are they based directly on experience in the firm or other institutions.

The other approaches taken by financial institutions for estimating operational risk are bottom-up measurement methodologies. The primary alternatives include scenario analysis and statistical or actuarial modeling.

Bottom-up scenario analysis uses simulation techniques to model the volatility of operating income and the flexibility of the cost base in light of adverse economic circumstances. The scenario analysis identifies and stresses to the limit the major business drivers of financial performance for each business activity. Probabilities are placed on how those drivers affect the operating profits for a large number of alternate scenarios. The operational risk capital for each activity driver is then calculated based on the volatility of operating profit and losses for a prescribed level of comfort.

Another bottom-up approach for measuring operational risk is to use actuarial science or statistical modeling. By gathering data on individual loss events, it is possible to build frequency and severity distributions for homogeneous types of risk. Monte Carlo simulation can then be used to calculate figures for risk capital at a statistical level of confidence.

To gain the maximum benefit from an actuarially based methodology, it is critically important that the processes that support the model provide value to line management in their own right. For example, the risk indicators that are used to reflect the state of current controls should be designed so that they form a robust, value-adding process that line management can use in their day-to-day activities. Second, it is necessary to collect relevant loss data in order to develop distributions for modeling.

The actuarial approach is appealing, though, because large and unexpected event losses are by definition low-frequency, high-severity events – precisely the type being measured by such an approach. Through scaling techniques, this approach is also more responsive to changes in the control environment, and it can lead institutions to be proactive in changing their insurance coverage.

The advantage of bottom-up approaches is that they are viewed as theoretically valid. They also:

- Provide detailed information that allows management to see their exposure to different types of risk (business and event risk) – not just a single overall figure
- Permit management to assess the magnitude of individual risk factors such as human activities, processes, and technology
- Support the development of an operational risk management program and
- Provide a transparent way to motivate staff to improve their management of operational risks.

Total economic capital

The aggregation of the various risks and the attributed economic capital is a major methodological issue. Economic capital requirements are usually computed separately for each type of risk (market, credit, and operational.) However, taking a consistent approach to confidence interval, time horizon, and exposure measurement simplifies the methodological issues. The question then becomes whether the individual capital allocations for each risk are simply aggregated[18] to arrive at a combined total economic capital, or whether the correlation[19] between market, credit, and operational risk should be included to arrive at the financial institution's total economic capital.

Not considering diversification in the determination of a financial institution's total economic capital would significantly overstate capital requirements. However, correlation across risk type is extremely difficult to measure. We (the authors) prefer to look at both alternatives and understand the impact of economic capital with and without the effect of correlation. We then assist the senior management of the financial institution in understanding the ramifications[20] and difficulties of each approach so they can arrive at a solution that fits their risk appetite.

Recently, the US Federal Reserve System Task Force conducted a review of the credit risk modeling and capital allocation processes of the major US banks (see Jones and Mingo, 1998). One of the findings was that the major US banks tended to estimate market, credit, and operational risk independently of each other. They calculated total economic capital by adding together the allocation for each type of risk. The banks were all aware that this piecemeal approach was not consistent with their underlying portfolio framework. However, given the difficulties in correctly estimating the complex interrelationships between risk types, the banks viewed the aggregation approach as a practical necessity.

The following illustrative tables demonstrate the difference in a financial institutions economic capital calculation. Both depict the difference in a financial institution's total capital level using a simple aggregation approach and an approach assuming correlation between market and credit risk within the financial institution. Table 23.2 depicts the difference by risk and Table 23.3 by major business line.

The simple aggregation of market, credit and operational risks that results in 1217.6 in Table 23.2 assumes perfect positive correlation. However, the total economic

Table 23.2 Total capital by risk

	Simple aggregation	Correlation
Credit	654.7	562.0
Market	120.8	103.7
Operational	442.1	442.1
Total economic capital	1217.6	1107.8

Table 23.3 Total capital by business activity

	Simple aggregation	Correlation
Wholesale banking	534.2	498.1
Retail	445.8	388.9
Asset management	237.6	220.8
Total firm	1217.6	1107.8

capital is actually less than the sum of the risks because there is some correlation or independence between the risks. Armed with the correlation factor between risks we can adjust the risks and arrive at new diversified total economic capital requirements of 1107.8. Note that the diversification credit of 109.8 has been spread among the risks.

Diversification also impacts the capital requirements of business activities in a financial institution. Table 23.3 highlights three major business activities. The simple aggregation approach assumes perfect positive correlation and results in a total economic capital requirement of 1217.6. However, most financial institutions go further and calculate the economic capital requirements on a fully diversified basis. This is a very important adjustment. Should a financial institution fail to take into account diversification the institution could end up attributing too much capital to a business unit and subsequently make it look unattractive from a performance perspective. As in Table 23.2, armed with calculating the correlation factor between business activities will permit us to weight the capital requirements by business unit and also the total firms capital requirement.

Some organizations look at a business both ways: first, based on the risks incurred without the diversification benefits of a larger company (this is most applicable for individual manager performance) and second, with correlation (this is applicable to more senior levels of management and overall strategic and capital planning).

Other capital concerns

Insurance risk

In some financial institutions, economic capital methodologies have to consider a specialized form of risk other than those already mentioned – insurance risk. This risk can be defined as the uncertainty arising from the frequency or magnitude of claims, and the uncertainty arising from the lapsing of in-force contracts or policies.

Insurance risk can also encompass unexpected long-term changes in mortality and morbidity levels that deviate from actuarial forecasts.

For unit-linked protection products (such as term insurance) any shift in the expected mortality or morbidity risks can be passed on to the policyholder in higher premium rates, which, in turn, affect the lapse rate. If there were any embedded value assets within the unit-linked product, additional modeling would be needed. The impact of a higher lapse rate on the embedded value asset would then need to be calculated, together with the one-year risk of a change in the mortality and morbidity rates.

In the case of annuity products, the risk arises from *improvement* in the mortality rates. If the improvement occurs, an estimate of the overall shift in the mortality rate will need to be modelled and its impact on the embedded value asset will then need to be calculated.

For general insurance products such as household, accident, health, and automobile insurance the unexpected risk is of catastrophic events that lead to large claims. The average, statistically expected claims ratio is known as the *expected claims*, and the volatility around the expected claims as the *unexpected claims*. Expected claims are a cost of doing business and would have been priced into the products. The risk associated with unexpected claims must be modeled and its impact calculated in terms of a reduction in profits from the financial institution's expected levels.

Portfolio theory

The essence of portfolio theory is the caution against purchasing a single asset with all our capital. The portfolio approach is quite different from a transaction-based approach. Diversification helps a financial institution minimize the probability of extreme outcomes. It also makes the risks of a portfolio significantly lower than the sum of the risks in the individual transactions.

Correlation is the basic parameter that determines the risk diversification of a portfolio of transactions, and it can play a major role in the calculation of economic capital. For instance, the addition of a new credit transaction may actually reduce the total credit capital required for the loan portfolio if it is negatively correlated with the rest of the portfolio's assets. At the same time, a transaction with positive correlation to the portfolio may add more capital to the portfolio than its individual capital requirement may initially indicate. In addition, the behavior of a trading portfolio depends not only on the individual volatility of the component positions but also on their covariance or correlation to one another. Negative covariance can also have a very dramatic effect by reducing portfolio risk, even if each of the individual positions exhibits a high level of risk. Hedging transactions are classic examples of negative covariance.

In an economic capital methodology, diversification can help reduce capital requirements. However, the constantly changing interaction between the various risks must be constantly remeasured and revalidated. Diversification requires that financial institutions understand the distinctions between transaction risks and portfolio risks. They must also understand the assumptions that are being made to estimate the probability of loss and the severity distributions for each potential loss. They must have a detailed knowledge of statistical methods to deal with the changing interaction between the various risks.

Regulatory capital considerations

The application of an economic capital methodology cannot ignore regulatory capital requirements. From a management standpoint it is important to know which business line is using up both economic and regulatory capital.

When economic capital is calculated and attributed to a business line, business lines that have regulatory capital requirements will be either higher or lower than the regulatory capital requirement. Additionally, the resulting total economic capital for the financial institution will be either higher or lower than the regulatory capital requirement.

At the total financial institution level, regulatory capital is a constraint and must be managed. In situations where attributed economic capital is more that regulatory capital requirement, no further action is required. Where capital is constrained, the financial institution may seek to reduce capital activities of a high user of regulatory capital, even though it may be economically profitable. In no circumstances should regulatory capital constraints be dealt with by increasing the attribution of economic capital to a business line.

The ideal situation for a financial institution is to rely on the economic capital results, but monitor the regulatory and book capital for inconsistencies and to address specific issues that may arise.

Applications of an economic capital framework

An economic capital framework enables a company to understand its business better and to manage its exposures proactively. It transforms the risk management process from *risk measurement* to *risk optimization*, with risk being managed to increase shareholder value and gain a competitive advantage. The key benefit of an economic capital framework is that it allows management to evaluate the performance of activities with widely differing risk/return profiles on a consistent and comparative basis. In this section, we will show how an economic capital framework facilitates the following activities:

- Risk-based pricing
- Refining the institution's credit processes and
- Controlling the institution's risk appetite.

Risk-based pricing

Traditionally, pricing of financial products is based on the cost of an individual transaction. The profitability of each transaction is calculated as the yield less costs and provisions for credit risk. A risk-adjusted economic capital-based process enables financial institutions to develop models that arrive at more strategic pricing of loan transactions. The target profitability is defined as a hurdle rate on economic capital. An economic capital-based pricing approach considers only those transactions that provide a higher return on capital than the hurdle rate.

Needless to say, risk-based pricing cannot be the only criterion. Transaction pricing should also consider such internal factors as strategic growth initiatives, relationship considerations, and synergy with other products, as well as external factors such as market penetration and competition. The market often overprices risk to top-quality borrowers and underprices weak borrowers (see Figure 23.4), yet it is difficult to charge significantly more than the accepted market price.

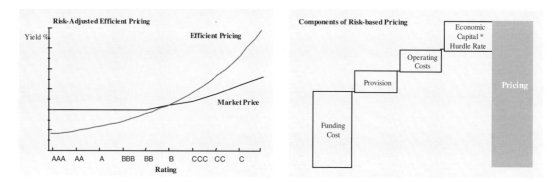

Figure 23.4 Risk-adjusted pricing.

The primary reason for this difference is regulatory capital. With the same regulatory capital requirements on high- and low-quality credits, banks charge the top credits more than a pure economic analysis would indicate to compensate for the capital tied up. At the lower end of the scale, some lenders always seem willing to lend to weak borrowers that push down market prices.

Since risk-based pricing includes a more complete view of the of the risks, a pricing model based on economic capital would differ from a market price as it is based upon a more rigorous approach. With a better understanding of risk, management can perceive the difference between the two prices, and make pricing decisions that maximize profitability and minimize risk. Such a financial institution could identify transactions in which risk is overpriced and seize opportunities to beat the competition. Conversely, knowledge that the market is underpricing risks can warn the institution about areas to avoid.

Consider the application of an economic capital approach to pricing strategies in the credit card business unit of a Latin American. This bank developed an enterprise-wide economic capital allocation methodology.

The credit card business had enjoyed double-digit growth for the past three years. The bank serviced three of the major international credit card brand names. The pricing policy that existed before the economic capital initiative did not discriminate by credit card type. When an economic capital study was performed using historical loan losses by card type, the bank realized that the riskiness differed for the various types of cards. As one might expect, the gold credit card users were, on average, less risky than those using the classic credit card. Some other differences were also observed across brand names (see Figure 23.5). These discrepancies gave rise to opportunities for discriminatory marketing strategy that ultimately could create greater shareholder value. For those cards that had larger returns than the bank's required hurdle rate, further investment in marketing was made to gain market share. Conversely, rate increases were applied to those cards that did not generate returns exceeding the hurdle rate.

The bank is now planning to implement a credit scoring process that will better reflect the riskiness of each individual credit card holder, allowing further refinement of its pricing across defined segments of its customer base.

With the emergence of new techniques that capture the effects of diversification in

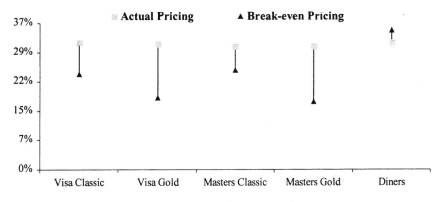

Figure 23.5   Pricing by product.

a portfolio, transactions can be examined in a portfolio context as well as individually. Such an approach provides a marginal transaction price that reflects levels of concentration and diversification in the existing portfolio. While a transaction may not look attractive to a financial institution on a stand-alone basis, the pricing may be acceptable given the correlation and diversification benefits it gives to the portfolio as a whole. With an economic capital-based pricing approach, hurdles can be targeted by transaction or by portfolio. While a transaction may be below the hurdle on a stand-alone basis, it may still be considered because it raises the profitability of the overall portfolio above the hurdle level.

If a transaction lowers the total economic capital required for the portfolio, the pricing would not have to be as high as it would be if the transaction were considered by itself or if it increased the total capital requirement for the institution. Thus, if we assume that the same capital requirements are used across institutions, a particular transaction's pricing may be more attractive to one institution than it is to another because of the different contents of their portfolios.

Refining credit processes

The economic capital process is an iterative process in which the capital calculations can be used to refine the institution's credit processes. By continuously refining such credit processes as provisioning, risk grading, and portfolio management, an institution can enhance the value it provides to its shareholders.

Provisioning

Financial institutions tend to set aside a reserve for credit losses, and it is this provision for losses which risk-adjusts income to arrive at risk adjusted returns. In comparison to traditional reserve provisioning based on portfolio characteristics with specific provisions for problem credits, a provisioning methodology based on individual loan ratings tied to expected loss levels provides a truer economic picture of a portfolio.

Financial institutions tend to reserve for credit losses using one of two provisioning methods and some apply specific provisions for potential losses. When financial institutions apply this approach, all extensions of credit are reviewed regularly and provisions are determined on a loan-by-loan basis in light of the credit characteristics of the borrower and the facility at the time of the review. Other financial institutions use statistical provisioning methods to determine the potential loss of a transaction or group of transactions on the basis of a historical average over a specific period of time.

Some financial institutions tend to reserve in excess of the level needed to cover expected losses. However, excessively conservative reserve measurements may be detrimental to the profitability of the firm and can create inconsistencies in comparisons across business lines or products. Economic capital methods – particularly when they are used in calculating expected losses – can provide institutions with a more accurate assessment of their capital and reserve requirements.

Risk grading

Risk grading is a prime example of a process that can be continuously improved using the results of the economic capital process. When developing capital requirements for credit risk, statistical analysis is highly dependent upon the risk grade or credit score. These risk grades are, in essence, a grouping of assets based upon an institution's opinion of the probability of loss. Some banks actually have an explicit link between their risk grades and expected loss ranges. Public rating agencies such as Moody's and Standard & Poor periodically publish default probabilities for each of their rating grades.

At the beginning of an economic capital process, most institutions can make an educated guess regarding the connection between their internal rating grades and estimates of default and loss. These guesses are based upon financial ratios, qualitative information, and data from public rating agencies. However, as the economic capital process continues, and as historical data is accumulated and credit changes are tracked, the institutions have a quantitative way of evaluating their ratings systems. For instance, outliers can be identified for upgrades or downgrades, changes can be made to the rating systems to adjust for conservatism or leniency, and additional rating grades may be added if necessary.

A more accurate risk grading system will, in turn, generate more accurate capital factors. In addition, an institution that has an economic capital-based approach will be better equipped to track its adherence to corporate risk tolerance policies and to report its risk position more accurately to shareholders and rating agencies.

Portfolio management

An economic capital process is an important tool for the effective management of credit portfolios. With such a process, the portfolio manager can better understand the risk composition and profitability of the portfolio – which segments of the portfolio enhance shareholder value and which ones destroy it. This information allows the portfolio manager to allocate resources to the appropriate areas and to set portfolio strategies. In addition to assisting in the transaction approval process by identifying the new transactions that would be beneficial to the portfolio, economic capital processes can identify exposures the institution needs to exit through sales, credit derivatives, securitization, or runoff. Thus, economic capital processes can help financial institutions make well-informed decisions in order to optimize their portfolios. By instituting a process that calculates portfolio-level capital requirements, an institution can identify the effects of any additional credit exposure upon the total capital requirements and the total risk position of the portfolio.

Controlling the risk appetite of the institution

Since by definition, risk appetite should be limited to the amount of capital a company can put aside to support a given business, economic capital plays a critical role in the process of setting the risk tolerance of the institution. Economic capital methodologies allow financial institutions to define their limit structure; manage their balance sheet exposures through sales, credit derivatives, securitization, or runoff; and control event risks.

Limit setting

The goal in setting limits should be to gain the maximum potential benefit from the risk capacity. Value-at-Risk limits, stop loss limits, credit exposure limits, and stress testing limits should all be aligned to ensure that existing risk exposures do not generate losses that exceed the economic capital allocation. Moreover, in order to optimize returns on economic capital, the limit structure should be dynamic enough to allow for periodic rebalancing to reflect changes in business strategy, budget variances, market volatility, regulatory rules, organization, or systems.

At many institutions, limits tend to be based upon intuition and qualitative rather than objective factors. By instituting a process to calculate economic capital, a financial institution can identify the effects of an additional exposure to the total capital requirements and total risk position of the portfolio. As an alternative to (or in addition to) the traditional 'hard limits' by customer, industry, rating or geographic region, institutions can take advantage of the economic capital process to implement 'soft limits' that are more flexible and more responsive to the current composition and actual risk of the portfolio.

In addition to understanding economic capital constraints, when setting and approving limits, the factors to consider should include business strategy, risk of the asset class, and the real diversification benefits to the organization. Firms that link their economic capital allocation process to their limit-setting process will be able to promote good risk taking and enhance shareholder value.

Securitization

The purpose of securitization is to transform illiquid assets into negotiable securities. Currently, well over $200 billion in assets are securitized, assets that, in times past, would have resided on the books of banks. Asset-backed securities are collateralized by loans and require high agency ratings, generally AA and AAA. Achieving these ratings requires credit enhancements insulating the senior security holders from defaults on the underlying loans. Generally, it is the sponsor that provides these credit enhancements, which can be via standby letters of credit to the conduit or the purchase of the most junior (subordinated) securities issued by the conduit. In return for providing the credit protection, as well as the loan origination and servicing functions, the financial institution lays claim to all residual spreads between the yields on the loans and the interest and non-interest cost of the conduit's securities, net of any loan losses. Thus, while securitization has reduced the cost of funding, financial institutions are taking on almost the same risk as they would have if the loans had been kept on the books of the bank.

Event risk management

The allocation of operational risk capital can be an effective behavior modification tool. With a capital allocation framework, business managers have an additional incentive to incorporate event risk (which is part of operational risk) into their decision-making process and take appropriate action.

Event risk figures, expressed as economic capital, can allow managers to make more informed decisions by quantifying the benefits of new technology systems or insurance programs – benefits that are traditionally expressed in qualitative terms. Economic capital methodologies also allow managers not only to measure the direct financial consequences of different investment alternatives but also to compare them in terms of reducing risk exposure. In the area of insurance, this information can be used to decide whether to buy insurance, how much coverage to purchase, what deductible should be established, and how much to pay for the program.

Applying economic capital methodologies to improve shareholder value

The use of economic capital-based methodologies extends far beyond pricing, credit processing, and risk appetite. These methodologies have assumed a central role in the strategic management processes of financial institutions, becoming tools that can help create shareholder value and competitive advantage in the marketplace.

The accepted theory of managing shareholder value creation (often called *value-based management*) suggests that share price is determined by a combination of growth, return and risk (see Haubenstock and Morisano, 1997). However, the commonly used models for shareholder value analysis and strategic planning typically consider growth and return prospects, including little, if any, systematic consideration of risk. When stock analysts and budgeters use free cash-flow models to simulate shareholder value, the only risk related component is the cost of capital used to discount future cash flows.

Just as shareholder value analysis and strategic planning ignore the element of risk, risk management processes tend to ignore the shareholder value component. Typically, these processes focus only on risk and return (see Figure 23.6). This paradox suggests that, although most people agree that the key drivers of shareholder value are growth, return, and risk, we have to conclude that these elements have not been well integrated into most analytic models or management processes.

Financial institutions need to distinguish between value-creating and value-destroying activities. They can do this only when senior executives recognize the dynamic interplay among growth, risk, and return. Each business unit creates value only when its total shareholder return exceeds the equity invested in the business. A positive spread implies that value is being added and a negative spread implies that value is being destroyed.

An economic capital-based shareholder value model

Shareholder value models require a forecast of the income statement (P&L) and balance sheet, and they include economic capital requirements. Planners and budgeters typically use either the book or regulatory definition for capital. We propose using an economic capital framework for analysing shareholder value.

For example, we can model a shareholder value analysis based on a six-year forecast of a P&L and a balance sheet (see Figure 23.7). The key drivers of shareholder value include assets and the major portions of the income statement. These are the

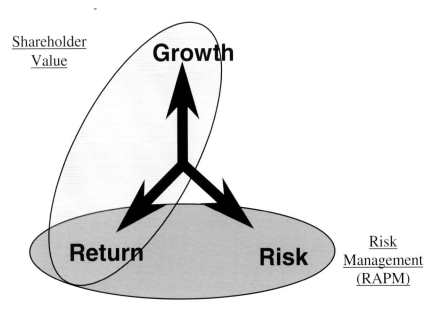

Figure 23.6 Strategic risk-adjusted return on capital.

factors proven to be the most significant in determining changes in value. The P&L and balance sheet are estimated as accurately as possible for a planning horizon of six years. The model includes a fade period that represents forecasts of earnings beyond the planning horizon at the cost of equity. (This period is needed for purposes of the model, since stock prices are based, not just upon current and future earnings, but upon the theoretical assumption that the financial institution will survive in perpetuity.)

In our proposed model, the row labelled 'Incremental capital' is an explicit forecast of risk-adjusted or economic capital. The model estimates free cash flow available as a dividend to shareholders. If a strategy includes moving up or down in average credit quality or changing market risk limits, the model can quantify the risk impact in terms of economic capital. If the company takes additional risks, it will need more economic capital, using up cash that then will not be available for distribution. Similarly, a decrease in economic capital frees up cash. The firm value represents the discounted value of the free cash flow in each period. The advantage of measuring in terms of economic capital is that it gives us a true risk-adjusted model that can be tailored to any risk profile.

Applications and examples

Economic capital-based approaches have been instrumental in creating shareholder value and competitive advantage in numerous instances. Such approaches have allowed financial institutions to make more informed decisions about their risk-taking activities, in such areas as:

- Managing capital resources efficiently to optimize shareholder value
- Managing share price expectations

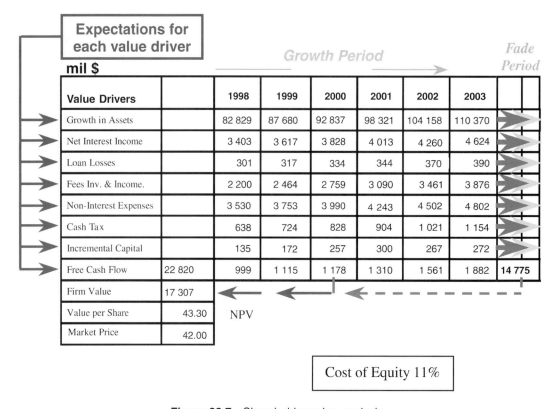

Expectations for each value driver mil $		Growth Period						Fade Period	
Value Drivers		1998	1999	2000	2001	2002	2003		
Growth in Assets		82 829	87 680	92 837	98 321	104 158	110 370		
Net Interest Income		3 403	3 617	3 828	4 013	4 260	4 624		
Loan Losses		301	317	334	344	370	390		
Fees Inv. & Income.		2 200	2 464	2 759	3 090	3 461	3 876		
Non-Interest Expenses		3 530	3 753	3 990	4 243	4 502	4 802		
Cash Tax		638	724	828	904	1 021	1 154		
Incremental Capital		135	172	257	300	267	272		
Free Cash Flow	22 820	999	1 115	1 178	1 310	1 561	1 882	**14 775**	
Firm Value	17 307								
Value per Share	43.30	NPV							
Market Price	42.00								

Cost of Equity 11%

Figure 23.7   Shareholder value analysis.

- Solving transfer pricing problems between countries and
- Linking performance measurement and compensation.

We will outline the benefits of an economic capital-based approach to each of these areas, and illustrate those benefits with case studies.

Managing capital resources to optimize shareholder value

To overcome competitive forces, a financial institution must understand how it uses its capital. Managing an institution's capital to invest assets more strategically is *not* simply an advantage but a business imperative. Proactively managing these activities includes aggressive pruning and asset redeployment on a never-ending basis. Leveraging a financial institution's capital base to build long-term value also requires its management to distinguish between value-creating and value-destroying investments.

Assessing an investment's potential value necessitates that a financial institution's management understands how to measure the profitability of its capital investments. To achieve this end, the financial institution must develop a capital management process encompassing four essential elements: a defined risk culture, organizational goals, a centralized decision-making infrastructure, and a performance measurement system. Those financial institutions that implement a dynamic process for the strategic management of capital – a process that encompasses these four elements – will deliver superior, sustainable returns to their shareholders.

Example

A major US money center bank has an economic capital-based process that serves as the foundation for planning, performance measurement, and capital allocation. The framework was adopted because it was easy to understand and because it could support performance reporting by product, organization, and business unit. Each business activity is assessed to determine whether it earns an adequate return for its level of risk. This review process has become a key decision-making tool for managing risk-taking activities, as well as ensuring that capital has been profitably deployed throughout the bank.

Each year during the planning process, all business units are ranked by their contribution to shareholder value, which is measured as return on equity less the cost of equity. Measuring performance by equity spread makes it relatively easy for the bank to identify units that create or destroy value in the business portfolio and to take appropriate action.

In one particular year, the strategic planning process revealed that a retail-lending business unit would achieve only a 13% return on risk-adjusted capital each year for the next three years. This was below the business unit's cost of equity hurdle rate of 15%, which the bank's senior management had established. Thus, every dollar invested in this business unit was dissipating shareholder value. Senior bank management initiated a review to determine the best course of action.

The review consisted of a comprehensive analysis of the unit's business strategy, risk profile, cost structure, and the opportunities presented in its business plan. Analysis revealed that the unit was lending primarily to high-risk customers. While the credit process was effective, marketplace pricing was very competitive, and the risk-adjusted returns for the unit were marginal. A further analysis of the retail lending unit's business plans indicated that their revenue was showing a growth rate of 6% compared to other areas of the bank, which were growing at a rate of 10% under the same economic conditions. Expenses for the unit were increasing at a rate of 3%, while other areas of the bank were holding expense growth flat. Clearly, the retail-lending unit would not be a major contributor of cash flow for the bank.

A review of the unit's customer list indicated that there were minimal cross-selling opportunities between the unit and other areas of the bank – substantiating the belief that the unit had very little overall strategic value to the bank. Market analysis revealed that competition was strong and a few large players dominated the marketplace. The retail-lending unit's share was just 2%. Scenario analysis indicated that even if the retail-lending unit could reduce costs and expand market share, the risk profile of the customers would not enable the unit to achieve a sustainable contribution to shareholder value over the long-term. There were no apparent product expansion possibilities or other opportunities to improve profitability.

The bank's senior management ultimately concluded that the retail lending unit's contribution could not be improved and that there was no way for the bank to prioritize the unit's long-term value for shareholders. Discussions were initiated regarding the possible divestiture or closing of the unit. Thought was given to the extent to which capital tied up in the unit could be redeployed into profitable businesses or used to buy back the bank's stock.

The bank eventually sold the retail-lending unit to a major competitor at a 150%

premium to book value. A portfolio analysis approach was used to determine how best to reallocate the retail lending unit's capital to other businesses that generated returns in excess of their cost of equity 'hurdle-rate' and to markets that could increase the bank's shareholder value. The additional capital gave two other retail units within the bank an opportunity to increase their market share and overall contribution. And the bank's revenue was improved by 3% from the sale of the unit.

Managing share price expectations

For a publicly traded company, the market's performance expectations and the company's ability to meet or manage those expectations can have a major impact on share price, whether those expectations were fair to begin with. Consequently, it is imperative that a financial institution be able to understand the drivers and assumptions behind stock analysts' projections, as well as the effects of such projections on the company's market value. An economic capital-based shareholder value model allows financial institutions to compare the impact of their own projections and those of investors and analysts on the share price. If the financial institution's current business plan will result in a market value that is above the value projected by external investors, there is no problem. However, if the market value is less aggressive, management may need to revise the business plan or to begin managing external expectations well in advance of reporting deadlines.

An economic capital-based shareholder value model also can be used to test scenarios in which a financial institution alters one or more of the drivers of shareholder value – growth, risk, and return. For instance, a financial institution can see the potential effects on its share price of asset growth strategies, rate or fee increases charged to its customers, or increases or decreases in economic capital due to changing customer profiles. Of course, the actual share price of a company is affected by many different factors, some of which are not covered by any financial shareholder value models – for instance, management change, industry conditions, and rumours. However, the models do give an indication of the general direction of share price movements and can serve as a basis for comparing differing scenarios.

Example

A publicly traded US regional bank has developed economic capital-based shareholder value models that estimate free cash flow for each of its business lines. The model results are aggregated to compute total shareholder value contribution for the entire institution. From industry stock analyst reports, the bank was able to garner information regarding the analysts' assumptions about the bank's profit and growth potential. By inputting this information into its shareholder value model, the bank found that the projected share price of the internal business plan was somewhat lower than the projection of the analysts.

The bank altered its business plan. It changed the targeted customer mix and introduced a cost reduction program. As a result of the planned changes, the bank was able to free up cash flow. Since this change in strategic direction came early enough in the cycle, the bank was able to meet its investors' expectations, thereby preserving its market value and garnering more respect from the analyst community.

Solving transfer pricing problems between countries

As the financial services sector continues to grow globally and financial service firms continue to 'go multinational', governments around the world are examining the implications of transfer pricing to assure that each country receives its fair share of the taxes generated by cross-border transactions. The close international scrutiny of transfer pricing underscores the need for reliable approaches for determining arm's length capital requirements (Morisano and Young, 1998).

Example

A study showed that two related securities firms in different countries are functionally equivalent and engage in many cross-border transactions with each other. (Cross-border affiliates often conduct trading operations that 'pass the book' from one affiliate – and securities market – to another.) This is known as *integrated trading* and is a further manifestation of the globalization of financial services. Integrated trading makes it difficult to account for each affiliate's operating profits. In such situations, the total profit of a given book must be split reasonably between the trading affiliates.

Traditional methods of allocating profits between affiliates have used expenditures or headcount involved in the trading, marketing, middle-office, and back-office functions. A cleaner approach to splitting profits in a globally integrated trading operation may be found in the financial theory that has proven to describe accurately the behavior of financial markets. This theory, known as the random walk hypothesis, assumes that successive returns are independent and that the returns are identically distributed over time.[21]

Applied to a global trading operation, the random walk model suggests that affiliates whose average trading skills are the same should not earn consistently different returns on a continuously traded book within a given year. Therefore, it is reasonable to split the profits of a trading book by assuming that each affiliate performed the same as the overall performance of the affiliates combined. (In other words, it is reasonable to assume that the return on common equity of each affiliate was the same in a given year, and was equal to the overall return on common equity earned by the trading book.)

Given this reasonable assumption, the profit split method can now be implemented using risk-adjusted profitability measurement to attribute capital and profit to an integrated global trading operation. The overall profit of the trading book can be allocated to each trading affiliate in proportion to the capital allocated to that affiliate by risk-adjusted profitability measurement. In this manner, a more refined profit split can be accomplished on the basis of sound financial theory.

Linking performance measurement and compensation

It is often said that people perform in response to the way they are being measured. In a shareholder value-based system, performance measurement includes not only the actual creation of value but also the results of day-to-day operations.

Institutions with mature risk-adjusted profitability measurement processes make an explicit link between risk-adjusted results and compensation. Many institutions have a '*balanced scorecard*' evaluation process in which one of the measures is financial performance. Financial performance is often measured in terms of revenue and risk-adjusted returns. Probably the most effective performance measure is shareholder value added – the dollars of profits in excess of a risk-adjusted return on capital hurdle rate. Linking performance measures to value creation encourages a culture of reward for performance and encourages business managers to manage their activities as if they were their own.

Example

At a major mortgage bank, an economic capital process currently serves as the foundation for performance measurement and incentive compensation. Before the implementation of the economic capital process, the mortgage bank was divided into three major divisions or silos, each headed by a steward. As the mortgage bank is privately held, the managers were unable to leverage stock price performance as a gauge of whether they were creating or destroying value for their owners. A historical review indicated that, on a risk-adjusted return basis, only one of the three units was adding value to the institution. The overall return on risk-adjusted capital was a paltry 10%.

Compensation at the mortgage bank was also based on achieving a profit goal for the year and discouraged any long-term value enhancing behavior. Compensation was also dominated by fixed pay (wages, retirement income, and medical benefits), which accounted for 90% of total compensation, while variable pay (profit sharing) accounted for 10%.

With the implementation of an economic capital process, managers are now assessed on whether they earn an adequate return for the level of risk incurred. Managers are ranked by their contribution to value added – the risk-adjusted return of the business less the cost of capital. A positive spread implies that value is being added and a negative spread implies that value is being destroyed.

A new incentive compensation package emphasizes value creation. Phantom stock was created for the firm, and each of the business units is valued quarterly. The new compensation package has increased the percentage of variable pay, and awards both short- and long-term stock options that are tied to performance.

Within three years of implementing the new risk-adjusted performance measurement process, two of the three divisions were creating value. The third turned out to be the major channel for bringing business into the company. The emphasis in that unit is on automation and cost reduction. The overall return on risk-adjusted capital for the mortgage bank has increased to 14%. This increase was brought about by a combination of business divestitures, acquisitions, and an emphasis on long-term planning.

Toward a value-based management process

Adopting a shareholder value model requires some changes in the financial institution's planning process. Fundamentally, there must be agreement that contribution to shareholder value is an important evaluation criterion, and that the company can benefit from using a shareholder value model to support its strategic planning process.

The very process of making a forecast of economic capital for entire businesses may be new to many institutions. In addition, the model implies a new mix of participants in the planning process. Along with strategic planning and finance, risk management and asset-liability management will probably have more active roles. The business units as well as corporate headquarters need to have access to the model to support their respective roles. Logistically, the sequence and timing of the planning process may require reevaluation to assure that all parties can provide the assumptions and inputs that are needed at the appropriate times.

Value-based management is a comprehensive approach that links day-to-day operations to the common goal of increasing shareholder value. Using the information that the model provides – and taking into consideration the strategic opportunities in the marketplace – a financial institution can make better-informed decisions about the allocation of its resources, ranging from capital to investments, people, and technology.

Conclusion

In this chapter we have endeavored to give a comprehensive overview of the concepts and issues involved in developing and implementing an economic capital approach. We have presented the need for a consistent and comprehensive economic capital process and have provided examples of risk-adjusted performance measurement and how it can improve a financial institution's value-based management process. We believe that economic capital allocation is a credible tool for financial institution decision makers and that the management objective at both a business unit and a corporate level should be to maximize risk in the context of adequate returns.

There is no single off-the-shelf solution for financial institutions that choose to implement economic capital and risk-adjusted performance measurement processes. Demand for these processes is growing, as institutions of all sizes and types are becoming literate about risk and the need to offensively use risk. Implementation is an individual matter, and institutions vary in the depth and breadth of their processes. Nor do process implementations occur overnight; but tend to evolve with time.

Yet no matter what the implementation challenges may be, the competitiveness of the markets does not allow institutions today the luxury of ignoring the necessity for risk-adjusted processes for both capital allocation and performance measurement.

Notes

[1] The financial services sector uses two common risk-adjusted profitability measurement models, risk-adjusted return on capital (RAROC) and return on risk-adjusted capital (RORAC.)

[2] In July 1988, the Bank for International Settlements (BIS) through its Committee on Banking Regulations and Supervisory Practices issued a framework for measuring capital adequacy and setting minimum capital standards for international banking activities. Regulatory capital standards attempt to measure risk capital according to a particular accounting standard.

[3] Furthermore, it is very important that the economic capital framework is compatible with the overall financial decision process for the financial institution.

[4] Both Standard & Poors and Moody's publish historical default information that can be used to assist an institution in selecting the desired level of confidence.

[5] Assuming a normal distribution, a 2.33 multiplier is statistically the 99th percentile.

[6] Market risk guidelines stipulate that a financial institution scale up the assets Value-at-Risk. The main issue with obtaining a long-term Value-at-Risk is that a company may not be able to forecast volatility for time horizons that are greater than 10 to 20 days.

[7] VaR, adjusted to a 10-day holding period, at three standard deviations level of confidence, multiplied by a factor (usually 3).

[8] The CAPM can be stated as follows: $K_e = R_f + \beta(R_m - R_f)$. Under CAPM, risk is divided into a 'systematic' component, being that part of return variability that is related to movements in an index of market returns, and an unsystematic component. The return expected from an asset is related to its systematic risk so that an asset which is uncorrelated with the market index (its beta factor equals zero) will be priced to provide investors with a return equal to that on a risk free asset.

[9] This was based on pioneering work done by Roger Ibbotson, whose *Stocks, Bonds, Bills, and Inflation (SBBI) Yearbook* provides authoritative historical data on the most important US asset classes. The data gives a comprehensive, historical view of the performance of capital market dating back to 1926.

[10] In 1996, the Bank for International Settlements (BIS) through its Committee on Banking Regulations and Supervisory Practices issued a framework for measuring market risk capital adequacy.

[11] For an in-depth discussion of Value-at-Risk see Jorion (1996).

[12] Developed by J. P. Morgan Bank in 1995. See the *RiskMetrics*™ *Technical Manual* (1995).

[13] BIS regulations call for holding capital equal to one-year for most trading instruments based on a scaling up of a 1-day or a 10-day Value-at-Risk.

[14] Liquidity refers to the ability to meet payments in an orderly, timely and cost-efficient manner.

[15] CreditMonitor is a tool developed by KMV, a consulting firm, which is capable of producing two key outputs for evaluating individual credits and the overall portfolio: expected default frequency and portfolio loss distributions.

[16] CreditMetrics™ is a portfolio credit risk management tool. J. P. Morgan and its co-sponsors published their CreditMetrics™ methodology 1997 and introduced a software tool, CreditManager™.

[17] CreditRisk+™ is a portfolio credit risk management framework design developed by Credit Suisse Financial Products in 1997.

[18] Assumes perfect independence between the risk components.

[19] Correlation is an indication of the degree of association between two or more activities. The value of the correlation coefficient is always between -1 and 1, and expresses how strong the relationship is between activities. When the correlation is perfect (1), credit defaults will lead to market defaults and vice versa.

[20] It is very hard for any financial institution to judge the stability of correlation assumption. As such, it is also very difficult to accept one correlation value over an extended time frame in attributing economic capital.

[21] A great deal of empirical support for the random walk hypothesis can be found in the finance literature. See, for instance, Solnik (1973), Taylor (1982) and Renshaw (1970).

References

Christofferson, P. F., Diebold, F. X. and Schuermann, T. (1998) 'Horizon problems and extreme events in financial risk management', *Federal Reserve Bank of New York Economic Policy Review*.

Haubenstock, M. and Morisano, F. (1997) 'Beyond loss avoidance to strategic risk management', *Banking Strategies*, July/August.

Jones, D. and Mingo, J. (1998) 'Industry practices in credit risk modelling and internal capital allocations', Board of Governors of the Federal Reserve System.

Jorien, P. (1996) *Value at Risk: The New Benchmark for Controlling Market Risk*, Irwin Professional Publishing, Chicago.

Markowitz, H. (1959) *Portfolio Selection: Effective Diversification of Investments*, Wiley, New York.

Marvin, S. (1996) 'Capital allocation: a study of current and evolving practices in selected banks', *OCC Staff Study 96-1*, December.

Morisano, F. and Young, J. (1998) 'Using risk-adjusted profitability measurement to resolve transfer pricing issues in financial services', *Tax Management Transfer Pricing Report*, **6,** No. 25, 8 April.

Renshaw, E. F. V. (1970) 'Simulating the Dow Jones industrial averages: a further test of the random walk hypotheses', *Financial Analysts Journal*, **26,** No. 4, 51–9, September/October.

RiskMetrics™ *Technical Manual* (1995) J. P. Morgan Bank, New York.

Sharpe, W. (1970) *Portfolio Theory and Capital Markets*, McGraw-Hill, New York.

Solnik, B. (1973) 'Note on the validity of the random walk for European stock prices', *Journal of Finance*, **XXVIII,** No. 5, 151–9, December.

Taylor, S. J. (1982) 'Tests of the random walk hypothesis against a price-trend hypothesis', *Journal of Financial and Quantitative Analysis*, **XVII,** No. 1, 37–62, March.

24

International regulatory requirements for risk management (1988–1998)

MATTIA L. RATTAGGI

Introduction

In the absence of financial intermediaries agents would find it costly, inefficient and even impossible to perform the activities actually carried out by these institutions. The existence of informational and time asymmetries as well as transaction costs are important explanatory elements for the existence of financial intermediaries.

Financial intermediaries are particularly prone to market inefficiencies. The first of these are negative externalities associated with failures. Such externalities stem from the fact that banks deal with the accepted means of payment of all economic transactions and that banks and financial intermediaries are closely linked through a complicated system of contracts. The regulation of financial intermediaries aims, therefore, at protecting investors, preserving market integrity and reducing systemic risk.

The international regulation of risk management originated in the 1980s, in a context of financial liberalization and industrial deregulation. Regulators switched their focus from the industry level to that of the financial firm. They introduced what came to be known as a market-friendly regulation.

Capital is a buffer against losses. Focusing on banking and on capital adequacy, regulators substituted the gearing ratio and the percentages-weighted assets approaches with a new paradigm, namely risk-based capital adequacy.

The international regulatory intervention on risk management has evolved since then, complementing quantitative capital adequacy rules with qualitative risk management organizational standards. It has taken an interindustrial dimension, involving security houses and insurance companies.

The conception of international regulatory requirements for risk management has always involved a close cooperation between the leading Basel Committee on Banking Supervision[1] and banks. More recently, cooperation has been widened to include the Technical Committee of the International Organization of Securities Commissions, the International Association of Insurance Supervisors and the related regulated firms. The approach has aimed at reaching homogenous standards in the international regulatory field.

National supervisory authorities have always received discretionary power in the implementation of the accords and guidelines. Only through the implementation at national level do regulatory requirements acquire legal force.

This chapter has two objectives. First, it aims at fulfilling the 'handbook' role. It therefore presents the necessary regulatory material to allow a financial intermediary to verify the degree of compliance of its risk management system. Second, it provides an overview of the underlying trends and tensions characterizing the evolution of international regulatory requirements for risk management.

Quantitative capital adequacy rules for banks

The implementation of a risk-based capital adequacy system has first required defining the risks and positions to be addressed. Since its conception, regulators have addressed both on- and off-balance sheet positions. The focus has first been on credit risk, in 1988, then on market risks.

The preparatory work on market risks was undertaken in collaboration with the Technical Committee of the International Organization of Securities Commissions. The reason for that lies in the capability of such rules of application to non-bank financial intermediaries as well. As far as the measurement methodology is concerned, the integration of market risks, in 1996, has been accompanied by a progressive reliance on banks' in-house risk measurement techniques. Their use has been subjected to qualitative, organizational, standards. The picture becomes completed by providing a definition of eligible capital and its relationship with the risks measured.

Capital requirements apply to internationally active banks on a world-wide consolidated basis. Unresolved critical issues underlying the presently implemented solution have ultimately led to the proposition of the pre-commitment approach.

The risks and positions addressed

International capital adequacy rules address credit risk, which is defined as the risk of counterparty failure on balance-sheet and off-balance-sheet positions. They also address market risks, which are defined as the risk of losses in on- and off-balance-sheet positions arising from fluctuations in market prices.

Credit risk[2]

The following on-balance-sheet positions and off-balance-sheet positions are addressed.

Balance-sheet positions

- *Category* (*i*)   Claims on domestic public-sector entities, excluding central government, and loans guaranteed, or collateralized, by securities issued by such entities (the portion of commercial loans fully guaranteed by these bodies should also be included in this category).

- *Category* (*ii*)
  - Claims on multilateral development banks (IBRD, IADB, AsDB, AfDB, EIB,

EBRD) and claims guaranteed, or collateralized, by securities issued by such banks (the portion of commercial loans fully guaranteed by these bodies should also be included in this category; the same holds for the fully covered part of claims collateralized by cash or by securities issued by OECD central governments, OECD non-central government public-sector entities or multilateral development banks).

– Claims on banks incorporated in the OECD and claims guaranteed by OECD incorporated banks (the portion of commercial loans fully guaranteed by these bodies should also be included in this category; the same may hold for the fully covered part of claims collateralized by cash or by securities issued by OECD central governments, OECD non-central government public-sector entities or multilateral development banks).

– Claims on securities firms incorporated in the OECD subject to comparable supervisory and regulatory arrangements, including risk-based capital requirements, and claims guaranteed by these securities firms.

– Claims on banks incorporated in countries outside the OECD with a residual maturity of up to one year and claims with a residual maturity of up to one year guaranteed by banks incorporated in countries outside the OECD.

– Claims on non-domestic OECD public-sector entities, excluding central government, and claims guaranteed, or collateralized, by securities issued by such entities (the portion of commercial loans fully guaranteed by these bodies is also to be included in this category; the same may hold for the fully covered part of claims collateralized by cash or by securities issued by OECD central governments, OECD non-central government public-sector entities or multilateral development banks).

– Cash items in process of collection.

- *Category (iii)* Loans fully secured by mortgage on residential property that is or will be occupied by the borrower or that is rented.

- *Category (iv)*
  – Claims on the private sector, claims on banks incorporated outside the OECD with a residual maturity of over one year; claims on central governments outside the OECD (unless denominated in national currency and funded in that currency).
  – Claims on commercial companies owned by the public sector; premises, plants and equipments and other fixed assets; real estate and other investments (including non-consolidated investment participations in other companies)
  – Capital instruments issued by other banks (unless deducted from capital) and all other assets.

Off-balance-sheet positions

- *Category (v)* Directed credit substitutes, e.g. general guarantees of indebtedness and acceptances; sale and repurchase agreements and asset sales with recourse, where the credit risk remains with the bank; forward asset purchases, forward deposits and partly-paid shares and securities, which represent commitments with certain drawdown.

- *Category (vi)* Certain transaction-related contingent items, e.g. performance bonds, bid bonds, warranties and standby letters of credit related to particular transactions; note issuance facilities and revolving underwriting facilities; other commitments with an original maturity of over one year.

- *Category (vii)* Short-term self-liquidating trade-related contingencies, e.g. documentary credits collateralized by the underlying shipments.

- *Category (viii)* Forwards, swaps, purchased options and similar derivative contracts.

Market risks[3]

The positions addressed are, first, instruments related to interest rates and equity. Only instruments belonging to the trading book are considered. Thus, a definition of the trading book has to be provided. Additionally, regulation distinguishes between two kinds of risks, namely, specific risk and general market risk. Their separate measurement constitutes the so-called 'building-block approach'. The other positions addressed are instruments related to foreign exchanges and commodity. These instruments are considered independently of them being part of the trading book or the banking book. A third section considers options of all kinds.

Trading book

The trading book consists of the bank's proprietary financial positions (including derivative products and off-balance-sheet instruments) intentionally held for short-term resale and/or which are taken on by the bank with the intention of benefiting in the short term from actual and/or expected differences between their buying and selling prices, or from other price or interest-rate variations, and positions in financial instruments arising from matched principal brokering and market making, or positions taken in order to hedge other elements of the trading book.

Banks are allowed some freedom to include in the measurement of market risk certain non-trading instruments on- or off-balance sheet which are deliberately used to hedge the trading activities, although these will not be subject to the capital charge for specific risk. Conversely, derivative products used to hedge positions in the banking book are not part of the trading book and are excluded from the market risk measure.

Following the building-block approach, interest rate-related instruments and equity-related instruments are evaluated in terms of two kind of risks, namely specific and general. Specific risk consists of the risk of loss caused by adverse price movements of the instrument (or of its derivatives) as a result of factors related to its issuer. General risk is the risk of loss caused by adverse market prices movements.

(i) *Interest rate-related instruments* The positions addressed are:

- Fixed-rate and floating-rate debt securities; instruments that behave like them, including non-convertible preference shares; convertible bonds, i.e. debt issues or preference shares that are convertible at a stated price into common shares of the issuer, if they are traded like debt securities
- Interest rate derivatives (options excluded) and off-balance-sheet instruments which react to changes in interest rates (e.g. FRAs, bond futures, interest rate swaps, forward foreign exchange positions).

In addition to specific and general market risks, regulatory requirements address basis risk (the risk that the relationship between the prices of two similar instruments will change) and gap risk as well.

(ii) *Equity-related instruments*   The positions addressed are:

- Positions in equities and instruments the market behavior of which is similar to that of equities (convertible securities, commitments to buy or sell equity securities)
- Derivative products other than options (futures and swaps on individual equities or stock indexes).

In the case of index contracts comprising a diversified portfolio of equities, regulatory requirements address execution risk as well.

Banking and trading books

(iii) *Foreign currency-related instruments*   Addressed are positions in foreign currencies, including gold.

(iv) *Commodities-related instruments*   Addressed are positions in commodities (including precious metals, but excluding gold), i.e. every physical product which is or can be traded on a secondary market. The risks covered are directional risk (determined by changes in spot prices arising from net open positions), forward gap and interest rate risk (generated by changes in forward prices arising from maturity mismatches) and basis risk (determined by changes in the price relationship between two similar commodities).

Options of all kinds

Regulatory requirements address delta risk (which measures the amount an option's price would be expected to change for a unit change in the price of the underlying), gamma risk (which is a measure of the amount delta would be expected to change in response to a unit change in the price of the underlying) and vega risk (which shows the amount an option's price would be expected to change in response to a unit change in the price volatility of the underlying instrument). In the case of interest rate-related options, banks may address rho risk as well (which shows the amount an option's price would be expected to change to reflect a change in market interest rates).

Interest rate-related instruments pertaining to the banking book have not been addressed in terms of quantitative capital adequacy rules (see below).

Measuring risks

How should risks be measured? The present regulatory system involves the application of a standardized methodology for measuring credit risk and allows a choice between a standardized methodology and the use of internal models for measuring market risks.

The co-existence of standardized measurement methods with the use of banks' proprietary models is the result of an on-going process. The structure of the section reflects this process by highlighting the standard methods for measuring both credit and market risks and by recalling the most important arguments of the discussion between risk managers and regulators that followed the publication of the standardized methodology for the measurement of market risks. This discussion ended with banks being given permission (under the fulfilment of a set of qualitative and quantitative conditions) to use internal models for measuring market risks.

The standard methods

The Basel Committee has provided a international standard measurement methodology both for credit and market risks.

Credit risk

A bank has to calculate the quantity 'risk-weighted assets' (rwa) by means of risk-weighting factors (rwf) for the four different categories of balance-sheet assets (A_i, $i = 1, \ldots, 4$) (see above).

Off-balance-sheet positions are taken into account by means of credit conversion factors. In the end, 'rwa' is the weighted sum of the values of the bank's holdings of each of the four categories of assets:

$$rwa = A_1\,rwf_1 + A_2\,rwf_2 + A_3\,rwf_3 + A_4\,rwf_4$$

The risk-weighting factors (balance-sheet positions) are set according to the categories specified above as follows:

Category (i):   0%, 10%, 20%, 50% (at national discretion)
Category (ii):   20%
Category (iii):   50%
Category (iv):   100%

The credit conversion factors (for off-balance-sheet positions) are set as follows:

Category (v):   100%
Category (vi):   50%
Category (vii):   20%

The credit conversion factors have to be multiplied by the weights applicable to the category of the counterpart for an on-balance sheet transaction (categories (i) to (iv)).

Category (viii):   Forwards, swaps, purchased options and similar derivative contracts

As far as these instruments are concerned, banks are exposed to credit risk only for the potential cost of replacing the cash flow (on contracts showing positive value) if the counterparty defaults. To compute the credit equivalent amount for these instruments, two methods are available: the current exposure method (a) and the original exposure method (b).

(a) According to the current exposure method, a bank should sum the total replacement cost (obtained by 'marking to market') of all its contracts with positive value and an amount for potential future credit exposure calculated on the basis of the total notional principal amount of its book, split by residual maturity according to a table of coefficients (see Table 24.1).[4]

Table 24.1 Coefficients for the current exposure method

Residual maturity	Interest rate	Exchange rate and gold	Equity	Precious metals except gold	Other commodities
One year or less	0.0%	1.0%	6.0%	7.0%	10.0%
Over one year to five years	0.5%	5.0%	8.0%	7.0%	12.0%
Over five years	1.5%	7.5%	10.0%	8.0%	15.0%

Banks engaged in forwards, swaps, purchased options or similar derivative contracts based on equities, precious metals except gold, or other commodities, have to apply this method.

(b) According to the original exposure method, the bank simply has to apply a set of conversion factors (see Table 24.2) to the notional principal amounts of each instrument (according to the nature of the instrument and its maturity).[5]

Table 24.2   Factors for the original exposure method

Maturity	Interest rate contracts	Exchange rate contracts and gold
One year or less	0.5%	2.0%
Over one year to two years	1.0%	5.0%
For each additional year	1.0%	3.0%

The computed credit equivalent amounts are eventually to be weighted according to the categories of counterparty set out above (see categories (i) to (iv)).

Related to the weighting aspect is the important issue of bilateral netting. This concerns the weighting of the net rather than the gross claims with the same counterparties arising out of the full range of derivatives contracts.

Banks are allowed to net transactions subject to any legally valid form of bilateral netting or form of novation. The bank needs to satisfy its national supervisor that it has:

- A netting contract or agreement with the counterparty
- Written and reasoned legal opinions that the relevant courts and administrative authorities would find the bank's exposure to be such a net amount under:
  - The law of the jurisdiction in which the counterparty is chartered
  - The law that governs the individual transactions and
  - The law that governs any contract or agreement necessary to effect the netting;
- Procedures in place to ensure that the legal characteristics of netting arrangements are kept under review.

Contracts containing walkaway clauses are not eligible for netting.

Banks using the current exposure method are required to compute credit exposure on bilaterally netted forward transactions by summing the net marked-to-market replacement cost (if positive) and an add-on based on the notional underlying principal.

Market risks

A bank needs first to consider the positions belonging to the trading book only (interest rate-related and equity-related instruments), then the positions which pertain to both the trading and the banking books (foreign exchange related and commodity related instruments), and finally options of all kinds. The two remaining sections provide information on the most important elements left open to national discretion and make clear how the different partial capital charges should be aggregated.

Trading book

According to the building block methodology, interest rate-related and equity-related instruments are evaluated twice, first in terms of specific risk, then in relation to general market risk.

(i) Interest rate-related instruments:

- *Specific risk* The instruments are ranked in five categories, according to the issuer. Each category has a specific capital charge (expressed in % of the market value of the instrument). The category 'government' includes all forms of government papers (e.g. bonds, Treasury bills). The capital charge for these instruments is nil. The category 'qualifying' includes securities issued by public sector entities and multilateral development banks as well as securities that are rated investment-grade). The capital charge will be 0.25% when the residual term to final maturity is 6 months or less; 1% when the residual term to final maturity lies between 6 months and 2 years; 1.6% when it exceeds 2 years. The remaining instruments are ranked under the category 'other' and receive the same specific capital charge as a private-sector borrower under the credit risk requirements (8%).
- *General market risk* The Basel Committee allows a choice between two methods, dubbed 'maturity method' and 'duration method' respectively. In both cases the capital charge consists of the sum of:

  – the net short or long position in the whole trading book
  – a small proportion of the matched positions in each time-band (known as 'vertical disallowance')
  – a larger proportion of the matched positions across different time-bands (the so-called 'horizontal disallowance')
  – a net charge for positions in options (whose calculation will be described below).

  In the maturity method long or short positions in debt securities and other sources of interest rate exposures including derivative instruments are slotted into a maturity ladder comprising thirteen time-bands (or fifteen, in the case of <3% coupon instruments) (see Table 24.3).[6] Floating rate instruments will

Table 24.3 Maturity method: time-bands and weights

Coupon 3% or >	Coupon <3%	Risk weight	Assumed changes in yield
1 month or less	1 month or less	0.00%	1.00
1 to 3 months	1 to 3 months	0.20%	1.00
3 to 6 months	3 to 6 months	0.40%	1.00
6 to 12 months	6 to 12 months	0.70%	1.00
1 to 2 years	1.0 to 1.9 years	1.25%	0.90
2 to 3 years	1.9 to 2.8 years	1.75%	0.80
3 to 4 years	2.8 to 3.6 years	2.25%	0.75
4 to 5 years	3.6 to 4.3 years	2.75%	0.75
5 to 7 years	4.3 to 5.7 years	3.25%	0.70
7 to 10 years	5.7 to 7.3 years	3.75%	0.65
10 to 15 years	7.3 to 9.3 years	4.50%	0.60
15 to 20 years	9.3 to 10.6 years	5.25%	0.60
Over 20 years	10.6 to 12 years	6.00%	0.60
	12 to 20 years	8.00%	0.60
	Over 20 years	12.50%	0.60

be allocated according to the residual term to the next repricing date. Opposite positions of the same amount in the same issues can be omitted. The same holds for closely matched swaps, forwards, futures and FRAs. The capital charge is arrived at by:

- Weighting the positions in each time-band by a factor designed to reflect their price sensitivity to assumed changes in interest rate (see Table 24.3)
- Adding a 10% charge on the smaller of the offsetting positions (to reflect basis risk and gap risk)
- Offsetting the weighted long and short positions in each time-band
- Conducting three rounds of horizontal offsetting (see Table 24.4).[7]

Table 24.4   Horizontal disallowances

Zones	Time-band	Within the zone	Between adjacent zones	Between zones 1/3
1	0–1 month	40%	40%	100%
1	1–3 months	40%	40%	100%
1	3–6 months	40%	40%	100%
1	6–12 months	40%	40%	100%
2	1–2 years	30%	40%	100%
2	2–3 years	30%	40%	100%
2	3–4 years	30%	40%	100%
3	4–5 years	30%	40%	100%
3	5–7 years	30%	40%	100%
3	7–10 years	30%	40%	100%
3	10–15 years	30%	40%	100%
3	15–20 years	30%	40%	100%
3	Over 20 years	30%	40%	100%

(a)   First between the net positions in each of three zones (0–1 year, 1–4 years, 4+ years). The lesser of the absolute values of the added long and short positions in the same zone is subject to the corresponding percentage.
(b)   The second round applies to the net positions in the three different zones. The lesser of the absolute values of the long and short positions between adjacent zones is subject to the corresponding percentage.
(c)   The third round concerns the net positions in zones 1 and 3. The lesser of the absolute values of the long and short positions between the two zones is subject to a 100% capital charge.

We follow the Basel Committee in providing a numerical example[8]. Let us suppose that a bank has the following positions (marked to market):

- A qualifying bond, $13.33 million, residual maturity 8 years, coupon 8%
- A government bond, $75 million, residual maturity 2 months, coupon 7%
- A interest rate payer swap $150 million, next fixing after 9 months, residual life 8 years
- A long position in interest rate future, $50 million, delivery after 6 months, life of underlying government security 3.5 years.

The first task consists of slotting the positions in the time-bands. Second, the positions need to be weighted. Then the calculation of the vertical and horizontal disallowances can take place (see Table 24.5).

Table 24.5 Numerical example

Time-bands (m: months, y: years)	Zones	Positions (in millions)	Weight (%)	Weighted positions (position × weight)/100	Vertical disallowance[a]	Horizontal disallowance 1[b]	Horizontal disallowance 2[c]	Horizontal disallowance 3[d]
1 m or less	1		0.00					
1 to 3 m	1	+75	0.20	+0.15				
3 to 6 m	1	−50	0.40	−0.20		+0.08		+1
6 to 12 m	1	+150	0.70	+1.05				
1 to 2 y	2		1.25					
2 to 3 y	2		1.75					
3 to 4 y	2	+50	2.25	+1.125			+0.45	
4 to 5 y	3		2.75					
5 to 7 y	3		3.25					
7 to 10 y	3	−150; +13.33	3.75	−5.625; +0.5	0.05			
10 to 15 y	3		4.50					
15 to 20 y	3		5.25					
Over 20 y	3		6.00					

[a] 10% of the lesser of the absolute values of the added (weighted) long and (weighted) long and (weighted) short positions in the same time-band (10% of 0.5 = 0.05).
[b] 40% of the lesser of the absolute values of the added long and short positions in the same zone (where there are more than one position): 40% of 0.2 = 0.08.
[c] 40% of the lesser of the absolute values of the long and short positions between adjacent zones 2 and 3 (40% of 1.125 = 0.45).
[d] 100% of the lesser of the absolute values of the long and short positions between distant zones 1 and 3 (100% of 1 = 1.00)

The total capital charge is computed as follow:

Overall net open position	3.00
Vertical disallowance	0.05
Horizontal disallowance 1	0.08
Horizontal disallowance 2	0.45
Horizontal disallowance 3	1.00
Total capital charge:	4.58

The duration method allows for the calculation of the price sensitivity of each position separately. The price sensitivity is comparable to the weighted position in the maturity ladder framework. The steps implied are, first, the computation of the price sensitivity of each instrument in terms of a change in interest rates provided by the Basel Committee (see Table 24.6).[9]

Let us suppose that a bank has the following positions (marked to market):

- A bond, $100 million, residual maturity 5 years, coupon 10%
- A bond, $19.19 million, residual maturity 3.5 years, coupon 2.75%

Table 24.6 Duration Method

Time-bands (m: months, y: years)	Zones	Positions (in millions)	Duration	Assumed change in yield (%)	Price sensitivity
1 m or less	1	...	...	1.00	...
1 to 3 m	1	...	...	1.00	...
3 to 6 m	1	...	...	1.00	...
6 to 12 m	1	...	...	1.00	...
1 to 1.9 y	2	...	...	0.90	...
1.9 to 2.8 y	2	...	...	0.80	...
2.8 to 3.6 y	2	19.19	3.21	0.75	0.462
3.6 to 4.3 y	3	...	...	0.75	...
4.3 to 5.7 y	3	100	3.79	0.70	2.653
5.7 to 7.3 y	3	...	...	0.65	...
7.3 to 9.3 y	3	...	...	0.60	...
9.3 to 10.6 y	3	...	...	0.60	...
10.6 to 12 y	3	...	...	0.60	...
12 to 20 y	3	...	...	0.60	...
Over 20 y	3	...	...	0.60	...

Basis risk is taken into account by subjecting long and short price sensitivities ('weighted positions' in Table 24.5) in each time-band to a 5% vertical disallowance. In the end the net position in each time-band is carried forward to perform the three rounds of horizontal disallowance (see Table 24.5).

- *The treatment of interest rate derivatives* (*options excluded*) In order to become subject to capital charges for specific and general market risks as described above, these instruments need first to be converted into market values of the principal amount of the underlying, or of the notional underlying. Futures and forward contracts are treated as a combination of a long and a short position in a notional government security; swaps are treated as two notional positions in government securities with relevant maturities.

  Thus, for instance, a receiver swap characterized by a maturity of 5 years, a fixed coupon of 4% and a first floating coupon fixed at 1%, will be decomposed in a long bond (maturity 5 years, coupon 4%) and a short bond (maturity 6 months, coupon 1%). Long and short positions in identical instruments with exactly the same issuer, coupon, currency and maturity may be excluded from the interest rate maturity framework.

  The use of two more sophisticated methods for calculating the positions to be included in the maturity or duration ladder is allowed to banks with large swap books:

1 A bank may slot into the general market risk framework the present values of the payments required by the swap, or
2 Allocate into the time-bands reproduced above the sensitivity of the net present value implied by the change in yield used in the maturity or duration methods.

The capital charge for general market risk stems from the slotting into the maturity ladder of the various categories of instruments. Interest rate and currency swaps, FRAs, forward foreign exchange contracts, futures on an interest rate index and interest rate futures are not subject to a specific risk capital charge. Futures contracts whose underlying is a debt security, or an index representing a basket of debt securities, are subject to a specific risk capital charge corresponding to the credit risk of the issuer.

(ii) Equity-related instruments:

- *Specific risk* To calculate the capital charge a bank sums all long positions and all short positions. The capital charge is 8% of the sum. In the event of a liquid and well-diversified portfolio the capital charge is 4%.
- *General market risk* The capital charge is 8% of the difference between the sum of the longs and the sum of the short positions.
- *The treatment of equity derivatives* (*options excluded*) In order to become subject to capital charges for specific and general market risks as described above, these instruments need first to be converted into positions in the relevant underlying, being it a individual equity or a portfolio of equities. Swaps will be treated as two notional positions. The offsetting rule applies to matched positions in each identical equity or stock index in each market. To cover execution risk, an additional capital charge of 2% will be levied on the net long or short position in an index contract comprising a diversified portfolio. The application of this additional charge will be modified in case of futures-related arbitrage strategies.[10]

Banking and Trading Books

The measurement systems address foreign currency-related and commodity-related instruments.

(iii) Foreign currency-related instruments:

To arrive at a capital charge for exposures in these positions a bank needs first to determine the net open position in each foreign currency by summing the following items:

- The net spot position (difference between all asset items and all liability items denominated in the currency in question)
- The net forward position (included currency futures and the principal on currency swaps not included in the spot position) valued at current spot market exchange rates
- Guarantees to be called
- Net future income/expenses not yet accrued but already fully hedged
- Any other item representing a profit or loss in foreign currencies.

Positions in composite currencies may be either treated as a currency or split into their component parts. Positions in gold need first to be converted at spot current rates into the relevant currency.

Accrued interest should be included as a position. Unearned but expected future interest (as well as anticipated expenses) may be excluded. Positions taken to hedge against the adverse effect of the exchange rate on the capital ratio might be excluded from the calculation above.[11] The net position in each foreign currency and in gold is then converted at spot rates into the reporting currency. The capital charge will be 8% of the higher of either the net long currency positions or the net short currency positions and 8% of the net position in gold.

(iv)   Commodity-related instruments

The Basel Committee allows the choice between two standard methods: the maturity ladder approach (a) and a simplified approach (b).

(a)   *The maturity ladder approach*   Under this method, banks express each spot and forward commodity position in terms of the standard physical unit of measurement (barrels, kilos, etc.). The net position in each commodity is then converted at current spot rates into the national currency. Each long and short position is slotted into the ladder according to its maturity. A separate maturity ladder will be used for each commodity.
   The capital charge is arrived at by multiplying matched long and short positions in each time-band by the corresponding spread rate (1.5%). The residual net position will be carried forward to offset exposures in time-bands that are further out, although a surcharge equal to 0.6% of the net positions carried forward will be added in respect of each time-band that the net position is carried forward. The resulting matched amount will be subject to the same 1.5% capital charge. This process will lead to either a only long or a only short position, to which a capital charge of 15% will apply. Commodity derivatives will be converted into notional commodities positions before be assigned to maturities. Commodity swaps will be incorporated as a series of positions equal to the notional amount of the contract, with one position corresponding with each payment on the swap and slotted into the maturity ladder accordingly. A payer swap would be a long position, a receiver swap would be a short position. The reproduction of the Basel Committee's numerical example simultaneously allows for the highlighting of the structure of the ladder (time-bands and spread rates) (see Table 24.7).[12]

(b)   *The simplified approach*   The calculation follows the ladder approach as far as the slotting of positions is concerned. The capital charge will be 15% of the net long or short position in each commodity. This charge covers directional risk. An additional capital charge equal to 3% of the bank's gross positions (long plus short) in each particular commodity is designed to cover basis risk, interest rate risk and forward gap risk.

Options of all kinds

The Basel Committee introduced a distinction between banks that use purchased options only and banks that also write options. The former may use the simplified approach, while banks pertaining to the second category should make use of an intermediate approach (delta-plus or scenarios).
   Banks strongly involved in trading should implement a comprehensive 'internal' risk management model (see over).

(a)   *Simplified approach*   Within this framework, the capital charge for long cash and long put, or short cash and long call, positions consists of the market value

Table 24.7   The maturity ladder approach

Suppose a bank has positions in only one commodity and that it has converted them at current spot rates into the national currency.

Time-bands	Position	Spread-rates	Capital calculation	Capital charge ($)
0–1 month	0	1.5%		
1–3 months	0	1.5%		
3–6 months		1.5%	($800 long + $ 800 short) × 1.5%	24
	Long $800		$200 short carried forward to 1–2	
	Short $1000		years time-band	
			$200 × 2 × 0.6%	2.4
6–12 months	0	1.5%		
1–2 years	Long $600	1.5%	($200 long + $200 short) × 1.5%	6
			$400 long carried forward to over	
			3 years	
			400 × 2 × 0.6	4.8
2–3 years	0	1.5%		
Over 3 years	Short $600	1.5%	($400 long + $400 short) × 1.5%	12
			Net position: $200	
			Capital charge: $200 × 15%	30
Total capital charge				79.2

of the underlying security (asset which would be received if the option were exercised) multiplied by the sum of specific and general market risk charges for the underlying (see above) less the amount the option is in the money (if any) bounded at zero.

Thus, for example, if a bank holds 100 shares currently valued at $10 each and a equivalent put option with a strike price of $11, the capital charge would be the market value of the shares position ($1000) multiplied by the sum of the 8% specific risk charge and the 8% general market risk charge, i.e. 16%, less the amount the option is in the money ($1) multiplied by the number of shares:

$$((100 \times \$10) \times 0.16) - ((\$11 - \$10) \times 100) = \$60 \text{ (capital charge)}$$

For long call or long put positions, the capital charge is the lesser of (1) the market value of the underlying securities multiplied by the sum of specific and general risk charges for the underlying and (2) the market value of the option.

(b) *Delta-plus method*   Banks may include within the standardized framework presented above the positions reported as the market value of the underlying multiplied by the delta (which measures the amount an option's price would be expected to change for a unit change in the price of the underlying).

Delta-equivalent (i.e. the market value of the underlying multiplied by the absolute value of the delta) options with debt securities or interest rates as underlying are slotted into the corresponding time-bands according to the two-legged approach. This requires one entry at the time the underlying contract takes effect and a second entry at the time the underlying contract matures.

Thus, for example, a bought call option on a June three-month interest-rate future is in April considered to be a long position with a maturity of five months and a short position with a maturity of two months. Similarly, the written option is slotted as a long position with a maturity of two months and a short position with a maturity of five months. Floating rate instruments with caps or floors are treated as a combination of floating rate securities and a series of European-style options. Thus the holder of a three-year floating rate bond indexed to six month LIBOR with a cap of 15% treats it as (1) a debt security that reprices in six months, and (2) a series of five written call options on a FRA with a reference rate of 15% (each with a negative sign at the time the underlying FRA takes effect and a positive sign at the time the underlying FRA matures).

Delta-equivalent options with equities as underlying are incorporated into the measure described above. Each national market is treated as a separate underlying. Delta-equivalent options with foreign currencies and gold as under-lyings are incorporated in the measure described above. Delta-equivalent options with commodities as underlying are incorporated in one of the measures described above. In order to calculate the total capital charge, however, banks should measure gamma (which is a measure of the amount delta would be expected to change in response to a unit change in the price of the underlying, providing therefore a indication of the difficulty of maintaining a delta-neutral portfolio) and vega as well (which shows the amount an option's price would be expected to change in response to a unit change in the price volatility of the underlying instrument).

For each individual option the capital charge for gamma risk (gamma impact) is calculated according to the following formula:

$$\frac{1}{2} \times \text{gamma} \times VU$$

VU (variation of the underlying of the option) is calculated as follows:

– For interest rate options: the market value of the underlying multiplied by the risk weights set out in Table 24.1 (see above)
– For options on equities: the market value of the underlying multiplied by 8%
– For foreign exchange and gold options: the market value of the underlying multiplied by 8%
– For options on commodities: the market value of the underlying multiplied by 15%.

The following positions are treated as the same underlying:

– Each time-band of Table 24.1, for interest rates
– Each national market, for equities and stock indices
– Each currencies pair and gold, for foreign currencies and gold
– Each individual commodity, for commodities.

The resulting (positive or negative) individual gamma impacts are then summed. Only the negative net gamma impact for each underlying is included in the calculation of the total gamma capital charge. The latter will consist of the sum of the absolute value of the net calculated negative gamma impacts.

The sum of the vegas for all options on the same underlying multiplied by a proportional shift in volatility of $\pm25\%$ provides the risk manager with the capital charges for volatility risk. The total capital charge for vega risk is the sum of the absolute value of the individual capital charges calculated for vega risk.

(c) *Scenario approach* The capital charge is based on scenario matrix analysis concerning changes in the option's underlying rate or price and the volatility of that rate or price. A bank needs to specify a fixed range of changes and needs to calculate, at various points along this grid, changes in the value of the option portfolio. A different matrix has to be set up for each individual underlying. The range of changes in the rates will be consistent with the assumed changes in yield set out in Table 24.1 (see above). The other price ranges are $\pm8\%$ for equities, $\pm8\%$ for foreign exchange and gold and $\pm15\%$ for commodities. For all risk categories, at least seven observations (including the current) should be used to divide the range into equally spaced intervals. Concerning the range of changes in the volatility of the underlying rate or price, a change equal to a shift in volatility of $+25\%$ and -25% will be applied.

   Once the matrix has been calculated, each cell contains the net profit or loss of the option. The capital charge will consist of the largest loss contained in the matrix.

National discretion

The specification of certain important aspects in the standardized measurement framework for market risks is left to national supervisors.

- As far as the calculation of the capital charge for specific risk on interest rate-related instruments is concerned, national supervisory authorities specify the kind of securities to be included in the category 'qualifying' as well as the offsetting possibilities for the category 'others'. In relation to the calculation of the capital charge for specific risk for a portfolio of equity-related instruments, national supervisors specify the criteria to be met for that portfolio to be considered liquid and well diversified. They may largely define 'structural positions' within the calculation of capital charge for foreign exchange-related instruments as well as the conditions under which a bank is exempted from any capital charge. National supervisory authorities detail the permission of netting between different sub-categories of the same commodity within the calculation of the capital charge for commodity risk. They may also specify some structural aspects related to the performance of a scenario matrix analysis within the calculation of a capital charge for option risks.
- As for risk measurement techniques, national supervisory authorities approve and monitor the choice, application, use and change of models for measuring the risk of (1) interest rate-related instruments, under the duration method, (2) foreign exchange-related instruments and (3) options (delta-plus and scenario approaches).

The overall capital charge (OCC)

The overall capital charge corresponds to the capital charges described above summed arithmetically.

Industry's criticism and the response of regulators

The International Convergence of Capital Measurement and Capital Standards (known as the Capital Accord) of 1988 relies on a standardized credit risk measurement methodology, which uniformly applies throughout the industry. The same holds for the standardized framework for measuring market risks included in the *Amendment to the Capital Accord to Incorporate Market risks* published in 1996, but already circulated as a proposal in 1993. In the 1993 proposal, the standardized framework for measuring market risks exhausted the paper. The present section therefore briefly recalls the dialectical process (between regulators and representatives of the banking industry) responsible for the inclusion, in the final version of 1996, of an alternative method for measuring market risks which allows banks to make use of their internal market risk measurement models.

The banking industry first reacted to the framework for measuring credit risk. It criticized the fact that the same risk factors apply to every loan granted to the private sector, when evidence shows that there are substantial differences in risk among such loans. It also argued that the proposed risk weights do not reflect some obvious determinants of credit risk such as risk concentrations in a specific asset category or particular obligor, industry or region.

These criticisms were reinforced when regulators proposed a standardized framework for measuring market risks. Bankers pointed to the fact that the approach assumes risks be additive, i.e. that the risks of a portfolio of assets can be measured by their weighted sum. They stressed that the approach could oblige banks to run two parallel systems for measuring market risks, one, the standardized framework, for regulatory purposes and another, based on sophisticated in-house models, for risk management purposes.

The idea, according to which a more accurate approach to risk measurement would be to apply portfolio theory (which allows each asset to have a different correlation with every other asset) and that regulators should rely on more accurate internal measurement systems rather than obliging banks to incur additional costs by running two parallel measurement systems, became a claim by the end of the consultative period on the 1993 proposal for the supervisory treatment of market risks.

For instance, the *Institute of International Finance* recommended 'that regulators exempt banks from implementation of the less precise regulatory model if the supervisors determine that the bank has superior internal measurement and control systems'.[13] The *British Bankers' Association* (1993) argued that by insisting that risk measures obtained from sophisticated methods be equivalent to those produced by more basic methods, regulators oblige banks strongly involved in the monitoring of market risks to run an additional method for regulatory purposes beside the one used in their risk management activity.

Regulators recognized that the standardized framework failed to take 'sufficient account of correlation and portfolio effects across instruments and markets, and did not reward risk diversification'.[14] They acknowledged as a strong argument the statement that 'proprietary risk management models developed by some of the more sophisticated banks produce far more accurate measures of market risk and that there would be costly overlaps if those banks were required to calculate their market risks in two different ways'.[15]

Allowing the use of internal models for regulatory purposes is to be seen as a natural consequence of the main pillar on which the whole modern regulatory approach to capital adequacy rests, namely, the reliance on the *riskiness* of positions rather than on their book-values. In this sense, it also follows that the permission to use internal risk measurement models for regulatory purposes has to be acknow-ledged as an ongoing process, suitable for further developments.

Banks' internal models[16]

As a basis for setting regulatory capital, the use of internal models has been allowed so far in relation to the measure of market risks only (with the exclusion of interest rate risk on banking book's positions). A bank is entitled to use internal models for measuring market risks once the national supervisory authority has given its explicit approval. Before approving the use of a bank's proprietary model, the supervisory authority may insist on a period of monitoring and live testing of the model. A set of quantitative and qualitative criteria governs the use of in-house models for calculating the capital charge for market risks. A particular rule has been devised for accounting for specific market risk. Once these elements have been reviewed, the calculation of the overall capital charge ensues.

Modeling and quantitative requirements

(i) A Value-at-risk (VaR) must be calculated on a daily basis, using a 99th percent-ile, one-tailed confidence interval and a 10-day holding period.

(ii) The historical observation period to be taken into account whenever measuring VaR has to cover minimally one year and the data set has to be updated at least once every three months. Whenever a upsurge in price volatility is experienced, supervisors may require the use of a shorter observation period. Banks may recognize empirical correlations within broad risk categories.

(iii) The VaR model must capture the non-linear price characteriztics of option positions. The set of risk factors of the bank's risk measurement system must capture the volatilities of the rates and prices underlying option positions (vega risk). If the option portfolios are large and/or complex, the bank has to measure the volatilities broken down by different maturities.

(iv) No particular type of VaR model is prescribed, provided that it takes into account the following risk factors:

- For interest rate-related instruments, the measurement system should model the yield curve by means of an established approach. In order to capture variation in the volatility of rates along the curve, the latter has to be divided into various maturity segments whose number will bear a relation to the nature of the trading strategy of the bank in question. The number will, however, not be smaller than six. To each segment a risk factor will be attached. A separate set of risk factors is required to capture spread risk.

- For exchange rate-related instruments and gold price the measurement system should incorporate a risk factor for each foreign currency in which the positions are denominated. There will therefore be a risk factor for each exchange rate involved.

- For equity-related instruments' prices a risk factor will be attached to each equity market. In the ideal case a bank should have risk factors for the volatility of each individual equity issue. As a minimum a bank is expected to design a risk factor which captures market-wide movements in equity prices. Positions in individual securities would then be expressed in beta equivalents relative to the market-wide index.

- For commodity-related instruments' prices the measurement system should incorporate a risk factor for each commodity price to which the bank is exposed. When the trading dimension is large, the bank will have to consider variation in the convenience yield (which measures the benefits derived from direct ownership of the physical commodity) between derivative positions and cash positions in the commodity.

Calculating the minimum capital charge

(i) The minimum capital requirement that each bank must meet on a daily basis, will be the higher of:

- Its previous day's VaR number measured according to the parameter specified above and
- An average of the daily VaR measures on each of the preceding sixty business days,

multiplied by a factor set by individual supervisory authorities.

(ii) The minimum multiplication factor equals 3. Banks will be charged with this minimum figure only if:
- The quality of the bank's risk management system fulfils the qualitative standards laid down below, and
- The model's backtesting results are satisfactory.

Let us consider first the backtesting issue[17] and then the qualitative standards.

(iii) The backtesting of a VaR model consists of periodically comparing the bank's daily VaR measures with the subsequent daily profit or loss. The calculation has to take place on a quarterly basis, using the most recent twelve months of data. The calculation of the VaR for backtesting purposes involves reference to a one-day holding period. This is meant to mitigate the so-called *contamination problem*, namely the fact that *ex-post* actual measures will be inevitably contaminated by changes in the portfolio composition during the holding period. A bank is then required to calculate the number of times out of 250 the trading outcomes were not covered by the VaR measures.

The more frequent the exceptions (after a minimum of 4), the higher will be the increase in the multiplication factor (see Table 24.8). The limit of the increase is set at 1.

The increase in the multiplication factor as set out in the yellow zone takes place unless the bank can demonstrate that such an increase is not warranted. To pursue this goal, a bank is invited to communicate to supervisors the underlying causes of the exceptions generated by the model. For example, it could be that the positions have been incorrectly fed into the model. This would leave the integrity of the model unaffected. Some exceptions could stem from the risk measurement not being pervasive enough. This would require some improvements in the model. The exceptions could also find their sources in the contamination problem (intra-day large money-losing change in positions). Supervisors will take these additional information into account to decide the appropriate course of action.

Table 24.8 Backtesting results and increases in the multiplication factor

Zones	Number of exceptions	Increase in the multiplication factor
Green	0	0.00
Green	1	0.00
Green	2	0.00
Green	3	0.00
Green	4	0.00
Yellow	5	0.40
Yellow	6	0.50
Yellow	7	0.65
Yellow	8	0.75
Yellow	9	0.85
Red	10 or more	1.00

Qualitative standards

(i) The bank must have a risk control unit in place. This unit must be independent from business trading units and should report to senior management directly. The unit is responsible for designing and implementing the bank's risk management system. It will produce daily reports regarding the output of the model. The reports will include an evaluation of the relationship between measures of risk exposure and trading limits. The unit will conduct the regular backtesting programme. A programme of stress testing must be in place and be reflected in the policies and limits set by senior management and the board of directors.

The scenarios examined in the stress testing exercise should cover the range of factors that can cause extraordinary losses in trading portfolios or make the control of risk in those portfolios very difficult. The goal is to shed light on the impact of such events on positions by evaluating the capacity of the bank's capital to absorb these large potential losses and by identifying the steps that might be taken to reduce the exposure and preserve the capital basis.

International guidelines distinguish between scenarios that do not require simulations by the bank (e.g. making information on the largest losses experienced during the reporting period available to supervisors) and scenarios that require a simulation by the bank. The latter should include testing the behavior of the present portfolio against past periods of significant disturbances (1987 equity crash, ERM crisis of 1992) incorporating both the large price movements and the sharp reduction in liquidity associated with these events. A bank should also evaluate the sensitivity of its exposure to changes in the assumptions about volatilities and correlations. In addition, a bank is encouraged to develop its own scenarios designed to capture the most adverse stress test given the characteristics of its portfolio. Results and methodology should be made available to supervisors.

The VaR model must be used in conjunction with internal trading and exposure limits. It must be closely integrated into the day-to-day risk management process of the bank and its output should be integrated into the process of planning, monitoring and controlling the bank's market risk profile. The measurement system must be well documented. The bank must permanently ensure that the operation of the risk measurement system complies with a documented set of internal policies, controls and procedures.

The board of directors and senior management must perform an active role in regarding risk control as an essential aspect of the business and by enforcing, when implied by the daily report, reductions of positions taken by traders as well as reductions in the bank's overall exposure. Senior management will periodically review the results of the stress-testing programme and prompt hedging steps whenever a particular vulnerability is revealed.

The risk management system must be independently reviewed by the bank's own internal auditors. The review should take place ideally at least once a year. It should include the activities of the business trading units and of the independent risk control unit. In particular, it should address the documentation, the organization of the risk control unit, the integration of market risk measures into daily risk management, the approval process for risk pricing models and valuation systems and the validation of any significant change in the process of measuring risks. Further, it must deal with the management information system, the accuracy of data sources, volatility and correlation assumptions, risk transformation calculations and the performing of the backtesting programme.

(ii) The model must be subject to external validation. The validation process involves, at a minimum:

- Verifying the internal validation processes described above
- Ensuring that the formulae used are validated by a qualified unit independent the trading area
- Checking the adequacy of the structure of internal models
- Checking the results of the backtesting programme
- Making sure that data flows and processes are transparent and accessible.

Capital adequacy for general and specific market risks

The use of internal models for setting capital against market risks is mostly supposed to replace the implementation of a standardized methodology for measuring general market risk only. If a model takes full account of the specific risk implied by interest rate-related instruments and equity securities, the total specific risk charge provided by it must minimally equal half of the charge calculated according to the standardized methodology. If the model takes only partial account of specific risk, the charge for specific market risk will stem from the standardized approach.

The overall capital charge (OCC)

This charge will correspond to the higher of the bank's previous day's VaR number, measured according to the parameter specified above, and an average of the daily VaR measures carried out on each of the preceding sixty business days, multiplied by the multiplication factor. This will minimally equal 3 or be adjusted by individual supervisory authorities following the backtesting results and the quality of the risk management system. The bank will then take into account the capital coverage of specific risk. This charge must minimally equal half of the charge calculated according to the standardized methodology. If this is not the case, the charge for specific market risk will entirely stem from the standardized approach.

Capital adequacy ratio and the definition of eligible capital

This section introduces the structure of the global minimum capital ratio for credit and market risks and addresses the definition of capital for regulatory purposes. The definition first proposed in 1988 to cover credit risk has been broadened to incorporate market risks, when the corresponding rules came into force in 1996.

The capital adequacy ratio

A bank needs first to consider credit risk by recalling the quantity 'risk-weighted assets' (rwa). Second, it has to deduce the amount stemming from debt and equity securities in the trading book as well as all positions in commodities. This leads to the quantity (RWA). The bank should then consider its market risks by recalling the overall capital charge (OCC) obtained either through the standardized framework or by using the internal model approach.

The capital charge for market risks (OCC) follows directly by merely relabeling the measured market risks; the one for credit risk should minimally equal 8% of RWA (obtained by prior risk-weighting the positions). To ensure consistency in the calculation of the global capital requirements (for credit and market risks), the measure of market risks has to be multiplied by the reciprocal value of the minimum capital percentage of RWA, namely 12.5.

The capital adequacy is eventually arrived at by making sure that the eligible capital for credit and market risks (EIC) (as defined below), divided by the RWA + OCC, equals 0.08.

$$EIC/(RWA + OCC) = 0.08$$

The definition of eligible capital

In calculating eligible capital (EIC), it is necessary first to calculate the bank's minimum capital requirement for credit risk. This makes it possible to determine how much remaining capital eligible for covering credit risk is available to support market risks.

Credit risk

The definition of the capital eligible for covering credit risk consists of two tiers: Tiers 1 and 2.

Tier 1, or core capital, is made up of permanent shareholders' equity (issued and fully-paid ordinary share/common stock and perpetual non-cumulative preference shares) and disclosed reserves created or increased from post-tax retained earnings (or other surplus, e.g. share premiums, retained profit, general reserves and legal reserves). General funds are also included provided that (1) they are made out of post-tax retained earnings or out of pretax earnings adjusted for all potential tax liabilities; (2) the funds and movements into or out of them are disclosed separately in the bank's published accounts; (3) the funds are available to the bank to meet losses for unrestricted and immediate use as soon as they occur.

Tier 2, or supplementary capital, includes undisclosed reserves, which have been passed through the profit and loss account and which are accepted by the supervisory authority, and revaluation reserves. Revaluation amount determined by law is admitted in Tier 2 if it reflects fully the possibility of fluctuation in the asset price and of its forced sale. In the case of latent revaluation reserves, the difference between historic cost book value and market value will be discounted by 55% to account for the potential volatility of such form of unrealized capital as well as for the notional tax charge on it. The supplementary capital also includes general provisions/general loan-loss reserves held against presently unidentified losses and hybrid (debt/equity) capital instruments. The latter should meet the following requirements: (1) be unsecured, subordinated and fully paid-up; (2) not be redeemable at the initiative of the holder or without the prior consent of the supervisory authority; (3) be available to participate in losses without the bank being obliged to cease trading; (4) they should allow the service of obligations to be deferred. Lastly, Tier 2 includes conventional unsecured subordinated term debt capital instruments with a minimum original fixed term to maturity of over five years and limited life redeemable preference shares.

Tier 2 cannot exceed 100% of Tier 1 and the subordinated term debt cannot be larger than 50% of Tier 1. Additionally, the eligible amount of general provisions/general loan-loss reserves bears a limit to the overall measured risk equal to 1.25 percentage points.

The value of the goodwill can be deduced from Tier 1. From the total capital a bank can deduce investments in unconsolidated banking and financial subsidiary companies as well as investments in the capital of other banks and financial institutions.

Market risks

To cover market risks, the eligible capital has been broadened, first, by broadening the scope of Tiers 1 and 2 and second, by introducing Tier 3. Tier 3 consists of short-term subordinated debt that is capable of becoming part of a bank's permanent capital and thus be available to absorb losses in the event of insolvency. It must (1) be unsecured, subordinated and fully paid up; (2) have an original maturity of at least two years; (3) not be repayable before the agreed repayment date (unless the national supervisory authority agrees); (4) be subject to a lock-in clause which stipulates that neither interest nor principal may be paid if this means the bank falling or remaining below its minimum capital requirement.

Tier 3 is to be used for the sole purpose of meeting a proportion of the capital requirements for market risks. The following condition has to be fulfilled: its use is limited to 250% of Tier 1 which is required to support market risks, i.e. a minimum of about 28.5% of market risks needs to be supported by Tier 1 capital not required to support risks in the remainder of the book. Additionally, Tier 2 may be substituted for Tier 3 up to 250% provided that Tier 2 does not exceed total Tier 1 and long-term subordinated debt does not exceed 50% of Tier 1 capital.

Pre-commitment

The focus switches here from the 'how it is' risk-based capital adequacy regulatory regime to the 'how could it be'.

The evolution of the regulatory treatment of market risks was marked by the introduction of the possibility for banks to use internal models for the calculation of market risks capital adequacy. This regulatory development has been surrounded by a lively debate, which can be reduced to a difference of attitude towards the possibility of the activity of risk management. The Pre-commitment approach can be interpreted with reference to this difference. The approach has been theoretically criticised and empirically tested.

Differing opinions about the possibility of risk management

Many of the perverse incentives associated with the implementation of the standard-ized measurement system (see above) surfaced again within the present internal models' framework. The minimum VaR multiplication factor of 3 is thought to provide arbitrarily excessive capital coverage. Should the capital coverage arrived at by means of the multiplication factor be higher than that generated by the standard framework, incentives against the development of more accurate internal models, and against the preservation of any in-built conservative element, would spring up. Oddly enough, banks could be penalized, rather than rewarded, for working on their risk management systems. In a extreme case, this could lead to a bank maintaining a second model only for the purpose of market risk-based capital calculation.

Attributing capital penalties according to the results of the backtesting exercise may also appear inappropriate. When model weaknesses are recognized, a bank can immediately take action to improve its VaR model. In contrast, the regulatory intervention may take effect less rapidly than the one of the bank and eventually impose a capital sanction deprived of its *raison d'être*.

The present internal model approach remains silent on the magnitude of the losses expected within the Value-at-Risk area. This could lead regulators to favor a model showing a 1% occurrence of a loss corresponding to 20% of the capital rather than a model showing a 2% occurrence of a loss corresponding to 3% of the capital.

Generally, backsliding into modeling by standardizing through the industry many of the parameters appears, to many, inconsistent with the premise that banks better know their market risks when it comes to modeling them.

The Basel Committee replies that the multiplication factor is designed to account for the fact that market price movements may differ from the statistical simplifications used in modeling. The past is not an accurate approximation of the future (models cannot adequately capture event risk arising from exceptional market circumstances) and the VaR estimate does not eliminate the possibility that the intraday trading may improve the overall risk exposure (contamination problem).

The Basel Committee recognized that banks know better the risks associated with their (portfolio of) positions. However, it regulated the use of internal models to make sure that the output in terms of capital is sufficient to absorb losses that could occur during the holding period. Thus, regulators basically look at the potential outcome of intraholding-period risk management activity in a negative way (as being likely to increase the overall risk exposure). This is because to them, the output of the model is the ending point of the market risks management story; i.e. its only purpose is to set regulatory capital.

To banks, on the other hand, the output of the model is the beginning of the market risks management story. A successful risk management activity relies on a positive attitude towards the potential outcome of the intraholding-period risk management activity. This is seen as being able to reduce the overall risk exposure, or to maintain it within reasonable limits.

These differing attitudes to the possibility of risk management activity provide a background for introducing the Pre-commitment approach and its critics.

The Pre-commitment approach

The Pre-commitment approach was introduced by Kupiec and O'Brien in 1995 as an alternative to the framework laid down by regulators for the use of internal models to set capital adequacy against market risks. These authors criticized the assumptions inherent in the Basel Committee's internal model approach, counterbalanced the pessimistic view on the risk consequences of intraholding-period trading activity and put forward the Pre-commitment approach.

Pitfall of the Basel internal models approach

The reliability of the Basel Committee's internal model approach rests on the assumption that a VaR model can accurately measure the bank's risk exposure over a 10-day holding period. It presupposes that long horizon risk estimates can be constructed from the banks' one-day risk measurement models. Kupiec and O'Brien made clear that risk managers arrive at long horizon risk estimates by either scaling the bank's estimated matrix of daily volatilities by 10 using the assumption of normality or by requiring the bank to estimate directly the 10-day covariance matrix of primitive asset returns.

Two difficulties complicate the extrapolation procedures: the true short-run distribution of primitive asset returns is not normal and the returns on primitive assets are very likely not instantaneously jointly normal, temporally independent and do not share the same distribution at each instant. As a consequence, the correct VaR measure will not be a simple multiple of the portfolio return's standard deviation.

Revaluing the possibility of risk management

Kupiec and O'Brien argued that intraholding-period trading activity may have a positive effect on the risk exposure. That is, the contamination of the holding period by intraperiod trading may really not be poisonous but just the antidote to poison.

Risk managers intervene on two levels: first, at the model level, by supplementing the model output with subjective judgements; second, at the level of positions, by adjusting the positions quickly to counteract either the consequences of large errors in estimating risk exposure or the consequences of an actual large exposure. Over lengthy regulatory holding periods, banks adjust their portfolios in response to market moves by making frequent adjustments to exposures, thus containing losses within management guidelines. In the words of Kupiec and O'Brien (1996, p. 64), 'the combined use of judgement and models is standard practice in daily risk management operations, and yet this interaction is [only one-sided, namely, negatively accounted] for in the internal models approach'.

The Pre-commitment approach

The Pre-commitment approach asks banks to '... pre-commit to a maximum potential loss on the trading portfolio over the regulatory holding period and ... commit capital to cover the maximum loss Pre-commitment' (Kupiec and O'Brien, 1995a, p. 47). The bank would choose its capital commitment, defined as a quantity that covers the maximum cumulative losses during the period rather than a daily requirement (Kupiec and O'Brien, 1996). A system of penalties in case '... of violation of the maximum loss Pre-commitment would give banks an incentive to manage their risk to stay within pre-commitments limits' (Kupiec and O'Brien, 1995a, p. 47). Regulators would review the chosen capital commitment, be satisfied that this figure was consistent with the bank's trading policy and risk management controls and make sure that qualitative risk management standards are implemented. The capital commitment could be publicly disclosed (Kupiec and O'Brien, 1995b). According to Kupiec and O'Brien (1996), the Pre-commitment approach would provide an efficient and less costly mechanism for achieving the adjustment in risk management supposedly to be induced by the actual multiplication factor.

All in all, the Pre-commitment approach rebalances the regulators accountancy of the possibility of risk management by duly recognizing the positive, i.e. risk reduction, side of the continuous combination of judgment and models in risk management activity. The approach has also the advantage of being result-oriented rather than process-oriented. It does not distinguish whether the losses originated from market mouvements, settlement failure, operational or legal problems). Therefore it generates a strong incentive for banks to identify, limit and control all these different risks (Jackson *et al.*, 1997).

Theoretical criticism and practical test

The Pre-commitment approach has been criticized on a theoretical basis and tested in practice.

The criticism

Gumerlock (1996) mitigated the hopes that the Pre-commitment approach could provide *the* solution to the calculation of adequate capital against market risks by highlighting that full reliance on bank decisions concerning the structuring of the VaR model and the monitoring of the exposure could overestimate the positive effects, i.e. risk-reduction effect, of continuous active risk management. In his words, the paradigm is one '... where losses are seen as happening in a time frame sufficient for management to respond with various kinds of stop-loss actions. [It] depends on firms with one-day value-at-risk models successfully conducting stop-loss trading activity to limit cumulative losses'. It is therefore appropriate for ordinary trading days only. It would not work during periods characterized by market shocks, i.e. it would not provide enough capital coverage in the system to avert systemic risks, the kind of events of interest to regulatory authorities. That is, Gumerlock rebalances again the possibility of risk management by weighting more heavily the potential negative, i.e. risk increase, side of the continuous combination of judgment and models in risk management activity.

Testing Pre-commitment

In the fourth quarter of 1996, the New York Clearing House organized a Precommitment pilot study in which a handful of banks took part.[18] Each bank submitted a Pre-commitment amount of capital at the start of each of the four quarters until the third quarter of 1997. They then compared the amount of precommitted capital for the period, with the actual *ex-post* trading profit and loss as reported to the firm's own regulator.

Never did a bank's result threaten the amount of capital precommitted. The ratio of precommitted capital to the actual periodic trading results appeared to vary among the banks, thus confirming the ability of the approach to account fully for the banks' subjective perception of the volatility of their earnings. The amount of capital banks chose to precommit appeared to be significantly less than the amounts required following the internal model approach of the Basel Committee (Shepheard-Walwyn, 1998).

In truth, the relevance of these results would need to be weighted by the number and magnitude of the volatility shocks which characterized the test period.

Risk management organization of financial intermediaries and disclosure recommendations

As shown in the case of the use of internal VaR models to set capital against market risks, international regulators acknowledged that quantitative rules are not alone sufficient to promote stability in the financial system. Qualitative standards to be met in the risk management organization as well as information disclosure are equally essential.

The presentation of the actual state of the regulation of interest rate risk management (a market risk) related to positions pertaining to the banking book provides a good transition from the preceding section to the more global subject of the regulation of the risk management of financial intermediaries and of disclosure recommendations. It introduces, in particular, the issues related to the measurement of risk for capital adequacy purposes faced by regulators whenever addressing capital adequacy for risks other than market risks on the trading book.

The Basel Committee's qualitative requirements prescribed in 1996 to banks that want to use internal models for setting capital against market risks on the trading book, reiterated and developed within the context of interest rate risk on the banking book (1997), find their origin in 1994. At that time, following other international forums, the Committee extensively addressed, in cooperation with the Technical Committee of the International Organization of Securities Commissions, the issue of risk management organizational standards to be met by financial intermediaries if they want to be active in the field of derivative activities.

To enhance market discipline, such that financial intermediaries that manage risk effectively are rewarded and financial intermediaries that do not are penalized, the Euro-currency Standing Committee of the Central Banks of the Group of Ten Countries, the Basel Committee on Banking Supervision and the Technical Committee of the International Organization of Securities Commissions, published disclosure recommendations and developed a framework for the transmission to supervisors of a more detailed information about derivatives and trading activities.

Interest rate risk management on the banking book

The regulation of interest rate risk management associated to positions pertaining to the banking book consists of a list of qualitative principles and does not prescribe, for the time being and for reasons to be mentioned, either a standardized risk measurement methodology (or models parameters setting) or, as a consequence, a quantitative risk-based capital charge.

The principles[19]

The principles for the management of interest rate risk are broadly in line with those prescribed for the use of internal models in the measurement of market risks in the trading book (see above) and with those making up the guidelines for the management of derivative risks (see below). The principles address the role of the board and senior management, the definition and content of risk policies and procedures, the main features of measurement and monitoring systems, the framework for internal controls and the information to be made available to supervisors.

The role of the board and senior management

'In order to carry out its responsibilities, the board of directors in a bank should approve strategies and policies with respect to interest rate risk management and ensure that senior management takes the steps necessary to monitor and control these risks. The board of directors should be informed regularly of the interest rate risk exposure of the bank in order to assess the monitoring and controlling of such risk.

Senior management must ensure that the structure of the bank's business and the level of interest rate risk it assumes are effectively managed, that appropriate policies and procedures are established to control and limit these risks, and that resources are available for evaluating and controlling interest rate risk.

Banks should clearly define the individuals and/or committees responsible for managing interest rate risk and should ensure that there is adequate separation of duties in key elements of the risk management process to avoid potential conflicts of interest. Banks should have risk measurement, monitoring and control functions with clearly defined duties that are sufficiently independent from position-taking functions of the bank and which report risk exposures directly to senior management and the board of directors. Larger or more complex banks should have a designated independent unit responsible for the design and administration of the bank's interest rate risk measurement, monitoring and control functions.'

Policies and procedures

'It is essential that banks' interest rate risk policies and procedures be clearly defined and consistent with the nature and complexity of their activities. These policies should be applied on a consolidated basis and, as appropriate, at the level of individual affiliates, especially when recognizing legal distinctions and possible obstacles to cash movements among affiliates.

It is important that banks identify the risks inherent in new products and activities and ensure these are subject to adequate procedures and controls before being introduced or undertaken. Major hedging or risk management initiatives should be approved in advance by the board or its appropriate delegated committee.'

Measurement and monitoring system

'It is essential that banks have interest rate risk measurement systems that capture all material sources of interest rate risk and that assess the effect of interest rate changes in ways that are consistent with the scope of their activities. The assumptions underlying the system should be clearly understood by risk managers and bank management.

Banks must establish and enforce operating limits and other practices that maintain exposures within levels consistent with their internal policies.

Banks should measure their vulnerability to loss under stressful market conditions – including the breakdown of key assumptions – and consider those results when establishing and reviewing their policies and limits for interest rate risk.

Banks must have adequate information systems for measuring, monitoring, controlling and reporting interest rate exposures. Reports must be provided on a timely basis to the bank's board of directors, senior management and, where appropriate, individual business line managers.'

Internal controls

'Banks must have an adequate system of internal controls over their interest rate risk management process. A fundamental component of the internal control system involves regular independent reviews and evaluations of the effectiveness of the system and, where necessary, ensuring that appropriate revisions or enhancements to internal controls are made. The results of such reviews should be available to the relevant supervisory authorities.'

Information for supervisory authorities

'Supervisory authorities should obtain from banks sufficient and timely information with which to evaluate their level of interest rate risk. This information should take appropriate account of the range of maturities and currencies in each bank's portfolio, including off-balance sheet items, as well as other relevant factors, such as the distinction between trading and non-trading activities. (. . .). Supervisors can use this basic information to perform their own assessments of a bank's exposure and risk profile'.[20]

Thus, for the first time, the Basel Committee suggests that supervisory authorities could actively and independently monitor the banks' level of interest rate risk in a quantitative way.

A closer look

The effects of changes in interest rates are usually evaluated from two complementary perspectives, earnings and economic value. In the former case, the focus is on the impact of changes in interest rates on periodically reported earnings (book values). In the second case, the focus is on the present value of all expected cash flows.

The risks involved are: repricing risk (related to differences in the maturity and repricing of banks' interest rate-related positions), yield curve risk (arising from unanticipated shifts of the yield curve), basis risk (stemming from imperfect correlation in the adjustment of the rates earned and paid on different instruments with similar repricing characteriztics) and option risk (typically embedded in many interest rate-related balance sheet instruments).

The Basel Committee does not prescribe, for the management of these market risks, either a standardized risk measurement methodology (or model parameters setting) or a quantitatively detailed risk-based capital charge. It simply comments that all banks should have enough capital to support interest rate risks. Why?

Providing an answer to this question allows for the drawing of a global picture about the interaction of bank proprietary risk measurement techniques with international industry risk-based capital requirements.

Standardization difficulties

The position of the Basel Committee in relation to the regulation of interest rate risk management on the banking book is dictated by the present difficulty of defining a measurement methodology which needs to be:

- Detailed enough to encompass the major risks related to balance-sheet interest rate-related positions and
- General enough to be uniformly proposed at national and international levels (as it is the case for the VaR for the trading book).

Non-maturing accounts like savings deposits and (Swiss) variable rate mortgages provide an insight into this problem. It is typical of these instruments that customers have the option to withdraw/prepay at any time and that banks can freely adjust the coupon they pay or get paid to a certain extent independently from changes in market rates. It is also typical of these instruments that they are not traded.

To model the cash flows associated to these positions, which is a precondition to perform a risk analysis from either the economic value or earnings perspectives, banks may employ either statistical methods or option pricing techniques. As an example of a statistical technique, banks attempt to replicate the development of the interest rate of a particular instrument with a combination of straight bonds (fixed cash flows) with different maturities and yields, in different proportions. The short-coming in this approach is that it poorly accounts for the customers' prepayment/withdraw option and for the option the banks have in fixing the coupon they pay or get paid. These behavioral options are simply pictured by means of the repricing strategy and cash flows structure implied by the composition (in staggered tranches) of the straight bonds making up the replicating portfolio.

Option pricing techniques allow for a better valuation. The method requires combining a prepayment/withdraw model and a coupon model with an interest rate model. The clients behavior regarding prepayment/withdraw is modeled on the basis of historical prepayment/withdraw records. The bank's behavior regarding the fixing of the coupon is equally modeled on the basis of historical records. The interest rate model provides future interest rate scenarios. The link of the coupon model with the interest rate model provides scenarios for the coupon. Both simulated future interest rate scenarios and coupon scenarios interact with the prepayment/withdraw model to come up, eventually, with modeled, scenario- (path-)dependent, cash flows.

The modeling of the customers' prepayment/withdraw option and of the coupon is largely dependent on the particular portfolio of clients of each bank and the economic environment in which the bank operates. Therefore, it cannot be easily generalized as an international detailed methodology. Furthermore, this method raises technical difficulties as far as the modeling of the coupon is concerned.

In the end it should be emphasized that the usual backtesting procedure (as stated for the use of internal models to set capital against market risks on the trading book) cannot be implemented for validating the models. These products are not traded, thus a historical series of market prices is missing.

As illustrated on the basis of modeling the balance sheet's embedded options of non-maturing accounts, the present proprietary risk measurement practice raises some new issues (validation through backtesting, enhanced bank-specific nature) regarding its generalization to an international methodology for setting risk-based capital adequacy.

Accordingly, the Basel Committee '... has set out principles for sound interest rate risk management rather than establishing a more standardized measure for interest rate risk', acknowledging '... that industry techniques for measuring and managing interest rate risk are continuing to evolve, particularly for products with uncertain cash flows or repricing dates, such as many mortgage-related products and retail deposits'.[21]

Banks' risk measurements and industry risk-based capital requirements

Risk-based capital adequacy regulation rests on the idea that capital should be judged adequate in relation to the riskiness of bank positions and not in relation to the nominal value of its positions. Banking industry risk-based capital requirements began with the standardized framework for measuring credit risk and market risks. The weakness of this framework is that it cannot adequately picture bank-specific risk profiles. The institutionalization of the use of Value-at-Risk methods has provided the basis for regulators to allow for the use of in-house models for measuring market risks.

Although conceding a certain degree of individuality, proposing a capital ratio throughout the international banking industry was only possible by standardizing many of the VaR parameters and multiplying its output (at least) by 3. Notwithstanding the fact that the use of internal models already necessitates regulatory one-to-one discussions and tests, the framework has still appeared inconsistent with the premise that banks better know their risks when it comes to measuring them (see above). The measurement of interest rate risk on the banking book shows a situation in which, for the time being, neither an institutionalized approach easily standardizable, nor backtestable models along the lines of VaR for the trading book do exist.

This global picture will have to be kept in mind when attempting at evaluating the prospects for risk-based capital adequacy and for the use of internal measurement models for other risks than market risks on the trading book.

Risk management guidelines for derivatives[22]

Concerns with the effective functioning and stability of financial markets expressed by both pratictioners and regulators following the huge development of the activity in derivative products were at the origin of the document *Derivatives: Practices and Principles* published by the Group of Thirty in 1993. One year after the Basel Committee on Banking Supervision and the Technical Committee of the International Organization of Security Commissions introduced the *Risk Management Guidelines for Derivative*, whose content would have been reiterated and developed in 1996 (*Qualitative Requirements for the Use of Internal Models in the Measurement of Market risks in the Trading Book*, see above) and, for banks, in 1997 (*Principles for the Management of Interest Rate Risk*, see above).

Bank and security supervisors ask the risk management organization of financial intermediaries active in both OTC and exchange-traded derivatives to comply with the following guidelines in five kinds of derivative-related risks.

Organizational standards

The guidelines address the oversight of the risk management process, the risk management process itself and the structure of internal controls and audits.

Board of directors, senior management and risk management functions

The board of directors should approve all significant policies and procedures relating to the management of risks of the whole institution as well as all significant changes to them. It should regularly be informed about the risk exposure and reevaluate these policies and procedures. The board should also entertain and foster discussions about the risk management process and the exposure between all the parties involved. The policies should be consistent with the business strategy, the capital strength, the management expertise and the firm's risk appetite.

Senior management has a more operative task, namely, making sure that there are adequate policies and procedures for conducting derivative operations, managing the risks (risk measure, risk reporting, risk taking limits and effective internal controls) and that there are sufficient resources and qualified staff.

Engagement in (new) derivative activities should not be approved prior to detailed analysis of the relevant financial products (including the legal aspects), markets, business strategies, reasonableness in relation to the overall firm's financial condition and capital level, availability of the necessary risk management human resources, risk management procedures, measurement and control systems.

It is important that the process of measuring, monitoring and controlling risks be performed independently of individuals conducting derivatives activities. Risk managers should independently report the exposure, should thoroughly understand the risks involved in the activities and be subject to a compensation policy unrelated to the performance of trading activities.

Risk measurement, risk limits, reporting and management review

The measurement and aggregation of risks should take place across trading and non-trading activities on an institution-wide basis to the fullest extent possible. The processes should be such as to enable coverage of all relevant risks on a timely basis (daily or on a real-time basis). Risk measurement should include the performance of stress tests, including worst-case scenarios and the effects of unusual changes in prices, in volatilities, in market liquidity as well as the possibility of the default of a large counterparty. These quantitative exercises should be accompanied by a qualitative assessment of the management actions to be taken under particular scenarios (e.g. contingency plans).

Risk measurement would be sterile if not compared with risk limits. Risk limits and risk taking guidelines should be set at an integrated institution-wide level for each type of risk involved. The guidelines should address the prompt treatment of exceptions to limits.

A timely management information system should be implemented firm-wide. The risk management function should monitor and report its risks measures to the senior management and to the board of directors in a non-technical and non-quantitative format. In dealer operations, exposures and profit and loss statements are to be reported on a daily basis to supervisors unrelated to the conduct of those activities.

The various building-blocks of the risk management process should be regularly (at least annually) reviewed, evaluated and updated to changes in the activities and in the market environment. The review process should include the limit structure and the models' underlying methodologies.

Internal controls and audits

A sound system of internal controls is a condition *sine qua non* for effective and efficient operations, reliable reporting and regulatory compliance. Internal controls should apply to all the aspects of the risk management process mentioned above. Internal auditors, in turn, should evaluate the effectiveness of internal controls, understanding, documenting, evaluating and testing them.

The risks addressed

Derivative activities involve the taking of five kinds of risks:

1 Credit risk (including settlement risk), defined as the risk that a counterparty fails to perform on an obligation to the institution.

2   Market risk, defined as the risk to an institution's financial condition resulting from adverse movements in the level or volatility of market prices.
3   Liquidity risks: one defined as the risk that an institution may not be able to unwind easily or offset a particular position at or near the previous market price and related to specific products or markets; the other defined as the risk that the institution will be unable to meet its payment obligations on settlement dates or in the event of margin calls (it is related to the general funding of the institution's derivatives activities).
4   Operational risk, defined (in the 1994 Basel Committee's paper) as the risk that deficiencies in information systems or internal controls result in unexpected losses. This risk, difficult to define properly, is associated with human errors, system failures and inadequate procedures and controls.
5   Legal risk, defined as the risk that contracts are not legally enforceable or documented correctly.

Derivatives and trading activities: public disclosure and supervisory information

Information disclosure is a hot topic among financial intermediaries. The existence of financial intermediaries is *also* explained with reference to informational asymmetries. However, financial markets function more efficiently when participants have better information about risks and returns. Also, an improved symmetry in the disclosure of information can help mitigate market disturbances by enhancing market discipline. The focus of regulators is therefore on favoring a harmonized disclosing practice, and on improving the content of the information disclosed, in order to fill the gap between the risk management information produced in-house and the information currently disclosed.

The 'history' of risk measurement for regulatory purposes, from standardized frameworks to internal models, from credit risk to interest rate risk on the banking book, has shown (if needed) that financial intermediaries know their risks best. As a consequence, internally generated risk management information may lie well ahead of, and be far more detailed than, the one implied by qualitative and quantitative regulatory guidelines. Aware of that, and in order to enhance further the prudential supervision of financial intermediaries, regulators have developed a framework for supervisory information about the risk management of derivatives and trading activities.

Public disclosure of derivatives and trading activities[23]

The recommendations define the broad characteriztics of the information to be disclosed. The information should be meaningful and understandable. It should preserve proprietary information and not be too burdensome. It should be such as to allow comparisons between firms. Eventually, the information should be timely and independently auditable. The information should encompass the risks incurred in trading and derivatives activities on a portfolio basis.

The qualitative side should cover the objectives and strategies of trading activities, the risk-taking philosophy and the way these activities fit into these objectives. It should enlarge on the organization of risk management and risk control and should provide a description of the major risks involved. Information about accounting and calculation methods should also be provided.

On the quantitative side, based on internal models, a financial intermediary should disclose information on models, assumptions, parameters, exposures and on the actual risk management performance. The information should be complemented with the impact on earnings of trading activities.

Supervisory information about derivatives and trading activities[24]

Supervisors have put forward a catalogue of information judged as important for evaluating derivative risks and a common minimum framework of information to which supervisors should have access. The latter appears to have been widely implemented by now. The data may be collected in several ways: by drawing from internal risk management systems, through on-site examinations, external audits, by means of special surveys or regular reporting procedures.

The information listed in the catalogue covers first credit risk. The focus is on OTC derivatives and on measures such as current and potential exposures (once enforceable netting agreements have been taken into account), risk concentration and counterparty quality. It includes, second, liquidity risk (market risk and funding risk). Third, it considers market risks, focusing on position data and on in-house estimates. The catalogue also comprises information about the impact of derivatives on an institution's earnings profile. Reference is made to trading income information (broken down by broad risk classes).

The common minimum information framework applies primarily to large, internationally active firms significantly involved in trading and derivative activities. The required information encompasses the scope and nature of an institution's involvement in the derivatives markets and the minimum data necessary to assess the market values, as well as the potential credit exposure, by broad risk categories. The framework also covers information on the notional amounts of derivatives by broad risk categories and by maturity as well as the counterparty credit risk. The credit quality of the counterparty, the impact of legally enforceable netting agreements, the use of collateral and guarantees are also part of the framework.

Cross-border and conglomerates supervision

The increasing globalization and integration of the financial services industry requires the supervision and regulation of risk management to overcome national boundaries and to embrace financial conglomerates. From the supervisory perspective, this implies institutionalizing cross-border banking supervision as well as financial conglomerates supervision.

Cross-border banking supervision

Modern international risk management regulatory requirements began in 1988, with the document *International Convergence of Capital Measurement and Capital Standards* (known as the capital accord on credit risk) of the Basel Committee on Banking Supervision.

The Basel Committee on Banking Supervision took up the 'implied' subject of cross-border supervision in 1990, when it provided practical guidance for setting up and managing information flows between national regulatory authorities. It further developed this aspect in 1992[25] by publishing minimum standards for the supervision of international banking groups and their cross-border establishments. The

Committee reaffirmed the necessity for supervisory authorities to cooperate on all prudential matters pertaining to international banking.

Specifically, it stated that 'all international banking groups and international banks should be supervized by a home country authority that capably performs consolidated supervision'.[26] This implies that the home country supervisor receives information on the banking group's global operations and that is capable of preventing corporate affiliations, should these hinder the effective supervision of the group. Also, 'the creation of a cross-border banking establishment should receive the prior consent of both the host country supervisory authority and the bank's and, if different, banking group's home country supervisory authority. ... Supervisory authorities should possess the right to gather information from cross-border banking establishments of the banks or banking groups for which they are the home country supervisor.... If a host country authority determines that any one of the foregoing minimum standards is not met to its satisfaction, that authority could impose restrictive measures deemed necessary to satisfy its prudential concerns consistent with these minimum standards, including the prohibition of the creation of banking establishments'.[27].

In 1996, the Basel Committee on Banking Supervision worked together with the Offshore Group of Banking Supervisors[28] to overcome difficulties experienced by national regulators in conducting cross-border supervision of international banks. The recommendations arrived at cover two sets of problems: (1) the home supervisors' access to information and (2) the implementation of the principle according to which all cross-border banking operations should be subject to effective home and host supervision.

1 To carry out effective consolidated supervision, home supervisors require quantitative and qualitative information about financial risks, risk management organization and control. The difficulties experienced originated from bank secrecy legislation and from impediments in conducting on-site inspections by home supervisors.
2 Home supervisors need to be able to assess the kind of supervision exercised by host supervisors. They need to assess all significant aspects of banking organization and operations related to business safety and soundness. The problems in this respect are related to the different interpretation given by host supervisors and home supervisors to the meaning of effective consolidated supervision.

The supervision of financial conglomerates

The Basel Committee on Banking Supervision took up this subject early in 1993, by inviting securities and insurance regulators (the Technical Committee of the International Organization of Securities Commissions and the International Association of Insurance Supervisors) to address the issues related to the supervision of financial conglomerates (defined as 'any group of companies under common control whose exclusive or predominant activities consist of providing significant services in at least two different financial sectors among banking, securities and insurance)'.[29] The 'Tripartite Group', which produced a substantial consultative report in 1995, gave rise to the Joint Forum on Financial Conglomerates[30] in 1996, with the aim to develop further the first report.

The objectives of the Forum were:

1 To review '...means to facilitate the exchange of information between supervisors within their own sectors and between supervisors in different sectors and [to] investigate legal or other barriers which could impede the exchange of information between supervisors within their own sectors and between supervisors in different sectors', and
2 To examine '...ways to enhance supervisory coordination, including the benefits and drawbacks to establishing criteria to identify and define the responsibilities of coordinator, and [to work] on developing principles toward the more effective supervision of regulated firms within financial conglomerates'.[31]

In 1998 the Joint Forum published a consultation document addressing the following issues: (1) capital adequacy, (2) information sharing, (3) coordination, (4) fit and proper principles and (5) a supervisory questionnaire.

1 The capital adequacy principles deal with the assessment of capital adequacy on a group-wide basis. The Forum first states that the measurement technique should detect and efficiently deal with situations:

> Where the same capital is used simultaneously as a buffer against risks in more than one legal entity (multiple gearing)
> Where the proceeds of debt issued by a parent is downstreamed in the form of equity
> Where multiple gearing stems from participations of unregulated intermediate holding companies in dependants or affiliates engaged in financial activities
> Where unregulated entities run risks related to activities otherwise subject to capital adequacy
> Characterized by participation in regulated dependants
> Where the treatment of minority and majority interests is not prudentially sound.

The Forum created three capital measurement techniques:

- *The building-block prudential approach.* This starts with the fully consolidated on- and off-balance sheet commitments split into four blocks: banks, insurance companies, securities firms and unregulated firms. The method involves comparing each block's capital level to its individual capital requirement. This allows for the identification of capital deficits. The regulatory capital requirements of each block (a proxy is used for the unregulated entity) is eventually compared with the aggregate amount of capital across the group.
- *The risk-based aggregation.* This requires adding together the solo capital requirements of the regulated blocks and a notional capital amount or capital norms for the unregulated block. Capital adequacy is arrived at by comparing the result with the group capital endowment.
- *The risk-based deduction method.* This makes use of unconsolidated regulatory data for each block to focus on the net assets of each related company. The book value of each participation in a dependant company is then replaced, in the balance sheet of the participating company, by the difference between the relevant share of the dependant's capital surplus or deficit.

2 The framework and principles for supervisory information sharing aim at facilitating and promoting communication between supervisors.

Understanding the structure of the conglomerate, whether the primary focus of its activity is on banking, on securities, on insurance, or equally shared among these three, is an essential prerequisite for determining how supervision and information sharing may be better organised.

Intense information sharing is essential for supervisors to understand the complexity of transactions that may be used to transfer risk and income within the group, to assess the soundness of controls within the conglomerate and to understand the influence of the dominant entity, the effectiveness of internal firewalls and the group-wide risk exposure. Information sharing should be flexible so as to enable a timely integration of structural development of the conglomerate. It should also cover information about the regulators' own objectives and approaches. As a consequence, information to a single supervisor should be such as to enable an effective supervision of each regulated entity residing within the conglomerate. Each supervisor should proactively interact with other supervisors in communicating and dealing with issues and developments of a material potentially adverse nature. Supervisors should foster an active, trustfully, information sharing cooperation among themselves.

3 The paper on coordination examines the question of the possible identification of a coordinator as well as elements that can help selecting and framing the role of it. The process of cooperation between regulators should be overviewed by a coordinator. Cooperation should be framed by arrangements making sure that certain information is provided in any situation. The existence of a coordinator should increase supervisors' ability to carry out their supervisory responsibilities. It should not in any case create among supervisors the perception of a shift in responsibilities.

4 The fit and proper principles attempt at making sure that supervisors of entities within financial conglomerates are able to exercise their responsibilities. Managers and directors of a entity exercising a material or controlling influence on the operations of other regulated entities should be subject to fitness and proprietary or other qualification tests organized by supervisors. The same holds for shareholders exerting a similar kind of influence. Supervisors of different entities should also be involved in the assessment procedure whenever managers or directors change entity within the conglomerate.

5 Through the elaboration of a questionnaire, the Joint Forum wants to assist supervisors in the process of understanding each others' objectives and approaches. The questionnaire aims at helping supervisors in understanding the objectives and practices and at facilitating the conclusion of arrangements for the exchange of information. The Joint Forum provides a matrix that can be used to capture responses to the questions. Each of the banking, securities and insurance supervisory agencies in those countries where the conglomerate has a significant presence should fill the questionnaire. The goal should be to allow for a comprehensive matching of supervisory structures to the conglomerates' business structures and to facilitate the identification of areas where specific attention is needed.

Conclusion

These closing remarks aim at discussing the current and likely developments in the field of international regulatory requirements for risk management.

Current developments

The present development of regulatory requirements for risk management unfolds along the lines indicated by the preceding three sections. With reference to the internationalization of risk management supervision, the application of supervisory principles is being enhanced on a world-wide basis (global core principles for banking supervision, development of risk management practices in emerging markets). Regarding the organization of firms' risk management, regulators are addressing other risks (operational risk management), strengthening existing measures (internal control systems) and suggesting ways of conduct (banks' interactions with highly leveraged institutions). Concerning quantitative capital adequacy rules, the standard method for setting capital against credit risk is being revised.

Global principles for effective banking supervision

Following the efforts to foster the world-wide application of bank risk management regulatory requirements, the Basel Committee published in 1997 twenty-five core principles for effective banking supervision.[32] The Committee worked closely with non-member supervisory authorities and suggested that international organizations such as the International Monetary Fund and the World Bank use the principles in assisting countries aiming at strengthening their supervisory activity. The goal is to promote global financial stability.

The principles enlarge (1) on the preconditions for effective banking supervision, licensing and structure, prudential regulations and requirements; (2) on the methods for ongoing banking supervision; (3) on information requirements; (4) on formal powers of supervisors and (5) on cross-border banking.

It is a regulatory challenge to establish efficient and pervasive risk management practices in financial intermediaries operating within emerging markets. Emerging markets distinguish themselves, among other things, because of the structure of their financial markets. In many countries, organized futures and options exchanges are non-existent. Risk management practice and regulation are frequently confined to credit risk. Market risks are not seen as key risk areas. Internal controls are frequently lacking.

Operational risk management, internal control systems and interactions with HLI

The Basel Committee on Banking Supervision has recently published a study on operational risk management.[33] The choice reflects the awareness of supervisors that proper management of this risk is essential to banking safety and soundness. Several significant losses could have been avoided if the banks had had a sound operational risk management in place. A lot remains to be done in this crucial field, as witnessed by the fact that even agreement over a definition of operational risk is still lacking (operational risk is mostly defined in terms of what remains after credit and market risks have been accounted for). The Basel Committee might come up with guidelines in the future, after an improved awareness of operational risk and identification of best practices.

The issue of internal controls pertains to operational risk management. In 1998, the Basel Committee issued a draft framework for the evaluation of internal control systems[34] describing the essential elements of a sound system for use by supervisors. The principles for its assessment cover the presence of effective management oversight, the existence of a control culture, the thorough performance of controls, the completeness of the risk assessment process, the reliability, timeliness and accessibility of all relevant information essential to decision making, the existence of an efficient communication network and the performance of controls, monitoring, audits, on a continuous basis.

In the aftermath of the Long Term Capital Management debacle the Basel Committee has made suggestions to financial institutions interacting with highly leveraged institutions (HLI). Quickly summarized, before entering into a relation with HLI, banks (1) should be confident of the reputation and creditworthiness of the institution, (2) should obtain comprehensive financial information on HLI (including both on- and off-balance-sheet items), (3) should develop measures of leverage relating to a measure of risk, (4) should impose tougher credit conditions, (5) should reject full collateralization of mark-to-market exposure as a risk management tool because it fails to eliminate exposure to declining market value of the pledged collateral.

Credit risk capital adequacy

A large consensus has emerged on the outdated character of the regulatory treatment of credit risk introduced in 1988.[36] The loan categories discussed in the Accord are too general and bear almost no relationship to risk. Thus, for instance, a unique risk weight for every private loan ignores the difference in the risk of a loan granted to a healthy company compared to the risk of a loan given to a firm close to bankruptcy. Also, lending to South Korea in 1999 requires much less capital than lending to a top AAA company (because South Korea is an OECD member).

Major banks have developed sophisticated VaR-derived credit risk modeling techniques. As a consequence, where these models suggest the required capital be lower than the regulatory capital, banks have incentives to convert these assets into tradable securities. On the other hand, where the models suggest the required capital be greater than the regulatory capital, banks have incentives to increase the proportion of these assets on their balance sheet.

The consensus on the outdated character of the Accord contrasts with the disagreement on how to reform it. The discussion has started. The most discussed issue so far relates to the use of proprietary models to set capital adequacy.

This orientation cannot surprise us. Based on risk, capital adequacy rules are logically asked to favor better informed and detailed banks' internal estimates over simple, standard risk measurement rules. On this basis, banks had successfully lobbied for the use of internal models to set capital against market risks. However, the discussion of the regulation of interest rate risk management on the banking book (see above) has shown that the use of internal models to set capital against risks others than market risks on the trading book raises new issues, namely the difficulty of validating the model by backtesting its output against historic market prices (because the latter are missing) and the enhanced bank-specific nature of these models, which complicates the process of standardizing its formulation to the whole industry.

The Basel Committee is evaluating the possibility of allowing the use of in-house models to set capital against credit risk. At the time of writing this conclusion (April 1999), it has produced a first report.[37] In the report it is acknowledged that '...credit risk models are not a simple extension of their market risk counterparts for two key reasons:

Data limitations: Banks and researchers alike report data limitations to be a key impediment to the design and implementation of credit risk models. Most credit instruments are not marked to market, and the predictive nature of a credit risk model does not derive from a statistical projection of future prices based on a comprehensive record of historical prices. The scarcity of the data required to estimate credit risk models also stems from the infrequent nature of default events and the longer-term time horizons used in measuring credit risk. Hence, in specifying model parameters, credit risk models require the use of simplifying assumptions and proxy data. The relative size of the banking book – and the potential repercussions on bank solvency if modeled credit risk estimates are inaccurate – underscore the need for a better understanding of a model's sensitivity to structural assumptions and parameter estimates.

Model validation: The validation of credit risk models is fundamentally more difficult than the backtesting of market risk models. Where market risk models typically employ a horizon of a few days, credit risk models generally rely on a time frame of one year or more. The longer holding period, coupled with the higher confidence intervals used in credit risk models, presents problems to model-builders in assessing the accuracy of their models. By the same token, a quantitative validation standard similar to that in the Market Risk Amendment would require an impractical number of years of data, spanning multiple credit cycles.'

Furthermore, the Basel Committee observed a range of *different practices* in the conceptual approaches to modelling. The differences include:

- The definition of credit loss (which encompasses the default-mode paradigm, in which a credit loss arises only if a borrower defaults within the planning horizon, and the mark-to-model paradigm, in which credit deterioration short of default is also incorporated)
- The chosen time horizons for monitoring credit risk
- The measurement of exposure and loss given default
- The aggregation of credit risk
- The measurement of the interdependence of factors that contribute to credit losses
- The measurement of the correlation between defaults and rating migrations.[39]

Hence the conclusion of the Committee that, for the time being, '...before a portfolio modeling approach could be used in the formal process of setting regulatory capital requirements for credit risk, regulators would have to be confident not only that models are being used to actively manage risk, but also that they are conceptually sound, empirically validated, and produce capital requirements that are comparable across institutions. At this time, significant hurdles, principally concerning data availability and model validation, still need to be cleared before these objectives can be met, and the Committee sees difficulties in overcoming these hurdles in the timescale envisaged for amending the Capital Accord.[40]

Among the existing alternative proposals it is worth mentioning the use of credit ratings as a proxy for the riskiness of loans. The problems is that only a few companies have ratings. The proposal could, however, find an application for sovereign risk.

Likely development

The interest in using internal risk models to set capital adequacy against credit risk (see above) should be evaluated taking into account the whole 'history' related to risk measurement for capital adequacy purposes as well as the studies over the effectiveness of risk-based capital adequacy. On this basis it is possible to appreciate fully some radical propositions about the regulation of bank capital which favor a further switch of regulation from complex capital adequacy rules to the quality of each banks' own internal risk management procedures. Mention of a possible development of international risk management regulation concludes the chapter.

Summing up the evolution of risk-based capital adequacy

The measurement of the riskiness of positions lies at the heart of the modern capital regulatory system. Accordingly, banks have asked for the use of their better informed in-house estimates to be permitted. This coherent vindication has been the driving force for the move from standardized methods to bank internal measurement techniques. The use of the latter is allowed as an optional to set regulatory capital against market risks on trading book (provided a set of qualitative requirements is met). Will the regulatory use of proprietary models be extended to risks other than market risks on the trading book? On which conditions?

The use of internal models for regulatory purposes must be accompanied by a minimum level of standardization throughout the industry. Otherwise the regulatory system would implode in a meaningless do-it-yourself-capital-regulation (full use of banks' specific internal models). Additionally, regulators will always need to increase (multiply) the output of internal model-based risk measures to account for model risk (the risk that market price movements may differ from the statistical simplifications used in modeling) and for the fact that the past is not an accurate approximation of the future (models cannot adequately capture event risk arising from exceptional market circumstances). Thus, enhancing the use of internal models following the modalities set down in the guidelines for the calculation of the capital charge against market risks goes hand in hand with the preservation of tensions between banks and regulators. These are nourished by the potential capital misallocation implied by the standardized elements of the regulatory risk measurement system, and can generate perverse behavioral incentives (i.e. incentives leading to an increase of the risk undertaken by a financial firm notwithstanding full regulatory compliance). Furthermore, the discussion of the regulation of interest rate risk management on the banking book and the first report on the use of in-house models to set capital against credit risk illustrated that there are products for which a internal risk measurement model standardizable for regulatory purposes might be difficult to define and to be introduced as an optional to simple standard rules.

The history of risk-based capital regulation appears therefore to be characterized by growing complexity, persistent tensions between risk managers and regulators and likely limitations concerning the regulatory use by banks of proprietary risk measurement models as an optional to simple standard rules along the lines set down in the guidelines for the calculation of the capital charge against market risks.

To complement the history summarized here is the fact that the positive effect of capital regulation on the risk-taking activity of banks has not yet been empirically confirmed. The studies show mixed results: analysing the likely effects of capital requirements on the portfolio selection of banks, economists cannot agree on whether the risk-taking activity of banks tends to increase or decrease. This situation does not help clarifying whether the benefits of international risk-based capital regulation offset its costs (which are undoubtedly positive).[41]

Promoting proactive risk management

Given the evolution of risk-based capital regulation, it is not surprising to find authors who propose to part with complex risk-based capital adequacy frameworks, set capital adequacy according to simple rules and concentrate on the quality of banks' own internal risk management procedures. Thus, Goodhart (1996) argued that 'the first line of defence must be the ... bank's own risk management.... It is, at the least, arguable that the route recently chosen by supervisors to apply risk-weightings to capital adequacy, though entirely understandable, has been *wrong*. It has led them into increasing complexity in a field where not only is it extraordinarily difficult to get the system right in principle, (and they have not done so), but the application of such rules to individual banks in different situations will not only be more expensive but also often less appropriate than those banks' own internal procedures. While a continuing dialogue between regulators and bankers on what is currently best practice in such risk-metrics is highly desirable, it would again seem wrong to try to fix and to impose the usage of particular models, or on particular ways of applying such models.... The emphasis in bank supervision should be placed on (a) public disclosure, (b) each bank's own internal risk control procedures. The concept that the authorities either can, or should, be capable of second-guessing management on the basis of better private channels of information should be refuted. ... There remains a strong case for the application of ... required capital ratios.... But such controls should be few and simple.'

Estrella (1998) approaches the problem by stressing the limitations embedded in the mechanical formulas used to determine adequate risk-based regulatory capital. Financial firms are social institutions. 'They have emerged ... as sets of rules that rest on a social context of common activity. These rules are not limited to formal laws, like banking ... regulations, but also include [dynamic and complex] conventions [whose importance] is pervasive.... How can we rely on static formulas if they have to be applied to a business that is continually changing? ... Obviously, the only way to keep pace is to change the formulas.... There is a danger that changes are now (and will continue to be) required with increasing frequency'. Estrella really points to the fact that complex formulas may have perverse side-effects and, most important, that formulas are bound to be always late in accounting for banking reality. 'It therefore seems advisable to avoid writing detailed mechanical formulas into statute and possibly even into regulation.... If mechanical formulas hold very little promise of identifying appropriate levels of regulatory capital, what else is there for regulators to turn to?' To this author, supervisors should give priority 'to determine whether the appropriate 'attitude and management' toward capital prevail in a firm, to focus on the way things are done ... while limiting reliance on mechanical formulas to a simple well-defined role.... looking ahead, a more adaptable approach could be obtained by a further shift in the focus of regulatory capital from mechanical formulas to supervision.'

In the face of a risk-based capital regulation characterized by growing complexity, persistent tensions between risk managers and regulators and likely limitations concerning the regulatory adoption of proprietary risk measurement models as an optional to simple standard rules, international risk management regulators might further complement defensive, industry-based, risk-based capital adequacy rules with preventive, firm-based, risk management best practices and information disclosure.

Two-tiered regulatory regime?

Stepping back from a complex, partially internal model-based, risk measurement regulatory system to simple rules in setting risk-based capital adequacy, and concentrating on the implementation of preventive risk management best practices might be a too radical and rough forecast of the possible development of international regulatory requirements for risk management. Presently it can be observed that:

1   The regulation of risk management is layered:

    (i)   National discretion is allowed at many regulatory levels

    (ii) *De-minimis* exemptions have been suggested at an international level (e.g. concerning capital requirements on foreign currency positions when these are judged 'negligible')

    (iii) A choice, linked to the level of sophistication of banks' risk management systems, already exists for setting capital against market risks (banks can chose between a standardized approach and the standardized use of proprietary models).

2   The prospective use of internal models to set regulatory capital against risks others than market risks on the trading book goes hand in hand with the difficulty of maintaining a 'traditional' validation process:

- Backtesting the output against historic market prices is problematic because these are missing
- Given the enhanced bank-specific nature of these models, standardizing its formulation at the level of the industry is complicated.

This suggests that it might be difficult to allow the regulatory use of these models in the context of the qualitative and validation requirements laid down in the *Amendment to the Capital Accord to Incorporate Market Risks* of 1996.[42]

3   The emphasis of regulators on capital adequacy is being complemented by a focus on preventive, firm-based, banks' own risk management practice which does not stop growing.

On this basis, supported by the actual polarization of the financial industry in large global players, on the one hand (merging process), and regional institutions, on the other, it is reasonable to mention a two-tiered risk management regulatory regime as a possible development of international regulatory requirements for risk management. Within this regime, large, sophisticated, financial institutions (core institutions) would be asked to meet higher regulatory standards and higher capital standards than other institutions. Core institutions would be allowed to make use of proprietary models (whenever available) to set regulatory capital against risks other than market risks, while other institutions would set capital following a set of readily understandable and simple rules.

The regulatory use of models by core institutions to set capital against risks other than market risks on the trading book would have to be somehow accurately validated and appropriately monitored in their structure and use. With respect to this point the suggested two-tiered regulatory regime would differentiate itself clearly from the present layered regulatory structure (see above, (1)).

Given the nature of the modeling of such risks, the use of proprietary models to set capital would require new working arrangements between risk managers, regulators, external and internal auditors. This would involve a sort of teamwork which should be specifically designed and structured to enable the highest level of judgmental objectivity regarding the model validation process and, more generally, concerning the whole set of qualitative regulatory standards involved.

To conclude, the major advantage of such a two-tiered regulatory regime would be the establishment of a relation between the potential systemic threat, and burden to individual investor, posed by core institutions and the level of sophistication and tightness of the applicable regulatory regime. Additionally, a two-tiered regulatory system would (1) avoid sophisticated banks incurring in the additional costs of maintaining a regulatory risk measurement system and a internal risk measurement system, (2) lessen the danger of development of behavioural incentives of a perverse nature, i.e. leading to an increase of the risk undertaken while complying with regulation, (3) maintain a high level of coherence within the risk management regulatory system, by allowing regulatory capital to be efficiently allocated through superior risk measurement systems whenever available, and (4) provide a institutional set up which fosters the interest of each market participant in developing better informed risk measurement techniques.

A whole study should be devoted to the topic of disclosure. Here, it will simply be noted that (1) there has been a lot of background work going on which has had a modest regulatory and also practical (only a handful of financial firms generously disclose financial, risk and capital information – although with great diversity yet) impacts so far, (2) disclosure is taking up two distinct channels, one directed towards the general public, another towards supervisory authorities, (3) modesty should drive expectations as far as the triggering of an effective market discipline is concerned. The working of the latter involves individual expectations and beliefs (i.e. the elements that govern the aggregated action of the demand side of the financial markets, supposed to exercise an effective discipline on the supply side). The point is that financial markets have been identified by a number of economists as being particularly prone to irrationality, diversity, behavioral volatility and as being the preferred environment for the 'animal spirits' to manifest. It is to be believed that humble progresses can only be expected from a concerted effort amongst all (groups of) market participants, from both the supply and demand sides, in the definition of a disclosure framework. Then it needs to be widely implemented and revised as risk management practice progresses.

Author's note

This chapter draws heavily (as it must) from the papers produced by the Basel Committee on Banking Supervision and from certain papers published by the Technical Committee of the International Organization of Securities Commissions (IOSCO).

The author has expressed his own views in the chapter.

Notes

[1] The Basel Committee on Banking Supervision was established at the end of 1974, following a series of currency and banking disturbances at international level. Founding fathers were the central-banks' governors of the Group of Ten countries. The countries currently represented

are Belgium, Canada, France, Germany, Italy, Japan, Luxembourg, the Netherlands, Sweden, Switzerland, the United Kingdom and the United States. The Committee seeks 'modalities for international cooperation in order to close gaps in the supervisory net and to improve supervisory understanding and the quality of banking supervision worldwide' (Compendium of documents produced by the Basel Committee on Banking Supervision, Basel Committee on Banking Supervision, 1997, p. 1) by exchanging information, improving the effectiveness of supervisory techniques and by setting minimum standards for capital adequacy.

[2] Basel Committee on Banking Supervision (1988, 1991, 1994a,b, 1995b, 1996d, 1998c).

[3] Basel Committee on Banking Supervision (1996a–c).

[4] Basel Committee on Banking Supervision (1997d, p. 78).

[5] Basel Committee on Banking Supervision (1997d, p. 79).

[6] Basel Committee on Banking Supervision (1996c, p. 12).

[7] *Ibid.*

[8] *Ibid.*, p. 51–2.

[9] *Ibid.*, p. 14.

[10] *Ibid*, p. 20.

[11] *Ibid*, p. 24.

[12] *Ibid*, p. 53.

[13] The Institute of International Finance (1993, p. iii).

[14] Basel Committee on Banking Supervision (1995a, p. 2).

[15] *Ibid.*

[16] Basel Committee on Banking Supervision (1996c, Part B).

[17] Basel Committee on Banking Supervision (1996a).

[18] Bank of America, Bankers Trust, Chase Manhattan, Citicorp, First Chicago NBD, First Union, J. P. Morgan, NationsBank, Fuji Bank and Swiss Bank Corporation.

[19] Basel Committee on Banking Supervision (1997a).

[20] *Ibid*, pp 3–5, 36.

[21] *Ibid*, p. 2.

[22] Basel Committee on Banking Supervision (1994c).

[23] Basel Committee on Banking Supervision (1995e, 1999c).

[24] Basel Committee on Banking Supervision (1995c, 1998e).

[25] Basel Committee on Banking Supervision (1992).

[26] *Ibid*, p. 24.

[27] *Ibid*, pp. 25–27.

[28] The group consists of the following member countries: Aruba, Bahamas, Bahrain, Barbados, Bermuda, Cayman Islands, Cyprus, Gibraltar, Guernsey, Hong Kong, Isle of Man, Jersey, Lebanon, Malta, Mauritius, Netherlands Antilles, Panama, Singapore and Vanuatu.

[29] Basel Committee on Banking Supervision (1995d, p. 1).

[30] The Joint Forum consists of an equal number of senior bank, insurance and securities supervisors from the following countries: Australia, Belgium, Canada, France, Germany, Italy, Japan, Netherlands, Spain, Sweden, Switzerland, the United Kingdom and the United States.

[31] Basel Committee on Banking Supervision (1998b, p. 1).

[32] Basel Committee on Banking Supervision (1997b).

[33] Basel Committee on Banking Supervision (1998h).

[34] Basel Committee on Banking Supervision (1998a).

[35] Basel Committee on Banking Supervision (1999a,b).

[36] Basel Committee on Banking Supervision (1988).

[37] Basel Committee on Banking Supervision (1999d).

[38] *Ibid*, pp. 1–2.

[39] *Ibid*, pp. 4–5.

[40] *Ibid*, p. 1.

[41] See Avery *et al.* (1988), Avery-Berger (1991), Berger *et al.* (1995), Boot-Greenbaum (1993),

Bradley *et al.* (1991), Cantor-Johnson (1992), Cole-Gunther (1995), Furlong-Keeley (1989), Gardener (1992), Gennotte-Pyle (1991), Gorton-Santomero (1990), Keeley-Furlong (1990), Keeton (1988), Kim-Santomero (1988), Koehn-Santomero (1980), Lackman (1986), Santomero-Watson (1977), Schaefer (1992), Sheldon (1995, 1996) and Wall-Peterson (1996).

[42] Basel Committee on Banking Supervision (1996c).

References

Allen, M. (1994) 'Building a role model', *Risk*, **7**, No. 9, September.

Avery, J. *et al.* (1988) 'Market discipline in regulating bank risk: new evidence from the capital markets', *Journal of Money, Credit, and Banking*, **20**, 597–610.

Avery, R. and Berger, A. (1991) 'Risk-based capital and deposit insurance reform', *Journal of Banking and Finance*, **15**, 847–74.

Basel Committee on Banking Supervision (1988) *International convergence of capital measurement and capital standards*, Bank for International Settlements, July.

Basel Committee on Banking Supervision (1990) *Information flows between banking supervisory authorities* (Supplement to the 'Basel Concordat' of May 1983), Bank for International Settlements, April.

Basel Committee on Banking Supervision (1991) *Amendment of the Basel capital accord in respect of the inclusion of general provisions/general loan-loss reserves in capital*, Bank for International Settlements, November.

Basel Committee on Banking Supervision (1992) *Minimum standards for the supervision of international banking groups and their cross-border establishments*, Bank for International Settlements, July.

Basel Committee on Banking Supervision (1993a) *Measurement of banks' exposure to interest rate risk*, Bank for International Settlements, April.

Basel Committee on Banking Supervision (1993b) Press statement, Bank for International Settlements, April.

Basel Committee on Banking Supervision (1994a) *Basel Capital Accord: the treatment of the credit risk associated with certain off-balance-sheet items*, Bank for International Settlements, July.

Basel Committee on Banking Supervision (1994b) *Amendment to the Capital Accord of July 1988*, Bank for International Settlements, July.

Basel Committee on Banking Supervision (1994c) *Risk management guidelines for derivatives*, Bank for International Settlements, July.

Basel Committee on Banking Supervision (1994d) *Prudential supervision of banks' derivatives activities*, Bank for International Settlements, December.

Basel Committee on Banking Supervision (1995a) *Proposal to issue a supplement to the Basel Capital Accord to cover market risks*, Bank for International Settlements, April.

Basel Committee on Banking Supervision (1995b) *Basel Capital Accord: treatment of potential exposure for off-balance-sheet items*, Bank for International Settlements, April.

Basel Committee on Banking Supervision (1995c) *Framework for supervisory information about the derivatives activities of banks and securities forms* (joint report by the Basel Committee on Banking Supervision and the Technical Committee of the IOSCO), Bank for International Settlements, May.

Basel Committee on Banking Supervision (1995d) *The supervision of financial con-*

glomerates (a report by the tripartite group of bank, securities and insurance regulators), Bank for International Settlements, July.

Basel Committee on Banking Supervision (1995e) *Public disclosure of the trading and derivatives activities of banks and securities firms*, Bank for International Settlements, November.

Basel Committee on Banking Supervision (1995f) Press statement, Bank for International Settlements, December.

Basel Committee on Banking Supervision (1995g) *Planned Supplement to the Capital Accord to Incorporate Market Risks (Consultative Proposal)*, Bank for International Settlements, April.

Basel Committee on Banking Supervision (1996a) *Supervisory framework for the use of 'backtesting' in conjunction with the internal models approach to market risk capital requirements*, Bank for International Settlements, January.

Basel Committee on Banking Supervision (1996b) *Overview of the amendment to the capital accord to incorporate market risks*, Bank for International Settlements, January.

Basel Committee on Banking Supervision (1996c) *Amendment to the capital accord to incorporate market risks*, Bank for International Settlements, January.

Basel Committee on Banking Supervision (1996d) *Interpretation of the capital accord for the multilateral netting of forward value foreign exchange transactions*, Bank for International Settlements, April.

Basel Committee on Banking Supervision (1996e) *The supervision of cross-border banking*, Bank for International Settlements, October.

Basel Committee on Banking Supervision (1996f) *Survey of disclosures about trading and derivatives activities of banks and securities firms* (joint report by the Basel Committee on Banking Supervision and the Technical Committee of the IOSCO), Bank for International Settlements, November.

Basel Committee on Banking Supervision (1997a) *Principles for the management of interest rate risk*, Bank for International Settlements, September.

Basel Committee on Banking Supervision (1997b) *Core principles for effective banking supervision*, Bank for International Settlements, September.

Basel Committee on Banking Supervision (1997c) *Survey of disclosures about trading and derivatives activities of banks and securities firms 1996*, Bank for International Settlements, November.

Basel Committee on Banking Supervision (1997d) *Compendium of documents produced by the Basel Committee on banking supervision*, Bank for International Settlements, April.

Basel Committee on Banking Supervision (1998a) *Framework for the evaluation of internal control systems*, Bank for International Settlements, January.

Basel Committee on Banking Supervision (1998b) *Supervision of financial conglomerates* (consultation documents), Bank for International Settlements, February.

Basel Committee on Banking Supervision (1998c) *Amendment to the Basel Capital Accord of July 1988*, Bank for International Settlements, April.

Basel Committee on Banking Supervision (1998d) *Consultative paper on the Basel Capital Accord*, Bank for International Settlements, April.

Basel Committee on Banking Supervision (1998e) *Supervisory Information Framework for derivatives and trading activities* (joint report by the Basel Committee on Banking Supervision and the Technical Committee of the IOSCO), Bank for International Settlements, September.

Basel Committee on Banking Supervision (1998f) *Framework for internal control systems in banking organisations*, Bank for International Settlements, September.

Basel Committee on Banking Supervision (1998g) *Enhancing bank transparency*, Bank for International Settlements, September.

Basel Committee on Banking Supervision (1998h) *Operational risk management*, Bank for International Settlements, September.

Basel Committee on Banking Supervision (1999a) *Banks' interactions with highly leveraged institutions*, Bank for International Settlements, January.

Basel Committee on Banking Supervision (1999b) *Sound practices for banks' interactions with highly leveraged institutions*, Bank for International Settlements, January.

Basel Committee on Banking Supervision (1999c) *Recommendations for public disclosure of trading and derivatives activities of banks and securities firms* (joint consultative paper by the Basel Committee on Banking Supervision and the Technical Committee of the IOSCO), Bank for International Settlements, February.

Basel Committee on Banking Supervision (1999d) *Credit risk modelling: current practices and applications*, Bank for International Settlements, April.

Beder, T. (1995) VAR: 'Seductive but dangerous', *Financial Analysts Journal*, September/October, 12–24.

Benston, G. (1992) 'International bank capital standards', in Gray, P. (ed.), *Research in International Business and Finance*, Vol. 9, *Emerging Challenges for the International Financial Service Industry*, JAI Press.

Berger, A. *et al.* (1995) 'The role of capital in financial institutions', *Journal of Banking and Finance*, **19**, 393–430.

Bernake, B. (1983) 'Non-monetary effects of the financial crisis in the propagation of the Great Depression', *American Economic Review*, **73**, 257–76.

Bliss, R. (1995) 'Risk-based bank capital: issues and solutions', *Economic Review – Federal Reserve Bank of Atlanta*, September/October, 32–40.

Boot, A. and Greenbaum, S. (1993) 'Bank regulation, reputation and rents: theory and policy implications', in Mayer, C. and Vives, X. (eds), *Capital markets and Financial Intermediation*, Cambridge University Press, 69–88.

Bradley, M. *et al.* (1991) 'Risk-weights, risk-based capital and deposit insurance', *Journal of Banking and Finance*, **15**, 875–93.

British Bankers' Association (1993) *The Supervisory Treatment of Market Risks – Comments on the Basel Consultative Paper*, London, October.

Cantor, R. and Johnson, R. (1992) 'Bank capital ratios, asset growth and the stock market', *Quarterly Review – Federal Reserve Bank of New York*, **17**, No. 3, Autumn, 10–24.

Cole, R. and Gunther, J. (1995) 'Separating the likelihood and timing of bank failure', *Journal of Banking and Finance*, **19**.

Crouhy, M., Galai, D. and Mark, R. (1998) 'The new 1998 regulatory framework for capital adequacy: 'standardised approach' versus 'internal models',' *Net Exposure*, 4 January (www.netexposure.co.uk).

Davidson, C. (1996) 'Wider horizons', *Risk*, **9**, No. 4, April, 55–59.

Derman, E. (1996) 'Model risk', *Risk*, **9**, No. 5, May, 34–37.

Elderfield, M. (1995) 'Capital incentives', *Risk*, **8**, No. 9, September.

Estrella, A. (1998) 'The future of regulatory capital: general principles and specific proposals', *Swiss Journal of Economics and Statistics*, **134** (4.2), 599–616.

Furlong, F. and Keeley, M. (1989) 'Capital regulation and bank risk-taking: a note', *Journal of Banking and Finance*, **13**, 883–91.

Gardener, E. P. M. (1992) *Capital Adequacy After 1992: the Banking Challenge*, Institute of European Finance, University College of North Wales, Research Papers in Banking and Finance, 11.

Garman, M. (1996) 'Improving on VAR', *Risk*, **9**, No. 5, 61–63.

Gennotte, G. and Pyle, D. (1991) 'Capital controls and bank risk', *Journal of Banking and Finance*, **15**, 805–24.

Giles, M. (1996) 'The domino effect – A survey of international banking', *The Economist*, 6 April.

Goodhart, C. A. E. (1996) 'Some regulatory concerns', *Swiss Journal of Economics and Statistics*, **132**, 613–36.

Gorton, G. and Santomero, A. (1990) 'Market discipline and bank subordinated debt', *Journal of Money, Credit and Banking*, **22**, 119–28.

Group of Thirty (1993) *Derivatives: Practices and Principles*, Washington, DC.

Gumerlock, R. (1996) 'Lacking commitment', *Risk*, **9**, No. 6, June, 36–39.

Hellwig, M. (1995) 'Systemic aspects of risk management in banking and finance', *Schweizerische Zeitschrift für Volkswirtschaft und Statistik*, Special Issue.

Herrig, R. and Litan, R. (1995) *Financial Regulation in the Global Economy*, The Brookings Institution, Washington, DC, pp. 107–8.

International Monetary Fund – Survey (1996) *Much is at Stake for G-7 in Today's Globalised World*, Washington DC, 15 July.

International Organization of Securities Commissions (1995) *The Implications for Securities Regulators of the Increased Use of Value at Risk Models by Securities Firms*, July.

International Organization of Securities Commissions (1997) *Financial Risk Management in Emerging Markets: Final Report*, November.

International Organization of Securities Commissions (1998a) *Risk Management and Control Guidance for Securities Firms and their Supervisors*, May.

International Organization of Securities Commissions (1998b) *Methodologies for Determining Minimum Capital Standards for Internationally Active Securities Firms which permit the Use of Models under Prescribed Conditions*, May.

Irwing, R. (1997) 'The internal question, *Risk*, July, 36–38.

Jackson, P., Maude, D. and Perraudin, W. (1995) *Capital requirement and value-at-risk analysis*, unpublished manuscript, Bank of England, October.

Jackson, P., Varotto, S. and Daripa, A. (1997) 'The Pre-commitment approach to setting capital requirements', *Financial Stability Review*, **3.**

Keeley, M. and Furlong, F. (1990) 'A re-examination of mean-variance analysis of bank capital regulation', *Journal of Banking and Finance*, **14**, 69–84.

Keeton, W. (1988) 'Substitutes and complements in bank risk-taking and the effectiveness of regulation', Federal Reserve Bank of Kansas City, Working Paper (December).

Kim, D. and Santomero, A. (1988) 'Risk in banking and capital regulation', *Journal of Finance*, **43**, 1219–33.

Koehn, M. and Santomero, A. (1980) 'Regulation of bank capital and portfolio risk', *Journal of Finance*, **35**, 1235–44.

Kupiec, P. and O'Brien, J. (1995a) 'Internal affairs', *Risk*, **8**, No. 5, May, 43–47.

Kupiec, P. and O'Brien, J. (1995b) 'Model alternative', *Risk*, **8**, No. 5, June, 37–41.

Kupiec, P. and O'Brien, J. (1996) 'Commitment is the key', *Risk*, **9,** No. 9, September, 60–64.

Kupiec, P. and O'Brien, J. (1998) 'The Pre-commitment approach: using incentives to set market risk capital requirements', *Net Exposure*, **4,** January.

Lackman, C. (1986) 'The impact of capital adequacy constraints on bank portfolios', *Journal of Business Finance and Accounting*, **13,** No. 4, 587–96.

Lane, W. *et al.* (1986) 'An application of the Cox proportional hazards model to bank failure', *Journal of Banking and Finance*, **10,** 511–31.

Lewis, M. K. (1995) *Financial Intermediaries*, International Library of Critical Writings in Economics, Vol. 43, Edward Elgar.

Lubochinsky, C. (1995) *Risk Analysis on Derivative Books and Implications for Regulations*, Caen University, Paris, mimeo.

Mahoney, J. (1995) *Empirical-based Versus Model-based Approaches to Value-at-Risk*, Federal Reserve Bank, New York, mimeo.

Matten, C. (1995) 'The capital allocation challenge for the banks', *Economic and Financial Prospects*, Basel, SBC, No. 4–5, October-November.

Merton, R. (1995) 'Financial innovation and the management and regulation of financial institutions', *Journal of Banking and Finance*, **19,** 461–81.

Prescott, E. (1997) 'The Pre-commitment approach in a model of regulatory banking capital', *Economic Quarterly – Federal Reserve Bank of Richmond*, **83/1,** Winter.

Santomero, A. and Watson, R. (1977) 'Determining an optimal capital standard for the banking industry', *Journal of Finance*, **32,** 1267–82.

Schaefer, S. (1992) 'Financial regulation: the contribution of the theory of finance', in Fingleton, J. (ed.), *The Internationalisation of Capital Markets and the Regulatory Response*, Graham and Trotman, pp. 149–66.

Scott-Quinn, B. and Walmsley, J. (1996) *Risk Management in International Securities Markets: are Today's Standards Appropriate?*, International Securities Market Association (ISMA), Zurich.

Sheldon, G. (1995) 'A limit-risk capital adequacy rule: an alternative approach to capital adequacy regulation for banks with an empirical application to Switzerland', *Swiss Journal of Economics and Statistics*, **131,** 773–805.

Sheldon, G. (1996) *Capital Adequacy Rules and Risk Behavior: An Empirical analysis*, University of Basel, LIU, mimeo.

Shepheard-Walwyn, T. (1998) 'The role of Precommitment in future capital regulation – the lessons of the New York pilot study, *Swiss Journal of Economics and Statistics*, **134** (4.2), 617–24.

Shepheard-Walwyn, T. and Litterman, R. (1998) 'Building a coherent risk measurement and capital optimisation model for financial firms', *Federal Reserve Bank of New York Conference*, February.

Shireff, D. (1995) 'Yes, you may pack your own parachute', *Euromoney*, May, 9–10.

Smithson, C. (1996a) 'Value-at-Risk (I)', *Risk*, **9,** No. 1, January, 25–27.

Smithson, C. (1996b) 'Value-at-Risk (II)', *Risk*, **9,** No. 2, February, 38–39.

Steil, B. (1994) *International Financial Market Regulation*, Wiley.

The Economist (1993) 'The sum, not the parts', London, December, 11.

The Institute of International Finance (1993) *Report of the Working Group on Capital Adequacy*, Washington, DC, October.

Thieke, G. (1994) 'On risk management process and how it relates to derivative activities, International Monetary Conference, London, June.

Wall, L. and Peterson, P. (1996) 'Banks' responses to binding regulatory capital requirements', *Economic Review – Federal Reserve Bank of Atlanta*, March/April, 1–17.

25

Risk transparency

ALAN LAUBSCH

Introduction

This chapter focuses on risk transparency, and the practical issues that arise in the process of risk reporting. The three major phases of risk reporting consist of (a) compiling position and market data in a timely manner, (b) applying appropriate methodologies to calculate risk (including stress testing), and (c) summarizing portfolio risks in a concise and complete manner.

The next section describes best practices for *risk reporting*. We will make suggestions for designing risk reports (i.e. format, content, and organization), and will show sample reports representing four types of companies: banks, hedge funds, asset managers, and traditional corporations.

The third section addresses *external reporting*. We will discuss emerging global standards for public risk disclosures of financial and non-financial companies, and show examples of actual risk disclosures from leading institutions. We will specifically review BIS disclosure recommendations and SEC disclosure requirements

Throughout this chapter, we will demonstrate how risk concepts are implemented in real solutions.

Risk reporting

Risk reporting process

Internal reporting

An efficient risk reporting process is the foundation for clear and timely communication of risk across an enterprise. Risk reports must be produced and distributed to many individuals and businesses. Risk reporting generally occurs at three organizational levels: the corporate, the business unit, and the individual trading desk level. Many risks that are managed at the trading desk level must be summarized in order to create meaningful information for management. Risk professionals design the format and content of these risk reports to suit the specific needs of each organizational level (see Figure 25.1).

Risk communication across the enterprise is summarized by Table 25.1. In addition to reporting on the three organizational levels, companies may have regional reporting (e.g. Deutsche Bank Asia) and legal entity reporting (e.g. J.P. Morgan Securities, Morgan Guaranty Trust Co.).

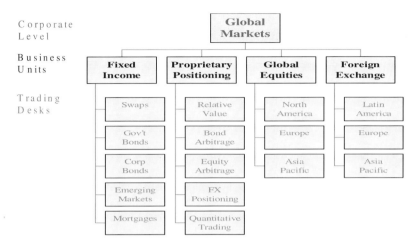

Figure 25.1 Typical organization of a global financial institution.

Table 25.1

Level	Aggregation	Report focus and content
Corporate	Firmwide	Senior managers focus on the total earnings volatility, market risk concentrations between business units, and stress testing. In addition to Value-at-Risk (VaR) numbers, senior managers appreciate written commentary on daily reports.
Business unit	Across trading desks	Business managers monitor risky outliers, large exposures, and yield curve positioning across trading desks.
Trading desk	Across accounts	Traders are interested in detailed risk summaries, hedging, marginal risk analysis, diversification, and individual risk positions.

Time scale

Reporting risk to senior management involves many timescales. Active financial institutions produce same-day market risk reports for discussion by senior managers, risk takers, and risk monitors. A company's Risk Management Committee (RMC) generally meets on a weekly to monthly basis to discuss macro risk exposures and trends in global financial markets. On a quarterly basis, board presentations analyze the firm's overall risk and performance relative to markets and peers.

External reporting

In addition to internal management reports, firms may be subject to regulatory risk reporting. There is also a clear trend toward greater voluntary disclosure of risks, as exemplified by several leading financial institutions' decision to reveal VaR statistics and histograms of trading results in their annual reports.[1] External reporting tends to be highly aggregated rather than instrument- or desk-specific.

Independent risk oversight

At many organizations, an independent risk oversight group is responsible for firmwide risk reporting.

How to use risk reports

Risk managers use firm-wide risk reports to quantify sources of risk across an organization and to estimate total exposure to financial markets. Risk reports at each level of the organization show whether risks are taken within prescribed **internal management limits** and **regulatory capital** constraints. Risk reports are also useful for evaluating risk-adjusted trading performance. Furthermore, risk reports are used for external disclosures to regulators, analysts, credit rating agencies, creditors, and the public.

An eagle-eye view of risk concentrations

Risk reporting is most useful at the corporate level because it can show the aggregation of risk across the entire firm and can highlight risk concentrations arising between separately managed business groups. For example, a daily report may point out unusually high exposure to European interest rates, due to similar positions in several trading desks in Paris, London, and New York. With comprehensive macro risk reporting, risk monitors have an eagle's perspective for identifying risk concentrations across the firm.

Macro risk analysis allows for more targeted and stable risk taking. For instance, if several desks are taking similar risks, risk managers may recommend unwinding or hedging of core positions. On the other hand, if many positions are offsetting, excess risk-taking capacity may be quickly allocated to select trading desks.

What type of information is required?

Significant investment in information infrastructure goes into building a sound risk measurement process. For measuring risk, two basic types of information are necessary: (a) position feeds and (b) market data.

- *Position feeds* Risk reporting systems require collection of position information for all portfolio positions. Given the sheer number of different financial instruments and transactions, this task can become overwhelming. Furthermore, positions may be tracked by many different systems, each with its own method of organizing information. For example, a risk manager of a large Canadian bank reported that his market risk system extracts position data from 70 different systems on a daily basis. In addition, feeds may be delayed or may provide insufficient information. In practice, it is not possible to assure a 100% accurate report of all positions at any point in time. Nonetheless, risk managers need to be confident that they can get a snapshot of the most significant portfolio risk exposures. A risk manager's ideal information infrastructure would include a comprehensive and real-time position data warehouse.
- *Market data* This consists of raw time series of **market rates**, **index levels**, and **prices**, and derived time series of **benchmark yield curves**, **spreads**, **implied volatilities**, **historical volatilities**, and **correlations**. Clean, complete, and timely market data is imperative for measuring risk. Often, data must be collected from several sources, then scrubbed to eliminate **outliers** and adjusted for **missing data points**. Furthermore, data should be snapped at the same time of day when possible. Procuring, cleaning, and organizing appropriate market data is a challenge for all active financial institutions.

Positions

Risk Report

Risk Engine

Market Data

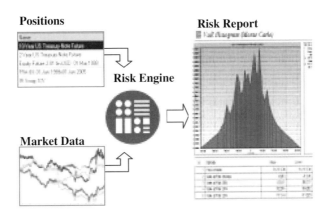

Figure 25.2 Risk information flow. Portfolio positions and market data are fed into a risk engine to generate risk reports, as illustrated here.

What makes a good risk report?

Risk reports should enhance risk communication across different levels of the firm, from the trading desk to the CEO. In this chapter, we focus on daily management VaR reporting. Public risk disclosures are discussed in the next section, credit exposure reporting in Appendix 3.

In order of importance, senior management reports should

- be timely
- be reasonably accurate
- highlight portfolio risk concentrations
- include a written commentary and
- be concise.

Risk reports must be timely

Risk management is a proactive discipline, and the time decay in the value of daily risk reports is high. Risk reports must therefore be timely and reflect current risk positions. For example, traders may look at instantaneous risk calculations, while senior trading desk managers may receive risk snapshots throughout the day. At J. P. Morgan, senior managers review the daily cross-firm risk report before close of business; it gives a rough snapshot of market risks toward the end of the trading day, when guidance can be provided to managers in the next time zone on risk appetite, position unwinding, or macro hedges.

Risk reports should be reasonably accurate

Risk management is not a precise science. The accurate prediction of risk is complicated by theoretical and practical constraints (e.g. unexpected events occur, certain risk factors may not be quantified due to expense or lack of data, market and position data may be delayed or incomplete, and risk methodologies are still evolving). Nonetheless, risk managers should strive to be as accurate as possible, given these constraints. The credibility of the risk management effort suffers if reports are considered inaccurate or unrealistic.

Timeliness versus accuracy

Risk managers may need to sacrifice some accuracy for timeliness. For example, many financial institutions use a same-day report for management purposes, even though they cannot reflect 100% of their positions. A financial control group generally processes a more complete next-day report to verify the accuracy of the previous same-day report. Red flags come up only if there are obvious differences between reports.

The chairperson of one global bank's daily market risk meeting puts it succinctly: 'Having mostly accurate information and people in the meeting who know what's missing is better than a fully accurate report one day too late.'

This practical focus illustrates an important difference between accounting and risk measurement: whereas accounting seeks to represent the past as accurately as possible, risk measurement seeks to capture conditions on the fly.

Risk reports should highlight risk concentrations

Risk reports should show risk concentrations by risk unit, asset class, and country. For interest rate 'curve' risk, it may be useful to look at risk by maturity bands. Risk can be viewed down to the instrument level and trader. Total portfolio VaR should be prominently displayed, and graphs of the entire distribution of potential returns should be available. VaR versus limits is also useful to include for management control.

The specific information in each internal management report varies by level of organization, from macro risk summaries at the corporate level, to detailed risk reports by specific instrument at the desk level, as shown Table 25.2.

Table 25.2

Report type	Content
Corporate level	• Shows total firmwide risk and summary of risk concentration among different business units, asset classes, and countries. • Breaks down VaR versus limits by business unit, asset class, and country. • May include commentary on size of market risk, significant risk concentrations, and interesting market developments. • May include legal entity and regional reports.

Business unit level	• Shows risk summary by trading desks, country, maturity band, and instrument type.
	 • Reports VaR versus limits by total business and individual desks.
	 • Optionally includes
	   – **Marginal VaR** report by desks, country, maturity band, and instrument type.
	   – **Cash flow Map** or **Present Value Report** by currency.

Desk level	• Shows detailed risk summary by instrument, position, and maturity band.
	 • Includes
	   – VaR versus limits by desk and trader.
	   – **Marginal VaR** report by instrument or instrument type.
	   – **Instrument Summary** report.
	   – **Cash flow Map** by currency.

Daily risk reports should include written commentary

Daily risk reports can be enhanced with a qualitative market risk commentary emphasizing notable market developments and risk positions. Often, risk monitors add the commentary after participating in a daily market risk discussion with risk takers and business managers. Commentaries should be brief and to the point (and distribution of the reports should not be slowed while a risk manager struggles with writer's block).

A sample daily market risk commentary

Global market volatility has continued to increase, with widening credit spreads and decreased liquidity for risky assets across Europe and the Americas. Trading volume across US fixed income was unusually low, and corporate bond traders note declining liquidity and increasing spreads due to a flight to quality. The firm's large inventory of corporates could suffer from further widening of spreads. Brazilian markets continue to bleed, with uncertainty surrounding impending fiscal reforms. While mostly FX hedged, the Emerging Markets desk is close to its $2MM VaR limits and could suffer large bond losses if Brazil is forced to raise interest rates to stem capital flight. A Latin American liquidity crunch could put pressure on Emerging Asia again, where the firm has long positions in THB, MYR, and SGD government paper. The FX desk reported significant trading by macro hedge funds, mostly short interest in long dated JPY/USD forwards and options. US equity markets continue to be volatile, with Internet stocks racing ahead. However the bank's direct equity exposure is currently low due to short SPX futures positions in proprietary trading which offset some systemic risk in market making books.

Market Risk Commentary, Wednesday, 17 March 1999

Written commentary is considered especially important for corporate managers, who may not be in touch with minute-by-minute developments on the trading floor. Written commentary adds color from the front lines, improves communication between the trading floor and the corporate office, and facilitates centralized risk management with decentralized position taking.

Risk reports should be concise

Keep summary risk reports to one page containing only essential risk information. No one has the time to be overwhelmed by thick reports full of numbers.

J. P. Morgan's 4:15 Report

Within our eight market-related global products, we have more than 120 risk-taking units spread over 14 locations spanning the globe. Our chairman rather likes the diversification this affords, but has a simple request: 'At the end of each day, tell me what our risks are and how we did.' Our answer is what we call our 4:15 Report – creatively named after a daily meeting at that time, which I typically chair, with senior managers from the main market units.

In a one-page snapshot, we have information on our positions and risk levels in every major market across all our products. There is also information on limits, P&Ls, and commentary on significant developments – all in plain English. And it is delivered each evening to all members of the corporate office, as well as to other

> key senior managers. This has proven to be a useful process to keep risks transparent, to keep communication flowing, and to keep all the key business managers' eyes focused on the same ball – our overall risk levels and performance.
>
> Steve Thieke, J. P. Morgan.

What are the major types of risk reports?

There are a several types of risk reports and measures, each with its own perspective of risk.

- The four major risk measures are **VaR, relative VaR, marginal VaR**, and **incremental VaR**.
- If Monte Carlo simulation or historical simulation is used to calculate risk, a full distribution of potential returns can be plotted to obtain a more elaborate perspective of potential outcomes.
- Stress test reports provide a measure of downside potential due to extreme market movements without prespecified loss probabilities.
- **VaR by counterparty** can be used to quantify potential credit exposure through market driven transactions.

Seven basic report types are widely use (see Table 25.3).

A number of closely related reports are commonly used with risk reports (see Table 25.4).

How do we organize a risk report?

Risk reporting depends on how a firm is organized, and is customized for each level of the organization. Risk reports should show which business units or desks are responsible for positions because it is important to connect exposures back to the risk taker. Therefore, risk reports must specify the most detailed level and then aggregate upwards.

Time dimensions in risk reporting

A company's risk exposures should be communicated on a regular basis. Non-financial companies should have at least monthly reviews of financial risks, while active financial companies should have daily discussions of risk taking. Table 25.5 shows the time dimensions of risk communication at a generic corporation.

In addition to these discussions, active financial institution may have meetings on a daily or weekly basis (Table 25.6).

Global bank case study

Background information

The VaR concept was pioneered by several leading US banks in the 1980s, and is now implemented in most global banks. In 1995, the Basel Committee on Banking Supervision approved VaR to satisfy market risk capital requirements.[2] Large banks tend to have the greatest market exposure to global interest rates and to a lesser extent FX and commodities. Equity market risk is growing as banks merge to become full-service financial institutions with equity under-writing and brokerage. Matrix

Table 25.3

Report type	Content and application

VaR	• VaR reports
	  − estimate the worst-case loss over a defined horizon with a specified confidence level; generally, a 1-day to 1-month horizon is used, and confidence intervals range from 90% to 99%.
	  − are used to measure portfolio risk concentrations
	  − may include VaR versus prespecified limits.
	• VaR may be
	  − analyzed in various dimensions: risk type (or asset class), country or region, maturity or duration band, instrument type or individual instrument, and counterparty;
	  − expressed in base currency or as percentage of notional or market value.

Return histogram	• When Monte Carlo simulation or historical simulation is used, risk reports often show a full histogram of simulated returns. The histogram's advantage is that it shows the full range of potential gains and losses, as opposed to only one specific loss statistic (e.g. a VaR number at 95% confidence yields no information about likely losses beyond that point, whereas a histogram enables you to calculate VaR at any confidence level).

Relative VaR	• Relative VaR
	  − measures risk relative to a prespecified benchmark and is expressed in absolute base currency amount or as a percentage
	  − is commonly used by investment managers with relative return objectives, such as mutual funds that track specific equity indices.

Marginal VaR	• Marginal VaR
	  − measures marginal contribution to portfolio risk and can be analyzed in the same dimensions as VaR; often graphed as a scattergram (e.g. marginal VaR versus VaR or PV)
	  − is useful for identifying and quantifying risk concentrations.

Stress test	• Stress test reports
	  − show the potential present value impact of prespecified scenarios or extreme market movements.
	  − are used to better capture event risk and are a useful complement to VaR analysis.

VaR by counterparty	• Reports VaR by trading counterparty, for estimating potential short-term credit exposure for market driven instruments like swaps, forwards, and options. • VaR by counterparty is used to monitor credit line usage.

organization structures are often used between regional and product managers. For example, Hong Kong equities trading may be the responsibility of the Asian regional manager and the Global Equities product manager.

VaR reporting typically happens at the corporate, business unit, and desk levels of the organization. Daily regional risk reports may also be produced in regional offices (e.g. Asia, Europe, and Americas). For example, Figure 25.4 is the organizational chart of a fictitious company, Global Bank, which is organized by product group and function. All business units are **market-making** groups, except Proprietary Positioning. In addition to daily risk reporting, banks have less frequent reporting that analyzes market trends, limits usage, risk performance, and projected credit exposure for market-driven instruments.

Table 25.4

Report type	Content and application
Present Value Report: provides the discounted net present value of cash flows	• Shows present value of cash flows in the same dimensions as VaR. • Can be used to estimate VaR as a percentage of PV.
Instrument Summary Report: shows instrument-specific information	• Shows information, such as price, notional value, net present value, duration, delta, vega, theta, and gamma. • Used by traders or desk managers interested in specific information.
Cash flow Map: summarizes net mapped cash flows for each currency	• Shows cash flows in designated maturity and currency buckets. • Is useful in understanding net yield curve positioning and can be used to design **macro hedges**.
Credit Exposure Report: shows credit exposures for market driven instrument	• Shows current and potential future credit exposure for market driven instruments, such as swaps, forwards, and purchased options. The three main exposure measures are *current*, *average*, and *peak exposure*. • Used by credit officers to monitor counterparty credit limit utilization.
P&L Report: shows daily mark-to-market (MTM) P&Ls of risk takers	• Compares the returns against the risks taken. For example, if a trader has a VaR of $1MM at 95% confidence and a 1-day horizon, actual returns should exceed VaR with 5% probability or about once in 20 trading days. • The returns are also used in backtesting the accuracy of VaR models.
Position Report: shows size and direction of positions	• Shows internal sources of risk: what positions generate the risk. • Often uses benchmark equivalents to reduce information overload (e.g. 2-year equivalents, C-Bond equivalents).
Market Information Report: shows market rates and indices	• Shows external sources of risk: what market changes generated P&Ls and risk. • Useful for understanding historical evolution of the markets and current conditions.

Corporate level report

The Corporate Level Report is discussed in a daily meeting by senior business managers, risk takers, and independent risk monitors, and then delivered to the CEO (see Figure 25.5).

Regional report

Additionally, regional reports are discussed by regional managers, risk takers, and risk monitors on a daily basis (see Figure 25.6).

Business unit report

Business unit reports may show more detail, for example VaR by instrument type and country (see Figure 25.7).

Desk level report

Desk level reports often contain specific information on positions. For example, see the VaR report for Corporate Bond Trading, which consists of two accounts: (a)

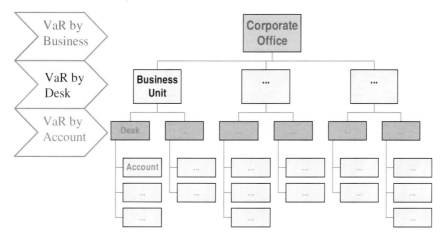

Figure 25.3 Risk reporting from the bottom up.

Table 25.5

Frequency	Risk forum
Monthly	• Corporate office and senior risk managers meet to discuss firmwide market risk profile (this is known as a 'market risk committee'). • Business risk reviews: The independent corporate risk management group and business managers perform these reviews.
Quarterly	• Firmwide risk profile review occurs at a board of directors meeting. • Risk return performance review is handled by a senior management group.
Ongoing	• Stress testing – Business level and firmwide (see Chapter 2). • Backtesting – Business level and firmwide (see Chapter 3). • Model risk reviews – Evaluation of pricing and risk models. • New product reviews – Evaluation of proposed new financial instruments.

Table 25.6

Frequency	Risk forum
Daily	• Management of risk by traders, businesses, and divisions • Same-day risk report of positions, risks, and total returns of global businesses • Meetings to discuss the same-day risk report, market events, and strategies
Weekly	• Local market risk committee meetings by regional office • Conference calls among senior risk managers • Review of counterparty credit exposure reports for market driven instruments

Interest Rate Hedges and (b) Corporates. Notice the underlying position and corresponding swap or futures hedge on the graph, and the summary VaR table showing the risk of each position in the Corporates and Hedges portfolios (see Figure 25.8).

Credit exposure reports

VaR can also be analyzed by counterparty to assess potential credit exposure due to market driven instruments (see Figure 25.9).

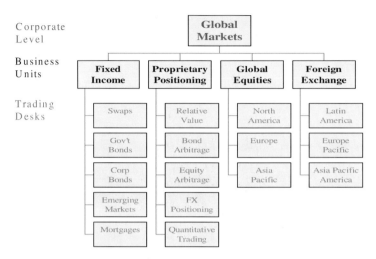

Figure 25.4   VaR reporting in an organization.

Stress reports

Banks perform regular stress tests from the desk to the corporate level. Traders may focus on the behavior of hedged portfolios by shocking specific market variables (such as instrument specific spreads) and the so called 'greeks' of option portfolios (e.g. delta, gamma, vega). Corporate level stress scenarios often consider broader macro scenarios that could have exacerbating effects throughout the firm's businesses. Table 25.7 is an a sample corporate level stress test for Global Bank.

Leveraged fund case study

Background information

There is a large variety of leveraged funds (or hedge funds), from the large Global Macro funds (e.g. Quantum, Tiger), to more specialized quantitative funds (e.g. DE Shaw, LTCM), regional funds, and risk arbitrage funds.

Leveraged funds are sophisticated investors with dynamic and complex trading strategies that can employ a full range of financial instruments. Since many funds are active users of derivatives, traditional notional measures of exposure are meaningless. Rigorous risk measurement and reporting is an essential discipline for these fund managers. Furthermore, in the aftermath of several spectacular fund blow-ups in 1998, regulators, lenders, and investors are requiring greater disclosure of risks.

External disclosures

For reporting risk to lenders and investors, hedge funds need to give a broader overview of risks without divulging specific instrument risks and directionality. For example, based on the internal management report in Figure 25.10, a hedge fund could choose to disclose only the total VaR of $4 001 746 without revealing regional risk details.

Internal management reporting

For internal management purposes, daily reports analyzing risk in several dimensions should be generated. Hedge funds often have very concentrated risks by position, so

Historical VaR Histogram

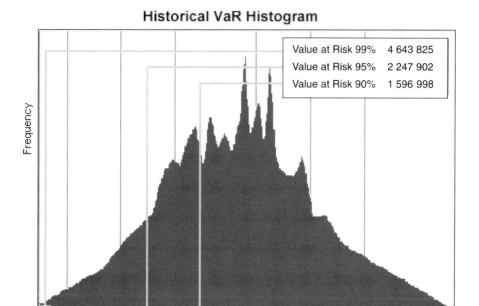

	Value at Risk 99%	4 643 825
	Value at Risk 95%	2 247 902
	Value at Risk 90%	1 596 998

95% VaR (1-day)	Aggregate	Diversi-fication benefit	Emerging markets	Fixed income	Foreign exchange	Global equities	Proprietary positioning
Aggregate	2 247 902	− 1 516 014	758 348	381 807	181 207	877 660	1 564 894
Diversification benefit	− 268 153	− 284 076			− 22 294		− 843 558
FX risk	354 187	− 93 236			79 449		367 974
Interest rate risk	1 307 719	− 979 818	758 348	381 807	124 052		1 023 330
Equity risk	595 424	− 1 040 659				877 660	758 423
Commodity risk	258 725						258 725

Comments
Proprietary positioning is taking large short positions in European Interest rates ($1 023 330 VaR) and equities ($758 423 VaR). On a firmwide basis, these short positions offset inventories held in Global Equities, Fixed Income and Emerging Markets. Hence the large *Diversification benefit* in the Interest rate risk and Equity risk categories.

Figure 25.5 Daily corporate VaR report.

risks are often viewed down to the instrument level. Hedge fund managers can use marginal VaR analysis to identify opportunities for unwinding positions to become more diversified (see Figure 25.11 to identify the 10 highest contributors to risk). Note that the highest stand-alone VaR (#5) is only the fifth highest contributor to risk.

VaR by maturity

For yield curve positioning, hedge funds are also interested in VaR by country and maturity band. Sometimes, curve risk is analyzed by duration instead of maturity band (see Figure 25.12).

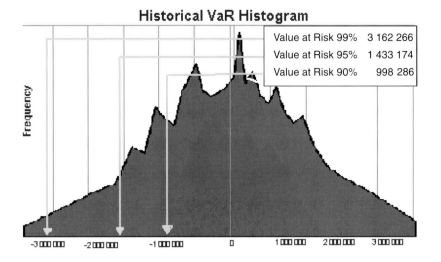

Historical VaR Histogram

	Value at Risk 99%	3 162 266
	Value at Risk 95%	1 433 174
	Value at Risk 90%	998 286

95% VaR (1-day)	Aggregate	Diversi- fication benefit	Fixed income	Foreign exchange	Global equities	Proprietary positioning
Aggregate	1 433 174	− 807 236	500 116	327 826	474 153	938 315
Diversification benefit	− 58 114		− 131 422	0	− 107 890	− 20 256
BEF	77 515	− 6 808	17 819		66 505	
CHF	55 205	− 269 500	139 500		185 205	
DEM	33 179	− 14 348	4 451		12 783	30 292
DKK	221 540	− 9 370	9 577		221 333	
ESP	615	− 25 211			3 475	22 351
EUR	567 650	− 117 737	139 004	327 826		218 557
FIM	56 163	− 5 225	13 852		47 535	
FRF	264 341	− 39 404	118 787		178 101	6 857
GBP	215 080	− 521 088	188 548		273 644	273 976

Comments
Large diversification benefit between Proprietary Positioning and Global Equities due to offsetting positions in GBP.

Figure 25.6 Daily European VaR report.

Investment manager case study

Background information

Investment managers can use VaR for capital allocation and risk-adjusted performance anal-ysis. Many investment managers are evaluated by Sharpe Ratio analysis, and have fixed capital that must be allocated to achieve a high return on risk. Investment managers therefore often analyze positions using Marginal VaR and VaR as a percentage of prevent value. Investment managers weigh expected returns of investments against incremental portfolio risk.

Investment managers also commonly use VaR to assess risk relative to a prespecified investment benchmark, such as the S&P 500 Index. VaR is a useful measure for both investment managers and upper management because it allows benchmark

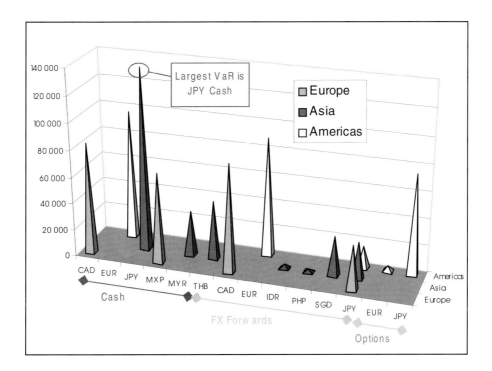

95% VaR (1-day)	Aggregate	*Diversification benefit*	FX Americas	FX Asia	FX Europe
Aggregate	298 533	*− 152 263*	196 261	180 531	74 004
Diversification benefit	*−494 541*		−69 207	−98 381	−208 113
Cash	214 011	*− 133 228*	114 747	135 823	96 669
CAD	83 460		83 460		
EUR	96 669				96 669
JPY	137 209			137 209	
MXP	67 381		67 381		
MYR	34 231			34 231	
THB	43 883			43 883	
FX forward	132 444	*− 75 048*	83 392	38 000	86 100
CAD	81 268		81 268		
EUR	89 157				89 157
IDR	3 309			3 309	
PHP	2 698			2 698	
SGD	29 644			29 644	
JPY	44 617	*− 33 422*	33 359	27 938	16 743
FX option	79 071	*− 63 361*		62 906	79 525
EUR	4 210				4 210
JPY	75 338				75 338

Comments
- Largest single FX exposure is unhedged long JPY cash position.
- FX Americas has concentrated CAD cash and forward positions.
- FX Europe has large long-dated JPY-options positions.
- Notice significant diversification within FX Europe, due to offsetting Euro Cash and Forward positions.

Figure 25.7 Global FX VaR report.

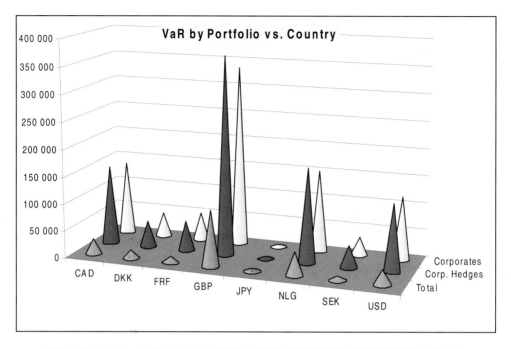

95% VaR	Total	Diversi-fication benefit	Hedges	Corporates
Total	157 365		677 000	633 065
Diversification benefit	*−84 736*	*−286 324*	*−242 115*	
CAD	29 172	*−255 453*	147 169	137 456
DKK	16 351	*−77 233*	49 423	44 161
FRF	11 828	*−94 516*	55 317	51 027
GBP	104 211	*−599 962*	368 691	335 482
JPY	684	*−7 178*	4 093	3 769
NLG	43 559	*−282 760*	174 408	151 911
SEK	8 447	*−65 126*	39 855	33 718
USD	27 849	*−214 175*	124 368	117 656

Comments
- All corporate bond positions are partially interest rate hedged, using swaps or futures. This can be seen from the large diversification benefit between Hedges and Corporates.
- Largest market risk is to GBP, due to large positions and significant spread risk between government and corporate issuers.

Figure 25.8   Corporate bond trading daily VaR.

definition in risk terms, which eliminates the need to create and rely on arbitrary percentage investment guidelines.

For example, to guide an investment manager using the S&P 500 benchmark, upper management can provide her with a single relative VaR limit instead of many figures defining a percentage maximum and minimum investment in every industry group. A relative VaR limit implies that deviation from a benchmark must remain below a threshold risk level.

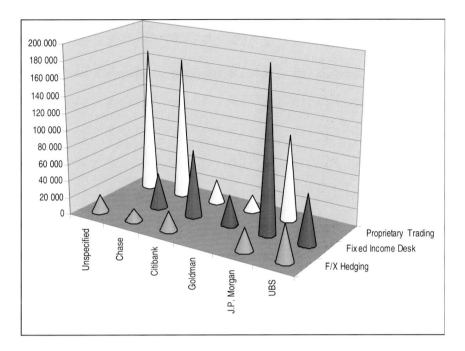

95% 1-week VaR	Total	F/X hedging	Fixed income desk	Proprietary trading
Total	476 207	64 394	341 693	294 593
Unspecified	170 377	20 565		170 673
Chase	166 035	14 572	40 584	166 026
Citibank	67 731	21 837	78 822	27 969
Goldman	38 943		35 201	18 578
J.P. Morgan	208 386	26 493	192 787	100 558
UBS	82 094	43 254	58 647	

Comments
- Largest counterparty exposure is to J. P. Morgan, due to large trades by Fixed Income and Proprietary Trading. There is a 5% chance that our exposure to J. P. Morgan will exceed $208 386 over 1 week.
- Fixed Income group Desk is generating the largest credit exposure ($341 693), followed by Proprietary Trading ($294 593).

Figure 25.9 VaR by counterparty.

While there are still no regulatory disclosure requirements, voluntary VaR disclosure can be a competitive advantage for investment managers who wish to differentiate themselves by providing clients with useful information. Some institutional clients specifically ask for VaR analysis, usually through custodians.

Relative VaR

For investment managers with a defined benchmark, relative VaR may be more relevant than stand-alone VaR. Relative VaR between two portfolios can be measured by calculating the net VaR of going long the original portfolio and shorting the benchmark portfolio. The performance of investment managers can be evaluated by comparing excess benchmark returns against relative VaR.[3]

Table 25.7   Quarterly global stress secario analysis.

Severity of event	Sample scenario	Likely market impact	Portfolio impact (in $ million)
Once in a year	Liquidity crisis (e.g. Oct '97 HKD attack and Brazil rate hike, Sep. '98 market turmoil and LTCM blowup)	Rates rise (50 to 100 bp) Spreads rise (20 to 100 bp) Equity indices drop (6%–10%) RMVI* increase (20%)	−25 −12 +20 −5 −21 total
Once in 5 years	Major currency devaluations and Emerging Markets turmoil (e.g. Brazil '99, Russia '98, S.E. Asia '97, Mexico '95)	Rates rise (100 to 200 bp) Spreads rise (40 to 200 bp) Equity indices drop (10%-20%) RMVI increase (30%)	−57 −22 +38 −8 −48 total
Once in a decade	Major financial sector crisis (e.g. US S&L '80s Crisis, Japan '90s, Asia '97)	Yield curve steepens (−100 to 300 bp) Spreads rise (60 to 300 bp) Equity indices drop (15%–25%) RMVI increase (40%)	−80 −43 +55 −15 −80 total
Once in 30 years	Major stock market crash (e.g. US '04, '29, '87)	Yield curve steepens (−100 to 400 bp) Spreads rise (100 to 500 bp) Equity indices drop (20%–30%) RMVI increase (60%)	−112 −61 +92 −23 −101 total
Once in a century	Major global depression, war and hyper inflation (e.g. World War I, II)	Yields rise (400 to 1000 bp) Spreads rise (200 to 1000 bp) Equity indices drop (25%–40%) Commodity prices rise (5% to 10%) RMVI increase (100%)	−260 −195 +238 +58 −40 −191 total

* RiskMetrics Volatility Index

Notes:

● The above stress tests reflect the firms's estimated exposure during a series of gross bear market events. Shocks assume daily worst-case movements, with no position unwinds. Stress tests only account for direct MTM changes of positions held in inventory and do not account for potential changes in underlying business volume (e.g. lower underwriting and secondary trading), or credit losses due to counterparty defaults. Note that totals add up to less than the individual components because individual losses are not simply additive.

● *RMVI* (RiskMetrics® Volatility Index) was used as a proxy to model implied volatility shocks on options positions (e.g. vega risk).

● Notice large positive gains in equity bear market scenarios, which is due to a very large short equity index futures position by the Proprietary Positioning group.

● The firm's largest bear market exposure comes from a large inventory of unhedged Eurobonds, which gives exposure to both interestrate and spread risk.

● Total direct exposure to extreme bear market scenarios is moderate with respect to capital, due to offsetting short equity positions by Proprietary Positioning. Indirect business volume exposure and credit concerns, however, may be substantial.

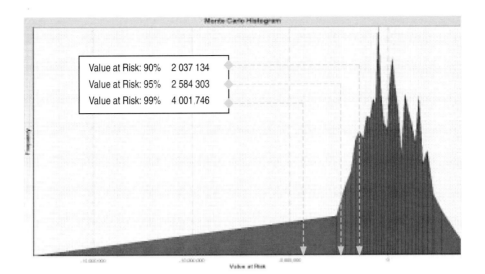

99% VaR (1-day)	Aggregate	Diversification benefit	FX Risk	Interest rate risk
Aggregate	4 001 746		2 790 699	3 643 519
Diversification benefit	*− 4 636 288*		*− 1 967 820*	*− 2 667 189*
North America	2 819 160	*− 541 971*	608 404	2 752 727
Central Europe	2 594 426	*− 1 007 867*	2 149 562	1 452 731
Japan	406 618	*− 88 710*	102 091	393 237
Australia	2 168 901	*− 650 670*	1 735 121	1 084 451
Emerging Asia	446 255	*− 96 523*	110 393	432 385
Latin America	11 343	*− 583*	851	11 075
Mid East & Africa	191 331	*− 44 868*	52 097	184 102

Comments

Long skewed tail due to short interest rate options. There is the potential for large losses if there is extreme divergence between US and European rates. However, overall VaR is well within tolerance. Large regional diversification is due to offsetting directional positions between US and Europe.

Figure 25.10   Global macro fund: regional VaR analysis.

Example

Table 25.8 is an example of an asset manager with three types of funds, each with its own benchmark.

External reporting

Figure 25.13 is a graph of VaR, benchmark VaR, and relative VaR for each of the three asset classes listed in column 1 of the table. VaR is expressed as a percentage of market value.

Internal management reporting

Relative VaR is useful for internal management reporting of positions. Deviations from bench-marks can be analyzed in many dimensions: deviation by duration, country allocation, and risk type (equity versus FX).

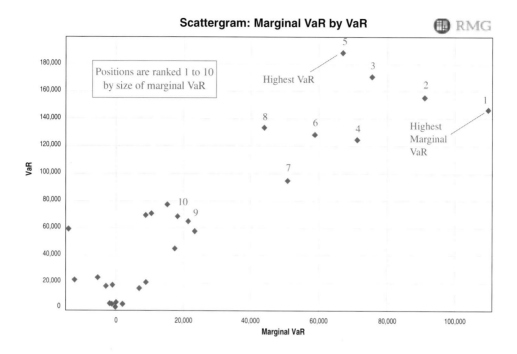

Figure 25.11 Marginal VaR analysis.

#	Marginal VaR	VaR	Position	#	Marginal VaR	VaR	Position
1	110 357	144 941	GBP 5Y Note	16	9 077	67 669	CAD 5Y Swap
2	91 761	153 574	IEP 5Y Swap	17	7 385	13 955	DKK 5Y Swap
3	76 052	169 057	GBP 5Y Swap	18	2 280	2 618	JPY 5Y Note
4	71 756	122 659	EUR 5Y Swap	19	297	3 040	BEF 5Y Swap
5	67 462	186 275	IEP 5Y Note	20	71	737	ESP 5Y Swap
6	59 199	126 304	AUD 5Y Note	21	4	61	ITL 5Y Swap
7	51 168	93 128	AUD 5Y Swap	22	−16	71	ITL 5Y Note
8	44 246	131 947	EUR 5Y Note	23	−47	814	ESP 5Y Note
9	23 675	55 657	NLG 5Y Swap	24	−795	1 662	JPY 5Y Swap
10	21 784	62 714	DEM 5Y Swap	25	−834	16 459	SEK 5Y Swap
11	18 544	66 755	DEM 5Y Note	26	−1 730	3 339	BEF 5Y Note
12	17 734	43 255	USD 5Y Swap	27	−2 810	15 984	SEK 5Y Note
13	15 304	75 613	CAD 5Y Note	28	−5 278	21 883	FRF 5Y Note
14	10 995	68 818	NLG 5Y Note	29	−12 089	20 297	DKK 5Y Note
15	9 286	18 694	FRF 5Y Swap	30	−13 996	57 444	USD 5Y Note

Internal reporting: relative risk

In Figure 25.14, we analyze how our international bond portfolio deviates from its benchmark country allocation.

Internal reporting: risk contribution

Investment managers can use incremental VaR to analyze portfolio diversification and identify undue concentrations. For example, Figure 25.15 uses incremental VaR to measure regional port-folio risk contributions.

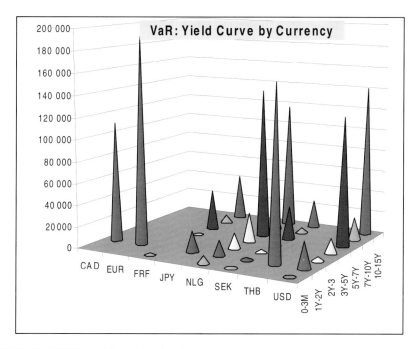

	Total	0–3M	1Y–2Y	2Y–3	3Y–5Y	5Y–7Y	7Y–10Y	10–15Y
Total	491 379	6 176	283 242	16 653	34 896	249 031	29 388	192 808
CAD	111 366		111 366					
EUR	191 925		191 925					
FRF	15 927	2 534				37 524	7 162	42 295
JPY	19 394		19 394					
NLG	336 498	7 366	14 521	14 330	27 341	138 783	19 775	117 195
SEK	73 095	1 475	2 821	2 853	5 732	30 755	4 502	26 117
THB	158 966		158 966					
USD	273 146		24 151	4 074	14 251	120 211	21 158	140 837

Comments
- VaR generated using RiskMetrics Monte Carlo simulation, 1-day horizon, 95% confidence.
- Largest exposure in Euro due to large short 2Y-position in asset swaps.
- Also significant Exposure to Kingdom of Thailand due to 2Y government bond position.

Figure 25.12 Global yield curve risk report.

Corporate case study

Background information

Fueled by globalization, capital markets fund raising, and regulatory prodding, VaR is making inroads with corporations. Enterprise-wide risk measurement is often more complex for corporates because of significant underlying non-financial exposures and accounting considerations. In addition to VaR, corporates may apply several related 'at-Risk' measures: Earnings-at-Risk (EaR), Earnings-Per-Shareat-Risk (EPSaR), and Cash-Flow-at-Risk (CFaR). Longer-horizon forecasting complications also arise, as corporations are interested in making quarterly or even annual projections of earnings volatility. These issues are addressed further in the *CorporateMetrics Technical Document* and the *LongRun Technical Document*.

Table 25.8

Fund	Investment objectives and constraints	Benchmark
Capital Preservation	Low risk profile, only short-term interest rate positioning allowed	US 3-month T-Bill
Global Bond Fund	Moderate risk profile, short- and long-term interest rate positioning and FX positioning	GBI+ Index*
Global Equities Fund	Aggressive risk profile with global equity and FX exposure	EAFE Index†

*GBI+ Index (Global Bond+ Index) is published by J. P. Morgan.
†EAFE Index (Europe Australia Far East Index) is published by Morgan Stanley.

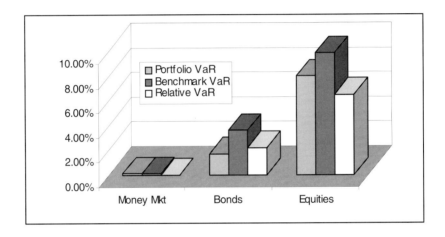

1-month 95% CL	Portfolio VaR	Benchmark VaR	Relative VaR	Relative VaR limit
Money market	0.1%	0.1%	0.0%	0.1%
Bonds	1.7%	3.6%	2.2%	3.4%
Equities	8.0%	9.9%	6.5%	6.7%

Comments
All portfolios are less aggressive than the benchmark in absolute VaR, indicating a cautious market view. While portfolios would outperform benchmarks if markets turn bearish, portfolios would underperform benchmarks in a bull market scenario. The relative VaR on equities is close to limits, showing that asset allocation deviates significantly from the benchmark. Deviation from the benchmark is due to under-weighting of Japanese equities.

Figure 25.13   Investment manager monthly VaR summary.

VaR has the most straightforward internal management application in a global corporate treasury, to measure FX and interest rate exposure. It can also be useful for companies that are sensitive to changes in commodity prices, such as airlines, manufacturers, steel producers, mining companies, and freight and shipping companies. For external disclosure requirements, VaR has been approved by the SEC as a measure of the risk of derivative positions.[4] One key advantage of using VaR for external reporting is that instrument-specific information need not be revealed.

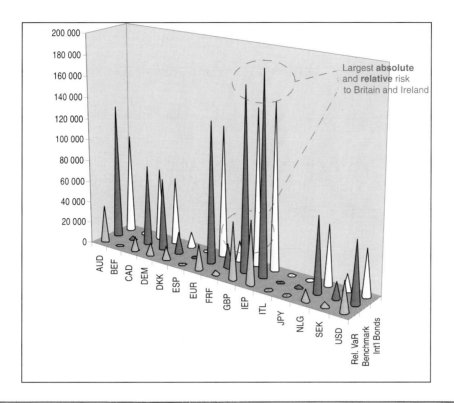

95% VaR (1-month)	Relative VaR	Diversification benefit	International bond benchmark	International bonds
Aggregate	98 504	− 1 055 612	656 783	497 333
Diversification benefit	− 155 702		− 290 437	− 300 872
AUD	34 528	− 184 904	126 304	93 128
BEF	559	− 5 820	3 339	3 040
CAD	12 696	− 30 586	75 613	67 669
DEM	11 226	− 118 244	66 755	62 714
DKK	12 558	− 21 694	20 297	13 955
ESP	142	− 1 409	814	737
EUR	23 383	− 231 222	131 947	122 659
FRF	4 116	− 36 461	21 883	18 694
GBP	52 864	− 261 134	169 057	144 941
IEP	58 237	− 281 612	186 275	153 574
ITL	11	− 121	71	61
JPY	356	− 3 923	2 618	1 662
NLG	10 563	− 113 912	68 818	55 657
SEK	4 836	− 27 607	15 984	16 459
USD	28 129	− 72 569	57 444	43 255

Comments
- Largest relative VaR positions are in GBP and IEP, due to country under-weighting.
- Overall VaR is lower than benchmark portfolio, expressing the fund's bearish view on the bond markets.
- Net relative VaR is well within the limit of USD 200 000.

Figure 25.14   Risk by country summary report.

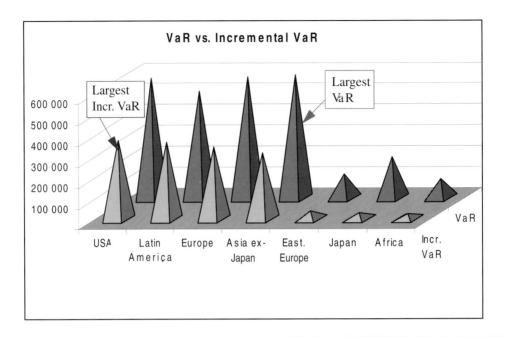

Risk contribution report	Present value	VaR	Incremental VaR	Contribution to risk
USA	71 774 216	574 194	378 341	25%
Latin America	10 258 887	512 944	369 626	25%
Europe	64 600 480	581 404	343 237	23%
Asia ex-Japan	12 693 840	589 734	317 346	21%
Eastern Europe	1 948 860	116 932	40 322	3%
Japan	19 569 450	195 694	30 068	2%
Africa	4 669 370	93 387	24 163	2%
Diversification benefit		*(1 161 186)*		
Aggregate	185 515 103	1 503 103	1 503 103	100%

Comments

- Even though Asia ex-Japan is the largest single relative VaR position, it is only the fourth largest contributor to risk, as measured by the percentage of incremental VaR (21%). The best 3 opportunities for reducing risk through hedges lie in the USA, Latin America, and Europe.
- **VaR** refers to 95% worst-case loss over 1 day due to adverse movements in market rates.
- Incremental VaR is the change in VaR that results when position size is increased by a small amount, multiplied by the portfolio weighting. The sum of all incremental VaRs add up to total diversified VaR.
- **Diversification benefit** is equal to diversified (aggregate) VaR minus the sum of all individual VaRs. It measures the risk reduction achieved through diversification (i.e. correlation being lower than 1) between risk categories.

Figure 25.15   Regional risk summary.

Airline example

Let's consider a US-based airline, Global Air, which is exposed to a host of business and financial risks. The airline has a centralized Treasury, which manages all financial risks, and three regional business groups, which are responsible for managing business risks (i.e. 'volumetric' risk related to operations and ticket sales). Each regional business is responsible for its own jet fuel procurement, while the

Treasury's Commodities Management group manages firmwide fuel price exposure centrally, with a mandate to keep annual Earnings-at-Risk (EaR) due to fuel price changes below a threshold amount. The Foreign Exchange group manages centralized FX exposures arising from international revenues and costs, and the Global Interest Rates group manages interest rate risk due to liabilities (see Figure 25.16).

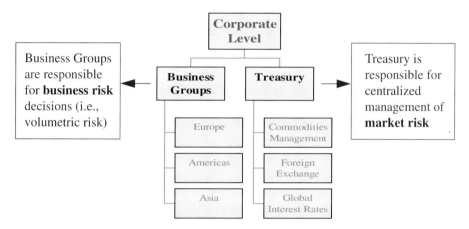

Figure 25.16 Global Air organizational chart.

We will focus on the market risks that Global Air faces. First, we will quantify EaR due to oil price sensitivity, then EaR due to all relevant market variables.

The Commodities Management trader in charge of designing a hedging program projects jet fuel consumption 1 month ahead, which is modeled as a short position in crude oil and unleaded gasoline. This assumes that the airline's P&L changes linearly with fuel prices[5] (i.e. all fuel price increases are absorbed by the airline, and fuel price decreases are direct savings to the airline). To cap downside, the trader purchases call options on oil futures. Instead of selling a put, she leaves the upside potential of oil prices falling uncapped. The payoff of this position is illustrated in the sliding scale: losses are capped after approximately 5% increase in oil prices, while profits from oil depreciation are uncapped. As Figure 25.17 illustrates, the net position after hedges resembles a long put option on oil. Notice that the airline only profits after a 2% depreciation, due to the premium paid on the purchased call option on oil futures.

Both underlying oil price sensitivities and derivatives hedges can be entered into a risk model for quantification of risk. The following risk reports analyze the net risk of this position.

Fuel VaR

The non-linear payoff from this exposure can be seen in the airline's commodity EaR report in Figure 25.18).

Total market risk

Next, we can aggregate FX risk from underlying operations and interest rate risk from the liabilities portfolio to calculate total market risk. We can then calculate the airline's total exposure to market risk (see Figure 25.19).

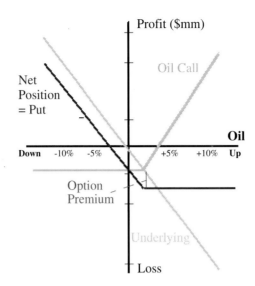

Figure 25.17   Airline sensitivity to oil price changes.

External disclosure of VaR

According to SEC disclosure requirements, a company has flexibility in how to disclose the VaR of its equities positions in terms of horizon and confidence level. Directionality and position-specific VaR need not be disclosed. Figure 25.20 might be the annual report disclosure of VaR for the airline.

Summary of risk reporting issues

To promote risk communication across the firm, risk reports should highlight risk concentrations in a timely and accurate manner. Keep daily summary reports to one page and consider enhancing it with a written commentary. There is an important organizational hierarchy to risk reporting, in that significant risk exposures must be channeled up from the risk taker to senior management through efficient risk reporting. Risk information should be customized for different levels of the organization, highlighting relevant dimensions of risk and identifying the risk-taking units.

There are different time dimensions to risk reporting. Active financial institutions use daily reports for active management of risks and monitoring of limits. Senior management look at monthly or quarterly reports for a more strategic view of risk performance, trends, capital allocation, and competitor analysis. Market risk reporting has become a necessity for banks, and is increasingly implemented by asset managers, hedge funds, and insurance companies, as well as traditional corporations.

External risk disclosures

Introduction

In addition to internal management reporting, companies are increasingly disclosing market risk to external entities: shareholders, regulators, analysts, lenders, and

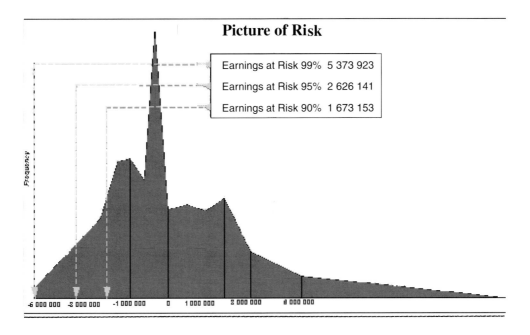

95% EaR (1-month)	Aggregate	Underlying	Commodity insurance
Aggregate	$2 626 141	12 618 318	4 319 514
Short crude oil	3 761 890	3 761 890	
Short unleaded	8 933 096	8 933 096	
Long crude call	1 560 172		1 560 172
Long unleaded Call	2 967 781		2 967 781

Comments
- Downside from Underlying positions (i.e. short fuel) is insured with long calls. Commodity Insurance reduced Underlying EaR by almost 80%, from 12 618 318 to 2 626 141. Notice that oil calls (i.e. insurance) reduces EaR by a greater amount than its stand-alone EaR (Commodity Insurance VaR = 4 319 514, EaR reduction = 9 992 177). Options have limited downside (i.e. the option premium) and unlimited upside (or insurance effect).
- Upside from oil prices falling is left uncapped, as shown by the long positive tail (right).

Figure 25.18 Total fuel EaR.

credit rating agencies. External disclosures vary greatly by country, industry, and company. Each central bank may impose risk reporting requirements on financial institutions within its jurisdiction. For example, in the United States, the Federal Reserve Bank regulates banks, and the SEC regulates securities firms and corporation. Beyond complying with required regulatory reporting, several leading institutions[6] have led the way with voluntary disclosures on market risk.

Emerging global standards for public disclosures

While there is no single global regulatory standard for risk reporting, the BIS has actively promoted risk disclosures by global financial institutions. Jointly with the Technical Committee of the International Organization of Securities Commissions (IOSCO), BIS issued 'Recommendations for Public Disclosure of Trading and

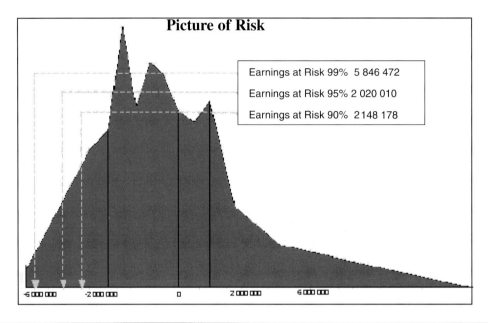

Picture of Risk

Earnings at Risk 99% 5 846 472

Earnings at Risk 95% 2 020 010

Earnings at Risk 90% 2 148 178

95% EaR (1-month)	Aggregate	Divers.benefit	Net commodities	Foreign exchange	Liabilities
Aggregate	2 825 816	− 1 686 054	2 626 141	1 102 734	782 994
Diversification benefit	− 1 554 109				− 318 736
Commodity risk	2 626 141		2 626 141		
Interest rate risk	495 300				495 300
FX risk	1 258 483	− 450 681		1 102 734	606 430

Comments
- The airline's largest concentration remains in commodities, even after hedges (2 626 141). The airline is also significantly exposed to foreign exchange (1 102 734) and, to a lesser extent, inter-est rates (781 994).
- Notice the large diversification benefit between risk classes due to low correlation between com-modity, interest rate, and foreign exchange rates (1 554 109).
- The distribution is positively skewed because losses due to rising oil prices are capped.

Figure 25.19 Firmwide EaR.

Derivatives Activities of Banks and Securities Firms'[7] with the following two general guidelines:

- First, institutions should provide financial statement users with a clear picture of their trading and derivatives activities. They should disclose meaningful summary information, both qualitative and quantitative, on the scope and nature of their trading and derivatives activities and illustrate how these activities contribute to their earnings profile. They should disclose information on the major risks associated with their trading and derivatives activities and their performance in managing these risks.
- Second, institutions should disclose information produced by their internal risk measurement and management systems on their risk exposures and their actual performance in managing these exposures. Linking public disclosure to the

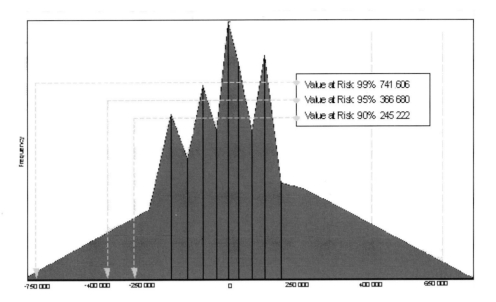

95% VaR (1-day)	31 December 1998	Average 1998	Maximum 1998	Minimum 1998
Commodity risk	$181 818	226 304	338 694	167 669
FX risk	$285 734	240 955	362 714	143 255
International rate risk	$139 542	144 941	223 737	122 659
Diversification benefit	*($240 414)*	*($241 256)*	NA	NA
Aggregate	$366 680	370 944	586 275	221 883

Comments
RiskMetrics historical simulation is used to calculate market risks, using 1 year of historical data.

Figure 25.20 VaR of derivatives.

internal risk management process helps ensure that disclosure keeps pace with innovations in risk measurement and management techniques.

Recommendations center on qualitative and quantitative disclosures, as shown in the next two sections.

General qualitative disclosures

Qualitative disclosures focus on the model and parameters used to measure risk and are based on the following guidelines:

- Discuss the methods used to measure and manage market risk
- Discuss how performance in managing market risks is assessed
- Describe the Major assumptions and parameters used by internal models necessary to understand an institution's market risk disclosures:
  - Type of model used
  - Portfolios covered by the model
  - Holding period

– Confidence level
– Observation period
- Discuss the method of aggregating risk exposures
- Discuss the method used to recognize correlations between market factors (e.g. correlation assumptions)
- Provide an overview of policies and procedures for validating internal models
- Provide an overview of policies and procedures for stress testing market risk
- Discuss changes in market risk exposure and risk management strategies from previous year

As an example of a qualitative disclosure, the following is Chase Manhattan's description of the risk measurement methodology from its 1998 *Annual Report*:

Chase Manhattan 1998 Annual Report
The VaR, a dollar amount, is a forward-looking estimate of the potential for loss. The VaR looks forward one trading day, and is calculated as the loss level expected to be exceeded with a 1 in 100 chance. The VaR methodology used at Chase is called historical simulation. Historical simulation assumes that actual observed historical changes in market indices such as interest rates, exchange rates and commodity prices reflect the future possible changes in those same rates and prices. In its daily VaR calculations, Chase's historical simul-tion provides different views of market risk in end-of-day positions, by aggregating positions by business, geography, currency or type of risk.

Statistical models of risk measurement, such as VaR, allow an objective, independent assessment of how much risk is actually being taken. Chase's historic simulation methodology permits consistent and comparable measurement of risk across instruments and portfolios, irrespective of the level of aggregation. Historical simulation also makes it easy to examine the VaR for any desired segment of the total portfolio and to examine that segment's contribution to total risk. The VaR calculations are performed for all management trading portfolios and market-risk related asset/liability management ('ALM') portfolios. Results are reported at various levels of detail by business unit and in aggregate.

General quantitative disclosures

Quantitative disclosures center on providing summary trading results and VaR statistics.

Market risk

- Provide summary quantitative information on market risk exposure based on internal methods used for measurement, with information on performance in managing those risks
- Provide daily information on profits and losses on trading activities, combined with daily value at risk numbers
- Provide summary VaR results on a weekly or monthly basis
- For those disclosing VaR data, provide high/low VaR
- For those disclosing VaR data, provide average VaR

- Discuss the results of scenario analysis or impact of rate shocks for traded portfolios
- Discuss the number of times (days) actual portfolio loss exceeded VaR
- For non-traded portfolios: provide summary VaR or EAR
- For non-traded portfolios: provide summary results of scenario analysis of impact of rate shocks

Sample quantitative risk disclosures

Table 25.9 outlines the major public market risk disclosures that are presented in the 1998 annual reports of Chase Manhattan, Citigroup, J.P. Morgan, UBS Warburg Dillon Read, and Credit Suisse First Boston.

Table 25.9

Public disclosures	Chase	Citi	JPM	UBS	CSFB
Confidence level	99%	99%	95%	99%	99%
Forecast horizon	1 day	1 day	1 day	1 day	1 day
Base currency	USD	USD	USD	CHF	CHF
Average, high, low VaR	Yes	Yes	Yes	Yes	Yes
VaR by risk category	Yes	Yes	Yes	Yes	Yes
Daily VaR graph	No	No	Yes	Yes	Yes
P&L versus VaR graph	No	No	No	Yes	Yes
Backtesting statistics	Yes	No	Yes	Yes	Yes
Histogram of daily P&L	Yes	No	Yes	Yes	Yes
Scenario analysis	No	Yes	No	No	No

Risk disclosures that exemplify reporting trends across the financial industry are highlighted below.

(a) Average, high and low VaR statistics are commonly disclosed in annual reports (see Tables 25.10 and 25.11).
(b) In addition to summary statistics, some firms, such as J.P. Morgan, provide a full history of aggregate daily portfolio VaR (see Figure 25.21).
(c) Trading results are commonly released in the form of a histogram (see Figure 25.22).
(d) Some firms publish a history of daily revenues, with VaR bands, as required by the BIS backtesting of internal models for market risk[8] (see Figure 25.23).

Voluntary risk disclosure for non-financial corporations

Increasingly, non-financial corporations provide the public with market risk disclosures. Voluntary disclosures are often perceived positively by the marketplace, because they demonstrate forward-looking financial management and a commitment to transparency. The ability to understand, measure, and manage market risk has become a competitive necessity for all global corporations.

Example 1   From Sony 1998 Annual Report

The financial instruments including financial assets and liabilities that Sony holds in the normal course of business are continuously exposed to fluctuations in markets, such as currency exchange rates, interest rates, and stock prices of investments. . . .

Table 25.10   Citigroup: 99% confidence 1-Day VaR

In millions of dollars	Citicorp			Salomon Smith Barney		
	31 Dec. 1998	1998 average	31 Dec. 1997	31 Dec. 1998	1998 average	31 Dec. 1997
Interest rate	$13	$16	$23	$75	$67	$57
Foreign exchange	7	8	8	3	17	12
Equity	5	7	8	15	9	11
All other (primarily commodity)	1	1	—	11	11	11
Covariance adjustment	(11)	(14)	(14)	(33)	(34)	(30)
Total	$15	$18	$25	$71	$70	$61

In millions of dollars	Citicorp		Salomon Smith Barney	
	High	Low	High	Low
Interest rate	25	10	75	62
Foreign exchange	16	3	26	3
Equity	13	4	15	5
All other (primarily commodity)	5	1	12	9

Source: BIS

Table 25.11   Chase Manhattan: 99% confidence 1-day VaR (trading portfolio only)

Year ended 31 December 1998 (in millions of dollars)	Marked-to-market trading portfolio			
	Average VaR	Minimum VaR	Maximum VaR	At 31 December 1998 VaR
Interest rate VaR	$22.8	$15.4	$36.8	$20.1
Foreign exchange VaR	8.6	2.2	21.6	2.3
Commodities VaR	3.6	2.3	5.0	2.6
Equities VaR	3.8	1.9	9.4	4.6
Less: Portfolio diversification	(13.1)	NM	NM	(8.9)
Total VaR	$27.7	$15.6	$44.9	$20.7

Source: BIS

Sony measures the effect of market fluctuations on the value of financial instruments and derivatives by using Value-at-Risk (herein referred to as 'VaR') analysis. VaR measures a potential maximum amount of loss in fair value resulting from adverse market fluctuations, for a selected period of time and at a selected level of confidence. Sony uses the variance/co-variance model in calculation of VaR. The calculation includes financial instruments such as cash and cash equivalents, time deposits, marketable securities, non-lease short- and long-term borrowings and debt, investments and advances and all derivatives including transactions for risk hedging held by Sony Corporation and consolidated subsidiaries. Sony calculates VaR for one day from the portfolio of financial instruments and derivatives as of March 31, 1998, at a confidence level of 95%.

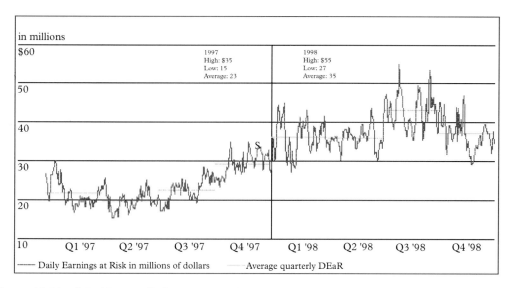

Figure 25.21 J. P. Morgan: Daily 95% VaR (or Daily-Earnings-at-Risk). Average DEaR or trading activities increased 65% over the previous year to $38 million, reflecting growth in market-making activities as well as in extreme increases in volatility from August through October. Since DEaR are used primarily as a measure of expected volatility of short-term trading positions, the model weights recent patterns of market volatility and correlations most heavily. As a result DEaR estimates changed rapidly in the August to October period of market turmoil.

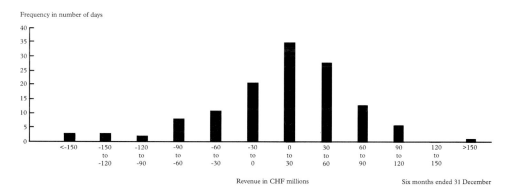

Figure 25.22 UBS Warburg Dillon Read: Trading revenue distribution.

Based on this assumption, Sony's consolidated VaR at 31 March 1998 is calculated to be 6.9 billion yen ($52 million), which indicates the potential maximum loss in fair value resulting from market fluctuations in one day at a 95% confidence level. By item, the VaR of currency exchange rate risk is calculated to be 7.2 billion yen ($55 million) which mainly consists of risks arising from the volatility of the exchange rates between yen and US dollars in which a relatively large amount of financial assets and liabilities and derivative transactions is main-tained. VaR of interest rate risk and stock price risk are calculated to be 3.4 billion yen ($26 million) and 3.3 billion yen ($25 million), respectively. The net VaR for Sony's entire portfolio is

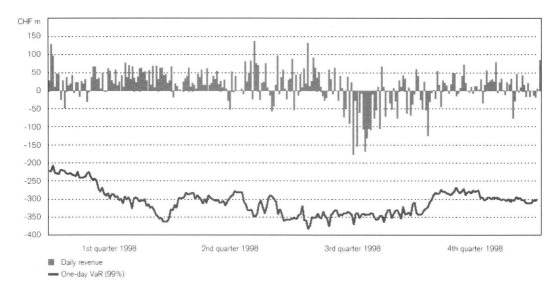

Figure 25.23 Credit Suisse First Boston: historical VaR versus revenue. Note: Credit Suisse First Boston's VaR vs. revenue band graph for 1998 shows an overly conservative VaR model. Revenues have a highly biased positive mean for the first two quarters of 1998, and even in the volatile 3rd quarter, realized losses never come close to VaR estimates. At 99% confidence, CSFB should expect 2 to 3 daily downside exceptions per year (i.e. 1% of 252 trading days).

smaller than the simple aggregate of VaR for each component of market risk. This is due to the fact that market risk factors such as currency exchange rates, interest rates, and stock prices are not completely independent, thus have the effect of offsetting a portion of overall profits and losses.

Example 2   From Procter & Gamble 1998 Annual Report

The Company is exposed to market risk, including changes in interest rates, currency exchange rates and commodity prices. To manage the volatility relating to these exposures on a consolidated basis, the Company nets the exposures to take advantage of natural offsets and enters into various derivative transactions for the remaining exposures pursuant to the Company's policies in areas such as counterparty exposure and hedging practices. The financial impacts of these hedging instruments are offset by corresponding changes in the underlying exposures being hedged. The Company does not hold or issue derivative financial instruments for trading-purposes.

Derivative positions are monitored using techniques including market value, sensitivity analysis and a value at risk model. The tests for interest rate and currency rate exposures discussed below are based on a variance/co-variance value at risk model using a one-year horizon and a 95% confidence level. The model assumes that financial returns are normally distributed and approximates the financial return for options and other non-linear instruments. The model also reflects the impact of correlation and diversification from holding multiple currency and interest rate instruments. Estimates of volatility and correlations of market factors are drawn from the J. P. Morgan RiskMetrics™ dataset as of June 30,1998. In cases where data is unavailable in RiskMetrics™, a reasonable approximation is included. The effect of these estimates did not significantly change the total value at risk.

The Company's market risk exposures relative to interest and currency rates, as discussed below, have not changed materially versus the previous reporting period. In addition, the Company is not aware of any facts or circumstances that would significantly impact such exposures in the near-term.

Interest Rate Exposure. . . . Based on the Company's overall interest rate exposure as of and during the year ended June 30, 1998, including derivative and other interest rate sensitive instruments, a near-term change in interest rates, within a 95% confidence level based on historical interest rate movements, would not materially affect the consolidated financial position, results of operations or cash flows.

Currency Rate Exposures.
Currency exposure. . . . Based on the Company's overall currency rate exposure as of and during the year ended June 30, 1998, including derivative and other foreign currency sensitive instruments, a near-term change in currency rates, within a 95% confidence level based on historical currency rate movements, would not materially affect the consolidated financial position, results of operations or cash flows.

Commodity Price Exposure. . . . Raw materials used by the Company are subject to price volatility caused by weather, supply conditions and other unpredictable factors. The Company uses futures and options contracts, primarily in food and beverage products, to manage the volatility related to certain of these exposures. Gains and losses relating to qualifying hedges of firm commitments or anticipated inventory transactions are deferred in prepaid expenses and are included in the basis of the underlying transactions. Commodity hedging activity is not material to the Company's consolidated financial position, results of operations or cash flows.

SEC disclosure requirements for derivatives

In 1997, the SEC recommended to its constituents to voluntarily report their derivative positions. As of June 1999, all members with a market cap of USD 2.5 billion or larger are required to report their derivative positions in one of three ways: (1) by listing their derivative positions in a tabular disclosure, (2) by providing sensitivity analyses, or (3) by reporting their exposures in VaR.[9] The companies are faced with the task of selecting one of the methods for reporting their market risk exposures.

Below are actual examples of the three types of market risk reporting options.

Tabular listing of derivative positions

From Tenneco 1998 Annual Report
In managing its foreign currency exposures, Tenneco identifies and aggregates naturally occurring offsetting positions and then hedges residual exposures through third party derivative contracts. The following table summarizes by major currency the notional amounts, weighted average settlement rates, and fair value for foreign currency forward purchase and sale contracts as of December 31, 1998. All contracts in the following table mature in 1999.

Sensitivity analysis of positions

From Texaco 1998 Annual Report:
Petroleum and Natural Gas Hedging

		Notional amount in foreign currency	Weighted average settlement rates	Fair value in US dollars
Belgian francs	Purchase	594	0.029	$17
	Sell	−644	0.029	−19
British pounds	Purchase	98	1.660	163
	Sell	−152	1.660	−252
Canadian dollars	Purchase	112	0.654	73
	Sell	−176	0.654	−115
Danish krone	Purchase	79	0.157	12
	Sell	—	—	—
French francs	Purchase	497	0.179	89
	Sell	−97	0.179	−17
German marks	Purchase	3	0.599	2
	Sell	−56	0.599	−33
Portuguese escudos	Purchase	1947	0.006	11
	Sell	−30	0.006	—
Spanish pesetas	Purchase	4545	0.007	32
	Sell	−325	0.007	−2
US dollars	Purchase	105	1.000	105
	Sell	−33	1.000	−33
Other	Purchase	395	0.043	17
	Sell	−719	0.068	−49
Total				$1

In 1998, the notional amount of open derivative contracts increased by $3423 million, mostly related to natural gas hedging.

For commodity derivatives permitted to be settled in cash or another financial instrument, sensitivity effects are as follows. At year-end 1998, the aggregate effect of a hypothetical 25% change in natural gas prices, a 15% change in crude oil prices and 16–21% change in petroleum product prices (dependent on product and location) would not materially affect our consolidated financial position, net income or cash flows.

VaR disclosure

From Dell 1998 Annual Report
Based on the Company's foreign exchange instruments outstanding at February 1, 1998, the Company estimates a maximum potential one-day loss in fair value of $12 million, using a Value-at-Risk ('VaR') model. The VaR model estimates were made assuming normal market conditions and a 95% confidence level. There are various types of modeling techniques that can be used in a VaR computation; the Company used a Monte Carlo simulation type model that valued its foreign currency instruments against a thousand randomly generated market price paths.

Summary

Increased regulatory scrutiny and public concern have stimulated a clear trend toward greater public disclosure of market risks, for both financial and non-financial corporations.

Several leading global financial firms have started voluntary disclosures of their market risk management methodology, including a range of VaR and trading results statistics, and sensitivity analysis. To avoid information overload, companies should limit disclosure to relevant information only. Relevant disclosure might include explanation of differences between reported accounting results and actual economic effects of hedges.

To encourage a broader range of institutions to disclose risks, BIS and IOSCO have jointly issued recommendations concerning voluntary global market risk disclosures. Regulatory agencies, in general, are also introducing mandatory disclosures.

In the United States, the SEC has required all non-bank members with a market capitalization of $2.5 billion or more to disclose derivative positions through tabular representation, sensitivity analysis or VaR. Other countries will surely follow, and risk disclosures are likely to become a standard for all major corporations.

There is a clear trend towards greater public risk disclosures. In the future, one might well expect mandatory or audited risk statements in a company's annual reports.

Index

KPMG GlobeRisk℠: Integrated risk management

KPMG is one of the world's leading global professional services firms and has a dominant position in providing financial sector consulting and advisory services to banking, investment and insurance clients.

KPMG's risk practice, GlobeRisk℠, has over 500 consultants located in all major financial markets across the globe specialising in Market Risk, Credit Risk, Operational Risk, Middle Office Operations and Risk IT

The types of services and solutions provided to our clients encompass the integration of risk across business strategy, organisation structures, management information and control environment. This is achieved through the effective identification, measurement, modelling and management of risk.

For more information please contact:

Martin E Titus +44 (0) 20 7311 5499
Partner, Chairman
KPMG GlobeRisk℠

Peter J Lore +1 732 530 6733
Global Sponsorship and
Website Co-ordinator

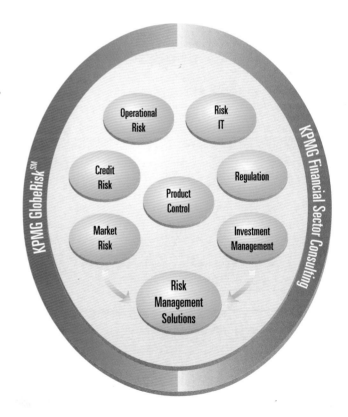

It's time for clarity.

REUTERS
Kondor+

Broad Coverage of Instruments
- Over 24 instruments including foreign exchange, money market, fixed income, and equities as well as exchange-traded and over-the-counter derivatives

Integration Capabilities
- Connectivity with front- and back-office systems
- Globally consolidated view of positions
- Unrivaled experience in open systems
- Access to real-time, historical and reference data

Real-Time Trading Tools
- Deal capture and real-time position-keeping
- Real-time valuation, mark-to-market and P/L
- Pricing tools, risk indicators, simulations and hedging recommendations
- Standard and customized reports
- Real-time global credit risk management

Powerful Risk Management Tools
- Risk measurement and performance analysis across all positions
- Multiple VAR methodologies (historical simulation, generalized covariance and RiskMetrics,™ Monte-Carlo), stress testing scenarios, relative risk analysis and benchmarking
- Global market, credit and settlement limits management

Toolkit Capabilities
- Integration of proprietary and third-party models
- Extension of data model
- Dynamic two-way interactions with third-party systems

A Reliable Partner
- Over 750 financial and application specialists in over 40 countries
- Continuous enhancements including client- and market-mandated functionality

  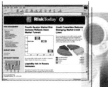

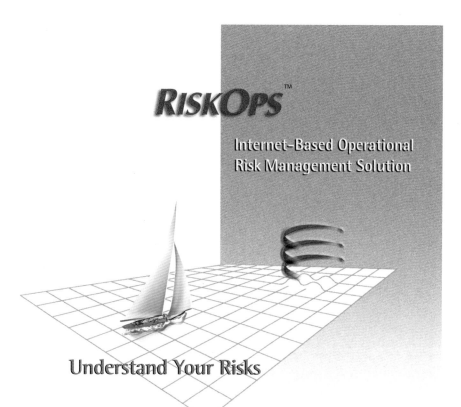